Administrative Law and Politics:
Cases and Comments

Second Edition

LIEF H. CARTER
University of Georgia

CHRISTINE B. HARRINGTON
New York University

HarperCollins*Publishers*

*For those who study and teach about democracy
in administrative law and politics.*

Sponsoring Editor: Catherine Woods
Project Coordination, Text and Cover Design: PC&F, Inc.
Production: Michael Weinstein
Compositor: PC&F, Inc.
Printer/Binder: R.R. Donnelley & Sons, Inc.
Cover Printer: Phoenix Color Corp.

Administrative Law and Politics: Cases and Comments, Second Edition
Copyright © 1991 by HarperCollins Publishers Inc.

Library of Congress Cataloging-in-Publication Data
Carter, Lief H.
    Administrative law and politics: cases and comments / Lief H.
Carter, Christine B. Harrington.
        p. cm.
    Includes bibliographical references and index
    ISBN 0-673-46031-2
    1. Administrative law—United States. I. Harrington, Christine
B. II. Title.
KF5402.C37, 1990
342.73′06—dc20
[347.3026]   90-5017
                                                                 CIP

97 98 99 10 9 8 7

Credits and Acknowledgments

Alfred C. Aman, Jr. From "Administrative Law in a Global Era," *73 Cornell Law Review 1101,* 1988. Reprinted by permission.

George D. Brandt. Excerpted by permission from "Due Process and Driver Licensing Suspension Hearings: What Do The States Do After *Love?*" 30 *Administrative Law Review,* 223 (1979), copyright American Bar Association.

Consumer Reports, "What the FTC Does," Copyright 1980 by Consumers Union of the United States, Inc., Mount Vernon, NY 10550. Reprinted by permission from *Consumer Reports,* March, 1980.

Charles Davis and Jonathan West. From "Jobs, Dollars and Gender," *18 Polity 138,* 1985. Reprinted by permission.

continued on page 621

CONTENTS

CHAPTER 12   The Law of Public Employment   431

PART IV   *Evaluating Administrative Law*   481

Skip

**CHAPTER 13   Six Blind People and an Elephant—A Hypothetical Symposium
on the Future of Administrative Law   483**

PREFACE

Administrative law is a complicated and vitally important part of our legal and political systems. Its effects fall on all of us, not just lawyers and judges. This book opens the door to the many mansions of administrative law for students, business people, and public servants—the non-lawyers whose lives are influenced by government and law every day.

For liberal arts students we hope this book does two things. It should alert them to the tremendous power administrative government uses to shape their lives, and it should teach the ways the legal system shapes this use of power. For students of business it provides information about the features of the legal and political process that so often seem to plunge them into a sea of rules and regulations. And for readers who practice or train to practice the work of public administrators, we hope this book will develop their confidence to navigate around the treacherous reefs of administrative law and procedure rather than to run aground through poor legal navigation or, worse, to remain at anchor in the harbor of inactivity, paralyzed by legal uncertainties. We hope, in other words, to help people in both public and private careers develop the confidence to make effective decisions efficiently because they know when they do and do not need to send an S.O.S. to a lawyer asking for professional help.

The majority of this book thus describes administrative law as clearly as possible for non-law students. Part I develops a working definition of administrative law and introduces theory for evaluating modern administrative law. Part II reviews the principal questions in the field, and Part III illustrates these questions in action in situations of practical interest to business people and public administrators alike. Part IV draws upon the knowledge readers have accumulated in the first three parts to evaluate critical issues in the field of administrative law.

None of us can make much conceptual sense of the world's confusion until we can fit what we see into some theoretical structure. Therefore this book emphasizes more than other texts what the rule of law means in modern government. We believe this focus will aid practitioner and academician alike. You will find our approach introduced and sketched in Part I, referred to in passing in Parts II and III, and fully defended in Part IV.

Judged by the theories of law and politics that we develop in this book, administrative law today lacks a unifying philosophical base. Some readers and teachers may applaud this normative emptiness on the premise that it permits pragmatic, incremental, and flexible development of policy. We disagree. This book, in other words, does take sides. At least users who disagree with our position will have what we hope is a clear evaluative standard to argue against.

The greatest effort in developing this book has come in deciding what to leave out. We have written for non-lawyers about a murky, sprawling, and underdeveloped field of law, a field containing many points about which law professors disagree, and many more that have the reputation for being (next to "estates in land") the most boring material ever taught in law school. So, some things have been omitted. Teachers and readers with strong administrative law backgrounds will have to accept that many of the more interesting legal puzzles—the *Wyman-Gordon* problem for example, and the APA's labyrinthian definitions of rules and rulemaking, orders and adjudication—do not appear here precisely because they are so interesting to law professors. Given our goals and strategy we have de-emphasized some classic cases, like *Crowell v. Benson*, because their contexts are complicated enough to confuse non-lawyers and because the law they state has little present practical significance. We have tried to use cases non-lawyers can digest. We have tried to diversify the kinds of federal and state agencies whose work the cases reveal in order to expand students' appreciation for the complexities of the administrative process.

A few more practical suggestions for learning and teaching from this book may be helpful. First, do not be surprised to find that the neat separation of the material into self-contained chapters breaks down, at least at the margins. This fuzziness is, we strongly suspect, in the nature of this unruly administrative law animal. Thus when you get to chapter 8 you will find material on adiministrative enforcement that overlaps the discussion in chapter 4 of administrative information-gathering. The problem of judicial inquiry into the mental process of the decider tends to pop up in many places, and so on.

Second, the richness, complexity and diversity of administrative law can entice writers and teachers to cover many points, exceptions and qualifications. This can create a choppy text, and a choppy academic course, of which students quickly tire. We have tried to avoid this evil (that is, we have tried to present solid chunks of digestible meat rather than endless snacks) by placing some reasonably important material in the "Exercises" section at the end of each chapter. We hope the chapter-end exercises and questions stimulate and aid effective teaching, but you do need to know that some of the items in these sections make points that some teachers and students will not want to neglect and which they will not find in the body of the book.

Finally, we have organized Part II roughly to follow the steps in an actual contested administrative action, from information-gathering to judicial review. College and graduate (MPA) students much appreciate this sequence. However, teachers who put judicial review at the theoretical front of their courses, a la Gellhorn, Byse, Strauss, Rakoff, and Schotland, for example, may prefer that students at least skim chapter 9 between chapters 2 and 3.

Lief Carter and Christine Harrington
July, 1990

Acknowledgments for the Second Edition by Christine Harrington

In the first edition Lief Carter acknowledged his many debts to those who taught him at Harvard Law School. I too wish to thank my academic grandparents of this book. In political science graduate school at the University of Wisconsin–Madison, I learned from David Fellman to see politics as a major force in shaping administrative law. I learned from Joel Handler how poor people, consumers, environmentalists, and others engaged in law reform became embattled with bureaucracies and embroiled in the politics of administrative law. As a research assistant for David Trubek, I worked at the Center for Public Representation in Madison, directed by Louise Trubek. There I observed how important administrative law and politics were to the Center's public-interest law struggles. From all of these graduate student experiences I realized how important it was to translate knowledge about law, which had become "professional-ized" by lawyers, into a language that would recapture the excitement and engagement in politics, administration, and law I saw among scholars of an earlier generation.

I first tried to do so with a small group of seniors majoring in political science at Vassar College. I thank them for reading more books than I have since dared to re-quire and for their patience with my naive project. Then my colleague Charles Noble and I received a small grant from Rutgers University–New Brunswick, to canvass the literatures in political science, public administration, public policy, political economy, regulatory history, and administrative law. With the assistance of Stuart Address, we put together a comprehensive set of materials on "Law and Administrative Regula-tion." I am indebted to Charles Noble, now at California State University–Long Beach, for his critical reading of American political economy and regulatory politics.

With this background, I approached preparing the second edition of this book. I owe many thanks to the students at New York University who have taken on the challenge to revitalize the study of administrative law in political science. In particular, I want to thank Nina Berman, now a law student at Harvard, and Larry Shapiro, a law student at Columbia, who as undergraduates were exceptionally fine research as-sistants. Peter Brigham, an undergraduate at Lake Forest College, also provided valua-ble assistance in the last instance, for which much thanks. Two graduate students, Kelley Bevans and Daniel Ward, who is now an assistant professor of political science at Rice University, helped analyze data on regulatory litigation and helped me identify future issues for the field.

Lief and I are fortunate that Albert Matheny, who helped improve the first edition, gave us critical feedback on the book and commented on the second edition as well. Martin Shapiro, from the University of California–Berkeley, also provided extremely useful and engaging suggestions for the manuscript. He has been influential in our thinking about the politics of administrative law; we vividly remember him at several academic conferences arguing that statutory law and regulatory politics are vitally im-portant but badly neglected arenas for studying jurisprudence and American politics. His insights about administrative jurisprudence, courts and agencies, and regulation have guided my own research on lawyers, legal ideology, and the constitution of the administrative state. John Brigham, University of Massachusetts–Amherst, also contributed to my thinking about an administrative law text. We share a life together and often teach administrative law in the same semester, so this topic is ever present in our relationship. Indeed, John's notion of what makes an administrative law text lively or deadly became an important standard for what to include in this edition.

Finally, we thank the series of editors who steered this book through the shark-infested seas of unregulated corporate buy-outs: John Covell, then at Little, Brown, who was followed by Richard Welna, Director of Advanced and Scholarly Publishing at Scott, Foresman, who was in turn followed by Lauren Silverman, Catherine Woods, Michael Weinstein, and the editorial staff at HarperCollins. We value their assistance and the superb production work under pressure by the PC&F staff in Hudson, N.H. In the end, of course, Lief and I assume responsibility for the text, but all of these people helped us interpret what an administrative law and politics text could be, and we gratefully acknowledge all these interpretive sources.

C.B.H.

PART I

The Rule of Law In Public Administration

CHAPTER 1

Why Administrative Law Matters

This book introduces you to one of the most important, exciting, and controversial fields of American politics: administrative law. Administrative law is society's "official" way of choosing how bureaucratic government should and should not make the important decisions that affect us all. At every level of government in the United States, from the small town to the federal, most day-to-day governmental decisions are enforced, and many are made, by public administrators. We live under regimes staffed largely by these unelected officials whom we call, sometimes pejoratively, *bureaucrats.* The United States political system has since its creation, however, taken seriously the idea that ours is a government of laws, not of men. Therefore legal rules and procedures play a key role in governing the work of these bureaucrats. Administrative law should matter to all citizens because it affects how public administrators tax us, regulate the safety of our environment, and touch many other aspects of our lives.

Administrative law has political consequences for all citizens, but it has even more immediate consequences for people who deal with government on a daily basis. Students of business know they will contend in their professional lives with much governmental control of their efforts. They want to know what protections the law affords them in this process. Students who now work or plan to work in public careers have an equally pragmatic reason for studying administrative law. They need a road map to help them find their way within the maze of rules and procedures they may confront on the job. This book teaches both the practical aspects of administrative law and the important political theories that underlie them.

The themes raised in this book touch central problems in American politics—how we came to have our present political system, how that system may fail to achieve the ends we expect of it, and what we may be able to do about such failures. Here, in nutshell form, are the five principal themes of this book. The first three, discussed in this chapter, set the stage for studying administrative law. Chapter 2 more fully explores the fourth and fifth.

Five Themes

1. The growth of government by public administrators is the most important legal and political innovation. The control of government by bureaucrats has existed in varying degrees in nearly all organized political systems. Some ancient cultures— Imperial Rome and some Chinese dynasties—developed surprisingly extensive

bureaucracies in order to assert political control over large territories.[1] Modern bureaucratic government has been shaped not so much by the drive to control territory as by the perspective that the free market economic system cannot meet important social needs. Administrative power grew to offset the tremendous economic, social, and political power that another form of organization—large business enterprises—accumulated in the last century. The voting farmers, workers, and consumers who felt oppressed by the power of big business demanded this.

2. Today the effects of administrative government influence us literally every moment of our lives. The character of administrative regulation, as well at its scope, is critical for understanding the development of the modern state.

3. Bureaucratic government has provided no utopian cure for the shortcomings of free enterprise. It has built-in tendencies that can lead it to treat individuals unfairly and to produce arbitrary and unjustifiable policies.

4. Administrative law seeks to reduce the tendencies toward arbitrariness and unfairness in bureaucratic government. It defines, for example, the procedures a bureaucracy must follow before it can revoke a business license. Administrative law is part of a political culture that values placing controls on the use of power, thus keeping the use of power within democratic boundaries.

5. Administrative law is a relatively new and open-ended field of law. This book reviews the key issues in the formation of administrative law. We also consider the political controversies that underlie its development and impact on American politics.

The remainder of this chapter elaborates the first three stage-setting themes. The last two themes will introduce administrative law itself in chapter 2.

Business and Government: A Brief History of the Origins of the Modern Administrative State

Political leaders from the beginning of recorded history have controlled their subjects through rules and government enforcement of rules. Most aspects of life have been regulated at some time in history—some have a history of regulation that begins in ancient times and continues to this century. For example, regulation of people who operate ferry boats can be traced back to 1900 B.C. In 1901, archeologists discovered ancient stone inscriptions now known as the Code of Hammurabi, king of Babylon. The code, a record of the legal rulings the king had made during his reign, contained 280 entries, carefully organized by subject matter. Twenty-five sections regulated a variety of professionals, among whom were ferrymen. Similarly, in the eighteenth century, one of the Maryland state legislature's first statutes authorized the state's county judges to set the maximum prices those ferrying passengers and cargo across the state's as yet unbridged waterways could charge. In 1838 Congress, after one too many explosions of steamboat boilers, created an agency to inspect steamboats for safety. Today, if you travel across northwestern Washington state, you will to cross Puget Sound by a state-operated ferry.

[1] See Thomas Metzger, *The Internal Organization of the Ch'ing Bureaucracy* (Cambridge, Mass.: Harvard University Press, 1973).

If a phenomenon—here the governmental control of the ferry business—occurs throughout human history, good reasons for it must exist. Public safety is one obvious reason. Another reason that applies to ancient Babylon, eighteenth-century Baltimore, and twentieth-century Bremerton, Washington, is perhaps less obvious: Once a society begins to follow the principle of division of labor, some people will gain control of natural monopolies. The person who controls the land where people find it safe to cross a river, or the person who has obtained the privilege of ferrying people, for a fee, across it along this route possesses a natural monopoly. He may charge not merely costs plus reasonable profit. He can charge whatever the customer is willing to pay, which may be much more. Farmers in ancient and modern times alike resent losing part of the value of their crop to such a monopolist, and they complain to their king or their government when they believe someone gouges them. The ferrying business, in other words, is an ancient example of a natural monopoly and hence of a free market failure.

But why should powerful kings listen to ordinary citizens? To honor the claims of such citizens often means ruling against the interests of the wealthy and powerful. What political advantage does a king gain by siding with the powerless? How can we explain the existence of regulation in the public interest? This is one of the great and complex question of politics, and one to which we can point out the beginnings of an answer: Some rulers are truly altruistic. Perhaps more frequently, rulers maintain their popularity in order to deter those who might try to take their throne from them by force. Furthermore, rulers throughout history have had to build and maintain the power to fight—to defend territory against outsiders at the very least and wage effective territorial conquests at best. History rather clearly indicates that rulers, while they may win battles, do not win wars when the bulk of the citizenry resists them or stops caring about the outcome. Thucydides's history of the losses of Athens to Sparta teaches this lesson. So does the United States defeat in Vietnam. To maintain political popularity and military strength, rulers must please not just the minority, those with wealth and power, but also the less wealthy majority that makes a political base and on whose morale the war effort depends.

Government throughout history has tried to balance the interests of those with power and those without it. Today we use words like *liberty, equality,* and *individual dignity* in our discussions of public policy. We want to believe that government serves all social interests. These values are indeed noble, but we must accept that governments honor them partly in self-defense, and we must remember that government's tendency in the long run is to please and to support, rather than obstruct, the interests of those who possess the most resources.

Administrative Government in the United States

Recall the Maryland statute just mentioned that authorized county judges to regulate ferry charges. Why would judges rather than administrators perform such tasks? This question has all of hindsight's blessings. We have a systematic sense of separation of functions today, but this separation has not always been so neat.

In the case of nearly every major change in government, politics, and society, no person or political body actually plans the change. (For well over one hundred years of English history, for example, it literally took an act of a special committee of

Parliament to get a divorce. When Henry VIII couldn't get a divorce from the Pope, he "authorized" Parliament to give him one. This event set a precedent the inertia of which lasted long after the absurdity of this procedure became evident.) The early authors of regulations—Hammurabi or the Maryland legislature—had no grand scheme of administrative government plotted out for the future. In Maryland, county judges possessed the primary legal responsibility of governing their counties. The legislature simply added the setting of ferry rates to their list of duties.

The early efforts of Congress to create administrative agencies had no grand design either. The first Congress of 1789 faced two problems for which the expedient solution at the time rather obviously seemed an office or agency. The first problem was to establish a way of estimating the duties importers would owe on goods they obtained in foreign countries. The second task responded to the various claims for pensions filed by soldiers "wounded and disabled during the late war." Congress created two agencies to solve those problems presumably because each problem would last for the foreseeable future and because some expertise and consistency from case to case would be desirable. Both organizations continue to this day.

In one sense these early agencies had very modest aims. They resulted not from any monumental political battles between the wealthy and the common man, but rather from an ordinary need to serve widely accepted public intests. Notice also how both these tasks fit squarely into the age-old reasons for government, to protect "us" (domestic producers, in this case) against "them" (foreign competition) and to encourage, in the case of veterans' claims, the willingness to fight.

The expansion of administrative government in the United States since 1789 did not follow anyone's plan. One relatively minor contemporary indication of this fact is that the various names of government offices—*Agency, Board, Commission, Administration, Bureau,* and so forth—tell you absolutely nothing about the office to which they attach.

Understanding the growth of administrative government, particularly in the twentieth century, requires review of some economic history. The producer of, say, Flemish harpsichords in Antwerp in the seventeenth century would have belonged to a guild. The agreements and customs of the guild controlled most aspects of the harpsichord trade: who could work, how many units per year they could produce, prices, wages, and the like. The introduction of so-called free competition would only upset this balance.

By the end of the eighteenth century, however, the concept of free and unlimited competition had risen from something devilish to something holy. In no small part because of Adam Smith's widely read *The Wealth of Nations* (1776), people in power began to undo self-imposed restrictions on who could produce how many of which goods. Freedom to compete was also the freedom to specialize, and in specializing and dividing labor lay the key to increasing the productivity of labor.

This idea seemed particularly benign in America, where the losers in the competitive game could presumably "go west" rather than starve. *Laissez faire,* the older French equivalent of the modern campaign slogan *get the government off our backs,* ruled so that the major nineteenth-century manufacturing, banking, and transportation businesses operated with tremendous freedom from either governmental or guild-imposed regulations. If anything, by the last half of the century government actively promoted business. Goverment promotion of business and protection of private property rights is itself a form of regulation, although we do not commonly use the term regulation in this sense. Laissez faire supports open competition among capitalists over government control of the economy, but it also relies on the state to protect private property rights and to enforce private business agreements such as contracts. Even Adam Smith recognized that the state played an important role in policing and maintaining order *for* the "free market."

Business bought some of this support with outright bribes. Standard Oil, a joke of the times put it, did everything to the Ohio legislature except refine it. Yet even without bribes the government would have assisted railroad and the lumber and cattle interests with huge grants of land. It would have maintained high tariffs, an anticompetitive policy disguised as promoting competition. Local police and the National Guard supported management with physical force in the 1892 Homestead steel strike. In 1894 the Pullman Company, bypassing a more progressive state government in Illinois, went straight to President Cleveland, who sent in the Army to break up the Pullman Strike.

For the bulk of the century, these forces converged to produce a remarkably unrestrained economy: mushrooming industrial technology, climaxing in the electrification of America; tremendously abundant natural resources easily exploited by well-capitalized large corporations; a thoroughly pro-business attitude by government; and a theory of laissez faire to call upon for support.

Well before the end of the century, however, this burst of economic freedom, this exception to the more usual course of economic history, began to die. The more successful businesses engaged in powerful domination of the less successful. And when economic panics (recessions or depressions we would call them today) struck, as they have throughout economic history, even more monopolizing occurred as investors created trusts to restore the blessed protection of the guilds.

Before the end of the century this unrestrained power had begun to impose such crushing costs on the average citizen that democratic politics inevitably sought to check it. Here, for example, is the farmer's point of view in 1891:

> Farmers are passing through the "valley and shadow of death"; farming as a business is profitless; values of farm products have fallen 50 per cent since the great war, and farm values have depreciated 25 to 50 per cent during the last ten years; farmers are overwhelmed with debts secured by mortgages on their homes, unable in many instances to pay even the interest as it falls due, and unable to renew the loans because securities are weakening by reason of the general depression; many farmers are losing their homes under this dreadful blight, and the mortgage mill still grinds. We are in the hands of a merciless power; the people's homes are at stake. . . .
>
> From this array of testimony the reader need have no difficulty in determining for himself "how we got here." The hand of the money changer is upon us. Money dictates our financial policy; money controls the business of the country; money is despoiling the people. . . . These men of Wall Street . . . hold the bonds of nearly every

state, county, city and township in the Union; every railroad owes them more than it is worth. Corners in grain and other products of toil are the legitimate fruits of Wall Street methods. Every trust and combine made to rob the people had its origin in the example of Wall Street dealers. . . . This dangerous power which money gives is fast undermining the liberties of the people. It now has the control of nearly half their homes, and is reaching out its clutching hands for the rest. This is the power we have to deal with.[2]

After the close of the Civil War, government was caught between popular cries like Mr. Peffer's and the appeal of the theory of free competition. The wealthy and influential supporters of free competition gained further strength because laissez faire appeared to fit so neatly into Darwin's theory of evolution. Herbert Spencer's *Social Statics* seemed to many to prove the necessity of free competition scientifically. (Indeed the term *survival of the fittest* was first Spencer's, later appropriated by Darwin.[3])

The logic of Social Darwinism suffers from a terminal defect, however. The laws of supply and demand produce the greatest good for the greatest number only when laborers, farmers, businessmen, and financiers can easily and quickly enter any market which promises them a better return than they currently get. It works only in the absence of monopolies. The lawyers, railroadmen, industrialists, and bankers who busily constructed trusts and monopolies defended their right to eliminate competition by invoking the rhetoric of free enterprise itself! It is surprising how few people appreciated the inconsistency at the time.

Caught in this ideological squeeze, state and federal governments wriggled inconclusively for decades before breaking free of the unworkable ideology. Between 1870 and 1874 four midwestern states, responding to strong pressure from their voting farmers, passed laws—the "Granger" laws—regulating the prices railroads, warehouses, and grain elevators could charge. In 1877 the United States Supreme Court upheld the constitutionality of these laws,[4] but within a decade the Court began to shift gears. Any time a state attempted to regulate charges for freight traveling through more than one state, the Court struck it down on the grounds that only Congress had constitutional power to do so. While its motives were ideological, the Court's move actually made economic sense, since a multitude of inconsistent state regulations was practically unworkable for something as complex as interstate railroad traffic.

In 1886 the Supreme Court held state regulation of interstate railroad traffic unconstitutional. Congress in 1887 responded by creating the Interstate Commerce Commission (ICC), the first modern regulatory agency. The Interstate Commerce Act prohibited a variety of discriminatory and unfair pricing practices. It required railroads to make their rates public and report them to the five-person agency. It required that rates be "reasonable and just," but did not grant to the ICC power to set railroad rates in so many words. The ICC was granted this power in 1906.

---

[2]From W. A. Peffer, *The Farmer's Side* (New York: D. Appleton & Co., 1891), 42 ff.

[3]John C. Greene, *The Death of Adam* (New York: Mentor, 1961), 295.

[4]*Munn v. Illinois*, 94 U.S. 113 (1876), *infra* 81.

This is unfortunate because by the end of the century the laissez faire philosophy dominated the political values of the justices of the Supreme Court. Having told the states that only Congress could regulate interstate rail rates, they then announced that Congress hadn't.[5] When the ICC issued a cease and desist order requiring railroads to lower rates, the railroads refused. The ICC possessed no enforcement power of its own, so it had to go to the courts seeking a judicially enforceable order. The courts did not cooperate. Of the first sixteen cases to reach the Supreme Court, the railroads won fifteen. In 1890 Congress passed the Sherman Antitrust Act with virtually no party opposition. The Supreme Court promptly ruled that it didn't apply to the oil or steel or sugar or any of the manufacturing monopolies because manufacturing was not part of the "commerce" Congress had constitutional power to control.

Why Modern Bureaucracy?

Why, given our modern understanding, was the Supreme Court wrong? What short-comings in free markets did the Court blindly fail to appreciate? Markets contain within them forces that push toward collusion, toward eliminating or reducing competition, toward monopoly. The conditions of the economists' perfect market—many buyers and sellers, ability to enter and exit a market rapidly, and complete information about market conditions available at all times to each buyer and seller—do not in fact occur very often. The trade in farm products through futures trading is often cited as an example of something close to a perfect market, but neither entering and leaving the business itself nor purchasing and selling farm land and machinery are rapid or easy. Former Oklahoma Senator Henry Bellmon reported in April of 1982 that he lost $100,000 in his cattle business in 1981. When the reporter asked why he didn't quit, he responded simply, "The reason you stay in farming is you can't get out."[6] As we know, farm prices fluctuate widely, often with such potentially ruinous consequences for farmers that the United States government has administered policies designed to control farm prices for the better part of this century.

The key to understanding the shortcomings of free markets lies in the fact that "free" markets do not necessarily possess the characteristics of perfect markets. A free market is simply a private market, an unregulated market. The real-world imperfections of markets lead some competitors to gain strength relative to others. Once a firm holds a position of market dominance it can then wield its market power to further increase its share, often in co-operative collusion with other businesses. This much the economic history of the post-Civil War period clearly teaches.

Other market shortcomings also deserve an explanation. Because free markets seem in economic history to go through boom and bust business cycles, modern government takes administrative steps to smooth the cycles out. Most modern central banking regulations, to say nothing of other monetary and fiscal policies, exist for this purpose. Furthermore, free markets have no mechanism that requires producers of goods to pay for indirect costs of production such as the costs imposed by air and water pollution. There is no incentive to control pollution because producers can sell a product for less if they do not have to recover pollution control costs as part of the selling

[5] *Cincinnati, New Orleans and Texas Pacific Railway Co. v. ICC*, 162 U.S. 184 (1896).

[6] The "Today" Show, National Broadcasting Company, 9 April 1982.

price of their products. Hence the creation of the Environmental Protection Agency (EPA).

Even when we imagine markets without tendencies to monopolize and production techniques that do not impose significant and unrecovered indirect costs, we still can identify evils that may call for regulation. To name the most obvious, people have a tendency to cheat. Sellers in medieval markets were tempted to use false weights. Promoters of new corporate schemes tend to inflate the optimistic side of the new venture and minimize its risks when they try to convince people to buy stock in the company. Hence the existence of the Securities and Exchange Commission (SEC). Government, in short, remains with us always because we are not angels.

None of these descriptions of free market shortcomings should surprise a reader with some economic background. Two other, and deeper, dimensions to the free market problem, however, may not be so obvious or familiar. First, in the United States' case, the administrative process plays such a major role because of increasing technological complexity. We live surrounded by very dangerous things—elevators, cars, airplanes, industrial wastes and chemical products, radioactivity, and recombinant DNA. To be sure, our lives are more secure than were the lives of those who lived and died before the advent of modern medicine. The point is that centuries ago people perceived many of the sources of insecurity to rest in the hands of the gods. People who view their lives theologically would more likely support the church than lobby to create regulatory agencies. Today people believe that, while they cannot control the safety of the things around them, somebody else—experts—can, and this explains much of the support for new governmental programs and agencies.

The second deeper dimension to the market problem is political. Markets do not fail or succeed in the abstract. Like most anything else in life, failure and success exist only in relation to standards. The standard by which the political culture of the United States judges the effectiveness of free markets is whether they augment or diminish *democracy*. Note the small *d*. In the past century American society has increasingly accepted the validity of the claims of average citizens, of workers, women, blacks, the poor, and other classes previously excluded from active political life. The spread of the franchise to these classes has increased the responsiveness of government to their claims, and these groups most keenly feel the effects of all of the free market's evils. Welfare programs, public education, and consumer protection all seek to promote the interests of those who feel the exploitative effects of business entreprenurial efforts most directly. The labor movement and the agencies like the National Labor Relations Board (NLRB) and state worker compensation commissions that support the labor movement fit the same category. In short, our commitment to equality of opportunity, coupled with an electorate containing many voters whose self-interest supports programs and candidates that favor those who cannot help themselves, has created a standard of free markets which makes their failures stand out in stronger relief than ever before. Administrative law matters because it is inextricably tied to the process we have chosen to realize our democratic dreams.

It took the first forty years of this century for the political process, with the courts very much at the rear, to work free of the impasse between economic fact and free enterprise ideology. The final move started with Theodore Roosevelt's presidency, during which Congress gave the ICC the specific power to regulate rates it had lacked. A year later, in 1907, Congress created the second major national regulatory agency, the Food and Drug Administration (FDA). The move ended only as World War II ended the Great Depression. Breaking the logjam has released a flow of new administrative agencies. In 1982 President Reagan urged a shift from national to state regulatory power, but there is little reason to believe that the amount of bureaucratic power in government will dramatically lessen, even if its locus shifts.

On the surface this history seems a fairly simple story. Powerful government—by kings, by the church, and occasionally by bureaucracies as in Rome and China—has been the norm during the development of civilization throughout the world. Laissez faire flourished only when an educated and industrious people seemed able to combine abundant natural resources with new technologies and new corporate business forms to accumulate capital and thus produce unlimited wealth without creating problems requiring governmental solutions. The problems appeared in due course, and government predictably reasserted its usual control, this time propelled by truly democratic forces.

But this history does not yet fully account for the creation of such a large bureaucracy. Why could the three traditional branches of government not handle the job? The Congress is not structured to do so. Members of Congress are essentially ombudspeople who try to help constituents with problems. When the problems seem serious enough, Congress passes law dealing with them. These functions don't leave any time for processing large volumes of routine claims, nor for elected officials is there much payoff for doing so. State legislatures, most of which still meet only a few weeks per year, have much less capacity to administer than does Congress.

The executive branch, of course, does contain the large majority of administrative employees, people who work in the regular chain of command in a department headed by a cabinet official. But Congress has often worried that partisan presidential politics and the tremendous presidential powers to exploit the office could seep into regulation of sensitive areas like transportation and communications. Besides, presidents come and go quite frequently, and with them their cabinet appointees. Coping with technologically complex problems needs continuing expertise and leadership.

Why not, then, leave the problems in the hands of the courts? Many state and all federal judges serve for life. Legislatures can create more judgeships any time they wish. Yet for a mix of reasons judges do not make good administrators. We have already seen how, at the very time the need for regulation became clear to the politicians at all levels, the courts resisted. Moreover, our judicial system, unlike the French legal system in which judges have played a strong regulatory role, works in ways that do not suit regulation well. Our judicial system specializes in resolving disputes between people or organizations *fairly*. It stresses the requirement that judges remain aloof and impartial. The laws of evidence strictly prohibit judges and juries from considering much potentially useful information. Our idea of "due process of law" drastically limits the way judges can communicate with the parties involved. The judge cannot call someone on the phone from his chambers and ask for the missing information in the case. Most important, judges cannot initiate investigations. They can constitutionally act only when injured parties bring cases to them, in a truly adversary format. The mechanics of our common law system require people with the best of legal claims to invest considerable money in litigation that often takes years to complete. The farmer, nickle-

and-dimed to death by high railroad rates, was in no position to gain judicial help even if the courts had been more sympathetic. Finally, courts cannot effectively cope with sudden dramatic jumps in the volume of work. In the 1967 Detroit riot and in the Washington, D.C., antiwar protests of the early seventies, the criminal courts practically broke down. The volume of administrative problems is so unpredictable, and the nature of abuses so potentially complex, that a static body of judges unable to specialize can deal neither efficiently nor effectively with regulatory problems.

Consider by contrast the administrative capacity that something as simple as a family or a small sorority needs to solve problems. Even simple problem-solving groups must be able to specialize, to divide labor, to manage limited resources by a budget, and to set priorities accordingly. Their members do not want to bog down in formalities of evidence. They want to be able to meet, haggle, compromise, experiment with a policy and quickly reject it if it fails. The communications network in any effective problem-solving group must not squelch feedback to policymakers from the field.

In other words, despite the curses leveled at "faceless bureaucracies" in political speeches, bureaucratic organizations have the characteristics that modern government requires. They have *continuity* that outlasts the political two- and four-year cycles. And unlike legislatures they have *memories* and the capacity to apply information from past experiences to new situations. Unlike courts, agencies routinely *divide labor* into more efficient specialities. They work, as courts do not and legislatures only partially do, with fairly fixed budgetary limits which require *priority setting and judicious compromising.* Finally, unlike courts, they are *proactive.* They have the *capacity to take sides,* to accept a mission, and to battle in the political arena to complete the mission successfully. Consider how necessary these administrative qualities are to the pursuit of consumer product safety, an area in which the free market has not performed very well.

In 1970 a temporary fact-finding body, the National Commission on Product Safety, reported to Congress some chilling facts about accidental deaths. Over 30,000 people are killed and over a half-million are injured annually from accidents around the home. At least 150,000 are seriously cut by broken glass alone, principally in windows and doors. Congress concluded from this report that this problem required a publicly funded administrative solution.

To cope with the problem of product safety, an organization must have the authority to initiate investigations to develop a clear idea of the greatest sources of actual harm around the home. It would need power to initiate specific investigations of suspicious products like rotary lawnmowers, not merely to show that they are dangerous, but also to devise the least costly design changes to reduce the danger. A governing agency needs the flexibility to negotiate and make some compromises with manufacturers if it is to accommodate competing interests satisfactorily. At the same time, however, it must develop a staff sufficiently independent from, yet familiar with, the businesses regulated to decide whether the information is reliable when provided by an industry presumably reluctant to be regulated.

Administrative government, like private business, exists to accomplish results. Both need the resources to do it. The legal system and the judicial process, on the other hand, exist primarily to preserve fairness. Fairness and efficiency, or getting on with the job, often collide with each other. This, as we have seen, is the main reason courts cannot assume the administrative burden directly.

The political debates over regulation are not simple either. It is important not to reduce the differences of opinion about regulation into pro and con positions toward government control of the economy. In addition, debates over regulation concern the provision of government benefits or entitlements. Administrative law therefore indirectly but powerfully shapes the role of government regulation of business and the scope and nature of the welfare state. The historical record shows that a multiplicity of interests demanded regulation at the turn of the century, and regulation has served conflicting sets of interests ever since. The following essay by Thomas K. McCraw, a historian, has become classic reading on this point for students of administrative politics. McCraw's survey of the literature on regulation in history, economics, political science, and law identifies competing understandings of regulation and emphasizes two models of regulation in the twentieth century: the public interest model and the capture model. Neither model entirely opposes government regulation, rather each provides political justifications for a particular theory of government regulation.

Regulation in America: A Review Article

Thomas K. McCraw
Business History Review 49 (1975): 159

With accelerating momentum over the last quarter-century, the subject of economic regulation by state and federal commissions has undergone rigorous reinterpretation. Although the process of revision is far from mature, studies in each relevant discipline—history, political science, law, and especially economics—have begun to reshape the terms of discussion and to advance alternative models of regulatory behavior. In so doing, they have questioned not only some long-held views of business-government relations, but also associated themes such as the nature and results of Progressive and New Deal reforms, the wisdom and efficacy of planned interference with market forces, and the character of the American polity itself.

Certain difficulties still block the formation of a satisfactory new synthesis. For one thing, the scope of "regulation" defies precise definition, since every economic activity is regulated in some degree.* Commissions of various types exist in all fifty states and throughout the federal establishment, but some have

little in common with others besides the presence of "board" or "commission" in their titles. Then too, regulation properly conceived includes structurally different (commissionless) but functionally similar roles played by institutions like the Antitrust Division of the Department of Justice and the price support apparatus of the Department of Agriculture. It also includes intra-industry regulatory mechanisms such as trade associations, rate bureaus, and price leadership systems. This essay will address only the commission aspects of regulation, beginning with two widely known but troublesome concepts or images: the "public interest" notion, and the recently dominant "capture" thesis. . . .

Public Interest

The "public interest" seems an unusually vague construct, indefinable and analytically counterproductive. Part of the problem comes from its multiple meanings and evolving redefinitions over time. In the nineteenth century, "public interest" enterprises had social overhead functions, such as banking, transportation, and several other industries later called "public utilities." Some of these enterprises combined great economic power with a propensity toward corruption, and they required regulation for the protection of potential victims. Others, notably railroads, tended toward "natural monopoly" and needed a surrogate for the lost discipline of the market. More recently,

---

*Even public utility regulation raises definitional issues. See James W. McKie, "Regulation and the Free Market: The Problem of Boundaries," *Bell Journal of Economics and Management Science,* I (Spring, 1970), 6–26.

still other industries, such as broadcasting and air transport, appeared to need regulation as an escape from chaotic or destabilizing competition, which injured not only themselves, but the public as well.

American law reflected these economic premises. Beginning in the nineteenth century and culminating in the *Nebbia* decision of 1934, the law marked off certain types of enterprises as "affected with a public interest" and therefore subject to a strong application of police power. . . .

In the political sense, insofar as it can be distinct from the legal or economic one, "public interest" has been roughly analogous to such phrases as "public good," and "common good," or "general welfare," expressing in the eighteenth and nineteenth centuries a conviction that the societal whole is greater than the sum of its parts, and by the mid-twentieth an intuition that consumer interests are more vital than they used to be. In political science, the notion is related to the theory of public goods, and also to pluralist thought, for which it serves as a point of departure.*

In a confusing amalgam of these usages, "public interest" is a thread of continuity at the heart of regulatory ideology, from its origins down to the present. The phrase "the public good," for example, appeared in the statute that created the first important regulatory tribunal, the Massachusetts Board of Railroad Commissioners, established in 1869 and dominated throughout its first decade by Charles Francis Adams, Jr. In commissions, Adams, like many others, detected "a new phase of representative government," made necessary by the unprecedented complexities of industrial technology. Commissions would take as their guide "the interest of the community," which informed regulators would harmonize with the interests of businesses. Unlike legislatures, the new agencies would sit continuously, investigating and deliberating within a universe of dispassionate expertise. Shunning turmoil, they would deal with industrial problems not as dramatic episodes, but as evolving processes calling for careful, meticulously considered responses. Statistics would replace emotions as the basis for action.†

For seven decades afterward, from the 1870s through the New Deal, state and federal commission regulation proliferated over railroads, gas and electric utilities, radio and television broadcasting, truck and air transport, and a few other enterprises. Although the reasons for regulations varied according to the industry involved, the notion of the "public interest" continued to dominate the rhetoric of reformers, the utterances of presidents, and the decisions of commissioners. It served as an ideological glue binding together the quasi-legislative, quasi-executive, quasi-judicial duties of regulators. In the 1930s, the doctrine reached its rhetorical zenith, a paradoxical result in view of the New Deal's frequent recognition of and assistance to private interest groups. Legislative draftmen inserted the phrase repeatedly into the flood of regulatory law that created the Federal Communications Commission, the Securities and Exchange Commission, and the Civil Aeronautics Authority (now Board). The "public interest" occurs a dozen times in the Communications Act, a dozen and a half in the Securities Exchange Act, and more than two dozen in the Civil Aeronautics Act, as a guide for regulators and as a justification for the immense discretionary powers those statutes bestowed.‡

The New Deal also produced the outstanding theoretical elaboration of administrative regulation, written by James Macauley Landis, a draftsman of both

---

*The concept is examined at length in Glendon Schubert, *The Public Interest* (Glencoe, Ill., 1960); Richard E. Flathman, *The Public Interest: An Essay Concerning the Normative Discourse of Politics* (New York, 1966); Carl J. Friedrich, ed., *The Public Interest* (Nomos V, New York, 1962); and Virginia Held, *The Public Interest and Individual Interests* (New York, 1970).

†Massachusetts *Acts and Resolves*, 1869, Chapter 408, Section 4, p. 701; Charles Francis Adams, Jr., "Boston, I," *North American Review*, CVI (January, 1868), 18, 25; Adams, "Railroad Inflation," *North American Review*, CVIII (January, 1869), 158, 163–164.

‡A typical declaration of the principle came from Commissioner Joseph B. Eastman of the ICC, who wrote to his colleagues in 1931: "For a long time I have quarreled with the idea that in a complaint case involving freight rates this Commission is merely a jury to decide between the parties upon the basis of the particular facts which they happen to bring to our attention in that case. The Commission is much more than that; it is an expert tribunal with a definite responsibility for the railroad rate structure of the country and its proper adjustment in the general public interest." ICC Docket No. 22876, May 4, 1931, Eastman Papers, Robert Frost Library, Amherst College, Amherst, Massachusetts.

the Securities Act and the Securities and Exchange Act. Pupil and friend of Felix Frankfurter, commissioner of the FTC and the SEC (and, later, dean of the Harvard Law School and member of the CAB), Landis was one of the brightest men of his time. In his Storrs Lectures at Yale, published in 1938 as *The Administrative Process*, he delivered the most eloquent celebration of commission regulation ever written. Recognizing the ambiguity of the "public interest," Landis nonetheless affirmed the validity and efficacy of broad administrative discretion founded on that doctrine.*

The "Capture" Image

Significantly, Landis devoted much of his analysis to a defense of regulation, for the idea had long since encountered critical attack. Deriving from many different sources and premises, this critique resolved into an alternative image of regulation at once more tough-minded, easily grasped, and above all more descriptive of what seemed to be going on within the regulatory agencies.

Early skeptics had questioned just how independent the regulatory machinery was likely to be, or should be. For one thing, the appointment of expert, nonpartisan regulators (or even bipartisian commissions) and their removal from the normal political process seemed a step toward elitism, away from the nation's democratic traditions. For another, genuine independence might be unsustainable against presidents or governors who wished to interfere with scientific deliberation, or thwart it through the appointment of cronies and hacks. Even more likely, considering what usually went on inside the lobbies of legislatures, regulated corporations could direct their potent economic influence as readily toward regulators as toward other public officials. These arguments, all related to experience as well as to deductive notions of "capture," persisted as a running debate throughout the Progressive Era. In 1925, President Calvin Coolidge symbolically crystallized the "capture" theme by appointing to the Federal Trade Commission a man (William E. Humphrey) who brought

a 3–2 majority against what most old progressives conceived as the "public interest." The ensuing despair brought loud protest, together with calls for the FTC's abolition from some of its erstwhile friends.[†]

The New Deal temporarily quieted criticism of this sort. Franklin D. Roosevelt appointed aggressive regulators like Landis and William O. Douglas, and attempted to undo history by firing Humphrey. Thus, during the thirties, intellectually respectable criticism of regulation came from other sources, many of them based on theoretical objections that held it to be "a headless fourth branch of government," unresponsive to executive leadership. It was to this kind of attack, rooted more in political science than in evidence of sellout, that Landis replied when he wrote *The Administrative Process*.[‡]

. . . Over the next two decades, observers noted that the CAB and FCC in particular seemed to follow doctrines that equated the "public interest" with whatever the most powerful elements of the communications and airline industries wanted. By the 1950s, scholars such as Samuel P. Huntington and Louis L. Jaffe had begun to analyze the ties between regulator and regulated, and the inherent flaws in regulatory thought. In 1955, Marver H. Bernstein published a devastating book that synthesized into a coherent whole all the diverse objections that had gathered force since the New Deal. And in 1960, James M. Landis, in a stunning turnaround, catalogued the breakdown of the regulatory system he himself had celebrated twenty-two years before.[§]

[†]G. Cullom Davis, "The Transformation of the Federal Trade Commission, 1914–1929," *Mississippi Valley Historical Review*, XLIX (December, 1962), 452 *ff.*

[‡]The Humphrey episode is examined in William E. Leuchtenburg, "The Case of the Contentious Commissioner: Humphrey's Executor v. U.S.," in Harold M. Hyman and Leonard W. Levy, eds., *Freedom and Reform: Essays in Honor of Henry Steele Commager* (New York, 1967), 276–312. The focus of Landis's attention is evident in *The Administrative Process*, 4.

[§]Huntington, "The Marasmus of the ICC: The Commission, the Railroads, and the Public Interest," *Yale Law Journal*, LXI (April, 1952), 467–509; Jaffe, "The Effective Limits of the Administrative Process: A Reevaluation," *Harvard Law Review*, LXVII (May, 1954), 1105–1135; Bernstein, *Regulating Business by Independent Commission* (Princeton, N.J., 1955); Landis, *Report on Regulatory Agencies to the President-Elect* (U.S., Senate, Committee on the Judiciary, 86th Cong., 2d sess., 1960).

---

*Landis, *The Administrative Process* (New Haven, Conn., 1938). On the "public interest," see especially 51–52.

By that time, the attack on regulation had become a staple of the broad re-evaluation of American institutions that began in the 1950s and reached maturity in the 1960s. Liberal reform as a whole underwent a searching critique and redefinition, its viability questioned by disillusioned analysts who looked beneath society's veneers and found the results of pluralist democracy ugly and repulsive. In a contest of prolonged national crisis and self-examination, the regulatory agencies remained prime targets. By the late 1960s, a common assumption held that the commissions, like so many American institutions, had sold out, that they had suffered "capture" by regulated interests, that the "public interest" had become a tragic joke.

Detail indictments quickly followed. Portraits of uniformly abysmal performance emerged from a series of immature, predictable, but incisive exposés published by the young associates of Ralph Nader. Less sensational but equally damning studies by other journalists and scholars suggested that however flawed the work of "Nader's Raiders" might be, their conclusions had merit. By the 1970s, the "public interest" as a credible standard for interpreting regulatory behavior had few defenders. In its place reigned the "capture" thesis, which was rapidly nearing the status of a truism, a cliché of both scholarship and popular perceptions. "If nearly a century of regulatory history tells us anything," observed economist Robert Heilbroner, "it is that the rules-making agencies of government are almost invariably captured by the industries which they are established to control."*

Historians and Regulation

Over much of the literature of "capture," one historian exerted a uniquely powerful influence.

Gabriel Kolko anticipated the crest of the thesis in each of his two books on regulation, *The Triumph of Conservatism* (1963), and *Railroads and Regulation* (1965). In Kolko's models, argued *a priori* and buttressed by impressive new evidence of the sort conventionally esteemed by historians, "capture" inhered in the American polity, because of the centrality of capitalist power. Thus, wrote Kolko, railroad men themselves "were the most important single advocates of federal regulation from 1877 to 1916." From the beginning, "the Interstate Commerce Commission entered into a condition of dependency on the railroads, and the railroads quickly begain relying on the Commission as a means of attaining their own ends." Even more startling, what was true of the railroads applied to American business in general: "Federal economic regulation was generally designed by the regulated interest to meet its own end, and not those of the public or the commonweal."†

Kolko's ideas failed to convince many of his colleagues. Some historians pointed out that he ignored contrary evidence and misunderstood basic economics; others argued that he fallaciously assumed a polarity between the public interest and private interests; still others asserted that even the selective evidence he did present, though useful, did not begin to sustain his thesis, in part because he often failed to distinguish what businessmen received from what they originally wanted.‡ Still, Kolko's books asked new, challenging questions, and neither the questions nor his evidence could be dismissed easily. . . . The Kolko model argued not only that "capture" inhered in the system from the outset, but also that the American political economy made the design and subsequent behavior of commissions inevitable, and therefore predictable. Such a theory had immense ap-

---

*Edward F. Cox, *et al., "The Nader Report" on the Federal Trade Commission* (New York, 1969), Robert Fellmeth, *The Interstate Commerce Omission* (New York, 1970); Mark J. Green, *The Closed Enterprise System* (New York, 1972); Green, ed., *The Monopoly Makers* (New York, 1973). Examples of additional critical literature include Louis M. Kohlmeier, Jr., *The Regulators: Watchdog Agencies and the Public Interest* (New York, 1969); and Paul W. MacAvoy, ed., *The Crisis of the Regulatory Commissions* (New York, 1970). The quotation is from Heilbroner, *et al., In the Name of Profit* (Garden City, N.Y., 1972), 239.

†Kolko, *Railroads and Regulation 1877-1916* (Princeton, N.J., 1965) 3, 233; Kolko, *The Triumph of Conservatism: A Reinterpretation of American History,* 1900–1916 (New York, 1963), 59.

‡A collection of Kolko criticism appears in Otis L. Graham, Jr., ed., *From Roosevelt to Roosevelt: American Politics and Diplomacy, 1901–1941* (New York, 1971), 70–109; see also Robert U. Harbeson, "*Railroads and Regulation, 1877–1916,* Conspiracy or Public Interest?" *Journal of Economic History,* XXVII (June, 1967), 230–242.

peal, the more so because it seemed a uniquely clear explanation of contemporary experience. Nor was the appeal confined to Kolko's ideological allies on the Left. His insistence that competition in the American economy was increasing at the turn of the twentieth century, and his implicit ideal of a decentralized society attracted admiration from many quarters, notably the "Chicago school" of free market economists.*

As "capture" became first an alternative to "public interest," then a cliché in its own right, questions arose about *its* validity. How could the Interstate Commerce Commission be simultaneously the captive of railroad, truck, and barge transporters, when these industries had overlapping markets and were partial competitors? In what sense was the Federal Power Commission the captive of the natural gas industry, whose field prices it regulated so stringently that production brought inadequate returns, leading to what critics called "regulation-induced shortages"?† How well did the "capture" thesis fit those few points of regulatory history where scholars had made detailed investigations? . . .

Benson's thesis was that . . . the origin of the ICC was a story of warring interest groups, no one of which represented the entire public or felt motivated by an ideology of the general welfare. Instead, economic men fought each other over the division of industrial spoils. Without regulation, the railroad magnates had the power to keep a disproportionate share for themselves, even during periods of instability within the industry. Benson's behavioral methodology, informed by pluralist theory from political science, cut

through the rhetoric of the period, and in the process demonstrated the inadequacy of both "public interest" and "capture" as models of the origins of national railroad regulation.‡

. . . In effect, [Albro Martin's] book [*Enterprise Denied*], together with a later article by Martin that clarified the controversy over pooling, totally inverted the thesis of Kolko's *Railroads and Regulation*. Whatever "capture" had occurred was the railroads by the ICC. Wherever Kolko had found "political capitalism" operating to the benefit of the industry, Martin discovered "archaic progressivism" undermining it. Where Kolko's implicit premise appeared to be the illegitimacy of the American polity, Martin's seemed to be the nonsense of regulatory meddling with a market system. . . . §

Taken as a whole, historical writing offers few clear patterns of regulatory behavior, except that it demonstrates the inadequacy of either "capture," the "public interest," or the two in tandem as satisfactory models. Most historians have emphasized the political aspects of regulation, with the one common conclusion that regulatory politics involved an intricate, complex struggle among intensely competitive interest groups, each using the machinery of the state whenever it could, to serve particularistic goals largely unrelated to "public interest" ideology except in the tactical sense.

Economists and Regulation

A continuing problem for both scholars and reformers has been the elusiveness of hard evidence concerning regulation's actual effects. Unlike their corporate counterparts, commissions issue no profit and

---

*Membership in the "Chicago school" is not a hard and fast category, but one important member is George J. Stigler . . . . Other Chicago-associated scholars apparently influenced by Kolko include Thomas G. Moore, *Freight Transportation Regulation: Surface Freight and the Interstate Commerce Commission* (Washington, D.C., 1972); and George W. Hilton, "The Consistency of the Interstate Commerce Act," *Journal of Law and Economics*, IX (October, 1966), 87 *ff*.

†This point is discussed briefly in James Q. Wilson, "The Dead Hand of Regulation," *The Public Interest*, XXV (Fall, 1971), 46–49; on the FPC, see Paul W. MacAvoy, "The Regulation-Induced Shortage of Natural Gas," *Journal of Law and Economics*, XIV (April, 1971), 167-199.

‡Benson, *Merchants, Farmers, and Railroads: Railroad Regulation and New York Politics*, 1850–1887 (Cambridge, Mass., 1955), 212, 245. An earlier work that included substantial analysis of nineteenth century state commissions in one area was Edward Chase Kirkland, *Men Cities and Transportation: A Study in New England History, 1820–1900* (2 vols., Cambridge, Mass., 1948). Benson's conclusion that railroad men supported regulation somewhat reluctantly was consistent with an earlier report by Thomas C. Cochran, in *Railroad Leaders 1845–1890: The Business Mind in Action* (Cambridge, Mass., 1953), 189–199.

§ Martin, *Enterprise Denied, passim*; Martin, "The Troubled Subject of Railroad Regulation in the Gilded Age—A Reappraisal," *Journal of American History*, LXI (September, 1974), 339–371.

loss statements telling in an instant whether the quarter or year has been good or bad. No regulatory agency lists its common stock on traders' exchanges, where a rise or fall might indicate success or failure. Nor do most commissioners, like elective politicians, face voters at regular intervals for endorsement or rejection. Consequently, the new attention that economists gave to regulation in the 1960s and 1970s had prodigious significance. In these studies, a "bottom line" appeared, purporting to provide quantitative assessments of regulation's impact.

Economists had long been interested in the subject. Institutional economics supplied some of the intellectual foundations of the commission movement, and prominent scholars like John R. Commons, William Z. Ripley, Balthasar H. Meyer, and Rexford G. Tugwell sometimes wrote regulatory laws, served on commissions or commission staffs, and made regulation an academic sub-discipline. By the 1930s, however, institutionalism had begun to wane, and the subsequent triumph of Keynesianism and macroeconomics inevitably made regulation a less exciting topic, prosaic in comparison with the glamour of fiscal policy, growth economics, and "fine tuning."

The studies emerging in the 1960s and 1970s grew less out of the old institutional tradition than from the intellectual revival of price theory, whose methods in themselves raised questions about the pricing functions exercised by state utility commissions and by Federal agencies such as the ICC, CAB, and Federal Power Commission. Adding a measure of ideology to the cold logic of price theory was the related work of scholars associated with the "Chicago school," whose near-worship of the market as allocator of resources led to a distaste for that very interference with market forces that lay at the heart of the commission movement. Irrespective of premises Left or Right, the explicit test for most economist was the performance of an industry under regulation. The collective conclusion, much more decisive than those of the empirically-oriented historians, held that regulation was an expensive failure. In a harsh summary verdict, one influential economist wrote in 1963: "What the regulatory commissions are trying to do is difficult to discover; what effect these commissions

actually have is, to a large extent, unknown; when it can be discovered, it is often absurd."*

The ICC, the oldest Federal commission, which had weathered innumerable storms and had by the 1930s attained a uniquely high reputation, was now found guilty of enormously costly errors. Its policies of minimum rate regulation, its reluctance to allow market forces to select optimal modes for particular freights, its custodial preservation of obsolete services, were ill serving the industries concerned and making a mockery of the "public interest." By the 1970s, "the immediate cost to the economy of such regulation-induced inefficiencies in surface freight transport is estimated at $4 billion to $10 billion a year." . . . †

Within the states, public utility commissions seemed to pursue unwise policies toward the electric power industry. One influential hypothesis held that

---

*Ronald H. Coase, "Comment," *American Economic Review*, LIV (May, 1964), 194. The rapid rise of interest in regulation among economists may be traced through two relatively new journals, both devoted largely to regulatory topics: the *Journal of Law and Economics*, and the *Bell Journal of Economics and Management Science*. A third indication is the large project begun in the late 1960s by the Brookings Institution, which resulted in a number of books on regulation, many of which are cited below.

†The quotation is from John R. Meyer and Alexander L. Morton, "A Better Way to Run the Railroads," *Harvard Business Review*, LII (July–August, 1974), 143, citing an unpublished paper by Thomas G. Moore. Moore's views are elaborated also in a book that conveniently surveys the literature of its subject: *Freight Transportation Regulation: Surface Freight and the Interstate Commerce Commission* (Washington, D.C., 1972). Important studies include John R. Meyer, Merton J. Peck, John Stenason, and Charles Zwick, *The Economics of Competition in the Transportation Industries* (Cambridge, Mass., 1959); Ann F. Friedlaender, *The Dilemma of Freight Transport Regulation* (Washington, D.C., 1969); George Wilson, *Essays on Some Unsettled Questions in the Economics of Transportation* (Bloomington, Ind., 1962); Wilson, "The Effect of Rate Regulation on Resource Allocation in Transportation," *American Economic Review*, LIV (May, 1964), 160–171; and Richard N. Farmer, "The Case for Unregulated Truck Transportation," *Journal of Farm Economics*, XLVI (May, 1964), 398–409. An interesting attempt to apply theory to early railroad experience is Paul W. MacAvoy, *The Economic Effects of Regulation: The Trunk-Line Railroad Cartels and the Interstate Commerce Commission Before 1900* (Cambridge, Mass., 1965).

regulation had no serious effect at all.* In an equally challenging argument, two scholars theorized that utilities tend to overcapitalize, and consequently to operate at outputs other than the optimal. This excessive-capitalization theory encouraged a host of spinoff studies, and gave its originators a type of immortality by incorporating their names into the phenomenon they described: "the Averch-Johnson effect." Still other scholars discovered additional errors common to state utility commissions.†

Economists tended to be less critical of those commissions with few or no pricing powers, but they hardly ignored them altogether. Scattered throughout the literature were indictments of the Federal Communications Commission, the Securities and Exchange Commission, state insurance commissions, and others. Sometimes regulation itself was held to inhibit technological innovation, a grievous charge to lay at the door of a uniquely American institution.‡

The distinctive contributions of the economists were their theoretically-based methodology, their quantification of regulatory inefficiencies, and their ability to predict probable effects of hypothetical changes in commission policy. Partly because their inquiries were typically less holistic than those of the historians, they were better able to keep a rigorous focus, and to specify precisely what it was they were try to show. On the other hand, they paid less attention to historical sequence and factual detail. Seldom did they attempt the kind of combined cultural and economic analysis so fruitful in the work of historians such as Ellis W. Hawley and Richard Hofstadter.§

A few economists did theorize about the entire regulatory process. One ambitious statement came from George J. Stigler, a leading member of the "Chicago school," who propounded a rudimentary model of regulation from its origins, through enactment, and into operation. Unhappy with assumptions that the "public interest" emerged automatically from regulation, Stigler showed equal impatience with the "capture" thesis: "This criticism seems to me exactly as appropriate as a criticism of the Great Atlantic and Pacific Tea Company for selling groceries, or as a criticism of a politician for currying popular support." In some respects, Stigler's was the Kolko model updated. Whatever "capture" had occurred was not so much of the commissions as it was of prior political power, which expressed itself through the creation of a regulatory mechanism. The new apparatus did not necessarily take the form of a commission, but could be an import quota system or tariff schedule. The virtue of Stigler's argument was its recognition that the regulatory process goes beyond purely economic

---

*George J. Stigler and Claire Friedland, "What Can Regulators Regulate? The Case of Electricity," *Journal of Law and Economics*, V (October, 1962), 1–16; see also Harold Demsetz, "Why Regulate Utilities?" *Journal of Law and Economics*, XI (April, 1968), 55–65. An enlightening discussion of the evolution of utility pricing theories is R. H. Coase, "The Theory of Public Utility Pricing and Its Application," *Bell Journal of Economics and Management Science*, I (Spring, 1970), 113–128. Elaborations of this theme may be found in any of several standard textbooks on public utility economics, one of the best of which is Alfred E. Kahn, *The Economics of Regulation* (2 vols., New York, 1970, 1971).

†Harvey Averch and L. L. Johnson, "Behavior of the Firm Under Regulatory Constraint," *American Economic Review*, LII (December, 1962), 1053-1069; discussions of the "A J effect" are summarized in William J. Baumol and Alvin K. Klevorick, "Input Choices and Rate-of-Return Regulation: An Overview of the Discussion," *Bell Journal of Economics and Management Science*, I (Autumn, 1970), 162–190.

‡The following are examples of recent scholarship on these topics: on the FCC, Roger G. Noll, Merton J. Peck, and John J. McGowan, *Economic Aspects of Television Regulation* (Washington, D.C., 1973); R. H. Coase, "The Federal Communications Commission," *Journal of Law and Economics*, II (October, 1959), 1–40; on technological aspects, William M. Capron, ed., *Technological Change in Regulated Industries* (Washington, D.C., 1971); on one aspect of SEC regulation, Jeffrey F. Jaffe, "The Effect of Regulation Changes on Insider Trading," *Bell Journal of Economics and Management Science*, V (Spring, 1974), 93–121; on state insurance commissions, Paul L. Joskow, "Car-

tels, Competition and Regulation in the Property-Liability Insurance Industry," *Bell Journal of Economics and Management Science*, IV (Autumn, 1973), 375–427.

§Many of the institutionalists did approach problems in this way, as have a few more recent economists such as J. K. Galbraith. For the historians, see, in particular, Hawley, *The New Deal and the Problem of Monopoly: A Study in Economic Ambivalence* (Princeton, N.J., 1966); and Hofstadter, "What Happened to the Antitrust Movement? Notes on the Evolution of an American Creed," in Earl F. Cheit, ed., *The Business Establishment* (New York, 1964), 113–151.

phenomena, that "the problem of regulation is the problem of discovering when and why an industry (or other group of like-minded people) is able to use the state for its purposes, or is singled out by the state to be used for alien purposes."*

Regulation in the Literature of Political Science and Law

An appropriate source of answers to Stigler's question would appear to be political science and law. As was the case in economics, the contributions from scholars in each of these two disciplines outnumbered those of historians, a logical circumstance considering that regulation is barely a century old, that it remains controversial, and that the commissions' embrace of legislative, executive, and judicial roles within a single institution raised theoretical and practical issues of keen interest to lawyers and students of government.

Although the characteristic approaches of the two disciplines were not identical, each one emphasized matters of procedure, responsibility, and equity. Where the distinctive method of historians was empirical, and of economists a theory-oriented testing of market efficiency, that of political scientists and lawyers centered on due process, legitimacy, and reform. The resulting scholarship fell into two broad categories. The first included a number of quasi-histories, written within a generation of the establishment of particular commissions and directed toward prescriptions for improvement as well as toward analysis. A second category focused on elaborations or critiques of interest group politics in America, and included books addressing the questions of "public interest" and "capture." This second category fitted into the pluralist versus anti-pluralist debate within both political science and law.

Three books on the Federal Trade Commission typified the first group, the prescriptive quasi-histories. In *The Federal Trade Commission: A Study in Administrative Law and Procedure*,[†] Gerard C. Henderson, a practicing lawyer, found the early FTC insufficiently judicial in its proceedings, sometimes guilty of unfairness, and ready to dissipate its energies in cases involving no broad public concern. Some of the same suggestions appeared in another study of the FTC, published in 1932 by Thomas C. Blaisdell.[‡] Anticipating much New Deal scholarship, Blaisdell found the commission's performance during the 1920s clearly unsatisfactory. The vague FTC Act implicitly identified competition *as* the "public interest," on the apparent assumption that competition in all cases promoted socially desirable results. Such a premise Blaisdell found controverted by American economic history. "Means were confused with ends," he wrote, in a comment significant not only for the FTC, but for other aspects of regulatory experience. . . .

In 1962, Henry J. Friendly updated these views, in a brief but important book entitled *The Federal Administrative Agencies: The Need for Better Definition of Standards*. Ending with a prescriptive chapter typical of regulatory scholarship, Friendly sought salvation through the creation of "a body of substantive law." Delineating the ways in which procedural delay denied justice, Friendly showed how due process carried to extremes could actually thwart the "public interest." Even so, he rejected the remedy of heavy reliance on presidential control over commissions recommended in the Landis report of 1960, and also in the extensive work of Emmette S. Redford, a leading figure among scholars of regulation within political science.[§] Displaying a faith in regulation consistent

---

*Stigler, "The Theory of Economic Regulation," *Bell Journal of Economics and Management Science*, II (Spring, 1971), 3–21. See also Stigler, "The Process of Economic Regulation," *The Antitrust Bulletin*, XVII (Spring, 1972), 207–235. A few other economists have attempted interdisciplinary approaches. See, for example, Roger G. Noll, "The Behavior of Regulatory Agencies," *Review of Social Economy*, XXIX (March, 1971), 15–19, and Paul L. Joskow, "Pricing Decisions of Regulated Firms: A Behavioral Approach," *Bell Journal of Economics and Management Science*, IV (Spring, 1973), 118–140.

†New Haven, Conn., 1924

‡Blaisdell, *The Federal Trade Commission: An Experiment in the Control of Business* (New York, 1932).

§Friendly, *The Federal Administrative Agencies: The Need for Better Definition of Standards* (Cambridge, Mass., 1962). Friendly was a Federal judge at the time. His book heavily footnoted, provided a convenient guide to the legal literature on administrative procedure, a topic I have only touched on in this discussion. Representative of the voluminous publications of Emmette S. Redford are *Administration of National Economic Control* (New York, 1952); *American Government and the Economy* (New York, 1965), and *The Regulatory Process: With Illustrations from Commercial Aviation* (Austin, Texas 1969).

with the book's dedication to Felix Frankfurter, a pioneer of legal scholarship and teaching in the field, Friendly concluded with an affirmation: "The administrative agencies have become a vital part of the structure of American government. Nothing is accomplished by merely negative criticism or by petulant proposals to abolish them."*

Such feelings echoed the tradition of reform-oriented scholarship emblematic of the 1930. . . . At the close of this productive decade of scholarship, Robert E. Cushman completed the broadest of the prescriptive quasi-histories, *The Independent Regulatory Commissions*, a massive study that grew out of Cushman's work on Franklin D. Roosevelt's Committee on Administrative Management.† Packed with suggestions for improvement, Cushman's book also contained a cross-national analysis of the American and British experiences in regulating business—a useful methodology mostly neglected since.

A landmark of regulation in the scholarship of political science was Marver H. Bernstein's book of 1955, *Regulating Business by Independent Commission.*‡ In a survey of the entire field, Bernstein weighed arguments for and against regulation and came down heavily on the negative side. Generalizing freely, the author propounded a "life cycle" theory, which held that commissions typically pass through successive phases, beginning with exuberant prosecution of mandate but ending with ossification and debility. In the area of

documentation, the book left something to be desired, but Bernstein's arguments seemed so thoughtful, reasonable, and self-assured that they practically set the terms for the critical attack that followed in the 1960s.

This attack, as noted above, came largely from economists and from reformers like "Nader's Raiders," who made heavy use of the economic literature and of the theories and arguments summarized by Bernstein. In political science, the analysis tended to become much broader, and to address issues of which regulation formed only a part. Especially noteworthy was the work of the critics of pluralism. Dismayed by the results of "broker-state" government in the New Deal pattern, unpersuaded by celebratory assurances from the 1950s writers that countervailing pressures from diverse interest groups yielded a genuine "public interest," these scholars detailed the distance between the aims of Progressive and New Deal reformers on the one hand, and the contemporary reality of American life on the other.

Three books both exemplified and influenced the anti-pluralist persuasion: Henry S. Kariel's *The Decline of American Pluralism*, Grant McConnell's *Private Power and American Democracy*, and Theodore J. Lowi's *The End of Liberalism.*§ The three differed in many particulars but held unanimously that pluralist theory disguised the exploitation of public authority by private groups for privates purposes. The "public interest," far from emerging automatically from the inter-group struggle, was simply lost in the shuffle. Regulated industries were the clients of their commissions. The American Farm Bureau Federation, in alliance with other powerful groups, dictated policy to the Department of Agriculture. Big Labor won big gains for itself, but often ignored the rest of society. Meanwhile, the "public interest" led nobody's list of priorities.

"Capture," in other words, applied not just to commissions but to the entire American polity. The system had degenerated from an original dream of constitutional democracy and the general welfare to a hopelessly fragmented mélange of small,

---

*Friendly, *The Federal Administrative Agencies*, 175; one example of the influence of Friendly's views may be found in William L. Cary (a former chairman of the SEC), *Politics and the Regulatory Agencies* (New York, 1967).

†Cushman, *The Independent Regulatory Commissions* (New York, 1941). The Committee, known popularly as the "Brownlow Committee," after its Chairman, Louis Brownlow, was one of a long series of *ad hoc* groups studying regulation and organization in the Federal establishment. Subsequent studies produced the Hoover Commission Report (numbers 1 and 2), the Landis Report, and the Ash Council Report.

‡Princeton, N.J., 1955. In the mid-1950s, there was nothing like a consensus on regulation within political science. Bernstein's views may be contrasted with those of Redford, *Administration of National Economic Control* (note 38 above), and of Robert E. Lane, *The Regulation of Businessmen* (New Haven, Conn., 1954). See also the uncritical quasi-history by James E. Anderson, *The Emergence of the Modern Regulatory State* (Washington, D.C., 1962).

§In the order listed: Stanford, Cal., 1961; New York, 1966; and New York, 1969.

autonomous constituencies sensitive only to self-interest. The tragedy was that the government had lent its authority to these constituencies, piece by sovereign piece, and that the pluralist postulate of universal access to power had encountered the incontrovertible fact that such access depended on systematic, articulate, well-funded organization. Some groups could not meet these tests. Unorganized or, as in the case of the poor, unorganizable, they stayed out in the cold, away from the American banquet.*

The anti-pluralist indictment inspired a variety of responses, some of them holding that the legal order in the United States had always provided mechanisms to protect the weak and unorganized. As one scholar put it in 1972, "probably never before in our history has legal policy been so supportive of the rights of individuals and groups affected by administrative action to be heard and to influence the action taken." To some writers, the advent of public interest law—an institutional adaption to some of the problems identified by the anti-pluralists—represented a hopeful sign that the existing system might yet work, given adequate funding for public interest lawyers.† . . .

An Assessment

The collective findings in history, economics, political science, and law have been sufficient to establish a few broad conclusions:

1. Neither "public interest" nor "capture," nor the two in combination adequately characterize the American experience with regulation over the last century. Sometimes regulation materialized with the support or even initiative of the industry involved (as with broadcasting), sometimes with the reluctant assent (as with the ICC), and sometimes against the rigid opposition (as with the Granger commissions and the SEC). Commissions often came into existence with broad popular support, sometimes amid obvious public apathy, but never in the face of mass-based, articulate opposition.

2. Once established, commissions did respond readily to pressures from organized interest groups. Such groups included not only the regulated industry, but also that industry's market elements (shippers, for example, in the case of the ICC), and occasionally the industry's labor force. Whenever actual "capture" by one of these elements did occur, it followed patterns not peculiar to commissions but common to a whole range of bureaucratic interdependency between government agencies and organized interest groups, whether in labor, agriculture, defense, or other private interests able to use the power of the state for their own profit.

3. Regulation in American has been a multifunctional pursuit, a circumstance that has offered scholars a choice, when they generalize about the regulatory process as a whole, between extreme caution on the one had, and extreme likelihood of error on the other. Regulation is best understood as an institution capable of serving diverse, even contradictory ends, some economic, some political, some cultural. Regulatory experience over the last century suggests several major ends or functions:
   a. the function of disclosure and publicity
   b. the function of cartelization
   c. the function of containing monopoly or oligopoly
   d. the function of economic harmony among industries
   e. the function of promotion or advocacy
   f. the function of legitimizing parts of the capitalist order
   g. the function of consumer protection.

. . . The functions could overlap, as in early railroad regulation, when efforts to control rates through disclosure and publicity aimed at stabilization and

---

*The solutions offered by the anti-pluralist varied, and in each book, the diagnosis seemed superior to the prescription. Lowi proposed a return to basic constitutional principles and the promotion of "juridicial democracy." McConnell suggested the strengthening of mechanisms that permitted the entire people to act as one. Invigoration of broad constituencies would limit the scope of "capture," promote citizen participation, and give substantive content to the "public interest."

†Carl A. Auerbach, "Pluralism aand the Administrative Process," *The Annals*, CD (March, 1972), 1. On public interest lawyers, see Simon Lazarus, *The Genteel Populists* (New York, 1974), Chapter 10; Joseph C. Goulden, *The Superlawyers* (New York, 1972), Chapter 10; and Richard C. Leone, "Public Interest Advocacy and the Regulatory Process," *The Annals*, CD (March, 1972), 46–58.

economic harmony. More often than not, regulatory functions among different commissions, and sometimes even within the same agency, could conflict. . . .

Despite the danger of internal inconsistency, regulators have identified whichever function they wished to emphasize at the moment with the "public interest." They could hardly have done otherwise. Almost nobody ever declares his hostility to the "public interest." Yet such rhetoric could go beyond either symbol or cant. . . . The "public interest," therefore, however defined, cannot remain static, even within the mind of an individual. Time makes it dynamic; and historians specialize in change over time. . . .

Multiple approaches are [also] essential for the realization of the major dividend available from the study of regulation: the illumination of that shadowy zone where public and private endeavors met and merged, where regulator and regulated experienced a confusion of identity and assumed each others' roles. Seldom in American history did the goals of private groups form a perfect identity with those of the rest of society, but seldom a perfect antithesis, either. Instead, sets of goals overlapped, now finely, now amply. Within the zones of overlap, private groups plausibly claimed service to society, and "capture" coexisted in fleeting calm with "public interest." Fleeting, because each zone suffered a double indeterminacy: who made the decisions, the public official or the businessman? And what were the precise boundaries of the zone? Constantly shifting from internal and external pressures, the zones formed arenas whose only permanent qualities were confusion, controversy, and uncertainty. Did a given action by a businessman or regulator denote the presence of "public interest," or of "capture"? Did it deserve congratulation, or condemnation? Prize, or prosecution?

The theme is ancient, of course, a continuous thread of American history back at least to the time of Hamilton. Writing twenty years ago, Robert A. Lively described "the incorrigible willingness of American public officials to seek the public good through private negotiations," and offered as a leading exhibit the early corporate enterprises promoted by the states.* In this sense, "capture" and "public interest" derived from a single source, and have been intertwined ever since. . . .

*Lively, "The American System: A Review Article," *Business History Review*, XXIX (March, 1955), 93.

An Overview of Theme One

The next section will give specific examples of modern regulatory government. Before turning there, one central point deserves repeating: The scope of public regulation has broadened, yet its emphasis today remains primarily where it was when the Congress founded the Interstate Commerce Commission a century ago. This emphasis focuses, now as then, on business economic power. Just as the ICC sought to offset the monopoly price-setting power of railroads, so today's Occupational Safety and Health Administration (OSHA) seeks to correct the business tendency to maintain unsafe work places, so today's Environmental Protection Agency (EPA) deals primarily with industrial pollution, both from factories and the automobiles and other machines factories produce, so today's Consumer Product Safety Commission (CPSC) seeks to force businesses to produce safer and more reliable products.

In comparing older regulations with newer kinds of regulation like OSHA and EPA, however, Alan Stone argues that the goals have changed somewhat.[7] Older regulation was premised on economic performance goals, such as price, costs, and profits, while post-New Deal regulation addresses intangible costs, such as pain and suffering—costs that Stone equates with social performance goals. The distinction between economic and social regulation captures the changing political orientations of the regulatory state.

[7] See Alan Stone, *Regulation and Its Alternatives* (Washington, D.C.: Congressional Quarterly Press, 1982).

While the distinction can be helpful, it is important not to overstate the difference between the two. We will see in later chapters how the contemporary debate over the use of a cost-benefit analysis in regulation is essentially a struggle over the weight that should be given to economic and social goals when regulating economic power.[8]

The Broad Reach of Administrative Action and Power

Just as Charles Dickens begins *A Christmas Carol* by telling his readers that they must believe that Marley was "dead as a doornail" in order to appreciate his story, you must believe in the tremendous reach and power of bureaucratic government in order to appreciate the importance of the study of administrative law. Here are just a few bits of data that document the twentieth-century administrative explosion.

- In 1930, 8 percent of the Gross National Product funded all national, state and local government, excepting only defense and foreign affairs. Today the figure is over 25 percent.
- At the end of the Korean War federal regulation limited itself primarily to fields such as: antitrust, finance, food and drug, labor relations, agriculture, transportation, and communication. Only twenty years later did a new set of agencies regulate a much wider spectrum of activity: energy, discrimination, environment, consumer protection, and so on—all this in addition to the even more costly non-regulatory functions of government: the postal service, social security, the national parks, and veterans' affairs.
- Between 1965 and 1975 alone, Congress created twenty-six new agencies.
- The federal bureaucracy now issues, approximately seven thousand rules and policy statements a year, two thousand of which legally bind the citizenry. By law, agencies must publish these actions in the *Federal Register,* which occupies more library shelf space than all the laws passed by Congress since it first met in 1789.
- Annually the Social Security Administration alone processes five million applications for social security benefits. Most of these raise no legal problems, yet the small fraction that does is twenty times greater in number than all the cases going to all the regular federal courts each year with the exception of bankruptcy cases.
- We now have approximately 576 regular federal trial judges,[9] but there are 1,075 federal administrative law judges,[10] 696 of whom work for the Social Security Administration.[11]
- Of the 186.3 million employed Americans, about 2.9 million work for the federal government, and over 14.4 million for state and local governments.[12]

[8] See Richard A. Harris and Sidney M. Milkis, *The Politics of Regulatory Change* (New York; Oxford University Press, 1989).

[9] This is the number of authorized U.S. district court judgeships according to the Federal Judicial Center, Washington, D.C., 1989.

[10] Administrative Law Judge Office, Washington, D.C., 1989.

[11] Ibid.

[12] *Monthly Labor Review*, February 1989 (Washington, D.C.: U.S. Department of Labor, Bureau of Labor Statistics).

How broad is the reach of bureaucratic government? Try this test. Think of all the ways government action affects the first hour of a typical person's day, during which we breathe, bathe, watch or listen to the morning news, eat a bowl of corn flakes, drive or take a bus somewhere. To us this first hour may seem as natural as the first hour of his day seemed to an American Indian five hundred years ago. Yet unlike the Indian's government, our government has by formal action regulated tehe quality of the air we breathe, the water we bathe in, the ingredients in our cereal, the labeling on the cereal box, the programming on radio and television, the prices of many of the things we consume, and so on. Often the government directly substitutes itself for private business, e.g., in selling clean water or running public hospitals. Americans swim in an ocean of publicly administered activities.

Illustrations

Two illustrations of the broad reach of bureaucratic power are the Federal Trade Commission and the Internal Revenue Service.

1. *The Federal Trade Commission*. The "FTC," created by Congress in 1914, carries the mandate to maintain free and fair competition in business. This book will reveal a good deal more of the FTC later because, after decades in which the agency actually did very little, the FTC has awakened in the last twenty years or so. Indeed, it has taken its job so seriously recently that since 1980 Congress has checked the FTC by vetoing some of its rules. Here is a *Consumer Reports* description of the FTC (March, 1980, p. 151):

> The Federal Trade Commission's job, assigned to it by Congress, is to step into the marketplace when necessary to keep consumers from being cheated. Congress laid the foundation of the FTC's authority in the original Federal Trade Commission Act of 1914, which declared "unfair methods of competition" to be unlawful. To make sure that relief from such methods would extend to consumers and not just injured businesses, the Wheeler-Lea Amendment, passed in 1938, added the words "unfair or deceptive acts or practices in commerce" to the Federal Trade Commission Act.
>
> Building on that mandate, Congress has steadily added to the agency's authority and workload over the years. Here are some things the FTC does to carry out Congressional mandates to aid consumers:
>
> - Prevent restraints of trade by business, such as price-fixing, boycotts, and anticompetitive mergers, all of which may raise prices to consumers.
> - Prevent unfair or deceptive advertising generally.
> - Specifically prohibit false or deceptive advertising for food, drugs, cosmetics, and medical devices.
> - Report on activities of the insurance industry in such areas as sales techniques, quality of information given to prospects, and value returned for each premium dollar.
> - Require that furs and clothing be accurately advertised and labeled.

- Require accurate quantitative and descriptive labeling of packaged items.
- Forbid mail-order firms to send unordered merchandise, then charge for it.
- Require lenders to give borrowers accurate and complete information about loan terms.
- Give consumers specific rights in correcting erroneous or disputed credit bills.
- Open up credit files to consumers so that misinformation can be challenged.
- Compel lessors of cars and other consumer goods to disclose leasing terms fully and accurately.
- Prohibit debt-collection agencies from harassing consumers.
- Enforce warranty standards.

You will see as the book proceeds, that agencies operate with many different procedures. The FTC's procedures are, however, typical enough to exhibit many of the terms and activities covered later. Here, therefore, is a brief and somewhat simplified description of that agency's procedures. One of the authors of this description, Professor Glen Robinson, has himself served as a commissioner of the Federal Communications Commission.

Federal Trade Commission Procedures

Robinson, Gellhorn, and Bruff
The Administrative Process
St. Paul: West Publishing Co., 1980, 440–442

The FTC's five members are appointed for seven-year terms which are staggered. Consequently, there is a continuing membership. The five commissioners must be politically balanced; that is, not more than three may be of the same political party. Most decisions are made by the agency as a body and, except for adjudicatory decisions and personnel or similarly sensitive matters, in public session. 5 U.S.C.A. § 552 (b) (open meetings requirement). The commissioners pass on all investigations at some point, on all complaints, on all settlements, and on all orders. Not all responsibilities are shared by the five commissioners, however. One commissioner is designated by the President as chairmain and serves in that capacity at the President's pleasure; the chairman is also principally

responsible for the administrative management of the agency.*

The internal organization of the Commission has been the subject of considerable study and controversy and has undergone frequent change. Currently, there are several administrative offices: general counsel, administrative law judges, policy planning, etc., to guide the administrative bureaucracy. Frequently these offices also exercise substantive roles. But the main substantive work of the FTC is developed by three operating bureaus: the Bureau of Consumer Protection (responsible for investigating and prosecuting false advertising and deceptive practices violations, guiding businessmen, educating the public, and preparing trade regulation rules); the Bureau of Competition (with similar responsibilities for antitrust enforce-

---

*In most agencies this internal administrative arrangement has worked tolerably well. This has not always been the case with the FTC, however, as when former chairman Paul Rand Dixon ignored the votes of three of his colleagues (and the abstention of the other) and filled vacant supervisory posts with "acting" appointees in order to circumvent their wishes.

ment); and the Bureau of Economics (responsible for preparing financial statistics, industry analysis, and economic evidence). In addition, the FTC maintains regional field offices in metropolitan areas around the country; they assist in preparing agency investigations and adjudications and also investigate and litigate actions with respect to local or regional trade practices.

While the discussion that follows is somewhat over-simplified, in the typical case the Commission's staff will receive a consumer or competitor complaint or determine after its own general inquiry to examine a particular practice. If the situation appears to warrant further action, an investigation is begun; the formality of the investigation varies, but it may involve the taking of testimony under oath before a staff attorney or the requesting of documents and reports under sections 6 and 9 of the FTC Act. Once the staff determines that it has sufficient facts to warrant action, it will seek Commission approval of a complaint, which will be assigned for hearing before an administrative law judge; the law judge will hear the case in much the same way that a case is tried before a judge in a typical trial court. After the hearing the law judge will prepare an initial decision which either party (the FTC staff attorney or the respondent) may

appeal to the commission. If it is not appealed, or if the Commission does not take the case on its own motion, the initial decision becomes the FTC's final order—and since no appeal was taken to the agency, it cannot be further questioned. If there is an appeal, the Commission will hear the matter as an appellate tribunal hears appeals from a trial court (except that the standard of "review" is much broader). If the FTC determines that a violation of law has occurred and that the case warrants, a cease and desist order will be issued. The order is usually not limited in time and may be enforced many years later. Most matters, however, are not taken to formal adjudication. The respondent will instead be given an informal opportunity to show that no violation has occurred or that a settlement and voluntary agreement to comply should be accepted. Similarly, if the legal question involves a widespread practice or there is no specific case before the Commission on which to consider the issue, the FTC may decide to rely on its rule-making powers, whereupon it will draft and announce a proposal, and after hearings may adopt a trade regulation rule. Such rules have the force of law and are enforced by penalty or civil redress proceeding as outlined above.

2. *The Internal Revenue Service.* The FTC is a so-called independent agency. Although the president appoints the five commissioners who compose it, the FTC does not operate within the direct chain of policy command headed by the president. It is in this sense independent, although as all agencies it feels the pulls and pressures of political life.[13] Other agencies do operate under the president within the more traditional executive departments, for example, the Department of the Treasury and the *Internal Revenue Service* (IRS), which operates within the Treasury, The IRS, as everyone knows, collects taxes, but the rules of the IRS also affect freedom of political speech and religion. Why? Because IRS regulations determine (a) whether an organization is not-for-profit, and thereby exempt from paying taxes, and (b) whether a citizen who contributes money to a cause can deduct the contribution from his or her taxes. IRS rules exempt schools, churches, charities, and the like from tax liability only if they spend no more than 20 percent of their budget (and never more than $500,000) on lobbying efforts designed to influence policy. Further, they may not "participate in or intervene in" election

[13]Beginning students of the administrative process often mistakenly assume that the "bureaucracy" is a monolithic branch of government immune from politics. Later sections of this book will show this is far from true. For a convincing proof that this is not so, see A. Lee Fritschler, *Smoking and Politics,* 2d ed. (Englewood Cliffs, N.J.: Prentice-Hall, Inc., 1975) and Theodore Lowi, *The End of Liberalism,* 2d ed. (New York: Norton & Co., 1979).

campaigns. They cannot endorse or evaluate candidates' records, even on matters that directly affect the organization's mission. But, particularly in the 1980 campaign year, churches claimed that the regulation prevented them from supporting certain causes. In Boston, the Roman Catholic Archbishop warned parishioners against voting for House candidates who supported abortions. The National Abortion Rights Action Committee in turn threatened to sue to challenge the tax-exempt status of the Catholic Church.[14]

These two examples of bureaucratic power, picked almost at random, could be multiplied well beyond the scope of this book. Figure 1.1 displays the simple number of main federal government agencies. It is awesome, but would be even more so if the chart included all state and local agencies as well.

There are three basic types of federal administrative agencies: (1) independent regulatory commissions; (2) agencies housed within a cabinet level department; and (3) agencies outside the formal structure of a cabinet department. Figure 1.2 shows the structure of one independent regulatory commission, the FTC. Following the creation of an independent commission by Congress, five or more commissioners are appointed by the president with the advice and consent of the Senate for staggered terms. One commissioner serves as the chair. Although commissions (e.g., FTC, NRC, FCC, SEC, EEOC, etc.) are technically within the executive branch of government, they can act more independent from presidential policy programs than officials in other types of agencies primarily because the president cannot remove commissioners without cause, whereas the president may remove heads of other agencies at his discretion. Figure 1.3 shows the structure of an agency, OSHA, that is within a cabinet level department, the Department of Labor. You will note that in addition to OSHA, the Department of Labor houses several other agencies, such as the Mine Safety and Health Administration, and Pension and Welfare Benefits Administration. Figure 1.4 shows the organization of the Environmental Protection Agency, an agency outside the formal structure of a cabinet department.

The Shortcomings of Regulatory Government

The third and final stage-setting theme discussed in this chapter explores and begins to explain what every reader already knows: administrative government has not satisfactorily resolved all of the problems created by modern, highly technological economies. Worse, some reasonably successful solutions have simultaneously created other problems of their own. For example, the Social Security system has successfully created a support system for millions of retired, disabled, and otherwise disadvantaged citizens. Yet the costs of the system, some argue, contributed substantially to huge projected budget deficits throughout the 1990s. Also the system lends itself to abuse by citizens who present false claims and by administrators who may withhold deserved benefits arbitrarily.

Some shortcomings in regulatory government will never disappear. Probably the most obvious of these results from inevitable economic change. An administrative program, structured and constrained by legislative mandates and its own goals and proce-

---

[14]"Churches, Politics, and the Tax Man," *Newsweek*, 6 October 1980, p. 46.

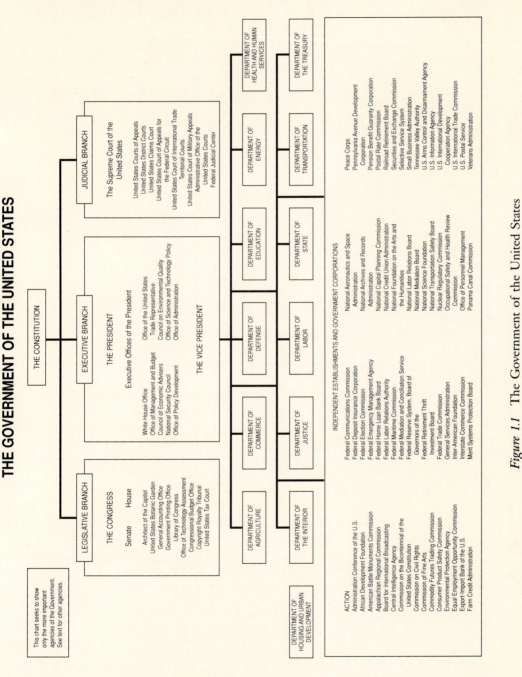

THE GOVERNMENT OF THE UNITED STATES

This chart seeks to show only the more important agencies of the Government. See text for other agencies.

THE CONSTITUTION

LEGISLATIVE BRANCH

THE CONGRESS

Senate | House

Architect of the Capitol
United States Botanic Garden
General Accounting Office
Government Printing Office
Library of Congress
Office of Technology Assessment
Congressional Budget Office
Copyright Royalty Tribunal
United States Tax Court

EXECUTIVE BRANCH

THE PRESIDENT

Executive Offices of the President

White House Office
Office of Management and Budget
Council of Economic Advisers
National Security Council
Office of Policy Development

Office of the United States
Trade Representative
Council on Environmental Quality
Office of Science and Technology Policy
Office of Administration

THE VICE PRESIDENT

JUDICIAL BRANCH

The Supreme Court of the United States

United States Courts of Appeals
United States District Courts
United States Claims Court
United States Court of Appeals for the Federal Circuit
United States Court of International Trade
Territorial Courts
United States Court of Military Appeals
Administrative Office of the United States Courts
Federal Judicial Center

DEPARTMENT OF AGRICULTURE

DEPARTMENT OF COMMERCE

DEPARTMENT OF DEFENSE

DEPARTMENT OF EDUCATION

DEPARTMENT OF ENERGY

DEPARTMENT OF HEALTH AND HUMAN SERVICES

DEPARTMENT OF HOUSING AND URBAN DEVELOPMENT

DEPARTMENT OF THE INTERIOR

DEPARTMENT OF JUSTICE

DEPARTMENT OF LABOR

DEPARTMENT OF STATE

DEPARTMENT OF TRANSPORTATION

DEPARTMENT OF THE TREASURY

INDEPENDENT ESTABLISHMENTS AND GOVERNMENT CORPORATIONS

ACTION
Administration Conference of the U.S.
African Development Foundation
American Battle Monuments Commission
Appalachian Regional Commission
Board for International Broadcasting
Central Intelligence Agency
Commission on the Bicentennial of the United States Constitution
Commission on Civil Rights
Commission of Fine Arts
Commodity Futures Trading Commission
Consumer Product Safety Commission
Environmental Protection Agency
Equal Employment Opportunity Commission
Export-Import Bank of the U.S.
Farm Credit Administration

Federal Communications Commission
Federal Deposit Insurance Corporation
Federal Election Commission
Federal Emergency Management Agency
Federal Home Loan Bank Board
Federal Labor Relations Authority
Federal Maritime Commission
Federal Mediation and Conciliation Service
Federal Reserve System, Board of Governors of the
Federal Retirement Thrift Investment Board
Federal Trade Commission
General Services Administration
Inter-American Foundation
Interstate Commerce Commission
Merit Systems Protection Board

National Aeronautics and Space Administration
National Archives and Records Administration
National Capital Planning Commission
National Credit Union Administration
National Foundation on the Arts and the Humanities
National Labor Relations Board
National Mediation Board
National Science Foundation
National Transportation Safety Board
Nuclear Regulatory Commission
Occupational Safety and Health Review Commission
Office of Personnel Management
Panama Canal Commission

Peace Corps
Pennsylvania Avenue Development Corporation
Pension Benefit Guaranty Corporation
Postal Rate Commission
Railroad Retirement Board
Securities and Exchange Commission
Selective Service System
Small Business Administration
Tennessee Valley Authority
U.S. Arms Control and Disarmament Agency
U.S. Information Agency
U.S. International Development Cooperation Agency
U.S. International Trade Commission
U.S. Postal Service
Veterans Administration

Figure 1.1 The Government of the United States

Source: The United States Government Manual 1988/89 (Washington, DC.: Government Printing Office, 1989), 21.

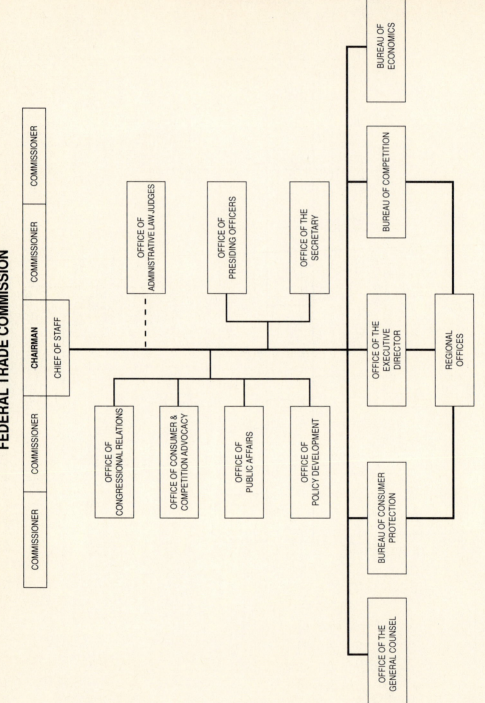

Figure 1.2   The Federal Trade Commission (FTC)

Source: The United States Government Manual 1988/89 (Washington, D.C.: Government Printing Office, 1989), 572.

DEPARTMENT OF LABOR

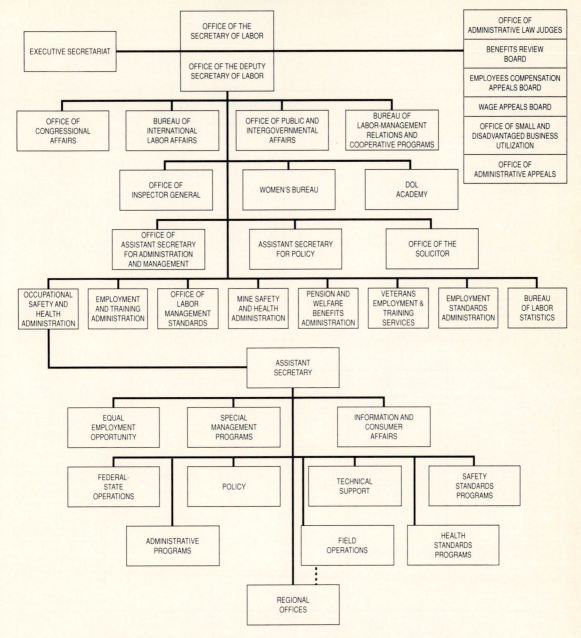

Figure 1.3   Cabinet Level Agency (OSHA in the Department of Labor)

Sources: The United States Government Manual 1988/89 (Washington, D.C.: Government Printing Office, 1989), 401, and *Federal Regulatory Directory*, 5th ed. (Washington, D.C.: Congressional Quarterly, Inc., 1988), 423.

ENVIRONMENTAL PROTECTION AGENCY

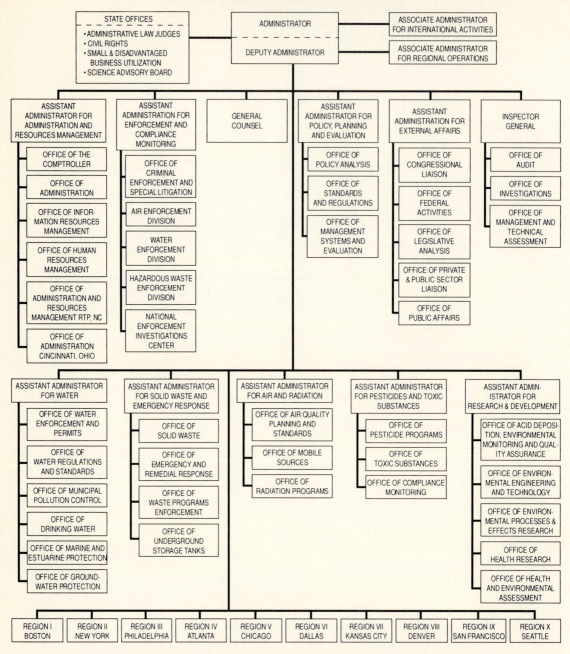

Figure 1.4   The Environmental Protection Agency (EPA)

Source: The United States Government Manual 1988/89 (Washington, D.C.: Government Printing Office, 1989), 526.

dures, does not automatically adjust to technological advances and changes in competition. The regulation of transportation began when railroads had a near monopoly on long-distance carrying of people and cargo. Many of the practices of transport regulation were carried over into the trucking and airline markets and retained there long after economists and businessmen realized that trucks, buses, trains, and airlines had created a much more competitive and self-regulating market than regulatory policy admitted. Only under President Carter in the late 1970s did serious deregulation of transportation begin.

The Dilemmas of Goal Attainment

Another and subtler inescapable shortcoming is the elusiveness of organizational goals. It may help to possess a mental picture of the objectives of administration, but it is essential to understand that goals are, far more often than not, the innocent-looking tip of a very extensive iceberg. It is tempting to draw on the American pragmatic tradition and expect government simply to figure out what needs doing and do it. In this view administration, either public or private, amounts to formulating goals, choosing the means that will achieve the goals, and then getting on with the job. But several harsh realities make that approach naive. The first harsh reality we may call the *level of goal formation* problem.

Promoting any good—the cleanliness of air, fair wages and healthy working conditions, the nutritional value of corn flakes, television programing that informs and entertains without corrupting—can constitute an administrative goal. So can the prevention of evils: blocking monopolistic mergers, deterring consumer fraud, minimizing traffic fatalities, and so forth. Conceived this way administrative policy goals are too numerous to count. Virtually every statute creating a federal or state administrative body sets forth, usually in flowery and imprecise language, the agency's mission.

Some analysts prefer to collapse all these goals into one goal: elected and appointed government officials alike should foster the public good. Unfortunately, people cannot agree what constitutes the public good or the "public interest," as discussed earlier by Thomas McCraw. Which serves the public good: building nuclear power plants to free ourselves from dependence on foreign energy sources? Or not building nuclear power plants to avoid both the risks of radiation damage and the tremendous expenses of such plants?

At this general level we encounter the second harsh reality. Goals stated broadly prevent us from seeing the trade-offs inherent in policy choices. A trade-off exists whenever people must sacrifice one good to attain another. Trade-offs contrast rather sharply with "good investments." A good investment of time or money raises the achievement of several goals simultaneously. For example, the devotion of athletic funds at a university to add seats to the football stadium may in the short term hurt the university's wrestling program or intramurals. However, if the university soon recovers the cost of construction and then uses the added revenue to increase support for unprofitable programs, no real trade-off occurs. But goods benefit in the long run. A trade-off, on the other hand, exists when one good is permanently lost, as in the trade-off between energy self-sufficiency and radiation safety. Thus one of the irksome things about goals is that they tend to fool us into thinking we live in a world without trade-offs, a world where we can have everything. In fact the useful administrators earn their pay because they must make difficult decisions about which good things we must sacrifice, and how much of them to sacrifice, in order to achieve other good things.

Goals also present themselves at different moral levels. Sometimes national security is not a controversial goal. Without giving it much thought we would nearly all agree that the United States fought for just causes in World War II. But did national security justify the steps taken by the West Coast military commander to, as it was said at the time, relocate Japanese-American *citizens* in something close to concentration camps? Did it justify U.S. intervention in Vietnam or Nicaragua? Stating goals does not in itself resolve disagreements about values. Goals are merely an expression of values.

Hugh Heclo, in his excellent descriptive study of middle- and upper-level federal administrators, lists the normative contradictions in government at the very beginning of his analysis. For Heclo the unresolvable tensions—between the norm of nonpartisanship and the norm of being responsive to citizen needs, between the obligation to behave in a legal and orderly fashion on one hand and to be creative and innovative on the other, and between the human instinct to be cooperative and loyal and at the same time not become corrupted—call for powerful leadership. His book describes how the current system fails to produce such leadership.[15] Jerry Mashaw notes similar normative contradictions among three administrative models: bureaucratic efficiency, professional judgment and fairness to clients and citizens.[16] Mashaw explains how the Social Security Administration's recent management efforts to limit the compensation awards of administrative law judges ran into resistance from the judges because management valued efficiency while the judges valued professional independence and fairness.

Consider now the human side of bureaucratic life. Our culture encourages us to develop and pursue our own personal goals, career advancement, good pay, and so forth. Much effort in any organization, be it a private corporation or an administrative agency, goes into keeping its workers happy by meeting as best it can their personal goals. Doing so not only consumes resources, it requires compromising some aspects of the organization's mission. For example, most prosecuting attorneys in our major population centers are recent graduates of law schools who seek trial experience. Because their superiors generally know this, they may not prevent some cases from going to trial even when the superior strongly suspects the case is too weak, in order to give the subordinate experience. Personnel training may undercut the value of fair prosecution.

Bureaucratic Pathologies

The psychological reality of the front-line human service agency or the school or a police department contains high levels of stress. Charles Goodsell's stimulating description of the reaction to stress in an Appalachian county welfare agency summarizes the point this way:

---

[15] Hugh Heclo, *A Government of Stangers* (Washington, D.C.: Brooking, 1977), 103 and 111.

[16] Jerry L. Mashaw, "Conflict and Compromise Among Models of Administrative Justice," *Duke Law Journal* 1981:181.

The concept of compression . . . refers to the stress of "heat" faced by service delivery workers. The manifestations of such stress are now being widely discussed around the country under the rubric of "burn-out." In the department studied perhaps a fifth of the workers exhibited symptoms associated with this syndrome, such as disillusionment, weariness, frustration, and demoralization.

When the subject of personal stress was explored in interviews with workers several factors surfaced. One universally identified by respondents is the activity known pejoratively as "paperwork." The completion of forms, the preparation of reports, and the arrangement for documentation involve an enormous amount of tedious clerical work, taking half or more of the worker's on-duty time (When inventoried, no less than 65 forms were found to be in use for financial assistance processing alone.)

A second origin of stress is clearly related, namely escalating caseloads. In recent years they have grown dramatically as a combined consequence of new programs, added accountability requirements, successful outreach activities, and only modest staff growth. Mandated deadlines for acting on benefit applications (ranging from 48 hours to 45 days) increase the pressure to produce. No overtime pay is available in the office to ease the time-bind. Low salaries generally (some receptionists and clerks are themsleves eligible for the Food Stamps they issue) offer little compensation for the pressures, and staff turnover is quite high.

To compound matters, some workers complain that in addition to enduring strains of time-crowded routine, they must live with the anxiety of being ready to face the unusual "incident." This is shouted verbal abuse at the office, tire slashings on home visits, or threatening phone calls at home. Drunks, armed men, and distraught or even deranged individuals must occasionally be dealt with. Personnel are cautioned to take no more chances than necessary, yet at the same time departmental norms forbid answering unpleasantness in kind—workers must simply "take it."[17]

Mismatches between economic and technological facts on the one hand and regulatory programs on the other exist. Compromise and negotiation among inconsistent organizational and individual goals and levels of attainment is one way of addressing the mismatch. Other shortcomings of administration may be susceptible to correction. Officials may choose ineffective managerial tactics for achieving goals. Legislatures may fail to provide enough funds for the most well-meaning of agencies to succeed. The following story illustrates both points all too well.

[17] Charles Goodsell, "Looking Once Again at Human Service Bureaucracy", *Journal of Politics* 43 (1981): 770, 771, footnotes omitted. For an excellent and disturbing book-length treatment of the problem, see Michael Lipsky, *Street Level Bureaucracy* (New York: Russell Sage, 1980).

In 1975, less than a hundred miles from Houston, Texas, construction began on the South Texas Nuclear Project. The Houston Lighting and Power Co. had hired the construction company of Brown and Root to construct a nuclear power plant by 1982 at a cost of $900 million. The cost overruns for this project were projected at several billion dollars; hence, like many other nuclear power plant projects, construction had to be suspended.

The construction of nuclear plants falls within the jurisdiction of the Nuclear Regulatory Commission (NRC) which, among many of its other duties, must insure that plants under construction actually meet the safety specification written into their designs. Bad welding of reinforcing bars or air bubbles in poured concrete restraining walls could cause a disaster.

How does the safety inspection system work? Very badly, it would seem. The NRC is so understaffed that its own personnel spend little time in the field performing on-site inspections. Therefore construction companies themselves actually hire and train and pay the people who do the day-to-day inspections. In the case of the South Texas Nuclear Project things went a little further. Here is an excerpt from an interview by George Crile, on assignment for CBS Television's "60 Minutes," of quality control inspector Dan Swayze, employee of Brown and Root, the prime contractor of the project, (Sunday, June 1, 1980);[18]

> *Swayze:* You can go down there in a few hours, and you can cite everything wrong with what they've done in a week. You're immediately surrounded by the superintendent, the general foreman, the foreman and the craft foreman for each individual craft participating in that pour.
>
> *Crile:* Well that's not intimidation, is it?
>
> *Swayze:* Well, when eight of them are huddled around you, and most of them are in pretty good shape, because they've been doing manual labor most of their lives, and they'd—well, what do you want me to say? Exactly what they say?
>
> *Crile:* Yes, Yeah.
>
> *Swayze:* Well, say "You son of a bitch, if you don't sign the bastard at eight o'clock, were going to kick your ass." Is that what you want? That's what they say . . .
>
> *Swayze:* It went from verbal, continuous harassment, verbal abuse. It finally reached a point in '77, in July, that we attempted to stop a pour for major deficiencies. They threatened to kill me. That night, they assaulted one of my inspectors. The next day—
>
> *Crile:* Physically assault a man?
>
> *Swayze:* Physically. Beat the hell out of him. Put him in the hospital for doing his job. The next day we took a vote. It was 100 percent. All the inspectors decided, "Obviously, they want us to do exactly nothing but fill paper out." We took a vote. We started filling out, and we did it for five months.

---

[18]"60 Minutes" excerpt © 1980 CBS Inc. All Rights Reserved. Reprinted by permission.

Crile: Are you saying for five months you did nothing?

Swayze: For five months we did no inspection whatsoever. We sat in
our office. We had radios. When they wanted a pour signed off,
we went down, the man assigned to that area went down, signed
the pour card, came back and played cards the rest of the day.

Crile: All the papers that bear your signature from that time are based
on—on fraudulent statements?

Swayze: Absolutely nothing. They are based on nothing.

Crile: How could you have done that?

Swayze: When you're hired to do a job, and they threaten to kill you,
and they start beating the hell out of the people that work for
you, what would you do?

On April 9, 1984, the NRC finally admitted officially that the independent self-
inspection procedure was deeply flawed. However, even before these facts came to
light an independent investigation of the Three Mile Island accident, initiated by the
NRC but headed by Mitchell Rogovin, a private Washington, D.C. attorney, had concluded:

We have found that the Nuclear Regulatory Commission itself is not
focused, organized or managed to meet today's needs. In our opinion
the commission is incapable, in its present configuration, of managing
a comprehensive national safety program for existing nuclear power
plants and those scheduled to come on line in the next few years adequate to ensure public health and safety.[19]

Note that the "fault" for this shortcoming does not necessarily lie with the NRC itself.
NRC funds are so limited that it may have had little alternative other than to adopt
the regulatory strategies illustrated by the South Texas fiasco.[20]

The final illustration of a bureaucratic shortcoming that need not inevitably occur
concerns the tendency of people in all sorts of settings, public and private, to advance
their self-interest at the expense of organizational needs. This reality can take the form
of outright bribery and other forms of corruption. Far more prevalent and perhaps
even more difficult to redress is the phenomenon of *agency capture* discussed in McCraw's
essay. In the process of governing, officials find themselves acting to protect or advance

[19]"Report on Nuclear Accident Holds Agency Is Unable to Insure Safety," *New York Times,* 25 January 1980,
p. A 13.

[20]Prior to the CBS exposure the NRC staff had begun to investigate the charges, which had come to its
attention when the intimidated inspectors complained to Congressman Gonzales of Texas. The NRC's investigation into the allegations concluded that the CBS charges were substantially correct, and that laxity on the part
of the existing NRC staff, not just understaffing, had contributed to the problem. The NRC did not halt all
construction. However, based on its own investigation, Houston Lighting and Power decided to terminate its
construction contract with Brown and Root. It has hired the Bechtel Corporation in its place. Construction
has therefore stopped. It is not certain that construction will ever resume. To get some further flavor of this
scandal, see "In the Matter of Houston Lighting and Power Company," *Nuclear Regulatory Commission Issuances*
12 (1980): 281.

the interests of those they govern. Capture differs from deliberate promotion, that is, when Congress by law authorizes an agency to protect and promote an industry as well as regulate it. The old Atomic Energy Commission operated under the mandate to promote the use of nuclear energy as well as to regulate it, a goal conflict that finally prompted the creation of the Nuclear Regulatory Commission that, underfunded though it was, did not suffer from a split administrative personality.

Capture occurs when agencies informally promote the very interests they are officially responsible for regulating. A Lee Fritschler's study, *Smoking and Politics*, describes why the FDA did not follow through on the surgeon general's determination that smoking correlated with a variety of illnesses this way:

> The Food and Drug Administration, the agency that the surgeon general suggested as the proper regulator of warning requirements, had demonstrated even less interest in the smoking and health issue that its sister agency, the PHS. The FDA's reluctance is due, according to Senator Neuberger's book, *Smoke Screen: Tobacco and the Public Welfare*, to a late Victorian episode in congressional politics. She claims that the item "tobacco" appeared in the 1890 edition of the *U.S. Pharmacopoeia*, an official listing of drugs published by the government. It did not appear in the 1905 or later editions, according to the senator, because the removal of tobacco from the *Pharmacopoeia* was the price that had to be paid to get the support of tobacco state legislators for the Food and Drug Act of 1906. The elimination of the word tobacco automatically removed the leaf from FDA supervision.
>
> The FDA was given what appeared to be another opportunity to concern itself with cigarette smoking when the Hazardous Substances Labeling Act was passed in 1960. It empowered the FDA to control the sale of substances which, among other things, had the capacity to produce illness to man through inhalation. Secretary Celebrezze suggested in a letter to the Senate that the act could be interpreted to cover cigarettes as "hazardous substances." In what had become characteristic behavior of HEW, however, the secretary went on to argue that it would be better to wait and let Congress amend the act to make it more explicit and thereby avoid controversy. Subsequently, Congress rejected such an amendment.
>
> The reluctance of the FDA could be traced to still other factors. During the early 1960s, the agency was having serious problems of its own. It suffered through some devastating investigations conducted by late Senator Estes Kefauver (D.-Tennessee). The hearings dealt with the pricing practices, safety, and monopoly aspects of the drug industry. One of the alarming revelations to emerge from the hearings was the extent to which the FDA was dominated and supported by that sector of the business community it was supposed to regulate, i.e., drug manufacturers and distributors. In what might have been simple

reflex action, the FDA found it easier to keep quit and follow Secretary Celebrezze's lead to continue to protect its good standing in the business community. The FDA found it expedient to ignore the cigarette health issue even though scientific indictments mounted in the early 1960s and other agencies began to take some action.[21]

Fritschler's fascinating study contrasts the FDA's refusal to tackle the tobacco health hazard with the willingness of the FTC to do so. It is remarkable how the differences in the effectiveness of agencies, including their susceptibility to capture, depend on the unique and often idiosyncratic combination of political forces, personalities, and leadership that characterize different agencies. To repeat a point made earlier, agencies may employ professional experts and Congress may label them "independent," but they are all deeply enmeshed in the political process.

Setting the Stage for the Study of Administrative Law

This chapter has emphasized the tremendous scope and power of administrative agencies of government. These agencies combine legislative, executive, and judicial functions. We ask and expect extraordinary accomplishments from modern government. We expect it to protect our personal safety. Obviously police and other law enforcement agencies do so, but so does the national defense establishment, the biggest single consumer of citizens' tax dollars. So do the Environmental Protection Agency, the Federal Aviation Agency (FAA), and the Occupational Safety and Health Administration. We expect government to assure social and economic justice, to protect smaller business efforts from the dominating power of larger ones, and to protect consumers, for whom the costs of gathering information are very high, against the tendency of businesses large and small to provide misleading information about their products. We expect welfare agencies to provide for the poor. We expect the Internal Revnue Service and state and local tax boards to collect tax money fairly. We expect the Federal Communications Commission (FCC) to allocate the limited number of bands in the spectrum of receivable radio waves equitably. We expect the National Science Foundation (NSF) to promote the acquisition of knowledge and the National Endowment for the Humanities (NEH) to promote the liberal arts. And on and on.

This chapter has also discussed the imperfections in the administrative process. These failings fall roughly into four categories. First, agencies charged with the task of protecting the general public by preventing certain monopolies from overcharging for their services have ended up promoting rather than regulating the same monopolies. Second, administrative decisions may be procedurally unfair. We shall meet an FTC chairman who gave speeches condemning a business while he sat in administrative judgment of that same business. Third, administration may be inefficient. And, fourth, we shall meet again the beleaguered NRC, which, despite the best of intentions and the most efficient possible use of its resources, still scares us because we fear it is ineffective.

[21]Fritschler, 34–35.

These imperfections as well as the others mentioned in this section are all embedded in a deeper political and legal structure that you will increasingly appreciate as you progress through this book. Agencies exist because, for a variety of reasons, legislatures delegate powers to administrative bodies for the purpose of creating and enforcing specific policies. However, politicians retain considerable influence in the bureaucratic process. Policy is often forged by interest groups, agencies, and legislators within the so-called iron triangle of compromise. Agencies often act cautiously, as the FDA did in response to growing evidence of the dangers of smoking. And agencies jockey for position among themselves for both authority and secure funding from year to year. Thus it is a mistake to assume that "bureaucracy" is a monolith, immune from political or legal influence. The real problem may arise not because agencies are relatively unresponsive to public claims, but because interest groups somtimes speak much louder than the public at large. You must judge by the end of this book the seriousness of the iron triangle's threat.

One final point. Eight years of the Reagan administration accelerated the trend toward *deregulation* which began in the late 1970s under the Democratic leadership of President Carter. The deregulation trend continues today with mixed implications. It is not clear whether deregulation relaxes administrative control in areas where goods and information in fact flow freely and competitively or whether deregulation policies have created new sets of regulations which privilege particular actors and interests in the "market place." The trend has already affected transportation and communications and is moving into energy and banking as well. Deregulation no doubt has changed the profile of administrative government.

In the United States, law plays a key role in determining both the process and substance of government. The concept that government must operate within legal limits is the core of our constitution itself, a document that structures and limits government and calls itself "the supreme law of the land." Administrative law matters because a system that adheres to the concept of the rule of law employs the courts and the constitutional and statutory principles courts enforce to check the shortcomings of government. Administrative law is not the only mechanism we possess for coping with the bureaucratic shortcomings this chapter has described, but it has become one of the most significant of those mechanisms. This is why administrative law matters. Now the stage is set to introduce administrative law. Chapter 2 proceeds to explain more precisely what administrative law and the rule of law mean and how they operate.

Exercises and Questions for Further Thought

1. Shortly after his inauguration, President Reagan sought to kill the Department of Energy's (DOE) proposed rules setting minimum standards for energy efficiency for home appliances including air-conditioning units. One argument advanced for doing so stated that the free market would solve the problem, i.e., that consumers would naturally buy the cheapest unit to operate over the long run. But officials of the Carrier Corporation, a well-known manufacturer of air-conditioning systems, argued that

every apartment house owner and every new home builder would have only an incentive to buy the lowest priced unit regardless of operating costs because the tenants or buyers, not the owners or builders, would pay the energy bills. What potential weakness in the free market system discussed above does this illustrate? What self-interested reasons might a corporation like Carrier have for supporting these rules? See "A Tale of Regulation," *Newsweek*, 2 March 1981, p. 31.

2. This chapter has pointed out that the free market economy model also depends on government to protect the interests of private property; hence it is wrong to contrast regulation against "free market" ideals. Regulation has different forms, some more proactive than others; social values about how government can best protect and create equality vary over time. Our perception of equality may change (i.e., people accept less inequality than before). Technology is a motive force in this change in perception, and is itself a major source of social problems. What characteristics of high technology might prevent free market choices or might limit the utility of the traditional private lawsuit for damages in tort from protecting citizens adequately?

3. Comment on the following statement:

> It is sometimes argued that we can solve collective problems not by
> regulating them or punishing them but simply charging fees for them.
> But there exists an inevitable conflict between private individual au-
> tonomy and the efficiency of economic systems. No matter how
> many fees the government might impose upon companies for the du-
> bious privilege of dumping pollutants in a river, a pricing-system
> method of social control will not induce companies to buy and oper-
> ate oxygenation equipment to revive a stream biologically killed from
> the polluting of prior years.

More generally, reflect on the nature of direct and indirect costs. Suppose it costs a manufacturer X dollars to combine raw materials and labor to produce a given quantity of steel. Then suppose that it would cost Y additional dollars per unit to dispose, properly and safely, of the by-products of this processing. Is it proper to say that the "costs of production" include both X and Y? Would an unregulated or underregulated industry necessarily pay X and Y and recover them through a unit sales price that reflects both? If not, who pays for the improper disposal of wastes and byproducts? If someone or some group pays the cost, it is clear the regulation forcing the consumers of steel to pay, in the main, transfers the cost from one to another segment of society. Is this alteration in who pays, then, the return we get on the dollars spent for waste regulation? Is it worth the regulatory cost? How can one calculate this worth? Is this not primarily a normative, hence political, question?

4. Despite the current move to deregulate the economy, many monopolies show no signs of disappearing. The medical profession continues to dominate the health industry, for example. Where business domination endures, we should expect such agencies as the FTC to continue seeking to offset monopolistic tendencies. Thus in 1979 the FTC issued an order preventing the American Medical Association (AMA) from interfering with doctors who choose to advertise their services to the public. As

you consider the regulatory goal of government to promote markets that are both competitive and equitable, try to formulate policy for the leasing of channels on space communications satellites. Do these satellites, operated by a handful of large private companies, represent a natural monopoly? If so, should the FCC allow companies like RCA to charge only their costs plus a reasonable return, perhaps at a first-come, first-served basis? Or should it permit RCA to charge what the market will bear? See, "FCC, in Shift, Permits RCA Unit to Lease Satellite Space at Flat Fee Based on Market," *Wall Street Journal,* 26 March 1982, p.2

5. This chapter has stressed the linkage between monopolistic power and the growth of government, but you should not neglect the reality that the profit motive in business leads some people, in both competitive and noncompetitive businesses, to cheat. How, for example, should government respond, if it all, to the case of the "University of Central Arizona," a two-person mail order house selling doctoral degree certificates to anyone who wanted to buy one? Is it significant that some people, especially in public education, increase their potential for job advancement if they can claim a graduate degree? What other areas of modern fraud can you think of?

6. This chapter has introduced several characteristics of the political environment of bureaucracy. It has noted that political influences on agencies are always potentially powerful, that agencies often work toward goals that cut against each other and jockey for position to achieve their own goals in a pragmatic, not a monolithic, independent, way. And we have seen that some agencies become captured by in interests they govern. How do the following news items illustrate these characteristics? The first is from the *Wall Street Journal* and the next from *Newsweek.*

> The Federal Communications Commission has decided to urge a federal judge to reject restrictions that the American Telephone and Telegraph Co. anti-trust settlement would place on Bell's local companies after they are shed.
>
> The proposed settlement, negotiated by AT&T and the Justice Department and currently under review by U.S. district Judge Harold Greene here, would bar the companies from offering anything other than local telephone service.[22]
>
> In many instances, deregulation represents a threat to established business. Consider the case of Aqua Slide 'n Dive Corp. of Brownsville, Texas. In 1976 the Consumer Product Saftey Commission [CPSC] issued a costly new rule governing the manufacture and installation of swimming-pool slides, and Aqua Slide, which previously controlled 90 percent of the domestic market, was soon enjoying a monopoly. So last year, when the Reaganites proposed to abandon the regulation, Aqua Slide began making waves. Faced with the threat of a lawsuit, the CPSC decided to let the rule stand even though there was no evidence that the standard had made swimming-pool slides any safer.

[22]"FCC Will Urge Judge to Reject Limits AT&T Accord Would Put on Units It Sheds," *Wall Street Journal,* 31 March 1982, p. 3.

One of the toughest regulatory decision of 1981 involved open warfare between two important industries. In an extremely controversial decision, National Highway Traffic Safety Administration director Raymond Peck rescinded a regulation requiring automakers to install air bags or automatic seat belts to protect passengers in the case of a crash. The decision, which will save the ailing auto industry approximately $1 billion a year, brought cheers from the automakers—and a storm of protest from consumer advocates. But the real threat to deregulation came from the insurance industry, which had hoped that passive restraints would reduce the cost of accident claims. "You're talking very big dollars," says Washington attorney Michael Sohn, who is representing the State Farm Mutual Automobile Insurance Co. in a suit to restore the standard.

Deregulation can also raise some highly charged emotional issues, as when the White House attempted to pare down rules designed to ensure that handicapped people have full access to public transportation and buildings. Soon after entering office, the Administration proposed to abolish the Architectural and Transportation Barriers Compliance Board, which established the access standards in the first place. Both Congress and handicapped groups were aghast. Compliance board chairman Mason Rose angrily vowed that the disabled would not return to "using back doors and freight elevators." Ultimately the board and the Administration struck a compromise in which 95 percent of the guidelines would remain intact. Only the most costly would be eliminated or deferred.

Sometimes deregulation works. At a November [1981] press conference, [President] Reagan mentioned the case of 3-year-old Katie Beckett of Cedar Rapids, Iowa, confined to a hospital because Federal rules barred Medicaid payments for less costly treatment at home. This month the Department of Health and Human Services is expected to change those rules—a move that will make life easier for 32,000 sick children—and save money as well.[23]

[23]"Mending the Rules," *Newsweek*, 11 January 1982, p. 51. Copyright 1982, by Newsweek, Inc. All Rights Reserved. Reprinted by permission.

CHAPTER 2

The Origins and Meaning of Administrative Law

Thus far this book about administrative law has said surprisingly little about its subject. This is because administrative law operates within such a complex political and economic context that it makes little sense to explain the law without learning at least a sketch of this context first. The three themes of chapter 1 examined aspects of this environment. We now turn to two main themes of administrative law itself.

The fourth theme is primarily descriptive and occupies all but the last of this chapter's six sections. This theme defines administrative law and illustrates it in action. Administrative law is one mechanism we possess for controlling and correcting administrative government. Political checks exercised in legislatures and executive offices are another mechanism. Administrative law, however, not only limits the authority of administrative government; it also gives legitimacy and authority to state actions. Therefore, as we describe administrative law, please think about the ways in which this body of law both *limits* administrative discretion and *empowers* administrative government.

The description of administrative law begins with a sketch of the legal process in general. It proceeds to show how administrative law differs from other branches of law and offers a brief history of administrative law in this century. This part of the chapter will distinguish, more particularly, between regulatory law and administrative law. Regulatory law includes such things as antitrust statutes and environmental protection policy. It is part of the machinery of governmental power. Administrative law by contrast states procedures for controlling that power. Administrative law regulates the regulators. It also empowers administrators to act. Administrative law is not the actual rules, decisions, and policies that administrators make. We often refer to these substantive rules as *regulatory laws.* Administrative law deals not primarily with the substance, the content, of policy outcomes but with the procedures of making policies. Administrative law focuses on the procedural problems of *fairness* in governmental decisionmaking. This distinction between administrative and regulatory law suggests that the process of making public policy is somehow separate from the substance of policy. While this distinction may be analytically useful at times, it is important for you to observe how particular procedures may or may not lead to certain substantive outcomes. The process may effect or even determine the kind of regulatory policies agencies like OSHA make and enforce. The values embedded in administrative law are no less neutral than the public policies reflected in regulatory law. One cannot understand the significance of procedural requirements or principles of administrative law apart from the substantive responsibilities of particular agencies and the means available to agencies for accomplishing their goals. The chapter next provides several illustrations of this point—illustrations that are classic cases that raise issues to be developed in later chapters. Therefore review them carefully.

The fifth and final theme, the most important in the book, tackles the important philosophical issues that lurk in any administrative law case and make the field so controversial. These problems deal with the capacity of law and courts to make a contribution to the quality of our lives. This theme evaluates whether and how well administrative law works. It asks among other things whether the rules and procedures courts have shaped today are adequate to offset the risks that technology, self-interested politicians, and businessmen may impose on society.

Before turning to the description of administrative law itself, let us alert you to the philosophical debate toward which the description points. We often say ours is a government of laws, not of men. The concept of the *rule of law* expresses this idea more formally. The rule of law means that government in the United States must operate within limits created by law. In its most familiar form the rule of law idea specifies that the government should not have too much power, that the bulk of human activity properly remains in private hands, that we should avoid a totalitarian police state. There are, however, applications of the rule of law concept that do not narrow power so much as they clarify and rationalize the use of power. The rule of law tries to keep the use of power open to participation by the governed. It seeks to call the use of power to public account and thus to prevent the emergence of the unresponsive and unfathomable bureaucratic caricature described in Franz Kafka's literary nightmares.

Administrative law refers to the way the legal system, primarily the courts, translates the philosophy of the rule of law into controls on bureaucratic power. But other philosophical queries creep in. American political philosophy may reject the idea of totalitarian and unresponsible government, but at the same time we know that the slogan that we are a government of laws, not of men, is a misleading oversimplification. Men and women, after all, make and enforce the laws. Furthermore the laws they make and enforce do not usually speak very clearly. Vague, ambiguous, and general laws leave much room for human discretion. To put it bluntly, law doesn't really limit government nearly as much as do the political, social, and economic choices of the legislators and judges who make and enforce the law. At first the judicial opinions you read in this book may appear as mechanical and inevitable constructions, like making a cake from a cookbook recipe. But as you learn more about the politics of administrative law you will be able to identify ways in which judges in each administrative law case search for and create theories about fairness, equality, and democracy in the relationship between citizen and government. How can we evaluate the wisdom of these theories? That is the crucial philosophical question in administrative law. It is the most important question in this book, and you must not lose sight of it.

What Is Law?

Law is one of several techniques people use to prevent or resolve conflicts. Unlike fighting, going to a counselor, or handling conflicts in another way, law is a process that starts by referring to rules and practices. The United States political system makes legal rules in four kinds of ways. Each of the four kinds of law contain both substantive and procedural rules.

1. *Statutes.* State legislatures and the Congress of the United States pass legislation after gathering information, debating the meaning of the evidence and the wording of the bill, and, in most cases, after compromising differing points of view in the final product. Statutes address social conditions and problems, for example, the threat of business monopoly, the need to prevent fraudulent advertising, or the desire to create and fund an agency charged with developing a technology to send people to the moon. Statutes speak for the future. Because legislators cannot tell precisely what shape the problem will take in the future and cannot predict what new methods of monopolizing trade or what new consumer fraud schemes people will dream up, statutes must address the future in general and flexible language. Since general and flexible statutory language cannot resolve specific cases (and because people deliberately violate clear rules), we keep courts open to interpret and apply statutory law in litigation.

Television dramas such as "L. A. Law" imply that all statutes define crimes and prescribe punishments for defendants whom the courts find guilty of committing them. In the United Sates, while nearly all crimes violate statutes, not all or even a majority of statutes create or define crimes. Statutes declare many kinds of policy. Each of the agencies whose work appears in this book gets its authority from the legislature through the statute that created it.

2. *Common Law.* In the old English legal system judges decided conflicts among citizens without statutes. If someone damaged your water wheel by banging it with their boat, if someone agreed to buy your cow and then broke their promise, if three of your pigs wandered into a neighbor's field and they refused to return them, judges willingly would decide these conflicts in the absence of a statute. Over the years these decisions came to constitute a body of *precedent* to which other judges would refer in deciding the cases that arose before them. The principles they eventually agreed on became the common law of tort, contract, property, and so on.

If today your dog gets loose and digs up the neighbor's garden of prizewinning flowers, if you agree to perform a service for an individual and then break your promise, or if you keep a package of valuable silver delivered to your home by mistake, judges in the United States will decide your legal responsibility in these situations and, if need be, how much you must pay or do to right any wrong done. Unless a statute supersedes, these judges will render a decision based on common-law principles of tort, contract, and property that resemble the judge-made law of England from earlies centuries.

Statutory law has more obvious relevance to administrative law because agencies are created by statutes and derive their powers from legislatures. Common law nevertheless has special significance for our purposes because it rests on the assumption that judges properly make law in the absence of legislative directions. Later chapters will show that judges behave and decide very much in the tradition of common law. Yet citizens, scholars, and judges disagree about how much lawmaking discretion judges ought to have in ruling on bureaucratic power.

3. *Constitutions.* Constitutions state the underlying rules for the operation of a political system. They create and govern the government. When it became clear that the original Articles of Confederation did not establish an effective form of government, the representatives from the colonies met in Philadelphia to create a new constitution. Gatherings of political leaders in the territories similarly drafted constitutions as these territories sought admission to the Union. Legislatures update constitutions by amendment. In some states this process is almost as simple as legislating. In the case of the national government, however, amendments must win approval from the Senate, the House of Representatives, and three-fourths of the states before they become part of the constitution.

Constitutional provisions also regulate the citizenry directly. This occurred with the prohibition amendment, and amendments to state constitutions do so more often. However, the bulk of constitutional law clearly defines not what citizens can and cannot do but what powers the government may or may not exercise. The first three articles of the United States Constitution, for example, prescribe a general structure for the three branches of government. They also detail some of the powers they may exercise: "Congress shall have power . . . to regulate commerce . . . among the several states," or "The President shall be Commander in Chief of the Army and Navy of the United States." You may already discern that if we care about limiting the power of bureaucratic government, and if the Constitution is the law that governs the government, then the Constitution by definition must play a central role in administrative law.

4. *Regulatory Law.* Congress makes statutes, judges create common law, constitutional conventions and the amendment process develop constitutions. The fourth and final kind of law takes an interesting twist. Administrative agencies make law. The FCC, by rule, limits the number of commercial broadcasting stations a company may own. The IRS, by rule, decides which groups need and need not pay taxes. The IRS creates tax law, and the FCC makes communications law. These laws regulate citizens. So do environmental law, antitrust law, and consumer protection law. Books have been written about each one of these fields of substantive law made by bureaucrats. *Administrative law, on the other hand, governs the bureaucrats themselves.* It focuses on matters of procedural law in contrast to substantive law. Yet, as we noted above, these two kinds of law may affect each other in important ways over time.

Administrative law applies legal principles from each of the four basic kinds of law. Thus administrative law tries to insure that agencies operate within their statutory limits. Its more important mission, however, applies the Constitution to the administrative process. Therefore we must take a second look at constitutional law.

Americans have long accepted the legal authority of the Constitution. Therefore let us agree that when the United States Constitution or the constitution of any state prohibits the government from doing something, it becomes just as illegal for the government to go ahead and do it as it is for a person to rob a bank in violation of criminal law.

No law means very much, however, if courts do not try to follow its meaning when making legal decisions. All law—statutory law, common law, constitutional law, and regulatory law— depends for legal force on the willingness of judges to make its provisions (or what judges believe are its provisions) stick. Therefore, when a constitution prohibits the government from depriving any person "of life, liberty, or property, without due process" as does the Fifth and Fourteenth amendments to the Constitution, courts must enforce this provision. Courts do so in lawsuits claiming that some governmental action violates this or that constitutional provision. This, in a nutshell, is the rule of law. If governments, including their administrative agencies, remained free to step beyond their legal boundaries whenever they wish, free of judicial interference, the rule of law itself would evaporate.

Unfortunately this description will mislead some. Constitutional law is not as straightforward. Does it, for example, violate "due process" to hold an accused person in jail simply because he is too poor to raise bail? Does government violate a woman's equal protection rights if it passes a law prohibiting abortions? Judges must *choose* or interpret what the vague, general, and ambiguous words in the Constitution mean in these and many other cases. Judges cannot avoid making up the law, or at least filling in the holes and clarifying the uncertainties, as they go along. Lawyers also supply judges with arguments why one particular interpretation of the Constitution is better than another; they, too, actively participate in the lawmaking. The following chapters spend a great deal of time studying what the judges have to say about administrative law but much less time on the words of the Constitution themselves. The classic question in political philosophy, "Who polices the policeman?", continues to stir political controversy. In administrative law, as elsewhere in law, social scientists claim that judges and lawyers *are* the police. This observation has provoked considerable debate about the power of judges and lawyers in a democratic society.

A First Look at the Development of Administrative Law

At the end of this book you will be in a better position to decide how satisfactorily the administrative law that courts have created polices bureaucratic power. Bear in mind, however, that administrative law is a remarkably new field. Courts have had just over fifty years to come to grips with the reality of bureaucratic power, so the presence of unsolved problems and confusing legal doctrine should not surprise us. Furthermore, we have seen that administrative agencies exist because, in part, courts are not well structured to make and implement administrative policy.

The legal profession has come to occupy a prominent role in regulatory politics and administrative lawmaking despite these differences. It is still puzzling how lawyers and judges acquired this position. The field of government administration originally presumed that public policy and administrative practices had to be free from the constraints of procedural legality. Indeed during the late nineteenth and early twentieth centuries, *non lawyers* such as traffic engineers, city planners, and businessmen practiced administrative law.[1] Also during the early period, the leadership of the American Bar Association (ABA), a private organization of lawyers established in 1879, raised questions about the constitutionality of administrative agencies on the grounds that

---

[1] See Louis L. Jaffe, "Law Making by Private Groups," *Harvard Law Review* 51 (1937):201, and Louis L. Jaffe, "Invective and Investigation in Administrative Law," *Harvard Law Review* 52, (1939): 1201.

Congress had unconstitutionally delegated its legislative authority to agencies and that these same agencies violated the principles of due process by adjudicating conflicts involving their own rules and regulations. By the early 1930s, the private bar lobbied Congress for a statute that would impose legal procedures on administrative agencies.[2] The politics of the ABA's design for administrative agencies emphasized the common-law view of fairness. The common-law definition of procedural fairness to the client was the main argument put forward by the private bar. It argued that agencies should be allowed to proceed, for example, to order rate reductions or cease and desist orders, only after following many of the judicial characteristics of a hearing. If agencies departed from the lawyers' model, as one did in the *Morgan* case reported later in this chapter, judges should strike down the agency's decision.

At the same time these debates were going on, a new flow of judicial blood came to the Supreme Court. William O. Douglas, former chairman of the SEC and law professor, and Felix Frankfurter, also formerly a law professor who had specialized in administrative problems and who had actively helped design the New Deal's response to the Great Depression, joined the Court. As President Franklin Roosevelt's appointees to the Court, they argued that the courts needed to give agencies more free reign to make decisions based on their own expertise, and they encouraged courts to defer to agencies' expertise in policymaking when possible.

Along with FDR's new appointments to the Supremet Court, a "new breed of lawyers" went to Washington to work for the government. Jerold Auerbach, a legal historian, argues that these lawyers were not from the same ethnic or racial backgrounds of traditional private lawyers who represented corporations.[3] New Deal agencies provided openings for black and Jewish lawyers who had not found opportunities in private practice. Women lawyers were less active in government agencies in part because law schools and the legal profession discriminated against women. The number of women lawyers does not increase significantly until the 1970s, with substantial pressure placed on law schools to admit qualified women. Today women comprise between 40–50 percent of entering law school classes. In the 1930s and 1940s the differences Auerbach finds between New Deal lawyers and private lawyers are among men. And despite difference in their class backgrounds and political orientations, Auerbach suggests that after the novelty of being a government lawyer wore off, the professional training and professional bonds between lawyers on both sides prevailed and a consensus on administrative procedure began to form.[4]

While some politicians and administrators agreed that a general administrative procedure statute might be useful, they disagreed over the extent to which the legislation should force agencies to act like courts. The ABA, having not fully endorsed the New Deal, pushed for the creation of an administrative law court to which all final

---

[2] See Louis G. Caldwell, "A Federal Administrative Court," *University of Pennsylvania Law Review* 84 (1936): 966.

[3] Jerold S. Auerbach, *Unequal Justice* (New York: Oxford University Press, 1976). Also see Fritz Morstein Marx, "The Lawyers' Role in Public Administration," *Yale Law Journal* 55 (1946):498, and Peter H. Irons, *The New Deal Lawyers* (Princeton, N.J.: Princeton University Press, 1982).

[4] Auerbach, 215. For a contrasting perspective see Frederick F. Blachly and Miriam E. Oatman, "Sabotage of the Administrative Process," *Public Administration Review* 6 (1946):213.

contested administrative decisions would go. Congress did not buy that idea, but it did pass the Walter-Logan Bill in 1940. This bill required the agencies to follow court-like procedures for nearly all administrative policymaking, thus formalizing much that agencies had informally done in the past. The bill also authorized the regular courts to review all agencies' decisions. Peter Woll describes the bill this way:

> The Walter-Logan bill privides an interesting example of the extent to which the legal profession was willing to go in forcing the administrative process into a judicial mold. With respect to the rule-making (legislative) functions of administrative agencies, the bill provided that "hereafter administrative rules and all amendments or modifications or supplements of existing rules implementing or filling in the details of any statute affecting the rights of persons or property shall be issued . . . only after publication of notice and public hearings." In addition to this extreme provision regarding rule-making, the bill provided that any "substantially interested" person could, within a three-year period, petition the agency for a reconsideration of any rule, and could furthermore demand a hearing. In this manner the bill attempted to enforce common-law due process, applicable only to adjudication, upon the legislative process of administrative agencies. It would have been equally appropriate to enforce judicial procedure upon Congress![5]

President Roosevelt vetoed the bill successfully. However in 1946 Congress passed the more modest version with the backing and support of the ABA—the Administrative Procedure Act (APA).[6] The act did not judicialize administrative action as thoroughly as did Walter-Logan. The APA (sec. 554) requires agencies to follow court-like hearings only when the legislation creating the agency expressly requires the agency to hold hearings. The APA also does not authorize judicial review of anything and everything the agency does (sec. 701a). This was a prudent move in light of the fact that the legislation creating some agencies specifically forbade judicial review and/or explicitly permitted the agencies to take certain steps at their own descretion.

Nonetheless, as Martin Shapiro points out, "American administrative procedures had been proceeding for 150 years without such a statute," and that this "fact is crucial to understanding the qualities of American administrative law that place it so firmly in the *intermediate realm*."[7] Shapiro uses the phrase "intermediate realm" to convey the idea that administrative law requires both constitutional and statutory interpretation. The passage of the APA in 1946 does not remove administrative law from this realm. Indeed, according to Shapiro, the APA "in theory does [not] provide a complete set

---

[5] Peter Woll, *Administrative Law: The Informal Process* (Berkeley: University of California Press, 1963), 18–19.

[6] See Appendix B. On 6 April 1982, the Senate approved, 94–0, the first substantial revision of the APA. More will be said of this bill later.

[7] Martin Shapiro, "The Supreme Court's 'Return' to Economic Regulation," *Studies in American Political Development*, 1 (1986): 102.

of procedures adequate to the needs of each agency and its clients. Instead it establishes a kind of residual body of procedural rules that come into play if the rules particular to any given agency are insufficient."[8]

Although the APA is but one source of administrative law, it has become an important document, like the U.S. Constitution, for administrative agencies. You will read cases that address specific portions of the APA, but by way of introducing you to the document let us mention four important areas of administration it governs: (1) *adjudication,* which deals with the process for hearing and deciding controversies; (2) *rulemaking,* which concerns the procedures for developing and amending regulatory rules; (3) *discretion of administrative agencies,* which is defined in the statute that creates an agency (i.e., the organic act) and reviewing courts must defer to the statute; and (4) *judicial review,* which establishes the standards that courts must apply when reviewing agency actions.

As you proceed through this book, particularly through the chapters that describe the law regulating formal adjudication and semiformal rulemaking, keep in mind that in many circumstances the APA permits agencies (as the Walter-Logan bill did not) to act informally without following any prescribed due process. Before cases reach the formal stage, many attempts to resolve them informally have usually occurred. The vast majority of cases never reach formal administrative decision levels at all. Does law need more aggressively to check possible abuses at informal administrative levels? Peter Woll wrote in the early 1960s:

> In summary, there is a trend in administrative law, perhaps indigenous to administrative adjudication, toward the development and utilization of informal procedure, characterized by correspondence, conference, and investigation rather than by procedure judicial in nature patterned upon the common law. . . . In terms of legal theory, a description and analysis of the use of informal procedure in administrative adjudication is important because it is a magnification of the general problem presented to legal theory by the development of administrative law.
> At the first line of defense, common-law theory demands that adjudication be handled by the courts; however, because this is evidently impossible in the modern administrative state, common-law theory demands the formalization of the administrative process in accordance with legal standards, with the opportunity for judicial review. Informal administrative adjudication, on the other hand, cannot be subjected to common-law forms by definition, nor are decisions made in this manner subject to judicial review, because of the legal doctrine of exhaustion of administrative remedy and more practical difficulties involved in taking a case to court. To the extent that informal procedure pervades the administrative process, a serious antithesis to the common law is present.[9]

[8] Ibid. Also see Martin Shapiro, *Who Guards the Guardians? Judicial Control of Administration* (Athens: GA: University of Georgia Press, 1988).

[9] Woll, 29–30.

Administrative Developments in the States

In most instances administrative power in the states has developed in response to the same pressures that moved the federal government to action. State legislators and state judges maintained that businesses "affected with a public interest" should and could be regulated. Both state and local governments licensed public houses, ferries, or other services even before federal regulations came along. Yet some interesting differences exist. In the last century, government, primarily state and local government, has increasingly controlled and operated the delivery of welfare services to the needy. Welfare broadly conceived operates not merely to aid poor families with dependent children (AFDC). It includes a variety of protections and services to those who for many reasons, such as being elderly, or disabled, cannot or do not earn a living.

At the turn of the century one of the most hotly debated welfare issues concerned the ability of a worker who was injured and incapacitated on the job to get some kind of compensation for the injury. Under common law, the employee who could no longer work could recover from the employer only after proving the employer's negligence caused his injury. If the accident simply happened, with neither party at fault, the employee lost. Often the employee could not discover enough about the employment situation to prove negligence to a jury, in which case he also lost.[10] To correct this problem many states passed worker's compensation laws requiring employers to insure against employee loss regardless of fault. To settle disputed claims, e.g., whether the injury really happened on the job or fully disabled the employee, states set up industrial accident boards.

In the most insightful study of such an agency to date, Philippe Nonet concluded that the legal model has come to dominate the state agency even more than at the federal level. Nonet believes the state administration may be overly legalized.

Administrative Justice

Philippe Nonet
New York: Russell Sage, 1969, Chapter 1

The architects of the welfare state had a characteristically narrow and negative conception of the role of law in government. To them, law evoked a system of rigid constraints that paralyzed initiative and prevented effective action to solve the problems of society. Government had to be freed from undue legalism, relieved of the burdensome formalism of legal procedure. It needed broader discretion in making and interpreting public policy. The growth of positive government would depend on the development of an alternative machinery, removed from the ambit of law, and free to "administer" policy in the light of public purposes. The informality and flexibility of the administrative process would provide the freedom needed for enlarging public authority. . . .

. . . A branch of the California Department of Industrial Relations, the Industrial Accident Commission (IAC) was responsible for administering state workmen's compensation laws, that is, the legislation governing the liability of employers for injuries occurring to employees in connection with their work.

---

[10]See James Weinstein, *The Corporate Ideal in the Liberal State, 1900–1918* (Boston: Beacon Press, 1968), 40–61.

Neither the IAC nor workmen's compensation has attracted much public or scholarly attention. Yet their creation in the early 1910s marks one of the major innovations of the welfare state, and their history dramatizes problems that have been central concerns of students of law and government.

Briefly, the history of the IAC is a story of transformation of a welfare agency into a court of law. Designed as an administrative authority, the early commission had a mandate for social action, aimed at improving the welfare of disabled workers by means of relief and rehabilitation. It had broad discretion in making and interpreting its policies, and enjoyed considerable freedom from procedural restraints and judicial review. Fifty years later, the agency has lost most of its early sense of initiative and public mission; it has acquired the outlook of a passive arbitrator, responsible only to those private interests of labor and industry it was originally meant to regulate. The IAC has become a highly self-conscious judicial body, largely removed from the concrete problems of welfare policy and governed by exacting standards of procedure. Its primary function is to hear and decide claims of right under a determinate set of laws.

As the agency changed, its modes of interpreting policy were increasingly legalized. Initially, the workmen's compensation was part of a broad program of social welfare, sharply divorced from the legal context of the employment relation. Although this legislation was developed and implemented by the IAC with considerable energy, it was interpreted in a way that was characteristically unsophisticated and narrow; and it was often enforced with little regard for the rights of affected persons. The history of workmen's compensation is one of growing detachment from public purposes, and progressive incorporation into the private law of employer and employee. Although this legalization revealed a loss of purpose on the part of the IAC, it also reflected an increased responsiveness to the claims of interested constituents and a steady enlargement of their rights. In the process, a set of administrative policies was infused with legal conceptions and took on the character of a body of law.

A striking feature of this evolution was the way it was affected by the changing character and capabilities of those whom workmen's compensation was meant to serve and protect. The early IAC was designed to reach workers who could not be counted upon to act as effective claimants and to bear the burden of promoting their interests. Workmen were then largely unorganized, politically resourceless, and highly vulnerable to the unrestrained power of employers; labor appeared unable to confront industry as an equal adversary. At this early state, administrative initiative was an alternative to partisan advocacy. Later, with the growth of organized labor, a passive and dependent constituency became an increasingly powerful and active participant. Unions found means of promoting among injured workers a more assertive consciousness of their rights, and developed a system of representation and advocacy that was capable of furthering their interests under the law. With the growing strength of labor, workmen's compensation became a focus of political conflict among organized interest groups, and the administrative process became an arena of continuing legal controversy.

You will encounter other illustrations of state as well as federal administration later in this book. You should ask whether the excessive legalization Nonet describes fits there as well.

To summarize, in its short history administrative law has developed along four tracks: administrative, judicial, constitutional, and statutory. The administrative track developed first out of procedures originating within the agencies. The APA gave statutory authority to these existing agency-made procedures. The judicial track depends on how judges interpret agency procedures. In the 1960s and 1970s nearly all of the current rules for notice and comment rulemaking were created in the common-law manner by court decisions not based on the wording of statutes or past procedural practices of agencies. The constitutional track also depends primarily on the judicial applications of the due process clauses that apply to all agencies at all levels of government. Much administrative law labors to articulate the circumstances in which agency procedures do or do not "deprive citizens of life, liberty or property without due process of law." The statutory track is somewhat more complicated. It includes judicial interpretations of the provisions in statutes that grant agency powers. For example, the next chapter presents a case in which the Supreme Court had to decide whether the Federal Power Act (FPA) required the Federal Power Commission (FPC) to eliminate racial discrimination by producers of electricity and natural gas. The statutory track also includes the generic administrative procedure acts at the national and state levels. These acts specify certain procedures that apply to many agencies, not just one. Several chapters to come focus on these provisions and judicial interpretations of them.

At this point beginning readers probably remain confused about the definition of administrative law. It is not regulatory law itself, but what is it? The next section provides three administrative law cases. All three involve the constitutional track of administrative law. You should study them with several goals in mind. First, familiarize yourself with the format and style of judicial opinions in general. Second, develop your skill in extracting the important points and conclusions from these cases. Third, think about the issues themselves. We say relatively little about the administrative law issues in these cases so that you can focus on the mechanics of analyzing cases. You can be sure, however, that these important questions of law will come up in many contexts in later chapters. Finally, relate these cases to the fundamental philosophical question in this book. Recall that this question concerns the role of the courts in governing the government and the effectiveness or ineffectiveness with which the courts play that role.

Adjudication and the Basics of Due Process: Three Illustrations

Adjudication is the focal point in any study of either the constitutional or statutory track of administrative law. This is so because laws so often contain uncertainties that courts ultimately must determine and announce what the laws mean; in addition, courts enforce laws. Fortunately, judges in our system have traditionally given reasons for their decisions. In this book you will find many references to judicial opinions giving reasons for their interpretations of the constitution and of the national and state administrative procedure statutes mentioned above. These statutes, like constitutions, govern how bureaucrats regulate us, and the courts have much to say about their meaning.

If you have not studied law by the *case method* before, you may still be struggling with some of the technical terms and concepts of legal analysis. The most important of these is the concept of *precedent*. Each judicial decision tries to justify itself so that it is consistent with an earlier similar decision. Each new decision also speaks to the future. To read a judicial opinion is therefore to read the law, just as much as reading a statutory clause. Students of cases need a method of abstracting and summarizing cases. I recommend the following: 1. Read the entire case through. 2. Reread the case noting in the following order as you read: (a) the key facts in the case; (b) the primary legal questions in the case; (c) the court's answer(s) to the question(s) ("holdings"); (d) the court's reasons for the holdings; (e) the argument of a dissenting opinion, if you believe it valuable. You will soon discover that the process of reasoning from precedents in law is not mechanical. The key to understanding holdings is to discover the normative, or value, judgments the judges make about the facts surrounding the case.

Morgan v. United States

304 U.S. 1 (1938) 6–1
+   Hughes, McReynolds, Brandeis, Butler, Stone, Roberts
–   Black
NP Cardozo, Reed

[In *Morgan* we have a complex set of facts that lead up to a legal dispute over whether regulated parties, in this case stockyard operators, were treated fairly by government administrators. In 1921, Congress authorized the secretary of agriculture to specify maximum "just and reasonable" charges that stockyard operators could set for their services. In the Packers and Stockyards Act of 1921, Congress instructed the secretary to do so only after a "full hearing." In 1930 the Department notified Morgan and other stockyard operators to appear for a hearing concerning their prices. The hearing, which had to be held twice due to the rapidly changing conditions in the Depression, took many months and accumulated a 10,000-page transcript of oral testimony and another 1,000 pages of statistical exhibits. Initially the secretary of agriculture did not personally review the hearing at all. He delegated to subordinates the job of listening to the oral arguments based on the hearing. In an earlier case involving Morgan the stockyard operators appealed to the Supreme Court claiming that they did not have a full or fair hearing because the decider had not reviewed the evidence. The Court agreed and sent the case back to the Department of Agriculture to try again.

Before the completion of the next round a new secretary was appointed. He did receive and review a list of 180 hearing findings organized by the department's Bureau of Animal Industries. The secretary made a few minor changes in the findings but otherwise approved them and ordered the stockyards to lower their prices. This time when the Court heard the case the stockyard operators had a new set of complaints. The Bureau of Animal Industries had been, in effect, the prosecutor in the case. For the secretary to rely only on its assessment of the issues seemed unfair to the stockyard operators. Also, the operators were not allowed to see the tentative report of the examiner in the hearing, so they had no basis for defining and making their final arguments, nor were they allowed to see the bureau's findings. The department, in effect, left them punching the air. Indeed, from the very beginning of the case, the department never formulated a specific complaint against the prices the stockyards charged.

The opinion of the Court that follows properly insists on basic administrative fairness. *Morgan*, although it is less than sixty years old, was one of the Court's first serious efforts to define administrative fairness in a modern administrative setting. In fact, the case had to go back twice more to the Court before the dust finally settled. As you read this first example of administrative law in action, try to imagine some additional potential defects in a hearing that would make it unfair.]

Mr. Chief Justice Hughes delivered the opinion of the Court.

The first question goes to the very foundation of the action of administrative agencies intrusted by the Congress with broad control over activities which in their detail cannot be dealt with directly by the Legislature. The vast expansion of this field of administrative regulation in response to the pressure of social needs is made possible under our system of adherence to the basic principles that the Legislature shall appropriately determine the standards of administrative action and that in administrative proceedings of a quasi-judicial character the liberty and property of the citizen shall be protected by the rudimentary requirements of fair play. These demand "a fair and open hearing," essential alike to the legal validity of the administrative regulation and to the maintenance of public confidence in the value and soundness of this important governmental process. Such a hearing has been described as an "inexorable safeguard." *St. Joseph Stock Yards Co. v. United States,* 298 U.S. 38, 73, 56, S. Ct. 720, 735, 80 L.Ed. 1033. [Other citations omitted] And in equipping the Secretary of Agriculture with extraordinary powers under the Packers and Stockyards Act, the Congress explicitly recognized and emphasized this recruitment by making his action depend upon a "full hearing." . . .

No opportunity was afforded to appellants for the examination of the findings . . . prepared in the Bureau of Animal Industry until they were served with the order. Appellants sought a rehearing by the Secreatry, but their application was denied on July 6, 1933, and these suits followed.

The part taken by the Secretary himself in the departmental proceedings is shown by his full and candid testimony. . . . He did not hear the oral argument. The bulky record was placed upon his desk and he dipped into it from time to time to get its drift. He decided that probably the essence of the evidence was contained in appellants' briefs. These, together with the transcript of the oral argument, he took home with him and read. He had several conferences with the Solicitor of the Department and with the officials in the Bureau of Animal Industry, and discussed the proposed findings. He testified that

he considered the evidence before signing the order. The substance of his action is stated in his answer to the question whether the order represented his independent conclusion, as follows: "My answer to the question would be that that very definitely was my independent conclusion as based on the findings of the men in the Bureau of Animal Industry. I would say, I will try to put it as accurately as possible, that it represented my own independent reactions to the findings of the men in the Bureau of Animal Industry."

Save for certain rate alterations, he "accepted the findings."

In the light of this testimony there is no occasion to discuss the extent to which the Secretary examined the evidence, and we agree with the Government's contention that it was not the function of the court to probe the mental processes of the Secretary in reaching his conclusions if he gave the hearing which the law required. The Secretary read the summary presented by appellants' briefs and he conferred with his subordinates who had sifted and analyzed the evidence. We assume that the Secretary sufficiently understood its purport. But a "full hearing"—a fair and open hearing—requires more than that. The right to a hearing embraces not only the right to present evidence, but also a reasonable opportunity to know the claims of the opposing party and to meet them. The right to submit argument implies that opportunity; otherwise the right may be but a barren one. Those who are brought into contest with the Government in a quasi-judicial proceeding aimed at the control of their activities are entitled to be fairly advised of what the Government proposes and to be heard upon its proposals before it issues its final command.

No such reasonable opportunity was accorded appellants. The administrative proceeding was initiated by a notice of inquiry into the reasonableness of appellants' rates. No specific complaint was formulated and, in a proceeding thus begun by the Secretary on his own initiative, none was required. Thus, in the absence of any definite complaint and in a sweeping investigation, thousands of pages of testimony were taken by the examiner and numerous complicated exhibits were introduced bearing upon all phases of the broad subject of the conduct of the market agencies. In the absence of any report by the examiner or any findings proposed by the Government, and thus without any concrete statement of the Government's claims, the parties approached the oral argument.

Nor did the oral argument reveal these claims in any appropriate manner. The discussion by counsel for the Government was "very general," as he said, in order not to take up "too much time." It dealt with generalities both as to principles and procedure. . . .

Congress, in requiring a "full hearing," had regard to judicial standards—not in any technical sense but with respect to those fundamental requirements of fairness which are of the essence of due process in a proceeding of a judicial nature. If in an equity cause, a special master or the trial judge permitted the plaintiff's attorney to formulate the findings upon the evidence, conferred ex parte with the plaintiff's attorney regarding them, and then adopted his proposals without affording an opportunity to his opponent to know their contents and present objections, there would be no hesitation in setting aside the report or decree as having been made without a fair hearing. The requirements of fairness are not exhausted in the taking or consideration of evidence, but extend to the concluding parts of the procedure as well as to the beginning and intermediate steps.

The answer that the proceeding before the Secretary was not of an adversary character, as it was not upon complaint but was initiated as a general inquiry, is futile. It has regard to the mere form of the proceeding and ignores realities. In all substantial respects, the Government acting through the Bureau of Animal Industry of the Department was prosecuting the proceeding against the owners of the market agen-cies. The proceeding had all the essential elements of contested litigation, with the Government and its counsel on the one side and the appellants and their counsel on the other. . . .

Again, the evidence being in, the Secretary might receive the proposed findings of both parties, each being notified of the proposals of the other, hear argument thereon, and make his own findings. But what would not be essential to the adequacy of the hearing if the Secretary himself makes the findings is not a criterion for a case in which the Secretary accepts and makes as his own the findings which have been prepared by the active prosecutors for the Government, after an ex parte discussion with them and without according any reasonable opportunity to the respondents in the proceeding to know the claims thus presented and to contest them. That is more than an irregularity in practice; it is a vital defect.

The maintenance of proper standards on the part of administrative agencies in the performance of their quasi-judicial functions is of the highest importance and in no way cripples or embarrasses the exercise of their appropriate authority. On the contrary, it is in their manifest interest. For, as we said at the outset, if these multiplying agencies deemed to be necessary in our complex society are to serve the purposes for which they are created and endowed with vast powers, they must accredit themselves by acting in accordance with the cherished judicial tradition embodying the basic concepts of fair play.

As the hearing was fatally defective, the order of the Secretary was invalid. In this view, we express no opinion upon the merits. The decree of the District Court is reversed. . . .

[Justice Black's dissenting opinion is omitted.]

When they finally finished, the *Morgan* cases had consumed nearly a decade of litigation. Indeed, two decades had passed since Congress passed the Packers and Stockyards Act, and by the early 1940s wartime conditions and the programs to deal with them made the act obsolete. One complaint aimed at the administrative process is that its cumbersome machinery allows wealthy interests with clever lawyers to delay the implementation of important policies for years. But how far can a bureaucracy go in the name of efficiency without denying a citizen due process of law? How close can an agency come to shooting first and asking questions later? Suppose a state welfare agency receives information that a recipient of welfare money is a drug addict.

Can the agency cut off the recipient's payments until he agrees to accept counseling and rehabilitation for drug addiction? What if the recipient insists he does not use drugs, that the agency has made a mistake? Should courts interpret the Due Process Clause so as to give the recipient a chance to prove his case in a hearing? If so, must the agency offer the hearing *before* it stops sending the checks? *Goldberg v. Kelly* (1970), the next case, addressed this last question.

While *Morgan* involved a federal statute and federal administration, *Goldberg* is a state case. Nevertheless, the Constitution and federal law still govern. This is because the Fourteenth Amendment requiring due process of law in state government is part of the Constitution. And the case reached the Supreme Court of the United States, not merely a state supreme court, because Article III of the Constitution gives the Supreme Court power to decide cases arising under the Constitution. There is further federal involvement: Because Congress has authorized the expenditure of federal funds to supplement state welfare programs, the federal government could impose conditions on how states administer the federal money. The Department of Health, Education, and Welfare (HEW) had prior to this case already required states to offer hearings. Whether these hearings had to precede termination as a constitutional matter remained, however, in doubt. Before *Goldberg,* the requirements of a fair termination hearing were also uncertain. Chapter 6 will cover the components of fair hearings more thoroughly, but a careful reading of both *Morgan* and *Goldberg* will allow you to anticipate many of these issues.

Goldberg also illustrates several characteristics of the judicial machinery that you need to master. First, recall that the *Morgan* opinion above closed with the sentence, "The decree of the District Court is reversed." What is the "District Court" and how does it differ from the Supreme Court? Both federal and state legal systems are hierarchies. Figure 2.1 shows the United States court system and path of appeals from federal trial courts (Federal District Courts), federal administrative agencies, and state courts to the appellate courts (U.S. Court of Appeals and the United States Supreme Court). Lawsuits usually begin in trial courts, where judges preside over a process of fact finding. Trials in our legal system try to find out who did what to whom. Deciding the meaning of law often enters the picture only at the edges, either because both sides agree about the meaning of the law or because the trial judge makes rather quick decisions about the law in order to keep the fact-finding process moving. The federal system refers to its trial courts as "District Courts." Hence the Supreme Court, which disagreed with the trial result in *Morgan,* "reversed" the District Court. In *Goldberg* the Supreme Court agreed with the trial court and affirmed its results in the case.

Second, if a party believes the trial judge applies the law incorrectly, that party can appeal to a higher appellate court. Appellate courts do not hold new trials. They accept as true the facts as the trial determined them. But they do resolve legal questions, sometimes affirming the trial court's legal decisions, sometimes reversing them. The U.S. Courts of Appeals hear most of the appeals from administrative agencies, although this was not the case in *Goldberg.*[11] Figure 2.2 is a map of the thirteen U.S. Courts

[11] See Woodford J. Howard, *Courts of Appeals in the Federal Judicial System: A Study of the Second, Fifth, and District of Columbia Circuits* (Princeton, N.J.: Princeton University Press, 1981).

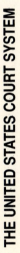
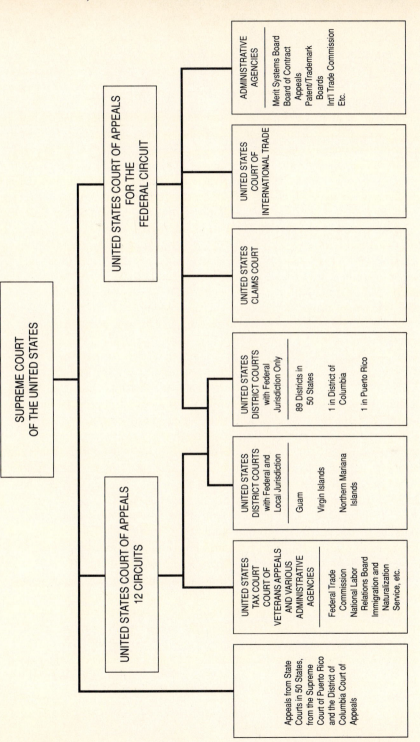

Figure 2.1 The United States Court System

Source: The United States Courts: Their Jurisdiction and Work (Washington, DC.: U.S. Administrative Office of the United States Courts, 1989), 3.

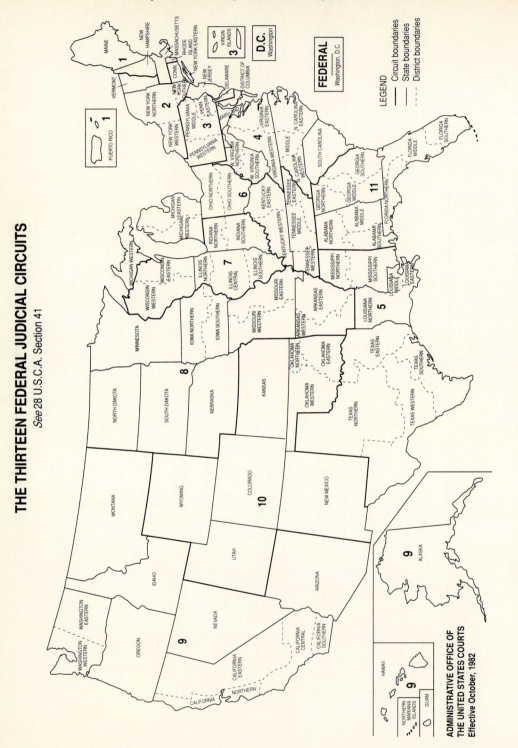

Figure 2.2   The Thirteen Federal Judicial Circuits (U.S. Courts of Appeals)

Source: The United States Courts: Their Jurisdiction and Work (Washington, D.C.: U.S. Administrative Office of the United States Courts, 1989), 5.

Table 2.1   Disposition of Administrative Appeals in the U.S. Courts of Appeals 1945–1985

Year	Total Cases Disposed	Without Hearing	With Hearing	With Hearing Affirmed	Reversed	Dismissed
1945	566	185	381	297 (78%)	81 (21%)	3 (1%)
1950	541	169	372	273 (74%)	77 (21%)	15 (4%)
1955	523	150	373	247 (66%)	107 (29%)	13 (3%)
1960	660	299	361	258 (71%)	91 (25%)	4 (1%)
1965	866	377	489	367 (75%)	95 (19%)	7 (1%)
1970	1248	584	664	527 (79%)	103 (16%)	16 (2%)
1975	1553	874	679	474 (70%)	146 (22%)	37 (5%)
1980	2210	1217	993	662 (67%)	222 (22%)	53 (5%)
1985	2485	1229	1256	953 (76%)	141 (11%)	57 (5%)

Sources: Christine B. Harrington, "Regulatory Reform: Creating Gaps and Making Markets," *Law & Policy* 10 (1988): 305: data derived from U.S. Administrative Office of the United States Courts, *Annual Reports*. A few cases categorized as "other" have been excluded from this table.

of Appeals, which are some times called *circuit* courts. The District of Columbia Court of Appeals decides a disproportionately high number of agency cases. Almost half of its docket are appeals from regulatory agencies. The ninth circuit also hears a substantial percentage of administrative appeals.[12] The circuit courts tend to affirm nearly three-quarters of the agency cases they hear. Table 2.1 show the disposition of administrative appeals in the circuit courts for 1945–85.

Third, unlike the *Morgan* excerpt above, the *Goldberg* opinion refers favorably to ideas it attributes to opinions in other cases. This reasoning from the example of other cases—precedents—is, as was said, an important part of legal reasoning. It is a habit inherited from common law. Remember in common law judges make decisions without referring to statutes at all. They try to keep their decisions consistent by making their results agree with results in similar cases. The reasons they give in their opinions become part of, and build up further, the body of common law. In many of the cases in this book you will see citations to other opinions. As you do, however, do not lose sight of the forest for the trees. It is the result in the case you read that matters.

Goldberg v. Kelly

397 U.S. 254 (1970) 6–3
+ Douglas, Harlan, Brennan, White, Marshall, Blackmun
− Black, Stewart, Burger

[Several residents of New York City, Kelly among them, received welfare payments under the federally assisted Aid to Families with Dependent Children program or the state's Home Relief program. They brought suit to prevent the termination of their welfare payments before a hearing had taken place. New York law did, however, allow an oral hearing before an independent state hearing officer *after* termination, at which

[12]See Christine B. Harrington, "Regulatory Reform: Creating Gaps and Making Markets," *Law & Policy* 10 (1988): 300–305.

time the recipient could offer oral evidence, cross-examine witnesses and have a record made of the hearing. If the recipient wins at this hearing he or she receives all the funds erroneously withheld.]

Mr. Justice Brennan delivered the opinion of the Court.

[T]he State Department of Social Services' Official Regulations . . . require that local social services officials proposing to discontinue or suspend a recipient's financial aid do so according to a procedure [which] . . . must include the giving of notice to the recipient of the reasons for a proposed discontinuance or suspension at least seven days prior to its effective date, with notice also that upon request the recipient may have the proposal reviewed by a local welfare official holding a position superior to that of the supervisor who approved the proposed discontinuance or suspension, and, further, that the recipient may submit, for purposes of the review, a written statement to demonstrate why his grant should not be discontinued or suspended. The decision by the reviewing official whether to discontinue or suspend aid must be made expeditiously, with written notice of the decision to the recipient. The section further expressly provides that "[a]ssistance shall not be discontinued or suspended prior to the date such notice or decision is sent to the recipient and his representative, if any, or prior to the proposed effective date of discontinuance or suspension, whichever occurs later." . . . [T]he New York City Department of Social Services promulgated Procedure No. 68-18. A caseworker who has doubts about the recipient's continued eligibility must first discuss them with the recipient. If the caseworker concludes that the recipient is no longer eligible, he recommends termination of aid to a unit supervisor. If the latter concurs, he sends the recipient a letter stating the reasons for proposing to terminate aid and notifying him that within seven days he may request that a higher official review the record, and may support the request with a written statement prepared personally or with the aid of an attorney or other person. If the reviewing official affirms the determination of ineligibility, aid is stopped immediately and the recipient is informed by letter of the reasons for the action. Appellees' challenge to this procedure emphasizes the absence of any provisions for the personal appearance of the recipient before the reviewing official, for oral presentation of evidence, and for confrontation and cross-examination of adverse witnesses. . . .

The constitutional issue to be decided, therefore, is the narrow one whether the Due Process Clause requires that the recipient be afforded an evidentiary hearing *before* the termination of benefits. The District Court held that only a pre-termination evidentiary hearing would satisfy the constitutional command, and rejected the argument of the state and city officials that the combination of the post-termination "fair hearing" with the informal pretermination review disposed of all due process claims.

For qualified recipients, welfare provides the means to obtain essential food, clothing, housing, and medical care. . . . [T]hus the crucial factor in this context—a factor not present in the case of the blacklisted government contractor, the discharged government employee, the taxpayer denied a tax exemption, or viturally anyone else whose governmental largesse is ended—is that termination of aid pending resolution of a controversy over eligibility may deprive an eligible recipient of the very means by which to live while he waits. Since he lacks independent resources, his situation becomes immediately desperate. His need to concentrate upon finding the means of daily subsistence, in turn, adversely affects his ability to seek redress from the welfare bureaucracy.

Moreover, important governmental interests are promoted by affording recipients a pre-termination evidentiary hearing. From its founding the nation's basic commitment has been to foster the dignity and well-being of all persons within its borders. We have come to recognize that forces not within the control of the poor contribute to their poverty. This perception, against the background of our traditions, has significantly influenced the development of the contemporary public assistance system. Welfare, by meeting the basic demands of subsistence, can help bring within the reach of the poor the same opportunities that are available to others to participate meaningfully in the life of the community. At the same time, welfare guards against the societal malaise that may flow from a widespread sense of unjustified frustration and insecurity. Public assistance, then, is not mere charity, but a means to "promote the general Welfare, and secure the Blessings of Liberty to ourselves and our Posterity." The same governmental interests which counsel the provision of welfare, counsel as well its uninterrupted provision to those eligible to receive it; pre-termination evidentiary hearings are indispensable to that end.

Appellant does not challenge the force of these considerations but argues that they are outweighed by countervailing governmental interests in conserving fiscal and administrative resources. These interests, the argument goes, justify the delay of any evidentiary hearing until after discontinuance of the grants. Summary adjudication protects the public fisc by stopping payments promptly upon discovery of reason to believe that a recipient is no longer eligible. Since most terminations are accepted without challenge, summary adjudication also conserves both the fisc and administrative time and energy by reducing the number of evidentiary hearings actually held.

We agree with the District Court, however, that these governmental interests are not overriding in the welfare context. The requirements of a prior hearing doubtless involve some greater expense, and the benefits paid to ineligible recipients pending decisions at the hearing probably cannot be recouped, since these recipients are likely to be judgment-proof. But the State is not without weapons to minimize these increased costs. Much of the drain on fiscal and administrative resources can be reduced by developing procedures for prompt pre-termination hearings and by skillful use of personnel and facilities. Indeed, the very provision for post-termination evidentiary hearing in New York's Home Relief program is itself cogent evidence that the State recognizes the primacy of the public interest in correct eligibility determinations and therefore in the provision of procedural safeguards. Thus, the interest of the eligible recipient in uninterrupted receipt of public assistance, coupled with the State's interest that his payments not be er-

roneously terminated, clearly outweighs the State's competing concern to prevent any increase in its fiscal and administrative burdens. . . .

We also agree with the District Court, however, that the pre-termination hearing need not take the form of a judicial or quasi-judicial trial. We bear in mind that the statutory "fair hearing" will provide the recipient with a full administrative review. Accordingly, the pre-termination hearing has one function only: to produce an initial determination of the validity of the welfare department's grounds for discontinuance of payments in order to protect a recipient against an erroneous termination of his benefits. . . . Thus, a complete record and a comprehensive opinion, which would serve primarily to facilitate judicial review and to guide future decisions, need not be provided at the pre-termination stage. We recognize, too, that both welfare authorities and recipients have an interest in relatively speedy resolution of questions of eligibility, that they are used to dealing with one another informally, and that some welfare departments have very burdensome caseloads. These considerations justify the limitation of the pre-termination hearing to minimum procedural safeguards, adapted to the particular characteristics of welfare recipients, and to the limited nature of the controversies to be resolved. We wish to add that we, no less than the dissenters, recognize the importance of not imposing upon the States or the Federal Government in this developing field of law any procedural requirements beyond those demanded by rudimentary due process.

"The fundamental requisite of due process of law is the opportunity to be heard." *Grannis v. Ordean,* 234 U.S. 385, 394 (1914). The hearing must be "at a meaningful time and in a meaningful manner." *Armstrong v. Manzo,* 380 U.S. 545, 552 (1965). In the present context these principles require that a recipient have timely and adequate notice detailing the reasons for a proposed termination, and an effective opportunity to defend by confronting any adverse witnesses and by presenting his own arguments and evidence orally. These rights are important in cases such as those before us, where recipients have challenged proposed terminations as resting on incorrect or misleading factual premises or on misapplication of rules or policies to the facts of particular cases.

We are not prepared to say that the seven-day notice currently provided by New York City is constitutionally insufficient per se, although there may be cases where fairness would require that a longer time be given. Nor do we see any constitutional deficiency in the content or form of the notice. New York employs both a letter and a personal conference with a caseworker to inform a recipient of the precise questions raised about his continued eligibility. Evidently the recipient is told the legal and factual bases for the Department's doubts. This combination is probably the most effective method of communicating with recipients.

The city's procedures presently do not permit recipients to appear personally with or without counsel before the official who finally determines continued eligibility. Thus a recipient is not permitted to present evidence to that official orally, or to confront or cross-examine adverse witnesses. These omissions are fatal to the constitutional adequacy of the procedures.

The opportunity to be heard must be tailored to the capacities and circumstances of those who are to be heard. It is not enough that a welfare recipient may present his position to the decision maker in writing or second-hand through his caseworker. Written submissions are an unrealistic option for most recipients, who lack the educational attainment necessary to write effectively and who cannot obtain professional assistance. Moreover, written submissions do not afford the flexibility of oral presentations; they do not permit the recipient to mold his argument to the issues the decision maker appears to regard as important. Particularly where credibility and veracity are at issue, as they must be in many termination proceedings, written submissions are a wholly unsatisfactory basis for decision. The second-hand presentation to the decision maker by the caseworker has its own deficiencies; since the caseworker usually gathers the facts upon which the charge of ineligibility rests, the presentation of the recipient's side of the controversy cannot safely be left to him. Therefore a recipient must be allowed to state his po-

sition orally. Informal procedures will suffice; in this context due process does not require a particular order of proof or mode of offering evidence. . . .

In almost every setting where important decisions turn on questions of fact, due process requires an opportunity to confront and cross-examine adverse witnesses. . . .

. . . What we said in *Greene v. McElroy*, 360 U.S. 474, 496-497 (1959) is particularly pertinent here:

> Certain principles have remained relatively immutable in our jurisprudence. One of these is that where governmental action seriously injures an individual, and the reasonableness of the action depends on fact finding, the evidence used to prove the Government's case must be disclosed to the individual so that he has an opportunity to show that it is untrue. While this is important in the case of documentary evidence, it is even more important where evidence consists of the testimony of individuals whose memory might be faulty or who, in fact, might be perjurers or persons motivated my malice, vindictiveness, intolerance, prejudice, or jealousy. We have formalized these protections in the requirements of confrontation and cross-examination. . . .

Welfare recipients must therefore be given an opportunity to confront and cross-examine the witnesses relied on by the department.

"The right to be heard would be, in many cases, of little avail if it did not comprehend the right to be heard by counsel." *Powell v. Alabama*, 287 U.S. 45, 68-69 (1932). We do not say that counsel must be provided at the pre-termination hearing, but only that the recipient must be allowed to retain an attorney if he so desires. . . .

Finally, the decision maker's conclusion as to a recipient's eligibility must rest solely on the legal rules and evidence adduced at the hearing. *Ohio Bell Tel. Co. v. PUC*, 301 U.S. 292 (1937). . . . To demonstrate compliance with this elementary requirement, the decision maker should state the reasons for his determination and indicate the evidence he relied on, cf. *Wichita R.R. & Light Co. v. PUC*, 260 U.S. 48,

57-59 (1922), though his statement need not amount to a full opinion or even formal findings of fact and conclusions of law. And, of course, an impartial decision maker is essential. Cf. *In re Murchison*, 349 U.S. 133 (1955); *Wong Yang Sung v. McGrath*, 330 U.S. 33, 45-46 (1950). We agree with the District Court that prior involvement in some aspects of a case will not necessarily bar a welfare official from acting as a decision maker. He should not, however, have particiapted in making the determination under review.

Affirmed.

Goldberg's extension of a due process requirement of an evidentiary hearing to routine state administrative matters initiated a dramatic change in administrative law, one which later chapters analyze in depth. A close reading of *Goldberg*, however, shows that the Court neglected to answer the most important question of all: *In what circumstances* does the Due Process Clause require this hearing? The nexe case did address the issue. Here the Court *denied* the recipient's claim to a pretermination hearing. You should use the techniques of case analysis discussed above to dig out the reasons for this denial.

Mathews v. Eldridge

424 U.S. 319 (1976) 6–2

+   Burger, Stewart, White, Blackmun, Powell, Rehnquist
–   Brennan, Marshall
NP   Stevens

[Eldridge had received Social Security benefits because he claimed he was completely disabled. The Social Security Administration determined after some years that Eldridge had recovered sufficiently to hold a job. It therefore terminated his Social Security benefit checks without holding an oral hearing. The details are reported in the opinion.]

Mr. Justice Powell delivered the opinion of the Court.

The issue in this case is whether the Due Process Clause of the Fifth Amendment requires that prior to the termination of Social Security disability benefit payments the recipient be afforded an opportunity for an evidentiary hearing. . . .

Cash benefits are provided to workers during periods in which they are completely disabled under the disability insurance benefits program created by the 1956 amendments to . . . the Social Security Act. . . . Eldridge was first awarded benefits in June 1968. In March 1972, he received a questionnaire from the state agency charged with monitoring his medical condition. Eldridge completed the questionnaire, indicating that his condition had not improved and identifying the medical sources, including physicians, from whom he had received treatment re-

cently. The state agency then obtained reports from his physician and psychiatric consultant. After considering these reports and other information in his file the agency informed Eldridge by letter that it had made a tentative determination that his disability had ceased in May 1972. The letter included a statement of reasons for the proposed termination of benefits, and advised Eldridge that he might request reasonable time in which to obtain and submit additional information pertaining to his condition.

In his written response, Eldredge disputed one characterization of his medical condition and indicated that the agency already had enough evidence to establish his disability. The state agency then made a final determination that he had ceased to be disabled in May 1972. This determination was accepted by the Social Security Administration (SSA), which notified Eldridge in July that his benefits would terminate after that month. The notification also advised him of his rights to seek reconsideration by the state agency of this initial determination within six months.

Instead of requesting reconsideration Eldridge commenced this action challenging the constitutional validity of the administrative procedures established by the Secreatry of Health, Education, and Welfare for assessing whether there exists a continuing disability. He sought an immediate reinstatement of benefits pending a hearing on the issue of his disability. . . . The Secretary moved to dismiss on the grounds that Eldridge's benefits had been terminated in accordance with valid administrative regulations and procedures and that he had failed to exhaust available remedies. . . .

. . . [The] District Court held that prior to termination of benefits Eldridge had to be afforded an evidentiary hearing of the type required for welfare beneficiaries under . . . the Social Security Act. . . . [T]he Court of Appeals for the Fourth Circuit affirmed. . . . We reverse. . . .

Procedural due process imposes constraints on governmental decisions which deprive individuals of "liberty" or "property" interests within the meaning of the Due Process Clause of the Fifth or Fourteenth Amendment. The Secretary does not contend that procedural due process is inapplicable to terminations of Social Security disability benefits. He recognizes, as has been implicit in our prior decisions, . . . that the interest of an individual in continued receipt of these benefits is a statutorily created "property" interest protected by the Fifth Amendment. . . . Rather, the Secretary contends that the existing administrative procedures . . . provide all the process that is constitutionally due before a recipient can be deprived of that interest.

This Court consistently has held that some form of hearing is required before an individual is finally deprived of a property interest. . . . the "right to be heard before being condemned to suffer grievous loss of any kind, even though it may not involve the stigma and hardships of a criminal conviction, is a principle basic to our society." . . . The fundamental requirement of due process is the opportunity to be heard "at a meaningful time and in a meaningful manner." Eldridge agrees that the review procedures available to a claimant before the initial determination of ineligibility becomes final would be adequate if disability benefits were not terminated until after the evidentiary hearing stage of the administrative process. The dispute centers upon what process is due prior to the initial termination of benefits, pending review.

In recent years this Court increasingly has had occasion to consider the extent to which due process requires an evidentiary hearing prior to the deprivation of some type of property interest even if such a hearing is provided thereafter. In only one case, *Goldberg v. Kelly*, . . . has the Court held that a hearing closely approximating a judicial trial is necessary. In other cases requiring some type of pretermination hearing as a matter of constitutional right the Court has spoken sparingly about the requisite procedures. . . .

These decisions underscore the truism that " '[d]ue process' unlike some legal rules, is not a technical conception with a fixed content unrelated to time, place, and circumstances." . . . "[D]ue process is flexible and calls for such procedural protections as the particular situation demands." . . . Accordingly, resolution of the issue whether the administrative procedures provided here are constitutionally sufficient requires analysis of the governmental and private interests that are affected. . . . More precisely, our prior decisions indicate that identification of the specific dictates of due process generally requires consideration of three distinct factors: first, the private interest that will be affected by the official action; second, the risk of an erroneous deprivation of such interest through the procedures used, and the probable value, if any, of additional or substitute procedural safeguards; and finally, the Government's interest, including the function involved and the fiscal and administrative burdens that the additional or substitute procedural requirement would entail. . . .

Despite the elaborate character of the administrative procedures provided by the Secretary, the courts below held them to be constitutionally inadequate concluding that due process requires an evidentiary hearing prior to termination. In light of the private and governmental interests at stake here and the nature of the existing procedures, we think this was an error.

Since a recipient whose benefits are terminated is awarded full retroactive relief if he ultimately prevails, his sole interest is in the uninterrupted receipt of this source of income pending final administrative decision on his claim. . . .

Only in Goldberg has the Court held that due process requires an evidentiary hearing prior to a temporary deprivation. It was emphasized there that welfare assistance is given to persons on the very margin of subsistence. . . . Eligibility for disability benefits, in contrast, is not based upon financial need. Indeed, it is wholly unrelated to the worker's income or support from many other sources, such as earnings of other family members, workmen's compensation awards, tort claims awards, savings, private insurance, public or private pensions, veterans' benefits, food stamps, public assistance, or the "many other important programs, both public and private, which contain provisions for disability payments affecting a substantial portion of the work force. . . ."

As Goldberg illustrates, the degree of potential deprivation that may be created by a particular decision is a factor to be considered in assessing the validity of any administrative decisionmaking process. . . . The potential deprivation here is generally likely to be less than in Goldberg, although the degree of difference can be overstated. . . . [T]o remain eligible for benefits a recipient must be "unable to engage in substantial gainful activity." . . .

As we recognized last Term, " . . . the possible length of wrongful deprivation of . . . benefits [also] is an important factor in assessing the impact of official action on the private interests." The Secretary concedes that the delay between a request for a hearing before an administrative law judge and a decision on the claim is currently between 10 and 11 months. Since a terminated recipient must first obtain a reconsideration decision as a prerequisite to invoking his right to an evidentiary hearing, the delay between the actual cutoff of benefits and final decision after a hearing exceeds one year.

In view of the torpidity of this administrative review process, . . . and the typically modest resources of the family unit of the physically disabled worker, the hardship imposed upon the erroneously terminated disability recipient may be significant. Still, the disabled worker's need is likely to be less than that of a welfare recipient. In addition to the possibility of access to private resources, other forms of government assistance will become available where the termination of disability benefits places a worker or his family below the subsistence level. . . . In view of these potential sources of temporary income, there is less reason here than in Goldberg to depart from the ordinary principle, established by our decisions, that something less than an evidentiary hearing is sufficient prior to adverse administrative action. . . .

An additional factor to be considered here is the fairness and reliability of the existing pretermination procedures, and the probable value, if any, of additional procedural safeguards. Central to the evaluation of any administrative process is the nature of the relevant inquiry. . . . In order to remain eligible for benefits the disabled worker must demonstrate by means of "medically acceptable clinical and laboratory diagnostic techniques" . . . that he is unable to "engage in any substantial gainful activity by reason of any *medically determinable* physical or mental impairment. . . ." . . . [emphasis supplied]. In short, a medical assessment of the worker's physical or mental condition is required. This is a more sharply focused and easily documented decision than the typical determination of welfare entitlement. In the latter case, a wide variety of information may be deemed relevant, and issues of witness credibility and veracity often are critical to the decisionmaking process. . . .

By contrast, the decision whether to discontinue disability benefits will turn, in most cases, upon "routine, standard, and unbiased medical reports by physician specialists," . . . concerning a subject whom they have personally examined. . . . To be sure, credibility and veracity may be a factor in the ultimate disability assessment in some cases. But procedural due process rules are shaped by the risk of error inherent in the truthfinding process as applied to the generality of cases, not the rare exceptions. The potential value of an evidentiary hearing, or even oral presentation to the decisionmaker, is substantially less in this context than in Goldberg. . . .

A further safeguard against mistake is the policy of allowing the disability recipient's representative full access to all information relied upon by the state agency. In addition, prior to the cutoff of benefits the agency informs the recipients of its tentative assessment, the reasons therefore, and provides a summary of the evidence that it considers most relevant. Opportunity is then afforded the recipient to submit additional evidence or arguments, enabling him to challenge directly the accuracy of information in his file as well as the correctness of the agency's tentative conclusions. These procedures . . . enable the recipient to "mold" his argument to respond to the precise issues which the decisionmaker regards as crucial. . . .

In striking the appropriate due process balance the final factor to be assessed is the public interest. This includes the administrative burden and other societal costs that would be associated with requiring, as a matter of constitutional right, an evidentiary hearing upon demand in all cases prior to the termination of disability benefits. The most visible burden would be the incremental costs resulting from the increased number of hearings and the expense of providing benefits to ineligible recipients pending decision. No one can predict the extent of the increase, but the fact that full benefits would continue until after such hearings would assure the exhaustion in most cases of this attractive option. Nor would the theoretical right of the Secretary to recover undeserved benefits result, as a practical matter, in any substantial offset to the added outlay of public funds. . . . [E]xperience with the constitutionalizing of government procedures suggests that the ultimate additional costs in terms of money and administrative burden would not be insubstantial.

Financial cost alone is not a controlling weight in determining whether due process requires a particular procedural safeguard prior to some administrative decision. But the Government's interest, and hence that of the public, in conserving scarce fiscal and administrative resources, is a factor that must be weighed. At some point the benefit of an additional safeguard to the individual affected by the administrative action and to society, in terms of increased assurance that the action is just, may be outweighed by the cost. Significantly, the cost of protecting those whom the preliminary administrative process has identified as likely to be found underserving may in the end come out of the pockets of the deserving since resources available for any particular program of social welfare are not unlimited. . . .

But more is implicated in cases of this type than ad hoc weighing of fiscal and administrative burdens against the interest of a particular category of claimants. The ultimate balance involves a determination as to when, under our constitutional system, judicial-type procedures must be imposed upon administrative action to assure fairness. We reiterate the wise admonishment of Mr. Justice Frankfurter that differences in the origin and function of administrative agencies "preclude wholesale transplantation of the rules of procedure, trial, and review which have evolved from the history and experience of courts." . . . The judicial model of an evidentiary hearing is neither a required, nor even the most effective, method of decisionmaking in all circumstances. The essence of due process is the requirement that "a person in jeopardy of serious loss [be given] notice of the case against him and opportunity to meet it." . . . All that is necessary is that the procedures be tailored, in light of the decision to be made, to "the capacities and circumstances of those who are to be heard," . . . to insure that they are given a meaningful opportunity to present their case. In assessing what process is due in this case, substantial weight must be given to the good-faith judgments of the individuals charged by Congress with the administration of social welfare programs that the procedures they have provided assure fair consideration of the entitlement claims of individuals. . . . This is especially so where, as here, the prescribed procedures not only provide the claimant with an effective process for asserting his claim prior to any administrative action, but also assure a right to an evidentiary hearing, as well as to subsequent judicial review, before the denial of his claim becomes final. . . .

We conclude that an evidentiary hearing is not required prior to the termination of disability benefits and that the present administrative procedures fully comport with due process. . . .

Reversed.

Mr. Justice Brennan, with whom Mr. Justice Marshall concurs, dissenting.

. . . I agree with the District Court and the Court of Appeals that, prior to termination of benefits, Eldridge must be afforded an evidentiary hearing of the type required for welfare beneficiaries. . . . I would add that the Court's consideration that a discontinuance of disability benefits may cause the recipient to suffer only a limited deprivation is no argument. It is speculative. Moreover, the very legislative deter-

mination to provide disability benefits, without any prerequisite determination of need in fact, presumes a need by the recipient which is not this Court's function to denigrate. Indeed, in the present case, it is indicated that because disability benefits were terminated there was a foreclosure upon the Eldridge home and the family's furniture was repossessed, forcing Eldridge, his wife and children to sleep in one bed. . . . Finally, it is also no argument that a worker, who has been placed in the untenable position of having been denied disability benefits, may still seek other forms of public assistance.*

*Eldridge, a truck driver, claimed in a post-termination hearing that his bad back prevented him from working. The administrative law judge ruled in his favor. Eldridge recovered back benefits in both senses!

The central legal issues in these three cases concern the rule of law itself, which we shall address shortly. To complete this chapter's descriptive theme, consider three background aspects of the legal process reflected in these cases. First, readers may wonder why these cases do not draw upon the requirements stated in *any* administrative procedure act. The answer regarding *Morgan* is simple. The Court decided the case before the federal APA was passed in 1946. As to the relatively recent cases, the APA does not apply because by its own words it does not cover welfare payment programs. The reason for this is complicated enough that we shall treat it separately in later chapters.

Second, students who have studied the legal process may wonder about the applicability of the doctrine of *stare decisis*. This doctrine encourages courts to follow the precedents in previous cases that *control*, that is, are factually similar to, the case in question. Thus one might expect *Goldberg* to control or dictate the result in *Mathews* and to suspect the Court of employing devious reasoning to reach the *Mathews* result. However, a close reading of *Mathews* shows that the Court believed the case did not factually resemble *Goldberg*. The conclusion—that Eldridge did not deserve an oral pretermination hearing because, he, unlike Kelly, could get other forms of public assistance while awaiting a post-termination hearing—is a choice on the part of the six-member majority to narrowly distinguish the two cases. Courts use judicial discretion to decide whether previous cases do or do not factually resemble the one before them.

Finally, recall the earlier point that regulatory law in large part responds to shortcomings the public perceives in the private economic system. You may ask yourself what welfare cases have to do with the shortcomings of free markets, but an important, if not obvious, linkage exists. Welfare programs exist *because* society has come to accept a public obligation to provide for those whom the private system does not, for a variety of reasons, support. For better or worse, once the obligation to provide relief becomes by political consensus a public responsibility, the Due Process Clause and the rule of law do affect how government carries the programs out.

Summary: What Is Administrative Law?

The agencies themselves, with varying amount of legal help from legislatures, create regulatory law. Administrative law comes primarily from judicial interpretations of legal statements prescribing the *procedures* agencies must follow. These come from constitutions, primarily but not exclusively from due process clauses, from administrative procedure statutes when they apply, and from the occasional clause within a statute creating an agency that prescribes a procedure to follow. In this last category falls the requirement for a "full hearing" adjudicated in *Morgan.* Regulatory law governs the citizenry; administrative law governs the government. We might say that administrative law governs the bureaucracy as other constitutional provisions govern the judicial, legislative, and presidential powers in government. With constitutional law, administrative law operates within the framework of political commitment to the rule of law. To this, the final theme of part I, we now turn.

The Rule of Law and the Role of Courts in Administrative Government

The philosophical concept of the rule of law plays a central role in administrative law because it has been a part of our liberal-legal political tradition since the founding of the nation and the adoption of our national constitution. It is a command to those who govern to obey the law and a command to all citizens to respect the law. Abraham Lincoln, in a speech he delivered as a young man, said:

> [L]et every man remember that to violate the law, is to trample on the blood of his father, and to tear the charter of his own, and his children's liberty. Let reverence for the laws be breathed by every American mother, to the lisping babe, that prattles on her lap; let it be taught in schools, in seminaries, and in colleges; let it be written in primers, spelling books, and in almanacs: let it be preached from the pulpit, proclaimed in legislative halls, and enforced in courts of justice. And, in short, let it become the political religion of the nation.... Reason, cold, calculating, unimpassioned reason, must furnish all the materials for our future support and defense. Let those materials be moulded into general intelligence, sound morality and, in particular, a reverence for the Constitution and laws.... [13]

In spite of Lincoln's appeal and the widespread honor given the rule of law, no single operational definition of the concept has won general acceptance either among scholars or the public. This book adopts one of several definitions of the practical

---

[13] Abraham Lincoln, "Address to the Young Men's Lyceum of Springfield, Illinois," 27 January 1838, from T. Harry Williams, ed., *Abraham Lincoln: Selected Speeches, Messages, and Letters* (New York: Rinehart & Co., 1957), 10, 14.

meaning of the rule of law. On this definition rests this book's most important assessments and conclusions about modern administrative law. Therefore let us make this definition as clear as possible by contrasting it with the definitions we reject.

Before describing the varying concepts of the rule of law and selecting among them, one further point needs coverage. While the rule of law as a philosophical matter urges all citizens to obey and respect the law, in operational terms the concept applies primarily to courts. The courts in our constitutional scheme have primary responsibility for deciding what laws mean as they decide concrete cases. The rule of law in operational terms states a role for the courts to play in applying the law in adjudicating cases. It commands judges to play an impartial role in government and politics, just as the rules of football, basketball, and baseball specify roles of impartiality for referees and umpires. But just what law do judges apply and how do they do so impartially? The answers to this question provide the various concepts of the rule of law.

1. *Constitutions are the supreme law of the land; the rule of law therefore requires courts to follow the constitution.* The difficulty with this view is that a constitution's words are often so broad, general, and ambiguous that they provide in themselves no limit on judicial discretion. To cite a due process requirement does not really constrain a judge or help define impartiality because a judge can assert that whatever he or she wishes to accomplish is or isn't due process. This pattern occurred during that point in our economic history when judges struck down a wide variety of social programs regulating business simply by asserting that they violated due process. To continue the analogy to referees, constitutions often say nothing more specific than would a basketball rule that commanded referees "to call a foul whenever a player does something dirty." Such a rule would leave referees free to define "dirty" as they choose.

2. *The rule of law requires judges to enforce statutes as written.* Some legislative language is concrete and clear, but very often it is no less general or ambiguous than the language of constitutions. In fact, statutory imprecision pops up particularly often in administrative law for the simple reason that if Congress could make clear law on a subject, it would not need to create a regulatory body in the first place. Part II of this book will reveal many instances in which Congress has merely commanded agencies "to regulate in the public interest." Also, the phrase *full hearing* is not much clearer than *due process.* In such circumstances judges are just as free under statutes as they are under constitutions to draw on their personal biases. And, if you criticize this argument by citing statutes that do state concrete and unambiguous provisions, you must recall that cases involving this statute usually do not reach the appellate courts precisely because the law is clear. Parties do not routinely invest thousands of dollars of legal fees in cases they expect to lose. For both parties to carry a suit forward, the law must be uncertain enough to lure both sides along by the chance of success.

3. *The rule of law requires judges to follow precedents.* This more limited version of the rule of law admits that judges simply draw on their biases in deciding cases for the first time. The restraint of law arises merely in the obligation to follow these decisions in future similar cases. The trouble here is that, as we saw in *Mathews's* treatment of *Goldberg,* judges are free to say a case is factually different from a previous case and hence escape the restraining influence of prior law.

4. *The rule of law refers to a philosophy of justice, not a concept of "following the law."* If we seek a test of judicial impartiality but cannot find it in the black and white letters of society's rules, a philosophy of justice may offer the only alternative. But which philosophy should judges choose? Should they attempt to articulate prominent social customs? Marxism? A natural law theory? We are on the right track but have yet to locate the proper philosophical train.

5. *The rule of law is a philosophy of compromise and balancing among social interests.* This statement pinpoints a common political as well as judicial approach to constitutional and administrative law problems. The Supreme Court selected this very test in its decision in *Mathews.* It said the costs in *Goldberg* of denying a hearing were greater than in *Mathews* because Eldridge could get welfare payments while he waited but Kelly could not. Many administrative law cases use the language of "balancing interests" because it conveys some idea of weighing interest and producing a fair outcome. But the balancing test usually leaves judges free to define the balance any way they wish. To be sure not all disabled recipients depend on the checks. But most do, and Eldridge certainly did. The costs to him may be less than to Kelly, but does the Court justify effectively that they are *enough* less to tip the balance the other way? Balancing will play a part in the judicial administrative law role, but it does not fully satisfy the obligation to the rule of law.

6. *The rule of law seeks to achieve fairness, rationality, and social equality by promoting public participation in decisionmaking.* Return to the Supreme Court's reasoning in *Morgan* and *Goldberg.* The requirements the cases call for do not leap out of the phrases *full hearing* or *due process of law.* These two opinions call for a set of procedures— confrontation, cross-examination, and so forth—designed to minimize the likelihood that a secretary of agriculture or a welfare supervisor will make the wrong decision in a case. They hope to offset the chances that laziness, the desire to preserve pride, loyalty to one party, biased views toward the facts or the parties, or any other common human failing will produce an irrational decision, that is, a decision not justified by the facts and the law. Legal disputes may be framed in certain ways so as to call for different judicial solutions. In *Mathews,* for example, the Court was concerned with balancing costs and benefits, which is very different from their approach in *Goldberg.* This perspective on the rule of law provides students of American politics and public administration with a guide for interpreting and evaluating the role of judges in administrative law. You will need to study several cases in the following chapters before you begin to feel comfortable with this approach.

This chapter's three cases combined with your own background in the study of American politics suggest one essential characteristic of how the rule of law should operate. Decisionmaking must in some, if not all, respects be an open and public process—open at least to the participation of those immediately affected, open at most to observation by the whole community. *Open* and *public* are not knee-jerk adjectives. They rest on an empirical assumption that when decisionmakers must decide and/or defend their decision in front of potential critics, they will less probably commit the errors that flow from laziness, bias, and the other sources of arbitrariness. The courts themselves attempt to meet this test by writing opinions justifying their results and exposing their reasoning to professional criticism. Public elections seek to push the

*Central to understanding administrative law.

legislative process toward openness. Two of the three cases above pushed toward openness. When the Court required the secretary of agriculture not to meet in private with the Bureau of Animal Industry in reaching a result, when the Court told a welfare office not to cut off a recipient of his or her only funds with which to finance a protest, the Court pushed the administrative decisionmaking process toward publicness.

Note here one critically important aspect of this definition of the rule of law. It does *not* ask the courts themselves to inquire so deeply into decisionmaking as to *guarantee* that the administrator reached the only possible correct decision on the facts. The courts are usually in a poorer position than the parties to judge what is substantively best. The courts' role is instead predominantly procedural. In this perspective the courts seek to insure that the process of decisionmaking minimizes the opportunity for presumptively arbitrary forces to work. It is precisely in this sense that administrative law chooses among theories of fairness. Yet as we discussed earlier in chapter 1, you will need to identify and evaluate the links between procedural fairness and substantive justice when analyzing legal opinions.

7. *The rule of law checks and shapes the power of government by formulating a legal rationality for decisionmaking.* Legal rationality does *not* boil down to a philosophy of compliance, nor is it a simple matter of following the rules or going by the book. Rules are general and judges choose how to apply them to specific cases.

To refine the concept, consider the definition of the "ideal of legality" offered by Philippe Nonet and Philip Selznick. They call it "maximum feasible reduction of arbitrariness."

> But the ideal of legality should not be confused with the paraphernalia of legalization—the proliferation of rules and procedural formalities. The bureaucratic patterns that pass for due process (understood as an "obstacle course") or for accountability (understood as compliance with official rules) are alien to responsive law. The ideal of legality needs to be conceived more generally and to be cured of formalism. In a purposive system legality is the progressive reduction of arbitrariness in positive law and its administration. To press for a maximum feasible reduction of arbitrariness is to demand a system of law that is capable of reaching beyond formal regularity and procedural fairness to substantive justice. That achievement, in turn, requires institutions that are competent as well as legitimate.[14]

The precise nature of legal rationality in administrative law will emerge through the pages of the book. While readers may disagree with each other and with us about the components of rationality, administrative law boils down to a dialogue or political debate about just what is procedurally fair in modern politics and government. Debates have more than one side, however. This book takes a position in the debate, as do all texts, but in the end you must develop the analytical skills and make reasoned judgments for yourself.

---

[14] *Law and Society in Transition: Toward Responsive Law* (New York: Harper Colophon, 1978), 107–108.

In this chapter and in the chapters in the second part of the book you will read many cases resolving many different kinds of legal disputes. Each one is, either implicitly or explicitly, a comment upon the nature of legal rationality and arbitrariness in government. The third and fourth parts of the book will draw on case examples to present a more complete examination of administrative law.

Exercises and Questions for Further Thought

1. The space limits of this book prevent it from covering all aspects of the administrative process itself. There are, however, some general categories of administrative agencies and classifications of their tasks that may help you decipher the facts and issues in cases to follow. It is moderately useful to differentiate the major *values* that drive administrative policies. These include (a) promoting personal safety, (b) assuring social and economic justice, and (c) reallocating wealth. Think of an agency or program in government that illustrates each of these values. Where, for example, does OHSA's regulation of toxic substances in the workplace fit in this scheme? Which of these values figure in the government programs in the three cases in this chapter?

Next, consider the *tools* of administration. The main administrative task is to shape events and influence behavior. In this regard the bureaucrat and the businessperson, the parent and the football coach, share the same task. How does any of us influence events and behavior? The most common way to control something is to claim ownership. Feudalism was a system of government built upon this idea. Kings claimed they and those beneath them literally possessed their kingdoms just as we possess automobiles and homes, at least once we pay off the loan. Today public or governmental ownership plays a less significant role than it once did, at least in Western civilization. But public ownership and management nevertheless remain an important governmental tool. Governments build and manage many things. The Tennessee Valley Authority, for example, controls flooding and produces energy by owning and managing resources.

The second main tool of government is regulation. Parents do not own their children, but they do regulate their behavior. The administrator may work with a more complex set of problems than the parent, but when they regulate, both will resort to one or a combination of these factors they hope will influence behavior: *prescription, promotion, permission,* and *prohibition.* The Federal Communications Commission *prescribes* that station operators must provide the FCC routinely with logs and other information about their daily programing. The National Science Foundation *promotes* scholarly research by giving money to the best research proposals. The Nuclear Regulatory Commission *permits* a nuclear power plant to begin operation if it has passed their safety tests. The FCC *prohibits* any company from owning more than the maximum number of station outlets promulgated in FCC rules. Think of others.

Is it not true that each public agency is a mix of values and tools but that the mix varies from agency to agency? What, for example, is the mix of values and tools in Amtrak? The Environmental Protection Agency? The Food Stamp program? Can you think of other mixes of values and tools in "real world" administrative agencies? Which mixes characterize the agencies in this chapter's three cases? Remember that these are policy values and official administrative tools. The people involved in any given decision may operate from very different personal values and use much more specific and subtle tools to achieve an immediate result.

2. Suppose an elected county "Commission" creates and funds a "County Health Department." The commissioners appoint a department head who in turn employs various subordinates, each with responsibility for a different kind of health problem. One such division is called the "Division of Animal and Livestock Diseases." The head of this division decides to issue the following rule, which the division head has published in the legal notice section of the local paper: "The maintaining of any pen or lot for the keeping of swine within 200 feet of any dwelling or potable water supply shall not be permitted."

A professor living in that town gives his son a pet piglet for Christmas. When the pig gets too smelly and unmanageable to live in its cardboard box in the house—that is, about December 26—the boy moves the pig under the house, where it lives in the crawlspace running the entire length of the house. Assume the family lets the pig out to play from time to time, and a cranky neighbor becomes offended by the sight. Assume also the pig badly startles more than one jogger trotting down the street late on winter afternoons.

Pigs are one of nature's most efficient converters of grain into meat, and this pig grows rapidly into the size, speed, and friendliness of a St. Bernard. The neighbor complains to the Health Department, and one March afternoon, a Ms. South, of the Animal and Livestock Disease Division, appears at the door. She informs the family that the pig must go because, she says, "You can't keep pigs in the county. It's against the law."

When the professor reads the rule she immediately sees she can make at least three arguments that the rule does not govern here:

(i) The crawlspace under the house is not a pen or lot for the keeping of the swine.
(ii) "Swine" is a plural word and does not cover keeping one pet pig.
(iii) The purpose of the rule is clearly to prevent noise and nose pollution, water pollution, and so on, and one pet pig simply cannot do the harm the act seeks to prevent. Therefore the rule does not apply.

List separately all the questions of (a) regulatory law and (b) administrative law this story might raise. Invent further facts if they will help.

3. After you have mastered the Court's handling of the legal questions in this chapter's three cases, try to identify how each majority opinion defines the problem of arbitrariness in public administration. Is there a difference in emphasis, particularly between *Mathews*, on one hand, and its two predecessors, on the other? Is it fair to say that *Mathews* is more concerned about the trade-off between fairness to the individual and cost to society? Is it not true that courts must consider this trade-off to avoid arbitrariness—that we cannot afford complete and total fairness to individuals at all times regardless of cost?

4. The three cases in this chapter all involve decisions about an individual's or a business enterprise's specific claims, rights, and interests. Where administrators decide the fortunes of an individual on the unique facts of his, her, or its case, they resemble

judges. As you may have guessed by now, the degree to which these judges must operate like actual judges in the legal system is one of the most common problems in the field. Think of other instances in which public officials act like judges. Does a teacher who assigns a grade in a class do so? Does a policewoman who makes a speeding arrest do so? How far would such decisions about the individuals be formalized? Also you should anticipate that agencies often act like legislatures, that is, they may promulgate rules covering entire industries. The Federal Trade Commission, for example, issued rules in 1964 requiring all cigarette labels to carry a health warning. Start thinking about the legal limits, if any, that the ideal of legality which Nonet and Selznick discuss should call for in administrative rulemaking.

5. Suppose exposure to a certain substance, asbestos, for example, is known to correlate with certain forms of cancer. What if a public agency charged with promoting public health rules that manufacturing plants, hotels, restaurants, and other public places must reduce exposure to asbestos as far as is technically feasible? If it is technically feasible to eliminate asbestos altogether, would it be arbitrary to do so? Does not this question depend on whether scientific evidence has shown that *any* exposure to asbestos might cause cancer? What if scientists need several more years of research before they can hope to answer this question? If this is so, would it be arbitrary for the health agency to "play it safe" or is it rational and not arbitrary to play it safe when the dangers are not yet fully known? Chapter 3 describes the Supreme Court's recent efforts to struggle with a closely related problem.

6. One important justification for judicial oversight of the administrative process is that the threat of judicial action and consequent exposure of wrongdoing to the public will motivate some to avoid the temptations of corruption in the first place. With this in mind, comment on the following story from the *Wall Street Journal:*

Houston's Tax Breaks Aimed at Business Require Immediate Remedy, Judge Rules

The *Wall Street Journal*
14 September 1981, p. 42

HOUSTON— A state court judge has issued a ruling that is forcing city officials there to confront a troublesome question: Have city tax assessors gone overboard in extending big tax breaks to big business?

Critics have long contended that this booming Texas town is run for and by big business—especially big oil. But it wasn't until mayoral candidate Noble Ginther, Jr. filed a lawsuit—accusing the city of omitting as much as $10 billion in "personal" property owned by big companies from the tax rolls in return for political favors—that the issue gained widespread public attention.

"We always knew that the big companies here weren't paying their fair share of the taxes," contends Ann Wheeler, head of the Greater Houston Tax Coalition, a taxpayers group. "But this town is ruled by big business, and we didn't think anybody could get them to pay up." . . .

But last week Judge Arthur Lesher issued a preliminary ruling that has caused considerable grief and embarrassment for Houston's corporate chieftains and city administrators. The judge ruled that tax breaks given to businesses and huge inequities in Houston's tax structure require immediate remedy. The judge issued a mandatory injunction ordering Houston's tax department to put all taxable personal property on the tax rolls, and he gave subpoena power to a special court-appointed "master" to see to it that the job gets done.

PART II

Elements of Modern
Administrative Law

CHAPTER 3

The Statutory Authority of Agencies

The sequence of the next six chapters roughly follows the sequence of steps leading to a final agency decision. Beginning students have no reason to know this pattern beforehand, so let us explain it here. Any agency action begins with an authorizing rule from an elected body. Usually this is a congressional statute, occasionally an executive order. Agencies have no constitutional status unless and until this statutory language creates them. This chapter explores the significance of statutory language. Chapter 4 addresses the next step—the gathering of information about problems needing administrative attention. Once an agency recognizes a problem exists, it may resolve it by informal means. Chapter 5 describes these informal procedures and in doing so introduces by comparison formal adjudication (chapter 6) and formal rulemaking (chapter 7). The next step, enforcement (chapter 8), prepares the way for judicial intervention, judicial review of administrative actions (chapter 9). Not all cases actually follow this sequence because courts review only a tiny fraction of administrative decisions, and sometimes the courts review early in the process. But it is a rough approximation.

One way the Constitution limits and defines government power is by separating it. Legislatures make laws. Presidents and governors execute laws by supervising the governmental machinery that applies the laws to practical stituations. The courts enforce the laws by resolving disputes about the meaning of laws in particular situations.

This division of state power we call the separation of powers doctrine. Although the Constitution only defines the powers of three branches of government, its scheme strongly implies an administrative process—the execution machinery—to work in the following way: legislatures must authorize by statute any sanction or control that government imposes on citizens. Administrative agency decisions are legally valid only when they conform to statutory authority. Therefore the task of the courts, and of administrative law, is to ensure that agencies act only with legislative permission, and of course within constitutional constraints. Judicial determination—whether an agency in fact operates within the scope of its statutory authority and the Constitution—leads us into issues of statutory and constitutional interpretation. When reviewing agency actions, how do courts interpret statutes and the Constitution?

The introductory chapters have already hinted that the system does not operate in a simple, clear-cut fashion. The allocation of government lawmaking is not a simple separation model. Courts order school desegregation, presidents order troops into combat in foreign countries, administrators make rules about environmental safety—all without any convincing proof of either statutory authorization or even political approval of the policy. Justice Robert Jackson once described administrative agencies in the following way:

> [Administrative agencies] have become a veritable fourth branch of Government, which has deranged our three-branch legal theories much as the concept of a fourth dimension unsettles our three-dimensional thinking. Courts have differed in assigning a place to these seemingly necessary bodies in our constitutional system. Administrative agencies have been called quasi-legislative, quasi-executive or quasi-judicial, as the occasion required, in order to validate their functions within the separation-of-powers scheme of the Constitution. The mere retreat to the qualifying "quasi" is implicit with confession that all recognized classifications have broken down, and "quasi" is a smooth cover which we draw over our confusion as we might use a counterpane to conceal a disordered bed.[1]

Justice Jackson's words remain apt. This chapter describes what remains of the statutory linkage between elected legislators and appointed administrators. Later chapters will illustrate the political negotiating between legislatures and agencies that takes place within the legal context.

Richard B. Stewart has explained why the simple separation model fails, and his description is worth digesting before turning to the details.[2] To put it curtly, many statutes do not in fact prescribe specific policies for the agencies to execute in the first place. Some legislation explicitly confers on agencies the discretion to make up their own policies. Other legislation may attempt to articulate general policy preferences in vague, general, or ambiguous language that does not translate directly into specific decisions. This statue of statutory nondirection can occur for several reasons. Not all problems have solutions. The political pressures on elected officials to do something about a problem are hard to resist, but when legislators don't have solutions, they tend to appoint a bureaucracy to find solutions. On the more pragmatic political side, a majority may agree a problem exists, but different minorities within the same majority may believe in different solutions. The legislative compromise may omit specific solution and establish general, vague and even ambiguous goals and guidelines. Finally, in the press of other business, legislators may simply not have the time or incentive to hammer out specifics on many issues. Thus the administrative law question for the courts concerns both the meaning of statutes (statutory interpretation) and the appropriate degree of administrative discretion under the statute. To this we now turn.

---

[1] *FTC v. Ruberoid Co.,* 343 U.S. 470, 487–488 (1952).

[2] "The Reformation of American Administrative Law," *Harvard Law Review* 88 (1975): 1669.

Political Perspectives on Regulation and Statutory Authority

Administrative agencies may receive little specific policy guidance from legislatures. Nevertheless constitutions indirectly affect the statutory basis of administration. For example, agencies cannot exist or operate without statutory authorization. The constitutional scheme in the United States gives legislatures practical control of the purse strings. A completely unpopular or runaway agency faces the possibility of finding itself meagerly provided for by the appropriations statutes. This constitutionally imposed statutory control of agencies through the power of the purse is extremely powerful, more often as a veiled threat than actual punishment.

Constitutional law, however, prevents legislatures from creating agencies by statute to perform impermissible tasks. If, for example, a legislature created a Citizen Censorship Committee for the Press (the CCCP) and empowered it to review in advance all publications and prohibit publication of those that were "not in the public interest," courts would most likely invalidate the legislation. Since 1931 the Supreme Court has held that virtually all forms of prior restraint violate the free press guarantees of the First and Fourteenth Amendments.[3]

The question of whether state legislatures or Congress can constitutionally delegate legislative powers to boards, commissions, and agencies is not simply a legal issue. Indeed, to comprehend the shifting judicial philosophies toward delegation it is important to first have a sense of the political controversy over government regulation. While this controversy continues today, the following Supreme Court cases—*Munn v. Illinois* (1876), *Lochner v. New York* (1905), and *NLBR v. Jones & Laughlin Steel Corp.* (1937)—illustrate how political perspectives shape legal interpretations of statutory authority.

Munn v. Illinois

94 U.S. 113 (1876) 7–2
+ Waite, Clifford, Swayne, Miller, Davis, Bradley, Hunt
− Field, Strong

[Article XIII of the Illinois Constitution, adopted in 1870, declared grain elevators to be "public warehouses" and gave the general assembly the power to pass legislation relating to the storage of grain. In 1871, the assembly passed an act creating a state commission for the purposes of establishing rates which warehouse owners could charge, requiring licenses to operate a warehouse, and other regulations governing the conduct of warehouse owners and operators. Munn & Scott, managers and proprietors of a grain warehouse in Chicago, were convicted and fined $100 for operating a ware-

---

[3] *Near v. Minnesota*, 283 U.S. 697 (1931). See *Nebraska Press Association v. Stuart*, 427 U.S. 539 (1976). "Prior restraint" is the legal term covering most forms of censorship. This rule does not prohibit punishing someone *after* they have published material in violation of law, e.g., military secrets.

house without a license and for charging farmers, whose grain they stored, prices higher than those specified by the commission. They sought review in the U.S. Supreme Court on a writ of error after failing to reverse this conviction in the Illinois Supreme Court.]

Chief Justice Waite delivered the opinion of the court.

The question to be determined in this case is whether the general assembly of Illinois can, under the limitations upon the legislative power of the States imposed by the Constitution of the United States, fix by law the maximum of charges for the storage of grain in warehouses at Chicago and other places in the State having not less than one hundred thousand inhabitants, "in which grain is stored in bulk, and in which the grain of different owners is mixed together, or in which grain is stored in such a manner that the identity of different lots or parcels cannot be accurately preserved."

It is claimed that such a law is repugnant—

1. To that part of sect. 8, art. 1, of the Constitution of the United States which confers upon Congress the power "to regulate commerce with foreign nations and among the several States;"
2. To that part of sect. 9 of the same article which provides that "no preference shall be given by any regulation of commerce or revenue to the ports of one State over those of another;" and
3. To that part of amendment 14 which ordains that no State shall "deprive any person of life, liberty, or property, without due process of law, nor deny to any person within its jurisdiction the equal protection of the laws."

We will consider the last of these objections first. . . .

The Constitution contains no definition of the word "deprive," as used in the Fourteenth Amendment. To determine its signification, therefore, it is necessary to ascertain the effect which usage has given it, when employed in the same or a like connection.

While this provision of the amendment is new in the Constitution of the United States, as a limitation upon the powers of the States, it is old as a principle of civilized government. It is found in Magna Charta, and, in substance if not in form, in nearly or quite all the constitutions that have been from time to time adopted by the several States of the Union. By the Fifth Amendment, it was introduced into the Cosntitution of the United States as a limitation upon the powers of the national government, and by the Fourteenth, as a guaranty against any encroachment upon an acknowledged right of citizenship by the legislatures of the States. . . .

When one becomes a member of society, he necessarily parts with some rights or privileges which, as an individual not affected by his relations to others, he might retain. "A body politic," as aptly defined in the preamble of the Constitution of Massachusetts, "is a social compact by which the whole people covenants with each citizen, and each citizen with the whole people, that all shall be governed by certain laws for the common good." This does not confer power upon the whole people to control rights which are purely and exclusively private, . . . but it does authorize the establishment of laws requiring each citizen to so conduct himself, and so use his own property, as not unnecessarily to injure another. This is the very essence of government, and has found expression in the maxim *sic utere tuo ut alienum non laedas* [so use your own as not to injure others]. From this source come the police powers, which, as was said by Mr. Chief Justice Taney in the *License Cases*, . . . "are nothing more or less than powers of government inherent in every sovereignty, . . . that is to say, . . . the power to govern men and things." Under these powers the government regulates the conduct of its citizens one towards another, and the manner in which each shall use his own property, when such regulation becomes necessary for the public good. In their exercise it has been customary in England from time immemorial, and in this country from its first colonization to regulate ferries, common carriers, hackmen, bakers, millers, wharfingers, innkeepers, &c., and in so doing to fix a maximum of charge to be made for services rendered, accommodations furnished, and articles sold. To this day, statutes are to be found in many of the States upon some or all these subjects;

and we think it has never yet been successfully contended that such legislation came within any of the constitutional prohibitions against interference with private property. With the Fifth Amendment in force, Congress, in 1820, conferred power upon the city of Washington "to regulate . . . the rates of wharfage at private wharves, . . . the sweeping of chimneys, and to fix the rates of fees therefor, . . . and the weight and quality of bread," . . . and, in 1848, "to make all necessary regulations respecting hackney carriages and the rates of fare of the same, and the rates of hauling by cartmen, wagoners, carmen, and draymen, and the rates of commission of auctioneers." . . .

From this it is apparent that, down to the time of the adoption of the Fourteenth Amendment, it was not supposed that statutes regulating the use, or even the price of the use, of private property necessarily deprived an owner of his property without due process of law. Under some circumstances they may, but not under all. The amendment does not change the law in this particular: it simply prevents the States from doing that which will operate as such a deprivation.

This brings us to inquire as to the principles upon which this power of regulation rests, in order that we may determine what is within and what without its operative effect. Looking, then, to the common law, from whence came the right which the Constitution protects, we find that when private property is "affected with a public interest, it ceases to be *juris privati* only." This was said by Lord Chief Justice Hale more than two hundred years ago, in his treatise *De Portibus Maris*, . . . and has been accepted without objection as an essential element in the law of property ever since. Property does become clothed with a public interest when used in a manner to make it of public consequence, and affect the community at large. When, therefore, one devotes his property to a use in which the public has an interest, he, in effect, grants to the public an interest in that use, and must submit to be controlled by the public for the common good, to the extent of the interest he has thus created. He may withdraw his grant by discontinuing the use; but, so long as he maintains the use, he must submit to the control. . . .

We . . . quote . . . the words of . . . eminent expounders of the common law, because, as we think, we find in them the principle which supports the legislation we are now examining. Of Lord Hale it was once said by a learned American judge,—

"In England, even on rights of prerogative, they scan his words with as much care as if they had been found in Magna Charta; and the meaning once ascertained, they do not trouble themselves to search any further." . . .

In later times, the same principle came under consideration in the Supreme Court of Alabama. That court was called upon in 1841, to decide whether the power granted to the city of Mobile to regulate the weight and price of bread was unconstitutional, and it was contended that "it would interfere with the right of the citizen to pursue his lawful trade or calling in the mode his judgment might dictate;" but the court said, "there is no motive . . . for this interference on the part of the legislature with the lawful actions of individuals, or the mode in which private property shall be enjoyed, unless such calling affects the public interest, or private property is employed in a manner which directly affects the body of the people. Upon this principle, in this State, tavern-keepers are licensed; . . . and the County Court is required, at least once a year, to settle the rates of inn-keepers. Upon the same principle is founded the control which the legislature has always exercised in the establishment and regulation of mills, ferries, bridges, turnpike roads, and other kindred subjects." *Mobile v. Yuille*, 3 Ala. N. S. 140.

From the same source comes the power to regulate the charges of common carriers, . . . [who] exercise a sort of public office, and have duties to perform in which the public is interested. . . . Their business is, therefore, "affected with a public interest," within the meaning of the doctrine which Lord Hale has so forcibly stated.

. . . Enough has already been said to show that, when private property is devoted to a public use, it is subject to public regulation. It remains only to ascertain whether the warehouses of these plantiffs in error, and the business which is carried on there, come within the operation of this principle.

For this purpose we accept as true the statements of fact contained in the elaborate brief of one of the counsel of the plantiffs in error. From these it appears that "the great producing region of the West and North-west sends its grain by water and rail to Chicago, where the greater part of it is shipped by vessel for transportation to the seaboard by the Great Lakes, and some of it is forwarded by railway to the Eastern ports. . . . Vessels, to some extent, are loaded in the Chicago harbor, and sailed through the St. Lawrence, directly to Europe. . . . The quantity [of grain] received in Chicago has made it the greatest grain market in the world. This business has created a demand for means by which the immense quantity of grain can be handled or stored, and these have been found in grain warehouses, which are commonly called elevators, because the grain is elevated from the boat or car, by machinery operated by steam, into the bins prepared for its reception, and elevated from the bins, by a like process, into the vessel or car which is to carry it on. . . . In this way the largest traffic between the citizens of the country north and west of Chicago and the citizens of the country lying on the Atlantic coast north of Washington is in grain which passes through the elevators of Chicago. In this way the trade in grain is carried on by the inhabitants of seven or eight of the great States of the West with four or five of the States lying on the sea-shore, and forms the largest part of inter-state commerce in these States. The grain warehouses or elevators in Chicago are immense structures, holding from 300,000 to 1,000,000 bushels at one time, according to size. They are divided into bins of large capacity and great strength. . . . They are located with the river harbor on one side and the railway tracks on the other; and the grain is run through them from car to vessel, or boat to car, as may be demanded in the course of business. It has been found impossible to preserve each owner's grain separate, and this has given rise to a system of inspection and grading, by which the grain of different owners is mixed, and receipts issued for the number of bushels which are negotiable, and redeemable in like kind, upon demand. This mode of conducting the business was inaugurated more than twenty years ago, and has grown to immense proportions. The railways have found it impracticable to own such elevators, and public policy forbids the transaction of such business by the carrier; the ownership has, therefore, been by private individuals, who have embarked their capital and devoted their industry to such business as a private pursuit."

In this connection it must also be borne in mind that, although in 1874 there were in Chicago fourteen warehouses adapted to this particular business, and owned by about thirty persons, nine business firms controlled them, and that the prices charged and received for storage were such "as have been from year to year agreed upon and established by the different elevators or warehouses in the city of Chicago, and which rates have been annually published in one or more newspapers printed in said city, in the month of January in each year, as the established rates for the year then next ensuing such publication." Thus it is apparent that all the elevating facilities through which these vast productions "of seven or eight great States of the West" must pass on the way "to four or five of the States on the sea-shore" may be a "virtual" monopoly.

Under such circumstances it is difficult to see why, if the common carrier, or the miller, or the ferryman, or the innkeeper, or the wharfinger, or the baker, or the cartman, or the hackney-coachman, pursues a public employment and exercise "a sort of public office," these plantiffs in error do not. They stand, to use again the language of their counsel, in the very "gateway of commerce," and take toll from all who pass. Their business most certainly "tends to a common charge, and is become a thing of public interest and use." Every bushel of grain for its passage "pays a toll, which is a common charge," and, therefore, according to Lord Hale, every such warehouseman "ought to be under public regulation, viz., that he . . . take but reasonable toll." Certainly, if any business can be clothed "with a public interest, and cease to be *juris privati* only," this has been. It may not be made so by the operation of the Constitution of Illinois or this statute, but it is by the facts.

We also are not permitted to overlook the fact that, for some reason, the people of Illinois, when they revised their Constitution in 1870, saw fit to make it the duty of the general assembly to pass laws "for the protection of producers, shippers, and receivers of grain and produce." . . . This indicates very clearly that during the twenty years in which this peculiar business had been assuming its present "immense proportions," something had occurred which led the whole body of the people to suppose that remedies such as are usually employed to prevent abuses by virtual monopolies might not be inappropriate here. For our purposes we must assume that, if a state of facts could exist that would justify such legislation, it actually did exist when the statute now under consideration was passed. For us the question is one of power, not of expediency. If no state of circumstances could exist to justify such a statute, then we may declare this one void, because in excess of the legislative power of the State. But if it could, we must presume it did. Of the propriety of legislative interference within the scope of legislative power, the legislature is the exclusive judge.

Neither is it a matter of any moment that no precedent can be found for a statute precisely like this. It is conceded that the business is one of recent origin, that its growth has been rapid, and that it is already of great importance. And it must also be conceded that it is a business in which the whole public has a direct and positive interest. It presents, therefore, a case for the application of a long-known and well-established principle in social science, and this statute simply extends the law so as to meet this new development of commercial progress. There is no attempt to compel these owners to grant the public an interest in their property, but to declare their obligations, if they use it in this particular manner. . . .

It is insisted, however, that the owner of property is entitled to a reasonable compensation for its use, even though it be clothed with a public interest, and that what is reasonable is a judicial and not a legislative question.

As has already been shown, the practice has been otherwise. In countries where the common law prevails, it has been customary from time immemorial for the legislature to declare what shall be a reasonable compensation under such circumstances, or, perhaps more properly speaking, to fix a maximum beyond which any charge made would be unreasonable. Undoubtedly, in mere private contracts, relating to matters in which the public has no interest, what is reasonable must be ascertained judicially. But this is because the legislature has no control over such a contract. So, too, in matters which do affect the public interest, and as to which legislative control may be exercised, if there are no statutory regulations upon the subject, the courts must determine what is reasonable. The controlling fact is the power to regulate at all. If that exists, the right to establish the maximum of charge, as one of the means of regulation, is implied. In fact, the common-law rule, which requires the charge to be reasonable, is itself a regulation as to price. Without it the owner could make his rates at will, and compel the public to yield to his terms, or forego the use.

But a mere common-law regulation of trade or business may be changed by statute. A person has no property, no vested interest, in any rule of the common law. That is only one of the forms of municipal law, and is no more sacred than any other. Rights of property which have been created by the common law cannot be taken away without due process; but the law itself, as a rule of conduct, may be changed at the will, or even at the whim, of the legislature, unless prevented by constitutional limitations. Indeed, the great office of statutes is to remedy defects in the common law as they are developed, and to adapt it to the changes of time and circumstances. To limit the rate of charge for services rendered in a public employment, or for the use of property in which the public has an interest, is only changing a regulation which existed before. It establishes no new principle in the law, but only gives a new effect to an old one.

We know that this is a power which may be abused but that is no argument against its existence. For protection against abuses by legislatures the people must resort to the polls, not to the courts. . . .

We come now to consider the effect upon this statute of the power of Congress to regulate commerce.

It was very properly said in the case of the *State Tax on Railway Gross Receipts*, 15 Wall. 293, that "it is not every thing that affects commerce that amounts to a regulation of it, within the meaning of the Constitution." The warehouses of these plantiffs in error are situated and their business carried on exclusively within the limits of the State of Illinois. They are used as instruments by those engaged in State as well as those engaged in inter-state commerce, but they are no more necessarily a part of commerce itself than the dray or the cart by which, but for them, grain would be transferred from one railroad station to another. Incidentally they may become connected with inter-state commerce, but not necessarily so. Their regulation is a thing of domestic concern, and, certainly, until Congress acts in reference to their inter-state relations, the State may exercise all the powers of government over them, even though in so doing it may indirectly operate upon commerce outside its immediate jurisdiction. We do not say that case may not arise in which it will be found that a State, under the form of regulating its own affairs, has encroached upon the exclusive domain of Congress in respect to inter-state commerce, but we do say that, upon the facts as they are represented to us in their record, that has not been done. . . .

Judgement affirmed.

Justice Field and Justice Strong dissented.

Justice Field. I am compelled to dissent from the decision of the court in this case, and from the reasons upon which that decision is founded. The principle upon which the opinion of the majority proceeds is, in my judgment, subversive of the rights of private property, heretofore believed to be protected by constitutional guaranties against legislative interference, and is in conflict with the authorities cited in its support. . . .

The declaration of the Constitution of 1870, that private buildings used for private purposes shall be deemed public institutions, does not make them so. The receipt and storage of grain in a building erected by private means for that purpose does not constitute the building a public warehouse. There is no magic in the language, though used by a constitutional convention, which can change a private business into a public one, or alter the character of the building in which the business is transacted. A tailor's

or a shoemaker's shop would still retain its private character, even though the assembled wisdom of the State should declare, by organic act or legislative ordinance, that such a place was a public workshop, and that the workmen were public tailors or public shoemakers. One might as well attempt to change the nature of colors, by giving them a new designation. The defendants were no more public warehousemen, as justly observed by counsel, than the merchant who sells his merchandise to the public is a public merchant, or the blacksmith who shoes horses for the public is a public blacksmith; and it was a strange notion that by calling them so they would be brought under legislative control. . . .

. . . The doctrine declared is that property "becomes clothed with a public interest when used in a manner to make it of public consequence, and affect the community at large;" and from such clothing the right of the legislature is deduced to control the use of the property, and to determine the compensation which the owner may receive for it. When Sir Matthew Hale, and the sages of the law in his day, spoke of property as affected by a public interest, and ceasing from that cause to be *juris privati* solely, that is, ceasing to be held merely in private right, they referred to property dedicated by the owner to public uses, or to property the use of which was granted by the government, or in connection with which special privileges were conferred. Unless the property was thus dedicated, or some right bestowed by the government was held with the property, either by specific grant or by prescription of so long a time as to imply a grant originally, the property was not accepted by any public interest so as to be taken out of the category of property held in private right. But it is not in any such sense that the terms "clothing property with a public interest" are used in this case. From the nature of the business under consideration—the storage of grain—which, in any sense in which the words can be used, is a private business, in which the public are interested only as they are interested in the storage of other products of the soil, or in articles of manufacture, it is clear that the court intended to declare that, whenever one devotes his property to a business which is useful to the public,—"affects the community at large,"— the legislature can regulate the compensation which the owner may receive for its use, and for his own services in connection with it." . . .

If this be sound law, if there be no protection, either in the principles upon which our republican government is founded, or in the prohibitions of the Constitution against such invasion of private rights, all property and all business in the State are held at the mercy of a majority of its legislature. The public has no greater interest in the use of buildings for the storage of grain than it has in the use of buildings for the residences of families, nor, indeed, any thing like so great an interest; and, according to the doctrine announced, the legislature may fix the rent of all tenements used for residences, without reference to the cost of their erection. If the owner does not like the rates prescribed, he may cease renting his houses. He has granted to the public, says the court, an interest in the use of the buildings, and "he may withdraw his grant by discontinuing the use; but, so long as he maintains the use, he must submit to the control." The public is interested in the manufacture of cotton, woollen, and silken fabrics, in the construction of machinery, in the printing and publication of books and periodicals, and in the making of utensils of every variety, useful and ornamental; indeed, there is hardly an enterprise or business engaging the attention and labor of any considerable portion of the community, in which the public has not an interest in the sense in which that term is used by the court in its opinion; and the doctrine which allows the legislature to interfere with and regulate the charges which the owners of property thus employed shall make for its use, that is, the rates at which all these different kinds of business shall be carried on, has never before been asserted, so far as I am aware, by any judicial tribunal in the United States. . . .

. . . If the constitutional guaranty extends no further than to prevent a deprivation of title and possession, and allows a deprivation of use, and the fruits of that use, it does not merit the encomiums it has received. Unless I have misread the history of the provision now incorporated into all our State constitutions, and by the Fifth and Fourteenth Amendments

into our Federal Constitution, and have misunderstood the interpretation it has received, it is not thus limited in its scope, and thus impotent for good. It has a much more extended operation than either court, State, or Federal has given to it. The provision, it is to be observed, places property under the same protection as life and liberty. Except by due process of law, no State can deprive any person of either. The provision has been supposed to secure to every individual the essential conditions for the pursuit of happiness; and for that reason has not been heretofore, and should never be, construed in any narrow or restricted sense.

No State "shall deprive any person of life, liberty, or property without due process of law," says the Fourteenth Amendment to the Constitution. . . .

By the term "liberty," as used in the provision, something more is meant than mere freedom from physical restraint or the bounds of a prison. It means freedom to go where one may choose, and to act in such manner, not inconsistent with the equal rights of others, as his judgment may dictate for the promotion of his happiness; that is, to pursue such callings and avocations as may be most suitable to develop his capacities, and give to them their highest enjoyment.

The same liberal construction which is required for the protection of life and liberty, in all particulars in which life and liberty are of any value, should be applied to the protection of private property. If the legislature of a State, under pretence of providing for the public good, or for any other reason, can determine, against the consent of the owner, the uses to which private property shall be devoted, or the prices which the owner shall receive for its uses, it can deprive him of the property as completely as by a special act for its confiscation or destruction. . . . The power of the State over the property of the citizen under the constitutional guaranty is well defined. The State may take his property for public uses, upon just compensation being made therefore. It may take a portion of his property by way of taxation for the support of the government. It may control the use and possession of his property, so far as may be necessary for the protection of the rights of others, and to secure to them the equal use and enjoyment of their property. The doctrine that each one must so use his own as not to injure his neighbor—*sic utere tuo ut alienum non laedas*—is the rule by which every member of society must possess and enjoy his property; and all legislation essential to secure this common and equal enjoyment is a legitimate exercise of State authority. Except in cases where property may be destroyed to arrest a conflagration or the ravages of pestilence, or be taken under the pressure of an immediate and overwhelming necessity to prevent a public calamity, the power of the State over the property of the citizen does not extend beyond such limits. . . .

There is nothing in the character of the business of the defendants as warehousemen which called for the interference complained of in this case. Their buildings are not nuisances; their occupation of receiving and storing grain infringes upon no rights of others, disturbs no neighborhood, infects not the air, and in no respect prevents others from using and enjoying their property as to them may seem best. The legislation in question is nothing less than a bold assertion of absolute power by the State to control at its discretion the property and business of the citizen, and fix the compensation he shall receive. The will of the legislature is made the condition upon which the owner shall receive the fruits of his property and

the just reward of his labor, industry, and enterprise. "That government," says Story, "can scarcely be deemed to be free where the rights of property are left solely dependent upon the will of a legislative body without any restraint. The fundamental maxims of a free government seem to require that the rights of personal liberty and private property should be held sacred." . . . The decision of the court in this case gives unrestrained license to legislative will. . . .

In the case decided by the Supreme Court of Alabama, where a power granted to the city of Mobile to license bakers, and to regulate the weight and price of bread, was sustained so far as regulating the weight of the bread was concerned, no question was made as to the right to regulate the price. . . . There is no doubt of the competency of the State to prescribe the weight of a loaf of bread, as it may declare what weight shall constitute a pound or a ton. But I deny the power of any legislature under our government to fix the price which one shall receive for his property of any kind. If the power can be exercised as to one article, it may as to all articles, and the prices of every thing, from a calico gown to a city mansion, may be the subject of legislative direction.

I am of opinion that the judgment of the Supreme Court of Illinois should be reversed.

Justice Strong concurred with Justice Field's dissent.

The political perspective advocated by Justice Field in his famous dissent in *Munn* became the Supreme Court's majority view on regulation by the late nineteenth century. With the appointment of six new justices to the Court between 1880 and 1890 and an aggressive effort by lawyers who represented business interests before the Court, laissez faire dominated judicial ideology.[4] Justice Field's dissent in *Munn* states this ideology clearly: "If a monopoly results [from the absence of state regulation] it is an outgrowth of 'entrepreneurial talent,' and such 'talent' should be protected by the judiciary." The Court's shift away from *Munn* directly attacked the view that government should protect the public from unfair business practices, such as monopolies with deprive consumers of market choices.

In *Chicago, Milwaukee and St. Paul R.R. Co. v. Minnesota* (1890),[5] several railroads challenged the constitutionality of an 1887 Minnesota statute regulating railroad rates. The Minnesota State Supreme Court upheld the statute based on the Court's reasoning

[4]See Benjamin Twiss, *Lawyers and the Constitution* (Princeton, N.J.: Princeton University Press, 1942).
[5]134 U.S. 418.

in *Munn*. On appeal, the U.S. Supreme Court overturned the statute, arguing that it stripped the power of a court to "stay the hands of the commission, if it [the commission] chooses to establish rates that are unequal and unreasonable." The Court not only objected to the commission's power to establish fair rates for privately owned railroads, but the Court also emphatically established the judiciary's authority to decide what constitutes a fair market rate. Thus regulatory schemes were attacked by industrial capitalists *and* the federal judges during the period when laissez faire economics influenced the judiciary's legal and political views on regulation (1890–1930s).

Lochner v. New York

198 U.S. 45 (1905) 5–4
+ Peckham, Brown, White, Fuller, Brewer
− Harlan, Holmes, White, Day

[In this case the Supreme Court reviewed the constitutionality of a New York state statute passed in 1897 that prohibited employment in a bakery for more than sixty hours a week or ten hours a day. Lochner, an employer, repeatedly violated this statute. He was convicted and the highest court in New York affirmed the conviction. He than appealed his conviction to the U.S. Supreme Court, arguing that the labor statute denied him "property" (i.e., profits made from the labor of those whom he employed in his bakery) without due process of law. Further he maintained that state regulation of working hours interfered with his "freedom of contract," allegedly protected under the Constitution. A five-member majority on the Court agreed with Lochner and struck down the New York labor law.

Lochner is a classic example of the influence of laissez-faire economic thought on judicial philosophy. The Court treated workers and bosses as if they were both equally free to make choices regarding how long they wanted to work and under what conditions. In this sense the case is often cited as an example of "legal formalism"; the school of jurisprudence that ignores the impact of economic and social inequalities on the "freedom" of individuals or groups. The dissenting opinions in this case, however, sharply dispute the validity of laissez-faire assumptions and their social Darwinian implications for the role of government in protecting the public interest.]

Justice Peckham delivered the opinion of the court.

The statute necessarily interferes with the right of contract between employer and employés, concerning the number of hours in which the latter may labor in the bakery of the employer. The general right to make a contract in relation to his business is part of the liberty of the individual protected by the Fourteenth Amendment of the Federal Constitution. . . . Under that provision no State can deprive any person of life, liberty or property without due process of law. The right to purchase or to sell labor is part of the liberty protected by this amendment, unless there are circumstances which exclude the right. There are, however, certain powers, existing in the sovereignty of each State in the Union, somewhat vaguely termed police powers, the exact description and limitation of which have not been attempted by the courts. Those powers, broadly stated and without, at present, any attempt at a more specific limitation, relate to the safety, health, morals and general welfare of the public. Both property and liberty are held on such reasonable conditions as may be imposed by the governing power of the State in the exercise of those powers, and with such conditions the Fourteenth Amendment was not designed to interfere. . . .

This court has recognized the existence and upheld the exercise of the police powers of the States in many cases which might fairly be considered as border ones. . . . Among the later cases where the state law has been upheld by this court is that of *Holden v. Hardy,* 169 U.S. 366. A provision in the act of the legislature of Utah was there under consideration, the act limiting the employment of workmen in all underground mines or workings, to eight hours per day, "except in cases of emergency, where life or property is in imminent danger." It also limited the hours of labor in smelting and other institutions for the reduction or refining of ores or metals to eight hours per day, except in like cases of emergency. The act was held to be a valid exercise of the police powers of the State. A review of many of the cases on the subject, decided by this and other courts, is given in the opinion. It was held that the kind of employment, mining, smelting, etc., and the character of the employés in such kinds of labor, were such as to make it reasonable and proper for the state to interfere to prevent the employés from being constrained by the rules laid down by the proprietors in regard to labor. . . .

It will be observed that, even with regard to the class of labor, the Utah statute provided for cases of emergency wherein the provisions of the statute would not apply. The statute now before this court has no emergency clause in it, and, if the statute is valid, there are no circumstances and no emergencies under which the slightest violation of the provisions of the act would be innocent. . . .

It must, of course, be conceded that there is a limit to the valid exercise of the police power by the State. There is no dispute concerning this general proposition. Otherwise the Fourteenth Amendment would have no efficacy and the legislatures of the States would have unbounded power, and it would be enough to say that any piece of legislation was enacted to conserve the morals, the health or the safety of the people; such legislation would be valid, no matter how absolutely without foundation the claim might be. The claim of the police power would be a mere pretext—become another and delusive name for the supreme sovereignty of the State to be exercised free from constitutional restraint. This is not contended for. In every case that comes before this court, therefore, where legislation of this character is concerned and where the protection of the Federal Constitution is sought, the question necessarily arises: Is this a fair, reasonable and appropriate exercise of the police power of the State, or is it unreasonable, unnecessary and arbitrary interference with the right of the individual to his personal liberty or to enter into those contracts in relation to labor which may seem to him appropriate or necessary for the support of himself and his family? Of course the liberty of contract relating to labor includes both parties to it. The one has as much right to purchase as the other to sell labor.

This is not a question of substituting the judgment of the court for that of the legislature. If the act be within the power of the State it is valid, although the judgment of the court might be totally opposed to the enactment of such a law. But the question would still remain: Is it within the police power of the State? and that question must be answered by the court.

The question whether this act is valid as a labor law, pure and simple, may be dismissed in a few words. There is no reasonable ground for interfering with the liberty of person or the right of free contract, by determining the hours of labor in the occupation of a baker. There is no contention that bakers as a class are not equal in intelligence and capacity to men in other trades or manual occupations, or that they are not able to assert their rights and care for themselves without the protecting arm of the State, interfering with their independence of judgment and of action. They are in no sense wards of the State. Viewed in the light of a purely labor law, with no reference whatever to the question of health, we think that a law like the one before us involves neither the safety, the morals nor the welfare of the public, and that the interest of the public is not in the slightest degree affected by such an act. The law must be upheld, if at all, as a law pertaining to the health of the individual engaged in the occupation of a baker. It does not affect any other portion of the public than those who are engaged in that occupation. Clean and wholesome bread does not depend upon whether the baker works but ten hours per day or only sixty hours a week. The limitation of the hours of labor does not come within the police power on that ground.

It is a question of which of two powers or rights shall prevail—the power of the State to legislate or the right of the individual to liberty of person and freedom of contract. The mere assertion that the subject relates though but in a remote degree to the public health does not necessarily render the enactment valid. The act must have a more direct relation, as a means to an end, and the end itself must be appropriate and legitimate, before an act can be held to be valid which interferes with the general right of an individual to be free in his person and in his power to contract in relation to his own labor. . . .

We think that there can be no fair doubt that the trade of a baker, in and of itself, is not an unhealthy one to that degree which would authorize the legislature to interfere with the right to labor, and with the right of free contract on the part of the individual, either as employer or employé. In looking through statistics regarding all trades and occupations, it may be true that the trade of a baker does not appear to be as healthy as some other trades, and is also vastly more healthy than still others. To the common understanding the trade of a baker has never been regarded as an unhealthy one. Very likely physicians would not recommend the exercise of that or of any other trade as a remedy for ill health. Some occupations are more healthy than others, but we think there are none which might not come under the power of the legislature to supervise and control the hours of working therein, if the mere fact that the occupation is not absolutely and perfectly healthy is to confer that right upon the legislative department of the Government. It might be safely affirmed that almost all occupations more or less affect the health. There must be more than the mere fact of the possible existence of some small amount of unhealthiness to warrant legislative interference with liberty. It is unfortunately true that labor, even in any department,

may possible carry with it the seeds of unhealthiness. But are we all, on that account, at the mercy of legislative majorities? A printer, a tinsmith, a locksmith, a carpenter, a cabinetmaker, a dry goods clerk, a bank's, a lawyer's or a physician's clerk, or a clerk in almost any kind of business, would all come under the power of the legislature, on this assumption. No trade, no occupation, no mode of earning one's living, could escape this all-pervading power, and the acts of the legislature in limiting the hours of labor in all employments would be valid, although such limitation might seriously cripple the ability of the laborer to support himself and his family. In our large cities there are many buildings into which the sun penetrates for but a short time in each day, and these buildings are occupied by people carrying on the business of bankers, brokers, lawyers, real estate, and many other kinds of business, aided by many clerks, messengers, and other employés. Upon the assumption of the validity of this act under review, it is not possible to say that an act, prohibiting lawyers' or bank clerks, or others, from contracting to labor for their employers more than eight hours a day, would be invalid. It might be said that it is unhealthy to work more than that number of hours in an apartment lighted by artificial light during the working hours of the day; that the occupation of the bank clerk, the lawyer's clerk, the real estate clerk, or the broker's clerk in such offices is therefore unhealthy, and the legislature in its paternal wisdom must, therefore, have the right to legislate on the subject of and to limit the hours for such labor, and if it exercises that power and its validity be questioned, it is sufficient to say, it has reference to the public health; it has reference to the health of the employés condemned to labor day after day in buildings where the sun never shines; it is a health law, and therefore it is valid, and cannot be questioned by the courts. . . .

. . . The act is not, within any fair meaning of the term, a health law, but is an illegal interference with the rights of individuals, both employers and employés, to make contracts regarding labor upon such terms as they may think best, or which they may agree upon with other parties to such contracts. Statutes of the nature of that under review, limiting the hours in which grown and intelligent men may labor to earn their living, are mere meddlesome interferences with the rights of the individual, and they are not saved from condemnation by the claim that they are passed in the exercise of the police power and upon the subject of the health of the individual whose rights are interfered with, unless there be some fair ground, reasonable in and of itself, to say that there is material danger to the public health or to the health of the employés, if the hours of labor are not curtailed. . . .

This interference on the part of the legislatures of the several States with the ordinary trades and occupations of the people seems to be on the increase. . . .

It is impossible for us to shut our eyes to the fact that many of the laws of this chapter, while passed under what is claimed to be the police power for the purpose of protecting the public health or welfare, are, in reality, passed from other motives. We are justified in saying so when, from the character of the law and the subject upon which it legislates, it is apparent that the public health or welfare bears but the most remote relation to the law. The purpose of a statute must be determined from the natural and legal effect of the language employed; and whether it is or is not repugnant to the Constitution of the United States must be determined from the natural effect of such statutes when put into operation, and not from their proclaimed purpose. . . .

. . . It seems to us that the real object and purpose were simply to regulate the hours of labor between the master and his employés (all being men, *sui juris*), in a private business, not dangerous in any degree to morals or in any real and substantial degree, to the health of the employés. Under such circumstances the freedom of master and employé to contract with each other in relation to their employment, and in defining the same, cannot be prohibited or interfered with, without violating the Federal Constitution.

The judgment of the Court of Appeals of New York as well as that of the Supreme Court and of the County Court of Oneida County must be reversed

and the case remanded to the County Court for further proceedings not inconsistent with this opinion.

Reversed.

Justice Harlan, with whom Justice White and Justice Day concurred, dissenting.

While this court has not attempted to mark the precise boundaries of what is called the police power of the State, the existence of the power has been uniformly recognized, both by the Federal and state courts.

All the cases agree that this power extends at least to the protection of the lives, the health and the safety of the public against the injurious exercise by any citizen of his own rights.

In *Patterson v. Kentucky*, 97 U.S. 501, after referring to the general principle that rights given by the Constitution cannot be impaired by state legislation of any kind, this court said: "It [this court] has, nevertheless, with marked distinctness and uniformity, recognized the necessity, growing out of the fundamental conditions of civil society, of upholding state police regulations which were enacted in good faith, and had appropriate and direct connection with that protection to life, health, and property which each State owes to her citizens." . . .

Speaking generally, the State in the exercise of its powers may not unduly interfere with the right of the citizen to enter into contracts that may be necessary and essential in the enjoyment of the inherent rights belonging to every one, among which rights is the right "to be free in enjoyment of all his faculties; to be free to use them in all lawful ways; to live and work where he will; to earn his livelihood by any lawful calling; to pursue any livelihood or avocation." This was declared in *Allgeyer v. Louisiana*, 165 U.S. 578, 589. But in the same case it was conceded that the right to contract in relation to persons and property or to do business, within a State, may be "regulated and sometimes prohibited, when the contracts or business conflict with the policy of the State as contained in its statutes"

So, as said in *Holden v. Hardy*, 169 U.S. 366, 391: "This right of contract, however, is itself subject to certain limitations which the State may lawfully impose in the exercise of its police powers. While this power is inherent in all governments, it has doubtless been greatly expanded in its application during the past century, owing to an enormous increase in the number of occupations which are dangerous, or so far detrimental to the health of the employés as to demand special precautions for their well-being and protection, or the safety of adjacent property." . . . Referring to the limitations placed by the State upon the hours of workmen, the court in the same case said [*Lawton v. Steele*, 152 U.S. 133]: "These employments, when too long pursued, the legislature has judged to be detrimental to the health of the employés, and, so long as there are reasonable grounds for believing that this is so, its decision upon this subject cannot be reviewed by the Federal courts."

The authorities on the same line are so numerous that further citations are unnecessary.

I take it to be firmly established that what is called the liberty of contract may, within certain limits, be subjected to regulations designed and calculated to promote the general welfare or to guard the public health, the public morals or the public safety. "The liberty secured by the Constitution of the United States to every person within its jurisdiction does not import," this court has recently said, "an absolute right in each person to be, at all times and in all circumstances, wholly freed from restraint. There are manifold restraints to which every person is necessarily subject for the common good." *Jacobson v. Massachusetts*, 197 U. S. 11.

Granting then that there is a liberty of contract which cannot be violated even under the sanction of direct legislative enactment, but assuming, as according to settled law we may assume, that such liberty of contract is subject to such regulations as the State may reasonably prescribe for the common good and the well-being of society, what are the conditions under which the judiciary may declare such regulations to be in excess of legislative authority and void? Upon this point there is no room for dispute; for, the rule is universal that a legislative enactment, Federal or state, is never to be disregarded or held

invalid unless it be, beyond question, plainly and palpably in excess of legislative power. In *Jacobson v. Massachusetts, supra*, we said that the power of the courts to review legislative action in respect of a matter affecting the general welfare exists *only* "when that which the legislature has done comes within the rule that if a statute purporting to have been enacted to protect the public health, the public morals or the public safety, has no real or substantial relation to those objects, or is, beyond all question, a plain, palpable invasion of rights secured by the fundamental law"—citing *Mugler v. Kansas*, 123 U.S. 623, 661; *Minnesota v. Barber*, 136 U. S. 313, 320: *Atkin v. Kansas*, 191 U. S. 207, 223. If there be doubt as to the validity of the statute, that doubt must therefore be resolved in favor of its validity, and the courts must keep their hands off, leaving the legislature to meet the responsibility for unwise legislation. If the end which the legislature seeks to accomplish be one to which its power extends, and if the means employed to that end, although not the wisest or best, are yet not plainly and palpably unauthorized by law, then the court cannot interfere. In other words, when the validity of a statute is questioned, the burden of proof, so to speak, is upon those who assert it to be unconstitutional. *McCulloch v. Maryland*, 4 Wheat. 316, 421.

Let these principles be applied to the present case. By the statute in question it is provided that, "No employé shall be required or permitted to work in a biscuit, bread or cake bakery or confectionery establishment more than sixty hours in any one week, or more than ten hours in any one day, unless for the purpose of making a shorter work day on the last day of the week; nor more hours in any one week than will make an average of ten hours per day for the number of days during such week in which such employé shall work."

It is plain that this statute was enacted in order to protect the physical well-being of those who work in bakery and confectionery establishments. It may be that the statute had its origin, in part, in the belief that employers and employés in such establishments were not upon an equal footing, and that the necessities of the latter often compelled them to submit to such exactions as unduly taxed their strength. Be this as it may, the statute must be taken as expressing the belief of the people of New York that, as a general rule, and in the case of the average man, labor in excess of sixty hours during a week in such establishments may endanger the health of those who thus labor. Whether or not this be wise legislation it is not the province of the court to inquire. Under our systems of government the courts are not concerned with the wisdom or policy of legislation. So that in determining the question of power to interfere with liberty of contract, the court may inquire whether the means devised by the State are germane to an end which may be lawfully accomplished and have a real or substantial relation to the protection of health, as involved in the daily work of the persons, male and female, engaged in bakery and confectionery establishments. But when this inquiry is entered upon I find it impossible, in view of common experience, to say that there is here no real or substantial relation between the means employed by the State and the end sought to be accomplished by its legislation. . . . Nor can I say that the statute has no appropriate or direct connection with that protection to health which each State owes to her citizens. . . . or that it is not promotive of health of the employés in question, . . . or that the regulation prescribed by the State is utterly unreasonable and extravagant or wholly arbitrary. . . . Still less can I say that the statute is, beyond question, a plain, palpable invasion of rights secured by the fundamental law. . . . Therefore I submit that this court will transcend its functions if it assumes to annul the statute of New York. It must be remembered that this statute does not apply to all kinds of business. It applies only to work in bakery and confectionery establishments, in which, as all know, the air constantly breathed by workmen is not as pure and healthful as that to be found in some other establishments or out of doors.

Professor Hirt in his treatise on the "Diseases of the Workers" has said: "The labor of the bakers is among the hardest and most laborious imaginable, because it has to be performed under conditions in-

jurious to the health of those engaged in it. It is hard, very hard work, not only because it requires a great deal of physical exertion in an overheated workshop and during unreasonably long hours, but more so because of the erratic demands of the public, compelling the baker to perform the greater part of his work at night, thus depriving him of an opportunity to enjoy the necessary rest and sleep, a fact which is highly injurious to his health." Another writer says: "The constant inhaling of flour dust causes inflammation of the lungs and of the bronchial tubes. The eyes also suffer through this dust, which is responsible for the many cases of running eyes among the bakers. The long hours of toil to which all bakers are subjected produce rheumatism, cramps and swollen legs. The intense heat in the workshops includes the workers to resort to cooling drinks, which together with their habit of exposing the greater part of their bodies to the change in the atmosphere, is another source of a number of diseases of various organs. Nearly all bakers are pale-faced and of more delicate health than the workers of other crafts, which is chiefly due to their hard work and their irregular and unnatural mode of living, whereby the power of resistance against disease is greatly diminished. The average age of a baker is below that of other workmen; they seldom live over their fiftieth year, most of them dying between the ages of forty and fifty. During periods of epidemic diseases the bakers are generally the first to succumb to the disease, and the number swept away during such periods far exceeds the number of other crafts in comparison to the men employed in the respective industries. When, in 1720, the plague visited the city of Marseilles, France, every baker in the city succumbed to the epidemic, which caused considerable excitement in the neighboring cities and resulted in measures for the sanitary protection of the bakers."

In the Eighteenth Annual Report by the New York Bureau of Statistics of Labor it is stated that among the occupations involving exposure to conditions that interfere with nutrition is that of a baker. . . . In that Report it is also stated that "from a social point of view, production will be increased by any change in industrial organization which diminishes the number of idlers, paupers and criminals. Shorter hours of work, by allowing higher standards of comfort and purer family life, promise to enhance the industrial efficiency of the wage-working class—improved health, longer life, more content and greater intelligence and inventiveness." . . .

Statistics show that the average daily working time among workingmen in different countries is, in Australia, 8 hours; in Great Britain, 9; in the United States, 9¾; in Denmark, 9¾; in Norway, 10; Sweden, France and Switzerland, 10½; Germany, 10¼; Belgium, Italy and Austria, 11; and in Russia, 12 hours.

We judicially know that the question of the number of hours during which a workman should continuously labor has been, for a long period, and is yet, a subject of serious consideration among civilized peoples, and by those having special knowledge of the laws of health. Suppose the statute prohibited labor in bakery and confectionery establishments in excess of eighteen hours each day. No one, I take it, could dispute the power of the State to enact such a statute. But the statute before us does not embrace extreme or exceptional cases. . . .

We also judicially know that the number of hours that should constitute a day's labor in particular occupations involving the physical strength and safety of workmen has been the subject of enactments by Congress and by nearly all of the States. Many, if not most, of those enactments fix eight hours as the proper basis of a day's labor.

I do not stop to consider whether any particular view of this economic question presents the sounder theory. What the precise facts are it may be difficult to say. It is enough for the determination of this case, and it is enough for this court to know, that the question is one about which there is room for debate and for an honest difference of opinion. There are many reasons of a weighty, substantial character, based upon the experience of mankind, in support of the theory that, all things considered, more than ten hours' steady work each day, from week to week, in a bakery or confectionery establishment, may endanger the health, and shorten the lives of the workmen, thereby diminishing their physical and mental capacity to serve the State, and to provide for those dependent upon them.

If such reasons exist that ought to be the end of this case, for the State is not amenable to the judiciary, in respect of its legislative enactments, unless such enactments are plainly, palpably, beyond all question, inconsistent with the Constitution of the United States. We are not to presume that the State of New York has acted in bad faith. Nor can we assume that its legislature acted without due deliberation, or that it did not determine this question upon the fullest attainable information, and for the common good. We cannot say that the State has acted without reason nor ought we to proceed upon the theory that its action is a mere sham. Our duty, I submit, is to sustain the statute as not being in conflict with the Federal Constitution, for the reason—and such is an all-sufficient reason—it is not shown to be plainly and palpably inconsistent with that instrument. Let the State alone in the management of its purely domestic affairs, so long as it does not appear beyond all question that it has violated the Federal Constitution. This view necessarily results from the principle that the health and safety of the people of a State are primarily for the State to guard and protect.

I take leave to say that the New York statute, in the particulars here involved, cannot be held to be in conflict with the Fourteenth Amendment, without enlarging the scope of the Amendment far beyond its original purpose and without bringing under the supervision of this court matters which have been supposed to belong exclusively to the legislative departments of the several States . . .

The judgment in my opinion should be affirmed.

Justice Holmes dissenting.

This case is decided upon an economic theory which a large part of the country does not entertain. If it were a question whether I agreed with that theory, I should desire to study it further and long before making up my mind. But I do not conceive that to be my duty, because I strongly believe that my agreement or disagreement has nothing to do with the right of a majority to embody their opinions in law. It is settled by various decisions of this court that state constitutions and state laws may regulate life in many ways which we as legislators might think as injudicious or if you like as tyrannical as this, and which equally with this interfere with the liberty to contract. Sunday laws and usury laws are ancient examples. A more modern one is the prohibition of lotteries. The liberty of the citizen to do as he likes so long as he does not interfere with the liberty of others to do the same, which has been a shibboleth for some well-known writers, is interfered with by school laws, by the Post Office, by every state or municipal institution which takes his money for purposes thought desirable, whether he likes it or not. The Fourteenth Amendment does not enact Mr. Herbert Spencer's Social Statics. The other day we sustained the Massachusetts vaccination law. *Jacobson v. Massachusetts*, 197 U. S. 11. . . . Two years ago we upheld the prohibition of sales of stock on margins or for future delivery in the constitution of California. *Otis v. Parker*, 187 U. S. 606. The decision sustaining an eight hour law for miners is still recent. *Holden v. Hardy*, 169 U. S. 366. Some of these laws embody convictions or predjudices which judges are likely to share. Some may not. But a constitution is not intended to embody a particular economic theory, whether of paternalism and the organic relation

of the citizen to the State or of *laissez faire*. It is made for people of fundamentally differing views, and the accident of our finding certain opinions natural and familiar or novel and even shocking ought not to conclude our judgment upon the question whether statutes embodying them conflict with the Constitution of the United States.

General propositions do not decide concrete cases. The decision will depend on a judgment or intuition more subtle than any articulate major premise. But I think that the proposition just stated, if it is accepted, will carry us far toward the end. Every opinion tends to become a law. I think that the word liberty in the Fourteenth Amendment is perverted when it is held to prevent the natural outcome of a dominant opinion, unless it can be said that a rational and fair man necessarily would admit that the statute proposed would infringe fundamental principles as they have been understood by the traditions of our people and our law. It does not need research to show that no such sweeping condemnation can be passed upon the statute before us. A reasonable man might think it a proper measure on the score of health. Men whom I certainly could not pronounce unreasonable would uphold it as a first instalment of a general regulation of the hours of work. Whether in the latter aspect it would be open to the charge of inequality I think it unnecessary to discuss.

In *Lochner* the Court gave private property interests priority over what a state legislature had defined as the public interest. The political and economic battle between these two sets of interests were at the core of the legal debate over regulation in the early twentieth century and continue to play an important role in today's debates. This debate did not consider replacing private property with state-owned industries, as in socialist countries. Rather the form of public regulation emerging at this time merely placed certain conditions (e.g., licensing, inspection, etc.) on industries affected by a public interest. Thus capitalism and state regulation were not fundamentally at odds with one another, but as James Weinstein argues, some corporate capitalists supported if they did not initiate regulatory programs in order to legitimate private economic and political interest as the "public interest," hence securing the long-term future of capitalism.[6] This position, of course, was not shared by all business groups. Indeed,

---

[6] See James Weinstein, *The Corporate Ideal in the Liberal State, 1900–1918* (Boston: Beacon Press, 1968). Also see Thomas McCraw's discussion of the capture thesis, *supra*, 15–16, 22–23.

while big business tended to provide the leadership for reform, forming associations that lobbied to create regulatory agencies such the case of the Federal Trade Commission (1914), the National Manufacturers Association, which represented small manufacturers, "dragged its feet until its membership was gradually converted to support" regulatory reforms.[7]

Although administrative law combines many different legal traditions (constitutional, statutory and judge-made law) whose own origins predate the twentieth century, with the development of the modern state administrative law came into its own. Prior to the 1930s major policy areas were ignored, were left entirely to the states, or were only marginally provided for by the federal government. Harry Scheiber, legal historian and professor of law at the University of California–Berkeley, notes that in 1929 national government expenditures ($2.6 billion) were one-third the amount spent by state and local governments. Ten years later, national spending had risen to $9 billion and surpassed state and local spending of $8.5 billion in 1939.[8]

Increased federal spending in this decade had both *quantitative* and *qualitative* results. The New Deal put into place a modern positive state, beginning with the 1933 Agricultural Adjustment Act and the National Industry Recovery Act. Until the Supreme Court struck them down in 1935, these two pieces of legislation brought agriculture and manufacturing within the scope of federal regulatory power. Other programs, however, survived judicial review by the conservative, laissez faire Supreme Court: the Tennessee Valley Authority instituted in 1933, the first natural resource and land management regional program under the federal government; the Social Security Act of 1935, the first national social entitlement program; the Works Progress Administration, created to provide government-financed employment programs administered by the states; and other areas of federal activity and regulation discussed in chapter 2.

In *National Labor Relations Board v. Jones & Laughlin Steel Corp.* (1937), the Supreme Court upheld the Wagner Act, which established the National Labor Relations Board (NLRB). Chief Justice Hughes's opinion for a five-member majority offers a legal solution to the political and economic debate over regulation—a solution that combines private property rights and public rights to protect the general health and welfare of society. Karl Klare, a law professor at Northeastern University, argues that the Court's solution was to "update legal consciousness and to make it more responsive to contemporary social exigencies—that is, to give a new life to the liberal legal order—while at the same time preserving its contradictions and mystification" about the relationship between capitalism and democracy.[9] As you read the Chief Justice Hughes' opinion, note how his New Deal jurisprudence, which combines protection for private and public rights, serves as a justification for an administrative process. At the same time, note how Hughes carves out a supervisory role for judiciary in administrative law.

---

[7] Weinstein, 92.

[8] Harry N. Scheiber, "From the New Deal to the New Federalism, 1933–1983," proceedings of a Conference at Boalt Hall School of Law, University of California, Berkeley, 16 April 1983, 2–4.

[9] Karl Klare "Judicial Deradicalizaton of the Wagner Act and the Origins of Modern Legal Consciousness, 1937-1941," *Minnesota Law Review* 62, (1978): 2806. Also see William E. Forbath "The Shaping of the American Labor Movement," *Harvard Law Review* 102 (1989): 1109.

National Labor Relations Board v. Jones & Laughlin Steel Corporation

301 U. S. 1 (1937) 5–4
+ Hughes, Stone, Brandeis, Roberts, Cardozo
- Sutherland, Van Devanter, McReynolds, Butler

Chief Justice Hughes delivered the opinion of the Court.

In a proceeding under the National Labor Relations Act of 1935, the National Labor Relations Board found that the respondent, Jones & Laughlin Steel Corporation, had violated the Act by engaging in unfair labor practices affecting commerce. The proceeding was instituted by the Beaver Valley Lodge No. 200, affiliated with the Amalgamated Association of Iron Steel and Tin Workers of America, a labor organization. The unfair labor practices charged were that the corporation was discriminating against members of the union with regard to hire and tenure of employment, and was coercing and intimidating its employees in order to interfere with their self-organization. The discriminatory and coercive action alleged was the discharge of certain employees.

The National Labor Relations Board, sustaining the charge, ordered the corporation to cease and desist from such discrimination and coercion, to offer reinstatement to ten of the employees named, to make good their losses in pay, and to post for thirty days notices that the corporation would not discharge or discriminate against members, or those desiring to become members, of the labor union. As the corporation failed to comply, the Board petitioned the Circuit Court of Appeals to enforce the order. The court denied the petition, holding that the order lay beyond the range of federal power. . . . We granted certiorari.

The scheme of the National Labor Relations Act—which is too long to be quoted in full—may be briefly stated. The first section sets forth findings with respect to the injury to commerce resulting from the denial by employers of the right of employees to organize and from the refusal of employers to accept the procedure of collective bargaining. There follows a declaration that it is the policy of the United States to eliminate these causes of obstruction to the free flow of commerce. The Act then defines the terms it uses, including the terms "commerce" and "affecting commerce." § 2. It creates the National Labor Relations Board and prescribes its organization. §§ 3–6. It sets forth the right of employees to self-organization and to bargain collectively through representatives of their own choosing. § 7. It defines "unfair labor practies." § 8. It lays down rules as to the representation of employees for the purpose of collective bargaining. § 9. The Board is empowered to prevent the described unfair labor practices affecting commerce and the Act prescribes the procedure to that end. The Board is authorized to petition designated courts to secure the enforcement of its orders. The findings of the Board as to the facts, if supported by evidence, are to be conclusive. If either party on application to the court shows that additional evidence is material and that there were reasonable grounds for the failure to adduce such evidence in the hearings before the Board, the court may order the additional evidence to be taken. Any person aggrieved by a final order of the Board may obtain a review in the designated courts with the same procedure as in the case of an application by the Board for the enforcement of its order. § 10. The Board has broad powers of investigation. § 11. Interference with members of the Board or its agents in the performance of their duties is punishable by fine and imprisonment. § 12. Nothing in the Act is to be construed to interfere with the right to strike. § 13. There is a separability clause to the effect that if any provision of the Act or its application to any person or circumstances shall be held invalid, the remainder of the Act or its application to other persons or circumstances shall not be affected. § 15. The particular provisions which are involved in the instant case will be considered more in detail in the course of the discussion.

The procedure in the instant case followed the statute. The labor union filed with the Board its verified charge. The Board thereupon issued its complaint against the respondent alleging that its action in discharging the employees in question constituted unfair labor practices affecting commerce within the meaning of § 8, subdivisions (1) and (3), and § 2, subdivisions (6) and (7) of the Act. Respondent, appearing specially for the purpose of objecting to the jurisdiction of the Board, filed its answer. Respondent admitted the discharges, but alleged that they were made because of inefficiency or violation of rules or for other good reasons and were not ascribable to union membership or activities. As an affirmative defense respondent challenged the constitutional validity of the statute and its applicability in the instant case. Notice of hearing was given and respondent appeared by counsel. The board first took up the issue of jurisdiction and evidence was presented by both the Board and the respondent. Respondent then moved to dismiss the complaint for lack of jurisdiction; and, on denial of that motion, respondent in accordance with its special appearance withdrew from further participation in the hearing. The Board received evidence upon the merits and at its close made its findings and order.

Contesting the ruling of the Board, the respondent argues (1) that the Act is in reality a regulation of labor relations and not of interstate commerce; (2) that the Act can have no application to the respondent's relations with its production employees because they are not subject to regulation by the federal government; and (3) that the provisions of the Act violate § 2 of Article III and the Fifth and Seventh Amendments of the Constitution of the United States. . . .

Summarizing the operations [of Jones & Laughlin Steel Corporation], the Labor Board concluded that the works in Pittsburgh and Aliquippa "might be likened to the heart of a self-contained, highly integrated body. They draw in the raw materials from Michigan, Minnesota, West Virginia, Pennsylvania in part through arteries and by means controlled by the respondent; they transform the materials and then pump them out to all parts of the nation through the vast mechanism which the respondent has elaborated."

To carry on the activities of the entire steel industry, 33,000 men mine ore, 44,000 men mine coal, 4,000 men quarry limestone, 16,000 men manufacture coke, 343,000 men manufacture steel, and 83,000 men transport its product. Respondent has about 10,000 employees in its Aliquippa plant which is located in a community of about 30,000 persons. . . .

. . . These employees were active leaders in the labor union. Several were officers and others were leaders of particular groups. Two of the employees were motor inspectors; one was a tractor driver; three were crane operators; one was a washer in the coke plant; and three were laborers. Three other employees were mentioned in the complaint but it was withdrawn as to one of them and no evidence was heard on the action taken with respect to the other two.

While respondent criticises the evidence and the attitude of the Board, which is described as being hostile toward employers and particularly toward those who insisted upon their constitutional rights, respondent did not take advantage of its opportunity to present evidence to refute that which was offered to show discrimination and coercion. In this situation, the record presents no ground for setting aside the order of the Board so far as the facts pertaining to the circumstances and purpose of the discharge of the employees are concerned. . . . We turn to the questions of law which respondent urges in contesting the validity and application of the Act.

First. The scope of the Act. —The Act is challenged in its entirety as an attempt to regulate all industry, thus invading the reserved powers of the States over their local concerns. . . .

We think it clear that the National Labor Relations Act may be construed so as to operate within the sphere of constitutional authority. The jurisdiction conferred upon the Board, and invoked in this instance, is found in § 10 (a), which provides:

"Sec. 10 (a). The Board is empowered, as hereinafter provided, to prevent any person from engaging in any unfair labor practice (listed in section 8) affecting commerce." . . .

There can be no question that the commerce thus contemplated by the Act (aside from that within a

Territory or the District of Columbia) is interstate and foreign commerce in the constitutional sense. . . .

. . . The grant of authority to the Board does not purport to extend to the relationship between all industrial employees and employers. Its terms do not impose collective bargaining upon all industry regardless of effects upon interstate or foreign commerce. It purports to reach only what may be deemed to burden or obstruct that commerce and, thus qualified, it must be construed as contemplating the exercise of control within constitutional bounds. . . . Whether or not particular action does affect commerce in such a close and intimate fashion as to be subject to federal control, and hence to lie within the authority conferred upon the Board, is left by the statute to be determined as individual cases arise. We are thus to inquire whether in the instant case the constitutional boundary has been passed.

Second. The unfair labor practices in question.—The unfair labor practices found by the Board are those defined in § 8, subdivisions (1) and (3). These provide:

Sec. 8. It shall be unfair labor practice for an employer—

"(1) To interfere with, restrain, or coerce employees in the exercise of the rights guaranteed in section 7."

"(3) By discrimination in regard to hire or tenure of employment or any term or condition of employment to encourage or discourage membership in any labor organization: . . . "

Section 8, subdivision (1), refers to § 7, which is as follows:

"Sec. 7. Employees shall have the right to self-organization, form, join, or assist labor organizations, to bargain collectively through representatives of their own choosing, and to engage in concerted activities, for the purpose of collective bargaining or other mutual aid or protection."

Thus in its present application, the statute goes no further than to safeguard the right of employees to self-organization and to select representatives of their own choosing for collective bargaining or other mutual protection without restraint or coercion by their employer.

That is a fundamental right. Employees have as clear a right to organize and select their representa-

tives for lawful purposes as the respondent has to organize its business and select its own officers and agents. Discrimination and coercion to prevent the free exercise of the right of employees to self-organization and representation is a proper subject for condemnation by competent legislative authority. Long ago we stated the reason for labor organizations. We said that they were organized out of the necessities of the situation; that a single employee was helpless in dealing with an employer; that he was dependent ordinarily on his daily wage for the maintenance of himself and family; that if the employer refused to pay him the wages that he thought fair, he was nevertheless unable to leave the employ and resist arbitrary and unfair treatment; that union was essential to give laborers opportunity to deal on an equality with their employer." . . . Fully recognizing the legality of collective action on the part of employees in order to safeguard their proper interests, we said that Congress was not required to ignore this right but could safeguard it. Congress could seek to make appropriate collective action of employees an instrument of peace rather than of strife. We said that such collective action would be a mockery if representation were made futile by interference with freedom of choice. Hence the prohibition by Congress of interference with the selection of representatives for the purpose of negotiation and conference between employers and employees, "instead of being an invasion of the constitutional right of either, was based on the recognition of the rights of both." *Texas & N. O. R. Co. v. Railway Clerks.* . . .

Third. The application of the Act to employees engaged in production.—The principle involved.—Respondent says that whatever may be said of employees engaged in interstate commerce, the industrial relations and activities in the manufacturing department of respondent's enterprise are not subject to federal regulation. The argument rests upon the proposition that manufacturing in itself is not commerce. . . .

The Government distinguishes these cases. The various parts of respondent's enterprise are described as interdependent and as thus involving "a great movement of iron core, coal and limestone along well-defined paths to the steel mills, thence through them, and thence in the form of steel products into the consuming centers of the country—a definite and well-understood course of business." . . .

. . . The congressional authority to protect interstate commerce from burdens and obstructions is not limited to transactions which can be deemed to be an essential part of a "flow" of interstate or foreign commerce. Burdens and obstructions may be due to injurious action springing from other sources. The fundamental principle is that the power to regulate commerce is the power to enact "all appropriate legislation" for "its protection and advancement" . . . to adopt measures "to promote its growth and insure its safety"; to foster, protect, control and restrain." . . . That power is plenary and may be exerted to protect interstate commerce "no matter what the source of the dangers which threaten it." . . .

Fourth. Effects of the unfair labor practice in respondent's enterprise. . . . It is obvious that it would be immediate and might be catastrophic. We are asked to shut our eyes to the plainest facts of our national life and to deal with the question of direct and indirect effects in an intellectual vacuum. Because there may be but indirect and remote effects upon interstate commerce in connection with a host of local enterprises throughout the country, it does not follow that other industrial activites do not have such a close and intimate relation to interstate commerce as to make the presence of industrial strife a matter of the most urgent national concern. When industries organize themselves on a national scale, making their relation to interstate commerce the dominant factor in their activities, how can it be maintained that their industrial labor relations constitute a forbidden field into which Congress may not enter when it is necessary to protect interstate commerce from the paralyzing consequences of industrial war? We have often said that interstate commerce itself is a practical conception. It is equally true that interferences with that commerce must be appraised by a judgment that does not ignore actual experience.

Experience has abundantly demonstrated that the recognition of the right of employees to self-organization and to have representatives of their own choosing for the purpose of collective bargaining is often an essential condition of industrial peace. Refusal to confer and negotiate has been one of the most prolific causes of strife. This is such an outstanding fact in the history of labor disturbances that it is a proper subject of judicial notice and requires no citation of instances. . . .

. . . Instead of being beyond the pale, we think that it presents in a most striking way the close and intimate relation which a manufacturing industry may have to interstate commerce and we have no doubt that Congress had constitutional authority to safeguard the right of respondent's employees to self-organization and freedom in the choice of representatives for collective bargaining.

Fifth. The means which the Act employs.—Questions under the due process clause and other constitutional restrictions.—Respondent asserts its right to conduct its business in an orderly manner without being subjected to arbitrary restraints. What we have said points to the fallacy in the argument. Employees have their correlative right to organize for the purpose of securing the redress of grievances and to promote agreements with employers relating to rates of pay and conditions of work. . . . Restraint for the purpose of preventing an unjust interference with that right cannot be considered arbitrary or capricious. The provision of § 9 (a) that representatives, for the purpose of collective bargaining, of the majority of the employees in an appropriate unit shall be the exclusive representatives of all the employees in that unit, imposes upon the respondent only the duty of conferring and negotiating with the authorized representatives of its employees for the purpose of settling a labor dispute. . . .

The Act does not compel agreements between employers and employees. It does not compel any agreement whatever. It does not prevent the employer "from refusing to make a collective contract and hiring individuals on whatever terms" the employer "may by unilateral action determine." The Act expressly provides in § 9 (a) that any individual employee or a group of employees shall have the right at any time to present grievances to their employer. The theory of the Act is that free opportunity for negotiation with accredited representatives of employees is likely to promote industrial peace and may bring about the adjustments and agreements which the Act in itself does not attempt to compel. . . . The Act does not interfere with the normal exercise of the right of the employer to select its employees or to discharge them. The employer may not, under cover of that right, intimidate or coerce its employees with respect to their self-organization and representation, and, on the other hand, the Board is not entitled to make its authority a pretext for interference with the right of discharge when that right is exercised for other reasons than such intimidation and coercion. The true purpose is the subject of investigation with full opportunity to show the facts. It would seem that when employers freely recognize the right of their employees to their own organizations and their unrestricted right of representation there will be much less occasion for controversy in respect to the free and appropriate exercise of the right of selection and discharge.

The Act has been criticised as one-sided in its application; that it subjects the employer to supervision and restraint and leaves untouched the abuses for which employees may be responsible; that it fails to provide a more comprehensive plan,—with better assurances of fairness to both sides and with increased chances of success in bringing about, if not compelling, equitable solutions of industrial disputes affecting interstate commerce. But we are dealing with the power of Congress, not with a particular policy or with the extent to which policy should go. We have frequently said that the legislative authority, exerted within its proper field, need not embrace all the evils within its reach. The Constitution does not forbid "cautious advance, step by step," in dealing with the evils which are exhibited in activities within the range of legislative power. . . . The question in such cases in whether the legislature, in what it does prescribe, has gone beyond constitutional limits.

The procedural provisions of the Act are assailed. But these provisions, as we construe them, do not offend against the constitutional requirements governing the creation and action of administrative bodies. See *Interstate Commerce Comm'n v. Louisville & Nashville R. Co.*, 227 U. S. 88, 91. The Act establishes standards to which the Board must conform. There must be complaint, notice and hearing. The Board must receive evidence and make findings. The findings as to the facts are to be conclusive, but only if supported by evidence. The order of the Board is subject to review by the designated court, and only when sustained by the court may the order be enforced. Upon that review all questions of the jurisdiction of the Board and the regularity of its proceedings, all questions of constitutional right or statutory authority, are open to examination by the court. We construe the procedural provisions as affording adequate opportunity to secure judicial protection against arbitrary action in accordance with the well-settled rules applicable to administrative agencies set up by Congress to aid in the enforcement of valid legislation. It is not necessary to repeat these rules which have frequently been declared. None of them appears to have been transgressed in the instant case. Respondent was notified and heard. It had opportunity to meet the charge of unfair labor practices upon merits, and by withdrawing from the hearing it declined to avail itself of that opportunity. The facts found by the Board support its order and the evidence supports the findings. Respondent has no just ground for complaint on this score.

The order of the Board required the reinstatement of the employees who were found to have been discharged because of their "union activity" and for the purpose of "discouraging membership in the union." That requirement was authorized by the Act. § 10 (c). . . .

Respondent complains that the Board not only ordered reinstatement but directed the payment of wages for the time lost by the discharge, less amounts earned by the employee during that period. This part of the order was also authorized by the Act. § 10 (c). It is argued that the requirement is equivalent to a money judgment and hence contravenes the Seventh Amendment with respect to trial by jury. The Seventh Amendment provides that "In suits at common law, where the value in controversy shall exceed twenty dollars, the right of trial by jury shall be preserved." The Amendment thus preserves the right which existed under the common law when the Amendment was adopted. . . .

The instant case is not a suit at common law or in the nature of such a suit. The proceeding is one unknown to the common law. It is a statutory proceeding. Reinstatement of the employee and payment for time lost are requirements imposed for violation of the statute and are remedies appropriate to its enforcement. The contention under the Seventh Amendment is without merit.

Our conclusion is that the order of the Board was within its competency and that the Act is valid as here applied. The judgment of the Circuit Court of Appeals is reversed and the cause is remanded for further proceedings in conformity with this opinion.
Reversed.

Justice McReynolds delivered the following dissenting opinion in the cases preceding:

Mr. Justice Van Devanter, Mr. Justice Sutherland, Mr. Justice Butler and I are unable to agree with the decisions just announced.

We conclude that these causes were rightly decided by the three Circuit Courts of Appeals and that their judgments should be affirmed. The opinions there given without dissent are terse, well-considered and sound. They disclose the meaning ascribed by experienced judges to what this Court has often declared, and are set out below in full.

Considering the far-reaching import of these decisions, the departure from what we understand has been consistently ruled here, and the extraordinary power confirmed to a Board of three, the obligation to present our views becomes plain.

The Court, as we think, departs from well-established principles followed in *Schechter Corp. v. United States*, 295 U.S. 495 (May, 1935) and *Carter v. Carter Coal Co.*, 298 U.S. 238 (May, 1936). Upon the authority of those decisions, the Circuit Courts of Appeals of the Fifth, Sixth and Second Circuits in the causes now before us have held the power of Congress under the commerce clause does not extend to relations between employers and their employees engaged in manufacture, and therefore the

Act conferred upon the National Labor Relations Board no authority in respect of matters covered by the questioned orders. . . .

. . . The precise question for us to determine is whether in the circumstances disclosed Congress has power to authorize what the Labor Board commanded the respondents to do. Stated otherwise, in the circumstances here existing could Congress by statute direct what the Board has ordered? General disquisitions concerning the enactment are of minor, if any, importance. . . .

. . . The Constitution still recognizes the existence of states with indestructible powers; the Tenth Amendment was supposed to put them beyond controversy.

We are told that Congress may protect the "stream of commerce" and that one who buys raw material without the state, manufacturers it therein, and ships the output to another state is in that stream. Therefore it is said he may be prevented from doing anything which may interfere with its flow.

This, too, goes beyond the constitutional limitations heretofore enforced. If a man raises cattle and regularly delivers them to a carrier for interstate shipment, may Congress prescribe the conditions under which he may employ or discharge helpers on the ranch? The products of a mine pass daily into interstate commerce; many things are brought to it from other states. Are the owners and the miners within the power of Congress in respect of the miners' tenure and discharge? May a mill owner be prohibited from closing his factory or discontinuing his business because so to do would stop the flow of products to and from his plant in interstate commerce? May employees in a factory be restrained from quitting work in a body because this will close the factory and thereby stop the flow of commerce? . . .

. . . Whatever effect any cause of discontent may ultimately have upon commerce is far too indirect to justify Congressional regulation. Almost anything—marriage, birth, death—may in some fashion affect commerce. . . .

The right to contract is fundamental and includes the privilege of selecting those with whom one is willing to assume contractual relations. This right is unduly abridged by the Act now upheld. A private owner is deprived of power to manage his own property by freely selecting those to whom his manufacturing operations are to be entrusted. We

think this cannot lawfully be done in circumstances like those here disclosed.

It seems clear to us that Congress has transcended the powers granted.

* Medical profession interest groups pressured legislators.

The courts have given more or less latitude to legislative regulation of business and economic matters, depending on their political views toward government regulation. The Court may express its views in regulation by deferring to "legislative widsom" and avoiding a more strict scrutiny of legislative motives. For example, in 1955 the Supreme Court upheld a statutory system for licensing ophthalmologists and optometrists with the curious consequence that an optician had to get a prescription before transferring a perfectly good set of lenses from a broken frame to a new frame. Said Justice Douglas, "The Oklahoma law may exact a needless, wasteful requirement in many cases, but it is for the legislature, not the courts, to balance the advantages and disadvantages of the new requirement."[10] However, the same constitutional principle governs both historical substantive due process and and the modern protection or noncommercial liberty and equality: legislatures cannot create agencies whose missions overstep constitutional limits.

The Delegation Doctrine

Constitutional barriers to the creation of the modern state in the twentieth century also concerned the issue of delegating legislative powers to administrative agencies. A strict reading of Article I of the Constitution and the principle of separation of powers establishes the doctrine that Congress may not delegate away the legislative powers that have been delegated to it by the Constitution: "All legislative powers herein granted shall be vested in the Congress of the United States." The Latin phrase *delegata potestas non potest delegari* means that powers delegated to Congress by the Constitution may not be redelegated. This is what we call the *nondelegation doctrine.*

However, the constitutional provision that all legislative powers shall be vested in the Congress does not forbid every form of delegation by Congress. Legislative powers granted to Congress also include the "implied powers" of Article I, section 8, which give Congress the necessary resources of flexibility and practicality to perform its legislative functions. The constitutional problem of delegation is therefore part of the Constitution itself. Our concern with delegation focuses on three questions:

1. Does Congress in fact possess the particular power that it purports to delegate? This question refers to the constitutionality of acts that delegate powers to other branches of government. Congress must first have the power before it can delegate it to another branch.

2. What are the conditions or guidelines for delegation?

[10] *Williamson v. Lee Optical Co.*, 348 U.S. 483, 487 (1955).

3. Do the actions of those officials to whom power is delegated fall within the scope of the statute which delegates authority?

We can begin to understand how the courts have addressed these questions, and hence given constitutional support for delegating authority to administrative agencies, by turning to an early case from 1892, *Field v. Clark*.[11] In this case, an exporting company challenged the constitutionality of the Reciprocal Tariff Act passed by Congress in 1890 on the grounds that it unconstitutionally delegated legislative powers to another branch of government. The act granted the president the authority to transfer certain articles (tea and sugar) from the duty-free list to the duty list if it was found that other countries were treating U.S. exports "unequally." The Supreme Court upheld the statute while reaffirming the nondelegation doctrine. The Court reasoned that Congress itself had said what duties would be charged to what products and thus it had established the policy which the president was to merely execute. The president's authority to make such determinations, the Court argued, did not delegate legislative power, but rather supplied *factual details* to activate an already established legislative policy.

Within twenty years of the *Field v. Clark* cases, the Supreme Court unanimously held in *United States v. Grimaud* (1911)[12] that officials may lawfully be given far greater authority than the power to recognize factual details which may be the triggering conditions for executing legislative policy. The Court admitted that it was difficult to define the line between legislative power to make laws and administrative authority to make regulations: "There is no analytical difference, no difference in kind, between the legislative function—of prescribing rules for the future that is exercised by the legislature or by the agency implementing the authority conferred by the legislature."[13] The Court concluded that the problem of distinguishing legislative policymaking from administrative duties could only be resolved by placing clear *limits* on the powers that are delegated to agencies.

In *Hampton & Co. v. United States* (1928)[14] the Supreme Court formulated a general rule for placing such limits on administration. The Court said that when reviewing challenges to statutory delegation, delegation should be upheld where Congress has provided agencies with an *intelligible principle* to follow. The intelligible principle standard gave broad powers of delegation to Congress, while at the same time seeming to serve as a limit on administrative authority. The Court justified broad delegation on the grounds that there were practical limits on legislative time and expertise, thus delegation was a "necessity" of modern government.

The necessity argument for delegation became central to the architects of the New Deal. Indeed, Congress's strategy for recovering from the Great Depression took the argument for broad regulation to its extreme when it authorized the president to approve codes of "fair competition" established by *private* trade associations and business

[11] 143 U.S. 649.

[12] 220 U.S. 506.

[13] *Ibid.*

[14] 276 U.S. 394.

executives. According to section 3 of the National Industrial Recovery Act, these private groups were to be "truly representative" of their industry, and the codes could not, at least on their face, work to put smaller operators out of business. Once final, the codes bound businesses with the force of law, and fines could be imposed on those who violated the codes. In *Schechter Poultry Corp. v. United States* (1935) the Supreme Court held this delegation unconstitutional.[15] The NRA, it said, set no limits or standards for the kinds of things the codes would cover. Worse, the statute prescribed no detailed procedures for actually making the codes. The act amounted to a legislative delegation of the entire process of making laws in this emergency to the executive and private enterprise. Such total delegation violates the constitutional requirement that Congress make the laws.

Since *Schechter*, opponents of bureaucratic power have often argued that an authorizing statute was so broad and standardless that it fell afoul of the Constitution. Yet the courts have, with a few state court exceptions, upheld all statutes against the charge of overbroad delegation. The Supreme Court has approved Congress's turning over to the secretary of the interior the job of determining how the competing states of Arizona and California should share the scarce waters of the Colorado River.[16] It upheld President Nixon's sudden imposition of wage and price controls in 1971.[17]

In theory the line the courts have drawn between *Schechter* and the permissible delegations makes sense. The delegation must be specific enough to allow the courts to discern the statute's limits and tell when the agencies have gone too far. Courts allow agencies to make law within these limits. Thus in the wage and price control case cited a moment ago, the late (and great) Judge Harold Leventhal stated:

> The key question is not answered by noting that the authority delegation is abroad. . . . The issue is whether the legislative description of the task assigned sufficiently marks the field within which the Administrator is to act so that it may be known whether he has kept within it in compliance with the legislative will. . . . The principle permitting a delegation of legislative power, if there has been sufficient demarcation of the field to permit a judgment whether the agency has kept within the legislative will, establishes a principle of accountability under which compatibility with the legislative design may be ascertained not only by Congress but by the courts and the public.[18]

Given the practical limits on legislative time and expertise, the courts really have no choice but to grant legislatures broad delegative authority. Most statutes meet the delegation test by defining a general area of policy concern—the regulation of broadcasting or interstate transportation, for example—and requiring the agency to do what

[15] 295 U.S. 495.

[16] *Arizona v. California*, 373 U.S. 546 (1963).

[17] *Amalgamated Meat Cutters etc. v. Connally*, 337 F. Supp. 737 (1971).

[18] 337 F. Supp. 737, 746.

is "reasonably necessary in the public interest." In practice, then, the delegations in *Schechter* and in *Arizona v. California* differ in degree more than kind, and not much in degree at that.[19]

Louis Jaffe, a Harvard law professor and an influential scholar in administrative law reform, discusses the concept of administration under the broad delegation model in the following essay.

The Illusion of the Ideal Administration

Louis L. Jaffe
Harvard Law Review 86 (1973): 1183

It is once again fashionable to advocate what may be called the "broad delegation model" of administrative agencies, as both a description of what agencies are and a prescription of what they ought to be. Professor Kenneth Davis, for example, believes that an administrator is to be given broad jurisdiction over a field; preferably, as a matter of principle the ends and means should not be highly defined by the legislature. The agency then proceeds to "regulate" in the "public interest"—to reach decisions on the major policy questions for which Congress "was neither equipped nor willing" to supply clear answers. At the same time, the theory goes, the administrator has the power and the *duty* continuously to evolve rules—partly as a way of doing a job, partly as a way of providing due process for affected interests. The emphasis here is on an administration as a ready, all-purpose, efficient mechanism, which legitimizes itself by reducing its discretion and power-potential through rulemaking.

This concept of administration provides a fertile ground in which criticisms of administrative agencies readily take root. The broader the power defined as appropriate for exercise by an agency, the greater the frustration of the critic who finds that the state of the regulated world is not to his tastes. The assumption that a vague delegation to regulate in the public interest yields a standard which is readily discoverable by an administrator provokes objection when results do not comport with one or another individual's concept of what the "public interest" requires. Thus, paradoxically, the more vague a delegation, the more likely the charge that an agency has failed to fulfill its congressional mandate.

To my mind, the broad delegation model is subject to numerous objections. It does not adequately or accurately describe the variety of processes which characterize administration. More important, it permits false implications and creates damaging expectations with respect to those agencies it does purport to describe. It assumes that "to regulate" has some meaning apart from the specific purposes of Congress, and that an objective has been established that is capable of disinterested and nonpolitical administration and amplifation by a body variously denominated as "independent," "expert," or "neutral." In my opinion, these assumptions are highly questionable, and the resulting failure to have a correct view of the phenomenon of administration in all its variety leads

---

[19] State Administrative law generally follows federal law on this matter. See *Chartiers Valley Joint Schools v. Allegheny Co. Board of School Directors*, 418 Pa. 520 (1965). In criminal law, which is mostly state law, a variation of the delegation doctrine retains some validity. The variation, called the vagueness doctrine, prevents legislatures from authorizing police to pick up anybody under loosely drawn vagrancy statutes. See *Papachristou v. City of Jacksonville*, 405 U.S. 156 (1972). One final delegation footnote which also involves state practices is the following: The courts do not require that agencies, as a matter of internal operations, adopt a separation of powers model. Thus in *Withrow v. Larkin*, 421 U.S. 35 (1975), the Supreme Court ruled that a state board charged with the task of licensing physicians could investigate charges, adjudicate them, and order suspensions of licenses all in one process involving the same personnel. See chapter 11.

to ill-founded and futile criticisms of the administrative process and the perpetuation of empty pieties. Ultimately, this refusal to face facts may consolidate the power of just those groups which it is the object of the critics to contain. The elaboration of the deficiencies of the broad delegation model will be the dominant theme of this essay. . . .

In a classic article published in 1887, Woodrow Wilson found that "large powers and unhampered discretion," which seemed to him to be "the indispensable conditions of responsibility,"* are the essence of administration. "There is not danger in power, if only it be not irresponsible. If it be divided, dealt out in shares to many, it is obscured; and if it be obscured, it is made irresponsible." In Wilson's view, the greater the power delegated the less likely it is that an administrative official will abuse it.[†]

It may be that if the delegate is highly visible, as is the President, broad powers promote responsibility. But especially in the inordinately complex administration of our day, visibility is low and constituencies ill-defined, so that our experience does not confirm Wilson's analysis.

A view almost totally opposed to Wilson's was advanced by Ernst Freund, a professor who did not aspire to power and did not become Governor of New Jersey and President of the United States. In his opinion, "with regard to major matters the appropriate sphere of delegated authority is where there are no controversial issues of policy or of opinion."[‡] Thus, a liberal delegation to regulate safety, a matter which is "purely technical," is permissible, though even here "direct statutory regulation may be preferred."[§]

Freund's model of administration may be seen as peculiarly reflecting a laissez-faire role for government. Freund believed that broad administrative powers would invariably be manipulated in one direction or another—in his time, he believed that it would in the direction of the wage earner, the consumer, the passenger who "will frankly and sincerely claim that his interest is identical with the public welfare."[‖] Though he would have preferred legislative solutions of such conflicts of interest, Freund recognized that administrative experiments were inevitable. His preference as to the character of such administration was much influenced by continental scholarship, with its concepts of administrative law and law in general. His ideal can be seen as equivalent to that of Max Weber[¶]—the rational bureaucracy as a more or less insulated, nonpolitical, expert hierarchy acting pursuant to an authoritative statement of ends and means. . . .

Freund's concept of administration seems to me very ill-conceived, given the degree of government involvement in the highly complex conditions of our own time. Lawmaking may appropriately take place in a variety of contexts—legislative, administrative, and judicial—each of which, by its structure or way of dealing with a problem, may have something to contribute. Freund's rigid limitation of policymaking to the legislature would make modern government impossible and would deprive us of many fruitful solutions.

The Depression and the collapse of confidence in laissez-faire and in minimum government triggered a rebirth of the Wilsonian notion of salvation by open-ended administration. Dean Landis' famous lectures, *The Administrative Process*,[**] espoused a paradigm of broad delegation which was the icon of the New Deal. His model was an organization with all the powers of government—legislative, executive, judicial—to make decisions in a field as the problems arose. The objectives were loosely defined; solutions were to be evolved by presumed experts. The assumed predicates were a body of technology relevant to the solution of problems in the field and a consequent self-

---

*Wilson, *The Study of Administration*, 2 Pol. Sci. Q. 197, 213 (1887) (reprinted in 56 Pol. Sci. Q. 481 (1941)).

[†]*Id.* at 214.

[‡]E. Freund, Administrative Powers over Persons and Property 218 (1928).

[§]*Id. See also id.* at 221 (delegated rulemaking "ought to be confined to noncontroversial matter of a technical character").

[‖]*Id.* at 31.

[¶]*See, e.g.,* M. Weber, The Theory of Social and Economic Organization 324-423 (T. Parsons ed. 1964).

[**]J. Landis, The Administrative Process (1938).

sufficiency or autonomy, implying an immunity from the political process. While reminiscent of the Weberian model of a bureaucracy thoroughly motored and controlled by rational elaboration, Landis' model administration derived its content and its authority, not from legislative or imperial dictates, but from an assumed comprehensive body of expertise available for the implementation of legislative grants of authority. One suspects that the description, coming as it did in the heyday of the New Deal from one of its most important intellectuals, included the subconscious assumption of an expertise informed by the values of the New Deal. As long as New Dealers were in control and a powerful public opinion supported them, the new agencies performed very well as judged by those who created them.*

But we came to see that the Landis model, if taken as generalization valid for all administrative agencies at all times, makes certain untenable assumptions: the existence in each case of relevant, value-free concepts, and an administration located at any given moment of time outside the political process, that is to say, outside or insulated from the power structure. It is ironic that two of the agencies so much relied on by Landis, the Federal Trade Commission and the Interstate Commerce Commission, were even when he wrote proving to be ineffective; indeed, the ICC was actually destructive of the economic health of the transportation industry.

Because these and other agencies did not keep pace with the demands made for progressive adaptation, the Landis theory gave ground to the "capture theory," which asserts that agencies become the captives of the industries which they are charged to regulate. This theory is still popular with pseudosophisticates, but the more instructed, I believe, see it as grossly exaggerating the germ of truth which it does indeed embody. The regulated—their interests and the pressures they exert—are very significant components in the power complex, but the theory focuses on them

to the exclusion of other components. It ignores as well as the truth in the Landis thesis that there are significant inputs from a bureaucracy as such: expertness, tradition, stability, and an organization one of whose values is the rationalized exercise of power. And so, a return to the classic Landis model of broad delegation has taken place.

. . . I would propose a view of administration which recognizes the peculiar political process which provides the milieu and defines the operation of each agency. The elements of this political process are common to all potential lawmaking activity—the intensity of a given problem, the degree to which it is felt throughout an organized and stable constituency, and the representation (or lack thereof) of varying interests within and without the lawmaking body. The significance of each of these elements and the manner of their interaction are unpredictable, and likely to vary with each successive problem. Often the outcome will be determined not by the abstracted merits of a situation, but by the character of certain interests which are cohesive and vociferous. The more important point for our purposes, however, is that the extent to which an agency is open—influenced by and responsive to a political process—is determined by the definiteness and specificity of the congressional expression of the agency's methods and objectives.

Taking the highly articulated scheme for tax administration as polar, one can proceed through a spectrum of agencies whose ends and means are less well defined and which, as a consequence, are to a greater or lesser extent centrally positioned in the uncertainties and structural deficiences of the political process. Where the ends and means of an agency's role are highly defined, elaborately rationalized—as is the case with tax or social security—the effects of the political process on the agency are marginal, though rationalization could never go so far as totally to exclude politically choice. In such agencies, the bureaucratic virtues and vices are predominant; highly rationalized administrations embody the advantages of stability, equality of treatment, order, comprehensibility and predictability, and the defects of rigidity and displacement of objectives by bureaucratic routine. Such agencies are to be judged in terms of their fair,

---

*Indeed, Landis recognized the role of a favorable public opinion. *See* J. Landis, The Administrative Process 61 (1938) ("The agency must have friends, friends who can give it substantial political assistance. . . . ").

uniform, and zealous application of well-articulated law; the very precision of the law may help to reduce pressures from the regulated. . . .

On the other hand, where in form or in substance the legislative design is incomplete, uncertain, or inchoate, a political process will take place in and around the agency, with the likely outcome a function of the usual variables which determine the product of lawmaking institutions. Each agency functions in a political milieu peculiar to itself, and reflects in its own way the virtues and vices or, if you will, the potential and limitations of a bureaucratic process. To the extent that an administration is an open one, it will have some potential for change and for meeting problems difficult to resolve or not yet ready to be resolved at other levels. To round out the portrait, it should be noted that the political framework in which the agency is situated is the primary, but not the only, factor determining the likelihood and nature of its action. Also revelant are technical elements—the state of information and the maturity of thinking on a given problem, and the rate of change in the area as it bears on the possibility of a stable solution. Finally, the potential for action may be greater or less, depending on the competence and political character of the agency's leadership, the talents and depth of its staff, and the esprit de corps, as it were, of the entire operation.

This analysis of agencies in terms of the political factors surrounding and affecting them leads me to question the notion that broad delegation is inherently preferable. It does not make sense to say that the burdens of the congressional workload and the pressure exerted by opposing political forces preclude a detailed legislative solution to a given problem, so that vague, general delegation is the better or the only alternative. The monumental detail of the tax code suggests that Congress can, and does, legislate with great specificity when it regards a matter as sufficiently important. Nor can a political conflict be avoided by relegating a problem to the care of an agency and invoking the talisman of "expertise." The effect of such a transfer of function is simply to shift the legislative process to a different level, and there is no reason to believe that the agency will be able to rise above power conflicts to achieve solutions that the legislature itself cannot or does not choose to provide. . . .

. . . The action or inaction of an agency acting under a broad delegation is often the result of the political process operating on the agency, and is, after all, all that can be expected. Indeed, the criticisms of administration must be recognized as themselves a component of the political process, and critics' invocation of the "public interest" as a standard with readily discoverable content should be viewed as but a useful tactic in the political debate.

Although the broad delegation model has become a statutory blueprint for administrative activity in the modern state, debate over its virtues and vices continues. Just as Jaffe questions those who would restrict statutory delegation, he cautions that we keep in mind the political factors surrounding administration and avoid adherence to simple models. Theodore Lowi, a political scientist at Cornell University, adds to Jaffe's political analysis of delegation by stressing the importance of representative democracy over the emergence of interest-group liberalism in the post-war period. In his book, *The End of Liberalism*,[20] Lowi argues against interest-group liberalism, or pluralism, as a method for making public policy. He proposes *juridical democracy* as an alternative to the realities of American pluralism where only those who have economic and political resources lobby Congress and administrative agencies to further their group or class interests. For Lowi, juridical democracy is a combination of strengthening the rule of law in administrative processes (versus the pressure of interest groups) and demanding more congressional input and oversight of administrative decisions.

[20]Theodore J. Lowi, *The End of Liberalism* 2d ed. (New York: W. W. Norton & Co., 1979).

Toward Juridical Democracy

Theodore J. Lowi
The End of Liberalism 2d ed. (New York:
W.W. Norton, 1979)

During the twentieth century, the United States became a united state. Given the world and national history of our troubled century, this was probably inevitable, and there is surely no turning back, assuming anyone remains who wants to turn back. But, the particular way we adjusted to historical forces was almost certainly not predetermined, and if we got to our present state by deliberate choices, we can get out of it the same way. If the corruption of modern democratic government began with the emergence of interest-group liberalism, reforms must be oriented toward the influences of that point of view. . . .

The End of Liberalism: A Four-Count Indictment

1. *Interest-group liberalism as public philosophy corrupts democratic government because it deranges and confuses expectations about democratic institutions.* Liberalism promotes popular decision-making but undermines popular decisions by misapplying the notion to the implementation as well as the formulation of policy. It derogates democratic rights by assuming they are being exercised when more people have merely been given access. Liberal practices reveal a basic disrespect for democracy. Liberal leaders do not wield the authority of democratic governments with the resoluteness born of confidence in the legitimacy or their positions, the integrity of their institutions, or the justness of the programs they serve. Quite the contrary, their approach betrays their convictions.

2. *Interest-group liberalism renders government impotent.* Liberals are copious in plans but irresolute in planning. Nineteenth-century liberalism had standards without plans—an anachronism even in its own time. But twentieth-century liberalism turned out to have plans without standards. Delegation of power was widely advertised as a counsel of strength but turned out to be a formula for weakness—an alienation of public domain, a gift of sovereignty to private satra-

pies. Because delegation of power turns out to be an imposition of impotence, it should render anachronistic the larger rationalization of interest-group liberalism. But doctrines are not organisms. They die only in combat, and no doctrine yet exists capable of doing the job.

3. *Interest-group liberalism demoralizes government, because liberal governments cannot achieve justice.* The question of justice has engaged the best minds for almost as long as there have been notions of state and politics, and since that time philosophers have been unable to agree on what justice is. But outside the ideal, in the realms of actual government and citizenship, the problem is simpler. In order to weigh and assess the quality of justice in our government, it is not necessary to define justice, because there is something about liberalism that prevents us from raising the question of justice at all. No matter what definition of justice is used, liberal governments cannot achieve justice because their policies lack the *sine qua non* of justice—that quality without which a consideration of justice cannot even be initiated. Considerations of justice in, or achieved by, an action cannot be made unless a deliberate and conscious attempt was made to derive the action from a preexisting general rule or moral principle governing such a class of actions. Therefore, any governing regime that makes a virtue of avoiding such rules puts itself outside the context of justice. . . .

4. *Interest-group liberalism corrupts democratic government in the degree to which it weakens the capacity of those governments to live by democratic formalisms.* Liberalism weakens democratic institutions by opposing formal procedure with informal bargaining. "Playing it by the book" is a role often unpopular in American war and sports literature precisely because it can be used to dramatize personal rigidity and the plight of the individual in collective situations. Because of the impersonality of formal procedures, there is inevitably a gap between form and reality. But this is something that can be seen in two directions, only one of which has been stressed in the literature on war, sports, and politics. The gap between form and reality gives rise to cynicism, for informality means

that some will escape their fate better than others. There has, as a consequence, always been cynicism toward public institutions in the United States; and this, too, is a good thing, since a little cynicism is the parent of healthy sophistication. However, when the informal is elevated to a positive virtue, and when the gap between the formal and the informal grows wider, and when the hard-won access of individuals and groups becomes a share of official authority, cynicism unavoidably curdles into distrust. Legitimacy can be defined as the distance between form and reality. How much spread can a democratic system tolerate and remain both democratic and legitimate? . . .

Interest-group liberalism possesses the mentality of a world universalized ticket-fixing. Destroy privilege by universalizing it. Reduce conflict by yielding to it. Redistribute power by the maxim of each according to his claim. Purchase support for the regime by reserving an official place for every major structure of power.

In the process, liberalism has promoted concentration of democratic authority but deconcentration of democratic power. Liberalism has opposed privilege in policy formulation only to foster it quite systematically in the implementation of policy. Liberalism has consistently failed to recognize, in brief, that in a democracy forms are important. In a medieval monarchy all formalisms were at court or manor. Democracy proves, for better or worse, that the masses like that sort of thing, too. And this is not a superficial preference.

Juridicial Democracy: Modest Proposals for Radical Reforms

These concluding comments are written for a time when political leaders have begun to see that the Second Republic, the regime of interest-group liberalism, is finished. At this time they persist in their search for distant explanations for the American distress, and usually the victims or the society get all the blame. But ultimately they must come to see that they, the leaders, are the problem, their belief system is the source of the pathology, and their policies will not succeed except at great economic and political cost. As this moment approaches, there will be an oppor-

tunity for fundamental changes. But these changes will have to be guided by a new public philosophy, and a new public philosophy does not come out of a package. It will emerge from a kind of political discourse in which few of us have engaged during the false consensus of our generation. As a contribution to this discourse, I offer *juridical democracy*.

. . . The need to define juridical democracy is to me a measure of the decline of law and of legitimate government in the United States. Juridical democracy is rule of law operating in institutions. Juridical democracy is a public philosophy which rejects informality as a criterion, accepting it only as a measure of the distance between reality and the ideal situation. Juridical democracy rejects realism; when reality and forms diverge, it is the reality that must first be attacked.

Juridical is not the same as judicial. In fact, many judicial rulings would not qualify as juridical because they have left the rule unclear and have thereby perpetuated dependence upon judges for resolution of future conflicts—until a clear leading rule is handed down. The juridical principle would build a public philosphy around the state, including the judiciary, and would concern itself with how and why the state must limit itself in the use of its power of coercion. The juridical principle therefore speaks to the powerless as well as the powerful. *The juridical principle is the only dependable defense the powerless have against the powerful.* In many cases the powerful would be immobilized if they had to articulate what they were going to do before they did it. On the other side, the juridical principle could relieve governments of many of their heaviest contemporary burdens. A delegation of power to the president or to agencies is in reality a delegation of personal responsibility for which there is almost never commensurate real power or consensus. . . . Moreover, the juridical principle would provide a basis for collective responsibility; the president or a specific agency would no longer be alone but would share responsibility with all those who supported the program from start to finish.

Juridical democracy is, however, two words; and each helps define the other. . . . On a host of issues, therefore, juridical democracy has very clear and profound substantive implications; it is not merely a procedural matter. On the other hand, there are many substantive issues upon which juridical democracy as a public philosophy would be silent, because no particular outcome would threaten to violate democratic notions of citizenship and equal treatment. In such cases, perhaps a majority of all cases, the only concern would be for the juridical—that is, the institutions of government ought to say what they are going to do to us before they do it; and if they cannot say they cannot act. . . .

THE JURIDICAL PRINCIPLE THROUGH JUDICIAL ACTION. Since all the proposals revolve around the effort to restore and expand the rule of law, it is natural to begin the design for a movement with proposals for judicial action. But the reader should not be misled by this ordering to the idea that all our problems can or will be resolved by proper judicial action. With that in mind, it is clear that the first and most important step toward juridical democracy, would involve revival of the still valid but universally disregarded rule in the Schechter case, where the Supreme Court declared the National Industrial Recovery Act void on the grounds that it had delegated legislative powers to the president without sufficiently defining the policy or criteria to guide the administrator. In other words, no rule of law, no agency. To accommodate interest-group liberal programs the Supreme Court created modern jurisprudence by giving full faith and credit to any expression that could get a majority vote in Congress. The Court's rule must once again become one of declaring invalid and unconstitutional any delegation of power to an administrative agency or to the president that is not accompanied by clear standards of implementation.

Restoration of the Schechter rule would be dramatic because it would mean an occasional confrontation between the Supreme Court and Congress. But there is no reason to fear judicial usurpation. Under present conditions, when Congress delegates without a shred of guidance, the courts usually end up rewriting many of the statutes in the course of construction. Since the Court's present procedure is always to find an acceptable meaning of a statute in order to avoid invalidating it, the Court is constantly legislating. In contrast, a blanket invalidation under the Schechter rule is tantamount to a court order for Congress to do its own work. Therefore the rule of law is a restraint upon rather than an expansion of judicial function. . . .

THE JURIDICAL PRINCIPLE BY PRESIDENTIAL ACTION. The first six presidents of the United States tended to use constitutional arguments to justify their vetoes of congressional bills. Andrew Jackson was the first president who vetoed bills simply because he considered them objectionable. But Jackson only vetoed twelve bills in his entire eight years as president, and as recently as President Grover Cleveland, constitutional arguments still tended to be preferred. Thus, even though modern presidents have disregarded constitutional arguments in their vetoes, there is ample precedent for a president's claim to a share of constitutional authority. . . .

The area where such a position is especially relevant is the president's obligation to see that the laws are faithfully executed. It would seem to me that the president is virtually obliged to veto a congressional enactment whenever Congress has not been clear enough about what should be executed, and how. The veto of a congressional enactment on the grounds that it said nothing would have the same effect as the Supreme Court's action under the Schechter rule. But there are additional advantages—vital ones: The Congress would have been told to go back and do its job properly. The public would be to that extent better informed about what Congress intends and what is expected of citizens. The level of debate and general political discourse would have been raised toward the question of congressional intentions. . . .

RULE OF LAW BY ADMINISTRATIVE FORMALITY. Schechter rules and presidential vetoes, even when forcefully applied in good faith, could never eliminate all the vagueness in legislative enactments and could never eliminate the need for delegation of power to administrative agencies. Ignorance of changing social conditions is important, although it is much overused as an alibi for malfeasance in legislative drafting.

Social pressure for some kind of quick action also interferes with drafting of a proper rule, even though this too is a much overused alibi. Nevertheless, even if it would often be impossible for Congress to live by the juridical principle despite sincere efforts to do so, there are at least two ways to compensate for that slippage and to bring these necessarily vague legislative formulations back to a much closer approximation of the juridical principle. The first of these is administrative formality. The second, to be taken up in the next section, is codification.

Administrative formality would simply be a requirement for early and frequent administrative rule-making. When an agency formulates a general rule it is without any question committing a legislative act. But in so doing, the agency is simply carrying out the responsibility delegated to it by Congress in the enabling statute for that agency, and is also carrying out the general intent of Congress as spelled out in the Administrative Procedure Act. This power to promulgate general rules has been validated by the Supreme Court. But the trouble is, few agencies do this, and even fewer like to do it. Most of the administrative rhetoric in recent years espouses the interest-group ideal of administration by favoring the norms of flexibility and decision by bargaining. Pluralism applied to administration usually takes the practical form of an attempt to deal with each case on its merits. But the ideal of case-by-case administration is in most instances a myth. Few persons affected by a decision have an opportunity to be heard. And each agency, regulatory or not, disposes of the largest proportion of its cases without any procedure at all, least of all by formal adversary processes. In practice, agencies end up with the worst of case-by-case adjudication *and* of rule-making. They try to work without rules in order to live with the loose legislative mandate, and then they try to treat their cases and practices as though they were operating under a rule. . . .

. . . A rule can be general and yet can gain clarity and practicality through the specific cases to which it is applied. It was precisely this ability to perceive the public policy implications in complex phenomena that explains our reliance on expert agencies in the first place. The rule in combination with the cases to which it applies can become a known factor in the everyday life of each client. In contrast, although there is an implicit rule in every bargained or adjudicated case, it cannot be known until the outcome of the bargain, and its later applications must be deciphered by lawyers representing potential cases. . . .

TOWARD RESTORATION OF CONGRESS: JURIDICAL DEMOCRACY THROUGH CODIFICATION The second approach to the problem of Congress's inherent inability to live by the juridical principle, codification, is highly consistent with and complementary to the first. Even if Congress is unable to provide good legislative guidelines at the time of the passage of the original organic act, there is no reason why Congress has to remain permanently incapable. The answer here is codification. Let us consider it in light of the modest proposition that Congress ought to be able to learn from its own experience.

Codification is nothing more than the effort to systematize, digest, and simplify all of the provisions of law relating to a particular subject. The most famous and successful effort at codification was probably that of the French law in 1804 (eventually called Code Napoleon to honor the emperor), which was sought because there were so many sources of law in France: Roman law in the south, customary law in the north, canon law over marriage and family, case law and government edict in an increasing number of areas by the time of the Revolution. Voltaire is said to have observed that travelers in France changed law as often as they changed horses. Demand for codification, beginning well before the Revolution, was a demand for consistency, for accessibility to common people, and for the dominance of the legislature in government. But codification does not require the extensive or rigid approach of the Code Napoleon. This simply defines the mechanism, and it is not a strange and new experience for the United States. . . .

A much richer experience with codification will be found in state law. For example, the state of New

York has had an active commission on law revision and codification at least since 1934. Many other states have similar commissions and each of these states seems to have gone much further than Congress in its effort to incorporate administrative and, especially, judicial decisions into later legislative enactments. Perhaps this is why there is more legal integrity in most state laws than in federal laws despite the lower average caliber of state legislators, the smaller professional staffs available to state legislators, and the lower average tenure and specialization of members of state legislatures. American Bar Association Committees have studied this problem as far back as 1914, and recommendations favoring codification of state or federal procedures and substantive clauses will be found in the work of certain legal scholars, most distinguished among them being Ernst Freund. Thus, if we do not engage in codification it is due to the ignorance and incompetence of contemporary legislators and not to anything inherently un-American. . . .

If Congress got regularly and routinely into the business of serious revision of its laws in light of administrative experience, it would then be perfectly possible for Congress to live according to the juridical principle and yet delegate broad powers to administrators. Everyone would be aware of the fact that the first enactment is only the beginning. Every administrator would be making decisions with an eye toward review of consistency, and every agency would have incentive to influence this process by promulgation of the early rules proposed in the the previous section. Every regulated corporation and individual would be pushing the regulatory agency toward general rulings and away from individual decisions because of the knowledge that these are likely to become legislation eventually. Finally, when these rulings are brought back to Congress and put through the regular legislative mill, they will not only be elevated in stature as law but very probably would go through further change and further clarification on their way back to the administrative agency. The regulator would then be participating in the legislative process in a way that is consonant with the Constitution and the juridical principle. This should definitely elevate the status of the regulator and at the same time would be far more honest and open from the standpoint of the regulated corporation and individual. . . .

SUNSET LAWS: A TENURE-OF-STATUTES ACT The juridical principle may be suffering most from the immortality of administrative agencies. Enabling legislation is as indefinite on agency duration as on substantive guidelines. Once an agency is established, its resources favor its own survival, and the longer agencies survive, the more likely they are to continue to survive. The only direct antidote to immortality would appear to be an attack upon the Frankenstein legislation creating each monster, and in that spirit the final reform proposal is for a general statute setting a Jeffersonian limit of from five to ten years on the life of every enabling act. The purpose of this reform is not merely to kill off superfluous and antiquated administrative agencies, desirable though that may be. The purpose is to provide an institutional means for facing up to the basic problem of juridical democracy—the absence of rule of law and the absence of real legislative power to impose it. The guillotine effect of a termination date on an agency enabling act is an opportunity for leverage in favor of imposing the clear rules of law the second time around that were impossible to impose in the original instance. As with codification, we can better live with bad organic laws if we are guaranteed another crack at them.

A termination date should not be considered a death sentence but an opportunity to learn from experience. This is why the notion of sunset is appropriate, because it implies a creative time during which the politics of the agency is likely to come unstuck and the opportunity for substantive reconsideration is most propitious. The termination date for the statute and program is, therefore, insufficient in itself and should not be judged alone. Everything depends upon what is made of the opportunity during those months when each agency is approaching its ultimate tenure, when it is likely to be politically most vulnerable. The sunset period is obviously the best period for codification of agency rules; one could easily imagine a tenure-of-statues act requiring that the renewal of an agency's enabling act should take the form of a new agency code.

Indeed, most agencies will survive the renewal process, and most will probably be able to avoid any serious alterations in the way they conduct their business. But each agency will be a different one if in the process its true nature has been exposed. My own hypothesis is that few agencies can withstand public scrutiny. And it is not a hypothesis but a certainty that the public will gain immensely from any effort,

even when unsuccessful, to codify past rulings and to enact them as a code to guide future conduct—until the next sunset. Those who prefer to be governed by rules rather than authority, must fear the present system, should be opposing almost all existing federal programs, and should be supporting any institution capable of providing rule of law—whether it is the aristocratic Supreme Court through judicial review or technocratic agencies that engage in early rule-making. But those who prefer their rules of law as enacted, at least in part, by elected assemblies should strongly prefer statutory tenure and codification.

Confining the Agency Within Its Statutory Limits

The next section of this chapter introduces the major problem of statutory authority in administrative law that courts have not, and cannot, finally resolve and lay aside: If legislatures must delegate within limits, then how do courts determine the limits and hold agencies within them? Since legislatures constantly modify agency authority, and because new questions regarding the limits of agency authority continuously arise and social problems and perceptions shift, courts continuously help agencies define their statutory authority.

Agencies of course have primary responsibility for determining their own statutory limits and acting within them. Because of the political pressures on them, many agencies do not choose to exercise all the powers that courts might hold the authorizing statues permit. The Federal Trade Commission, for example, choose not to exercise rulemaking powers for the first half-century of its existence, even though its statute authorized it to "prevent" certain evils and prevention arguably requires rulemaking. In the following case the agency in question interpreted its authority a certain way and the courts upheld its interpretation. It is an example of how the Court has upheld agency authority to make substantive decisions within the scope of delegated authority.

NAACP et al. v. Federal Power Commission

425 U.S. 662 (1976) 8–0

+ Brennan, Stewart, White, Blackmun, Powell, Rehnquist, Stevens, Burger
NP Marshall

[In 1972 the National Association for the Advancement of Colored People and several other organizations petitioned the Federal Power Commission (FPC). They asked the Commission to issue a rule "requiring equal employment opportunity and nondiscrimination in the employment practices of its regulatees." The Federal Power Act, as amended by the Natural Gas Act, charges the FPC with responsibility to set just and reasonable prices for the sale of electricity and natural gas. Its regulations must, by statute, "serve the public interest." The petitioners claimed that racial discrimination was a costly practice and that the statutes therefore authorized the FPC to prevent it as part of its rate-controlling power. They also claimed that racial discrimination contradicted the public interest, whether it added to the cost of energy or not, and therefore that the commission possessed statutory authority to prevent it. The FPC refused the request, and the plantiffs went to court to compel such a rule.]

Justice Stewart delivered the opinion of the Court.

The question presented is not whether the elimination of discrimination from our society is an important national goal. It clearly is. The question is not whether Congress could authorize the Federal Power Commission to combat such discrimination. It clearly could. The question is simply whether or to what extent Congress did grant the Commission such authority. Two possible statutory bases have been advanced to justify the conclusion that the Commission can or must concern itself with discriminatory employment practices on the part of the companies it regulates. . . .

Without necessarily endorsing the specific identification of the costs "arguably within" the Commission's "range of concern," we agree with the basic conclusion of the Court of Appeals on this branch of the case. The Commission clearly has the duty to prevent its regulatees from charging rates based upon illegal, duplicative, or unnecessary labor costs. To the extent that such costs are demonstrably the product of a regulatee's discriminatory employment practices, the Commission should disallow them. For example, when a company complies with a backpay award resulting from a finding of employment discrimination in violation of Title VII of the Civil Rights Act of 1964, 42 U.S.C. § 2000e *et seq.*, it pays twice for work that was performed only once. The amount of the backpay award, therefore, can and should be disallowed as an unnecessary cost in a ratemaking proceeding.

To the extent that these and other similar costs, such as attorney's fees, can be or have been demonstrably quantified by judicial decree or the final action of an administrative agency charged with consideration of such matters, the Commission clearly should treat these costs as it treats any other illegal, unnecessary, or duplicative costs. We were told by counsel during oral argument that the Commission would routinely disallow the costs of a backpay award resulting from an order of the National Labor Relations Board or the decree of a court based upon a finding of an unfair labor practice. The governing principle is no different in the area of discriminatory employment practices.

As a general proposition it is clear that the Commission has the discretion to decide whether to approach these problems through the process of rulemaking, individual adjudication, or a combination of the two procedures. *SEC v. Chenery Corp.*, 332 U.S. 194, 202–203. The present Commission practice, we are told, is to consider such questions only in individual ratemaking proceedings, under its detailed accounting procedures. Assuming that the Commission continues that practice, it has ample authority to consider whatever evidence and make whatever inquiries are necessary of illegitimate costs because of racially discriminatory employment practices. . . .

The Court of Appeals rejected the broader argument based upon the statutory criterion of "public interest," and we hold that it was correct in doing so. This Court's cases have consistently held that the use of the words "public interest" in a regulatory statute is not a broad license to promote the general public welfare. Rather, the words take meaning from the purposes of the regulatory legislation. . . .

Thus, in order to give content and meaning to the words "public interest" as used in the Power and Gas Acts, it is necessary to look to the purposes for which the Acts were adopted. In the case of the Power and Gas Acts it is clear that the principal purpose of those Acts was to encourage the orderly development of plentiful supplies of electricity and natural gas at reasonable prices. While there are undoubtedly other subsidiary purposes contained in these Acts, the parties point to nothing in the Acts or their legislative histories to indicate that the elimination of employment discrimination was one of the purposes that Congress had in mind when it enacted this legislation. The use of the words "public interest" in the Gas and Power Acts is not a directive to the Commission to seek to eradicate discrimination, but, rather, is a charge to promote the orderly production of plentiful supplies of electric energy and natural gas at just and reasonable rates.

It is useful again to draw on the analogy of federal labor law. No less than in the federal legislation defining the national interest in ending employment discrimination, Congress in its earlier labor legislation unmistakably defined the national interest in free collective bargaining. Yet it could hardly be supposed that in directing the Federal Power Commission to be guided by the "public interest," Congress thereby instructed it to take original jurisdiction over the processing of charges of unfair labor practices on the parts of its regulatees.

We agree, in short, with the Court of Appeals that the Federal Power Commission is authorized to consider the consequences of discriminatory employment practices on the part of its regulatees only insofar as such consequences are directly related to the Commission's establishment of just and reasonable rates in the public interest. Accordingly, we affirm the judgment before us.

It is ordered.

Statutes creating agencies usually state the kinds of procedures agencies should follow in reaching decisions. Recall, for example, that in *Morgan* the Court took seriously Congress's call for a "full hearing." Just as the Court in the previous case helped define the limits to the policies the FPC could adopt, the following case requires an agency to stick to the procedures required by the agency's authorizing statute. This case is an example of agency authority to set standards and the legitimacy of the process by which those standards are set.

Moss v. Civil Aeronautics Board

430 F.2d 891 (D.C. Cir. 1970) 3–0

[In the late 1960s John E. Moss, U.S. Representative from California, and 31 other representatives filed suit against the Civil Aeronautics Board (CAB). They charged that the board had followed a practice of setting air fares that avoided the procedures required by the Federal Aviation Act to hold a public hearing about fares, a hearing that the air fare-paying public might attend. The act required interstate air carriers to charge fares according to a fare list (*tariff*) filed with and approved by the CAB. The tariffs and therefore the fares may change only after public notice and hearings. The act requires the board to "take into consideration, among other factors . . .

1. The effect of such rates upon the movement of traffic;
2. The need in the public interest of adequate and efficient transportation of persons and property by air carriers at the lowest cost consistent with the furnishing of such service;
3. Such standards respecting the character and quality of service to be rendered by air carriers as may be prescribed by or pursuant to law;
4. The inherent advantages of transportation by aircraft; and
5. The need of each carrier for revenue sufficient to enable such air carrier, under honest, economical, and efficient management, to provide adequate and efficient air carrier service."

The statute does not, however, require the hearing until after the board suspends an existing or proposed new tariff.

Moss alleged that the board staff avoided the requirement for a hearing in the following way. The staff would meet unofficially—*ex parte* is the technical term, one you may remember from *Morgan*—with representatives from the airlines at the initial stage of the proceedings. They would discuss fares and related matters without any hearing. The board staff would then comment upon the proposed new rates and on the upcoming review. In doing so it would announce its own suggestions for fares based on the informal discussions. The airlines would then quickly change their request as necessary to conform to the board's suggestions. The board, being content with the result, would not suspend the new tariff at all and thus never trigger the public hearing stage. At this point outsiders had no way of verifying that the board had decided consistently with the statutory criteria listed above.]

J. Skelly Wright, Circuit Judge:

Petitioners complain that the Board effectively "determined" rates, within the meaning of Sections 1002(d) and 1002(e), to be charged by the air carriers without proper notice and hearings as required by Section 1002(d) and without taking into account the rate-making factors enumerated in Section 1002(e). The Board admits that it would have been required to act in accordance with subsections (d) and (e) if its actions amounted to the making of rates. The Board, however, contends that it was not required to adhere to the standards of subsections (d) and (e) because, as the formal title of its September 12 order ("Order of Investigation and Suspension") indicates, it was not determining rates but only exercising its power under Section 1002(g) to suspend, pending a more complete investigation, the rates initially filed by the carriers in August.

The Board also admits that immediatley after its September 12 order the airlines withdrew their August tariffs and filed new tariffs listing rates based directly on and in conformity with that order. But the Board disclaims any legal responsibility for the rates listed in the carriers' September tariffs. According to the Board, the detailed outline of the rate structure which it "proposed to accept" in its September 12 order was not an attempt to prescribe or determine rates for the future within the meaning of the statute, but merely served to explain to the carriers—as required by the statute—the Board's reasons for suspending the August filings. The Board points out that the carriers were not legally bound by the September 12 order of the Board to file a new tariff and list rates based on its formula. Therefore, the Board argues, even though the carriers did precisely what the Board indicated in its September 12 order should be done, the resulting rates are carrier-made rates for which the Board is not to be held accountable. . . .

As a practical matter, the Board's order amounted to the prescription of rates because, as the Board admits, the pressures on the carriers to file rates conforming exactly with the Board's formula were great, if not actually irresistible. All the carriers had indicated an urgent need for an immediate increase in revenues; the Board had made it clear, by threatening to use its power to suspend proposed rates, that only rates conforming to its detailed model would be accepted and not suspended. It explicitly stated that it would "consider fares produced by the formula as a 'just and reasonable' ceiling, and any fare in excess of this ceiling would be viewed *prima facie* as outside the realm of justness and reasonableness and would ordinarily be suspended and ordered investigated." Any carrier wanting to file higher tariffs would be dissuaded, not only by the indications in the order that only those tariffs meeting the standards set down by the Board would be accepted, but also by the Board's explicit statement that increases would be considered only "where strong justification was shown." . . .

The Board has pointed to no case in which the Board or Commission has set out such a complete and detailed scheme for making rates which it wanted filed and in which a court has held that the resulting rates were carrier-made rates. Even a cursory reading of the order makes it clear that the Board told the carriers what rates to file; it set forth a step-by-step formula requiring major changes in rate-making practices and in rates which it expected the carriers to adopt. And the Board concededly took this action after closed sessions with carrier representatives, without statutory public hearings and, according to petitioners, without reference to the rate-making standards of the statute.

If, as the Board argues, the rates resulting from this procedure are carrier-made, rather than agency-made, the public would not only be fenced out of its role in rate-making, but judicial review of the Board's actions would be severely limited. On appeal agency-made rates are tested against the Act's explicit rate-making procedures. Thus a court must decide whether, in determining rates, the Board has properly observed the statutory procedures and taken into account the factors which Congress has said should be considered when rates are made. If the statutory plan has been complied with, the court can then determine whether substantial evidence in the record supports the Board's rates. Here the Board has in effect determined rates and the record made in so doing is inadequate for judicial review. By contrast, if the tariffs filed pursuant to the Board's order of September 12 are not Board-determined rates, judicial review is practically nonexistent. Aggrieved parties can object to carrier-made rates and ask the Board to investigate them, but the Board's refusal to investigate would be reviewable only for an abuse of discretion. And, of course, it would be very difficult indeed to apply this limited standard of review to a record made in large part behind closed doors.

Moreover, the Board's suspension authority, on which it relies for justification of its actions in this case, is totally insulated from judicial review. It is this power which the Board uses to work its will in rate-making rather than the judicially reviewable statutory rate-making plan designed by Congress to protect the public. In the absence of a compelling justification for the Board's admitted practice of making rates by use of its suspension power, we cannot

help but conclude that the Board is only seeking to avoid the strict requirements of the rate-making portion of the statute and the resulting more stringent judicial review. No requirement of Board operation or policy of the Act seems to support the Board's blatant attempt to subvert the statute's scheme.

The Board has argued that to hold it accountable for these rates would "hobble the administrative process," seemingly because it feels that the procedures required by Sections 1002(d) and 1002(e) of the Act do not permit the Board to respond quickly enough to meet the immediate revenue needs of the carriers in times of rapidly rising costs. While we recognize that under the statute the Board has an obligation to afford the carriers sufficient revenues, that obligation cannot become a *carte blanche* allowing the Board to deal only with the carriers and disregard the other factors, such as the traveling public's interest in the lowest possible fares and high standards of service, which are also enumerated in the Act as rate-making criteria.

Furthermore, we see no inconsistency between adhering to the statutory plan and awarding a speedy increase in carrier revenues. The statute does not require a complete, time-consuming, scholarly and theoretical review of all aspects of rate-making before the Board passes upon proposals which are submitted. The Board is expected to use its experience gleaned from ongoing studies and investigations in its day-to-day activities, and it can act with reasonable speed as long as it affords public notice, holds a proper hearing, and takes the statutory factors into account when it determines rates. In any case, ignoring the general public's interests in order to better serve the carriers is not the proper response to the difficulties supposedly created by an outdated or unwieldly statutory procedure. After all, there is more to rate-making than providing carriers with sufficient revenue to meet their obligations to their creditors and to their stockholders.

In short, we simply do not agree with the Board that abdication from its proper supervisory role under the statute need be the result of today's holding requiring the Board to comply with the statute in rate-making. We would be sympathetic, for example, to instances in which the Board felt that compelling circumstances required it to act without complete information before an investigation is completed. Any approval of rates under such conditions would be subject to revision once more complete information is obtained. We would liken such emergency Board action to the interim approval which Judge Tamm recently remarked upon, in a somewhat different context. Speaking for the court: he said:

" . . . [Our] assessment of the Board's findings should be bifurcated, with different standards applied to the findings relating to full and interim approval. That is, the fact that interim approval is useful primarily in situations in which the Board needs to act expeditiously . . . but lacks sufficient information to determine authoritatively whether the agreement as a whole will serve the public interest, indicates that our review of the findings supporting the interim approval should be relatively limited. Since the Board in electing to order an interim approval is essentially saying that . . . further data gleaned from practical experience is necessary to an enlightened determination of the public interest, a reviewing court can do little more than ask whether this conclusion is reasonable and based upon substantial evidence. . . . "

We fully recognize that a carrier's exigent economic circumstances at times will make it necessary for the Board to act on the basis of incomplete data. But we emphatically reject any intimation by the Board that its responsibilities to the carriers are more important that its responsibilities to the public. Board action must always comply with the procedural requirements of the statute and must always be based on an assessment of the relevant available data, with due consideration given to all the factors enumerated in the statute, which factors taken together make up the public interest. . . .

Since the record shows, as the Board admits, that the public notice and hearing requirements of Section 1002(d) were not observed in issuing the order of September 12, that order is invalid and the tariffs filed by the carriers based thereon are unlawful. Under the circumstances, this case is remanded to the Board for further proceedings.

So ordered.

Before proceeding further, reflect on the role of Judge Wright believes courts should play in the administrative process. It is an active role in at least two respects. The CAB did not technically violate the letter of its statute, but the court insisted that the CAB had violated its spirit. Second, the court perceived that spirit as protecting the public interest, not just the airline's interest. The concept of legality we introduced in part calls for publicly observable procedures in order to minimize arbitrariness. Judge Wright's approaches is squarely within that tradition.

The Role of Courts in Statutory Interpretation

One of the most perplexing questions in administrative law involves statutory interpretation.[21] This is particularly evident in regulatory cases involving scientific research and conflicting data on the subject under regulation. Saccharin, asbestos, benzene, radiation, and other substances have appeared in recent news reports in association with various diseases. When such research findings appear, environmental groups, health organizations and members of Congress instruct agencies to take steps to minimize the danger. The problem is perplexing because while data may establish an association, it often cannot distinguish between safe and unsafe levels of exposure. As a result, Congress's statutory instructions to agencies may be highly uncertain, so uncertain

[21]For an overview of theories of statutory interpretations see Cass R. Sunstein, "Interpreting Statutes in the Regulatory State," *Harvard Law Review* 103 (1989): 405.

as to amount to no more than an instruction to the agencies to *do something*, the something being unspecified.

A command to do something about a health problem does not violate the delegation doctrine because the Congress does create limits to the action of the agencies invovled. The Food and Drug Administration and the Occupational Safety and Health Administration are limited by statute in the sense they cannot regulate airline safety or safety in the homes. They do not have the carte blanche power the Court rejected in *Schechter*. The problem lies in choosing between playing it safe and prohibiting exposures that are suspected but not proven to cause problems, on the one hand, and insisting on proof before forcing businesses to make costly changes on the other. In the statute creating OSHA, Congress waffled on this choice. We have included portions of the OSHA statute in Appendix D so that you can get an idea of what statutes look like and begin to comprehend the kind of issues agencies and courts face when interpreting a statute. The statutory language of the OSHA statute leaves the choice open, so open it is hard to tell if any statutory command exists it all.

How should the courts interpret such statutory "guidelines"? Leave all issues to the discretionary judgment of administrative officials, or insist on rational proof? These questions have become all the more pressing with the passage of social and economic regulatory statutes in the 1960s and 1970s. Statutes passed during these decades have been characterized as having very broadly stated aspirational goals—"to provide safe and healthful employment," alongside very specific but incomplete standards and criteria—a "standard which most adequately assures, to the extent feasible, on the basis of the best available evidence." Neither regulatory agencies nor courts have settled on a formula for interpreting statutes.

The majority and dissenting opinions in the following cases reveal how divided the Court is in its response to these questions. In addition, the disputes and the disputants in these cases provide insight into the role of administrative agencies in political controversy over regulation during the Reagan administration. That agencies, such as OSHA and EPA, are now under attack by public interest groups, representatives of labor, and environmental coalitions signifies how important politics is in determining administrative practices. Broad delegation may lead to very different regulatory policies depending on whether New Deal politics and welfare-state building are on the national agenda, or whether deregulation and efforts to dismantle the welfare state guide the exercise of delegated powers.

Industrial Union Department v. American Petroleum Institute

448 U.S. 607 (1980) 5–4
+   Burger, Stewert, Stevens
+/-   Powell, Rehnquist
-    Brennan, White, Marshall, Blackmun

[The Occupational Safety and Health Act of 1970 delegates broad authority to the secretary of labor to promulgate standards to ensure safe and healthful working conditions for the nation's workers. Section 3 of the act defines an "occupational safety and health standard" as a standard that is "reasonably necessary or appropriate to provide safe and health employment." Where toxic materials or harmful physical agents are concerned, a standard must also comply with section 6(b)(5), which directs the secretary to "set the standard which most adequately assures, to the extent feasible, on the basis of the best available evidence, that no employee will suffer material impairment of health or functional capacity." When the toxic material of harmful physical agent is a carcinogen, the secretary has taken the position that no safe exposure level can be determined and that section 6(b)(5) requires him to set an exposure limit at the lowest technologically feasible level that will not impair the viability of the industries regulated.

The Occupational Safety and Health Administration is charged with regulating work environments in the interest of worker safety and health; the Industrial Union Department within OSHA executes this function of the agency. Benzene, a known carcinogen, had previously been permitted by OSHA regulation to exist in the air of a work place in a concentration not in excess of 10 ppm. At a later date, OSHA lowered the permitted concentration to 1 ppm in the belief that lower concentrations would lead to a lower incidence of leukemia. In so doing, OSHA acted upon the assumption that its authorizing statute directed that the level should be set at a safe level or at the lowest level feasible if a safe level cannot be determined. The American Petroleum Institute (API) brought suit challenging both OSHA's interpretation of the statute and its factual basis for the reduction in concentration. The appellate court held for the API. OSHA then brought its case to the Supreme Court.]

Stevens, J. for the Court:

The critical issue at this point in the litigation is whether the Court of Appeals was correct in refusing to enforce the 1 ppm exposure limit on the ground that it was not supported by appropriate findings.

Any discussion of the 1 ppm exposure limit must, of course, begin with the Agency's rationale for imposing that limit.

The evidence in the administrative record of adverse effects of benzene exposure at 10 ppm is sketchy at best. . . . The Agency made no finding that . . . any . . . empirical evidence, or any opinion testimony demonstrated that exposure to benzene at or below the 10 ppm level had ever in fact caused leukemia. . . .

In the end OSHA's rationale for lowering the permissible exposure limit to 1 ppm was based not on any finding that leukemia has ever been caused by exposure to 10 ppm of benzene and that it will not be caused by exposure to 1 ppm, but rather on a series of assumptions indicating that some leukemias might result from exposure to 10 ppm and that the

number of cases might be reduced by reducing the exposure level to 1 ppm. In reaching the result, the Agency first unequivocally concluded that benzene is a human carcinogen. Second, it concluded that industry had failed to prove that there is a safe threshold level of exposure to benzene below which no excess leukemia cases would occur. In reaching this conclusion OSHA rejected industry contentions that certain epidemiological studies indicating no excess risk of leukemia among workers exposed at levels below 10 ppm were sufficient to establish that the threshold level of safe exposure was at or above 10 ppm. It also rejected an industry witness' testimony that a dose-response curve could be constructed on the basis of the reported epidemiological studies and that this curve indicated that reducing the permissible exposure limit from 10 to 1 ppm would prevent at most one leukemia and one other cancer death every six years.

Third, the Agency applied its standard policy with respect to carcinogens, concluding that, in the absence of definitive proof of a safe level, it must be assumed that any level above zero presents some increased risk of cancer. As the federal parties point out in their brief, there are a number of scientists and public health specialists who subscribe to this view, theorizing that a susceptible person may contract cancer from the absorption of even one molecule of a carcinogen like benzene. . . .

Fourth, the Agency reiterated its view of the Act, stating that it was required by § 6(b)(5) to set the standard either at the level that has been demonstrated to be safe or at the lowest level feasible, whichever is higher. If no safe level is established, as in this case, the Secretary's interpretation of the statute automatically leads to the selection of an exposure limit that is the lowest feasible. Because of benzene's importance to the economy, no one has ever suggested that it would be feasible to eliminate its use entirely, or to try to limit exposures to the small amounts that are omni-present. Rather, the Agency selected 1 ppm as a workable exposure level . . . and then determined that compliance with that level was technologically feasible and that "the economic impact of . . . [compliance] will not be such as to threaten the financial welfare of the affected firms or the general economy." . . . It therefore held that 1 ppm was the minimum feasible exposure level within the meaning of § 6(b)(5) of the Act.

Finally, although the Agency did not refer in its discussion of the pertinent legal authority to any duty to identify the anticipated benefits of the new standard, it did conclude that some benefits were likely to result from reducing the exposure limit from 10 ppm to 1 ppm. This conclusion was based, again, not on evidence, but rather on the assumption that the risk of leukemia will decrease as exposure levels decrease . . .

It is noteworthy that at no point in its lengthy explanation did the Agency quote or even cite § 3(8) of the Act. It made no finding that any of the provisions of the new standard were "reasonably necessary or appropriate to provide safe or healthful employment and places of employment." Nor did it allude to the possibility that any such finding might have been appropriate. . . .

Our resolution of the issues in these cases turns, to a large extent, on the meaning of and the relationship between § 3(8), which defines a health and safety standard as a standard that is "reasonably necessary and [sic] appropriate to provide safe of healthful employment" and § 6(b)(5), which directs the Secretary in promulgating a health and safety standard for toxic materials to "set the standard which most adequately assures, to the extent feasible, on the basis of the best available evidence, that no employee will suffer material impairment of health or functional capacity. . . ."

In the Government's view, § 3(8)'s definition of the term "standard" has no legal significance or at best merely requires that a standard not be totally irrational. It takes the position that § 6(b)(5) is controlling and that it requires OSHA to promulgate a standard that either gives an absolute assurance of safety for each and every worker or reduces exposures to the lowest level feasible. The Government interprets "feasible" as meaning technologically achievable at a cost that would not impair the viability of the industries subject to the regulation. The respondent industry representatives, on the other hand, argue that the Court of Appeals was correct in holding that the "reasonably necessary and appropriate" language of § 3(8), along with the feasibility requirement of § 6(b)(5), requires the Agency to quantify both the costs and the benefits of a proposed rule and to conclude that they are roughly commensurate.

In our view, it is not necessary to decide whether either the Government or industry is entirely correct. For we think it is clear that § 3(8) does apply to all permanent standards promulgated under the Act and that it requires the Secretary, before issuing any standard, to determine that it is reasonably necessary and appropriate to remedy a significant risk of material health impairment. Only after the Secretary has made the threshold determination that such a risk exists with respect to a toxic substance, would it be necessary to decide whether § 6(b)(5) requires him to select the most protective standard he can consistent with economic and technological feasibility, or whether, as respondents argue, the benefits of the regulation must be commensurate with the costs of its implementation. Because the Secretary did not make the required threshold finding in these cases, we have no occasion to determine whether costs must be weighed against benefits in an appropriate case.

Under the Government's view, § 3(8), if it has any substantive content at all, merely requires OSHA to issue standards that are reasonably calculated to produce a safer or more healthy work environment. . . . apart from this minimal requirement of rationality, the Government argues that § 3(8) imposes no limits on the Agency's power, and thus would not prevent it from requiring employers to do whatever would be "reasonably necessary" to eliminate all risks of any harm from their workplaces. With respect to toxic substances and harmful physical agents, the Government takes an even more extreme position. Relying on § 6(b)(5)'s direction to set a standard "which most adequately assures . . . that no employee will suffer material impairment of health or functional capacity," the Government contends that the Secretary is required to impose standards that either guarantee workplaces that are free from any risk of material health impairment, however small, or that come as close as possible to doing so without running entire industries.

If the purpose of the statute were to eliminate completely and with absolute certainty any risk of serious harm, we would agree that it would be proper for the Secretary to interpret §§ 3(8) and 6(b)(5) in this fashion. But we think it clear that the statute was not designed to require employers to provide absolutely risk-free workplaces whenever it is technologically feasible to do so, so long as the cost is not great enough to destroy an entire industry. Rather, both the language and structure of the Act, as well as its legislative history, indicate that it was intended to require the elimination, as far as feasible, of significant risks of harm.

By empowering the Secretary to promulgate standards that are "reasonably necessary or appropriate to provide safe or healthful employment and places of employment," the Act implies that, before promulgating any standard, the Secretary must make a finding that the workplaces in question are not safe. But "safe" is not the equivalent of "risk-free." There are many activities that we engage in every day—such as driving a car or even breathing city air—that entail some risk of accident or material health impairment; nevertheless, few people would consider these activities "unsafe." Similarly, a workplace can hardly be considered "unsafe" unless it threatens the workers with a significant risk of harm.

Therefore, before he can promulgate any permanent health or safety standard, the Secretary is required to make a threshold finding that a place of employment is unsafe—in the sense that significant risks are present and can be eliminated or lessened by a change in practices. This requirement applies to permanent standards promulgated pursuant to § 6(b)(5), as well as to other types of permanent standards. For there is no reason why § 3(8)'s definition of a standard should not be deemed incorporated by reference into § 6(b)(5). The standards promulgated pursuant to § 6(b)(5) are just one species of the genus of standards governed by the basic requirement. That section repeatedly uses the term "standard" without suggesting any exception from, or qualification of, the general definition; on the contrary, it directs the Secretary to select "*the* standard"—that is to say, one of various possible alternative that satisfy the basic definition in § 3(8)—that is most protective. Moreover, requiring the Secretary to make a threshold finding of significant risk is consistent with the scope of the regulatory power granted to him by § 6(b)(5), which empowers the Secretary to promulgate standards, not for chemicals and physical agents generally, but for "*toxic* materials" and "*harmful* physical agents."

This interpretation of §§ 3(8) and 6(b)(5) is supported by the other provisions of the Act. Thus, for example, § 6(g) provides in part that "[i]n determining the priority for establishing standards under this section, the Secretary shall give due regard to the urgency of the need for mandatory safety and health standards for particular industries, trades, crafts, occupations, businesses, workplaces or work environments." The Government has expressly acknowledged that this section requires the Secretary to undertake some cost-benefit analysis before he promulgates any standard, requiring the elimination of the most serious hazards first. If such an analysis must precede the promulgation of any standard, it seems manifest that Congress intended, at a bare minimum, that the Secretary find a significant risk of harm and therefore a probability of significant benefits before establishing a new standard.

Section 6(b)(8) lends additional support to this analysis. That subsection requires that, when the Secretary substantially alters an existing consensus standard, he must explain how the new rule will "better effectuate" the purposes of the Act. If this requirement was intended to be more than a meaningless formality, it must be read to impose upon the Secretary the duty to find that an existing national consensus standard is not adequate to protect workers from a continuing and significant risk of harm. Thus, in this case, the Secretary was required to find that exposures at the current permissible exposure level of 10 ppm present a significant risk of harm in the workplace.

In the absence of a clear mandate in the Act, it is unreasonable to assume that Congress intended to give the Secretary the unprecedented power over American industry that would result from the Government's view of §§ 3(8) and 6(b)(5), coupled with OSHA's cancer policy. Expert testimony that a substance is probably a human carcinogen—either because it has caused cancer in animals or because individuals have contracted cancer following extremely high exposures—would justify the conclusion that the substance poses some risk of serious harm no matter how minute the exposure and no matter how many experts testified that they regarded the risk as insignificant. That conclusion would in turn justify pervasive regulation limited only by the constraint of feasibility. In light of the fact that there are literally thousands of substances used in the workplace that have been identified as carcinogens or suspect carcinogens, the Government's theory would give OSHA power to impose enormous costs that might produce little, if any, discernible benefit. . . .

The legislative history also supports the conclusion that Congress was concerned, not with absolute safety, but with the elimination of significant harm. . . .

Given the conclusion that the Act empowers the Secretary to promulgate health and safety standards only where a significant risk of harm exists, the critical issue becomes how to define and allocate the burden of proving the significance of the risk in a case such as this, where scientific knowledge is imperfect and the precise quantification of risks is therefore impossible. The Agency's position is that there is substantial evidence in the record to support its conclusion that there is no absolutely safe level for a carcinogen and that, therefore, the burden is properly on industry to prove, apparently beyond a shadow of a doubt, that there *is* a safe level for benzene exposure. The Agency argues that, because of the uncertainties in this area, any other approach would render it helpless, forcing it to wait for the leukemia deaths that it believes are likely to occur before taking any regulatory action.

We disagree. As we read the statute, the burden was on the Agency to show, on the basis of substantial evidence, that it is at least more likely than not that long-term exposure to 10 ppm of benzene presents a significant risk of material health impairment. Ordinarily, it is the proponent of a rule or order who has the burden of proof in administrative proceedings. . . . In some cases involving toxic substances, Congress has shifted the burden of proving that a particular substance is safe onto the party opposing the proposed rule. The fact that Congress did not follow this course in enacting OSHA indicates that it intended the Agency to bear the normal burden of establishing the need for a proposed standard.

In this case OSHA did not even attempt to carry its burden of proof. The closest it came to making a finding that benzene presented a significant risk of harm in the workplace was its statement that the benefits to be derived from lowering the permissible exposure level from 10 to 1 ppm were "likely" to be "appreciable." The Court of Appeals held that this finding was not supported by substantial evidence. Of greater importance, even if it were supported by substantial evidence, such a finding would not be sufficient to satisfy the Agency's obligations under the Act. . . .

Contrary to the Government's contentions, imposing a burden on the Agency of demonstrating a significant risk of harm will not strip it of its ability to regulate carcinogens, nor will it require the Agency to wait for deaths to occur before taking any action.

First, the requirement that a "significant" risk be identified is not a mathematical straitjacket. It is the Agency's responsibility to determine, in the first instance, what it considers to be a "significant" risk. Some risks are plainly acceptable and others are plainly unacceptable. If, for example, the odds are one in a billion that a person will die from cancer by taking a drink of chlorinated water, the risk clearly could not be considered significant. On the other hand, if the odds are one in a thousand that regular inhalation of gasoline vapors that are 2% benzene will be fatal, a reasonable person might well consider the risk significant and take appropriate steps to decrease or eliminate it. Although the Agency has no duty to calculate the exact probability of harm, it does have an obligation to find that a significant risk is present before it can characterize a place of employment as "unsafe."

Thus, so long as they are supported by a body of reputable scientific thought, the Agency is free to use conservative assumptions in interpreting the data with respect to carcinogens, risking error on the side of overprotection rather than underprotection.

Finally, the record in this case and OSHA's own rulings on other carcinogens indicate that there are a number of ways in which the Agency can make a rational judgment about the relative significance of the risks associated with exposure to a particular carcinogen. . . .

. . . In this case the record makes its perfectly clear that the Secretary relied squarely on a special policy for carcinogens that imposed the burden on industry of proving the existence of a safe level of exposure, thereby avoiding the Secretary's threshold responsibility of establishing the needs for more stringent standards. In so interpreting his statutory authority, the Secretary exceeded his power.

The judgment of the Court of Appeals remanding the petition for review to the Secretary for further proceedings is affirmed.

Justice Marshall, with whom Justice Brennan, Justice White, and Justice Blackmun join, dissenting.

In cases of statutory construction, this Court's authority is limited. If the statutory language and legislative intent are plain, the judicial inquiry is at an end. Under our jurisprudence, it is presumed that ill-considered or unwise legislation will be corrected through the democratic process; a court is not permitted to distort a statute's meaning in order to make it conform with the Justices' own views of sound social policy. . . .

Today's decision flagrantly disregards these restrictions on judicial authority. The plurality ignores the plain meaning of the Occupational Safety and Health Act of 1970 in order to bring the authority of the Secretary of Labor in line with the plurality's own views of proper regulatory policy. The unfortunate consequence is that the Federal Government's efforts to protect American workers from cancer and other crippling diseases may be substantially impaired. . . .

In this case the Secretary of Labor found, on the basis of substantial evidence, that (1) exposure to benzene creates a risk of cancer, chromosomal damage, and a variety of nonmalignant but potentially fatal blood disorders, even at the level of 1 ppm; (2) no safe level of exposure has been shown; (3) benefits in the form of saved lives would be derived from the permanent standard; (4) the number of lives that would be saved could turn out to be either substantial or relatively small; (5) under the present state of scientific knowledge, it is impossible to calculate even in a rough way the number of lives that would be saved, at least without making assumptions that would appear absurd to much of the medical community; and (6) the standard would not materially harm the financial condition of the covered industries. The Court does not set aside any of these findings. Thus, it could not be plainer that the Secretary's decision was fully in accord with his statutory mandate "most adequately [to] assur[e] . . . that no employee will suffer material impairment of health or functional capacity. . . ."

The plurality's conclusion to the contrary is based on its interpretation of 29 U.S.C. § 652(8), which defines an occupational safety and health standard as one "which requires conditions . . . reasonably necessary or appropriate to provide safe or healthful employment. . . ." According to the plurality, a standard is not "reasonably necessary or appropriate" unless the Secretary is able to show that it is "at least more likely than not," that the risk he seeks to regulate is a "significant" one. . . . Nothing in the statute's language or legislative history, however, indicates that the "reasonably necessary or appropriate" language should be given this meaning. Indeed, both demonstrate that the plurality's standard bears no connection with the acts or intentions of Congress and is based only on the plurality's solicitude for the welfare of regulated industries. And the plurality uses this standard to evaluate not the agency's decision in this case, but a strawman of its own creation.

Unlike the plurality, I do not purport to know whether the actions taken by Congress and its delegates to ensure occupational safety represent sound or unsound regulatory policy. The critical problem in cases like the ones at bar is scientific uncertainty. While science has determined that exposure to benzene at levels above 1 ppm creates a definite risk of health impairment, the magnitude of the risk cannot be quantified at the present time. The risk at issue has hardly been shown to be insignificant; indeed, future research may reveal that the risk is in fact considerable. But the existing evidence may frequently be inadequate to enable the Secretary to make the threshold finding of "significance" that the Court requires today. If so, the consequence of the plurality's approach would be to subject American workers to a continuing risk of cancer and other fatal diseases, and to render the Federal Government powerless to take protective action on their behalf. Such an approach would place the burden of medical uncertainty squarely on the shoulders of the American worker, the intended beneficiary of the Occupational Safety and Health Act. . . .

Because today's holding has no basis in the Act, and because the Court has no authority to impose its own regulatory policies on the Nation, I dissent.

Congress enacted the Occupational Safety and Health Act as a response to what was characterized as "the grim history of our failure to heed the occupational health needs of our workers."* The failure of voluntary action and legislation at the state level . . . had resulted in a "bleak" and "worsening" situation in which 14,500 persons had died annually as a result of conditions in the workplace. In the four years preceding the Act's passage, more Americans were killed in the workplace than in the contemporaneous Vietnam War. . . . The Act was designed as "a safety bill of rights for close to 60 million workers." Its stated purpose is "to assure so far as possible every working man and woman in the Nation safe and healthful working conditions and to preserve our human resources." . . .

The Act is enforced primarily through two provisions. First, a "general duty" is imposed upon employers to furnish employment and places of employment "free from recognized hazards that are causing or are likely to cause death or serious physical harm." . . . Second, the Secretary of Labor is authorized to set "occupational safety and health standards," defined as standards requiring "conditions, or the adoption or use of one or more practices, means, methods, operations, or processes, reasonably necessary or appropriate to provide safe or healthful employment and places of employment." . . .

The legislative history of the Act reveals Congress' particular concern for health hazards of "unprecedented complexity" that had resulted from chemicals whose toxic effects "are only now being discovered." . . . "Recent scientific knowledge points to hitherto unsuspected cause-and-effect relationships between occupational exposures and many of the so-called chronic diseases—cancer, respiratory ailments, allergies, heart disease, and others." . . . Members of Congress made repeated references to the dangers posed by carcinogens and to the defects in our knowledge of their operation and effect. One of the primary purposes of the Act was to ensure regulation of these "insidious 'silent' killers." . . .

The authority conferred by § 655(b)(5), however, is not absolute. The subsection itself contains two primary limitations. The requirement of "material" impairment was designed to prohibit the Secretary from regulating substances that create a trivial hazard to affected employees. Moreover, all standards promulgated under the subsection must be "feasible." During the floor debates Congress expressed concern

*Legislative History of the Occupational Safety and Health Act of 1970 (Committee Print compiled for the Senate Committee on Labor and Public Welfare), p. iii (1971) (Foreword by Sen. Williams) (hereinafter Leg. Hist.).

that a prior version of the bill, not clearly embodying the feasibility requirement, would require the Secretary to close down whole industries in order to eliminate risks of impairment. This standard was criticized as unrealistic. The feasibility requirement was imposed as an affirmative limit on the standard-setting power.

The remainder of § 655(b)(5), applicable to all safety and health standards, requires the Secretary to base his standards "upon research, demonstrations, experiments, and such other information as may be appropriate." In setting standards, the Secretary is directed to consider "the attainment of the highest degree of health and safety protection for the employee" and also "the latest available scientific data in the field, the feasibility of the standards, and experience gained under this and other health and safety laws."

The Act makes provision for judicial review of occupational safety and health standards promulgated pursuant to § 655(b)(5). The reviewing court must uphold the Secretary's determinations if they are supported by "substantial evidence in the record considered as a whole." It is to that evidence that I now turn. . . .

The plurality's discussion of the record in this case is both extraordinarily arrogant and extraordinarily unfair. It is arrogant because the plurality presumes to make its own factual findings with respect to a variety of disputed issues relating to carcinogen regulation. . . . It should not be necessary to remind the Members of this Court that they were not appointed to undertake independent review of adequately supported scientific findings made by a technically expert agency. And the plurality's discussion is unfair because its characterization of the Secretary's report bears practically no resemblance to what the Secretary actually did in this case. Contrary to the plurality's suggestion, the Secretary did not rely blindly on some Draconian carcinogen "policy." . . . If he had, it would have been sufficient for him to have observed that benzene is a carcinogen, a proposition respondents do not dispute. Instead, the Secretary gathered over 50 volumes of exhibits and testimony and offered a detailed and evenhanded discussion of the relationship between exposure to benzene at all recorded exposure levels and chromosomal damage, aplastic anemia, and leukemia. In that discussion he evaluated, and took seriously, respondents' evidence of a safe exposure level. . . .

The hearings on the proposed standard were extensive, encompassing 17 days from July 19 through August 10, 1977. The 95 witnesses included epidemiologists, toxicologists, physicians, political economists, industry reprensentatives, and members of the affected work force. Witnesses were subjected to exhaustive questioning by representatives from a variety of interested groups and organizations. . . .

Considerable evidence showed an association between benzene and nonmalignant blood disorders at low exposure levels. . . . Because of the absence of adequate data, a dose-response curve showing the relationship between benzene exposure and blood disorders could not be constructed. There was considerable testimony, however, that such disorders had resulted from exposure to benzene at or near the current level of 10 ppm and lower. The Secretary concluded that the current standard did not provide adequate protection. He observed that a "safety factor" of 10 to 100 was generally used to discount the level at which a casual connection had been found in existing studies. Under this approach, he concluded that, quite apart from any leukemia risk, the permissible exposure limit should be set at a level considerably lower than 10 ppm.

Finally, there was substantial evidence that exposure to benzene caused leukemia. The Secretary concluded that the evidence established that benzene was a carcinogen. A causal relationship between benzene and leukemia was first reported in France in 1897, and since that time similar results had been found in a number of countries, including Italy, Turkey, Japan, Switzerland, the Soviet Union, and the United States. The latest study, undertaken by the National Institute for Occupational Safety and Health (NIOSH) in the 1970's, reported a fivefold excess over the normal incidence of leukemia among workers exposed to benzene at industrial plants in Ohio. There was testimony that this study seriously understated the risk.

The Secretary reviewed certain studies suggesting that low exposure levels of 10 ppm and more did not cause any excess incidence of leukemia. Those studies, he suggested, suffered from severe methodological defects, as their authors frankly acknowledged. Finally, the Secretary discussed a study suggesting a statistically significant excess in leukemia at levels of 2 to 9 ppm. He found that, despite certain deficiencies in the study, it should be considered as consistent with other studies demonstrating an excess leukemia risk among employees exposed to benzene. . . .

. . . The Secretary offered a detailed discussion of the role that economic considerations should play in his determination. He observed that standards must be "feasible," both economically and technologically. In his view the permanent standard for benzene was feasible under both tests. The economic impact would fall primarily on the more stable industries, such as petroleum refining and petrochemical production. . . . These industries would be able readily to absorb the costs or to pass them on to consumers. None of the 20 affected industries, involving 157,000 facilities and 629,000 exposed employees, . . . would be unable to bear the required expenditures. . . . He concluded that the compliance costs were "well within the financial capability of the covered industries." . . . An extensive survey of the national economic impact of the standard, undertaken by a private contractor, found first-year operating costs of between $187 and $205 million, recurring annual costs of $34 million, and investment in engineering controls of about $266 million. Since respondents have not attacked the Secretary's basic conclusions as to cost, the Secretary's extensive discussion need not be summarized here.

Finally, the Secretary discussed the benefits to be derived from the permanent standard. During the hearings, it had been argued that the Secretary should estimate the health benefits of the proposed regulation. To do this he would be required to construct a dose-response curve showing, at least in a rough way, the number of lives that would be saved at each possible exposure level. Without some estimate of benefits, it was argued, the Secretary's decisionmaking would be defective. During the hearings an industry witness attempted to construct such a

dose-response curve. Restricting himself to carcinogenic effects, he estimated that the proposed standard would save two lives every six years and suggested that this relatively minor benefit would not justify the regulation's costs. . . .

The Secretary concluded that, in light of the scientific uncertainty, he was not required to calculate benefits more precisely. In any event he gave "careful consideration" to the question of whether the admittedly substantial costs were justified in light of the hazards of benzene exposure. He concluded that those costs were "necessary" in order to promote the purposes of the Act. . . .

. . . The Secretary's determinations must be upheld if supported by "substantial evidence in the record considered as a whole." . . . This standard represents a legislative judgment that regulatory action should be subject to review more stringent than the traditional "arbitrary and capricious" standard for informal rulemaking. We have observed that the arbitrary and capricious standard itself contemplates a searching "inquiry into the facts" in order to determine "whether the decision was based on a consideration of the relevant factors and whether there has been a clear error of judgment." *Citizens to Preserve Overton Park v. Volpe*, 401 U. S. 402, 416 (1971). Careful performance of this task is especially important when Congress has imposed the comparatively more rigorous "substantial evidence" requirement. As we have emphasized, however, judicial review under the substantial evidence test is ultimately deferential. . . . The agency's decision is entitled to the traditional presumption of validity, and the court is not authorized to substitute its judgment for that of the Secretary. If the Secretary has considered the decisional factors and acted in conformance with the statute, his ultimate decision must be given a large measure of respect. . . .

The plurality is insensitive to three factors which, in my view, make judicial review of occupational safety and health standards under the substantial evidence test particularly difficult. First, the issues often reach a high level of technical complexity. In such circumstances the courts are required to immerse themselves in matters to which they are unaccustomed by training or experience. Second, the factual issues with which the Secretary must deal are frequently not subject to any definitive resolution. . . . Causal connections and theoretical extrapolations may be uncertain. Third, when the question involves determination of the acceptable level of risk, the ultimate decision must necessarily be based on considerations of policy as well as empirically verifiable facts. Factual determinations can at most define the risk in some statistical way; the judgment whether that risk is tolerable cannot be based solely on a resolution of the facts.

The decision to take action in conditions of uncertainty bears little resemblance to the sort of empirically verifiable factual conclusions to which the substantial evidence test is normally applied. Such decisions were not intended to be unreviewable; they too must be scrutinized to ensure that the Secretary has acted reasonably and within the boundaries set by Congress. But a reviewing court must be mindful of the limited nature of its role. See *Vermont Yankee Nuclear Power Corp. v. NRDC*, 435 U. S. 519 (1978). It must recognize that the ultimate decision cannot be based solely on determinations of fact, and that those factual conclusions that have been reached are ones which the courts are ill-equipped to resolve on their own. . . .

The plurality avoids this conclusion through reasoning that may charitably be described as obscure. According to the plurality, the definition of occupational safety and health standards as those "reasonably necessary or appropriate to provide safe or healthful . . . working conditions" requires the Secretary to show that it is "more likely than not" that the risk he seeks to regulate is a "significant" one. . . .

The plurality suggests that under the "reasonably necessary" clause, a workplace is not "unsafe" unless the Secretary is able to convince a reviewing court that a "significant" risk is at issue. . . . That approach is particularly embarrassing in this case, for it is contradicted by the plain language of the Act. The plurality's interpretation renders utterly superfluous the first sequence of § 655(b)(5), which, as noted above, requires the Secretary to set the standard "which most adequately assures . . . that no employee will suffer material impairment of health." Indeed, the plurality's interpretation reads that sentence out of the Act. By so doing, the plurality makes the test for standards regulating toxic substances and harmful physical agents substantially identical to the test for standards generally—plainly the opposite of what Congress intended. And it is an odd canon of construction that would insert in a vague and general definitional clause a threshold requirement that overcomes the specific language placed in a standard-setting provision. The most elementary principles of statutory construction demonstrate that precisely the opposite interpretation is appropriate. . . . In short, Congress could have provided that the Secretary may not take regulatory action until the existing scientific evidence proves the risk at issue to be "significant," but it chose not to do so.

The plurality's interpretation of the "reasonably necessary or appropriate" clause is also conclusively refuted by the legislative history. While the standard-setting provision that the plurality ignores received extensive legislative attention, the definitional clause received *none at all*. An earlier version of the Act, . . . did not embody a clear feasibility constraint and was not restricted to toxic substances or to "material" impairments. The "reasonably necessary or appropriate" clause was contained in this prior version of the bill, as it was at all relevant times. In debating this version, Members of Congress repeatedly expressed concern that it would require a risk-free universe. . . . The definitional clause was not mentioned at all, an omission that would be incomprehensible if Congress intended by that clause to require the Secretary to quantify the risk he sought to regulate in order to demonstrate that it was "significant." . . .

The plurality ignores applicable canons of construction, apparently because it finds their existence inconvenient. But as we stated quite recently, the inquiry into statutory purposes should be "informed by an awareness that the regulation is entitled to deference unless it can be said not to be a reasoned and supportable interpretation of the Act." *Whirlpool Corp. v. Marshall*, 445 U. S. 1, 11 (1980). Can it honestly be said that the Secretary's interpretation of the Act is "unreasoned" or "unsupportable"? And as we stated in the same case, "safety legislation is to be liberally construed to effectuate the congressional purpose." . . . The plurality's disregard of these principles gives credence to the frequently voiced criticism that they are honored only when the Court finds itself in substantive agreement with the agency action at issue.

In short, today's decision represents a usurpation of decisionmaking authority that has been exercised by and properly belongs with Congress and its authorized representatives. The plurality's construction has no support in the statute's language, structure, or legislative history. The threshold finding that the plurality requires is the plurality's own invention. It bears no relationship to the acts or intentions of Congress, and it can be understood only as reflecting the personal views of the plurality as to the proper allocation of resources for safety in the American workplace. . . .

In recent years there has been increasing recognition that the products of technological development may have harmful effects whose incidence and severity cannot be predicted with certainty. The responsibility to regulate such products has fallen to administrative agencies. Their task is not an enviable one. Frequently no clear causal link can be established between the regulated substance and the harm to be averted. Risks of harm are often uncertain, but inaction has considerable costs of its own. The agency must decide whether to take regulatory action against possibly substantial risks or to wait until more definitive information becomes available—a judgment which by its very nature cannot be based solely on determinations of fact.

Those delegations, in turn, have made on the understanding that judicial review would be available to ensure that the agency's determinations are supported by substantial evidence and that its actions do not exceed the limits set by Congress. In the Occupational Safety and Health Act, Congress expressed confidence that the courts would carry out this important responsibility. But in these cases the plurality has far exceeded its authority. The plurality's "threshold finding" requirement is nowhere to be found in the Act and is antithetical to its basic purposes. "The fundamental policy questions appropriately resolved in Congress . . . are *not* subject to re-examination in the federal courts under the guise of judicial review of agency action," *Vermont Yankee Nuclear Power Corp. v. NRDC*, 435 U.S. . . . (emphasis in original). Surely this is no less true of the decision to ensure safety for the American worker than the decision to proceed with nuclear power. . . .

Because the approach taken by the plurality is so plainly irreconcilable with the Court's proper institutional role, I am certain that it will not stand the test of time. In all likelihood, today's decision will come to be regarded as an extreme reaction to a regulatory scheme that, as the Members of the plurality perceived it, imposed an unduly harsh burden on regulated industries. But as the Constitution "does not enact Mr. Herbert Spencer's Social Statics," *Lochner v. New York*, 198 U.S. 45, 75 (1905) (Holmes, J., dissenting), so the responsibility to scrutinize federal administrative action does not authorize this Court to strike its own balance between the costs and benefits of occupational safety standards. I am confident that the approach taken by the plurality today, like that in *Lochner* itself, will eventually be abandoned, and that the representative branches of government will once again be allowed to determine the level of safety and health protection to be accorded to the American worker.

American Textile Manufacturers Institute v. Donovan

101 S. Ct. 2478, 452 U.S. 490 (1981) 5–3
+   Brennan, White, Marshall, Blackmun, Stevens
−   Stewart, Burger, Rehnquist
NP Powell

[In this case, the issues and facts are similar to those of the benzene case but revolve on a slightly different point. The concentration of cotton dust, which causes byssinosis in those exposed to it, was set at a limit held by OSHA to be the safest for the textile workers that was technologically feasible—a requirement of the Occupational Safety and Health Act. The textile industry challenged the rule based on its belief that the word *feasible* implied a cost-benefit analysis and that the results of that analysis would take precedence over absolute reliance on a standard set solely with concern for the workers' health uppermost in mind. In a word, the issue was whether *feasible* meant "within the realm of possibility" or "within the realm of economic practicality."]

Brennan, J., for the Court:

The principal question presented in this case is whether the Occupational Safety and Health Act requires the Secretary, in promulgating a standard, . . . , to determine that the costs of the standard bear a reasonable relationship to its benefits. Petitioners urge not only that OSHA must show that a standard addresses a significant risk of material health impairment, . . . but also that OSHA must demonstrate that the reduction in risk of material health impairment is significant in light of the costs of attaining that reduction. . . . Respondents on the other hand contend that the Act requires OSHA to promulgate standards that eliminate or reduce such risks "to the extent such protection is technologically and economically feasible." . . . To resolve this debate, we must turn to the language, structure, and legislative history of the Occupational Safety and Health Act.

The starting point of our analysis is the language of the statute itself. . . . Section 6(b)(5) of the Act, 29 U.S.C. § 655(b)(5) (emphasis added), provides: "The Secretary, in promulgating standards dealing with toxic materials or harmful physical agents under this subsection, shall set the standard which most adequately assures, to the extent feasible," on the basis of the best available evidence that no employee will suffer material impairment of health or functional capacity event if such employee has regular exposure to the hazard dealth with by such standard for the period of his working life."

Although their interpretations differ, all parties agree that the phrase "to the extent feasible" contains the critical language in § 6(b)(5) for purposes of this case.

The plain meaning of the word "feasible" supports respondents' interpretation of the statute. According to Webster's Third New International Dictionary of the English Language, "feasible" means "capable of being done, executed, or effected." Id., at 831 (1976). Accord, The Oxford English Dictionary 116 (1933) ("Capable of being done, accomplished or carried out"); Funk & Wagnalls New "Standard" Dictionary of the English Language 903 (1957) ("That may be done, performed or effected"). Thus, § 6(b)(5) directs the Secretary to issue the standard that "most adequately assures . . . that no employee will suffer material impairment of health," limited only by the extent to which this is "capable of being done." In effect then, as the Court of Appeals held, Congress itself defined the basic relationship between costs and benefits, by placing the "benefit" of worker health above all other considerations save those making attainment of this "benefit" unachievable. Any standard based on a balancing of costs and benefits by the Secretary that strikes a different balance than that struck by Congress would be inconsistent with the command set forth in § 6(b)(5). Thus, cost-benefit analysis by OSHA is not required by the statute because feasibility analysis is. . . .

Even though the plain language of § 6(b)(5) supports this construction, we must still decide whether § 3(8), the general definition of an occupational safety and health standard, either alone or in tandem with § 6(b)(5), incorporates a cost-benefit requirement for standards dealing with toxic materials or harmful physical agents. Section 3(8) of the Act, 29 U.S.C. § 652(8) (emphasis added), provides: The term 'occupational safety and health standard' means a standard which requires conditions, or the adoption or use of one or more practices, means, methods, operations, or processes, reasonably necessary or appropriate to provide safe or healthful employment and places of employment."

Taken alone, the phrase "reasonably necessary or appropriate" might be construed to contemplate some balancing of the costs and benefits of a standard. Petitioners urge that, so construed, § 3(8) engrafts a cost benefit analysis requirement on the issuance of § 6(b)(5) standards, even if § 6(b)(5) itself does not authorize such analysis. We need not decide whether § 3(8), standing alone, would contemplate some form of cost-benefit analysis. For even if it does, Congress specifically chose in § 6(b)(5) to impose separate and additional requirements for issuance of a subcategory of occupational safety and health standards dealing with toxic materials and harmful physical agents: it required that those standards be issued to prevent material impairment of health to the extent feasible. Congress could reasonably have concluded that health standards should be subjected to different criteria than safety standards because of the special problems presented in regulating them. . . .

Agreement with petitioners' argument that § 3(8) imposes an additional and overriding requirement of cost-benefit analysis on the issuance of § 6(b)(5) standards would eviscerate the "to the extent feasible" requirement. Standards would inevitably be set at the level indicated by cost-benefit analysis, and not at the level specified by § 6(b)(5). . . . We cannot believe that Congress intended the general terms of § 3(8) to countermand the specific feasibility requirement of § 6(b)(5). Adoption of petitioners' interpretation would effectively write § 6(b)(5) out of the Act. We decline to render Congress's decision to include a feasibility requirement nugatory, thereby offending the well-settled rule that all parts of a statute, if possible, are to be given effect. Congress did not contemplate any further balancing by the agency for toxic material and harmful physical agents standards, and we should not "impute to Congress a purpose to paralyze with one hand what it sought to promote with the other."

. . . The legislative history of the Act, while concededly not crystal clear, provides general support for respondents' interpretation of the Act. The Congressional reports and debates certainly confirm that Congress meant "feasible" and nothing else in using that term. . . .

Not only does the legislative history confirm that Congress meant "feasible" rather than "cost-benefit" when it used the former term, but it also shows the Congress understood that the Act would create substantial costs for employers, yet intended to impose such costs when necessary to create a safe and healthful working environment. Congress viewed the costs of health and safety as a cost of doing business. . . .

Section 6(f) of the Act provides that "[t]he determinations of the Secretary shall be conclusive if supported by substantial evidence in the record considered as a whole." 29 U.S.C. § 655(f). Petitioners contend that the Secretary's determination that the Cotton Dust Standard is "economically feasible" is not supported by substantial evidence in the record considered as a whole. In particular, they claim (1) that OSHA underestimated the financial costs necessary to meet the Standard's requirements; and (2) that OSHA incorrectly found that the Standard would not threaten the economic viability of the cotton industry.

In statutes with provisions virtually identical to § 6(f) of the Act, we have defined substantial evidence as "such relevant evidence as a reasonable mind might accept as adequate to support a conclusion." . . . The reviewing court must take into account contradictory evidence in the record . . . , but "the possibility of drawing two inconsistent conclusions from the evidence does not prevent an administrative agency's finding from being supported by substantial evidence," . . . Therefore, our inquiry is not to determine whether we, in the first instance, would find OSHA's findings supported by substantial evidence. Instead we turn to OSHA's findings and the record upon which they were based to decide whether the Court of Appeals "misapprehended or grossly misapplied" the substantial evidence test. . . .

After estimating the cost of compliance with the Cotton Dust Standard, OSHA analyzed whether it was "economically feasible" for the cotton industry to bear this cost. OSHA concluded that it was, finding that "although some marginal employers may shut down rather than comply, the industry as a whole will not be threatened by the capital requirements of the regulation." . . . In reaching this conclusion on the Standard's economic impact, OSHA made specific findings with respect to employment, energy consumption, capital financing availability, and profitability. . . . To support its findings, the agency relied primarily on RTI's comprehensive investigation of the Standard's economic impact. . . .

The Court of Appeals found that the agency "explained the economic impact it projected for the textile industry," and that OSHA has "substantial support in the record for its . . . findings of economic feasibility for the textile industry." . . . On the basis of the whole record, we cannot conclude that the Court of Appeals "misapprehended or grossly misapplied" the substantial evidence test. . . .

When Congress passed the Occupational Safety and Health Act in 1970, it chose to place pre-eminent value on assuring employees a safe and healthful working environment, limited only by the feasibility of achieving such an environment. We must measure the validity of the Secretary's actions against the requirements of that Act. For "[t]he judicial function does not extend to substantive revision of regulatory policy. That function lies elsewhere—in Congressional and Executive oversight or amendatory legislation." . . .

Accordingly, the judgment of the Court of Appeals is affirmed. . . .

Justice Stewart, dissenting.

. . . Because I believe that OSHA failed to justify its estimate of the cost of the Cotton Dust Standard on the basis of substantial evidence, I would reverse the judgment before us without reaching the question whether the Act requires that a standard, beyond being economically feasible, must meet the demands of a cost-benefit examination.

The simple truth about OSHA's assessment of the cost of the Cotton Dust Standard is that the agency never relied on any study or report purporting to predict the cost to industry of the Standard finally adopted by the agency. OSHA did have before it one cost analysis, . . . which attempted to predict the cost of the final Standard. However, as recognized by the Court, . . . the agency flatly rejected that prediction as a gross overestimate. The only other estimate OSHA had, the Hocutt-Thomas estimate prepared by industry researchers, was not designed to predict the cost of the final OSHA Standard. Rather, it assumed a far less stringent and inevitably far less costly standard for all phases of cotton production except roving. . . . The agency examined the Hocutt-Thomas study, and concluded that it too was an overestimate

of the costs of the less stringent standard it was addressing. I am willing to defer to OSHA's determination that the Hocutt-Thomas study was such an overestimate, conceding that such subtle financial and technical matters lie within the discretion and skill of the agency. But in a remarkable non sequitur, the agency decided that because the Hocutt-Thomas study was an overestimate of the cost of a less stringent standard, it could be treated as a reliable estimate for the more costly final Standard actually promulgated, never rationally explaining how it came to this happy conclusion. This is not substantial evidence. It is unsupported speculation. . . .

Justice Rehnquist, with whom The Chief Justice joins, dissenting.

A year ago I stated my belief that Congress in enacting § 6(b)(5) of the Occupational Safety and Health Act of 1970 unconstitutionally delegated to the Executive Branch the authority to make the "hard policy choices" properly the task of the legislature. *Industrial Union Dept. v. American Petroleum Institute*, 448 U.S. 607, 671 (1980) (concurring in judgment). Because I continue to believe that the Act exceeds Congress' power to delegate legislative authority to nonelected officials, see *J. W. Hampton & Co. v. United States*, 276 U.S. 394 (1928), . . . I dissent. . . .

Throughout its opinion, the Court refers to § 6(b)(5) as adopting a "feasibility standard" or a "feasibility requirement." . . . But as I attempted to point out last Term in *Industrial Union Dept. v. American Petroleum Institute*, . . . the "feasibility standard" is no standard at all. Quite the contrary, I argued there that the insertion into § 6(b)(5) of the words "to the extent feasible" . . . rendered what had been a clear, if somewhat unrealistic, statute into one so vague and precatory as to be an unconstitutional delegation of legislative authority to the Executive Branch. Prior to the inclusion of the "feasibility" language, § 6(b)(5) simply required the Secretary to "set the standard which most adequately assures, on the basis of the best available professional evidence, that no employee will suffer any impairment of health." . . . Had that statute been enacted, it would undoubtedly support the result the Court reaches in these cases, and it would not have created an excessive delegation problem. The Secretary of Labor would quite clearly have been authorized to set exposure standards without regard to any kind of cost-benefit analysis.

But Congress did not enact that statute. The legislative history of the Act reveals that a number of Members of Congress, such as Senators Javits, Saxbe, and Dominick, had difficulty with the proposed statute and engaged Congress in a lengthy debate about the extent to which the Secretary should be authorized to create a risk-free work environment. Congress had at least three choices. It could have required the Secretary to engage in a cost-benefit analysis prior to the setting of exposure levels, it could have prohibited cost-benefit analysis, or it could have permitted the use of such an analysis. Rather than make that choice and resolve that difficult policy issue, however, Congress passed. Congress simply said that the Secretary should set standards "to the extent feasible." . . .

In believing that § 6(b)(5) amounts to an unconstitutional delgation of legislative authority to the Executive Branch, I do not mean to suggest that Congress, in enacting a statute, must resolve all ambiguities or must "fill in all of the blanks." Even the neophyte student of government realizes that legislation is the art of compromise, and that an important, controversial bill is seldom enacted by Congress in the form in which it is first introduced. It is not unusual for the various factions supporting or opposing a proposal to accept some departure from the language they would prefer and to adopt substitute language agreeable to all. But that sort of compromise is a far cry from this case, where Congress simply abdicated its responsibility for the making of a fundamental and most difficult policy choice. . . . That is a "quintessential legislative" choice and must be made by the elected representatives of the people, not by nonelected officials in the Executive Branch.

Chevron v. Natural Resources Defense Council, Inc., et al.

467 U.S. 837 (1984) 6–0
+   Brennan, White, Burger, Blackmun, Powell, Stevens
NP   Marshall, Rehnquist, O'Connor

[The Clean Air Act Amendments of 1977 require states that have not met the national air quality standards, set by the EPA, to establish a permit program regulating "new or modified major stationary sources" of air pollution. In 1981, the EPA made regulations on how to implement the permit requirement, allowing a state to adopt a plantwide definition of the term "stationary source." This means that plants with several pollution-emitting devices may only need to modify one piece of equipment without meeting the permit conditions if the modification does not increase the total emission from the plant. Such an interpretation allows a state to treat all of the pollution-emitting devices within the same industrial grouping as though they were encased within a single "bubble."

The Natural Resources Defense Council, a national environmental public interest organization, challenged EPA's "bubble concept" as contrary to what Congress envisioned as a "stationary source" in its amendments to the Clean Air Act.]

Justice Stevens delivered the opinion for the Court.

II

When a court reviews an agency's construction of the statute which it administers, it is confronted with two questions. First, always, is the question whether Congress has directly spoken to the precise question at issue. If the intent of Congress is clear, that is the end of the matter; for the court as well as the agency, must give effect to the unambiguously expressed intent of Congress. If, however, the court determines Congress has not directly addressed the precise question at issue, the court does not simply impose its own construction on the statute, as would be necessary in the absence of an administrative interpretation. Rather, if the statute is silent or ambiguous with respect to the specific issue, the question for the court is whether the agency's answer is based on a permissible construction of the statute.

If Congress has explicitly left a gap for the agency to fill, there is an express delegation of authority to the agency to elucidate a specific provision of the statute by regulation. Such legislative regulations are given controlling weight unless they are arbitrary, capricious, or manifestly contrary to the statute. Sometimes the legislative delegation to an agency on a particular question is implicit rather than explicit. In such a case, a court may not substitute its own construction of a statutory provision for a reasonable interpretation made by the administration of an agency.

We have long recognized that considerable weight should be accorded to an executive department's construction of a statutory scheme it is entrusted to administer, and the principle of deference to administrative interpretations . . .

In light of these well-settled principles it is clear that the Court of Appeals misconceived the nature of its role in reviewing the regulations at issue. Once it determined, after its own examination of the legislation, that Congress did not actually have an intent regarding the applicability of the bubble concept to the permit program, the question before it was not whether in its view the concept is "inappropriate in the general context of a program designed to improve air quality, but whether the Administrator's view that it is appropriate in the context of this particular program is a reasonable one. Based on the examination of the legislation and its history which follows, we agree with the Court of Appeals that Congress did not have a specific intention on the applicability of the bubble concept in these cases, and conclude that the EPA's use of that concept here is a reasonable policy choice for the agency to make. . . .

III

In the 1950's and the 1960's Congress enacted a series of statutes designed to encourage and to assist the States in curtailing air pollution. . . . The Clean Air Amendments of 1970, . . . "sharply increased federal authority and responsibility in the continuing effort to combat air pollution," . . . but continued to assign "primary responsibility for assuring air quality" to the several States. . . . Section 109 of the 1970 Amendments directed the EPA to promulgate National Ambient Air Quality Standards (NAAQS's) and § 110 directed the States to develop plans (SIP's) to implement the standards within specified deadlines. In addition, § 111 provided that major new sources of pollution would be required to conform to technology-based performance standards; the EPA was directed to publish a list of categories of sources of pollution and to establish new source performance standards (NSPS) for each. Section 111(e) prohibited the operation of any new source in violation of a performance standard.

Section 111(a) defined the terms that are to be used in setting and enforcing standards of performance for new stationary sources. It provided:

"For purposes of this selection:

. . .

"(3) The term 'stationary source' means any building, structure, facility, or installation which emits or may emit any air pollutant." . . .

In the 1970 Amendments that definition was not only applicable to the NSPS program required by § 111, but also was made applicable to a requirement, of § 110 that each state implementation plan contain a procedure for reviewing the location of any proposed new source and preventing its construction if it would preclude the attainment or maintenance of national air quality standards.

In due course, the EPA promulgated NAAQS's, approved SIP's, and adopted detailed regulations governing NSPS's for various categories of equipment. In one of its programs, the EPA used a plantwide definition of the term "stationary source." In 1974, it issued NSPS's for the nonferrous smelting industry that provided that the standards would not apply to the modification of major smelting units if their increased emissions were offset by reductions in other portions of the same plant. . . .

The 1970 legislation provided for the attainment of primary NAAQS's by 1975. In many areas of the country, particularly the most industrialized States, the statutory goals were not attained. In 1976, the 94th Congress was confronted with this fundamental problem, as well as many others respecting pollution control. As always in this area, the legislative struggle was basically between interests seeking strict schemes to reduce pollution rapidly to eliminate its social costs and interests advancing the economic concern that strict schemes would retard industrial development with attendant social costs. The 94th Congress, confronting these competing interests, was unable to agree on what response was in the public interest: legislative proposals to deal with nonattainment failed to command the necessary consensus.

In light of this situation, the EPA published an Emissions Offset Interpretative Ruling in December 1976, . . . to "fill the gap," as respondents put it, until Congress acted. The Ruling stated that it was intended to address "the issue of whether and to what extent national air quality standards established under the Clean Air Act may restrict or prohibit growth of major new or expanded stationary air pollution sources." . . . In general, the Ruling provided that "a major new source may locate in an area with air quality worse than a national standard only if stringent conditions can be met." . . . The Ruling gave primary emphasis to the rapid attainment of the statute's environmental goals. Consistent with that emphasis, the construction of every new source in nonattainment areas had to meet the "lowest achievable emission rate" under the current state of the art for that type of facility. . . . The 1976 Ruling did not, however, explicitly adopt or reject the "bubble concept." . . .

IV

The Clean Air Act Amendments of 1977 are a lengthy, detailed, technical, complex, and comprehensive response to a major social issue. A small portion of the statute . . . expressly deals with nonattainment areas. The focal point of this controversy is one phrase in that portion of the Amendments.

Basically, the statute required each State in a nonattainment area to prepare and obtain approval of a new SIP by July 1, 1979. . . .

Most significantly for our purposes, the statute provided that each plan shall

"(6) require permits for the construction and operation of new or modified major stationary sources in accordance with section 173" . . . .

Before issuing a permit, § 173 requires (1) the state agency to determine that there will be sufficient emissions reductions in the region to offset the emissions from the new source and also to allow for reasonable further progress toward attainment, or that the increased emissions will not exceed an allowance for growth established pursuant to § 172(b)(5); (2) the applicant to certify that his other sources in the State are in compliance with the SIP, (3) the agency to determine that the applicable SIP is otherwise being implemented, and (4) the proposed source to comply with the lowest achievable emission rate (LAER).

The 1977 Amendments contain no specific reference to the "bubble concept." Nor do they contain a specific definition of the term "stationary source," though they do not disturb the definition of "stationary source" contained in § 111(a)(3), applicable by the terms of the Act to the NSPS program. Section 302(j), however, defines the term "major stationary source" as follows:

"(j) Except as otherwise expressly provided, the terms 'major stationary source' and 'major emitting facility' mean any stationary facility or source of air pollutants which directly emits, or has the potential to emit, one hundred tons per year or more of any air pollutant (including any major emitting facility or source of fugitive emissions of any such pollutant, as determined by rule by the Administrator)."

V

The legislative history of the portion of the 1977 Amendments dealing with nonattainment areas does not contain any specific comment on the "bubble concept" or the question whether a plantwide definition of a stationary source is permissible under the permit program. It does, however, plainly disclose that in the permit program Congress sought to accommodate the conflict between the economic interest in permitting capital improvements to continue and the environmental interest in improving air quality. Indeed, the House Committee Report identified the economic interest as one of the "two main purposes" of this section of the bill. . . .

The portion of the Senate Committee Report dealing with nonattainment areas states generally that it was intended to "supersede the EPA administrative approach," and that expansion should be permitted if a State could "demonstrate that these facilities can be accommodated within its overall plan to provide for attainment of air quality standards." . . .

The Senate Report notes the value of "case-by-case review of each new or modified major source of pollution that seeks to locate in a region exceeding an ambient standard," explaining that such a review "requires matching reductions from existing sources against emissions expected from the new source in order to assure that introduction of the new source will not prevent attainment of the applicable standard by the statutory deadline." . . . This description of a case-by-case approach to plant additions, which emphasizes the net consequences of the construction or modification of a new source, as well as its impact on the overall achievement of the national standards, was not, however, addressed to the precise issue raised by these cases.

VI

As previously noted, prior to the 1977 Amendments, the EPA had adhered to a plantwide definition of the term "source" under a NSPS program. After adoption of the 1977 Amendments, proposals for a plantwide definition were considered in at least three formal proceedings.

In January 1979, the EPA considered the question whether the same restriction on new construction in nonattainment areas that had been included in its December 1976 Ruling should be required in the revised SIP's that were scheduled to go into effect in July 1979. After noting that the 1976 Ruling was ambiguous on the question "whether a plant with a number of different processes and emission points would be considered a single source," . . . the EPA, in effect, provided a bifurcated answer to that question. In those areas that did not have a revised SIP in effect by July 1979, the EPA rejected the plantwide definition; on the other hand, it expressly concluded that the plantwide approach would be permissible in certain circumstances if authorized by an approved SIP. . . .

In April, again in September 1979, the EPA published additional comments in which it indicated that revised SIP's could adopt the plantwide definition of source in nonattainment areas in certain circumstances. . . . On the latter occasion, the EPA made a formal rulemaking proposal that would have permitted the use of the "bubble concept" for new installations within a plant as well as for modifications of existing units. It explained:

> "'Bubble' Exemption: The use of offsets inside the same source is called the 'bubble.' EPA proposes use of the definition of 'source' (see above) to limit the use of the bubble under nonattainment requirements. . . ."

Significantly, the EPA expressly noted that the word "source" might be given a plantwide definition for some purposes and a narrower definition for other purposes. . . .

> "Source means any building structure, facility, or installation which emits or may emit any regulated pollutant. 'Building, structure, facility or installation' means plant in PSD areas and in nonattainment areas except where the growth prohibitions would apply or where no adequate SIP exists or is being carried out."

The EPA's summary of its proposed Ruling discloses a flexible rather than rigid definition of the term "source" to implement various policies and programs. . . .

In August 1980, however, the EPA adopted a regulation that, in essence, applied the basic reasoning of the Court of Appeals in these cases. The EPA took particular note of the two then-recent Court of Appeals decisions, which had created the bright-line rule that the "bubble concept" should be employed in a program designed to maintain air quality but not in one designed to enhance air quality. Relying heavily on those cases, EPA adopted a dual definition of "source" for nonattainment areas that required a permit whenever a change in either the entire plant, or one of its components, would result in a significant increase in emissions even if the increase was completely offset by reductions elsewhere in the plant. The EPA expressed the opinion that this interpretation was "more consistent with congressional intent" than the plantwide definition because it "would bring in more sources or modifications for review," . . . but its primary legal analysis was predicated on the two Court of Appeals decisions.

In 1981 a new administration took office and initiated a "Government-wide reexamination of regulatory burdens and complexities." . . . In the context of that review, the EPA reevaluated the various arguments that had been advanced in connection with the proper definition of the term "source" and concluded that the term should be given the same definition in both nonattainment areas and PSD areas.

In explaining its conclusion, the EPA first noted that the definitional issue was not squarely addressed in either the statute or its legislative history and therefore that the issue involved an agency "judgment as how to best carry out the Act." . . . It then set forth several reasons for concluding that the plantwide definition was more appropriate. It pointed out that the dual definition "can act as a disincentive to new investment and modernization by discouraging modifications to existing facilities" and "can actually retard progress in air pollution control by discouraging replacement of older, dirtier processes or pieces of equipment with new, cleaner ones." . . . Moreover, the new definition "would simplify EPA's rules by using the same definition of 'source' for PSD, nonattainment new source review and the construction

moratorium. This reduces confusion and inconsistency." . . . Finally, the agency explained that additional requirements that remained in place would accomplish the fundamental purposes of achieving attainment with NAAQS's as expeditiously as possible. These conclusions were expressed in a proposed rulemaking in August 1981. . . .

VII

We are not persuaded that parsing of general terms in the text of the statute will reveal an actual intent of Congress. We know full well that this language is not dispositive; the terms are overlapping and the language is not precisely directed to the question of the applicability of a given term in the context of a larger operation. To the extent any congressional "intent" can be discerned from this language, it would appear that the listing of overlapping, illustrative terms was intended to enlarge, rather than to confine, the scope of the agency's power to regulate particular sources in order to effectuate the policies of the Act. . . .

More importantly, that history plainly identifies the policy concerns that motivated the enactment; the plantwide definition is fully consistent with one of those concerns—the allowance of reasonable economic growth—and, whether or not we believe it most effectively implements the other, we must recognize that the EPA has advanced a reasonable explanation for its conclusion that the regulations serve the environmental objectives as well. . . .

Our review of the EPA's varying interpretations of the word "source"—both before and after the 1977 Amendments—convinces us that the agency primarily responsible for administering this important legislation has consistently interpreted it flexibly—not in a sterile textual vacuum, but in the context of implementing policy decisions in a technical and complex arena. The fact that the agency has from time to time changed its interpretation of the term "source" does not, as respondents argue, lead us to conclude that no deference should be accorded the agency's interpretation of the statute. An initial agency interpretation is not instantly carved in stone. On the contrary, the agency, to engage in informed rulemaking, must consider varying interpretations and the wisdom of its policy on a continuing basis. Moreover, the fact that the agency has adopted different definitions in different contexts adds force to the argument that the definition itself is flexible, particularly since Congress has never indicated any disapproval of a flexible reading of the statute.

Significantly, it was not the agency in 1980, but rather the Court of Appeals that read the statute inflexibly to command a plantwide definition for programs designed to maintain clean air and to forbid such a definition for programs designed to improve air quality. The distinction the court drew may well be a sensible one, but our labored review of the problem has surely disclosed that it is not a distinction that Congress ever articulated itself, or one that the EPA found in the statute before the courts began to review the legislative work product. We conclude that it was the Court of Appeals, rather than Congress or any of the decisionmakers who are authorized by Congress to administer this legislation, that was primarily responsible for the 1980 position taken by the agency. . . .

The arguments over the policy that are advanced in the parties' briefs create the impression that respondents are now waging in a judicial forum a specific policy battle which they ultimately lost in the agency and in the 32 jurisdictions opting for the "bubble concept," but one which was never waged in Congress. Such policy arguments are more properly addressed to legislators or administrators, not to judges.

In these cases, the Administrator's interpretation represents a reasonable accommodation of manifestly competing interests and is entitled to deference: the regulatory scheme is technical and complex, the agency considered the matter in a detailed and reasoned fashion, and the decision involves reconciling conflicting policies. Congress intended to accommodate both interests, but did not do so itself on the level of specificity presented by these cases. Perhaps that body consciously desired the Administrator to strike the balance at this level, thinking that those with great expertise and charged with responsibility for administering the provision would be in a better position to do so; perhaps it simply did not consider the question at this level; and perhaps Congress was unable to forge a coalition on either side of the question, and those on each side decided to take their chances with the scheme devised by the agency. For judicial purposes, it matters not which of these things occurred.

Judges are not experts in the field, and are not part of either political branch of the Government. Courts must, in some cases, reconcile competing political interests, but not on the basis of the judges' personal policy preferences. In contrast, an agency to which Congress has delegated policymaking responsibilities may, within the limits of that delegation, properly rely upon the incumbent administration's views of wise policy to inform its judgments. While agencies are not directly accountable to the people, the Chief Executive is, and it is entirely appropriate for this political branch of the Government to make such policy choices—resolving the competing interest which Congress itself either inadvertently did not resolve, or intentionally left to be resolved by the agency charged with the administration of the statute in light of everyday realities.

When a challenge to an agency construction of a statutory provision, fairly conceptualized, really centers on the wisdom of the agency's policy, rather than whether it is a reasonable choice within a gap left open by Congress, the challenge must fail. In such a case, federal judges—who have no constituency—have a duty to respect legitimate policy choices made by those who do. The responsibilities for assessing the wisdom of such policy choices and resolving the struggle between competing views of the public interest are not judicial ones: "Our Constitution vests such responsibilities in the political branches." . . .

We hold that the EPA's definition of the term "source" is a permissible construction of the statute which seeks to accommodate progress in reducing air pollution with economic growth. . . .

The judgment of the Court of Appeals is reversed.

It is so ordered.

Congressional and Executive Control over the Exercise of Statutory Authority

Two major changes in the state's structure have resulted from broad delegation. One is the increase and consolidation of power in the executive branch. The second is the creation and institutionalization of power in administrative agencies. The political irony of this expansion and redistribution of governmental power is that "while Congress was legislating to occupy new policy areas formerly left outside the national government's realm of responsibilities, Congress was allowing its own authority to erode significantly."[22] We now often refer to this as the *self-inflicted wound*—Congress plays an important role in creating the institutional conditions for its own loss of a significant role in policymaking. It would be a mistake, however, to focus only on what powers Congress lost and the powers the president and administrative agencies gained with the rise of the administrative state. The judicial branch has also gained new powers from broad delegation. Courts are active agents in defining the legal boundaries of agencies (also see chapter 9) and in interpreting the role of the president and Congress in administrative policymaking. Courts decide the nature and scope of control these two branches of government have in the administrative process.

In this final section we focus on executive and legislative controls over the exercise of statutory authority by agencies. It is difficult to talk only about the Court's treatment of one branch of government because, as you will see in the cases below, many administrative law cases that come before the Court concern conflicts over which branch has statutory or constitutional power over agency actions. To fully understand executive and legislative controls over agencies, we need to think about the *institutional relationships* between the branches of government. What is the theory of separation of powers in administrative law? To what extent do Congress and president share responsibility for supervising administrative procedures and policies? To what extent has broad delegation by Congress limited its own role in the administrative process? How important are the political branches of government in regulating the regulators?

The expansion of the state during the New Deal resulted in a fundamental shift in our constitutional structure. The issues related to agency accountability to elected official, discussed by Jaffe and Lowi, are as important today as they were during the New Deal period. The creation of new social and environmental agencies in the mid-1960s and 1970s, such as the Equal Employment Opportunity Commission (1964), the Environmental Protection Agency (1970), the Occupational Safety and Health Administration (1970), and the Consumer Product Safety Commission (1972), again raise the old problem of making nonelected bureaucrats accountable to a democratic polity.

Congress has developed a number of devices for monitoring agency decisions. One example is the National Environmental Policy Act (NEPA), which since 1969 has required that certain agencies provide environmental impact statements to identify and analyze the consequences of their decisions on the environment. Environmental im-

---

[22]Scheiber, 3.

pact statements have been important documents for helping Congress refashion its policy goals and amend statutes. A more direct mechanism for monitoring agency actions is the *legislative veto*. A legislative veto is a statutory provison that allows Congress to veto decisions by administrators. The first legislative veto provision Congress enacted was in 1932. Between 1932 and 1983 it is estimated that Congress inserted 295 veto-type procedures in 196 different statutes. In 1983, the Supreme Court addressed the constitutionality of the legislative veto in *Immigration and Naturalization Service v. Chadha.*

Immigration and Naturalization Service v. Chadha

462 U.S. 919 (1983) 7–2
+ Burger, Brennan, Marshall, Blackmun, Powell, Stevens, O'Connor
– White, Rehnquist

[Jagdish Rai Chadha, an East Indian who held a British passport, came to the United States in 1966 on a nonimmigrant student visa. His visa expired in 1972, and he was required by the Immigration and Naturalization Service (INS) to show cause why he should not be deported for having "remained in the United States for a longer time than permitted." Upon submitting his application for a suspension of deportation to the INS, the immigration judge ordered that Chada's deportation be suspended and that he be allowed to remain in the United States as a permanent resident alien. In the Immigration and Nationality Act Congress delegated the major responsibility for enforcement to the Attorney General, who is obligated by the statute to provide Congress with a "detailed statement of the facts and pertinent provisions of law" in all cases where the Attorney General recommends suspension of deportation. Congress gave itself the authority in the statute to veto the Attorney General's decision. In 1975 Representative Eilberg, chair of the House of Representatives Judiciary Subcommittee on Immigration, Citizenship, and International Law, introduced a resolution to overturn the Attorney General's decision. This resolution was passed by the subcommittee and the House of Representatives. If Congress had not acted, the Attorney General's decision would have been final and Chadha would have been able to remain in the United States. Chadha challenged the constitutionality of the resolution. Seven members of the Supreme Court agreed with Chadha and ruled that the legislative veto was unconstitutional. Justice White's dissent supports the veto as a legitimate and necessary check on administrative discretion.]

Chief Justice Burger delivered the opinion of the Court.

III

We turn now to the question whether action of one House of Congress under § 244(c)(2) violates strictures of the Constitution. We begin, of course, with the presumption that the challenged statute is valid. . . .

"Since 1932, when the first veto provision was enacted into law, 295 congressional veto-type procedures have been inserted in 196 different statutes as follows: from 1932 to 1939, five statutes were affected; from 1940–49, nineteen statutes; between 1950–59, thirty-four statutes; and from 1960–69, forty-nine. From the year 1970 through 1975, at least one hundred sixty-three such provisions were included in eighty-nine laws." Abourezk, The Congressional Veto: A Contemporary Response to Executive Encroachment on Legislative Prerogatives, 52 Ind. L. Rev. 323, 324 (1977) . . .

Explicit and unambiguous provisions of the Constitution prescribe and define the respective functions of the Congress and of the Executive in the legislative process. Since the precise terms of those familiar provisions are critical to the resolution of these cases, we set them out verbatim. Article I provides:

> "All legislative Powers herein granted shall be vested in a Congress of the United States, which shall consist of a Senate and House of Representatives." Art. I, § 1. . . .
> "Every Bill which shall have passed the House of Representatives *and* the Senate, *shall*, before it becomes a law, be presented to the President of the United States . . . ." Art. I § 7, cl. 2 . . .
> "*Every* Order, Resolution, or Vote to which the Concurrence of the Senate and House of Representatives may be necessary (except on a question of Adjournment) *shall be* presented to the President of the United States; and before the Same shall take Effect, *shall be* approved by him, or being disapproved by him, *shall be* repassed by two thirds of the Senate and House of Representatives, according to the Rules and Limitations prescribed in the Case of a Bill." Art. I, § 7, cl. 3. . . .

These provisions of Art. I are integral parts of the constitutional design for the separation of powers. We have recently noted that "[t]he principle of separation of powers was not simply an abstract generalization in the minds of the Framers: it was woven into the document that they drafted in Philadelphia in the summer of 1787." *Buckley v. Valeo*, 424 U.S., at 124. Just as we relied on the textual provision of Art. II, § 2, cl. 2, to vindicate the principle of separation of powers in *Buckley*, we see that the purposes underlying the Presentment Clauses, Art. I, § 7, cls. 2, 3, and the bicameral requirement of Art. I, § 1,

and § 7, cl. 2, guide our resolution of the important question presented in these cases. The very structure of the Articles delegating and separating powers under Arts. I, II, and III, exemplifies the concept of separation of powers, and we now turn to Art. I.

B
The Presentment Clauses

. . . The decision to provide the President with a limited and qualified power to nullify proposed legislation by veto was based on the profound conviction of the Framers that the powers conferred on Congress were the powers to be most carefully circumscribed. It is beyond doubt that lawmaking was a power to be shared by both Houses and the President. In The Federalist No. 73 (H. Lodge ed. 1888), Hamilton focused on the President's role in making laws:

> "If even no propensity had ever discovered itself in the legislation body to invade the rights of the Executive, the rules of just reasoning and theoretic propriety would of themselves teach us that the one ought not to be left to the mercy of the other, but ought to possess a constitutional and effectual power of self-defence".

See also The Federalist No. 51 . . .

The President's role in the lawmaking process also reflects the Framers' careful efforts to check whatever propensity a particular Congress might have to enact oppressive, improvident, or ill-considered measures.

C
Bicameralism

The bicameral requirement of Art. I, §§ 1, 7, was of scarcely less concern to the Framers than was the Presidential veto and indeed the two concepts are interdependent. By providing that no law could take effect without the concurrence of the prescribed majority of the Members of both Houses, the Framers reemphasized their belief, already remarked upon in connection with the Presentment Clauses, that legislation should not be enacted unless it has been carefully and fully considered by the Nation's elected officials. In the Constitutional Convention debates on the need for a bicameral legislature, James Wilson, later to become a Justice of this Court, commented:

> "Despotism comes on mankind in different shapes, sometimes in an Executive, sometimes in a military, one. Is there danger of a Legislative depotism? Theory & practice both proclaim it. If the Legislative authority be not restrained, there can be neither liberty nor stability; and it can only be restrained by dividing it within itself, into distinct and independent branches. In a single house there is no check, but the inadequate one, of the virtue & good sense of those who compose it." 1 Farrand 254.

. . . These observations are consistent with what many of the Framers expressed, none more cogently than Madison in pointing up the need to divide and disperse power in order to protect liberty:

> "In republican government, the legislative authority necessarily predominates. The remedy for this inconveniency is to divide the legislature into different branches; and to render them, by different modes of election and different principles of action, as little connected with each other as the nature of their common functions and their common dependence on the society will admit." The Federalist No. 51, p324. (H. Lodge ed. 1888) . . .

See also The Federalist No. 62.

IV

The Constitution sought to divide the delegated powers of the new Federal Government into three defined categories, Legislative, Executive, and Judicial, to assure, as nearly as possible, that each branch of government would confine itself to it its assigned responsibility. The hydraulic pressure inherent within each of the separate Branches to exceed the outer limits of its power, even to accomplish desirable objectives, must be resisted.

Although not "hermetically" sealed from one another, *Buckley v. Valeo*, 424 U.S., at 121, the powers delegated to the three Branches are functionally identifiable. When any Branch acts, it is presumptively exercising the power the Constitution has delegated to it. See *J. W. Hampton & Co. v. United States*, 276 U.S. 394, 406 (1928). When the Executive acts, he presumptively acts in an executive or administrative capacity as defined in Art. II. And when, as here, one House of Congress purports to act, it is presumptively acting within its assigned sphere.

Beginning with this presumption, we must nevertheless establish that the challenged action under § 244(c)(2) is of the kind to which the procedural requirements of Art. 1, § 7, apply. Not every action taken by either House is subject to the bicameralism and presentment requirements of Art. I. Whether actions taken by either House are, in law and fact, an exercise of legislative power depends not on their form but upon "whether they contain matter which is properly to be regarded as legislative in its character and effect." S. Rep. No. 1335, 54th Cong., 2d Sess., 8 (1897).

Examination of the action taken here by one House pursuant to § 244(c)(2) reveals that it was essentially legislative in purpose and effect. In purporting to exercise power defined in Art. 1, § 8, cl. 4., to "establish an uniform Rule of Naturalization," the House took action that had the purpose and effect of altering the legal rights, duties, and relations of persons, including the Attorney General, Executive Branch officials and Chadha, all outside the Legislative Branch. Section 244(c)(2) purports to authorize one House of Congress to require the Attorney General to deport an individual alien whose deportation otherwise would be canceled under § 244. The one-House veto operated in these cases to overrule the Attorney General and mandate Chadha's deportation; absent the House action, Chadha would remain in the United States. Congress has *acted* and its action has altered Chadha's status.

The legislative character of the one-house veto in these cases is confirmed by the character of the congressional action it supplants. Neither the House of Representatives nor the Senate contends that, absent the veto provision in § 244(c)(2), either of them, or both of them acting together, could effectively require the Attorney General to deport an alien once the Attorney General, in the exercise of legislatively delegated authority, had determined the alien should remain in the United States. . . .

The nature of the decision implemented by the one-House veto in these cases further manifests its legislatve character. After long experience with the clusmy, time-consuming private bill procedure, Congress made a deliberate choice to delegate to the Executive Branch, and specifically to the Attorney General, the authority to allow deportable aliens to remain in this country in certain specified circumstances. It is not disputed that this choice to delegate authority is precisely the kind of decision that can be implemented only in accordance with the procedures set out in Art. I. Disagreement with the Attorney General's decision on Chadha's deportation — that is, Congress' decision to deport Chadha — no less than Congress' original choice to delegate to the Attorney General the authority to make that decision, involves determinations of policy that Congress can implement in only one way; bicameral passage followed by presentment to the President. Congress must abide by its delegation of authority until that delegation is legislatively altered or revoked.*

Finally, we see that when the Framers intended to authorize either House of Congress to act alone and outside of its prescribed bicameral legislative role, they narrowly and precisely defined the procedure for such action. There are four provisions in the Constitution, explicit and unambiguous, by which one House may act alone with the unreviewable force of law, not subject to the President's veto:

(a) The House of Representatives alone was given the power to initate impeachments. Art. I, § 2, cl. 5;

(b) The Senate alone was given the power to conduct trials following impeachment on charges initiated by the House and to convict following trial. Art. I, § 3, cl. 6;

(c) The Senate alone was given unreviewable power to approve or to disapprove Presidential appointments. Art. II, § 2, cl. 2;

(d) The Senate alone was given unreviewable power to ratify treaties negotiated by the President. Art. II, § 2, cl. 2

Clearly, when the Draftsmen sought to confer special powers on one House, independent of the other House, or of the President, they did so in explicit, unambiguous terms. . . .

. . . The bicameral requirement, the Presentment Clauses, the President's veto, and Congress' power to override a veto were intended to erect enduring checks on each Branch and to protect the people from the improvident exercise of power by mandating certain prescribed steps. To preserve those checks, and maintain the separation of powers, the carefully defined limits on the power of each Branch must not be eroded. To accomplish what has been attempted by one House of Congress in this case requires action in conformity with the express procedures of the Constitution's prescription for legislative action: passage by a majority of both Houses and presentment to the President.

The veto authorized by § 244(c)(2) doubtless has been in many respects a convenient shortcut; the "sharing" with the Executive by Congress of its authority over aliens in this manner is, on its face, an appealing compromise. In purely practical terms, it is obviously easier for action to be taken by one House without submission to the President; but it is crystal clear from the records of the Convention, contemporaneous writings and debates, that the Framers ranked other values higher than efficiency." . . .

. . . With all the obvious flaws of delay, untidiness, and potential for abuse, we have not yet found a better way to preserve freedom than by making the exercise of power subject to the carefully crafted restraints spelled out in the Constitution. . . .

V

We hold that the congressional veto provision in § 244(c)(2) is severable from the Act and that it is

---

*This does not mean that Congress is required to capitulate to "the accretion of policy control by forces outside its chambers." Javits & Klein, Congressional Oversight and the Legislative Veto: A Constitutional Analysis, 52 N. Y. U. L. Rev. 455, 462 (1977). The Constitution provides Congress with abundant means to oversee and control its administrative creatures. Beyond the obvious fact that Congress ultimately controls administrative agencies in the legislation that creates them, other means of control, such as durational limits on authorizations and formal reporting requirements, lie well within Congress' constitutional power. See *id.*, at 460–461; Kaiser, Congressional Action to Overturn Agency Rules: Alternatives to the "Legislative Veto," 32 Ad. L. Rev. 667 (1980). . . .

unconstitutional. Accordingly, the judgment of the Court of Appeals is Affirmed.

Justice Powell, concurring in the judgment.

Justice Rehnquist, with whom Justice White joins, dissenting.

A severability clause creates a presumption that Congress intended the valid portion of the statute to remain in force when one part is found to be invalid. A severability clause does not, however, conclusively resolve the issue. . . . Because I believe that Congress did not intend the one-House veto provision of § 244(c)(2) to be severable, I dissent.

By severing § 244(c)(2), the Court permits suspension of deportation in a class of cases where Congress never stated that suspension was appropriate. I do not believe we should expand the statute in this way without some clear indication that Congress intended such an expansion. . . .

Justice White, dissenting.

Today the Court not only invalidates § 244(c)(2) of the Immigration and Nationality Act, but also sounds the death knell for nearly 200 other statutory provisions in which Congress has reserved a "legislative veto." For this reason, the Court's decision is of surpassing importance. And it is for this reason that the Court would have been well advised to decide the cases, if possible, on the narrower grounds of separation of powers, leaving for full consideration the constitutionality of other congressional review statutes operating on such varied matters as war powers and agency rulemaking, some of which concern the independent regulatory agencies.

The legislative veto developed initially in response to the problems of reorganizing the sprawling Government structure created in response to the Depression. The Reorganization Acts established the chief model for the legislative veto. When President Hoover requested authority to reorganize the Government in 1929, he coupled his request that the "Congress be willing to delegate its authority over the problem (subject to defined principles) to the Executive" with a proposal for legislative review. He proposed that the Executive "should act upon approval of a joint com-

mittee of Congress or with the reservation of power of revision by Congress within some limited period adequate for its consideration." Public Papers of the Presidents, Herbert Hoover, 1929, p. 432 (1974). Congress followed President Hoover's suggestion and authorized reorganization subject to legislative review. . . . Although the reorganization authority reenacted in 1933 did not contain a legislative veto provision, the provision returned during the Roosevelt administration and has since been renewed numerous times. Over the years, the provision was used extensively. Presidents submitted 115 Reorganization Plans to Congress of which 23 were disapproved by Congress pursuant to legislative veto provisions. . . .

Shortly after adoption of the Reorganization Act of 1939, . . . Congress and the President applied the legislative veto procedure to resolve the delegation problem for national security and foreign affairs. World War II occasioned the need to transfer greater authority to the President in these areas. The legislative veto offered the means by which Congress could confer additional authority while preserving its own constitutional role. During World War II, Congress enacted over 30 statutes conferring powers on the Executive with legislative veto provisions. President Roosevelt accepted the veto as the necessary price for obtaining exceptional authority.

Over the quarter century following World War II, Presidents continued to accept legislative vetos by one or both Houses as constitutional, while regularly denouncing provisions by which congressional Committees reviewed Executive activity.* The legislative veto balanced delegations of statutory authority in new areas of governmental involvement: for the space program, international agreements on nuclear energy, tariff arrangements, and adjustment of federal pay rates.

---

*Presidential objections to the veto, until the veto by President Nixon of the War Powers Resolution, principally concerned bills authorizing Committee vetoes. As the Senate Subcommittee on Separation of Powers found in 1969, "an accommodation was reached years ago on legislative vetoes exercised by the entire Congress or by one House, [while] disputes have continued to arise over the committee form of the veto." S. Rep. No. 91–549, p. 14 (1969). . . .

During the 1970's the legislative veto was important in resolving a series of major constitutional disputes between the President and Congress over claims of the President to broad impoundment, war, and national emergency powers. The key provision of the War Power Resolution, . . . authorizes the termination by concurrent resolution of the use of armed forces in hostilities. A similar measure resolved the problem posed by Presidential claims of inherent power to impound appropriations. Congressional Budget and Impoundment Control Act of 1974, . . . In conference, a compromise was achieved under which permanent impoundments, termed "rescissions," would require approval through enactment of legislation. In contrast, temporary impoundments, or "deferrals," would become effective unless disapproved by one House. This compromise provided the President with flexibility, while preserving ultimate congressional control over the budget.* . . .

In the energy field, the legislative veto served to balance broad delegations in legislation emerging from the energy crisis of the 1970's.† . . .

. . . It is an important if not indispensable political invention that allows the President and Congress to resolve major constitutional and policy differences, assures the accountability of independent regulatory agencies, and preserves Congress' control over lawmaking. Perhaps there are other means of accommodation and accountability, but the increasing reliance of Congress upon the legislative veto suggests that the alternatives to which Congress must now turn are not entirely satisfactory.‡

The history of the legislative veto also makes clear that it has not been a sword with which Congress has struck out to aggrandize itself at the expense of the other branches—the concerns of Madison and Hamilton. Rather, the veto has been a means of defense, a reservation of ultimate authority necessary if Congress is to fulfill its designated role under Art. I as the Nation's lawmaker. While the President has often objected to particular legislative vetoes, generally those left in the hands of congressional Committees, the Executive has more often agreed to legislative review as the price for a broad delegation of authority. To be sure, the President may have preferred unrestricted power, but that could be precisely why Congress thought it essential to retain a check on the exercise of delegated authority. . . .

If the legislative veto were as plainly unconstitutional as the Court strives to suggest, its broad ruling today would be more comprehensible. But, the constitutionality of the legislative veto is anything but clear-cut. The issue divides scholars, courts, Attorneys General, and the two other branches of the National Government. . . .

The reality of the situation is that the constitutional question posed today is one of immense difficulty over which the Executive and Legislative Branches . . . That disagreement stems from the silence of the Constitution on the precise question: The Constitution does not directly authorize or prohibit the legislative veto. Thus, our task should be to determine whether the legislative veto is consistent with the purposes of Art. I and the principles of separation of powers which are reflected in that Article and throughout the Constitution. . . .

. . . These is no question that a bill does not become a law until it is approved by both the House and the Senate, and presented to the President. . . .

. . . The power to exercise a legislative veto is not the power to write new law without bicameral approval or Presidential consideration. The veto must be authorized by statute and may only negative what an Executive department or independent agency has proposed. On its face, the legislative veto no more allows one House of Congress to make law than does the Presidential Veto confer such power upon the President. . . .

---

*The Impoundment Control Act's provision for legislative review has been used extensively. Presidents have submitted hundreds of proposed budget deferrals, of which 65 have been disapproved by resolutions of the House or Senate with no protest by the Executive. . . .

†The veto appears in a host of broad statutory delegations concerning energy rationing, contingency plans, strategic oil reserves, allocation of energy production materials, oil exports, and naval petroleum reserve production.

‡While Congress could write certain statutes with greater specificity, it is unlikely that this is a realistic or even desirable substitute for the legislative veto. The controversial nature of many issues would prevent Congress from reaching agreement on many major problems if specificity were required in their enactments. . . .

The Court heeded this counsel in approving the modern administrative state. The Court's holding today that all legislative-type action must be enacted through the lawmaking process ignores that legislative authority is routinely delegated to the Executive Branch, to the independent regulatory agencies, and to private individuals and groups. . . .

The wisdom and the constitutionality of these broad delegations are matters that still have not been put to rest. But for present purposes, these cases establish that by virtue of congressional delegation, legislative power can be exercised by independent agencies and Executive departments without the passage of new legislation. For some time, the sheer amount of law—the substantive rules that regulate private conduct and direct the operation of government—made by the agencies has far outnumbered the lawmaking engaged in by Congress through the traditional process. There is no question but that agency rulemaking is lawmaking in any functional or realistic sense of the term. . . .

If Congress may delegate lawmaking power to independent and Executive agencies, it is most difficult to understand Art. I as prohibiting Congress from also reserving a check on legislative power for itself. Absent the veto, the agencies receiving delegations of legislative or quasi-legislative power may issue regulations having the force of law without bicameral approval and without the President's signature. It is thus not apparent why the reservation of a veto over the exercise of that legislative power must be subject to a more exacting test. In both cases, it is enough that the initial statutory authorizations comply with the Art. I requirements. . . .

The Court also takes no account of perhaps the most relevant consideration: However resolutions of disapproval under § 244(c)(2) are formally characterized, in reality, a departure from the status quo occurs only upon the concurrence of opinion among the House, Senate, and President. . . .

The central concern of the presentment and bicameralism requirements of Art. I is that when a departure from the legal status quo is undertaken, it is done with the approval of the President and both Houses of Congress—or, in the event of Presidential veto, a two-thirds majority in both Houses. This interest is fully satisfied by the operation of § 244(c)(2). The President's approval is found in the Attorney General's action in recommending to Congress that the deportation order for a given alien be suspended. The House and the Senate indicate their approval of the Executive's action by not passing a resolution of disapproval within the statutory period. Thus, a change in the legal status quo—the deportability of the alien—is consummated only with the approval of each of the three relevant actors. The disagreement of any one of the three maintains the alien's preexisting status: the Executive may choose not to recommend suspension; the House and Senate may each veto the recommendation. . . .

Thus understood, § 244(c)(2) fully effectuates the purposes of the bicameralism and presentment requirements. . . .

. . . At no place in § 244 has Congress delegated to the Attorney General any final power to determine which aliens shall be allowed to remain in the United States. Congress has retained the ultimate power to pass on such changes in deportable status. . . .

. . . [I]t may be said that this approach leads to the incongruity that the two-House veto is more suspect than its one-House brother. Although the idea may be initially counterintuitive, on close analysis, it is not at all unusual that the one-house Veto is of more certain constitutionality than the two-House version. If the Attorney General's action is a proposal for legislation, then the disapproval of but a single House is all that is required to prevent its passage. Because approval is indicated by the failure to veto, the one-House veto satisfies the requirement of bicameral approval. The two-House version may present a different question. . . .

. . . [I]t may be objected that Congress cannot indicate its approval of legislative change by inaction. In the Court of Appeals' view, inaction by Congress "could equally imply endorsement, acquiescence, passivity, indecision, or indifference," . . . and the Court appears to echo this concern. This objection appears more properly directed at the wisdom of the legislative veto than its constitutionality. The Constitution does not and cannot guarantee that legislators will carefully scrutinize legislation and deliberate before acting. In a democracy it is the electorate that holds the legislators accountable for the wisdom of their choices. . . .

The Court of Appeals struck § 244(c)(2) as violative of the constitutional principle of separation of powers. . . .

. . . [T]he history of the separation-of-powers doctrine is also a history of accommodation and practicality. Apprehensions of an overly powerful branch have not led to undue prophylactic measures that handicap the effective working of the National Government as a whole. The Constitution does not contemplate total separation of the three branches of Government. *Buckley v. Valeo*, 424 U.S. 1, 121 (1976). . . .

I do not suggest that all legislative vetoes are necessarily consistent with separation-of-powers principles. A legislative check on an inherently executive function, for example, that of initiating prosecutions, poses an entirely different question. But the legislative veto device here—and in many other settings—is far from

an instance of legislative tyranny over the Executive. It is a necessary check on the unavoidably expanding power of the agencies, both Executive and independent, as they engage in exercising authority delegated by Congress. . . .

I regret that I am in disagreement with my colleagues on the fundamental questions that these cases present. But even more I regret the destructive scope of the Court's holding. It reflects a profoundly different conception of the Constitution than that held by the courts which sanctioned the modern administrative state. Today's decision strikes down in one fell swoop provisions in more laws enacted by Congress than the Court has cumulatively invalidated in its history. I fear it will now be more difficult to "insur[e] that the fundamental policy decisions in our society will be made not by an appointed official but by the body immediately responsible to the people," *Arizona v. California*, 373 U.S. 546, 626 (1963) (Harlan, J., dissenting in part). I must dissent.

In the next case, *Bowsher v. Synar* (1986), the meaning of the separation of powers principle in the administration process generated a dispute over whether the Comptroller General functions primarily as as agent of Congress or the president in an elaborate statutory scheme to reduce the federal budget. Both the majority opinion and the two dissents rely on a set of cases dealing with the power of the president to remove administrators and to make appointments. The Court applies its past interpretations of presidental removal powers (*Myers v. United States*, 1926; *Humphrey's Executor v. United States*, 1935; and *Weiner v. United States*, 1958) and presidential appointments powers (*Buckley v. Valeo*, 1976) to the issues raised in *Bowsher v. Synar*. Therefore as you read *Bowsher*, you will learn how the Court has ruled on the issues of removal and appointments. Both of these powers enable the president to influence the administrative process. How expansive are these powers according to the Court? To what extent are administrative agencies protected from the political agendas of presidents?

Bowsher v. Synar

106 S. Ct. 3181 (1986) 7–2
+ Burger, Brennan, Marshall, Powell, Rehnquist, Stevens, O'Connor
− White, Blackmun

[Congress passed the Balanced Budget and Emergency Deficit Control Act in 1985, also known as the Gramm-Rudman-Hollings Act, for the purpose of developing an administrative process to enforce deficit reductions. The act set a "maximum deficit amount" for federal spending each year between 1986 and 1991 and established a mechanism for administering this plan. The directors of the Office of Management and Budget (OMB) and the Congressional Budget Office (CBO) were required independently to estimate the federal budget deficit for the upcoming year and calculate "the budget reduction necessary to ensure that the deficit does not exceed the maximum deficit amount." The directors were then to report their estimates to the Comptroller General (head of the General Accounting Office), who reports to the president, who then issues an order mandating the spending reduction specified by the Comptroller General. The statute provided that Congress may then legislate reduction in spending, but if it does not, the president's "sequestration order" becomes effective, and the spending reduction included in that order are made.

Members of Congress who voted against the act filed a complaint seeking declaratory relief and the National Treasury Employees Union also sued alleging injury by automatic cuts in cost-of-living increases.]

Chief Justice Burger delivered the opinion of the Court.

The question presented by these appeals is whether the assignment by Congress to the Comptroller General of the United States of certain functions under the Balanced Budget and Emergency Deficit Control Act of 1985 violates the doctrine of separation of powers. . . .

III

. . . Even a cursory exmination of the Constitution reveals the influence of Montesquieu's thesis that checks and balances were the foundation of a structure of government that would protect liberty. The Framers provided a vigorous legislative branch and a separate and wholly independent executive branch, with each branch responsible ultimately to the people. The Framers also provided for a judicial branch equally independent with "[t]he judicial Power . . . extend[ing] to call Cases, in Law and Equity, arising under this Constitution, and the Laws of the United States." Art. III, § 2.

Other, more subtle, examples of separated powers are evident as well. Unlike parliamentary systems such as that of Great Britain, no person who is an officer of the United States may serve as a Member of the Congress. Art. I, § 6. Moreover, unlike parliamentary systems, the President, under Article II, is responsible not to the Congress but to the people, subject only to impeachment proceedings which are exercised by the two Houses as representatives of the people. Art. II, § 4. And even in the impeachment of a President the presiding officer of the ultimate tribunal is not a member of the legislative branch, but the Chief Justice of the United States. Art. I, § 3.

That this system of division and separation of powers produces conflicts, confusion, and discordance at times is inherent, but it was deliberately so structured to assure full, vigorous and open debate on the great issues affecting the people and to provide avenues for the operation of checks on the exercise of governmental power.

The Constitution does not contemplate an active role for Congress in the supervision of officers charged with the execution of the laws it enacts. The President appoints "Officers of the United States" with the "Advice and Consent of the Senate. . . ." Article II, § 2. Once the appointment has been made and confirmed, however, the Constitution explicitly provides for removal of Officers of the United States by Congress only upon impeachment by the House of Representatives and conviction by the Senate. An impeachment by the House and trial by the Senate can rest only on "Treason, Bribery or other high Crimes and Misdemeanors." Article II, § 4. A direct congressional role in the removal of officers charged with the execution of the laws beyond this limited one is inconsistent with separation of powers.

This was made clear in debate in the First Congress in 1789. When Congress considered an amendment to a bill establishing the Department of Foreign

Affairs, the debate centered around whether the Congress "should recognize and declare the power of the President under the Constitution to remove the Secretary of Foreign Affairs without the advice and consent of the Senate. [*Myers v. United States* 272 U.S. 52 (1925)]. James Madison urged rejection of a congressional role in the removal of Executive Branch officers, other than by impeachment, saying in debate:

> "Perhaps there was no argument urged with more success, or more plausibly grounded against the Constitution, under which we are now deliberating, than that founded on the mingling of the Executive and Legislative branches of the Government in one body. It has been objected, that the Senate have too much of the Executive power even, by having a control over the President in the appointment to office, Now, shall we extend this connexion between the Legislative and Executive departments, which will strengthen the objection, and diminish the responsibility we have in the head of the Executive?" 1 Annals of Cong. 380.

Madison's position ultimately prevailed, and a congressional role in the removal process was rejected. This "Decision of 1789" provides "contemporaneous and weighty evidence" of the Constitution's meaning since many of the Members of the first Congress "had taken part in framing that instrument." *Marsh v. Chambers*, 463 U.S. 783 (1983).

This Court first directly addressed this issue in *Myers v. United States*. . . . At issue in *Myers* was a statute providing that certain postmasters could be removed only "by and with the advice and consent of the Senate." The President removed one such postmaster without Senate approval, and a lawsuit ensued. Chief Justice Taft, writing for the Court, declared the statute unconstitutional on the ground that for Congress to "draw to itself, or to either branch of it, the power to remove or the right to participate in the exercise of that power . . . would be . . . to infringe the constitutional principle of the separation of governmental powers." *Id.*, at 161.

A decade later, in *Humphrey's Executor v. United States*, 295 U.S. 602 (1935), . . . relied upon heavily by appellants, a Federal Trade Commissioner who had been removed by the President sought back pay. *Humphrey's Executor* involved an issue not presented either in the *Myers* case or in this case—*i.e.*, the power of Congress to limit the President's powers of removal of a Federal Trade Commissioner. 295 U.S., at 630. . . . The relevant statute permitted removal "by the President," but only "for inefficiency, neglect of duty, or malfeasance in office." Justice Sutherland, speaking for the Court, upheld the statute, holding that "illimitable power of removal is not possessed by the President [with respect to Federal Trade Commissioners]." 295 U.S., at 628–629. . . . The Court distinguished *Myers*, reaffirming its holding that congressional participation in the removal of executive officers is unconstitutional. Justice Sutherland's opinion for the Court also underscored the crucial role of separated powers in our system:

> "The fundamental necessity of maintaining each of the three general departments of government entirely free from the control or coercive influence, direct or indirect, of either of the others, has often been stressed and is hardly open to serious question. So much is implied in the very fact of the separation of the powers of these departments by the Constitution; and in the rule which recognizes their essential co-equality." 295 U.S., at 629-630 . . .

The Court reached a similar result in *Weiner v. United States*, 357 U.S. 349 . . . (1958), concluding that, under *Humphrey's Executor*, the President did not have unrestrained removal authority over a member of the War Crimes Commission.

In light of these precedents, we conclude that Congress cannot reserve for itself the power of removal of an officer charged with the execution of the laws except by impeachment. To permit the execution of the laws to be vested in an officer answerable only to Congress would, in practical terms, reserve in Congress control over the execution of laws. As the District Court observed, "Once an officer is appointed, it is only the authority that can remove him, and not the authority that appointed him, that he must fear and, in the performance of his functions, obey." 626 F.Supp., at 1401. The structure of the Constitution does not permit Congress to execute the laws; it follows that Congress cannot grant to an officer under its control what it does not possess.

Our decision in *INS v. Chadha*, 462 U.S. 919, . . . (1983), supports this conclusion. . . . To permit an officer controlled by Congress to execute the laws would be, in essence, to permit a congressional veto. Congress could simply remove, or threaten to remove, an officer for executing the laws in any fashion found to be unsatisfactory to Congress. This kind of congressional control over the execution of the laws, *Chadha* makes clear, is constitutionally impermissible.

The dangers of congressional usurpation of Executive Branch functions have long been recognized. "[T]he debates of the Constitutional Convention, and the Federalist Papers, are replete with expressions of fear that the Legislative Branch of National Government will aggrandize itself at the expense of the other two branches." *Buckley v. Valeo*, 424 U.S. 1, (1976). . . . Indeed, we also have observed only recently that "[t]he hydraulic pressure inherent within each of the separate Branches to exceed the outer limits of its power, even to accomplish desirable objectives, must be resisted." *Chadha*, 462 U.S., at 951. . . . With these principles in mind, we turn to consideration of whether the Comptroller General is controlled by Congress.

IV

. . . Appellants urge that the Comptroller General performs his duties independently and is not subservient to Congress. We agree with the District Court that this contention does not bear close scrutiny.

The critical factor lies in the provisions of the statute defining the Comptroller General's office relating to removability. Although the Comptroller General is nominated by the President from a list of three individuals recommended by the Speaker of the House of Representatives and the President pro tempore of the Senate . . . and confirmed by the Senate,

he is removable only at the initiative of Congress. He may be removed not only by impeachment but also by Joint Resolution of Congress "at any time" resting on any one of the following bases:

"(i) permanent disability;

"(ii) inefficiency;

"(iii) neglect of duty;

"(iv) malfeasance; or

"(v) a felony or conduct involving moral turpitude."

31 U.S.C. § 703(e)(1).

This provision was included, as one Congressman explained in urging passage of the Act, because Congress "felt that [the Comptroller General] should be brought under the sole control of Congress, so that Congress at the moment when it found he was inefficient and was not carrying on the duties of his office as he should and as the Congress expected, could remove him without long, tedious process of a trial by impeachment." 61 Cong. Rec. 1081 (1921). . . .

Justice White contends that "[t]he statute does not permit anyone to remove the Comptroller at will; removal is permitted only for specified cause, with the existence of cause to be determined by Congress following a hearing. Any removal under the statute would presumably be subject to post-termination judicial review to ensure that a hearing had in fact been held and the finding of cause for removal was not arbitrary." . . .

. . . [T]he dissent's assessment of the statute fails to recognize the breadth of the grounds for removal. The statute permits removal for "inefficiency," "neglect of duty," or "malfeasance." These terms are very broad and, as interpreted by Congress, could sustain removal of a Comptroller General for any number of actual or perceived transgressions of the legislative will. The Constitutional Convention chose to permit impeachment of executive officers only for "Treason, Bribery, or other high Crimes and Misdemeanors." It rejected language that would have permitted impeachment for "maladministration," with Madison arguing that "[s]o vague a term will be equivalent to a tenure during pleasure of the Senate." 2 Farrand 550. . . .

. . . Surely no one would seriously suggest that judicial independence would be strengthened by allowing removal of federal judges only by a joint resolution finding "inefficiency," "neglect of duty," or "malfeasance." . . .

This much said, we must also add that dissent is simply in error to suggest that the political realities reveal that the Comptroller General is free from influence by Congress. . . . Congress created the office because it believed that it "needed an officer, responsible to it alone, to check upon the application of public funds in accordance with appropriations." H. Mansfield, The Comptroller General: A Study in the Law and Practice of Financial Administration 65 (1939).

It is clear that Congress has consistently viewed the Comptroller General as an officer of the Legislative Branch. The Reorganization Acts of 1945 and 1949, for example, both stated that the Comptroller General and the GAO are "a part of the legislative branch of the Government." 59 Stat. 616; 63 Stat. 205. Similarly, in the Accounting and Auditing Act of 1950, Congress required the Comptroller General to conduct audits "as an agent of the Congress." 64 Stat. 835.

Over the years, the Comptrollers General have also viewed themselves as part of the Legislative Branch. In one of the early Annual Reports of Comptroller General, the official seal of his office was described as reflecting:

> "the independence of judgment to be exercised by the General Accounting Office, subject to the control of the legislative branch . . .
> The combination represents an agency of the Congress independent of other authority auditing and checking the expenditures of the Government as required by law and subjecting any questions arising in that connection to quasi-judicial determination." GAO Ann.Rep. 5–6 (1924).

Later, Comptroller General Warren, who had been a member of Congress for 15 years before being appointed Comptroller General, testified that: "During most of my public life, . . . I have been a member of the legislative branch. Even now, although heading a great agency, it is an agency of the Congress, and *I am an agent of the Congress.*" . . .

Against this background, we see no escape from the conclusion that, because Congress had retained removal authority over the Comptroller General, he may not be entrusted with executive powers. The remaining question is whether the Comptroller General has been assigned such powers in the Balanced Budget and Emergency Deficit Control Act of 1985.

V

. . . The primary responsibility of the Comptroller General under the instant Act is the preparation of a "report." . . .

In preparing the report, the Comptroller General is to have "due regard" for the estimates and reductions set forth in a joint report submitted to him by the Director of CBO and the Director of OMB, the President's fiscal and budgetary advisor. However, the Act plainly contemplates that the Comptroller General all will exercise his independent judgment and evaluation with respect to those estimates. . . .

[W]e view these functions as plainly entailing execution of the law in constitutional terms. Interpreting a law enacted by Congress to implement the legislative mandate is the very essence of "execution" of the law. . . .

The executive nature of the Comptroller General's functions under the Act is revealed in § 252(a)(3) which gives the Comptroller General the ultimate authority to determine the budget cuts to be made. Indeed, the Comptroller General commands the President himself to carry out, without the slightest variation (with exceptions not relevant to the constitutional issues presented) the directive of the Comptroller General. . . .

VII

No one can doubt that Congress and the President are confronted with fiscal and economic problems of unprecedented magnitude, but "the fact that a given law or procedure is efficient, convenient, and useful in facilitating functions of government, standing alone, will not save it if it is contrary to the Constitution. Convenience and efficiency are not the primary objectives — or the hallmarks — of democratic government. . . . " *Chadha, supra,* 462 U.S., at 944. . . .

We conclude the District Court correctly held that the powers vested in the Comptroller General under § 251 violate the command of the Constitution that the Congress play no direct role in the execution of the laws. Accordingly, the judgment and order of the District Court are affirmed.

Our judgment is stayed for a period not to exceed 60 days to permit Congress to implement the fall-back provisions.

Justice Stevens, with whom Justice Marshall joins, concurring in the judgment.

The fact that Congress retained for itself the power to remove the Comptroller General is important evidence supporting the conclusion that he is a member of the Legislative Branch of the Government. Unlike the Court, however, I am not persuaded that the congressional removal power is either a necessary, or a sufficient, basis for concluding that his statutory assignment is invalid.

As Justice White explains, . . . Congress does not have the power to remove the Comptroller General at will, or because of disagreement with any policy determination that he may be required to make in the administration of this, or any other, Act. The statute provides a term of 15 years for the Comptroller General; it further provides that he must retire upon becoming 70 years of age, and that he may be removed at any time by impeachment or by "joint resolution of Congress, after notice and an opportunity for a hearing, only for — (i) permanent disability; (ii) inefficiency; (iii) neglect of duty; (iv) malfeasance; or (v) a felony or conduct involving moral turpitude." 31 U.S.C. § 703(e)(1)(B). Far from assuming that this provision creates a " 'here-and-now subservience' " respecting all of the Comptroller General's actions, *ante,* at 3189, n. 5 (quoting District Court), we should presume that Congress will adhere to the law — that it would only exercise its removal powers if the Comptroller General were found to be permanently disabled, inefficient, neglectful, or culpable of malfeasance, a felony, or conduct involving moral turpitude.

The notion that the removal power at issue here automatically creates some kind of "here-and-now subservience" of the Comptroller General to Congress is belied by history. There is no evidence that Congress has ever removed, or threatened to remove, the Comptroller General for reasons of policy. Moreover, the President has long possessed a comparable power to remove members of the Federal Trade Commission, yet it is universally accepted that they are independent of, rather than subservient to, the President in performing their official duties. . . .

To be sure, there may be a significant separation of powers difference between the President's *exercise* of carefully circumscribed removal authority and Congress' *exercise* of identically circumscribed removal authority. But the *Humphrey's Executor* analysis at least demonstrates that it is entirely proper for Congress to specify the qualifications for an office it has created, and that the prescription of what might be termed "dereliction-of-duty" removal standards does not itself impair the independence of the official subject to such standards.

The fact that Congress retained for itself the power to remove the Comptroller General thus is not necessarily an adequate reason for concluding that his role in the Gramm-Rudman-Hollings budget reduction process is unconstitutional. It is, however, a fact that lends support to my ultimate conclusion that, in exercising his functions under this Act, he serves as an agent of the Congress.

I concur in the judgment.

Justice White, dissenting.

The Court, acting in the name of separation of powers, takes upon itself to strike down the Gramm-Rudman-Hollings Act, one of the most novel and far-reaching legislative responses to a national crisis since the New Deal. The basis of the Court's action is a solitary provision of another statute that was passed over sixty years ago and has lain dormant since that time. I cannot concur in the Court's action. . . . I will, address the wisdom of the Court's willingness to interpose its distressingly formalistic view of separation of powers as a bar to the attainment of governmental objectives through the means chosen by the

Congress and the President in the legislative process established by the Constitution. . . .

Before examining the merits of the Court's argument, I wish to emphasize what it is that the Court quite pointedly and correctly does *not* hold: namely, that "executive" powers of the sort granted the Comptroller by the Act may only be exercised by officers removable at will by the President. The Court's apparent unwillingness to accept this argument, which has been tendered in this Court by the Solicitor General, is fully consistent with the Court's longstanding recognition that it is within the power of Congress under the "Necessary and Proper" Clause, Art. 1, § 8, to vest authority that falls within the Court's definition of executive power in officers who are not subject to removal at will by the President and are therefore not under the President's direct control. See *e.g.*, *Humphrey's Executor v. United States*, 295 U.S. 602, . . . (1935); *Wiener v. United States*, 357 U.S. 349, . . . (1958). In an earlier day, in which simpler notions of the role of government in society prevailed, it was perhaps plausible to insist that all "executive" officers be subject to an unqualified presidential removal power, see *Myers v. United States*, 272 U.S. 52 . . . (1926); but with the advent and triumph of the administrative state and the accompanying multiplication of the tasks undertaken by the Federal Government, the Court has been virtually compelled to recognize that Congress may reasonably deem it "necessary and proper" to vest some among the broad new array of governmental functions in officers who are free from the partisanship that may be expected of agents wholly dependent upon the President.

The Court's recognition of the legitimacy of legislation vesting "executive" authority in officers independent of the President does not imply derogation of the President's own constitutional authority—indeed, duty—to "take Care that the Laws be faithfully executed," Art. II, § 3, for any such duty is necessarily limited to a great extent by the content of the laws enacted by the Congress. As Justice Holmes put it, "The duty of the President to see that the laws be executed is a duty that does not go beyond the laws or require him to achieve more than Congress sees fit to leave within his power." *Myers v. United States*,

272 U.S., at 177 . . . (Holmes, J., dissenting). Justice Holmes perhaps overstated his case, for there are undoubtedly executive functions that, regardless of the enactments of Congress, must be performed by officers subject to removal at will by the President. Whether a particular function falls within this class or within the far larger class that may be relegated to independent officers "will depend upon the character of the office." *Humphrey's Executor*, 295 U.S., at 631. . . .

It is evident (and nothing in the Court's opinion is to the contrary) that the powers exercised by the Comptroller General under the Gramm-Rudman Act are not such that vesting them in an officer not subject to removal at will by the President would in itself improperly interfere with Presidential powers. Determining the level of spending by the Federal Government is not by nature a function central either to the exercise of the President's enumerated powers or to his general duty to ensure execution of the laws; rather, appropriating funds is a peculiarly legislative function, and one expressly committed to Congress by Art. 1, § 9, which provides that "[n]o Money shall be drawn from the Treasury, but in Consequence of Appropriations made by Law." . . . Delegating the execution of this legislation—that is, the power to apply the Act's criteria and make the required calculations—to an officier independent of the President's will does not deprive the President of any power that he would otherwise have or that is essential to the performance of the duties of his office. Rather, the result of such a delegation, from a standpoint of the President, is no different from the result of more traditional forms of appropriation: under either system, the level of funds available to the Executive branch to carry out its duties is not within the President's discretionary control. . . .

. . . [T]he question remains whether, as the Court concludes, the fact that the officer to whom Congress has delegated the authority to implement the Act is removable by a joint resolution of Congress should require invalidation of the Act. . . . I cannot accept, . . . that the exercise of authority by an officer removable for cause by a joint resolution of Congress is analogous to the impermissible execution of the law by Congress itself, nor would I hold that the congressional role in the removal process renders the Comptroller an "agent" of the Congress, incapable of receiving "executive" power.

In *Buckley v. Valeo*, . . . the Court held that Congress could not reserve to itself the power to appoint members of the Federal Election Commission, a body exercising "executive" power. *Buckley*, however, was grounded on a textually based separation of powers argument whose central premise was that the Constitution requires that all "Officers of the United States" (defined as "all persons who can be said to hold an office under the government," . . . whose appointment is not otherwise specifically provided for elsewhere in its text be appointed through the means specified by the Appointments Clause, Art. II, § 2, cl. 2 — that is, either by the President with the advice and consent of the Senate or, if Congress so specifies, by the President alone, by the courts, or by the head of a department. The *Buckley* Court treated the Appointments Clause as reflecting the principle that "the Legislative Branch may not exercise executive authority," . . . but the Court's holding was merely that Congress may not direct that its laws be implemented through persons who are its agents in the sense that it chose them; the Court did not pass on the legitimacy of other means by which Congress might exercise authority over those who execute its laws. Because the Comptroller is not an appointee of Congress but an officer of the United States appointed by the President with the advice and consent of the Senate, *Buckley* neither requires that he be characterized as an agent of the Congress nor in any other way calls into question his capacity to exercise "executive" authority. . . .

The deficiencies in the Court's reasoning are apparent. First, the Court badly mischaracterizes the removal provision when it suggests that it allows Congress to remove the Comptroller for "executing the laws in any fashion found to be unsatisfactory"; in fact, Congress may remove the Comptroller only for one or more of five specified reasons, which "although not so narrow as to deny Congress any leeway, circumscribe Congress' power to some extent by providing a basis for judicial review of congressional removal."

Ameron, Inc. v. United States Army Corps of Engineers, 787 F.2d 875, 895 (CA3 1986) (Becker, J., concurring in part). Second, and more to the point, the Court overlooks or deliberately ignores the decisive difference between the congressional removal provision and the legislative veto struck down in *Chadha:* under the Budget and Accounting Act, Congress may remove the Comptroller only through a joint resolution, which by definition must be passed by both Houses and signed by the President. See *United States v. California,* 332 U.S. 19, . . . (1947). In other words, a removal of the Comptroller under the statute *satisfies the requirements of bicameralism and presentment laid down in Chadha.* The majority's citation of *Chadha* for the proposition that Congress may only control the acts of officers of the United States "by passing new legislation," *ante* at 3192, in no sense casts doubt on the legitimacy of the removal provision, for that provision allows Congress to effect removal only through action that constitutes legislation as defined in *Chadha.* . . .

The statute does not permit anyone to remove the Comptroller at will; removal is permitted only for specified cause, with the existence of cause to be determined by Congress following a hearing. Any removal under the statute would presumably be subject to post-termination judicial review to ensure that a hearing had in fact been held and that the finding of cause for removal was not arbitrary. . . . These procedural and substantive limitations on the removal power militate strongly against the characterization of the Comptroller as a mere agent of Congress by virtue of the removal authority. . . . Removal authority limited in such a manner is more properly viewed as motivating adherence to a substantive standard established by law than as inducing subservience to the particular institution that enforces that standard. . . .

More importantly, the substantial role played by the President in the process of removal through joint resolution reduces to utter insignificance the possibility that the threat of removal will induce subservience to the Congress. . . .

The practical result of the removal provision is not to render the Comptroller unduly dependent upon or subservient to Congress, but to render him one of the most independent officers in the entire federal establishment. Those who have studied the office agree that the procedural and substantive limits on the power of Congress and the President to remove the Comptroller make dislodging him against his will practically impossible. As one scholar put it nearly fifty years ago, "Under the statute the Comptroller General, once confirmed, is safe so long as he avoids a public exhibition of personal immortality, dishonesty, or failing mentality." H. Mansfield, The Comptroller General 75–76 (1939. The passage of time has done little to cast doubt on this view: of the six Comptrollers who have served since 1939, none has been threatened with, much less subjected to, removal. Recent students of the office concur that "[b]arring resignation, death, physical or mental incapacity, or extremely bad behavior, the Comptroller General is assured his tenure if he wants it, and not a day more." F. Mosher, The GAO 242 (1979). . . .

Realistic consideration of the nature of the Comptroller General's relation to Congress thus reveals that the threat to separation of powers conjured up by the majority is wholly chimerical. The power over removal retained by the Congress is not a power that is exercised outside the legislative process as established by the Constitution, nor does it appear likely that it is a power that adds significantly to the influence Congress may exert over executive officers through other, undoubtedly constitutional exercises of legislative power and through the constitutionally guaranteed impeachment power. . . .

The majority's contrary conclusion rests on the rigid dogma that, outside of the impeachment process, any "direct congressional role in the removal of officers charged with the execution of the laws . . . is inconsistent with separation of powers." Reliance on such an unyielding principle to strike down a statute posing no real danger of aggrandizement of congressional power is extremely misguided and insensitive to our constitutional role. The wisdom of vesting "executive" powers in an officer removable by joint resolution may indeed be debatable—as may be the wisdom of the entire scheme of permitting an unelected official to revise the budget enacted by Congress—but

such matters are for the most part to be worked out between the Congress and the President through the legislative process, which affords each branch ample opportunity to defend its interests. . . . [T]he role of this Court should be limited to determining whether the Act so alters the balance of authority among the branches of government as to pose a genuine threat to the basic division between the lawmaking power and the power to execute the law. Because I see no such threat, I cannot join the Court in striking down the Act.

I dissent.

Justice Blackmun, dissenting.

However wise or foolish it may be, that statute unquestionably ranks among the most important federal enactments of the past several decades. I cannot see the sense of invalidating legislation of this magnitude in order to preserve a cumbersome, 65-year-old removal power that has never been exercised and appears to have been all but forgotten until this litigation.

In the absence of express statutory direction, I think it is plain that, as both Houses urge, invalidating the Comptroller General's functions under the Deficit Control Act would frustrate congressional objectives far more seriously than would refusing to allow Congress to exercise its removal authority under the 1921 law. The majority suggests that the removal authority plays an important role furthering Congress' desire to keep the Comptroller General under its control. . . .

Indeed, there is a little evidence that Congress as a whole was very concerned in 1921—much less in 1985 or during the intervening decades—with its own ability to control the Comptroller General. The committee reports on the 1921 Act and its predecessor bills strongly suggest that what was critical to the legislators was not the Comptroller General's subservience to Congress, but rather his independence from the President. . . .

I do not claim that the 1921 removal provision is a piece of statutory deadwood utterly without contemporary significance. But it comes close. Rarely if ever invoked even for symbolic purposes, the removal provision certainly pales in importance be-side the legislative scheme the Court strikes down today—an extraordinarily far-reaching response to a deficit problem of unprecedented proportions.

Because I believe that the constitutional defect found by the Court cannot justify the remedy it has imposed, I respectfully dissent.

Exercises and Questions for Further Thought

1. Do you believe the Court's reasoning in *Industrial Union Department v. American Petroleum Institute* and *American Textile Manufactures Institute v. Donovan* differ? If so, how? Do you think Congress should have created more specific statutory instructions for the secretary?

2. Is Justice Marshall right when he says the Supreme Court's ruling in *Industrial Union Department v. American Petroleum Institute*, "flagrantly disregards . . . restrictions on judicial authority"? Is it fair to compare the Court's opinion in this case with the Court's perspective on regulation in *Lochner*? In his dissent, Justice Marshall suggests they are similar. Why? How "activist" do you think the conservative majorities were in *Lochner* and in the benzene case? Is Justice Marshall any less "activist"? For a description of the politics of OSHA see Charles Noble, *Liberalism at Work: the Rise and Fall of OSHA* (Philadelphia: Temple University Press, 1986).

3. Why do you think the Court in *Chevron v. Natural Resources Defense Council* supported the EPA's interpretation of the Clean Air Act Amendments? Compare the Court's reasoning in this case with the majority opinion in *Industrial Union Department v. American Petroleum Institute*.

4. Do the Supreme Court's interpretations of statutes discussed in this chapter adopt Theodore Lowi's proposal for "juridical democracy"? To what extent is Lowi's proposal a standard for statutory interpretation?

5. The Federal Trade Commission Act empowers the FTC to "prevent unfair methods of competition in commerce, and unfair or deceptive acts or practices in commerce." In 1971 the FTC published in the Federal Register a "trade regulation rule" announcing that failure to post octane ratings of gasoline on gasoline pumps at service stations was an unfair method of competition and an unfair and deceptive act or practice under the statute. Do you think the statute delegated authority to the FTC to announce such a specific rule? See *National Petroleum Refiners Association v. Federal Trade Commission*, 482 F.2d 672 (1973), for the opinion. Since you have presumably noticed the stickers announcing octane ratings today on most pumps, you know how the case came out. The word *prevent* is the key statutory word here. Why? Would you reach a similar result if the CAB started setting air fares by rule?

6. An act of Congress states that "the Secretary of State may grant and issue passports . . . under such rules as the President shall designate and prescribe for and on behalf of the United States. . . . " Mr. Rockwell Kent sought but failed to obtain a passport under a regulation duly issued by the secretary of state which stated that passports would be denied to Communists and to those whose travel might advance the Communist movement. Is this statute an unconstitutional delegation of legislative power? Kent brought his objection to the Supreme Court, which in 1958 held 5–4, that the

secretary wrongfully withheld the passport. The Court did *not* find the delegation unconstitutional. What other legal reason do you suppose the Court did give for reaching this result? See *Kent v. Dulles*, 357 U.S. 116 (1958).

7. In recent year scientists have debated heatedly the potential dangers that may lurk in the new field of genetic engineering. The National Institute of Health, a federal agency, his proposed regulating and thus limiting recombinant DNA research. Would doing so violate the First Amendment's protections of free expression?[23]

8. The Office of Information and Regulatory Affairs (OIRA) was created as part of the Paperwork Reduction Act of 1980 (PL 96-551). "Under executive orders issued by President Reagan in 1981 and 1983, OIRA reviewed all major regulatory actions of other federal agencies to ensure that they met administration guidelines for cost effectiveness. Its reviews in many instances led to substantial revisions in health and environmental regulations."[24] Witnesses from OSHA testified under subpoena before the Senate Labor and Human Resources Committee in 1988 that OMB had interfered with formaldehyde health standards limiting employer responsibility and delayed standards for viruses, such as hepatitis B and AIDS."[25]

These are just a few examples of political influence in the administrative process. Consider Jaffe's discussion of the New Deal and these more recent instances of partisanship in administration. How influential should presidents be in the formulation of administrative policy?

[23] See Ira Carmen, "The Constitution in the Laboratory," *Journal of Politics* 43 (1981): 737, and Richard Delgado and David Miller, "God, Galileo and Government," *Washington Law Review* 53 (1978): 363.

[24] *Congressional Quarterly Almanac* 42, 1983: 26.

[25] *Congressional Quarterly Weekly Report*, vol. 46 no. 17, 23 April 23, 1988, p. 1109.

CHAPTER 4

Information and Administration

Once Congress creates an agency and expresses its responsibilities in a statute, the agency must begin to gain power over the environment it seeks to influence. Knowledge is power, says the adage. This chapter reviews some of the more common methods government officials use to gain power over their environment by getting information about it. However, the adage cuts two ways. The concept of limited government at least implies that citizens need information about government operations before they can check its power. Administrative law therefore includes statutory policies concerning information itself. These policies prescribe methods of investigation and compulsion of testimony to get information into government hands. At the same time, through sunshine laws (laws requiring political decisions to be made in public) and freedom of information statutes, they channel information to the governed.

Investigations

Most government information is acquired from the regulated industries themselves or the individuals who receive government benefits. Regulators talk to the regulated in order to learn about what they are doing. For example, the government collects information on industrial practices and keeps records on the medical status of people receiving Medicare. Sometimes information is communicated in an informal manner and on a voluntary basis. At other points in the regulatory process, the submission of written materials may be required. Regulators mix with the regulated in order to know enough to make short-term decisions and long-range policies. Herein lie potential sources of conflict. Does the government depend too heavily on those whom it is supposed to be regulating? In the process of giving information to the government are trade secrets jeopardized?[1] To what extent do individuals incriminate themselves when they provide the government with information?

The basic rules for administrative investigations have the same constitutional origins as do the more familiar rules governing police searches, seizures, and interrogations. The Fourth Amendment prohibits "unreasonable searches and seizures," and the Fifth Amendment prohibits government from compelling people to give evidence against themselves. In one of the earlier cases on the subject, *FTC v. American Tobacco Co.,*

---

[1] See *Ruckelshaus, Administrator, U.S. EPA v. Monsanto Co.,* 467 U.S. 986 (1984).

the Supreme Court denied to the commission broad "fishing expedition" powers.[2] The FTC had ordered two tobacco companies to produce "all letters and telegrams received by the Company from, or sent by it to, all of its" customers throughout the year 1921. The agency had no specific knowledge that the papers would reveal evidence of wrong-doing. The Court's opinion held that the Fourth Amendment prohibited the government from forcing a business at any time to produce anything merely on the suspicion that this might reveal something amiss. Speaking for the Court, Justice Holmes referred to such acts on the part of agencies as "fishing expeditions" in violation of the constitutional protection against "unreasonable searches and seizures."

There are, however, important differences between a police search, triggered by a reported crime and the possibility of the search leading to criminal arrest, and an administrative investigation, which may have a fundamentally cooperative objective. Thus the inspection of a meatpacking plant's sanitary and safety conditions is not done to send the packers to jail for a violation but rather, at least initially, to suggest steps the packer must take to improve sanitation and safety. The Internal Revenue Service audit, though it contains many anxious and aggravating moments, rarely produces a civil or criminal charge. It merely requires the taxpayer to document and support the claims on the tax return and to pay up when his documentation fails.

Because of these differences, courts have backed away from *American Tobacco's* implication that the strict rules of criminal investigation cover agencies. Businesses are not specifically protected by the Fifth Amendment's self-incrimination provisions regarding, for example, allegations of unfair labor practices.[3] Regarding the entry of government officials onto private property without permission or warrant, however, the Fourth Amendment influence remains fairly strong.

On-site inspections authorized by law cover hundreds of kinds of business operations. City housing inspectors may seek to enter an apartment building to see if the number of tenants exceeds the maximum permitted by the building's occupancy permit. Firefighters need to inspect schools and office buildings to assure compliance with fire codes. Welfare officials may want to visit the homes of welfare recipients to see if those drawing welfare checks actually live in poverty. The two cases reported next bring you up to date on the law of administrative inspections.

Wyman v. James

400 U.S. 309 (1971) 6–3
+ Burger, Black, Harlan, Stewart, White, Blackmun
- Douglas, Brennan, Marshall

[James had, two years in the past, applied for and received Aid for Dependent Children (AFDC) for her son and herself. It was the policy (based on statute) of the New York Department of Social Services to have a caseworker visit the homes of the AFDC

[2] 264 U.S. 298 (1924).

[3] *Oklahoma Press Co. v. Walling,* 327 U.S. 186 (1946).

recipients to make determinations about the continued eligibility of the recipient and about the need for other available services. Upon being informed by mail of an impending visit, James notified the department that she would provide information, but would not allow a home visit. In a pretermination hearing, James and her attorney reiterated their stand. A notice of termination was subsequently issued. James brought suit to continue her eligibility on the Fourth Amendment grounds that a home visit is a search without a warrant. She prevailed in the lower courts. Please note the special meaning of the word *reasonable* in the context of search and seizure law. It is not simply a synonym for *rationality*.]

Justice Blackmun delivered the opinion of the Court.

When a case involves a home and some type of official intrusion into that home, as this case appears to do, an immediate and natural reaction is one of concern about Fourth Amendment rights and the protection which that Amendment is intended to afford. Its emphasis indeed is upon one of the most precious aspects of personal security in the home: "The right of the people to be secure in their persons, houses, papers, and effects. . . ." This Court has characterized that right as "basic to a free society." . . .

In *Camara* Mr Justice White, after noting that the "translation of the abstract prohibition against 'unreasonable searches and seizures' into workable guidelines for the decision of particular cases is a difficult task," went on to observe: "Nevertheless, one governing principle, justified by history and by current experience, has consistently been followed: except in certain carefully defined classes of cases, a search of private property without proper consent is 'unreasonable' unless it has been authorized by a valid search warrant." 387 U.S., at 528–529.

If . . . we were to assume that a caseworker's home visit, before or subsequent to the beneficiary's initial qualification for benefits, somehow (perhaps because the average beneficiary might feel she is in no position to refuse consent to the visit), and despite its interview nature, does possess some of the characteristics of a search in the traditional sense, we nevertheless conclude that the visit does not fall within the Fourth Amendment's proscription. This is because it does not descend to the level of unreasonableness. It is unreasonableness which is the Fourth Amendment's standard. . . .

There are a number of factors that compel us to conclude that the home visit proposed for Mrs. James is not unreasonable:

1. The public's interest in this particular segment of the area of assistance to the unfortunate is protection and aid for the dependent child whose family requires such aid for that child. The focus is on the *child* and, further, it is on the child who is *dependent*. There is no more worthy object of the public's concern. . . .

2. The agency, with tax funds provided from federal as well as from state sources, is fulfilling a public trust. The State, working through its qualified welfare agency, has appropriate and paramount interest and concern in seeing and assuring that the intended and proper objects of that tax-produced assistance are the ones who benefit from the aid it dispenses. . . .

3. One who dispenses purely private charity naturally has an interest in and expects to know how his charitable funds are utilized and put to work. The public, when it is the provider, rightly expects the same. It might well expect more, because of the trust aspect of public funds, and the recipient, as well as the caseworker, has not only an interest but an obligation.

4. The emphasis of the New York statutes and regulations is upon the home, upon "close contact" with the beneficiary, upon restoring the aid recipient "to a condition of self-support," and upon the relief of his distress. The federal emphasis is no different. It is upon "assistance and rehabilitation," upon maintaining and strengthening family life, and upon "maximum self-support and personal independence

consistent with the maintenance of continuing parental care and protection" . . .

5. The home visit, it is true, is not required by federal statute or regulation. But it has been noted that the visit is "the heart of welfare administration"; that it affords "a personal, rehabilitative orientation, unlike that of most federal programs"; and that the "more pronounced service orientation" effected by Congress with the 1956 amendments to the Social Security Act "gave redoubled importance to the practice of home visiting." Note, Rehabilitation, Investigation and Welfare Home Visit, 79 Yale L.J. 746, 748 (1970). The home visit is an established routine in states besides New York.

6. The means employed by the New York agency are significant. Mrs. James received written notice several days in advance of the intended home visit. The date was specified. Section 134a of the New York Social Services Law, effective April, 1967, . . . sets the . . . tone. Privacy is emphasized. The applicant-recipient is made the primary source of information as to eligibility. Outside informational sources, other than public records, are to be consulted only with the beneficiary's consent. Forcible entry or entry under false pretenses or visitation outside working hours or snooping in the home are forbidden. . . .

7. Mrs. James, in fact, on this record presents no specific complaint of any unreasonable intrusion of her home and nothing that supports an inference that the desired home visit had as its purpose the obtaining of information as to criminal activity. She complains of no proposed visitation at an awkward or retirement hour. She suggest no forcible entry. She refers to no snooping. She describes no impolite or reprehensible conduct of any kind. She alleges only, in general and nonspecific terms, that on previous visits and, on information and belief, on visitation at the home of other aid recipients, "questions concerning personal relationships, beliefs and behavior are raised and pressed which are unnecessary for a determination of continuing eligibility." Paradoxically, this same complaint could be made of a conference held elsewhere than in the home, and yet this is what is sought by Mrs. James. . . .

8. We are not persuaded, as Mrs. James would have us be, that all information pertinent to the issue of eligibility can be obtained by the agency through an interview at a place other than the home, or as the District Court majority suggested, by examining a lease or a birth certificate, or by periodic medical examinations, or by interviews with school personnel. . . .

9. The visit is not one by police or uniformed authority. It is made by a caseworker of some training whose primary objective is, or should be, the welfare, not the prosecution, of the aid recipient for whom the worker has profound responsibility. . . .

10. The home visit is not a criminal investigation, does not equate with a criminal investigation, and despite the announced fears of Mrs. James and those who would join her, is not in aid of any criminal proceeding. If the visitation serves to discourage misrepresentation of fraud, such a byproduct of that visit does not impress upon the visit itself a dominant criminal investigative aspect. And if the visit should, by chance, lead to the discovery of fraud and a criminal prosecution should follow, then, even assuming that the evidence discovered upon the home visitation is admissible, an issue upon which we express no opinion, that is a routine and expected fact of life and a consequence no greater than that which necessarily ensues upon any other discovery by a citizen of criminal conduct. . . .

It seems to us that the situation is akin to that where an Internal Revenue Service agent, in making a routine civil audit of a taxpayer's income tax return, asks that the taxpayer produce for the agent's review some proof of a deduction the taxpayer has asserted to his benefit in the computation of his tax. If the taxpayer refuses, there is, absent fraud, only a disallowance of the claimed deduction and a consequent additional tax. The taxpayer is fully within his "rights" in refusing to produce the proof, but in maintaining and asserting those rights a tax detriment results and it is a detriment of the taxpayer's own making. So here Mrs James has the "right" to refuse the home visit, but a consequence in the form of cessation of aid, similar to the taxpayer's resultant additional tax, flows from the refusal. The choice is entirely hers, and nothing of constitutional magnitude is involved.

Camara v. Municipal Court, 387 U.S. 523 (1967) and its companion case, *See v. City of Seattle*, 387 U.S. 541 (1967), both by a divided Court, are not inconsistent with our result here. Those cases concerned, respectively, a refusal of entry to city housing inspectors checking for a violation of a building's occupancy permit, and a refusal of entry to a fire department representative interested in compliance with a city's fire code. In each case a majority of this Court held that the Fourth Amendment barred prosecution for refusal to permit the desired warrantless inspection. *Frank v. Maryland*, 359 U.S. 360 (1959), a case that reached an opposing result and that concerned a request by a health officer for entry in order to check the source of rat infestation, was *pro tanto* overruled. Both *Frank* and *Camara* involved dwelling quarters. *See* had to do with a commercial warehouse.

But the facts of the three cases are significantly different from those before us. Each concerned a true search for violations. *Frank* was a criminal prosecution for the owner's refusal to permit entry. So, too, was *See*. *Camara* had to do with a writ of prohibition sought to prevent an already pending criminal prosecution. The community welfare aspects, of course, were highly important, but each case arose in a criminal context where a genuine search was denied and prosecution followed.

In contrast, Mrs. James is not being prosecuted for her refusal to permit the home visit and is not about to be so prosecuted. . . . The only consequence of her refusal in that the payment of benefits ceases. Important and serious as this is, the situation is no different than if she had exercised a similar negative choice initially and refrained from applying for AFDC benefits.

Reversed. . . .

Justice Douglas, dissenting.

. . . [T]he right of privacy which the Fourth protects is perhaps as vivid in our lives as the rights of expression sponsored by the First. If the regime under which Barbara James lives were enterprise capitalism as, for example, if she ran a small factory geared into the Pentagon's procurement program, she certainly would have a right to deny inspectors access to her home unless they came with a warrant.

Is a search of her home without a warrant made "reasonable" merely because she is dependent on government largesse?

Judge Skelly Wright has stated the problem succinctly:

> Welfare has long been considered the equivalent of charity and its recipients have been subjected to all kinds of dehumanizing experiences in the government's effort to police its welfare payments. In fact, over half a billion dollars are expended annually for administration and policing in connection with the Aid to Families with Dependent Children program. Why such large sums are necessary for administration and policing has never been adequately explained. No such sums are spent policing for the government subsidies granted to farmers, airlines, steamship companies, and junk mail dealers, to name but a few. The truth is that in this subsidy area society has simply adopted a double standard, one for aid to business and the farmer and a different one for welfare. Poverty, Minorities, and Respect for Law, 1970 Duke L.J. 425, 437–438.

If the welfare recipient was not Barbara James but a prominent, affluent cotton or wheat farmer receiving benefit payments for not growing crops, would not the approach be different? Welfare in aid of dependent children, like social security and unemployment benefits, has an aura of suspicion. There doubtless are frauds in every sector of public welfare whether the recipient be a Barbara James or someone who is prominent or influential. But constitutional rights—here the privacy of the *home*—are obviously not dependent on the poverty or on the affluence of the beneficiary. . . .

It may be that in some tenements one baby will do service to several women and call each one "mom."

It may be that other frauds, less obvious, will be perpetrated. But if inspectors want to enter the precincts of the home against the wishes of the lady of the house, they must get a warrant. The need for exigent action as in cases of "hot pursuit" is not present for the lady will not disappear; nor will the baby.

I would place the same restrictions on inspectors entering the *homes* of welfare beneficiaries as are on inspectors entering the *homes* of those on the payroll of government, or the *homes* of those who contract with the government, or the *homes* of those who work for those having government contracts. The values of the *home* protected by the Fourth Amendment are not peculiar to capitalism as we have known it; they are equally relevant to the new form of socialism which we are entering. Moreover, as the numbers of functionaries and inspectors multiply, the need for protection of the individual becomes indeed more essential if the values of a free society are to remain.

What Lord Acton wrote Bishop Creighton about the corruption of power is increasingly pertinent today: "I cannot accept your canon that we are to judge Pope and King unlike other men, with a favourable presumption that they did no wrong. If there is any presumption it is the other way against holders of power, increasing as the power increases. Historic responsibility has to make up for the want of legal responsibility. Power tends to corrupt and absolute power corrupts absolutely. Great men are almost always bad men, even when they exercise influence and not authority: still more when you superadd the tendency or the certainty of corruption by authority."

The bureaucracy of modern government is not only slow, lumbering, and oppressive; it is omnipresent. It touches everyone's life at numerous points. It pries more and more into private affairs, breaking down the barriers that individuals erect to give them some insulation from the intrigues and harassments of modern life. Isolation is not a constitutional guarantee; but the sancity of the sanctuary of the *home* is such—as marked and defined by the Fourth Amendment, *McDonald v. United States*, 335 U.S. 451, 453. What we do today is to depreciate it.

I would sustain the judgement of the three-judge court in the present case.

Prior to the decision in *Wyman* the Court had moved to narrow the range of permissible warrantless inspections. Note that *Frank*, *Camara*, and *See* all involved some form of criminal prosecution for refusal. In *Wyman* the private citizen did not run the risk of prosecution merely for refusing entry, and in this case the court approves a warrantless inspection. Ask yourself whether this distinction is so important. What if the inspection uncovers evidence of a regulatory violation or of some unambiguously criminal behavior? Are the inspectors forbidden from acting on what they see or reporting it to others?

In the next case, *Marshall v. Barlow's Inc.* (1978), the Court addresses the issue of whether OSHA may carry out warrantless searches of private businesses. The Court rules against OSHA and in so doing further narrows the authority of administrative agencies to carry out certain types of warrantless searches. After reading *Marshall*, compare how the Court treats Fourth Amendment issues in the context of inspecting business premises versus a welfare recipient's home. Why is the state's authority greater in the area of welfare regulation? Should businesses be subject to on-site inspections without notice or warrants in order to protect the safety and health of the workers they employ?

Marshall v. Barlow's Inc.

436 U. S. 307 (1978) 5–3
+ Burger, Stewart, White, Marshall, Powell
– Blackmun, Rehnquist, Stevens
NP Brennan

[The Occupational Safety and Health Act of 1970 empowers agency officials to carry out warrantless searches of the work area of any employment facility within OSHA's jurisdiction for safety hazards and violations of OSHA regulation. An OSHA inspector went to the customer service area of Barlow's Inc., an electrical and plumbing company in Pocatello, Idaho, and informed the president and general manager that their company had "turned up in the agency's selection process." Although no specific complaint had been received by OSHA indicating that Barlow's Inc. had violated OSHA regulations, the inspector asked to enter the business area. After Mr. Barlow refused OSHA's request, a federal district court ordered that Barlow admit the inspector. Barlow refused OSHA entry and sought injunctive relief againt the warrantless search.]

Justice White delivered the opinion of the Court.

I

The Secretary urges that warrantless inspections to enforce OSHA are reasonable within the meaning of the Fourth Amendment. Among other things, he relies on § 8 (a) of the Act, 29 U. S. C. § 657 (a), which authorizes inspection of business premises without a warrant and which the Secretary urges represents a congressional construction of the Fourth Amendment that the courts should not reject. Regrettably, we are unable to agree.

The Warrant Clause of the Fourth Amendment protects commercial buildings as well as private homes. To hold otherwise would belie the origin of that Amendment, and the American colonial experience. An important forerunner of the first 10 Amendments to the United States Constitution, the Virginia Bill of Rights, specifically opposed "general warrants, whereby an officer or messenger may be commanded to search suspected places without evidence of a fact committed." The general warrant was a recurring point of contention in the Colonies immediately preceding the Revolution. The particular offensiveness it engendered was acutely felt by the merchants and businessmen whose premises and products were in spected for compliance with the several parliamentary revenue measures that most irritated the colonists. . . .

This Court has already held that warrantless searches are generally unreasonable, and that this rule applies to commercial premises as well as homes. In *Camara v. Municipal Court*, 387 U. S. 523 (1967), we held: "[E]xcept in certain carefully defined classes of cases, a search of private property without proper consent is 'unreasonable' unless it has been authorized by a valid search warrant."

On the same day, we also ruled: "As we explained in *Camara*, a search of private houses is presumptively unreasonable if conducted without a warrant. The businessman, like the occupant of a residence, has a constitutional right to go about his business free from unreasonable official entries upon his private commercial property. The businessman, too, has that right placed in jeopardy if the decision to enter and inspect for violation of regulatory laws can be made and enforced by the inspector in the field without official authority evidenced by a warrant." *See v. City of Seattle*, 387 U.S. 541 (1967).

These same cases also held that the Fourth Amendment prohibition against unreasonable searches protects against warrantless intrusions during civil as well as criminal investigations. . . . The reason is found in the "basic purpose of this Amendment . . . [which] is to safeguard the privacy and security of individuals against arbitrary invasions by governmental officials." *Camara, supra,* at 528. If the government intrudes on a person's property, the privacy interest suffers whether the government's motivation is to investigate violations of criminal laws or breaches of other statutory or regulatory standards. It therefore appears that unless some recognized exception to the warrant requirement applies, *See* v. *Seattle* would require a warrant to conduct the inspection sought in this case.

The Secretary urges that an exception from the search warrant requirement has been recognized for "pervasively regulated business[es]," *United States v. Biswell,* 406 U. S. 311, 316 (1972), and for "closely regulated" industries "long subject to close supervision and inspection." *Colonnade Catering Corp. v. United States,* 397 U. S. 72, 74, 77 (1970). These cases are indeed exceptions, but they represent responses to relatively unique circumstances. Certain industries have such a history of government oversight that no reasonable expectation of privacy, see *Katz v. United States,* 389 U. S. 347, 351–352 (1967), could exist for a proprietor over the stock of such an enterprise. Liquor *(Colonnade)* and firearms *(Biswell)* are industries of this type; when an entrepreneur embarks upon such a business, he has voluntarily chosen to subject himself to a full arsenal of governmental regulation.

. . . "A central difference between those cases [*Colonnade* and *Biswell*] and this one is that businessmen engaged in such federally licensed and regulated enterprises accept the burdens as well as the benefits of their trade, whereas the petitioner here was not engaged in any regulated or licensed business. The businessman in a regulated industry in effect consents to the restrictions placed upon him." *Almeida-Sanchez v. United States,* 413 U. S. 266, 271 (1973). . . .

[T]he Secretary attempts to support a conclusion that all businesses involved in interstate commerce have long been subjected to close supervision of employee safety and health conditions. But the degree of federal involvement in employee working circumstances has never been of the order of specificity and pervasiveness that OSHA mandates. It is quite un-

convincing to argue that the imposition of minimum wages and maximum hours on employers who contracted with the Government . . . prepared the entirety of American interstate commerce for regulation of working conditions to the minutest detail. Nor can any but the most fictional sense of voluntary consent to later searches be found in the single fact that one conducts a business affecting interstate commerce; under current practice and law, few businesses can be conducted without having some effect on interstate commerce. . . .

The critical fact in this case is that entry over Mr. Barlow's objection is begin sought by a Government agent. Employees are not being prohibited from reporting OSHA violations. What they observe in their daily functions is undoubtedly beyond the employer's reasonable expectation of privacy. The Government inspector, however, is not an employee. Without a warrant he stands in no better position than a member of the public. What is observable by the public is observable, without a warrant, by the Government inspector as well. The owner of a business has not, by the necessary utilization of employees in his operation, thrown open the areas where employees alone are permitted to the warrantless scrutiny of Government agents. That an employee is free to report, and the Government is free to use, any evidence of noncompliace with OSHA that the employee observes furnishes no justification for federal agents to enter a place of business from which the public is restricted and to conduct their own warrantless search.

II

. . . Because "reasonableness is still the ultimate standard," *Camara v. Municipal Court,* . . . the Secretary suggests that the Court decide whether a warrant is needed by arriving at a sensible balance between the administrative necessities of OSHA inspections and the incremental protection of privacy of business owners a warrant would afford. . . .

The Secretary submits that warrantless inspections are essential to the proper enforcement of OSHA because they afford the opportunity to inspect without prior notice and hence to preserve the advantages of surprise. While the dangerous conditions outlawed by the Act include strutural defects that cannot be quickly hidden or remedied, the Act also regulates a myriad of safety details that may be amenable to speedy alteration or disguise. The risk is that during the interval between an inspector's initial request to search a plant and his procuring a warrant following the owner's refusal of permission, violations of this latter type could be corrected and thus escape the inspector's notice. . . .

We are unconvinced, however, that requiring warrants to inspect will impose serious burdens on the inspection system or the courts, will prevent inspections necessary to enforce the statute, or will make them less effective. In the first place, the great majority of businessmen can be expected in normal course to consent to inspection without warrant; the Secretary has not brought to this Court's attention any widespread pattern of refusal. . . .

Whether the Secretary proceeds to secure a warrant or other process, with or without prior notice, his entitlement to inspect will not depend on his demonstrating probable cause to believe that conditions in violation of OSHA exist on the premises. Probable cause in the criminal law sense is not required. For purposes of an administrative search such as this, probable cause justifying the issuance of a warrant may be based not only on specific evidence of an existing violation but also on a showing that "reasonable legislative or administrative standards for conducting an . . . inspection are satisfied with respect to a particular [establishment]." *Camara v Municipal Court.* A warrant showing that a specific business has been chosen for an OSHA search on the basis of a general administrative plan for the enforcement of the Act derived from neutral sources such as, for example, dispersion of employees in various types of industries across a given area, and the desired frequency of searches in any of the lesser divisions of the area, would protect an employer's Fourth Amendment rights. We doubt that the consumption of enforcement energies in the obtaining of such warrants will exceed manageable proportions.

Nor do we agree that the incremental protections afforded the employer's privacy by a warrant are so

marginal that they fail to justify the administrative burdens that may be entailed. The authority to make warrantless searches devolves almost unbridled discretion upon executive and administrative officers, particularly those in the field, as to when to search and whom to search. A warrant, by contrast, would provide assurances from a neutral officer that the inspection is reasonable under the Constitution, is authorized by statute, and is pursuant to an administrative plan containing specific neutral criteria. . . . These are important functions for a warrant to perform, functions which underlie the Court's prior decisions that the Warrant Clause applies to inspections for compliance with regulatory statutes. . . .

III

We hold that Barlow's was entitled to a declaratory judgement that the Act is unconstitutional insofar as it purports to authorize inspections without warrant or its equivalent and to an injunction enjoining the Act's enforcement to that extent. The judgment of the District Court is therefore affirmed.

So ordered.

Justice Stevens with whom Justice Blackmun and Justice Rehnquist join, dissenting.

The Fourth Amendment contains two separate Clauses, each flatly prohibiting a category of governmental conduct. . . .

In cases involving the investigation of criminal activity, the Court has held that the reasonableness of a search generally depends upon whether it was conducted pursuant to a valid warrant. . . . There is, however, also a category of searches which are reasonable within the meaning of the first Clause even though the probable-cause requirement of the Warrant Clause cannot be satisfied. . . . The regulatory inspection program challenged in this case, in my judgement, falls within this category.

 . . . The routine OSHA inspections are, by definition, not based on cause to believe there is a violation on the premises to be inspected. Hence, if the inspections were measured against the requirements of the Warrant Clause, they would be automatically and unequivocally unreasonable.

The Court's approach disregards the plain language of the Warrant Clause and is unfaithful to the balance struck by the Framers of the Fourth Amendment— "the one procedural safeguard in the Constitution that grew directly out of the events which immediately preceded the revolutionary struggle with England." This preconstitutional history includes the controversy in England over the issuance of general warrants to aid enforcement of the seditious libel laws and the colonial experience with writs of assistance issued to facilitate collection of the various import duties imposed by Parliament. The Framers' familiarity with the abuses attending the issuance of such general warrants provided the principal stimulus for the restraints on arbitrary governmental intrusions embodied in the Fourth Amendment.

Fidelity to the orginal understanding of the Fourth Amendment, therefore, leads to the conclusion that the Warrant Clause has no application to routine, regulatory inspections of commercial premises. If such inspections are valid, it is because they comport with the ultimate reasonableness standard of the Fourth Amendment. . . .

Even if a warrant issued without probable cause were faithful to the Warrant Clause, I could not accept the Court's holding that the Government's inspection program is constitutionally unreasonable because it fails to require such a warrant procedure. In determining whether a warrant is a necessary safeguard in a given class of cases, "the Court has weighed the public interest against the Fourth Amendment interest of the individual . . . " *United States v. Martinez-Fuerte*, 428 U. S., at 555. Several considerations persuade me that this balance should be struck in favor of the routine inspections authorized by Congress.

Congress has determined that regulation and supervision of safety in the workplace furthers an important public interest and that the power to conduct warrantless searches is necessary to accomplish the safety goals of the legislation. In assessing the public interest side of the Fourth Amendment balance, however, the Court today substitutes its judgement for that of Congress on the question of what inspection authority is needed to effectuate the purposes of the Act. . . .

The Court's analysis does not persuade me that Congress' determination that the warrantless-inspection power as a necessary adjunct of the exercise of the regulatory power is unreasonable. It was surely not unreasonable to conclude that the rate at which employers deny entry to inspectors would increase if covered businesses, which may have safety violations on their premises, have a right to deny warrantless entry to a compliance inspector. . . . [E]ven if it were true that many employers would not exercise their right to demand a warrant, it would provide little solace to those charged with administration of OSHA; faced with an increase in the rate of refusals and the added costs generated by futile trips to inspection sites where entry is denied, officials may be compelled to adopt a general practice of obtaining warrants in advance. . . .

Finally, the Court would distinguish the respect accorded Congress' judgement in *Colonnade* and *Biswell* on the ground that businesses engaged in the liquor and firearms industry " 'accept the burdens as well as the benefits of their trade. . . . ' " In the Court's view, such businesses consent to the restrictions placed upon them, while it would be fiction to conclude that a businessman subject to OSHA consented to routine safety inspection. In fact, however, consent is fictional in both contexts. Here, as well as in *Biswell*, businesses are required to be aware of and comply with regulations governing their business activities. In both situations, the validity of the regulations depends not upon the consent of those regulated, but on the existence of a federal statute embodying a congressional determination that the public interest in the health of the Nation's work force or the limitation of illegal firearms traffic outweighs the businessman's interest in preventing a Government inspector from viewing those areas of his premises which relate to the subject matter of the regulation. . . .

I respectfully dissent.

The courts have held that evidence illegally obtained by officials may not be used in criminal proceedings. This is called the *exclusionary rule*. Since the 1960s, when the Supreme Court applied the exclusionary rule to state criminal procedures in *Mapp v. Ohio*[4] and *Miranda v. Arizona*,[5] there have been a number of significant exceptions to the rule, thus allowing the admission of evidence obtained without a search warrant in certain instances. These developments bother civil libertarians, who argue that together the exceptions have substantially eroded the general principle and led to the denial of Fourth Amendment protections. Political conservatives, on the other hand, argue that exceptions are desirable to give law enforcement officials the flexibility they need in apprehending criminal suspects.

In the field of administrative law, the question of what evidence can be obtained and used for purposes of enforcing regulatory rules is equally controversial. The next two cases provide you with a background on the constitutional issues surrounding the gathering of evidence by inspectors. These cases also demonstrate how divided the Supreme Court is over the question of applying the exclusionary rule to administrative proceedings.

Immigration and Naturalization Service v. Lopez-Mendoza et al.

468 U.S. 1032 (19984) 5–4

+ O'Connor, Burger, Blackmun, Powell, Rehnquist
− Brennan, White, Marshall, Stevens

[The question in this case is whether evidence obtained during an unlawful arrest can be used in a civil deportation hearing. INS agents arrested Adan Lopez-Mendoza in 1976 at a transmission repair shop in San Mateo, California, where he worked. The INS agents did not have a warrant to search the premise or to arrest any individuals. Over the objection of the proprietor, the agents spoke with Lopez-Mendoza. He gave his name, said he was from Mexico, and indicated that he did not have close ties in the United States. The agents arrested him and initiated deportation proceedings against him. Another worker, Sandoval-Sanchez, was also arrested on the premises. At the deportation hearing Sandoval-Sanchez contended that he was not aware that he had a right to remain silent. The immigration judge found both individuals deportable and ruled that the legality of the arrests was not relevant to a deportation proceedings. Lopez-Mendoza and Sandoval-Sanchez appealed the ruling to the Ninth Circuit Court of Appeals, which vacated the orders of deportation and remanded the case to a lower court for determination of whether their Fourth Amendment rights had been violated by the arrest and whether the evidence obtained was admissible in the deportation proceeding.]

[4]367 U.S. 643 (1961).

[5]384 U.S. 436 (1966).

Justice O'Connor announced the judgement of the Court and delivered the opinion of the Court.

II

A deportation proceeding is a purely civil action to determine eligibility to remain in this country, not to punish an unlawful entry, though entering or remaining unlawfully in this country is itself a crime. . . . The deportation hearing looks prospectively to the respondent's right to remain in this country in the future. Past conduct is relevant only insofar as it may shed light on the respondent's right to remain. . . .

A deportation hearing is held before an immigration judge. The judge's sole power is to order deportation; the judge cannot adjudicate guilt or punish the respondent for any crime related to unlawful entry into or presence in this country. Consistent with the civil nature of the proceeding, various protections that apply in the context of a criminal trial do not apply in a deportation hearing. The respondent must be given "a reasonable opportunity to be present at [the] proceeding," but if the respondent fails to avail himself of that opportunity the hearing may proceed in his absence. . . . In many deportation cases the INS must show only identity and alienage; the burden then shifts to respondent to prove the time, place, and manner of his entry. . . . A decision of deportability need be based only on "reasonable, substantial, and probative evidence." . . . required only "clear, unequivocal and convincing" evidence of the respondent's deportability, not proof beyond a reasonable doubt. . . . In short, a deportation hearing is intended to provide a streamlined determination of eligibility to remain in this country, nothing more. The purpose of deportation is not to punish past transgressions but rather to put an end to a continuing violation of the immigration laws.

III

The "body" or identity of a defendant or respondent in a criminal or civil proceeding is never itself suppressible as a fruit of an unlawful arrest, even if it is conceded that an unlawful arrest, search, or interrogation occurred. See *Gerstein v. Pugh,* 420 U.

S. 103, 119 (1975). . . . A similar rule applies in forfeiture proceedings directed against contraband or forfeitable property. . . .

On this basis alone the Court of Appeals' decision as to respondent Lopez-Mendoza must be reversed. At his deportation hearing Lopez-Mendoza objected only to the fact that he had been summoned to a deportation hearing following an unlawful arrest; he entered no objection to the evidence offered against him. . . .

IV

Respondent Sandoval-Sanchez has a more substantial claim. He objected not to his compelled presence at a deportation proceeding, but to evidence offered at that proceeding. The general rule in a criminal proceeding is that statements and other evidence obtained as a result of an unlawful, warrantless arrest are suppressible if the link between the evidence and the unlawful conduct is not too attenuated. *Wong Sun v. United States,* 371 U. S. 471 (1963). The reach of the exclusionary rule beyond the context of a criminal prosecution, however, is less clear. Although this Court has once stated in dictum that "[i]t may be assumed that evidence obtained by the [Labor] Department through an illegal search and seizure cannot be made the basis of a finding in deportation proceedings," *United States ex rel. Bilokumsky v. Tod,* 263 U. S. 149 (1923), the Court has never squarely addressed the question before. . . .

In *United States v. Janis,* 428 U. S. 433 (1976), this Court set forth a framework for deciding in what types of proceeding application of the exclusionary rule is appropriate. Imprecise as the exercise may be, the Court recognized in *Janis* that there is no choice but to weigh the likely social benefits of excluding unlawfully seized evidence against the likely costs. On the benefit side of the balance "the 'prime purpose' of the [exclusionary] rule, if not the sole one, 'is to deter future unlawful police conduct,'" quoting *United States v. Calandra,* 414 U. S. 338, 347 (1974). On the cost side there is the loss of often probative evidence and all of the secondary costs that flow from the less accurate or more cumbersome adjudication that therefore occurs.

At stake in *Janis* was application of the exclusionary rule in a federal civil tax assessment proceeding following the unlawful seizure of evidence by state, not federal, officials. The Court noted at the outset that "[i]n the complex and turbulent history of the rule, the Court never has applied it to exclude evidence from a civil proceeding, federal or state." . . . Two factors in *Janis* suggested that the deterrence value of the exclusionary rule in the context of that case was slight. First, the state law enforcement officials were already "punished" by the exclusion of the evidence in the state criminal trial as a result of the same conduct. . . . Second, the evidence was also excludable in any federal criminal trial that might be held. Both factors suggested that further application of the exclusionary rule in the federal civil proceeding would contribute little more to the deterrence of unlawful conduct by state officials. On the cost side of the balance, *Janis* focused simply on the loss of "concededly relevant and reliable evidence." . . . The Court concluded that, on balance, this cost outweighed the likely social benefits achievable through application of the exclusionary rule in the federal civil proceeding. . . .

The likely deterrence value of the exclusionary rule in deportation proceedings is difficult to assess. On the one hand, a civil deportation proceeding is a civil complement to a possible criminal prosecution, and to this extent it resembles the civil proceeding under review in *Janis*. The INS does not suggest that the exclusionary rule should not continue to apply in criminal proceedings against an alien who unlawfully enters or remains in this country, and the prospect of losing evidence that might otherwise be used in a criminal prosecution undoubtedly supplies some residual deterrent to unlawful conduct by INS officials. But it must be acknowledged that only a very small percentage of arrests of aliens are intended or expected to lead to criminal prosecutions. Thus the arresting officer's primary objective, in practice, will be to use evidence in the civil deportation proceeding. Moreover, here, in contrast to *Janis*, the agency officials who effect the unlawful arrest are the same officials who subsequently bring the deportation action. As recognized in *Janis*, the exclusionary rule is likely to be most effective when applied to such "intrasovereign" violations.

Nonetheless, several other factors significantly reduce the likely deterrent value of the exclusionary rule in a civil deportation proceeding. First, regardless of how the arrest is effected, deportation will still be possible when evidence not derived directly from the arrest is sufficient to support deportation. As the BIA has recognized, in many deportation proceedings "the sole matters necessary for the Government to establish are the respondent's identity and alienage—at which point the burden shifts to the respondent to prove the time, place and manner of entry." . . . Since the person and identity of the respondent are not themselves suppressible, the INS must prove only alienage, and that will sometimes be possible using evidence gathered independently of, or sufficiently attenuated from, the original arrest. . . . The INS's task is simplified in this regard by the civil nature of the proceeding. As Justice Brandeis stated: "Silence is often evidence of the most persuasive character. . . . [T]here is no rule of law which prohibits officers charged with the administration of the immigration law from drawing an inference from the silence of one who is called upon to speak. . . . A person arrested on the preliminary warrant is not protected by a presumption of citizenship comparable to the presumption of innocence in a criminal case. There is no provision which forbids drawing an adverse inference from the fact of standing mute." *United States ex rel. Bilokumsky v. Tod*, 263 U. S., at 153–154.

The second factor is a practical one. In the course of a year the average INS agent arrests almost 500 illegal aliens. Brief for Petitioner 38. Over 97.5% apparently agree to voluntary deportation without a formal hearing. . . . Among the remainder who do request a formal hearing (apparently a dozen or so in all, per officer, per year) very few challenge the circumstances of their arrests. As noted by the Court of Appeals, "the BIA was able to find only two reported immigration cases since 1899 in which the [exclusionary] rule was applied to bar unlawfully seized evidence, only one other case in which the rule's application was specifically addressed, and fewer than fifty BIA proceedings since 1952 in which a Fourth

Amendment challenge to the introduction of evidence was even raised." . . . Every INS agent knows, therefore, that it is highly unlikely that any particular arrestee will end up challenging the lawfulness of his arrest in a formal deportation proceeding. When an occasional challenge is brought, the consequences from the point of view of the officer's overall arrest and deportation record will be trivial. In these circumstances, the arresting officer is most unlikely to shape his conduct in anticipation of the exclusion of evidence at a formal deportation hearing.

Third, and perhaps most important, the INS has its own comprehensive scheme for deterring Fourth Amendment violations by its officers. Most arrests of illegal aliens away from the border occur during farm, factory, and other workplace surveys. Large numbers of illegal aliens are often arrested at one time, and conditions are understandably chaotic. . . . To safeguard the rights of those who are lawfully present at inspected workplaces the INS has developed rules restricting stop, interrogation, and arrest practices. . . . These regulations require that no one be detained without reasonable suspicion of illegal alienage, and that no one be arrested unless there is an admission of illegal alienage or other strong evidence thereof. New immigration officers receive instruction and examination in Fourth Amendment law, and others receive periodic refresher courses in law. . . . Evidence seized through intentionally unlawful conduct is excluded by Department of Justice policy from the proceeding for which it was obtained. See Memorandum from Benjamin R. Civiletti to Heads of Offices, Boards, Bureaus and Divisions, Violations of Search and Seizure Law (Jan. 16, 1981). The INS also has in place a procedure for investigating and punishing immigration officers who commit Fourth Amendment violations. See Office of General Counsel, INS, U. S. Dept. of Justice, The Law of Arrest, Search, and Seizure for Immigration Officers 35 (Jan. 1983). The INS's attention to Fourth Amendment interests cannot guarantee that constitutional violations will not occur, but it does reduce the likely deterrent value of the exclusionary rule. Deterrence must be measured at the margin.

Finally, the deterrent value of the exclusionary rule in deportation proceedings is undermined by the avail-

ability of alternative remedies for institutional practices by the INS that might violate Fourth Amendment rights. The INS is a single agency, under central federal control, and engaged in operations of broad scope but highly repetitive character. The possibility of declaratory relief against the agency thus offers a means for challenging the validity of INS practices, when standing requirements for bringing such an action can be met. . . .

. . . On the other side of the scale, the social costs of applying the exclusionary rule in deportation proceedings are both unusual and significant. The first cost is one that is unique to continuing violations of the law. . . .

Presumably no one would argue that the exclusionary rule should be invoked to prevent an agency from ordering corrective action at a leaking hazardous waste dump if the evidence underlying the order had been improperly obtained, or to compel police to return contraband explosives or drugs to their owner if the contraband had been unlawfully seized. . . . Sandoval-Sanchez is a person whose unregistered presence in this country, without more, constitutes a crime. His release within our borders would immediately subject him to criminal penalties. His release would clearly frustrate the express public policy against an alien's unregistered presence in this country. Even the objective of deterring Fourth Amendment violations should not require such a result. The constable's blunder may allow the criminal to go free, but we have never suggested that it allows the criminal to continue in the commission of an ongoing crime. When the crime in question involves unlawful presence in this country, the criminal may go free, but he should not go free within our borders.

Other factors also weigh against applying the exclusionary rule in deportation proceedings. . . .

The average immigration judge handles about six deportation hearings per day. . . . Neither the hearing officers nor the attorneys participating in those hearings are likely to be well versed in the intricacies of Fourth Amendment law. The prospect of even occasional invocation of the exclusionary rule might significantly change and complicate the character of these proceedings. . . . This sober assessment of the exclusionary rule's likely costs, by the agency that would have to administer the rule in at least the administrative tiers of its application, cannot be brushed off lightly.

The BIA's concerns are reinforced by the staggering dimension of the problem that the INS confronts. Immigration officers apprehend over one million deportable aliens in this country every year. . . . A single agent may arrest many illegal aliens every day. Although the investigatory burden does not justify the commission of constitutional violations, the officers cannot be expected to compile elaborate, contemporaneous, written reports detailing the circumstances of every arrest. . . . Fourth Amendment suppression hearings would undoubtedly require considerably more, and the likely burden on the administration of the immigration laws would be correspondingly severe.

Finally, the INS advances the credible argument that applying the exclusionary rule to deportation proceedings might well result in the suppression of large amounts of information that had been obtained entirely lawfully. INS arrests occur in crowded and confused circumstances. Though the INS agents are instructed to follow procedures that adequately protect Fourth Amendment interests, agents will usually be able to testify only to the fact that they followed INS rules. The demand for a precise account of exactly what happened in each particular arrest would plainly preclude mass arrests, even when the INS is confronted, as it often is, with massed numbers of ascertainably illegal aliens, and even when the arrests can be and are conducted in full compliance with all Fourth Amendment requirements.

In these circumstances we are persuaded that the *Janis* balance between costs and benefits comes out against applying the exclusionary rule in civil deportation hearings held by the INS. By all appearances the INS has already taken sensible and reasonable steps to deter Fourth Amendment violations by its officers, and this makes the likely additional deterrent value of the exclusionary rule small. The costs of applying the exclusionary rule in the context of civil deportation hearings are high. In particular, application of the exclusionary rule in cases such as Sandoval-Sanchez', would compel the courts to release from custody persons who would then immediately

resume their commission of a crime through their continuing, unlawful presence in this country. "There comes a point at which courts, consistent with their duty to administer the law, cannot continue to create barriers to law enforcment in the pursuit of a supervisory role that is properly the duty of the Executive and Legislative Branches." *United States v. Janis*, 428 U. S., at 459. That point has been reached here.

V

We do not condone any violations of the Fourth Amendment that may have occurred in the arrests of respondents Lopez-Mondoza or Sandoval-Sanchez. . . . Our conclusions concerning the exclusionary rule's value might change, if there developed good reason to believe that Fourth Amendment violations by INS officers were widespread. . . . Finally, we do not deal here with egregious violations of Fourth Amendment or other liberties that might transgress notions of fundamental fairness and undermine the probative value of the evidence obtained. . . . At issue here is the exclusion of credible evidence gathered in connection with peaceful arrests by INS officers. We hold that evidence derived from such arrests need not be suppressed in an INS civil deportation hearing.

The judgment of the Court of Appeals is therefore Reversed.

Justice Brennan, dissenting.

. . . I believe the basis for the exclusionary rule does not derive from its effectiveness as a deterrent, but is instead found in the requirements of the Fourth Amendment itself. My view of the exclusionary rule would, of course, require affirmance of the Court of Appeals. In this case, federal law enforcement officers arrested respondents Sandoval-Sanchez and Lopez-Mendoza in violation of their Fourth Amendment rights. The subsequent admission of any evidence secured pursuant to these unlawful arrests in civil deportation preceedings would, in my view, also infringe those rights. The Government of the United States bears an obligation to obey the Fourth Amendment; that obligation is not lifted simply because the law enforcement officers were agents of the

Immigration and Naturalization Service, nor because the evidence obtained by those officers was to be used in civil deportation proceedings.

Justice White, dissenting.

. . . [T]here is no principled basis for distinguishing between the deterrent effect of the rule in criminal cases and in civil deportation proceedings. The majority attempts to justify the distinction by asserting that deportation will still be possible when evidence not derived from the illegal search or seizure is independently sufficient. . . . However, that is no less true in criminal cases. The suppression of some evidence does not bar prosecution for the crime, and in many cases even though some evidence is suppressed a conviction will nonetheless be obtained.

The majority also suggests that the fact that most aliens elect voluntary departure dilutes the deterrent effect of the exclusionary rule. . . . However, that fact no more diminishes the importance of the exclusionary sanction than the fact that many criminal defendants plead guilty dilutes the rule's deterrent effect in criminal cases. The possibility of exclusion of evidence quite obviously plays a part in the decision whether to contest either civil deportation or criminal prosecution. Moreover, in concentrating on the incentives under which the individual agent operates to the exclusion of the incentives under which the agency as a whole operates neglects the "systemic" deterrent effect that may lead the agency to adopt policies and procedures that conform to Fourth Amendment standards. . . .

The majority believes "perhaps most important" the fact that the INS has a "comprehensive scheme" in place for deterring Fourth Amendment violations by punishing agents who commit such violations. . . . Since the deterrent function of the rule is furthered if it alters either "the behavior of individual law enforcement officers or the policies of their departments," . . . it seems likely that it was the rule's deterrent effect that led to the programs to which the Court now points for its assertion that the rule would have no deterrent effect.

The suggestion that alternative remedies, such as civil suits, provide adequate protection is unrealistic. Contrary to the situation in criminal cases, once the Government has improperly obtained evidence against an illegal alien, he is removed from the country and is therefore in no position to file civil actions in federal courts. Moreover, those who are legally in the country but are nonetheless subjected to illegal searches and seizures are likely to be poor and uneducated, and many will not speak English. It is doubtful that the threat of civil suits by these persons will strike fear into the hearts of those who enforce the Nation's immigration laws.

It is also my belief that the majority exaggerates the costs associated with applying the exclusionary rule in this context. Evidence obtained through violation of the Fourth Amendment is not automatically suppressed, and any inquiry into the burdens associated with application of the exclusionary rule must take that fact into account. . . .

Finally, the majority suggests that application of the exclusionary rule might well result in the suppression of large amounts of information legally obtained because of the "crowded and confused circumstances" surrounding mass arrests. . . . Rather than constituting a rejection of the application of the exclusionary rule in civil deportation proceedings, however, this argument amounts to a rejection of the application of the Fourth Amendment to the activities of INS agents. . . . The Court may be willing to throw up its hands in dismay because it is administratively inconvenient to determine whether constitutional rights have been violated, but we neglect our duty when we subordinate constitutional rights to expediency in such a manner. Particularly is this so when, as here, there is but a weak showing that administrative efficiency will be seriously compromised.

In sum, I believe that the costs and benefits of applying the exclusionary rule in civil deportation proceedings do not differ in any significant way from the costs and benefits of applying the rule in ordinary criminal proceedings. . . . Accordingly, I dissent.

[Justice Marshall, dissenting opinion omitted.]
[Justice Stevens, dissenting opinion omitted.]

Dow Chemical Company v. United States

206 U.S. S.Ct. 1819 (1986) 5–4

+   Burger, White, Rehnquist, Stevens, O'Connor
−/+ Brennan, Marshall, Blackmun, and Powell concurred with the majority
       in Part III and filed a dissenting opinion.

[In 1978, EPA enforcement officials made an on-site visit to the 2,000-acre chemical manufacturing plant in Midland, Michigan, owned by Dow Chemical Company. The company consented to the EPA inspection. However, a subsequent inspection request was denied. EPA did not seek an administrative search warrant, but hired a commercial aerial photographer who took pictures of the facility while flying in lawful navigable airspace. When Dow Chemical Company found out about the photographs, it filed a suit against the EPA alleging that the EPA had violated its Fourth Amendment rights and had exceeded its statutory investigative authority. The U.S. Court of Appeals for the Sixth Circuit upheld EPA's actions, and Dow Chemical appealed this ruling to the U.S. Supreme Court.]

Chief Justice Burger delivered the opinion of the Court.

II

The photographs at issue in this case are essentially like those commonly used in map-making. Any person with an airplane and an aerial camera could readily duplicate them. In common with much else, the technology of photography has changed in this century. These developments have enhanced industrial processes, and indeed all areas of life; they have also enhanced law enforcement techniques. Whether they may be employed by competitors to penetrate trade secrets is not a question presented in this case. Governments do not generally seek to appropriate trade secrets of the private sector, and the right to be free of appropriation of trade secrets is protected by law.

Dow nevertheless relies heavily on its claim that trade secret laws protect it from any aerial photography of this industrial complex by its competitors, and that this protection is relevant to our analysis of such photography under the Fourth Amendment. That such photography might be barred by state law with regard to competitors, however, is irrelevant to the questions presented here. State tort law governing unfair competition does not define the limits of the Fourth Amendment. . . . The Government is seeking these photographs in order to regulate, not to compete with, Dow. If the Government were to use the photographs to compete with Dow, Dow might have a Fifth Amendment "taking" claim. . . . Hence, there is no prohibition of photographs taken by a casual passenger on an airliner, or those taken by a company producing maps for its map-making purposes.

III

Congress has vested in EPA certain investigatory and enforcement authority, without spelling out precisely how this authority was to be exercised in all the myriad circumstances that might arise in monitoring matters relating to clean air and water standards. When Congress invests an agency with enforcement and investigatory authority, it is not necessary to identify explicitly each and every technique that may be used in the course of executing the statutory mission. Aerial observation authority, for example, is not usually expressly extended to police for traffic control, but it could hardly be thought necessary for a legislative body to tell police that aerial observation could be employed for traffic control of a metropolitan area, or to expressly authorize police to send messages to ground highway patrols that a particular over-the-road truck was traveling in excess of 55 miles per hour. Common sense and ordinary human experience teaches that traffic violators are apprehended by observation.

Regulatory or enforcement authority generally carries with it all the modes of inquiry and investigation traditionally employed or useful to execute the authority granted. Environmental standards such as clean air and clean water cannot be enforced only in libraries and laboratories, helpful as those institutions may be.

Under § 144(a)(2), the Clean Air Act provides that "upon presentation of . . . credentials," EPA has a "right of entry to, upon, or through any premises." 42 U.S.C. § 7414(a)(2)(A). Dow argues this limited grant of authority to enter does not authorize any aerial observation. In particular, Dow argues that unannounced aerial observation deprives Dow of its right to be informed that an inspection will be made or has occurred, and its right to claim confidentiality of the information contained in the places to be photographed, as provided in § 114(a) and (c), 42 U.S.C. § 7414(a),(c). It is not claimed that EPA has disclosed any of the photographs outside the agency.

Section 114(a), however, appears to expand, not restrict, EPA's general powers to investigate. Nor is there any suggestion in the statute that the powers conferred by this section are intended to be exclusive. There is no claim that EPA is prohibited from taking photographs from a ground-level location accessible to the general public. The EPA, as a regulatory and enforcement agency, needs no explicit statutory provision to employ methods of observation commonly available to the public at large: we hold that the use of aerial observation and photography is within the EPA's statutory authority.

IV

We turn now to Dow's contention that taking aerial photographs constituted a search without a warrant, thereby violating Dow's rights under the Fourth Amendment. . . .

. . . Plainly a business establishment or an industrial or commercial facility enjoys certain protections under the Fourth Amendment. See *Marshall v. Barlow's, Inc.*, 436 U.S. 307 (1978); *See v. City of Seattle*, 387 U.S. 541 (1967).

. . . [T]he Court has drawn a line as to what expectations are reasonable in the open areas beyond the curtilage of a dwelling; "open fields do not provide the setting for those intimate activities that the [Fourth] Amendment is intended to shelter from governmental interference or surveillance." . . . In *Oliver*, we held that "an individual may not legitimately demand privacy for activities out of doors in fields, except in the area immediately surrounding the home." . . . To fall within the open fields doctrine the area "need be neither 'open' nor a 'field' as those terms are used in common speech." . . .

Dow plainly has a reasonable, legitimate, and objective expectation of privacy within the interior of its covered buildings, and it is equally clear that expectation is one society is prepared to observe. . . . Moreover, it could hardly be expected that Dow would erect a huge cover over a 2,000-acre tract. In contending that its entire enclosed plant complex is an "industrial curtilage," Dow argues that its exposed manufacturing facilities are analogous to the curtilage surrounding a home because it has taken every possible step to bar access from ground level.

. . . The intimate activities associated with family privacy and the home and its curtilage simply do not reach the outdoor areas or spaces between structures and buildings of a manufacturing plant.

Admittedly, Dow's enclosed plant complex, like the area in *Oliver*, does not fall precisely within the "open fields" doctrine. The area at issue here can perhaps be seen as falling somewhere between "open fields" and curtilage, but lacking some of the critical characteristics of both. . . .

We pointed out in *Donovan v. Dewey*, 452 U.S. 594 (1981), that the Government has "greater latitude to conduct warrantless inspections of commercial property" because "the expectation of privacy that the owner of commercial property enjoys in such property differs significantly from the sanctity accorded an individual's home." We emphasized that unlike a homeowner's interest in his dwelling, "[t]he interest of the owner of commercial property is not one in being free from any inspections." . . . And with regard to regulatory inspections, we have held that "[w]hat is observable by the public is observable without a warrant, by the Government inspector as well." *Marshall v. Barlow's, Inc.* . . .

. . . Here, EPA was not employing some unique sensory device that, for example, could penetrate the walls of buildings and record conversations in Dow's plants, offices or laboratories, but rather a conventional, albeit precise, commercial camera commonly used in map-making. . . .

It may well be, as the Government concedes, that surveillance of private property by using highly sophisticated surveillance equipment not generally available to the public, such as satellite technology, might be constitutionally proscribed absent a warrant. But the photographs here are not so revealing of intimate details as to raise constitutional concerns. Although they undoubtedly give EPA more detailed information that naked-eye views, they remain limited to an outline of the facility's buildings and equipment. The mere fact that human vision is enhanced somewhat, at least to the degree here, does not give rise to constitutional problems. An electronic device to penetrate walls or windows so as to hear and record confidential discussions of chemical formulae or other trade secrets would raise very different and far more serious questions. . . .

We hold that the taking of aerial photographs of an industrial plant complex from navigable airspace is not a search prohibited by the Fourth Amendment. Affirmed.

Justice Powell, with whom Justice Brennan, Justice Marshall, and Justice Blackmun join, concurring in Part III, and dissenting.

The Fourth Amendment protects private citizens from arbitrary surveillance by their Government. For nearly twenty years, this Court has adhered to a standard that ensured that Fourth Amendment rights would retain their vitality as technology expanded the Government's capacity to commit unsuspected intrusions into private areas and activities. Today, in the context of administrative aerial photography of commercial premises, the Court retreats from that standard. . . . Such an inquiry will not protect Fourth Amendment rights, but rather will permit their gradual decay as technological advances.

Fourth Amendment protection of privacy interests in business premises "is . . . based upon societal expectations that have deep roots in the history of the Amendment." *Oliver v. United States*, 466 U.S. 170 (1984). In *Marshall v. Barlow's, Inc.*, 436 U.S. 307 (1978), we observed that the "particular offensiveness" of the general warrant and writ of assistance, so despised by the Framers of the Constitution, "was acutely felt by the merchants and businessmen whose premises and products were inspected" under their authority. . . . Against that history, "it is untenable that the ban on warrantless searches was not intended to shield places of business as well as of residence." . . . Our precedents therefore leave no doubt that proprietors of commercial premises, including corporations, have the right to conduct their business free from unreasonable official intrusion. . . .

. . . [W]here Congress has made a reasonable determination that a system of warrantless inspections is necessary to enforce its regulatory purpose, and where "the federal regulatory presence is sufficiently comprehensive and defined that the owner of commercial property cannot help but be aware that his property will be subject to periodic inspections," warrantless inspections may be permitted. . . . This exception does not apply here. The Government does not contend, nor does the Court hold, that the Clean Air Act authorizes a warrantless inspection program that adequately protects the privacy interests of those whose premises are subject to inspection.

. . . The exception we have recognized for warrantless inspections, limited to pervasively regulated businesses, see *Donovan v. Dewey, United States v. Biswell*, 406 U.S. 311 (1972); *Colonnade Catering Corp. v. United States*, 397 U.S. 72 (1970), is not founded solely on the differences between the premises occupied by such businesses and homes, or on a conclusion that administrative inspections do not intrude on protected privacy interests and therefore do not implicate Fourth Amendment concerns. Rather, the exception is based on a determination that the reasonable expectation of privacy that the owner of a business does enjoy may be adequately protected by the regulatory scheme itself. . . .

III

Since our decision in *Katz v. United States*, the question whether particular governmental conduct constitutes a Fourth Amendment "search" has turned on whether that conduct intruded on a constitutionally protected expectation of privacy. . . .

An expectation of privacy is reasonable for Fourth Amendment purposes if it is rooted in a "source outside of the Fourth Amendment, either by reference to concepts of real or personal property law or to understandings that are recognized and permitted by society." *Rakas v. Illinois*, 439 U.S. 128, (1978). Dow argues that, by enacting trade secret laws, society has recognized that it has a legitimate interest in preserving the privacy of the relevant portions of its open-air plants. As long as Dow takes reasonable steps to protect its secrets, the law should enforce its right against theft or disclosure of those secrets.

. . . Accordingly, Dow has a reasonable expectation of privacy in its commercial facility in the sense required by the Fourth Amendment. EPA's conduct in this case intruded on that expectation because the aerial photography captured information that Dow had taken reasonable steps to preserve as private.

Access to Information Held by Government

As you will recall from Thomas McCraw's article (chapter 1), the regulation literature regularly confirms that government agencies are often captured by the industries they regulate. Citizens have little information about and limited access to the regulatory process when it is dominated by informal negotiations between agencies and the industries they regulate.[6] Acknowledgement of the vast power private interests exercise over public policy prompted a wave of reforms in the mid-1960s and 1970s—what we might call *counter-capture reforms.* Public interest advocates, such as Ralph Nader,[7] organized a citizens' movement—*the public interest movement*—which continues today to support efforts to expand public access and participation in the regulatory process as an antidote to corporate capture.[8]

Courts play a role in supporting public interest reforms in the administrative process by broadening standing, expanding notice and comment periods, and developing the requirement that the agency's record all the facts used in making an agency decision (see chapter 9).[9] Congress has imposed additional reforms limiting the extent to which

[6] See Samuel Huntington, "The Marasmus of the ICC: The Commission, the Railroad and the Public Interest," *Yale Law Journal* 61 (1952): 467; M. H. Bernstein, *Regulating Business by Independent Commission* (Princeton, N.J.: Princeton University Press, 1955); and Grant McConnel, *Private Power and American Democracy* (New York: Vintage Books, 1966).

[7] See Ralph Nader, *Public Interest Perspective: The Next Four Years* (Washington, D.C.: Public Citizen, 1977).

[8] See Joel F. Handler, *Social Movements and the Legal System* (New York: Academic Press, 1978); David Vogel, "Promoting Pluralism: The Politics of the Public Interest Movement," *Political Science Quarterly* 95 (1981): 608; and Michael W. McCann, *Taking Reform Seriously: Perspectives on Public Interest Liberalism* (Ithaca, N.Y.: Cornell University Press, 1986).

[9] See J. Delong, "Informal Rulemaking and the Integration of Law and Policy," *Virginia Law Review* 65 (1979): 257.

agencies and interested parties can engage in private decisionmaking by requiring agencies to hold meetings in public (the Government Sunshine Act 1976), by prohibiting ex parte decisions (Administrative Procedure Act 1976), and by increasing access to information (the Freedom of Information Act 1966). These reforms, coupled with procedural due process expansions during the early 1970s (chapter 2), seek to expand citizen participation in decisionmaking and reduce the influence of regulated industries over administrative discretion.

The Freedom of Information Act (FOIA)[10] is the most significant law for expanding access to information about the government. This statute allows citizens to request copies of documents submitted to and held by the government. Unless provisions of the act expressly exempt the document, it must be released. A version of the present law was added to the Administrative Procedure Act (APA). Initially the act required no specific deadlines for compliance through disclosure, and this toothless law was rarely enforced.[11] In 1974 Congress amended the act to require the agency to decide within ten days whether to comply. If the agency refuses, the petitioner can now take the issue directly to court.

A fairly typical use of FOIA occurred when Procter and Gamble required about 20,000 documents from the Center for Disease Control. These documents are part of P&G's strategy to exonerate itself from liability for deaths and illness caused by toxic shock syndrome allegedly related to use of P&G's Rely tampon. This effort has cost the company over one million dollars.[12]

The Freedom of Information Act lists nine categories of documents exempt from the disclosure requirement:

1. Information "specifically authorized under criteria established by an Executive order to be kept secret in the interest of national defense or foreign policy"
2. Internal personnel rules and practices
3. Material specifically exempted by other statutory provisions
4. Trade secrets and business information deemed confidential or privileged
5. Inter- and intra-agency memoranda
6. Personnel and medical files
7. Law enforcement records
8. Banking records
9. Geological and geophysical data concerning mineral wealth

There is a considerable amount of litigation over the meaning and scope of these nine exemptions. FOIA case law has become an important area of federal administrative law practice. In particular, three exemptions (2, 5, and 6) are regularly the subject

---

[10]See Appendix B, the Administrative Procedure Act, Sec. 552.

[11]See Ralph Nader, "Freedom From Information: The Act and the Agencies," *Harvard Civil Rights–Civil Liberties Law Review* 5 (1970): 1.

[12]"Rely Counterattack," *Wall Street Journal*, 26 June 1981, p. 25. The average individual citizen or small business does not have Procter and Gamble's financial capacity to pay for reproduction of large quantities of government documents. Standards and procedures for fee waivers are discussed by John E. Bonine, "Public Interest Fee Waivers Under the Freedom of Information Act," *Duke Law Journal* 1981 (April, 1981): 213.

of litigation. These exemptions are often used by agencies when they deny access to government documents. Agencies claim that protecting the public's right to information under FOIA must be balanced against an individual's right to privacy.[13] In other words, agencies sometimes uses an individual's right to privacy in order to shield the government from having to release documents about its own activities. This occurred in the next case, *Department of the Air Force v. Rose* (1976). The government claimed that it did not have to release materials because they fell within exemptions 2 and 6. The next case, *Taxation With Representation Fund v. Internal Revenue Service* (1981), is an example of how the courts have interpreted exemption 5 which deals with inter- and intra-agency memoranda. Both cases are also good examples of the kind of arguments agencies use to avoid disclosing government documents.

Department of the Air Force v. Rose

425 U.S. 352 (1976) 5–3

  per curiam
- Burger, Blackmun, Rehnquist
NP Stevens

[Student law review editors at New York University Law School, researching an article on the U.S. Air Force Academy honor code, were denied access to case summaries of honors and ethics hearings even if it would not identify any individuals. The law students brought a suit seeking disclosure of these hearing summaries under the FOIA. The Department of the Air Force argued that the summaries were "matters . . . related solely to the internal personnel rules and practices of an agency" and included information from "personnel files"; thus they should be protected from mandatory disclosure under exemptions 2 and 6.]

II

Our discussion may conveniently begin by again emphasizing the basic thrust of the Freedom of Information Act . . . We canvassed the subject at some length three years ago in *EPA v. Mink*, 410 U.S. 73 (1973), and need only briefly review that history here. The Act revises § 3, the public disclosure section, of the Administrative Procedure Act (1964 ed.). The revision was deemed necessary because "Section 3 was generally recognized as falling far short of its disclosure goals and came to be looked upon more as a withholding statute than a disclosure state." *Mink, supra*. Congress therefore structured a revision whose basic purpose reflected "a general philosophy of full agency disclosure unless information is exempted under clearly delineated statutory language." . . . To make crystal clear the congressional objective—in the words of the Court of Appeals, "to pierce the veil of administrative secrecy and to open agency action to the light of public scrutiny," . . . Congress provided in § 552(c) that nothing in the Act should be read to "authorize withholding of information or limit the availability of records to the public, except as specifically stated. . . . " Consistently with that objective, the Act repeatedly states "that official information shall be made available 'to the public,' for public in-

---

[13]The Privacy Act of 1974 prohibits disclosure of any kind of retrievable information about an individuals—information such as an individual's name or other means of identification. Exemption 6 of the FOIA is not as restrictive.

spection.'" *Mink, supra.* There are, however, exemptions from compelled disclosure. They are nine in number and are set forth in § 552(b). But these limited exemptions do not obscure the basic policy that disclosure, not secrecy, is the dominant objective of the Act. . . . We need not consider in this case the applicability of Exemption 2 in such circumstances, however, because, as the Court of Appeals recognized, this is not a case "where knowledge of administrative procedures might help outsiders to circumvent regulations or standards. Release of the [sanitized] summaries, which constitute quasi-legal records, poses no such danger to the effective operation of the Codes at the Academy." . . . Indeed, the materials sought in this case are distributed to the subjects of regulation, the cadets, precisely in order to assure their compliance with the known content of the Codes. . . .

. . . What we have said of the military in other contexts has equal application here: it "constitutes a specialized community governed by a separate discipline from that of the civilian," *Orloff v. Willoughby,* 345 U.S. 83 (1953), in which the internal law of command and obedience invests the military officer with "a particular position of responsibility." *Parker v. Levy,* 417 U.S. 733 (1974). Within this discipline, the accuracy and effect of a superior's command depends critically upon the specific and customary reliability of subordinates, just as the instinctive obedience of subordinates depends upon the unquestioned specific and customary reliability of the superior. The importance of these considerations to the maintenance of a force able and ready to fight effectively renders them undeniably significant to the public role of the military. Moreover, the same essential integrity is critical to the military's relationship with its civilian direction. Since the purpose of the Honor and Ethics Codes administered and enforced at the Air Force Academy is to ingrain the ethical reflexes basic to these responsibilities in future Air Force officers, and to select out those candidates apparently unlikely to serve these standards, it follows that the nature of this instruction — and its adequacy or inadequacy — is significantly related to the substantive public role of the Air Force and its Academy. Indeed, the public's stake in the operation of the Codes as they affect the training of future Air Force officers and their military careers is underscored by the Agency's own proclamations of the importance of cadet-administered Codes to the Academy's educational and training program. . . .

. . . [W]e think that, at least where the situation is not one where disclosure may risk circumvention of agency regulation, Exemption 2 is not applicable to matters subject to such a genuine and significant public interest. The exemption was not designed to authorize withholding of all matters except otherwise secret law bearing directly on the propriety of actions of members of the public. Rather, the general thrust of the exemption is simply to relieve agencies of the burden of assembling and maintaining for public inspection matter in which the public could not reasonably be expected to have an interest. The case summaries plainly do not fit that description. They are not matter with merely internal significance. They do not concern only routine matters. Their disclosure entails no particular administrative burden. We therefore agree with the Court of Appeals that, given the Senate interpretation, "the Agency's withholding of the case summaries (as edited to preserve anonymity) cannot be upheld by reliance on the second exemption." . . .

IV

Additional questions are involved in the determination whether Exemption 6 exempts the case summaries from mandatory disclosure as "personnel and medical files and similar files the disclosure of which would constitute a clearly unwarranted invasion of personal privacy." The first question is whether the clause "the disclosure of which would constitute a clearly unwarranted invasion of personal privacy" modifies "personnel and medical files or only "similar files." The Agency argues that Exemption 6 distinguishes "personnel" from "similar" files, exempting all "personnel files" but only those "similar files" whose disclosure constitutes "a clearly unwarranted invasion of personal privacy," and that the case summaries sought here are "personnel files." . . .

. . . [W]e find nothing in the wording of Exemption 6 or its legislative history to support the Agency's claim that Congress created a blanket exemption for personnel files. Judicial interpretation has uniformly reflected the view that no reason would exist for nondisclosure in the absence of a showing of a clearly unwarranted invasion of privacy, whether the documents are filed in "personnel" or "similar" files. . . . Congressional concern for the protection of the kind of confidential personal data usually included in a personnel file is abundantly clear. But Congress also made clear that nonconfidential matter was not to be insulated from disclosure merely because it was stored by an agency in its "personnel" files. Rather, Congress sought to construct an exemption that would require a balancing of the individual's right of privacy against the preservation of the basic purpose of the Freedom of Information Act "to open agency action to the light of public scrutiny." The device adopted to achieve that balance was the limited exemption, where privacy was threatened, for "clearly unwarranted" invasions of personal privacy.

. . . Congress enunciated a single policy, to be enforced in both cases by the courts, "that will involve a balancing" of the private and public interests. . . .

. . . Congress' recent action in amending the Freedom of Information Act to make explicit its agreement with judicial decisions requiring the disclosure of nonexempt portions of otherwise exempt files is consistent with this conclusion. Thus, 5 U.S.C. § 552(b) (1970 ed., Supp. V) now provides that "[a]ny reasonably segregable portion of a record shall be provided to any person requesting such record after deletion of the portions which are exempt under this subsection." And § 552(a)(4)(B) (1970 ed., Supp. V) was added explicitly to authorize *in camera* inspection of matter claimed to be exempt "to determine whether such records or *any part* thereof shall be withheld." (Emphasis supplied.) The Senate Report accompanying this legislation explains, without distinguishing "personnel and medical files" from "similar files," that its effect is to require courts "to look beneath the label on a file or record when the withholding of information is challenged. . . .

" . . . [W]here files are involved [courts will] have to examine the records themselves and require disclosure of portions to which the purposes of the exemption under which they are withheld does not apply." S. Rep. No. 93–854, p. 32 (1974).

The remarks of Senator Kennedy, a principal sponsor of the amendments, make the matter even clearer. "For example, deletion of names and identifying characteristics of individuals would in some cases serve the underlying purpose of Exemption 6, which exempts 'personnel and medical files and similar files the disclosure of which would constitute a clearly unwarranted invasion of privacy.' " 120 Cong. Rec. 17018 (1974).

In so specifying, Congress confirmed what had perhaps been only less clear earlier. For the Senate and House Reports on the bill enacted in 1966 noted specifically that Health, Education, and Welfare files, Selective Service files, or Veterans' Administration files, which as the Agency here recognizes were clearly included within the congressional conception of "personnel files," were nevertheless intended to be subject to mandatory disclosure in redacted form if privacy could be sufficiently protected. . . .

Moreover, even if we were to agree that "personnel files" are wholly exempt from any disclosure under Exemption 6, it is clear that the case summaries sought here lack the attributes of "personnel files" as commonly understood. Two attributes of the case summaries require that they be characterized as "similar files." First, they relate to the discipline of cadet personnel, and while even Air Force Regulations themselves show that this single factor is insufficient to characterise the summaries as "personnel files," it supports the conclusion that they are "similar." Second, and most significantly, the disclosure of these summaries implicates similar privacy values; for as said by the Court of Appeals, . . . "identification of disciplined cadets—a possible consequence of even anonymous disclosure—could expose the formerly accused men to lifelong embarrassment, perhaps disgrace, as well as pratical disabilities, such as loss of employment or friends." . . . But these summaries, collected only in the Honor and Ethics Code reading files and the Academy's honor records, do not contain the "vast amounts of personal data," . . . which constitute the kind of profile of an individual ordinarily to be found in his personnel file: showing, for example, where he was born, the names of his parents, where he has lived from time to time, his high school or other school records, results of examinations, evaluations of his work performance. Moreover, access to these files, is not drastically limited, as is customarily true of personnel files, only to supervisory personnel directly involved with the individual (apart from the personnel department itself), frequently thus excluding even the individual himself. On the contrary, the case summaries name no names except in guilty cases, are widely disseminated for examination by fellow cadets, contain no facts except such as pertain to the alleged violation of the Honor or Ethics Codes, and are justified by the Academy solely for their value as an educational and instructional tool the better to train military officers for discharge of their important and exacting functions. Documents treated by the Agency in such a manner cannot reasonably be claimed to be within the common and congressional meaning of what constitutes a "personnel file" under Exemption 6.

In striking the balance whether to order disclosure of all or part of the case summaries, the District Court, in determining whether disclosure will entail a "clearly unwarranted" invasion of personal privacy, may properly discount its probability in light of Academy tradition to keep identities confidential within the Academy. Respondents sought only such disclosure as was consistent with this tradition. Their request for access to summaries "with personal references or other identifying information deleted," respected the confidentality interests embodied in Exemption 6. As the Court of Appeals recognized, however, what constitutes identifying information regarding a subject cadet must be weighed not only from the viewpoint of the public, but also from the vantage of those who would have been familiar, as fellow cadets or Academy staff, with other aspects of his career at the Academy. Despite the summaries' distribution within the Academy, many of this group with earlier access to summaries may never have identified a particular cadet, or may have wholly forgotten his encounter with Academy discipline. And the risk to the privacy interests of a former cadet, particularly one who has remained in the military, posed by his identification by otherwise unknowing former colleagues or instructors cannot be rejected as trivial. We nevertheless conclude that consideration of the policies underlying the Freedom of Information Act, to open public bus-

iness to public view when no "clearly unwarranted" invasion of privacy will result, requires affirmance of the holding of the Court of Appeals, . . . that although "no one can guarantee that all those who are 'in the know' will hold their tongues, particularly years later when time may have eroded the fabric of cadet loyalty," it sufficed to protect privacy at this stage in these proceedings by enjoining the District Court, . . . that if in its opinion deletion of personal references and other identifying information "is not sufficient to safeguard privacy, then the summaries should not be disclosed to [respondents]." We hold, therefore, in agreement with the Court of Appeals, "that the in camera procedure [ordered] will further the statutory goal of Exemption Six: a workable compromise between individual rights 'and the preservation of public rights to Government information.'" . . .

To be sure, redaction cannot eliminate all risks of identifiability, as any human approximation risks some degree of imperfection, and the consequences of exposure of identity can admittedly be severe. But redaction is a familiar technique in other contexts and exemptions to disclosure under the Act were intended to be practical workable concepts, *EPA v. Mink* . . . ; S. Rep. No. 813, p. 5; H.R. Rep. No. 1497, p. 2. Moreover, we repeat, Exemption 6 does not protect against disclosure every incidental invasion of privacy—only such disclosures as constitute "clearly unwarranted" invasions of personal privacy.

Affirmed.

Chief Justice Burger, dissenting.

If "hard cases make bad law," unusual cases surely have the potential to make even worse law. Today, on the basis of a highly unusual request for information about a unique governmental process, a military academy honor system, the Court interprets definitively a substantial and very significant part of a major federal statute governing the balance between the public's "right to know" and the privacy of the individual citizen.

In my view, the Court makes this case carry too much jurisprudential baggage. Consequently, the basic congressional intent to protect a reasonable balance between the availability of information in the custody of the Government and the particular individual's right of privacy is undermined. . . .

 . . . Having acknowledged the necessity of such a balance, however, the Court, in my view, blandly ignores and thereby frustrates the congressional intent by refusing to weigh, realistically, the grave consequences implicit in release of this particular information, in any form, against the relatively inconsequential claim of "need" for the material alleged in the complaint.

 . . . The stigma which our society imposes on the individual who has accepted such a position of trust and abused it is not erasable, in any realistic sense, by the passage of time or even by subsequent exemplary conduct. The absence of the broken sword, the torn epaulets, and the Rogue's March from our military ritual does not lessen the indelibility of the stigma. . . . Indeed, the mode of punitive separation as the result of court-martial is the same for both officers and cadets—dismissal. . . .

 Admittedly, the Court requires that, before release, these documents be subject to *in camera* inspection with power of excising parts. But, as the Court admits, any such attempt to "sanitize" these summaries would still leave the very distinct possibility that the individual would still be identifiable and thereby injured. In light of Congress' recent manifest concern in the Privacy Act of 1974, 5 U.S.C. § 552a (1970 ed., Supp. V), for "governmental respect for the privacy of citizens . . . ," S. Rep. No. 93–1183, p. 1 (1974), it is indeed difficult to attribute to Congress a willingness to subject an individual citizen to the risk of possible severe damage to his reputation simply to permit law students to invade individual privacy to prepare a law journal article. Its definition of a "clearly unwarranted invasion of personal privacy" as equated with "protect[ing] an individual's private affairs from *unnecessary* public scrutiny . . . ," S. Rep. No. 813, 89th Cong., 1st Sess., 9 (1965) (emphasis supplied), would otherwise be rendered meaningless.

 Moreover, excision would not only be ineffectual in accomplishing the legislative intent of protecting an individual's affairs from unnecessary public scrutiny, but it would place an intolerable burden upon a district court which, in my view, Congress never intended to inflict. Although the 1974 amendments

to the Freedom of Information Act require that "[a]ny reasonable segregable portion of a record . . . ," 5 U.S.C. § 552(b) (1970 ed., Supp. V), otherwise exempt, be provided, there is nothing in the legislative history of the original Act or its amendments which would require a district court to construct, in effect, a new document. Yet, the excision process mandated here could only require such a sweeping reconstruction to the material that the end product would constitute an entirely new document. No provision of the Freedom of Information Act contemplates a federal district judge acting as a "rewrite editor" of the original material.

 If the Court's holding is indeed a fair reflection of congressional intent, we are confronted with a "split-personality" legislative reaction, by the conflict between a seeming passion for privacy and a comparable passion for needless invasions of privacy.

 Accordingly, I would reverse the judgment of the Court of Appeals.

Justice Blackmun, dissenting.

 I cannot accept the rationale of the Court of Appeals majority that the existence of a "substantial potential for public interest outside the Government," 495 F. 2d 261, 265 (1974), makes these case summaries any less related "solely" to internal personnel rules and practices. Surely, public interest, which is secondary and a by-product, does not measure "sole relationship," which is a primary concept. These summaries involve the discipline, fitness, and training of cadets. They are administered and enforced on an Academy-limited basis by the cadets themselves, and they exist wholly apart from the formal system of courts-martial and the Uniform Code of Military Justice.

 Finally, I note the Court's candid recognition of the personal risks involved. . . . Today's decision, of course, now makes those risks a reality for the cadet, "particularly one who has remained in the military," and the risks are imposed upon the individual in return for a most questionable benefit to the public and personal benefit to respondent Rose. So often the pendulum swings too far.

 I fear that the Court today strikes a severe blow to the Honor Codes, to the system under which they operate, and to the former cadets concerned. It is sad to see these old institutions mortally wounded and passing away and individuals placed in jeopardy and embarrassment for lesser incidents long past.

I would reverse the judgment of the Court of Appeals.

[Justice Rehnquist, dissenting opinion omitted.]

Taxation With Representation Fund v. Internal Revenue Service

646 F. 2d 666, U.S.C.A., D.C. Cir. (1981) 3–0

[The Taxation With Representation Fund (TWRF) asked the IRS to permit it to inspect and copy three types of documents: General Counsel Memoranda (GCM); Technical Memoranda (TM); and Action on Decisions (AODs). IRS refused their request, claiming that all of the requested memoranda and indices were protected from disclosure under Exemption 5. After exhausting all administrative remedies, TWRF filed a FOIA suit.]

Judge Harry T. Edward, Circuit Judge.

The issues raised by this appeal require this court's consideration for the first time whether certain records of the Internal Revenue Service ("IRS") may be withheld from public disclosure pursuant to Exemption 5 of the Freedom of Information Act ("FOIA"), 5 U.S.C. § 552(b)(5). Exemption 5 of the FOIA protects "inter-agency or intra-agency memorandums or letters which would not be available by law to a party other than an agency in litigation with the agency." 5 U.S.C. § 552(b)(5). While Exemption 5 has been construed generally to exempt those documents normally privileged in the civil discovery contest, the focus of this litigation is the "deliberative process" privilege portion of Exemption 5. . . .

I

In order to get a clear understanding of the issues at stake here, it is essential to focus on the disputed documents which are the subject of this appeal. To this end, in this section we will first describe GCMs, TMS and AODs, and explain the function and significance of each document in IRS decisionmaking processes, and then outline the procedural history of this case.

Descriptions of the Documents

1. General Counsel's Memoranda (GCMs)
General Counsel's Memoranda are:
legal memorandums from the Office of Chief Counsel to the Internal Revenue Service prepared in response to a formal request for legal advice from the Assistant Commissioner (Technical). They are primarily prepared by attorneys in the Interpretative Division of the Office of Chief Counsel and usually addressed to the Office of the Assistant Commissioner (Technical) in connection with the review of proposed private letter rulings, proposed technical advice memorandums, and proposed revenue rulings (hereinafter proposed determinations) of the Service. . . .

A completed GCM is forwarded to the Office of the Assistant Commissioner (Technical), who uses the memorandum to determine "what positions will be taken in the proposed revenue ruling, proposed private letter ruling, or proposed technical advice memorandum." . . .

If differences arise between the positions of the Office of Assistant Commissioner (Technical) and the Office of Chief Counsel, the differences "are generally reconciled on an informal basis before the adoption of the revenue ruling, private letter ruling, or technical advice memorandum in question." . . .

Completed GCMs are then copied and distributed to key officials within the Internal Revenue Service, including the Office of Chief Counsel. . . .

IRS personnel who confer or negotiate on tax liability matters with taxpayers may refer to GCMs for guidance as to the positions to take in such negotiations. During such negotiations, IRS staff members do not typically state that a particular position is required by a GCM, nor do agency personnel provides copies of GCMs to taxpayers. . . . In addition, IRS personnel are instructed by section 4245.3(3) of the Internal Revenue Manual that GCMs should not be used "as precedents in the disposition of other cases but may be used as a guide with other research material in formulating a district office position on an issue." . . . However, GCMs are frequently cited by staff attorneys in the Office of Chief Counsel in subsequent GCMs "to insure consistency, avoid duplication of research, provide a reference source, and update earlier memorandums when a position on an issue is sustained, modified, or changed within the Office of Chief Counsel." . . .

2. Technical Memoranda (TMs)

Technical Memoranda are memoranda from the Commissioner of the Internal Revenue Service to the Assistant Secretary of the Treasury (Tax Policy). . . . The TMs at issue in this case are drafted by attorneys in the Legislation and Regulations Division of the Office of Chief Counsel in connection with the preparation of proposed Treasury decisions or regulations. . . .

3. Actions On Decisions (AODs)

Actions on Decisions are legal memoranda prepared by attorneys in the Tax Litigation Division and directed to the Chief Counsel whenever the IRS loses a case in the Tax Court, a Federal District Court, the Court of Claims, or the United States Court of Appeals. . . .

The record in unclear as to whether AODs recommending appeal are also reviewed by the Assistant Commissioner (Technical). However, there is some evidence to indicate that these AODs are printed and distributed along with all other AODs. . . .

II

Exemption 5, which is the focus of this litigation, protects

> inter-agency or intra-agency memorandums or letters which would not be available by law to a party other than an agency in litigation with the agency. 5 U.S.C. § 552(b)(5).

Given the literal language of Exemption 5, it is not surprising that the courts have construed this exemp-

tion to encompass the protections traditionally afforded certain documents pursuant to evidentiary privileges in the civil discovery context. . . .

The deliberative process privilege protects "confidential intra-agency advisory opinions . . . disclosure of which would be injurious to the consultative functions of government." . . . As was recently noted by Judge Wald in *Coastal States*, the deliberative process privilege is "unique to government" and

> has a number of purposes: it serves to assure that subordinates within an agency will feel free to provide the decision-maker with their uninhibited opinions and recommendations without fear of later being subject to public ridicule or criticism; to protect against premature disclosure of proposed policies before they have been finally formulated or adopted; and to protect against confusing the issues and misleading the public by dissemination of documents suggesting reasons and rationales for a course of action which were not in fact the ultimate reasons for the agency's action.

. . . Thus, the privilege protects documents reflecting advisory opinions, recommendations, and deliberations comprising part of a process by which governmental decisions and policies are formulated, as well as other subjective documents that reflect the personal opinions of the writer prior to the agency's adoption of a policy. . . .

Notwithstanding these significant policy considerations underscoring the necessity that materials reflecting the deliberative process be protected, this exception to the general disclosure mandate of FOIA should be construed "as narrowly as consistent with efficient Government operation." *EPA v. Mink*, 410 U.S. 73 (1973) . . . Thus, the courts have developed over the years certain specific limitations regarding the types of documents that are protected by the deliberative process privilege.

"Predecisional" Versus "Post-Decisional" Documents and Inquiries Concerning the "Working Law of the Agency"

Exemption 5 does not apply to final agency actions that constitute statements of policy or final opinions that have the force of law, or which explain actions that an agency has already taken. . . . Nor does Exemption 5 protect communications that implement an established policy of an agency. . . . This latter limitation on Exemption 5 grew out of the Supreme Court's approval in *Sears* of the distinction drawn by lower courts between "predecisional communications, which are privileged, and communications made after the decision and designed to explain it, which are not." . . .

Predecisional documents are thought generally to reflect the agency "give-and-take" leading up to a decision that is characteristic of the deliberative process; whereas *post-decisional* documents often represent the agency's position on an issue, or explain such a position, and thus may constitute the "working law" of an agency. Accordingly, the courts have recognized little public interest in the disclosure of "reasons supporting a policy which an agency has rejected, or . . . reasons which might have supplied, but did not supply, the basis for a policy which was actually adopted on a different ground." . . . However, the courts have recognized a strong public interest in the disclosure of reasons that *do* supply the basis for an agency policy actually adopted. As noted by the Supreme Court in *Sears:*

> Exemption 5, properly construed, calls for "disclosure of all 'opinions and interpretations' which embody the agency's effective law and policy, and the withholding of all papers which reflect the agency's group thinking in the process of working out its policy and determining what its law shall be." Davis, The Information Act: A Preliminary Analysis, 34 U.Chi.L. Rev. 761, 797 (1967); Note, Freedom of Information Act and the Exemption for Intra-Agency Memoranda, 86 Harv.L. Rev. 1047 (1973). . . .

While the predecisional/post-decisional dichotomy is useful as a starting point in distinguishing documents that are privileged from documents that are not, we must be careful not to lose sight of the primary thrust of the exemption in making these distinctions. Predecisional documents are not exempt merely because they are predecisional; they must also be part of the deliberative process by which a decision is made. . . .

Function and Significance of the Document in the Agency Decisionmaking Process

One way of determining whether a document in fact constitutes the "working law" of an agency is to consider the function and significance of the document in the agency's decisionmaking process. . . .

III

Having reviewed the existing case law on the subject, we now turn to consider the application of the deliberative process privilege portion of Exemption 5 to the documents here in dispute.

Documents Not Covered by This Opinion

For the reasons hereafter discussed, we affirm the judgment of the District Court, *except* with respect to the following documents:

GCMs that are never distributed. The GCMs that are the focus of this litigation are documents that are revised to reflect the final position of the Assistant Commissioner (Technical) and are widely distributed throughout the agency. As we note below, such documents can find no protection from disclosure in Exemption 5. However, there may be situations where a GCM is merely considered and rejected by the Assistant Commissioner (Technical); in such instances— assuming that the unapproved document is never released for publication throughout the agency—the document would remain predecisional and/or purely deliberative, and thus protected under Exemption 5. We do not mean to suggest otherwise in this opinion.

TMs pertaining to proposed Treasury decisions or regulations that have never been approved. . . . [T]he record is unclear as to what is done with TMs related to decisions and regulations that are never approved. We emphasize that this opinion covers only those TMs which, as a form of "legislative history," are issued in connection with decisions and regulations that have been approved by Treasury. We can find no compelling evidence or reason to support the disclosure of other TM documents, which would appear to be purely predecisional and deliberative in the absence of approval by Treasury of the related decision or regulation.

AODs recommending appeals of pending cases. The record is somewhat unclear as to whether AODs recommending appeal are approved by the Assistant Commissioner (Technical), and whether such AODs ever contain discussions of litigation strategy. Indeed, it is not even entirely clear whether AODs recommending appeal are published and distributed in the same fashion as other AODs; nor is it clear whether these documents state "tentative" or "final" positions of the agency. In the absence of findings with respect to these points, we are unwilling to approve the District Court's order covering AODs recommending appeal. We will therefore remand for further consideration and appropriate findings by the District Court.

GCMs, TMs and AODs for which disclosure is sought at a "predecisional" stage. As our opinion will make clear, the documents subject to disclosure here include materials that reflect the "working law" of the agency, in the form of final opinions, instructions or advice to staff, interpretative reports (explaining decisions or regulations), and the like. We are mindful of the fact that at various predecisional stages in the decisionmaking processes described, a GCM, TM or AOD may be nothing more than a purely deliberative/predecisional document. During the course of these predecisional stages, the documents are thus protected from disclosure under Exemption 5. Once adopted and released, however, the final documents are subject to disclosure under FOIA. In other words, this opinion merely reconfirms the point made in *Coastal States,* that

> even if the document is predecisional at the time it is prepared, it can lose that status if it is adopted, formally or informally, as the agency position on an issue or is used by the agency in its dealings with the public.

617 F.2d at 866.

GCMs Subject to Disclosure

Excluding those GCM documents referred to above in section III. A., we hereby affirm the judgment of the District court requiring disclosure under

FOIA of the specific GCMs heretofore described in section I.

As noted in our discussion above, GCMs are memoranda from the Chief Counsel to the Commissioner written originally for the purpose of guiding the Assistant Commissioner (Technical) concerning substantive issues on proposed revenue rulings, private letter rulings, and technical advice memoranda. The evidence also reveals that the same qualities that make these memoranda useful to the Assistant Commissioner (Technical) recommend the memoranda to agency lawyers for legal research and to agency field personnel in need of guidance in dealing with the public on certain tax liability issues. Moreover, the fact that earlier GCMs are constantly updated to reflect the current status of an issue within the Office of Chief Counsel, combined with the "reconcilation" of positions taken by the Chief Counsel in GCMs with those ultimately adopted by the decisionmaker in the formal rulings, eliminates whatever deliberative character these documents may have had prior to their being "updated" or "reconciled." In essence, after a decision has been reached, a completed GCM becomes an expression of agency policy.

The GCM explains rulings issued by the Assistant Commissioner, and its serves as an interpretative guide and research tool for agency personnel. We are thus persuaded that GCMs function as a body of "working law" within the IRS. . . .

In holding that GCMs are not exempt from disclosure as deliberative documents, we do not ignore the test of decisional authority posed in *Renegotiation Board,* and recently expanded upon by this court in *Coastal States* and *Brinton.* That test looks to whether a document was issued by a body possessing the authority to make the final decision as to which the document pertains. *Coastal States* and *Brinton* posit as a rule of thumb that "final" materials tend to flow from a superior with policymaking authority to a subordinate who carries out policy, while "deliberative" materials typically flow from a subordinate to a superior official. . . .

TMs Subject to Disclosure

We find that much of the same reasoning developed in our discussion of GCMs is applicable with respect to TMs because of the similarity in function and treatment of these two documents. The District Court's finding that TMs explain the reasons behind the adoption of final agency action is clearly supported by the record.

The record is replete with evidence indicating that TMs pertaining to regulations and decisions approved by Treasury may be fairly equated with "legislative history" accompanying a newly enacted statute. Indeed, there is even evidence to the effect that a TM may tell more about a regulation than the regulation itself. . . .

Moreover, these explanatory memoranda are systematically filed under the Treasury Decision number to which they pertain and can be gotten "simply by looking at one of the tax services." . . . The record also reveals that TMs are made available in the Legislation and Regulation Divisions for research by lawyers within the agency and IRS personnel who confer and negotiate with the public. . . . As in the case of GCMs, these documents have been informally adopted by the agency as explanations of its policy, and are used by personnel within the agency as the "working law" of the agency. We therefore agree with the District Court's conclusion that, except with respect to the documents listed in section III. A., *supra*, TMs are not exempt from disclosure under FOIA.

AODs Subject to Disclosure

Finally, excluding those AODs referred to in section III. A. above (certain ones of which will be the subject of further review upon remand), we affirm the judgment of the District Court requiring disclosure of AODs.

Prior to publication and distribution, an AOD recommending "no appeal" is approved by the Assistant Commissioner (Technical). The AOD may be revised or withdrawn to correspond to changes in agency policy or positions. Final AODs are widely disseminated to agency personnel for use in legal research and in conferring with the public.

AODs that opt for "no appeal"– including cases of acquiescence or nonacquiescence – clearly pertain to the law that will be applied by the agency henceforth, and the explanations contained therein constitute explanations of the agency's "final" legal position on an issue. We conclude, therefore, that given the undisputed evidence at hand, final AODs recommending "no appeal" cannot possibly be viewed as deliberative/predecisional documents. On the authority of *Sears*, discussed at length, *supra*, we believe that the conclusion is inescapable that these documents are not protected from disclosure under Exemption 5.

So ordered.

Until quite recently lawyers and courts tended to assume that these exemptions exhausted the field. That is, immediate disclosure was mandatory unless the document fit one of the nine categories. But in *Federal Open Market Committee of the Federal Reserve System v. Merrill*, 443 U.S. 340 (1978), the Supreme Court seemed to pull some of the teeth out of the act. Here the Court allowed the Federal Reserve to delay releasing information that fell into none of the nine categories. The Court adopted the so-called weighing the harm argument and determined that the harm of release, in this case of information about financial markets, justified the delay. Why Congress, through its own careful construction of the nine exemptions, had not presumably already done this weighing remained unclear.

Several other serious problems in the interpretation of the nine exemptions have also developed in the past decade. For example, section 6(b)(1) of the Consumer Product Safety Act specifies that thirty days before the Consumer Product Safety Commission makes public information concerning a product defect, it must supply such information to the manufacturer or private labeler of the product and give it a chance to respond. What if, under the FOIA, citizens petitioned for the release of information and the CPSC agrees to do so? Does 6(b)(1) qualify as an exemption from FOIA under the third FOIA exception listed above? If it does, would the manufacturers of the products have legal authority to sue to prevent the commission from releasing the information? The Court in 1980 answered both questions in the affirmative.[14]

The bulk of recent comment upon and analysis of the FOIA has been decidely critical. FBI Director William Webster, complained in the late 1970s that the act was too strong, requiring expenditure of millions of dollars annually. The FBI alone employs over 200 people to process FOIA requests.[15]

These FOIA complications, when combined with the debate whether the act is too strong or too weak, compel the conclusion that Congress has not fine-tuned its information policy. Information is not a thing that belongs in a policy class by itself. Information is content, facts and ideas about government programs as complex and varied as the myriad of government programs themselves. An excerpt from one of the more judicious statements of the inadequacies of federal information policy follows.[16]

A Proposal for a Comprehensive Restructuring of the Public Information System

Charles Koch and Barry Rubin
Duke Law Journal 1 (1979)

. . . Although the drafters of the FOIA recognized the necessity of balancing the need for a smoothly operating government against the needs of public access, they made no effort to integrate the public information system into the overall functioning of the government. Consequently, perhaps the greatest failure of the present information system is the unneccessary friction between it and other government operations. The public information system created by the Act, as interpreted by the courts, focuses only on the release of documents in government files. The irrebuttable presumption is that free-wheeling disclosure of information will always be in the public interest. The drafters did not leave room for either the courts or the agencies to modify or individualize this broad public interest determination.

The only provisions recognizing the necessity of protecting government operations are the Act's exemptions. Some of the exemptions, especially those involving internal documents and investigatory files, were the result of government operation analysis. These exemptions could have been used to enable the courts ot merge the Information Act access system into overall government operations. However, even with a sensitive approach to the needs of government, the Act does not provide sufficient flexibility to allow the courts to integrate disclosure of information into the machinery of government. Curing this failure will require thoughtful legislative analysis. Initially, Congress must recognize that evaluation of the Act's performance requires consideration not only of the public interest but also of the Act's overall impact on the performance of government. At present, the Act interferes with the government's ability to react to the needs of its citizenry and it has an adverse impact on individual agency functions. It thus prevents officials from performing primary duties that Congress has also deemed to be in the public interest. . . .

---

[14]*CPSC v. GTE Sylvania, Inc.* 447 U.S. 102 (1980). See also *Chrysler Corp. v. Brown*, 441 U.S. 281 (1979).

[15]See James Reston, Jr., "The Jonestown Papers," *New Republic*, April 25, 1981.

[16]See also "A Model for Determining the Publication Requirements of Section 552 (a)(1) of the Administrative Procedure Act," *University of Michigan Journal of Law Reform* 13 (1980): 515.

Not all states have freedom of information statutes. Some that do not nevertheless have a more general category of openness known as *sunshine laws.* These laws, more informatively called *public meeting laws,* rest on the assumption that so-called executive sessions, study sessions, and closed sessions of agency members produce results more pragmatic than informed citizens would easily accept. Interesting issues arise where, as usual, the general statute does not anticipate the specific case.

Chapter two concluded with seven different ways of defining "the rule of law." The sixth of these equated the rule of law with public participation. The "sunshine" reform movement has sought to achieve this goal very explicitly. This movement to require open meetings began at the state level in the early 1960s. It was not until 1976 that Congress passed the federal Sunshine Act,[17] which requires that multimember federal agencies open their meetings to the public. The act defines "meetings" as deliberations of at least a quorum, which must be open to the public if the deliberations will affect agency policy. However, there are ten exemptions to the Sunshine Act, seven of which are similar to the FOIA exemptions. If a majority of the officials at a meeting vote in favor of closing a meeting for one of the following reasons, the public will be excluded:

1. Meeting concerns information that is vital to the national defense or foreign policy
2. Meeting concerns internal personnel rules and practices
3. Material discussed is specifically exempted by other statutory provisions
4. Trade secrets and business information deemed confidential or privileged
5. Open meeting would invade personal privacy
6. Meeting concerns law enforcement records
7. Meeting concerns banking records
8. Matters discussed involve accusing a person of a crime or formally censuring a person
9. Open meeting would frustrate implementation of a proposed agency action if prematurely known
10. Meeting concerns the agency's participation in formal rulemaking or litigation

Just as litigation over the meaning of FOIA exemptions raises the issues of public access, government secrecy, and personal privacy, so too does the litigation over the meaning of the Sunshine Act exemptions focus attention on conflicts over excluding the public from government meetings in a democratic society. Although important decisions that influence the direction of government policy are not always made in formal meetings, we know that one way of checking the informal power structure is to make officials accountable for their decisions in a public setting. This is the philosophy of the public interest movement, and thus we find that often those who challenge closed meetings are public interest groups, such as Common Cause. In the next case, *Nuclear Regulatory Commission v. Common Cause* (1982), Circuit Court Judge Skelly Wright rejects efforts by the NRC to close its meetings under Exemption 9. Judge Wright describes the theory of democratic participation that underlies the Sunshine Act, and he gives judicial supports for this theory in his interpretation of Exemption 9.

[17]5 U.S.C. § 552b.

Nuclear Regulatory Commission v. Common Cause

674 F.2d 921, U.S.C.A., D.C. Cir. (1982) 3–0

[This case involves three unrelated cases that were consolidated on appeal. In each case the Nuclear Regulatory Commission (NRC) closed its meetings to discuss the agency's budget proposal and announced that the sessions would be closed to the public. The NRC relied mainly on Exemption 9 of the Sunshine Act, which permits closing of meetings if the agency decides that premature disclosure would be "likely to significantly frustrate implementation of a proposed agency action," but also cited Exemptions 2 and 6. In all three cases, a representative of Common Cause, a public interest consumer organization, was excluded from the meetings. Common Cause filed suit seeking a declaratory judgment that closure of the meetings had violated the Sunshine Act. It asked for an injunction ordering the release of the transcripts of each meeting and an order to the NRC to permit Common Cause to attend future Commission meetings "that are similar in nature" to those meetings they closed.]

J. Skelly Wright, Circuit Judge.

In these cases we must decide an important unresolved issue: whether any of the statutory exemptions from the Sunshine Act apply to agency budget deliberations. Interpreting the statutory language in light of the legislative history and underlying policies of the Act, we conclude that there is no blanket exemption for agency meetings at any stage of the budget preparation process. The availability of exemptions for specific portions of budgetary discussions must be determined upon the facts of each case.

. . . We strike down the District Court's injunction of July 2, 1981 because it is too vague to satisfy the standards of Rule 65(d) [of the Federal Rules of Civil Procedure].* Reaching the substantive Sunshine Act issues, we conclude that none of the exemptions to the Sunshine Act provides any blanket exception for budget discussion at any stage—preliminary staff budget briefings, markup/reclama meetings, or meetings to prepare reclama to OMB. On the basis of our inspection of the transcripts of the Commission's two closed meetings, we decide that no portion of either

meeting is exempt from disclosure, and we therefore order that the full transcripts be released.

III. Sunshine Act and the Budget Process

A. THE PURPOSES OF THE SUNSHINE ACT. Congress enacted the Sunshine Act to open the deliberations of multi-member federal agencies to public view. It believed that increased openness would enhance citizen confidence in government, encourage higher quality work by government officials, stimulate well-informed public debate about government programs and policies, and promote cooperation between citizens and government. In short, it sought to make government more fully accountable to the people. In keeping with the premise that "government should conduct the public's business in public," the Act established a general presumption that agency meetings should be held in the open. Once a person has challenged an agency's decision to close a meeting, the agency bears the burden of proof. Even if exempt subjects are discussed in one portion of a meeting, the remainder of the meeting must be held in open session.

The Act went farther than any previous federal legislation in requiring openness in government. In general the Sunshine Act's exemptions parallel those in the Freedom of Information Act (FOIA), but there is an important difference. Unlike FOIA, which spe-

---

*Rule 65(d) requires: "Every order granting an injunction and every restraining order shall set forth the reasons for its issuance; shall be specific in terms; shall describe in reasonable detail, and not by reference to the complaint or other document, the act or acts sought to be restrained. . . . "

cifically exempts "predecisional" memoranda and other documents on the premise that government cannot "operate in a fishbowl," the Sunshine Act was designed to open the predecisional process in multi-member agencies to the public. During the legislative process a number of federal agencies specifically objected to the Sunshine Act's omission of an exemption for predecisional deliberations. Congress deliberately chose to forego the claimed advantages of confidential discussions among agency heads at agency meetings.

Express language in the Sunshine Act also demonstrates that Congress did not intend to follow the FOIA pattern for predecisional discussions at agency meetings. . . .

Notwithstanding the omission of a deliberative process privilege from the Sunshine Act, the Commission asks us to hold that the deliberative process leading to formulation of an agency's budget request is exempt from the Sunshine Act. To resolve this question, we must examine the statutory underpinnings of the budget process and the specific exemptions from the Sunshine Act which the Commission invokes.

B. THE BUDGET AND ACCOUNTING ACT OF 1921. The Budget and Accounting Act, 42 Stat. 21 (1921), was designed to centralize formulation of the Executive Branch budget. Previously Congress had received "uncompared, unrelated, and unrevised" estimates from individual departments and agencies, "representing the personal views and aspirations of bureau chiefs[.]" S.Rep. No. 524, 66th Cong., 2d Sess. 6 (1920). The disadvantages of this uncoordinated system led Congress to delegate to the President exclusive authority to submit budgetary requests on behalf of the Executive Branch. 31 U.S.C. § 15 (1976). Congress thereby sought to enhance the government's ability to control the overall level of expenditures and to choose among conflicting priorities.

The Commission contends that the Budget and Accounting Act mandates secrecy in the budget formulation process, and that the Sunshine Act must therefore be construed to permit closing of agency budget meetings. . . . We find this statutory argument unpersuasive.

The Commission first relies on the President's authority, under the Budget and Accounting Act, to prescribe rules and regulations for preparation of the budget, 31 U.S.C. § 16 (1976), and on the "longstanding practice of confidentiality for Executive Branch discussions leading to the formulation of the President's Budget." . . . The statute, however, makes no reference to confidentiality, nor does it authorize the President to prescribe budgetary rules and regulations without regard to the requirements of other federal statutes. The President's rulemaking authority under 31 U.S.C. § 16 is therefore subject to the specific requirements of the Sunshine Act. . . .

Second, the Commission reasons that the congressional goal of centralized budget formulation cannot be achieved without secrecy. If the proposals of individual agencies must be adopted in public, it suggests, development of the presidential budget would be "fragmented" and the President's discretion to choose among alternatives would be impaired. . . . This contention reads too much into the 1921 Act, which simply requires that the President submit a single, unified Executive Branch budget proposal to Congress for consideration. It does not prescribe any method by which he must develop the consolidated budget figures which he submits. Nor does it require that the President's proposals be the only budgetary information available to the public. Even if agencies discuss their budget proposals at public sessions, the President remains capable of revising agency requests and combining them into a unified budget.

Indeed, the Sunshine Act itself affords persuasive evidence that Congress did not intend to allow presidential claims of confidentiality under the Budget and Accounting Act to override the Sunshine Act's specific provisions regarding openness and secrecy. Exemption 3, a provision which received extensive consideration in both houses, allows closing of a meeting or portion of a meeting which would "disclose matters specifically exempted from disclosure by statute," provided that such statute requires that matters be withheld from the public in such a manner as to leave no discretion on the issue, or establishes particular criteria for withholding or refers to particular types of matters to be withheld.

5 U.S.C. § 552b(c)(3)(1976). The Budget and Accounting Act of 1921, which contains no explicit references to confidentiality, does not qualify under the strict requirements of Exemption 3.

Therefore, the budget process is exempt from the open meeting requirement, in whole or in part, only if it fits within the terms of other specific Sunshine Act exemptions.

C. No Blanket Exemption for Budget Meetings. Exceptions to the Sunshine Act's general requirement of openness must be construed narrowly. H.R.Rep.No. 94-880 (part 1), 94th Cong., 2 Sess. 2 (1976). Congress rejected the approach of establishing "functional categories" of agency business whose discussion could automatically be closed to the public. Instead the Sunshine Act provides for an examination of each item of business to ascertain whether it may be closed under the terms of one of ten specific exemptions. *Pacific Legal Foundation v. Council on Environmental Quality*, 636 F.2d 1259, 1265 (D.C.Cir.1980). Exemptions must be interpreted in light of Congress' intention that agencies must "conduct their deliberations in public to the greatest extent possible." S.Rep.No. 94-354, *supra*, at 11. Nevertheless the Commission claims that Exemption 9(B) permits closing of agency budget meetings in their entirety.

Exemption 9(B) permits closing of meetings to prevent "premature disclosure" of information whose disclosure would be likely to "significantly frustrate implementation of a proposed agency action." For two reasons, the precept of narrow construction applies with particular force to this exemption, upon which the Commission principally relies. First, as we have seen, Congress decided not to provide any exemption for predecisional deliberations because it wished the process of decision as well as the results to be open to public view. . . . Yet the agencies may attempt to seize upon the language of Exemption 9(B) to avoid

the perceived discomfort and inconvenience that are, in the words of one commentary, "inherent in the open meeting principle . . . ." R. Berg & S. Klitzman, An Interpretive Guide to the Government in the Sunshine Act 24 (1978). Second, an overly broad construction of Exemption 9(B), which applies to all agencies subject to the Act, would allow agencies to "circumvent the spirt of openness which underlies this legislation." S.Rep.No. 94-354, *supra*, at 20.

The language of the exemption is not self-explanatory; we therefore turn to the legislative history for guidance. The House and Senate committee reports give four concrete examples of Exemption 9(B) situations. First, an agency might consider imposing an embargo on foreign shipment of certain goods; if this were publicly known, all of the goods might be exported before the agency had time to act, and the effectiveness of the proposed action would be destroyed. . . . Second, an agency might discuss whether to approve a proposed merger; premature public disclosure of the proposal might make it impossible for the two sides to reach agreement. . . . Third, disclosure of an agency's proposed strategy in collective bargaining with its employees might make it impossible to reach an agreement. Fourth, disclosure of an agency's terms and conditions for purchase of real property might make the proposed purchase impossible or drive up the price. . . .

We construe Exemption 9(B) to cover those situations delineated by the narrow general principles which encompass all four legislative examples. In each of these cases, disclosure of the agency's proposals or negotiating position could affect private decisions by parties other than those who manage the federal government — exporters, potential corporate merger partners, government employees, or owners of real property. The private responses of such persons might damage the regulatory or financial interests of the government as a whole, because in each case the agency's proposed action is one for which the agency takes final responsibility as a governmental entity.

The budget process differs substantially from the examples given by the House and Senate reports. Disclosure of the agency's discussions would not affect private parties' decisions concerning regulated activity or dealings with the government. Rather, the Commission contends that opening budget discussions to the public might affect political decisions by the President and OMB. In addition, disclosure would not directly affect "agency action" for which the Commission has the ultimate responsibility. Instead, the Commission fears that disclosure of its time-honored strategies of item-shifting exaggeration, and fall-back positions would give it less leverage in its "arm's length" dealings with OMB and the President, who make the final budget decisions within the Executive Branch. The Commission argues that it would thereby be impaired in its competition with other government agencies—which also serve the public and implement federal legislation—for its desired share of budgetary resources. It is not clear, however, whether the interests of the government as a whole, or the public interest, would be adversely affected.

Moreover, in the budget context the public interest in disclosure differs markedly from its interest in the four situations described in the committee reports. In those cases disclosure would permit either financial gain at government expense or circumvention of agency regulation. In contrast, disclosure of budget deliberations would serve the affirmative purposes of the Sunshine Act: to open government deliberations to public scrutiny, to inform the public "what facts and policy considerations the agency found important in reaching its decision, and what alternatives it considered and rejected," and thereby to permit "wider and more informed public debate of the agency's policies . . . ." S.Rep.No. 94 354, *supra*, at 5–6.

The budget deliberation process is of exceptional importance in agency policymaking. The agency heads must review the entire range of agency programs and responsibilities in order to establish priorities According to the Commission, a budget meeting "candidly consider[s] the merits and efficiencies of on-going or expected regulatory programs or projects" and then "decides upon the level of regulatory activities it proposes to pursue . . . ." These decisions, the government contends, have a significant impact on "the Commission's ability to marshal regula-

tory powers in a manner which insures the greatest protection of the public health and safety with the most economical use of its limited resources." . . .

D. PARTICULARIZED EXEMPTIONS. The Sunshine Act contains no express exemption for budget deliberations as a whole, and we do not read such an exemption into Exemption 9(B). We recognize, nevertheless, that specific items discussed at Commission budget meetings might be exempt from the open meetings requirement of the Act, and might justify closing portions of Commission meetings on an individual and particularized basis. After examining the transcripts of the Commission's closed meetings of July 27, 1981 and October 15, 1981, however, we conclude that none of the subject matter discussed at either meeting comes within any of the exemptions cited by the Commission. The Commission must therefore release the full transcripts of these meetings to the public. . . .

Our *in camera* inspection of the transcripts of the July 27, 1981 and October 15, 1981 Commission meetings leads us to conclude that Exemption 9(B) does not support withholding of any portion of the transcripts.

2. EXEMPTION 2. The Commission also relies on Exemption 2—matters that "relate solely to the internal personnel rules and practices of an agency[,]" 5 U.S.C. § 552b(c)(2) (1976)—to justify closing portions of budget meetings. Under the Commission's interpretation, Exemption 2 includes discussions of allocation of personnel among programs, evaluations of the performance of offices and projects within the Commission, and consideration of more economical schemes of "internal management." . . . This construction is belied by the statutory language and legislative history of Exemption 2.

The language in Exemption 2 to the Government in the Sunshine Act is virtually identical with that in Exemption 2 to the Freedom of Information Act. 5 U.S.C. § 552(b)(2) (1976). The conference report on the Sunshine Act expressly adopts the standards of *Dep't of Air Force v. Rose*, 425 U.S. 352, (1976), the leading Supreme Court decision interpreting Exemption 2 of FOIA. . . . Under this standard, personnel-related discussions at budget meetings fall squarely outside the scope of the exemption.

Budget allocations inevitably impinge on personnel matters, because government cannot implement programs without personnel. Salaries and wages are a sizable proportion of the Commission's budget. But budget decisions regarding personnel cutbacks, and evaluations of the prior performance of offices and programs, do not relate *solely* to "internal personnel rules and procedures." Discussions of possible administrative cost savings through adoption of new "internal management" techniques also fall beyond the narrow confines of Exemption 2, because they deal with the impact of budget cuts on the Commission's ability to carry out its responsibilities. . . .

3. EXEMPTION 6. The government invoked Exemption 6 to justify its decisions to close both meetings at issue; it no longer claims that the exemption protects any of the deliberations at the October 15 meeting. Exemption 6 protects information of a personal nature whose disclosure would constitute "an unwarranted invasion of personal privacy[.]" 5 U.S.C. § 552b(c)(6) (1976). The agency contends that this exemption protects discussion of "an individual manager's particular qualifications, characteristics and professional competence in connection with a budget request for that particular manager's program." . . . This contention is unsupported by the legislative history of the Sunshine Act.

Exemption 6 applies to information of a personal nature, including discussions of a person's health, drinking habits, or financial circumstances. It provides greater protection to private individuals, including applicants for federal grants and officials of regulated private companies, and to low-level government employees, than to government officials with executive responsibilities. . . . It was not intended to shelter substandard performance by government executives. The Senate report expressly noted that "if the discussion centered on the alleged incompetence with which a Government official has carried out his duties it might well be appropriate to keep the meeting open, since in that case the public has a special interest in knowing how well agency employees are carrying out their public responsibilities." Exemption 6, the report added, "must not be used by an agency to shield itself from political controversy involving the agency and its employees about which the public should be informed." . . . These policy considerations apply *a fortiori* in the budget process, in which the performance of individual executives may affect the Commission's willingness to allocate budgetary resources to particular regulatory programs.

Given the narrow scope of Exemption 6 as applied to managerial officials, we hold that no portion of the discussion at the July 27, 1981 meeting was covered by Exemption 6. The Commission's discussion of individual performance was limited to managerial officials with executive responsibility.

E. COMPLIANCE WITH THE SUNSHINE ACT. Our *in camera* inspection of the transcripts of the July 27, 1981 and October 15, 1981 Commission meetings does not show that any portion of either meeting may be withheld from the public under any of the asserted exemptions to the Sunshine Act. We therefore order the Commission to release the transcripts to the public. 5 U.S.C. § 552b(f)(2) (1976). The transcripts shall be made available in a place readily accessible to the public, and copies shall be furnished to any person at the actual cost of duplication. *Id.*

If in the future the Commission wishes to close all or any portion of a budget meeting, the statute requires it to announce its intention and to give a brief statement of its reasons. If any person objects to closing of the meeting, he may file a civil action in the District Court to compel the Commission to comply with the statute. He may include an application for interlocutory relief in his complaint, if the meeting has not yet been held. The District Court should act promptly on any motion for interim relief to avoid frustration of the purposes of the Sunshine Act through delay. In its decision on the merits the District Court may examine *in camera* the transcripts of closed agency meetings and may issue such relief as it deems appropriate, with due regard for orderly administration and the public interest.

IV. Conclusion

For the reasons stated in this opinion the District Court's injunction issued July 2, 1981 and its contempt finding made on September 9, 1981 are vacated. Because the Commission has not carried its burden of proving that the July 27, 1981 and October 15, 1981 meetings were lawfully closed, the Commission shall release the transcripts of those meetings to the public forthwith.

So ordered.

Consider finally the operation of the Privacy Act (1974) which, like the FOIA, is part of the Administrative Procedure Act. The statute's title can mislead. It does *not* prevent the government from gathering information about people and thereby invading their privacy. It seeks instead to allow a citizen to learn what the government knows about his private life. (see *Department of the Air Force v. Rose, supra,* at p.182).

As you might guess, criminal investigations, CIA records, and other similarly sensitive materials are exempted from the Privacy Act. Unless exempted, an agency must provide a method for citizens to inspect records, e.g., about their financial affairs, and correct any demonstrable errors therein. It also requires the agency not to use the information for other than stated purposes and prohibits it from providing the information to others without the citizen's consent. See section 552a of the APA in Appendix B.

Exercises and Questions for Further Thought

1. How valid is Justice Douglas's point, dissenting in *Wyman*, that our legal system grants a narrower presumption of innocence to the poor than to those believed by some to be more respectable citizens? Do the punishments (or lack of them) given to the Watergate participants bear on this point? If some inequity exists, is this a valid basis for a legal decision? Why or why not?

2. Investigations for administrative purposes occasionally raise problems of entrapment. In 1981 IRS agents obtained a search warrant and seized eight boxes of books and records from the home of Mr. and Mrs. William Jones. The judge issued the warrant based on the information gathered in the following manner:

In an attempt to reveal and combat the growing proportion of businesses which fail to report accurately their total income, the IRS instituted an undercover "Business Opportunities Project." Targets of these projects are businesses that keep two sets of books, one reflecting the *reported* income and a second set documenting the *real* income, which is the reported income plus the skimmed cash upon which the individual pays no taxes.

Agents working for these "projects" pose as prospective buyers of businesses with a high cash flow, thereby likely candidates for cash skimming. These undercover agents contact brokers and sellers and indicate their interest in "skimming" after acquiring a suitable business.

Once contact with an owner is established, the agent wins confidence and is shown the second set of books documenting the true cash flow of the business. Caught in one such trap, the Joneses revealed to an IRS agent documents showing an additional $25,000 unreported income per year.

While IRS officials claim a need for such projects, attorneys for targets of these projects assert that the tactics are illegal entrapments.

Comment upon the legal and ethical acceptability of this practice.[18]

3. The Supreme Court has argued that regulators should use cost-benefit analysis to determine the scope of an agency's authority to gather information when it conflicts with individual rights. The Court has also said that in weighing these interests it will take into account the difference between criminal and civil penalties which may result from agency inspections. After reading *Wyman* and *INS v. Lopez-Mendoza*, how valid do you think the criminal/civil distinction is for the individuals in these cases? What harm results from a civil proceeding based on evidence obtained through an agency inspection? Does the Court apply this distinction in *Marshall v. Barlow's?* Do welfare recipients and chemical companies have the same "expectation of privacy?" Discuss the social and political "costs and benefits" of applying the exclusionary rule to administrative proceedings.

4. Theodore Lowi and others have argued that one major failing in our political system arises because Congress fails to make laws specific enough to channel administrative power precisely and thus reduce the potential influence of interest groups on the administrative process (chapter 3). If FOIA, particularly its nine exceptions, illustrates a concrete and specific directive to administrative agencies, argue from this example that the cure, legislative specificity, is worse than the disease.

5. In this chapter we have discussed two efforts by the public interest movement to revive pluralism by increasing public access to agency information and decision-making. To what extent do the exemptions to FOIA and the Sunshine Act work against the public interest reforms for strengthening participatory democracy?

[18]See *Wall Street Journal*, 23 December 1981, p. 13.

CHAPTER 5

Informality and Formality in Administrative Law

The next three chapters teach what is without doubt the most difficult side of administrative law to master. Before you yawn and close the book, let us assure you that there will be light at the end of this tunnel. Once you have mastered the concepts set out here, they will seem simple and logical. As with learning to do long division or finding square roots of numbers, once the light clicks on, you will have no trouble keeping the concepts clearly in focus.

These three chapters review the legal procedures required to adjudicate (the judicial side of public administration) and to make administrative rules (the legislative side of adminstration). These procedures are the most familiar aspects of administrative law. For reasons you will shortly understand, most judicial opinions in administrative law focus on legal controls and requirements that govern these two processes. Students who only learn administrative law from cases tend to think that these two processes occupy the bulk of administrator's time, that they are the main thing public administration is "about."

Administrators do more than adjudicate controversies and make rules to guide their future behavior, however. While the formal procedures for adjudication and rulemaking are better documented, a host of less familiar *informal procedures* make up the daily activities of administrators. We think that you can best learn the full range of administrative procedure by locating different kinds of procedures on a continuum of legal formality. The least formal are those that administrators can make with the least concern for legal limits, that is, with the most discretion. The most formal are those decisions that must conform to the most extensive and detailed procedural requirements prescribed by statutes and the courts.

No decision is ever entirely free of legal limits, of course. Murder is rarely an acceptable tool of administrative policy. In the everyday practice of administration, however, administrators make most decisions informally, without significant legal constraints on what to decide or how to decide it.

But what, precisely, is the complication that makes this material difficult for non-lawyers? It is that adjudication and rulemaking, the standard staples of administrative law, can fall *anywhere* on the continuum. You will see that the trick is to identify how many and what kinds of formalities the law requires in a given set of circumstances, regardless of whether the law labels the problem rulemaking or adjudication.

It is important to understand that informality, discretion, and the raw exercise of political power historically predate legal constraints. Recall that the rule of law is a surprisingly recent development in Western civilization. Administrative law over the years has moved to increase administrative formalities. To appreciate the development of formality within administrative law, it is best to understand the informal political seas from which the new life form emerged.

To help you pull these materials together we have constructed the continuum of informality and formality in administrative law in Appendix A, page 545. We have put it at the end of the book because it helps put in perspective cases that arise in many chapters. You will recognize some of the cases, but not all of them, and the adjudication/rulemaking distinction may befuddle you until you have mastered chapters 5 through 7.

The next section gives some examples of informal administration. It may appear contradictory to study administrative decisions unbounded by law in a book on administrative law. A danger does indeed lurk here. To discuss in detail the nonlegal side of administration would quickly expand this book beyond its scope and your patience. Although the great majority of criminal prosecutions are resolved informally through the prosecutor's use of discretion and plea bargaining, the principles of criminal law and the politics that shape these principles provide a context for bargaining in the shadow of the law. Thus there is a link between the formal and informal aspects of criminal law practice, and this link is also apparent in other fields of law, such as administrative law.

Just as in criminal justice, which is really one kind of public administration, so in noncriminal administration eighty percent or more of daily activity is on the informal half of the continuum.[1] However, studying informal administration and law is not a contradiction precisely because the potential for formalizing the informal by imposing legal constraints on it always exist. At the same time when courts affirm the authority of agencies to make informal decisions or use informal procedure such as mediation, they are giving legal authority to the informal dimension of administration. Whether and how much to formalize an informal process has been the central problem in virtually every case thus far reported in this book. The Department of Agriculture acted less formally before *Morgan* than afterward. The welfare recipient had no pretermination hearing before *Goldberg*.

Obviously if the central issue in administrative law is whether to push an administrative procedure toward the formal end of the continuum, this chapter cannot dispose of all that passes for informal administration. You are merely alerted to keep this continuum in mind as you make your way through the legal requirements described in later chapters.

Examples of Informal Administration

1. The commissioners of the FTC decide to act to eliminate abuses in the undertaking business. They may proceed either by bringing actions against individual viola-

[1]James O. Freedman, *Crisis and Legitimacy* (New York: Columbia University Press, 1978), 10.

tors by charging them with unfair business practices in specific instances (an adjudication strategy) or by writing rules and applying them to all undertakers (a rulemaking strategy). In the case of the FTC, at least, the *choice* between the two is entirely at the discretion of the commissioners.

2. A hospital reports to a state health agency that a patient has suffered from the toxic poisoning known as botulism. The hospital has traced the offending organism to a certain brand of canned meat. The health agency, without further investigation, orders all grocers to pull the brand from their shelves immediately.

3. Officials at the Internal Revenue Service decide to audit automatically all returns in which the taxpayer claims the costs of operating a yacht as a deductible business expense. They also decide to shift personnel from the review of estate tax returns to the review of income tax returns. Both IRS decisions are discretionary.

4. During the Vietnam war buildup, a man just out of school unexpectedly receives his notice to report for his preinduction physical examination three weeks later. He wants to join the Peace Corps instead, and needs to delay induction long enough for the Peace Corps to process his application. In a phone conservation with his local Selective Service Board, the board representative gives him detailed but "unofficial" instructions on how to delay taking the physical exam long enough for the Peace Corps to process his application.

5. After a female administrator in the U.S. Department of Justice reports to the head of her division that she has been sexually harassed by her male supervisor, the division head tells her "not to worry about it" because he will "speak to her supervisor informally about the matter." The division head goes to the supervisor's office and discusses the complaint of sexual harassment informally and confidentially. The male supervisor agrees not to harass sexually the people he works with, including the woman who made the complaint. The division head's decision not to advise a federal employee of her rights under Title VII of the Civil Rights Act of 1964 to bring legal actions against her supervisor and the Deparment of Justice, and his decision to talk informally to the male supervisor about the complaint both exercise administrative discretion.

In all five illustrations administrators made decisions not to apply formal rules or enforce written regulations. Yet in each instance the administrator acted in the capacity of a government official.

Informal Administration in Rulemaking and Adjudication

The journey out of this morass of specific instances starts with a very important step. When an agency *adjudicates* an issue, the courts have often stated that the United States Constitution does impose some legal formalities. In other words, adjudication can rarely be entirely discretionary. When an agency makes rules, however, the Constitution does not necessarily require any legal procedures, and the Administrative Procedure Act (APA) in section 553, exempts some classes of rulemaking from its legal requirements. In adjudication, court rulings that seem to deny a person's claim for legal formalities on closer inspection usually say that the person has a proper claim, but not yet, not this early in the game.[2] This is the gist of *Mathews v. Eldridge* and *Wyman v. James*. But in rulemaking situations, in the absence of statutory legal requirements, courts may approve discretionary agency decisions now and forever.

Thus the first step is to distinguish rulemaking and adjudication. To help clarify the distinction, begin by thinking of the difference between the legal outputs of legislatures and of courts. Legislatures make statutes—rulemaking—that speak to a general class of citizens, often to all adults. Courts, on the other hand, make judgments—adjudication—that resolve the interests of specific parties by assessing a set of facts unique to them and their dispute. The following case, *Bi-Metallic Investment Co. v. State Board of Equalization of Colorado* (1915), is the Supreme Court's classic case on distinguishing rulemaking and adjudication. Although this case is pre-APA, it serves as the Court's understanding of the difference between rulemaking and adjudication even after the APA.

Bi-Metallic Investment Co. v. State Board of Equalization of Colorado

239 U.S. 44 (1915) 9–0

+ White, McKenna, Holmes, Day, Hughes, Van Devanter, Lamar, Pitney, McReynolds

[The Supreme Court of Colorado had upheld the order of the State Board of Equalization raising the tax valuation of all taxable property in Denver by an across-the-board forty percent. The decision by the board was unilateral and without any prior hearings where those adversely affected could present their case. The petitioner, the owner of property in Denver, brought this suit claiming that it had suffered loss of property through increased taxation without an opportunity to be heard. It asserted that this constituted a deprivation of property without due process of law in violation of the Fourteenth Amendment, and asked that the board's order be set aside.]

Justice Holmes delivered the opinion of the Court.

For the purposes of decision we assume that the constitutional question is presented in the baldest way—that neither the plaintiff nor the assessor of Denver, who presents a brief on the plaintiff's side, nor any representative of the city and county, was given an opportunity to be heard, other than such as they may have had by reason of the fact that the time of meeting of the boards is fixed by law. On this assumption it is obvious that injustice may be suffered if some property in the county already has been valued at its full worth. But if certain property has been valued at a rate different from that generally prevailing in the county the owner has had his opportunity to protest and appeal as usual in our system of taxation. *Hagar v. Reclamation District*, 111 U.S. 701, 709, 710, so that it must be assumed that the property owners in the county all stand alike. The question then is whether all individuals have a constitutional right to be heard before a matter can be decided in which all are equally concerned—here, for instance, before a superior board decides that the local taxing officers have adopted a system of underevaluation throughout a county, as notoriously often has been the case. The answer of this court in the *State Railroad Tax Cases*, 92 U.S. 575, at least as to any further notice,

---

[2]Courts also deny claims for adjudication when they conclude that the claimant possesses no legal interest that merits protection. The personnel cases discussed in chapter 12 illustrate the point well.

was that it was hard to believe that the proposition was seriously made.

Where a rule of conduct applies to more than a few people it is impracticable that every one should have a direct voice in its adoption. The Constitution does not require all public acts to be done in town meeting or an assembly of the whole. General statutes within the state power are passed that affect the person or property of individuals, sometimes to the point of ruin, without giving them a chance to be heard. Their rights are protected in the only way that they can be in a complex society, by their power, immediate or remote, over those who make the rule. If the result in this case had been reached as it might have been by the State's doubling the rate of taxation, no one would suggest that the Fourteenth Amendment was violated unless every person affected had been allowed an opportunity to raise his voice against it before the body entrusted by the state constitution with the power. In considering this case in this court we must assume that the proper state machinery has been used, and the question is whether, if the state constitution had declared that Denver had been undervalued as compared with the rest of the State and had decreed that for the current year the valuation should be forty percent higher, the objection now urged could prevail. It appears to us that to put the question is to answer it. There must be a limit to individual argument in such matters if government is to go on. In *Londoner v. Denver*, 210 U.S. 373, 385, a local board had to determine "whether, in what amount, and upon whom" a tax for paving a street should be levied for special benefits. A relatively small number of persons was concerned, who were exceptionally affected, in each case upon individual grounds, and it was held that they had a right to a hearing. But that decision is far from reaching a general determination dealing only with the principle upon which all the assessments in a county had been laid.

In due course we shall see that the line between adjudication and rulemaking becomes more blurred the closer we study it. Nevertheless the classic *Bi-Metallic* case states two critical distinguishing factors. First, does the agency action affect a small specifically identified number of people whom the agency can feasibly hear without sinking under this burden? Second, does the agency decision depend at least in part on facts about specific people and their cases such that an individual, if given some right to be heard, might show the agency it made a factual mistake in his case? Note how the decision to cut off an individual's welfare payments on the basis of some facts about the individual falls in the adjudication category. On the other side, an IRS decision to audit the tax returns of all taxpayers in a certain category, e.g., people who claim deductions for operating yachts, fall in the rulemaking category. The IRS cannot feasibly hear all potentially interested yacht owners, and no one yacht owner possesses the facts that might prove that auditing *all* yacht owners is a bad policy. The decision to raise all property values an equal amount falls in this same rulemaking category.

Adjudication at the Informal End of the Continuum

The more formal adjudication becomes, the more it resembles trial procedures before an impartial judge. For both historical and practical reasons agencies have never used lay juries, but in most other respects a formal administrative "trial" resembles a trial before a judge in the judicial system. Sections 554, 556, and 557 of the APA prescribe the features of a hearing at the federal level, procedures that agencies must sometimes follow in rulemaking as well as adjudication if statutes require. However, many decisions regarding the interests of specific parties in concrete fact situations do not require a formal trial. The constitutional due process requirements of *Goldberg v. Kelly* together with the statutory requirements of the APA mark the formal end of our continuum. The next few pages show that courts often permit much less formality than *Goldberg* seems to require, and sometimes none at all.

Goldberg remains the Supreme Court's most complete statement of the Constitution's due process requirements for adjudication. It has triggered much comment and research, including Dean Paul Verkuil's careful review of the nature of informal adjudication in just a few agencies in the federal government. We reproduce much of it here not merely to show that much informal adjudication occurs but to give beginning students a sense of the vastness of federal activity. The article also teaches that the bureaucratic world hardly marches in lockstep with the occasional pronouncements of the Supreme Court. Despite its density the article is therefore worth reading. Veteran students of public affairs may wish to skim parts of this study. Do, however, take note of Verkuil's list of the ten *Goldberg* ingredients. Chapter 6 will explain each in more detail.

A Study of Informal Adjudication Procedures

Paul Verkuil
University of Chicago Law Review 43 (1976):
739, 757–71

Since there are so many different ways the federal government adjudicates informally, the study, conducted in the summer of 1975, was designed to reduce the observation process to manageable size. In order to establish a controlled setting, four agencies were selected for study in terms of four typical informal adjudication categories. The agencies selected were the Departments of Agriculture (USDA), Commerce, Housing and Urban Development (HUD), and the Interior. The categories selected were: (1) grants, benefits, loans, and subsidies; (2) licensing, authorizing, and accrediting; (3) inspecting, grading, and auditing; and (4) planning, policy making, and economic development. The resulting "four-by-four" study was intended to permit comparison of intra- and inter-agency behavior in informal adjudication.

The study focused on forty-two individual programs in the four categories, with the bulk of the programs falling in the first two categories. The study of each program involved direct contact by the author with responsible agency personnel, usually government lawyers with backgrounds in the particular programs and their attendant procedures. Each contact person was provided with a written request for information (a procedural "checklist") which was further explained in follow-ups both in person and by telephone. As the data requested were received, they were compiled according to the checklist paragraphs. From these compilations summaries by program and by agency were produced.

One goal of this empirical phase was to determine how much impact emerging notions of procedural due process were having upon the process of informal adjudication. To measure this awareness more precisely, the individual procedural ingredients mandated in *Goldberg* were isolated and tabulated with respect to each of the programs studied. *Goldberg* has been described as requiring the following ten ingredients:

1. timely and adequate notice;
2. confronting adverse witnesses;
3. oral presentation of arguments;
4. oral presentation of evidence;
5. cross-examination of adverse witnesses;
6. disclosure to the claimant of opposing evidence;

7. the right to retain an attorney;
8. a determination on the record of the hearing;
9. a statement of reasons for the determination and an indication of the evidence relied on; and
10. an impartial decision maker.*

The survey data will be presented first by program in descending order of the number of *Goldberg* ingredients; then, after noting some significant procedural innovations and other practices worthy of comment, the data will be summarized and cross-tabulated.

A. Presentation by Ingredients

The ten *Goldberg* procedural ingredients were present in their entirety in only two of the forty-two programs studied. Both of these programs are administered by the Department of Agriculture, and involve category one (grants, benefits, loans, and subsidies). They are disqualification of recipients under the food stamp program, and establishment of agricultural marketing quotas. Since the food stamp program has social goals similar to the welfare program, it is not suprising that the full *Goldberg* ingredients should be provided. On the other hand, the other USDA program presents an

---

* See *Goldberg v. Kelly*, 397 U.S. 254, 267–71 (1970). The ten ingredients extracted from *Goldberg* are substantially as identified by Professor Davis. See K. Davis [*Administrative Law*, 5th ed. (St. Paul: West Publishing Co., 1973)] at 288. Their enumeration is not uncontroversial, however. Professor Clark Byse, in discussions with the author, has interpreted ingredient 6 to be of no independent vitality (i.e., as a discovery device) but rather to be only the inevitable consequence of providing ingredients 3, 4, and 5. He would, therefore, find only nine *Goldberg* ingredients. This survey, however, proceeds on the assumption that ingredient 6 has separate meaning as a discovery device, and agency procedures will be measured against its requirements. For a quick overview, the following statistical summary should be helpful. Of the forty-two programs studied, two provided all ten *Goldberg* ingredients, five provided nine, two provided eight, four provided seven, one provided six, one provided five, nine provided four, thirteen provided three, three provided two, and two provided none. These totals were taken from operative procedural regulations, which do not exist for the last two programs. . . . Alternatively stated, the summary by ingredient shows forty of the functions provided ingredient 1, ten ingredient 2, twenty-one ingredient 3, twelve ingredient 4, nine ingredient 5, ten ingredient 6, sixteen ingredient 7, eight ingredient 8, thirty-seven ingredient 9, and thirty-eight ingredient 10.

---

unexpectedly elaborate procedural mechanism. USDA currently sets quotas for support payments to farmers who produce tobacco, peanuts, and extra-long staple cotton. These quotas are set initially by local county committees. Upon receiving notification of his quota, a dissatisfied farmer has fifteen days to apply for review before the local review committee, which is composed of three farmers appointed from the farmer's locality by the Secretary of Agriculture. The hearing before this committee contains the full *Goldberg* ingredients. Judicial review of the committee's decision, based upon the substantial evidence test, may be had within fifteen days in the United States district court or a state court of record.

Four programs, all administered by the Department of Agriculture, have procedures containing nine of the ten *Goldberg* ingredients. Two of the programs have every ingredient by number 8 (a determination resting solely on the record of the hearing): reparations proceeedings under the Packers and Stockyards Act (PSA) and under the Perishable Agricultural Commodities Act (PACA). Both resist classification within the four categories of informal adjudication established at the outset. Essentially, the Department of Agriculture exacts reparations for farmers injured by the unfair conduct of packers, stockyards, and dealers in perishable agricultural commodities (fresh fruits and vegetables). The informal adjudication procedures established by the Department for making these reparations decisions offer useful insights into the informal adjudication process. Of particular interest is the fact that the reparation proceedings under both acts provide for a *Goldberg*-type (nine ingredient) oral hearing and a shortened procedure which is much more summary in form. In addition the Department engages in an informal settlement stage before either procedural route is undertaken. Attorneys in the Department's Office of General Counsel are responsible for administering the reparation proceedings. They first investigate all claims, conduct the oral or shortened hearings at field offices, and prepare recommended decisions for the judicial officer, who reviews the transcript of the record and renders the final agency decision. There does not appear to be any articulated policy for excluding the *Goldberg* requirement for a determination on the record from the otherwise elaborate oral hearings, unless it is that the judicial officer who renders the final decision is not the hearing officer and that the order itself is not directly reviewable.

The two other Department of Agriculture programs that provide nine of the *Goldberg* ingredients are in the licensing and inspection categories; revocation or suspension of veterinary accreditations and withdrawal of approval of markets or facilities under the animal quarantine laws. In both cases the missing procedural ingredient is number six, disclosure to claimant of opposing evidence, which is precluded by explicit department policy.

There were two programs with eight *Goldberg* ingredients: debarring of "responsibility connected" employees of licensees who violate the Perishable Agricultural Commodities Act from future employment with PACA licensees, a procedure that omits ingredients 2 (confrontation) and 5 (cross-examination); and issuing permits under the Offshore Shrimp Fisheries Act, a Commerce program that omits ingredients 6 (disclosure of opposing evidence) and 8 (determination on the record). The "responsibly connected" debarment determination has for a long time been made by the Chief of the Regulatory Branch of the Fruit and Vegetable Division, USDA, without any established procedural regulations. Nonetheless, in the cases where the initial determination is questioned, the division provides the debarred employee with an informal hearing containing each of the *Goldberg* ingredients except confrontation and cross-examination. Recently, however, the division's procedures for determining who is a "responsible employee" have come under judicial scrutiny, and significant changes may be necessary in the future.

Four programs operated under procedures with seven of the *Goldberg* ingredients: removal of grain inspectors' licenses under the United States Grain Standards Act (a USDA function); debarment of lender-builders, appraisers, and attorneys under the Federal Housing Administration (HUD); issuance of permits under the Antiquity Act (Interior); and grants and loans by the Bureau of Indian Affairs (Interior).

The first program fails to provide ingredients 3 (oral argument), 6 (disclosure of opposing evidence), and 10 (impartial decision maker); the second fails to provide 2 (confrontation), 5 (cross-examination), and 6 (disclosure of opposing evidence); the third also omits ingredients 2, 5, and 8; and the fourth omits ingredients, 2, 4, (oral presentation of evidence), and 5.

One program has procedures with six *Goldberg* ingredients. Retailer disqualification under the food stamp program is a USDA function that omits ingredients 2 (confrontation), 4 (oral presentation of evidence), 5 (cross-examination), and 8 (determination on the record). Retailers may be disqualified under the Food Stamp Act for irregularities such as selling ineligible items or discounting stamps for cash. The disqualification can be for up to three years. It should be noted that the procedures for retailer disqualifications are considerably less formal than for disqualifications of food stamp recipients. The decisions are made by a single official (the Chief, Retailer-Wholesaler Branch, Food Stamp Division) in an effort, according to USDA, to obtain uniformity of treatment for retailers throughout the nation. This official reviews case summaries from local officials who collect information, issue notices of charges, and allow the retailer and his counsel to make an oral and written explanation of the charge. The retailer is entitled to administrative review of any order of disqualification. Approximately 49 percent of the retailers seek this review, which represents the final agency decision. In the last five years 182 retailers have sought judicial review.

One program had five *Goldberg* ingredients; leasing of oil, gas, and coal deposits. The program is in the Department of the Interior and has an informal procedure with ingredients, 1, 6, 7, 9, and 10.

Over one-half of the forty-two programs studied (twenty-two) provided procedures with either four or three of the *Goldberg* ingredients. Of the nine programs with four ingredients, all but one had ingredients 1, 3, 9, and 10; of the thirteen programs with three ingredients, all had ingredients 1, 9, and 10. Thus the distinction between eight of the nine four-ingredient programs and the thirteen three-ingredient programs is the addition of oral argument (ingredient

3) to the minimal adversary informal procedures of notice, a statement of reasons, and an impartial decision maker. The eight four-ingredient programs are: loans by the Farmers Home Administration (USDA); public works grants, business development loans, and technical assistance grants by the Economic Development Administration (Commerce); financial guarantees to developers of new communities (HUD); establishment of estuarine sanctuaries (Commerce); master planning for new parks (Interior); and planning for outer continental shelf oil and gas leasing (Interior). The thirteen three-ingredient programs include seven programs within the Department of Commerce; three within the Department of Interior; and three within HUD.

The preponderance of these three- and four-ingredient programs is in the categories of grants and benefits or planning and policymaking. Each of the four agencies studied has programs within these classifications, with Commerce the leader at eleven programs.

Three programs surveyed provided procedures with two of the *Goldberg* ingredients; in each case those ingredients are 1 (notice) and 10 (impartial decision maker). These programs are auditing of money grants for outdoor recreation (Interior); voluntary inspection of fish products (Commerce); and inspection for lead base paint and structural defects on public housing (HUD). Since each program involves inspections, it is not surprising that the adversary procedural ingredients are held to a minimum.

The two remaining programs have no designated procedures, and for the purposes of this study they are categorized as having none of the *Goldberg* ingredients. Both these programs are in the Department of Agriculture: meat and poultry inspections and plant quarantine certifications. . . .

Let us highlight four implications of Verkuil's study. First, the survey reveals a range of administrative adjudicatory formality that is all the more surprising because the study involves only a small minority of federal programs and agencies. Second, most of these procedures have been adopted by the agencies at their own discretion. They are not the results of court orders or statutory prescriptions. Third, please be reassured that this chapter only introduces the ten *Goldberg* ingredients. You *should* at this point feel some frustration about the terminology Verkuil uses, for example, the meaning of a *determination on the record* or *an impartial decision maker.* The next chapters will flesh out these concepts.

The fourth and most important implication is a particularly important principle of modern administrative law raised by the survey. How, you may have asked, can agencies get away with adjudications less formal than *Goldberg* requires? The answer is that the courts have not only used the so-called balancing test to decide whether, at a given point, any hearing is legally necessary. They have also said that the circumstances of many types of adjudication permit use of fewer than all ten ingredients, even when some hearing is required. This form of balancing is less explicitly cost-benefit than the *Mathews* analysis. The how-many-ingredients balance tries to assess which ingredients are suited to the needs of the parties in the situation.[3]

Thus in *Goss v. Lopez*, 419 U.S. 565 (1975), students were suspended from school for allegedly disrupting classes and fighting. They received no hearing prior to their suspension. The Supreme Court ruled that the school administration erred by failing to allow the students at least to tell their side in an informal give-and-take with school

---

[3] "Without saying so directly, the Court set *Goldberg's* rigid model aside and replaced it with an admittedly vague procedural balancing test." Paul Verkuil, "The Emerging Concept of Administrative Procedure", *Columbia Law Review* 78 (1978): 258, 288.

officials. The Court in effect required an approximation of the first four ingredients but no more. Note that the Court did not require an impartial decisionmaker. It did, however, state that the minimal hearing was suitable in education because hearings could have educational value for students regardless of their outcomes.

Hence the *Goldberg* decision has not produced a single set of criteria that all informal adjudication must meet. In fact, when all ten elements are present, an agency is very close to the formal end of the continuum. The Supreme Court seems to have concluded that the Constitution demands varying amounts of formality depending on the nature of the problem, and no single set of criteria will necessarily ever be applied. The next case shows just how informal adjudication can become.

Board of Curators of the University of Missouri et. al. v. Horowitz

435 U.S. 78 (1978) 5–4
+   Burger, Stewart, Powell, Rehnquist, Stevens
+/–   Brennan, White, Marshall, Blackmun

[Horowitz, a medical student, was placed on academic probation at the end of her first year in medical school for poor clinical performance and a deficiency in personal hygiene. The same situation existed at the end of her second year and she was dropped from school. She brought suit claiming procedural due process had not been afforded her since she had been given no opportunity to rebut the evidence against her at a hearing. The Eighth Circuit Court of Appeals, reversing the district court, held this procedure violated due process].

Justice Rehnquist delivered the opinion of the Court.

We granted certiorari to consider what procedures must be accorded to a student at a state educational institution whose dismissal may constitute a deprivation of "liberty" or "property" within the meaning of the Fourteenth Amendment. We reverse the judgment of the Court of Appeals. . . .

Respondent was admitted with advanced standing to the Medical School in the fall of 1971. During the final years of a student's education at the school, the student is required to pursue in "rotational units" academic and clinical studies pertaining to various medical disciplines such as obstetrics-gynecology, pediatrics, and surgery. Each student's academic performance at the School is evaluated on a periodic basis by the Council on Evaluation, a body composed of both faculty and students, which can recommend various actions including probation and dismissal. The recommendations of the Council are reviewed by the

Coordinating Committee, a body composed solely of faculty members, and must ultimately be approved by the Dean. Students are not typically allowed to appear before either the Council or the Coordinating Committee on the occasion of their review of the student's academic performance.

In the spring of respondent's first year of study, several faculty members expressed dissatisfaction with her clinical performance during a pediatrics rotation. The faculty members noted respondent's "performance was below that of her peers in all clinical patient-oriented settings," that she was erratic in her attendance at clinical sessions, and that she lacked a critical concern for personal hygiene. Upon the recommendation of the Council on Evaluation, respondent was advanced to her second and final year on a probationary basis.

Faculty dissatisfaction with respondent's clinical performance continued during the following year.

For example, respondent's docent, or faculty adviser, rated her clinical skills as "unsatisfactory." In the middle of the year, the Council again reviewed respondent's academic progress and concluded that respondent should not be considered for graduation in June of that year; furthermore, the Council recommended that, absent "radical improvement," respondent be dropped from the school.

Respondent was permitted to take a set of oral and practical examinations as an "appeal" of the decision not to permit her to graduate. Pursuant to this "appeal," respondent spent a substantial portion of time with seven practicing physicians in the area who enjoyed a good reputation among their peers. The physicians were asked to recommend whether respondent should be allowed to graduate on schedule, and, if not, whether she should be dropped immediately or allowed to remain on probation. Only two of the doctors recommended that respondent be graduated on schedule. Of the other five, two recommended that she be immediately dropped from the school. The remaining three recommended that she not be allowed to graduate in June and be continued on probation pending further reports on her clinical progress. Upon receipt of these recommendations, the Council on Evaluation reaffirmed its prior position.

The Council met again in mid-May to consider whether respondent should be allowed to remain in school beyond June of that year. Noting that the report on respondent's recent surgery rotation rated her performance as "low-satisfactory," the Council unanimously recommended that "barring receipt of any reports that Miss Horowitz has improved radically, [she] not be allowed to re-enroll in the . . . School of Medicine." The Council delayed making its recommendation official until receiving reports on other rotations; when a report on respondent's emergency rotation also turned out to be negative, the Council unanimously reaffirmed its recommendation that respondent be dropped from the school. The Coordinating Committee and the Dean approved the recommendation and notified respondent, who appealed the decision in writing to the University's Provost for Health Sciences. The Provost sustained the school's actions after reviewing the record compiled during the earlier proceedings. . . .

In *Goss v. Lopez*, 419 U.S. 565 (1975), we held that due process requires, in connection with the suspension of a student from public school for disciplinary reasons, "that the student be given oral or written notice of the charges against him, and if he denies them, an explanation of the evidence the authorities have and an opportunity to present his side of the story." Id., at 581. The Court of Appeals apparently read *Goss* as requiring some type of formal hearing at which respondent could defend her academic ability and performance. All that *Goss* required was an "informal give-and-take" between the student and the administrative body dismissing him that would, at least, give the student "the opportunity to characterize his conduct and put it in what he deems the proper context." But we have frequently emphasized that "[t]he very nature of due process negates any concept of inflexible procedures universally applicable to every imaginable situation." *Cafeteria Workers v. McElroy*, 367 U.S. 886, 895, (1961). The need for flexibility is well illustrated by the significant difference between the failure of a student to meet academic standards and the violation by a student of valid rules of conduct. This difference calls for far less stringent procedural requirements in the case of an academic dismissal.

Since the issue first arose 50 years ago, state and lower federal courts have recognized that there are distinct differences between decisions to suspend or dismiss a student for disciplinary purposes and similar actions taken for academic reasons which may call for hearings in connection with the former but not the latter. Thus, in *Barnard v. Inhabitants of Shelburne*, 216 Mass. 19, 102 N.E. 1095 (1913), the Supreme Judicial Court of Massachusetts rejected an argument, based on several earlier decisions requiring a hearing in disciplinary contexts, that school officials must also grant a hearing before excluding a student on academic grounds. According to the court, disciplinary cases have "no application. . . . Misconduct is a very different matter from failure to attain a standard of excellence in studies. A determination as to the fact involves investigation of a quite different kind. A public hearing may be regarded as helpful to the ascertainment of misconduct and useless or harmful in finding out the truth as to scholarship. . . . "

Reason, furthermore, clearly supports the perception of these decisions. A school is an academic institution, not a courtroom or administrative hearing room. In *Goss,* this Court felt that suspensions of students for disciplinary reasons have a sufficient resemblance to traditional judicial and administrative factfinding to call for a "hearing" before the relevant school authority. While recognizing that school authorities must be afforded the necessary tools to maintain discipline, the Court concluded:

> [I]t would be a strange disciplinary system in an educational institution if no communication was sought by the disciplinarian with the student in an effort to inform him of his dereliction and to let him tell his side of the story in order to make sure that an injustice is not done. . . .
>
> [R]equiring effective notice and informal hearing permitting the student to give his version of the events will provide a meaningful hedge against erroneous action. At least the disciplinarian will be alerted to the existence of disputes about facts and arguments about cause and effect. 419 U.S., at 580, 583–584.

Even in the context of a school disciplinary proceeding, however, the Court stopped short of requiring a formal hearing since "further formalizing the suspension process and escalating its formality and adversary nature may not only make it too costly as a regular disciplinary tool but also destroy its effectiveness as a part of the teaching process." Id., at 583.

Academic evaluations of a student, in contrast to disciplinary determinations, bear little resemblance to the judicial and administrative factfinding proceedings to which we have traditionally attached a full-hearing requirement. In *Goss,* the school's decision to suspend the students rested on factual conclusions that the individual students had partcipated in demon-

strations that had disrupted classes, attacked a police officer, or caused physical damage to school property. The requirement of a hearing, where the student could present his side of the factual issue, could under such circumstances "provide a meaningful hedge against erroneous action." Ibid. The decision to dismiss respondent, by comparison, rested on the academic judgment of school officials that she did not have the necessary clinical ability to perform adequately as a medical doctor and was making insufficient progress toward that goal. Such a judgment is by its nature more subjective and evaluative than the typical factual questions presented in the average disciplinary decision. Like the decision of an individual professor as to the proper grade for a student in his course, the determination whether to dismiss a student for academic reasons requires an expert evaluation of cumulative information and is not readily adapted to the procedural tools of judicial or administrative decisionmaking.

Under such circumstances, we decline to ignore the historic judgment of educators and thereby formalize the academic dismissal process by requiring a hearing. The educational process is not by nature adversary; instead it centers around a continuing relationship between faculty and students, "one in which the teacher must occupy many roles — educator, adviser, friend, and, at times, parent-substitute," *Goss v. Lopez,* 419 U.S., at 594 (Powell, J., dissenting). This is especially true as one advances through the varying regimes of the educational system, and the instruction becomes both more individualized and more specialized. In *Goss,* this Court concluded that the value of some form of hearing in a disciplinary context outweighs any resulting harm to the academic environment. Influencing this conclusion was clearly the belief that disciplinary proceedings, in which the teacher must decide whether to punish a student for disruptive or insubordinate behavior, may automatically bring an adversary flavor to the normal student-teacher relationship. The same conclusion does not follow in the academic context. . . .

The judgment of the Court of Appeals is therefore reversed.

(B) when the agency for good cause finds (and incorporates the
finding and a brief statement of reasons therefor in the rules issued)
that notice and public procedure thereon are impracticable, unnecessary, or contrary to the public interest.

(c) After notice required by this section, the agency shall give interested persons an opportunity to participate in the rule making
through submission of written data, views, or arguments with or
without opportunity for oral presentation. After consideration of the
relevant matter presented, the agency shall incorporate in the rules
adopted a concise general statement of their basis and purpose. When
rules are required by statute to be made on the record after opportunity for an agency hearing, sections 556 and 557 of this title apply
instead of this subsection.

Notice and comments are the core of how regulators pass rules.

(d) The required publication or service of a substantive rule shall
be made not less than 30 days before its effective date, except—

(1) a substantive rule which grants or recognizes an exemption or
relieves a restriction;

(2) interpretative rules and statements of policy; or

(3) as otherwise provided by the agency for good cause found and
published with the rule.

(e) Each agency shall give an interested person the right to petition
for the issuance, amendment, or repeal of a rule.

The section is well salted with exceptions to the requirement of notice and comment, and we shall discuss these exceptions momentarily. Before doing so, however,
a bit more background is necessary. First, some statutes creating or defining agency
responsibilities create their own rulemaking procedures, which preempt the APA. The
most prominent of these today is the Federal Trade Commission Improvement Act
of 1975. Occasionally a statute requires a full trial-type hearing for rulemaking. This
brings into play the provisions of APA sections 554, 556, and 557. These rules primarily
govern formal adjudication and are described in chapter 6. Second, you should be
aware that the Model State Administrative Procedure Act, included in Appendix C,
particularly sections three through seven, states fewer exceptions than the federal act
and seems to give citizens somewhat greater voice in the making of such rules. Finally,
chapter 7 of this book will discuss what section 553 of the APA does require, plus
extra requirements that some courts have added for constitutional reasons in rulemaking proceedings.

Some of section 553's exceptions hardly surprise us. Section (a)(1)'s military and
diplomatic affairs may require such speed and secrecy that the advance notice and comments gathering process could devastate the policy's effectiveness. Other exceptions
are less obvious and will benefit from some illustrations.

1. *Section (a)(2): Matter Relating to Public Property.* The Bureau of Reclamation,
which operated a federal hydroelectric dam and sold the power at low rates, decided
to reallocate the electricity. A city cut off from this low-cost power supply sued

claiming that the bureau should have held a 553-type hearing. The Court denied the claim because the dam and the power were federal public property.[5]

2. *Section (a)(2): Matter Relating to Grants.* Without following 553 procedures, the Federal Highway Administration set standards that states must meet to receive federal highway funds. Since these funds are grants, the Court approved the agency's action.[6]

3. *Section (b)(A): Notice and Hearing Not Required for Interpretative Rules.* The secretary of labor issued a rule denying immigrant status to people, including domestic servants, whose work might deny a job to an American citizen able and willing to perform it. Plaintiffs sought immigrant status for their alien maid and challenged the rule for the lack of a hearing. The Court upheld the rule because it was an interpretation of the policy stated in the section 212(a)(14) of the Immigration and Nationality Act.[7]

4. *Section (b)(B): Notice Not Required When Contrary to the Public Interest.* During President Nixon's wage and price freeze, announced on August 15, 1971, the White House and the Cost of Living Council issued many executive orders and regulations regarding wages and prices. Some businesses who raised prices in the face of these rules claimed that the rules had no legal effect because no advance notice had been given. Courts held that the delay required by 553 would encourage businesses to raise their prices in advance of the effective date of the freeze and that 553 procedures would therefore hurt the public interest.[8]

These examples show that the APA leaves much room for discretionary administrative policymaking. Indeed, these exceptions seem potentially elastic enough to allow agencies to avoid 553 whenever they so desire. Agencies could do this by simply calling any rule an interpretation of its authorizing statute, or a statement of general policy, or by claiming that notice would hurt the national interest. Courts have resisted such stretching of these words. Especially where the "interpretative rule" loophole threatens to expand, courts have insisted either that the agency be interpreting specific legislative language, or that it follow notice and comment proceedings whenever the rule has a substantial negative impact on specific interests.[9]

Legal Problems in Informal Administration

In a sense every legal issue in administrative law wrestles with the question, "How much formality is enough?" This was, after all, the problem in *Morgan, Goldberg,* and *Horowitz.* A few issues do, however, arise out of informality itself, and this chapter concludes by examining one of the more perplexing of these, the problem of administrative *estoppel.* To introduce the case, review the example above of the informal advice

---

[5] *City of Santa Clara v. Kleppe,* 418 F. supp. 1243 (1976). And see *Lodge 1647 and Lodge 1904, American Federation of Government Employees v. McNamara,* 291 F. Supp. 286 (1968) describing a federal personnel matter exempt from 553.

[6] *Center for Auto Safety v. Cox,* 580 F.2d 689 (1978).

[7] *Pesikoff v. Secretary of Labor,* 501 F.2d 757 (1974).

[8] See *DeRieux v. Five Smiths, Inc.,* 499 F.2d 1321 (1974).

[9] See *Chrysler Corp. v. Brown,* 441 U.S. 281 (1979).

given by the Selective Service employee, page 203. She in effect said, "If you take a certain course of action, you won't be drafted before the Peace Corps has a chance to consider your application." But what if the Selective Service Board's policies say something different, or if the board simply reneges on the advice, even though it was accurate when given? Can the disappointed citizen require an administrative agency to act consistently with its informal advice, even if that advice is mistaken or superseded? Does giving incorrect advice informally "estop," that is, preclude, the government from enforcing its actual policies upon the misinformed citizen? This raises the related question of when an agency becomes legally obligated to follow its own informal decisions. In the context of studying informal administration, we are interested in what recourse, if any, people have against informal decisions that turn out to be at odds with agency policy.

Federal Crop Insurance Corp. v. Merrill

332 U.S. 380 (1947) 5–4

+ Vinson, Reed, Frankfurter, Murphy, Burton
− Black, Rutledge, Jackson, Douglas

[Merrill had inquired of the Federal Crop Insurance Corporation, which is completely government-owned, as to whether spring wheat planted on land that had grown winter wheat was insurable under the Federal Crop Insurance Act. Being assured that it was, Merrill planted the spring wheat and found it subsequently destroyed by drought. The corporation refused to pay since its regulations prohibited the insuring of reseeded crops. Merrill brought suit to collect claiming he had been misled by the government. The Idaho courts sustained Merrill's contention.]

Justice Frankfurter delivered the opinion of the Court.

We brought this case here because it involves a question of importance in the administration of the Federal Crop Insurance Act. . . .

The case no doubt presents phases of hardship. We take for granted that, on the basis of what they were told by the Corporation's local agent, the respondents reasonably believed that their entire crop was covered by petitioner's insurance. And so we assume that recovery could be had against a private insurance company. But the Corporation is not a private insurance company. It is too late in the day to urge that the Government is just another private litigant, for purposes of charging it with liability, whenever it takes over a business theretofore conducted by private enterprise or engages in competition with private ventures. Government is not partly public or partly private, depending upon the governmental pedigree of the type of particular activity or the man-

ner in which the Government conducts it. The Government may carry on its operations through conventional executive agencies or through corporate forms especially created for defined ends. *See Keifer & Keifer v. Reconstruction Finance Corp.*, 306 U.S. 381, 390, 59 S. Ct. 516, 83 L. Ed. 784. Whatever the form in which the Government functions, anyone entering into an arrangement with the Government takes the risk of having accurately ascertained that he who purports to act for the Government stays within the bounds of his authority. The scope of this authority may be explicitly defined legislation, properly exercised through the rule-making power. And this is so even though, as here, the agent himself may have been unaware of the limitations upon his authority. . . .

If the Federal Crop Insurance Act had by explicit language prohibited the insurance of spring wheat which is reseeded on winter wheat acreage, the ignorance of such a restriction, either by the respondents or the Corporation's agent, would be immaterial and recovery could not be had against the Corporation for loss of such reseeded wheat. Congress could hardly define the multitudinous details appropriate for the business of crop insurance when the Government entered it. Inevitably "the terms and conditions" upon which valid governmental insurance can be had must be defined by the agency acting for the Government. And so Congress had legislated in this instance, as in modern regulatory enactments it so often does, by conferring the rule-making power upon the agency created for carrying out its policy. . . .

Accordingly, the Wheat Crop Insurance Regulations were binding on all who sought to come within the Federal Crop Insurance Act, regardless of actual knowledge of what is in the Regulations or of the hardship resulting from innocent ignorance. The oft-quoted observation in *Rock Island, Arkansas & Louisiana R. Co. v. United States*, 254 U.S. 141, 143, 41 S.Ct. 55, 56, 65 L. Ed. 188, that "Men must turn square corners when they deal with the Government," does not reflect a callous outlook. It merely expresses the duty of all courts to observe the conditions defined by Congress for charging the public treasury. The "terms and conditions" defined by the Corporation, under authority of Congress, for creating liability on the part of the Government preclude recovery for the loss of the reseeded wheat no matter with what good reason the respondents thought they had obtained insurance from the Government. Indeed, not only do the wheat regulations limit the liability of the Government as if they had been enacted by Congress directly, but they were in fact incorporated by reference in the application, as specifically required by the Regulations.

We have thus far assumed, as did the parties here and the courts below, that the controlling regulation in fact precluded insurance coverage for spring wheat reseeded on winter wheat acreage. It explicitly states that the term "wheat crop shall not include . . . winter wheat in the 1945 crop year, and spring wheat which has been reseeded on winter wheat acreage in the

1945 crop year." Sec. 414–37 (v) of Wheat Crop Insurance Regulations, 10 F.R. 1591. The circumstances of this case tempt one to read the regulation, since it is for us to read it, with charitable laxity. But not even the temptations of a hard case can elude the clear meaning of the regulation. It precludes recovery for "spring wheat which has been reseeded on winter wheat acreage in the 1945 crop year." Concerning the validity of the regulation, as "not inconsistent with the provisions" of the Federal Crop Insurance Act, no question has been raised.

The Judgement is reversed and the cause remanded for further proceedings not inconsistent with this opinion.

Reversed.

Justice Black, and Justice Rutledge, dissent.
Justice Jackson, dissenting.

It was early discovered that fair dealing in the insurance business required that the entire contract between the policyholder and the insurance company be embodied in the writings which passed between the parties, namely the written application, if any, and the policy issued. It may be well enough to make some types of contracts with the Government subject to long and involved regulations published in the Federal Register. To my mind, it is an absurdity to hold that every farmer who insures his crops knows what the Federal Register contains or even knows that there is such a publication. If he were to peruse this voluminous and dull publication as it is issued from time to time in order to make sure whether anything has been promulgated that affects his rights, he would never need crop insurance, for he would never get time to plant any crops. Nor am I convinced that a reading of technically-worded regulations would enlighten him much in any event . . .

It is very well to say that those who deal with the Government should turn square corners. But there is no reason why the square corners should constitute a one-way street.

Justice Douglas joins in this opinion.

Estoppel cases like *Merrill* raise the ancient problem expressed in the maxim, "Ignorance of the law excuses no man." If one need not turn square corners, then farmers who lose uninsured crops can falsely claim that someone on the phone told them they had insurance and succeed. The opposite result from the one reached in *Merrill* thus could encourage fraud.

Exercises and Questions for Further Thought

1. Review the Model State APA rulemaking provisions in Appendix C. If they had been in effect when the *Bi-Metallic* case arose, would the Colorado board have had to follow a different course from the one they actually used in this situation?

2. Suppose that a state law providing for the licensing of race horse trainers states that the license of any trainer will be immediately and automatically suspended if, following a race, a urine test on a horse in his care shows the horse to have been drugged. Suppose a trainer who has just had his license suspended sues to have his license reinstated, at least pending a hearing on the merits of the case in which he presents his side of the story. He cites *Goldberg*. What result would the court reach? See *Barry v. Barchi*, 99 S.Ct. 2642 (1979).

[handwritten margin note: Trainer lost - he received a post-suspension hearing - Court cited Mathews. Trainer failed to maintain control.]

3. Do you agree with the philosophy that "men must turn square corners when they deal with the government"? Why or why not?

4. The next two chapters will further clarify the elements of adjudication and rulemaking and articulate the differences and similarities more fully. You should note here, however, that, when requiring a hearing, courts do not consider the costs an administrative action may impose. The *Bi-Metallic* tax decision imposed a much greater cost on people than did the tax decision in *Londoner v. Denver*, cited by Justice Holmes in *Bi-Metallic*, yet the court required a hearing only in *Londoner*. Is it wise for courts to ignore this difference? Why or why not?

5. Technological advances create some new possibilities for relatively informal adjudication. Try to imagine how administrators might use computer hook-ups for gathering data. For an assessment of hearings by telephone see Corsi and Hurley, *"Pilot Study Report on the Use of the Telephone in Administrative Fair Hearings,"* *Administrative Law Review* 31 (1979):485.

[handwritten margin note: People w/ expertise tend to have the upper hand.]

6. Suppose a grade-school principal adopts a policy that permits the spanking of a student with a wooden paddle for violation of certain well-defined school rules. Assume that the principal communicates the paddling policy in advance to students and their parents. A student was paddled on accusation of violating a school rule. No hearing was provided prior to the paddling. Through his parents, the student brought suit claiming, for himself and other students who might receive future paddlings, that due process required a hearing with at least some of the *Goldberg* ingredients before execution of punishment. Should their view prevail? In *Ingraham v. Wright*, 430 U.S. 651 (1977), it did not. A student paddled without justification can at common law bring a tort action against the school for assault and battery. Does this fact affect your analysis in *Ingraham*? Why or why not?

[handwritten note: Justice White dissented: Severe beatings had taken place. A mistake cannot be taken back. A prisoner cannot be subjected to paddling.]

CHAPTER 6

Formal Elements of a Hearing

The time has come to halt the journey into the forest of administrative law long enough to look at a map of the terrain. The first five chapters have described a great variety of administrative actions. Each time an agency acts we try to discover the various ways law controls the decisionmaking process. Three kinds of laws may control any given action. In previous chapters we have said that there are at least four *sources* of administrative law (administrative, judicial, constitutional, and statutory). Here we want to discuss three *kinds* of laws that may control any given action, be that action taken by an agency or a court.

Controlling Law

Constitutional Law

Both the federal government, through the Fifth Amendment, and the state governments, through the Fourteenth Amendment, must afford their citizens *due process of law.* If the courts decide that an agency action falls in the rulemaking category, then, under *Bi-Metallic's* reasoning, the Due Process Clause does not come into play. Agencies may, as far as the Constitution goes, simply announce rules following whatever discretionary informal procedure they wish. Such instances mark the informal end of our legal continuum. If, on the other hand, a court feels an agency action has some of the qualities of adjudication—that it speaks to a relatively manageable group of people whose participation might improve the quality of the decisionmaking process—the courts say due process requires agencies to do something to insure fairness to the person or people affected. We have seen that this something may, depending on the judicial analysis of the specific situation, require a formal hearing in which the agency observes the *Goldberg* conditions. But we have seen how courts have applied *Goldberg* quite narrowly and that the Supreme Court has permitted some very informal adjudicatory procedures, particularly in the school discipline cases of *Goss* and *Horowitz.* This due process law of administration frustrates beginning and expert students of administrative law alike. The case-by-case analysis does not give administrators clear guidance across the full range of adjudicative problems.

The Supreme Court's failure, at the present point in the development of administrative law, to articulate clear constitutional principles to guide adjudication raises the suspicion that the justices have no philosophy of administrative due process at all. The suspicion grows when we ask whether the degree of informality the Court may permit at the informal end of the continuum adequately protects the interests of citizens. Before condemning the Court on such grounds, however, we must recognize that the Court is a political body. That is, nine people with potentially strong but divergent views on legal issues must accommodate those views sufficiently to keep the Court, their collective selves, functioning. Individual justices may have detailed and precise administrative law philosophies, such as Justice White's theory of administration articulated in his lengthy dissenting opinion in *INS v. Chadha, supra* at 147. However, as in the *Chadha* case, such philosophies do not necessarily produce majority opinions that state any one of them. By the early 1980s the bulk of the justices who decided *Goldberg* had left the Court, but their replacements, under the leadership of two conservative chief justices, Warren Burger and William Rehnquist, have not yet managed to hammer out a strong consensus on detailed constitutional principles of administrative law. In this period of groping uncertainty and disagreement, legal ambiguity may be unavoidable. The situation need not endure, and at this writing we are observing a growing trend toward the reduction of due process protection in administrative settings.

The Statutes Creating and Authorizing Agencies to Act

Any time a legislature creates an agency by statute, and any time it chooses to amend agency power by statute, that legislature can prescribe both what the agency does and how it shall do it. Legislatures need not pay attention to the due process distinction between rulemaking and adjudication as long as they do not prescribe *less* than due process requires. In other words, legislatures may require fully formal hearings for rulemaking, or perhaps something in the middle of the continuum, as Congress did for the FTC in the Federal Trade Commission Improvement Act. The same statutes may specify adjudicatory procedures. If the agency's statute requires a formal hearing for either rulemaking or adjudication, then the agency must follow the Administrative Procedure Act's (APA) formal hearing requirements, to which we turn in a moment. Before doing so, however, please recall another entirely separate point about creating and authorizing statutes: These statutes, but not the Constitution nor the APA, define what the agency may do as well as how it proceeds. Courts may step in, as chapter 3 showed, to overrule agency action that does not fit within the power delegated to the agency by statute.

The Administrative Procedure Act

The APA uses the rulemaking/adjudication distinction, but on close inspection this is not the APA's most important contribution. The APA does not so much distinguish rulemaking and adjudication as it defines the elements of a hearing when it is required. Section 556, for example, defines some procedural elements of a formal hearing that apply to *both* rulemaking and adjudication whenever the authorizing statute calls for a hearing "on the record" (section 554(a)). If the agency authorizing statute does not call for "adjudication . . . to be determined on the record after opportunity for an agency hearing?" (section 554(a)), then the APA has little influence on the agency's adjudication and we fall back on the vague constitutional due process tests.[1] By contrast, the

---

[1] Compare section 1(2) and section 9 of the Model State APA (Appendix C) to the federal APA (Appendix B).

APA *does* require a rulemaking procedure when the agency's authorizing statute is silent. Section 553 states the nature of such "notice and comment" hearings along with the exceptions (see chapter 5) where agencies need not follow notice and comment procedures. The 553 machinery is much less formal than that of a formal hearing.

In summary, each of these three kinds of laws (constitutional, statutory, and the APA) may prescribe that an agency follow one or more procedural elements, regardless of the rulemaking or adjudicative character of the administrative action. This chapter makes little effort to teach you how to tell *when* any given element is legally necessary. Instead it describes what each element means when, for whatever reason, the law does require it or an agency voluntarily adopts the element on its own. For example, both kinds of APA hearings, "notice and comment" and "formal," require *notice,* and this chapter reports what notice means in both contexts.

A Threshold Question: What Triggers Formal Adjudication Under the APA?

We have seen that, for the formal hearing provisions of the APA to come into play, an agency's authorizing statute must require it. More specifically, section 554(a) "applies . . . in every case of adjudication required by statute to be determined *on the record* after opportunity for an agency hearing . . . " (emphasis added). What if the authorizing statute calls for a hearing but fails to state explicitly that the hearing must be on the record? In some case, courts will refuse to decide simply on the basis of the presence or absence of the magic words *on the record* in the authorizing statute. Courts may look to the legislative history of the statute in order to determine if formal adjudication is required.[2]

Marathon Oil Co. v. Environmental Protection Agency
564 F.2d 1253, U.S.C.A., 9th Cir. (1977) 3–0

[The petitioner claimed that an EPA regulation concerning effluent limits for the transfer of oil was defective since it resulted from a hearing in which rulemaking standards were used. Marathon claimed that the adverse impact suffered coupled with the disputable nature of the facts justifying the rule made the hearing adjudicatory in impact and, thus, called for fuller protections than those available in a rulemaking setting.]

Sneed, Circuit Judge.

In setting out procedures that an agency must follow in making "adjudicatory" determinations, Congress recognized that certain administrative decisions closely resemble judicial determinations and, in the interest of fairness, require similar procedural protections. These "quasi-judicial" proceedings determine the specific rights of particular individuals or entities. And, like judicial proceedings, the ultimate decision often turns, in large part, on sharply-disputed factual issues. As a result, such APA procedures as cross-examination of key witnesses are needed both

---

[2]See *United States v. Independent Bulk Transport Co.,* 480 F. Supp. 474 (1979).

for the protection of affected parties and to help achieve reasoned decisionmaking. At the opposite end of the pole are agency determinations that depend less on the resolution of factual disputes and more on the drawing of policy: such "rulemaking" decisions must by necessity be guided by more informal procedures. See *Bi-Metallic Investment Co. v. State Board of Equalization*, 239 U.S. 441, 36 S. Ct. 141, 60 L. Ed. 372 (1915). According to the Attorney General's Manual on the APA, issued shortly after the APA was passed,

the entire act is based upon [this] dichotomy between rule making and adjudication . . . . Rule making . . . is essentially legislative in nature, not only because it operates in the future but also because it is primarily concerned with policy considerations . . . . Typically, the issues relate not to the evidentiary facts, as to which the veracity and demeanor of witnesses would often be important, but rather to the policymaking conclusions to be drawn from the facts . . . . Conversely, adjudication is concerned with the determination of past and present rights and liabilities . . . . In such proceedings, the issues of fact are often sharply controverted. [Attorney General's Manual on the Administrative Procedure Act, at 14–15 (1947).]

Working from this basic dichotomy, the setting of effluent limitations under section 402 of the Control Act is clearly "adjudicatory" in nature and requires the special protections of sections 554, 556 and 557 of the APA. Unlike, for example, section 304 proceedings which lead to the promulgation of industry-wide effluent limitation guidelines and which are in large measure policy-making, section 402 proceedings focus on whether particular effluent limitations are currently practicable for individual point sources. As the instant proceeding well demonstrates, the factual questions involved in the issuance of section 402 permits will frequently be sharply disputed. Adversarial hearings will be helpful, therefore, in guaranteeing both reasoned decisionmaking and meaningful judicial review. In summary, the proceedings were conducted in order "to adjudicate disputed facts in particular cases," not "for the purpose of promulgating policy-type rules or standards." The protections of sections 554, 556 and 557 of the APA are therefore particularly appropriate. . . .

Moreover, whether the formal adjudicatory hearing provisions of the APA apply to specific administrative processes does not rest on the presence or absence of the magical phrase "on the record." Absent congressional intent to the contrary, it rests on the substantive character of the proceedings involved. The 79th Congress' purpose in limiting the APA provisions to determinations made "on the record" after opportunity for a hearing was not to provide future Congresses with a talisman that they would use to signify whether or not sections 554, 556 and 557 of the APA should apply. It was to limit the sections' applications to those types of adjudications, discussed above, needing special procedural safeguards. The APA defines "adjudication" broadly as an agency process leading to a final disposition "other than rulemaking." 5 U.S.C. § § 551(6)–(7) (1970). But not all "non-rulemakings" are "adjudications" of the nature outlined above and calling for special protective proceedings. Thus, Congress inserted section 554's prefatory language cited by the EPA to exclude from the residual definition of adjudication "governmental functions, such as the administration of loan programs, which traditionally have never been regarded as adjudicative in nature and as a rule have never been exercised through other than business procedures." Attorney General's Manual, supra, at 40. . . .

In summary, the crucial question is not whether particular talismanic language was used but whether the proceedings under review fall within that category of quasi-judicial proceedings deserving of special procedural protections. . . . "[I]t would be a disservice to our form of government and to the administrative process itself if the courts should fail, so far as the terms of the Act warrant, to give effect to its remedial purposes where the evils it aimed at appear." *Wong Yang Sung v. McGrath* [339 U.S. 33 (1950)]. . . .

Remanded.

Marathon won. They felt the procedure should be adjudicatory.

Criticism. APA adjudication is a poor way to make decisions. It allows private wealthy interests to stall, to buy time.

Because the two cases involve different agencies and different authorizing statutes they do not directly clash. The EPA must operate one way, the Coast Guard another. But there is a real philosophical tension between the two cases. The first emphasizes administrative efficiency while the second emphasizes fairness. This tension, evident in the lower court APA "threshold" decisions, closely resembles the tensions in the Supreme Court's due process decisions. Note that, just as in *Mathews* and *Horowitz*, so in this threshold case, the courts end up making vague case-by-case judgment calls. These results may be justifiable, but courts have not yet provided a convincing justification.

The Components of a Hearing

We shall follow Paul Verkuil's list of the *Goldberg* ingredients (see pages 206–207) as a means to structure this section. Since you are familiar with the components of due process as described in *Goldberg*, we draw on them to review the comparable APA requirements.

Timely and Adequate Notice

The concept of notice really lies at the heart of the problem of fairness in any judging situation. Individuals and organizations subject to government regulation want to know in advance what rules the government will apply to them. Both APA hearing procedures, section 553(b) and section 554(b), stress adequate notice, and even the most informal constitutional adjudications, for example, that of *Horowitz* and *Goss*, presume that the citizen knows what the government claims they did wrong and knows it in time to do something about it if he or she wishes. You will note that the APA provisions insure that the citizen learns the mechanics of the hearing in their case—when and where they will be heard. But the essence of fair notice has to do with substance, the terms of the proposed rule, and the matters of fact and law asserted in adjudication.

Disclosure of Opposing Evidence and Opportunity to Confront and Cross-examine Adverse Witnesses

The second, fifth, and sixth items on the *Goldberg* list are closely related to each other. These requirements deal not with the charge of wrongdoing but with the proof of wrongdoing. Under the conventional theory of rulemaking, of course, no charge of wrongdoing arises, therefore section 553 does not on its face provide any opportunity to challenge the evidence on the side one opposes. This conventional theory is under attack, and we shall examine that attack in chapter 7. For now, consider how important these three elements are in a case judging a person's security clearance, a prerequisite for working for a private company that produced goods for the armed forces. In *Greene v. McElroy* (1959), the Defense Department withdrew the plaintiff Greene's security clearance based on "confidential information" which it refused to provide him.[3] Although the case was decided on narrower grounds, Chief Justice Earl Warren in his opinion for the Court stated:

---

[3] 360 U.S. 474. Recall that the Court quoted this passage approvingly in *Goldberg, supra*, at 64.

Certain principles have remained relatively immutable in our jurisprudence. One of these is that where governmental action seriously injures an individual, and the reasonableness of the action depends on fact findings, the evidence used to prove the Government's case must be disclosed to the individual so that he has an opportunity to show that it is untrue. While this is important in the case of documentary evidence, it is even more important where the evidence consists of the testimony of individuals whose memory might be faulty or who, in fact, might be perjurers or persons motivated by malice, vindictiveness, intolerance, prejudice, or jealousy. We have formalized these protections in the requirements of confrontation and cross-examination. They have ancient roots. They find expression in the Sixth Amendment which provides that in all criminal cases the accused shall enjoy the right "to be confronted with the witnesses against him." This Court has been zealous to protect these rights from erosion. It has spoken out not only in criminal cases, . . . but also in all types of cases where administrative and regulatory action were under scrutiny. . . . Nor, as it has been pointed out, has Congress ignored these fundamental requirements in enacting regulatory legislation. . . .

Greene was not an APA-based decision. Given Chief Justice Warren's ringing statement, we might expect the APA to require these elements emphatically in formal hearings. In fact the APA speaks to this issue with a curiously soft voice, saying merely in section 556(d): "A party is entitled to present his case or defense by oral or documentary evidence, to submit rebuttal evidence, and to conduct such cross-examination as may be required for a full and true disclosure of the facts." While under this provision administrative law judges have considerable control over rebuttal and cross-examination, the custom has been to afford ample opportunity in formal hearings to cross examine and rebut. Also, section 556(e) states that "When an agency decision rests on official notice of a material fact not appearing in the evidence in the record, a party is entitled, on timely request, to an opportunity to show the contrary." The implication is that the agency would allow the same opportunity regarding facts in the record as in fact they customarily do.

Oral Presentation of Arguments and Evidence

The APA itself, as the excerpt from 556(d) above shows, does not necessarily permit claimants to present their position orally before the agency. The result is that when a person claims a right to be heard orally, courts will fall back on the due process analysis of *Goldberg*. However, formal hearings generally do allow ample oral presentations if the parties insist. Furthermore, the APA unambiguously protects the opportunity to present one's case in writing. This forms the *comment* part of the notice and comment requirements for rulemaking; in many rulemaking situations the comments of interested parties run many hundreds of pages. In formal hearings written submission of evidence accomplishes in most cases the same result as oral presentation. Through written depositions, a questionnaire version of examination, and cross-examination of witnesses, parties can usually introduce the same information as oral situations allow.

[handwritten margin note: written presentations are always protected, but oral ones are not in all cases.]

A lawyer may be able to contribute at a private hearing more than at some administrative hearings.

The Right to Retain an Attorney

Unlike criminal cases, where the government must provide lawyers for people who cannot afford them, the right to an attorney in administrative proceedings only covers the right to hire and pay for legal assistance.[4] When the federal government regulates private business activities we need not worry that a party may not be able to afford a lawyer. But in precisely the situation described by *Goldberg* – welfare cases – parties will not usually be able to afford counsel, and therefore the "right" to hire an attorney does little good. The absence of counsel for the indigent in administrative matters even includes decisions made by the administrative personnel of probation offices and parole boards about criminals.[5]

The right to hire and pay for attorneys can, of course, only be exercised by those who have sufficient economic resources. The majority of Americans cannot easily afford representation of their interests by attorneys in administrative processes. Interest groups litigating in the public interest, such as the National Resources Defense Council (NRDC) and the Environmental Defense Fund (EDF), provide legal representation for citizens concerned about cleaning up and protecting the environment. These nonprofit organizations depend on contributions from the public for some of their expenses, but they depend more heavily on court-awarded attorneys' fees for covering their litigation costs. The following article by political scientists Karen O'Connor and Lee Epstein describes public policy changes in awarding attorneys' fees. The article also discusses different interest group theories that political scientists have developed to explain interest-group behavior and politics.

Bridging the Gap between Congress and the Supreme Court: Interest Groups and the Erosion of the American Rule Governing Awards of Attorneys' Fees

Karen O'Connor and Lee Epstein
Western Political Quarterly 38 (1985): 238.

Erosion of the American rule governing awards of attorneys' fees is an important legal-political development. For more than 170 years, Congress and the Supreme Court clung to the view that prevailing parties were not entitled to recover their costs or attorneys' fees when they successfully advanced their claims on the merits. In 1964 this situation changed dramatically; passage of Title II of the Civil Rights Act coupled with a subsequent expansive Supreme Court interpretation of that provision, quickly led to erosion of the rule. . . .

The Evolution of the American Rule

Either by statute or in equity, English courts traditionally have awarded litigation costs to prevailing parties. American courts and legislatures, however, did not follow suit. In fact, in the United States, "the litigant, win, lose, or draw, [paid] his own lawyer" (Derfner 1980: 15). Rejection of this tradition stands in sharp contrast to the colonists' adoption of most other English common law traditions (Newberg 1980: 15–17). Yet, many theories have been offered to explain rejection of "attorney subsidies." Some, for example, have pointed to the prevalent distrust of lawyers noting that attorneys symbolized the worst facets of

---

[4]APA, Section 555(b).

[5]See *Gagnon v. Scarpelli*, 411 U.S. 778 (1973).

British rule (Falcon 1973: 379–81; *Yale Law Journal* 1940: 699–701). Thus, it was not surprising that the colonies and subsequently the states, drafted laws that severely limited fee awards. . . . While this is the most widely accepted explanation for the rejection of the English rule, others have posited that colonists believed that the rule was "undemocratic" because it limited the poor's access to the courts as they could not risk liability for attorneys' fees (*Hastings Law Journal* 1973: 733). Still, another reason offered was that early fee legislation specified the exact dollar amount of awards that soon became meaningless as a result of inflation (Ehrenzweig 1966: 792; McCormick 1931: 619).

Regardless of the reasons why the English rule was not adopted, the "American rule" as it has come to be known generally has stood as a bar to recovery of plaintiffs' costs in litigation. Thus, as historically applied, the American rule prohibits the recovery of attorneys' fees unless there is a specific statute empowering the courts to make such an award.

Since 1796 when the Supreme Court first examined the attorneys' fees issue in *Arcambel v. Wiseman*, it consistently has enforced the view that in the absence of specific statutory provisions, the federal courts would not award attorneys' fees to prevailing plaintiffs. In response to this judicial interpretation, Congress periodically has provided for awards of attorneys' fees in specific pieces of legislation. Until the 1960s, however, the vast majority of these allowed for recovery to the prevailing party in only highly technical areas of economic relations. These provisions varied; some required the courts to award attorneys' fees while others left awards to the discretion of the presiding judge.

In the 1960s, a major change occurred in congressional policy toward attorneys' fees. Recognition of the fact that the resources of the federal government would be inadequate to enforce fully the provisions contained in sections of the Civil Rights Act of 1964, Congress, at the urgings of the NAACP, the ACLU, the National Lawyers Guild, and other organizations, voted to include specific authorizations for awards of attorneys' fees. Specifically, Title II of the Act stated that: "In any action pursuant to this title, the court,

in its discretion may allow the prevailing party other than the United States a reasonable attorney's fee as part of the costs. . . ." Congress' inclusion of that attorneys' fees provision thus institutionalized the notion that private enforcement of civil rights laws was necessary because the U.S. government lacked the resources to pursue the problem adequately. This is known as the private attorney general concept.

The full import of the private attorney general concept was realized in *Newman v. Piggie Park Enterprises, Inc.* in 1968. *Newman* was a lawsuit filed under Title II of the Civil Rights Act of 1964 by the NAACP Legal Defense Fund (LDF) to enjoin the actions of five drive-in restaurants and a sandwich shop that refused to serve black patrons. After a U.S. Court of Appeals enjoined the practice, the LDF sought a writ of certiorari to the U.S. Supreme Court on the question of the proper construction of Title II's attorneys' fees authorization. In a per curiam opinion, the Court, following the lead of Congress, endorsed the private attorney general concept. The Court stressed that:

> When the Civil Rights Act of 1964 was passed, it was evident that enforcement would prove difficult and that the nation would have to rely in part upon private litigation as a means of securing broad compliance with the law.
>
> When a plaintiff brings an action under that Title [II], he cannot recover damages. If he obtains an injunction, he does so not for himself alone but also as a "private attorney general," vindicating a policy that Congress considered of the highest priority (390 U.S. at 401–402).

Thus, according to the Court, those who sued on behalf of others and not simply as individuals could recover the cost of their attorneys fees' from the private party found guilty of discrimination prohibited by the act.

This ruling immediately was hailed by civil rights leaders as a major victory and viewed as one that would facilitate litigation brought in the public interest. According to Roy Wilkins, then Executive Director of the NAACP, *Newman* would make "it possible for poor persons denied services to file suit without fear of having to pay legal fees beyond their means" (*New York Times* 1968: 30).

Even more important, perhaps, was that *Newman* was partially responsible for the proliferation of liberal interest groups dedicated to securing policy change through litigation. The Ford Foundation, for example, recognizing the potential of *Newman*, began to provide seed money for the establishment of diverse kinds of interest groups dedicated to using the courts as well as for the creation of litigating arms within "traditional" interest groups (McKay 1977) with the expectation that they would contribute to and increase their own budgets through recovery of attorneys' fees. . . . This attitude led to the phenomenal growth of these kinds of interest groups. As revealed in Figure 1 below, following *Newman* through 1974, more than 50 new groups were created to litigate on behalf of the public interest.

Not only did the number of these groups increase, but as Ford expected, so did the proportion of their annual operating budgets derived from attorneys' fees awards. Between 1972 and 1975, attorneys' fees as a source of funding increased almost fourfold. By 1975, the NAACP LDF, for example, received $550,000 of its 3 million dollar operating budget from attorneys' fees (Settle and Weisbrod 1978: 534–36).

The proliferation of these firms and the expectation that they could recover their operating expenses subsequently led to a dramatic increase in litigation being initiated by "private attorneys general." And, even though *Newman* involved fee recovery for race discrimination litigation, most interpreted the decision to apply to all areas of public interest law. Buttressing this assumption was the fact that Congress was beginning to include specific authorizations providing for attorneys' fees recovery in most major pieces of legislation of interest to existing groups. For example, most environmental laws passed since 1970 included provisions allowing the court to award reasonable attorneys' fees to prevailing parties. Thus, in the period after *Newman*, it appeared that the vi-

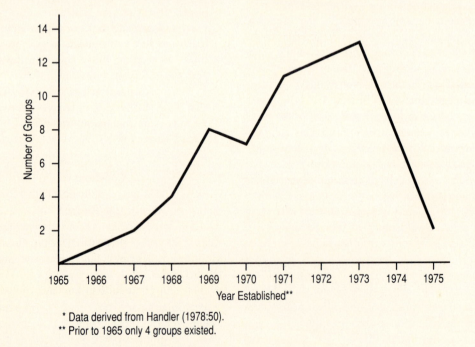

* Data derived from Handler (1978:50).
** Prior to 1965 only 4 groups existed.

Figure 6.1 Year of Establishment of 72 Interest Groups That Lobby the Court*

tality of the American rule was seriously in doubt; Congress, the Court, and various interest groups accepted the private attorney general interpretation.

In 1975, the Supreme Court, however, severed this alliance and dealt litigating groups, whose coffers by this time were extremely dependent on fee awards (Witt 1975), a severe blow in *Alyeska Pipeline Service Co. v. Wilderness Society.* In *Alyeska*, the Wilderness Society, the Environmental Defense Fund (EDF), and the Friends of the Earth, represented by the Center for Law and Social Policy (CLSP), a D.C. based public interest law firm, had successfully sued to stop the Secretary of the Interior from issuing permits necessary for the construction of the trans-Alaska pipeline. Litigation on the merits, however, was terminated after Congress amended the Mineral Leasing Act to allow issuance of the permit. After passage of that amendment, the CLSP attempted to recoup its attorneys' fees from the Pipeline Company. Its lawyers argued that they had acted as private attorneys general, litigating on behalf of the public interest. The Court of Appeals accepted this argument and allowed the CLSP to recover one-half of the fees to which it was entitled, over $100,000 for more than 4,000 hours of legal work. In its opinion, the Court of Appeals held that:

> . . . respondents had acted to vindicate "important statutory rights of all citizens . . . ," had ensured that the governmental system functioned properly, and were entitled to attorneys' fees lest the great cost of litigation of this kind, particularly against well-financed defendants such as Alyeska, deter private parties desiring to see the laws protecting the environment properly enforced (495 F.2d 1029).

The Court further noted that:

> It may well be that counsel serve organizations like [respondents] for compensation below that obtainable in the market because they believe the organizations further a public interest. Litigation of this sort should not have to rely on the charity of counsel any more than it should rely on the charity of parties volunteering to serve as private attorneys

general. The attorneys who worked on this case should be reimbursed the reasonable value of their services, despite the absence of any obligations on the part of [respondents] to pay attorneys' fees (495 F.2d 1037).

In a 5 to 2 decision, the U.S. Supreme Court rejected this reasoning. Writing for the Court, Justice Byron White presented a lengthy history of the relations between Congress and the courts on the issue of attorneys' fees provisions. On the basis of that analysis, Justice White concluded that attorneys' fees were not recoverable absent specific statutory authorization. Thus, since Congress had not included specific provisions allowing for recovery in any of the statutes relied on by CLSP, the Court of Appeals award was reversed.

In *Alyeska*, Justice White recognized, however, that prevailing sentiment favored erosion of the American rule. Not only did he note numerous law review articles, lower court decisions, and congressional hearings concerning the advisability of abandoning the American rule, he also claimed that:

> It is also apparent from our national experience that the encouragement of private action to implement public policy has been viewed as desirable in a variety of circumstances. But the rule followed in our courts with respect to attorneys' fees has survived. It is deeply rooted in our history and in congressional policy. . . .

The reaction from interest groups was immediate; organizations throughout the country claimed that *Alyeska* had sounded the death knell for public interest law. As noted by Charles Halpern, a founder of CLSP, "Until *Alyeska* . . . I would have probably said that attorneys' fee awards were the number one factor in the future of public interest law financing" (Quote in Witt 1975: 35). Similarly, Sid Wolinsky of Public Advocates in San Francisco noted:

> It increases our burden about tenfold. The decision is an unmitigated disaster for the legal profession. It expressly and implicitly recognizes the law as a place for money-grubbers only.

If you can get an award, or if your client can afford to pay you a fat fee, then you are welcome in U.S. courts. But if you want to do something as lowly as advance the public interest, then you are clearly discouraged from coming into the courts. (Quoted in Witt 1975: 35.)

Thus, just as Justice White predicted, *Alyeska* was perceived by numerous groups as a severe deterrent to the initiation of litigation by "private attorneys general."

Other public interest lawyers were less pessimistic about the decision, realizing that there was still one institution potentially sympathetic to their cause—Congress. According to Bruce Terris, a D.C. based, public interest attorney:

Perhaps now the issue will be so squarely focused before Congress that it will act . . . I don't think this ruling was the most devastating thing in the world. It did halt a trend, but it's best to go through Congress, not the courts, to establish attorneys' fee awards. I'm hopeful that since Congress has been challenged by the courts to make clear what it wants, that's what it will do. (Quoted in Witt 1975: 35–38.)

Unwilling to rely on Congress to accept the Court's cue, however, leaders of these organizations immediately went to Congress to ask for a more favorable policy proclamation. After hearings early in 1976, where numerous groups including the National Organization for Women, the Consumers Union of the United States, the Consumer Federation of America, the Center for National Policy Review, several Nader groups, the Mental Health Law Project, and the Southern Poverty Law Center testified or submitted statements, Congress passed the Civil Rights Attorneys' Fees Awards Act of 1976. The Act provided for awards of attorneys' fees at a court's discretion to participants bringing actions under all civil rights legislation passed since 1876. Under the terms of this Act, plaintiffs could recover fees from the states as well as from private parties. And, even though this Act

failed to permit prevailing plaintiffs to recover their fees from the federal government, Congress still claimed that the purpose of the Act was "to remedy anomalous gaps in our civil rights laws created by the U.S. Supreme Court's recent decision in *Alyeska* and to achieve consistency in our civil rights laws."

While Congress passed the Attorneys' Fees Act at the urgings of several groups, taking their cue from Justice White in *Alyeska*, these same groups perceived the gap in the 1976 law and began to pressure Congress for legislation that would allow them to recover attorneys' fees awards from the federal government. Yet, because of the potentially tremendous costs to the federal government, passage of this type of blanket legislation required far longer pressure.

During the period from 1976 to 1980, however, interest groups and environmentalists in particular were able to convince Congress to add such provisions to legislation allowing for recovery from the U.S. government on a piecemeal basis. The 1976 Toxic Substance Control Act, for example, allows the party challenging the federal government to recover fees whether or not they actually win the entire suit. Finally in 1980, Congress succumbed to the wishes of interest groups and passed the all encompassing Equal Access to Justice Act, which "authorizes the federal government to pay attorneys' fees for individual and small businesses that defend themselves against 'overreaching' government actions." (Jackson 1982: 680).

Since passage of the Civil Rights Attorneys' Fees Awards and Equal Access to Justice Acts, interest groups have taken full advantage of their provisions. Some groups claim to derive up to 50 percent of their operating budgets from these awards. In fact, in some instances, groups that have lost most of the major issues in a case on the merits have been able to recoup their costs in later attorneys' fees proceedings. Groups that have been able to do so, even though they lost the case in principle, have considered these "wins" in the final analysis because no money was lost (Sherwood 1981).

Yet, the success of these groups in translating adverse judicial decisions into favorable congressional legislation has prompted some members of the Reagan administration to seek to limit recovery of fees against the federal government. Specifically, Michael Horowitz, legal advisor to the Office of Management and Budget, has proposed legislation that would limit the hourly dollar amounts that attorneys and interest groups could recover for their services (Horowitz 1983). Horowitz believes that such legislation is necessary because "liberal groups have come to rely on attorneys fees awards as a 'permanent financing mechanism' " (Jackson 1982: 680).

While liberal interest groups plan to lobby against the Horowitz plan, conservative interest groups wholeheartedly endorse proposals for limits on fee awards. Groups such as the Washington and Pacific Legal Foundations believe that they should not accept fee awards because their financial "support must come from the public" (Popeo 1982; Momboisse 1982).

Even if liberal interest groups are able to fight off challenges from the Reagan administration and conservative groups, they may still face erosion of their congressional victories from the Court—the institution that thus far has most often limited those victories. During its 1982 term, for example, the Supreme Court decided two cases that revealed the justices' disinclination to construe specific statutory fee awards provisions liberally. In the first, *Hensley v. Eckerhart*, the Court rejected claims made by Legal Services of Eastern Missouri, the NAACP Legal Defense Fund, the Lawyers Committee for Civil Rights Under Law, and the ACLU concerning construction of the Civil Rights Attorneys' Fees Awards Act. The Court held that the Act's authorization of attorneys' fees to prevailing parties meant that fees were recoverable only for the time spent on successful portions of the suit. Later, in July 1983, the Supreme Court further limited the application of an attorneys' fees authorization contained in the Clean Air Act. *Ruckelshaus v. Sierra Club, et al.* arose out of litigation in which the Sierra Club and the Environmental Defense Fund (EDF) questioned air pollution control standards promulgated by the Environmental Protection Agency (EPA). While the EDF and the Sierra Club lost the case on the merits, they petitioned the Court of Appeals of the District of Columbia to recover their attorneys'

fees. Even though neither group prevailed on the merits of the case, the Court of Appeals awarded $45,000 to the Sierra Club and $46,000 to the EDF. The EPA then asked the Supreme Court to review this decision to determine whether the award was appropriate given that neither group had won any part of the challenge.

Although the Clean Air Act stated that a court could award attorneys' fees "whenever it determined that such an award is appropriate," the Supreme Court chose to construe that provision narrowly. Writing for the Court, Justice Rehnquist stated that, "absent some degree of success on the merits by the claimants it is not appropriate for a federal court to award attorneys' fees" (51 U.S.L.W. at 5136).

Justices Stevens, Brennan, Marshall, and Blackmun strongly dissented from this interpretation of the Act. Writing for the dissenters, Justice Stevens noted that:

> If one reads that statute and its legislative history without any strong predisposition in favor or against the "American Rule" endorsed by the Court in *Alyeska Pipeline Service Co. v. Wilderness Society*, and repeatedly rejected by Congress thereafter, the answer is really quite plain—and it is not the one the Court engrafts on the statute. (51 U.S.L.W. at 5136.)

Thus, once again, interest groups may be forced back to Congress to overcome these adverse judicial decisions.

Analysis

There is no question that the demise of the American rule has acted as an incentive for groups to deepen their involvement in the judicial process. Even several justices of the U.S. Supreme Court have noted this trend.* One justice, in particular, noted that the Court is literally "swamped" by these kinds of suits and that there is a "ceiling on how much time [the Court] can give to these issues."

*Interviews were conducted by the authors with five Supreme Court justices during the 1983–84 academic year.

Yet beyond the readily observable implications of the importance of the fee shifting issue, is that it provides support for key elements of several theories that have been offered to explain interest group behavior. E. E. Schattschneider (1935, 1960), for example, argued that pressure groups attempt to achieve their goals by expanding or contracting what he termed the scope of conflict. According to Schattschneider, different kinds of groups attempt to meet this challenge in different ways. "The most powerful special interests" (1960:40) want to keep the scope of conflict private, that is, they know they will fare best, given their resources when government is excluded from the conflict. In contrast, "losers in the private conflict involve public authority in the struggle" (1960:40). In Schattschneider's terms, these "weak" groups must "socialize conflict" before they can achieve their goals. To accomplish socialization, weak groups must enlarge the scope of the conflict by bringing other, likeminded groups into the fray so that they can alter the bias of the political system in their favor.

Schattschneider's theory, then, provides a powerful lens for viewing policy changes in the awards of attorneys' fees. Groups initially desiring such awards could be classified as "losers" because of their very nature: the ideas to which they adhere ("equality, consistency, equal protection of the laws, justice, liberty . . ." (1960: 7) — and their continual inability to convince the judiciary to award them these fees. Thus, to succeed, these weak groups were forced to socialize the issue of attorneys' fees by mobilizing to pressure Congress for change. There, they could take advantage of a bias in the political system, a bias that favors groups who retain lobbyists in Washington, D.C. (1935: 164–84). Those groups who early on fought for inclusion of an attorneys' fees provision in the Civil Rights Act of 1964 well fit this description in that they could call on their experienced lobbyists to attend congressional hearings, an activity that Schattschneider has noted as inherently biased toward groups with these resources.

Once the rule was initially altered, "weak" groups continued to socialize the conflict. This task was clearly facilitated by the fact that the alteration in the rule itself had led to the creation of more groups, which in turn further expanded the scope of the conflict. In fact, by the time Congress passed the Civil Rights Attorneys' Fees Awards Act of 1976, the scope of the conflict had been sufficiently enlarged so as to realter the "balance of forces." This, in turn, led to continued policy change.

While elements of Schattschneider's theory well explain how liberal groups expanded the scope of the conflict to create policy change, David Truman's (1951) "disturbance theory" provides a useful perspective for framing the current struggle in this area. Truman's theory suggests that groups will form to dissipate societal disturbances in order to restore equilibrium. Truman, for example, claimed that employer associations formed to restore the equilibrium that had been unbalanced after unions began to become a power force in society. Currently, a new set of organizations, formed to "restore" a balance in the field of public interest law, has vowed to support plans limiting fee awards. Many of these conservative firms are "frustrated," believing that liberals have benefited far too much from the legislation they so ably urged. Thus, just as Truman predicted, a new wave of organizations arose to fight what they view as a political inequity.

Our findings in this study also provide support for the notions enunciated by scholars examining issues of group maintenance. More specifically, as Jeffrey M. Berry (1977) and Jack Walker (1983) have both noted, public interest groups depend upon outside sources to maintain themselves. By seeking such support, public interest groups overcome the "free rider" problem inherent in the economic groups discussed by Mancur Olson (1965). As Walker has noted, "during recent years group leaders learned how to cope with the public goods dilemma not by inducing large numbers of new members to join their groups through the manipulation of selective benefits, but by locating important new sources of funding outside the immediate membership" (1983: 397). Once again, our findings lend support to this idea. As liberal groups pushed for further alteration in the American rule, the Ford Foundation entered the conflict as the political patron of these groups: it began to provide seed money for public interest law firms with the expectation that they would contribute to their own maintenance through the recovery of attorneys' fees.

In sum, the importance of the fee shifting issue goes beyond immediate appearances: it provides an interesting lens by which to view and then bridge existing theories of interest group behavior. Clearly, as Schattschneider predicted, policy change came about when affected groups sought to expand the scope of the conflict. Their ability to obtain their goals in such short order was largely determined by their success in socializing the conflict, e.g., an ever growing number of groups repeatedly pressured Congress. In other words, numbers count for something in the political process: the more groups that can be brought in on one side of a conflict, the greater the chances are for their success.

This task was facilitated by the fact that political patrons such as the Ford Foundation saw the utility in providing funding for organizations that could help to maintain themselves by pursuing the activity for which they were created in the first instance. Thus, a combination of theories help to explain how and why these groups succeeded.

Truman's disturbance theory, however, would lead us to expect that these groups may not continue to enjoy further expansions of the rule. Conservatives, perceiving an imbalance in the process, are leading efforts to modify the rule. If these new forces can unite in numbers, as did their liberal counterparts, then they too may be able to force change. Any diminution in attorneys' fee recovery provisions in turn would lead to reprivatization of the scope of the conflict, and the cycle would start anew.

Cases

Alyeska Pipeline Service Co. v. Wilderness Society, 95 S.Ct. 1612. 1975.

Arcambel v. Wiseman, 3 U.S. (3 Dall.) 306. 1796.

Hensley v. Eckerhart, 51 U.S.L.W. 4552. 1983.

Mills v. Electric-Auto Lite Co., 396 U.S. 375. 1976.

Newman v. Piggie Park Enterprises, Inc., 390 U.S. 400. 1968.

Ruckelshaus v. Sierra Club, 51 U.S.L.W. 5132. 1983.

Trustees v. Greenough, 307 U.S. 161. 1882.

Vaughan v. Atkinson, 369 U.S. 527. 1962.

References

BERRY, J. M. 1977. *Lobbying for the People*. Princeton: Princeton University Press.

DERFNER, M. F. 1980. "The Civil Rights Attorneys' Fees Awards Act of 1976." In H. Newberg, ed., *Public Interest Practice and Fee Awards*. New York. Practising Law Institute.

EHRENZWEIG, A. 1966. "Reimbursement of Counsel Fees and the Great Society." *California Law Review* 54: 1619.

FALCON, R. 1973. "Award of Attorneys' Fees in Civil Rights and Constitutional Litigation." *Maryland Law Review* 33: 379.

FORD FOUNDATION. 1973. *The Public Interest Law Firm: New Voices for New Constituencies*. New York: Ford Foundation.

HANDLER, J. 1978. "The Public Interest Law Industry." In B. Weisbrod et. al., eds., *Public Interest Law*. p. 50, Berkeley: University of California Press.

HASTINGS LAW JOURNAL. 1973. "Awarding Attorneys' Fees to the 'Private Attorney General': Judicial Green Light to Private Litigation in the Public Interest." *Hastings Law Journal* 24: 733.

HOROWITZ, M. 1983. Interview conducted in Washington, D.C.

JACKSON, D. 1982. "Paying Lawyers to Sue the Government— An Expense that OMB Could Do Without." *National Journal* (April 17): 680.

McCORMICK, D. 1931. "Counsel Fees and Other Expenses of Litigation as an Element of Damages." *Minnesota Law Review* 15: 619.

McKAY, R. 1977. *Nine for Equality Under Law: Civil Rights Litigation*. New York: Ford Foundation.

MOMBOISSE, R. 1982. Interview with Managing Attorney, Pacific Legal Foundation in Washington, D.C.

NEW YORK TIMES. 1968. "High Court Orders Defendants to Pay Rights Case Fees." *New York Times* (March 19): 30.

NEWBERG, H. 1980. *Public Interest Practice and Fee Awards*. New York. Practising Law Institute.

O'CONNOR, K., and L. EPSTEIN. 1983. "The Rise of Conservative Interest Group Litigation." *Journal of Politics* 45: 479.

OLSON, M. 1965. *The Logic of Collective Action*. Cambridge: Harvard University Press.

POPEO, D. 1982. Interview with General Counsel, Washington Legal Foundation in Washington, D.C.

SCHATTSCHNEIDER, E. E. 1935. *Politics, Pressures and the Tariff*. New York: Prentice-Hall.

———. 1960. *The Semi-Sovereign People*. New York. Holt, Rinehart, and Winston.

SETTLE, R., and B. A. WEISBROD. 1978. "Financing Public Interest Law: An Evaluation of Alternative Financing

Arrangements." In B. Weisbrod et al., eds., *Public Interest Law*, p. 534. Berkeley: University of California Press.

SHERWOOD, P. 1981. Interview with Staff Attorney, NAACP Legal Defense Fund in New York City, N.Y.

TRUMAN, D. B. 1951. *The Governmental Process*. New York: Knopf.

WALKER, J. 1983. "The Origins and Maintenance of Interest Groups in America," *American Political Science Review* 77: 390.

WITT, E. 1975. "After Alyeska: Can the Contender Survive." *Juris Doctor*: 35.

YALE LAW JOURNAL. 1940. "Distribution of Legal Expense Among Litigants." *Yale Law Journal* 49: 699.

The contemporary political struggle over whether the state and private parties should pay attorneys' fees to prevailing parties in public interest litigation takes place in the courtroom and in legislative halls. The economics of funding public interest litigation does require mobilizing support for the political values at stake in litigation. The next case, *Walters v. National Association of Radiation Survivors* (1985), illustrates how the Supreme Court has responded to the issues of access to litigation and litigation resources, such as attorney's fee reimbursement, in administrative law. In this case the Court rejected the right to have counsel appointed at Veterans Administration hearings for disabilities caused by exposure to radiation during atomic bomb tests.

Walters v. National Association of Radiation Survivors

105 S.Ct. 3180 (1985) 6–3

+ Burger, White, Blackmun, Powell, Rehnquist, O'Connor
- Brennan, Marshall, Stevens

[Veterans' organizations, veterans, and a veteran's widow brought action challenging the constitutionality of a statutory provision that imposed a $10 maximum fee to be paid an attorney or agent who represents a veteran before the Veterans Administration seeking benefits for service-connected death or disability. The plaintiffs claimed that the fee limitation denied them any "realistic opportunity" to obtain legal representation in presenting their claims to the VA and hence violated their rights under the Due Process Clause of the Fifth Amendment and under the First Amendment freedom of speech clause. The District Court for the Northern District of California agreed and issued a nationwide "preliminary injunction" prohibiting the enforcement of the fee limitation. The Administrator of Veterans Affairs appealed the District Court's decision.]

Justice Rehnquist delivered the opinion of the Court.

I

Congress has by statute established an administrative system for granting service-connected death or disability benefits to veterans. . . . The amount of the benefit award is not based upon need, but upon service connection—that is, whether the disability is causally related to an injury sustained in the service—and the degree of incapacity caused by the disability.

Appellees here are two veterans' organizations, three individual veterans, and a veteran's widow. The two veterans' organizations are the National Association of Radiation Survivors, an organization principally concerned with obtaining compensation for its members for injuries resulting from atomic bomb tests, and Swords to Plowshares Veterans Rights Organization, an organization particularly devoted to the concerns of Vietnam veterans. The complaint contains no further allegation with respect to the numbers of members in either organization who are veteran claimants. Appellees did not seek class certification. . . .

. . . To understand fully the posture in which the case reaches us it is necessary to discuss the administrative scheme in some detail.

Congress began providing veterans pensions in early 1789, and after every conflict in which the nation has been involved Congress has, in the words of Abraham Lincoln, "provided for him who has borne the battle, and his widow and his orphan." The VA was created by Congress in 1930, and since that time has been responsible for administering the congressional program for veterans' benefits. In 1978, the year covered by the report of the Legal Services Corporation to Congress that was introduced into evidence in the District Court, approximatley 800,000 claims for service-connected disability or death and pensions were decided by the 58 regional offices of the VA. Slightly more than half of these were claims for service-connected disability or death, and the remainder were pension claims. Of the 800,000 total claims in 1978, more than 400,000 were allowed, and some 379,000 were denied. Sixty-six thousand of these denials were contested at the regional level; about a quarter of these contests were dropped, 15% prevailed on reconsideration at the local level, and the remaining 36,000 were appealed to the [Board of Veterans' Appeals] BVA. At that level some 4,500, or 12%, prevailed, and another 13% won a remand for further proceedings. Although these figures are from 1978, the statistics in evidence indicate that the figures remain fairly constant from year to year.

As might be expected in a system which processes such a large number of claims each year, the process prescribed by Congress for obtaining disability benefits does not contemplate the adversary mode of dispute resolution utilized by courts in this country. It is commenced by the submission of a claim form to the local veterans agency, which form is provided by the VA either upon request or upon receipt of notice of the death of a veteran. Upon application a claim generally is first reviewed by a three-person "rating board" of the VA regional office—consisting of a medical specialist, a legal specialist, and an "occupational specialist." A claimant is "entitled to a hearing at any time on any issue involved in a claim . . . ." 38 CFR § 3.103(c) (1984). Proceedings in front of the rating board "are ex parte in nature," § 3.103(a); no Government official appears in opposition. The principal issues are the extent of the claimant's disability and whether it is service connected. The board is required by regulation "to assist a claimant in developing the facts pertinent to his claim," § 3.103(a), and to consider any evidence offered by the claimant. See § 3.103(b). In deciding the claim the board generally will request the applicant's Armed Service and medical records, and will order a medical examination by a VA hospital. Moreover, the board is directed by regulation to resolve all reasonable doubts in favor of the claimant. § 3.102.

After reviewing the evidence the board renders a decision either denying the claim or assigning a disability "rating" pursuant to detailed regulations developed for assessing various disabilities. Money benefits are calculated based on the rating. The claimant is notified of the board's decision and its reasons, and the claimant may then initiate an appeal by filing a "notice of disagreement" with the local agency. If the local agency adheres to its original decision it must then provide the claimant with a "statement of the case"—a written description of the facts and applicable law upon which the board based its determination—so that the claimant may adequately present his appeal to the BVA. Hearings in front of the BVA are subject to the same rules as local agency hearings—they are *ex parte*, there is no formal questioning or cross-examination, and no formal rules of evidence apply. . . . The BVA's decision is not subject to judicial review. . . .

The process is designed to function throughout with a high degree of informality and solicitude for the claimant. There is no statute of limitations, and a denial of benefits has no formal res judicata effect; a claimant may resubmit as long as he presents new facts not previously forwarded. . . . Perhaps more importantly for present purposes, however, various veterans' organizations across the country make available trained service agents, free of charge, to assist claimants in developing and presenting their claims. These service representatives are contemplated by the VA statute, 38 U.S.C. § 3402, and they are recognized as an important part of the administrative scheme. . . .

III

Judging the constitutionality of an Act of Congress is properly considered " 'the gravest and most delicate duty that this Court is called upon to perform,' " *Rostker v. Goldberg*, 453 U.S. 57, 64 . . . , (1981), and we begin our analysis here with no less deference than we customarily must pay to the duly enacted and carefully considered decision of a coequal and representative branch of our Government. Indeed one might think, if anything, that more deference is called for here; the statute in question for all relevant purposes has been on the books for over 120 years. . . . We think that the District Court went seriously awry in assessing the constitutionality of § 3404.

Appellees' first claim, accepted by the District Court, is that the statutory fee limitation, as it bears on the administrative scheme in operation, deprives a rejected claimant or recipient of "life, liberty or property, without due process of law" . . . by depriving him of representation by expert legal counsel. Our decisions establish that "due process" is a flexible concept—that the processes required by the Clause with respect to the termination of a protected interest will vary depending upon the importance attached to the interest and the particular circumstances under which the deprivation may occur. See *Mathews, supra*, 424 U.S., at 334. . . . (1972). In defining the process necessary to ensure "fundamental fairness" we have recognized that the Clause does not require that "the procedures used to guard against an erroneous deprivation . . . be so comprehensive as to preclude any possibility of error," *Mackey v. Montrym*, 443 U.S. 1 . . . (1979), and in addition we have emphasized that the marginal gains from affording an additional procedural safeguard often may be outweighed by the societal cost of providing such a safeguard. See *Mathews*, 424 U.S., at 348. . . .

These general principles are reflected in the test set out in *Mathews*, which test the District Court purported to follow, and which requires a court to consider the private interest that will be affected by the official action, the risk of an erroneous deprivation of such interest through the procedures used, the probable value of additional or substitute procedural safeguards, and the government's interest in adhering to the existing system. . . .

The Government interest, which has been articulated in congressional debates since the fee limitation was first enacted in 1862 during the Civil War, has been this: that the system for administering benefits should be managed in a sufficiently informal way that there should be no need for the employment of an attorney to obtain benefits to which a claimant was entitled, so that the claimant would receive the entirety of the award without having to divide it with a lawyer. . . . While Congress has recently considered proposals to modify the fee limitation in some respects, a Senate Committee Report in 1982 highlighted the body's concern that "any changes relating to attorneys' fees be made carefully so as not to induce unnecessary retention of attorneys by VA claimants and not to disrupt unnecessarily the very effective network of nonattorney resources that has evolved in the absence of significant attorney involvement in VA claims matters." S.Rep. No. 97-466, p. 49 (1982). Although this same Report professed the Senate's belief that the original stated interest in protecting veterans from unscrupulous lawyers was "no longer tenable," the Senate nevertheless concluded that the fee limitation should with a limited exception remain in effect, in order to "protect claimants' benefits" from being unnecessarily diverted to lawyers.

In the face of this congressional commitment to the fee limitation for more than a century, the District Court had only this to say with respect to the governmental interest:

"The government has neither argued nor shown that lifting the fee limit would harm the government in any way, except as the paternalistic protector of claimants' supposed best interests. To the extent the paternalistic role is valid, there are less drastic means available to ensure that attorneys' fees do not deplete veterans' death or disability benefits." 589 F.Supp., at 1323.

It is not for the District Court or any other federal court to invalidate a federal statute by so cavalierly dismissing a long-asserted congressional purpose. If "paternalism" is an insignificant Government interest, then Congress first went astray in 1792, when by its Act of March 23 of that year it prohibited the "sale, transfer or mortgage . . . of the pension . . . [of a] soldier . . . before the same shall become due." Acts of Congress long on the books, such as the Fair Labor Standards Act, might similarly be described as "paternalistic"; indeed, this Court once opined that "[s]tatutes of the nature of that under review, limiting the hours in which grown and intelligent men may labor to earn their living, are mere meddlesome interferences with the rights of the individual . . . ." *Lochner v. New York*, 198 U.S. 45 . . . (1905). That day is fortunately long gone, and with it the condemnation of rational paternalism as a legitimate legislative goal.

There can be little doubt that invalidation of the fee limitation would seriously frustrate the oft-repeated congressional purpose for enacting it. Attorneys would be freely employable by claimants to veterans' benefits, and the claimant would as a result end up paying part of the award, or its equivalent, to an attorney. But this would not be the only consequence of striking down the fee limitation that would be deleterious to the congressional plan.

A necessary concomitant of Congress' desire that a veteran not need a representative to assist him in making his claim was that the system should be as informal and nonadversarial as possible. This is not to say that complicated factual inquiries may be rendered simple by the expedient of informality, but surely Congress desired that the proceedings be as informal and nonadversarial as possible. The regular introduction of lawyers into the proceedings would be quite unlikely to further this goal. . . .

Thus, even apart from the frustration of Congress' principal goal of wanting the veteran to get the entirety of the award, the destruction of the fee limitation would bid fair to complicate a proceeding which Congress wished to keep as simple as possible. It is scarcely open to doubt that if claimants were permitted to retain compensated attorneys the day might come when it could be said that an attorney might indeed be necessary to present a claim properly in

a system rendered more adversary and more complex by the very presence of lawyer representation. It is only a small step beyond that to the situation in which the claimant who has a factually simple and obviously deserving claim may nonetheless feel impelled to retain an attorney simply because so many other claimants retain attorneys. And this additional complexity will undoubtedly engender greater administrative costs, with the end result being that less Government money reaches its intended beneficiaries.

. . . It would take an extraordinarily strong showing of probability of error under the present system — and the probability that the presence of attorneys would sharply diminish that possibility — to warrant a holding that the fee limitation denies claimants due process of law. We have no hesitation in deciding that no such showing was made out on the record before the District Court.

As indicated by the statistics set out earlier in this opinion, more than half of the 800,000 claims processed annually by the VA result in benefit awards at the regional level. An additional 10,000 claims succeed on request for reconsideration at the regional level, and of those that do not, 36,000 are appealed to the BVA. Of these, approximately 16% succeed before the BVA. It is simply not possible to determine on this record whether any of the claims of the named plaintiffs, or of other declarants who are not parties to the action, were wrongfully rejected at the regional level or by the BVA, nor is it possible to quantify the "erroneous deprivations" among the general class of rejected claimants. If one regards the decision of the BVA as the "correct" result in every case, it follows that the regional determination against the claimant is "wrong" in the 16% of the cases that are reversed by the Board.

Passing the problems with quantifying the likelihood of an erroneous deprivation, however, under *Mathews* we must also ask what value the proposed additional procedure may have in reducing such error. In this case we are fortunate to have statistics that bear directly on this question, which statistics were addressed by the District Court. These unchallenged statistics chronicle the success rates before the BVA depending on the type of representation of the claimant, and are summarized in the following figures taken from the record.

Ultimate Success Rates Before the
Board of Veterans' Appeals by
Mode of Representation

American Legion 16.2%
American Red Cross..............16.8%
Disabled American Veterans...16.6%
Veterans of Foreign Wars.......16.7%
Other nonattorney.................15.8%
No representation 15.2%
Attorney/Agent 18.3%

The District Court opined that these statistics were not helpful, because in its view lawyers were retained so infrequently that no body of lawyers with an expertise in VA practice had developed, and lawyers who represented veterans regularly might do better than lawyers who represented them only *pro bono* on a sporadic basis. The District Court felt that a more reliable index of the effect lawyers would have on the proceedings was a statistical study showing success of various representatives in appeals to discharge review boards in the uniformed services—statistics that showed a significantly higher success rate for those claimants represented by lawyers as compared to those claimants not so represented.

We think the District Court's analysis of this issue totally unconvincing, and quite lacking in the deference which ought to be shown by an federal court in evaluating the constitutionality of an Act of Congress. We have the most serious doubt whether a competent lawyer taking a veteran's case on a *pro bono* basis would give less than his best effort, and we see no reason why experience in developing facts as to causation in the numerous other areas of the law where it is relevant would not be readily transferable to proceedings before the VA. Nor do we think that lawyers' success rates in proceedings before military boards to upgrade discharges—proceedings which are not even conducted before the VA, but before military boards of the uniformed services—are to be preferred to the BVA statistics which show reliable success by mode of representation in the very type of proceeding to which the litigation is devoted.

The District Court also concluded, apparently independently of its ill-founded analysis of the claim statistics, (1) that the VA processes are procedurally, factually, and legally complex, and (2) that the VA system presently does not work as designed, particularly in terms of the representation afforded by VA personnel and service representatives, and that these representatives are "unable to perform all of the services which might be performed by a claimant's own paid attorney." . . . Unfortunately the court's findings on "complexity" are based almost entirely on a description of the plan for administering benefits in the abstract, together with references to "complex" cases involving exposure to radiation or agent orange, or post-traumatic stress syndrome. The court did not attempt to state even approximately how often procedural or substantive complexities arise in the run-of-the mine case, or even in the unusual cases. The VA procedures cited by the court do permit a claimant to prejudice his rights by failing to respond in a timely manner to an agency notice of denial of an initial claim, but despite this possibility there is nothing in the District Court's opinion indicating that these procedural requirements have led to an unintended forfeiture on the part of a diligent claimant. On the face of the procedures, the process described by the District Court does not seem burdensome: one year would in the judgment of most be ample time to allow a claimant to respond to notice requesting a response. In addition, the VA is required to read any submission in the light most favorable to the claimant, and service representatives are available to see that various procedural steps are complied with. It may be that the service representative cannot, as the District Court hypothesized, provide all the services that a lawyer could, but there is no evidence in the record that they cannot or do not provide advice about time limits.

The District Court's opinion is similarly short on definition or quantification of "complex" cases. If this term be understood to include all cases in which the claimant asserts injury from exposure to radiation or agent orange, only approximately 3 in 1,000 of the claims at the regional level and 2% of the appeals to the BVA involve such claims. Nor does it appear that all such claims would be complex by any fair definition of that term: at least 25% of all agent orange cases and 30% of the radiation cases, for example, are disposed of because the medical examination reveals no disability. What evidence does appear in the record indicates that the great majority of claims involve simple questions of fact, or medical questions relating to the degree of a claimant's disability; the record also indicates that only the rare case turns on a question of law. There are undoubtedly "complex" cases pending before the VA, and they are undoubtedly a tiny fraction of the total cases pending. Neither the District Court's opinion nor any matter in the record to which our attention has been directed tells us more than this. . . .

[W]here, as here, the only interest protected by the Due Process Clause is a property interest in the continued receipt of Government benefits, which interest is conferred and terminated in a nonadversary proceeding, these precedents are of only tangential relevance. Appellees rely on *Goldberg v. Kelly,* 397 U.S. 254 . . . (1970), in which the . . . Court said that "counsel can help delineate the issues, present the factual contentions in an orderly manner, conduct cross-examination, and generally safeguard the interests of the recipient." *Id.,* at 270–271. . . . But in defining the process required the Court also observed that "the crucial factor in this context . . . is that termination of aid pending resolution of a controversy over eligibility may deprive an *eligible* recipient of the very means by which to live while he waits. . . . His need to concentrate upon finding the means for daily subsistence, in turn, adversely affects his ability to seek redress from the welfare bureaucracy." *Id.,* at 264 . . . (emphasis in original).

We think that the benefits at stake in VA proceedings, which are not granted on the basis of need, are more akin to the Social Security benefits involved in *Mathews* than they are to the welfare payments upon which the recipients in *Goldberg* depended for their daily subsistence. Just as this factor was dispositive in *Mathews* in the Court's determination that no evidentiary hearing was required prior to a temporary deprivation of benefits, 424 U.S., at 342–343, so we think it is here determinative of the right to employ counsel. Indeed, there appears to have been no stated policy on the part of New York in *Goldberg* against

permitting an applicant to divide up his welfare check with an attorney who had represented him in the proceeding; the procedures there simply prohibited personal appearance of the recipient with or without counsel and regardless of whether counsel was compensated, and in reaching its conclusion the Court relied on agency regulations allowing recipients to be represented by counsel under some circumstances. . . .

This case is further distinguishable from our prior decisions because the process here is not designed to operate adversarially. While counsel may well be needed to respond to opposing counsel or other forms of adversary in a trial-type proceeding, where as here no such adversary appears, and in addition a claimant or recipient is provided with substitute safeguards such as a competent representative, a decision-maker whose duty it is to aid the claimant, and significant concessions with respect to the claimant's burden of proof, the need for counsel is considerably diminished. We have expressed similar concerns in other cases holding that counsel is not required in various proceedings that do not approximate trials, but instead are more informal and nonadversary. . . .

IV

Finally, we must address appellees' suggestion that the fee limitation violates their First Amendment rights. . . . There are numerous conceptual difficulties with extending the cited cases to cover the situation here; for example, those cases involved the rights of unions and union members to retain or recommend counsel for proceedings where counsel were allowed to appear, and the First Amendment interest at stake was primarily the right to associate collectively for the common good. In contrast, here the asserted First Amendment interest is primarily the individual interest in best prosecuting a claim, and the limitation challenged applies across-the-board to individuals and organizations alike.

But passing those problems, appellees' First Amendment arguments, at base, are really inseparable from their due process claims. The thrust is that they have been denied "meaningful access to the courts" to present their claims. This must be based in some notion that VA claimants, who presently are allowed to speak in court, and to have someone speak for them, also have a First Amendment right to pay their surrogate speaker, beyond that questionable proposition, however, even as framed appellees' argument recognizes that such a First Amendment interest would attach only in the absence of a "meaningful" alternative. . . . [W]e concluded that appellees had such an opportunity under the present claims process, and that significant Government interests favored the limitation on "speech" that appellees attack. Under those circumstances appellees' First Amendment claim has no independent significance. The decision of the District Court is accordingly reversed.

Justice O'Connor, with whom Justice Blackmun joins, concurring. [Omitted.]

Justice Brennan, with whom Justice Marshall joins, dissenting.

. . . Contrary to the Court's assertion, there is much more than a "semantic difference" between a finding of likelihood of success sufficent to support preliminary relief and a final holding on the merits. . . . Until today, the Court always has recognized that district court findings on "likelihood of success on the merits" are *not* "tantamount to decisions on the underlying merits"; the two are "significantly different." *University of Texas v. Camenisch*, 451 U.S. 390 . . . (1981). Preliminary injunctions are granted on the basis of a broad "balance of factors" determined through "procedures that are less formal and evidence that is less complete than in a trial on the merits," and the parties are accorded neither "a full opportunity to present their case nor . . . a final judicial decision based on the *actual* merits of a controversy." *Id.*, at 395–396 . . . (emphasis added). District court orders granting preliminary injunctions may therefore be reviewed only on an abuse-of-discretion standard: an appellate court may conclude that the district court's preliminary relief sweeps too broadly, or is based on an improper balancing of hardships, or even that the likelihood of success has been overdrawn. . . .

. . . The Court focuses on the *Mathews* factors of the risk of an erroneous decision through the current procedures and the probable value of additional safeguards. The Court rummages through the partially developed record and seizes upon scattered evidence introduced by the Government on the eve of the preliminary-injunction hearing—evidence that never has been tested in a trial on the merits—and pronounces that evidence "reliable" and compelling. . . . The conclusion is preordained: the statutes give the appellees "an opportunity under the present claims process" to "make a meaningful presentation" without an attorney's assistance, and the District Court's "holding" of unconstitutionality must therefore be reversed. . . .

This brand of constitutional adjudication is extraordinary. Whereas Justice O'Connor faithfully adheres to the limited role of appellate judges in reviewing preliminary injunctions and thereby departs from the purposes of § 1252, the opinion for the Court seizes upon the underlying purposes of § 1252 in order to evade the well-established rule prohibiting appellate courts from even purporting to "intimate . . . view[s]" on the ultimate merits when reviewing preliminary injunctions granted on likelihood of success. . . . If the opinion for the court turns out to be more than an unfortunate aberration, it will threaten a fundamental transformation of the equitable process of granting preliminary relief in cases challenging the constitutionality of Government action. Individual litigants seeking such relief on grounds of irreparable injury and a balancing of hardships will essentially be required to confront the Government with both hands tied behind their backs: if they successfully obtain such relief, this Court will immediately intervene pursuant to § 1252 to review the "holding" of unconstitutionality, will make *de novo* findings that selected evidence is "reliable," will castigate the individuals for failing to adduce sufficient evidence to support the "merits" of the "holding," and will issue a ringing proclamation that the challenged statute is constitutional. . . .

Justice Stevens, with whom Justice Brennan and Justice Marshall join, dissenting.

The Court does not appreciate the value of individual liberty. It may well be true that in the vast majority of cases a veteran does not need to employ a lawyer . . . and that the system of processing veterans benefit claims, by and large, functions fairly and effectively without the participation of retained counsel. . . . Everyone agrees, however, that there are at least some complicated cases in which the services of a lawyer would be useful to the veteran and, indeed, would simplify the work of the agency by helping to organize the relevant facts and to identify the controlling issues. . . . What is the reason for denying the veteran the right to counsel of his choice in such cases? The Court gives us two answers: First, the paternalistic interest in protecting the veteran from the consequences of his own improvidence. . . . and second, the bureaucratic interest in minimizing the cost of administering the benefit program. . . . I agree that both interests are legitimate, but neither provides an adequate justification for the restraint on liberty imposed by the $10-fee limitation. . . .

. . . The language in § 3405, particularly the use of the words "directly or indirectly," apparently would apply to consultations between a veteran and a lawyer concerning a claim that is ultimately allowed, as well as to an appearance before the agency itself. In today's market, the reasonable fee for even the briefest conference would surely exceed $10. Thus, the law that was enacted in 1864 to protect veterans from unscrupulous lawyers—those who charge excessive fees—effectively denies today's veteran access to *all* lawyers who charge reasonable fees for their services.

The Court's opinion blends its discussion of the paternalistic interest in protecting veterans from unscrupulous lawyers and the bureaucratic interest in minimizing the cost of administration in a way that implies that each interest reinforces the other. Actually the two interests are quite different and merit separate analysis.

In my opinion, the bureaucratic interest in minimizing the cost of administration is nothing but a red herring. Congress has not prohibited lawyers from participating in the processing of claims for benefits and there is no reason why it should. The complexity of the agency procedures can be regulated by limiting the number of hearings, the time for argument, the length of written submissions, and in

other ways, but there is no reason to believe that the *agency's* cost of administration will be increased because a claimant is represented by counsel instead of appearing *pro se.* The informality that the Court emphasizes is desirable because it no doubt enables many veterans, or their lay representatives, to handle their claims without the assistance of counsel. But there is no reason to assume that lawyers would add confusion rather than clarity to the proceedings. As a profession, lawyers are skilled communicators dedicated to the service of their clients. Only if it is assumed that the average lawyer is incompetent or unscrupulous can one rationally conclude that the efficiency of the agency's work would be undermined by allowing counsel to participate whenever a veteran is willing to pay for his services. I categorically reject any such assumption.

The fact that a lawyer's services are unnecessary in most cases, and might even be counterproductive in a few, does not justify a total prohibition on their participation in all pension claim proceedings. . . .

The paternalistic interest in protecting the veteran from his own improvidence would unquestionably justify a rule that simply prevented lawyers from overcharging their clients. Most appropriately, such a rule might require agency approval, or perhaps judicial review, of counsel fees. It might also establish a reasonable ceiling, subject to exceptions for especially complicated cases. In fact, I assume that the $10-fee limitation was justified by this interest when it was first enacted in 1864. But time has brought changes in the value of the dollar, in the character of the legal profession, in agency procedures, and in the ability of the veteran to proceed without the assistance of counsel. . . .

. . . It is evident from what I have written that I regard the fee limitation as unwise and an insult to the legal profession. It does not follow, however, that it is unconstitutional. The Court correctly notes that the presumption of constitutionality that attaches to every Act of Congress requires the challenger to bear the burden of demonstrating its invalidity. . . .

The fact that the $10-fee limitation has been on the books since 1864 does not, in my opinion, add any force at all to the presumption of validity.

Surely the age of the *de jure* segregation at issue in *Brown v. Board of Education*, 347 U.S. 483 . . . (1954), or the age of the gerrymandered voting districts at issue in *Baker v. Carr*, 369 U.S. 186 . . . (1962), provided no legitimate support for those rules. In this case, the passage of time, instead of providing support for the fee limitation, has effectively eroded the one legitimate justification that formerly made the legislation rational. The age of the statute cuts against, not in favor of, its validity.

It is true that the statute that was incorrectly invalidated in *Lochner* provided protection for a group of workers, but that protection was a response to the assumed disparity in the bargaining power of employers and employees, and was justified by the interest in protecting the health and welfare of the protected group. It is rather misleading to imply that a rejection of the *Lochner* holding is an endorsement of rational paternalism as a legitimate legislative goal. . . . But in any event, the kind of paternalism reflected in this statute as it operates today is irrational. It purports to protect the veteran who has little or no need for protection, and it actually denies him assistance in cases in which the help of his own lawyer may be of critical importance.

But the statute is unconstitutional for a reason that is more fundamental than its apparent irrationality. What is at stake is the right of an individual to consult an attorney of his choice in connection with a controversy with the Government. In my opinion that right is firmly protected by the Due Process Clause of the Fifth Amendment and by the First Amendment. . . .

The fundamental error in the Court's analysis is its assumption that the individual's right to employ counsel of his choice in a contest with his sovereign is a kind of second-class interest that can be assigned a material value and balanced on a utilitarian scale of costs and benefits. . . .

Unfortunately, the reason for the court's mistake today is all too obvious. It does not appreciate the value of individual liberty.

I respectfully dissent.

A Determination on the Record of the Hearing and Statement of Reasons and Material Evidence

The eighth and ninth *Goldberg* ingredients discussed now, plus the final ingredient in the next subsection, focus our attention on the process by which agencies actually reach decisions. You will recall that the APA distinguishes between its two main forms of hearings in terms of the presence or absence of the on-the-record requirement. Section 553 imposes no obligation on the agency to decide one way rather than another. After gathering comments and making its decision the agency must "adopt a concise general statement of their basis and purpose" (553)(c), but it need not show that it reached the decision on the basis of the comments.

In formal trial-type hearings, however, agencies must satisfy courts that they have reached any given result on the basis of information formally presented on the record. The opportunity to appear, give arguments, cross-examine opposing witnesses, and so forth does not suffice. The agency must show, after all this has ended and some person or group must sit down and decide what it all means, that the decision does arise from the evidence in the case itself, not from some secret or other off-the-record source. This issue of course was central in *Morgan*. The communications between the Bureau of Animal Industries and the secretary of agriculture were not on the record.

These findings requirements are often called the *substantial evidence* test. It is a test of reasonableness. If the decisionmaker's conclusions necessarily require facts X, Y, and Z to be true, then the record of the hearing must contain credible, that is, believable, evidence that X, Y, and Z are true. Note that this test requires much less proof than does the requirement of proof of guilt "beyond a reasonable doubt" in criminal cases. It is also weaker than the preponderance test of the evidence in civil court cases. The following essay reviews some of the philosophy underlying the findings requirements.

Note: Administrative Findings Under Section 8(c)

Virginia Law Review 51 (1965): 459, 462.

The most obvious reason for requiring findings is that government should not operate in secret. The acts of the sovereign should be done in the open, subject to comment and criticism. Of course, the lack of findings to support an administrative act does not make the effects of the act any less discoverable, but the process by which the decision was reached is part of the process of government, and a basic premise of the APA is that insofar as possible the entire process of government should be revealed.

The parties, and losing parties especially, have a right to know as fully as possible the grounds upon which their case was decided. . . . The parties need to know the basis of a decision if they are to prepare intelligently for agency review of the decision of a subordinate officer, or for reconsideration by the agency of its own decision, or for judicial review.

Findings are the essential basis of proper judicial review of administrative action. The respective roles of agency and court have ever been hard to define, but the court is responsible at least for seeing that the agency acts within its discretion and not arbitrarily or capriciously. Before the court can do this it must know the basis for the administrative decision. . . .

Another reason for requiring findings is that the doctrines of stare decisis, res judicata, and law of the case depend on the clarity of previous decisions. . . . Only adequate findings will reveal whether a decision was on the merits, what issues were actually decided, and what policies were involved.

Practically, additional benefits will result from an agency's explication of its decisions, particularly of important policy decisions. When the parties dealing with an agency know exactly what it has decided and why, there is likely to be less duplicative litigation on the same point. Often adjudication could be avoided if the agency initially would make clear its position. While abbreviated findings might seem expedient to the overworked agency at the moment, they may create greater workloads in the long run.

Finally, it should be recognized that inadequate disclosure and careless writing of opinions, possible indicia of a careless decision, will hardly engender in the public mind confidence in the studied competence and expertise which supposedly justify the relaxed procedures and wide discretion allowed administrative agencies. . . .

While disclosure is the basis of the foregoing considerations, another broad policy underlies the findings requirement which does not directly involve disclosure—the policy of insuring thorough consideration by the agency of its decisions. Anyone is less likely to act arbitrarily or capriciously if he is required to set down with some particularity the reasons for his action. It is all too easy to be arbitrary through mere inadvertence because the thought given to the action was insufficient to uncover all the factors involved. Requiring the agency to publish its reasoning fully not only decreases the likelihood that issues will be neglected: it may also prompt a reexamination of assumptions essential to the rationale which are overlooked until it is reduced to writing. The reasons for requiring findings may thus be classed under two main headings: the policy of disclosure and the policy of insuring thorough agency consideration.

Before proceeding further we must clarify a critical point. The APA itself leaves agencies some flexibility in structuring the outlines of the formal hearing process. Section 557(b) permits agencies to use an administrative law judge to conduct the initial hearing and to make findings and potentially final decisions. But the agency members themselves may also conduct this trial-type hearing. And in some instances the agency members may conduct a second hearing in the process of reviewing the decision of the administrative law judge. In these formal procedures both the judge and the agency itself must comply with the APA.

Most federal formal trial-type hearings do begin with an administrative law judge. States, operating under due process requirements and sometimes their own administrative procedure acts, also frequently use this division of labor. The relationship between the initial fact finder and the final decisionmaker has posed one of the most controversial legal issues surrounding the "on the record" requirement. Obviously a decider cannot, after the hearing but before the decision, get on the phone and consult anybody he or she wishes about the issues. In fact the APA, section 557, now quite strictly prohibits all forms of off-the-record *ex parte* communications in formal hearings. But what if the decider does some independent reading? What if the decider looks up past similar cases for ideas and approaches that might tip the balance? What if the final decider sits down with the initial fact finder and discusses the case, not to review new or secret facts but simply to develop wise solutions? We never forbid conventional judges from doing library research or discussing cases with their clerks or even having clerks author opinions for them. Are these practices any more sinful in administrative law? The following case discusses the reasoning for prohibiting *ex parte* communications in the administrative process.

Mazza v. Cavicchia

Supreme Court of New Jersey
15 N.J. 498 (1954) 5–2

[Mazza operated a hotel and restaurant which possessed an on-premises consumption liquor license. The license was revoked because the operator allowed lewd activity and the sale of contraceptives to take place on the premises. Both acts violated state rules governing the operation of businesses authorized by license to sell liquor by the drink. A hearing before the Division on Alcoholic Beverage Control on the validity of the charge was held and Mazza's license was suspended for 180 days on the basis of the record developed at the hearing. However, Mazza was not provided a copy of the proceedings that were used as the basis of the decision. The lower court in the face of Mazza's challenge upheld the validity of the decision and Mazza appealed to the state supreme court.]

The opinion of the court was delivered by Vanderbilt, C.J.

Mazza appeals here asserting that his constitutional rights have been infringed, N.J. Const. 1947, Art. VI, Sec. V, par. 1, clause (a), in that he was denied due process and a fair hearing before the Division [of Alcohol Beverage Control]. It is unnecessary for us to determine each of the points raised because we are of the opinion that by reason of the failure to supply the appellant with a copy of the hearer's secret report to the Director [of the Division] the appellant was deprived of his right to due process and a fair hearing before the administrative tribunal. . . .

The crucial point in the pending appeal is whether

the failure to supply the appellant with a copy of the hearer's secret report to the Director constitutes reversible error.

It was conceded at the oral argument in the [lower court] as well as in this court that "The hearer in fact files a report of his conclusions with the Director, although there is no official and public rule which requires it, and no notice of the submission of the report is given to the affected licensee."

It is argued in the brief of the respondent Director that his determination was made "upon the basis of his own independent findings and not by a subordinate." This, however, is not saying that the hearer's report was not used by him in the process of deciding the case. Nowhere in the record before us is it stated that he failed to read and otherwise utilize the hearer's confidential report. Every inference is entirely to the contrary. The respondent's brief concedes that hearers' reports have been consistently used since the inception of the agency in 1933. Is it not inconceivable that the Director should have insisted on having hearer's reports for 21 years and yet not used them in preparing his decisions? Is it reasonable to suppose that they merely served the function speciously assigned to them in the respondent's brief:

"The hearer's report serves merely to save the Director the time-consuming effort involved in the mechanical task of dictating his decision. The report has neither official status nor binding force. While it normally accompanies the record submitted to the Director for decision, the preparation of the report, so far as its place in the determinative action of the Director is concerned, could well await the Director's determination made after examination of the complete record."

What possible purpose could the consistent submission of such reports for 21 years have served, but to furnish the Director a key to the facts and the law of each case? . . .

In any proceeding that is judicial in nature, whether in a court or in an administrative agency, the process of decision must be governed by the basic principle of the exclusiveness of the record. "Where a hearing is prescribed by statute, nothing must be taken into account by the administrative tribunal in arriving at

its determination that has not been introduced in some manner into the record of the hearing." . . . Unless this principle is observed, the right to a hearing itself becomes meaningless. Of what real worth is the right to present evidence and to argue its significance at a formal hearing, if the one who decides the case may stray at will from the record in reaching his decision? Or consult another's findings of fact, or conclusions of law, or recommendations or even hold conferences with him? . . .

It should be borne in mind that the danger of unfairness in this type of procedure is particularly great in an agency in which there is such a high degree of concentration of prosecuting and judicial functions in the one agency. . . .

It is as much to the advantage of the Division as to private parties before it that the public have confidence in the fairness of its procedure. Whatever inconvenience the agency may suffer in modifying its practice (and one wonders how great it will really be) will be more than offset by the increased trust which the public will have in the justness of its procedure. . . .

Jacobs, J., with whom Burling, J., agrees, dissenting.

In the proper discharge of our function of judicial review we should examine the proceedings with full recognition that the Division of Alcoholic Beverage Control is part of a coordinate branch of government and that its administrator has the same capacity for the wholesome administration of justice in his lawful sphere as judges have in theirs. Thus viewed, the record leaves little room for doubt that the appellant was fairly charged, tried and found guilty on the basis of compelling evidence, and that his liquor license was justly suspended in strict compliance with all statutory and constitutional requirements. . . .

. . . [N]o request was ever made on the licensee's behalf to examine the hearer's analysis and recommendation and, in any event, the Director did not rely upon them. The record may be searched in vain for any suggestion to the contrary and the Director's opinion states unequivocally that he had "examined and reexamined the entire record" before him and that, having done so he was "thoroughly convinced that a careful reading of the testimony and evidence could lead any dispassionate, discerning person to but one conclusion, namely, that the testimony of the Division's agent truthfully represents the facts in all material and probative respects." Further on, he states that "on the basis of the full testimonial record, revealingly corroborated by all of the attendant circumstances, I am convinced that the violations were committed as charged herein." There is no contention advanced by the licensee that the Director did not personally study all of the testimony and evidence as he says he did. . . .

. . . [I]n the first Morgan case . . . Chief Justice Hughes took pains to point out that evidence may be taken by an examiner and "may be sifted and analyzed by competent subordinates." . . .

It would seem that the majority have mistakenly dealt with the instant proceeding as one in which the Director went beyond the strict record. Even in that situation, however, this court recently held that the administrative determination will not be upset in the absence of a showing of prejudice. . . . [T]he setting aside of the licensee's suspension disregards the essential justice of the proceeding and the important public interests involved, and tends to impose upon the Director, though the legislature has declined to do so, rigid judicial notions as to the precise form of procedural routine to be followed by him. . . .

Both *Mazza*, as an illustration of state law, and the federal APA seem to take a very tough line prohibiting *ex parte* influences. Some have argued that a tough line is needed because the officials can so easily fake (or give the appearance of) deciding on the record when in fact they do not.

The Impartial Decisionmaker

At first glance you might expect this last category of legal formality to pose the fewest legal puzzles of any issue in this chapter. After all, the very essence of judging is impartiality. But on closer look we see that partiality and bias take several forms. Some biases are unavoidable. Some—the Environmental Protection Agency's statutory obligation to protect the environment, for example—are required by law. Congress delegates powers to agencies so that they may implement and enforce legislative policies that are meant to serve a particular mission.

All people, judges included, hold certain values about policy that merge into our views about law. The Warren Court judges shared values about the moral rightness of treating citizens equally without regard to race. These feelings—so different from those at the end of the previous century—caused them to forbid school segregation under the Equal Protection Clause in *Brown v. Board of Education*, 347 U.S. 484 (1954). Judges cannot avoid having values about such matters, and it is desirable that law adapt and change as a democratic society brings new values to bear on political and legal questions.

In the administrative world the "rightness" of some values is every bit as strong as in our conventional courts. For example, Congress created the EPA to protect the environment. To do this job, legally commanded by Congress, we can hardly expect the agency to show no interest in or worse yet a bias against protecting the environment.

Other more specific types of bias exist that administrative law seeks properly to prevent. These biases concern the extent to which decisionmakers close their minds to the facts of the specific cases and issues before them. It is one thing to favor clean rivers and quite another to jump to the conclusion, without looking at the facts, that

Exxon is not responsible for polluting the waters of the Alaska coast subsequent to an oil tanker "spill" in 1989. The following cases describe two kinds of improper bias. The first is called *prejudgment*. A judge prejudges a case when evidence suggests he has, for whatever reasons, reached a decision in the case before hearing the facts. This accusation is less often leveled at administrative law judges in the federal system than at the politically appointed members of the agency themselves who make the final decisions.

The second form of bias is called *improper interest in the result*. Do we suspect that the decider stands to gain in any systematic way—perhaps financially or politically—by deciding a certain way? Unlike the prejudgment problem, which depends on evidence in the case itself, improper interest occurs when the judge in theory is in a position to benefit. In a classic case in this area the Supreme Court held that a mayor in charge of a small town's financial fortunes could not sit as traffic judge if the fines in traffic court supported the town's budget.[6] *Gibson v. Berryhill*, below, treats the same problem

---

Gibson v. Berryhill

411 U.S. 564 (1973) 9–0

+ Burger, Douglas, Brennan, Stewart, White, Marshall, Blackmun, Powell, Rehnquist

[A section of an Alabama statute that had previously allowed private companies to practice optometry by employing optometrists was subsequently repealed. However, one of the affected companies, Lee Optical, continued to employ its optometrists and let those optometrists practice. The Alabama Optometric Association, composed solely of practitioners in private practice, filed charges with the Alabama Board of Optometry, also composed solely of optometrists in private practice, asking that the licenses of optometrists employed by Lee be revoked for unprofessional conduct in abetting Lee in the practice of illegal optometry. After a delay in which the board successfully sought court enforcement to stop Lee from operating, the board prepared to hear the charges. The affected optometrists sued in federal district court to restrain the board from acting since its composition would tend to deny the affected optometrists a fair hearing. A special three-judge district court sustained the optometrists' contention.]

Intended to cut off "main street" optometrists would benefit from a win in this case.

Justice White delivered the opinion of the Court.

The District Court thought the Board to be impermissibly biased for two reasons. First, the Board had filed a complaint in state court alleging . . . charges . . . substantially similar to those pending against appellees before the Board. . . .

Secondly, the District court determined that the aim of the Board was to revoke the licenses of all optometrists in the State who were employed by business corporations such as Lee, and that these optometrists accounted for nearly half of all the optometrists practicing in Alabama. Because the Board

[6] *Ward v. Village of Monroeville*, 409 U.S. 57 (1972).

of Optometry was composed solely of optometrists in private practice for their own account, the District Court concluded that success in the Board's efforts would possibly redound to the personal benefit of members of the Board, sufficiently so that . . . the Board was constitutionally disqualified from hearing the charges filed against the appellees.

The District Court apparently considered either source of possible bias—prejudgment of the facts or personal interest—sufficient to disqualify the members of the Board. Arguably, the District Court was right on both scores, but we need reach, and we affirm, only on the latter ground of possible personal interest.

It is sufficiently clear from our cases that those with substantial pecuniary interest in legal proceedings should not adjudicate these disputes. *Tumey v. Ohio,* 273 U.S. 510 (1927). And *Ward v. Village of* Monroeville, 409 U.S. 57 (1972), indicates that the financial stake need not be as direct or positive as it appeared to be in *Tumey.* It has also come to be the prevailing view that "[m]ost of the law concerning disqualification because of interest applies with equal force to . . . administrative adjudicators." K. Davis, Administrative Law Text § 12.04, p. 250 (1972), and cases cited. The District Court proceeded on this basis and, applying the standards taken from our cases, concluded that the pecuniary interest of the members of the Board of Optometry had sufficient substance to disqualify them, given the context in which this case arose. As remote as we are from the local realities underlying this case and it being very likely that the District Court has a firmer grasp of the facts and of their significance to the issues presented, we have no good reason on this record to overturn its conclusion and we affirm it. . . .

The next case raises the important due process issue whether the agency can ignore an administrative law judge's decision and if so on what basis. *Cinderella Career and Finishing Schools, Inc. v. FTC* (1970) is a good illustration of the two-level federal processes mentioned in section 557 of the APA. Agencies generally retain the power to make the final decision. It need not agree with the administrative law judge's decision.

Cinderella Career and Finishing Schools, Inc. v. Federal Trade Commission

425 F.2d 583, U.S.C.A., D.C. Cir. (1970) 3–0

[Cinderella, a private vocational school, was charged by the Federal Trade Commission with making exaggerated advertising claims for the career benefits to be gained by attending its courses. After an in-depth hearing (50 witnesses, 200 exhibits) contained in 1,810 pages of testimony, the hearing examiner (now called an *administrative law judge*) ruled in favor of Cinderella. The FTC reversed the hearing examiner on some of the charges, and in so doing ignored all the testimony and relied completely on its own evaluation of the ads. Additionally, the chairman of the FTC made a speech during the commission's review of the case indicating indirectly that he had already made up his mind that Cinderella was in the wrong. Cinderella brought suit challenging the decision for lack of due process in the consideration of the evidence and for possible prejudgment on the part of the chairman. All emphases in the material were added by Judge Tamm.]

Tamm, Circuit Judge.

We are faced with two principal issues on this appeal: whether the action of the Commission in reversing the hearing examiner comports with standards of due process, and whether then Chairman Paul Rand Dixon should have recused himself from participation in the review of the initial decision due to public statements he had previously made which allegedly indicated pre-judgment of the case on his part. . . .

In their final decision the Commissioners first criticized the hearing examiner for his handling of some of the testimony, stating that "[f]rom the initial decision it appears that the examiner ignored some of this testimony and some of it was given little or no weight because the examiner either questioned the credibility of the witness or considered their testimony hearsay." . . . The Commissioners themselves then proceeded to ignore all testimony completely: "[I]n view of our decision to independently analyze—and without assistance from consumer or other witnesses—the challenged advertisements and their impact . . . *it becomes unnecessary to review the testimony of these expert and consumer witnesses*." . . . Later in the opinion they again noted that "for the reasons stated above *the Commission will rely on its own reading and study of the advertisements to determine whether the questioned representation has the capacity to deceive*." . . . The hearing examiner in a Federal Trade Commission proceeding has both the right and duty to make determinations concerning the credibility of witnesses and the exclusion of hearsay evidence; while the Commissioners may review those determinations on appeal, in light of the record, they may not choose to ignore completely the testimony adduced at the hearing.

A further example of the Commissioners' determination to make a de novo review of the advertisements rather than considering the record as developed during the hearing is the statement that: "A review of the examiner's initial decision has persuaded the members of the Commission *to examine firsthand and independently* the challenged representations contained in respondents' advertisements rather than relying on the analysis thereof contained in the initial decision."

. . . Not only do we find this conduct on the part of the Commissioners a violation of their own rules and hence of due process, but we also seriously question their ability to make the determination called for without the aid of the testimony in the record. . . . "The Commission, as stated in its opinion . . . , *evaluated Cinderella's advertising entirely on the basis of its own study of the material. It found no need to resolve the conflicting expert and consumer testimony in the record* bearing upon the meaning of the advertisements."

. . . We are unable to find any authority for their proposition—that a sixteen-day hearing may be completely ignored if the Commissioners are dissatisfied with the result reached by their hearing examiner. . . .

We think it as preposterous for the Commission to claim a right to ignore that evidence and, with more daring than prudence, to decide a case de novo as it would be for this court to claim a right to ignore the findings of fact and conclusions of law of a district in a proceeding here, substituting the judgment of this court on a cold record for that of the finder of the fact below. . . .

[W]hile the appeal from the examiner's decision was pending before him, Chairman [of the Commission] Dixon made a speech . . . in which he stated:

. . . *What about carrying ads that offer college educations in five weeks*, fortunes by raising mushrooms in the basement, getting rid of pimples with a magic lotion, *or becoming an airline hostess by attending a charm school?* . . . *Granted that newspapers are not in the advertising policing business, their advertising managers are savvy enough to smell deception when the odor is strong enough.* . . .

[T]here is in fact and law authority in the Commission, acting in the public interest, to alert the public to *suspected violations* of the law by *factual press releases* whenever the Commission shall have reason to believe that a respondent is engaged in activities made unlawful by the Act. . . . " This does not give individual Commissioners license to prejudge cases or to make speeches which give the appearance that the case has been prejudged. Conduct such as this may have the effect of entrenching a Commissioner in a position which he has publicly stated, making it difficult, if not impossible, for him to reach a different conclusion in the event he deems it necessary to do so after consideration of the record. There is a marked difference between the issuance of a press release which states that the Commission has filed a complaint because it has "reason to believe" that there have been violations, and statements by a Commissioner after an appeal has been filed which give the appreareance that he has already prejudged the case and that the ultimate determination of the merits will move in predestined grooves. While these two situations—Commission press releases and a Commissioner's pre-decision public statements—are similar in appearance, they are obviously of a different order of merit.

Chairman Dixon, sensitive to theory but insensitive to reality, made the following statement in declining to recuse himself from this case after petitioner requested that he withdraw:

> As . . . I have stated . . . this principle "is not a rigid command of the law, compelling disqualification for trifling causes, but a consideration addressed to the discretion and sound judgment of the administrator himself in determining whether, irrespective of the law's requirements, he should disqualify himself."

. . . If this is a question of "discretion and judgment," Commissioner Dixon has exercised questionable discretion and very poor judgment indeed, in directing his shafts and squibs at a case awaiting his official action. We can use his own words in telling Commissioner Dixon that he has acted "irrespective of the law's requirements." . . .

The test for disqualification has been succinctly stated as being whether "a disinterested observer may conclude that [the agency] has in some measure adjudged the facts as well as the law of a particular case in advance of hearing it." . . .

[T]he Sixth Circuit was required to reverse a decision of the FTC because Chairman Dixon refused to recuse himself from the case even though he had served as Chief Counsel and Staff Director to the Senate Subcommittee which made the initial investigation into the production and sale of the "wonder drug" tetracycline. . . . Incredible though it may seem, the court was compelled to note in that case that:

> [T]he Commission is a fact-finding body. As Chairman, Mr. Dixon sat with the other members as triers of the facts and *joined in making the factual determination* upon which the order of the Commission is based. *As counsel for the Senate Subcommittee, he had investigated and developed many of these same facts.* [American Cyanamid Co. v. F.T.C., 363 F.2d 757 (1966) at 767.]

. . . It is appalling to witness such insensitivity to the requirements of due process; it is even more remarkable to find ourselves once again confronted with a situation in which Mr. Dixon, pouncing on the most convenient victim, has determined either to distort the holdings in the cited cases beyond all reasonable interpretation or to ignore them altogether. We are constrained to this harshness of language because of Mr. Dixon's flagrant disregard of prior decisions.

The rationale for remanding the case despite the fact that former Chairman Dixon's vote was not necessary for a majority is well established. Litigants are entitled to an impartial tribunal whether it consists of one man or twenty and there is no way which we know of whereby the influence of one upon the others can be quantitatively measured. . . . [W]e vacate the order of the Commission and remand with instructions that the Commissioners consider the record and evidence in reviewing the initial decision, without the participation of Commissioner Dixon. . . .

Administrative law judges (ALJs) serve as the central decisionmakers in formal administrative adjudication. While not much is known about the hiring process for ALJs or how they function, in recent years they have become the focal point of political efforts to implement the regulatory policies of the Reagan and Bush administrations. Martin Tolchin, a journalist for the *New York Times*,, describes how efforts by the Bush administration to reduce social security costs compromise the independence of ALJs working for the Social Security Administration. Before discussing the controversy surrounding ALJs and policy implementation, read the following essay by Jeffrey S. Lubbers, a staff attorney for the Administrative Conference of the United States, a governmental body that conducts research on federal administrative procedures. Lubbers's article describes the selection process for ALJs and discusses some of the criticisms of this process.

Federal Administrative Law Judges: A Focus on Our Invisible Judiciary

Jeffrey S. Lubbers
Administrative Law Review 33 (1981): 109.

Administrative law judges are employed by executive departments and independent agencies to conduct hearings and make decisions in proceedings in which administrative determinations must be based on the records of trial-type hearings. An ALJ's decision may be, and often is, the final decision of the agency without further proceedings if there is no appeal to, or review on the motion of, the agency. . . .

When compared with the role of judges of the federal courts, the role of ALJs in our governmental system is less visible, and, as one would guess, less well understood. The federal judge is, after all, the personification of the judicial branch of the government: a robed authority figure who can demand and receive respect and obeisance even from presidents. Federal judges are guaranteed life tenure by the Constitution; there is little reason to question their independence. The significance of their decisions, which are regularly published and widely accessible, is clearly comprehensible within the context of the familiar three-tier structure of the federal court system (i.e., district courts, courts of appeals, and the Supreme Court). ALJs, on the other hand, in spite of being called judges and functioning as such, are subject to doubts about their independence due in part to their employment status as agency personnel. Furthermore, few agencies systematically publish decisions of their ALJs, and the significance of an ALJ's "decision" as a determinant of his agency's decision or final action varies markedly from agency to agency.

The position of administrative law judge (formerly called "hearing examiner"*) did not even exist until the Administrative Procedure Act (APA) was enacted in 1946. Prior to the APA, there were no reliable safeguards to ensure the objectivity and judicial capability of presiding officers in formal administrative proceedings. Ordinarily these officers were subordinate employees chosen by the agencies, and the power of the agencies to control and influence such personnel made questionable the contention of any agency that its proceedings assured fundamental fairness. Furthermore, the role of the presiding officer in an agency's decisional process was often unclear; many agencies would ignore the officer's decisions without giving reasons, and enter their own de novo decisions. The APA was designed to correct these conditions. Reshaping the role of the "hearing examiner" was a crucial precondition to both of these basic reforms.

The APA spelled out the powers and duties of these so-called examiners as presiding officers. By giving the Civil Service Commission the authority to determine their qualifications and compensation, the APA attempted to insure their competence, impartiality and independence. The basic structure of the 1946 Act remains unchanged today.

As to the independence issue, the Act lodges in the Office of Personnel Management (OPM, the successor of the Civil Service Commission) exclusive authority for the initial examination and certification for selection of ALJs. In addition, ALJs receive compensation as prescribed only by OPM, independently of agency recommendations or ratings, and they can be removed by the agency which employs them only when good cause is established before the Merit Systems Protection Board after opportunity for hearing. The APA also requires that the ALJs' functions be conducted in an impartial manner and provides that if a disqualification petition is filed against an ALJ in any case, the agency must determine that issue on the record, and as part of the decision in that case. The Act also prescribes that an ALJ may not be responsible to, or subject to supervision by, anyone performing investigative or prosecutorial functions for an agency. This "separation of functions" requirement is designed to prevent the investigative or prosecutorial arm of an agency from controlling a hearing or influencing the ALJ. Finally, to insure that the ALJs are well insulated from improper agency pressure and controls, the APA contains two other

---

*The APA originally used the term "examiner." This was changed to "hearing examiner" in the 1966 codification of the Act. After a long campaign by the examiners, the title was changed to administrative law judge by the Civil Service Commission on August 19, 1972. The APA was subsequently so amended in 1978. Pub. L. No. 95–251.

provisions designed to make the ALJ at least semi-independent of the employing agency: ALJs are to be assigned to their cases in rotation so far as is practicable; and they may not perform their duties inconsistently with their roles as ALJs. . . .

Since the passage of the Administrative Procedure Act, the U.S. Civil Service Commission (now OPM) has been exclusively responsible for the initial examination, certification for selection, and compensation of ALJs. . . .

There are several important interrelated facets of the selection and appointment process. The Office of Personnel Management through its Office of Administrative Law Judges administers the recruitment, evaluation, and selection of those eligible to be appointed as ALJs. OPM has determined the minimum level of qualifying experience which an individual must have to be eligible. In addition OPM conducts interviews, administers a test of writing ability, evaluates the qualifying experience of all applicants who meet the minimum experience requirements, and scores each of them on a scale of 100 points. Those who score 80 points or above become "eligibles" and are ranked (highest scores at the top) on registers maintained by OPM from which the agencies make their appointments. The office maintains two registers; one at the GS-16 grade level, the other at GS-15. This is done because OPM has created ALJ positions at both of these levels. ALJ positions in a majority of those agencies which employ ALJs (including most of the major agencies engaged in economic regulation) are at the GS-16 level. The positions in the remaining four agencies (including the Social Security Administration which employs over half of all ALJs) are at the GS-15 level. . . .

In order to qualify as an ALJ, the applicant must be an attorney and have seven or more years of "qualifying experience," at least two of which must be within the seven-year period immediately preceding the date of the application. Qualifying experience means primarily (1) judicial experience; (2) the preparation, trial, hearing or review of formal administrative law cases at the federal, state, or local level; or (3) the preparation and trial or appeal of cases in courts of unlimited or original jurisdiction.

The ALJ applicant must consent to having inquiries (referred to by OPM as "vouchers") sent to about 20 individuals having personal knowledge of the applicant's experience, professional abilities, and qualifications (e.g., supervisors, judges, law partners, co-counsel and opposing counsel). The applicant also must demonstrate writing ability by preparing, under OPM supervision, a sample opinion which is examined for clarity, conciseness and legal soundness. Finally, the applicant must participate in an oral interview before a special panel composed of an official of OPM, a practicing attorney, and an official of an administrative agency.*

. . . After the panel completes the interview and reviews the writing sample, it may recommend an adjustment of the tentative eligibility rating score, although in practice adjustments are minor (nearly always less than five points). The director of the Office of ALJs may, in his discretion, accept, reject, or modify the recommendation. The former director estimated that about 72 percent of all applicants are rated ineligible. Approximately 32 percent of all applicants fail to pass the threshold because they lack one or more of the minimum experience requirements, about 36 percent fail to establish tentative eligibility by scoring below 79 points after the first two ratings are totaled, and 4 percent have their score lowered below 80 after evaluation by a special panel.

. . . [T]he agencies' appointment power is restricted by a statutory requirement known as the "rule of three" which is applicable to all competitive civil service jobs in the federal government. Under this requirement, when an agency requests a list of eligibles, OPM must certify enough names from the top of the register to permit the agency to consider at least three names per appointment to each vacancy. The agency is then obliged to make its selection from those three who have the highest scores and are actually available for appointment. As will be shown, the Veterans Preference Act tends to make the "rule of three" even more restrictive on agency choice. . . .

---

*The attorney is usually, but not always, nominated by the Administrative Law Section of the ABA.

. . . The Act provides that an eligible applicant . . . who meets certain requirements as a wartime veteran of the armed services is entitled to 5 (10 in the case of a disabled veteran) additional points above his scored rating. Since there is only a 20-point spread on scores among all ALJ eligibles (from 80 to 100), the addition of 5 to 10 veterans preference points to any score can change by many places an eligible's ranking on the register. . . . Actual selection statistics confirm this. OPM has testified that from 1970 to 1979, of the 793 ALJs appointed, 593 (74.8 percent) were veterans.

The impact of veterans preference on the register ranking combined with the "rule of three" has led to criticism of the ALJ selection system as keeping many outstanding candidates, especially women, at the bottom of the register and as discouraging others from even applying. The Administrative Conference has recommended that both the extra points and the selection preference requirement for veterans be repealed with respect to the certification and selection of ALJs, and that agencies be permitted to appoint an ALJ from among the highest ten ranked eligibles who are on the register at the time of selection.

. . . [M]any agencies have sought to avoid the restrictions upon their appointment of ALJs through the procedure of "selective certification." Using this process, an agency . . . is permitted to appoint specially certified eligibles without regard to their ranking in relation to other eligibles on the register who lack the special certification. For example, the Federal Communications Commission (FCC) has arranged with OPM for special certification of eligibles who can show:

> [t]wo years of experience in the preparation, presentation, or hearing of formal cases, or in making decisions on the basis of the record of such hearings, originating before governmental regulatory bodies at the Federal, state, or local level, *in the field of communications law.**

The result of this selective certification procedure is to establish, in effect, separate registers for those eligibles who have specialized experience. Announcement No. 318 lists the following agencies as utilizing selective certification for appointees from the GS-16 register. Department of Agriculture, Civil Aeronautics Board, Federal Communications Commission, Federal Energy Regulatory Commission, Department of Labor, Interstate Commerce Commission, National Labor Relations Board, and Securities and Exchange Commission. Only three agencies utilize selective certification for appointment from the GS-15 register: Bureau of Alcohol, Tobacco and Firearms, Social Security Administration (positions in Puerto Rico only) and U.S. Coast Guard. The possible benefits of selective certification to the agencies which have arranged for it are obvious, and those agencies have in fact utilized it extensively. A study made for the Civil Service Commission in 1974 reported that "approximately 82 percent of the ALJs in the agencies using selective certification attained their positions through its use."

The practice of selective certification has been the subject of criticism on the grounds that it severely limits opportunities for generalist applicants and that it leads to "inbreeding" among an agency's ALJs through biasing the selection process in favor of the agency's own staff attorneys who are most likely to meet the specialized experience criteria.† . . .

Whether inbreeding actually poses a problem, beyond appearances, is however, debatable. One agency which relies heavily upon selective certification, the National Labor Relations Board, steadfastly continues to defend the board's need to utilize the practice and maintains that the practicing labor-management bar also supports its retention. In regulatory agencies, on the other hand, where a pro-enforcement attitude may more strongly pervade, the judges' agency background may be a matter of greater concern to the practicing bar.

Selective certification does not apply solely to government attorneys, of course: attorneys in private

---

*U.S. Office of Personnel Management, Announcement No. 318 (emphasis added). The special qualifications for all agencies utilizing selective certification are set forth in the announcement.

†*See generally* Miller, *The Vice of Selective Certification in the Appointment of Hearing Examiners,* 20 Ad. L. Rev. 477 (1968).

practice have the same opportunity to be specially certified as do agency staff attorneys. However, it appears that private attorneys who have specialized expertise in law practice within areas of ALJ selective certification have little interest in forsaking their practice to become ALJs. The percentage of private attorneys on the GS-16 register has fluctuated in recent years, but very few private attorneys listed on the register are specially certified. In March 1980 there were 220 eligibles on the GS-16 register; twenty-three were private attorneys and only two were specially certified.

It seems clear that selective certification represents a response by OPM to agencies' complaints about the restrictions upon their power to appoint ALJs with particularized expertise. The policy does strike a sort of balance with the restrictiveness of the applicable provisions of the Veterans Preference Act and the "rule of three," but whether it strikes an optimum balance, whether it enhances the quality or productivity of the ALJs, and whether it unduly discriminates against "generalist" eligibles remain much debated questions. The agencies utilizing selective certification generally favor its continuation, generalist eligibles oppose it, and others have urged its modification.

I share the Administrative Conference's belief that the objective of selective certification could be achieved without closing the door to highly qualified generalists by changing the process of ALJ certification and selection. Under its recommendation, eligibles would be awarded extra rating points for specialized experience of the kind now recognized for selective certification; a pool of the ten, rather than three, highest ranking eligibles on the register would be certified for agency selection; and, by amendment of the Veterans Preference Act, the agency would be free to select any eligible in the certified pool even if there were a higher-rated veteran in the pool. . . .

. . . [M]any fewer private attorneys tend to apply than do federal agency lawyers. One can only assume that the limited salary potential for ALJs is a major factor in this. ALJs' salaries like those of other top governmental officers are limited by a statutory ceiling. As of October 1980 a GS-15's salary ranged from $44,547 to the ceiling of $50,112 and a GS-16 was

at the ceiling. Apparently this salary level is not high enough to attract many specialized practitioners from the private bar. Indeed as far back as 1974, the then director of the Office of ALJs expressed the opinion that ALJ service was also gradually losing its appeal to specially qualified agency staff attorneys in relation to the more lucrative lure of private practice. . . .

Thirty-five years after the passage of the Administrative Procedure Act the administrative law judge is a strong and flourishing institution. Both the number of judges and the number of agencies using them have been growing yearly. Their status and functions have been enhanced by a long series of decisions of federal courts reviewing administrative agency decision making. And they themselves have organized an effective professional association—the Federal Administrative Law Judges Conference (FALJC).* Nevertheless, in recent years questions about the recruitment, selection, utilization, independence, and competence of the ALJ have been asked with increasing, rather than decreasing, frequency. . . .

In the last twenty-five years a number of proposals have been advanced for a unified administrative trial court, or at least a centralized corps of judges to be used, but not employed or housed by the agencies.† Recently the movement has intensified. . . . In 1976 former ABA President Bernard Segal called for the creation of an independent ALJ corps in a speech to the ABA. Since then, the concept has garnered much support from ALJs themselves while the employing agencies tend to oppose the idea. In addition, with the creation of the Occupational Safety and Health Review Commission and Federal Mine Safety and Health Review Commission as adjudicative commissions, staffed with ALJs and independent of the

---

*The FALJC is the only independent association of ALJs. The ABA's Section of Judicial Administration has organized a conference of ALJs, and the numerous ALJs in the Department of HHS have also formed their own association of ALJs.

†*See, e.g.,* Hector, *Problems of the CAB and the Independent Regulatory Commissions,* 69 Yale L.J. 931 (1960); Minow, *Suggestions for Improvement of the Administrative Process: Letter to President Kennedy from Newton N. Minow, Chairman, Fed. Communications Comm'n,* 15 Ad. L. Rev. 146 (1963); Hoover Comm'n on the Executive Branch of Government, Legal Services and Procedures 87–88 (1955).

Department of Labor, Congress has shown itself to be increasingly sensitive to the value of having judges who are free from any influence of the enforcement agency.

Such proposals raise structural questions that go to the heart of our administrative process. Proponents of the corps idea bear the burden of attending to the details of its proposed implementation. . . . The very size and balkanization of the burgeoning administrative judiciary and the variety of matters it now handles would hinder any attempt to rapidly transform it into a coherent corps. On the other hand, the prospect of increased unification remains attractive because of its potential administrative efficiency, enhancement of the perception (at least) of judicial independence, and the facilitation of uniformity in administrative procedures and in productivity norms. I hope therefore that the unified corps concept can receive intensive scrutiny in the next several years, and that Congress can authorize a limited experiment by which amenable agencies can draw upon a separately appointed and administered corps of ALJs. . . .

Judges Who Decide Social Security Claims Say Agency Goads Them to Deny Benefits

Martin Tolchin
New York Times, 8 January 1989.

Many of the judges who decide claims for Government disability and health insurance charge that they are being harassed by the Social Security Administration in an effort to reduce costs.

"We have gotten allegations from administrative law judges of coercion, threatened transfers and other kinds of pressures," said Representative Barney Frank, Democrat of Massachusetts, who is chairman of a House Judiciary subcommittee that will hold hearings on the allegations next month.

'The harassment is all in the interest of keeping awards down for sick and needy people," Mr. Frank said.

The agency denies that it harasses the law judges. It says it monitors them to increase their productivity and reduce costs.

"We're not aware of any allegations of harassment," said Phil Gambino, chief spokesman for the Social Security Administration. "We recognize and support the need for independence."

But through their national organization, the Association of Administrative Law Judges, a number of judges have said the Social Security Administration imposes a monthly quota of cases and retaliates against those who do not meet it. Some say the agency also punishes those who award benefits it considers excessive.

Russell Barone, an administrative law judge in Chicago, said the agency recently turned down his request for a transfer to Buffalo because he had decided an average of only 31 cases a month instead of 37.

Paul Rosenthal of Newport Beach, Calif., the former chief administrative law judge at the Social Security Administration, said that as punishment for an effort to increase the judges' top salaries, now $71,377 a year, he was ordered not to accept an award from the American Bar Association in 1986. The award commended Mr. Rosenthal and the agency's judges for "outstanding efforts to protect the integrity of administrative adjudication within their agency."

Mr. Rosenthal said his persistent efforts on behalf of the law judges led the agency to demote him in March 1987. He retired last month.

Louis D. Enoff, the agency's Deputy Commissioner for Programs, said some agency officials considered the Bar Association award an insult to the Social Security Administration, feeling that it took the judges' side in their dispute with the agency. But he said he was unaware that Mr. Rosenthal had been ordered not to accept the award.

The judges, who have lifetime tenure, are part of a national corps, hired by Federal agencies to decide disputes involving eligibility and awards under Government programs. Their status is similar to that of Federal judges under a law that deems them "independent and secure in their tenure and compensation."

Of 1,034 administrative law judges, 696 work for the Social Security Administration, where they hear appeals from people denied disability or health insurance benefits. There are about 300,000 such hearings a year.

Charges of harassment have been made by judges working for other agencies, but the judges assert that the Social Security Administration is the worst offender.

In 1982 the agency began to review the decisions of all judges who allowed benefits in 70 percent of their decisions or more. It warned them that if their performance did not change, "other steps" would be considered.

That policy drew sharp criticism from Congress and brought a lawsuit from the Association of Administrative Law judges. The agency dropped the review procedure in 1984, and the lawsuit was dismissed, although a Federal district judge in Chicago said the policy had "created an untenable atmosphere of tension and unfairness" that could have compromised the independence of the judges.

But some judges say the agency still exerts indirect pressure to hold down the benefits. The agency has taken away secretaries and lawyers reporting to individual judges, replacing them with personnel pools that the judges say remain under the agency's authority and are sometimes manipulated to discipline them. The agency says the move was needed for greater efficiency, but some judges say the net effect was to take away their independence and ability to act impartially.

"The Social Security Administration doesn't treat judges like judges," said Nahum Litt, the chief administrative law judge at the Department of Labor. "They treat them as other employees."

Mr. Litt said the problem arose from a conflict between budget-minded agency officials and judges who are supposed to be disinterested in the fiscal effects of their rulings.

"The agency has consistently tried to control the ability of A.L.J.'s to function as independent adjudicators," said Ronald J. Bernoski, an administrative law judge in Milwaukee who is secretary of the law judges' association.

W. C. Lynch, a Social Security Administration law judge in Eugene, Ore., who is a member of the association's board of directors, said, "There is a wealth of evidence that if an A.L.J. incurs the ire of the Social Security Administration, he very likely would not get certain assignments, travel arrangements, transfers and other things that he wanted. It's not too subtle."

Both men testified last month at a hearing of the House Ways and Means Committee, but only after being publicly assured that the agency would not punish them for their testimony.

The Informalism of Formal Administrative Hearings

Throughout this chapter we have seen how administrative procedures combines informal and formal aspects. Recall Justice Rehnquist's description of the administrative scheme Congress established for the Board of Veterans' Appeals in *Walters v. National Association of Radiation Survivors* (1985). In denying veterans the right to more than $10 for attorneys' fees, Justice Rehnquist argued that the administrative process "should be as informal and nonadversarial as possible." Since the retreat from *Goldberg,* beginning in the mid-to-late 1970s, there has been a reform movement calling for greater informalism in administrative procedure. In chapter 7 we will describe the political origins of this movement more specifically and analyze its impact on administrative rulemaking. We conclude this chapter by calling attention to the extent to which informal procedures are *formally* part of the administrative process. In other words, you should understand that a formal element of an administrative hearing is its informal procedure.

To illustrate, a number of grievance procedures used by universities to deal with sexual harassment complaints combine informal and formal procedures. Following the successful efforts by the women's movement to classify sexual harassment as a form of sex discrimination prohibited under Title VII of the Civil Rights Act of 1964,[7] the Equal Employment Opportunity Commission published guidelines in 1980 defining sexual harassment. Those guidelines read as follows:

EEOC GUIDELINES ON DISCRIMINATION BECAUSE OF SEX[8]

§ 1604.11 Sexual harassment.

(a) Harassment on the basis of sex is a violation of Sec. 703 of Title VII.* Unwelcome sexual advances, requests for sexual favors, and other verbal or physical conduct of a sexual nature constitute sexual harassment when (1) submission to such conduct is made either explicitly or implicitly a term or condition of an individual's employment, (2) submission to or rejection of such conduct by an individual is used as the basis for employment decisions affecting such individual, or (3) such conduct has the purpose or effect of unreasonably interfering with an individual's work performance or creating an intimidating, hostile, or offensive working environment.

(b) In determining whether alleged conduct constitutes sexual harassment, the Commission will look at the record as a whole and at the totality of the circumstances, such as the nature of the sexual advances and the context in which the alleged incidents occurred. The determination of the legality of a particular action will be made from the facts, on a case by case basis.

(c) Applying general Title VII principles, an employer, employment agency, joint apprenticeship committee or labor organization (hereinafter collectively referred to as "employer") is responsible for its acts and those of its agents and supervisory employees with respect to sexual harassment regardless of whether the specific acts complained of were authorized or even forbidden by the employer and regardless of whether the employer knew or should have known of their occurrence. The Commission will examine the circumstances of the particular employment relationship and the job functions performed by the individual in determining whether an individual acts in either a supervisory or agency capacity.

*The principles involved here continue to apply to race, color, religion or other origin.

[7] See Catharine A. MacKinnon, *Sexual Harassment of Working Women* (New Haven, Conn.: Yale University Press, 1979).

[8] See Billie Wright and Linda Weiner, *The Lecherous Professor* (Boston: Beacon Press, 1984) 189–193.

(d) With respect to conduct between fellow employees, an employer is responsible for acts of sexual harassment in the workplace where the employer (or its agents or supervisory employees) knows or should have known of the conduct, unless it can show that it took immediate and appropriate corrective action.

(e) An employer may also be responsible for the acts of non-employees, with respect to sexual harassment of employees in the workplace, where the employer (or its agents or supervisory employees) knows or should have known of the conduct and fails to take immediate and appropriate corrective action. In reviewing these cases the Commission will consider the extent of the employer's control and any other legal responsibility which the employer may have with respect to the conduct of such non-employees.

(f) Prevention is the best tool for the elimination of sexual harassment. An employer should take all steps necessary to prevent sexual harassment from occurring, such as affirmatively raising the subject, expressing strong disapproval, developing appropriate sanctions, informing employees of their right to raise and how to raise the issue of harassment under Title VII, and developing methods to sensitize all concerned.

(g) Other related practices: Where employment opportunities or benefits are granted because of an individual's submission to the employer's sexual advances or requests for sexual favors, the employer may be held liable for unlawful sex discrimination against other persons who were qualified for but denied that employment opportunity or benefit.

As you read the University of Massachusetts at Amherst Sexual Harassment Policy, reprinted below, consider the following questions. Does this university's procedure satisfy the EEOC Guidelines? If, so why? If not, why not? What impact does the informal process have on the formal procedures? The University of Massachusetts' policy states that there are two modes of resolution for formal complaints—mediation and a hearing. How is mediation different from a hearing in this context? And finally, think about what impact mediation, an informal procedure, has on the formal hearing process.

University of Massachusetts at Amherst Sexual Harassment Policy (1988)

Preamble

The University of Massachusetts at Amherst is committed to providing faculty, staff and students with an environment where they may pursue their careers or studies without being sexually harassed. Sexual harassment, as here defined, is a violation of Title VII of the 1964 Civil Rights Act. For the purposes of this policy, it is defined as follows:

Unwelcomed sexual advances, requests for sexual favors, and other verbal or physical conduct of a sexual nature constitute sexual harassment when: 1) submission to such conduct is made either explicitly or implicitly a term or condition of an individual's employment or academic work; or 2) submission to or rejection of such conduct by an individual is used as the basis for employment or academic decisions affecting such individual; or 3) such conduct has the purpose or effect of unreasonably interfering with an individual's work performance or creating an intimidating, hostile or offensive working or academic environment.

In determining whether an alleged incident constitutes sexual harassment, those entrusted with administering this policy will look at the totality of the circumstances, such as the nature of the sexual advances and the context in which the alleged incidents occurred. The determination of a suitable penalty will be made from a finding of fact on a case-by-case basis and from any record of previous sexual harassment by the respondent.

Procedure

The Office of Affirmative Action will be responsible for administering this policy and its procedures. The Director of Affirmative Action will serve as Chair of the Sexual Harassment Board. The University's Vice Chancellors will see that all supervisors on the Amherst campus receive information and training concerning sexual harassment and the responsibilities of supervisors when complaints are received.

I. PURPOSE AND SCOPE. This grievance procedure is intended to provide a fair, prompt and reliable determination about whether the University's sexual harassment policy has been violated. It is available to anyone who, at the time of the alleged harassment, was either employed by or enrolled at the University of Massachusetts at Amherst. No University employee or student is exempt from the jurisdiction of this policy.

In most instances, the complaint will be the victim of the alleged harassment. However, the University reserves the right to initiate a formal complaint against an employee or student when the alleged victim is unwilling or unable to serve as a complainant, but is willing and able to serve as a witness. The Chair of the Sexual Harassment Board will determine when the University should press charges against a respondent and, in such instances, the Chair, with the approval of the Chancellor, will designate who will present the University's case.

As in any grievance procedure, justice requires that the legal rights as well as the right to academic freedom of the complainant and the respondent be fully assured. The University will make every effort to protect these rights and will undertake no action that threatens or compromises them.

This procedure is not intended to impair or limit the right of anyone to seek a remedy available under state or federal law. A complainant may file a complaint with an external agency to meet state and federal agency deadlines without jeopardizing his or her right to a University hearing. However, if a complainant seeks relief outside the University, the University will not be obliged to continue processing a grievance while the case is being considered by an outside agency or court.

If the respondent in a formal grievance is an undergraduate student, the Dean of Students will be notified, and a hearing process as described in the undergraduate *Code of Student Conduct* will be initiated. Graduate student respondents will be referred to the Dean of the Graduate School (or his or her designee) who will provide a hearing process analogous to the one described in the undergraduate *Code of Student Conduct*.

If the respondent is a member of the Chancellor's staff, the Chancellor will serve the role described for the respondent's Vice Chancellor in this procedure.

II. THE SEXUAL HARASSMENT BOARD. The Chancellor will appoint a Sexual Harassment Board of twenty-five members, each for a term of three years which may be renewed. The members will include at least: four faculty members, four members of the professional staff, four classified employees, four undergraduate students, and four graduate students. The Director of the Office of Affirmative Action will chair the Board. Without ten working days of receiving a formal complaint, the Chair will name three members from the Board to constitute the Hearing Panel. At least one member of each Panel will be drawn from the complainant's and respondent's respective constituencies (that is, graduate or undergraduate student, faculty member, professional staff, or classified employee). The Chair will designate one member to serve as the Presiding Officer.

The members of the panel will act at all times to preserve confidentiality. Once each year, new panel members will participate in a workshop designed to educate them about the issues encompassing sexual harassment as well as to the procedures for conducting a sexual harassment hearing which are described below.

III. DEADLINES. A complainant will have twelve months following an incident to file a complaint unless he or she can show good reason (as determined by the Chair of the Sexual Harassment Board) for having that deadline waived. The people charged with administering this process will endeavor to meet all deadlines, but failure to do so will not prevent the process from continuing. The complainant or the respondent must demonstrate to the Chair's satisfaction some prejudice stemming from a delay before this process will be stopped. Deadlines cited in this document are intended to serve as outside limits for actions to occur. In the interest of the parties concerned, all maters should be handled as expeditiously as possible.

If a respondent fails to answer a charge or to participate in a hearing concerning sexual harassment, his or her Vice Chancellor will be notified of that fact by the Chair of the Sexual Harassment Board. Failure to respond to a charge or to appear at a hearing will be considered a breach of an employee's or student's responsibility. Furthermore, a respondent will not prevent this process from proceeding by his or her silence or absence. Failure to respond may result in the hearing proceeding solely on the basis of the complainant's testimony and evidence.

A complainant may withdraw a charge after it has been filed, provided the respondent agrees to the withdrawal.

IV. RETALIATION. No individual will be penalized by the University or by any person for participating in the procedures described here. Since retaliation is a violation of federal Civil Rights law concerning sexual harassment, any act of retaliation directed against either a complainant or a respondent will be subject to this grievance procedure. Complaints of retaliation should be addressed to the Chair of the Sexual Harassment Board, who will advise the grieving party of his or her rights in this matter. The Affirmative Action Office will assist the victim of retaliation in preparing a complaint which will then be processed in the same manner as a sexual harassment complaint.

V. INFORMAL PROCESS. Persons with sexual harassment complaints are encouraged to consult first with the Affirmative Action Office to learn about the options and resources available to them.

In some circumstances informal resolution of a complaint (prior to filing a grievance) may be more satisfactory than directly proceeding to a formal grievance. Agencies for informal resolutions may include, but are not limited to, any one or more of the following: consultation and action at the department level; mediation through the Ombuds Office, the Mediation Project or any other appropriate agency; advice and assistance of legal counsel; advice and assistance of the Department of Public Safety.

VI. FILING A COMPLAINT. Any individual who chooses to file a formal sexual harassment complaint should do so in the Affirmative Action Office within twelve months of the incident. The Office will advise complainants about the formal grievance procedure as well as possible sanctions and forms of relief. When appropriate, the Office may also recommend counseling or other support services which provide victim assistance.

The Office will maintain a record of all complaints received, including complainants' and respondents' names, and the outcome of proceedings, including sacntions imposed. At the end of every academic year the Office will prepare an annual report of statistics and relevant commentary for the Executive Vice Chancellor. As far as possible, the report will contain no information which could lead to identification of the parties. The annual report will be available to faculty, staff and students upon request to the Executive Vice Chancellor.

VII. FORMAL PROCEDURE. A complainant may file a formal complaint immediately or may do so after efforts to reach an informal settlement prove unsuccessful.

The complaint will be written on a standard form by the complainant with the assistance of the Affirmative Action Office; it will state clearly and concisely the complainant's description of the incident; it will also indicate any remedy sought. The complaint must be signed by the complainant. Remaining neutral, the Office will send the respondent a copy of the complaint within five working days after it is received. A copy of the complaint will also be sent to the respondent's Vice Chancellor.

The respondent will have ten working days to respond in writing. The Affirmative Action Office will be available to assist with the preparation of the response to the complaint. This statement, written on a standard form, will contain full and specific responses to each claim in the complaint, admitting, denying or explaining the complainant's allegations. The respondent must sign his or her statement which will then be appended to the original complaint. Within three working days, the Affirmative Action Office will forward both statements to the complainant, the respondent, the respondent's Vice Chancellor, and the Chair of the Sexual Harassment Board.

There will be two modes of resolution for formal complaints. A complaint may be settled through mediation or through a hearing. If the complainant and respondent agree to pursue mediation, they will be referred to the Ombudsperson. Remaining neutral, the Ombudsperson will consult and advise both the complainant and the respondent about the mediation process. If the Ombudsperson perceives any conflict of interest in the case, or upon request of either party, the Ombudsperson will name an alternative mediator who is acceptable to all parties.

If the mediation results in a mutually acceptable agreement, copies of the agreement will be forwarded to the Affirmative Action Office. If the mediation does not result in an agreement, the case will be returned to the Affirmative Action Office for a hearing.

When a hearing is requested, the Chair of the Sexual Harassment Board will name three members from the Board to constitute a Hearing Panel within ten working days after receiving the request.

VIII. THE HEARING PANEL. Before a Hearing Panel is convened, each party to the proceeding will have the right to object to the appointment of any panel member on the grounds that that member's participation would jeopardize the party's right to a fair and reliable hearing. The Chair of the Sexual Harassment Board will determine whether objections have merit and will judge whether a panel member will be seated.

Before any case is heard by the Hearing Panel, the complainant and the respondent, along with their advocates (if desired, in accordance with Section IX), will meet with the Presiding Officer of the Hearing Panel to attempt to clarify the issues and to define the areas of disagreement. To encourage a fair and focused hearing, the Presiding Officer will notify the Hearing Panel at the start of the proceedings about the points of agreement and disagreement.

The Hearing Panel will hear testimony and consider evidence related to the complaint. The panel will determine whether the University policy on sexual harassment has been violated, and, if so, will recommend appropriate penalty and relief to the Chair of the Sexual Harassment Board.

Duties and Powers of the Presiding Officer and the Hearing Panel

The Presiding Officer will:

1. ensure an orderly presentation of all evidence;
2. ensure that the proceedings are accurately recorded; and
3. see that a fair and impartial decision based on the issues and evidence presented at the hearing is issued by the Hearing Panel no later than ten working days after the conclusion of the hearing or, when written arguments are submitted, ten working days after their submission.

The Hearing Panel will:

1. conduct a fair and impartial hearing which ensures all the rights of all parties involved;
2. define issues of contention;
3. receive and consider all relevant evidence which reasonable people customarily rely upon in the conduct of serious business;
4. ask relevant questions of the complainant, respondent, and any witness if needed to elicit information which may assist the Hearing Panel in making a decision;
5. ensure that the complainant and respondent have full opportunity to present their claims orally or in writing and to present witnesses and evidence which may establish their claims;
6. continue the hearing to a subsequent date if necessary to permit either party to produce additional evidence, witnesses, or other relevant materials;
7. change the date, time or place of the hearing on its own motion or for good reason shown by either party, and with due notice to all parties;
8. permit both parties to submit written arguments within ten working days from the conclusion of the hearing;
9. rule by majority on all questions of fact, interpretations of rules, regulations and policies, recommendations for penalties and relief, and any requests that are made during the hearing.

The Hearing Panel may consult with University Counsel or have his or her assistance at the hearing.

IX. THE HEARING. The Hearing is intended to provide an opportunity to determine whether University policy has been violated. Both parties will be given a full and fair hearing. The proceeding, although formal, is not a court proceeding and the Hearing Panel will not be bound by the procedures and rules of evidence of a court of law. In most instances, complainants and respondents will be expected to speak for themselves. The Hearing Panel will hear and admit evidence which it believes is pertinent to the case.

The Hearing Panel will conduct its hearings by the following procedures:

1. Unless otherwise agreed by a majority of the Panel, a closed hearing will be held within ten working days after the Hearing Panel has been appointed.
2. The complainant and respondent will have the opportunity to hear all testimony, to examine all evidence, to respond to any testimony, and to present evidence and witnesses which advance arguments relevant to the issues in contention.
3. Each party will have the right to be accompanied and advised by two people at any stage of the proceedings; one or both may be an attorney. However, advisors will not address the Hearing Panel directly except in special cases, and with permission of the Panel.
4. If either party is a member of a collective bargaining unit, the advisors mentioned above may, upon the request of the party, be representatives of his or her union. However, neither party will be required to be advised by a union representative. When there is no request for union representation by a member of a union, the union will be notified that a hearing has been scheduled and will be allowed to send an observer.
5. The hearing will be recorded on tape by the Hearing Panel and the tapes will become the property of the University. Subsequently, either party may have supervised access to the tapes by application to the Director of Affirmative Action.

The proceedings before the Hearing Panel will be as follows:

1. The Presiding Officer will read the charge(s) and ask the respondent to either admit or challenge the allegation(s).
2. The complainant may present a brief opening statement, followed by the same from the respondent.
3. The Hearing Panel will give each party the opportunity to present all relevant evidence.
4. Each party may make a concluding statement to the Hearing Panel.
5. If either party wishes to submit any written argument after the hearing, he or she will notify the Presiding Officer within two working days

after the hearing. The written argument will be submitted within ten working days after the hearing's conclusion.

6. A Hearing Panel, by a majority vote of its members, may make other rules concerning the procedure of a hearing which it deems appropriate and consistent with this Sexual Harassment policy.

X. DECISION OF THE HEARING PANEL. After all the evidence and testimony is presented, the Hearing Panel will convene for private deliberations to determine whether the University's policy on sexual harassment has been violated. If the panel finds that the policy has not been violated, that fact will be registered in all University records pertaining to the case in the Ombuds Office, the Office of Affirmative Action, and the office of the respondent's Vice Chancellor. If it has been violated, the Hearing Panel will prepare findings and will recommend a penalty for the respondent and relief for the complainant. The findings of fact as well as the recommended penalty and relief will be based solely on the testimony and evidence presented at the hearing.

The penalty should reflect the severity of the harassment. The penalties may include, but will not be limited to, any one or combination of the following: verbal admonition, written warning placed in the respondent's personnel file, probation, suspension without pay, demotion, removal from administrative duties within a department, and dismissal. The Hearing Panel may also make appropriate recommendations, such as professional counseling, and may recommend relief for the complainant which reinstates and restores, as much as possible, the aggrieved party.

The Hearing Panel will forward its findings and recommended penalty and relief to the Chair of the Sexual Harassment Board. The Chair of the Sexual Harassment Board will review the recommended penalty and any University records of the respondent's past sexual harassment violations. The Chair will adjust the Hearing Panel's recommended penalty to take into account any record of previous sexual harassment by the respondent. Any revision of the penalty, along with written reasons for the revision, will be affixed to the Hearing Panel's decision.

Within three working days after receiving the Panel's findings and recommendation, the Chair of the Sexual Harassment Board will forward these, a record of the hearing, and any recommended adjustment of the penalty to the respondent's Vice Chancellor. The Vice Chancellor will render his or her written decision to the complainant, the respondent, and the Chair of the Sexual Harassment Board no later than fifteen working days after receiving the complete record of the hearing. The Vice Chancellor will be responsible for determining and implementing both the penalty and relief. The Vice Chancellor's determination of penalty and relief (including the dates by which each will be implemented) will also be submitted in writing to the complainant, the respondent, and the Chair of the Sexual Harassment Board.

XI. REVIEW. Within ten working days after the complainant and the respondent receive a written copy of the Vice Chancellor's decision, the respondent, the complainant or the Chair of the Sexual Harassment Board may request a review by submitting a written petition to the Executive Vice Chancellor. (When the respondent is an employee in Academic Affairs, the Chancellor will review the decision.) The petition will set forth in detail the specific grounds upon which review is sought. The Executive Vice Chancellor will forward a copy of the petition to the Chair of the Sexual Harassment Board, the Hearing Panel, and both parties. The Executive Vice Chancellor will review the record of the case—the taped record of the hearing, documents considered by the Panel, the Panel's findings and recommendations, and any record of previous offenses—and may modify or vacate a Vice Chancellor's decision. The Executive Vice Chancellor may, for example, decide that the Panel's findings are unsupported by a preponderance of evidence, or that some aspect of the process violated an individual's legal rights, academic freedom, or these procedures.

The Executive Vice Chancellor may: a) affirm or revise the decision of the Vice Chancellor; or b) request specific findings from the Panel; or c) remand the case to the Chair of the Sexual Harassment Board for a new hearing. In the couse of review, the Executive Vice Chancellor may consult with University Counsel who will have access to the complete record of the case.

The Executive Vice Chancellor will render a written decision within fifteen working days after receipt of the petition for review, the decision of the Vice Chancellor, and the complete record of the Hearing Panel. The Executive Vice Chancellor's decision will be sent to the Vice Chancellor, the complainant, the respondent, the Hearing Panel, and the Chair of the Sexual Harasssment Board. The Executive Vice Chancellor's decision will constitute final University disposition of the matter.

XII. RECORDS. Records of all formal mediations, hearings, and reviews will be kept by the Office of Affirmative Action. The records will be available to:

the Chair of the Sexual Harassment Board,
the Ombudsperson,

a respondent's Vice Chancellor,
the Executive Vice Chancellor, or
the Chancellor

a) when determining an appropriate procedure or penalty for a subsequent sexual harassment complaint, or b) when a complaint of retaliation is made, or c) when a decision is reviewed, or d) when a respondent is a candiate for a supervisory position.

The records will also be available to University Counsel if needed for any proceeding related to these policies or procedures, whether internal to the University or in any judicial or administrative proceeding in which the University, its trustees, officers, employees or agents are a party.

XIII. STANDARD OF PROOF. A violation of this sexual harassment policy will be found only where there is a preponderance of evidence that a violation has occurred. The Hearing Panel, the Vice Chancellors and the Executive Vice Chancellor will be bound to make their determinations based on this standard of proof.

Exercises and Questions for Further Thought

1. After the Supreme Court announced its opinion in the *Morgan* case the secretary of agriculture was so incensed that he wrote a letter to the *New York Times* publicly criticizing the Court's position. The same secretary had then to reconsider the case after the Supreme Court remanded it. Should his letter disqualify him from reconsidering the issues? See *United States v. Morgan*, 313 U.S. 409 (1941).

2. The Employment Standards Administration imposes and collects civil fines from those who illegally employ child laborers. Federal law requires that the fines thus collected be turned over to the administration to help reimburse its enforcement costs. Is this legally permissible? What if the fines thus collected amount to less than 1 percent of the ESA's annual budget? What if in an average year the ESA underspends its budget so that it refunds to the Treasury at the end of the year an average of 5 percent of its budget authorization? See *Marshall v. Jerrico, Inc.*, 446 U. S. 238 (1980).

Acting as prosecutors, not judges

3. One of the classic early judicial interpretations of the APA occurred in *Wong Yang Sung v. McGrath*, 339 U.S. 33, and 94 L. Ed. 616 (1950). You should read this case both to enrich your appreciation of the APA's early history and because the Court, through Justice Jackson, speaks with a clarity amd moral vigor too often missing in recent judicial pronouncements on the APA.

4. Review APA section 554(d)'s restrictions on *ex parte* communications in formal hearings. At first glance the section seems to write the *Morgan* result into law. It prevents the administrative law judge from consulting others about the facts of the case off the record without giving the parties a chance to rebut, and it prohibits the investigator or prosecutor from influencing the final decision. Note, however, that the politically appointed members of the agencies, who make the final decisions, are exempted from 554(d).

5. One of the attractions of employment with government is that it provides effective and marketable training for future private careers. Part of the marketability of this experience consists simply in the fact that former employees know and are often friendly with agency personnel who remain. Should there be limits on participation by former employees? See the 1978 Ethics in Government Act as described in Thomas D. Morgan, "Appropriate Limits on Participation by a Former Agency Official in Matters Before an Agency," *Duke Law Journal* 1980: 1. Note this matter is not confined to adjudication. Why?

6. Administrative law judges, like trial judges sitting without juries in complex cases, write opinions explaining and justifying their findings. So do the members of the administrative boards themselves who make final decisions. Obviously these written opinions can and do create a body of precedent that agencies could theoretically follow just as common law courts follow judicial precedents. In administrative adjudication it is permissible for agencies to decide case by citing "rules" which consist of principles announced in previous adjudications. Throughout its history the National Labor Relations Board (NLRB) has made labor law in just this way. Is this just, particularly in cases where such rules are applied retroactively? See *Brooks v. NLRB*, 348 U.S. 96 (1954). Once the decision has been announced, should courts *require* agencies to follow these principles in the future under the common law doctrine of stare decisis, or should agencies possess the flexibility to change their "common law?" See *Office of Communications of the United Church of Christ v. FCC*, 590 F.2d 1062 (1978).

CHAPTER 7

Ambiguities in Rulemaking Procedures

Chapters 5 and 6 provided a general outline of the law of administrative procedure. The Constitution itself would seem to require no particular process, since when an agency makes a rule it simply acts on behalf of the legislature, and legislatures have no constitutional obligation to hold hearings or provide interested citizens a chance to comment on proposed laws. From this perspective the law of rulemaking in a given situation depends only upon what statutes call for. If authorizing statutes call for a full hearing, then the agency must follow the formal hearing requirements discussed in the last chapter. If a statute calls for something more than notice and comment but less than a formal hearing, as does recent legislation governing the Federal Trade Commission, then the agency must do whatever the statute requires.[1] And if the authorizing statute is silent, then the agency must follow APA section 553 notice and comment requirements unless one of the exceptions applies.

This chapter introduces a serious complication in that seemingly straightforward summary. This complication boils down to a single question. Given that it is possible for agencies to accomplish their objectives by following *either* the rulemaking *or* the adjudication route, should an agency be permitted to escape the formalities of a hearing by simply switching the name they give to what they do? Consider the following.

What if, instead of investigating the allegations against the Cinderella Finishing School through a trial-type hearing, the FTC simply listed all the charges against Cinderella and, after notice and written comment, issued a rule prohibiting any "finishing school" from doing any of these things? The rule would be general—it would apply to all finishing schools—and it would impose no legal liability (at that point, anyway) on Cinderella. But would that be fair to Cinderella? If Cinderella persisted in those practices, the cards would then be stacked against it, since in the hearing at that point they would appear to violate the new FTC rule. Cinderella would not have the oppor-

---

[1] Thus in the proceeding to regulate children's advertising on television under the "Magnuson-Moss Act" the plantiffs won a court order to disqualify the Chairman of the FTC. The court held the chairman, Michael Pertschuk, had prejudged the issue very much as his predecessor had done in *Cinderalla. Association of National Advertisers v. FTC*, 460 F. Supp. 996 (1978). An appellate court reversed, but Pertschuk excused himself anyway.

tunity afforded to it in the actual case to show the administrative law judge that its practices were not deceptive.

This chapter deals with the basic problem we have just illustrated. Unlike the past two chapters, which drew a large map of the law in this field, this chapter explores one dark jungle on the map.

Is Rulemaking a Desirable Administrative Strategy?

Professor Kenneth C. Davis, whom judges quote more often than any other administrative law scholar, has called simple notice and comment rulemaking "perhaps one of the greatest inventions of modern government."[2] These procedures permit agencies to gather and examine any information they wish. Their judgment need not depend on the information generated by contending parties on the record of a hearing. Any and all citizens and groups are free to submit evidence. Furthermore, the agency would seem to be free to seek out what it feels is useful information, either from experts on its own staff or from specialists elsewhere. Because no lengthy trial occurs, agencies may reach decisions quickly, that is, in a matter of months rather than years. And in one sense such decisions are fairer because they hold no one at fault for past practices. They work toward the future and allow those whom the rule governs to conform to it without paying the costs of elaborate legal proceedings.

Agency power to issue rules has, however, engendered fear in some that agencies will usurp legislative power. During the New Deal period, which laid the foundation for modern administration, politicians expressed concern that agencies with legislative rulemaking authority could become far too powerful. You will recall that the Walter-Logan bill sponsored by the American Bar Association, required much more formal public hearing, than the APA. And the simple analogy that agencies need no rulemaking limits because they act in a legislative manner breaks down because legislators submit directly to elections but bureaucrats do not. By the 1960s, however, the fears of administrative dictatorships were replaced by fears of administrative ineffectiveness. The fear that rulemaking administrators would become all-powerful was no doublt somewhat exaggerated from the beginning. After all, adjudication in agencies duplicates to a large extent the work of courts. Many agencies were created with implied rulemaking power *because* case-by-case judicial adjudication, as in antitrust law, failed to solve the social problem. The judicial move to acknowledge and encourage administration through rulemaking rather than adjudication gathered strength in the 1960s. Rulemaking received a major boost in 1973 in the following landmark case.

[2] *Administrative Law* (St. Paul: West Publishing Co., 1973), 243.

United States v. Florida East Coast Railway, Inc.

*553 Rulemaking case.

410 U.S. 224 (1973) 6–2

+ Burger, Brennan, White, Marshall, Blackmun, Rehnquist
− Douglas, Stewart
NP Powell

[In the 1960s the Interstate Commerce Commission became concerned about a shortage of railroad freight cars. In order to encourage railroad corporations to buy more cars for their own use (as opposed to hoping to lease available cars from other lines) the ICC by rule adopted "incentive per diem rates" that one line would have to pay for the use of another line's rolling stock. The ICC tried to set these rates high enough to make it more economical for lines to buy new cars and thus alleviate the shortage. However, the Interstate Commerce Act, Section 1 (14)(a), required the ICC to make such rules and regulations of freight car service "after hearing." In past cases the ICC had in fact followed the formal trial-type procedures. Thus the issue was whether the words "after hearing" required a formal hearing or only notice and comment under 553. The ICC had used 553 in this instance.]

Justice Rehnquist.

We here decide that the Commission's proceeding was governed only by § 553 . . . and that appellees received the "hearing" required by § 1 (14)(a) of the Interstate Commerce Act.

. . . Here, the Commission promulgated a tentative draft of an order, and accorded all interested parties 60 days in which to file statements of position, submissions of evidence, and other relevant observations. The parties had fair notice of exactly what the Commission proposed to do, and were given an opportunity to comment, to object, or to make some other form of written submission. The final order of the Commission indicates that it gave consideration to the statements of the two appellees here. Given the "open-ended" nature of the proceedings, and the Commission's announced willingness to consider proposals for modification after operating experience had been acquired, we think the hearing requirement of § 1 (14)(a) of the Act was met.

Appellee railroads cite a number of our previous decisions dealing in some manner with right to a hearing in an administrative proceeding. Although appellees have asserted no claim of constitutional deprivation in this proceeding, some of the cases they rely upon expressly speak in constitutional terms, while others are less than clear as to whether they depend upon the Due Process Clause of the Fifth and Fourteenth Amendments to the Constitution, or upon generalized principles of administrative law formulated prior to the adoption of the Administrative Procedure Act.

Morgan v. United States, 304 U.S. 1 (1938), is cited in support of appellees' contention that the Commission's proceedings were fatally deficient. That opinion describes the proceedings there involved as "quasi-judicial," id., at 14, and thus presumably distinct from a rulemaking proceeding such as that engaged in by the Commission here. But since the order of the Secretary of Agriculture there challenged did involve a form of ratemaking, the case bears enough resemblance to the facts of this case to warrant further examination of appellees' contention. The administrative procedure in *Morgan* was held to be defective primarily because the persons who were to be affected by the Secretary's order were found not to have been adequately apprised of what the Secretary proposed to do prior to the time that he actually did it. Illustrative of the Court's reasoning is the following passage from the opinion:

The right to a hearing embraces not only the right to present evidence but also a reasonable opportunity to know the claims of the opposing party and to meet them. The right to submit argument implies that opportunity; otherwise the right may be but a barren one. Those who are brought into contest with the Government in a quasi-judicial proceeding aimed at the control of their activities are entitled to be fairly advised of what the Government proposes and to be heard upon its proposals before it issues its final command . . .

The proceedings before the Secretary of Agriculture had been initiated by a notice of inquiry into the reasonableness of the rates in question, and the individuals being regulated suffered throughout the proceeding from its essential formlessness. The Court concluded that this formlessness denied the individuals subject to regulation the "full hearing" that the statute had provided.

Assuming, arguendo, that the statutory term "full hearing" does not differ significantly from the hearing requirement of § 1 (14)(a), we do not believe that the proceedings of the Interstate Commerce Commission before us suffer from the defect found to be fatal in *Morgan*. Though the initial notice of the proceeding by no means set out in detail what the Commission proposed to do, its tentative conclusions and order of December 1969, could scarcely have been more explicit or detailed. All interested parties were given 60 days following the issuance of these tentative findings and order in which to make appropriate objections. Appellees were "fairly advised" of exactly what the Commission proposed to do sufficiently in advance of the entry of the final order to given them adequate time to formulate and to present objections to the Commission's proposal. *Morgan*, therefore, does not aid appellees . . .

The basic distinction between rulemaking and adjudication is illustrated by this Court's treatment of two related cases under the Due Process Clause of the Fourteenth Amendment. In *Londoner v. Denver*, cited in oral argument by appellees, 210 U.S. 373 (1908), the Court held that due process had not been accorded a landowner who objected to the amount assessed against his land as its share of the benefit resulting from the paving of a street. Local procedure had accorded him the right to file a written complaint and objection, but not to be heard orally. This Court held that due process of law required that he "have the right to support his allegations by argument however brief, and, if need be, by proof, however informal." Id., at 386. But in the later case of *Bi-Metallic Investment Co. v. State Board of Equalization*, 239 U.S. 441 (1915), the Court held that no hearing at all was constitutionally required prior to a decision by state tax officers in Colorado to increase the valuation of all taxable property in Denver by a substantial percentage. The Court distinguished *Londoner* by stating that there a small number of persons "were exceptionally affected, in each case upon individual grounds." . . .

Later decisions have continued to observe the distinction adverted to in *Bi-Metallic Investment Co.*, supra. In *Ohio Bell Telephone Co. v. Public Utilities Comm'n*, 301 U.S. 292, 304–305 (1937), the Court noted the fact that the administrative proceeding there involved was designed to require the utility to refund previously collected rate charges. The Court held that in such a proceeding the agency could not, consistently with due process, act on the basis of undisclosed evidence that was never made a part of the record before the agency. The case is thus more akin to *Louisville & Nashville R. Co.*, [227 U.S. 88 (1913)] than it is to this case. *FCC v. WJR*, 337 U.S. 265 (1949), established that there was no across-the-board constitutional right to oral argument in every administrative proceeding regardless of its nature. While the line dividing them may not always be a bright one, these decisions represent a recognized distinction in administrative law between proceedings for the purpose of promulgating policy-type rules or standards, on the one hand, and proceedings designed to adjudicate disputed facts in particular cases on the other.

Here, the incentive payments proposed by the Commission in its tentative order, and later adopted in its final order, were applicable across the board to all of the common carriers by railroad subject to the Interstate Commerce Act. No effort was made to single out any particular railroad for special consideration based on its own peculiar circumstances. Indeed, one of the objections of appellee Florida East Coast was that it and other terminating carriers should have been treated differently from the generality of the railroads. But the fact that the order may in its effects have been thought more disadvantageous by some railroads than by others does not change its generalized nature. Though the Commission obviously relied on factual inferences as a basis for its order, the source of these factual inferences was apparent to anyone who read the order of December 1969. The factual inferences were used in the formulation of a basically legislative-type judgment, for prospective application only, rather than in adjudicating a particular set of disputed facts.

The Commission's procedure satisfied both the provisions of § 1 (14)(a) of the Interstate Commerce Act and of the Administrative Procedure Act, and were not inconsistent with prior decisions of this Court, We, therefore, reverse the judgment of the District Court, and remand the case so that it may consider those contentions of the parties that are not disposed of by this opinion.

It is so ordered.

Justice Douglas, with whom Justice Stewart concurs, dissenting.

The present decision makes a sharp break with traditional concepts of procedural due process. The Commission order under attack is tantamount to a rate order. Charges are fixed that nonowning railroads must pay owning railroads for boxcars of the latter that are on the tracks of the former . . . This is the imposition on carriers by administrative fiat of a new financial liability. I do not believe it is within our traditional concepts of due process to allow an administrative agency to saddle anyone with a new rate, charge, or fee without a full hearing that includes the right to present oral testimony, cross-examine witnesses, and present oral argument. That is required by the Administrative Procedure Act, 5 U.S.C. § 556

(d); § 556 (a) states that § 556 applies to hearings required by § 553. Section 553 (c) provides that § 556 applies "[w]hen rules are required by statute to be made on the record after opportunity for an agency hearing." A hearing under § 1 (14)(a) of the Interstate Commerce Act fixing rates, charges, or fees is certainly adjudicatory, not legislative in the customary sense.

The question is whether the Interstate Commerce Commission procedures used in this rate case "for the submission of . . . evidence in written form" avoided prejudice to the appellees so as to comport with the requirements of the Administrative Procedure Act. . . .

The more exacting hearing provisions of the Administrative Procedure Act, 5 U. S. C. §§ 556–557, are only applicable, of course, if the "rules are required by statute to be made on the record after opportunity for an agency hearing." *Id.*, § 553 (c).

. . . The rules in question here established "incentive" per diem charges to spur the prompt return of existing cars to make the acquisition of new cars financially attractive to the railroads. Unlike those we considered in *Allegheny-Ludlum*, these rules involved the creation of a new finacial liability. Although quasi-legislative, they are also adjudicatory in the sense that they determine the measure of the financial responsibility of one road for its use of the rolling stock of another road. The Commission's power to promulgate these rules pursuant to § 1 (14)(a) is conditioned on the preliminary *finding* that the supply of freight cars to which the rules apply is inadequate. Moreover, in fixing incentive compensation once this threshold finding has been made, the Commission "shall give consideration to the national level of ownership of such type of freight car and to other factors affecting the adequacy of the national freight car supply . . . "

. . . I . . . find a clear mandate that where, as here, ratemaking must be based on evidential facts, § 1 (14)(a) requires that full hearing which due process normally entails. . . .

Accordingly, I would hold that appellees were not afforded the hearing guaranteed by § 1 (14)(a) of the Interstate Commerce Act and 5 U. S. C. §§ 553, 556, and 557, and would affirm the decision of the District Court.

Legislative and Adjudicative Rulemaking

Today courts, scholars, politicians, and agencies themselves widely approve the idea of administration through rulemaking. The ambiguities and criticisms arise in the practical implementation of section 553. You can appreciate the problem better by reviewing all the formalities described in chapter 6 that Section 553 does *not* require. It does not, above all, require a decision "on the record." This means that, to suppose an extreme case, an agency could ignore all of the submitted comments. The agency members could, in theory, let one of the interests appear in a secret session in the agency conference room and decide only on the basis of this information. Or the Office of Management and Budget could call and threaten to cut the agency's recommended appropriation for the next fiscal year unless the agency reached a decision the White House desired.[3]

Recall that the opinion in *Morgan* condemned *ex parte*, off-the-record fact finding. The potential unfairness of *ex parte* communications lies at the heart of the rulemaking jungle. Despite the *Bi-Metallic* principle and despite the fact that section 553 imposes no such limit on rulemaking, some courts have imposed fairness requirements on rulemaking.

One of the first cases to do so was *Sangamon Valley Television Corp. v. United States*, decided in 1959.[4] Appreciation of this case requires some background knowledge of the work of the Federal Communication Commission. Whenever two or more companies compete for the right to operate a television channel in a certain location, the FCC would hold a hearing. The FCC did not, however, hold hearings in deciding, based in part on scientific data about interference among stations, which channels should operate in which cities. These it announced after informal rulemaking proceedings in its "Table of Television Channel Assignments." At the beginning of this story Sangamon was competing with another company, in an adjudicatory hearing, for the license to operate VHF Channel 2 in Springfield, Illinois. Another company, headed by Mr. Tenenbaum, owned a much less potentially profitable UHF channel in St. Louis. Because St. Louis had the larger potential audience, the FCC was persuaded to consider switching the UHF channel to Springfield and moving Channel 2 to St. Louis. Both before and after the notice of this proposed rule was published, Tenenbaum repeatedly visited the FCC commissioners in their offices to urge that the channels be switched. Since he would lose the UHF channel he felt he would have the inside track to getting the license for the more profitable Channel 2 once it was transferred to St. Louis. Tenenbaum did not stop there. He sent each commissioner Thanksgiving and Christmas

---

[3] The Johnson administration in the mid-1960s apparently put pressure on the Civil Aeronautics Board to give preferential treatment to all-cargo air carriers in order to sustain their capacity to support the Vietnam war effort. The CAB adopted controversial rulemaking proceedings to allow only all-cargo carriers to sell space on a "blocked" discount basis. The rule, upheld by the Court of Appeals, is described in *American Airlines v. CAB*, 359 F.2d 624 (1966). See Lief Carter, *The Blocked Space Controversy*, unpublished third year thesis, Harvard Law School, 1965.

[4] 269 F.2d 221.

turkeys. Both he and his attorney sent letters containing information about the proposed rule privately to the FCC.

Now consider the case from Sangamon's perspective. The rulemaking process blocked them from their opportunity to operate a profitable VHF station, Channel 2, and there was certainly reason to believe that a hidden, off-the-record process which they could not examine or influence could have affected the outcome. The FCC had, in effect, managed to employ a rulemaking proceeding to accomplish an adjudiciary result. Sangamon therefore sued to set aside the reassignment of Channel 2 to St. Louis. The Court agreed with Sangamon.

It held that "whatever the proceeding may be called it involved not only allocation of TV channels among communities but also resolution of conflicting private claims to a valuable privilege . . . [Therefore] basic fairness requires such a proceeding be carried out in the open."[5] The opinion thus helped create a distinction between purely legislative rulemaking and rulemaking with adjudicatory overtones.

Since *Sangamon* the law has sometimes extended its principle and sometimes limited it. In the most expansionary decision of all, *Home Box Office, Inc. v. FCC,* 567 F.2d 9 (1977), the Court of Appeals for the District of Columbia ruled that, regardless of the legislative character of rulemaking, all *ex parte* communication must cease once the notice of rulemaking is published.[6] *Home Box Office* got generally poor reviews by the legal critics. Nathaniel Nathanson, reporting to the Administrative Conference, said the decision "carries the concept of improper *ex parte* communications far beyond that previously entertained by the Congress, the courts and most of the federal administrative agencies."[7] *Home Box Office's* position was undercut in what is today the Supreme Court's most powerful statement on the problem of rulemaking, the *Vermont Yankee* case. The case does not directly involve *ex parte* communications, but rather the general degree to which courts can require agencies to supplement 553 with other due process requirements.

Beginning in the mid-1960s into the 1970s, a new judicial consciousness about administrative policymaking emerged called *hybrid rulemaking.* The philosophy of hybrid rulemaking is that courts should require agencies to develop an evidentiary basis for a decision that is less formal than a full-fledged trial-type hearing but more substantial than traditional notice and comment requirements. Judge Bazelon's decision for the D.C. Circuit Court of Appeals, in *Natural Resources Defense Council v. Nuclear Regulatory Commission* (1976) is a classic endorsement of hybrid rulemaking. His decision was overturned on appeal by the U.S. Supreme Court in *Vermont Yankee Nuclear Power Corp. v. Natural Resources Defense Council* (1978). Since that Supreme Court decision it appears that hybrid rulemaking has come under attack, resulting in a judicial prefer-

---

[5] *Id.* at 224. On remand from the appellate court Tenenbaum was vindicated. See L. Jaffe and N. Nathanson, *Administrative Law* (Boston: Little, Brown & Co., 1961), 684–85.

[6] John Robert Long, "Comment: Ex Parte Contacts in Informal Rule Making: The Bread and Butter of Administrative Procedure," *Emory Law Journal* 27 (1978): 293, 303–4.

[7] "Report to the Select Committee on Ex Parte Communications in Informal Rulemaking Proceedings," *Administrative Law Review* 30 (1978):377,379. See also generally, Paul Verkuil, "The Emerging Concept of Administrative Procedure," *Columbia Law Review* 78 (1978):258; Long, *"Comment,"* above, and Glenn T. Carberry, *"Ex Parte* Communications in Off-the-Record Administrative Proceedings: A Proposed Limitation on Judicial Innovation," *Duke Law Review* 1980:65.

ence for the less formal mode of rulemaking. These two opinions, however, represent divergent legal responses to the question of how formal agency rulemaking should be. These two opinions also reflect an underlying political debate about agency rulemaking. How much authority should administrative "experts" have over policymaking in a democratic society? How shall we hold agencies accountable for their decisions? To what extent do formal or informal procedures for agency rulemaking insure that participation by interested parties, such as public interest groups, is meaningful?

We address these important questions by examining both the legal and political dimensions of rulemaking. We compare the legal and political perspectives offered by Judge Bazelon with the Supreme Court's unanimous opinion written by Justice Rehnquist in the *Vermont Yankee* cases. We then analyze agency adjudication and rulemaking as policymaking paradigms. Here we include an article by Colin S. Diver, professor of law at Boston University. Diver discusses the historical and political uses of administrative policymaking through rulemaking and adjudication. He argues that the shift toward greater use of rulemaking resulted from reform efforts to democratize administrative procedure.

Natural Resources Defense Council v. Vermont Yankee Nuclear Power Corp.

547 F.2d 633, U.S.C.A., D. C. Cir. (1976) 3–0

[This case involves one of the most controversial areas of public policy today—the safety of nuclear power plants. The Atomic Energy Commission (now the Nuclear Regulatory Commission) is charged by law to grant operating licenses to nuclear plants only after safe operation is assured. The commission of course must insure the safe construction of the plants themselves, but the problem of what to do with the waste products of nuclear generation also imposes risks on the public. When the Vermont Yankee Nuclear Power Corp. sought an operating license in this case, no specific plan for the long-term disposal of nuclear wastes existed. By rulemaking, the AEC finessed the problem. Relying only on vague but optimistic promises that scientists would find a solution to the waste disposal problem soon (but lacking any of the scientific and technical details on how it would be solved) the AEC's "spent fuel cycle rule" announced that the nuclear waste safety problem would not itself prevent the AEC from issuing operating licenses to plants.

During the rulemaking process an environmental group, the National Resources Defense Council, sought to discover the full range of evidence the AEC possessed about the waste disposal safety problem. It also sought to cross-examine witnesses and otherwise challenge the evidence before the AEC. The AEC refused.]

Bazelon, Chief Judge.

It is undisputed that a reactor licensing is a "major Federal action significantly affecting the quality of the human environment" which requires a "detailed" environmental impact statement under § 102(2)(c) of NEPA, [National Environmental Policy Act], 42 U.S.C. § 4332(2)(C). That section requires an impact statement to consider, *inter alia,*

> (ii) any adverse environmental effects which cannot be avoided should the proposal be implemented, . . .

(v) any irreversible and irretrievable commitments of resources which would be involved in the proposed action should it be implemented.

The plain meaning of this language encompasses radioactive wastes generated by the operations of a nuclear power station, just as it does the stack gases produced by a coal-burning power plant.

Nor are the wastes generated by the subject reactor *de minimis.* We were informed at argument that the Vermont Yankee plant will produce approximately 160 pounds of plutonium wastes annually during its 40-year life span. Plutonium is generally accepted as among the most toxic substances known; inhalation of a single microscopic particle is thought to be sufficient to cause cancer. Moreover, with a half-life of 25,000 years, plutonium must be isolated from the environment for 250,000 years before it becomes harmless. Operation of the facility in question will also produce substantial quantities of other "high-level" radioactive wastes in the form of strontium-90 and cesium-137 which, with their shorter, 30-year half-lives, must be isolated from the environment for "only" 600 to 1000 years. . . .

The Board agreed that "there will be an incremental environmental effect ultimately resulting from the operation of this reactor as the result of the operation of whatever reprocessing and disposal grounds may from time to time be used during the life of the plant." In its opinion, however, these effects were too "contingent and presently indefinable" to be evaluated at the time of licensing in view of the 40-year expected life of the reactor. The Board wrote:

. . . The possibility that improved technology may be developed during the 40-year life span of a reactor does not render consideration of environmental issues too speculative, as the Board appears to suggest. NEPA's requirement for forecasting environmental consequences far into the future implies the need for predictions based on existing technology and those developments which can be extrapolated from it. . . .

The second argument advanced by the Board is that licensing proceedings for reprocessing plants are a more "appropriate proceeding" in which to weigh the environmental effects of reprocessing and waste

disposal. . . . Licensing of a reprocessing plant or waste disposal facility is itself a "major Federal action" affecting the environment which requires a NEPA statement. The real question posed by the Board's opinion is whether the environmental effects of the wastes produced by a nuclear reactor may be ignored in deciding whether to build it because they will later be considered when a plant is proposed to deal with them. To answer this question any way but in the negative would be to misconstrue the fundamental purpose of NEPA. Once a series of reactors is operating, it is too late to consider whether the wastes they generate should have been produced, no matter how costly and impractical reprocessing and waste disposal turn out to be; all that remain are engineering details to make the best of the situation which has been created. NEPA's purpose was to break the cycle of such incremental decision-making. . . .

The order granting a full-term license for the Vermont Yankee plant is hereby remanded to await the outcome of further proceedings in the rulemaking, discussed hereafter. . . .

An "informal rulemaking hearing" of the "legislative-type" was scheduled [by the NRC] to receive comments in the form of "oral or written statements." By subsequent notice, the Commission designated a three-member hearing board to preside, and reiterated, "The procedural format for the hearing will follow the legislative pattern, and no discovery or cross-examination will be utilized." 38 Fed.Reg. 49 (Jan. 3, 1973).

The primary argument advanced by the public interest intervenors is that the decision to preclude "discovery or cross-examination" denied them a meaningful opportunity to participate in the proceedings as guaranteed by due process. They do not question the Commission's authority to proceed by informal rulemaking, as opposed to adjudication. They rely instead on the line of cases indicating that in particular circumstances procedures in excess of the bare minima prescribed by the Administrative Procedure Act, 5 U.S.C. § 553, may be required.

The Government concedes that "basic considerations of fairness may under exceptional circumstances" require additional procedures in "legislative-type proceedings," but contends that the procedures here were more than adequate. Thus, we are called upon to decide whether the procedures provided by the agency were sufficient to ventilate the issues.

A few general observations are in order concerning the role of a court in this area. Absent extraordinary circumstances, it is not proper for a reviewing court to prescribe the procedural format which an agency must use to explore a given set of issues. Unless there are statutory directives to the contrary, an agency has discretion to select procedures which it deems best to compile a record illuminating the issues. Courts are no more expert at fashioning administrative procedures than they are in the substantive areas of responsibility which are left to agency discretion. What a reviewing court can do, however, is scrutinize the record as a whole to insure that genuine opportunities to participate in a meaningful way were provided, and that the agency has taken a good, hard look at the major questions before it.

We have sometimes suggested that elucidation of certain types of issues, by their very nature, might require particular procedures, including cross-examination. In fact, we have been more concerned with making sure that the record developed by agency procedures discloses a thorough ventilation of the issues than with what devices the agency used to create the dialogue. . . .

. . . A reviewing court must assure itself not only that a diversity of informed opinion was heard, but that it was genuinely considered . . . Since a reviewing court is incapable of making a penetrating analysis of highly scientific or technical subject matter on its own, it must depend on the agency's expertise, as reflected in the statement of basis and purpose, to organize the record, to distill the major issues which were ventilated and to articulate its reasoning with regard to each of them.

An agency need not respond to frivolous or repetitive comment it receives. However, where apparently significant information has been brought to its attention, or substantial issues of policy or gaps in its reasoning raised, the statement of basis and purpose must indicate why the agency decided the criticisms were invalid. Boilerplate generalities brushing aside detailed criticism on the basis of agency "judgment" or "expertise" avail nothing; what is required is a reasoned response, in which the agency points to particulars in the record which, when coupled with its reservoir of expertise, support its resolution of the controversy. An agency may abuse its discretion by proceeding to a decision which the record before it will not sustain, in the sense that it raises fundamental questions for which the agency has adduced no reasoned answers.

With these observations in mind, we turn to our examination of this record. . . .

The only discussion of high-level waste disposal techniques was supplied by a 20-page statement by Dr. Frank K. Pittman, Director of the AEC's Division of Waste Management and Transportation. This statement, delivered during the oral hearings, was then incorporated, often verbatim, into the revised version of the Environmental Survey published after the comment period. . . .

Dr. Pittman proceeded to describe for the first time in public the "design concepts" for a federal surface repository for retrievable storage of high-level waste. This is essentially a warehouse in which sealed canisters containing cylinders of solidified nuclear wastes can be stored in water-filled basins recessed into the ground on a temporary basis (up to 100 years), until such time as a permanent waste disposal scheme is devised, when they can be removed. While the "intended life" of the facility is only 100 years, some high-level wastes must be isolated for up to 250,000 years. . . . Therefore, the Environmental Survey states, without further explanation, that in the future a "permanent" Federal repository for "geologic storage of high-level wastes" will be established and that the "Federal government will have the obligation to maintain control over the site *in perpetuity*." . . .

Until recently the AEC planned to dispose of wastes by burying them deep inside abandoned salt mines. These plans were postponed indefinitely after a series of technical difficulties, including the discovery the salt mines might be susceptible to underground flooding. The Revised Environmental Survey devotes two sentences to recounting how prior waste disposal plans fared:

It was planned to construct a Federal repository in a salt mine for long-term geological storage of solid high-level wastes by the mid 1970's. However, subsequent events have deferred the site selection and construction of such a facility. . . .

Dr. Pittman's description of the new plan—now also postponed indefinitely—to build a surface storage facility can only fairly be described as vague, but glowing. . . . In less than two pages, he set out a very general description of what the facility is supposed to do, accompanied by several schematic drawings. . . .

. . . [W]ithout benefit of details, Dr. Pittman offers conclusory reassurances that the proposed facility will be designed so that the possibility of a "meltdown" can be dismissed as "incredible." . . .

There is no discussion of how "adequate human surveillance and maintenance" can be assured for the periods involved, nor what the long-term costs of such a commitment are, nor of the dangers if surveillance is not maintained. Nor is any explanation offered for Dr. Pittman's optimism regarding bedded salt as a disposal method, since the problems which have surfaced and delayed that program are not mentioned. Nor does the statement anywhere describe what "other acceptable geologic disposal concepts" are under consideration.

Based on Dr. Pittman's statement, the Revised Environmental Survey concludes that the resources consumed in waste storage will be minimal, that "under normal conditions" no radioactivity will be released, and that the possibility of a serious accident is "incredible." In short, based on the information in Dr. Pittman's statement, the Commission concluded that the future environmental effects from the disposal of high-level nuclear wastes are negligible . . .

We do not dispute these conclusions. We may not uphold them, however, lacking a thorough explanation and a meaningful opportunity to challenge the judgments underlying them. Our duty is to insure that the reasoning on which such judgments depend, and the data supporting them, are spread out in detail on the public record. Society must depend largely on oversight by the technically-trained members of the agency and the scientific community at large to monitor technical decisions. The problem with the conclusory quality of Dr. Pittman's statement—and the complete absence of any probing of its underlying basis—is that it frustrates oversight by anyone: Commission, intervenors, court, legislature or public . . .

Although the vagueness of the presentation regarding waste disposal made detailed criticism of its specifics impossible, . . . the public interest intervenors did offer a number of more general comments concerning the Commission's approach. They criticized the Commission for a general "failure to distinguish between design objectives on the one hand and performance on the other," . . . noting that no consideration had been given actual experience with storage of wastes generated by weapons production. . . . They also questioned confident assertions by the AEC that long-term waste management is feasible, laying particular stress on the immense time periods involved which mock human institutions: . . .

They reiterated repeatedly that the problems involved are not merely technical, but involve basic philosophical issues concerning man's ability to make commitments which will require stable social structures for unprecedented periods.

The intervenors pointed out that storing wastes aboveground places a premium on stable human institutions for monitoring and surveillance, . . . that until plans for long-term disposal in the salt beds at Lyons, Kansas fell through, . . . , the agency had itself rejected the idea of surface storage because of the surveillance problems. . . .

. . . The Commission disposed of these issues summarily in its statement of basis and purpose accompanying the promulgation of the rule without attempting to articulate responses to any of the points which had been raised regarding waste disposal: . . .

. . . Not only were the generalities relied on in this case not subject to rigorous probing—in any form—but when apparently substantial criticisms were brought to the Commission's attention, it simply ignored them or brushed them aside without answer. Without a thorough exploration of the problems involved in waste disposal, including past mistakes, and a forthright assessment of the uncertainties and differences in expert opinion, this type of agency action cannot pass muster as reasoned decisionmaking.

Many procedural devices for creating a genuine dialogue on these issues were available to the agency—including informal conferences between intervenors and staff, document discovery, interrogatories, technical advisory committees comprised of outside experts with differing perspectives, limited cross-examination, funding independent research by intervenors, detailed annotation of technical reports, surveys of existing literature, memoranda explaining methodology. We do not presume to intrude on the agency's province by dictating to it which, if any, of these devices it must adopt to flesh out the record. It may be that no combination of the procedures mentioned above will prove adequate, and the agency will be required to develop new procedures to accomplish the innovative task of implementing NEPA through rulemaking. On the other hand, the procedures the agency adopted in this case, if administered in a more sensitive, deliberate manner, might suffice. Whatever techniques the Commission adopts, before it promulgates a rule limiting further consideration of waste disposal and reprocessing issues, it must in one way or another generate a record in which the factual issues are fully developed.

. . . NEPA does not guarantee a particular outcome on the merits; rather, the statute mandates only a "careful and informed decisionmaking process" to enlighten the decisionmaker and the public. In the rulemaking context, that requires the Commission to identify and address information contrary to its own position, to articulate its reasoning and to specify the evidence on which it relies. The Commission may well reach the same conclusion on remand. But if it does so on such a record, the Congress, the courts, and the public will all know where we stand.

It has become a commonplace among proponents of nuclear power to lament public ignorance. The public—the "guinea pigs" who will bear the consequences of either resolution of the nuclear controversy—is apprehensive. But public concern will not be quieted by proceedings like the present . . .

Separate Statement of Chief Judge Bazelon:

I add a word of my own on some of the broader implications of Judge Tamm's concurrence.

I agree that courts should be reluctant to impose particular procedures on an agency. For example, requiring cross-examination in a rulemaking proceeding is radical therapy, which may cause the patient to suffer a slow, painful death . . . But I reject the implication that any techniques beyond rudimentary notice and comment are needless "over-formalization" of informal rulemaking . . . Unhappily, no such bright line can be drawn between rulemaking and adjudicatory proceedings.

The purpose of rulemaking was to allow public input on policy, whereas adjudication was designed to resolve disputed facts. . . . However, in response to the "paralysis" of the administrative process in the last decade, rulemaking has been expanded into fact-intensive areas previously thought to require adjudicatory procedures. Administrative proceedings are now common which do not fit neatly into either the rulemaking or adjudicatory category. These new proceedings are "hybrids" in the sense that involve issues of general applicability which can be treated efficiently only in generic proceedings, but nonetheless involve factual components of such relative importance that a greater assurance of accuracy is required than that which accompanies notice and comment procedures."*

The need for reliable fact-finding does not necessarily imply transplanting trial-type procedures. Factual issues in hybrid proceedings tend to be complex scientific or technical ones involving mathematical or experimental data, or other "legislative facts" peculiarly inappropriate for trial-type procedures. Agencies should innovate procedural formats responsive to the new problems created by hybrid rulemaking . . .

Of course, important differences remain *from the standpoint of a reviewing court*. I am convinced that in highly technical areas, where judges are institutionally incompetent to weigh evidence for themselves, a focus on agency procedures will prove less intrusive, and more likely to improve the quality of

---

*The development of scientific or technical standards is a prime example. These decisions may involve both assessing scientific evidence, and also a "legislative" or policy component as to what level of risk is "safe," and how uncertainties are to be valued. See Handler, *A Rebuttal: The Need for a Sufficient Scientific Base for Governmental Regulation*, 43 Geo. Wash. L. Rev. 808, 809 (1975).

decisionmaking, than judges "steeping" themselves "in technical matters to determine whether the agency has exercised a reasoned discretion." *See Ethyl Corp. v. EPA*, 176 U.S.App.D.C. 373, 541 F.2d 1, No. 73–2205 (1976) (en banc) (Bazelon, C. J., concurring), cert. denied, 526 U.S. 941, (1976).

Tamm, Circuit Judge, separate statement concurring in result:

. . . [T]he inadequacy of the record demands that we remand this case to the Commission in order to ensure that it has taken a hard look at the waste storage issue. I cannot, however, without qualification, endorse the approach the majority has taken to reach this result or its suggested disposition on remand.

The majority appears to require the Commission to institute further procedures of a more adversarial nature than those customarily required for informal rulemaking by the Administrative Procedure Act, 5 U.S.C. § 553 (1970). The Commission chose to proceed by "hybrid" rulemaking below, allowing petitioners to present oral arguments before the Commission and subjecting participants to questions, but not permitting participants to cross-examine. . . . By so proceeding the Commission exceeded the minimum procedural requirements of section 553. In my view, the deficiency is not with the *type* of proceeding below, but with the completeness of the record generated. More procedure will not, in this case, guarantee a better record, and a better record can be generated without reopening the oral proceeding at this time . . .

I am also troubled by two other aspects of the majority opinion. First, I am distressed because I believe the majority opinion fails to inform the Commission in precise terms what it must do in order to comply with the court's ad hoc standard of review. The majority sends the waste storage issue back to the Commission for a "thorough ventilation." This

language, of course, means very little in procedural terms. In order to aid the Commission in filling in the gaps in the record, the majority enumerates a number of procedural alternatives in varying degrees of formality, some less intrusive into agency prerogatives than others . . . The Commission is thus left to decide which to adopt, further confused by the majority's statement . . . I believe it almost inevitable that, after fully considering the problems and alternative methods of waste disposal and storage, the Commission will reach the same conclusion and therefore see little to be gained other than delay from imposing increased adversarial procedures in excess of those customarily required.

This brings me to my second, related concern with the majority's approach. I believe the majority's insistence upon increased adversariness and procedural rigidity, uneasily combined with its non-direction toward any specific procedures, continues a distressing trend toward over-formalization of the administrative decisionmaking process which ultimately will impair its utility. As Judge Wright has recently noted, the administrative response to overuse of judicial imposition of such ad hoc procedural refinements is easily foreseeable. Fearing reversal, administrators will tend to overformalize, clothing their actions "in the full wardrobe of adjudicatory procedures," until the advantages of informal rulemaking as an administrative tool are lost in a heap of judicially imposed procedure. Wright, *The Courts and the Rulemaking Process: The Limits of Judicial Review,* 59 Cornell L. Rev. 375, 387–88 (1974). The majority's reliance upon the so-called "hybrid rulemaking" cases for its conclusion that the procedures prescribed by section 553 are inadequate for resolution of the complex issues involved in this case and its insistence that the Commission adopt more formal adversary procedures are, I believe, misplaced. . . .

Vermont Yankee Nuclear Power Corp. v. Natural Resources Defense Council, Inc.

435 U.S. 519 (1978) 7–0
+ Burger, Brennan, Stewart, White, Marshall, Rehnquist, Stevens
NP Blackmun, Powell

[The following opinion contains the necessary background information on this case.]

Justice Rehnquist delivered the opinion of the Court.

In 1946, Congress enacted the Administrative Procedure Act, which as we have noted elsewhere was not only "a new basic and comprehensive regulation of procedures in many agencies," *Wong Yang Sung v. McGrath,* 339 U.S. 33 (1950), but was also a legislative enactment which settled "long-continued and hard-fought contentions, and enacts a formula upon which opposing social and political forces have come to rest." Section 553 of the Act, dealing with rulemaking, requires that " . . . notice of proposed rulemaking shall be published in the Federal Register . . . ," describes the contents of that notice, and goes on to require in subsection (c) that after the notice the agency "shall give interested persons an opportunity to participate in the rulemaking through submission of written data, views, or arguments with or without opportunity for oral presentation. After consideration of the relevant matter presented, the agency shall incorporate in the rules adopted a concise general statement of their basis and purpose." 5 U.S.C.A. § 553. Interpreting this provision of the Act in *United States v. Allegheny-Ludlum Steel, Corp.* 406 U.S. 742 (1972), and *United States v. Florida East Coast Railroad Co.,* 410 U.S. 224 (1973), we held that generally speaking this section of the Act established the maximum procedural requirements which Congress was willing to have the courts impose upon agencies in conducting rulemaking procedures. Agencies are free to grant additional procedural rights in the exercise of their discretion, but reviewing courts are generally not free to impose them if the agencies have not chosen to grant them. This is not to say necessarily that there are no circumstances which would ever justify a court in overturning agency action because of a failure to employ procedures beyond those

required by the statute. But such circumstances, if they exist, are extremely rare. . . .

It is in the light of this background of statutory and decisional law that we granted certiorari to review two judgments of the Court of Appeals for the District of Columbia Circuit because of our concern that they had seriously misread or misapplied this statutory and decisional law cautioning reviewing courts against engrafting their own notions of proper procedures upon agencies entrusted with substantive functions of Congress. . . .

[B]efore determining whether the Court of Appeals reached a permissible result, we must determine exactly what result it did reach, and in this case that is no mean feat. Vermont Yankee argues that the court invalidated the rule because of the inadequacy of the procedures employed in the proceedings. Respondent NRDC, on the other hand, labeling petitioner's view of the decision a "straw man," argues to this Court that the court merely held that the record was inadequate to enable the reviewing court to determine whether the agency had fulfilled its statutory obligation. . . .

After a thorough examination of the opinion itself, we conclude that while the matter is not entirely free from doubt, the majority of the Court of Appeals struck down the rule because of the perceived inadequacies of the procedures employed in the rulemaking proceedings. The court first determined the intervenors' primary argument to be "that the decision to preclude 'discovery or cross-examination' denied them a meaningful opportunity to participate in the proceedings as guaranteed by due process" . . . The court also refrained from actually ordering the agency to follow any specific procedures, but there is little doubt in our minds that the ineluctable mandate of the court's decision is that the procedures afforded during the hearings were inadequate. This conclusion is particularly buttressed by the fact that after the court examined the record, . . . and declared it insufficient, the court proceeded to discuss at some length the necessity for further procedural devices or a more "sensitive" application of those devices employed during the proceedings . . .

In prior opinions we have intimated that even in a rulemaking proceeding when an agency is making a " 'quasi-judicial' " determination by which a very small number of persons are " 'exceptionally affected, in each case upon individual grounds,' " in some circumstances additional procedures may be required in order to afford the aggrieved individuals due process. *United States v. Florida East Coast R. Co.*, 410 U.S. 224, 242–245, quoting from *Bi-Metallic Investment Co. v. State Board of Equalization*, 239 U.S. 441, 446 (1915). It might also be true, although we do not think the issue is presented in this case and accordingly do not decide it, that a totally unjustified departure from well settled agency procedures of long standing might require judicial correction.

But this much is absolutely clear. Absent constitutional constraints or extremely compelling circumstances "the administrative agencies should be free to fashion their own rules of procedure and to pursue method of inquiry capable of permitting them to discharge their multitudinous duties."

Respondent NRDC argues that § 553 of the Administrative Procedure Act merely establishes lower procedural bounds and that a court may routinely require more than the minimum when an agency's proposed rule addresses complex or technical factual issues or "issues of great public import." We have, however, previously shown that our decisions reject this view.

We also think the legislative history, even the part which it cites, does not bear out its contention . . . Congress intended that the discretion of the agencies and not that of the courts be exercised in determining when extra procedural devices should be employed.

There are compelling reasons for construing § 553 in this manner. In the first place, if courts continually review agency proceedings to determine whether the agency employed procedures which were, in the court's opinion, perfectly tailored to reach what the court perceives to be the "best" or "correct" result, judicial review would be totally unpredictable. And the agencies, operating under this vague injunction to employ the "best" procedures and facing the threat of reversal if they did not, would undoubtedly adopt full adjudicatory procedures in every instance. Not only would this totally disrupt the statutory scheme, through which Congress enacted "a formula upon which opposing social and political forces have come to rest," *Wong Yang Sung v. McGrath, supra*, at 40, but all the inherent advantages of informal rulemaking would be totally lost.

Secondly, it is obvious that the court in this case reviewed the agency's choice of procedures on the basis of the record actually produced at the hearing, and not on the basis of the information available to the agency when it made the decision to structure the proceedings in a certain way. This sort of Monday morning quarterbacking not only encourages but almost compels the agency to conduct all rulemaking proceedings with the full panoply of procedural devices normally associated only with adjudicatory hearings.

Finally, and perhaps most importantly, this sort of review fundamentally misconceives the nature of the standard for judicial review of an agency rule. The court below uncritically assumed that additional procedures will automatically result in a more adequate record because it will give interested parties more of an opportunity to participate and contribute to the proceedings. But informal rulemaking need not be based solely on the transcript of a hearing held before an agency. Indeed, the agency need not even hold a formal hearing. See 5 U.S.C.A., § 553(c). Thus, the adequacy of the "record" in this type of proceeding is not correlated directly to the type of procedural devices employed, but rather turns on whether the agency has followed the statutory mandate of the Administrative Procedure Act or other relevant statutes. If the agency is compelled to support the rule which it ultimately adopts with the type of record produced only after a full adjudicatory hearing, it simply will have no choice but to conduct a full adjudicatory hearing prior to promulgating every rule. In sum, this sort of unwarranted judicial examination of perceived procedural shortcomings of a rulemaking proceeding can do nothing but seriously interfere with that process prescribed by Congress . . .

Reversed and remanded.

Justice Rehnquist's opinion does not officially shut the door on the power of the courts to supplement 553 with due process requirements, like the opportunity to cross-examine or the prohibition against ex parte communications, in adjudicatory-like rulemaking. His language does preserve the distinction between legislative and adjudicative rulemaking. Nevertheless the opinion dramatically narrows the door's opening. This is because Rehnquist implies that adjudicatory rulemaking requiring constitutional as well as 553 standards is rare in administrative action. In fact, as the *Sangamon* decision defined it, adjudicative rulemaking is very common. Most administrative rules, at least those that 553 does not itself exempt, do depend on factual considerations on which reasonable people disagree and which an adversary process might illuminate. More important, most rules resolve "conflicting private claims to a valuable privilege." What if the AEC had announced a rule refusing to license further nuclear power plants until the spent fuel problem had been solved? What if it had followed the *same* procedure on the *same* issue but decided differently? We can imagine that Vermont Yankee's lawyers would try to invoke the *Sangamon* doctrine precisely because the rule would deny them their valuable privilege of operating their power plant.

So far you have seen that agencies do not make a simple choice between adjudication or rulemaking when they make policy. Both rulemaking and adjudication vary in formality. Judge Bazelon argues that the NRC should be required to carry out a more formal rulemaking process (i.e., hybrid rulemaking) than the NRC and the Supreme Court support. Hence the decision about which administrative procedure to use for making policy cannot be resolved abstractly. Colin S. Diver, in his article reprinted below, explores the political implications of different policymaking approaches. He argues in favor of rulemaking over adjudication on the ground that it has the potential to expand participation in agency decisionmaking. However, Diver questions whether the Supreme Court's decision in the *Vermont Yankee* case , the *Benzene*[9] case, and the *Cotton Dust*[10] case have undercut the democratic character of policymaking through rulemaking.

[9] *Industrial Union Department, AFL-CIO v. American Petroleum Institute* U.S. 607 (1980); see chapter 3, pp. 122–132.

[10] *American Textile Manufacturers Institute, Inc. v. Donovan* 101 C (1981); see chapter 3, pp. 132–136.

Policymaking Paradigms in Administrative Law

Colin S. Diver
Harvard Law Review 95 (1981):393.

Administrative law is, in essence, a search for a theory of how public policy should be made. Two powerful traditions mark the boundaries of that search. On one side, we leave the choice among competing values to a largely unstructured process of pulling and hauling by individuals directly accountable to the citizenry. On the other side, we demand a highly structured process of party-controlled proof and argument before a neutral arbiter to resolve disputes over the application of rules to specific facts. Between these extremes is that vast landscape we call policymaking—the reconciliation and elaboration of lofty values into operational guidelines for the daily conduct of society's business.

. . . [D]espite the difficulty of articulating an affirmative model, our implicit vision of policymaking—embedded in the myriad pronouncements of reviewing courts and authorizing legislatures—has shifted over the past twenty years. My thesis is that this transformation can best be understood as a movement from an "incrementalist" model of policymaking to one of "comprehensive rationality." As most prominently developed by Charles Lindblom,* comprehensive rationality and incrementalism represent two competing models of the policymaking process. Each has its own internal logic: comprehensive rationality is structural, static, prophylactic; incrementalism is organic, dynamic, remedial.

The genius of these models for our purposes is that each prescribes a way of thinking and acting sufficiently abstract to encompass the extraordinarily diverse forms of administrative lawmaking. The central questions these models address, moreover, are precisely those that administrative law must answer. Which problems should we try to solve? How do

we define them? What evidence should be required to support a decision? Who should take part in the decision? How should it be implemented? How can it be challenged? These questions supply grist enough for many mills, from practical politics to academic discourse. But the collective efforts of legislatures and courts to answer them furnish a revealing glimpse at society's view of how policy should be made.

This Article . . . argues that these decisions clarify the relationship between the public participation required for comprehensively rational agency decisionmaking and the substantive choices that agencies must make . . .

I. Two Models of the Policymaking Process

A. COMPREHENSIVE RATIONALITY. Comprehensive rationality entails four steps. First, the decisionmaker must specify the goal he seeks to attain. Second, he must identify all possible methods of reaching his objective. Third, he must evaluate how effective each method will be in achieving the goal. Finally, he must select the alternative that will make the greatest progress toward the desired outcome.

Only a superhuman decisionmaker could faithfully adhere to the ideal of comprehensive rationality. He would have to be able to identify goals unambiguously, which would sometimes require reconciliation of numerous competing objectives. He would need a Jovian imagination to conceive of every possible means to attain his goals. Finally, he would have to anticipate the precise consequences of adopting each alternative and to invent a metric that permits comparison among them.

The techniques of "policy analysis"† have helped to reduce the gap between rationalist ideals and administrative practice. Probability theory, for example, enables analysts to cope with the omnipresent reality of uncertainty . . .

---

*See D. Braybrooke & C. Lindblom, *A Strategy of Decision* (1963); C. Lindblom, *The Intelligence of Democracy* (1965); Lindblom, "The Science of 'Muddling Through,'" 19 *Pub. Ad. Rev.* 79 (1959).

†Useful overviews of the "policy analysis" field include. A. Meltsner, *Policy Analysts in the Bureaucracy* (1976); *Public Expenditures and Policy Analysis* (R. Haveman & J. Margolis eds. 1970); E. Quade, *Analysis for Public Decisions* (1975); E. Stokey & R. Zeckhauser, *A Primer for Policy Analysis* (1978); A. Wildavsky, *Speaking Truth to Power: The Art and Craft of Policy Analysis* (1979).

In the administrative domain . . . the solution to this dilemma has been to fall back on a principle derived from democratic theory: the policymaker must promote only those goals specified by the politically responsible legislature. Although, as students of statutory interpretation know all too well, this suggestion provides only the roughest of road maps, it at least demarks the quadrant in which to wander.

B. INCREMENTALISM. An alternative model of how policy should be made is "incrementalism." This model has three characteristic features. First, policymaking is piecemeal and tightly restricted in scope. Policymakers consider only a handful of alternatives, which differ only slightly from each other and from the status quo. For each alternative, moreover, analysts consider only a limited range of future consequences. They routinely exclude remote or uncertain consequences, even though those consequences might prove momentous. Second, the process is dynamic and remedial. Policymaking becomes a series of small adjustments and avowedly temporary "fixes." Errors are corrected and problems are solved; lofty visions of some preferred social state play no part. Finally, incrementalism is decentralized. Policy is made by many actors at many levels of government and indeed in the society at large. In such a system, policy is a sequence of reactions as much to changes in the positions of other participants as to changes in the outside world.

As a theory of how public policy is *in fact* made, incrementalism draws from two disciplines: psychological decision theory and organization theory. Psychologists have long argued that people use a fairly simple cybernetic feedback-response system, rather than classically rational inquiry, to solve many complex problems. Organization theory, in turn, highlights the importance of both conflicts among individuals and bureaucratic routines on decisionmaking by corporate bodies. For our purposes, however, incrementalism is useful not merely as a description of reality, but as a legitimate normative competitor to the synoptic paradigm. To be sure, its prescriptive quality rests in part on its asserted realism, but it derives most of its moral force from its perceived ability to accommodate value conflicts more effectively than

comprehensive rationality. Rather than disposing of conflict by authoritative fiat, it diffuses conflict by attending in sequence to differing values. Even if this strategy merely masks conflict under the pretense of responsiveness, it arguably enhances the acceptability of the outcomes it produces . . .

II. *The Golden Age of Incrementalism*

The three decades from the New Deal to the mid-1960's were the halcyon days of incrementalist thought in administrative law. Agencies made policy in fits and starts. "Policy" was a shifting set of working hypotheses, alternately announced, modified, withdrawn, and resurrected. Generic principles emerged from the gloom, only to slip again into the shadows. Regulators were reactive, tentative, evasive, indefinite.*

This description is a caricature but, like all caricatures, grounded in reality. What most distinguishes this period is the extent to which legislatures and courts tolerated—and indeed supported—incremental decisionmaking. Courts rarely objected to agencies' penchant for announcing policy through the flexible medium of adjudicative orders rather than through generic rulemaking. Although courts occasionally applauded the idea of rulemaking, they regularly sustained the announcement of policy through adjudication.† Indeed, the very authority to make binding rules was long in doubt for several agencies. Not until 1968 could the Federal Power Commission be sure of its power to use rulemaking to set rates for a whole class of natural gas producers,‡ and

---

*See, e.g., H. Friendly, *The Federal Administrative Agencies: The Need for Better Definition of Standards* (1962); Jaffe, "The Illusion of the Ideal Administration," 86 Harv. L. Rev. 1183 (1973); Jaffe, "Book Review," 65 *Yale L.J.* 1068 (1956).

†See, e.g., SEC v. Chenery Corp. (Chenery II), 332 U.S. 194 (1947); NLRB v. Pease Oil Co., 279 F.2d 135 (2d Cir. 1960); Leedom v. International Bhd. of Elec. Workers, Local Union No. 108, 278 F.2d 237, 243 (D.C. Cir. 1960). This fact did not stop a few courts from overturning adjudicative policy changes because of unfair retroactive impacts. E.g., NLRB v. Guy F. Atkinson Co., 195 F.2d 141 (9th Cir. 1952).

‡Permian Basin Area Rate Cases, 390 U.S. 747 (1968). The FPC's power to use an acknowledged rulemaking authority to impose requirements upon statutory "hearing" rights had been affirmed only four years earlier in FPC v. Texaco Inc., 377 U.C. 33 (1964).

not until 1973 did the Federal Trade Commission have clear authority to make binding rules about trade practices.* In other contexts, the courts showed their discomfort with the idea of strictly applied rules by insisting that agencies make explicit provision for exemptions. . . .

. . . By sticking closely to the facts in particular cases, agencies could shelter themselves from judicial disapproval. Moreover, the courts encouraged rapid change in policy by applying to agency actions a relaxed conception of stare decisis, estoppel, and res judicata. . . .

. . . In principle, adjudicators can extend policy as much or as little as they wish in a single decision. In practice, however, administrators, like judges, ordinarily attempt to extend policy no further than needed to dispose of the issues at hand. For one thing, the typical adjudication is not well suited to serve as a springboard for expansive policymaking. For another, going beyond the case at hand requires the agency to expend resources investigating additional factual and policy issues. A private litigant is rarely willing to assist in that effort, for the benefits will accrue primarily to others. Indeed, a litigant seeking prompt results has a keen interest in minimizing the scope of investigation. The agency will itself often share this desire, leading it to suppress any inclination to extend its policymaking. Heavy administrative reliance on adjudication, then, reflects a preference for making policy by margin-dependent choice. Limiting the issues to those presented by the immediate facts helps to ensure that changes in policy will occur in modest shifts rather than bold departures.

Reviewing courts might have weighed in against this conservative tendency by demanding more comprehensive analysis of policy options. They could have

required that individual decisions fit into a larger strategy explicitly tailored to maximize the agency's objectives. In fact, however, courts generally held agency actions to only a weak standard of rationality. Agencies were under no duty to consider all possible alternatives. They were expected only to demonstrate that their policies were "rational" in an almost trivial sense—more likely than not to promote a permissible goal—rather than "rational" in the policy analyst's sense of "producing the greatest net benefit." Perhaps one should not be surprised that courts so recently burned by second-guessing legislative policy judgments should be shy of closely scrutinizing administrative ones. . . .

Elaboration of policy through decisions in individual cases is inherently a dynamic process. Policy emerges as the gradual accretion of adjudicative deposits. Moreover, the meaning of old decisions is constantly subject to reinterpretation. Values thought salient to a decision become dormant when the decision is next cited; values once ignored suddenly emerge. By encouraging reliance on the adjudicative mode, Congress and the courts implicitly endorsed sequential policy development.

The common law policymaking so typical of the earlier period is also remedial in that it focuses more on the removal of irritants than on the attainment of ideals. Under such a regime, only demands for relief from claimed existing inadequacies provide a reason to make new policy. . . .

Occasionally, of course, agencies in the pre-1965 period engaged in rulemaking. Yet judicial attitudes toward that practice displayed a similar attachment to defeasible rules. Thus, the Administrative Procedure Act apparently contemplated that informal rules would most commonly be reviewed by collateral attacks on their legality in enforcement hearings. In such proceedings, it was assumed, the challenger could assail the rule as applied to his particular situation. With this backstop, the rules themselves could be developed by informal means. The Act's minimal notice and comment requirements were regarded solely as "instruments for the education of the administrator."

Moreover, reviewing courts were markedly uneasy about the use of hard-and-fast rules to foreclose opportunities to litigate issues in an individualized

---

*National Petroleum Refiners Ass'n v. FTC, 482 F.2d 672 (D.C. Cir. 1973), *cert. denied*, 415 U.S. 951 (1974). Indeed at one time courts expressed serious doubts about agencies' authority to make "law." Courts tended either to refuse to review agency decisions, *see e.g.*, Lem Moon Sing v. United States, 158 U.S. 538, 546 (1895); Fong Yue Ting v. United States, 149 U.S. 698, 714–15 (1893); Ekiu v. United States, 142 U.S. 651, 660 (1892); Decatur v. Paulding, 39 U.S. (14 Pet.) 497, 516 (1840), or to subject their decisions to trial de novo, *see, e.g.*, Ng Fung Ho v. White, 259 U.S. 276, 284–85 (1922); Ohio Valley Water Co. v. Ben Avon Borough, 253 U.S. 287, 289 (1920).

fashion. Although early decisions permitted use of rulemaking to cut back issues previously open to litigation, they implied that the agency must offer an explicit mechanism for obtaining exemptions in particular cases. This unanimity in the attitudes of Congress and the courts suggests that both sought to cast rulemaking in the mold of common law adjudication. With this emphasis, rules take on the flavor of adjudicatively developed presumptions, generic and sweeping in terms, but tentative in application. Even rulemaking—that most decidedly synoptic of policy devices—was thus conceived as an incrementalist mechanism. . . .

Adjudication necessarily implies decentralization in the making of policy. A host of administrative law judges exercise considerable de facto law-giving power in their role as issuers of initial decisions. To the extent that initial decisions are not reviewed, they become the final decisions of the agency. Even when these decisions are reviewed within the agency, they often shape the agency's perception of policy issues and alternatives.

Policymaking through adjudication, moreover, is reviewed by a broader swath of the judiciary than is rulemaking. Judicial review of rulemaking is typically restricted to the appellate courts—and indeed, largely to the District of Columbia Circuit—whereas jurisdiction to review adjudications tends to be distributed more evenly by judicial level and geography.

More important than the decentralization of decisionmaking is the fragmentation of responsibility for setting the agenda. A system of policymaking by adjudication, especially one that relies heavily on private initiation, delegates to a wide constituency the task of identifying policy questions. Early regulatory programs in such industries as public utilities, transportation, and communications reinforced this tendency. Viewed by many as protectionist measures for the benefit of a favored industry, these programs relied almost exclusively on the initiative of regulated firms. Licensing schemes most clearly evince this mentality: private parties must approach the agency with a specific request for permission. In rate regulation, too, the burden of initiation ordinarily falls on the regulated party. An administrative process that parties must initiate is almost inevitably an incremental one. It is thus no accident that the age of incrementalism was also an era in which licensing and rate approval were the dominant regulatory instruments.

The same reactive attitude spilled over into other regulatory contexts as well. The NLRB is the most conspicuous example. Throughout its history the Board has refused to use its minimal rulemaking power, and has acted as little more than an umpire in disputes between organized labor and management. Even an agency like the FTC, although charged with seeking out and undoing evil, often adopted a reactive posture. Until recently, for example, it allowed its regulatory agenda to be set almost exclusively by the complaints of disgruntled competitors.

In some contexts, moreover, the courts affirmatively encourged this social fragmentation of policymaking. Implication of private rights of action to enforce regulatory statutes—at its zenith in the 1960's—best illustrates this phenomenon. By recognizing a private cause of action, courts invite the countless customers and competitors of regulated firms to set the regulatory agenda. Private self-interest thus competes on at least equal terms with an administrator's conception of the public interest in the formation of policy. . . .

To be sure, administrative incrementalism had its share of critics from the very beginning of the modern era.* The chorus of disaffection began to swell, however, in the 1960's. Presidential commissions,† jurists, and academics‡ all lamented the incoherence of much regulatory policy. The product of many agencies' deliberations, these critics argued, was not a flexible policy, but no policy at all—a paper veneer behind which rank favoritism or obsequiousness could flourish. Even when agencies produced discernible policy,

---

*See, e.g., President's Comm'n on Administrative Management, Report with Studies of Administrative Management in the Federal Government 41 (1937); Huntington, "The Marasmus of the ICC: The Commission, the Railroads, and the Public Interest," 61 Yale L.J. 467 (1952).

†See Landis, Report on Regulatory Agencies to the President-Elect (1960); Report of the President's Advisory Council on Executive Organization, A New Regulatory Framework (1971).

‡E.g., K. Davis, Discretionary Justice (1969); M. Edelman, The Symbolic Uses of Politics 22–66 (1964); T. Lowi, The End of Liberalism, 92–126 (2d ed. 1979).

the incremental method often extorted a high price in the great uncertainty it imposed on a public seeking guidance for its own conduct. Representatives for the unorganized public—self-appointed or otherwise—added both decibels and political clout to the protests.* Business as usual at the administrative agencies, they said, excluded the "real" beneficiaries of many programs—consumers, workers, the poor and infirm—from participation in policy development.

The cumulative effect of these criticisms was a formidable onslaught on the whole structure of administrative regulation. By no means were all of these criticisms addressed specifically to aspects of the incrementalist paradigm. But that paradigm had become associated with an increasingly discredited regime of cartel-like economic regulation medium and messages were by then inextricably linked. . . .

III. The Triumph of Comprehensive Rationality

Beginning in the mid-1960's and accelerating rapidly during the early years of the 1970's, a new consensus about policymaking began to emerge. The key doctrinal shift was enhanced emphasis on rulemaking as a method of formulating policy. . . . Besides granting rulemaking power in new regulatory statutes, Congress increasingly resorted to "action-forcing" techniques to compel prospective adoption of policies. The courts as well threw their weight behind the greater use of rulemaking. Instances of judicial insistence on rulemaking, though rare, accumulated rapidly enough to provide rulemaking enthusiasts like Kenneth Culp Davis the basis for discerning a general tendency.† Courts invoked in a variety of legal grounds—due process,‡ organic statutes and internal

agency procedures,§ or abuse of discretion‖—for divining an obligation to proceed by rulemaking. Some cases merely vacated specific agency orders as inadequately justified,¶ while others directly commanded the agency to initiate rulemaking proceedings.** . . .

. . . More exacting judicial review of substantive agency decisions accompanied greater procedural formality. The very label used to describe modern judicial review of policymaking—the "hard look doctrine"†† —captures the spirit of this information. Reviewing courts are no longer willing to affirm based on the intuitive plausibility of the link between the policy announced and the statutory standard. And the agency can no longer be content with just any alternative that advances its goal; it must be prepared to demonstrate the alternative's superiority over others advanced by outside participants or conceived by the agency itself. To enforce that requirement, courts examined, often in painstaking detail, the agency's factual predicate, analytic methodology, and chain of reasoning.

As judicial review became more rigorous, it focused more on review of the rule itself than on its subsequent applications. Further judicial relaxation of standing and ripeness barriers opened the courthouse doors to preenforcement review of rules once expected to be challenged only in enforcement proceedings. . . .

. . . In short, the doctrinal reformation attempts to embody, in legally enforceable rules of administrative conduct, the prescriptive model of comprehensive rationality. A comparison of that paradigm's

---

*See, e.g., E. Cox, R. Fellmeth & J. Schulz, 'The Nader Report' on the Federal Trade Commission (1969); R. Fellmeth, The Interstate Commerce Commission (1970).

†Davis, "Administrative Law Surprises in the Ruiz Case," 75 Colum. L. Rev. 823, 827–28 (1975).

‡E.g., Soglin v. Kauffman, 418 F.2d 163, 168 (7th Cir. 1969); Holmes v. New York City Hous. Auth. 398 F.2d 262,264–65 (2d Cir. 1968); Hornsby v. Allen, 326 F.2d 605, 609–10 (5th Cir. 1964); cf. Amsterdam, "Perspectives on the Fourth Amendment," 58 Minn. L. Rev. 349 (1974) (arguing that police searches and seizures should be invalidated unless conducted in accordance with rules.)

§E.g., Morton v. Ruiz, 415 U.S. 199, 231–36 (1974).

‖E.g., Bahat v. Sureck, 637 F.2d 1315, 1317 (9th Cir. 1981); Ruangswang v. INS, 591 F.2d 39, 46 (9th Cir. 1978).

¶See, e.g., Morton v. Ruiz, 415 U.S. 199, 230–38 (1974); Bahat v. Sureck, 637 F.2d 1315 (9th Cir. 1981); cf. United States v. Bryant, 439 F.2d 643,652 (D.C. Cir. 1971) (requiring police rulemaking).

**E.g., Rockbridge v. Lincoln, 449 F.2d 567 (9th Cir. 1971); Holmes v. New York City Hous. Auth., 398 F.2d 262 (2d Cir. 1968).

††See Greater Boston Television Corp. v. FCC, 444 F.2d 841, 850–53 (D.C. Cir. 1970), cert. denied, 403 U.S. 923 (1971); Environmental Defense Fund, Inc. v. Ruckelshaus, 439 F.2d 584 (D.C. Cir. 1971); Leventhal, "Environmental Decisionmaking and the Role of the Courts," 122 U. Pa. L. Rev. 509 (1974).

central features with contemporary doctrine demonstrates the closeness of the fit. . . .

A more precise specification of regulatory goals has been the goal or byproduct of many recent developments in administrative law. . . . Indeed, some observers have described new regulatory agencies such as the Environmental Protection Agency or the Occupational Safety and Health Administration as "single-purpose" agencies.* . . .

The courts too have contributed in a modest but appreciable way to the clarifaction of statutory goals. The federal courts have not followed the advice of some distinguished commentators to revive the nondelegation doctrine as a tool for invalidating generous statutory grants of authority.† But they have invoked the doctrine explicitly on several recent occasions to limit severely a statute's interpretation,‡ and have more frequently appeared to have nondelegation in mind when they imposed similar limitations without explicitly mentioning the doctrine. . . .

When neither Congress nor the courts have themselves been prepared to delineate the agency's tradeoff function, they have increasingly required the agencies to do so. Many of the rulemaking formalities recently imposed by Congress and reviewing courts have aimed at compelling agencies to specify their goals more articulately. The agency's notice of proposed rulemaking must clearly identify the objective to be attained, and the rule's statement of basis and purpose must show how the agency's action serves that objective. Similarly, courts have increasingly

demanded explanation even in adjudications not customarily thought to require procedural formalities.

In a number of contexts, Congress has explicitly required agencies to consider numerous options when making policy. NEPA requires agencies contemplating any "major Federal actions significantly affecting [the environment]" to consider "alternatives to the proposed action." Several recent regulatory statutes contain similar requirements. The Consumer Product Safety Commission, for example, is required by its organic act to investigate, as part of its rulemaking function, "any means of achieving the [desired] objective . . . while minimizing adverse effects" on competition or commercial practices. The Toxic Substances Control Act goes so far as to specify seven alternative approaches to regulating hazardous chemicals that the EPA must consider before adopting a rule; the EPA must choose the "least burdensome" requirement that provides "adequate" protection against risks to health and the environment.

The courts have abetted these legislative efforts to broaden administrators' policymaking vision. Besides merely opening up rulemaking to wider outside participation, courts have tried to open the decisionmaker's mind as well by insisting that the agency respond to the significant issues raised by public comment. A parallel trend is discernible in judicial review of licensing and other "adjudicative" proceedings involving prospective policy decisions. . . .

. . . The most demanding aspect of the synoptic paradigm is the care with which it requires policymakers to consider the consequences of each policy option. The quest to satisfy that requirement has produced a host of sophisticated analytical techniques—cost-benefit analysis, cost-effectiveness analysis, risk assessment, and systems analysis—which have now infiltrated the legal framework for policymaking. Congress has increasingly required use of these techniques. Several recent regulatory statutes expressly call for cost-benefit analysis or risk assessment of the policy options under consideration. For example, the National Forest Management Act of 1976 requires the Secretary of Agriculture to "formulate and implement . . . a process for estimating long-terms [sic]

---

* *See generally* Ackerman & Hassler, (discussion of EPA); Weaver, "Regulation, Social Policy and Class Conflict," in *Regulating Business: The Search for an Optimum* 193 (Inst. for Contemp. Stud. 1978) (new regulatory agencies are significantly different from the older agencies).

† *See, e.g.,* J. Ely, *Democracy and Distrust* 131–34 (1980); Gewirtz, "The Courts, Congress, and Executive Policy-Making: Notes on Three Doctrines," 40 *Law & Contemp. Probs.,* Summer 1976, at 46, 49–65; McGowan, "Congress, Court, and Control of Delegated Power," 77 *Colum. L. Rev.* 1119, 1127–30 (1977); Wright, "Beyond Discretionary Justice," 81 *Yale L.J.* 575, 581–87 (1972).

‡ *E.g.,* Industrial Union Dep't, AFL-CIO v. American Petroleum Inst., 448 U.S. 607, 645–46 (1980) (Stevens J., concurring); National Cable Television Ass'n v. United States, 415 U.S. 336, 342 (1974).

costs and benefits" in order to justify a forest management plan. The Consumer Product Safety Commission's product safety rules must "express in the rule itself the risk of injury which the standard is designed to eliminate or reduce." . . .

Cost-benefit analysis, moreover, has been the centerpiece of the Carter and Reagan Administrations' regulatory reform programs. The Reagan program, for example, requires executive agencies to prepare a "Regulatory Impact Analysis" of all "major" rules, including a description of all potential costs and benefits and "[a] determination of the potential net benefits of the rule."* Moreover, the Reagan order forbids any regulatory action, whether "major" or minor, by executive agencies unless "the potential benefits to society . . . outweigh the potential costs to society" and the alternative chosen to achieve the goal maximizes the aggregate net benefit to society.† These executive programs and comparable features of pending regulatory reform legislation‡ most dramatically illustrate the triumph of microeconomics analysis in the current vision of how agency policy should be made.

The allure of analysis has turned many a judicial head as well. Reviewing courts have insisted that agencies probe the implications of their policy choices. Not only must administrators attend to consequences suggested by public comment; courts will also frequently require them to seek out and analyze other possible consequences of their actions. Although most courts do not demand explicit quantification unless the statute so requires, several have nonetheless called for a qualitative comparison of good and bad consequences. Even if the courts have not universally endorsed specific analytic techniques, they have typically demanded a thorough and expansive approach consistent with the synoptic ideal. . . .

IV. Comprehensive Rationality in the Supreme Court

As the 1970's drew to a close, then, comprehensive rationality had attracted an impressive following. To be sure, incrementalism still flourished in various bureaucratic backwaters, but it enjoyed little favor at administrative law's most stylish addresses: the White House, Capitol Hill, and the federal courthouses. Congress seemed increasingly committed to action-forcing regulatory legislation, rigorous analysis, and aggressive judicial review. Presidential regulatory reform programs virtually defied cost-analysis. And federal appeals courts continued to chastise administrative policymakers for the narrowness of their vision and the shallowness of their inquiry.

Amid this undiluted enthusiasm, the Supreme Court kept its counsel. Its affair with comprehensive rationality has been strangely mercurial—now ardent, now coolly distant. A trio of recent decisions involving nuclear energy and occupational health display this mercurial quality. A careful reading of the opinions reveals a fundamental allegiance to the synoptic paradigm, although each opinion hints at a reluctance to impose upon administrators a specific conception of rationality. In *Vermont Yankee*,§ the Court attempted to dissociate comprehensive rationality from the excesses of expanded public participation in administrative decisionmaking, while in its *Benzene*‖ and *Cotton Dust*¶ opinions it refined the meaning of rationality as a strategy for combatting occupational disease.

---

*Exec. Order No. 12,291, § 3(d), 46 Fed. Reg. 13,193, 13,194 (1981). A "major" rule is one that is likely to result in an "annual effect on the economy of $100 million or more," causes a "major increase" in cost and prices, or has "significant adverse effects" on competition or employment. *Id.* § 3(d), 46 Fed. Reg. at 13,193. See generally Bliss, "Regulatory Reform: Toward a More Balanced and Flexible Federal Agency Regulation," 8 *Pepperdine L. Rev.* 619 (1981).

†Exec. Order No. 12,291, § 2, 46 Fed. Reg. at 13,193.

‡*E.g.*, S. 755, 96th Cong., 1st Sess. § 602 (1979); S. 262, 96th Cong., 1st Sess. § 602 (1979). S. 755 opens, significantly, with the words: "To make regulations more cost-effective." S. 755, 96th Cong., 1st Sess. preamble (1979). The required regulatory analysis would entail an assessment of "projected benefits" and "adverse economic effects," *id.* § 602(c)(3), reconciled with the alternatives considered, *id.* § 602(c)(4). *See also* S. 1080, 97th Cong., 1st Sess. (1981) (proposing a regulatory impact analysis for all "major" rules); H.R. 746, 97th Cong., 1st Sess (1981).

§Vermont Yankee Nuclear Power Corp. v. Natural Resources Defense Council, Inc., 435 U.S. 519 (1978).

‖Industrial Union Dep't, AFL-CIO v. American Petroleum Inst., 448 U.S. 607 (1980).

¶American Textile Mfrs. Inst. v. Donovan, 101 S. Ct. 2478 (1981).

A. VERMONT YANKEE AND PUBLIC PARTICIPATION IN RULEMAKING. . . .

Writing for a unanimous Court, Justice Rehnquist seized the occasion to level a broadside at the procedural creativity of lower federal courts in rulemaking cases. . . . Reviewing courts were not, the Court admonished, to stray beyond the "statutory minima" of section 553 of the Administrative Procedure Act in order to "impose upon the agency [their] own notion of which procedures are 'best' or most likely to further some vague, undefined public good."* On the surface, then, *Vermont Yankee* seemed a defeat for the synoptic movement, and it has been widely criticized as such. "Hybrid" rulemaking procedures, after all, had become integrally associated, in the minds of many reformers, with the drive for increased analytic rigor.

Yet rather than signaling a return to incrementalist muddling, the decision merely refines the synoptic paradigm. Although challenging one tenet of the analysts' creed—hybrid rulemaking—the decision expressly reaffirms another: on-the-record judicial review of rulemaking. And it leaves untouched an elaborate structure of synoptic devices, such as the "hard look" doctrine and rigorous enforcement of section 553's explicit procedural obligations.

More fundamentally, *Vermont Yankee* expresses the Court's unease, not with lower court efforts to rationalize policymaking, but with their attempts to democratize it in ways incompatible with the synoptic paradigm. The central object of the Court's wrath was the appeals court's insistence that the anti-nuclear intervenors have "a meaningful opportunity to participate in the proceedings." Although it left the choice of particular procedures to the NRC, the lower court had demanded a "genuine dialogue" between the NRC and the opponents of nuclear power. It was this emphasis that "public concern . . . be quieted" that seems to have troubled the Supreme Court most deeply. The Court's quarrel is thus not with synoptic analysis, but rather with one of its most persistent camp followers: broadened public participation.

Expanded participation in administrative policymaking has been linked closely to the doctrinal transformation of administrative law since the mid-1960s.[†] Many of the landmark decisions of the transitional era exhibit powerful democratic as well as rationalist impulses.[‡] Public participation, like rationalism, was a common response to the felt inadequacies of incrementalist decisionmaking. Participation was a cure for the myopia of the incrementalist administrator, unable to see beyond the parties before him to the full range of public interests affected by his decisions. This "agency capture" was reinforced by the incrementalist instinct to consider only minor deviations from the status quo and by the judicial deference to agency policy choices. Conversely, opening the agency to all those affected by its decisions would broaden its focus while obviating the need for close judicial scrutiny of substantive agency choices.

But the values of participation and rationality, intertwined as they have been in the literature and in political agrument, are nonetheless distinct. Public participation can, of course, promote rationality by enlarging the policymaker's field of vision, reducing his burden of investigation, and disciplining his substantive biases. But in the eyes of a confirmed synopticist, it can just as easily subordinate to the tyranny of selective self-interest any dispassionate search for utopian solutions. The urge to satisfy a multitude of conflicting interests may force administrators to make decisions based on expediency or an ad hoc evaluation of "all the relevant circumstances." The chances of achieving rational policy through the advocacy of various affected interests may therefore be doubtful.

Far from being incompatible, adherence to the synoptic paradigm and distrust of participatory process go hand in hand. Many economists who strenuously defend comprehensive rationality as a goal, for example, see the reality of policymaking as nothing more

---

[†]*See generally* Gelhorn, "Public Participation in Administrative Proceedings," 81 *Yale L.J.* 359 (1972) (intervention in agency decisionmaking); Stewart, *supra* note 8.

[‡]*E.g.*, National Welfare Rights Org. v. Finch, 429 F. 2d 725 (D.C. Cir. 1970); Office of Communication of the United Church of Christ v. FCC, 359 F.2d 944 (D.C. Cir. 1966); Scenic Hudson Preservation Conference v. FPC, 354 F.2d 608 (2d Cir. 1965), *cert. denied*, 384 U.S. 941 (1966).

Id. at 548, 549.

than competition among influential partisans for self-ish objectives. Indeed, participatory procedures are more consistent with the incrementalist's impulse to accommodate conflicting values than with the policy analyst's penchant for objectivity. It should be remembered that the leading metaphor for comprehensive rationality is not the spirited debate of the town meeting but the scientist's lonely search for truth. . . .

B. BENZENE, COTTON DUST, AND THE ARTICULATION OF POLICY GOALS. Having purged itself of participatory heresies, a court that truly worshipped at the synoptic altar would seize the next opportunity to reaffirm the four central tenets of rationalist dogma: independent specification of goals, identification of alternatives, rigorous analysis of consequences, and optimization through informed choice. A pair of celebrated challenges to federal occupational health standards presented the Supreme Court with just such an opportunity.

The first of these, *Industrial Union Department, AFL-CIO v. American Petroleum Institute (Benzene)*, involved an attack on the Occupational Safety and Health Administration's controversial standard for workplace exposure to benzene, a conceded carcinogen. OSHA had lowered the permissible threshold exposure level from ten parts per million to one part per million, a modification that the petrochemical industry said would impose costs far exceeding the benefits produced.

Although no opinion commanded a majority of the Court, each of the Justices voting to strike down the OSHA standard relied on synoptic, rather than incrementalist, arguments. Justice Stevens' plurality opinion interpreted the Occupational Safety and Health Act to require OSHA to make an affirmative finding of "a significant risk of harm and therefore a probability of significant benefit" before establishing, or even modifying, a mandatory health standard. . . . Applying the Court's newly fashioned yardstick, Justice Stevens found wanting the agency's decision to lower the benzene threshhold. In doing so, he expressly rejected what he perceived to be an undocumented presumption by the agency that there is no safe level of exposure to carcinogens like benzene. This rejection of a factually undocumented

hypothesis illustrates another judicial habit typical of the synoptic era. An incrementalist judge would almost certainly have accepted—as Justice Marshall, in dissent, did in fact accept—a working hypothesis of this sort, backed by a plausible claim of administrative expertise and the prospect of later review and modification. But in a synoptic world of remorseless, one-shot decisions that impose unavoidable consequences, there is no place for casual presumptions.

In a concurring opinion, Chief Justice Burger supported the remand so that the Secretary of Labor could "retrace his steps with greater care and consideration"—insisting, in essence, on the "hard look" doctrine's requirement of adequate justification. And although the Chief Justice seemed uneasy with the plurality's searching review of a "policy judgment," the implicit distinction between the substantive correctness of the policy judgment and the adequacy of the offered explanation can, in the hands of a comprehensive rationalist, shrink to nothing. . . .

. . . Finally, Justice Rehnquist displayed his own loyalty to the comprehensive rationalist standard, albeit in an unconventional fashion. Finding the statutory standard impenetrable, he proposed to invoke the nondelegation doctrine to nullify the statute altogether. This doctrinally extraordinary approach would command Congress to define clear and consistent goals for each regulatory program, against which the rationality of all subsequent actions could be tested.

For all its internal doctrinal confusion, then, the *Benzene* case reveals a strong majority allegiance to the synoptic ideal. This allegiance was again expressed, though more equivocally, in the Court's affirmance of OSHA's cotton dust standard in *American Textile Manufacturers Institute, Inc. v. Donovan (Cotton Dust)*. In *Cotton Dust*, the Court decided the question left unresolved in *Benzene*—whether the Act requires OSHA to analyze the costs and benefits of proposed standards for toxic substances. Writing for a 5-3 majority, Justice Brennan held that it did not.

Although the Court's refusal to require cost-benefit analysis might seem a clear defeat for the analytic movement, the Court's substitute standard—"technologically and economically feasible"—if anything specifies the regulatory objective more precisely.

Congress, said the Court in a virtual echo of *Overton Park*, had already balanced the interests and had elevated health to a preeminent position.

To be sure, the majority opinion does contain uncertain portents for the analytic paradigm. Devoted rationalists might be particularly troubled by Justice Brennan's reliance on congressional silence to support his rejection of cost-benefit analysis. . . . In *Cotton Dust*, the Court did not reject the practice of rationalism but simply deferred to a different practitioner.

V. Striking the Proper Balance

The Supreme Court's recent decisions in nuclear energy and occupational health may thus be read to endorse the main tenets of comprehensive rationality. Yet they communicate, by their very ambivalence, a tempering of enthusiasm for the synoptic credo. And surely some moderation is warranted. . . . At its best, comprehensive rationality makes ravenous demands on agencies' limited investigative resources and cognitive faculties. Judged by its demanding standards, policymakers are virtually defenseless against reproof for falling short. Reviewing courts, beguiled by the idea of optimal choice, must struggle to resist finding reversible error in any agency's analytical process. At its worst, comprehensive rationality merely masks the decisionmaker's private biases under a legitimizing facade of objectivity and analytic rigor.*

. . . A growing body of disaster stories,† coupled with mounting attacks on the ethical and conceptual foundations of comprehensive rationality,‡ has greatly increased public awareness of its failings. But the proper response to that awareness is less clear. Our social philosophy exhibits a troublesome tendency to vacillate between polar extremes. The so-lution to synoptic failures it not a blind retreat to incrementalism. What is needed is a sense of balance, a recognition of the finite reach of our means. We need not cast all our weight on one side, for incrementalism and comprehensive rationality each offer unique advantages as well as conspicuous limitations. A fully mature theory of policymaking should be able to accommodate both, with each as master in its appropriate realm.

The singular advantage of incrementalism is its ability to accommodate uncertainty and diversity. Where comprehensive rationality tortures fundamental value conflicts into an uncomfortable and often illusory truce, incrementalism creates a quasi-market for their serial reconciliation. While non-incrementalist policies are doomed to rigidity by the very political over-selling needed to launch them, the modesty of incremental undertakings enables them more readily to adapt to novel circumstances. Where the synoptic method erects a flimsy bulwark of false certainty against the tide of technical and social change, incrementalism deals only with the present, leaving tomorrow to tomorrow.

Yet the incremental method is not wholly preferable to comprehensive rationality even when uncertainty and conflict prevail. As doubt and strife intensify, incrementalism increasingly taxes the resources of the decisionmaker. To accommodate diverse preferences while adjusting to changing circumstances demands more and more organizational slack. Resources husbanded by avoiding ex ante policy specification can be consumed in spades by a process of ex post policy elaboration. Even more important, incrementalism can succeed only as long as its remedial apparatus functions smoothly. . . .

These considerations suggest the following principles to guide architects of administrative policymaking. The synoptic paradigm should be the preferred way to make policy in relatively stable environments. Given contemporary ferment in regulatory and social policy, examples are somewhat difficult to find. Such examples might include fair labor standards, licensure qualifications for the practice of various occupations, or safety standards for commercial transportation. . . . One important implication of this first principle is that synoptic decisionmaking will often

---

*Cf. Kennedy, "Cost-Benefit Analysis of Entitlement Problems: A Critique," 33 *Stan L. Rev.* 387, 411 (1981) (labeling efficiency analysis "simply a language for carrying on political or ethical discussion").

†*E.g.*, R. Tobin, *The Social Gamble* (1979); Ackerman & Hassler; Margolis, "The Politics of Auto Emissions," 49 *Pub. Interest* 3 (1977); see also "Boundaries of Analysis" (H. Feiveson, F. Sinden & R. Socolow eds. 1976) (the Tocks Island dam controversy).

‡J. Mendeloff, *Regulating Safety: An Economic and Political Analysis of Occupational Safety and Health Policy* 63–80 (1979); Kelman, *Cost-Benefit Analysis—An Ethical Critique*, Reg., Jan.–Feb. 1981, at 33.

become more appropriate as a regulatory regime matures than it was in its infancy. Technical uncertainty is likely to be greatest and public opinion most polarized at the beginning of a new policy initiative. . . .

Even in unstable environments, comprehensive rationality should be favored when either of two additional conditions exists. The first is when small errors in policy can cause irreversible or even catastrophic harm. Some current examples are the regulation of nuclear power plant safety and nuclear fuel cycle, and the regulation of carcinogenic substances in food, consumer products, the environment, and the workplace. Protection of endangered species has similarly high stakes, if not the same intensity of public concern. It is more difficult to classify regulation of conventional nontoxic air and water pollutants. At some point, an incremental increase in pollution may cause a transformation in the ecological balance. Normally, however, adverse environmental outcomes are sufficiently detectable and reversible to be amenable to incrementalist repair.

Synoptic treatment is also appropriate is those policy regimes involving egregious—and irremediable—misallocations of political power among persons most intimately affected. This factor is prominent in such administrative programs as regulation of immigration and naturalization, public assistance, housing and nutritional services for the poor, antidiscrimination regulation, and programs for native Americans. Because the intended beneficiaries of these programs have little access to political power, legal advice, and self-help, they are often unable to participate in any agency proceeding. Therefore only the synoptic model, in which the decisionmaker *must* consider all interests—including those not immediately before him—can give adequate protection to these beneficiaries.

This leaves a large reservoir of public issues better suited to the incrementalist model. These government functions must live with acute technical uncertainty or heightened value conflict, but without the risk of irreversible catastrophe or irremediable inequalities. One can draw likely candidates from numerous fields of regulation: nonnuclear energy, production and use, broadcasting, collective bargaining, anticompetitive and deceptive business practices, and most safety hazards (but not necessarily health hazards) in consumer products, workplaces, and transportation. Many of these areas, such as energy and safety regulation, involve a high degree of technological uncertainty. Others, like collective bargaining and workplace accident prevention, involve sharply focused conflict not easily amenable to generic resolution.

The foregoing discussion sketches a method for choosing intelligently between the incremental and synoptic models. There remains the question of who—Congress, the courts, or the agencies—should make that choice. My candidate is the agencies themselves. Choosing an approach to public policy often involves close calls of the sort that agencies are generally best equipped to make. Finetuning of these choices, on the other hand, should be the job of the courts.

But what of Congress? Recently, the Supreme Court has twice chastised lower courts for imposing on agencies a particular policy technique not explicitly authorized by Congress . . . Congress cannot anticipate every change in technology, values, or resources that might dictate a change in lawmaking technique. The courts, by contrast, are better able to provide the calibration needed to ensure that agencies respond to those changes. Today's courts should demand a synoptic approach to controlling nuclear wastes or workplace carcinogens, for example, not out of a strained search for legislative intent, but out of respect for the potentially devastating consequences of narrowminded incremental decisions. In general, courts should use the principles . . . to monitor agency choices of procedures, while according those choices the deference they deserve.

The debates over the degree of formality of the rulemaking process have inevitably followed the growing tendency to use rulemaking for formulating policy. The *Vermont Yankee* cases and Diver's article lay out the legal and political terrain of this debate. To summarize, the central questions debate: (1) what role should courts play in reviewing rulemaking procedures, a topic we will explore further in chapter 9; (2) what kind of rulemaking procedures will most likely encourage consideration of alternative policy options and enhance public knowledge of substantive issues, such as nuclear power and nuclear weapons production; and (3) what degree of authority should administrators have over the process of policy formation?

Although Judge Bazelon and Justice Rehnquist give us different answers to these questions, both urge agencies to develop devices that will create a dialogue about regulation. The most ambitious and potentially most influential reform of agency rulemaking currently under way is called *regulatory negotiation*. In the article below, one of us, Professor Harrington, describes regulatory negotiation and examines the political implications of this legal reform. Regulatory negotiation is an informal rulemaking process that uses private mediators to negotiate and mediate conflicts between parties *before* an agency gives "notice and comment" in the *Federal Register* on a proposed rule. Regulatory negotiation has been promoted by reformers who find fault with more formal rulemaking processes, like hybrid rulemaking, and who want to reduce legal challenges to administrative rules. They maintain that one way of achieving this is to establish a consensus among "interested parties" before announcing a proposed rule. Yet, just as Diver questions whether Supreme Court decisions, such as the *Vermont Yankee* case, have limited democratic participation in administrative policymaking, Harrington's article questions the extent to which regulatory negotiation privatizes the rulemaking process and signifies a return to the model of interest group liberalism which Lowi so aptly criticized more than two decades ago.

Regulatory Reform: Creating Gaps and Making Markets

Christine B. Harrington
Law & Policy 10 (1988):293.

. . . Alternative dispute resolution techniques, such as mediation and arbitration, have been proposed for courts, in part, as a response to the perceived dispute resolution "crisis" of the courts. Informal dispute resolution is said to be a less adversarial and hence more effective method for resolving a range of disputes. . . .

The most ambitious, potentially most influential, and certainly the least examined expansion of the reform to date is taking place in administrative agencies. In this setting the reform is called "regulatory negotiation," a process for developing agency rules by negotiation among the parties affected by regulation. Recommendations issued by the Administrative Conference of the United States (ACUS) encourage agencies to "review the areas that they regulate to determine the potential for the establishment and use of dispute resolution mechanisms by private organizations as an alternative to direct agency action" (ACUS, 1986: 11930). . . . Facilitators, or mediators, are selected from outside the agency to help the parties reach an agreement on a rule. Once a consensus is reached, the rule will be published in the Federal Register and a period for public notice and comment is set. Examples of federal agency negotiated rulemaking are: Environmental Protection Agency penalties for heavy engine manufacturers who fail to comply with the requirement of the Clean Air Act, exemptions from pesticide licensing regulations, rules governing the removal of absestos in public schools, and standards for residential woodburning stoves; Federal Aviation Administration regulations dealing with maximum flight time and minimum rest period for pilots; and Occupational Safety and Health

Administration standards governing exposure to benzene and methylenedianiline.

The use of private mediators in the regulatory rulemaking process raises many questions about the influence of private interests on public policy. Questions of this sort have already been raised in the debates over civil settlement. Political scientists and legal scholars have taken issue with the new claim that private settlement is always a desirable alternative to public adjudication (Resnik, 1982; Fiss, 1984; Provine, 1986; Kritzer, 1986). In the case of civil settlement, and the legal process more generally, this debate is over whether the judiciary should be in the business of making public policy. There is less attention to this element of formalism in the area of administrative regulation. Indeed, given the history of regulation, the shift to informal negotiation is a curious development because the regulatory process is much less clearly associated with the ideals of formalism than the civil courts. Even the so-called "judicialization" of the administrative process, following the passage of the Administrative Procedure Act in 1946 (Seidman and Gilmour, 1986) and during the early 1970s (Funston, 1974), did not seek to replicate the adversarial nature of the judicial process. Despite differences between the role of agencies and courts in shaping public policy, administrative capacity like court capacity is a current focus of scholarly attention and reform.

Institutional capacity, however, is a problematic variable in plotting the relationship between law and politics. This approach construes legal processes and institutions as instruments of politics and describes reform strategies based on an instrumental view of law.* This paper takes another approach by adding to the conventional picture of politics and law the construction of social relations in dispute processing

ideology.† In doing so, I argue for a new approach to the relationship between law and politics; an approach that shows the constitutive role of law in politics. This is a perspective shared by a growing body of interdisciplinary research on law.‡ At this point in its development, judging the impact of alternative dispute resolution on regulation would be premature. This is, however, an appropriate time to examine the conceptualization of state-market relations embedded in this reform. In this sense, processes indicate the relationship between political, economic and legal power. These reform institutions tell us about the role of law in organizing state-market relations. Dispute processes, such as regulatory negotiation, not only serve political and economic interests, they also help constitute those interests. . . .

II. Reforming Regulation through Dispute Processing

. . . Alternative dispute resolution reforms in civil, criminal, and administrative settings are linked by a shared anti-adversarial approach to dispute processing. In these three areas, conventional practices are

---

*Instrumental concepts of law are found in both orthodox Marxist and Legal Realist analyses of law. For orthodox Marxists, law is a tool of the dominant classes used to maintain and reproduce their power in society. For Legal Realists, law is a tool that can be used for engineering social reform. Both perspectives treat law as an instrument of politics having little or no authority independent from its use in politics.

†Dispute processing ideology refers to the structure of values presupposed in justifications for this reform and expressed through its practice. These values shape the way in which social relations are conceptualized and evaluated. This concept of ideology differs from what Michael McCann views as the "common pejorative use of 'ideology' to imply conceptual dogmatism, irrationalism, or naivete" (1986: 21). For a more elaborate discussion of concepts of ideology in legal research see Hunt (1985).

‡A constitutive concept of law differs from an instrumental concept in that law is seen as having power to frame politics. Legal processes, doctrine and institutions shape political possibilities. Recent examples of theoretical and empirical work on a constitutive approach to law include: Robert Gordon's study of lawyer's work as ideology views "every legal practice—from drafting a complaint for simple debt to writing a constitution—[as] makes a contribution to building a general ideological scheme or political language out of such explaining and rationalizing conceptions" (1983: 72); Maureen Cain's analysis of work of civil courts as "conceptive ideological work: using old rules to generate new ways of thinking, of making sense of, and thereby of constituting ideologically new and emergent material forms" (1983: 131); and John Brigham's research on social movements as "constituted in legal terms when they see the world in those terms and organize themselves accordingly . . . Legal forms are evident in the language, purposes, and strategies of movement activity as practices" (1987b: 306).

portrayed as highly adversarial closed systems that prevent parties from addressing the underlying issues of a dispute. Traditional dispute processing structures (e.g. courts and administrative agencies) are characterized as essentially passive institutions acting as umpires who determine the outcome (win-lose) of a battle between two opposing sides. This description of conventional dispute processes emphasizes the limits of legalism and sharpens the boundary between expectations of fairness, associated with formal justice, and what legalism can actually deliver.

A fundamental premise of the alternative dispute resolution movement is that there is a "gap" between the promise and the capacity of formal justice. This perceived gap is the product of an idealized conception of formal justice. Used as the standard for evaluating institutional practices, this ideal becomes the criterion for judging institutional capacity. The ideal itself is treated as nonproblematic, separate from its social meaning and its historic functions. Locating the limits of legalism in an idealized conception of formal justice creates a gap which then underlies the claim for alternative dispute resolution. The reform then seeks to reduce the "gap" by using law (i.e. legal institutions and legal processes) as a tool for social change. For example, Richard Stewart observes that "Although public interest litigation was designed to reduce the gap between regulatory goals and their implementation and enforcement, in many instances it actually may have increased the gap" (Stewart, 1985: 679). Gaps of this sort have become the principal justification for mobilizing new legal reforms, including regulatory negotiation.

A. CONVENTIONAL REGULATORY RULEMAKING. Despite a trend towards the judicialization of the administrative process in the last twenty years, the relative informality of administrative regulation remains. Agencies such as the Environmental Protection Agency bargain regularly with affected parties. In fact, before the EPA publishes a proposed rule which it believes will be controversial, EPA officials notify Congress, industry, environmentalists, and state and local officials. For some time the agency has operated on the belief that informal discussions with affected parties will help resolve controversy (Comment, 1981).

The informal character of administrative regulation is also found in the image of agency capture . . . The capture thesis focuses on informal negotiations between regulator and regulated because it is believed that informal bargaining enhances the power of private interests over public policy.

The capture thesis prompted a wave of reforms in the 1970s—what we might call counter-capture reforms. . . .

. . . [C]hanges in the approach to agency policymaking came about in the 1970s as a response to a particular type of regulation—social regulation. The rise of social regulation, such as environmental, consumer, health and safety regulation, expanded the scope of regulation from one industry to many. Unlike the economic regulation of the New Deal agencies, social regulation is generic. It mandates that agencies regulate the conduct of firms across industrial sectors instead of within a specific industry. Consequently agencies engaged in social regulation often use rulemaking instead of adjudication in order to establish a uniform rule and "economize on decision costs" (Diver, 1981).

Rulemaking institutionalized greater interest group and citizen participation than adjudication. Citizens and groups could comment on a proposed rule made through the rulemaking process whereas participation in adjudication was limited to those who challenged an agency decision. At the same time that agencies were shifting to a rulemaking approach the public interest law movement sought to expand the impact of participation in rulemaking by demanding that agencies do more than afford interested parties the opportunity to be heard. They sought to require that agencies engage in a more probing factfinding process and establish a record responding to alternative policy proposals. . . .

Where public interest reforms expanded the right of direct participation in the rulemaking process these reforms challenged the New Deal model of administrative expertise by transforming the agency from protector of the public interest to umpire assessing competing claims. Informal agreement on an agency rule has less chance of being established in the case of social regulation, it is argued, because a rule, for example on exposure to toxic substances in the work place affects many industries, and the procedures are too adversarial. Today, this approach to regulatory decisionmaking is criticized for promoting "costly litigation because it decreases the opportunity for the development of long-term continuing relationships between regulator and regulated" (Stewart, 1985: 655).

Efforts to reduce agency capture have been somewhat successful where regulatory practices have created an unfriendly environment for the development of long-term continuing relationships. Yet, advocates of regulatory negotiation maintain that the economic and social costs of litigation are too high a price to pay for regulating private interests. They say that by "encouraging and empowering regulatees to challenge agency decision making in an effort to enhance the political legitimacy of the rulemaking process, Congress and the courts have increased the complexity, cost, and time it takes to generate rules that can be implemented" (Susskind and McMahon, 1985: 136). A debilitating complexity is the linchpin to the ideology of this reform.

B. NEGOTIATED RULEMAKING. According to ACUS recommendations, regulatory negotiation may be initiated by either an agency or one of its constituencies. The agency designates a "neutral convenor," a private mediator or facilitator, whose job is to identify the interested parties and relevant issues. First the convenor undertakes a "feasibility analysis" to establish whether or not the parties, including agency actors, will agree to negotiate a rule. In a number of cases the agency will empanel the interested parties as an advisory committee under authority from the Federal Advisory Committee Act of 1976 (FACA). If negotiations produce agreement between parties, a rule will be announced in the Federal Register.

As with other proposals for alternative dispute resolution, the advocates are very enthusiastic about the advantages of rulemaking by negotiation. They see the following advantages: (1) negotiated rulemaking

offers the parties direct participation in the process; (2) the mediator is more active in "outreach" to the parties affected by the regulation than in the "customary rulemaking route" (Harter, 1984: 4); (3) the parties will be engaged in direct substantive decisions rather than appearing as expert witnesses providing testimony before the agency; (4) the costs of participation are reduced because the parties need not prepare "defensive research" (Harter, 1982); and (5) the quality of participation is richer because the parties are in a setting that provides incentives to rank their concerns. . . .

The emphasis on increased participation through a negotiation process appears to respond to the age-old criticism about the failure of a responsive bureaucracy in a democratic policy. . . .

[Yet] it is significant that those who criticize the expansion of party participation under the public interest law reforms in the 1970s are now calling for regulatory negotiation as a way of enhancing party involvement in the regulatory process. This fact suggests that participation alone is not the central value, but rather the form of participation is the pivotal point of debate. Thus, the parties to negotiated rulemaking, including the state, become the "experts" who exercise regulatory discretion.

Regulatory negotiation turns away from traditional measures for restricting agency discretion, such as more stringent due process requirements, and instead brings a private mediator/facilitator into the process. Harter explains that an outside mediator "enhances the appearance of neutrality and has control over the calendar and the ability to move in ways that may be different for an insider" (1984: 4). A private nonpartisan convenor, it is argued, is preferable to the sponsoring agency who will be viewed as "suspect by the potential participants" (Susskind and McMahon, 1985: 163). Here, the process blunts the power of traditional public authority in the name of neutrality. Yet, advocates deny that regulatory negotiation delegates public authority to private parties. They claim that agencies participate in the process and have the equivalent of a veto over a "consensus." Here, the state becomes simply one of the participants. Its veto is not special. It is in this sense that regulatory negotiation shares a market conception with deregulation, an issue we will address later.

Still, many questions about delegating public authority remain. Will negotiations be open to the public? Regulatory negotiation groups constituted as advisory committees under the FACA are required to hold their plenary meetings in public, but caucuses and work group sessions may be held privately.* A related question concerns the scope of judicial review for negotiated regulation. Advocates propose a less stringent standard of revierw, one which narrowly focuses on the process of negotiation, rather than the adequacy of the substantive rule. Judicial review is valued only in so far as it may "enhance the efficiency and perceived legitimacy of the rulemaking process" (*Ibid.*, 165). . . .

*Reformers still feel there are some problems with the due process based ex parte rules of the FACA, which require open meetings. They contend that the parties should be able to close the meetings "when appropriate," because parties might "reasonably" be reluctant to engage in negotiations if they thought that positions they might raise would be held against them later. Efforts to establish negotiated rulemaking and civil settlement pursuant to statutory authorization are currently proposed as remedies to the ex parte rule.

III. The "Crisis" of Regulatory Litigation

. . . My study of regulatory litigation rates is based on data collected from the Annual Report of the Administrative Office of the U.S., which started categorizing administrative appeals in 1937. . . .

Figure 7.1 shows cases filed in the U.S. Circuit Courts of Appeals per 100,000 people from 1945 to 1985. Overall the trend is toward an increase in appellate case filing since 1960. Administrative appeals, however, do not increase at the same pace as other appellate litigation, particularly private civil and U.S. civil cases where over time the increases are most dramatic. A comparison of the percent change in filings per 100,000 people shows that between 1960 and 1965, when the trend upward begins, administrative appeals increase by 39% whereas other kinds of appellate litigation increases from 57% (bankruptcy) to 85% (criminal) (see Table 7.1). Although there is considerable fluctuation in bankruptcy and criminal appellate cases from 1960 to 1980, there is a steady increase in administrative, private civil, and U.S. civil filings in this period. Administrative appeals increase slightly faster (39.5%)

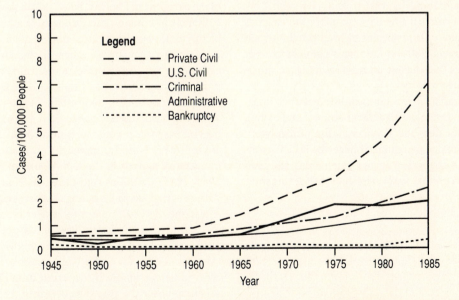

Figure 7.1   Cases Filed in the U.S. Court of Appeals per 100,000 People, 1945–1985

Table 7.1   Variability of Filings in the U.S. Courts of Appeals, 1945–1985*
(% Change in Filings per 100,000 People)

	Administrative	Private Civil	Criminal	U.S. Civil	Bankruptcy
1945–1950	− 15.8	+ 28.1	− 44.4	− 6.1	− 52.9
1950–1955	+ 9.4	4.1	+ 105.0	− 6.5	+ 12.5
1955–1960	+ 17.1	+ 11.8	− 17.1	− 10.2	− 22.2
1960–1965	+ 39.0	+ 62.4	+ 85.3	+ 61.4	+ 57.1
1965–1970	+ 33.3	+ 71.0	+ 106.3	+ 49.3	− 9.1
1970–1975	+ 39.5	+ 27.5	+ 49.2	+ 30.2	+ 10.0
1975–1980	+ 22.6	+ 48.8	− 0.5	+ 47.8	+ 54.5
1980–1985	+ 2.3	+ 57.4	+ 8.3	+ 38.2	+ 158.8

Data derived from the Annual Reports of the Administrative Office of the United States and the Statistical Abstract of the United States.

than private civil (27.5%) and U.S. civil (30.2%) filings between 1970–1975.* Private civil, U.S. civil, and bankruptcy filings outpace administrative appeals from 1975 to 1985.

Over the past fifteen years, when reformers claim there has been significant increase in regulatory litigation, the smallest increase in appellate filing has been in administrative appeals. Administrative appeals increased 75% from 1970 to 1985, compared with a 340% increase in bankruptcy; 199% increase in private civil; 166% increase in U.S. civil; and 79% increase in criminal appeals. Lows as the increase was during these years, it begins to level off almost entirely between 1980 and 1985 with a growth rate that constitutes the smallest increase in appellate filings of any category (2%). . . .

Rather than sharp increases in regulatory litigation there appears to be a redistribution of cases within the circuit courts and a concentration of regulatory litigation in one particular circuit—the D.C. Circuit. Procedural changes in agency rulemaking and judicial review are less likely explanations for this shift,

however, than are jurisdictional changes or changes in the organization of the regulatory bar.

Over the past fifteen years regulatory litigation has actually declined as a percentage of cases filed in the U.S. Courts of Appeals (see Figure 7.2). In 1940, administrative appeals constituted 23% of the cases filed in the circuit courts; in 1985, administrative appeals constitute 10% of the cases filed. From 1955 to 1960, administrative appeals increased slightly from 16% to 19%; then, by 1965 they dropped back to 16% of the circuit court's docket. Since 1960 a slow decline continues in administrative appeals as a percentage of the total appellate courts' filings. . . .

Has judicial support for agency decision weakened over the past fifteen years? Are the courts reversing more agency decisions and thus perhaps encouraging more appeals? We do not have data on the percentage of agency decisions appealed, but we do have data on how the circuit courts treat those cases that are appealed. Table 7.2 shows the disposition of administrative appeals in the U.S. Courts of Appeals, 1945–1985. On the average, the circuit courts affirm 73% of agency decisions during this forty year period. The highest level of support for agency decision was in 1970 (79%); the lowest level of support was in 1955 (66%). The range of fluctuation in support levels over this period is not great, and certainly there appears to be no significant deviation from the norm or average over the past fifteen years. . . . Here we also find that the circuit courts provide stability if not legitimacy for agency rules.

*The growth in administrative appeals between 1970 and 1975 might be attributed to the establishment of new regulatory agencies such as the EPA and OSHA in this period. Initial challenges of agency authority and decisionmaking procedures are common ways of shaping agency practices (Shapiro, 1968). Thus, following the creation of new agencies, such as those in the 1970s, we would expect an increase in legal activity. The Administrative Office data categorizes appeals from these new agencies as "other" until 1976.

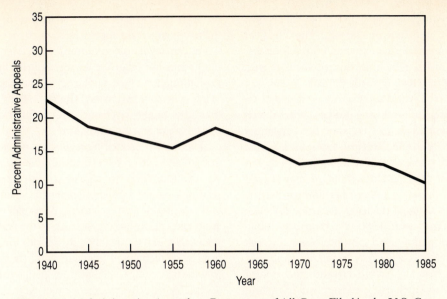

Figure 7.2   Administrative Appeals as Percentage of All Cases Filed in the U.S. Courts of Appeals: 1940–1985

Table 7.2   Disposition of Administrative Appeals in the U.S. Courts of Appeals, 1945–1985*

Year	Total Cases Disposed	Without Hearing	With Hearing	With Hearing Affirmed	Reversed	Dismissed
1945	566	185	381	297 (78%)	81 (21%)	3 (1%)
1950	541	169	372	273 (74%)	77 (21%)	15 (4%)
1955	523	150	373	247 (66%)	107 (29%)	13 (3%)
1960	660	299	361	258 (71%)	91 (25%)	4 (1%)
1965	866	377	489	367 (75%)	95 (19%)	7 (1%)
1970	1248	584	664	527 (79%)	103 (16%)	16 (2%)
1975	1553	874	679	474 (70%)	146 (22%)	37 (5%)
1980	2210	1217	993	662 (67%)	222 (22%)	53 (5%)
1985	2485	1229	1256	953 (76%)	141 (11%)	57 (5%)

Data derived from the Annual Reports of the Administrative Office. Few cases are categorized as "other," and therefore have been excluded from this table

IV. The Political Economy of Regulatory Negotiation

The contemporary reform movement creates a picture of regulatory litigation that is not supported by an empirical study of litigation rates. The pace of regulatory litigation has not increased sharply in the last fifteen years nor has judicial support for agency rules weakened. These findings provide us with a socio-legal context for analyzing the construction of a regulatory litigation "crisis" and the constitution of new regulatory relations through dispute processing reform. That is, rather than conclude that these findings identify a fundamental flaw in the logic of regulatory negotiation, I argue that from the empirical study of regulatory litigation we identify the conception of law which underlies this reform. The "crisis" in regulatory litigation is constructed from a formalist conception of law which, in this instance, equates conventional rulemaking with the rule of law.

For example, hybrid rulemaking is treated as an adversarial litigation-inducing process, rather than a resource that may in fact enhance the bargaining power of certain parties. Recourse to litigation, which became more viable with the development of hybrid rulemaking and the hard look standard, may expand the terms of disputing rather than limit or narrow the process to a formal challenge of agency rules (see Mather and Yngvesson, 1980–81). From a sociological view of disputing and dispute processing, the lack of sharp increases in regulatory litigation over the last fifteen years may be attributed to the expansion of dispute options with the development of hybrid rulemaking including settlement to avoid litigation. This formalist concept of law and the "crisis" of regulatory litigation organizes new "markets," new arenas of competition, for regulatory policymaking (see Hurst, 1982) under the guise of a new partnership between the state and private interests.

A. COMMUNICATION IN THE MARKET. Why does this anti-adversarial campaign persist in the face of regulatory politics that call for a turn away from an expansionist state through deregulation? On the one hand, anti-adversarial processes for administrative rulemaking and deregulation both minimize state intervention. Yet, attacks on regulatory litigation focus on the need for more direct participation by interested parties. Traditional rulemaking came under attack in the late 1970s. The attack focused on social regulation and targeted "its economic inefficiency in failing to discriminate between low-cost and high-cost compliance activity" (Rabin, 1986: 1318; also see Breyer, 1982; Derthick and Quirk, 1985). Advocates of regulatory negotiation built on this critique, but emphasized procedural inefficiencies accompanying social regulation rather than the substance of what was being regulated. The anti-regulation mood of the late 1970s was directed at administrative activity that went beyond the policing model. If deregulation is

no more than a "preference for the less intrusive of the two mainstream approaches that characterize the American regulatory tradition—a preference for a ubiquitous but relatively narrow policing model of regulation over a mixed policing-cartelization system of administrative governance" (Rabin, 1986: 1318–19), then how might we characterize the political economy of regulatory negotiation?

The market created by regulatory negotiation is not an "alternative" to regulation; rather it applies a very traditional view of regulation to new regulatory relations—social regulation. There are many points in the conventional regulatory process where negotiation takes place, linking tradition to the reform. We know that parties create opportunities for negotiation by challenging a regulation and then offering to withdraw their challenge in exchange for a more acceptable rule that the agency will agree to publish as their proposed rule. This type of negotiation, called "sequential negotiation," has been characterized as more adversarial than regulatory negotiation. Regulatory negotiation is bargaining that is explicitly structured to work toward accommodating differences before a formal rule challenge is made. Regulatory negotiation, may complement existing rulemaking practices by emphasizing negotiation prior to setting an agency rule,* but does it change the political philosophy of agency regulation?

Underlying the argument for regulatory negotiation is an old image of the market. That image is one of the state withdrawing from its regulatory role as a welfare state so that the self-balancing market sys-

---

*Proposals for early "settlement" procedures, such as regulatory negotiation, may add another layer to "an already too protracted process" (Gaba, 1985: 111). Will the use of a private facilitator/mediator create additional delays and more bureaucracy? What assurances are there that all interested parties will have the opportunity to participate? Once time and resources have been expended to convene the parties, some of them, including the agency, may reject the rule, thus wasting scarce resources. Finally, there is even the possibility that the courts will strike down the rule for failing to meet the "hard look" test. Some have also argued that regulatory negotiation may actually increase the role of appellate courts by requiring them to determine who the interested parties are, what form of participation is appropriate, and what procedural rule will govern the consensus process (Wald, 1985: 24).

tem can reassert itself. Rather than speak directly about markets, however, the language of regulatory negotiation is about communications between the parties. The market-place of ideas, as it were, malfunctions in an adversarial rulemaking setting because it produces distorted dialogue—dialogue between lawyers who make "flat arguments for extreme positions based on defensive research" (Harter, 1982: 22). The adversarial process is criticized for not giving the parties an opportunity to communicate directly with one another.

B. RULEMAKING IN THE MINIMALIST STATE. The vision of state-market relations is one in which self-balancing incentives operate to express and accommodate conflict and overcome private and public coercion. Voluntary compliance is the primary goal to be strengthened with this regulatory reform. The state becomes one of the interested parties in regulatory negotiation because it is seen as being too biased to police effectively the market and achieve high levels of voluntary compliance. A private mediator, instead, plays the policing role of facilitating a consensus among the parties—a consensus on voluntary compliance.

Regulatory negotiation may not articulate a strong anti-statist stance, but elements of anti-statism are evident in the negotiator's role. The traditional model of regulation is concerned with controlling agency discretion and protecting private interests from unwarranted government intrusion. Regulatory negotiation appears to be a strategy of this sort. Yet, once an agency commits itself to the negotiation process, its role changes from "umpire" to interested party and the state's role in the process also changes. From the point negotiations begin, political legitimacy derives not from the accountability of public authorities or even from the publicness of the process; instead, the process of sharing in making the "ultimate judgement" about the rules is said to provide political legitimacy to regulatory negotiation.

The model of regulatory negotiation, according to its proponents, reconciles the tension in democratic theory between public accountability and private interests. It does so by returning to a minimalist theory of the state. The process for expressing and managing political demands is supposed to replicate an idealized version of interest representation, while it is also more democratic and more efficient. By inviting affected groups to negotiate rules, we are told, the agency replicates a social microcosm, or the interest balancing process that underlies current rulemaking procedures (Comment, 1981).

The minimalist state and interest group theory are familiar combinations in American politics. Together they constitute a laissez-faire theory of the economy and a pluralist image of politics. In regulatory negotiation, groups advance their claims not only to the state but to all other groups participating in rulemaking. This produces a notion of "balancing interests" that is very similar to the market notion of economic exchange—each group receives some of what it wants in negotiation (win-win outcome), but no group receives everything (win-lose outcome). Interest representation has long been part of the politics of dispute processing reform and American politics. Theodore Lowi described "interest group liberalism" as a theory of interest representation in his analysis of post-New Deal public philosophy (1979). Lowi argued that the model of interest group liberalism rested on the following assumptions: 1) all interests are organized; 2) organized interests have representatives who answer and check other organized groups; and 3) the state insures access to organized groups and ratifies the "agreements and adjustments worked out among the competing leaders" (*Ibid.*, 51). He further noted that interest group liberalism resembled the pluralist model of modern political science. The assumptions of this model have been subject to considerable criticism within political science over the past two decades. Most significantly, critics of pluralism argue that organized groups do not compete among themselves, as assumed by the market theory of the economy. Instead, the most powerful groups have institutionalized their interests by forming a partnership with the state (Kariel, 1961; McConnell, 1966; Lowi, 1979).

Social movement litigation strategies were employed by public interest law reformers in the 1970s to remedy "institutionalized pluralism" (Handler,

1978). Advocacy representation was the principal method they adopted for redistributing resources to social-reform groups. This method was used in the regulatory arena as well as the courts. Although reformers such as Ralph Nader criticized regulatory capture for resembling institutionalized pluralism, the political philosophy of interest representation was retained by the public interest law movement.* Law reformers sought to use legal advocacy in effect to make pluralism work.

Regulatory negotiation is another interest representation approach to making pluralism work. It differs from the social-reform litigation approach in its return to the informal bargaining style of interest group liberalism. Regulatory negotiation seems to reproduce what Lowi and others so forcefully criticized interest group liberalism for—substituting an informal process for meaningful political debate over the values of regulation. For example, Susskind and McMahon's description of two cases where regulatory negotiation was used to develop EPA rules glorifies the process of consensus building, but says little about the issues in dispute or the substantive outcomes of the dispute process (1985). Indeed, Judge Patricia Wald of the District of Columbia Circuit Court of Appeals has argued that negotiated regulation may subvert the substantive policy goals of regulation since the consensus of "agreed-upon rules might not be a reasonable product of the original statute" (1985:22).

Regulatory negotiation does not, however, replicate all aspects of interest group liberalism. It cannot be said of this reform, as Lowi said of interest group liberalism, that "the role of government is one of insuring access to the most effectively organized, and

of ratifying the agreements and adjustments worked out among the competing leaders"(1979: 51). The repudiation of New Deal regulation during the Public Interest era may have transformed the role of agencies from "expert" to umpire. However, regulatory negotiation does not simply shift the role of agencies as third party intervenor from umpire to facilitator, it puts a private party into what was formerly a public position. Under this arrangement, the state relinquishes the more direct policing role of interest group liberalism. The parties, including the state, become the "experts" controlling regulatory discretion over public policy.

Regulatory negotiation reconstitutes the public philosophy of interest group liberalism in a theory of political legitimacy associated with a minimalist state. I have argued that regulatory negotiation does not reproduce all aspects of the market theory of the economy and a pluralist image of democratic politics. With the replacement of the state's role as third-party intervenor by a private mediator, regulatory negotiation is not simply a return to interest group liberalism. . . . State power, expressed as the authority to exercise agency discretion, is not removed from the regulatory process. It would be a mistake to ignore the extent to which regulatory negotiation depends on the state for legitimacy. And it would be a mistake to overlook the indirect rule of the state through the accommodation of [private interests]. The silence of the state is an expression of state power and an aspect of a minimalist state that has not been identified in earlier critiques of interest group pluralism and the accompanying call for "juridical democracy" (e.g., see Lowi, 1979).

*Private interests have always played some role in the regulatory process. Both liberals and conservatives have tolerated, and at times even encouraged, the delegation of power to private parties. Yet agency dependency on private interest has also been troubling for both liberals and conservatives. In a capitalist democracy, agency dependency is politically ambiguous. On the one hand, it is encouraged. Power is delegated to interested and affected private parties allowing them to participate in making public policy. On the other hand, agency dependency on private interests cuts against the public interest mission of many agencies. The counter-capture reforms of the 1970s sought to reorganize agency discretion and limit dependency on industry regulated interests. Their approach to curbing agency dependency, however, turned toward an even more expansive role for private interests.

References

ADMINISTRATIVE OFFICE OF THE UNITED STATES: *Reports of the Annual Meetings* (various years). Washington, D.C.

BRIGHAM, J. 1987a. *The Cult of the Court.* Philadelphia: Temple University Press.

BRIGHAM, J. 1987b. "Right, Rage, and Remedy: Forms of Law in Political Discourse," in *Studies in American Political Development.* Vol. 2. New Haven: Yale University Press.

BREYER, S. 1982. *Regulation and Its Reform.* Cambridge: Harvard University Press.

CAIN, M. 1983. "Where Are the Disputes?: A Study of the First Instance Civil Court in the U.K.," in M. Cain and

K. Kulcsan (eds.) *Disputes and the Law*. Budapest: Akademiai Kiado.

COMMENT. 1981. "Rethinking Regulation: Negotiation as an Alternative to Traditional Rulemaking," *Harvard Law Review* 99: 1871.

DERTHICK, M. and P. J. QUIRK. 1985. *The Politics of Deregulation*. Washington, D.C.: The Brookings Institution.

DIVER, C. S. 1981. "Policymaking Paradigms in Administrative Law," *Harvard Law Review* 95: 393.

FISS, O. 1984. "Against Settlement," *Yale Law Journal* 93: 1073.

FUNSTON, R. 1974. "Judicialization of the Administrative Process," *American Politics Quarterly* 2: 38.

GABA, J. M. 1985. "Internal Rulemaking by Settlement Agreement," *Georgetown Law Journal* 73:1241.

GORDON, R.W. 1983. "Legal Thought and Legal Practice in the Age of American Enterprise, 1870–1920," in G. Gelson (ed.) *Professions and Professional Ideologies in America*. Chapel Hill: University of North Carolina Press.

HANDLER J. F. 1978. *Social Movements and the Legal System*. New York: Academic Press.

HARTER, P. J. 1982. "Negotiating Regulations: A Cure for Malaise," *Georgetown Law Journal* 71: 1.

HARTER, P. J. 1984. "Status Report on Project on 'The Uses of Alternative Means of Dispute Resolution in the Administrative Process'," Memorandum to Committee on Administration of the Administrative Conference of the U.S., Washington, D.C., November 19, 1984.

HUNT, A. 1985. "The Ideology of Law: Advances and Problems in Recent Applications of the Concept of Ideology to the Analysis of Law," *Law & Society Review* 9: 11.

HURST, J. W. 1982. *Law and Markets in United States History: Different Modes of Bargaining Among Interests*. Madison: University of Wisconsin.

KARIEL, H. S. 1961. *The Decline of American Pluralism*. Stanford: Stanford University Press.

KRITZER, H. M. 1986. "Adjudication to Settlement: Shading in the Gray," *Judicature* 70: 161.

LOWI, T. J. 1979. *The End of Liberalism*. 2nd ed. New York: W.W. Norton & Company.

MCCANN, M. W. 1986. *Taking Reform Seriously: Perspectives on Public Interest Liberalism*. Ithaca: Cornell University Press.

MCCONNELL, G. 1966. *Private Power and American Democracy*. New York: Vintage Books.

PROVINE, M. D. 1986. "Managing Negotiated Justice: Settlement Procedures in the Courts," prepared for the Conference on Judicial Administration Research Rockefeller College, State University of New York at Albany, June 16–18, 1986.

RABIN, R. L. 1986. "Federal Regulation in Historical Perspective," *Stanford Law Review* 38: 1189.

RESNIK, J. 1982. "Managerial Judges," *Harvard Law Review* 96: 374.

SEIDMAN, H. and R. GILMOUR 1986. *Politics, Position, and Power: from the Positive to the Regulatory State*. 4th ed. New York: Oxford University Press.

SHAPIRO, M. 1968. *The Supreme Court and Administrative Agencies*. New York: Free Press.

STEWART, R. B. 1985. "The Discontents of Legalism: Interest Group Relations in Administrative Regulation," *Wisconsin Law Review* 1985: 655.

SUSSKIND, L. and G. MCMAHON. 1985. "The Theory and Practice of Negotiated Rulemaking," *The Yale Journal of Regulation* 3: 133.

WALD, P. M. 1985. "Negotiation of Environmental Disputes: A New Role for the Courts?" *Columbia Journal of Environmental Law* 10:1.

Will the recent political shift toward deregulation change the law governing administrative procedure? We conclude this chapter by discussing the effect of deregulation on agency rulemaking procedures. Under the Reagan administration we witnessed several efforts by federal regulatory agencies to implement the philosophy of deregulation. In *Motor Vehicle Manufactures Assn. v. State Farm Mutual Automobile Ins. Co.* (1983), the Supreme Court held that the National Highway Traffic Safety Administration (NHTSA) could not carry out its policy agenda of deregulation by discarding rules NHTSA had made, requiring manufacturers to install air bags in cars, without going through a rulemaking process. This case demonstrates how changing political perspectives on regulation can affect agency rulemaking procedures. After you read *Motor Vehicle Manufacturers Assn. v. State Farm Mutual Automobile Ins. Co.*, you will have been exposed to a wide range of political perspectives on agency rulemaking procedures—ranging from the public interest movement's push for hybrid rulemaking to the Reagan administration's efforts to rescind rules in order to implement such new policies as deregulation. All these cases and commentary on the legal and political dimensions of the administrative policymaking process implicitly ask: how does agency rulemaking function to democratize the regulatory process? If a new regime comes to Washington and advocates deregulation, should administrative procedures conform to those policy goals?

Handwritten margin notes: Public agencies must be bound by their own rules. Why did the agency change its mind?

Motor Vehicles Manufacturers Association v. State Farm Mutual Automobile Insurance Co.

103 S. Ct. 2856 (1983) 5–4
+　　Brennan, White, Marshall, Blackmun, Stevens
+/–　Burger, Powell, Rehnquist, O'Connor

[The National Highway Traffic Safety Act of 1966 directs the Secretary of Transportation to issue motor vehicle safety standards that "shall be practicable, shall meet the need for motor vehicle safety, and shall be stated in objective terms." After numerous rulemaking notices, NHTSA established a rule requiring new motor vehicles produced after September 1982 to be equipped with "passive restraints," such as seatbelts. In 1981, NHTSA rescinded the requirement. Insurance companies petitioned for review of the rescinding order.]

Justice White delivered the opinion of the Court.

The development of the automobile gave Americans unprecedented freedom to travel, but exacted a high price for enhanced mobility. Since 1929, motor vehicles have been the leading cause of accidental deaths and injuries in the United States. In 1982, 46,300 Americans died in motor vehicle accidents and hundreds of thousands more were maimed and injured. While a consensus exists that the current loss of life on our highways is unacceptably high, improving safety does not admit to easy solution. In 1966, Congress decided that at least part of the answer lies in improving the design and safety features of vehicle itself. But much of the technology for building safer cars was undeveloped or untested. . . . This task called for considerable expertise and Congress responded by enacting the National Traffic and Motor Vehicle Safety Act of 1966 (Act). . . . The Act, created for the purpose of "reduc[ing] traffic accidents and deaths and injuries to persons resulting from traffic accidents," . . .

The Act . . . authorizes judicial review under the provisions of the Administrative Procedure Act (APA) . . . of all "orders establishing, amending, or revoking a Federal motor vehicle safety standard," . . . Under this authority, we review today whether NHTSA acted arbitrarily and capriciously in revoking the requirement in Motor Vehicle Standard 208 that new motor vehicles produced after September 1982 be equipped with passive restraints to protect the safety of the occupants of the vehicle in the event of a collision. Briefly summarized, we hold that the agency failed to present an adequate basis and explanation for rescinding the passive restraint requirement and that the agency must either consider the matter further or adhere to or amend Standard 208 along lines which its analysis supports.

I

The regulation whose rescission is at issue bears a complex and convoluted history. Over the course of approximately 60 rulemaking notices, the requirement has been imposed, amended, rescinded, reimposed, and now rescinded again.

As originally issued by the Department of Transportation in 1967, Standard 208 simply required the installation of seatbelts in all automobiles. . . . It soon became apparent that the level of seatbelt use was too low to reduce traffic injuries to an acceptable level. The Department therefore began consideration of "passive occupant restraint systems"– devices that do not depend for their effectiveness upon any action taken by the occupant except that necessary to operate the vehicle. Two types of automatic crash protection emerged: automatic seatbelts and airbags. The automatic seatbelt is a traditional safety belt, which when fastened to the interior of the door remains attached without impeding entry or exit from the vehicle, and deploys automatically without any action on the part of the passenger. The airbag is an inflatable device concealed in the dashboard and steering column. It automatically inflates when a sensor indicates that deceleration forces from an accident have exceeded a preset minimum, then rapidly deflates to dissipate those forces. The lifesaving potential of these devices was immediately recognized, and in 1977, after substantial on-the-road experience with both devices, it was estimated by NHTSA that passive restraints could prevent approximately 12,000 deaths and over 100,000 serious injuries annually. . . .

In 1969, the Department formally imposed a standard requiring the installation of passive restraints, . . . thereby commencing a lengthy series of proceedings. In 1970, the agency revised Standard 208 to include passive protection requirements, and in 1972, the agency amended the Standard to require full passive protection for all front seat occupants of vehicles manufactured after August 15, 1975. . . . On review, the agency's decision to require passive restraints was found to be supported by "substantial evidence" and upheld. *Chrysler Corp. v. Department of Transportation,* 472 F.2d 659 (CA6 1972).

In preparing for the upcoming model year, most cars makers chose the "ignition interlock" option, a decision which was highly unpopular, and led Congress to amend the Act to prohibit a motor vehicle safety standard from requiring or permitting compliance by means of an ignition interlock or a continuous buzzer designed to indicate that safety belts were not in use. . . . The 1974 Amendments also provided that any safety standard that could be satisfied by a system other than seatbelts would have to be submitted to Congress where it could be vetoed by concurrent resolution of both Houses. . . .

The effective date for mandatory passive restraint systems was extended for a year until August 31, 1976. . . . But in June 1976, Secretary of Transportation William T. Coleman Jr., initiated a new rulemaking on the issue. . . . After hearing testimony and reviewing written comments, Coleman extended the optional alternatives indefinitely and suspended the passive restraint requirement. Although he found passive restraints technologically and economically feasible, the Secretary based his decision on the expectation that there would be widespread public resistance to the new systems. He instead proposed a demonstration project involving up to 500,000 cars installed with passive restraints, in order to smooth the way for public acceptance of mandatory passive restraints at a later date. . . .

Coleman's successor as Secretary of Transportation disagreed. Within months of assuming office, Secretary Brock Adams decided that the demonstration project was unnecessary. He issued a new mandatory passive restraint regulation, known as Modified Standard 208 [1977]. . . . The Modified Standard mandated the phasing in of passive restraints beginning with large cars in model year 1982 and extending to all cars by model year 1984. The two principal systems that would satisfy the Standard were airbags and passive belts; the choice of which system to install was left to the manufacturers. . . . The Standard also survived scrutiny by Congress, which did not exercise its authority under the legislative veto provision of the 1974 Amendments.

Over the next several years, the automobile industry geared up to comply with Modified Standard 208. . . .

In February 1981, however, Secretary of Transportation Andrew Lewis reopened the rulemaking due to changed economic circumstances and, in particular, the difficulties of the automobile industry. . . . Two months later, the agency ordered a one-year delay in the application of the Standard to large cars, extending the deadline to September 1982, . . . and at the same time, proposed the possible rescission of the entire Standard. . . . After receiving written comments and holding public hearings, NHTSA issued a final rule (Notice 25) that rescinded the passive restraint requirement contained in Modified Standard 208.

II

In a statement explaining the rescission, NHTSA maintained that it was no longer able to find, as it had in 1977, that the automatic restraint requirement would produce significant safety benefits. . . . This judgment reflected not a change of opinion on the effectiveness of the technology, but a change in plans by the automobile industry. In 1977, the agency had assumed that airbags would be installed in 60% of all new cars and automatic seatbelts in 40%. By 1981 it became apparent that automobile manufacturers planned to install the automatic seatbelts in approximately 99% of the new cars. For this reason, the lifesaving potential of airbags would not be realized. Moreover, it now appeared that the overwhelming majority of passive belts planned to be installed by manufacturers could be detached easily and left that way permanently. . . .

State Farm Mutual Automobile Insurance Co. and the National Association of Independent Insurers filed petitions for review of NHTSA's rescission of the passive restraint Standard. The United States Court of Appeals for the District of Columbia Circuit held that the agency's rescission of the passive restraint requirement was arbitrary and capricious. . . . 680 F.2d 206 (1982). While observing that rescission is not unrelated to an agency's refusal to take action in the first instance, the court concluded that, in this case, NHTSA's discretion to rescind the passive restraint requirement had been restricted by various forms of congressional "reaction" to the passive restraint issue. . . .

III

Unlike the Court of Appeals, we do not find the appropriate scope of judicial review to be the "most troublesome question" in these cases. Both the Act and the 1974 Amendments concerning occupant crash protection standards indicate that motor vehicle safety standards are to be promulgated under the informal rulemaking procedures of the Administrative Procedure Act. 5 U.S.C. § 553. The agency's action in promulgating such standards therefore may be set aside if found to be "arbitrary, capricious, an abuse of discretion, or otherwise not in accordance with law." . . . *Citizens to Preserve Overton Park v. Volpe*

401 U.S. 402. . . . (1971). . . . We believe that the rescission or modification of an occupant-protection standard is subject to the same test. . . .

Petitioner Motor Vehicle Manufacturers Association (MVMA) disagrees, contending that the rescission of an agency rule should be judged by the same standard a court could use to judge an agency's refusal to promulgate a rule in the first place—a standard petitioner believes considerably narrower than the traditional arbitrary-and-capricious test. We reject this view. The Act expressly equates orders "revoking" and "establishing" safety standards; neither that Act nor the APA suggests that revocations are to be treated as refusals to promulgate standards. Petitioner's view would render meaningless Congress' authorization for judicial review of orders revoking safety rules. Moreover, the revocation of an extant regulation is substantially different than a failure to act. Revocation constitutes a reversal of the agency's former views as to the proper course. . . . Accordingly, an agency changing its course by rescinding a rule is obligated to supply a reasoned analysis for the change beyond that which may be required when an agency does not act in the first instance.

In so holding, we fully recognize that "[r]egulatory agencies do not establish rules of conduct to last forever," *American Trucking Assns., Inc. v. Atchison, T. & S.F.R. Co.*, 387 U.S. 397 . . . (1967), and that an agency must be given ample latitude to "adapt their rules and policies to the demands of changing circumstances." *Permian Basin Area Rate Cases*, 390 U.S. 747. . . . But the forces of change do not always or necessarily point in the direction of deregulation. In the abstract, there is no more reason to presume that changing circumstances require the rescission of prior action, instead of a revision in or even the extension of current regulation. If Congress established a presumption from which judicial review should start, that presumption—contrary to petitioners' views—is not *against* safety regulation, but *against* changes in current policy that are not justified by the rulemaking record. . . .

. . . Normally, an agency rule would be arbitrary and capricious if the agency has relied on factors which Congress has not intended it to consider, entirely failed to consider an important aspect of the problem, offered an explanation for its decision that runs counter to the evidence before the agency, or is so implausible that it could not be ascribed to a difference in view or the product of agency expertise. The reviewing court should not attempt itself to make up for such deficiences; we may not supply a reasoned basis for the agency's action that the agency itself has not given. . . . For purposes of these cases, it is also relevant that Congress required a record of the rulemaking proceedings to be compiled and submitted to a reviewing court, . . . and intended that agency findings under the Act would be supported by "substantial evidence on the record considered as a whole." . . .

IV

The Court of Appeals correctly found that the arbitrary-and-capricious test applied to rescissions of prior agency regulations, but then erred in intensifying the scope of its review based upon its reading of legislative events. It held that congressional reaction to various versions of Standard 208 "raise[d] doubts" that NHTSA's rescission "necessarily demonstrates an effort to fulfill its statutory mandate," and therefore the agency was obligated to provide "increasingly clear and convincing reasons" for its action. . . .

This path of analysis was misguided and the inferences it produced are questionable . . . While an agency's interpretation of a statute may be confirmed or ratified by subsequent congressional failure to change that interpretation, . . . in the cases before us, even an unequivocal ratification—short of statutory incorporation—of the passive restraint standard would not connote approval or disapproval of an agency's later decision to rescind the regulation. That decision remains subject to the arbitrary-and-capricious standard. . . .

V

. . . The first and most obvious reason for finding the rescission arbitrary and capricious is that NHTSA apparently gave no consideration whatever to modifying the Standard to require that airbag technology be utilized. . . . Automatic belts were added as a means of complying with the Standard because they were believed to be as effective as airbags in achieving the goal of occupant crash protection. . . .

The agency has now determined that the detachable automatic belts will not attain anticipated safety benefits because so many individuals will detach the mechanism. Even if this conclusion were acceptable in its entirety, . . . standing alone it would not justify any more than an amendment of Standard 208 to disallow compliance by means of the one technology which will not provide effective passenger protection. It does not cast doubt on the need for a passive restraint standard or upon the efficacy of airbag technology. . . .

. . . At the very least this alternative way of achieving the objectives of the Act should have been addressed and adequate reasons given for its abandonment. But the agency not only did not require compliance through airbags, it also did not even consider the possibility in its 1981 rulemaking. Not one sentence of its rulemaking statement discusses the airbags-only option. . . . We have frequently reiterated that an agency must cogently explain why it has exercised its discretion in a given manner, and we reaffirm this principle again today.

The automobile industry has opted for the passive belt over the airbag, but surely it is not enough that the regulated industry has eschewed a given safety device. For nearly a decade, the automobile industry waged the regulatory equivalent of war against the airbag and lost—the inflatable restraint was proved sufficiently effective. Now the automobile industry has decided to employ a seatbelt system which will not meet the safety objectives of Standard 208. This hardly constitutes cause to revoke the Standard itself. Indeed, the Act was necessary because the industry was not sufficiently responsive to safety concerns. The Act intended that safety standards not depend on current technology and could be "technology-forcing" in the sense of inducing the development of superior safety design. . . .

Petitioners also invoke our decision in *Vermont Yankee Nuclear Power Corp. v. Natural Resources Defense Council, Inc.*, 435 U.S. 519 . . . (1978), as though it were a talisman under which any agency decision is by definition unimpeachable. Specifically, it is submitted that to require an agency to consider an airbags-only alternative is, in essence, to dictate to the agency the procedures it is to follow. Petitioners both misread

Vermont Yankee and misconstrue the nature of the remand that is in order. In *Vermont Yankee*, we held that a court may not impose additional procedural requirements upon an agency. We do not require today any specific procedures which NHTSA must follow. Nor do we broadly require an agency to consider all policy alternatives in reaching decision. It is true that rulemaking "canot be found wanting simply because the agency failed to include every alternative device and thought conceivable by the mind of man . . . regardless of how uncommon or unknown that alternative may have been. . . ." *Id.*, at 551. . . . But the airbag is more than a policy alternative to the passive restraint Standard; it is a technological alternative within the ambit of the existing Standard. We hold only that given the judgment made in 1977 that airbags are an effective and cost-beneficial lifesaving technology, the mandatory passive restraint rule may not be abandoned without any consideration whatsoever of an airbags-only requirement. . . .

In these cases, the agency's explanation for rescission of the passive restraint requirement is *not* sufficient to enable us to conclude that the rescission was the product of reasoned decisionmaking. To reach this conclusion, we do not upset the agency's view of the facts, but we do appreciate the limitations of this record in supporting the agency's decision. We start with the accepted ground that if used, seatbelts unquestionably would save many thousands of lives and would prevent tens of thousands of crippling injuries. Unlike recent regulatory decisions we have reviewed, *Industrial Union Dept. v. American Petroleum Institute*, 448 U.S. 607 . . . (1980); *American Textile Mfrs. Institute, Inc. v. Donovan*, 452 U.S. 490 . . . (1981), the safety benefits of wearing seatbelts are not in doubt, and it is not challenged that were those benefits to accrue, the monetary costs of implementing the Standard would be easily justified. We move next to the fact that there is no direct evidence in support of the agency's finding that detachable automatic belts cannot be predicted to yield a substantial increase in usage. The empirical evidence on the record, consisting of surveys of drivers of automobiles equipped with passive belts, reveals more than a doubling of the usage rate experienced with manual belts. Much of the agency's rulemaking statement—and much of the controversy in these cases—centers on the conclusions that should be drawn from these studies. The agency maintained that the doubling of seatbelt usage in these studies could not be extrapolated to an across-the-board mandatory standard because the passive seatbelts were guarded by ignition interlocks and purchasers of the tested cars are somewhat atypical. Respondents insist these studies demonstrate that Modified Standard 208 will substantially increase seatbelt usage. We believe that it is within the agency's discretion to pass upon the generalizability of these field studies. This is precisely the type of issue which rests within the expertise of NHTSA, and upon which a reviewing court must be most hesitant to intrude.

But accepting the agency's view of the field tests on passive restraints indicates only that there is no reliable real-world experience that usage rates will substantially increase. . . .

The agency is correct to look at the costs as well as the benefits of Standard 208. The agency's conclusion that the incremental costs of the requirements were no longer reasonable was predicated on its prediction that the safety benefits of the regulation might be minimal. Specifically, the agency's fears that the public may resent paying more for the automatic belt systems is expressly dependent on the assumption that detachable automatic belts will not produce more than "negligible safety benefits." *Id.*, at 53424. When the agency reexamines its findings as to the likely increase in seatbelt usage, it must also reconsider its judgment of the reasonableness of the monetary and other costs associated with the Standard. In reaching its judgment, NHTSA should bear in mind that Congress intended safety to be the pre-eminent factor under the Act. . . .

By failing to analyze the continuous seatbelts option in its own right, the agency has failed to offer the rational connection between facts and judgment required to pass muster under the arbitrary-and-capricious standard. . . . While the agency is entitled to change its view on the acceptability of continuous passive belts, it is obligated to explain its reasons for doing so.

... Accordingly, we vacate the judgment of the Court of Appeals and remand the case to that court with directions to remand the matter to the NHTSA for further consideration consistent with this opinion.

So ordered.

Justice Rehnquist, with whom the Chief Justice Burger, Justice Powell, and Justice O'Connor join, concurring in part and dissenting in part.

I join Parts I, II, III, IV, and V-A of the Court's opinion. In particular, I agree that, since the airbag and continuous spool automatic seatbelt were explicitly approved in the Standard the agency was rescinding, the agency should explain why it declined to leave those requirements intact. In this case, the agency gave no explanation at all. Of course, if the agency can provide a rational explanation, it may adhere to its decision to rescind the entire Standard.

I do not believe, however, that NHTSA's view of detachable automatic seatbelts was arbitrary and capricious. The agency adequately explained its decision to rescind the Standard insofar as it was satisfied by detachable belts. . . .

. . . The agency chose not rely on a study showing a substantial increase in seatbelt usage in cars equipped with automatic seatbelts *and* an ignition interlock to prevent the car from being operated when the belts were not in place *and* which were voluntarily purchased with this equipment by consumers. . . . It is reasonable for the agency to decide that this study does not support any conclusion concerning the effect of automatic seatbelts that are installed in all cars whether the consumer wants them or not and are not linked to an ignition interlock system. . . .

. . . The agency's changed view of the standard seems to be related to the election of a new President [Reagan] of a different political party [Republican]. It is readily apparent that the responsible members of one administration may consider public resistance and uncertainties to be more important than do their counterparts in a previous administration. A change in administration brought about by the people casting their votes is a perfectly reasonable basis for an executive agency's reappraisal of the costs and benefits of its programs and regulations. As long as the agency remains within the bounds established by Congress,* it is entitled to assess administrative records and evaluate priorities in light of the philosophy of the administration.

---

*Of course, a new administration may not choose not to enforce laws of which it does not approve, or to ignore statutory standards in carrying out its regulatory functions. But in this case, as the Court correctly concludes, *ante*, at 2867–2868, Congress has not required the agency to require passive restraints.

Exercises and Questions for Further Thought

1. Review one more time the *Morgan* case in chapter 2. Suppose the case arose under the modern APA but the other statutory law was the same. Suppose further that the Secretary of Agriculture announced a new set of prices after section 553 notice and comment hearings only. If the packers challenged the procedure, how would Justice Rehnquist rule? Does his statement in the rail car leasing case necessarily reveal how he would decide that issue, particularly after his opinion in *Vermont Yankee?*

2. Suppose a state liquor agency determined by rule that no liquor store could remain open after 10:00 p.m. in any town containing a public college, junior college, or university. Suppose this state to be covered by the Model State Administrative Procedure Act in Appendix C. In what circumstances would ex parte communication be forbidden in this rulemaking? Start with section 13 and work back through the definitions you will need to solve this puzzle.

3. Consider the political characteristics and implications of Justice Rehnquist's positions in *Vermont Yankee* and his dissent in *Motor Vehicles Manufacturers Assn. v. State Farm Mutual Automobile Ins. Co.*, Justice Rehnquist is generally classified as a proponent of judicial self-restraint, and both of these decisions seek to reduce the oversight of the courts in the administrative process. But he is also by reputation a conservative, an Arizona Republican appointed by President Nixon. Is it not fair to say that both these decisions are pro-government? Can we best explain Justice Rehnquist's position by pointing out that free enterprise benefited by the policies he allows the agencies to pursue, or are other less ideological factors perhaps at work?

4. By statute the Federal Aviation Administration may suspend the license of any commercial airline pilot for safety's sake. The statute gives the pilot an opportunity to be heard first. The FAA also has power to issue "reasonable rules . . . to provide adequately for national security and safety in air commerce." Following only 553 rulemaking proceedings the Administrator, the one-man head of the FAA, issued a rule that automatically terminated the licenses of commercial pilots at the age of 60. The pilots brought suit claiming they had been denied their opportunity to be heard. The Administrator stated that the age of 60 was as defensible a cut-off as any and that the FAA did not have the resources to evaluate the health of every pilot frequently enough to catch the many health problems that crop up past that age. What decision should a court reach in this suit?[11]

5. It is a maxim of jurisprudence that legislation does not affect actions that occurred prior to the passage of the statute. That is, legislation is not applied retroactively. Should administrative rules be applied retroactively by the agencies that create them? Courts have permitted some retroactive applications and have used the familiar rubric of balancing costs and benefits. See *Tennessee Gas Pipeline Co. v. Federal Energy Regulation Commission*, 606 F.2d 1094 (1979).

[11] See *Air Line Pilots Association v. Quesada*, 276 F.2d 892 (1960).

CHAPTER 8

Enforcement of Administrative Policy

This chapter completes the book's description of the actions and processes common to administrative governance. Enforcement is the last step an agency can take to achieve its policy goals. Any remaining changes in policy or action will occur in the courts in the course of judicial review of agency action, discussed in the next chapter. This chapter does not limit itself to a single focal point or theme. Some of the issues raised here have appeared with varying specificity in earlier chapters, and some, particularly enforcement through revocation and threat of revocation of licenses, will appear again later. This chapter seeks primarily to fill in descriptive details so students will be familiar with the routines of administrative action.

Administrative Law and the Problem of Compliance

The word *enforcement* evokes pictures of police officers with drawn guns using force itself to apprehend law violators and by this example to deter others from violating law in the future. To confine enforcement to the use of force would, however, cause us to miss most of the activities of the legal system that produce compliance with law. In administrative law we must begin by broadening the concept of enforcement to include the full array of administrative actions that encourage compliance with statutory policy created by the legislature, compliance with rules made by agencies, and compliance with adjudicatory outcomes directed at individual parties. These three levels of compliance tend to succeed one another. That is, to the extent statutory policy or administrative rules are clear and complied with, adjudication (itself an enforcement process) becomes less likely. Thus the best introduction to enforcement begins with a brief review of compliance itself.

Compliance occurs when actions are consistent with legal commands. If a rule speaks generally or ambiguously in a policy area—and we have seen how and why many administrative statutes are general and ambiguous—it is not realistic to expect compliance because the rule provides no guide against which to test compliance's presence or absence. This is particularly true in much regulatory policy which, as we have seen, delegates to agencies the obligation to develop the rules of conduct specific enough to command compliance. Thus in administrative law, just as in criminal law or any body of rules, government policies can change social practices. The question naturally arises: Which kind of policies are more effective in producing high levels of compliance? As you might have guessed, the answer is contingent on a number of social factors (i.e., legal, political, and economic) that can vary from one regulatory context to another.[1] Here, in summary form, is a list of conditions that we often associate with different degrees of regulatory compliance. In some settings the significance of one condition, such as the power of the regulated parties, may be more important than the severity of the sanction in determining whether regulatory compliance will be high or low. As you read this list, think about the relationship between these conditions and consider the extent to which they may impact differently on different regulatory contexts.

1. *Rules.* Compliance varies with the following characteristics of rules:
   a. the clarity with which a rule describes the people covered by it;
   b. the clarity with which the rule assigns responsibility to specific individuals to enforce the rule;
   c. the clarity of the sanction imposed for noncompliance;
   d. the severity of the sanction.
2. *Enforcers.* Compliance varies with the following characteristics of those who enforce or implement a rule or policy:
   a. the extent to which enforcers in fact know it is their responsibility to enforce;
   b. the extent to which enforcers feel the command to enforce is legitimate and proper;
   c. the extent to which enforcers believe the command to enforce is consistent with their operational objectives as well as their personal objectives and ambitions;
   d. the capacity of enforcers to devote resources to the enforcement task.
3. *Beneficiaries.* Beneficiaries include consumers of products of regulated businesses. Often the general public benefits, as in the case of reduced air and water pollution. Compliance varies with the following characteristics of the beneficiaries of public policy:
   a. the extent to which beneficiaries perceive the benefits they receive and the amount of value they put on them;
   b. the resources beneficiaries possess to promote the enforcement process;
   c. the extent to which beneficiaries believe enforcers will listen to their specific complaints about instances of noncompliance.
4. *Regulated Parties.* Compliance varies with the following characteristics of those whose behavior the rule or policy seeks to affect:
   a. the extent to which the regulated perceive a command that requires or proscribes specific behaviors;
   b. the extent to which the regulated define the command as legitimate and proper;
   c. the extent to which the regulated lack resources to prevent detection and/or block enforcement;

---

[1]For a good introductions to the different perspectives on regulatory compliance see Deborah A. Stone, *Policy Paradox and Political Reason* (Glenview, Il: Scott, Foresman/Little, Brown, 1988). For work that addresses particular regulatory compliance problems, see Eugene Bardach and Robert A. Kagan, eds., *Social Regulation: Strategies for Reform* (San Francisco: Institute for Contemporary Studies, 1982).

d. the benefits to the regulated of noncompliance relative to the cost of the sanction if imposed;

e. the extent to which the regulated believe that a sanction will be applied once noncompliance has been detected.

These categories hardly exhaust the problem of enforcement and compliance.[2] They do, however, explain a satisfyingly large part of legal and illegal practices we observe in society. This compliance model helps us understand many of the phenomena we have already uncovered in administrative government. The Federal Trade Commission delayed for decades regulating through rulemaking because it doubted the legitimacy of the process (2b) and because consumer group beneficiaries were poorly organized (3a and 3b). You can explain the Nuclear Regulatory Commission's failure to police the South Texas Nuclear Project in terms of its resource shortages (2d and 4c & d), and so on.

The rest of this chapter focuses on three specific characteristics of enforcement implicit in the compliance model. These are the nature of sanctions (costs) that administrators can impose, the devices administrators may use short of formal adjudication or criminal prosecution to pressure people to comply, and the role of citizens in enforcing government policies through litigation.

The Nature of Administrative Sanctions

A sanction is a cost imposed for noncompliance. Section 551 (10) of the APA defines sanctions to include:

(A) prohibition, requirement, limitation, or other condition affecting the freedom of a person;

(B) withholding of relief;

(C) imposition of penalty or fine;

(D) destruction, taking, seizure, or withholding of property;

(E) assessment of damages, reimbursement, restitution, compensation, costs, charges, or fees;

(F) requirement, revocation, or suspension of a license; or

(G) taking other compulsory or restrictive action.

As the compliance model indicates, the nature and effectiveness of sanctions depend not so much on the label we put on the sanction as on the likelihood that it will be imposed for noncompliance and the hardship it imposes on the party. Whether oil shippers prevent oil spills more effectively depends on whether the Coast Guard's civil fine of a few hundred dollars, reduced by the fact that not all oil spills are detected and attributable, makes it profitable for the company to make the effort to reduce spills. Here are more illustrations of administrative sanctions.

[2]For an exhaustive treatment see F. Zimring and G. Hawkins, *Deterrence* (Chicago: University of Chicago Press, 1973).

Cutting Funds or Other Financial Aids

[handwritten margin note: Company could pass fine on to the consumer. There is a point at which the fine is too high to pass on.]

Cutting funds has been a major enforcement tool in areas, particularly education, that have grown to depend on federal support. Desegregation in many parts of the country, for example, occurred less because of Supreme Court rulings than because of the threat to withdraw educational funds.[3] In 1982 the Environmental Protection Agency threatened to cut off hundreds of millions of dollars of federal aid after finding that a dozen major United States cities had failed to comply with clean air laws. The cutoffs would occur through withholding future federal grants for construction of highways and sewers in Pittsburgh, Chicago, Houston, and other major cities. This was not the first time such a major cutoff occurred to enforce environmental rules. In 1980 the Carter administration cut off $850 million for eight communities that failed to create mandatory inspection programs for automobile pollution-control equipment.[4]

Loss of License

This sanction raises such a serious threat that it is covered in a separate chapter. Licenses range from the driver's permit, with which we are all familiar, to occupational, professional, and other business licenses. To operate without a license exposes the citizen in most cases to immediate criminal liability, which makes the sanction potentially effective *if,* as the compliance model suggests, the perceived risks of detection are reasonably high.

Administrative Fines

Administrative fines can be a serious financial threat. For example, in 1983 the NRC, with Congress's permission, sought to increase nuclear safety by levying six-figure fines.[5]

Criminal Sanctions

While agency actions rarely impose criminal penalties, these penalties always loom as a background threat. Even if an agency has no direct authority to seek criminal penalties in court, courts under their contempt power possess the authority to fine or jail those who refuse a court order to obey an agency. In some areas of policy the authorizing statutes prescribe criminal penalties for violations. This is true of one of our oldest regulatory policies, antitrust law, though the FTC and the justice department have, and usually prefer, the option of proceeding civilly in such cases. Similarly, most readers know that the IRS possesses the power to seek criminal penalties for tax fraud, as do the taxing authorities in the states. No agency can impose and enforce criminal penalties alone. Criminal penalties result only from proceedings in the regular courts.[6]

---

[3] See Rodgers and Bullock, *Coercion to Compliance* (Lexington, Mass.: Lexington Books, 1976).

[4] "EPA Threatens Cutoff of Road, Sewer Aid. . . . " *Wall Street Journal,* 5 April 1982, 5.

[5] "NRC Staff Proposes Boston Edison Pay Record $550,000 for Alleged Violations," *Wall Street Journal,* 20 January 1982, 17.

[6] For a discussion of the political barriers to imposing criminal penalties against corporations, see Marshall B. Clinard and Peter C. Yeager, *Corporate Crime* (New York: Free Press, 1980).

Economic Sanctions

In addition to the other sanctions listed in the Administrative Procedure Act (APA), above, agencies whose programs involve financial decisions can use economic sanctions to achieve policy aims. Thus the Carter administration made procurement policies a part of its inflation-reduction strategy. Agencies were exhorted not to purchase from those who had significantly raised prices. The late Department of Health, Education, and Welfare often made minority participation a prerequisite for receiving various community development funds. Finally, IRS has denied tax-exempt status to certain institutions, schools primarily, that practice racial segregation or otherwise offend public policy goals.

Administrative Enforcement Techniques

The detailed techniques of enforcement vary from agency to agency. To describe them in combination with all the available sanctions would require a book exclusively on enforcement. This description outlines the five most common forms.[7]

1. Consent Settlements

Prior to formal adjudication, and usually with the threat of adjudication looming, the parties negotiate a consent settlement. In a large agency such as the FTC, where the five commissioners do not themselves do the negotiating, the agency head or heads will review and tentatively accept, reject, or modify the settlement. The settlement is then communicated to all interested parties who have an opportunity to react informally to the tentative agreement. After a specified period the agreement becomes effective. At this point the agreement has all the legal effect of a formal order arising from adjudication. If a party to the agreement violates it in the future, the agency may seek summarily to impose penalties for violations.

Agencies benefit from consent settlements because they avoid the time and expense of adjudication but produce a legally binding result. The private parties also save time and money. Additionally they make no admission of formal violation and avoid the possible embarrassment of having a formal hearing find them in violation.

2. Advisory Opinions

When a party seeks information regarding the lawfulness of a proposed action, advisory opinions are used. Under certain conditions agencies adopt internal procedures for issuing advisory opinions. In such circumstances agencies routinely honor their advisory opinions.

3. Industry Guides

To develop guidelines dealing with either problematic practices in a variety of business contexts or a practice in a specific industry, agencies use industry guides. These guides

---

[7] This section is based on the more detailed review of FTC enforcement in G. Robinson, W. Gellhorn, and C. Bruff, *The Administrative Process* (St. Paul: West Publishing Co., 1980), 544–607.

have no force of law and therefore do not necessarily follow APA notice and comment procedures. The FTC has, however, normally invited comment, and has even sponsored "trade practice conferences" in which industry representatives meet and try to agree on a voluntary code to deal with a problem. The commission might, for example, seek a conference to develop voluntary standards for the use of the descriptive term "light" in reference to lower calorie beer and wine.

4. Cease and Desist Orders

Adjudication, unless it entirely exonerates the position of the citizen in question, results in an order. In fact, section 551(7) defines adjudication in these terms: "'adjudication' means agency process for the formulation of an order." Section 551(6) defines *order* as "the whole or a part of a final disposition, whether affirmative, negative, injunctive, or declaratory in form, of an agency in a matter other than rulemaking but including licensing." Not all orders are cease and desist orders. An order can impose any of the sanctions listed in section 551(10), above. A cease and desist order specifies certain actions which the party must not take in the future. It is therefore sometimes called a *negative* order. The effect of this order imposes no punishment for any prior illegal practice and, except for the added costs of the hearing, produces the same sanctions as a consent decree.

5. Affirmative Disclosure and Other Corrective Orders

When an agency believes that a business has actively misled its customers, through advertising or other promotional materials, it can by order require the business to correct the misinformation. In *J. B. Williams Co. v. FTC*, 381 F.2d 884 (1967), the appellate court upheld an FTC order requiring Geritol commercials to disclose that most fatigue does not result from iron deficiency anemia, the only cause that Geritol plausibly could alleviate. And in *Warner-Lambert Co. v. FTC*, 562 F. 2d 749 (1977), the appellate court required the makers of Listerine to state that their product would not prevent colds or sore throats or lessen their severity. The FTC had also ordered Warner-Lambert to state in their advertisement that this disclaimer was "contrary to prior advertising." The court modified the FTC's order by removing this corrective statement. It held the corrective statement was punitive. Punitive sanctions are appropriate in cases of deliberate deception and bad faith. However, the court noted that Listerine had been promoted for a hundred years as a cold preventative or remedy and that for the bulk of that time the claim was, at least according to the facts on the record of the hearing, made in good faith. Listerine was required to spend as much money advertising that the product did not prevent colds as it spent, between April 1962 and March 1972, on its advertisement that Listerine did prevent or alleviate colds.

Enforcement and Political Resistance

When administrative action poses an immediate threat, through the enforcement of sanctions, to citizens' economic or personal interests, private citizens and groups are most likely to seek political support in Congress to block action. The pattern of lobbying Congress to block enforcement of certain programs has increased significantly since 1970. Since 1975 Congress and individual legislators have, by attaching amendments to appropriations bills and by threatening to reduce IRS's own appropriations, curtailed national enforcement of several IRS policies designed to reduce tax avoidance and evasion. Some of Congress's meddling with the IRS raises serious constitutional questions. However, few if any administrative agencies are powerful enough to bring lawsuits to test Congress's power to intervene without increasing legislative ire.[8] Part IV returns to this problem.

Citizen Initiation of Agency Enforcement

Private citizens and interest groups have the right to bring their own actions in court to enforce statutory policies for which administrative agencies are responsible. Enforcement suits that citizens initiate differ somewhat from suits which challenge the orders or rules of an agency.[9] In the next case, *Environmental Defense Fund* v. *Ruckelshaus* (1971), an environmental organization brought a suit against the Secretary of Agriculture for failing to take actions authorized by Congress. Citizen suits to enforce governmental policy are an outgrowth of the public interest movement and its efforts to monitor agency decisions and *nondecisions*. However, citizens may sue private parties as well. For example, in *Gwaltney of Smithfield* v. *Chesapeake Bay Foundation, Inc. and Natural Resources Defense Council* (1987), two environmental organizations filed suit against a meat-packing company for violating pollution regulations of the Clean Water Act. While Congress delegated the responsibility for enforcing the Clean Water Act to the EPA, many environmental groups have argued that the EPA, particularly under the direction of the Reagan and Bush administrations, has failed to prosecute violators and hence has contributed to the noncompliance problem.

Although it is important to consider citizen suits as one method of enforcing government policy, we also need to be aware of how citizen groups have used litigation to enforce policy. What kind of sanctions did the citizen organizations in these cases seek to impose against those who failed to comply with government policies? In what sense are citizen suits more powerful as agents of political mobilization (i.e., arousing public awareness of regulatory noncompliance) than as tools of regulatory enforcement? Because the courts have been involved in interpreting legislation that grants citizens the authority to bring such suits, the answers to these questions in part turn on legal opinions about citizens suits. In the next two cases you have an opportunity to examine, once again, how the politics of administrative law are shaped by the legal ideology of courts.

[8] See Archie Parnell, "Congressional Interference in Agency Enforcement: The IRS Experience," *Yale Law Journal* 89 (1980):1360.

[9] See Comment, "Private Enforcement and Rulemaking Under the Federal Trade Commission Act," *Northwestern Law Review* 69 (1974):462.

Environmental Defense Fund v. Ruckelshaus

439 F. 2d 584, U.S.C.A., D.C. Cir. (1971) 2–1

[The Federal Insecticide, Fungicide, and Rodenticide Act (FIFRA) provides that certain pesticides must be registered with the Secretary of Agriculture and that they must conform to the statutory standards of product safety which requires that they "not cause unreasonable adverse effects on the environment." The act also provides for a trial-type adjudication process for removing pesticides that failed to conform to the standards. In addition, the act authorizes the Secretary to suspend registration when "necessary to prevent imminent hazard to the public." The Environmental Defense Fund submitted a petition to the Secretary in 1969 to do just that with the pesticide DDT. The Secretary refused to suspend the federal registration of the pesticide DDT, and no action was taken. The Environmental Defense Fund challenged the Secretary's decision.]

Not notice and comment.

Chief Judge Bazelon.

This is a petition for review of an order of the Secretary of Agriculture, refusing to suspend the federal registration of the pesticide DDT or to commence the formal administrative procedures that could terminate that registration. We conclude that the order was based on an incorrect interpretation of the controlling statute, and accordingly remand the case for further proceedings.

I

At the outset, we reject respondents' contention that this court lacks jurisdiction to entertain the petition . . . In the ordinary case, the administrative process begins when the Secretary issues a notice of cancellation to the registrant. The matter may then be referred, at the request of the registrant, to a scientific advisory committee, and to a public hearing, before the Secretary issues the order that effectively cancels or continues the registration. Instead of issuing a notice of cancellation, the Secretary may alternatively initiate the process by summarily suspending a registration, when "necessary to prevent imminent hazard to the public." . . . The suspension order thus operates to afford interim relief during the course of the lengthy administrative proceedings . . .

On May 28, 1970, this court concluded that the Secretary's silence on the request for suspension was equivalent to a denial of that request, and that the denial was reviewable as a final order, because of its immediate impact on the parties.[*] The court remanded the case to the Secretary for a fresh determination on the question of suspension and for a statement of the reasons for his decision. With respect to the request for cancellation notices, we similarly remanded for a decision on the record or for a statement of reasons for deferring the decision, but we reserved judgment on the question whether there was presently a decision ripe for review in this court. We rejected the suggestion that petitioners lack standing to seek review of the action of the Secretary, and that the decisions with respect to suspension and cancellation are committed by law to the unreviewable discretion of the Secretary.

II

We do not find in the FIFRA any conclusive indication that Congress intended to limit review to those orders made after advisory committee proceedings and a public hearing . . . In the first place, statutory review is available to persons other than the manufacturer, who may have no right to call for advisory committee proceedings or a public hearing. In the second place, the manufacturer himself may in some circumstances be entitled to judicial review

---

[*]*EDF v. Hardin*, 428 F.2d 1098.

of an administrative determination that is not subject to further consideration in subsequent administrative proceedings. In either case, the lack of a committee report and a hearing record may limit the scope of review, but it does not preclude review entirely.

Nor can we find in the statutory scheme any support for the *Nor-Am* distinction between orders granting and denying suspension. For the administrative proceedings that follow suspension are equally available after a refusal to suspend. If the Secretary orders suspension, the proceedings are expedited; otherwise they may follow in due course after he issues cancellation notices. In either event, there is a prospect of further administrative action, but that prospect does not resolve for us the question of reviewability. The subsequent proceedings are designed solely to resolve the ultimate question whether cancellation is warranted, and not to shed any further light on the question whether there is a sufficient threat of "imminent hazard" to warrant suspension in the interim . . .

III

. . . [A] decision of the Secretary to issue cancellation notices is not reviewable, because it merely sets in motion the administrative process that terminates in a reviewable final order. An unqualified refusal to issue notices, on the other hand, operates with finality as an administrative rejection of the claim that cancellation is required.

If the Secretary had simply refused to issue the requested notices of cancellation, we would have no difficulty concluding that his order was a final order, ripe for review in this court in accordance with the FIFRA. Here, however, the Secretary has taken the position that investigations are still in progress, that final determinations have not yet been made concerning the uses for which cancellation notices have not yet issued. Therefore, with respect to the cancellation notices, we treat the petition as a request for relief in the nature of mandamus, to compel the Secretary to issue notices as required by statute.

The FIFRA . . . language vests discretion in the Secretary to determine whether an article is in compliance with the act, and to decide what action should

be taken with respect to a nonconforming article. Nevertheless, his decisions are reviewable for abuse of discretion . . .

. . . The stated purpose of the amendment was to protect the public by removing from the market any product whose safety or effectiveness was doubted by the Secretary. The legislative history supports the conclusion that Congress intended any substantial question of safety to trigger the issuance of cancellation notices, shifting to the manufacturer the burden of proving the safety of his product.

. . . [W]hen Congress creates a procedure that gives the public a role in deciding important questions of public policy, that procedure may not lightly be sidestepped by administrators. The cancellation decision does not turn on a scientific assessment of hazard alone. The statute leaves room to balance the benefits of a pesticide against its risks. The process is a delicate one, in which greater weight should be accorded the value of a pesticide for the control of disease, and less weight should be accorded its value for the protection of a commercial crop. The statutory scheme contemplates that these questions will be explored in the full light of a public hearing and not resolved behind the closed doors of the Secretary. There may well be countervailing factors that would justify an administrative decision, after committee consideration and a public hearing, to continue a registration despite a substantial degree of risk, but those factors cannot justify a refusal to issue the notices that trigger the administrative process.

In this case the Secretary has made a number of findings with respect to DDT. On the basis of the available scientific evidence he has concluded that (1) DDT in large doses has produced cancer in test animals and various injuries in man, but in small doses its effect on man is unknown; (2) DDT is toxic to certain birds, bees, and fish, but there is no evidence of harm to the vast majority of species of nontarget organisms; (3) DDT has important beneficial uses in connection with disease control and protection of various crops. These and other findings led the Secretary to conclude "[t]hat the use of DDT should continue to be reduced in an orderly, practicable manner which will not deprive mankind of uses which are essential to the public health and welfare. To this end there should be continuation of the comprehensive study of essentiality of particular uses and evaluations of potential substitutes."

. . . [W]hen, [the Secretary] reaches the conclusion that there is a substantial question about the safety of a registered item, he is obliged to initiate the statutory procedure that results in referring the matter first to a scientific advisory committee and then to a public hearing. We recognize, of course, that one important function of that procedure is to afford the registrant an opportunity to challenge the initial decision of the Secretary. But the hearing, in particular, serves other functions as well. Public hearings bring the public into the decision-making process, and create a record that facilitates judicial review. If hearings are held only after the Secretary is convinced beyond a doubt that cancellation is necessary, then they will be held too seldom and too late in the process to serve either of those functions effectively. . . .

IV

. . . Petitioners do not challenge the Secretary's determination of the kinds of harm that may be associated with DDT. They argue that his estimate of the probability that harm will occur is too low, in light of available reports of scientific studies. They also argue that he has set the standard of proof too high, in light of the clear legislative purpose. On the first point, we think it appropriate in the circumstances of this case to defer to the administrative judgment. We have neither an evidentiary record, nor the scientific expertise, that would permit us to review the Secretary's findings with respect to the probability of harm. We have found no error of law that infects the Secretary's inferences from the scientific data. And we have recognized that it is particularly appropriate to defer to administrative findings of fact in reviewing a decision on a question of interim relief.

The second part of the petitioners' challenge, however, is entirely appropriate for judicial consideration at this time. The formulation of standards for suspension is entrusted to the Secretary in the first instance, but the court has an obligation to ensure that the administrative standards conform to the legislative purpose, and that they are uniformly applied in individual cases. . . .

. . . We stand on the threshold of a new era in the history of the long and fruitful collaboration of administrative agencies and reviewing courts. For many years, courts have treated administrative policy decisions with great deference, confining judicial attention primarily to matters of procedure. On matters of substance, the courts regularly upheld agency action, with a nod in the direction of the "substantial evidence" test, and a bow to the mysteries of administrative expertise. Courts occasionally asserted, but less often exercised, the power to set aside agency action on the ground that an impermissible factor had entered into the decision, or a crucial factor had not been considered. Gradually, however, that power has come into more frequent use, and with it, the requirement that administrators articulate the factors on which they base their decisions.

Strict adherence to that requirement is especially important now that the character of administrative litigation is changing. As a result of expanding doctrines of standing and reviewability, and new statutory causes of action, courts are increasingly asked to review administrative action that touches on fundamental personal interests in life, health, and liberty. These interests have always had a special claim to judicial protection, in comparison with the economic interests at stake in a ratemaking or licensing proceeding.

To protect these interests from administrative arbitrariness, it is necessary, but not sufficient, to insist on strict judicial scrutiny of administrative action. For judicial review alone can correct only the most egregious abuses. Judicial review must operate to ensure that the administrative process itself will confine and control the exercise of discretion. Courts should require administrative officers to articulate the standards and principles that govern their discretionary decisions in as much detail as possible. Rules and regulations should be freely formulated by administrators, and revised when necessary. Discretionary decisions should more often be supported with findings of fact and reasoned opinions. When administrators provide a framework for principled decision-making, the result will be to diminish the importance of judicial review by enhancing the integrity of the administrative process, and to improve the quality of judicial review in those cases where judicial review is sought.

Remanded for further proceedings consistent with this opinion.

Robb, Circuit Judge (dissenting):
In my view the majority opinion substitutes the judgment of this court for the judgment of the Secretary in a matter committed to his discretion by law. This action is taken without the benefit of any administrative hearing in which the validity of the petitioner's forebodings and the soundness of the Secretary's discretionary action might be tested. In effect, the court is undertaking to manage the Department of Agriculture. Finding nothing in the statutes that gives us such authority I respectfully dissent.

Gwaltney of Smithfield v. Chesapeake Bay Foundation, Inc. and Natural Resources Defense Council

98 L. Ed 2d 306 (1987) 6–3
+   Burger, Brennan, White, Marshall, Rehnquist, Blackmun
+/– Stevens, Scalia, O'Connor

[The Clean Water Act of 1972 permits citizens to bring suits to enforce the provisions of the act. A meat-packing company in Virginia, Gwaltney of Smithfield, repeatedly violated the conditions of a pollutant discharge permit issued pursuant to the act. Two environmental groups filed suit in district court alleging that the company had violated and would continue to violate the act. The company moved for the dismissal of the action for want of subject-matter jurisdiction, but the district court ruled that citizens could bring enforcement actions on the basis of past violations under the act. The U.S. Court of Appeals for the Fourth Circuit affirmed this ruling. The U.S. Supreme Court granted review.]

There was some question as to whether the federal courts had jurisdiction.

Justice Marshall delivered the opinion of the Court.
In this case, we must decide whether § 505(a) of the Clean Water Act, also known as the Federal Water Pollution Control Act, . . . confers federal jurisdiction over citizen suits for wholly past violations.

I

The Clean Water Act . . . was enacted in 1972 "to restore and maintain the chemical, physical, and biological integrity of the Nation's waters." . . . In order to achieve these goals, . . . of the Act makes unlawful the discharge of any pollutant into navigable waters except as authorized by specified sections of the Act. . . .

One of these specified sections . . . is § 402, which establishes the National Pollutant Discharge Elimination System (NPDES). . . . Pursuant to it, . . . the Administrator of the Environmental Protection Agency (EPA) may issue permits authorizing the discharge of pollutants in accordance with specified conditions. . . . each State may establish and administer its own permit program if the program conforms to federal guidelines and is approved by the Administrator. . . .

The holder of a federal NPDES permit is subject to enforcement action by the Administrator for failure to comply with the conditions of the permit. The Administrator's enforcement arsenal includes administrative, civil, and criminal sanctions. . . . The holder of a state NPDES permit is subject to both federal and state enforcement action for failure to comply. . . . In the absence of federal or state enforcement, private citizens may commence civil actions against any person "alleged to be in violation of" the conditions of either a federal or state NPDES permit. . . . If the citizen prevails in such an action, the court may order injunctive relief and/or impose civil penalties payable to the United States Treasury. . . .

The Commonwealth of Virginia established a federally approved state NPDES program administered by the Virginia State Water Control Board (Board). . . . In 1974, the Board issued an NPDES permit to ITT-Gwaltney authorizing the discharge of seven pollutants from the company's meat-packing plant on the Pagan River in Smithfield, Virginia. The permit, which was reissued in 1979 and modified in 1980, established effluent limitations, monitoring requirements, and other conditions of discharge. In 1981, petitioner Gwaltney of Smithfield acquired the assets of ITT-Gwaltney and assumed obligations under the permit.

Between 1981 and 1984, petitioner repeatedly violated the conditions of the permit by exceeding effluent limitations on five of the seven pollutants covered. These violations are chronicled in the Discharge Monitoring Reports (DMRs) that the permit required petitioner to maintain. . . . The most substantial of the violations concerned the pollutants fecal coliform, chlorine, and total Kjeldahl nitrogen (TKN). Between October 27, 1981, and August 30, 1984, petitioner violated its TKN limitation 87 times, its chlorine limitation 34 times, and its fecal coliform limitation 31 times. . . . Petitioner installed new equipment to improve its chlorination system in March 1982, and its last reported chlorine violation occurred in October 1982. . . . Petitioner installed an upgraded wastewater treatment system in October 1983, and its last reported TKN violation occurred on May 15, 1984. . . .

Respondents Chesapeake Bay Foundation and Natural Resources Defense Council, two nonprofit corporations dedicated to the protection of natural resources, sent notice in February 1984, to Gwaltney, the Administrator of EPA, and the Virginia State Water Control Board, indicating respondents' intention to commence a citizen suit under the Act based on petitioner's violations of its permit conditions. Respondents proceeded to file this suit in June 1984 . . .

II

A

It is well settled that "the starting point for interpreting a statute is the language of the statute itself." . . . The Court of Appeals concluded that the "to be in violation" language of § 505 is ambiguous, whereas petitioner asserts that it plainly precludes the construction adopted below. We must agree with the Court of Appeals that § 505 is not a provision in which Congress' limpid prose puts an end to all dispute. But to acknowledge ambiguity is not to conclude that all interpretations are equally plausible. The most natural reading of "to be in violation" is a requirement that citizen-plantiffs allege a state of either continuous or intermittent violation — that is, a reasonable likelihood that a past polluter will continue to pollute in the future. Congress could have phrased its requirement in language that looked to the past ("to have violated"), but it did not choose this readily available option.

Respondents urge that the choice of the phrase "to be in violation," rather than phrasing more clearly directed to the past, is a "careless accident," the result of a "debatable lapse of syntactical precision." . . . But the prospective orientation of that phrase could not have escaped Congress' attention. Congress used identical language in the citizen suit provisions of several other environmental statutes that authorize only prospective relief. . . .

Respondents seek to counter this reasoning by observing that Congress also used the phrase "is in violation" in § 309(a) of the Act, which authorizes the Administrator of EPA to issue compliance orders. . . . That language is incorporated by reference in § 309(b), which authorizes the Administrator to bring civil enforcement actions. Because it is little questioned that the Administrator may bring enforcement actions to recover civil penalties for wholly past violations, respondents contend, the parallel language of § 309(a) and § 505(a) must mean that citizens, too, may maintain such actions.

Although this argument has some initial plausibility, it cannot withstand close scrutiny and comparison of the two statutory provisions. The

Administrator's ability to seek civil penalties is not discussed in either § 309(a) or § 309(b); civil penalties are not mentioned until § 309(d), which does not contain the "is in violation" language . . . The citizen suit provision suggests a connection between injunctive relief and civil penalties that is noticeably absent from the provision authorizing agency enforcement. A comparison of § 309 and § 505 thus supports rather than refutes our conclusion that citizens, unlike the Administrator, may seek civil penalties only in a suit brought to enjoin or otherwise abate an ongoing violation.

B

Our reading of the "to be in violation" language of § 505(a) is bolstered by the language and structure of the rest of the citizen suit provisions in § 505 of the Act. These provisions together make plain that the interest of the citizen-plaintiff is primarily forward-looking.

One of the most striking indicia of the prospective orientation of the citizen suit is the pervasive use of the present tense throughout § 505. A citizen suit may be brought only for violation of a permit limitation "which is in effect" under the Act. . . . Citizen-plaintiffs must give notice to the alleged violator, the Administrator of EPA, and the State in which the alleged violation "occurs." . . . A Governor of a State may sue as a citizen when the Administrator fails to enforce an effluent limitation "the violation of which is occurring in another State and is causing an adverse effect on the public health or welfare in his State." . . . The most telling use of the present tense is in the definition of "citizen" as "a person . . . having an interest which is or may be adversely affected" by the defendant's violations of the Act. . . . This definition makes plain what the undeviating use of the present tense strongly suggests: the harm sought to be addressed by the citizen suit lies in the present or the future, not in the past. . . .

. . . Adopting respondent's interpretation of § 505's jurisdictional grant would create a . . . disturbing anomaly. The bar on citizen suits when governmental enforcement action is under way suggests that the citizen suit is meant to supplement rather than to supplant governmental action. The legislative history of the Act reinforces this view of the role of the citizen suit. The Senate Report noted that "[t]he Committee intends the great volume of enforcement actions [to] be brought by the State," and that citizen suits are proper only "if the Federal, State, and local agencies fail to exercise their enforcement responsibility." S Rep No. 92–414, p 64 (1971). . . . Permitting citizen suits for wholly past violations of the Act could undermine the supplementary role envisioned for the citizen suit. This danger is best illustrated by an example. Suppose that the Administrator identified a violator of the Act and issued a compliance order under § 309(a). Suppose further that the Administrator agreed not to assess or otherwise seek civil penalties on the condition that the violator take some extreme corrective action, such as to install particularly effective but expensive machinery, that it otherwise would not be obliged to take. If citizens could file suit, months or years later, in order to seek the civil penalties that the Administrator chose to forgo, then the Administrator's discretion to enforce the Act in the public interest would be curtailed considerably. The same might be said of the discretion of state enforcement authorities. Respondents' interpretation of the scope of the citizen suit would change the nature of the citizens' role from interstitial to potentially intrusive. We cannot agree that Congress intended such a result.

C

The legislative history of the Act provides additional support for our reading of § 505. Members of Congress frequently characterized the citizen suit provisions as "abatement" provisions or as injunctive measures . . .

Moreover, both the Senate and House Reports explicitly connected § 505 to the citizen suit provisions authorized by the Clean Air Act, which are wholly injunctive in nature. . . .

III

Our conclusion that § 505 does not permit citizen suits for wholly past violations does not necessarily dispose of this lawsuit, as both lower courts recognized. The District Court found persuasive the fact that "[respondents]" allegation in the complaint, that Gwaltney was continuing to violate its NPDES permit when plaintiffs filed suit[,] appears to have been made fully in good faith." 611 F Supp, at 1549, n 8. On this basis, the District Court explicity held, albeit in a footnote, that "even if Gwaltney were correct that a district court has no jurisdiction over citizen suits based entirely on unlawful conduct that occurred entirely in the past, the Court would still have jurisdiction here." Ibid. The Court of Appeals acknowledged, also in a footnote, that "[a] very sound argument can be made that [respondents'] allegations of continuing violations were made in good faith," 791 F2d, at 308, n 9, but expressly declined to rule on this alternative holding. Because we agree that § 505 confers jurisdiction over citizen suits when the citizen-plaintiffs make a good-faith allegation of continuous or intermittent violation, we remand the case to the Court of Appeals for further consideration.

Petitioner argues that citizen-plaintiffs must prove their allegations of ongoing noncompliance before jurisdiction attaches under § 505. . . . We cannot agree. The statute does not require that a defendant "be in violation" of the Act at the commencement of suit; rather, the statute requires that a defendant be "*alleged* to be in violation." . . . Our acknowledgement that Congress intended a good-faith allegation to suffice for jurisdictional purposes, however, does not give litigants license to flood the courts with suits premised on baseless allegations. Rule 11 of the Federal Rules of Civil Procedure, which requires pleadings to be based on good-faith belief, formed after reasonable inquiry, that they are "well grounded in fact," adequately protects defendants from frivolous allegations.

Petitioner contends that failure to require proof of allegations under § 505 would permit plaintiffs whose allegations of ongoing violation are reasonable but untrue to maintain suit in federal court even though they lack constitutional standing. Petitioner reasons that if a defendant is in complete compliance with the Act at the time of suit, plaintiffs have suffered no injury remediable by the citizen suit provisions of the Act. Petitioner, however, fails to recognize that our standing cases uniformly recognize that allegations of injury are sufficient to invoke the jurisdiction of a court. In Warth v. Seldin, 422 US 490 . . . (1975), for example, we made clear that a suit will not be dismissed for lack of standing if there are sufficient "allegations of fact"—not proof—in the complaint or supporting affidavits. This is not to say, however, that such allegations may not be challenged. In United States v SCRAP, 412 US 699 . . . (1973), we noted that if the plaintiffs' "allegations [of standing] were in fact untrue, then the [defendants] should have moved for summary judgment on the standing issue and demonstrated to the District Court that the allegations were sham and raised no genuine issue of fact." If the defendant fails to make such a showing after the plaintiff offers evidence to support the allegation, the case proceeds to trial on the merits, where the plaintiff must prove the allegations in order to prevail. But the Constitution does not require that the plaintiff offer this proof as a threshold matter in order to invoke the District Court's jurisdiction.

Petitioner also worries that our construction of § 505 would permit citizen-plaintiffs, if their allegations of ongoing noncompliance become false at some later point in the litigation because the defendant begins to comply with the Act, to continue nonetheless to press their suit to conclusion. According to petitioner, such a result would contravene both the prospective purpose of the citizen suit provisions and the "case or controversy" requirement of Article III. Longstanding principles of mootness, however, prevent the maintenance of suit when "there is no reasonable expectation that the wrong will be repeated.' " . . . In seeking to have a case dismissed as moot, however, the defendant's burden "is a heavy one." . . . The defendant must demonstrate that it is "*absolutely clear* that the allegedly wrongful behavior could not reasonably be expected to recur." . . . (emphasis added). Mootness doctrine thus protects defendants from the maintenance of suit under the Clean Water Act based solely on violations wholly unconnected to any present or future wrongdoing, while it also protects plaintiffs from defendants who seek to evade sanction by predictable "protestations of repentance and reform." . . .

Because the court below erroneously concluded that respondents could maintain an action based on wholly past violations of the Act, it declined to decide whether respondents' complaint contained a good-faith allegation of ongoing violation by petitioner. We therefore remand the case for consideration of this question. The judgment of the Court of Appeals is vacated, and the case is remanded for further proceedings consistent with this opinion.

It is so ordered.

Justice Scalia, with whom Justice Stevens and Justice O'Connor join, concurring in part and concurring in the judgment.

I join Parts I and II of the Court's opinion. I cannot join Part III because I believe it misreads the statute to create a peculiar new form of subject matter jurisdiction.

The Court concludes that subject matter jurisdiction exists under § 505 if there is good-faith allegation that the defendant is "in violation." Thereafter, according to the Court's interpretation, the plaintiff can never be called on to prove that jurisdictional allegation. . . . This creates a regime that is not only extraordinary, but to my knowledge utterly unique. I can think of no other context in which, in order to carry a lawsuit to judgment, allegations are necessary but proof of those allegations (if they are contested) is not. The Court thinks it necessary to find that Congress produced this jurisprudential anomaly because any other conclusion, in its view, would read the word "alleged" out of § 505. It seems to me that, quite to the contrary, it is the Court's interpretation that ignores the words of the statute.

Section 505(a) states that "any citizen may *commence* a civil action on his own behalf . . . against any person . . . who is alleged to be in violation . . . " (emphasis added). There is of course nothing unusual in the proposition that only an allegation is required to *commence* a lawsuit. Proof is never required, and could not practicably be required, at that stage. From this clear and unexceptionable language of the statute, one of two further inferences can be made: (1) The inference the Court chooses, that the requirement for commencing a suit is the same as the requirement for maintaining it, or (2) the inference that, in order to maintain a suit the allegations that are required to commence it must, if contested, be proven. It seems to me that to favor the first inference over the second is to prefer the eccentric to the routine. It is well ingrained in the law that subject matter jurisdiction can be called into question *either* by challenging the sufficiency of the allegation *or* by challenging the accuracy of the jurisdictional facts alleged. . . . Had Congress intended us to eliminate the second form of challenge, and to create an extraordinary regime in which the jurisdictional fact consists of a good-faith belief, it seems to me it would have delivered those instructions in more clear fashion than merely specifying how a lawsuit can be commenced.

In my view, therefore, the issue to be resolved by the Court of Appeals on remand of this suit is not whether the allegation of a continuing violation on the day suit was brought was made in good faith after reasonable inquiry, but whether the petitioner was in fact "in violation" on the date suit was brought . . .

Even if the Court were correct that no evidence of a state of noncompliance has to be produced to survive a motion for dismissal on grounds of subject matter jurisdiction, such evidence would still be required in order to establish the plaintiff's standing. While Gwaltney did not seek certiorari (or even appeal to the Circuit Court) on the denial of its motion to dismiss for lack of standing, it did raise the standing issue before us here, . . . and we in any event have an independent obligation to inquire into standing where it is doubtful. . . . If it is undisputed that the defendant was in a state of compliance when this suit was filed, the plaintiff would have been suffering no remediable injury in fact that could support suit. The constitutional requirement for such injury is reflected in the statute itself, which defines "citizen" as one who has "an interest which is or may be adversely affected." . . .

We conclude the chapter with an article by two political scientists, John T. Scholz and Feng Heng Wei, who examine conflicting political demands on OSHA's enforcement policies between 1976 and 1983 for all fifty states. Scholz and Wei test four hypotheses about the effect of political, economic and bureaucratic forces on agency enforcement actions. They find that different enforcement strategies, such as targeting nonserious violations, issuing citations, or focusing on serious violations, correspond to state-level political and bureaucratic characteristics. In addition they emphasize that the daily contacts between agencies and interest groups play an important role in determining enforcement activities. The article helps you to understand the interaction of complex forces at work in the process of regulatory enforcement. Whether these enforcement activities lead to increased levels of compliance with OSHA regulations is not our immediate concern here. However you should think about the possible links between our previous discussion of compliance and the following study of agency enforcement practices.[10]

Regulatory Enforcement in a Federal System

John T. Scholz and Fent Heng Wei
American Political Science Review
80 (1986):1249.

Two contrasting images of public bureaucracy have dominated the study of federal agencies, particularly those responsible for regulatory enforcement. One image focuses on central control over agency structure, tasks, and budgets and emphasizes the importance of elected officials and pressure groups in determining bureaucratic behavior. The other image, more dominant in the field of public administration, focuses on the nature of the policy task and the organizational characteristics of a bureaucracy and notes that organizational imperatives dominate the actions of public bureaucracies. . . .

Both images are rooted in the classical distinction between political and administrative questions that lies at the base of democratic theory. Political officials acquire the authority to settle political questions through the electoral process, while bureaucrats are delegated authority to settle administrative questions because of their technical expertise. . . .

Our study of OSHA probes the degree to which its enforcement activities vary in response to political and task differences among states. OSHA provides an excellent subject because it undertakes or supervises extensive enforcement actions of a relatively similar nature in all states, because its regulations have remained relatively stable during the period of study, and because its inspectors had developed a reputation in its early years of being legalistic and unresponsive to important task factors (Bardach and Kagan, 1982), making it a difficult test case for enforcement responsiveness. Because we are primarily concerned with the responsiveness of established enforcement agencies, we included state-level enforcement data from 1976 to 1983, the period after the problems of OSHA's formative years had diminished. During this period few new laws and organizational tasks were imposed on OSHA, and yet there were differences among states and considerable changes in political and task factors expected to affect enforcement (Centaur Associates, 1985). Before presenting the results of our analysis, we will discuss hypotheses concerning (1) the political factors likely to influence OSHA, (2) the task factors likely to influence OSHA, (3) the instrumental and symbolic enforcement responses

---

[10]For additional discussion of regulatory enforcement see Suzanne Weaver, *Decision to Prosecute: Organization and Public Policy in the Antitrust Division* (Cambridge: MIT Press, 1977), Eugene Bardach and Robert A. Kagan, *Going by the Book: The Problem of Regulatory Unreasonableness* (Philadelphia: Temple University Press, A Twentieth Century Fund Report, 1982); and R. Shep Melnick, *Regulation and the Courts: The Case of the Clean Air Act* (Washington, D.C.: Brookings Institution, 1983), particularly chap. 7.

available to OSHA, and (4) the comparative responsiveness of federal and state agencies that enforce OSHA regulations.

Hypothesis 1. Agencies respond to changes in multiple political environments.

The primary hypothesis to be tested in this study is that bureaucracies respond rationally to multiple political and task signals from their environment, altering activities in different time periods and geographic regions according to these signals. Given the complex structure of American politics and the multiple paths of influence over government agencies, however, it is not at all clear which political signals the agency should be expected to follow. A narrow legalistic view of democratic authority would presumably argue that only federal elected officials should influence federal bureaucracies like OSHA, and only through legitimate policy channels. Thus, the party affiliation and ideological inclination of a state's congressional contingent should have an overall impact on aggregate national enforcement levels but not on the the particular level of enforcement in the given state. . . .

A pragmatic agency, however, is likely to respond to the more subtle concerns of congressmen for their particular districts by initiating more intensive enforcement efforts in areas and industries where congressmen hope to maintain strong labor support and by developing more cooperative enforcement programs in areas and industries where business backing is important to congressmen. Such variation in enforcement may, in some instances, reflect conscious strategies by agency leadership to gain or maintain support from particular elected officials but may also reflect the local enforcement official's inclination to take advantage of an elected official's willingness to provide local leadership and implementation resources. The first strategy attempts to increase the agency's formal resources (budgets and statutory authority) while the second attempts to increase external resources provided by outside groups. Of course, the second strategy is aimed not only at elected officials but also at interest groups, whose resources are required to supplement formal resources (Bardach, 1977; Pressman and Wildavsky, 1976; Selznick,

1966), particularly given the chronic insufficiency of the enforcement resources allocated to OSHA and other regulatory agencies to establish a credible enforcement threat (McCaffrey, 1982; Mendeloff, 1979; Smith, 1976). . . .

Local interest group support can be even more important to enforcement officals than the support of local elected officals because their members can directly help or hinder enforcement. Enforcement agencies routinely meet with affected organizations at various levels to discuss inspection procedures, conflicting interpretations of regulations, and other enforcement problems. In addition, the act establishing OSHA, like most other regulatory enforcement legislation, provides several points at which individuals from affected business and labor organizations directly affect the enforcement process. Labor representatives, for example, can increase the likelihood that violations will be found and penalized by filing complaints with OSHA alleging violations in their workplace and by accompanying OSHA officials during inspections. Although all workers have the right to file complaints anonymously, complaints are most likely to be filed when systematically encouraged by active unions.

Business, on the other hand, can increase the cost of enforcement actions—thus reducing the level of enforcement activities—in many ways, particularly by appealing citations to the special appellate body, the OSHA Review Commission. As appeals increase, inspectors must spend more time carefully documenting citations and preparing testimony. In addition, appeals boards almost automatically reduce fines and dismiss some citations: for example, during one period in California, penalties were cut by an average of 50%, according to CAL-OSHA officials. . . .

If agency responses are assumed to be rational, the signals to which OSHA responds provides some clues about the relative importance of formal and informal resources to the agency. To the extent that local resources are more important for enforcement than formal resources, direct actions by interest groups and local election networks should have a measurable impact on enforcement activities. Even state legislators and governors are then likely to have some influence over federal policies. To the extent that central resources are most important, only political forces filtered through Congress, relevant congressional committees, and the president should affect the distribution of enforcement activities, and task conditions should be a primary cause for enforcement variation between states. . . .

. . . To measure the political effect of a state's congressional contingent, we assume that congressmen who vote more frequently for prolabor positions in Congress are also more likely to seek higher levels of enforcement in the district. We therefore calculate a prolabor ideological index for each state contingent based on the mean difference between trade union Committee on Political Education (COPE) (prolabor voting) and National Association of Manufacturers (NAM) (probusiness voting) scores for all senators and congressmen from the state.

At the state level, ideological indicators like COPE and NAM scores are not consistently available. Given the prolabor nature of OSHA enforcement and the long-standing alliances of business with the Republicans and labor with the Democrats, we assume that Democratic governors and legislators are more likely to seek higher levels of enforcement. Although this simplification does not do justice to the diversity of partisan alignments in state politics, partisanship is used frequently in a similar manner in state policy studies. . . .

For interest groups, we expect the level of enforcement activities to vary directly with the support provided by labor and inversely with the resistance offered by business. We include the number of worker complaints per 1,000 industrial workers filed with OSHA as the best available measure of the direct activity of labor to influence enforcement. . . .

In summary, we expect that OSHA enforcement will be most vigorous during periods of and in states with high levels of labor complaints and more Democratic and prolabor elected officials than probusiness and Republican ones, although we are uncertain whether responsiveness will be more significant for legislative or executive officials at the state or federal level.

Hypothesis 2. Agencies respond to changes in task environments.

Economic models of enforcement note that enforcement efficiency requires the shifting of resources among enforcement arenas with different task characteristics until marginal returns in each area are equal (Stigler, 1970). Thus, in order to obtain maximum political credit for implementing the formal tasks assigned by central political authorities with a given budget, an agency would vary its enforcement activities over time in different states to reflect differences in task-related conditions affecting the return on enforcement activities.

However, organizational and political problems limit an agency's ability to adapt to changes in task-related factors. Implementation research has emphasized the difficulty agencies face in assembling and coordinating effective routines to accomplish any task (Bardach, 1977), even for modest policy goals in relatively tranquil political environments (Pressman and Wildavsky, 1976). Once effective routines have been established, organizational rationality requires that they be standardized, that variation be minimized, and that core technologies (in OSHA, for producing and processing citations) be buffered from environmental fluctuations (Thompson, 1967), all of which reduce the variation to be expected in enforcement due to task differences. Thus, task responsiveness becomes diluted by organizational necessities.

Conflicting political signals further reduce an agency's political task responsiveness. First, the centrifugal force of local political pressures and the bureaucratic interests of local operating units pose a problem that federal agencies frequently solve through standardizing procedures and output beyond the requirements for organization efficiency (Kaufman, 1960). Professional standards, acceptable measures of task output and of task-related differences in local conditions, and agreement on the causal relationships between agency activities and outcomes (e.g., between OSHA's enforcement efforts and the reduction of risk) generally aid agencies in preserving the discretion of local operating units to vary output in response to local conditions. In compact urban agencies delivering standard services like fire protection and road maintenance, for example, technical decision routines have been found to determine the difference in level of service among an agency's service areas. Political differences between areas had less of an effect for these professionalized services (Levy et al., 1974) but a greater effect on less-professionalized urban bureaucracies; bureaucratic decision rules had less of an effect on less-professionalized urban bureaucracies (Jones, 1981: Jones et al., 1977). Because federal agencies like OSHA generally have less-developed professionalism, less-established technologies, greater organizational problems imposed by broader mandates and jurisdictions, and more complex political environments than urban agencies, task responsiveness becomes more questionable. For OSHA in particular, the contentiousness of the political environment and the difficulty in establishing appropriate task-related justifications for different levels of enforcement decrease the likelihood of task-related responsiveness.

Two testable decision rules about the efficient use of scarce resources emerged from interviews with enforcement officials as potential indicators of task responsiveness for OSHA. First, we expect that enforcement activities will be highest where industrial accidents rates are highest because enforcement professionals tend to believe that enforcement resources are most effectively deployed where high accident rates indicate that safety problems are more numerous. Accident rates affect inspectors, who look at past accident records of firms during inspections and who tend to look harder, to cite more of the detected violations, and to assess maximum penalties in firms with higher accident rates. Similarly, OSHA managers are aware of aggregate accident figures and know that they will be criticized when rates go up. As a measure of accident rates, annual safety and health incident rates were aggregated at the state level from annual Bureau of Labor Statistics survey data for the years 1974–1983.

Second, we expect that enforcement should be sensitive to general economic conditions despite the strict statutory language requiring inspectors to cite any observed violation regardless of economic conditions. In informal interviews, OSHA enforcement officials at all levels expressed concern about contributing to unemployment when times are bad and seemed inclined to give firms more leeway when the business cycle was down. They are more willing to be aggressive when business is good and employment is less a problem because firms have greater resources to respond and workers are more likely to support the efforts of OSHA inspectors. Furthermore, OSHA is less politically vulnerable to business complaints during good times than during bad times. Annual state data on unemployment and per capita income were collected to test the effect of economic conditions on enforcement actions. We expect enforcement to be inversely related to unemployment and positively related to income. . . .

It is possible that task variables such as accident rates and economic conditions will affect enforcement indirectly by increasing political demands for enforcement (Moe, 1985a). . . .

Hypothesis 3. Agencies tend to respond instrumentally to task changes and symbolically to political changes.

Agencies can respond to political and task influences with activities that vary in their costs and their perceived likelihood of producing desired effects. Given the number of external factors affecting the industrial accident rates OSHA is charged with moderating (Mendeloff, 1979; Smith, 1976), political oversight of OSHA—as of most agencies—is based on measures of enforcement activities rather than on outcomes (e.g., accident rates). Because the relative effectiveness of different activities is not well established, particularly for those not actively involved in the process, bureaucrats may have considerable discretion in deciding which activity to increase to satisfy increased political demand. The hypothesis to be tested here is that bureaucrats will respond to political demands by changing lower-cost, "symbolic" output that may help generate the desired political support, even if it may have no effect on accidents, but will respond to task factors with "instrumental" output that agency professionals consider to be more likely to affect outcomes, even though it is also more costly. In organizational terms, responsive bureaucrats cope with the political environment by buffering critical enforcement activities and with the task environment by monitoring task changes and routinely altering critical activities to adapt to changes. . . .

. . . [W]e expect that political responsiveness will be most pronounced for inspections and nonserious citations, while task responsiveness will be more evident for serious citations and penalties. To test this hypothesis, state-level enforcement data on inspections, citations and penalties were collected from annual OSHA enforcement reports, with serious and nonserious citations and penalties recorded separately. . . .

Hypothesis 4. State agencies are more responsive than federal agencies.

OSHA provides a unique opportunity to compare the responsiveness of state and federal bureaucracies performing the same task because authorized state agencies are allowed to enforce the federal law if OSHA certifies that state programs are at least as effective as the federal counterpart. Twenty-two states chose this option for most of the period under study. The summary data for political and task variables . . . indicate that the labor force in state-program states is considerably more involved in OSHA enforcement, yet the states tend to be somewhat more Republican. They are smaller and slightly richer, with somewhat higher unemployment and accident rates. The differences in political and task factors are minor compared with the differences in standardized enforcement measures . . . where states with state programs consistently score higher than states with federal programs.

Why some states chose to pay approximately 50% of the costs for the right to enforce OSHA regulations with state agencies is not clear from this data. Most analysts agree that states assume regulatory responsibility with the expectation that the state bureaucracy would be more responsive to state conditions, presumably to business interests assumed to

dominate at the state level (Marvel, 1982; Williams and Matheny, 1984). . . .

The expected difference in task responsiveness between the two programs in less clear, particularly because the difference in civil service systems and professionalism is not well known. Some argue that the characteristics that increase the political penetrability of state bureaucracies also decrease professional concerns with statutory goals (Marlow, 1981; Marvel, 1982). Professional prestige, salaries, civil service protection, training, and career opportunities are generally assumed to be better in federal than in state enforcement programs. However, complaints of legalistic, "nit-picking" enforcement by federal OSHA, particularly in its early years, indicate that the federal agency was dominated by inflexible, standardized decision routines that provided little room for professional task responsiveness (Bardach and Kagan, 1982; Smith, 1976). To test whether state and federal programs differed significantly in political and task responsiveness for our data set, a standard dummy variable analysis was used to estimate the difference in slopes and intercepts of the two different groups of states. . . .

Agency Responsiveness to Multiple Political Signals

Two conclusions about political responsiveness stand out clearly from the analysis. First, OSHA exhibited a remarkable responsiveness to all political factors [described above]. . . .

Second, the direct interest group measure for labor clearly exerted the most consistent influence on enforcement activities, significantly affecting every activity. The magnitude of labor's impact on enforcement during the period is more difficult to compare with other variables because the variables have no common scale of measurement and because inferences about relative impacts based on regression coefficients are statistically problematic due to multicollinearity and measurement error problems (Moe, 1985, p. 1109). . . . For example, the impact on total penalties in the state program of an increase equivalent to the standard deviation would amount to $816 for labor complaints, compared with $65 for Congress,—$31 for state legislatures, $12 for accident rates, and—$8 for unemployment. This effect is even greater than the—$195 change representing the entire effect of the Reagan administration. Using this crude test, labor's impact on all enforcement variables is considerably greater than that of other variables, although we cannot claim from this test that the difference is of statistical significance. The consistency and magnitude of the effect of labor on all enforcement actions underscores the importance of direct enforcement resources provided by interest groups. We suspect that a measure of direct business actions would similarly be quite important in shaping enforcement actions.

PRESIDENTIAL ADMINISTRATION. The results confirm the importance of presidential influence over administrative actions (Chubb, 1985; Moe, 1982, 1985a). Both the Carter and Reagan administrations were primarily concerned with reducing OSHA's early reputation as a "nit-picking" agency that repeatedly cited insignificant violations while ignoring more serious ones. In response, OSHA significantly reduced the penalties associated with nonserious violations in the years following the Ford administration, although, surprisingly, the number of nonserious citations was not significantly reduced in response to Reagan and actually increased under Carter. The Carter administration, reflecting the traditional Democratic affiliation with labor interests, shifted penalties from nonserious to more serious safety-related violations, resulting in no significant decrease in total penalties. The Reagan administration, reflecting the traditional Republican concern with business interests, reduced penalties for nonserious citations by even greater amounts without a corresponding increase in penalties for serious citations, leading to a significant decline in total penalties as well.

. . . [T]he enforcement data suggest that presidential administrations may be able to increase OSHA activities in state-program states (as Carter did) more readily than they can decrease them (as Reagan attempted). The drop in serious violations and in total penalties during the Reagan years (the 1982 and 1983

fiscal years) was much more dramatic for the federal program than for the state programs, while the initial rise in serious violations under Carter (fiscal year 1978) was more dramatic for state programs. This result supports the importance of the statutory provision that provides that federal OSHA set minimum but not maximum enforcement levels for state programs.

CONGRESS. A prolabor congressional delegation increased nonserious and total penalties in both state- and federal-program states but increased nonserious citations only in federal-program states. Given the lack of direct congressional authority over the state programs, it is surprising that only nonserious citations exhibited significantly greater responsiveness for the federal program compared with state programs. . . . The similar effect on both state and federal penalty activities suggests that the resources provided by local electoral networks are more important to agencies than formal resources controlled by Congress.

Although studies of the Federal Trade Commission (Weingast and Moran, 1983) and the National Labor Relations Board (Moe, 1985a) found that congressional committee membership had a significant effect on aggregate national enforcement actions, no significant influence was found on state-level OSHA enforcement activities. The measures of party identification of OSHA's oversight committee members (1 for each Democrat, −1 for each Republican, and 0 for states with no members) for Senate, House, and combined committee membership were insignificant in all equations and, therefore, dropped from the final estimates presented in Table 8.1. . . . It should be noted that OSHA officials firmly deny any informal influence of elected officials at the local level, but the pervasive influence of local interest group actions combined with the likely influences of local electoral networks indicate the need for further studies of the complex, subtle interactions between political and bureaucratic institutions at the local level.

STATE GOVERNORS AND LEGISLATORS. As expected, states with Democratic governors had significantly

Table 8.1 Enforcement Activity Response to Political and Task Factors

Factors	Inspections	Citations		Penalties		
		Nonserious	Serious	Nonserious	Serious	Total
Political Factors						
Carter (FYs 1978–81)	1.09	2.49	1.40*	−50.17*	70.58	−49.63
Reagan (FYs 1982–83)	5.22	−2.43	.87	−129.67*	−283.67	−195.58*
Governor	1.98*	10.30*	.26	95.42*	35.13	116.69*
Congress						
State	.04	.01	.01	1.06*	−.39	1.45*
Federal	.02	.17*	.00	.98*	1.01	2.18*
State legislature						
State	.32*	.58*	−.02	1.14	−1.92	−1.95*
Federal	.03*	−.28*	−.03	−3.11	−5.46	−2.18
Labor						
State	5.23*	7.46*	1.01*	68.38*	161.24*	207.23*
Federal	1.01*	−3.62*	.53*	−22.35*	124.13*	187.36*
Task Factors						
Accidents						
State	.23	.63	−.06	5.90*	10.68*	7.55*
Federal	−.00	−.28	.01	−4.51*	5.59*	.62*
Unemployment						
State	−.02	.19	−.01*	3.90*	−1.98*	−3.89*
Federal	−.06	−.07	−.01*	.42	−1.47*	−.39
Income						
State	.00	.03*	.00	−.00	.02	.15
Federal	−.00	−.01*	−.00	−.15	−.19	−.06
Intercept Terms						
State program	−42.35*	−197.98*	6.63	−769.00	303.87	−436.82
Federal program	34.43*	135.20	11.81	1317.13	1858.47	595.46
R^2 (uncorrected)	.64	.62	.45	.43	.50	.54

Source: Data provided by the Occupational Safety and Health Administration from their computerized data base for federal states and from annual reports for state-program states.

Note: . . . The figures are estimated regression coefficients from the pooled data for all 50 states from 1976 through 1983, calculated by the Parks method . . . .

*Statistically significant at the .05 level (t test), with 383 degrees of freedom for t statistics. Underscoring indicates that the difference between the state and federal programs is statistically significant at the .05 level.

more enforcement actions in almost every category, presumably because of the governor's proximity to administrative channels, both federal and state . . .

LABOR. As noted, direct labor interaction through the filing of complaints had the most consistent effect on all enforcement output. State programs were significantly responsive for all output, and the federal program showed positive responsiveness for everything but nonserious citations and penalties. These negative relationships must be understood in conjunction with the positive relationship for serious citations and penalties because higher levels of labor complaints appear to induce a shift in resources from nonserious citations to serious ones with considerably higher penalties (thus the higher total penalties despite the decline in nonserious penalties). This tradeoff in the federal program may reflect successful attempts by management to improve the productivity of OSHA's complaint responses, which in the early 1970s were considered by many to have unduly dominated the determination of inspection targets in areas where unions were most active. In the state programs, no such tradeoff takes place, suggesting that sufficient enforcement resources are available to attend to both serious and nonserious violations.

Agency Responsiveness to Task Signals

The response to task signals was significant but less consistent than the response to political signals . . . [The] findings support the argument that symbolic responses are reserved for changes in elected officials, while instrumental responses in key enforcement activities are reserved for task environment changes relevant to formal statutory objectives. The impressively robust effect of labor on all activities indicates that consistent, day to day contacts between interest groups and the enforcement bureaucracy bring the most consistent responses, both symbolic and instrumental.

Higher accident rates, the task variable most directly related to OSHA's statutory goals, brought significant increase in all penalties except for nonserious violations in the federal program, where the same tradeoff discussed previously for labor appears to decrease penalties for nonserious violations as attention is focused on serious violations. Higher unemployment, the most relevant measure of business cycle activity, led to the expected reduction in serious citations and serious penalties. Here the tradeoff between serious and nonserious penalties is evident even for the state program, where a greater number of serious violations apparently get reclassified and penalized as nonserious when higher unemployment signals an adverse business climate, leading to the negative coefficient for serious penalties and the positive coefficient for nonserious penalties. Higher per capita income affects only nonserious citations and has an unexpected negative effect in federal programs. The poor performance of this indicator probably reflects confounding relationships between per capita income and government budgets as well as industrial development and related business/union political strengths.

Responsiveness of OSHA State Agencies and the Federal Agency to Political and Task Signals

The results in Table 1 provide strong evidence that, for OSHA enforcement, state bureaucracies are considerably more responsive than the federal bureaucracy to all task and political factors, with the expected exception of Congress . . .

Thus, the greater responsiveness of state agencies to political and task demands apparently produces the observed higher mean level of enforcement by state agencies. . . . In sum, bureaucrats in both programs respond to different levels of political and task conditions, but state program bureaucrats respond with greater changes in output and with fewer constrained tradeoffs between serious and nonserious violations.

Conclusion

The image of public bureaucracy reflected in this study is that of an organization that responds rationally to political demands but does so in a complex, federalist environment in which statutory commands and oversight by central institutions provide only one set of conflicting signals. The role of federal agencies in the American policy process is not simply one of translating central political decisions into organizationally efficient routines because central institutions seldom can provide the bureaucracy with sufficient resources for such implementation. Instead, the creative role of the bureaucracy requires the development of organizationally feasible tasks that will gain and maintain sufficient support from critical actors in multiple operational arenas without undermining central support needed for formal budgets and statutory adjustments.

Thus, bureaucracy plays the important and seldom-recognized role of integrating political demands made at various levels of the American federalist system by incrementally adapting central policies to fit into varied and changing local conditions. . . . As agencies adjust and modify routines in response to pressures from groups with formal and informal resources, the political system "learns" which policy interventions work and what they can do. Changes in central policies and oversight by central institutions provide only one input into this process, one that the agency itself helps shape through its strategic responses.

Understanding the responsiveness of bureaucracies to the range of political and task factors in their environment is an important step in understanding the role of federal agencies in the policy process. This study of OSHA indicates that even the relatively isolated enforcement routines for standardized national regulations respond consistently to daily interactions with interest groups involved in the enforcement process. Professional reactions to statutory concerns, represented in the study by accident and unemployment rates, also elicited strong instrumental responses, while responses to elected officials tended to emphasize more symbolic actions. The smaller size and greater flexibility of state bureaucracies allowed greater responsiveness than was observed in the federal bureaucracy.

References

BARDACH, EUGENE. 1977. *The Implementation Game*. Boston: MIT Press.

BARDACH, EUGENE, and ROBERT A. KAGAN. 1982. *Going By the Book: The Problem of Regulatory Unreasonableness*. Philadelphia: Temple University Press.

CENTAUR ASSOCIATES. 1985. *The Impact of OSHA's Recent Enforcement Activities*. Washington, D.C.: Centaur Associates.

CHUBB, JOHN E. 1985. "The Political Economy of Federalism." *American Political Science Review*. 79:994–1015.

JONES, BRYAN D. 1981. "Party and Bureaucracy: The Influence of Intermediary Groups on Urban Policy Service Delivery." *American Political Science Review*, 75:688–700.

JONES, BRYAN D., SAADIA R. GREENBURG, CLIFFORD KAUFMAN, and JOSEPH DREW. 1977. "Bureaucratic Response to Citizen-Initiated Contacts: Environmental Enforcement in Detroit." *American Political Science Review*, 71: 148–65.

JONES, CAROL ADAIRE. 1984. "Agency Enforcement and Company Compliance Behavior: An Empirical Study of the OSHA Asbestos Standard." Unpublished Manuscript.

KAUFMAN, HERBERT. 1960. *The Forest Ranger: A Study in Administrative Behavior*. Baltimore: Johns Hopkins University Press.

LEVY, FRANK, ARNOLD J. MELTSNER, and AARON WILDAVSKY. 1974. *Urban Outcomes*. Berkeley: University of California Press.

MARLOW, MICHAEL L. 1981. "The Impact of Different Government Units in the Regulation of the Workplace Environment." *Public Choice*, 37:349–56.

MARVEL, MARY K. 1982. "The Economics of Enforcement: The Case of OSHA." *Journal of Economics and Business*," 34:165–71.

MARVEL, MARY K., 1982. "Implementation and Safety Regulation: Variations in Federal and State Administration under OSHA." *Administration and Society*, 14:15–33.

MCCAFFREY, DAVID. 1982. *OSHA and the Politics of Health Regulation*. New York: Plenum Press.

MCCAFFREY, DAVID.. 1983. "An Assessment of OSHA's Recent Effects on Injury Rates." *Journal of Human Resources*, 18:131–46.

MENDELOFF, JOHN. 1979. *Regulating Safety: An Economic and Political Analysis of Occupational Safety and Health Policy*. Cambridge, MA: MIT Press.

MOE, TERRY M. 1982. "Regulatory Performance and Presidential Administration." *American Journal of Politics*, 26:197–224.

MOE, TERRY M. 1985a. "Control and Feedback in Economic Regulation: The Case of the NLRB." *American Political Science Review*, 79:1094–1116.

PRESSMAN, JEFFREY, and AARON WILDAVSKY. 1976. *Implementation*. Boston: MIT Press.

SELZNICK, PHILLIP. 1966. *TVA and the Grassroots*. New York: Harper and Row.

SMITH, ROBERT S. 1976. *The Occupational Safety and Health Act: Its Goals and Its Achievements*. Washington, D.C.: American Enterprise Institute.

THOMPSON, JAMES D. 1967. *Organizations in Action*. New York: McGraw Hill.

WEINGAST, BARRY R. and MARK J. MORAN. 1983. "Bureaucratic Discretion or Congressional Control: Regulatory Policymaking by the Federal Trade Commission." *Journal of Political Economy*, 91:765–800.

WILLIAMS, BRUCE A., and ALBERT R. MATHENY, 1984. "Testing Theories of Social Regulation: Hazardous Waste Regulation in the American States." *Journal of Politics*, 46:428–58.

Exercises and Questions for Further Thought

1. Should private citizens and interest groups be granted a right of their own to bring actions in court to enforce statutory policies for which administrative agencies are responsible? On one hand, this could offset the problem of capture. On the other hand, judicial decisions might contradict or interfere with the orderly development of agency policy.

2. The model of compliance described in this chapter helps explain the dynamics of regulation. It also serves another less obvious but more important purpose, one which you should begin to think about now. The principles of administrative law announced in appellate court decisions either succeed or fail to shape administrative behavior effectively because of the pushing and pulling of the very same forces in the compliance model that affect regulatory compliance. Think of any case covered thus far that imposes a behavioral constraint on administrators. Then speculate about the forces pushing toward and away from administrative compliance. You should differentiate the compliance of a governmental party to the case, from the extent to which other agencies similarly situated will voluntarily adopt the policies expressed in the opinion.

3. An excellent illustration of the influence of "beneficiaries" of regulatory decisions developed when a number of companies, interest groups, and regulators went to court to stop execution of the settlement of the Department of Justice's antitrust suit against American Telephone and Telegraph Company. Large corporate users of the local telephone companies that AT&T must sell and the state regulatory authorities fear that the companies sold will be so "stripped" of assets and burdened with liabilities that they will fail to provide adequate service. What other current or recent examples of beneficiaries affecting policy implementation can you think of?

CHAPTER 9

Judicial Review

The previous chapters in this part have moved you along a path—a path that starts at the point where a statute authorizes agency action. It then passes through information-gathering to informal and formal decisionmaking and enforcement. In this chapter we arrive at the last phase of any administrative decision, its success or failure if and when a judge reviews its legality.

Actually the path is not usually so straight. We have already studied cases where courts reviewed administrative decisions before any enforcement occurred. And some decisions—the Nuclear Regulatory Commission's green light to operate nuclear plants before the waste disposal problem was solved, for example—don't create a need to enforce anything. The result permits the agency to proceed with its plans. Nevertheless the path does end with judicial review because courts tend to have the last word. The only avenue open from the courts goes to Congress, which has set aside judicial administrative law rulings only rarely. Chapters 10 through 12, part III, do not take the path further. Instead they illustrate three important areas of administrative law that raise questions on the path we have already traveled.

Because courts potentially have the last word in all cases, this chapter is as important as any in the book. It describes the ground rules governing the process by which courts have reached all the decisions you read in this or any other legal casebook. Although constitutions, administrative procedure acts, and authorizing statutes help define administrative law, such legal pronouncements do not answer every contingency. We have already discussed the role of judicial interpretation and you should have a good background at this point for now examining more precisely the role of courts in reviewing administrative agency decisions. Judges create judicial concepts and principles in the process of reviewing administrative decisions. These concepts often reappear in an agency's own justifications for its actions. In this respect administrative law resembles other sites of law where judicial pronouncements become embedded in the way institutions, such as agencies, present themselves.

This chapter covers the two major components of judicial review. One concerns the ground rules—ripeness, standing, mootness, exhaustion, and primary jurisdiction—for obtaining *access* to judicial review of agency decisions. These rules govern when courts will review agency decisions. Courts play an important role in shaping the very rules that determine when they will review agency decisions and under what circumstances. The second component, hinted at in earlier chapters, concerns the *scope* of judicial review. There is considerable disagreement about how deferential courts should be toward administrative discretion. In the *Vermont Yankee* cases you compared Judge Bazelon's opinion, calling for greater judicial scrunity of agency rulemaking, with Justice Rehnquist's opinion, reversing the Court of Appeals decision and narrowing the scope of judicial review. The scope of judicial review is also an important issue in many judicial opinions about statutory interpretation, such as *Chevron v. NRDC,* 1984 (chapter 3). This chapter articulates the various dimensions of this fundamental problem.

Here are some typical scope of review questions:

1. How much deference should courts give to an agency's interpretation of its own statutory authority?
2. When an agency, either in rulemaking or adjudication, finds certain facts and incorporates them into its decision, how willingly should judges dispute the facts the agency found? How freely should judges substitute their own interpretation of the facts for the agency's interpretation?
3. How aggressively should courts force agencies to give detailed factual justification for their decisions?

Controversy surrounds the scope of judicial review in part for historical reasons. At the time of the final political triumph of the New Deal there existed among lawyers, students of law, and government a consensus that administrators could cope with the problems of economic regulation better than either legislatures or courts. Administrators, they believed, could combine expert training with effective information gathering techniques to shape wise policy closely and continuously without constant political interference. Since courts lacked these virtues, they should not actively oppose administrative choices the way they opposed so much administrative policy in the fifty years before 1937. If these assumptions about administrative superiority held true in practice, then courts should intervene only to prevent violations of the Constitution itself and to block administrative actions that lacked any legislative authorization.

The consensus that courts should defer to agency expertise, information processing, and impartiality has since the New Deal come unglued for several reasons. Let us review them briefly. The first of these—agency capture—we have already discussed at length. An industry that an agency tries to regulate so controls the flow of information and expertise to the agency and develops such close interpersonal relationships with agency staff (in no small part by offering good jobs to agency staff) that the agency in the end protects an industry more than it regulates it. The second deficiency is that many agencies have to accommodate quite inconsistent philosophies about the agency's mission. Some who work for the Social Security Administration feel the organization should try to ease human misfortunes, while others in the same organization place cost control at the top of their priority list. Third, we have learned that agencies cannot mechanically implement clear public policy. Much is left to discretion, and agencies do not always use it wisely. A law that calls for regulating the communications industry "in the public interest" more resembles an empty balloon that the Federal Communications Commission may inflate as much as it desires without explicit legislative guidance. You can see how the extent to which we trust the administrative process to avoid these pitfalls will influence how judges should answer questions of judicial scope such as the three listed above.

Part IV will again address these problems in more detail. For this chapter's purposes, you need only appreciate that *one* plausible way to cope with increasing doubts about administrative performance is to increase judicial surveillance of it. We do not have to believe that judges are somehow magically better administrators to justify judicial review. We need merely accept the wisdom in H. L. Mencken's observation that conscience is the small voice within us that tells us that someone may be looking.

Access to Judicial Review

We turn now to the first and most general problem of judicial review. Courts, like any other branch of government, face constitutional limits on their power. Courts of course say what the law is, but they have not automatically interpreted their power so as to expand it to the maximum. For gatekeeping reasons, that is, to reduce their workload to manageable proportions, judges have denied themselves power to intervene.

Article III, section 2, of the Constitution confers on federal courts jurisdiction in "cases" and "controversies." The courts have consistently interpreted these two jurisdiction-granting words to cover only the power to decide lawsuits. A lawsuit exists only when a plaintiff files a complaint against a defendant and the court gains jurisdictional power over the defendant to force him to answer the complaint in court. This process creates a genuine legal disagreement. We call this the *requirement of adversariness.* Where parties disagree about the case, they presumably will present their best evidence, their best arguments, in court asserting why they should win. For a court to reach out and decide a case without getting the best evidence from both sides increases the risk that courts will make mistakes.

In practice, although there are some specific exceptions in the laws of some states, judges take for granted that they may act only to resolve lawsuits. The interesting legal issues today deal not with the mere existence of a lawsuit, but with whether the suit is adversarial enough to fall within Article III's grant of power. Thus in the extreme case where two sides agree to sue each other, but both really hope for the same result, the "case and controversy" requirement is not met.[1] Other issues are not quite so obvious, and this section examines five of these.

You may initially think these five issues are mere legal technicalities, issues for lawyers to handle with no significance for administrators themselves. However, these topics—ripeness, standing, mootness, exhaustion, and primary jurisdiction—do involve important assumptions about the role of courts in modern government. A restrictive definition of ripeness or standing, for example, necessarily eliminates some occasions for judicial review. These five items primarily affect only the timing of judicial review in legal theory, but in the practice of law, just as in love and politics, timing affects whether some things happen at all.

1. Ripeness and the Presumption of Reviewability

What if a person or corporation or government agency has made a decision that will affect others when it is implemented but has not yet begun to implement it? Should

---

[1] Cf. *Muskrat v. United States,* 219 U.S. 346 (1911).

courts wait until the harm has happened before calling the case adversarial enough to hear, or should courts intervene to examine whether the harm is legally permissible before it happens? How much or how far before it happens? These questions deal with how *ripe* a legal contest must be to deserve judicial scrutiny. Judges who believe courts should avoid interfering with the administrative process will require much ripeness. Hence it is not surprising to find that one of the strongest judicial statements in favor of judicial review of administration simultaneously requires only a moderate ripening of the harm before courts can review a decision.

As you read this next case try to identify the harm the drug companies will suffer if the courts refuse to intervene at this point in the proceedings. Does this harm make the issue real and substantial enough to assure a fully adversary proceeding? Also, try to articulate the ways judicial intervention at this stage might impair the regulatory process. Note the majority's argument that both sides can benefit from a ruling at this time.[2]

Abbott Laboratories, Inc. v. Gardner

387 U.S. 136 (1967) 8–0

\+   Warren, Black, Douglas, Harlan, Stewart, Clark, White, Fortas

NP Brennan   *dissented*

[Congress in 1962 required manufacturers of prescription drugs to print the "established," i.e., generic, name of the drug along with the manufacturer's own proprietary brand name on drug labels, in advertisements, and in other printed materials. The commissioner of the Food and Drug Administration required the drug manufacturers to print the generic name alongside the brand name every time the brand name appeared, not just once or at the top of the label or other material. Before the FDA made any effort to enforce this regulation a group of thirty-seven drug manufacturers, of which Abbott Laboratories was the first alphabetically listed, asked the courts to declare the regulation void for exceeding the statutory authority granted the FDA.]

Justice Harlan delivered the opinion of the Court.

The injunctive and declaratory judgement remedies are discretionary, and courts traditionally have been reluctant to apply them to administrative determinations unless these arise in the context of a controversy "ripe" for judicial resolution. Without undertaking to survey the intricacies of the ripeness doctrine it is fair to say that its basic rationale is to prevent the courts, through avoidance of premature adjudication, from entangling themselves in abstract disagreements over administrative policies, and also to protect the agencies from judicial interference until an administrative decision has been formalized and its effects felt in a concrete way by the challenging parties. The problem is best seen in a two-fold aspect, requiring us to evaluate both the fitness of the issues for judicial decision and the hardship to the parties of withholding court consideration.

As to the former factor, we believe the issues presented are appropriate for judicial resolution at this time. First, all parties agree that the issue tendered is a purely legal one: whether the statute was properly construed by the Commissioner to require the established name of the drug to be used every time the proprietary name is employed. Both sides moved for summary judgement in the District Court,

---

[2] See also *Koehring Co. v. Adams*, 605 F.2d 280 (1979), and *City of Rochester v. Bond*, 603 F.2d 927 (1979).

Statute requiring safety equipment in vehicles used on public roads.

and no claim is made here that further administrative proceedings are comtemplated. It is suggested that the justification for this rule might vary with different circumstances, and that the expertise of the Commissioner is relevant to passing upon the validity of the regulation. This of course is true, but the suggestion overlooks the fact that both sides have approached this case as one purely of congressional intent, and that the Government made no effort to justify the regulation in factual terms.

Second, the regulations in issue we find to be "final agency action" within the meaning of § 10 of the Administrative Procedure Act, 5 U.S.C. § 704, as construed in judicial decisions. An "agency action" includes any "rule," defined by the Act as "an agency statement of general or particular applicability and future effect designed to implement, interpret, or prescribe law or policy," §§ 2(c), 2(g), 5 U.S.C. §§ 551(4), 551(13). The cases dealing with judicial review of administrative actions have interpreted the "finality" element in a pragmatic way. Thus in *Columbia Broadcasting System v. United States*, 316 U.S. 407, 62 S. Ct. 1194, 86 L. Ed. 1563, a suit under the Urgent Deficiencies Act, 38 Stat. 219, this Court held reviewable a regulation of the Federal Communications Commission setting forth certain proscribed contractual arrangements between chain broadcasters and local stations. The FCC did not have direct authority to regulate these contracts, and its rule asserted only that it would not license stations which maintained such contracts with the networks. Although no license had in fact been denied or revoked, and the FCC regulation could properly be characterized as a statement only of its intentions, the Court held that "Such regulations have the force of law before their sanctions are invoked as well as after. When as here they are promulgated by order of the Commission and the expected conformity to them causes injury cognizable by a court of equity, they are appropriately the subject of attack. . . ." 316 U.S., at 418–419. . . .

Again, in *United States v. Storer Broadcasting Co.*, 351 U.S. 192, 76 S. Ct. 763, 100 L. Ed. 1081, the Court held to be a final agency action within the meaning of the Administrative Procedure Act an FCC regulation announcing a Commission policy that it would not issue a television license to an applicant already owning five such licenses, even though no specific application was before the Commission. The Court stated: "The process of rulemaking was complete. It was final agency action . . . by which Storer claimed to be 'aggrieved.'" 351 U.S. at 198.

We find decision in the present case following a fortiori from these precedents. The regulation challenged here, promulgated in a formal manner after announcement in the Federal Register and consideration of comments by interested parties is quite clearly definitive. There is no hint that this regulation is informal, see *Helco Products Co. v. McNutt*, 78 U.S. App. D.C. 71, . . . or only the ruling of a subordinate official, see *Swift & Co. v. Wickham*, D.C., 230 F. Supp. 398, 409, affd, 2 Cir., 364 F.2d 241, or tentative. It was made effective upon publication, and the Assistant General Counsel for Food and Drugs stated in the District Court that compliance was expected . . .

This is also a case in which the impact of the regulations upon the petitioners is sufficiently direct and immediate as to render the issue appropriate for judicial review at this stage. These regulations purport to give an authoritative interpretation of a statutory provision that has a direct effect on the day-to-day business of all prescription drug companies; its promulgation puts petitioners in a dilemma that it was the very purpose of the Declaratory Judgement Act to ameliorate. As the District Court found on the basis of uncontested allegations, "Either they must comply with the every time requirement and incur the costs of changing over their promotional material and labeling or they must follow their present course and risk prosecution." 228 F. Supp. 855, 861. The regulations are clear-cut, and were made effective immediately upon publication; as noted earlier the agency's counsel represented to the District Court that immediate compliance with their terms was expected. If petitioners wish to comply they must change all their labels, advertisements, and promotional materials; they must destroy stocks of printed matter; and they must invest heavily in new printing type and new supplies. The alternative to compliance—continued use of material which they believe in good faith meets the statutory requirements, but which clearly does not meet the regulation of the Commissioner—may be even more costly. That course would risk serious criminal and civil penalties for the unlawful distribution of "misbranded" drugs.

It is relevant at this juncture to recognize that petitioners deal in a sensitive industry, in which public confidence in their drug products is especially important. To require them to challenge these regulations only as a defense to an action brought by the Government might harm them severely and unnecessarily. Where the legal issue presented is fit for judicial resolution, and where a regulation requires an immediate and significant change in the plaintiffs' conduct of their affairs with serious penalties attached to noncompliance, access to the courts under the Administrative Procedure Act and the Declaratory Judgment Act must be permitted, absent a statutory bar or some other unusual circumstance, neither of which appears here. . . .

The Government further contends that the threat of criminal sanctions for noncompliance with a judicially untested regulation is unrealistic; the Solicitor General has represented that if court enforcement becomes necessary, "the Department of Justice will proceed only civilly for an injunction . . . or by condemnation." We cannot accept this argument as a sufficient answer to petitioners' petition. This action at its inception was properly brought and this subsequent representation of the Department of Justice should not suffice to defeat it.

Finally, the Government urges that to permit resort to the courts in this type of case may delay or impede effective enforcement of the Act. We fully recognize the important public interest served by assuring prompt and unimpeded administration of the Pure Food, Drug, and Cosmetic Act, but we do not find the Government's argument convincing. First, in this particular case, a pre-enforcement challenge by nearly all prescription drug manufacturers is calculated to speed enforcement. If the Government prevails, a large part of the industry is bound by the decree; if the Government loses, it can more quickly revise its regulation. . . .

Lastly, although the Government presses us to reach the merits of the challenge to the regulation in the event we find the District Court properly entertained this action, we believe the better practice is to remand the case to the Court of Appeals for the Third Circuit to review the District Court's decision that the regulation was beyond the power of the Commissioner.

Reversed and remanded.

2. Standing

Professor Paul Freund once described Justice Harlan's opinions as possessing the qualities of fine, well-aged wine. Harlan's opinion in *Abbott Labs* makes satisfyingly clear that, despite the traditional view that courts must simply insure adversariness when they intervene, these doctrines—ripeness and presumption of reviewability—really accomplish more. They insure that the facts are fully developed and that the parties will address the law in point, not in tangential or speculative matters. The standing requirement pursues the same objectives as does ripeness. The standing concept applies throughout the legal system, so we may begin to explore it with an example less abstract than those typical of administrative law.

Suppose a couple plans to marry. Two months before the wedding date a drunken driver negligently strikes the man in a crosswalk. He suffers such serious injuries that the couple must postpone the wedding for a year. The law recognizes the man's legal capacity to bring suit to recover from the drunk driver for his injuries, but the woman has no standing to do so for him because she has not received the injury and she has no legally recognized relationship with him at this time. Standing doctrine thus judicially recognizes the claims of plaintiffs *directly injured* by the defendant. Note the important related point that while the driver's action may have caused her harm in an obvious way, she has no standing to recover for the hurt to herself, either. If the man earned $200,000 a year and by postponing the marriage she lost a year of sharing that money with him, she would suffer a real and measurable loss, but indirectly, not directly, from the defendant's negligent act.

Until 1968 the Court had consistently refused standing to taxpayer suits. In that year the Court granted limited standing to taxpayers if their suits met two requirements. First, taxpayer-plaintiffs had to challenge a specific congressional enactment made under the taxing and spending clause of Article I, section 8, of the Constitution. Second, they had to allege that the government violated some specific constitutional limitation on its taxing and spending power. In this case, plaintiffs gained standing to challenge expenditure of tax money that aided private schools operated by religious groups.[3]

In administrative law the requirements for standing are generally not as strict as they are for constitutional claims. Section 702 of the Administrative Procedure Act (APA) grants a person standing if she has been "aggrieved by [an] agency action within the meaning of the relevant statute." In *Association of Data Processing Service Organizations, Inc. v. Camp* (1970), Justice Douglas spells out the rationale for granting standing to parties before administrative tribunals if their claims are within a "zone of interest" as compared to the more narrow requirement that parties demonstrate "direct injury."

Association of Data Processing Service Organization, Inc. v. Camp

397 U.S. 150 (1970) 7–2
+ 	Burger, Black, Douglas, Harlan, Stewart, Marshall, Blackmun
+/– 	Brennan, White

[The Association of Data Processing Service Organizations challenged a ruling by the Comptroller of the Currency permitting national banks to provide data processing services as part of their banking services. The lower court dismissed the suit on the grounds that the petitioners lacked standing and the Court of Appeals affirmed.]

Justice Douglas delivered the opinion of the Court.
Generalizations about standing to sue are largely worthless as such. One generalization is, however, necessary and that is that the question of standing in the federal courts is to be considered in the framework of Article III which restricts judicial power to "cases" and "controversies." As we recently stated in *Flast* v. *Cohen*, 392 U.S. 83, 101, "[I]n terms of Article III limitations on federal court jurisdiction, the question of standing is related only to whether the dispute sought to be adjudicated will be presented

in an adversary context and in a form historically viewed as capable of judicial resolution." *Flast* was a *taxpayer's* suit. The present is a *competitor's* suit. And while the two have the same Article III starting point, they do not necessarily track one another.

The first question is whether the plaintiff alleges that the challenged action has caused him injury in fact, economic or otherwise. There can be no doubt but that petitioners have satisfied this test. The petitioners not only allege that competition by national banks in the business of providing data processing

[3] *Flast v. Cohen*, 392 U.S. 83 (1968).

services might entail some future loss of profits for the petitioners, they also allege that respondent American National Bank & Trust Company was performing or preparing to perform such services for two customers for whom petitioner Data Systems, Inc., had previously agreed or negotiated to perform such services . . .

Those tests were based on prior decisions of this Court, such as *Tennessee Power Co. v. TVA*, 306 U.S. 118, where private power companies sought to enjoin TVA from operating, claiming that the statutory plan under which it was created was unconstitutional. The court denied the competitors' standing, holding that they did not have that status "unless the right invaded is a legal right,—one of property, one arising out of contract, one protected against tortious invasion, or one founded on a statute which confers a privilege." *Id.*, at 137–138.

The "legal interest" test goes to the merits. The question of standing is different. It concerns, apart from the "case" or "controversy" test, the question whether the interest sought to be protected by the complainant is arguably within the zone of interests to be protected or regulated by the statute or constitutional guarantee in question. Thus the Administrative Procedure Act grants standing to a person "aggrieved by agency action within the meaning of a relevant statute." 5 U.S.C. § 702. That interest, at times, may reflect "aesthetic, conservational, and recreational" as well as economic values. *Scenic Hudson Preservation Conf. v. FPC*, 354 F. 2d 608, 616; *Office of Communication of United Church of Christ v. FCC*, 123 U.S. App. D.C. 328, 334–340, 359 F. 2d 994, 1000–1006. A person or a family may have a spiritual stake in First Amendment values sufficient to give standing to raise issues concerning the Establishment Clause and the Free Exercise Clause. *Abington School District v. Schempp*, 374 U.S. 203. We mention these noneconomic values to emphasize that standing may stem from them as well as from the economic injury on which petitioners rely here. Certainly he who is "likely to be financially" injured, *FCC v. Sanders Bros. Radio Station*, 309 U.S. 470, 477, may be a reliable private attorney general to litigate the issues of the public interest in the present case.

Apart from Article III jurisdictional questions, problems of standing, as resolved by this Court for its own governance, have involved a "rule of self-restraint." *Barrows v. Jackson*, 346 U.S. 249, 255. Congress can, of course, resolve the question one way or another, save as the requirements of Article III dictate otherwise. *Muskrat v. United States*, 219 U.S. 346.

Where statutes are concerned, the trend is toward enlargement of the class of people who may protest administrative action. The whole drive for enlarging the category of aggrieved "persons" is symptomatic of that trend. In a closely analogous case we held that an existing entrepreneur had standing to challenge the legality of the entrance of a newcomer into the business, because the established business was allegedly protected by a valid city ordinance that protected it from unlawful competition. *Chicago v. Atchison, T. & S. F. R. Co.*, 357 U.S. 77, 83–84. . . .

. . . There is great contrariety among administrative agencies created by Congress as respects "the extent to which, and the procedures by which, different measures of control afford judicial review of administrative action." *Stark v. Wickard*, 321 U.S. 288, 312 (Frankfurter, J., dissenting). The answer, of course, depends on the particular enactment under which review is sought. . . .

We read § 701 (a) as sympathetic to the issue presented in this case. As stated in the House Report:

> The statutes of Congress are not merely advisory when they relate to administrative agencies, any more than in other cases. To preclude judicial review under this bill a statute, if not specific in withholding such review, must upon its face give clear and convincing evidence of an intent to withhold it. The mere failure to provide specially by statute for judicial review is certainly no evidence of intent to withhold review. H. R. Rep. No. 1980, 79th Cong., 2d Sess., 41.

There is no presumption against judicial review and in favor of administrative absolutism (see *Abbott Laboratories v. Gardner*, 387 U.S. 136, 140), unless that purpose is fairly discernible in the statutory scheme. . . .

We find no evidence that Congress in either the Bank Service Corporation Act or the National Bank Act sought to preclude judicial review of administrative rulings by the Comptroller as to the legitimate scope of activities available to national banks under those statutes. Both Acts are clearly "relevant" statutes within the meaning of § 702. The Acts do not in terms protect a specified group. But their general policy is apparent; and those whose interests are directly affected by a broad or narrow interpretation of the Acts are easily indentifiable. It is clear that petitioners, as competitiors of national banks which are engaging in data processing services, are within that class of "aggrieved" persons who, under § 702, are entitled to judicial review of "agency action."

Whether anything in the Bank Service Corporation Act or the National Bank Act gives petitioners a "legal interest" that protects them against violations of those Acts, and whether the actions of respondents did in fact violate either of those Acts, are questions which go to the merits and remain to be decided below.

We hold that petitioners have standing to sue and that the case should be remanded for a hearing on the merits.

Reversed and remanded.

Justice Brennan, with whom Justice White joins, concurring in the result and dissenting.

I concur in the result in [this] case but dissent from the Court's treatment of the question of standing to challenge agency action.

The Court's approach to standing, set out in *Data Processing*, has two steps: (1) since "the framework of Article III . . . restricts judicial power to 'cases' and 'controversies,'" the first step is to determine "whether the plaintiff alleges that the challenged action has caused him injury in fact"; (2) if injury in fact is alleged, the relevant statute or constitutional provision is then examined to determine "whether the interest sought to be protected by the complainant is arguably within the zone of interests to be protected or regulated by the statute or constitutional guarantee in question."

My view is that the inquiry in the Court's first step is the only one that need be made to determine standing. I had thought we discarded the notion of any additional requirement when we discussed standing solely in terms of its constitutional content in *Flast v. Cohen*, 392 U.S. 83 (1968). By requiring a second, nonconstitutional step, the Court comes very close to perpetuating the discredited requirement that conditioned standing on a showing by the plaintiff that the challenged governmental action invaded one of his legally protected interests. . . .

Before the plaintiff is allowed to argue the merits, it is true that a canvass of relevant statutory materials must be made in cases challenging agency action. But the canvass is made, not to determine *standing*, but to determine an aspect of *reviewability*, that is, whether Congress meant to deny or to allow judicial review of the agency action at the instance of the plaintiff.* The Court in the present cases examines the statutory materials for just this purpose but only after making the same examination during the second step of its standing inquiry. Thus in *Data Processing* the Court determines that the petitioners have standing because they alleged injury in fact and because "§ 4 [of the Bank Service Corporation Act of 1962] arguably brings a competitor within the zone of interests protected by it." The Court then determines that the Comptroller's action is reviewable at the instance of the plaintiffs because "[b]oth [the Bank Service Corporation Act and the National Bank Act] are clearly 'relevant' statutes within the meaning of [the Administrative Procedure Act, 5 U.S.C. § 702 (1964 ed., Supp. IV)]. The Acts do not in terms protect a specified group. But their general policy is apparent; and those whose interests are directly affected by a broad or narrow interpretation of the Acts are easily identifiable. . . .

---

*Reviewability has often been treated as if it involved a single issue: whether agency action is conclusive and beyond judicial challenge by anyone. In reality, however, reviewability is equally concerned with a second issue: whether the *particular* plaintiff then requesting review may have it. See the Administrative Procedure Act, 5 U.S.C. §§ 701 (a) and 702 (1964 ed., Supp. IV). Both questions directly concern the extent to which persons harmed by agency action may challenge its legality.

I submit that in making such examination of statutory materials an element in the determination of standing, the Court not only performs a useless and unnecessary exercise but also encourages badly reasoned decisions, which may well deny justice in this complex field. When agency action is challenged, standing, reviewability, and the merits pose discrete, and often complicated, issues which can best be resolved by recognizing and treating them as such.

Although *Flast v. Cohen* was not a case challenging agency action, its determination of the basis for standing should resolve that question for all cases. We there confirmed what we said in *Baker v. Carr*, 369 U.S. 186, 204 (1962), that the "gist of the question of standing" is whether the party seeking relief has "alleged such a personal stake in the outcome of the controversy as to assure that concrete adverseness which sharpens the presentation of issues upon which the court so largely depends for illumination of difficult . . . questions." "In other words," we said in *Flast*, "when standing is placed in issue in a case, the question is whether the person whose standing is challenged is a proper party to request an adjudication of a particular issue" and not whether the controversy it otherwise justiciable, or whether, on the merits, the plaintiff has a legally protected interest that the defendant's action invaded. 392 U.S., at 99–100. The objectives of the Article III standing requirement are simple: the avoidance of any use of a "federal court as a forum [for the airing of] generalized grievances about the conduct of government," and the creation of a judicial context in which "the questions will be framed with the necessary specificity, . . . the issues . . . contested with the necessary adverseness and . . . the litigation . . . pursued with the necessary vigor to assure that the . . . challenge will be made in a form traditionally thought to be capable of judicial resolution." . . .

Just two years after the *Data Processing* case, the Supreme Court in *Sierra Club v. Morton*[4] indicated that it did not intend to expand standing as far as many had thought the Court did in *Data Processing*. Instead, the Supreme Court applied the requirement of direct injury in an administrative law case. The Sierra Club, an organization devoted to environmental protection, complained that the United States Forest Service failed to comply with federal rules designed to protect forest environments when it approved the development by Walt Disney Enterprises of a major resort in the Mineral King Valley of California's Sierra Nevada Mountains. The Club claimed to be "adversely affected or aggrieved by agency action" (APA section 702). The Court dismissed the claim for lack of standing because "nowhere in the pleadings or affidavits did the Club state that its members use Mineral King for any purpose, much less that they use it in any way that would be significantly affected by the proposed actions of the [government].[5] Section 702, said the Court, requires "that the party seeking review be himself among the injured.[6]

This result might seem a setback to the ability of citizen's groups to protest governmental action, but in practice it has not been. The Sierra Club amended its suit to allege that its members used the valley and would be affected by changing it. The Disney project died.

Nonetheless standing law today allows a considerably wider class of citizens to bring suits than it did less than twenty years ago. Richard Stewart has argued that "any class of interests which the administrator is required by statute (either implicitly or explicitly)

---

[4] 405 U.S. 727 (1972) 5–2 see Justice Douglas's and Justice Blackmun's dissenting opinions.

[5] Id.. at 735.

[6] Ibid.

to consider in framing agency policy is entitled to standing."[7] The Supreme Court has never stated the point quite so boldly, but, as the next case shows, the Court reaches equally broad results. The case illustrates a modern and quite liberal interpretation of the standing doctrine.

United States v. Students Challenging Regulatory Agency Procedures

412 U.S. 669 (1973) 8–0
+   Brennan, Stewart, Blackmun
+/–   Douglas, White, Marshall, Burger, Rehnquist
NP   Powell

[SCRAP, a public interest group composed of five law school students with the avowed mission of improving the quality of the environment, brought suit for injunctive relief to stop the Interstate Commerce Commission from enforcing a set of orders allowing increased freight charges on the nation's railroads. In its claim to standing, SCRAP alleged that the increased rates would cause their members to pay more for goods carried by the railroads and thus lead to a higher use of throwaway products in lieu of the more expensive durable goods typically carried by railroads. The increased use of throwaway items would, in turn, lead to more litter in national parks. This result would cause the members of SCRAP to pay more taxes to finance the increased need for cleanup operations. Additionally, the increased use of throwaway items would demand the use of additional natural resources that would harm the natural areas that members of SCRAP, avid outdoor enthusiasts, used for recreation. The trial court agreed with the students and enjoined the ICC from permitting the railroads to raise their rates.]

Justice Stewart delivered the opinion of the Court.

The appellants challenge the appellees' standing to sue, arguing that the allegations in the pleadings as to standing were vague, unsubstantiated and insufficient under our recent decision in *Sierra Club v. Morton*. . . . . The appellees respond that unlike the petitioner in *Sierra Club*, their pleadings sufficiently alleged that they were "adversely affected" or "aggrieved" within the meaning of [Sec 702] of the Administrative Procedure Act . . . and they point specifically to the allegations that their members used the forests, streams, mountains, and other resources in the Washington metropolitan area for camping, hiking, fishing, and sightseeing, and that this use was disturbed by the adverse environmental impact caused by the nonuse of recyclable goods brought about by a rate increase on those commodities. . . .

The petitioner in *Sierra Club*, "a large and long-established organization, with a historic commitment to the cause of protecting our Nation's natural heritage from man's depredations," . . . sought a declaratory judgement and an injunction to restrain federal officials from approving the creation of an extensive ski-resort development in the scenic Mineral King Valley of the Sequoia National Forest. The Sierra Club claimed standing to maintain its "public interest" lawsuit because it had " 'a special interest in the conservation and [the] sound maintenance of the national parks, game refuges and forests of the country. . . . ' " . . . We hold those allegations insufficient.

[7] Richard Stewart, "The Reformation of American Administrative Law," *Harvard Law Review* 88 (1975):1699.
Also see Mark Tushnet, "The New Law of Standing: A Plea for Abandonment," *Cornell Law Review* 62 (1977):1.

Relying upon our prior decisions . . . we held that [Sec. 702] of the APA . . . "injury in fact" . . . made it clear that standing was not confined to those who could show "economic harm," although both *Data Processing* and *Barlow* had involved that kind of injury. Nor, we said, could the fact that many persons shared the same injury be sufficient reason to disqualify from seeking review of an agency's action any person who had in fact suffered injury. . . .

In *Sierra Club*, though, we went on to stress the importance of demonstrating that the party seeking review be himself among the injured, for it is this requirement that gives a litigant a direct stake in the controversy and prevents the judicial process from becoming no more than a vehicle for the vindication of the value interests of concerned bystanders. No such specific injury was alleged in *Sierra Club*. In that case the asserted harm "will be felt directly only by those who use Mineral King and Sequoia National Park, and for whom the aesthetic and recreational values of the area will be lessened by the highway and ski resort," . . . yet "[t]he Sierra Club failed to allege that it or its members would be affected in any of their activities or pastimes by the . . . development." . . . Here, by contrast, the appellees claimed that the specific and allegedly illegal action of the Commission would directly harm them in their use of the natual resources of the Washington Metropolitan Area.

Unlike the specific and geographically limited federal action of which the petitioner complained in *Sierra Club*, the challenged agency action in this case is applicable to substantially all of the Nation's railroads, and thus allegedly has an adverse environmental impact on all the natural resources of the country. Rather than a limited group of persons who used a picturesque valley in California, all persons who utilize the scenic resources of the country, and indeed all who breathe its air, could claim harm similar to that alleged by the environmental groups here. But we have already made it clear that standing is not to be denied simply because many people suffer the same injury. Indeed some of the cases on which we relied in *Sierra Club* demonstrated the patent fact that persons across the Nation could be adversely affected by major governmental actions. . . . To deny standing to persons who are in fact injured simply because many others are also injured, would mean that the most injurious and widespread Government actions could be questioned by nobody. We cannot accept that conclusion.

But the injury alleged here is also very different from that at issue in *Sierra Club* because here the alleged injury to the environment is far less direct and perceptible. The petitioner there complained about the construction of a specific project that would directly affect the Mineral King Valley. Here, the Court was asked to follow a far more attenuated line of causation to the eventual injury of which the appellees complained—a general rate increase would allegedly cause increased use of nonrecyclable commodities as compared to recyclable goods, thus resulting in the need to use more natural resources to produce such goods, some of which resources might be taken from the Washington area, and resulting in more refuse that might be discarded in national parks in the Washington area. The railroads protest that the appellees could never prove that a general increase in rates would have this effect, and they contend that these allegations were a ploy to avoid the need to show some injury in fact.

Of course, pleadings must be something more than an ingenious academic exercise in the conceivable. A plaintiff must allege that he has been or will in fact be perceptibly harmed by the challenged agency action, not that he can imagine circumstances in which he could be affected by the agency's action. And it is equally clear that the allegations must be true and capable of proof at trial. But we deal here simply with the pleadings in which the appellees alleged a specific and perceptible harm that distinguished them from other citizens who had used the natural resources that were claimed to be affected. If, as the railroads now assert, these allegations were in fact untrue, then the appellants should have moved for summary judgment on the standing issue and demonstrated to the District Court that the allegations were sham and raised no genuine issue of fact. We cannot say on these pleadings that the appellees could not prove their allegations which, if proved, would place them squarely among those persons injured in fact by the Commission's action, and entitled under the clear import of *Sierra Club* to seek review. The District Court was correct in denying the appellants' motion to dismiss the complaint for failure to allege sufficient standing to bring this lawsuit. . . .

[Reversed on other grounds.]

Note the *SCRAP* opinion's assertion that standing depends on what might arguably be true. The law of standing does not require plaintiffs to prove their actual case in order to gain the right to prove their case. It merely gives plaintiffs a chance to prove their case, which in the end *SCRAP* did not. To gain standing, plaintiffs must show a second element in addition to direct legal injury. The injury must also be substantial. Since the harm to any single individual is not very substantial if the cost of shipping empty beer cans increases a few cents a ton, *SCRAP* establishes a precedent that expands standing for interest groups.

The substantial injury criteria often comes into question in regulatory cases either because the nature of the injury is not yet fully realized or because the parties alleging injury are not directly involved in the regulatory scheme. The latter we call *third-party suits*. The have become more common with the advent of the public interest movement.[8] The last standing case we include, *Duke Power Co. v. Carolina Environmental Study Group* (1978) is technically not a third-party suit, but it does involve public interest organizations who attempted to employ a broad concept of standing to challenge the limited liability law governing nuclear power plant accidents.

Duke Power Co. v. Carolina Environmental Study Group

98 S. Ct. 2620 (1978) 6–3
+   Burger, Brennan, White, Marshall, Blackmun, Powell
+/– Stewart, Rehnquist, Stevens

[Duke Power Company and the Nuclear Regulatory Commission were sued by environmental organization and their members who lived in areas where Duke Power proposed to build a nuclear power plant. The environmental organizations challenged the constitutionality of the Price-Anderson Act, which imposed a $560 million limitation on liability for nuclear accidents. Plaintiffs maintained that this limitation restricted their common-law remedies for injuries caused by nuclear power plants, thus taking their property without due process of law and violating their equal protection rights. The district court upheld plaintiffs' standing, and Duke Power appealed this ruling directly to the Supreme Court.]

Chief Justice Burger delivered the opinion of the Court.
We turn first to consider the kinds of injuries the District Court found the appellees suffered. It discerned two categories of effects which resulted from the operation of nuclear power plants in potentially dangerous proximity to appellees' living and working environment. The immediate effects included: (a) the production of small quantities of non-natural radiation which would invade the air and water; (b) a "sharp increase" in the temperature of two lakes presently used for recreational purposes resulting from the use of the lake waters to produce steam and to

---

[8] See Cass R. Sunstein, "Interest Groups in American Public Law," *Stanford Law Review* 38 (1985):29

cool the reactor; (c) interference with the normal use of the waters of the Catawba River; (d) threatened reduction in property values of land neighboring the power plants; (e) "objectively reasonable" present fear and apprehension regarding the "effect of the increased radioactivity in air, land and water upon [appellees] and their property, and the genetic effects upon their descendants"; and (f) the continual threat of "an accident resulting in uncontrolled release of large or even small quantities of radioactive material" with no assurance of adequate compensation for the resultant damage. . . .

For purposes of the present inquiry, we need not determine whether all the putative injuries identified by the District Court, particularly those based on the possibility of a nuclear accident and the present apprehension generated by this future uncertainty, are sufficiently concrete to satisfy constitutional requirements. . . . Certainly the environmental and aesthetic consequences of the thermal pollution of the two lakes in the vicinity of the disputed power plants is the type of harmful effect which has been deemed adequate in prior cases to satisfy the "injury in fact" standard. See *United States v. SCRAP* . . . *Sierra Club v. Morton.* And the emission of non-natural radiation into appellees' environment would also seem a direct and present injury. . . .

The more difficult step in the standing inquiry is establishing that these injuries "fairly can be traced to the challenged action of the defendant," *Simon v. Eastern Ky. Welfare Rights Org.*, 426 U.S., at 41 . . . or put otherwise, that the exercise of the Court's remedial powers would redress the claimed injuries. . . . The District Court discerned a "but for" causal connection between the Price-Anderson Act, which appellees challenged as unconstitutional, "and the construction of the nuclear plants which the [appellees] view as a threat to them." . . . Particularizing that causal link to the facts of the instant case, the District Court concluded that "there is a substantial likelihood that Duke would not be able to complete the construction and maintain the operation of the McGuire and Catawba Nuclear Plants but for the protection provided by the Price-Anderson Act." *Id.*, at 220.

These findings, which, if accepted, would likely satisfy the second prong of the constitutional test for standing as elaborated in *Simon*, are challenged on two grounds. First, it is argued that the evidence presented at the hearing, contrary to the conclusion reached by the District Court, indicated that the McGuire and Catawba nuclear plants would be completed and operated without the Price-Anderson Act's limitation on liability. And second, it is contended that the Price-Anderson Act is not, in some essential sense, the "but for" cause of the disputed nuclear power plants and resultant adverse effects since if the Act had not been passed Congress may well have chosen to pursue the nuclear program as a Government monopoly as it had from 1946 until 1954. We reject both of these arguments.

The District Court's finding of a "substantial likelihood" that the McGuire and Catawba nuclear plants would be neither completed nor operated absent the Price-Anderson Act rested in major part on the testimony of corporate officials before the Joint Committee on Atomic Energy (JCAE) in 1956–1957 when the Price-Anderson Act was first considered and again in 1975 when a second renewal was discussed. During the 1956–1957 hearings, industry spokesmen for the utilities and the producers of the various component parts of the power plants expressed a categorical unwillingness to participate in the development of nuclear power absent guarantees of a limitation on their liability. . . . By 1975, the tenor of the testimony had changed only slightly. While large utilities and producers were somewhat more equivocal about whether a failure to renew Price-Anderson would entail their leaving the industry, the smaller producers of component parts and architects and engineers—all of whom are essential to the building of the reactors and generating plants—considered renewal of the Act as the critical variable in determining their continued involvement with nuclear power. . . . Duke Power itself, in its letter to the Committee urging extension of the Act, cited recent experiences with suppliers and contractors who were requiring the inclusion of cancellation clauses in their contracts to take effect if the liability-limitation provisions were eliminated. *Id.*, at 217. . . .

. . . Considering the documentary evidence and the testimony in the record, we cannot say we are left with "the definite and firm conviction that" the finding by the trial court of a substantial likelihood that the McGuire and Catawba nuclear power plants would be neither completed nor operated absent the Price-Anderson Act is clearly erroneous; and, hence, we are bound to accept it. . . .

It is further contended that in addition to proof of injury and of a causal link between such injury and the challenged conduct, appellees must demonstrate a connection between the injuries they claim and the constitutional rights being asserted. This nexus requirement is said to find its origin in *Flast v. Cohen*, 392 U.S. 83 . . . (1968), where the general question of taxpayer standing was considered:

> "The nexus demanded of federal taxpayers has two aspects to it. First, the taxpayer must establish a logical link between that status and the type of legislative enactment attacked.
> . . . Secondly, the taxpayer must establish a nexus between that status and the precise nature of the constitutional infringement alleged." *Id.*, at 102, 88 S. Ct., at 1954.

. . . Since environmental and health injuries claimed by appellees are not directly related to the constitutional attack on the Price-Anderson Act, such injuries, the argument continues, cannot supply a predicate for standing. We decline to accept this argument.

The major difficulty with the argument is that it implicitly assumes that the nexus requirement formulated in the context of taxpayer suits has general applicability in suits of all other types brought in the federal courts. No cases have been cited outside the context of taxpayer suits where we have demanded this type of subject-matter nexus between the right asserted and the injury alleged, and we are aware of none. . . . We . . . cannot accept the contention that, outside the context of taxpayers' suits, a litigant must demonstrate something more than injury in fact and a substantial likelihood that the judicial relief requested will prevent or redress the claimed injury to satisfy the "case or controversy" requirement of Art. III.

. . . Given our conclusion that, in general, limiting liability is an acceptable method for Congress to utilize in encouraging the private development of electric energy by atomic power, candor requires acknowledgment that whatever ceiling figure is selected will, of necessity, be arbitrary in the sense that any choice of a figure based on imponderables like those at issue here can always be so characterized. This is not, however, the kind of arbitrariness which flaws otherwise constitutional action. When appraised in terms of both the extremely remote possibility of an accident where liability would exceed the limitation and Congress' now statutory commitment to "take whatever action is deemed necessary and appropriate to protect the public from the consequences of" any such disaster, 42 U.S.C § 2210(e) (1970) ed., Supp. V), we hold the congressional decision to fix a $560 million ceiling at this stage in the private development and production of electric energy by nuclear power, to be within permissible limits and not violate of due process.

Justice Stewart, concurring in the result.

On the issue of standing, the Court relies on the "present" injuries of increased water temperatures and low-level radiation emissions. Even assuming that but for the Act the plant would not exist and therefore neither would its effects on the environment, I cannot believe that it follows that the appellees have standing to attack the constitutionality of the Act. Apart from a "but for" connection in the loosest sense of that concept, there is no relationship at all between the injury alleged for standing purposes and the injury alleged for federal subject-matter jurisdiction.

Surely a plaintiff does not have standing simply because his challenge, if successful, will remove the injury relied on for standing purposes *only* because it will put the defendant out of existence. Surely there must be *some* direct relationship between the plaintiff's federal claim and the injury relied on for standing. . . . An interest in the local water temperature does not, in short, give these appellees standing to bring a suit under 28 U.S.C. § 1331 (1976 ed.) to challenge the constitutionality of a law limiting liability in an unrelated and as-yet-to-occur major nuclear accident.

For these reasons, I would remand these cases to the District Court with instructions to dismiss the complaint.

Justice Rehnquist, with whom Justice Stevens joins, concurring in the judgment.

I can understand the Court's willingness to reach the merits of this case and thereby remove the doubt which has been cast over this important federal statute. In so doing, however, it ignores established limitations on district court jurisdiction as carefully defined in our statutes and cases. Because I believe the preservation of these limitations is in the long run more important to this Court's jurisprudence than the resolution of any particular case or controversy, however important, I too would reverse the judgment of the District Court, but would do so with instructions to dismiss the complaint for want of jurisdiction. . . .

Justice Stevens, concurring in the judgment. [omitted]

3. Mootness

A case becomes moot when the harm affecting the plaintiff somehow ceases during the course of litigation. For example, when Marco DeFunis challenged the decision of the University of Washington's law school to deny his admission even though the school admitted nonwhite students with lower numerical scores than DeFunis's, the lower court ordered DeFunis admitted to the school. By the time this reverse discrimination issue reached the United States Supreme Court, DeFunis was close to completing his final year. The law school conceded that, regardless of the Court's decision, it would grant DeFunis a degree when he completed the requirements for it. The Court held the case moot as a result.[9]

4. Exhaustion of Administrative Remedies

The ripeness doctrine and the law requiring that plaintiffs exhaust their chances for administrative remedies are sometimes virtually indistinguishable. A difference does exist, however. A case that is unripe is somehow incomplete. Further facts need to be developed or rules interpreted, and thus the court does not have the final problem necessarily before it. Exhaustion is narrower. A decision is final. A potential or actual harm has taken clear shape. Yet the agency itself may provide relief from the harm the plaintiff fears.[10] Exhaustion is thus primarily a gatekeeping rule, one designed to avoid work for courts unless and until it becomes unavoidable.

5. Primary Jurisdiction

In a complex bureaucracy, and expecially in one that has grown piecemeal as our governmental bureaucracies have done, the authorities and jurisdictions of agencies overlap and in some cases overlap subject-matter jurisdiction of the courts themselves. *Primary jurisdiction* is a traffic-light doctrine designed to steer cases in one direction. For example, in 1975 the Sunflower Electric Cooperative charged the Kansas Power and Light

[9]*DeFunis v. Odegaard*, 416 U.S. 312 (1974). See *Roe v. Wade*, 410 U.S. 113 (1973), for different results regarding the mooting effect of the termination of a pregnancy on a lawsuit challenging a statute imposing criminal penalties for performing an abortion.

[10]Also see *Bowen v. City of New York*, 106 S. Ct. 2022 (1986), where the Supreme Court unanimously held that the rules of exhaustion do not apply to claimants under the Social Security Administration's disability provisions if plaintiff alleges an irregularity in the agency's proceedings.

Company and several other utilities in federal district court with conspiring to monopolize the exchange of power in violation of the Sherman Antitrust Act. The defendants asked the court, under the primary jurisdiction doctrine, to refuse to hear the case because the Federal Power Commission had authority over rate setting for electricity. The trial court agreed to do so because the FPC possessed special competence in the matter. The appellate court reversed. The FPC, it held, had no authority to address antitrust matters directly and had no particular experience with such matters. Besides, the FPC had no direct authority to regulate the practice of energy exchange that the plaintiffs accused the defendants of illegally monopolizing. Since courts traditionally hear antitrust cases and because an inconsistency between a judicial and an agency ruling might, but probably would not, occur, the appellate court ordered the trial court to hear the antitrust case.[11]

The rules of judicial reviewability discussed in this section may seem technical or legalistic, but they affect the openness and rationality of the bureaucratic system just as powerfully as do the principles of rulemaking and adjudication themselves. Indeed the rules of ripeness, standing, etc., at bottom form another instance of judicial balancing. The reviewability rules balance the degree of injury suffered, the obviousness of the potential administrative error, the lack of a chance to gain relief elsewhere than in the courts, and the importance of judicial intervention to clarify law for the future. As each of these factors increases in magnitude, judicial intervention becomes more appropriate.[12]

The Scope of Judicial Review

Sections 701 to 706 of the APA appear to shape court review of administrative action significantly, but in practice these sections for the most part reiterate preexisting law. For example, the result in *Sierra Club* purported to rest on section 702, but the Court could have reached the same result easily under general principles of standing. Similarly section 701(a) suggests that Congress possesses power by statute to prevent judicial review of some actions. But Article III of the Constitution appears to grant the same power to Congress.

Can Congress erase federal court jurisdiction to hear constitutional questions themselves, including those involving important civil rights? This question has become a hotly debated political issue. Recent cases have tried to avoid directly confronting the problem by interpreting statutes limiting jurisdiction narrowly. Thus section 211(a) of Title 38 of the United States Code reads: "the decisions of the Administrator [of the Veterans' Administration] of any question of law or fact under any law administered by the Veterans' Administration providing benefits for veterans . . . shall be final and conclusive and no . . . court of the United States shall have the power or jurisdiction to review such decision. . . ." When the administrator denied veterans' benefits to

---

[11] *Sunflower Electric Coop. v. Kansas Power and Light Co., et al.*, 603 F.2d 791 (1979).

[12] See Gary Cheedes, *"Understanding Judicial Review of Federal Agency Action,"* University of Richmond Law Review 12 (1978):469.

a conscientious objector, the conscientious objector challenged the decision in court on religious freedom grounds. The Supreme Court accepted jurisdiction by treating his claim as one *under* the Constitution and not *under* section 211(a) at all. The plaintiff lost on the merits.[13]

As a practical matter Congress usually says nothing about reviewability of administrative decisions in authorizing legislation. The statutory language that does exist often reiterates APA language and/or *Abbott Labs's* presumption of reviewability. Occasionally, however, Congress imposes specific time limits for the reviewability by courts of administrative rules. For example, the Clean Air Act Amendments of 1977 allow only sixty days from the time it becomes official to contest a rule. But what if a rule's defects and the hardship it imposes only become clear when, perhaps much later, the rule is applied and enforced? Several courts have refused to honor the statutory time limit in such instances.[14]

Reviewing Agency Action Committed to Agency Discretion

Two more aspects of judicial review require attention. The first involves the interpretation of section 701(a). When does a statute "preclude judicial review," 701(a)(1)? When is "agency action committed to agency discretion by law," 701(a)(2)? How do these sections differ? The second aspect examines the scope of judicial review. Just how aggressively should courts question agency conclusions of fact and interpretations of law? Section 706 permits *some* inquiry into both law and facts, and you should review that section in Appendix B (The Federal Administrative Procedure Act) before reading further in this chapter.

The *Overton Park* case, which follows, deals with both problems and thus shows you the link between the questions of *whether judicial review* and *how much judicial review*.

Citizens to Preserve Overton Park v. Volpe

401 U.S. 402 (1971) 8–0

+ Burger, Black, Harlan, Brennan, Stewart, White, Marshall, Blackmun

NP Douglas

[The Department of Transportation (DOT) planned to construct a section of Interstate 40 through Overton Park in Memphis and had acquired both the right-of-way and the approval of local officials. When constructed, the interstate would effectively sever one part of the park from the other. The secretary of DOT was authorized by statute to approve the routing of interstates through public parks only if no "feasible and prudent" alternate route existed. Further, if no "feasible and prudent" alternative could be found, the secretary was directed by statute to approve construction only

---

[13]*Johnson v. Robison*, 415 U.S. 361 (1974).

[14]See Frederick Davis, "Judicial Review of Rulemaking: New Patterns and New Problems," Duke Law Journal (1981):279.

[if there had been every effort to plan for a minimum of harm to the park. When the secretary did approve the construction without any factual findings in his decision to the effect that all possible alternatives were not feasible and that harm to the park had been minimized, the citizens group brought suit claiming a violation of the secretary's statutory authority. The district court entered summary judgment for the secretary and was affirmed by the appellate court.]

Opinion of the Court by Justice Marshall, announced by Justice Stewart.

The growing public concern about the quality of our natural environment has prompted Congress in recent years to enact legislation designed to curb the accelerating destruction of our country's natural beauty. We are concerned in this case with § 4 (f) of the Department of Transportation Act of 1966, as amended, and § 18 (a) of the Federal-Aid Highway Act of 1968, . . . 23 U.S.C. § 138 . . . (hereafter § 138). These statutes prohibit the Secretary of Transportation from authorizing the use of federal funds to finance the construction of highways through public parks if a "feasible and prudent" alternative route exists. If no such route is available, the statutes allow him to approve construction through parks only if there has been "all possible planning to minimize harm" to the park. . . ."

Petitioners contend that the Secretary's action is invalid without such formal findings and that the Secretary did not make an independent determination but merely relied on the judgment of the Memphis City Council. They also contend that it would be "feasible and prudent" to route I-40 around Overton Park either to the north or to the south. And they argue that if these alternative routes are not "feasible and prudent," the present plan does not include "all possible" methods for reducing harm to the park. Petitioners claim that I-40 could be built under the park by using either of two possible tunneling methods,* and they claim that, at a minimum, by using advanced drainage techniques the expressway could be depressed below ground level along the en-

---

*Petitioner argue that either a bored tunnel or a cut-and-cover tunnel, which is a fully depressed route covered after construction, could be built. Respondents contend that the construction of a tunnel by either method would greatly increase the cost of the project, would create safety hazards, and because of increases in air pollution would not reduce harm to the park.

tire route through the park including the section that crosses the small creek.

Respondents argue that it was unnecessary for the Secretary to make formal findings, and that he did, in fact, exercise his own independent judgment which was supported by the facts. In the District Court, respondents introduced affidavits, prepared specifically for this litigation, which indicated that the Secretary had made the decision and that the decision was supportable. These affidavits were contradicted by affidavits introduced by petitioners, who also sought to take the deposition of a former Federal Highway Administrator who had participated in the decision to route I-40 through Overton Park.

The District Court and the Court of Appeals found that formal findings by the Secretary were not necessary and refused to order the deposition of the former Federal Highway Administrator because those courts believed that probing of the mental processes of an administrative decisionmaker was prohibited. And, believing that the Secretary's authority was wide and reviewing courts' authority narrow in the approval of highway routes, the lower courts held that the affidavits contained no basis for a determination that the Secretary had exceeded his authority.

We agree that formal findings were not required. But we do not believe that in this case judicial review based solely on litigation afffidavits was adequate.

A threshold question—whether petitioners are entitled to any judicial review—is easily answered. Section 701 of the Administrative Procedure Act, 5 U.S.C. § 701 . . . , provides that the action of "each authority of the Government of the United States," which includes the Department of Transportation, is subject to judicial review except where there is a statutory prohibition on review or where "agency action is committed to agency discretion by law." In this case, there is no indication that Congress sought to prohibit judicial review and there is most certainly no "showing of 'clear and convincing evidence' of a . . . legislative intent" to restrict access to judicial review. *Abbott Laboratories v. Gardner*, 387 U.S. 136, 141 (1967). . . .

Similarly, the Secretary's decision here does not fall within the exception for action "committed to agency discretion." This is a very narrow exception. Berger, Administrative Arbitrariness and Judicial Review, 65 Col. L. Rev. 55 (1965). The legislative history of the Administrative Procedure Act indicates that it is applicable in those rare instances where "statutes are drawn in such broad terms that in a given case there is no law to apply." . . .

Section 4 (f) of the Department of Transportation Act and § 138 of the Federal-Aid Highway Act are clear and specific directives. Both the Department of Transportation Act and the Federal-Aid Highway Act provided that the Secretary "shall not approve any program or project" that requires the use of any public parkland "unless (1) there is no feasible and prudent alternative to the use of such land, and (2) such program includes all possible planning to minimize harm to such park. . . ." . . . This language is a plain and explicit bar to the use of federal funds for construction of highways through parks—only the most unusual situations are exempted.

Despite the clarity of the statutory language, respondents argue that the Secretary has wide discretion. They recognize that the requirement that there be no "feasible" alternative route admits of little administrative discretion. For this exemption to apply the Secretary must find that as a matter of sound engineering it would not be feasible to build the highway along any other route. Respondents argue, however, that the requirement that there be no other "prudent" route requires the Secretary to engage in a wide-ranging balancing of competing interests. They contend that the Secretary should weigh the detriment resulting from the destruction of parkland against the cost of other routes, safety considerations, and other factors, and determine on the basis of the importance that he attaches to these other factors whether, on balance, alternative feasible routes would be "prudent."

But no such wide-ranging endeavor was intended. It is obvious that in most cases considerations of cost, directness of route, and community disruption will indicate that parkland should be used for highway construction whenever possible. Although it may be necessary to transfer funds from one jurisdiction to another, there will always be a smaller outlay required from the public purse when parkland is used since the public already owns the land and there will be no need to pay for right-of-way. And since people do not live or work in parks, if a highway is built on parkland no one will have to leave his home or give up his business. Such factors are common to substantially all highway construction. Thus, if Congress intended these factors to be on an equal footing with preservation of parkland there would have been no need for the statutes.

Congress clearly did not intend that cost and disruption of the community were to be ignored by the Secretary. But the very existence of the statutes indicates that protection of parkland was to be given paramount importance. The few green havens that are public parks were not to be lost unless there were truly unusual factors present in a particular case or the cost or community disruption resulting from alternative routes reached extraordinary magnitudes. If the statutes are to have any meaning, the Secretary cannot approve the destruction of parkland unless he finds that alternative routes present unique problems.

Plainly, there is "law to apply" and thus the exemption for action "committed to agency discretion" in inapplicable. But the existence of judicial review is only the start: the standard for review must also be determined. For that we must look to § 706 of the Administrative Procedure Act, 5 U.S.C. § 706. . . . , which provides that a "reviewing court shall . . . hold unlawful and set aside agency action, findings, and conclusions found" not to meet six separate standards. In all cases agency action must be set aside if the action was arbitrary, capricious, an abuse of discretion, or otherwise not in accordance with law" or if the action failed to meet statutory, procedural, or constitutional requirements. 5 U.S.C. §§ 706 (2)(A), (B), (C), (D). . . .

In certain narrow, specifically limited situations, the agency action is to be set aside if the action was not supported by "substantial evidence." And in other equally narrow circumstances the reviewing court is to engage in a *de novo* review of the action and set it aside if it was "unwarranted by the facts." 5 U.S.C. §§ 706 (2) (E), (F). . . .

Petitioners argue that the Secretary's approval of the construction of I-40 through Overton Park is subject to one or the other of these latter two standards of limited applicability. First, they contend that the "substantial evidence" standard of § 706 (2) (E) must be applied. In the alternative, they claim that § 706 (2) (F) applies and that there must be a *de novo* review to determine if the Secretary's action was "unwarranted by the facts." Neither of these standards is, however, applicable.

Review under the substantial-evidence test is authorized only when the agency action is taken pursuant to a rulemaking provision of the Administrative Procedure Act itself, 5 U.S.C. § 553 . . . , or when the agency action is based on a public adjudicatory hearing. See 5 U.S.C. §§ 556, 557. . . . The Secretary's decision to allow the expenditure of federal funds to build I-40 through Overton Park was plainly not an exercise of a rulemaking function. See 1 K. Davis, Administrative Law Treatise § 5.01 (1958). And the only hearing that is required by either the Administrative Procedure Act or the statutes regulating the distribution of federal funds for highway construction is a public hearing conducted by local officials for the purpose of informing the community about the proposed project and eliciting community views on the design and route. 23 U.S.C. § 128. . . . The hearing is nonadjudicatory, quasi-legislative in nature. It is not designed to produce a record that is to be the basis of agency action—the basic requirement for substantial-evidence review. . . .

Petitioners' alternative argument also fails. *De novo* review of whether the Secretary's decision was "unwarranted by the facts" is authorized by § 706 (2)(F) in only two circumstances. First, such *de novo* review is authorized when the action is adjudicatory in nature and the agency factfinding procedures are inadequate. And, there may be independent judicial factfinding when issues that were not before the agency are raised in a proceeding to enforce nonadjudicatory agency action. . . . Neither situation exists here.

Even though there is no *de novo* review in this case and the Secretary's approval of the route of I-40 does not have ultimately to meet the substantial-evidence test, the generally applicable standards of § 706 require the reviewing court to engage in a substantial inquiry. Certainly, the Secretary's decision is entitled to a presumption of regularity. . . . But that presumption is not to shield his action from a thorough, probing, in-depth review.

The court is first required to decide whether the Secretary acted within the scope of his authority. . . . This determination naturally begins with a delineation of the scope of the Secretary's authority and discretion. L. Jaffe, Judicial Control of Administration Action 359 (1965). As has been shown, Congress has specified only a small range of choices that the Secretary can make. Also involved in this initial inquiry is a determination of whether on the facts the Secretary's decision can reasonably be said to be within that range. The reviewing court must consider whether the Secretary properly construed his authority to approve the use of parkland as limited to situations where there are no feasible alternative routes or where feasible alternative routes involve uniquely difficult problems. And the reviewing court must be able to find that the Secretary could have reasonably believed that in this case there are no feasible alternatives or that alternatives do involve unique problems.

Scrutiny of the facts does not end, however, with the determination that the Secretary has acted within the scope of his statutory authority. Section 706 (2)(A) requires a finding that the actual choice made was not "arbitrary, capricious, an abuse of discretion, or otherwise not in accordance with law." . . . To make this finding the court must consider whether the decision was based on a consideration of the relevant factors and whether there has been a clear error of judgment. Although this inquiry into the facts is to be searching and careful, the ultimate standard of review is a narrow one. The court is not empowered to substitute its judgment for that of the agency.

The final inquiry is whether the Secretary's action followed the necessary procedural requirements. Here the only procedural error alleged is the failure of the Secretary to make formal findings and state his reason for allowing the highway to be built through the park.

Undoubtedly, review of the Secretary's action is hampered by his failure to make such findings, but the absence of formal findings does not necessarily require that the case be remanded to the Secretary. Neither the Department of Transportation Act nor the Federal-Aid Highway Act requires such formal findings. Moreover, the Administrative Procedure Act requirements that there be formal findings in certain rulemaking and adjudicatory proceedings do not apply to the Secretary's action here. See 5 U.S.C. §§ 553 (a)(2), 554 (a). . . . [T]here is an administrative record that allows the full, prompt review of the Secretary's action that is sought without additional delay which would result from having a remand to the Secretary.

That administrative record is not, however, before us. The lower courts based their review on the litigation affidavits that were presented. These affidavits were merely *"post hoc* rationalizations," *Burlington Truck Lines v. United States*, 371 U.S. 156, 168–169 (1962), which have traditionally been found to be an inadequate basis for review. *Burlington Truck Lines v. United States, supra; SEC v. Chenery Corp.*, 318 U.S. 80, 87 (1943). And they clearly do no constitute the "whole record" compiled by the agency: the basis for review required by § 706 of the Administrative Procedure Act. . . .

Thus it is necessary to remand this case to the District Court for plenary review of the Secretary's decision. That review is to be based on the full administrative record that was before the Secretary at the time he made his decision. But since the bare record may not disclose the factors that were considered or the Secretary's construction of the evidence it may be necessary for the District Court to require some explanation in order to determine if the Secretary acted within the scope of his authority and if the Secretary's action was justifiable under the applicable standard.

The court may require the administrative officials who participated in the decision to give testimony explaining their action. Of course, such inquiry into the mental processes of administrative decisionmakers is usually to be avoided. *United States v. Morgan*, 313 U.S. 409, 422 (1941). And where there are administrative findings that were made at the same time as the decision, as was the case in *Morgan*, there must be a strong showing of bad faith or improper behavior before such inquiry may be made. But here there are no such formal findings and it may be that the only way there can be effective judicial review is by examining the decisionmakers themselves. See *Shaughnessy v. Accardi*, 349 U.S. 280 (1955).

The District Court is not, however, required to make such an inquiry. It may be that the Secretary can prepare formal findings including the information required by DOT Order 5610.1 that will provide an adequate explanation for his action. Such an explanation will, to some extent, be a *"post hoc rationalization"* and thus must be viewed critically. If the District Court decides that additional explanation is necessary, that court should consider which method will prove the most expeditious so that full review may be had as soon as possible.

Reversed and remanded.

Later- the trial judge did not feel the decision was based on this record. Volpe ordered another look - ended the project.

The Hard Look Standard

In the mid-1960s, as courts began to respond to the public interest movement's efforts to limit agency discretion or at least require that agencies demonstrate they have examined all possible alternatives before proposing a particular regulation, the *hard look standard* emerged as the appropriate criteria for courts to apply when reviewing agency decisions. This standard for judicial review is rooted in early cases, such as *SEC v. Chenery*, 332 U.S. 194 (1947) requiring an agency to provide substantial explanation for an exercise of its discretion, but it was further developed at the height of the public interest reform movement (mid-1960s to early 1970s). The set of earlier cases, reprinted below, established the contemporary judicial rational for the hard look standard. The Court applied the scope of judicial review under the hard look standard in the previous case, *Overton Park*, so you should be somewhat familiar with it. However, since it has been the subject of much controversy recently, we provide more background on this doctrine. These next two cases are also good examples of the dialogue that takes place between courts and agencies during judicial review proceedings. Note how the Court of Appeals instructs the Federal Power Commission (FPC) in *Scenic Hudson Preservation Conference (I)* and then ask yourself how well the FPC followed those instructions in *Scenic Hudson Preservation Conference (II)*. Did the hard look standard in this case lead to a different policy, or did it merely enable the FPC to better justify its policy choice? How "hard" is the hard look standard? Does it go too far in expanding the scope of judicial review, or is it in the end a means for strengthening the credibility and hence authority of agency decisions?

Scenic Hudson Preservation Conference v. Federal Power Commission (I)

354 F.2d 608, U.S.C.A., 2d Cir. (1965) 3–0

[The Scenic Hudson Preservation Conference, a conservationist organization, petitioned to set aside three orders of the Federal Power Commission (FPC) concerning the construction of a hydroelectric project on the Hudson River, called the Storm King Project.]

Hays, Circuit Judge.

I

The Storm King project is to be located in an area of unique beauty and major historical significance. The highlands and gorge of the Hudson offer one of the finest pieces of river scenery in the world. . . . Petitioners' contention that the Commission must take these factors into consideration in evaluating the Storm King project is justified by the history of the Federal Power Act.

The Federal Water Power Act of 1920 . . . (now Federal Power Act, 16 U.S.C. § 791a et seq.), was the outgrowth of a widely supported effort on the part of conservationists to secure the enactment of a complete scheme of national regulation which would promote the comprehensive development of the nation's water resources. . . .

In recent years the Commission has placed increasing emphasis on the right of the public to "out-door recreational resources." 1964 F.P.C. Report 69. Regulations issued in 1963, for the first time, required the inclusion of a recreation plan as part of a license application. . . . The Commission has recognized gener-

ally that members of the public have rights in our recreational, historic and scenic resources under the Federal Power Act. . . .

IV

The Federal Power Commission argues that having intervened "petitioners cannot impose an affirmative burden on the Commission." But, as we have pointed out, Congress gave the Federal Power Commission a specific planning responsibility. . . . The totality of a project's immediate and long-range effects, and not merely the engineering and navigation aspects, are to be considered in a licensing proceeding. . . .

In this case, as in many others, the Commission has claimed to be the representative of the public interest. This role does not permit it to act as an umpire blandly calling balls and strikes for adversaries appearing before it; the right of the public must receive active and affirmative protection at the hands of the Commission.

This court cannot and should not attempt to substitute its judgment for that of the Commission. But we must decide whether the Commission has correctly discharged its duties, including the proper fulfillment of its planning function in deciding that the "licensing of the project would be in the overall public interest." The Commission must see to it that the record is complete. The Commission has an affirmative duty to inquire into and consider all relevant facts. . . .

In addition to the Commission's failure to receive or develop evidence concerning the gas turbine alternative, there are other instances where the Commission should have acted affirmatively in order to make a complete record.

The Commission neither investigated the use of interconnected power as a possible alternative to the Storm King project, nor required Consolidated Edison to supply such information. The record sets forth Consolidated Edison's interconnection with a vast network of other utilities, but the Commission dismissed this alternative by noting that "Con Edison is relying fully upon such interconnections in estimating its future available capacity." However, only ten pages later in its opinion the Commission conceded:

> "Of significant importance, in our opinion, is the absence in the record, or the inadequacy, of information in regard to Con Edison's future interconnection plans; its plans, if any, for upgrading existing transmission lines to higher voltages; and of its existing transmission line grid in this general area and its future plans." . . .

. . . There is no evidence in the record to indicate that either the Commission or Consolidated Edison ever seriously considered this alternative. Nor is there any evidence that a combination of devices, for example, gas turbine and interconnections, were considered. . . . The failure of the Commission to inform itself of these alternatives cannot be reconciled with its planning responsibility under the Federal Power Act.

In its March 9 opinion the Commission postponed a decision on the transmission route to be chosen until the May 1965 hearings were completed. Inquiry into the cost of putting lines underground was precluded because the May hearings were limited to the question of overhead transmission routes. The petitioners'

April 26, 1965 motion to enlarge the scope of the May hearing was denied. The Commission insisted that the question of underground costs had been "extensively considered." We find almost nothing in the record to support this statement. . . .

. . . At the time of its original hearings, there was sufficient evidence before the Commission concerning the danger to fish to warrant further inquiry. . . .

Just after the Commission closed its proceedings in November the hearings held by the New York State Legislative Committee on Natural Resources alerted many fisherman groups to the threat posed by the Storm King project. On December 24 and 30, January 8, and February 3 each of four groups, concerned with fishing, petitioned for the right to intervene and present evidence. They wished to show that the major spawning ground for the distinct race of Hudson River striped bass was in the immediate vicinity of the Storm King project and not "much farther upstream" as inferred by Dr. Perlmutter, the one expert witness called by Consolidated Edison; to attempt to prove that, contrary to the impression given by Dr. Perlmutter, bass eggs and larvae float in the water, at the mercy of currents; that due to the location of the spawning ground and the Hudson's tidal flow, the eggs and larvae would be directly subject to the influence of the plant and would be threatened with destruction; that "no screening device presently feasible would adequately protect these early stages of fish life" and that their loss would ultimately destroy the economicaly valuable fisheries. . . . The Commission rejected all these petitions as "untimely," and seemingly placing great reliance on the testimony of Dr. Perlmutter, concluded:

> "The project will not adversely affect the fish resources of the Hudson River provided adequate protective facilities are installed."

Although an opportunity was made available at the May hearings for petitioners to submit evidence on protective designs, the question of the adequacy of *any* protectice design was inexplicably excluded by the Commission.

The licensing order of March 9 and the two orders of May 6 are set aside, and the case remanded for further proceedings.

Scenic Hudson Preservation Conference v. Federal Power Commission (II)

453 F.2d 463, U.S.C.A., 2d Cir. (1971) 4–1, *en banc*

[Following the remand, the Federal Power Commission again granted Con Edison a license, but for a slightly different project (a pumped storage project) than the one licensed in the previous case. Once again the Scenic Hudson Preservation Conference petitioned for review.]

Hays, Circuit Judge.

The new proceedings have produced a project that is different in some ways from the project that was before this court in 1965.

The functional elements of the project remain the same. It is still to be the largest pumped storage plant in the world and its principal function, to provide energy for peak load periods, is unchanged. The proposed location is the same as that previously proposed, the Hudson River at approximately river mile 56.5, about 40 miles north of New York City at Storm King Mountain near Cornwall, New York. . . .

The petitions in this case are occasioned by the "grave concern" aroused among conservationist groups by the Storm King project. . . . The petitions allege lack of compliance with the terms of our earlier remand, absence of substantial evidence to support the Commission's findings, and failure to comply with statutory mandates. We find, however, that the Commission has fully complied with our earlier mandate and with the applicable statutes and that its findings are supported by substantial evidence. In view of the extensive powers delegated to the Commission and the limited scope of review entrusted to this court, it is our duty to deny the petitions.

I

. . . The scope of review of the Commision's exercise of its authority and responsibility is narrowly limited. The Act, § 313 (b), provides that "[t]he finding of the Commission as to the facts, if supported by substantial evidence, shall be conclusive." 16 U.S.C. § 825*l*(b). . . .

Petitioners . . . argue, [that a] different standards ought to prevail with respect to issues arising in an environmental context.* There is an effort to find a basis for this position in our earlier remand in *Scenic Hudson* and in cases which have taken a similar approach. See, *e.g.,* Citizens to Preserve Overton Park, Inc. v. Volpe, 401 U.S. 402, (1971). . . .

To read these cases as sanctioning a new standard of judicial review for findings on matters of environmental policy is to misconstrue both the holdings in the cases and the nature of our remand in *Scenic Hudson*. An element common to all these cases was the failure of an agency or other governmental authority to give adequate consideration to the environmental factors in the situations with which they were presented. In Citizens to Preserve Overton Park, Inc. v. Volpe, . . . for example, the Court remanded the case to the district court to determine whether the Secretary of Transportation's decision "was based on a consideration of the relevant factors." The Court pointed out that "[a]lthough this inquiry into the facts is to be searching and careful, the ultimate standard of review is a narrow one. . . .

In our opinion in *Scenic Hudson, supra,* remanding the 1965 orders of the Commission, we were careful to make it clear that we were raising no question of change in the basic standard of administrative review and that the purpose of our remand was only to require the proper performance of its functions by the Commission. . . .

Where the Commission has considered all relevant factors, and where the challenged findings, based on such full consideration, are supported by substantial evidence, we will not allow our personal views

*Sive, Some Thoughts of an Environmental Lawyer in the Wilderness of Administrative Law, 70 Colum. L. Rev. 612 (1970), seeks to provide support for such a position.

as to the desirability of the result reached by the Commission to influence us in our decision. . . .

II

. . . On January 25, 1966, acting on our remand, the Commission ordered that further proceedings be commenced before a Hearing Examiner. In that order the Commission said:

> "We do not understand the Court's order as restricting any further proceedings to the specific matters on which it found the present record insufficient to support our previous determinations and we do not believe it would be in the public interest to do so. The record in the first two hearings in the proceeding will, of course, be part of the present hearing. But all parties will be free to offer timely presentations of evidence on all matters relevant to the question whether a license should be granted."

The hearings were commenced on November 14, 1966 and with several brief recesses, were concluded on May 23, 1967. A motion of the State of Connecticut's Board of Fisheries and Game to intervene was subsequently granted, and further hearings were held on the issue of the protection of fish. These hearings were closed on October 16, 1967. On August 6, 1968, the Hearing Examiner issued his Initial Decision recommending that Con Ed be granted a 50 year license for the project. On November 19, 1968, the proceedings were reopened in response to a petition by the City of New York to intervene and introduce evidence on possible hazards to its Catskill Aqueduct. At this proceeding, further evidence was taken on the alternative site in Palisades Interstate Park. The Hearing Examiner issued a Supplemental Initial Decision on December 23, 1969, which concluded that the project did not endanger the Aqueduct and that the alternative site was "not a proper and preferable alternative location for applicant's projected project." In all other respects, except for minor items, the Initial Decision remained unchanged.

The proceedings on remand involved 100 hearing days, the testimony of some sixty expert witnesses, and the introduction of 675 exhibits. The record comprises more than 19,000 pages. Both the Hearing Examiner and the Commissioner arranged with the parties to visit the proposed site and the surrounding area before rendering their decisions.

On August 19, 1970, the Commission issued its decision. In its opinion the Commission reviewed the power needs of the area served by Con Ed and considered possible alternatives to the Storm King project in terms of reliability, cost, air and noise pollution, and overall environmental impact. Concluding that there was no satisfactory alternative, the Commission evaluated the environmental effects of the project itself. It held that the scenic impact would be minimal, that no historic site would be adversely affected, that the fish would be adequately protected and that the proposed park and scenic overlook would enhance recreational facilities. . . .

We find that the proceedings of the Commission and its report meet the objections upon the basis of which we remanded the earlier determination. Examination of the Commission's conclusions and the evidence on which the conclusions are based establishes that the Commission has complied with our instructions and that the evidence supporting the Commission's conclusions amply meets the statutory requirement of substantiality.

A. "Alternative plans"

The Commission gave detailed and comprehensive consideration to alternatives. Its initial statement of the basic issues of the case before it and the manner of its subsequent dealing with those issues demonstrates that there is no sound basis for petitioners' contention that the Commission's approach was too narrow.

> "The weighing of social values required by the concept of the public convenience and necessity in this case involves on the one hand the alleged greater and much needed reliability, economic savings, and anti-air pollution benefits which this project offers compared with any feasible alternative, and on the other hand the alleged aesthetic and environmental

detriment the project would impose on an area of great scenic, natural and historic value." . . .

B. *"The conservation of natural resources, the maintenance of natural beauty, and the preservation of historic sites."*

The Commission gave extended consideration to the environmental aspect of our remand order. Testimony was taken from "a veritable 'Who's Who' of conservation, each witness discussing a different facet of this esoteric and subjective matter." The Commission said: "[O]ur conclusion that the license must issue does not rest upon any discounting of the case made by the intervenors relating to the natural beauty, historical significance, and spiritual qualities of the Storm King Mountain in its setting." Its essential finding in this regard was that the Cornwall project, as modified by the Commission to make any structures not buried "as unobtrusive as ingenuity can make them," constitutes "no real impairment of the environmental and scenic aspects of the Highlands."

The original plan for the project provided for a powerhouse that would be 80 per cent underground. The project licensed by the Commission now calls for the powerhouse to be completely underground. While in an area visually part of Storm King Mountain, the powerhouse would not be under the mountain itself but in the Village of Cornwall "on a small river-bottom foothill." . . .

The Commission's criticisms led to the substantial modification of the recreational aspects of the project. Con Ed's original proposal included an information center and recreation area to be located in the vicinity of the powerhouse site. These features were eliminated by the Commission. The Commission approved the construction of a riverfront park and a scenic overlook. The park is to be built on the rock excavated from the site of the power plant. It would be located in that part of the river to the north and west of the project adjacent to the shoreline. This 57 acre mile-long recreational facility, to be linked by two bridges to the Town of Cornwall to which it will be transferred upon completion, is to consist of play area, picnic sites, shelters, and sanitary facili-

ties. The scenic overlook is to occupy a 36 acre tract abutting State Highway 9–W, and would also include picnic stites. The Commission found that the overlook would enable visitors to enjoy "the scenic vistas of the Hudson River" and "will not seriously or substantially impinge on the scenic historic or environmental qualities of the area." . . .

The thrust of petitioners' arguments is that the principle of preservation of scenic beauty permits of no intrusion at all into this area and that, therefore, no power plant, no matter how innocuous, may be built. This is clearly a policy determination which, whatever may be our personal views, we do not have the power to impose on the Commission. The Commission has complied with the terms of our remand by giving careful and thorough consideration to the impact of the project on the environment. The conclusions it has reached are supported by substantial evidence. . . .

Oakes, Circuit Judge (dissenting).

If this case came to us without environmental overtones and with no threat to the water supply of the largest city in the United States, I would be constrained to take the viewpoint of the majority. . . .

It is also true, of course, that the courts cannot quarrel with the Congressional policy impliedly expressed in Sections 207 and 311 of the Federal Power Act, that puts great emphasis on "adequate service," 16 U.S.C. § 824f, the "cost of generation. . . . " and "the development of navigation, industry, commerce, and the national defense," 16 U.S.C. § 825j.

On the other hand Congress has now placed a measure of responsibility with the FPC, and the other federal agencies, to take environmental factors into account. The FPC also has its own duties, specified in Section 10(a) of the Federal Power Act, 16 U.S.C. § 803(a), to issue a license to use water power only when the project will be best adapted for "beneficial public uses, including recreational purposes." And indeed as Judge Learned Hand once put it, although in reference to agency interpretation of statutes:

In spite of the plenitude of discussion in recent years as to how far courts must defer to the rulings of an adminstrative tribunal, it is doubtful whether in the end one can say more than that there comes a point at which the courts must form their own conclusions. Before doing so they will, of course,—like the administrative tribunals themselves—look for light from every quarter, and after all crannies have been searched, will yield to the adminstrative interpretation in all doubtful cases; but they can never abdicate. Niagara Falls Power Co., v. FPC, 137 F.2d 787, 792 (2d Cir. 1943).

. . . Finally, while judicial deference to administrative expertise is required, not every agency is expert in every aspect of science, technology, aesthetics or human behavior. Universal Camera Corp. v. NLRB, 340 U.S. 474, 476, . . . (1951); see l. Jaffe, Judicial Control of Administrative Action 576 et seq. (1965). As Professor Jaffe has said, " . . . expertness is not a magic wand which can be indiscriminately waved over the corpus of an agency's findings to preserve them from review." Id. at 613; see also 4 K. Davis, Administrative Law Treatise § 30.07 (1958).

With these considerations in mind, I dissent. I dissent because I think the FPC acted arbitrarily, abusing its discretion while purporting to act under the mandate of this court in *Scenic Hudson, supra*; because its findings in respect to the Catskill Aqueduct are inconsistent and insufficient; because its findings as to the effect of the project upon New York City air pollution are incomplete and fail to take into account relevant factors; and because the Commission's findings and conclusions show that it has not really followed the mandates of the National Environmental Policy Act of 1969, Pub.L. 91–190 (Jan 1, 1970), 42 U.S.C. §§ 4321–4347.

The City of New York has pointed out, in opposition to the license granted by the FPC, that the Storm King (sometimes called "Cornwall") project

powerhouse is proposed to be built only 140 feet from the Moodna Tunnel section of the Catskill Aqueduct. This aqueduct is one of three systems supplying water to New York City. It is a gravity-flow aqueduct over 50 years old, conveying aproximately 40 per cent of the city's average daily water supply from the Ashokan Reservoir, 100 miles north of the city to the Kensico Reservior, 15 miles north of the city line. Those who may remember the effects of severe droughts in the 1940's and the 1960's on the New York City water supply must realize the importance of such a vast quantity of water to the city, and imagine the consequences of its disruptions. . . .

Several of the commission's own "findings" on the danger to the Aqueduct tend to support the City's position and not the applicant's, and most of the commision's findings on the Aqueduct are couched in terms of uncertainty. . . .

. . . The Findings fail to convince me that there is no substantial risk to the Aqueduct. . . .

. . . The mere recitation of testimony by the Federal Power Commission does not amount to the making of findings. . . . If the structural integrity is unknown to the City or any of its witnesses, presumably it is also unknown to the commission and to Consolidated Edison's witnesses. The burden is not on the City to prove that the Aqueduct will not break, but on the applicant to prove and the commission to find no danger to public "life, health and property." . . .

. . . This being the second opportunity the commission has had to follow the mandate of this court, and it having failed to do so as I suggest above, I would conclude, as did then Circuit Judge Burger in an FCC case, "that it will serve no useful purpose to ask the Commission to reconsider the Examiner's actions and its own Decision and Order. . . . " Office of Communication of the United Church of Christ v. FCC, 425 F.2d 543, 550 (D.C.Cir. 1969). I would therefore reverse, without a remand.

Since the *Scenic Hudson Preservation Conference* cases, the Court appears to be shifting its position on the scope of judicial review. In *Chevron* v. *NRDC* (1984) (chapter 3), the Court called for a more deferential stance towards agency interpretation of statutory provisions. The Court said when Congress directly addresses the precise question at issue, courts are not supposed to be very deferential to agencies. However, when Congress has not addressed the question, then the Court said there should be considerable deference to agency interpretation.[15] The last case in this section, *Heckler v. Chaney* (1985), indicates how far the current Court is willing to erode the hard look standard of review. This case concerns judicial review of an agency's decision not to take action. In announcing that the "presumption of unreviewability" applies to agency *inaction*, the Court moved further away from the jurisprudence of the hard-look standard. In an era of conservative deregulation, federal agencies appear less enthusiastic about carrying out the policy missions of regulatory statutes born in the liberal political environment of the 1960s and 1970s. These same political conditions have led to the growth of citizen suits seeking judicial intervention and review of agencies' refusals to act.[16]

Heckler v. Chaney

> 470 U.S. 821 (1985) 9–0
>
> + Burger, Brennan, White, Marshall, Blackmun, Powell, Rehnquist, Stevens, O'Connor

[Prison inmates convicted of capital offenses and sentenced to death by lethal injection of drugs petitioned the Food and Drug Administration (FDA), alleging that the use of drugs for these purposes violated the Federal Food, Drug, and Cosmetic Act (FDCA). They requested the FDA to enforce the act so as to prevent the use of drugs for lethal injection. The FDA refused the request, and the inmates sued in federal district court. The lower court held that "nothing in the FDCA indicated an intent to circumscribe the FDA's enforcement discretion or to make it reviewable." The Court of Appeals for the D.C. Circuit reversed, holding that the FDA's refusal to take enforcement action was reviewable and that their decision was an abuse of discretion. Secretary of Health and Human Service Heckler appealed this ruling to the Supreme Court.]

Justice Rehnquist delivered the opinion of the Court.

I

Respondents have been sentenced to death by lethal injection of drugs under the laws of the States of Oklahoma and Texas. Those States, and several others, have recently adopted this method for carrying out the capital sentence. Respondents first petitioned the FDA, claiming that the drugs used by the States for this purpose, although approved by the FDA for the medical purposes stated on their labels, were not approved for use in human executions. They alleged that the drugs had not been tested for the purpose for which they were to be used, and that, given that the drugs would likely be administered by untrained personnel, it was also likely that the drugs would not

---

[15] For an interesting criticism of *Chevron* and of those scholars who argue for judicial dererence to administrative interpretation, see Cass R. Sunstein's comments in "Judicial Review of Administrative Action in a Conservative Era," *Administrative Law Review* 39 (1987):366.

[16] See Barry Boyer and Errol Meidinger, "Privatizing Regulatory Enforcement: A Preliminary Assessment of Citizen Suits Under Federal Environmental Law," *Buffalo Law Review* 34 (1985):833.

induce the quick and painless death intended. They urged that use of these drugs for human execution was the "unapproved use of an approved drug" and constituted a violation of the Act's prohibitions against "misbranding."* . . . [T]hey requested the FDA to affix warnings to the labels of all the drugs stating that they were unapproved and unsafe for human execution, to send statements to the drug manufacturers and prison administrators stating that the drugs should not be so used, and to adopt procedures for seizing the drugs from state prisons and to recommend the prosecution of all those in the chain of distribution who knowingly distribute or purchase the drugs with intent to use them for human execution.

The FDA Commissioner responded, refusing to take the requested actions. The Commissioner . . . conclud[ed] that FDA jurisdiction in the area was generally unclear but in any event should not be exercised to interfere with this particular aspect of state criminal justice systems. . . .

II

The Court of Appeals' decision addressed three questions: (1) whether the FDA had jurisdiction to undertake the enforcement actions requested, (2) whether if it did have jurisdiction its refusal to take those actions was subject to judicial review, and (3) whether if reviewable its refusal was arbitrary, capricious, or an abuse of discretion. In reaching our conclusion that the Court of Appeals was wrong, however, we need not and do not address the thorny question of the FDA's jurisdiction. For us, this case turns on the important question of the extent to which determinations by the FDA *not to exercise* its enforcement authority over the use of drugs in interstate commerce may be judicially reviewed. That decision in turn involves the construction of two separate but necessarily interrelated statutes, the APA and the FDCA.

The APA's comprehensive provisions for judicial review of "agency actions" are contained in 5 U.S.C.

§§ 701–706. Any person "adversely affected or aggrieved" by agency action, see §702, including a "failure to act," is entitled to "judicial review thereof," as long as the action is a "final agency action for which there is no other adequate remedy in a court," see §§ 704. The standards to be applied on review are governed by the provisions of § 706. But before any review at all may be had, a party must first clear the hurdle of § 701(a). That section provides that the chapter on judicial review "applies, according to the provisions thereof, except to the extent that—(1) statutes preclude judicial review; or (2) agency action is committed to agency discretion by law." Petitioner urges that the decision of the FDA to refuse enforcement is an action "committed to agency discretion by law" under § 701(a)(2).

This Court has not had occasion to interpret this second exception in § 701(a) in any great detail. On its face, the section does not obviously lend itself to any particular construction; indeed, one might wonder what difference exists between § (a)(1) and § (a)(2). The former section seems easy in application; it requires construction of the substantive statute involved to determine whether Congress intended to preclude judicial review of certain decisions. That is the approach taken with respect to § (a)(1) in cases such as *Southern R. Co., v. Seaboard Allied Milling Corp,* 442 U.S. 444 (1979), and *Dunlop v. Bachowski,* 421 U.S., at 567. But one could read the language "committed to agency discretion *by law*" in § (a)(2) to require a similar inquiry. In addition, commentators have pointed out that construction of § (a)(2) is further complicated by the tension between a literal reading of § (a)(2), which exempts from judicial review those decisions committed to agency "discretion," and the primary scope of review prescribed by § 706(2)(A)—whether the agency's action was "arbitrary, capricious, or an *abuse of discretion.*" How is it, they ask, that an action committed to agency discretion can be unreviewable and yet courts still can review agency actions for abuse of that discretion? See 5 K. Davis, Administrative Law § 28:6 (1984) (hereafter Davis); Berger, Administrative Arbitrariness and Judicial Review, 65 Colum. L. Rev. 55, 58 (1965). The APA's legislative history provides little help on

*See 21 U.S.C. §352(f): "A drug or device shall be deemed to be misbranded . . . [u]nless its labeling bears (1) adequate directions for use. . . . "

this score. Mindful, however, of the common-sense principle of statutory construction that sections of a statute generally should be read "to give effect, if possible, to every clause . . . ,"see *United States v. Menasche*, 348 U.S. 528, 538–539 (1955), we think there is a proper construction of § (a)(2) which satisfies each of these concerns.

This Court first discussed § (a)(2) in *Citizens to Preserve Overton Park v. Volpe*, 401 U.S. 402 (1971). . . . Interested citizens challenged the Secretary's approval under the APA, arguing that he had not satisfied the substantive statute's requirements. This Court first addressed the "threshold question" of whether the agency's action was at all reviewable. After setting out the language of § 701(a), the Court stated:

"In this case, there is no indication that Congress sought to prohibit judicial review and there is most certainly no 'showing of "clear and convincing evidence" of a . . . legislative intent' to restrict access to judicial review. *Abbott Laboratories v. Gardner*, 387 U.S. 136, 141 (1967). . . .

Similarly, the Secretary's decision here does not fall within the exception for action 'committed to agency discretion.' This is a very narrow exception. . . . The legislative history of the Administrative Procedure Act indicates that it is applicable in those rare instances where 'statutes are drawn in such broad terms that in a given case there is no law to apply.' S. Rep. No. 752, 79th Cong., 1st Sess., 26 (1945)." *Overton Park, supra*, at 410.

The above quote answers several of the questions raised by the language of § 701(a), although it raises others. First, it clearly separates the exception provided by § (a)(1) from the § (a)(2) exception. The former applies when Congress has expressed an intent to preclude judicial review. The latter applies in different circumstances; even where Congress has not affirmatively precluded review, review is not to be had if the statute is drawn so that a court would have no meaningful standard against which to judge the agency's exercise of discretion. In such a case, the statute ("law") can be taken to have "committed" the decisionmaking to the agency's judgement absolutely. This

construction avoids conflict with the "abuse of discretion" standard of review in § 706—if no judicially manageable standards are available for judging how and when an agency should exercise its discretion, then it is impossible to evaluate agency action for "abuse of discretion." In addition, this construction satisfies the principle of statutory construction mentioned earlier, by identifying a separate class of cases to which § 701 (a)(2) applies.

To this point our analysis does not differ significantly from that of the Court of Appeals. That court purported to apply the "no law to apply" standard of *Overton Park*. We disagree, however, with that court's insistence that the "narrow construction" of § (a)(2) required application of a presumption of reviewability even to an agency's decision not to undertake certain enforcement actions. Here we think the Court of Appeals broke with tradition, case law, and sound reasoning.

Overton Park did not involve an agency's refusal to take requested enforcement action. It involved an affirmative act of approval under a statute that set clear guidelines for determining when such approval should be given. Refusals to take enforcement steps generally involve precisely the opposite situation, and in that situation we think the presumption is that judicial review is not available. This Court has recognized on several occasions over many years that an agency's decision not to prosecute or enforce, whether through civil or criminal process, is a decision generally committed to an agency's absolute discretion. See *United States v. Batchelder*, 442 U.S. 114 . . . (1979); *United States v. Nixon*, 418 U.S. 683, . . . (1974); *Vaca v. Sipes*, 386 U.S. 171 . . . (1967); *Confiscation Cases*, 7 Wall. 454 (1869). This recognition of the existence of discretion is attributable in no small part to the general unsuitability for judicial review of agency decisions to refuse enforcement.

The reasons for this general unsuitability are many. First, an agency decision not to enforce often involves a complicated balancing of a number of factors which are peculiarly within its expertise. Thus, the agency must not only assess whether a violation has occurred, but whether agency resources are best spent on this violation or another, whether the agency is likely to succeed if it acts, whether the particular enforcement action requested best fits the agency's overall policies, and, indeed, whether the agency has enough resources to undertake the action at all. . . . The agency is far better equipped than the courts to deal with the many variables involved in the proper ordering of its priorities. Similar concerns animate the principles of administrative law that courts generally will defer to an agency's construction of the statute it is charged with implementing, and to the procedures it adopts for implementing that statute. See *Vermont Yankee Nuclear Power Corp. v. Natural Resources Defense Council, Inc.*, 435 U.S. 519 (1978); *Train v. Natural Resources Defense Council, Inc.*, 421 U.S. 60 (1975).

In addition to these administrative concerns, we note that when an agency refuses to act it generally does not exercise its *coercive* power over an individual's liberty or property rights, and thus does not infringe upon areas that courts often are called upon to protect. . . . Finally, we recognize that an agency's refusal to institute proceedings shares to some extent the characteristics of the decision of a prosecutor in the Executive Branch not to indict—a decision which has long been regarded as the special province of the Executive Branch, inasmuch as it is the Executive who is charged by the Constitution to "take Care that the Laws be faithfully executed." U.S. Const., Art. II, § 3. . . .

III

. . . Respondents nevertheless present three separate authorities that they claim provide the courts with sufficient indicia of an intent to circumscribe enforcement discretion. Two of these may be dealt with summarily. First, we reject respondents' argument that the Act's substantive prohibitions of "misbranding" and the introduction of "new drugs" absent agency approval, see 21 U.S.C. §§ 352(f)(1), 355, supply us with "law to apply." These provisions are simply irrelevant to the agency's discretion to refuse to initiate proceedings.

We also find singularly unhelpful the agency "policy statement" on which the Court of Appeals placed great reliance. We would have difficulty with this statement's vague language even if it were a properly adopted agency rule. Although the statement indicates that the agency considered itself "ob-ligated" to take certain investigative actions, that language did not arise in the course of discussing the agency's discretion to exercise its enforcement power, but rather in the context of describing agency policy with respect to unapproved uses of approved drugs by physicians. . . .

Respondents' third argument, based upon § 306 of the FDCA, merits only slightly more consideration. That section provides:

> "Nothing in this chapter shall be construed as requiring the Secretary to report for prosecution, or for the institution of libel or injunction proceedings, minor violations of this chapter whenever he believes that the public interest will be adequately served by a suitable written notice or ruling." 21 U.S.C. § 336.

Respondents seek to draw from this section the negative implication that the Secretary is *required* to report for prosecution all "major" violations of the Act, however those might be defined, and that it therefore supplies the needed indication of an intent to limit agency enforcement discretion. We think that this section simply does not give rise to the negative implication which respondents seek to draw from it. The section is not addressed to agency proceedings designed to discover the existence of violations, but applies only to a situation where a violation has already been established to the satisfaction of the agency. We do not believe the section speaks to the criteria which shall be used by the agency for investigating *possible* violations of the Act.

. . . The fact that the drugs involved in this case are ultimately to be used in imposing the death penalty must not lead this Court or other courts to import profound differences of opinion over the meaning of the Eighth Amendment to the United States Constitution into the domain of administrative law.

The judgement of the Court of Appeals is reversed.

Justice Brennan, concurring.

Today the Court holds that individual decisions of the Food and Drug Administration not to take enforcement action in response to citizen requests are presumptively not reviewable under the Administrative Procedure Act, 5 U.S.C. §§ 701–706. I concur in this decision. This general presumption is based on the view that, in the normal course of events, Congress intends to allow broad discretion for its administrative agencies to make particular enforcement decisions, and there often may not exist readily discernible "law to apply" for courts to conduct judicial review of non-enforcement decisions. See *Citizens to Preserve Overton Park* v. *Volpe*. . . .

I also agree that, despite this general presumption, "Congress did not set agencies free to disregard legislative direction in the statutory scheme that the agency administers." *Ante,* at 833. . . .

Justice Marshall, concurring in the judgement.

Easy cases at times produce bad law, for in the rush to reach a clearly ordained result, courts may offer up principles, doctrines, and statements that calmer reflection, and a fuller understanding of their implications in concrete settings, would eschew. In my view, the "presumption of unreviewability" announced today is a product of that lack of discipline that easy cases make all too easy. The majority, eager to reverse what it goes out of its way to label as an "implausible result," not only does reverse, as I agree it should, but along the way creates out of whole cloth the notion that agency decisions not to take "enforcement action" are unreviewable unless Congress has rather specifically indicated otherwise. Because this "presumption of unreviewability" is fundamentally at odds with rule-of-law principles firmly embedded in our jurisprudence, because it seeks to truncate an emerging line of judicial authority subjecting enforcement discretion to rational and principled constraint, and because, in the end, the presumption may well be indecipherable, one can only hope that it will come to be understood as a relic of a particular factual setting in which the full implications of such a presumption were neither confronted nor understood.

I write separately to argue for a different basis of decision: that refusals to enforce, like other agency actions, are reviewable in the absence of a "clear and convincing" congressional intent to the contrary, but that such refusals warrant deference when, as in this case, there is nothing to suggest that an agency with enforcement discretion has abused that discretion.

. . . The "tradition" of unreviewability upon which the majority relies is refuted most powerfully by a firmly entrenched body of lower court case law that holds reviewable various agency refusals to act. This case law recognizes that attempting to draw a line for purposes of judicial review between affirmative exercises of coercive agency power and negative agency refusals to act, . . . is simply untenable; one of the very purposes fueling the birth of administrative agencies was the reality that governmental refusal to act could have just as devastating an effect upon life, liberty, and the pursuit of happiness as coercive governmental action. As Justice Frankfurter, a careful and experienced student of administrative law, wrote for this Court, "any distinction, as such, between 'negative' and 'affirmative' orders, as a touchstone of jurisdiction to review [agency action] serves no useful purpose." *Rochester Telephone Corp. v. United States,* 307 U.S. 125, 143 (1939). The lower courts, facing the problem of agency inaction and its concrete effects more regularly than do we, have responded with a variety of solutions to assure administrative fidelity to congressional objectives: a demand that an agency explain its refusal to act, a demand that explanations given be further elaborated, and injunctions that action "unlawfully withheld or unreasonably delayed," 5 U.S.C. § 706, be taken. . . . Whatever the merits of any particular solution, one would have hoped the Court would have acted with greater respect for these efforts by responding with a scalpel rather than a blunderbuss.

[T]he Court . . . implies far too narrow a reliance on positive law, either statutory or constitutional, . . . as the sole source of limitations on agency discretion not to enforce. In my view, enforcement discretion is also channelled by traditional background understandings against which the APA was enacted and which Congress hardly could be thought to have intended to displace in the APA. . . . Congress should not be presumed to have departed from principles of rationality and fair process in enacting the APA. Moreover, the agency may well narrow its own enforcement discretion through historical practice, from which it should arguably not depart in the absence of explanation, or through regulations and informal action. Traditional principles of rationality and fair process do offer "meaningful standards" and "law to apply" to an agency's decision not to act, and no presumption of unreviewability should be allowed to trump these principles. . . .

The problem of agency refusal to act is one of the pressing problems of the modern administrative state, given the enormous powers, for both good and ill, that agency inaction, like agency action, holds over citizens. As *Dunlop v. Bachowski*, 421 U.S. 560 (1975), recognized, the problems and dangers of agency inaction are too important, too prevalent, and too multifaceted to admit of a single facile solution under which "enforcement" decisions are "presumptively unreviewable." Over time, I believe the approach announced today will come to be understood, not as mandating that courts cover their eyes and their reasoning power when asked to review an agency's failure to act, but as recognizing that courts must approach the substantive task of reviewing such failures with appropriate deference to an agency's legitimate need to set policy through the allocation of scarce budetary and enforcement resources. Because the Court's approach, if taken literally, would take the courts out of the role of reviewing agency inaction in far too many cases, I join only the judgment today.

Reviewing Questions of Fact and Questions of Law

Section 706 (2) seems to divide the scope of review into two neat categories, review of questions of law (A–D) and review of questions of fact (E and F). We can for analytical purposes follow this formal division, but in practice the formality breaks down. Decisions, both in agencies and in courts, really occur when the decider brings together facts and law. To evaluate a decision effectively one must examine facts and law in combination, not isolation.[17]

Reviewing the Evidence

One of the mercifully more settled areas of administrative law concerns the amount of deference courts should give to agency findings of fact. During the first part of this century, when courts actively sought to protect private economic interests against governmental interference, courts often insisted that they must exercise independent judgment about evidence in cases threatening property and related *vested* rights. To require *de novo* review in all such cases, however, would paralyze the administrative process. With the advent of the modern administrative state courts are much more deferential.

This deference takes two paths. First, courts do not hold agencies to the same rules that limit the admissibility of evidence in courts. Hearsay evidence is admissible and may, depending on how convincing it is in context, rise to the level of substantial evidence.[18] Similarly, while an appellate court might require a new trial if the trial judge allowed irrelevant and immaterial evidence into the record, courts will not set aside an agency finding that does so as long as other substantial evidence supports the finding.

[17] Compare Section 15(g) of the Model State APA (Appendix C).

[18] In *Carroll v. Knickerbocker Ice Co.*, 218 N.Y. 435, 113 N.E. 507 (1916) the court set aside a workmen's compensation award because the only evidence submitted was based on hearsay testimony. The court concluded that "there must be a residuum of legal evidence to support the claim before an award can be made." This is known as the residuum rule.

The second path considers how much freedom the courts should allow agencies in weighing the evidence. In criminal trials the jury must believe the accused's guilt beyond a reasonable doubt. In civil trials the decision is based on the preponderance of the evidence. But in administrative law substantial evidence may be considerably less. Courts will not set aside a result even though an inconsistent and inherently more convincing interpretation of the evidence could be drawn. A conclusion from the facts, in other words, may be hotly disputed without being necessarily arbitrary, unreasonable, or capricious, and courts generally let reasonable but debatable conclusions stand. This practice depends on the assumption that the agency's decision has a history of administrative expertise behind it but the judge's view of the same factual dispute does not.

Universal Camera Corp. v. National Labor Relations Board

340 U.S. 474 (1951) 7–2
+   Vinson, Reed, Frankfurter, Jackson, Burton, Clark, Minton
+/–   Black, Douglas

[In this case an employee, one Mr. Chairman, was fired from his job as a supervisory employee at Universal Camera. He claimed he was fired for giving testimony to the National Labor Relations Board (NLRB) favoring recognition of a new union in the plant. The company claimed he was fired for various other reasons, including an insubordinate refusal to discipline an employee and for accusing his boss of being drunk. The charges were heard in an adjudicatory hearing. The examiner at the hearing, who heard all the conflicting testimony firsthand, decided that the evidence did not support the charge that Chairman was fired because he gave prounion testimony. Therefore the company did not have to reinstate him. After reviewing the full record the NLRB reached the opposite conclusion and ordered him reinstated. It is significant that Chairman gave his prounion testimony on 30 November 1943, but the company did not finally fire him until 24 January 1944. The alleged acts of insubordination all occurred *after* 30 November 1943.]

Justice Frankfurter delivered the opinion of the Court.

The essential issue raised by this case . . . is the effect of the Administrative Procedure Act and the legislation colloquially known as the Taft-Hartley Act, 5 U.S.C.A. § 1001 et seq.; 29 U.S.C.A. § 141 et seq., on the duty of Courts of Appeals when called upon to review orders of the National Labor Relations Board.

The Court of Appeals for the Second Circuit granted enforcement of an order directing, in the main, that petitioner reinstate with back pay an employee found to have been discharged because he gave testimony under the Wagner Act, 29 U.S.C.A. § 151 et seq., and cease and desist from discriminating against any employee who files charges or gives testimony under that Act. The court below, Judge Swan dissenting, decreed full enforcement of the order. . . .

Want of certainty in judicial review of Labor Board decisions partly reflects the intractability of any formula to furnish definiteness of content for all the impalpable factors involved in judicial review. But in part doubts as to the nature of the reviewing power and uncertainties in its application derive from history, and to that extent an elucidation of this history may clear them away.

The Wagner Act provided: "The findings of the Board as to the facts, if supported by evidence, shall be conclusive" Act of July 5, 1935, § 10(e), 49 Stat.

449, 454, 29 U.S.C. § 160(e), 29 U.S.C.A. § 160(e). This Court read "evidence" to mean "substantial evidence." *Washington. V & M. Coach Co. v. Labor Board,* 301 U.S. 142, . . . and we said that "[s]ubstantial evidence is more than a mere scintilla. It means such relevant evidence as a reasonable mind might accept as adequate to support a conclusion." *Consolidated Edison Co. v. National Labor Relations Board*, 305 U.S. 197, 229 . . . Accordingly, it "must do more than create a suspicion of the existence of the fact to be established. . . . [I]t must be enough to justify, if the trial were to a jury, a refusal to direct a verdict when the conclusion sought to be drawn from it is one of fact for the jury." *National Labor Relations Board v. Columbian Enameling & Stamping Co.*, 306 U.S. 292, 300. . . .

The very smoothness of the "substantial evidence" formula as the standard for reviewing the evidentiary validity of the Board's findings established its currency. But the inevitably variant applications of the standard to conflicting evidence soon brought contrariety of views and in due course bred criticism. Even though the whole record may have been canvassed in order to determine whether the evidentiary foundation of a determination by the Board was "substantial," the phrasing of this Court's process of review readily lent itself to the notion that it was enough that the evidence supporting the Board's result was "substantial" when considered by itself. It is fair to say that by imperceptible steps regard for the fact-finding function of the Board led to the assumption that the requirements of the Wagner Act were met when the reviewing court could find in the record evidence which, when viewed in isolation, substantiated the Board's findings. This is not to say that every member of this Court was consciously guided by this view or that the Court ever explicitly avowed this practice as doctrine. What matters is that the belief justifiably arose that the Court had so construed the obligation to review. . . .

[In addition,] [t]he final report of the Attorney General's Committee . . . submitted in January, 1941 . . . concluded that "[d]issatisfaction with the existing standards as to the scope of judicial review derives largely from dissatisfaction with the fact-finding

procedures now employed by the administrative bodies." Departure from the "substantial evidence" test, it thought, would either create unnecessary uncertainty or transfer to courts the responsibility for ascertaining and assaying matters the significance of which lies outside judicial competence. Accordingly, it recommended against legislation embodying a general scheme of judicial review.

Three members of the Committee registered a dissent. Their view was that the "present system or lack of system of judicial review" led to inconsistency and uncertainty. They reported that under a "prevalent" interpretation of the "substantial evidence" rule "if what is called 'substantial evidence' is found anywhere in the record to support conclusions of fact, the courts are said to be obliged to sustain the decision without reference to how heavily the countervailing evidence may preponderate—unless indeed the stage of arbitrary decision is reached. Under this interpretation, the courts need to read only one side of the case and, if they find any evidence there, the administrative action is to be sustained and the record to the contrary is to be ignored." Their view led them to recommend that Congress enact principles of review applicable to all agencies not excepted by unique characteristics. One of these principles was expressed by the formula that judicial review could extend to "findings, inferences, or conclusions of fact unsupported, upon the whole record, by substantial evidence." So far as the history of this movement for enlarged review reveals, the phrase "upon the whole record" makes its first appearance in this recommendation of the minority of the Attorney General's Committee. This evidence of the close relationship between the phrase and the criticism out of which it arose is important, for the substance of this formula for judicial review found its way into the statute books when Congress with unquestioning—we might even say uncritical—unanimity enacted the Administrative Procedure Act. . . .

Similar dissatisfaction with too restricted application of the "substantial evidence" test is reflected in the legislative history of the Taft-Hartley Act. The bill as reported to the House provided that the "findings of the Board as to the facts shall be conclusive unless it is made to appear to the satisfaction of the court either (1) that the findings of the fact are against the manifest weight of the evidence, or (2) that the findings of fact are not supported by substantial evidence." The bill left the House with this provision. Early committee prints in the Senate provided for review by "weight of the evidence" or "clearly erroneous" standards. But, as the Senate Committee Report relates, "it was finally decided to conform the statute to the corresponding section of the Administrative Procedure Act where the substantial evidence test prevails. In order to clarify any ambiguity in that statute, however, the committee inserted the words 'questions of fact, if supported by substantial evidence *on the record considered as a whole.* . . . ' "

This phraseology was adopted by the Senate. The House conferees agreed. They reported to the House: "It is believed that the provisions of the conference agreement relating to the courts' reviewing power will be adequate to preclude such decisions as those in *N.L.R.B. v. Nevada Consol. Copper Corp.*, 316 U.S. 105, . . . without unduly burdening the courts." The Senate version became the law.

It is fair to say that in all this Congress expressed a mood. And it expressed its mood not merely by oratory but by legislation. As legislation that mood must be respected, even though it can only serve as a standard for judgment and not as a body of rigid rules assuring sameness of application. Enforcement of such broad standards implies subtlety of mind and solidity of judgment. But it is not for us to question that Congress may assume such qualities in the federal judiciary.

From the legislative story we have summarized, two concrete conclusions do emerge. One is the identity of aim of the Administrative Procedure Act and the Taft-Hartley Act regarding the proof with which the Labor Board must support a decision. The other is that now Congress has left no room for doubt as to the kind of scrutiny which a court of appeals must give the record before the Board to satisfy itself that the Board's order rests on adequate proof.

It would be mischievous word-playing to find that the scope of review under the Taft-Hartley Act is any different from that under the Administrative Procedure Act. The Senate Committee which reported the review clause of the Taft-Hartley Act expressly indicated that the two standards were to conform in this regard, and the wording of the two Acts is for purposes of judicial administration identical. And so we hold that the standard of proof specifically required of the Labor Board by the Taft-Hartley Act is the same as that to be exacted by courts reviewing every administrative action subject to the Administrative Procedure Act.

Whether or not it was ever permissible for courts to determine the substantiality of evidence supporting a Labor Board decision merely on the basis of evidence which in and of itself justified it, without taking into account contradictory evidence or evidence from which conflicting inferences could be drawn, the new legislation definitively precludes such a theory of review and bars its practice. The substantiality of evidence must take into account whatever in the record fairly detracts from its weight. This is clearly the significance of the requirement in both statutes that courts consider the whole record. Committee reports and the adoption in the Administrative Procedure Act of the minority views of the Attorney General's Committee demonstrate that to enjoin such a duty on the reviewing court was one of the important purposes of the movement which eventuated in that enactment. . . .

We conclude, therefore, that the Administrative Procedure Act and the Taft-Hartley Act direct that courts must now assume more responsibility for the reasonableness and fairness of Labor Board decisions than some courts have shown in the past. Reviewing courts must be influenced by a feeling that they are not to abdicate the conventional judicial function. Congress has imposed on them responsibility for assuring that the Board keeps within reasonable grounds. That responsibility is not less real because it is limited to enforcing the requirement that evidence appear substantial when viewed, on the record as a whole, by courts invested with the authority and enjoying the prestige of the Courts of Appeals. The Board's findings are entitled to respect; but they must nonetheless be set aside when the record before a Court of Appeals clearly precludes the Board's decision from being justified by a fair estimate of the worth of the testimony of witnesses or its informed judgment on matters within its special competence or both. . . .

The decision of the Court of Appeals is assailed on two grounds. It is said (1) that the court erred in holding that it was barred from taking into account the report of the examiner on questions of fact insofar as the report was rejected by the Board, and (2) that the Board's order was not supported by substantial evidence on the record considered as a whole, even apart from the validity of the court's refusal to consider the rejected portions of the examiner's report.

The latter contention is easily met. . . . [I]t is clear from the court's opinion in this case that it in fact did consider the "record as a whole," and did not deem itself merely the judicial echo of the Board's conclusion. . . . On such a record we could not say that it would be error to grant enforcement.

The first contention, however, raises serious questions to which we now turn. . . .

The direction in which the law moves is often a guide for decision of particular cases, and here it serves to confirm our conclusion. However halting its progress, the trend in litigation is toward a rational inquiry into truth, in which the tribunal considers everything "logically probative of some matter requiring to be proved." Thayer, A Preliminary Treatise on Evidence, 530. This Court has refused to accept assumptions of fact which are demonstrably false, even when agreed to by the parties. Machinery for discovery of evidence has been strengthened; the boundaries of judicial notice have been slowly but perceptibly enlarged. It would reverse this process for courts to deny examiners' findings the probative force they would have in the conduct of affairs outside a courtroom.

We do not require that the examiner's findings be given more weight than in reason and in the light of judicial experience they deserve. The "substantial evidence" standard is not modified in any way when the Board and its examiner disagree. We intend only to recognize that evidence supporting a conclusion may be less substantial when an impartial, experienced examiner who has observed the witnesses and lived with the case has drawn conclusions different from the Board's than when he has reached the same conclusion. The findings of the examiner are to be considered along with the consistency and inherent probability of testimony. The significance of his report, of course, depends largely on the importance of credibility in the particular case. To give it this significance does not seem to us materially more difficult than to heed the other factors which in sum determine whether evidence is "substantial."

We therefore remand the cause to the Court of Appeals. On reconsideration of the record it should accord the findings of the trial examiner the relevance that they reasonably command in answering the comprehensive question whether the evidence supporting the Board's order is substantial. But the court need not limit its reexamination of the case to the effect of that report on its decision. We leave it free to grant or deny enforcement as it thinks the principles expressed in this opinion dictate.

Judgment vacated and cause remanded.

Reviewing the Law

National Labor Relations Board v. Hearst Publications, Inc.

322 U.S. 111 (1944) 8–1
+ Stone, Black, Reed, Frankfurter, Douglas, Murphy, Jackson, Rutledge
− Roberts

[The issue in this case was whether "newsboys" are independent contractos with a newspaper or are to be considered employees of the newspaper. Only employees are protected by the Wagner Act. The NLRB had found them to be employees. This finding was challenged by the newspaper.]

Justice Rutledge delivered the opinion of the Court.

. . . The papers are distributed to the ultimate consumer through a variety of channels, including independent dealers and newsstands often attached to drug, grocery or confectionery stores, carriers who make home deliveries, and newsboys who sell on the streets of the city and its suburbs. Only the last of these are involved in this case.

The newsboys work under varying terms and conditions. They may be "bootjackers," selling to the general public at places other than established corners, or they may sell at fixed "spots." They may sell only casually or part-time, or full-time; and they may be employed regularly and continuously or only temporarily. The units which the Board determined to be appropriate are composed of those who sell full-time at established spots. Those vendors, misnamed boys, are generally mature men, dependent upon the proceeds of their sales for their sustenance, and frequently supporters of families. Working thus as news vendors on a regular basis, often for a number of years, they form a stable group with relatively little turnover, in contrast to schoolboys and others who sell as bootjackers, temporary and casual distributors.

Overall circulation and distribution of the papers are under the general supervision of circulation managers. But for purposes of street distribution each paper has divided metropolitan Los Angeles into geographic districts. Each district is under the direct and close supervision of a district manager. His function in the mechanics of distribution is to supply the newsboys in his district with papers which he obtains from the publisher and to turn over to the publisher the receipts which he collects from their sales, either directly or with the assistance of "checkmen" or "main spot" boys. The latter, stationed at the important corners or "spots" in the district, are newsboys who, among other things, receive delivery of the papers, redistribute them to other newsboys stationed at less important corners, and collect receipts from their sales. For that service, which occupies a minor portion of their working day, the checkmen receive a small salary from the publisher. The bulk of their day, however, they spend in hawking papers at their "spots" like other full-time newsboys. A large part of the appropriate units selected by the Board for the News

and the Herald are checkmen who, in that capacity, clearly are employees of those papers.

The newsboys' compensation consists in the difference between the prices at which they sell the papers and the prices they pay for them. The former are fixed by the publishers and the latter are fixed either by the publishers or, in the case of the News, by the district manager. In practice the newsboys receive their papers on credit. They pay for those sold either sometime during or after the close of their selling day, returning for credit all unsold papers. Lost or otherwise unreturned papers, however, must be paid for as though sold. Not only is the "profit" per paper thus effectively fixed by the publisher, but substantial control of the newsboys' total "take home" can be effected throught the ability to designate their sales areas and the power to determine the number of papers allocated to each. While as a practical matter this power is not exercised fully, the newsboys' "right" to decide how many papers they will take is also not absolute. In practice, the Board found, they cannot determine the size of their established order without cooperation of the district manager. And often the number of papers they must take is determined unilaterally by the district managers.

In addition to effectively fixing the compensation, respondents in a variety of ways prescribe, if not the minutiae of daily activities, at least the broad terms and conditions of work. This is accomplished largely through the supervisory efforts of the district managers, who serve as the nexus between the publishers and the newsboys. The district managers assign "spots" or corners to which the newsboys are expected to confine their selling activities. Transfers from one "spot" to another may be ordered by the district manager for reasons of discipline or efficiency or other cause. Transportation to the spots from the newspaper building is offered by each of the respondents. Hours of work on the spots are determined not by the impersonal pressures of the market, but to a real extent by explicit instructions from the district managers. Adherence to the prescribed hours is observed closely by the district managers or other supervisory agents of the publishers. Sanctions, varying in severity from reprimand to dismissal, are visited on the tardy and the delinquent. By similar supervisory controls minimum standards of diligence and good conduct while at work are sought to be enforced. However wide may be the latitude for individual initiative beyond those standards, district managers' instructions in what the publishers apparently regard as helpful sales technique are expected to be followed. Such varied items as the manner of displaying the paper, of emphasizing current features and headlines, and of placing advetising placards, or the advantages of soliciting customers at specific stores or in the traffic lanes are among the subjects of this instruction. Moreover, newsboys are furnished with sales equipment, such as racks, boxes and change aprons, and advertising placards by the publishers. In this pattern of employment the Board found that the newsboys are an integral part of the publishers' distribution system and circulation organization. And the record discloses that the newsboys and checkmen feel they are employees of the papers and respondents' supervisory employees, if not respondents themselves, regard them as such.

In addition to questioning the sufficiency of the evidence to sustain these findings, respondents point to a number of other attributes characterizing their relationship with the newsboys and urge that on the entire record the latter cannot be considered their employees. They base this conclusion on the argument that by common-law standards the extent of their control and direction of the newsboys' working activities creates no more than an "independent contractor" relationship and that common-law standards determine the "employee" relationship under the Act. . . .

The principal question is whether the newsboys are "employees." Because Congress did not explicitly define the term, respondents say its meaning must be determined by reference to common-law standards. In their view "common-law standards" are those the courts have applied in distinguishing between "employees" and "independent contractors" when working out various problems unrelated to the Wagner Act's purposes and provisions.

The argument assumes that there is some simple, uniform and easily applicable test which the courts have used, in dealing with such problems, to determine whether persons doing work for others fall in one class or the other. Unfortunately this is not true. . . . Few problems in the law have given greater variety of application and conflict in results than the cases arising in the borderland between what is clearly an employer-employee relationship and what is clearly one of independent entrepreneurial dealing. . . .

Two possible consequences could follow. One would be to refer the decision of who are employees to local state law. The alternative would be to make it turn on a sort of pervading general essence distilled from state law. Congress obviously did not intend the former result. It would introduce variations into the statute's operation as wide as the differences the forty-eight states and other local jurisdictions make in applying the distinction for wholly different purposes. Persons who might be "employees" in one state would be "independent contractors" in another. They would be within or without the statute's protection depending not on whether their situation falls factually within the ambit Congress had in mind, but upon the accidents of the location of their work and the attitude of the particular local jurisdiction in casting doubtful cases one way or the other. Persons working across state lines might fall in one class or the other, possibly both, depending on whether the Board and the courts would be required to give effect to the law of one state or of the adjoining one, or to that of each in relation to the portion of the work done within its borders.

Both the terms and the purposes of the statute, as well as the legislative history, show that Congress had in mind no such patchwork plan for securing freedom of employees' organization and of collective bargaining. The Wagner Act is federal legislation, administered by a national agency, intended to solve a national problem on a national scale. It is an Act, therefore, in reference to which it is not only proper, but necessary for us to assume, "in the absence of a plain indication to the contrary, that Congress . . . is not making the application of the federal act dependent on state law." . . .

Whether, given the intended national uniformity, the term "employee" includes such workers as these newsboys must be answered primarily from the history, terms and purposes of the legislation. . . . It will not do, for deciding this question as one of uniform national application, to import wholesale the traditional common-law conceptions or some distilled essence of their local variations as exclusively controlling limitations upon the scope of the statute's effectiveness. To do this would be merely to select some of the local, hairline variations for nation-wide application and thus to reject others for coverage under the Act. That result hardly would be consistent with the statute's broad terms and purposes. . . .

The mischief at which the Act is aimed and the remedies it offers are not confined exclusively to "employees" within the traditional legal distinctions separating them from "independent contractors." Myriad forms of service relationship, with infinite and subtle variations in the terms of employment, blanket the nation's economy. Some are within this Act, others beyond its coverage. Large numbers will fall clearly on one side or on the other, by whatever test may be applied. But intermediate there will be many, the incidents of whose employment partake in part of the one group, in part of the other, in varying proportions of weight. And consequently the legal pendulum, for purposes of applying the statute, may swing one way or the other, depending upon the weight of this balance and its relation to the special purpose at hand.

Unless the common-law tests are to be imported and made exclusively controlling, without regard to the statute's purposes, it cannot be irrelevant that the particular workers in these cases are subject, as a matter of economic fact, to the evils the statute was designated to eradicate and that the remedies it affords are appropriate for preventing them or curing their harmful effects in the special situation. . . .

It is not necessary in this case to make a completely definitive limitation around the term "employee." That task has been assigned primarily to the agency created by Congress to administer the Act. Determination of "where all the conditions of the relation require protection" involves inquiries of the Board charged with this duty. Everyday experience in the administration of the statute gives it familiarity with the circumstances and backgrounds of employment relationships in various industries, with the abilities and needs of the workers for self organization and collective action, and with the adaptability of collective bargaining for the peaceful settlement of their disputes with their employers. The experience thus acquired must be brought frequently to bear on the question who is an employee under the Act. Resolving that question, like determining whether unfair labor practices have been committed, "belongs to the usual administrative routine" of the Board. . . .

In making that body's determination as to the facts in these matters conclusive, if supported by evidence, Congress entrusted to it primarily the decision whether the evidence establishes the material facts. Hence in reviewing the Board's ultimate conclusions, it is not the court's function to substitute its own inferences of fact for the Board's, when the latter have support in the record. Undoubtedly questions of statutory interpretation, especially when arising in the first instance in judicial proceedings, are for the courts to resolve, giving appropriate weight to the judgment of those whose special duty is to adminster the questioned statute. But where the question is one of specific application of a broad statutory term in a proceeding in which the agency administering the statute must determine it initially, the reviewing court's function is limited. Like the commissioner's determination under the Longshoremen's & Harbor Workers' Act, that a man is not a "member of a crew" . . . or that he was injured "in the course of his employment" . . . and the Federal Communications Comission's determination that one company is under the "control" of another . . . , the Board's determination that specified persons are "employees" under this Act is to be accepted if it has "warrant in the record" and a reasonable basis in law.

In this case the Board found that the designated newsboys work continuously and regularly, rely upon their earnings for the support of themselves and their families, and have their total wages influenced in large measure by the publishers who dictate their buying and selling prices, fix their markets and control their supply of papers. Their hours of work and their efforts on the job are supervised and to some extent prescribed by the publishers or their agents. Much of their sales equipment and advertising materials is furnished by the publishers with the intention that it be used for the publisher's benefit. Stating that "the primary consideration in the determination of the applicability of the statutory definition is whether effectuation of the declared policy and purposes of the Act comprehend securing to the individual the rights guaranteed and protection afforded by the Act," the Board concluded that the newsboys are employees. The record sustains the Board's findings and there is ample basis in the law for its conclusion. . . . Reversed and remanded.

Justice Roberts, dissenting opinion.

. . . I think it plain that newsboys are not "employees" of the respondents within the meeting and intent of the National Labor Relations Act. When Congress, in § 2(3), said "The term 'employee' shall include any employee, . . ." it stated as clearly as language could do it that the provisions of the Act were to extend to those who, as a result of decades of tradition which had become part of the common understanding of our people, bear the named relationship. Clearly also Congress did not delegate to the National Labor Relations Board the function of defining the relationship of employment so as to promote what the Board understood to be the underlying purpose of the statute. The question who is an employee, so as to make the statute applicable to him, is a question of the meaning of the Act and, therefore, is a judicial and not an administrative question. . . .

The Court's classic opinion in *Hearst* shows how questions of law and fact inevitably merge. Whether newsboys are or are not independent contractors is, of course, a legal conclusion. But the conclusion in turn depends on the facts, on what newsboys do and whether their degree of economic power vis-a-vis their employers really typifies those of most independent contractors. On the inevitable merging of law and fact in the decisional process, the Hearst company refused to recognize and bargain collectively with a properly elected union representing newsboys. It insisted that newsboys were independent contractors and not "employees" at all. Therefore, they were not covered by the National Labor Relations Act. The NLRB decided that the newsboys were employees within the meaning of the act, but the lower court on review held that at common law the newsboys were independent contractors and not employees protected by the act. The question before the Supreme Court therefore was whether the agency, here the NLRB, possessed any expertise or other quality that gave its conclusions on matters of law special weight or credibility. This case arose before the adoption of the APA, but its influence is still strong.

In the following work Professors Mashaw and Merrill, with some assistance from the late Judge Harold Levanthal, have provided a wise analysis of the law-fact interplay.

Scope of Review: Introduction to the American Public Law System

Jerry L. Mashaw and Richard A. Merrill
St. Paul: West Publishing Co., 1975,
pp. 786–788

. . . [T]he law-fact distinction presents obvious conceptual difficulties. The part of administrative decisionmaking that seems to raise the most difficult questions for administrators and for reviewing courts—the application of law to facts—is not exclusively the decision of a question of law or the finding of facts. To take a prosaic example, reasonable men may easily agree both on the abstract definition of "negligence" (the failure to act prudently under the circumstances) as well as on the operative facts of a given case; yet they may and often do disagree about whether those facts fit the legal definition, i.e., establish negligence on the part of the defendant. Is the conclusion in a particular case that the defendant was or was not negligent a conclusion of law or of fact? Obviously, it is at once neither . . . and both. Similar sorts of judgments abound in administrative decisionmaking; for example, an FTC determination that practices are "unfair or deceptive"; an NLRB determination that an employer has "interfered with," "restrained" or "coerced" employees in their exercise of collective rights; or an FCC determination that the award of a broadcast license to one of two competing applicants better serves "the public interest."

Finally, even if conceptual difficulties did not undermine the law-fact dichotomy in many situations, we would be likely to doubt that the relationship between administrative agencies that exercise widely varying administrative functions and courts that review their activities in many types of proceedings should or could be based on bipolar tests. We know that in construing statutes, courts often give significant weight to the interpretations of responsible administrators. Because the interpretation of a statute is clearly a question of law, administrators are thus conceded an important role in deciding at least some types of legal questions. Indeed, our experience with a wide range of agencies leaves no doubt that administrators may be "law determiners" as well as "fact finders." The issue for reviewing courts therefore becomes one of determining the permissible range of administrative lawmaking and deciding whether a particular action falls within that range.

This is not to say that the form in which a claim of administrative illegality is presented to a reviewing court has no bearing on the court's resolution of the dispute. But the formulation of the question is only one of the factors that will influence the degree to which judicial review becomes penetrating rather than perfunctory. Judicial review of administrative action may be as much art as science, as much "feel" and "flavor" as formal structure and analysis. This view was elaborated by Judge Harold Leventhal, one of the judiciary's most insightful students of administrative law, in *Greater Boston Television Corp. v. FCC*, 444 F.2d 841 [850-852] (D.C.Cir. 1970), *cert. denied*, 406 U.S. 950 (1972). The case involved review of the FCC's renewal of a broadcast license for which the appellant had been an unsuccessful competing applicant:

Approaching this case as we have with full awareness of and responsiveness to the court's "supervisory" function in review of agency decision, it may be appropriate to take note of the salient aspects of that review. It begins at the threshold, with enforcement of the requirement of reasonable procedure, with fair notice and opportunity to the parties to present their case. It continues into examination of the evidence and agency's findings of facts, for the court must be satisfied that the agency's evidentiary fact findings are supported by substantial evidence, and provide rational support for the agency's inferences of ultimate fact. Full allowance must be given not only for the opportunity of the agency . . . to observe the demeanor of the witnesses, but also for the reality that agency matters typically involve a kind of expertise—sometimes technical in a scientific sense, sometimes more a matter of specialization in kinds of regulatory programs. . . . A court does not depart from its proper function when it undertakes a study of the record, hopefully perceptive, even as to the evidence on technical and specialized matters, for this enables the court to penetrate to the underlying decisions of the agency, to satisfy itself that the agency has exercised a reasoned discretion, with reasons that do not deviate from or ignore the ascertainable legislative intent. . . .

Assuming consistency with law and the legislative mandate, the agency has latitude not merely to find facts and make judgments, but also to select the policies deemed in the public interest. The function of the court is to assure that the agency has given reasoned consideration to all the material facts and issues. This calls for insistence that the agency articulate with reasonable clarity its reasons for decision, and identify the significance of the crucial facts, a course that tends to assure that the agency's policies effectuate general standards, applied without unreasonable discrimination. . . .

Its supervisory function calls on the court to intervene not merely in case of procedural inadequacies, or bypassing of the mandate in the legislative charter, but more broadly if the court becomes aware, especially from a combination of danger signals, that the agency has not really taken a "hard look" at the salient problems, and has not genuinely engaged in reasoned decisionmaking. If the agency has not shirked this fundamental task, however, the court exercises restraint and affirms the agency's action even though the court would on its own account have made different findings or adopted different standards. . . .

The process thus combines judicial supervision with a salutary principle of judicial restraint, an awareness that agencies and courts together constitute a "partnership" in furtherance of the public interest, and are "collaborative instrumentalities of justice." The court is in a real sense part of the total administrative process, and not a hostile stranger to the office of first instance.

Exercises and Questions for Further Thought

How important is record? Depends on the statute.

1. Some of the problems of judicial review discussed in this chapter involve questions of statutory interpretation and thus extend the principles discussed in chapter 3. The main issue concerns the extent courts should defer to agency interpretations of their own statutes. Apply the principles in *Universal Camera* and *Hearst* to the benzene, cotton dust, or *Chevron v. NRDC* cases in chapter 3. Did the Court employ any of them? Should it have? Also, ask yourself whether *Overton Park* does not implicitly retreat from the principle in *Hearst*. Does *Heckler v. Chaney* affirm the principles of *Hearst*? If the NLRB was presumptively correct, why wasn't Secretary Volpe? Does the difference lie in the presence of a reviewable record in *Hearst* but not in *Overton Park*?

2. We commented that the influence of the *Hearst* decision remains strong in administrative law today. However, in 1980, the Supreme Court upheld a lower court *reversal* of an NLRB classification of faculty members at Yeshiva University as "professional employees." The Court held that faculty members were managers, not workers, and therefore their efforts to organize were not covered by the National Labor Relations Act. The majority said the case raised a "mixed" question "of fact and law." Does this distinguish the case from *Hearst*? See *NLRB v. Yeshiva University*, 444 U.S. 672 (1980).

3. Would it have been permissible for the Supreme Court to decide George Eldridge's claim (*Mathews v. Eldridge*) against him for failure to exhaust administrative remedies? Why or why not? *No - his was a constitutional issue - immediate hearing.*

4. A federal statute provides that "where the father or one or more sons or daughters of a family were killed in action or died in line of duty while serving in the Armed Forces . . . , the sole surviving son of such family shall not be inducted for [military] service." McKart, a sole surviving son, was called up for his preinduction military physical exam after his mother died. Selective Service had concluded that the statute did not apply in these circumstances. Without reporting for his physical and without exhausting any other administrative remedy, McKart sued to have this statutory interpretation set aside. Should courts defer to agency expertise on this matter? See *McKart v. United States*, 395 U.S. 185 (1969).

5. The courts in the early part of this century gave relatively little credence to claims of superior administrative fact-gathering capacity and expertise. As a result courts often

permitted full trials in court of the issues already resolved by the agency. Only under the Roosevelt Court was begun the withdrawal of the presumption of complete, or "de novo," judicial review and the insistence upon deference to administrative findings. In this perspective Justice Frankfurter's opinion in *Universal Camera* served to further bolster the credibility of fact finding by administrative law judges. But does this opinion go too far? Is it not plausible, based on experience with many such cases and consistent with achieving the policy goals of the nation's new labor laws, that the NLRB itself might believe that Chairman was "set up" by his superiors? Is it not plausible that experienced NLRB members might conclude that management had hounded Chairman into taking unwise actions, or that in such uncertain cases labor law ought to presume this to be true unless the company can show it isn't? Recall that *Vermont Yankee* and the current trend in administrative law is to defer to discretionary agency actions.

6. Law school students of administrative law learn to differentiate several forms of "judicial review of law" problems. These deserve brief mention here. First, courts distinguish questions of agency statutory interpretation from those of clearly delegated agency policymaking, and more aggressively review the former, often called interpretive rules. Second, courts are less likely to review legal conclusions when the questions involve technical matters, for example, of contract interpretation, which are presumably well-informed by the agency's special technical expertise on the matter. Where does the *Hearst* case fall in the scheme just outlined?

7. During the New Deal, political liberals supported deference to agency decision-making in part because the Court repeatedly applied the philosophy of laissez faire to strike down government regulation. Administrative agencies developed and implemented New Deal policies at a time when courts opposed these policies. Today we find that a politically conservative Supreme Court is limiting judicial review of agency actions and inactions. Hence, like the New Deal liberals, conservatives support agency discretion. Discuss this administrative law/politics paradox. Is it just simply a change in the guard—conservatives are now dominating national politics and are in the majority on the Supreme Court—which explains the current support for administrative authority? Consider the difference between Justice Rehnquist's majority opinion and Justice Marshall's concurring opinion in *Heckler v. Chaney*. In this case, conservatives and liberal justices deferred to administrative interpretation, but their reasoning for doing so differed substantially. How would you describe the difference between contemporary political liberal and conservative jurisprudence on judicial review of agency action and inaction?

PART III

Practical Problems in Administrative Law

Liability of the State and of Individual Officials for Legal Wrongs

The three chapters in this part apply law to several recurring problems in public administration. These chapters describe practical applications of some of the legal principles prior chapters explained. For example, chapter 11, on licensing problems ranging from drivers' licenses to licenses for nuclear power plants, and chapter 12, which treats personnel decisions, extend your appreciation for the varying requirements of a hearing. These three chapters, and particularly chapter 10, also introduce some new legal principles that students of administration need to know but that don't neatly fit elsewhere in the book. Despite differences of emphasis, these chapters fit together because each describes a problem that occurs at all levels of government, from the most powerful agencies in Washington, D.C., to the smallest towns in Wisconsin.

Responsibilities and Liabilities in Law

Up to this point we have focused mainly on the legal responsibilities of administrators. These are the things administrators ought to do in a given set of circumstances: hold a trial-type hearing, publish the draft of the proposed rule in the *Federal Register*, conduct an informal give and take with students before expelling them, and so forth. Nearly all the cases covered thus far declare such responsibilities for the first time. That is, they state in a context of ambiguous and uncertain law that "from now on in circumstances similar to those of this case the law shall require . . . " You can finish the sentence differently to suit each case.

The issue of liability raises a different question. Assuming the agency or officials have a clear legal responsibility and fail to perform it, how shall it or they compensate for this legal failure, this legal wrong? In all cases where courts declare new responsibilities, and in some cases stating previously clear legal responsibilities, the first judicial step merely instructs the agency to follow judicial orders. No question of compensation or liability would arise unless and until the agency refused to follow the orders.

In other circumstances, however, courts decide that people or institutions are liable to provide some compensation for their past wrongs. When a court finds someone liable for a past wrong it usually requires him to pay money damages and/or take actions to prevent the harm from continuing. The idea of liability is so common in many branches of law that lawyers and students take it for granted almost from the outset. The law of contract simultaneously defines a legally binding contract and states the damages someone who breaches the contract may have to pay or the actions they must take. The tort law of negligence holds that the wrongdoer must pay for the damages the wrong caused. And criminal law adds a set of compensations paid to society—fines, jail and prison sentences, and the rare execution—for those convicted of offending society's criminal statutes.

Public administrators and governments today are in many legal respects held to virtually the same level of liability as any private citizen. No matter how incensed Chairman Dixon may have been at the advertisements of the Cinderella Finishing School, he would be just as liable in tort as a private citizen if he had in his anger punched Cinderella's president in the nose, just as criminally liable if he had gunned the president down.

With some important exceptions—the police officer's legal authority to kill, for example—the criminal law applies equally to all of us. General books on the subject cover it fully, and it needs no special attention here. At the other extreme, the law of government contracting in many of its operating details does not simply follow general contract law or the Uniform Commercial Code, and it is so complex that sheer lack of space prohibits treatment here. Tort law falls somewhere in between. Torts are direct harms to people and property. They include (in addition to negligence) assault, battery, false imprisonment, libel, slander, and so forth. For curious historical reasons, courts have not held governments in the United States to ordinary tort liability, but by statute and recent court decisions the tort liability of government has expanded. In one controversial area, the responsibility to protect the civil rights of citizens, the government and its officials have a broader liability than have private citizens.

Liabilities and Responsibilities Distinguished: An Important Illustration

Before turning to the main business of this chapter, we consider a celebrated legal issue that will allow you to pin down the difference between responsibility and liability. The legal issue concerns the responsibility of public officials to present testimony and other tangible evidence they possess in court when properly subpoenaed to do so. The issue, as you may already have spotted, gained its celebrity in the Nixon tapes case, and remains a lively one.

In the course of the trials arising from the 1972 burglary of the Democratic party offices in the Watergate complex, the trial court subpoenaed tape recordings in President Nixon's possession. Nixon insisted that the tapes were protected by the doctrine of executive privilege and that he therefore had no legal responsibility to present them. The Supreme Court held him legally obligated to produce them.[1] It said in part:

---

[1] *United States v. Nixon*, 418 U.S. 683, 706 (1974).

However, neither the doctrine of separation of powers, nor the need for confidentiality of high level communications, without more, can sustain an absolute, unqualified presidential privilege of immunity from judicial process under all circumstances. The President's need for complete candor and objectivity from advisers calls for great deference from the courts. However, when the privilege depends solely on the broad, undifferentiated claim of public interest in the confidentiality of such conversations, a confrontation with other values arises. Absent a claim of need to protect military, diplomatic or sensitive national security secrets, we find it difficult to accept the argument that even the very important interest in confidentiality of presidential communications is significantly diminished by production of such material for *in camera* inspection with all the protection that a district court will be obliged to provide.

You might think that if a president of the United States must produce evidence in court, then everyone must do so, there being no stronger claim than that of executive privilege. In reality the law does protect stronger claims. If the president or any administrator refused to testify on the grounds that the testimony would incriminate him, the courts would honor the refusal. President Nixon invoked no such claim, and the Court ordered him to produce the materials. He did so, and the rest is history. But what if Nixon had refused to produce? Here the difference between responsibility and liability surfaces. The president's case occupies the unique position that he is only liable, as long as he is president, to impeachment and removal from office. Nixon's was the rare case in which the courts could impose no liability on him for refusing. Only the Congress could do so.

Tort Liability of Government for Acts of Officials

When a court concludes that a private person or institution has committed a tort, a wrong directed against the plaintiff or the plaintiff's property, the court then normally awards some money to the plaintiff. In some instances the court simply tries to estimate the dollar equivalent of the plaintiff's losses and to make compensation. Where, for example, the plaintiff loses property in an auto accident caused by the defendant's fault, the damages will cover the property the plaintiff lost. Where personal injury occurs, however, courts may award for pain and suffering as well as direct medical expenses, which makes the damages less certain. Furthermore, in some cases — libel and slander are typical — the plaintiff's tangible damages are very hard to estimate. The law complicates these issues further by permitting judges to award punitive damages to plaintiffs, damages designed more to prevent such wrongs in the future than to compensate the plaintiff.

The law of tort has two goals: to compensate for losses caused by others and to deter people from engaging in behavior that may cause harm.[2] You might therefore

[2] See G. Edward White, *Tort Law in America: An Intellectual History* (New York: Oxford University Press, 1980).

assume that either individual government officials or the government as a separate legal entity should meet the same standard of care toward people as does anyone else. Indeed one could argue that our concept of the ideal of legality commands the state to owe a duty of care to its citizens that is *higher* than citizens owe each other. Yet American law went in virtually the opposite direction. Borrowing the English principle that "the king can do no wrong," the courts held that people could sue the government in tort only when the government by statute gave them permission to do so. This doctrine of "sovereign immunity" would seem particularly out of place in a governmental system formed in rebellion against a monarchy, in a system whose constitution prohibits titles of nobility. Nevertheless, until Congress adopted the Federal Tort Claims Act (FTCA) in 1946, tort suits against the federal government got nowhere in court. In the strictest legal sense the government simply could not commit a tort because no law recognized the possibility. Congress did pass many "private bills" to compensate victims of government torts. In fact, one purpose for Congress's adopting the FTCA was to get rid of this time-consuming duty.[3]

Arguments in favor of the doctrine of sovereign immunity do exist. A lawsuit filed by one private citizen against another is a costly and time-consuming process. Often the defendant must cease pursuing some course of action pending the suit's resolution. But if a government is sovereign over its citizens, citizens cannot, by the definition of sovereignty, stop government dead in its track by going to court.[4] Besides, lawsuits raise the possibility that the sovereign's treasury will have to pay damages, or its employees perform services, consequences that could hamper effective public administration. These arguments do have some merit. However, ask yourself in the cases set out below whether Congress and the courts have struck a wise balance between the needs of sovereignty and administrative effectiveness, and the rule of law and the ideal of legality. Is not the essence of democracy that law *does* limit the authority of the sovereign?

The FTCA on first reading seems to strike a proper balance. Its most pertinent part reads: "The United States shall be liable, respecting the provisions of this title relating to tort claims, in the same manner and to the same extent as a private individual under like circumstances." Note that the act only creates liability for the government as a separate legal entity. It creates no individual liability of the officials themselves. The act, at least according to one plausible reading of these words, would seem to apply the private rules of tort to public actions: If you negligently drive your truck at work into someone else's truck, your company is liable to pay the damages; so also, when a soldier negligently drives an army tank into another, the government must pay the damages. In *Feres v. United States*, 340 U.S. 135 (1950), one of the first judicial interpretations of the act, the Supreme Court rejected this plausible reading. It said that the act only covered the government when it did the sorts of things private people do. Since there exists no private army, navy, air force, FBI, etc., the act did not cover

---

[3] See Peter H. Schuck, *Suing Government: Citizen Remedies for Official Wrongs* (New Haven, Conn.: Yale University Press, 1983).

[4] See Phillip J. Cooper, "The Supreme Court on Government Liability: The Nature and Origins of Sovereign and Official Immunity," *Administration and Society* 16 (1984): 257.

the negligence of soldiers and police. We shall see that the *Feres* doctrine has diminished, but Congress created the tort liability of law enforcement officials only in 1974.[5]

The original FTCA contained several exceptions. The most important excludes from coverage claims "based upon the exercise or performance or the failure to exercise or perform a discretionary function or duty on the part of a federal agency or an employee of the Government, whether or not the discretion involved be abused." Three years after the Supreme Court, in *Feres*, narrowly interpreted the coverage of the FTCA, it interpreted this exception very broadly. The "accordion words" in this exception are *discretionary function* and *discretion*. Expanded to their furthest, these words could cover every choice anyone makes. We have discretion to buy peas or beans for dinner, discretion whether to drink coffee or the whiskey that might cause us to injure another negligently as we drive home. Interpreted this broadly, the exception would swallow up the statute. Most narrowly, we can define governmental discretion as the top level of policymaking, whether by the White House or by the regulatory commissions themselves. While officially taking a position closer to the narrow interpretation, the Court actually applied the concept far more broadly than its words suggest.

The Court took this position in *Dalehite v. United States*, 346 U.S. 15 (1953). Henry G. Dalehite and 559 others died in the tragic explosion at Texas City, Texas. The explosion took place on the waterfront during the handling and loading of ammonium nitrate fertilizer for shipment, under a United States government aid program, to postwar France. Dalehite's heirs and others in the consolidated case filed personal and property claims for $200,000,000. The negligence claim rested on several causal factors. In general, under tort law one acts negligently when one fails to use the standard of care a reasonable and prudent person would adopt in the circumstances. Here it was alleged that the fertilizer, which had been coated with a flammable substance to prevent it from caking in the bags, was not properly handled because it was not properly labeled so as to warn its handlers of the fire danger. We can assume that a court would have found a private company that proceeded in this fashion negligent and liable.

However, the packaging and shipping of the fertilizer were part of a government program. The Court interpreted *discretion* to cover all the judgmental or policy decisions made by experts at a planning rather than an operational level of government. It said, "The acts found to have been negligent were thus performed under the discretion of a plan developed at a high level under a direct delegation of plan-making authority from the apex of the Executive Department. The establishment of this plan . . . clearly required the exercise of expert judgment."[6] The plaintiffs lost, though eventually, as had some but not all prior victims of governmental negligence, they received some compensation by virtue of a special private bill passed by Congress to compensate them. This of course put the burden of compensation back on congressional shoulders.

The case nicely illustrates the inevitable open-endedness of legal reasoning. The judgment depends much less on formal legal analysis than on deeply ingrained judicial hunches and values. The judges in this close (four-to-three) majority presumably

---

[5] See Howard Ball, "The U.S. Supreme Court's Glossing of the Federal Tort Claims Act: Statutory Construction and Veterans' Tort Action," *Western Political Quarterly* 41 (1988):529.

[6] 346 U.S. 15, 39–40.

felt a primary obligation to the treasury of the United States and the taxpayers who support it. They refused to authorize the expenditure of large sums because Congress had not clearly approved their doing so. Yet judges starting with different values and hunches would reach the opposite result. Judges who believe that those who are injured through no fault of their own should not bear the cost of the loss because others *have* been at fault might have ordered the government to pay. Judges might further believe (1) that making those at fault pay for losses they cause will encourage greater care and less harm in the long run, and (2) that the fairest social response to catastrophic loss is to spread the loss to the entire population, either through insurance covered by many thousands of premiums or through the government supported by taxpayers. These judges might feel even more compelled to require that the government should pay for the loss here. The fact that the decision to ship fertilizer to France was "discretionary" in this view simply does not change the reasons why the government should reimburse honest citizens for their losses in this disaster.

In the years since *Dalehite* the pendulum has swung away from the narrowest interpretations, and now we are witnessing it return to the narrow reading. Here are four illustrative cases. The distinction between decisions made at the planning versus operational levels does remain and is generally accepted. The real problem in *Dalehite*, then, is that the actual and proximate causes of the fire, the bad labeling and careless handling of the bags, really occurred at the operational, not the planning level. However, establishing a link between an alleged injury and government action requires more than sorting out the facts. Indeed, judicial interpretation of "the facts" in all four government tort liability cases determines whether the government has met its "duty of care" or not. As you read these cases pay close attention to the judicial process of constructing liability through the interpretation of facts. You will see how the expansion of government liability in *Indian Towing Co., Inc. v. U.S.* (1955) and *Griffin v. U.S.* (1974) rests on a welfare-state theory of the government's obligation to its citizens. According to this theory, once the state decides to become involved in certain activities, such as regulating lighthouses and inspecting vaccines, the state has an affirmative obligation to protect its citizens from negligent actions by government officials. In contrast, you will see how in *Allen v. United States* (1987) and *DeShaney v. Winnebago County Social Services*, (1989), the courts have undermined this theory in recent years by reducing the scope of the state's obligation and reinstating the narrow interpretation, articulated in *Dalehite*, of citizen rights under the Federal Tort Claims Act.

Indian Towing Co., Inc. v. United States

350 U.S. 61 (1955) 5–4
+ Warren, Black, Frankfurter, Douglas, Harlan
− Reed, Burton, Clark, Minton

[A towed barge belonging to the Indian Towing Company went aground on an island in the Mississippi River and its cargo of fertilizer was damaged. The company alleged that the grounding was due solely to the failure of the Coast Guard–operated warning light on the island. The company brought suit under the Federal Tort Claims Act to recover the damages it suffered, claiming that the light's failure was due to: (1) the failure of responsible Coast Guard officials to check the light's battery and sun relay system; (2) the failure of a chief petty officer to inspect electrical connections exposed to the weather; (3) the failure to check the light for a period of 24 days before the grounding; and (4) the failure to repair the light or give warning that it wasn't working. The company alleged also that there was a loose connection that could have been discovered with a proper inspection. The district court and Fifth Circuit found for the government.]

Justice Frankfurter delivered the opinion of the Court. The relevant provisions of the Federal Tort Claims Act are 28 U.S.C. §§ 1346(b), 2674, and 2680(a):

§ 1346(b). " . . . the district courts . . . shall have exclusive jurisdiction of civil actions on claims against the United States, for money damages, accruing on and after January 1, 1945, for injury or loss of property, or personal injury or death caused by the negligent or wrongful act or omission of any employee of the Government while acting within the scope of his office or employment, under circumstances where the United States, if a private person, would be liable to the claimant in accordance with the law of the place where the act or omission occurred."

§ 2674. The United States shall be liable . . . in the same manner and to the same extent as a private individual under like circumstances, but shall not be liable for interest prior to judgment or for punitive damages."

§ 2680. "The provisions of this chapter and section 1346(b) of this title shall not apply to—

"(a) Any claim based upon an act or omission of an employee of the Government, exercising due care, in the execution of a statute or regulation, whether or not such statute or regulation be valid, or based upon the exercise or performance or the failure to exercise or perform a discretionary function or duty on the part of a federal agency or an employee of the Government, whether or not the discretion involved be abused."

The question is one of liability for negligence at what this Court has characterized the "operation level" of governmental activity. *Dalehite v. United States*, 346 U.S. 15, 42. The Government concedes that the exception of § 2680 relieving from liability for negligent "exercise of judgment" (which is the way the Government paraphrases a "discretionary function" in § 2680(a)) is not involved here, and it does not deny that the Federal Tort Claims Act does provide for liability in some situations on the "operational level" of its activity. But the Government contends that the language of § 2674 (and the implications of § 2680) imposing liability "in the same manner and to the same extent as a private individual under like circumstances . . . " must be read as excluding liability in the performance of activities which private persons do not perform. Thus, there would be no liability for negligent performance of "uniquely governmental functions." The Government reads the statute as if it imposed liability to the same extent as would be imposed on a private individual "under the same circumstances." But the statutory language is "under like circumstances," and it is horn-book tort law that one who undertakes to warn the public of danger and thereby induces reliance must perform his "good Samaritan" task in a careful manner.

Furthermore, the Government in effect reads the statute as imposing liability in the same manner as if it were a municipal corporation and not as if it were a private person, and it would thus push the courts into the "non-governmental"–"governmental" quagmire that has long plagued the law of municipal corporations. A comparative study of the cases in the forty-eight States will disclose an irreconcilable conflict. More than that, the decisions in each of the States are disharmonious and disclose the inevitable chaos when courts try to apply a rule of law that is inherently unsound. The fact of the matter is that the theory whereby municipalities are made amenable to liability is an endeavor, however awkward and contradictory, to escape from the basic historical doctrine of sovereign immunity. The Federal Tort Claims Act cuts the ground from under that doctrine . . .

While the Government disavows a blanket exemption from liability for all official conduct furthering the "uniquely governmental" activity in any way, it does claim that there can be no recovery based on the negligent performance of the activity itself, the so-called "end-objective" of the particular governmental activity. Let us suppose that the Chief Petty Officer going in a Coast Guard car to inspect the light on Chandeleur Island first negligently ran over a pedestrian; later, while he was inspecting the light, he negligently tripped over a wire and injured someone else; he then forgot to inspect an outside connection and that night the patently defective connection broke and the light failed, causing a ship to go aground and its cargo of triple super phosphate to get wet; finally the Chief Petty Officer on his way out of the lighthouse touched a key to an uninsulated wire to see that it was carrying current, and the spark he produced caused a fire which sank a nearby barge carrying triple super phosphate. Under the Government's theory, some of these acts of negligence would be actionable, and some would not. But is there a rational ground, one that would carry conviction to minds not in the grip of technical obscurities, why there should be any difference in result? The acts were different in time and place but all were done in furtherance of the officer's task of inspecting the lighthouse and in furtherance of the Coast Guard's task in operating a light on Chandeleur Island. Moreover, if the United States were to permit the operation of private lighthouses—not at all inconceivable—the Government's basis of differentiation would be gone and the negligence charged in this case would be actionable. Yet there would be no change in the character of the Government's activity in the places where it operated a lighthouse, and we would be attributing bizarre motives to Congress were we to hold that

it was predicating liability on such a completely fortuitous circumstance—the presence or absence of identical private activity.

While the area of liability is circumscribed by certain provisions of the Federal Tort Claims Act, see 28 U.S.C. § 2680, all Government activity is inescapably "uniquely governmental" in that it is performed by the Government. In a case in which the Federal Crop Insurance Corporation, a wholly Government-owned enterprise, was sought to be held liable on a crop-insurance policy on the theory that a private insurance company would be liable in the same situation, this Court stated: "Government is not partly public or partly private, depending upon the governmental pedigree of the type of a particular activity or the manner in which the Government conducts it." *Federal Crop Insurance Corp. v. Merrill*, 332 U.S. 380, 383–384. On the other hand, it is hard to think of any governmental activity on the "operational level," our present concern, which is "uniquely governmental," in the sense that its kind has not at one time or another been, or could not conceivably be, privately performed . . .

The Coast Guard need not undertake the lighthouse service. But once it exercised its discretion to operate a light on Chandeleur Island and engendered reliance on the guidance afforded by the light, it was obligated to use due care to make certain that the light was kept in good working order; and, if the light did become extinguished, then the Coast Guard was further obligated to use due care to discover this fact and to repair the light or give warning that it was not functioning. If the Coast Guard failed in its duty and damage was thereby caused to petitioners, the United States is liable under the Tort Claims Act.

The Court of Appeals for the Fifth Circuit considered *Feres v. United States*, 340 U.S. 135, and *Dalehite v. United States*, 346 U.S. 15, controlling. Neither case is applicable. *Feres* held only that "the Government is not liable under the Federal Tort Claims Act for injuries to servicemen where the injuries arise out of or are in the course of activity incident to service. Without exception, the relationship of military personnel to the Government has been governed exclusively by federal law." 340 U.S., at 146. And see *Brooks*

v. United States, 337 U.S. 49. The differences between this case and *Dalehite* need not be labored. The governing factors in *Dalehite* sufficiently emerge from the opinion in that case.

Reversed.

Justice Reed, with whom Justice Burton, Justice Clark, and Justice Minton join, dissenting.

The question of the liability of the United States for this negligence depends on the scope and meaning of the Federal Tort Claims Act. The history of the adoption of that Act has heretofore been thoroughly explained. Before its enactment, the immunity of the Government from such tort actions was absolute. The Act authorized suits against the Government under certain conditions. . . .

In *Feres v. United States*, 340 U.S. 135, we passed upon the applicability of the Act to claims by members of the armed services injured through the negligence of other military personnel. . . . [I]n *Feres* the Court was of the view that the Act does not create new causes of action theretofore beyond the applicable law of torts. So, in determining whether an action for negligence in maintaining public lights is permissible, we must consider whether similar actions were allowed by the law of the place where the negligence occurred, prior to the Tort Claims Act, against public bodies otherwise subject to suit.

Dalehite v. United States, 346 U.S. 15, 42, followed the reasoning of *Feres*. . . . These two interpretive decisions have not caused Congress to amend the Federal Tort Claims Act. As a matter of fact, the catastrophe that gave rise to the *Dalehite* case was subsequently presented to Congress for legislative relief by way of compensation for the losses which resulted, as found by the trial court, partly from the negligence of the Coast Guard. Throughout the reports, discussion and enactment of the relief act, there was no effort to modify the Tort Claims Act so as to change the law, in any respect, as interpreted by this Court in *Feres* and *Dalehite*. . . . One cannot say that when a statute is interpreted by this Court we must follow that interpretation in subsequent cases unless Congress has amended the statute. . . . [W]e should continue to hold, as a matter of *stare decisis* and as the normal rule, that inaction of Congress, after a well-known and important decision of common knowledge, is "an aid in statutory construction . . . useful at times in resolving statutory ambiguities." *Helvering v. Reynolds*, 313 U.S. 428, 432. The nonaction of Congress should decide this controversy in the light of the previous rulings. The reasons which led to the conclusions against creating new and novel liabilities in the *Feres* and *Dalehite* cases retain their persuasiveness.

Griffin v. United States

500 F.2d 1059, U.S.C.A., 3rd Cir. (1974) 2–1–0

[Mrs. Griffin had become a quadriplegic as a result of a faulty lot (Lot 56) of polio vaccine. She settled out of court with the manufacturer of the vaccine but went to court with a suit under the Federal Tort Claims Act charging negligence on the part of the Division of Biological Standards (DBS) of the Department of Health, Education, and Welfare, which had routinely inspected the lot and let it be distributed for public use. Subsequent tests proved Lot 56 did not meet federal standards for release to public use. The District Court awarded Mrs. Griffin damages in excess of $2,000,000.]

Rosenn, Circuit Judge.

The threshold question confronting us is whether this action is barred because of the "discretionary function" exception to the Torts Claims Act . . .

The Government contends that the decision to release Lot 56 involved the exercise of a discretionary function. It argues that the determination called for by the regulation . . . that the neurovirulence of a particular lot does not exceed that of the "reference strain" involves the exercise of judgment. It maintains that Congress intended, by the discretionary function exception, § 2680(a), to exclude all claims "arising from acts of a regulatory nature."

We believe that the construction of 2680(a) urged upon us by the Government is too broad. Activity of any consequence is rarely without its judgmental component. The effect of accepting the Government's contention would effectively immunize all Governmental activity from judicial review except the most ministerial acts. In its landmark decision, *Dalehite v. United States,* . . . the Supreme Court explicitly recognized that not all activity involving judgment is necessarily encompassed within the Act's exception: "The 'discretion' protected by the section is not that of the judge—a power to decide within the limits of positive rules of law subject to judicial review. It is the discretion of the executive or the administrator to act according to one's judgment of the best course, a concept of substantial historical ancestry in American law . . ." The decisions held discretionary in *Dalehite* involved, at minimum, some consideration as to the feasibility or practicability of Government programs . . . Such decisions involved considerations of public policy, calling for a balance of such factors as cost of Government programs against the potential benefit. The Court stated: "[The discretionary function] also includes determinations made by executives or administrators in establishing plans, specifications or schedules of operations. Where there is room for *policy* judgment and decision, there is discretion." [Emphasis supplied.] . . . Where decisions have not involved policy judgments as to the public interest, the courts have not held the decisions to be immune from judicial review . . .

To determine the applicability of the discretionary function exception, therefore, we must analyze not merely whether judgment was exercised but also whether the nature of the judgment called for policy considerations . . .

Plaintiffs, in the instant case, challenge solely the manner by which the regulation was implemented. They contend that in approving a particular lot, Lot 56, for release to the public, DBS failed to comply with the standard established by the Surgeon General.

The issue before us, therefore, is whether the implementation of regulation 73.114(b)(1)(iii) by DBS involved a "discretionary function." To decide this question we must first determine exactly what the regulation required be done in determining whether to release a particular lot.

The crucial action in approving a particular test lot for polio vaccine manufacture was the determination that the neurovirulence of the test lot "[did] not exceed" that of the NIH "reference strain." The regulation required a "comparative analysis" of the monkey neurovirulence test results of a particular test lot with the monkey neurovirulence test results of the reference strain. The regulation enumerates five criteria as evidence of neurovirulence: the number of animals showing lesions characteristic of poliovirus infection, the number of animals showing lesions other than those characteristic of poliovirus infection, the severity of the lesions, the degree of dissemination of the lesions, and the rate of occurrence of paralysis not attributable to the mechanical injury resulting from inoculation trauma.

Plaintiffs contend that the test lot could not be approved if it exceeded the reference strain with respect to any *one* of the five enumerated criteria. Under this interpretation of the regulation DBS could not approve a lot which minimally exceeded the reference strain with respect to any one criterion, even if DBS considered that criterion the poorest indicia of neurovirulence of the enumerated criteria, and even though the test lot was far superior to the reference strain with respect to the other four criteria.

We do not agree with this construction of the regulation. The regulation merely lists five criteria as evidence of neurovirulence and calls for a "comparative analysis." DBS has consistently construed the regulation as permitting it to weight the criteria in accordance with the degree to which it believed each criterion reflected neurovirulence.

The Supreme Court has stated on another occasion: "Since this involves an interpretation of an administrative regulation a court must necessarily look to the administrative construction of the regulation if the meaning of the words used is in doubt . . . [T]he ultimate criterion is the administrative interpretation, which becomes of controlling weight unless it is plainly erroneous or inconsistent with the regulation." *Bowles v. Seminole Rock and Sand Co.*, 325 U.S. 410, 413–414 (1945). We find the DBS interpretation of the regulation to allow weighting of the five criteria of neurovirulence neither "plainly erroneous" nor "inconsistent with the regulation."

We acknowledge that under DBS' construction of the regulation, the implementation called for a judgment determination as to the degree to which each of the enumerated criteria indicated neurovirulence in monkeys. The judgment, however, was that of a professional measuring neurovirulence. It was not that of a policy-maker promulgating regulations by balancing competing policy considerations in determining the public interest. Neither was it a policy planning decision nor a determination of the feasibility or practicability of a government program. At issue was a scientific, but not policy-making, determination as to whether each of the criteria listed in the regulation was met and the extent to which each such fac-

tor accurately indicated neurovirulence. DBS' responsibility was limited to merely executing the policy judgments of the Surgeon General. It had no authority to formulate new policy in the immunization program.

Where the conduct of the Government employees in implementing agency regulations required only performance of scientific evaluation and not the formulation of policy, we do not believe that the conduct is immunized from judicial review as a "discretionary function." As Judge Waterman of the Second Circuit has stated: "The fact that judgments of government officials occur in areas requiring professional expert evaluation does not necessarily remove those judgments from the examination of courts by classifying them as discretionary functions under the Act." *Hendry v. United States*, 418 F.2d 774, 783 (2d Cir. 1969) . . .

The case will be remanded for proceedings consistent with this opinion.

Allen v. United States

816 F.2d 1417, U.S.C.A., 10th Cir. (1987) 3–0

[In a class action against the United States, some twelve hundred named plaintiffs alleged five hundred deaths and injuries resulted from radioactive fallout from open-air atomic bomb testing in Nevada during the 1950s and 1960s. The district court selected and tried twenty-four of these claims in order to find a common legal framework for the rest. The district court ruled against the government on nine claims and in favor of the government on fourteen claims, leaving one outstanding claim.]

Logan, Circuit Judge.

In 1950 the AEC [Atomic Energy Commission] chose an area in Nevada as a testing site. The President approved this choice. Thereafter, between 1951 and 1962, eight series of open-air tests were conducted, with the President approving each series of tests. Over one hundred atomic bombs were detonated.

Each test explosion was executed according to detailed plans which the AEC officially reviewed and adopted. Separate plans for protecting the public, and for providing the public with appropriate information, were also adopted by the AEC. To actually execute the plans, however, the AEC delegated some

of its authority. The AEC selected a "Test Manager" for each test series, who had some day-to-day discretion. The Test Manager could, for example, postpone a given test because of adverse weather conditions. The Test Manager in turn delegated authority to a Radiological Safety Officer (a "Radsafe Officer") who was in charge of implementing plans to avoid radiation dangers, and a Test Information Officer who was in charge of implementing plans to provide public information on the tests. Both the Radsafe Officer and the Test Information Officer also had some day-to-day discretion in performing their duties.

At trial, as a basis for government liability, plaintiffs singled out the alleged failure of the government, especially of the Radsafe Officers and the Test Information Officers, to fully monitor offsite fallout exposure and to fully provide needed public information on radioactive fallout. The district court focused on these two failures in finding government liability. . . .

The Federal Tort Claims Acts (FTCA) authorizes suits for damages against the United States

> "for injury or loss of property, or personal injury or death caused by the negligent or wrongful act or omission of any employee of the Government while acting within the scope of his office or employment, under circumstances where the United States, if a private person, would be liable to the claimant in accordance with the law of the place where the act or omission occurred."

28 U.S.C. § 1346(b). In such suits, the United States is liable "in the same manner and to the same extent as a private individual under like circumstances." 28 U.S.C. 2674. Suit is not allowed, however, for any claim

> "based upon an act or omission of an employee of the Government, exercising due care, in the execution of a statute or regulation, whether or not such statute or regulation be valid, or *based upon the exercise or performance or the failure to exercise or perform a discretionary function or duty* on the part of a federal agency or an employee of the Government, *whether or not the discretion involved be abused.*"

28 U.S.C. § 2680(a) (emphasis added). The key term, "discretionary function," is not defined. For over thirty-five years the federal courts have been attempting to define it.

Plaintiffs in the present case attempted to distinguish between the discretionary initiation of government programs, at the highest levels of administration, and the decisions involved in carrying out programs, at lower levels. Plaintiffs argued that while low-level decisions may involve some "judgment," they do not fall within the discretionary function exception of 2680(a). *See, e.g., Indian Towing Co. v. United States,*

350 U.S. 61, . . . (1955) (reference to "operational level" of activity; no immunity found for government-failure to operate lighthouse). The district court agreed, basing its finding of government liability squarely on a distinction between high-level and low-level governmental activity. . . .

After the district court judgment in the present case, the Supreme Court decided *United States v. S.A. Empresa de Viacao Aerea Rio Grandense (Varig Airlines),* 467 U.S. 797 . . . (1984), in which it explicitly rejected distinctions based on the administrative level at which the challenged activity occurred. In *Varig,* various plaintiffs brought an FTCA suit against the United States, claiming that the Federal Aviation Administration (FAA) had negligently implemented plane inspection and design certification programs, allowing improper flammable materials and a defective heater system to be used to construct a specific Boeing 707 and a specific DeHavilland Dove. The planes in question caught fire and burned, killing most of those on board. The Supreme Court held, however, that the United States was immune from suit. The Court found that the contested FAA actions constituted the performance of a "discretionary function," exempt under 28 U.S.C. 2680(a) from potential FTCA liability. . . .

The plaintiffs in *Varig* focused on "low-level" decisions in their suit. They challenged the actual issuance by the FAA of design approval certificates for two plane types, the decision to enforce FAA standards with a particular "spot-check" system, and the actual plane inspections that were and were not carried out under that system. . . . The Supreme Court found that each of these actions constituted a discretionary function, immune from suit under 2680(a). . . . The Court emphasized that it is "the nature of the conduct, rather than the status of the actor, that governs whether the discretionary function exception applies in a given case." *Varig,* 467 U.S. at 813. . . .

On appeal, plaintiffs contend that the AEC, in planning and conducting its monitoring and information programs, was not making the kind of policy judgments protected by § 2680(a). They point to the general statutory provisions instructing the AEC to consider public health and safety, and claim that these broad congressional directives leave no further room for discretion. We disagree.

In the case before us, as in *Varig,* the government actors had a general statutory duty to promote safety; this duty was broad and discretionary. In the case before us it was left to the AEC, as in *Varig* it was left to the Secretary of Transportation and the FAA, to decide exactly *how* to protect public safety. If anything, the obligation imposed on the FAA to protect public safety was greater and the discretion granted to the FAA by Congress was less, in the circumstances reviewed by *Varig,* than the comparable obligation imposed and discretion available to the AEC in the present case. . . . We cannot say that what was protected by the Supreme Court in *Varig* is now subject to liability.

Plaintiffs further contend that, even if the initial discretion granted by the AEC by statute was broad, test site personnel violated the AEC's own policy directives by failing to implement adequate protective measures. We cannot accept this argument either. Neither the plaintiffs nor the district court have been able to point to a single instance in which test site personnel ignored or failed to implement specific procedures mandated by the AEC for monitoring and informing the public. Indeed, the district court's conclusions appear to be based, at least in part, on perceived inadequacies in the AEC's radiological safety and information plans themselves. The court relied heavily on a 1954 report to the AEC by the Committee to Study Nevada Proving Grounds which was moderately critical of the measures taken up to that point to inform and warn the public. . . . The stated objective of this report, however, was "[t]o be a basis for Commission decisions on future policy." . . . The operational plans the district court considered deficient embody those AEC policy decisions. As such, these plans clearly fall within the discretionary function exception.

Government liability cannot logically be predicated on the failure of test-site personnel to go beyond what the operational plans specifically required them to do. If, as the plaintiffs maintain, the AEC delegated "unfettered authority" to a Test Manager and his subordinates to implement public safety programs, this simply compels the conclusion that those officers exercised considerable discretion. Their actions, accordingly, also fall within the discretionary function exception.

It is irrelevant to the discretion issue whether the AEC or its employees were negligent in failing to adequately protect the public . . . When the conduct at issue involves the exercise of discretion by a government agency or employee, § 2680(a) preserves governmental immunity "whether or not the discretion involved be abused." For better or worse, plaintiffs here "obtain their 'right to sue from Congress [and] necessarily must take it subject to such restrictions as have been imposed.' " *Dalehite v. United States,* 346 U.S. 15. . . .

. . . The *Dalehite* plaintiffs, like the present plaintiffs, were unable to point to any instances in which government employees acted negligently in performing specific, mandatory duties. The *Dalehite* plaintiffs instead argued primarily, just as the present plaintiffs argue here, that at various points the government could have made better plans, and that the government failed to fully investigate the hazards of the dangerous material involved and to fully inform and warn the nearby populace. . . .

The Supreme Court in *Dalehite* found every contested government decision, action, and omission to be the performance of a discretionary function, exempt from suit under § 2680(a): the cabinet-level decision to export the fertilizer, the lower-level failure to fully test for explosive properties, the Field Director's fertilizer production plan, the actual production of the fertilizer in accordance with the government specifications, and the specific decisions to bag the fertilizer at a certain temperature and to label the fertilizer in a certain way . . . The various actions and omissions of the Coast Guard, supervising the actual loading of the ships, were also exempted, as was the general failure to warn the nearby populace of potential dangers. . . .

. . . Given the Court's holding in *Dalehite,* reaffirmed in *Varig,* we must conclude that the government is immune from liability for the failure of the AEC administrators and employees to monitor radioactivity more extensively or to warn the public more fully than they did. . . .

Our decision here adheres to the principle enunciated by the Supreme Court of broad sovereign immunity. An inevitable consequence of that sovereign immunity is that the United States may escape legal responsibility for injuries that would be compensible if caused by a private party. There remain administrative and legislative remedies; we note the express authorization under 42 U.S.C. § 2012(i) for the government to make funds available for damages suffered by the public from nuclear incidents. Nonetheless, judicial reluctance to recognize the some-

times harsh principle of sovereign immunity explains much of the tangle of the prior FTCA cases . . .

For the above reasons, we find all challenged actions surrounding the government atomic bomb tests in the 1950s and 1960s to be immune from suit, as the performance by a federal agency of a "discretionary function," protected by § 2680(a).

We reverse the district court's decision with regard to those nine claims in which the government was found to have liability and remand for further proceedings consistent with this opinion.

McKay, Circuit Judge, concurring: [omitted].

DeShaney v. Winnebago County Department of Social Services

103 L Ed 2d 249 (1989) 6–3

+ Rehnquist, White, Stevens, O'Connor, Scalia, Kennedy
- Brennan, Marshall, Blackmun

[A four-year-old boy in Winnebago County, Wisconsin was severely beaten by his natural father, causing brain damage and requiring his placement in an institution for the profoundly retarded for the rest of his life. The boy, Joshua DeShaney, and his mother, Melody DeShaney, brought suit against the County's Department of Social Services (DSS) and individual DSS employees, alleging that they failed to intervene to protect him against a known risk of violence and thus deprived him of his liberty without due process of law. The district court and the Court of Appeals for the Seventh Circuit held that a state agency's failure to render protective services to persons within its jurisdiction does not violate the due process clause of the Fourteenth Amendment. The DeShaneys appealed to the U.S. Supreme Court.]

Chief Justice Rehnquist delivered the opinion of the Court.

I

The facts of this case are undeniably tragic. Petitioner Joshua DeShaney was born in 1979. In 1980, a Wyoming court granted his parents a divorce and awarded custody of Joshua to his father, Randy DeShaney. The father shortly thereafter moved to Neenah, a city located in Winnebago County, Wisconsin, taking the infant Joshua with him. There he entered into a second marriage, which also ended in divorce.

The Winnebago County authorities first learned that Joshua DeShaney might be a victim of child abuse in January 1982, when his father's second wife complained to the police, at the time of their divorce, that he had previously "hit the boy causing marks and [was] a prime case for child abuse." . . . The Winnebago County Department of Social Services (DSS) interviewed the father, but he denied the accusations, and DSS did not pursue them further. In January 1983, Joshua was admitted to a local hospital with multiple bruises and abrasions. The examining physician suspected child abuse and notified DSS, which immediately obtained an order from a Wisconsin juvenile court placing Joshua in the temporary custody of the hospital. Three days later, the county convened an ad hoc "Child Protection Team"—consisting of a pediatrician, a psychologist, a police detective, the county's lawyer, several DSS case workers, and various hospital personnel—to consider Joshua's situation. At this meeting, the Team decided that there was insufficient evidence of child abuse to retain Joshua in the custody of the court. The Team did, however, decide to recommend several measures to protect Joshua, including enrolling him in a preschool program, providing his father with certain counselling services, and encouraging his father's girlfriend to move out of the home. Randy DeShaney entered into a voluntary agreement with DSS in which he promised to cooperate with them in accomplishing these goals.

Based on the recommendation of the Child Protection Team, the juvenile court dismissed the child protection case and returned Joshua to the custody of his father. A month later, emergency room personnel called the DSS caseworker handling Joshua's case to report that he had once again been treated for suspicious injuries. The caseworker concluded that there was no basis for action. For the next six months, the caseworker made monthly visits to the DeShaney home, during which she observed a number of suspicious injuries on Joshua's head; she also noticed that he had not been enrolled in school and that the girlfriend had not moved out. The caseworker dutifully recorded these incidents in her files, along with her continuing suspicions that someone in the DeShaney household was physically abusing Joshua, but she did nothing more. In November 1983, the emergency room notified DSS that Joshua had been treated once again for injuries that they believed to be caused by child abuse. On the caseworker's next two visits to the DeShaney home, she was told that Joshua was too ill to see her. Still DSS took no action.

In March 1984, Randy DeShaney beat 4-year-old Joshua so severely that he fell into a life-threatening coma. Emergency brain surgery revealed a series of hemorrhages caused by traumatic injuries to the head inflicted over a long period of time. Joshua did not die, but he suffered brain damage so severe that he

is expected to spend the rest of his life confined to an institution for the profoundly retarded. Randy DeShaney was subsequently tried and convicted of child abuse. . . .

Because of the inconsistent approaches taken by the lower courts in determining when, if ever, the failure of a state or local governmental entity or its agents to provide an individual with adequate protective services constitutes a violation of the individual's due process rights . . . and the importance of the issue to the administration of state and local governments, we granted certiorari. . . .

II

The Due Process Clause of the Fourteenth Amendment provides that "[n]o State, shall . . . deprive any person of life, liberty, or property, without due process of law." Petitioners contend that the State deprived Joshua of his liberty interest in "free[dom] from . . . unjustified intrusions on personal security," see *Ingraham v. Wright*, 430 US 651, 673 . . . (1977), by failing to provide him with adequate protection against his father's violence. The claim is one invoking the substantive rather than procedural component of the Due Process Clause; petitioners do not claim that the State denied Joshua protection without according him appropriate procedural safeguards, see *Morrissey v. Brewer*, 408 US 471 . . . (1972).[*]

But nothing in the language of the Due Process Clause itself requires the State to protect the life, liberty, and property of its citizens against invasion by private actors. The Clause is phrased as a limitation on the State's power to act, not as a guarantee of certain minimal levels of safety and security . . . [I]ts language cannot fairly be extended to impose an affirmative obligation on the State to ensure that

---

[*]Petitioners also argue that the Wisconsin child protection statutes gave Joshua an "entitlement" to receive protective services in accordance with the terms of the statute, an entitlement which would enjoy due process protection against state deprivation under our decision in Board of Regents v. Roth, 408 US 564. . . . (1972). . . . But this argument is made for the first time in petitioners' brief to this Court: it was not pleaded in the complaint, argued to the Court of Appeals as a ground for reversing the District Court, or raised in the petition for certiorari. We therefore decline to consider it here.

those interests do not come to harm through other means. Nor does history support such an expansive reading of the constitutional text. . . . Its purpose was to protect the people from the State, not to ensure that the State protected them from each other. The Framers were content to leave the extent of governmental obligation in the latter area to the democratic political processes.

Consistent with these principles, our cases have recognized that the Due Process Clauses generally confer no affirmative right to governmental aid, even where such aid may be necessary to secure life, liberty, or property interests of which the government itself may not deprive the individual. See, e.g., *Harris v. McRae*, 448 US 297 . . . (1980). . . . As we said in *Harris v. McRae*, "[a]lthough the liberty protected by the Due Process Clause affords protection against unwarranted *government* interference . . . , it does not confer an entitlement to such [governmental aid] as may be necessary to realize all the advantages of that freedom." 448 US, at 317–318 . . . (emphasis added). If the Due Process Clause does not require the State to provide its citizens with particular protective services, it follows that the State cannot be held liable under the Clause for injuries that could have been averted had it chosen to provide them.* As a general matter, then, we conclude that a State's failure to protect an individual against private violence simply does not constitute a violation of the Due Process Clause.

Petitioners contend, however, that even if the Due Process Clause imposes no affirmative obligation on the State to provide the general public with adequate protective services, such a duty may arise out of certain "special relationships" created or assumed by the State with respect to particular individuals. . . . Petitioners argue that such a "special relationship" existed here because the State knew that Joshua faced a special danger of abuse at his father's hands, and specifically proclaimed, by word and by deed, its intention to protect him against that

danger. . . . Having actually undertaken to protect Joshua from this danger—which petitioners concede the State played no part in creating—the State acquired an affirmative "duty," enforceable through the Due Process Clause, to do so in a reasonably competent fashion. Its failure to discharge that duty, so the argument goes, was an abuse of governmental power that so "shocks the conscience," *Rochin v. California*, 342 US 165 . . . (1952), as to constitute a substantive due process violation. . . .

We reject this argument. It is true that in certain limited circumstances the Constitution imposes upon the State affirmative duties of care and protection with respect to particular individuals. In *Estelle v. Gamble*, 429 US 97 . . . (1976), we recognized that the Eighth Amendment's prohibition against cruel and unusual punishment, made applicable to the States through the Fourteenth Amendment's Due Process Clause, *Robinson v. California*, 370 US 660 . . . (1962), requires the State to provide adequate medical care to incarcerated prisoners. . . . We reasoned that because the prisoner is unable " 'by reason of the deprivation of his liberty [to] care for himself,' " it is only " 'just' " that the State be required to care for him. . . .

In *Youngberg v. Romeo*, 457 US 307 . . . (1982), we extended this analysis beyond the Eighth Amendment setting, holding that the substantive component of the Fourteenth Amendment's Due Process Clause requires the State to provide involuntarily committed mental patients with such services as are necessary to ensure their "reasonable safety" from themselves and others . . .

But these cases afford petitioners no help. Taken together, they stand only for the proposition that when the State takes a person into its custody and holds him there against his will, the Constitution imposes upon it a corresponding duty to assume some responsibility for his safety and general well-being. . . . The rationale for this principle is simple enough: when the State by the affirmative exercise of its power so restrains an individual's liberty that it renders him unable to care for himself, and at the same time fails to provide for his basic human needs—e.g., food, clothing, shelter, medical care, and reasonable safety—it transgresses the substantive limits on

---

*The State may not, of course, selectively deny its protective services to certain disfavored minorities without violating the Equal Protection Clause. See *Yick Wo v. Hopkins*, 118 US 356 . . . (1886). But no such argument has been made here.

state action set by the Eighth Amendment and the Due Process Clause. . . . The affirmative duty to protect arises not from the State's knowledge of the individual's predicament or from its expressions of intent to help him, but from the limitation which it has imposed on his freedom to act on his own behalf. . . .

Petitioners concede that the harms Joshua suffered did not occur while he was in the State's custody, but while he was in the custody of his natural father, who was in no sense a state actor. While the State may have been aware of the dangers that Joshua faced in the free world, it played no part in their creation, nor did it do anything to render him any more vulnerable to them. That the State once took temporary custody of Joshua does not alter the analysis, for when it returned him to his father's custody, it placed him in no worse position than that in which he would have been had it not acted at all; the State does not become the permanent guarantor of an individual's safety by having once offered him shelter. Under these circumstances, the State had no constitutional duty to protect Joshua.

It may well be that, by voluntarily undertaking to protect Joshua against a danger it concededly played no part in creating, the State acquired a duty under state tort law to provide him with adequate protection against that danger . . . But the claim here is based on the Due Process Clause of the Fourteenth Amendment, which, as we have said many times, does not transform every tort committed by a state actor into a constitutional violation. . . .

Judges and lawyers, like other humans, are moved by natural sympathy in a case like this to find a way for Joshua and his mother to receive adequate compensation for the grievous harm inflicted upon them. But before yielding to that impulse, it is well to remember once again that the harm was inflicted not by the State of Wisconsin, but by Joshua's father. The most that can be said of the state functionaries in this case is that they stood by and did nothing when suspicious circumstances dictated a more active role for them. In defense of them it must also be said that had they moved too soon to take custody of the son away from the father, they would likely have been met with charges of improperly intruding into the

parent-child relationship, charges based on the same Due Process Clause that forms the basis for the present charge of failure to provide adequate protection.

The people of Wisconsin may well prefer a system of liability which would place upon the State and its officials the responsibility for failure to act in situations such as the present one. They may create such a system, if they do not have it already, by changing the tort law of the State in accordance with the regular law-making process. But they should not have it thrust upon them by this Court's expansion of the Due Process Clause of the Fourteenth Amendment.

Affirmed.

Justice Brennan, with whom Justice Marshall and Justice Blackmun join, dissenting.

"The most that can be said of the state functionaries in this case," the Court today concludes, "is that they stood by and did nothing when suspicious circumstances dictated a more active role for them." . . . Because I believe that this description of respondents' conduct tells only part of the story and that, accordingly, the Constitution itself "dictated a more active role" for respondents in the circumstances presented here, I cannot agree that respondents had no constitutional duty to help Joshua DeShaney.

It may well be, as the Court decides . . . that the Due Process Clause as construed by our prior cases creates no general right to basic governmental services. That, however, is not the question presented here; indeed, that question was not raised in the complaint, urged on appeal, presented in the petition for certiorari, or addressed in the briefs on the merits. No one, in short, has asked the Court to proclaim that, as a general matter, the Constitution safeguards positive as well as negative liberties.

This is more than a quibble over dicta; it is a point about perspective, having substantive ramifications. In a constitutional setting that distinguishes sharply between action and inaction, one's characterization of the misconduct alleged under § 1983 may effectively decide the case. Thus, by leading off with a discussion (and rejection) of the idea that the Constitution imposes on the States an affirmative duty to take basic care of their citizens, the Court foreshadows — perhaps even preordains — its conclusion that no duty existed even on the specific facts before us. This initial discussion establishes the baseline from which the Court assesses the DeShaneys' claim . . .

The Court's baseline is the absence of positive rights in the Constitution and a concomitant suspicion of any claim that seems to depend on such rights. From this perspective, the DeShaneys' claim is first and foremost about inaction (the failure, here, of respondents to take steps to protect Joshua), and only tangentially about action (the establishment of a state program specifically designed to help children like Joshua). And from this perspective, holding these Wisconsin officials liable . . . would seem to punish an effort that we should seek to promote.

I would begin from the opposite direction. I would focus first on the action that Wisconsin *has* taken with respect to Joshua and children like him rather than on the actions that the State failed to take. Such a method is not new to this Court. Both *Estelle v. Gamble* and *Youngberg v. Romeo* began by emphasizing that the States had confined J. W. Gamble to prison and Nicholas Romeo to a psychiatric hospital. This initial action rendered these people helpless to help themselves or to seek help from persons unconnected to the government. . . . Cases from the lower courts also recognize that a State's actions can be decisive in assessing the constitutional significance of subsequent inaction . . .

In striking down a filing fee as applied to divorce cases brought by indigents, see *Boddie v. Connecticut,* 401 US 371 . . . (1971), and in deciding that a local government could not entirely foreclose the opportunity to speak in a public forum, see, e.g., *Schneider v. State,* 308 US 147 . . . (1939); *Hague v. CIO,* 307 US 496, (1939); *United States v. Grace,* 461 US 171 . . . (1983), we have acknowledged that a State's actions — such as the monopolization of a particular path of relief — may impose upon the State certain positive duties. Similarly, *Shelley v. Kraemer,* 334 US 1 . . . (1948), and *Burton v. Wilmington Parking Authority,* 365 US 715 . . . (1961), suggest that a State

may be found complicit in an injury even if it did not create the situation that caused the harm . . .

. . . To put the point more directly, these cases signal that a State's prior actions may be decisive in analyzing the constitutional significance of its inaction. I thus would locate the DeShaneys' claims within the framework of cases like *Youngberg* and *Estelle,* and more generally, *Boddie* and *Schneider,* by considering the actions that Wisconsin took with respect to Joshua.

Wisconsin has established a child-welfare system specifically designed to help children like Joshua. Wisconsin law places upon the local departments of social services such as respondent . . . a duty to investigate reported instances of child abuse. . . . While other governmental bodies and private persons are largely responsible for the reporting of possible cases of child abuse, . . . Wisconsin law channels all such reports to the local departments of social services for evaluation and, if necessary, further action. . . . Even when it is the sheriff's office or police department that receives a report of suspected child abuse, that report is referred to local social services departments for action, . . . the only exception to this occurs when the reporter fears for the child's *immediate* safety. . . . In this way, Wisconsin law invites — indeed, directs — citizens and other governmental entities to depend on local departments of social services such as respondent to protect children from abuse.

The specific facts before us bear out this view of Wisconsin's system of protecting children. Each time someone voiced a suspicion that Joshua was being abused, that information was relayed to the Department for investigation and possible action. . . . (As to the extent of the social worker's involvement in and knowledge of Joshua's predicament, her reaction to the news of Joshua's last and most devastating injuries is illuminating: "I just knew the phone would ring some day and Joshua would be dead." 812 F2d 298, 300 (CA7 1987).)

Even more telling than these examples is the Department's control over the decision whether to take steps to protect a particular child from suspected abuse. While many different people contributed information and advice to this decision, it was up to the people at DSS to make the ultimate decision . . . whether to disturb the family's current arrangements. . . . When Joshua first appeared at a local hospital with injuries signaling physical abuse, for example, it was DSS that made the decision to take him into temporary custody for the purpose of studying his situation—and it was DSS, acting in conjunction with the Corporation Counsel, that returned him to his father. . . . Unfortunately for Joshua DeShaney, the buck effectively stopped with the Department. . . .

. . . Through its child-welfare program, . . . the State of Wisconsin has relieved ordinary citizens and governmental bodies other than the Department of any sense of obligation to do anything more than report their suspicions of child abuse to DSS. If DSS ignores or dismisses these suspicions, no one will step in to fill the gap. Wisconsin's child-protection programs thus effectively confined Joshua DeShaney within the walls of Randy DeShaney's violent home until such time as DSS took action to remove him. Conceivably, then, children like Joshua are made worse off by the existence of this program when the persons and entities charged with carrying it out fail to do their jobs.

It simply belies reality, therefore, to contend that the State "stood by and did nothing" with respect to Joshua. . . . Through its child-protection program, the State actively intervened in Joshua's life and, by virtue of this intervention, acquired ever more certain knowledge that Joshua was in grave danger. These circumstances, in my view, plant this case solidly within the tradition of cases like *Youngberg* and *Estelle* . . .

I would allow Joshua and his mother the opportunity to show that respondents' failure to help him arose, not out of the sound exercise of professional judgment that we recognized in *Youngberg* as sufficient to preclude liability, . . . but from the kind of arbitrariness that we have in the past condemned. See, e.g., *Daniels v. Williams*, 474 US 327 . . . (1986).

. . . *Youngberg's* deference to a decisionmaker's professional judgment ensures that once a caseworker has decided, on the basis of her professional training and experience, that one course of protection is preferable for a given child, or even that no special protection is required, she will not be found liable for the harm that follows . . . Moreover, that the Due Process Clause is not violated by merely negligent conduct . . . means that a social worker who simply makes a mistake of judgment under what are admittedly complex and difficult conditions will not find herself liable in damages under § 1983. . . .

. . . My disagreement with the Court arises from its failure to see that inaction can be every bit as abusive of power as action, that oppression can result when a State undertakes a vital duty and then ignores it. Today's opinion construes the Due Process Clause to permit a State to displace private sources of protection and then, at the critical moment, to shrug its shoulders and turn away from the harm that it has promised to try to prevent. Because I cannot agree that our Constitution is indifferent to such indifference, I respectfully dissent.

Justice Blackmun, dissenting.

Today, the Court purports to be the dispassionate oracle of the law, unmoved by "natural sympathy." . . . But, in this pretense, the Court itself retreats into a sterile formalism which prevents it from recognizing either the facts of the case before it or the legal norms that should apply to those facts. As Justice Brennan demonstrates, the facts here involve not mere passivity, but active state intervention in the life of Joshua DeShaney—intervention that triggered a fundamental duty to aid the boy once the State learned of the severe danger to which he was exposed.

The Court fails to recognize this duty because it attempts to draw a sharp and rigid line between action and inaction. But such formalistic reasoning has no place in the interpretation of the broad and stirring clauses of the Fourteenth Amendment. Indeed, I submit that these clauses were designed, at least in part, to undo the formalistic legal reasoning that infected antebellum jurisprudence, which the late Professor Robert Cover analyzed so effectively in his significant work entitled *Justice Accused* (1975).

Like the antebellum judges who denied relief to

fugitive slaves, . . . the Court today claims that its decision, however harsh, is compelled by existing legal doctrine. On the contrary, the question presented by this case is an open one, and our Fourteenth Amendment precedents may be read more broadly or narrowly depending upon how one chooses to read them. Faced with the choice, I would adopt a "sympathetic" reading, one which comports with dictates of fundamental justice and recognizes that compassion need not be exiled from the province of judging. . . .

Poor Joshua! Victim of repeated attacks by an irresponsible, bullying, cowardly, and intemperate father, and abandoned by respondents who placed him in a dangerous predicament and who knew or learned what was going on, and yet did essentially nothing except, as the Court revealingly observes, ante, at —, 103 L Ed 2d 257, "dutifully recorded these incidents in [their] files." It is a sad commentary upon American life, and constitutional principles—so full of late of patriotic fervor and proud proclamations about "liberty and justice for all," that this child, Joshua DeShaney, now is assigned to live out the remainder of his life profoundly retarded. Joshua and his mother, as petitioners here, deserve—but now are denied by this Court—the opportunity to have the facts of their case considered in the light of the constitutional protection that 42 USC § 1983 [42 USCS § 1983] is meant to provide.

Qualified Personal Liability in Tort of Government Officials

The tort law covered thus far has carved out areas of liability for the government itself. Damages awarded in such cases come from the public treasury, hence from public revenues. It is a given in the modern doctrine of most tort laws that the existence of potential liability if anything encourages citizens to use greater thoughtfulness and care in their daily actions, and no obvious reasons suggest the same dynamic should not affect public officials.

The law of individual liability has, like the law of governmental liability, moved, though in a halting and unfinished fashion, toward recognizing and honoring private tort claims. In *Barr v. Mateo*, 360 US 564 (1959), the Supreme Court articulated a blanket exemption for individual liability at common law. The case received considerable scholarly criticism at the time, and since then the Court has, without directly overruling *Barr*, moved in the opposite direction. The Court has relied on the distinction between violations of common law and violations of constitutional rights, a distinction reinforced by the classic principle of *Marbury v. Madison* and by a provision of the Civil Rights Act of 1871, 42 U.S. Code Section 1983, which permits actions against individual state officials. This provision states:

> Every person who, under color of any statute, ordinance, regulation, custom, usage, of any State or Territory, subjects, or causes to be subjected, any citizen of the United States or other person within the jurisdiction thereof to the deprivation of any rights, privileges, or immunities secured by the Constitution and laws, shall be liable to the party injured in an action at law, suit in equity, or other proper proceeding for redress.

The next case nicely summarizes the legal history preceding the finding of qualified personal liability under section 1983, but it is hardly the final word in this particularly unsettled branch of administrative law.

Butz v. Economou

438 U.S. 478 (1978) 5–4

+   Brennan, White, Marshall, Blackmun, Powell
+/–   Stewart, Burger, Renhquist, Stevens

[Economou controlled a commodity futures brokerage firm that had been the subject of a hearing before the Commodity Exchange Authority of the Department of Agriculture for its failure to maintain required records. The firm lodged a suit to enjoin the hearing but lost. As a result of the hearing, the firm's license to trade was revoked. Later, however, in response to a second complaint lodged by the firm, the Second Circuit ordered the license reinstated because the firm had not been adequately warned of its deficiency prior to the hearing. This third case was brought before the results of the hearing were finalized and named the secretary of agriculture and his subordinates who participated in the hearing and decisionmaking as defendants in a ten-point complaint charging a violation of constitutional rights. The district court dismissed the case citing the immunity of federal officials. The Second Circuit reversed holding that only a qualified immunity, similar to that granted state officials, was available.]

Justice White delivered the opinion of the Court.

. . . The single submission by the United States on behalf of petitioners is that all of the federal officials sued in this case are absolutely immune from any liability for damages even if in the course of enforcing the relevant statutes they infringed respondent's constitutional rights and even if the violation was knowing and deliberate. Although the position is earnestly and ably presented by the United States, we are quite sure that it is unsound and consequently reject it.

In *Bivens v. Six Unknown Fed. Narcotics Agents*, 403 U.S. 388 (1971), the victim of an arrest and search claimed to be violative of the Fourth Amendment brought suit for damages against the responsible federal agents. Repeating the declaration in *Marbury v. Madison*, 1 Cranch 137, 163 (1803), that " '[t]he very essence of civil liberty certainly consists in the right of every individual to claim the protection of the laws,' " 403 U.S., at 397, and stating that "[h]istorically, damages have been regarded as the ordinary remedy for an invasion of personal interests in liberty," *id.*, at 395, we rejected the claim that the plaintiff's remedy lay only in the state court under state law, with the Fourth Amendment operating merely to nullify a defense of federal authorization. We held that

a violation of the Fourth Amendment by federal agents gives rise to a cause of action for damages consequent upon the unconstitutional conduct. . . .

Bivens established that compensable injury to a constitutionally protected interest could be vindicated by a suit for damages invoking the general federal-question jurisdiction of the federal courts, but we reserved the question whether the agents involved were "immune from liability by virtue of their official position," and remanded the case for that determination. On remand, the Court of Appeals for the Second Circuit, as has every other Court of Appeals that has faced the question, held that the agents were not absolutely immune and that the public interest would be sufficiently protected by according the agents and their superiors a qualified immunity.

In our view, the Courts of Appeals have reached sound results. We cannot agree with the United States that our prior cases are to the contrary and support the rule it now urges us to embrace. Indeed, as we see it, the Government's submission is contrary to the course of decision in this Court from the very early days of the Republic.

The Government places principal reliance on *Barr v. Matteo*, 360 U.S. 564 (1959). In that case, the acting director of an agency had been sued for malicious defamation by two employees whose suspension for misconduct he had announced in a press release. The defendant claimed an absolute or qualified privilege, but the trial court rejected both and the jury returned a verdict for plaintiff.

In the 1958 Term, the Court granted certiorari in *Barr* "to determine whether in the circumstances of this case petitioner's claim of absolute privilege should have stood as a bar to maintenance of the suit despite the allegations of malice made in the complaint." . . . The Court was divided in reversing the judgment of the Court of Appeals, and there was no opinion for the Court. The plurality opinion inquired whether the conduct complained of was among those "matters committed by law to [the official's] control" and concluded, after an analysis of the specific circumstances, that the press release was within the "outer perimeter of [his] line of duty" and was "an appropriate exercise of the discretion which an officer of that rank must possess if the public service is to function effectively." . . . The plurality then held that under *Spalding v. Vilas*, 161 U.S. 483 (1896), the act was privileged and that the officer could not be held liable for the tort of defamation despite the allegations of malice. *Barr* clearly held that a false and damaging publication, the issuance of which was otherwise within the official's authority, was not itself actionable and would not become so by being issued maliciously. The Court did not choose to discuss whether the director's privilege would be defeated by showing that he was without reasonable grounds for believing his release was true or that he knew that it was false, although the issue was in the case as it came from the Court of Appeals.

Barr does not control this case. It did not address the liability of the acting director had his conduct not been within the outer limits of his duties, but from the care with which the Court inquired into the scope of his authority, it may be inferred that had the release been unauthorized, and surely if the issuance of press releases had been expressly forbidden by statute, the claim of absolute immunity would not have been upheld. The inference is supported by the fact that Mr. Justice Stewart, although agreeing with the principles announced by Mr. Justice Harlan, dissented and would have rejected the immunity claim because the press release, in his view, was not action in the line of duty. 360 U.S., at 592. It is apparent also that a quite different question would have been presented had the officer ignored an express statutory or constitutional limitation on his authority.

Barr did not, therefore, purport to depart from the general rule, which long prevailed, that a federal official may not with impunity ignore the limitations which the controlling law has placed on his powers. The immunity of federal executive officials began as a means of protecting them in the execution of their federal statutory duties from criminal or civil actions based on state law. See *Osborn v. Bank of the United States*, 9 Wheat. 738, 865–866 (1824).[*] A federal official who acted outside of his federal statutory authority would be held strictly liable for his trespassory acts. For example, *Little v. Barreme*, 2 Cranch 170 (1804), held the commander of an American warship liable in damages for the seizure of a Danish cargo ship on the high seas. Congress had directed the President to intercept any vessels reasonably suspected of being en route *to* a French port, but the President had authorized the seizure of suspected vessels whether going *to* or *from* French ports, and the Danish vessel seized was en route *from* a forbidden destination. The Court, speaking through Mr. Chief Justice Marshall, held that the President's instructions could not "change the nature of the transaction, or legalize an act which, without those instructions, would have been a plain trespass." . . . Although there was probable cause to believe that the ship was engaged in traffic with the French, the seizure at issue was not among that class of seizures that the Executive had been authorized

---

[*] Mr. Chief Justice Marshall explained: "An officer, for example, is ordered to arrest an individual. It is not necessary, nor is it usual, to say that he shall not be punished for obeying this order. His security is implied in the order itself. It is no unusual thing for an act of congress to imply, without expressing, this very exemption from State control. . . . The collectors of the revenue, the carriers of the mail, the mint establishment, and all those institutions which are public in their nature, are examples in point. It has never been doubted that all who are employed in them are protected while in the line of duty; and yet this protection is not expressed in any act of congress. It is incidental to, and is implied in, the several acts by which these institutions are created, and is secured to the individuals employed in them by the judicial power alone. . . . "

by statute to effect. See also *Wise v. Withers*, 3 Cranch 331 (1806).

Bates v. Clark, 95 U.S. 204 (1877), was a similar case. The relevant statute directed seizures of alcoholic beverages in Indian country, but the seizure at issue, which was made upon the orders of a superior, was not made in Indian country. The "objection fatal to this class of defenses is that in that locality [the seizing officers] were utterly without any authority in the premises" and hence were answerable in damages. . . .

In *Spalding v. Vilas*, 161 U.S. 483 (1896), on which the Government relies, the principal issue was whether the malicious motive of an officer would render him liable in damages for injury inflicted by his official act that otherwise was within the scope of his authority. The Postmaster General was sued for circulating among the postmasters a notice that assertedly injured the reputation of the plaintiff and interfered with his contractual relationships. The Court first inquired as to the Postmaster General's authority to issue the notice. In doing so, it "recognize[d] a distinction between action taken by the head of a department in reference to matters which are manifestly or palpably beyond his authority, and action having more or less connection with the general matters committed by law to his control or supervision." . . .

Concluding that the circular issued by the Postmaster General "was not unauthorized by law, nor beyond the scope of his official duties," the Court then addressed the major question in the case—whether the action could be "maintained because of the allegation that what the officer did was done maliciously?" . . . Its holding was that the head of a department could not be "held liable to a civil suit for damages on account of official communication made by him pursuant to an act of Congress, and in respect of matters within his authority," however improper his motives might have been. . . . Because the Postmaster General in issuing the circular in question "did not exceed his authority, nor pass the line of his duty," *id.*, at 499, it was irrelevant that he might have acted maliciously.

Spalding made clear that a malicious intent will not subject a public officer to liability for performing his authorized duties as to which he would otherwise not be subject to damages liability. But *Spalding* did not involve conduct manifestly or otherwise beyond the authority of the official, nor did it involve a mistake of either law or fact in construing or applying the statute.[*] It did not purport to immunize officials who ignore limitations on their authority imposed by law. . . .

Insofar as cases in this Court dealing with the immunity or privilege of federal officers are concerned, this is where the matter stood until *Barr v. Matteo*. There, as we have set out above, immunity was granted even though the publication contained a factual error, which was not the case in *Spalding*. The plurality opinion and judgment in *Barr* also appear—although without any discussion of the matter—to have extended absolute immunity to an officer who was authorized to issue press releases, who was assumed to know that the press release he issued was false and who therefore was deliberately misusing his authority. Accepting this extension of immunity with respect to state tort claims, however, we are confident that *Barr* did not purport to protect an official who has not only committed a wrong under local law, but also violated those fundamental principles of fairness embodied in the Constitution. Whatever level of protection from state interference is appropriate for federal officials executing their duties under federal law, it cannot be doubted that these officials, even when acting pursuant to congressional authorization, are subject to the restraints imposed by the Federal Constitution.

The liability of officials who have exceeded constitutional limits was not confronted in either *Barr*

---

[*]Mr. Justice Brennan, dissenting in *Barr v. Matteo*, 360 U.S., at 587 n. 3, emphasized this point: "The suit in *Spalding* seems to have been as much, if not more, a suit for malicious interference with advantageous relationships as a libel suit. The Court reviewed the facts and found no false statement. See 161 U.S., at 487–493. The case may stand for no more than the proposition that where a Cabinet officer publishes a statement, not factually inaccurate, relating to a matter within his Department's competence, he cannot be charged with improper motives in publication. The Court's opinion leaned heavily on the fact that the contents of the statement (which were not on their face defamatory) were quite accurate, in support of its conclusion that publishing the statement was within the officer's discretion, foreclosing inquiry into his motives. . . ."

or *Spalding.* Neither of those cases supports the Government's position. Beyond that, however, neither case purported to abolish the liability of federal officers for actions manifestly beyond their line of duty; and if they are accountable when they stray beyond the plain limits of their statutory authority, it would be incongruous to hold that they may nevertheless willfully or knowingly violate constitutional rights without fear of liability.

Although it is true that the Court has not dealt with this issue with respect to federal officers,* we have several times addressed the immunity of state officers when sued under 42 U.S.C. § 1983 for alleged violations of constitutional rights. These decisions are instructive for present purposes. . . .

Pierson v. Ray, 386 U.S. 547 (1967), decided that § 1983 was not intended to abrogate the immunity of state judges which existed under the common law and which the Court had held applicable to federal judges in *Bradley v. Fisher*, 13 Wall. 335 (1872). *Pierson* also presented the issue "whether immunity was available to that segment of the executive branch of a state government that is . . . most frequently exposed to situations which can give rise to claims under § 1983 — the local police officer." *Scheuer v. Rhodes*, 416 U.S., at 244–245. Relying on the common law, we held that police officers were entitled to a defense of "good faith and probable cause," even though an arrest might subsequently be proved to be unconstitutional. We observed, however, that "[t]he common law has never granted police officers an absolute and unqualified immunity, and the officers in this case do not claim that they are entitled to one." . . .

In *Scheuer v. Rhodes, supra,* the issue was whether "higher officers of the executive branch" of state governments were immune from liability under § 1983 for violations of constitutionally protected rights. . . . There, the Governor of a State, the senior and subordinate officers of the state National Guard, and

a state university president had been sued on the allegation that they had suppressed a civil disturbance in an unconstitutional manner. We explained that the doctrine of official immunity from § 1983 liability, although not constitutionally grounded and essentially a matter of statutory construction, was based on two mutually dependent rationales: "(1) the injustice, particularly in the absence of bad faith, of subjecting to liability an officer who is required, by the legal obligations of his position, to exercise discretion; (2) the danger that the threat of such liability would deter his willingness to execute his office with the decisiveness and judgment required by the public good." . . . The opinion also recognized that executive branch officers must often act swiftly and on the basis of factual information supplied by others, constraints which become even more acute in the "atmosphere of confusion, ambiguity, and swiftly moving events," created by a civil disturbance. . . .

Although quoting at length from *Barr v. Matteo*, we did not believe that there was a need for absolute immunity from § 1983 liability for these high-ranking state officials. Rather the considerations discussed above indicated:

> [I]n varying scope, a qualified immunity is available to officers of the executive branch of government, the variation being dependent upon the scope of discretion and responsibilities of the office and all the circumstances as they reasonably appeared at the time of the action on which liability is sought to be based. It is the existence of reasonable grounds for the belief formed at the time and in light of all the circumstances, coupled with good-faith belief, that affords a basis for qualified immunity of executive officers for acts performed in the course of official conduct. . . .

Subsequent decisions have applied the *Scheuer* standard in other contexts. In *Wood v. Strickland*, 420 U.S. 308 (1975), school administrators were held entitled to claim a similar qualified immunity. A school board member would lose his immunity from a § 1983 suit only if "he knew or reasonably should have known that the action he took within his sphere of official

---

Doe v. McMillan, 412 U.S. 306 (1973), did involve a constitutional claim for invasion of privacy — but in the special context of the Speech or Debate Clause. The Court held that the executive officials would be immune from suit only to the extent that the legislators at whose behest they printed and distributed the documents could claim the protection of the Speech or Debate Clause.

responsibility would violate the constitutional rights of the student affected, or if he took the action with the malicious intention to cause a deprivation of constitutional rights or other injury to the student." . . .

We agree with the perception . . . that, in the absence of congressional direction to the contrary, there is no basis for according to federal officials a higher degree of immunity from liability when sued for a constitutional infringement as authorized by *Bivens* than is accorded state officials when sued for the identical violation under § 1983. The constitutional injuries made actionable by § 1983 are of no greater magnitude than those for which federal officials may be responsible. The pressures and uncertainties facing decisionmakers in state government are little if at all different from those affecting federal officials. We see no sense in holding a state governor liable but immunizing the head of a federal department; in holding the administrator of a federal hospital immune where the superintendent of a state hospital would be liable; in protecting the warden of a federal prison where the warden of a state prison would be vulnerable; or in distinguishing between state and federal police participating in the same investigation. Surely, *federal* officials should enjoy no greater zone of protection when they violate *federal* constitutional rules than do *state* officers.

The Government argues that the cases involving state officials are distinguishable because they reflect the need to preserve the effectiveness of the right of action authorized by § 1983. But as we discuss more fully below, the cause of action recognized in *Bivens v. Six Unknown Fed. Narcotics Agents*, 403 U.S. 388 (1971), would similarly be "drained of meaning" if federal officials were entitled to absolute immunity for their constitutional transgressions. . . .

Moreover, the Government's analysis would place undue emphasis on the congressional origins of the cause of action in determining the level of immunity. It has been observed more than once that the law of privilege as a defense to damages actions against officers of Government has "in large part been of judicial making." . . .

The presence or absence of congressional authorization for suits against federal officials, is, of course, relevant to the question whether to infer a right of action for damages for a particular violation of the Constitution. In *Bivens*, the Court noted the "absence of affirmative action by Congress" and therefore looked for "special factors counseling hesitation." . . .

Absent congressional authorization, a court may also be impelled to think more carefully about whether the type of injury sustained by the plaintiff is normally compensable in damages . . . and whether the courts are qualified to handle the types of questions raised by the plaintiff's claim. . . .

But once this analysis is completed, there is no reason to return again to the absence of congressional authorization in resolving the question of immunity. Having determined that the plaintiff is entitled to a remedy in damages for a constitutional violation, the court then must address how best to reconcile the plaintiff's right to compensation with the need to protect the decisionmaking processes of an executive department. Since our decision in *Scheuer* was intended to guide the federal courts in resolving this tension in the myriad factual situations in which it might arise, we see no reason why it should not supply the governing principles for resolving this dilemma in the case of federal officials. The Court's opinion in *Scheuer* relied on precedents dealing with federal as well as state officials, analyzed the issue of executive immunity in terms of general policy considerations, and stated its conclusion, quoted *supra*, in the same universal terms. The analysis presented in that case cannot be limited to actions against state officials.

Accordingly, without congressional directions to the contrary, we deem it untenable to draw a distinction for purposes of immunity law between suits brought against state officials under § 1983 and suits brought directly under the Constitution against federal officials. The § 1983 action was provided to vindicate federal constitutional rights. That Congress decided, after the passage of the Fourteenth Amendment, to enact legislation specifically requiring state officials to respond in federal court for their failures to observe the constitutional limitations on their powers is hardly a reason for excusing their federal counterparts for the identical constitutional transgressions. To create a system in which the Bill of Rights monitors more closely the conduct of state officials than it does that of federal officials is to stand the constitutional design on its head. . . .

As we have said, the decision in *Bivens* established that a citizen suffering a compensable injury to a constitutionally protected interest could invoke the general federal-question jurisdiction of the district courts to obtain an award of monetary damages against the responsible federal official. As Mr. Justice Harlan, concurring in the judgment, pointed out, the action for damages recognized in *Bivens* could be a vital means of providing redress for persons whose constitutional rights have been violated. The barrier of sovereign immunity is frequently impenetrable. Injunctive or declaratory relief is useless to a person who has already been injured. "For people in Bivens' shoes, it is damages or nothing."

Our opinion in *Bivens* put aside the immunity question; but we could not have contemplated that immunity would be absolute. If, as the Government argues, all officials exercising discretion were exempt from personal liability, a suit under the Constitution could provide no redress to the injured citizen, nor would it in any degree deter federal officials from committing constitutional wrongs. Moreover, no compensation would be available from the Government, for the Tort Claims Act prohibits recovery for injuries stemming from discretionary acts, even when that discretion has been abused.

The extension of absolute immunity from damages liability to all federal executive officials would seriously erode the protection provided by basic constitutional guarantees. The broad authority possessed by these officials enables them to direct their subordinates to undertake a wide range of projects—including some which may infringe such important personal interests as liberty, property, and free speech. It makes little sense to hold that a Government agent is liable for warrantless and forcible entry into a citizen's house in pursuit of evidence, but that an official of higher rank who actually orders such a burglary is immune simply because of his greater authority. Indeed, the greater power of such officials affords a greater potential for a regime of lawless conduct. Extensive Government operations offer opportunities for unconsti-

tutional action on a massive scale. In situations of abuse, an action for damages against the responsible official can be an important means of vindicating constitutional guarantees. . . .

There remains the task of applying the foregoing principles to the claims against the particular petitioner-defendants involved in this case. Rather than attempt this here in the first instance, we vacate the judgment of the Court of Appeals and remand the case to that court with instructions to remand the case to the District Court for further proceedings consistent with this opinion.

So ordered.

Justice Rehnquist, with whom The Chief Justice, Justice Stewart, and Justice Stevens join, concurring in part and dissenting in part.

I concur in that part of the Court's judgment which affords absolute immunity to those persons performing adjudicatory functions within a federal agency . . . those who are responsible for the decision to initiate or continue a proceeding subject to agency adjudication . . . and those agency personnel who present evidence on the record in the course of an adjudication. . . . I cannot agree, however, with the Court's conclusion that in a suit for damages arising from allegedly unconstitutional action federal executive officials, regardless of their rank or the scope of their responsibilities, are entitled to only qualified immunity even when acting within the outer limits of their authority. The Court's protestations to the contrary notwithstanding, this decision seriously misconstrues our prior decisions, finds little support as a matter of logic or precedent, and perhaps most importantly, will, I fear, seriously "dampen the ardor of all but the most resolute, or the most irresponsible, in the unflinching discharge of their duties," *Gregoire v. Biddle*, 177 F. 2d 579, 581 (CA2 1949) (Learned Hand, J.).

Most noticeable is the Court's unnaturally constrained reading of the landmark case of *Spalding v. Vilas*, 161 U.S. 483 (1896). The Court in that case did indeed hold that the actions taken by the Postmaster General were within the authority conferred upon him by Congress, and went on to hold that even though he had acted maliciously in carrying out the duties conferred upon him by Congress he was protected by official immunity. But the Court left no doubt that it would have reached the same result had it been alleged that official acts were unconstitutional. . . . The court today attempts to explain away that language by observing that *Spalding* indicated no intention to overrule *Kendall v. Stokes*, 3 How. 87 (1845), or *Wilkes v. Dinsman*, 7 How. 89 (1849).-

. . . In short, *Spalding* clearly and inescapably stands for the proposition that high-ranking executive officials acting within the outer limits of their authority are absolutely immune from suit.

. . . No one seriously contends [in this case] that the Secretary of Agriculture or the Assistant Secretary, who are being sued for $32 million in damages, had wandered completely off the official reservation in authorizing prosecution of respondent for violation of regulations promulgated by the Secretary for the regulation of "futures commission merchants," 7 U.S.C. § 6 (1976 ed.). This is precisely what the Secretary and his assistants were empowered and required to do. That they would on occasion be mistaken in their judgment that a particular merchant had in fact violated the regulations is a necessary concomitant of any known system of administrative adjudication; that they acted "maliciously" gives no support to respondent's claim against them unless we are to overrule *Spalding*.

The Court's attempt to distinguish *Spalding* may be predicated on a simpler but equally erroneous concept of immunity. . . .

Putting to one side the illogic and impracticability of distinguishing between constitutional and common-law claims for purposes of immunity, which will be discussed shortly, this sort of immunity analysis badly misses the mark. It amounts to saying that an official has immunity until someone alleges he has acted unconstitutionally. But that is no immunity at all: The "immunity" disappears at the very moment when it is needed. The critical injury in determining whether an official is entitled to claim immunity is not whether someone has in fact been injured by his action; that is part of the plaintiff's case in chief. The immunity defense turns on whether the action was

one taken "when engaged in the discharge of duties imposed upon [the official] by law," *Spalding*, 161 U.S., at 498, or in other words, whether the official was acting within the outer bounds of his authority. Only if the immunity inquiry is approached in this manner does it have any meaning. That such a rule may occasionally result in individual injustices has never been doubted, but at least until today, immunity has been accorded nevertheless. . . .

The Court also suggests in sweeping terms that the cause of action recognized in *Bivens* would be " 'drained of meaning' if federal officials were entitled to absolute immunity for their constitutional transgressions." *Ante*, at 501. But *Bivens* is a slender reed on which to rely when abrogating official immunity for Cabinet-level officials. In the first place, those officials most susceptible to claims under *Bivens* have historically been given only a qualified immunity. . . .

My biggest concern, however, is not with the illogic or impracticality of today's decision, but rather with the potential for disruption of Government that it invites. The steady increase in litigation, much of it directed against governmental officials and virtually all of which could be framed in constitutional terms, cannot escape the notice of even the most casual observer. From 1961 to 1977, the number of cases brought in the federal courts under civil rights statutes increased from 296 to 13,113. See Director of the Administrative Office of the United States Courts Ann. Rep. 189, Table 11 (1977); Ann. Rep. 173, Table 17 (1976). It simply defies logic and common experience to suggest that officials will not have this in the back of their minds when considering what official course to pursue. It likewise strains credulity to suggest that this threat will only inhibit officials from taking action which they should not take in any event. It is the cases in which the grounds for action are doubtful, or in which the actor is timid, which will be affected by today's decision.

The Court, of course, recognizes this problem and suggests two solutions. First, judges, ever alert to the artful pleader, supposedly will weed out insubstantial claims. *Ante*, at 507. That, I fear, shows more optimism than prescience. Indeed, this very case, unquestionably frivolous in the extreme, belies any hope in that direction. And summary judgment of affidavits and the like is even more inappropriate when the central, and perhaps only, inquiry is the official's state of mind. See C. Wright, Law of Federal Courts 493 (3d ed. 1976) (It "is not feasible to resolve on motion for summary judgment cases involving state of mind"); *Subin v. Goldsmith*, 224 F 2d 753 (CA2 1955).

The second solution offered by the Court is even less satisfactory. The Court holds that in those special circumstances "where it is demonstrated that absolute immunity is essential for the conduct of the public business," absolute immunity will be extended. *Ante*, at 507. But this is a form of "absolute immunity" which in truth exists in name only. If, for example, the Secretary of Agriculture may never know until inquiry by a trial court whether there is a possibility that vexatious constitutional litigation will interfere with his decisionmaking process, the Secretary will obviously think not only twice but thrice about whether to prosecute a litigious commodities merchant who has played fast and loose with the regulations for his own profit. Careful consideration of the rights of every individual subject to his jurisdiction is one thing; a timorous reluctance to prosecute any of such individuals who have a reputation for using litigation as a defense weapon is quite another. Since Cabinet officials are mortal, it is not likely that we shall get the precise judgmental balance desired in each of them, and it is because of these very human failings that the principles of *Spalding*, 161 U.S., at 498, dictate that absolute immunity be accorded once it be concluded by a court that a high-level executive official was "engaged in the discharge of duties imposed upon [him] by law." . . .

History will surely not condemn the Court for its effort to achieve a more finely ground product from the judicial mill, a product which would both retain the necessary ability of public officials to govern and yet assure redress to those who are the victims of official wrongs. But if is such a system of redress for official wrongs was indeed capable of being achieved in practice, it surely would not have been rejected by this Court speaking through the first Mr. Justice Harlan in 1896, by this Court speaking through the second Mr. Justice Harlan in 1959, and by Judge Learned Hand speaking for the Court of Appeals for the Second Circuit in 1948. These judges were not inexperienced neophytes who lacked the vision or the ability to define immunity doctrine to accomplish that result had they thought it possible. Nor were they obsequious toadies in their attitude toward high-ranking officials of coordinate branches of the Federal Government. But they did see with more prescience than the Court does today, that there are inevitable trade-offs in connection with any doctrine of official liability and immunity. They forthrightly accepted the possibility that an occasional failure to redress a claim of official wrongdoing would result from the doctrine of absolute immunity which they espoused, viewing it as a lesser evil than the impairment of the ability of responsible public officials to govern.

But while I believe that history will look approvingly on the motives of the Court in reaching the result it does today, I do not believe that history will be charitable in its judgment of the all but inevitable result of the doctrine espoused by the Court in this case. That doctrine seeks to gain and hold a middle ground which, with all deference, I believe the teachings of those who were at least our equals suggest cannot long be held. That part of the Court's present opinion from which I dissent will, I fear, result in one of two evils, either one of which is markedly worse than the effect of according absolute immunity to the Secretary and the Assistant Secretary in this case. The first of these evils would be a significant impairment of the ability of responsible public officials to carry out the duties imposed upon them by law. If that evil is to be avoided after today, it can be avoided only by a necessarily unprincipled and erratic judicial "screening" of claims such as those made in this case, an adherence to the form of the law while departing from its substance. Either one of these evils is far worse than the occasional failure to award damages caused by official wrongdoing, frankly and openly justified by the rule of *Spalding v. Vilas, Barr v. Matteo*, and *Gregoire v. Biddle*.

It is futile to summarize the law of official liability and immunity at this stage in its development. Nevertheless, students who hold or contemplate holding public positions, or students of politics and American government who are interested in the nature of state power, should pay particular attention to the standard of reasonableness articulated in the *Wood* case and cited approvingly in *Butz*. The test, whether an administrator reasonably should have known that his act or decision would violate a constitutional right, is very similar to common law tests employed for many years in conventional tort law. It gives officials a personal incentive to care about constitutional principles but does not demand the impossible of them. Whether the Court will eventually overrule *Barr* and extend the test to nonconstitutional violations remains an open possibility.

Exercises and Questions for Further Thought

1. What if a judge, federal or state, misapplies or ignores a valid constitutional claim of a party in litigation? Should that judge be held individually liable under the theory of *Butz*? Should the standard applied to judges in the regular judicial system also apply to administrative law judges? How do you think the current Chief Justice Rehnquist would answer this question given his dissenting opinion in *Butz*?

2. In *United States v. Union Trust Co.*, 221 F.2d 62 (1954), plaintiffs sought to recover damages suffered when two small aircraft collided while approaching a runway. The air traffic controller, a government employee, had given each pilot permission to land on the same runway at the same time. Under the law of *Feres*, what decision would the court reach? Under *Dalehite*? Under more recent decisions? Is it appropriate to describe air traffic controllers' decisions as "discretionary"? Why or why not?

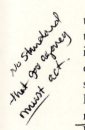

3. Not only do the recent government tort liability cases signal a movement back to the narrow view of governmental liability under the FTCA (as stated in *Dalehite*), the Supreme Court's refusal to hold officials liable for *inaction* also leads to a narrow interpretation of state power. How accurate do you find Chief Justice Rehnquist's view of state power in the *DeShaney* case? Compare his perspective on the state's obligation, subsequent to the provision of services, with Justice Brennan's dissent in that case. In what sense is the majority opinion in the *DeShaney* case similar to the Court's unanimous opinion in *Heckler v. Chaney*, 1985 (*supra*, p. 366)? Why do you think Justices Brennan, Marshall, and Blackmun concurred with the majority in *Heckler*, but dissented in *DeShaney*?

4. Recent regulatory reforms, such as regulatory negotiation (chapter 7), echo Justice Rehnquist's sentiments in his *Butz* dissent—the potential disruption of government caused by litigation against it is reason to limit government tort liability. What are the advantages of making litigation *more* accessible to the public, as opposed to less, in the area of tort liability? In a democracy, does litigation function as one way for citizens to hold public officials accountable? How accountable should public officials be in a democratic state? Consider the relationship between liability principles and due process values discussed in previous chapters.

5. For further discussion of the issues raised in this chapter, see the collection of excellent essays in *Law and Contemporary Problems*, Vol. 42, No. 1, 1978. See particularly the comments of Professor Jerry Mashaw, beginning at page 8, and of Professor Mancur Olson, beginning at page 67, for differing criticisms of absolute common law official immunity. Note Olson's point that the rule in *Barr* may be necessary to avoid an unmanageable overload of cases in our already overloaded court system. For a comparative government treatment of the subject, see Leon Hurwitz, *The State as Defendant* (Westport, Conn: Greenwood Press, 1981).

Mashaw - gov will protect its own unless liability rules are clear.

CHAPTER 11

Licensing

The next two chapters allow readers to see how administrative law principles are developed in familiar settings. Of all the governmental activities covered by administrative law, readers have most likely experienced the licensing process. We refer to the familiar and often nerve-wracking process nearly all teenagers experience—getting a driver's license. And adults live in varying degrees of awareness that they could lose their drivers' licenses in certain circumstances.

Licenses for drivers are the most common kind of license, and we shall see that the circumstances in which licenses may be revoked have yielded some of the most stimulating materials in due process adjudication. Readers may be misled, however, if they take the driver's license as a model of all licensing problems. One of the interesting facets of governmental licensing is that it covers an astonishing range of issues and serves several quite different purposes. Many illustrations have already appeared in this book. *Vermont Yankee* dealt with a problem of safety in nuclear generated power that environmental groups felt should have been resolved prior to granting operating licenses. The Federal Communication Commission holds the keys to nearly guaranteed profits for those who receive the limited and prized licenses to operate television stations in metropolitan areas.

The Varieties of Licensing Programs

A license is a grant of governmental permission to do something. In most cases operating without permission leads directly to criminal prosecution. Obviously the law governing the grant of permission to operate a citizen's band radio in one's car addresses a different breed of problem than those raised in the assessment of whether a nuclear plant is designed and constructed to operate within acceptable safety margins. To help conceptualize the different species of licensing programs, consider the following four licensing categories.

1. Control of Public Resources

To operate a concession stand in a public park the concessionaire must get a license. To cut timber legally from a national forest, lumbermen must get permission from the United States Forest Service. Licensing in these instances seeks primarily to exert extra leverage to induce private interests to operate in ways consistent with the public agency's plans and policies. In varying degrees all licenses in all circumstances serve as a sanction to insure compliance according to the model developed in chapter 8, but in this category regulating public resources is usually the primary goal. This task concerns the allocation of public resources and sets limits for aesthetics, safety, and other reasons. For years businessmen and politicians, even some economists, believed that the market would not sustain safe and healthy use of the public airways by commercial airlines. Hence the Civil Aeronautics Board issued two kinds of licenses: licenses to operate at all and licenses to operate on specific routes. That process has ended. The CAB officially expired in 1985. Whether or not market forces have been better able to run the commercial air industry is highly questionable today.

2. Fair Allocation of Limited Resources

Licensing policy must cope with the interaction between technology and natural resources. In chapter 5 Paul Verkuil mentioned in passing the government program for licensing coastal shrimp fishermen. The theory here is familiar to commercial and recreational fishermen and hunters. The number of people who use our natural resources, if not limited, sooner or later would exhaust or destroy our natural resources. The number of radio airways for which it is economical to design and sell receivers has also been deemed a limited resource, hence the work of the FCC. Note here the need for fair procedure does matter. If Smith wins permission to gain from nature while Jones loses, the process of deciding must make a plausible claim of fairness. Often simple principles, such as *first come, first served*, suffice to achieve acceptable fairness, but this of course depends on the subject matter. (The FCC considered and rejected a program of awarding licenses by lottery.)[1]

3. Assurance of Competence in Complex and Dangerous Occupations

As in the first category, this type of licensing program seeks by law to limit the number of people in a market, but the objective is not to limit or control them per se; it is, as in the case of doctors, lawyers, pharmacists, and the like, to regulate their competence. The need arises both because incompetence in such fields can cause great harm and because consumers lack the training necessary to judge competence themselves.[2]

4. Maintenance of Public Order

The differences between the third and fourth categories is one primarily of degree. Poor automobile driving can cause as much harm as medical malpractice. So can an overabundance of alcoholic beverages, which gave rise to the law limiting the number of suppliers. The license requirement for drivers and liquor sellers, however, does not carry with it the same detailed tests and standards of performance presumed to increase the competence of the professions. The tests and requirements are relatively

[1] In 1982, Congress passed legislation (HR 3239-PL 97-259) authorizing the FCC to establish licensing lottery rules. The FCC declared this process "unworkable." See *Congressional Quarterly Almanac* 38 (1982): 338.

[2] See Kenneth M. Meier, *Regulation: Politics, Bureaucracy, and Economics* (New York: St. Martin's Press, 1985), in particular chapter 7.

straightforward. In the case of professional licensing the candidate must show mastery of large quantities of complex material. The qualifying process plays a large part in achieving the goals. Where the license seeks to maintain public order, it is the threat of losing the license that produces the greater sanctioning effect. Liquor stores refuse to sell to minors not because of professional training in a "liquor school" but because of the threat of detection and loss of license.

Licensing as Adjudication

Granting, denying, or revoking licenses obviously depends on specific facts about specific parties. Licensing clearly qualifies as adjudication and therefore requires due process protections, regardless of what administrative procedure statutes or authorizing statutes may require. But here two problems arise. First, licensing programs serve different goals and range in complexity from nuclear energy to citizen's band radios. The same procedures are hardly necessary for all types of licenses. Second, there may in some cases be a very substantial difference in the hardship imposed by denying an application for a license and revoking one previously granted and used in business. If a businessperson invests in the liquor business, if a restaurant is capitalized based on projected receipts from alcohol as well as food, the revocation of the license may put the person out of business altogether. But if the Nuclear Regulatory Commission does not establish a licensing procedure for the proposed national high-level radioactive waste dump in Yucca Mountain, Nevada, the U.S. Department of Energy will not then build a repository for the existing waste generated by private nuclear power and government nuclear weapons facilities, let alone future waste. Should the due process protection for revocation be greater than the protections in initial license decisions, at least where the initial decisions are not "life or death" business matters?

The Administrative Procedure Act (APA), Section 558, requires formal adjudication for denial, termination, or revocation of licenses, but in 554(d)(A) exempts initial applications for licenses from 558's hearing procedures. When a nuclear power company seeks an operating license or a broadcaster seeks a television station license, millions, perhaps billions, of dollars are at stake. Authorizing statutes and due process requirements generally provide full-hearing protections in such cases. The interesting administrative law questions in licensing arise at the more mundane levels of auto licensing, occupational licensing, and the like. Because the majority of readers will more often deal with state and local licensing activities, the cases and discussion in this chapter focus exclusively on state licensing programs.

Hornsby v. Allen

326 F.2d 605, U.S.C.A., 5th Cir. (1964) 2–1

[Mrs. Hornsby applied for a license to operate a retail liquor store in Atlanta. Even though her character and the store's proposed location met the stated requirements for the granting of a license, her application was denied by the city council. No reasons were given for the denial. Mrs. Hornsby brought suit claiming that such a denial without stated reasons constituted a violation of due process. Additionally, she charged that the Fourteenth Amendment was also violated, since either one of the two aldermen in the ward where the store was to be located could veto the application whatever its merits. The district court dismissed the case as not falling under the Fourteenth Amendment because it centered on a so-called political question concerning the motives of a legislative body, and because no charge of discrimination was made. Mrs. Hornsby appealed.]

Tuttle, Chief Judge.

At the outset, we note our disagreement with the district court's classification of the challenged actions as purely those of a legislative body; we do not conceive the denial of an application for a license to be an act of legislation. Although there is disagreement on the matter, we prefer the view that licensing proper is an adjudicative process. Thus when a municipal or other governmental body grants a license it is an adjudication that the applicant has satisfactorily complied with the prescribed standards for the award of that license. Similarly the denial of a license is based on an adjudication that the applicant has not satisfied those qualifications and requirements. On the other hand, the prescription of standards which must be met to obtain a license is legislation, since these standards are authoritative guides for future conduct derived from an assessment of the needs of the community. A government agency entrusted with the licensing power therefore functions as a legislature when it prescribes these standards, but the same agency acts as a judicial body when it makes a determination that a specific applicant has or has not satisfied them.

Since licensing consists in the determination of factual issues and the application of legal criteria to them — a judicial act — the fundamental requirements of due process are applicable to it. Due process in administrative proceedings of a judicial nature has been said generally to be conformity to fair practices of Anglo-Saxon jurisprudence, which is usually equated with adequate notice and a fair hearing. Although strict adherence to the common-law rules of evidence at the hearing is not required the parties must generally be allowed an opportunity to know the claims of the opposing party, to present evidence to support

their contentions, and to cross-examine witnesses for the other side. Thus it is not proper to admit *ex parte* evidence, given by witnesses not under oath and not subject to cross-examination by the opposing party. *A fortiori*, the deciding authority may not base its decision on evidence which has not been specifically brought before it; the findings must conform to the evidence adduced at the hearing. Furthermore, the Supreme Court has said that an administrative order "cannot be upheld merely because findings might have been made and considerations disclosed which would justify its order. . . . There must be such a responsible finding." . . .

Also, the Supreme Court has held that the arbitrary refusal to grant a license or permit to one group when other groups have obtained permits under similar circumstances constitutes a denial of equal protection of the law. . . .

Neither is the assertion that liquor may be a menace to public health and welfare a sufficient answer to Mrs. Hornsby's allegations. The potential social undesirability of the product may warrant absolutely prohibiting it, or as the Aldermanic Board has done to some extent here, imposing restrictions to protect the community from its harmful influences. But the dangers do not justify depriving those who deal in liquor, or seek to deal in it, of the customary constitutional safeguards. Indeed, the great social interest in the liquor industry makes an exceptionally strong case for adherence to proper procedures and access to judicial review in licensing the retail sale of liquor . . . judications on the basis of merit. The first step toward insuring that these expectations are realized is to require adherence to the standards of due process; absolute and uncontrolled discretion invites abuse. . . .

It follows that the trial court must entertain the suit and determine the truth of the allegations. If it develops that no ascertainable standards have been established by the Board of Aldermen by which an applicant can intelligently seek to qualify for a license, then the court must enjoin the denial of licenses under the prevailing system and until a legal standard is established and procedural due process provided in the liquor store licensing field.

The judgment is reversed.

Impartial Decisionmakers in Licensing

Recall from chapter 6 that impartiality has two components. Decisionmakers must neither prejudge the issue before them before considering the facts on the record, nor decide cases in which they stand to benefit personally more from one outcome than the other. It was for the latter reason that the Supreme Court struck down the method of licensing optometrists in Alabama in *Gibson v. Berryhill*. The next case addresses both components of impartiality. Notice particularly that the same people who investigate also make an important decision about the termination of a license. This phenomenon is called *combination of functions*.

Withrow et al. v. Larkin

421 U.S. 35(1975) 9–0

+ Burger, Douglas, Brennan, Stewart, White, Marshall, Blackmun, Powell, Rehnquist

[The state of Wisconsin enacted statues specifying offenses for which a physician may have his license to practice suspended by an examining board. Larkin, a physician in Milwaukee, was charged by the board with fee-splitting, practicing under an alias, and allowing an unlicensed physician to practice at his Milwaukee clinic. The board, supported by the district court, held an investigatory hearing. This hearing allowed appellee to introduce evidence but not to cross-examine witnesses. Larkin's attorney, but not Larkin himself, was present. As a result of that hearing, the board notified appellee that it had the facts and would hold a contested hearing to determine if Larkin should have his license suspended. Larkin sought and obtained an order from the district court restraining the board from holding the hearing. Based on the Due Process Clause of the Fourteenth Amendment, however, the board, with district court support, held another investigatory hearing in which it found probable cause to start the revocation of license process and to initiate criminal charges. A three-judge district court noted a serious federal question and enjoined enforcement of the licensing statutes against Larkin. The board appealed.]

Justice White delivered the opinion of the Court.

The District Court framed the constitutional issue, which it addressed as being whether "for the board temporarily to suspend Dr. Larkin's license at its own contested hearing on charges evolving from its own investigation would constitute a denial to him of his rights to procedural due process." . . . The question was initially answered affirmatively, and in its amended judgment the court asserted that there was a high probability that appellee would prevail on the question. Its opinion stated that the "state medical examining board [did] not qualify as [an independent] decisionmaker [and could not] properly rule with regard to the merits of the same charges it investigated and, as in this case, presented to the district attorney." . . . We disagree. On the present record, it is quite unlikely that appellee would ultimately prevail on the merits of the due process issue presented to the District Court, and it was an abuse of discretion to issue the preliminary injunction.

Concededly, a "fair trial in a fair tribunal is a basic requirement of due process." *In re Murchison*, 349 U.S. 133, 136 (1955). This applies to administrative agencies which adjudicate as well as to courts. *Gibson v. Berryhill*, 411 U.S. 564, 579 (1973). Not only is a biased decisionmaker constitutionally unacceptable but "our system of law has always endeavored to prevent even the probability of unfairness." . . . In pursuit of this end, various situations have been identified in which experience teaches that the probability of actual bias on the part of the judge or decisionmaker is too high to be constitutionally tolerable. Among these cases are those in which the adjudicator has a pecuniary interest in the outcome and in which he has been the target of personal abuse or criticism from the party before him.

The contention that the combination of investigative and adjudicative functions necessarily creates an unconstitutional risk of bias in administrative adjudication has a much more difficult burden of persuasion to carry. It must overcome a presumption of honesty and integrity in those serving as adjudicators; and it must convince that, under a realistic appraisal of psychological tendencies and human weakness, conferring investigative and adjudicative powers on the same individuals poses such a risk of actual bias or prejudgment that the practice must be forbidden if the guarantee of due process is to be adequately implemented.

Very similar claims have been squarely rejected in prior decisions of this Court. . . .

This Court has also ruled that a hearing examiner who has recommended findings of fact after rejecting certain evidence as not being probative was not disqualified to preside at further hearings that were required when reviewing courts held that the evidence had been erroneously excluded. . . . The Court of Appeals had decided that the examiner should not again sit because it would be unfair to require the parties to try "issues of fact to those who may have prejudged them . . . ." But this Court unanimously reversed, saying: "Certainly it is not the rule of judicial administration that, statutory requirements apart, . . . a judge is disqualified from sitting in a retrial because he was reversed on earlier rulings. We find no warrant for imposing upon administrative agencies a stiffer rule, whereby examiners would be disentitled to sit because they ruled strongly against a party in the first hearing." . . .

More recently we have sustained against due process objection a system in which a Social Security examiner has responsibility for developing the facts and making a decision as to disability claims, and observed that the challenge to this combination of functions "assumes too much and would bring down too many procedures designed, and working well, for a governmental structure of great and growing complexity." . . .

That is not to say that there is nothing to the argument that those who have investigated should not then adjudicate. The issue is substantial, it is not new, and legislators and others concerned with the operations of administrative agencies have given much attention to whether and to what extent distinctive administrative functions should be performed by the same persons. No single answer has been reached. Indeed, the growth, variety, and complexity of the administrative processes have made any one solution highly unlikely. Within the Federal Government itself, Congress has addressed the issue in several different ways, providing for varying degrees of separation from complete separation of functions to virtually none at all. For the generality of agencies, Congress has been content with § 5 of the Administrative Procedure Act, 5 U.S.C. § 554(d), which provides that no employee engaged in investigating or prosecuting may also participate or advise in the adjudicating function, but which also expressly exempts from this prohibition "the agency or a member or members of the body comprising the agency."

It is not surprising, therefore, to find that "[t]he case law, both federal and state, generally rejects the idea that the combination [of] judges [and] investigating functions is a denial of due process . . . ." 2 K. Davis, Administrative Law Treatise § 13.02, p. 175 (1958). Similarly, our cases, although they reflect the substance of the problem, offer no support for the bald proposition applied in this case by the District Court that agency members who participate in an investigation are disqualified from adjudicating. The incredible variety of administrative mechanisms in this country will not yield to any single organizing principle . . . When the Board instituted its investigative procedures, it stated only that it would investigate whether proscribed conduct had occurred. Later in noticing the adversary hearing, it asserted only that it would determine if violations had been committed which would warrant suspension of appellee's license. Without doubt, the Board then anticipated that the proceeding would eventuate in an adjudication of the issue; but there was no more evidence of bias or the risk of bias or prejudgment than inhered in the very fact that the Board had investigated and would now adjudicate. Of course, we should be alert to the possibilities of bias that may lurk in the way particular procedures actually work in practice. The processes utilized by the Board, however, do not in themselves contain an unacceptable risk of bias. The investigative proceeding had been closed to the public, but appellee and his counsel were permitted to be present throughout; counsel actually attended the hearings and knew the facts presented to the Board. No specific foundation has been presented for suspecting that the Board had been prejudiced by its investigation or would be disabled from hearing and deciding on the basis of the evidence to be presented at the contested hearing. The mere exposure to evidence presented in nonadversary investigative procedures is insufficient in itself to impugn the fairness of the Board members at a later adversary hearing. Without a showing to the contrary, state administrators "are assumed to be men of conscience and intellectual discipline, capable of judging a particular controversy fairly on the basis of its own circumstances." *United States v. Morgan*, 313 U.S. 409, 421 (1941).

We are of the view, therefore, that the District Court was in error when it entered the restraining order against the Board's contested hearing and when it granted the preliminary injunction based on the untenable view that it would be unconstitutional for the Board to suspend appellee's license "at its own contested hearing on charges evolving from its own investigation . . . ." The contested hearing should have been permitted to proceed. . . .

The judgment of the District Court is reversed and the case is remanded to that court for further proceedings consistent with this opinion. . . .

In assessing *Withrow* you should consider two ways in which the situation differs from that in *Cinderella* and *Gibson*. Both these cases set aside *final* decisions in which bias may have entered. The *Withrow* decision affects matters at a more preliminary stage. Second, as Justice White points out, no *specific* evidence of bias was introduced. In reasoning similar to the later *Horowitz* case, the Court presumes that "professional" decisions are impartial and valid in the absence of specific evidence.

Professional Standards in Licensing

How much weight should the presumption that professionals are wise and impartial because they are professionals carry? In the post-Watergate era there can be no serious dispute that professionals do not always think and act virtuously. The danger of course is that a strong presumption of professional virtue will screen judgments by professionals on nonprofessional grounds from view. The next two cases show that the Supreme Court does not blindly approve all "professional" judgments.

Schware v. Board of Bar Examiners

353 U.S. 232 (1957) 8–0
+   Warren, Black, Frankfurter, Douglas, Burton, Clark, Harlan, Brennan
NP Whittaker

[Schware, aspiring to be an attorney, applied in 1953 to take the Bar Examination in New Mexico. His application was denied. At a subsequent formal hearing before the examining board, he was informed that his application was denied because of his use of aliases, his arrest record, and his membership in a subversive organization. These events occurred in the 1930s. Since then Schware had kept a clean record, and had served honorably in World War II. He also received support at the hearing from a rabbi, a member of the bar, and his law school while the board neither called witnesses nor introduced evidence. Schware appealed the board's continued denial as a violation of the Due Process Clause of the Fourteenth Amendment, but the New Mexico Supreme Court upheld the board's decision.]

Justice Black delivered the opinion of the Court.

The question presented is whether petitioner, Rudolph Schware, has been denied a license to practice law in New Mexico in violation of the Due Process Clause of the Fourteenth Amendment to the United States Constitution.

A State cannot exclude a person from the practice of law or from any other occupation in a manner or for reasons that contravene the Due Process or Equal Protection Clause of the Fourteenth Amendment . . . A State can require high standards of qualification, such as good moral character or proficiency in its law, before it admits an applicant to the bar, but any qualification must have a rational connection with the applicant's fitness or capacity to practice law. . . . Obviously an applicant could not be excluded merely because he was a Republican or a Negro or a member of a particular church. Even in applying permissible standards, officers of a State cannot exclude an applicant when there is no basis for their finding that he fails to meet these standards, or when their action is invidiously discriminatory . . .

Here the State concedes that Schware is fully qualified to take the examination in all respects other than good moral character. Therefore the question is whether the Supreme Court of New Mexico on the record before us could reasonably find that he had not shown good moral character.

There is nothing in the record which suggests that Schware has engaged in any conduct during the past 15 years which reflects adversely on his character. The New Mexico Supreme Court recognizes that he "presently enjoys good repute among this teachers, his fellow students and associates and in his synagogue." . . . The undisputed evidence in the record shows Schware to be a man of high ideals with a deep sense of social justice. Not a single witness testified that he was not a man of good character. . . .

The State contends that even though the use of aliases, the arrests, and the membership in the Communist Party would not justify exclusion of petitioner from the New Mexico bar if each stood alone, when all three are combined his exclusion was not unwarranted. We cannot accept this contention. In the light of petitioner's forceful showing of good moral character, the evidence upon which the State relies—the arrests for offenses for which petitioner was neither tried nor convicted, the use of an assumed name many years ago, and membership in the Communist Party during the 1930s—cannot be said to raise substantial doubts about his present good moral character. There is no evidence in the record which rationally justifies a finding that Schware was morally unfit to practice law. . . .

Reversed.

Cord v. Gibb

Supreme Court of Virginia
254 S.E.2d 71 (1979) 7–0

[The background of the case is succinctly explained in this short opinion.]

Per Curiam.

This is an appeal by Bonnie C. Cord . . . from an order denying her the certificate of honest demeanor or good moral character required by Code § 54–60 as a prerequisite to her right to take the bar examination conducted by the Virginia Board of Bar Examiners . . .

Cord, a 1975 law school graduate, was admitted by examination to practice law in the District of Columbia that same year. After engaging in private practice for a period of 13 months, Cord accepted a position as an Attorney-Advisor with an agency of the federal government. She was still employed in that capacity on the date she petitioned for the required certificate. At that time Cord was a member, in good standing, of The District of Columbia Bar, The Bar Association of the District of Columbia, and the American Bar Association.

The court below, as required by the second paragraph of Code § 54–60, appointed three practicing attorneys to make an investigation of the moral character and fitness of Cord and to report their findings to the court.

In their written report, the attorneys disclosed that they had completed their investigation, which included a personal interview with Cord and contacts with her former employers. The reports also related that petitioner, in her interview, stated that she had jointly purchased a home in a rural area of Warren County with Jeffrey Blue, and that she and Blue jointly resided there. Two of the investigating attorneys reported that they were of the opinion that from the standpoint of "moral character and fitness," Cord was qualified to take the bar examination. One of the investigating attorneys, believing that Cord's living arrangement affected her character and fitness, recommended that the required certificate not be issued.

After reviewing this report, the trial court convened [a] . . . hearing to allow Cord to present further evidence in support of her petition. At this hearing four of Cord's neighbors, all of whom were aware of her living arrangement, vouched for her good moral character, integrity and acceptance in the community. All these witnesses testified that Cord's living arrangement, while generally known in the community, was not a "matter of discussion within the community" and that her admission to practice law would not reflect adversely on the organized bar.

In addition to this testimony, the court received and considered a letter written by Cord's nearest neighbor attesting to her "high character" and acceptance in the community. The court also received and considered letters from three practicing attorneys in the District of Columbia with whom Cord had been associated while in private law practice. Each of these letters vouched for Cord's professional competence, integrity and good moral character in such terms as "she is of the highest moral character both professionally and personally" and "Bonnie, during the thirteen months that she was associated with this firm, always demonstrated the highest possible morals, both professionally and personally."

In its order the trial court, while finding that Cord met the statutory requirements for taking the bar examination in all other respects, refused to issue the certificate of honest demeanor or good moral character "on the grounds that the living arrangement of Applicant would lower the public's opinion of the Bar as a whole." In applying this standard in lieu of the statutory standard, the trial court erred.

Whether a person meets the "honest demeanor, or good moral character" standard of Code § 54–60 is, of course, dependent upon the construction placed on those terms. The United States Supreme Court, recognizing that a state may require "high standards of qualification, such as good moral character or proficiency in its law, before it admits an applicant to the bar," has held that such qualifications, to pass constitutional muster, must have a "rational connection with the applicant's fitness to practice law." *Schware v. Board of Bar Examiners* . . .

Except for Cord's statement that she and a male to whom she was not married jointly owned and resided in the same dwelling, the record is devoid of any evidence which would otherwise reflect unfavorably on Cord's professional competence, honest demeanor and good moral character. In fact, the evidence of a number of responsible citizens in the community where Cord resides establishes that she is of good character and honest demeanor. Likewise,

the letters received from Cord's former employers vouch for her good moral character, as well as her professional competence.

While Cord's living arrangement may be unorthodox and unacceptable to some segments of society, this conduct bears no rational connection to her fitness to practice law. It cannot, therefore, serve to deny her the certificate required by Code § 54–60.

Accordingly, we hold the trial court erred in refusing to issue to petitioner a certificate of honest demeanor or good moral character. The order below will be reversed and the case will be remanded with direction that the trial court forthwith issue the certificate requested by petitioner.

Reversed and remanded.

Schware and *Cord* both defend constitutional rights derived from the First Amendment—freedom of political belief and freedom of association. The Court has since World War II treated these and related freedoms as more central or primary in constitutional philosophy than the rights of due process. These primary civil rights have received vigorous judicial protection. When such constitutional constraints do not arise in licensing cases, courts tend to give licensing boards considerably more discretion in weighing the facts of cases before them. To this we now turn.

Discretionary Analysis of the Facts: The Case of the Driver's License

In 1971 the Supreme Court announced a significant application of *Goldberg v. Kelly's* due process philosophy.[3] The case involved a decision by the state of Georgia to suspend a driver's license because the driver failed to carry liability insurance as required by Georgia law. The Court required the state to give the driver a presuspension hearing comparable to that awarded Kelly. The Court discounted the artificial notion that a license is a privilege rather than a right, noting simply that drivers have an obvious interest, often a financial one, in their ability to drive, and that this interest qualified for constitutional protection. The additional expenses of such hearings were not to be balanced away against the value of due process protections.

The Court in *Bell v. Burson* rejected the argument that Georgia could suspend the license without a hearing because the statute operated automatically, that is, required no finding of fact. The Court noted a number of facts that would, if found true at a hearing, make suspension unnecessary. These would include a finding by a trial court that the driver was not responsible for the accident and hence not liable for damages, or a showing that, if liable, the driver had paid off the judgment.

[3] *Bell v. Burson*, 402 U.S. 535, opinion by Justice Brennan.

The same requirement would seem to apply to point system suspensions of revocations of licenses. Though superficially automatic in application, point system decisions could involve a variety of disputed factual questions. These could include (1) convictions counted against the driver belonging to another driver of the same or similar name; (2) erroneous entry of conviction or judgment in traffic court records; (3) improper calculation of points, or (4) failure to grant point credits properly earned. In the following case the Supreme Court refused to extend *Bell* to point system cases. The result is to rely on the accuracy of the discretionary analysis of the case by the hearing officials. This may be unjust to the driver, but as you read the case try to identify a serious roadblock this ruling may impose for improving traffic safety.

Dixon v. Love

431 U.S. 105 (1977) 8–0
+   Burger, Stewart, White, Brennan, Marshall, Blackmun, Stevens
NP   Rehnquist

[Love, a truck driver, had his driver's license suspended by the state of Illinois following three convictions on driving charges within a twelve-month period. Subsequently convicted of driving while his license was suspended, another suspension was levied. After both suspensions had expired, Love was twice convicted of speeding and arrested on a third speeding charge—all within a period of seven months—but some years after his suspensions had expired. While awaiting the results from the third charge, the appellee received a notice from the state informing him that his license would be revoked for over a year if he were convicted of a third violation. Love was convicted on the third charge, and his license was revoked with no prior hearing under an administrative rule made by the Illinois secretary of state under a broad grant of statutory discretion. The rule makes no provision for a hearing until after the action is taken. Love challenged that rule and the district court agreed.]

Justice Blackmun delivered the opinion of the Court.

The issue in this case is whether Illinois has provided constitutionally adequate procedures for suspending or revoking the license of a driver who repeatedly has been convicted of traffic offenses. The statute and administrative regulations provide for an initial summary decision based on official records, with a full administrative hearing available only after the suspension or revocation has taken effect.

The case centers on § 6–206 of the Illinois Driver Licensing Law (c. 6 of the Illinois Vehicle Code). The section is entitled "Discretionary authority to suspend or revoke license or permit." It empowers the Secretary of State to act "without preliminary hearing upon a showing by his records or other sufficient evidence" that a driver's conduct falls into any one of 18 enumerated categories. . . .

Pursuant to his rulemaking authority under this law . . . the Secretary has adopted administrative regulations that further define the bases and procedures for discretionary suspensions. These regulations generally provide for an initial summary determination based on the individual's driving record. The Secretary has established a comprehensive system of assigning "points" for various kinds of traffic offenses, depending on severity, to provide an objective means of evaluating driving records.

One of the statutorily enumerated circumstances

justifying license suspension or revocation is conviction of three moving traffic offenses within a 12-month period. This is one of the instances where the Secretary, by regulation, has provided a method for determining the sanction according to the driver's accumulated "points."

Another circumstance, specified in the statute, supporting suspension or revocation is where a licensee

[h]as been repeatedly involved as a driver in motor vehicle collisions or has been repeatedly convicted of offenses against laws and ordinances regulating the movement of traffic, to a degree which indicates lack of ability to exercise ordinary and reasonable care in the safe operation of a motor vehicle or disrespect for the traffic laws and the safety of other persons upon the highway. . . .

Here again the Secretary has limited his broad statutory discretion by an administrative regulation. This regulation allows suspension or revocation, where sufficient points have been accumulated to warrant a second suspension within a 5-year period. The regulation concludes flatly: "A person who has been suspended thrice within a 10-year period shall be revoked."

Section 6–206(c)(1) requires the Secretary "immediately" to provide written notice of a discretionary suspension or revocation under this statute, but no prior hearing is required. Within 20 days of his receiving a written request from the licensee, the Secretary must schedule a full evidentiary hearing for a date "as early as practical" in either Sangamon County or Cook County, as the licensee may specify. . . . The final decision of the Secretary after such hearing is subject to judicial review in the Illinois courts. . . . In addition, a person whose license is suspended or revoked may obtain a restricted permit for commercial use or in case of hardship. . . .

It is clear that the Due Process Clause applies to the deprivation of a driver's license by the State: "Suspension of issued licenses . . . involves state action that adjudicates important interests of the licensees. In such case the licenses are not to be taken away without

that procedural due process required by the Fourteenth Amendment." *Bell v. Burson*, 402 U.S., at 539, 91 S. Ct., at 1589.

It is equally clear that a licensee in Illinois eventually can obtain all the safeguards procedural due process could be thought to require before a discretionary suspension or revocation becomes final. Appellee does not challenge the adequacy of the administrative hearing, noted above. . . . The only question is one of timing. This case thus presents an issue similar to that considered only last Term in *Mathews v. Eldridge*, . . . namely, "the extent to which due process requires an evidentiary hearing prior to the deprivation of some type of property interest even if such a hearing is provided thereafter." We may analyze the present case, too, in terms of the factors considered in *Eldridge*:

[I]dentification of the specific dictates of due process generally requires consideration of three distinct factors: first, the private interest that will be affected by the official action; second, the risk of an erroneous deprivation of such interest through the procedures used, and probable value, if any, of additional or substitute procedural safeguards; and finally, the Government's interest, including the function involved and the fiscal and administrative burdens that the additional or substitute procedural requirement would entail. . . .

The private interest affected by the decision here is the granted license to operate a motor vehicle. Unlike the social security recipients in *Eldridge*, who at least could obtain retroactive payments if their claims were subsequently sustained, a licensee is not made entirely whole if his suspension or revocation is later vacated. On the other hand, a driver's license may not be so vital and essential as are social insurance payments on which the recipient may depend for his very subsistence. . . . The Illinois statute includes special provisions for hardship and for holders of commercial licenses, who are those most likely to be affected by the deprival of driving privileges. . . . We therefore conclude that the nature of the private interest here is not so great as to require us "to depart from the ordinary principle, established by our decisions, that something less than an evidentiary hearing is sufficient prior to adverse administrative action." . . .

Moreover, the risk of an erroneous deprivation in the absence of a prior hearing is not great. Under the Secretary's regulations, suspension and revocation decisions are largely automatic. Of course, there is the possibility of clerical error, but written objection will bring a matter of that kind to the Secretary's attention. In this case appellee had the opportunity for a full judicial hearing in connection with each of the traffic convictions on which the Secretary's decision was based. Appellee has not challenged the validity of those convictions or the adequacy of his procedural rights at the time they were determined. . . . Since appellee does not dispute the factual basis for the Secretary's decision, he is really asserting the right to appear in person only to argue that the Secretary should show leniency and depart from his own regulations. Such an appearance might make the licensee feel that he has received more personal attention, but it would not serve to protect any substantive rights. We conclude that requiring additional procedures would be unlikely to have significant value in reducing the number of erroneous deprivations.

Finally, the substantial public interest in administrative efficiency would be impeded by the availability of a pretermination hearing in every case. Giving licensees the choice thus automatically to obtain a delay in the effectiveness of a suspension or revocation would encourage drivers routinely to request full administrative hearings. . . . Far more substantial than the administrative burden, however, is the important public interest in safety on the roads and highways, and in the prompt removal of a safety hazard . . .

We conclude that the public interests present under the circumstances of this case are sufficiently visible and weighty for the State to make its summary initial decision effective without a predecision administrative hearing.

The present case is a good illustration of the fact that procedural due process in the administrative setting does not always require application of the judicial model. When a governmental official is given the power to make discretionary decisions under a broad statutory standard, case-by-case decisionmaking may not be the best way to assure fairness. Here the Secretary commendably sought to define the statutory standard narrowly by the use of his rule-making authority. The decision to use objective rules in this case provides drivers with more precise notice of what conduct will be sanctioned and promotes equality of treatment among similarly situated drivers. The approach taken by the District Court would have the contrary result of reducing the fairness of the system, by requiring a necessarily subjective inquiry in each case as to a driver's "disrespect" or "lack of ability to exercise ordinary and reasonable care."

The judgment of the District Court is reversed. It is so ordered.

Justice Stevens, Justice Marshall, and Justice Brennan, concurring [omitted].

Isn't real due process as being assessed in few the point s few

In an article critical of the decision in *Dixon v. Love*, George D. Brandt, Chief of the Adjudication Branch of the National Highway Traffic Safety Administration, argues that the best method of improving traffic safety lies in correcting the behavior of problem drivers. This, he believes, requires a highly skilled staff of traffic advisors who possess the flexibility to negotiate specific driving limitations in individual cases. Such a program will involve discretion and therefore will necessarily need to include *Goldberg* protections. But Brandt goes further and challenges the notion that professionalism requires less due process. He believes that *Bell* was causing a slow but profound change in the training and caliber of traffic safety officers. *Dixon*, he fears, may have stopped this trend and set back traffic safety in the process.

Due Process and Driver Licensing Suspension Hearings: What Do the States Do after *Love*?

George D. Brandt
Administrative Law Review 30 (1979):223

Since license withdrawal is the ultimate weapon in the arsenal to deter violations and accidents, it is better used as a threat instead of being imposed. With this threat held in reserve, driver improvement efforts through probation and the issuance of restricted licenses may encourage improved driver performance. Professor John H. Reese, in his definitive study on driver licensing administration, concluded that a point system has no utility as a highway safety measure unless "beneficial effects" can be demonstrated from the remedial action taken. . . .

Since only a few states have developed an effective driver licensing agency hearing authority capability, there are not many models to discuss. New York has fourteen safety referees throughout the state. All of the referees spend two to three weeks in training before conducting any hearings. Pretermination point-system suspension hearings are tape recorded with evidence submitted formally into the record and all testimony given under oath. Considerable time is devoted by the referees in reviewing the driver's record to allow the driver to discuss or challenge it. At the end of the hearing the driver may explain his need for a license. The safety referee has considerable latitude in case disposition. He can issue a "restricted use license" to a person, such as Love, whose driver's license has been suspended and is necessary to his employment. The applicant for a "restricted use license" may be required to attend a driver rehabilitation program as a condition of issuance.

[A] NHTSA study made a number of recommendations for the upgrading of the nation's driver licensing agency hearing authority. Ten of the more significant ones are as follows:

1. That the authority to withdraw the driver license and to conduct driver license hearings be vested with the administrative agency responsible for issuing and controlling driver licenses;

2. That state legislatures delegate sufficient authority to driver licensing agencies to support their conduct of these hearings and the subsequent administrative decisions concerning license withdrawals;

3. That Administrative Procedures Acts be adopted and made applicable to driver license withdrawal proceedings;

4. That an independent unit responsible for conducting "trial-type" hearings be established;

5. That action be taken by each driver licensing agency to ensure that drivers are heard before licenses are withdrawn;

6. That formal hearing procedures be used in "trial-type" hearings involving contested facts;

7. That first appeals be made to the agency;

8. That appeals to a court of law be made on the record;

9. That trained specialists serve as hearing officers;

10. That the hearing officer position be a senior level position in the agency.

Regardless of whether the hearing officers are attorneys or trained senior licensing agency officials, the legal profession (particularly state assistant attorney generals who work or are assigned to motor vehicle departments and department counsel) has a responsibility to assist driver licensing agencies to upgrade all license suspension hearing officer activities, including point-system suspensions. This should mean, as a minimum, the creation of an independent hearing officer unit within the licensing agency. This upgrading may be difficult to accomplish in the face of bureaucratic inertia, the lack of an understanding of what needs to be done and budgetary constraints.

First, if a jurisdiction can pay a driver improvement analyst a maximum salary of $15,000 a year, why pay experienced, qualified, hearing officers as much as $25,000 a year? Second, even though courts have no interest or expertise in driver license suspension cases, some jurisdictions will continue to postpone the development of a qualified hearing officer cadre through the use of de novo court appeal. This will exacerbate current court case delay and backlog problems. Third, jurisdictions may interpret *Love* to justify continued use of point-system suspension authority without providing the problem driver with a pretermination "opportunity to be heard" and additional driver improvement benefits.

In conclusion, the effect of the U.S. Supreme Court's decision in *Love*, relying on *Mathew's* balancing of interests approach, may be to eviscerate pretermination hearing requirements in most driver licensing suspension and revocation cases. While the Court distinguished *Love* from *Bell* on the grounds that it was a point-system mandatory revocation involving limited contested facts, the reality is otherwise. The Court did not rest its decision on such narrow grounds. Instead, the Court found the interests of efficiency, highway safety effectiveness and fairness to be better served without a pretermination hearing.

The Court in *Love* stressed that a motorist faced with license suspension or revocation could rebut the agency's determination in writing. The Court held that "requiring an inquiry in each case on a driver's disrespect or lack of ability to exercise ordinary and reasonable care" would reduce fairness. The "personal attention" the court found so repugnant is the essence of state driver licensing agency action aimed at improved driver behavior and highway safety. Oral statements before an impartial hearing officer by the driver improvement analyst and the motorist on these issues are the central features of this process.

The use by the Court of "prompt removal of a safety hazard" as justification for summary suspension in *Love* was illusory. The Court knew that professional drivers, such as Love, were treated with leniency under the Illinois law. This lenient treatment led the Court to require "something less than an evidentiary" pretermination hearing. The Court was not aware of the body of highway safety knowledge which recommends the integration of license withdrawal action with referral to driver improvement and the issuance of hardship or restricted licenses. This integration can be accomplished both fairly and effectively through hearings conducted by an impartial hearing officer. Summary suspension or revocation action which permits only written comment is inadequate.

The Court, in backing off from the due process principles established in *Goldberg* and its progeny, such as *Bell*, needs to be fully aware of the nation's current driver licensing agency hearing capability. In approximately half of the states, hearing officers have neither the authority to make a decision nor issue an order and few states have hearing officers who are properly trained. In only three out of twenty-two states with hearing officers do lawyers constitute all or most of the staff. For the Court to sanction the use of written comment only in point-system suspension or revocation cases supports the pre-Bell situation among driver licensing agencies.

The states need to develop an independent, qualified, driver licensing agency hearing officer unit with the authority to handle all hearing requirements both formal and informal. This would include rendering decisions and issuing orders in point-system and other license suspension actions. In support of this unit, states should adopt the following five-point program:

1. a notice to drivers of a pending license withdrawal action, and a statement of reasons and due process rights,
2. an opportunity to pretermination hearings in point-system suspension or revocation cases,
3. pretermination hearings before hearing officers who do not also serve as driver improvement analysts,
4. employment of hearing officers who occupy senior level positions in the driver licensing agency, and
5. hearing officer training in due process, traffic law and adjudicatory procedures, and driver behavior and highway safety.

The establishment of an independent driver licensing hearing officer unit within the agency would go a long way toward ensuring impartiality. The professionalization of hearing officers, either by employing predominately legal personnel or through training, is also important. New York has employed professional, trained, hearing officers to hear point-system suspension cases. They have the authority under an administrative point system to suspend or place drivers on restrictive status and require attendance at a driver improvement program. This combines the best features of administrative rulemaking and individual case-by-case decisionmaking that is necessary to improve driver performance. . . .

Exercises and Questions for Further Thought

Cind, Gibs—evidence of prejudgement,
personal gain.
No such evidence in
Larkin.

1. The text distinguished *Withrow v. Larkin* from *Cinderella* and *Gibson* on the basis that the latter two cases contained specific evidence of bias. What precisely was that evidence and why does it rightly call for closer judicial inspection than the Court gave Dr. Larkin's case?

Yes. Can require
license. It must be
reasonable. Cost low,
time & place restrictions
minimal.

2. Can the government insist that individuals receive a license before exercising First Amendment freedoms, particularly before freely exercising their religion? What if religious beliefs call for door-to-door evangelizing and sale of religious tracts and an ordinance requires an license for all door-to-door selling? See *Jones v. Opelika*, 316 U.S. 584 (1942) and *Murdock v. Pennsylvania*, 319 U.S. 105 (1943).

3. Should a board of medical examiners that excludes chiropractors be presumed impartial in cases where chiropractors seek licenses to practice?

4. The granting and revoking of licenses by the state to regulate certain professions is many times the responsibility of a "board of examiners." Suppose you were a practitioner of a certain licensed profession and your profession's examining board instituted proceedings against you for "unprofessional conduct." Further, suppose that the statute authorizing the Board to act used those same words in describing reasons why licenses can be revoked. However, the statute goes no further and does not describe exactly what unprofessional conduct is. What *constitutional* defense do you think would be helpful to your case? How would you distinguish your situation from the time-honored usage in military law of the phrase *conduct unbecoming an officer and a gentleman* or the provision in the Constitution that the president may be impeached or for *high crimes and misdemeanors*? What if your state operates under an administrative procedures act that has been judicially interpreted to require agencies to make rules to flesh out legislation? How would that affect your constitutional defense? Would it give you a statutory defense in addition to or in lieu of the constitutional defense? To see how an actual court handled these issues, see *Megdal v. Oregon State Board of Dental Examiners*, 605 P.2d 273 (1980).

Probably means
what the President
thinks it means.

Dentist had tried to commit
fraud on his records. Standards
were too vague for the courts to
convict him.

CHAPTER 12

The Law of Public Employment

Thus far the presentation has centered on relationships between administrative agencies and parties outside the agency that the agency affects. These outsiders include individuals, like welfare recipients, with almost client-like relationships to the agency; large regulated corporations—commercial broadcasters, for example—that often cooperate with their regulators to reap the protective benefits of regulation; and lobbying groups such as the Sierra Club or the Environmental Defense Fund that form at least in part to block administrative actions that harm their causes.

Administrative law seeks to structure minimum standards of accuracy, rationality, and fairness in these relationships. However, agencies have great power over the employees within the agencies as well. Since the Due Process Clause of the Constitution makes no distinction between fairness to insiders and to outsiders, the same problems of accuracy, rationality and fairness apply to decisions about personnel.

Actually the law of public employment illustrates three important pratical aspects of administrative law. The first, which we shall cover only briefly, is historical. Some of the first statutory efforts to control administrative practice of any kind involved personnel. The Pendleton Act of 1883, in creating the United States Civil Service Commission, recognized the need to rationalize the appointment of employees and to regulate their political obligations so as to eliminate the irrationalities of the spoils system.

The second area of administrative law that personnel cases particularly well illustrate deals with the constitutional requirements for hearings. We have traced the effects of *Goldberg* on several welfare cases that followed it and have seen its decline in the field of education, but the *Goldberg* philosophy has had an even more substantial impact on law dealing with personnel. The federal Administrative Procedure Act and most state acts do not cover matters of internal management, including employment, so the law that governs lies on the constitutional track of administrative law.

Finally, public employment law returns us to an issued raised only briefly in part I. Agencies need not merely comply with administrative procedure acts and employ processes that are "due," they must additionally avoid violating any other provision of the Constitution. We shall see that the courts often tie the constitutional protections of free speech and due process together in the employment area. Also, agencies must not practice racial and sexual discrimination in personnel matters. The last section of this chapter will describe how public employers cope with antidiscrimination laws.

The Development of Civil Service

American history is full of nearly forgotten stories of political courage. One of these concerns Chester A. Arthur. As head of the port of New York for many years, he openly supported the machine system of politics and its method of maintaining loyalty by distributing the spoils of political success to the faithful. He stalwartly supported one of New York's leading spoilers of the day, Senator Roscoe Conkling. Arthur became vice-president under James Garfield in 1881. Garfield soon offended the Conkling crowd by refusing to make many of the spoils appointments they recommended. Four months after the election a frustrated and presumably mad office-seeker associated with the Conkling crowd fatally shot President Garfield.

On assuming the presidency, Arthur, sincerely shocked by the assassination, turned against the spoils system, and with much general public support, promoted adoption of the Pendleton Act. Only 14,000 employees were initially covered by the act. However, by an interesting political dynamic, politicians steadily expanded its scope. This occurred because the act permitted the president by executive order to expand its coverage. As new presidents took office, they deliberately expanded the act to cover their own *political* appointees so as to freeze them in their jobs after the president's term ended.

The Pendleton Act itself provided few modern legal protections. Justice Rehnquist, in *Arnett v. Kennedy,* noted the very limited nature of its protections:

> While the Pendleton Act is regarded as the keystone in the present arch of Civil Service legislation, by present-day standards it was quite limited in its application. It dealt almost exclusively with entry into the federal service and hardly at all with tenure, promotion, removal, veterans' preference, pensions and other subjects addressed by subsequent Civil Service legislation. The Pendleton Act provided for the creation of a Classified Service, and required competitive examination for entry into that service. Its only provision with respect to separation was to prohibit removal for the failure of an employee in the classified service to contribute to a political fund or to render any political service.
>
>   For 16 years following the effective date of the Pendleton Act, this last-mentioned provision of the Act appears to have been the only statutory or regulatory limitation on the right of the Government to discharge classified employees.[1]

The first tentative move toward due process in the handling of government employees came with the Lloyd–LaFollette Act of 1913. This act gave the employee threatened with dismissal the right to respond to the charges that occasioned his dismissal. But the right to respond in a hearing was made contingent on the wishes of the superior making the removal, and the potential for arbitrariness thus remained strong.

Neither the Pendleton Act nor the Lloyd–LaFollette Act seriously addressed the

---

[1]416 U.S. 134 (1974). *Arnett* itself held that due process did not require a hearing prior to the employee's termination.

full range of issues that may surround the decision to terminate an employee. This is because at common law one's possession of a job, including a job with the government, constituted a privilege, not a constitutionally protected right. For our purposes the simplest way to conceive of a legal privilege is to assume that it exists only to the extent a contract creates it. In the field of employment, a worker would have the privilege of working for the government only to the extent a legally binding contract would obligate the government to pay the employee for work done. For a variety of reasons the contracts of employment and the contractual common law on which they rested normally permitted governmental employers to fire employees on relatively short notice and without any necessary showing of cause.[2] As long as a government job remained a legal privilege, due process questions simply did not arise. And this brings us to the second and most important of this chapter's illustrations of administrative law in practice.

The Constitutional Requirements of a Termination Hearing

In 1964 Professor Charles Reich of Yale published an article entitled "The New Property."[3] In it he insisted that the modern state had amassed so much financial power, particularly in its welfare aid programs, that the old legal rights/privileges distinction no longer was wise social policy. A job with the government, a welfare check, a research grant, have all replaced the forms of property, like farm land, that the Founders sought to protect through the Due Process Clause. Reich argued that by establishing public employment, contracts, services, and so forth, the state itself created expectations that it would provide such benefits to citizens qualified to receive them. Reich reasoned that if the state denied these benefits without due process, it would violate the expectations it had created. Therefore due process protections belong in welfare and employment terminations. *Goldberg v. Kelly* was widely viewed as a positive legal response to Reich's call. A few years later the rights/privilege doctrine began to fade in employment termination cases. The classification of statutory entitlements as property stimulated a growing number of legal claims as the scope of governmental responsibilities expanded. The area of government employment fostered many of the early claims to entitlement.[4] The cases described here involve state but not federal action; due process clauses cover both levels of government.

In June 1972 the Supreme Court decided cases in which two college professors, neither of whom had official tenure, were fired without a hearing. In the first case, *Board of Regents v. Roth*, David Roth was hired for his first teaching job as an assistant professor of political science at Wisconsin State University at Oshkosh.[5] His contract

---

[2] *Bailey v. Richardson*, 341 U.S. 918 (1951).

[3] *Yale Law Journal* 73 (1964): 733.

[4] For an extended description and analysis of constitutional property see John Brigham, *Property and the Politics of Entitlement.* (Philadelphia: Temple University Press, 1990).

[5] 408 U.S. 564 (1972).

ran for one year. The university refused to rehire him for a second year. It gave no reasons for its decision. Its own system rules did not require it to do so. Roth alleged that he was not renewed because he had publicly criticized the university's administration and that therefore not to rehire him violated his freedom of speech. The Court held that Roth had no property right to be rehired. If the university had publicly criticized Roth by stating why he was not rehired, reasons that might injure his chances for future employment, then the Court stated he would have at least a right to some of the *Goldberg* protections. Similarly he would be protected if he had some informal promise of tenure or of contract renewal. Roth failed to meet either of these conditions and lost. The Court did not therefore thoroughly analyze his freedom of speech claim.

The second case, decided the same day and set out below, involved rather different facts. Note the importance of the interaction between free speech and due process claims.

Perry et al. v. Sindermann

408 U.S. 593 (1972) 5–3

+ Burger, Stewart, White, Blackmun, Rehnquist
- Douglas, Brennan, Marshall
NP Powell

[Sindermann, faculty member of Odessa (Texas) Junior College, had been employed on a series of one-year contracts for six years previously at other Texas junior colleges and for three years at Odessa when he came into conflict with the college's board of regents in his advocacy of the elevation of the college to four-year status. He actively criticized the regents, and an advertisement critical of the regents appeared in a newspaper over his name. Further, in his elected capacity as president of the Texas Junior College Teachers Association, he had occasion to miss classes in order to testify before the state legislature. At the end of his fourth year, the regents voted not to offer him another one-year contract. The regents made comments on Sindermann's alleged insubordination in a press release, but provided neither an official statement of the reason for the nonrenewal of the contract nor the opportunity of a hearing where Sindermann could try to rebut any charges. Sindermann brought suit alleging violation of his First Amendment right to free speech and Fourteenth Amendment right to due process in the form of a hearing. The district court granted summary judgment against Sindermann, but the appellate court reversed.]

Justice Stewart delivered the opinion of the Court.

The first question presented is whether the respondent's lack of a contractual or tenure right to re-employment, taken alone, defeats his claim that the nonrenewal of his contract violated the First and Fourteenth Amendments. We hold that it does not.

For at least a quarter-century, this Court has made clear that even though a person has no "right" to a valuable governmental benefit and even though the government may deny him the benefit for any number of reasons, there are some reasons upon which the government may not rely. It may not deny a benefit to a person on a basis that infringes his constitutionally protected interests—especially, his interest in freedom of speech. For if the government could deny a benefit to a person because of his constitutionally protected speech or associations, his exercise of those freedoms would in effect be penalized and inhibited. This would allow the government to "produce a result which [it] could not command directly." *Speiser v. Randall*, 357 U.S. 513, 526. Such interference with constitutional rights is impermissible. . . .

Thus, the respondent's lack of a contractual or tenure "right" to re-employment for the 1969–1970 academic year is immaterial to his free speech claim. Indeed, twice before, this Court has specifically held that the nonrenewal of a nontenured public school teacher's one-year contract may not be predicated on his exercise of First and Fourteenth Amendment rights. *Shelton v. Tucker* . . . , *Keyishian v. Board of Regents*. . . . We reaffirm those holdings here.

In this case, of course, the respondent has yet to show that the decision not to renew his contract was, in fact, made in retaliation for his exercise of the constitutional right of free speech. The District Court foreclosed any oppportunity to make this showing when it granted summary judgment. Hence, we cannot now hold that the Board of Regents' action was invalid.

But we agree with the Court of Appeals that there is a genuine dispute as to "whether the college refused to renew the teaching contract on an impermissible basis—as a reprisal for the exercise of constitutionally protected rights." 430 F.2d, at 943. The respondent has alleged that his nonretention was based on his testimony before legislative committees and his other public statements critical of the Regents' policies. And he has alleged that this public criticism was within the First and Fourteen Amendments' protection of freedom of speech. Plainly, these allegations present a bona fide constitutional claim. For this Court has held that a teacher's public criticism of his superiors on matters of public concern may be constitutionally protected and may, therefore, be an impermissible basis for termination of his employment. *Pickering v. Board of Education*. . . .

The respondent's lack of formal contractual or tenure security in continued employment at Odessa Junior College, though irrelevant to his free speech claim, is highly relevant to his procedural due process claim. But it may not be entirely dispositive.

We have held today in *Board of Regents v. Roth* . . . , that the Constitution does not require opportunity for a hearing before the nonrenewal of a nontenured teacher's contract, unless he can show that the decision not to rehire him somehow deprived him of an interest in "liberty" or that he had a "property" interest in continued employment, despite the lack of tenure or a formal contract. In *Roth* the teacher had not made a showing on either point to justify summary judgment in his favor.

Similarly, the respondent here has yet to show that he has been deprived of an interest that could invoke procedural due process protection. As in *Roth*, the mere showing that he was not rehired in one particular job, without more, did not amount to a showing of a loss of liberty. Nor did it amount to a showing of a loss of property.

But the respondent's allegations—which we must construe most favorably to the respondent at this stage of the litigation—do raise a genuine issue as to his interest in continued employment at Odessa Junior College. He alleged that this interest, though not secured by a formal contractual tenure provision, was secured by a no less binding understanding fostered by the college administration. In particular, the respondent alleged that the college had a de facto tenure program, and that he had tenure under that program. He claimed that he and others legitimately relied upon an unusual provision that had been in the college's official Faculty Guide for many years:

> Teacher Tenure: Odessa College has no tenure system. The Administration of the College wishes the faculty member to feel that he has permanent tenure as long as his teaching services are satisfactory and as long as he displays a cooperative attitude toward his co-workers and his superiors, and as long as he is happy in his work.

Moreover, the respondent claimed legitimate reliance upon guidelines promulgated by the Coordinating Board of the Texas College and University System that provided that a person, like himself, who had been employed as a teacher in the state college and university system for seven years or more has some form of job tenure. Thus, the respondent offered to prove that a teacher with his long period of service at this particular State College had no less a "property" interest in continued employment than a formally tenured teacher at other colleges, and had no less a procedural due process right to a statement of reasons and a hearing before college officials upon their decision not to retain him.

We have made clear in *Roth, supra,* at 571–572, that "property" interests subject to procedural due process protection are not limited by a few rigid, technical forms. Rather, "property" denotes a broad range of interests that are secured by "existing rules or understandings." . . . A person's interest in a benefit is a "property" interest for due process purposes if there are such rules or mutually explicit understandings that support his claim of entitlement to the benefit and that he may invoke at a hearing. . . .

A written contract with an explicit tenure provision clearly is evidence of a formal understanding that supports a teacher's claim of entitlement to continued employment unless sufficient "cause" is shown. Yet absence of such an explicit contractual provision may not always foreclose the possibility that a teacher has a "property" interest in re-employment. For example, the law of contracts in most, if not all, jurisdictions long has employed a process by which agreements, though not formalized in writing, may be "implied." . . . Explicit contractual provisions may be supplemented by other agreements implied from "the promisor's words and conduct in the light of the surrounding circumstances." . . . And, "[t]he meaning of [the promisor's] words and acts is found by relating them to the usage of the past." . . .

A teacher, like the respondent, who has held his position for a number of years, might be able to show from the circumstances of this service—and from other relevant facts—that he has a legimate claim of entitlement to job tenure. Just as this Court has found there to be a "common law of a particular industry or of a particular plant" that may supplement a collective-bargaining agreement, *Steelworkers v. Warrior & Gulf Co.,* 363 U.S. 574, 579, so there may be an unwritten "common law" in a particular university that certain employees shall have the equivalent of tenure. This is particularly likely in a college or university, like Odessa Junior College, that has no explicit ten-

ure system even for senior members of its faculty, but that nonetheless may have created such a system in practice. See C. Byse & L. Joughin, Tenure in American Higher Education 17–28 (1959).

In this case, the respondent has alleged the existence of rules and understandings, promulgated and fostered by state officials, that may justify his legitimate claim of entitlement to continued employment absent "sufficient cause." We disagree with the Court of Appeals insofar as it held that a mere subjective "expectancy" is protected by procedural due process, but we agree that the respondent must be given an opportunity to prove the legitimacy of his claim of such entitlement in light of "the policies and practices of the institution." . . . Proof of such a property interest would not, of course, entitle him to reinstatement. But such proof would obligate college officials to grant a hearing at his request, where he could be informed of the grounds for his nonretention and challenge their sufficiency. . . .

Affirmed.

Justice Brennan, with whom Justice Douglas joins, dissenting in part [omitted].

Justice Marshall, dissenting in part.

. . . I agree with Part I of the Court's opinion holding that respondent has presented a bona fide First Amendment claim that should be considered fully by the District Court. But, for the reasons stated in my dissenting opinion in *Board of Regents v. Roth,* . . . I would modify the judgment of the Court of Appeals to direct the District Court to enter summary judgment for respondent entitling him to a statement of reasons why his contract was not renewed and a hearing on disputed issues of fact.

[*Portions from Justice Marshall's dissenting opinion in* Board of Regents v. Roth:]

. . . This Court has long maintained that "the right to work for a living in the common occupations of the community is of the very essence of the personal freedom and opportunity that it was the purpose of the [Fourteenth] Amendment to secure." *Truax v. Raich,* 239 U.S. 33, 41 (1915) (Hughes, J.). It has also established that the fact that an employee has no contract guaranteeing work for a specific future period does not mean that as the result of action by the government he may be "discharged at any time for any reason or for no reason." *Truax v. Raich, supra,* at 38.

In my view, every citizen who applies for a government job is entitled to it unless the government can establish some reason for denying the employment. This is the "property" right that I believe is protected by the Fourteenth Amendment and that cannot be denied "without due process of law." And it is also liberty—liberty to work—which is the "very essence of the personal freedom and opportunity" secured by the Fourteenth Amendment. . . .

Employment is one of the greatest, if not the greatest, benefits that governments offer in modern-day life. When something as valuable as the opportunity to work is at stake, the government may not reward some citizens and not others without demonstrating that its actions are fair and equitable. And it is procedural due process that is our fundamental guarantee of fairness, our protection against arbitrary, capricious, and unreasonable government action. . . .

It may be argued that to provide procedural due process to all public employees or prospective employees would place an intolerable burden on the machinery of government. Cf. *Goldberg v. Kelly, supra.* The short answer to that argument is that it is not burdensome to given reasons when reasons exist. Whenever an application for employment is denied, an employee is discharged, or a decision not to re-hire an employee is made, there should be some reason for the decision. It can scarcely be argued that government would be crippled by a requirement that the reason be communicated to the person most directly affected by the government's action.

Where there are numerous applicants for jobs, it is likely that few will choose to demand reasons for not being hired. But, if the demand for reasons is exceptionally great, summary procedures can be devised that would provide fair and adequate information to all persons. As long as the government has a good reason for its actions it need not fear disclosure. It is only where the government acts improperly that procedural due process is truly burdensome. And that is precisely when it is most necessary.

It might also be argued that to require a hearing and a statement of reasons is to require a useless act, because a government bent on denying employment to one or more persons will do so regardless of the procedural hurdles that are placed in its path. Perhaps this is so, but a requirement of procedural regularity at least renders arbitrary action more difficult. Moreover, proper procedures will surely eliminate some of the arbitrariness that results, not from malice, but from innocent error. "Experience teaches. . . . that the affording of procedural safeguards, which by their nature serve to illuminate the underlying facts, in itself often operates to prevent erroneous decisions on the merits from occurring." *Silver v. New York Stock Exchange,* 373 U.S. 341, 366 (1963). When the government knows it may have to justify its decisions with sound reasons, its conduct is likely to be more cautious, careful, and correct.

Professor Gellhorn put the argument well:

"In my judgment, there is no basic division of interest between the citizenry on the one hand and officialdom on the other. Both should be interested equally in the quest for procedural safeguards. I echo the late Justice Jackson in saying: 'Let it not be overlooked that due process of law is not for the sole benefit of an accused. It is the best insurance for the Government itself against those blunders which leave lasting stains on a system of justice'—blunders which are likely to occur when reasons need not be given and when the reasonableness and indeed legality of judgments need not be subjected to any appraisal other than one's own. . . ." Summary of Colloquy on Administrative Law, 6 J. Soc. Pub. Teachers of Law 70, 73 (1961).

Accordingly, I dissent.

Compare the reasoning in *Perry* with the decision of the Court in the following case, *Bishop v. Wood et al.,* a case again dealing with the concept of a property right in a particular job.

Bishop v. Wood et al.

426 U.S. 341 (1976) 5–4

+ Burger, Stewart, Powell, Rehnquist, Stevens
– Brennan, White, Marshall, Blackmun

[Bishop, a tenured police officer in the city of Marion, North Carolina, was terminated without a hearing by the city manager (Wood). The termination took place
privately and at the termination Wood informed Bishop of the reasons behind his severance. The termination was done on the authority of a city ordinance that specified
a permanent employee may be fired if the employee's work is substandard, or the employee is negligent, inefficient, or unfit to perform the requisite duties. Bishop brought
suit claiming, *inter alia*, that his period of service with the city (three years) and his
status as a permanent employee vested him with a property right in his job that entitled him to a pretermination hearing. The Court held that a property right is established by ordinance or by an implied contract. The crux of the case then became the
interpretation of the city ordinance governing the dismissal of city employees and the
Court held that, in this case, the ordinance did not vest Bishop with a property right
in his job, notwithstanding his tenure and length of service.]

Justice Stevens delivered the opinion of the Court.

The questions for us to decide are (1) whether petitioner's employment status was a property interest
protected by the Due Process Clause of the Fourteenth
Amendment, and (2) assuming that the explanation
for his discharge was false, whether that false explanation deprived him of an interest in liberty protected
by that Clause.

Petitioner was employed by the city of Marion
as a probationary policeman on June 9, 1969. After
six months he became a permanent employee. He
was dismissed on March 31, 1972. He claims that
he had either an express or an implied right to continued employment.

A city ordinance provides that a permanent employee may be discharged if he fails to perform work
up to the standard of his classification, or if he is negligent, inefficient, or unfit to perform his duties.* Peti-

tioner first contends that even though the ordinance
does not expressly so provide, it should be read to
prohibit discharge for any other reason, and therefore to confer tenure on all permanent employees.
In addition, he contends that his period of service,
together with his "permanent" classification, gave him
a sufficient expectancy of continued employment to
constitute a protected property interest.

A property interest in employment can, of course,
be created by ordinance, or by an implied contract.
In either case, however, the sufficiency of the claim
of entitlement must be decided by reference to state
law. The North Carolina Supreme Court has held
that an enforceable expectation of continued public
employment in that State can exist only if the employer, by statute or contract, has actually granted
some form of guarantee. . . . Whether such a guarantee has been given can be determined only by an examination of the particular statute or ordinance in
question.

*Article H, § 6, of the Personnel Ordinance of the city of Marion,
reads as follows:

Dismissal. A permanent employee whose work is not satisfactory
over a period of time shall be notified in what way his work is deficient and what he must do if his work is to be satisfactory. If a permanent employee fails to perform work up to the standard of the
classification held, or continues to be negligent, inefficient, or unfit

to perform his duties, he may be dismissed by the City Manager.
Any discharged employee shall be given written notice of his discharge
setting forth the effective data and reasons for his discharge if he shall
request such a notice.

On its face the ordinance on which petitioner relies may fairly be read as conferring such a guarantee. However, such a reading is not the only possible interpretation; the ordinance may also be construed as granting no right to continued employment but merely conditioning an employee's removal on compliance with certain specified procedures. We do not have any authoritative interpretation of this ordinance by a North Carolina state court. We do, however, have the opinion of the United States District Judge who, of course, sits in North Carolina and practiced law there for many years. Based on his understanding of state law, he concluded that petitioner "held his position at the will and pleasure of the city." This construction of North Carolina law was upheld by the Court of Appeals for the Fourth Circuit, albeit by an equally divided court. In comparable circumstances, this Court has accepted the interpretation of state law in which the District Court and the Court of Appeals have concurred even if an examination of the state-law issue without such guidance might have justified a different conclusion.

In this case, as the District Cout construed the ordinance, the City Manager's determination of the adequacy of the grounds for discharge is not subject to judicial review; the employee is merely given certain procedural rights which the District Court found not to have been violated in this case. The District Court's reading of the ordinance is tenable; it derives some support from a decision of the North Carolina Supreme Court, *Still v. Lance* . . . ; and it was accepted by the Court of Appeals for the Fourth Circuit. These reasons are sufficient to foreclose our independent examination of the state-law issue.

Under that view of the law, petitioner's discharge did not deprive him of a property interest protected by the Fourteenth Amendment. . . .

Petitioner's claim that he has been deprived of liberty has two components. He contends that the reasons given for his discharge are so serious as to constitute a stigma that may severely damage his reputation in the community; in addition, he claims that those reasons were false.

In our appraisal of petitioner's claim we must accept his version of the facts since the District Court granted summary judgment against him. His evidence established that he was a competent police officer; that he was respected by his peers; that he made more arrests than any other officer on the force; that although he had been criticized for engaging in high-speed pursuits, he had promptly heeded such criticism; and that he had a reasonable explanation for his imperfect attendance at police training sessions. We must therefore assume that his discharge was a mistake and based on incorrect information.

In *Board of Regents v. Roth*, 408 U.S. 564, we recognized that the nonretention of an untenured college teacher might make him somewhat less attractive to other employers, but nevertheless concluded that it would stretch the concept too far "to suggest that a person is deprived of 'liberty' when he simply is not rehired in one job but remains as free as before to seek another." . . . This same conclusion applies to the discharge of a public employee whose position is terminable at the will of the employer when there is no public disclosure of the reasons for the discharge.

In this case the asserted reasons for the City Manager's decision were communicated orally to the petitioner in private and also were stated in writing in answer to interrogatories after this litigation commenced. Since the former communication was not made public, it cannot properly form the basis for a claim that petitioner's interest in his "good name, reputation, honor, or integrity" was thereby impaired. And since the latter communication was made in the course of a judicial proceeding which did not commence until after petitioner had suffered the injury for which he seeks redress, it surely cannot provide retroactive support for his claim. A contrary evaluation of either explanation would penalize forthright and truthful communication between employer and employee in the former instance, and between litigants in the latter.

Petitioner argues, however, that the reasons given for his discharge were false. Even so, the reasons stated to him in private had no different impact on his reputation than if they had been true. And the answers to his interrogatories, whether true or false, did not cause the discharge. The truth or falsity of the City Manager's statement determines whether or not his decision to discharge the petitioner was correct or prudent, but neither enhances nor diminishes petitioner's claim that his constitutionally protected interest in liberty has been impaired. A contrary evaluation of his contention would enable every discharged employee to assert a constitutional claim merely by alleging that his former supervisor made a mistake.

The federal court is not the appropriate forum in which to review the multitude of personnel decisions that are made daily by public agencies. We must accept the harsh fact that numerous individual mistakes are inevitable in the day-to-day administration of our affairs. The United States Constitution cannot feasibly be construed to require federal judicial review for every such error. In the absence of any claim that the public employer was motivated by a desire to curtail or to penalize the exercise of an employee's constitutionally protected rights, we must presume that official action was regular and, if erroneous, can best be corrected in other ways. The Due Process Clause of the Fourteenth Amendment is not a guarantee against incorrect or ill-advised personnel decisions.

The judgment is affirmed.

Justice Brennan, with whom Justice Marshall concurs, dissenting.

. . . Today the Court effectively destroys even that last vestige of protection for "liberty" by holding that a State may tell an employee that he is being fired for some nonderogatory reason, and then turn around and inform prospective employers that the employee was in fact discharged for a stigmatizing reason that will effectively preclude future employment.

. . . [R]espondents should be required to accord petitioner a due process hearing in which he can attempt to vindicate his name; this further expansion of those personal interests that the Court simply writes out of the "life, liberty, or property" Clauses of the Fifth and Fourteenth Amendments is simply another curtailment of precious constitutional safeguards that marks too many recent decisions of the Court.

I also fully concur in the dissenting opinions of Mr. Justice White and Mr. Justice Blackmun, which forcefully demonstrate the Court's error in holding that petitioner was not deprived of "property" without

due process of law. I would only add that the strained reading of the local ordinance, which the Court deems to be "tenable," *ante,* at 347, cannot be dispositive of the existence *vel non* of petitioner's "property" interest. There is certainly a federal dimension to the definition of "property" in the Federal Constitution; cases such as *Board of Regents v. Roth, supra,* held merely that "property" interests encompass those to which a person has "a legitimate claim of entitlement," 408 U.S., at 577, and *can* arise from "existing rules or understandings" that derive from "an independent source *such* as state law." *Ibid.* (emphasis supplied). But certainly, at least before a state law is definitively construed as not securing a "property" interest, the relevant inquiry is whether it was objectively reasonable for the employee to believe he could rely on continued employment. Cf. *ibid.* ("It is a purpose of the ancient institution of property to protect those claims upon which people rely in their daily lives, reliance that must not be arbitrarily undermined.") At a minimum, this would require in this case an analysis of the common practices utilized and the expectations generated by respondents, and the manner in which the local ordinance would reasonably be read by respondents' employees. These disputed issues of fact are not meet for resolution, as they were on summary judgment, and would thus at a minimum require a remand for further factual development in the District Court.

These observations do not, of course, suggest that a "federal court is . . . the appropriate forum in which to review the multitude of personnel decisions that are made daily by public agencies." *Ante,* at 349. However, the federal courts *are* the appropriate forum for ensuring that the constitutional mandates of due process are followed by those agencies of government making personnel decisions that pervasively influence the lives of those affected thereby; the fundamental premise of the Due Process Clause is that those procedural safeguards will help the government avoid the "harsh fact" of "incorrect or ill-advised personnel decisions." *Ante,* at 350. Petitioner seeks no more than that, and I believe that his "property" interest in continued employment and his "liberty" interest in his good name and reputation dictate that he be accorded procedural safeguards before those interests are deprived by arbitrary or capricious government action.

Justice White, with whom Justice Brennan, Justice Marshall, and Justice Blackmun join, dissenting [omitted].

Justice Blackmun, with whom Justice Brennan joins, dissenting [omitted].

Bishop v. Wood retreats from the protections created in *Perry,* but the retreat is not immediately obvious. Superficially the absence of any public criticism of Officer Bishop, at least prior to the litigation, might seem to make his case indistinguishable from that of Assistant Professor Roth. The argument's logic begins to collapse, however, if you consider further the implication of the city's dismissal ordinance. Because Bishop was a "nonprobationary" employee, the world knows that he was dismissed not simply for budget tightening or other managerial reasons unrelated to his performance. He must have been dismissed because his superiors thought his work was "negligent, inefficient or unfit" because the dismissal ordinance requires such a belief. The ordinance appears to give Bishop some protected tenure in his job. Therefore, prior to litigation, the act of dismissing him has communicated to the public negative information that could hurt the officer's chances of future employment.

The case may additionally bother us because it does not give employees with some real expectation that their jobs are permanent a chance to disprove the factual basis of the case for termination. The case against the employee can be totally false. Note that in the law of employment termination just as in the law of academic discipline the Court has retreated from *Goldberg* itself. Ask yourself whether the loss of a job and the loss of welfare support are so different from the perspective of the aggrieved citizen. If a welfare recipient deserves all ten *Goldberg* protections before a payment cutoff, why should an employee fired from public service deserve none of them?

The nature of the hearing required when a property right is found to exist, either when removal is a result of a constitutionally protected action on the part of the employee or when the employee's reputation and/or ability to secure other employment is impaired, has, like so many other questions in administrative law, received only case-by-case judicial treatment. Differing decisions from different courts concerning the strictness of the separation of judicial and prosecutorial functions, the degree of openness in a hearing, and the necessity for confrontation and cross-examination, have made the law of personnel hearings ambiguous.

For exactly that reason, most levels of government have gone beyond the Court's prescriptions in providing for hearings. The Civil Service Reform Act of 1978 provides an illustration of this trend. This act provides for a two-tier hearing process if the employee wishes to avail himself or herself of it. Section 7513 of the act requires that an employee who is to be removed, suspended for more than fourteen days, reduced in pay or grade, or laid off for thirty days or less be provided with certain protections at the agency level. Specifically, the employee is entitled to:

1. At least thirty days advance written notice setting forth the reasons for the action. The requirement is waived if the employee is believed to have committed a crime for which imprisonment is a possible punishment.
2. Not less than seven days to answer the charges orally and/or in writing to include the submission of affidavits or other documentary evidence.
3. Representation by an attorney or other person.
4. Receipt of a written decision and the reasons for it at the earliest practicable date.

Additionally, at the discretion of the agency, the employee may be afforded a hearing which can be a replacement for provision 2 above. Even further, but again at the discretion of the agency, the hearing may be in addition to the provisions of number 2.

The second tier of the process described in section 7701 of the act begins with the employee's statutorily created right to appeal the decision of the agency under the procedures above to the Merit System Protection Board—the employee protection arm of the federal civil service system. When this occurs the board may hear the case itself or assign the hearing to an administrative law judge or to an employee of the board. In the hearing, a transcript must be maintained and the employee may be represented by an attorney or other representative. Thus, while the courts have not mandated a hearing in all instances, the federal government has gone beyond the minimum set by the courts to afford all covered employees the opportunity for such a hearing. Further, the act provides that the decisions of the Merit System Protection Board may be judicially reviewed—in effect, a third tier of review.

A recent illustration of how the Supreme Court has interpreted state public employment procedures for dismissal is *Cleveland Board of Education v. Loudermill* (1985). As you read this case pay attention to the Court's interpretation of the relationship between the substantive aspect of employment as a property right and the procedural requirements for protecting that right. Prior to *Loudermill*, the Court developed a line of reasoning suggesting that property rights are defined by and conditioned on the legislature's choice of procedure for its deprivation (see *Arnett* v. *Kennedy*, 416 U.S. 134, 1974). In *Arnett* the Court said: "[W]here the grant of a substantive right is inextricably intertwined with the limitations on the procedures which are to be employed in determining that rights, a litigant in the position of appellee must take the bitter with the sweet."[6] By linking the scope of procedural protection to the substantive nature of property interests, legislatures could erode the value of entitlements simply by specifying limited procedural protection for termination of employment. In *Loudermill* the Court majority rejects this theory and affirms a constitutional due process requirement for statutory entitlements.

Cleveland Board of Education v. Loudermill

470 U.S. 532 (1985) 7–2

+   Burger, White, Blackmun, Powell, Stevens, O'Connor, Marshall
+/−   Brennan
−   Rehnquist

[In 1979, James Loudermill stated on a job application that he had never been convicted of a felony. In 1981, he was fired from his security guard job with the Cleveland Board of Education after the Board discovered that he had been convicted of grand larceny in 1968. Loudermill was not afforded an opportunity to respond to the charge of dishonesty or to challenge his dismissal. Loudermill filled an appeal with the Cleveland Civil Service Commission stating that he had thought his conviction for grand larceny

[6]416 U.S. 134, at 152–154.

[handwritten margin note: Can be compared to Mathews v. Eldridge. He is entitled to a pre-termination hearing, even just a chance to be heard, need not be elaborate. If there is a termination after a hearing state law applies. Statute rules. Yet statute is not enough before termination.]

was for a misdemeanor, not a felony. The hearing referee recommended he be reinstated, but after hearing argument the full commission upheld Loudermill's dismissal. Loudermill filed suit in federal court alleging that the Ohio law was unconstitutional because it did not provide public employees with an opportunity to respond to charges against them prior to dismissal, thus depriving liberty and property without due process. The district court denied his claim; however, the Court of Appeals for the Sixth Circuit reversed. The Supreme Court granted certiorari.]

Justice White delivered the opinion of the Court.

II

Property interests are not created by the Constitution, "they are created and their dimensions are defined by existing rules or understandings that stem from an independent source such as state law . . . ." *Board of Recents v. Roth*, . . . at 577. . . . The Ohio statute plainly creates such an interest. Respondents were "classified civil service employees," Ohio Rev. Code Ann. § 124.11 (1984), entitled to retain their positions "during good behavior and efficient service," who could not be dismissed "except . . . for . . . misfeasance, malfeasance, or nonfeasance in office," § 124.34.* The statute plainly supports the conclusion, reached by both lower courts, that respondents possessed property rights in continued employment. . . .

The . . . Board argues, however, that the property right is defined by, and conditioned on, the legislature's choice of procedures for its deprivation. . . . The Board stresses that in addition to specifying the grounds for termination, the statute sets out procedures by which termination may take place. The procedures were adhered to in these cases. According to petitioner, "[t]o require additional procedures would in effect expand the scope of the property interest itself." *Id.*, at 27. . . .

This argument, which was accepted by the District Court, has its genesis in the plurality opinion

in *Arnett v. Kennedy*, 416 U.S. 134 (1974). *Arnett* involved a challenge by a former federal employee to the procedures by which he was dismissed. The plurality reasoned that where the legislation conferring the substantive right also sets out the procedural mechanism for enforcing that right, the two cannot be separated:

> "The employee's statutorily defined right is not a guarantee against removal without cause in the abstract, but such a guarantee as enforced by the procedures which Congress has designated for the determination of cause.
>
> "[W]here the grant of a substantive right is inextricably intertwined with the limitations on the procedures which are to be employed in determining that right, a litigant in the position of appellee must take the bitter with the sweet." *Id.*, at 152-154.

This view garnered three votes in *Arnett*, but was specifically rejected by the other six Justices. See *id.*, at 166–167 (Powell, J., joined by Blackmun, J.,); *id.*, at 177–178, 185 (White, J.,); *id.*, at 211 (Marshall, J., joined by Douglas and Brennan, JJ.). Since then, this theory has at times seemed to gather some additional support. See *Bishop v. Wood*, 426 U.S. 341, 355–361 (1976) (White, J., dissenting); *Goss v. Lopez*, 419 U.S., at 586–587 (Powell, J., joined by Burger, C.J., and Blackmun and Rehnquist, JJ., dissenting). More recently, however, the Court has clearly rejected it. In *Vitek v. Jones*, 445 U.S. 480, 491 (1980), we pointed out that "minimum [procedural] requirements [are] a matter of federal law, they are not diminished by the fact that the State may have specified its own procedures that it may deem adequate for determining the preconditions to adverse official action." This conclusion was reiterated in *Logan v. Zimmerman*

---

*The relevant portion of § 124.34 provides that no classified civil servant may be removed except "for incompetency, inefficiency, dishonesty, drunkenness, immoral conduct, insubordination, discourteous treatment of the public, neglect of duty, violation of such sections or the rules of the director of administrative services or the commission, or any other failure of good behavior, or any other acts of misfeasance, malfeasance, or nonfeasance in office."

Brush Co., 455 U.S. 422, 432 (1982), where we reversed the lower court's holding that because the entitlement arose from a state statute, the legislature had the prerogative to define the procedures to be followed to protect entitlement.

In light of these holdings, it is settled that the "bitter with the sweet" approach misconceives the constitutional guarantee. If a clearer holding is needed, we provide it today. The point is straightforward: the Due Process clause provides that certain substantive rights—life, liberty, and property—cannot be deprived except pursuant to constitutionally adequate procedures. The categories of substance and procedure are distinct. Were the rule otherwise, the Clause would be reduced to a mere tautology. "Property" cannot be defined by the procedures provided for its deprivation any more than can life or liberty. The right to due process "is conferred, not by legislative grace, but by constitutional gurantee. While the legislature may elect not to confer a property interest in [public] employment, it may not constitutionally authorize the deprivation of such an interest, once conferred, without appropriate procedural safeguards." . . .

III

. . . The need for some form of pretermination hearing, recognized in these cases, is evident from a balancing of the competing interests at stake. These are the private interest in retaining employment, the governmental interest in the expeditious removal of unsatisfactory employees and the avoidance of administrative burdens, and the risk of an erroneous termination. See *Mathews v. Eldridge*, 424 U.S. 319, 335 (1976).

The case before us illustrates these considerations. . . . [I]n light of the referee's recommendation, . . . we cannot say that a fully informed decisionmaker might not have exercised its discretion and decided not to dismiss him, notwithstanding its authority to do so. In any event, the termination involved arguable issues, and the right to a hearing does not depend on a demonstration of certain success. . . .

The governmental interest in immediate termination does not outweigh these interests. . . . [A]ffording the employee an opportunity to respond prior to termination would impose neither a significant administrative burden nor intolerable delays. Furthermore, the employer shared the employee's interest in avoiding disruption and erroneous decisions; and until the matter is settled, the employer would continue to receive the benefit of the employee's labors. It is preferable to keep a qualified employee on than to train a new one. A governmental employer also has an interest in keeping citizens usefully employed rather than taking the possibly erroneous and counterproductive step of forcing its employees onto the welfare rolls. Finally, in those situations where the employer perceives a significant hazard in keeping the employee on the job, it can avoid the problem by suspending with pay.

IV

The foregoing considerations indicate that the pretermination "hearing," though necessary, need not be elaborate. We have pointed out that "[t]he formality and procedural requisites for the hearing can vary, depending upon the importance of the interests involved and the nature of the subsequent proceedings." *Boddie v. Connecticut*, 401 U.S., at 378. See *Cafeteria Workers v. McElroy*, 367 U.S. 886, 894–895 (1961). In general, "something less" than a full evidentiary hearing is sufficent prior to adverse administrative action. *Mathews v. Eldridge*, 424 U.S., at 343. Under state law, respondents were later entitled to a full administrative hearing and judicial review. The only question is what steps were required before the termination took effect.

In only one case, *Goldberg v. Kelly*, 397 U.S. 254 (1970), has the Court required a full adversarial evidentiary hearing prior to adverse governmental action. However, as the *Goldberg* Court itself pointed out, see *id.*, at 264, that case presented significantly different considerations than are present in the context of public employment. . . .

The essential requirements of due process, and all that respondents seek or the Court of Appeals required, are notice and an opportunity to respond. The opportunity to present reasons, either in person or in writing, why proposed action should not be taken is a fundamental due process requirement.

See Friendly, "Some Kind of Hearing," 123 U. Pa. L. Rev. 1267, 1281 (1975). The tenured public employee is entitled to oral or written notice of the charges against him, an explanation of the employer's evidence, and an opportunity to present his side of the story. . . . To require more than this prior to termination would intrude to an unwarranted extent on the government's interest in quickly removing an unsatisfactory employee. . . .

VI

We conclude that all the process that is due is provided by a pretermination opportunity to respond, coupled with post-termination administrative procedures as provided by the Ohio statute. Because respondents allege in their complaints that they had no chance to respond, the District Court erred in dismissing for failure to state a claim. The judgment of the Court of Appeals is affirmed, and the case is remanded for further proceedings consistent with this opinion.

So ordered.

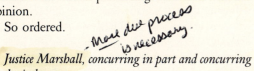 *More due process is necessary.*

Justice Marshall, concurring in part and concurring in the judgment.

I agree wholeheartedly with the Court's express rejection of the theory of due process, urged upon us by the petitioner Boards of Education, that a public employee who may be discharged only for cause may be discharged by whatever procedures the legislature chooses. I therefore join Part II of the opinion for the Court. I also agree, that before discharge, the respondent employees were entitled to the opportunity to respond to the charges against them (which is all they requested), and that the failure to accord them that opportunity was a violation of their constitutional rights. Because the Court holds that the respondents were due all the process they requested, I concur in the judgment of the Court.

I write separately, however, to reaffirm my belief that public employees who may be discharged only for cause are entitled, under the Due Process Clause of the Fourteenth Amendment, to more than respondents sought in this case. I continue to believe that *before the decision is made to terminate an employee's wages,*

the employee is entitled to an opportunity to test the strength of the evidence "by confronting and cross-examining adverse witnesses and by presenting witnesses on his own behalf, whenever there are substantial disputes in testimonial evidence," *Arnett v. Kennedy,* 416 U.S. 134, 214 (1974) (Marshall, J., dissenting). Because the Court suggests that even in this situation due process requires no more than notice and an opportunity to be heard before wages are cut off, I am not able to join the Court's opinion in its entirety. . . .

. . . The opinion for the Court does not confront this reality. I cannot and will not close my eyes today—as I could not 10 years ago—to the economic situation of great numbers of public employees, and to the potentially traumatic effect of a wrongful discharge on a working person. Given that so very much is at stake, I am unable to accept the Court's narrow view of the process due to a public employee before his wages are terminated, and before he begins the long wait for a public agency to issue a final decision in his case.

Justice Brennan, concurring in part and dissenting in part.

Today the Court puts to rest any remaining debate over whether public employers must provide meaningful notice and hearing procedures before discharging an employee for cause. . . .

Accordingly, I concur in Parts I–IV of the Court's opinion. I write separately to comment on two issues the Court does not resolve today, and to explain my dissent from the result in Part V of the Court's opinion.

First, the Court today does not prescribe the precise form of required pretermination procedures in cases where an employee disputes the *facts* proffered to support his discharge. . . .

Factual disputes are not involved in these cases, however, and the "very nature of due process negates any concept of inflexible procedures universally applicable to every imaginable situation." *Cafeteria Workers v. McElroy,* 367 U.S. 886, 895 (1961). . . .

The second issue not resolved today is that of administrative delay. In holding that Loudermill's administrative proceedings did not take too long, the Court plainly does *not* state a flat rule that 9-month delays in deciding discharge appeals will pass constitutional scrutiny as a matter of course. . . . The holding in Part V is merely that, in this particular case, Loudermill failed to allege facts sufficient to state a cause of action, and not that nine months can never exceed constitutional limits.

[handwritten: Think Court is adding to the statute. Would generate huge # of cases. No consistency to judgements]

Justice Rehnquist, dissenting.

In *Arnett v. Kennedy*, 416 U.S. 134 (1974), six Members of this Court agreed that a public employee could be dismissed for misconduct without a full hearing prior to termination. A plurality of Justices agreed that the employee was entitled to exactly what Congress gave him, and no more. . . .

. . . We ought to recognize the totality of the State's definition of the property right in question, and not merely seize upon one of several paragraphs in a unitary statute to proclaim that in that paragraph the State has inexorably conferred upon a civil service employee something which it is powerless under the United States Constitution to qualify in the next paragraph of the statute. This practice ignores our duty under *Roth* to rely on state law as the source of property interests for purposes of applying the Due Process Clause of the Fourteenth Amendment. While it does not impose a federal definition of property, the Court departs from the full breadth of the holding in *Roth* by its selective choice from among the sentences the Ohio Legislature chooses to use in establishing and qualifying a right.

Having concluded by this somewhat tortured reasoning that Ohio has created a property right in the respondents in these cases, the Court naturally proceeds to inquire what process is "due" before the respondents may be divested of that right. This customary "balancing" inquiry conducted by the Court in these cases reaches a result that is quite unobjectionable, but it seems to me that it is devoid of any principles which will either instruct or endure. The balance is simply an ad hoc weighing which depends to a great extent upon how the Court subjectively views the underlying interests at stake. The results in previous cases and in these cases have been quite unpredictable. To paraphrase Justice Black, today's balancing act requires a "pretermination opportunity to respond" but there is nothing that indicates what tomorrow's will be. *Goldberg v. Kelly*, 397 U.S. 254, 276 (1970) (Black, J., dissenting). The results from today's balance certainly do not jibe with the result in *Goldberg* or *Mathews v. Eldridge*, 424 U.S. 319 (1976). The lack of any principled standards in this area means that these procedural due process cases will recur time and again. Every different set of facts will present a new issue on what process was due and when. One way to avoid this subjective and varying interpretation of the Due Process Clause in cases such as these is to hold that one who avails himself of government entitlements accepts the grant of tenure along with its inherent limitations.

Because I believe that the Fourteenth Amendment of the United States Constitution does not support the conclusion that Ohio's effort to confer a limited form of tenure upon respondents resulted in the creation of a "property right" in their employment, I dissent.

Other Constitutional Protections for Public Employees

The cases in the previous section struggle to determine when a termination requires some kind of hearing and which of the *Goldberg* ingredients such hearings should include. A major difference between due process protection and the protections of other constitutional rights is that in the latter case courts themselves may make the final decision about whether the employee keeps the job.

We have already seen, in *Perry* and in *Loudermill*, that the Court is only partially sensitive to the harsh reality of political life. Modern politics contains its own equivalent of the oft-told ancient tendency in which the king beheads the bearer of bad tidings. People who speak out against superiors tend to get fired. Because the First Amendment protects free speech, employees fired for exercising that right have persuaded trial courts to order their reinstatement. Courts similarly order reinstatement of those fired for discriminatory reasons, which we shall discuss shortly.

The Court's protection of political freedom reached further in *Elrod v. Burns.*[7] Here, when a Democrat defeated a Republican for Sheriff of Cook County, Illinois, he fired all those deputies who refused to shift to the Democratic party or otherwise support the party and win the dubious sponsorship of an established Democrat. Citing *Perry*, among other cases, the Court struck down this practice, stating in part:

> Patronage practice falls squarely within the prohibitions of . . . *Perry*. Under that practice, public employees hold their jobs on the condition that they provide, in some acceptable manner, support for the favored political party. The threat of dismissal for failure to provide that support unquestionably inhibits protected belief and association, and dismissal for failure to provide support only penalizes its exercise. The belief and association which Government may not ordain directly are achieved by indirection. And regardless of how evenhandedly these restraints may operate in the long run, after political office has changed hands several times, protected interests are still infringed and thus the violation remains.
>
> Although the practice of patronage dismissals clearly infringes First Amendment interests, our inquiry is not at an end, for the prohibition on encroachment of First Amendment protections is not an absolute. Restraints are permitted for appropriate reasons. . . . [I]f conditioning the retention of public employment on the employee's support of the in-party is to survive constitutional challenge, it must further some vital government end by a means that is least restrictive of freedom of belief and association in achieving that end, and the benefit gained must outweigh the loss of constitutionally protected rights.
>
> One interest which has been offered in justification of patronage is the need to insure effective government and the efficiency of public employees. It is argued that employees of political persuasions not the same as that of the party in control of public office will not have the incentive to work effectively and may even be motivated to subvert the incumbent administration's efforts to govern effectively. We are not persuaded. The inefficiency resulting from the wholesale replacement of large numbers of public employees every time political office changes hands belies this justification. And the prospect of dismissal after an election in which the incumbent party has lost is only a dis-

---

[7] 427 U.S. 347 (1976), reaffirmed by 5–4 vote in *Rutan et al. v. Republican Party of Illinois, et al.*, 58 U.S.L.W. 4872 (1990).

incentive to good work. Further, it is not clear that dismissal in order to make room for a patronage appointment will result in replacement by a person more qualified to do the job since appointment often occurs in exchange for the delivery of votes, or other party service, not job capability. More fundamentally, however, the argument does not succeed because it is doubtful that the mere difference of political persuasion motivates poor performance; nor do we think it legitimately may be used as a basis for imputing such behavior. . . . At all events, less drastic means for insuring government effectiveness and employee efficiency are available to the State. Specifically, employees may always be discharged for good cause, such as insubordination or poor job performance, when those bases in fact exist. . . .

A second interest advanced in support of patronage is the need for political loyalty of employees, not to the end that effectiveness and efficiency be insured, but to the end that representative government not be undercut by tactics obstructing the implementation of policies of the new administration, policies presumably sanctioned by the electorate. The justification is not without force, but is nevertheless inadequate to validate patronage wholesale. Limiting patronage dismissals to policymaking positions is sufficient to achieve this governmental end. Nonpolicymaking individuals usually have only limited responsibility and are therefore not in a position to thwart the goals of the in-party. . . .

Right of Privacy

The Supreme Court in 1965, in *Griswold v. Connecticut*, 381 U.S. 479, suggested that the Constitution protects a "penumbra" of rights, rights implied by but not stated in the Bill of Rights itself. One of these has loosely been called the *right of privacy*. Should such a right prevent employers from setting standards for dress and hair length of employees?

Kelley v. Johnson

425 U.S. 238 (1976) 6–2

+ Burger, Stewart, White, Blackmun, Powell, Rehnquist
− Brennan, Marshall
NP Stevens

[Johnson, a Suffolk County, New York, policeman brought suit against county authorities to stop them from enforcing a regulation limiting the length of a policeman's hair. His claim was that such a regulation deprived him of his liberty under the Fourteenth Amendment to regulate his own personal appearance. The district court dismissed his suit but the Second Circuit reversed.]

Justice Rehnquist delivered the opinion of the Court.

Section 1 of the Fourteenth Amendment to the United States Constitution provides in pertinent part: "[No State] shall . . . deprive any person of life, liberty, or property, without due process of law."

This section affords not only a procedural guarantee against the deprivation of "liberty," but likewise protects substantive aspects of liberty against unconstitutional restriction by the State.

The "liberty" interest claimed by respondent here, of course, is distinguishable from those protected by the Court in *Roe v. Wade*, 410 U.S. 113 (1973); *Eisenstadt v. Baird*, 405 U.S. 438 (1972); *Stanley v. Illinois*, 405 U.S. 645 (1972); *Griswold v. Connecticut* . . . and *Meyer v. Nebraska*, 262 U.S. 390 (1923). Each of those cases involved a substantial claim of infringement on the individual's freedom of choice with respect to certain basic matters of procreation, marriage, and family life. But whether the citizenry at large has some sort of "liberty" interest within the Fourteenth Amendment in matters of personal apperance is a question on which this Court's cases offer little, if any, guidance. We can, nevertheless, assume an affirmative answer for purposes of deciding this case, because we find that assumption insufficient to carry the day for respondent's claim.

Respondent has sought the protection of the Fourteenth Amendment not as a member of the citizenry at large, but on the contrary as an employee of the police force of Suffolk County, a subdivision of the State of New York. While the Court of Appeals made passing reference to this distinction, it was thereafter apparently ignored. We think, however, it is highly significant. In *Pickering v. Board of Education*, 391 U.S. 563, 568 (1968), after noting that state employment may not be conditioned on the relinquishment of First Amendment rights, the Court stated that "[a]t the same time it cannot be gainsaid that the State has interests as an employer in regulating the speech of its employees that differ significantly from those it possesses in connection with regulation of the speech of the citizenry in general." More recently, we have sustained comprehensive and substantial restrictions upon activities of both federal and state employees

lying at the core of the First Amendment. . . . If such state regulations may survive challenges based on the explicit language of the First Amendment, there is surely even more room for restrictive regulations of state employees where the claim implicates only the more general contours of the substantive liberty interest protected by the Fourteenth Amendment. . . .

The promotion of safety of persons and property is unquestionably at the core of the State's police power, and virtually all state and local governments employ a uniform police force to aid in the accomplishment of that purpose. Choice of organization, dress, and equipment for law enforcement personnel is a decision entitled to the same sort of presumption of legislative validity as are state choices designed to promote other aims within the cognizance of the State's police power. . . . Thus the question is not, as the Court of Appeals conceived it to be, whether the State can "establish" a "genuine public need" for the specific regulation. It is whether respondent can demonstrate that there is no rational connection between the regulation, based as it is on petitioner's method of organizing its police force, and the promotion of safety of persons and property.

We think the answer here is so clear that the District Court was quite right in the first instance to have dismissed respondent's complaint. Neither this Court, the Court of Appeals, nor the District Court is in a position to weigh the policy arguments in favor of and against a rule regulating hair styles as a part of regulations governing a uniformed civilian service. The constitutional issue to be decided by these courts is whether petitioner's determination that such regulations should be enacted is so irrational that it may be branded "arbitrary," and therefore a deprivation of respondent's "liberty" interest in freedom to choose his own hair style. *Williamson v. Lee Optical Co.*, 348 U.S. 483, 487–488 (1955). The overwhelming majority of state and local police of the present day are uniformed. This fact itself testifies to the recognition by those who direct those operations, and by the people of the States and localities who directly or indirectly choose such persons, that similarity in appearance of police officers is desirable. This choice may be based on a desire to make police officers readily recognizable to the members of the public, or a desire for the esprit de corps which such similarity is felt to inculcate within the police force itself. Either one is a sufficiently rational justification for regulations so as to defeat respondent's claim based on the liberty guaranty of the Fourteenth Amendment. . . .

Reversed.

Justice Powell, concurring [omitted].

Justice Marshall, with whom Justice Brennan joins, dissenting.

. . . I think it clear that the Fourteenth Amendment does indeed protect against comprehensive regulation of what citizens may or may not wear. And I find that the rationales offered by the Court to justify the regulation in this case are insufficient to demonstrate its constitutionality. Accordingly, I respectfully dissent. . . .

. . . [W]e have observed that "[l]iberty under law extends to the full range of conduct which the individual is free to pursue." *Bolling v. Sharpe*, 347 U.S. 497, 499 (1954). See also *Poe v. Ullman*, 367 U.S. 497, 543 (1961) (Harlan, J., dissenting). It seems to me manifest that that "full range of conduct" must encompass one's interest in dressing according to his own taste. An individual's personal apperance may reflect, sustain, and nourish his personality and may well be used as a means of expressing his attitude and lifestyle.* In taking control over a citizen's personal appearance, the government forces him to sacrifice substantial elements of his integrity and identity as well. To say that the liberty guarantee of the Fourteenth Amendment does not encompass matters of personal appearance would be fundamentally inconsistent with the values of privacy, self-identity, autonomy, and personal integrity that I have always assumed the Constitution was designed to protect. See *Roe v.*

*While the parties did not address any First Amendment issues in any detail in this Court, governmental regulation of a citizen's personal appearance may in some circumstances not only deprive him of liberty under the Fourteenth Amendment but violate his First Amendment rights as well. *Tinker v. Des Moines School Dist.*, 393 U.S. 503 (1969).

Wade, 410 U.S. 113 (1973); *Stanley v. Georgia*, 394 U.S. 557, 564 (1969); *Griswold v. Connecticut*, 381 U.S. 479, 485 (1965); *Olmstead v. United States*, 277 U.S. 438, 478 (1928) (Brandeis, J., dissenting).

If little can be found in past cases of this Court or indeed in the Nation's history on the specific issue of a citizen's right to choose his own personal appearance, it is only because the right has been so clear as to be beyond question. When the right has been mentioned, its existence has simply been taken for granted. For instance, the assumption that the right exists is reflected in the 1789 congressional debates over which guarantees should be explicitly articulated in the Bill of Rights. I. Brant, The Bill of Rights 53–67 (1965). There was considerable debate over whether the right of assembly should be expressly mentioned. Congressman Benson of New York argued that its inclusion was necessary to assure that the right would not be infringed by the government. In response, Congressman Sedgwick of Massachusetts indicated:

"If the committee were governed by that general principle . . . they might have declared that *a man should have a right to wear his hat if he pleased* . . . but [I] would ask the gentleman whether he thought it necessary to enter these trifles in a declaration of rights, *in a Government where none of them were intended to be infringed.*" Id., at 54–55 (emphasis added).

Thus, while they did not include it in the Bill of Rights, Sedgwick and his colleagues clearly believed there to be a right in one's personal appearance. And, while they may have regarded the right as a trifle as long as it was honored, they clearly would not have so regarded it if it were infringed. . . .

To my mind, the right in one's personal appearance is inextricably bound up with the historically recognized right of "every individual to the possession and control of his own person," *Union Pacific R. Co. v. Botsford*, 141 U.S. 250, 251 (1891), and, perhaps even more fundamentally, with "the right to be let alone—the most comprehensive of rights and the right most valued by civilized men." *Olmstead v. United States, supra*, at 478 (Brandeis, J., dissenting). In an increasingly crowded society in which it is already extremely difficult to maintain one's identity and personal integrity, it would be distressing, to say the least, if the government could regulate our personal appearance unconfined by any constitutional strictures whatsoever. . . .

The Court cautions us not to view the hair-length regulation in isolation, but rather to examine it "in the context of the county's chosen mode of organization for its police force." *Ante*, at 247. While the Court's caution is well taken, one should also keep in mind, as I fear the Court does not, that what is ultimately under scrutiny is neither the overall struc- ture of the police force nor the uniform and equipment requirements to which its members are subject, but rather the regulation which dictates acceptable hair lengths. The fact that the uniform requirement, for instance, may be rationally related to the goals of increasing police officer "identifiability" and the maintenance of esprit de corps does absolutely nothing to establish the legitimacy of the hair-length regulation. I see no connection between the regulation and the offered rationales and would accordingly affirm the judgment of the Court of Appeals.

When the government places conditions on public employment that conflict with an individual's privacy rights, the courts apply a "balancing test." As the dissenting opion in *Kelley v. Johnson* makes clear, some members of the current Court disagree not only with the outcome of the majority's weighing process, but with the very idea that fundamental rights, such as privacy, should be "balanced" against governmental interests. The controvery over privacy as a constitutional right is grounded in very different interpretations about what rights are protected by the Constitution. While the Court in *Roe v. Wade*, 410 U.S. 113 (1973), affirmed the interpretation of privacy in *Griswold v. Connecticut*, (previous page), a new conservative majority on the Court has indicated that that right may no longer be fundamental at least for women who seek abortions from public hospitals (*Webster v. Reproductive Health Services*, 109 S. Ct. 1739 (1989).[8] The right to privacy is under attack not only in the area of abortion but in other areas directly effecting the rights of public employees—among them mandatory drug testing. The drug policies of the Reagan and Bush administrations target public employees. Should the right of privacy prevent the government from implementing a mandatory drug screening program for public employees?

National Treasury Employees Union et al. v. Von Raab

109 S. Ct. 1384 (1989) 5–4
+ Rehnquist, White, Blackmun, O'Connor, Kennedy
– Marshall, Brennan, Scalia, Stevens

[In 1986, the Commissioner of the United States Customs Service announced that certain employees would be subject to a drug testing program designed to detect the presence of marijuana, cocaine, opiates, amphetamines, and phencyclidine. These

---

[8] Citing the *DeShaney v. Winnebago Country Department of Social Services, supra* at p. 398, Chief Justice Rehnquist upheld provisions of a Missouri law that make it "unlawful for any public employee within the scope of his employment to perform or assist an abortion, not necessary to save the life of the mother," section 188.210: "our cases have recognized that the due process clauses generally confer no affirmative right to governmental aid, even where such aid may be necessary to secure life, liberty or property interests of which the government itself may not deprive the individual."

employees included those who sought transfer or promotion in the following positions: (1) jobs directly involving the interdiction of illegal drugs; (2) jobs requiring the carrying of firearms; and (3) jobs requiring the handling of classified materials. The National Treasury Employee Union filed suit alleging that the drug testing program violated the Fourth Amendment rights of these federal employees. The district court agreed and enjoined the drug testing program. The Court of Appeals for the Fifth Circuit reversed. The union appealed to the Supreme Court.]

Justice Kennedy delivered the opinion of the Court.

I

The United States Customs Service, a bureau of the Department of the Treasury, is the federal agency responsible for processing persons, carriers, cargo, and mail into the United States, collecting revenue from imports, and enforcing customs and related laws. . . . An important responsibility of the Service is the interdiction and seizure of contraband, including illegal drugs. In 1987 alone, Customs agents seized drugs with a retail value of nearly 9 billion dollars. . . . In the routine discharge of their duties, many Customs employees have direct contact with those who traffic in drugs for profit. Drug import operations, often directed by sophisticated criminal syndicates, *United States v. Mendenhall*, 446 US 544 . . . (1980) (Powell, J., concurring), may be effected by violence or its threat. As a necessary response, many Customs operatives carry and use firearms in connection with their official duties. . . .

In December 1985, respondent, the Commissioner of Customs, established a Drug Screening Task Force to explore the possibility of implementing a drug screening program within the Service. After extensive research and consultation with experts in the field, the Task Force concluded "that drug screening through urinalysis is technologically reliable, valid and accurate." Citing this conclusion, the Commissioner announced his intention to require drug tests of employees who applied for, or occupied, certain positions within the Service. The Commissioner stated his belief that "Customs is largely drugfree," but noted also that "unfortunately no segment of society is immune from the threat of illegal drug use." . . .

In May 1986, the Commissioner announced implementation of the drug-testing program. Drug tests were made a condition of placement or employment for positions that meet one or more of three criteria. [see description above.] . . .

. . . An independent contractor contacts the employee to fix the time and place for collecting the sample. On reporting for the test, the employee must produce photographic identification and remove any outer garments, such as a coat or a jacket, and personal belongings. The employee may produce the sample behind a partition, or in the privacy of a bathroom stall if he so chooses. To ensure against adulteration of the specimen, or substitution of a sample from another person, a monitor of the same sex as the employee remains close at hand to listen for the normal sounds of urination. Dye is added to the toilet water to prevent the employee from using the water to adulterate the sample.

Upon receiving the specimen, the monitor inspects it to ensure its proper temperature and color, places a tamper-proof custody seal over the container, and affixes an identification label indicating the date and the individual's specimen number. The employee signs a chain-of-custody form, which is initialed by the monitor, and the urine sample is placed in a plastic bag, sealed, and submitted to a laboratory.

Customs employees who test positive for drugs and who can offer no satisfactory explanation are subject to dismissal from the Service. Test results may not, however, be turned over to any other agency, including criminal prosecutors, without the employee's written consent. . . .

. . . We now affirm so much of the judgment of the court of appeals as upheld the testing of employees directly involved in drug interdiction or required to carry firearms. We vacate the judgment to the extent it upheld the testing of applicants for positions requiring the incumbent to handle classified materials, and remand for further proceedings.

II

In *Skinner v. Railway Labor Executives' Assn.*, 103 L Ed 2d 639, 109 S Ct —, decided today, we hold that federal regulations requiring employees of private railroads to produce urine samples for chemical testing implicate the Fourth Amendment, as those tests invade reasonable expectations of privacy. Our earlier cases have settled that the Fourth Amendment protects individuals from unreasonable searches conducted by the Government, even when the Government acts as an employer, . . . and, in view of our holding in *Railway Labor Executives* that urine tests are searches, it follows that the Customs Service's drug testing program must meet the reasonableness requirement of the Fourth Amendment.

While we have often emphasized, and reiterate today, that a search must be supported, as a general matter, by a warrant issued upon probable cause, . . . our decision in *Railway Labor Executives* reaffirms the longstanding principle that neither a warrant nor probable cause, nor, indeed, any measure of individualized suspicion, is an indispensable component of reasonableness in every circumstance. . . . 103 L Ed 2d 639, 109 S Ct—. See also *New Jersey v. T.L.O.*, 469 US 325 . . . (1985); *United States v. Martinez-Fuerte*, 428 US 543 . . . (1976). As we note in *Railway Labor Executives*, our cases establish that where a Fourth Amendment intrusion serves special governmental needs, beyond the normal need for law enforcement, it is necessary to balance the individual's privacy expectations against the Government's interests to determine whether it is impractical to require a warrant or some level of individualized suspicion in the particular context. . . . 103 L Ed 2d 639, 109 S Ct.—.

It is clear that the Customs Service's drug testing program is not designed to serve the ordinary needs of law enforcement. Test results may not be used in a criminal prosecution of the employee without the employee's consent. The purposes of the program are to deter drug use among those eligible for promotion to sensitive positions within the Service and to prevent the promotion of drug users to those positions. These substantial interests, no less than the Government's concern for safe rail transportation at issue in *Railway Labor Executives*, present a special need that may justify departure from the ordinary warrant and probable cause requirements.

A

Petitioners do not contend that a warrant is required by the balance of privacy and governmental interests in this context, nor could any such contention withstand scrutiny. We have recognized before that requiring the Government to procure a warrant for every work-related intrusion "would conflict with 'the common-sense realization that government offices could not function if every employment decision became a constitutional matter.' " . . . *New Jersey v. T.L.O., supra,* at 340.

Even if Customs Service employees are more likely to be familiar with the procedures required to obtain a warrant than most other Government workers, requiring a warrant in this context would serve only to divert valuable agency resources from the Service's primary mission. The Customs Service has been entrusted with pressing responsibilities, and its mission would be compromised if it were required to seek search warrants in connection with routine, yet sensitive, employment decisions.

Furthermore, a warrant would provide little or nothing in the way of additional protection of personal privacy. A warrant serves primarily to advise the citizen that an intrusion is authorized by law and limited in its permissible scope and to interpose a neutral magistrate between the citizen and the law enforcement officer "engaged in the often competitive enterprise of ferreting out crime." *Johnson v. United States*, 333 US 10 (1948). . . . Under the Customs program, every employee who seeks a transfer to a covered position knows that he must take a drug test, and is likewise aware of the procedures the Service must follow in administering the test. A covered employee is simply not subject "to the discretion of the official in the field." *Camara v. Municipal Court*, 387 US 523 . . . (1967). The process becomes automatic when the employee elects to apply for, and thereafter pursue, a covered position. Because the Service does not make a discretionary determination to search based on a judgment that certain conditions are present, there are simply "no special facts for a neutral magistrate to evaluate." . . .

. . . Our Cases teach, . . . that the probable-cause standard " 'is peculiarly related to criminal investigations.' " . . . In particular, the traditional probable-cause standard may be unhelpful in analyzing the reasonableness of routine administrative functions . . . especially where the Government seeks to *prevent* the development of hazardous conditions or to detect violations that rarely generate articulable grounds for searching any particular place or person. . . . Our precedents have settled that, in certain limited circumstances, the Government's need to discover such latent or hidden conditions, or to prevent their development, is sufficiently compelling to justify the intrusion on privacy entailed by conducting such searches without any measure of individualized suspicion. E.g., *Railway Labor Executives*, . . . 103 L Ed 2d 639, 109 S Ct—. We think the Government's need to conduct the suspicionless searches required by the Customs program outweighs the privacy interests of employees engaged directly in drug interdiction, and of those who otherwise are required to carry firearms.

The Customs Service is our Nation's first line of defense against one of the greatest problems affecting the health and welfare of our population. We have adverted before to "the veritable national crisis in law enforcement caused by smuggling of illicit narcotics." *United States v. Montoya de Hernandez*, 473 US 531 . . . (1985). . . . The record in this case confirms that, through the adroit selection of source locations, smuggling routes, and increasingly elaborate methods of concealment, drug traffickers have managed to bring into this country increasingly large quantities of illegal drugs. The record also indicates, and it is well known, that drug smugglers do not hesitate to use violence to protect their lucrative trade and avoid apprehension.

Many of the Service's employees are often exposed to this criminal element and to the controlled substances they seek to smuggle into the country. The physical safety of these employees may be threatened, and many may be tempted not only by bribes from the traffickers with whom they deal, but also by their own access to vast sources of valuable contraband seized and controlled by the Service. The Commis-

sioner indicated below that "Customs [o]fficers have been shot, stabbed, run over, dragged by automobiles, and assaulted with blunt objects while performing their duties." . . . At least nine officers have died in the line of duty since 1974. . . .

It is readily apparent that the Government has a compelling interest in ensuring that front-line interdiction personnel are physically fit, and have unimpeachable integrity and judgment. Indeed, the Government's interest here is at least as important as its interest in searching travelers entering the country. We have long held that travelers seeking to enter the country may be stopped and required to submit to a routine search without probable cause, or even founded suspicion, "because of national self protection reasonably requiring one entering the country to identify himself as entitled to come in, and his belongings as effects which may be lawfully brought in." *Carroll v. United States*, 267 US 132, . . . (1985). The public interest demands effective measures to bar drug users from positions directly involving the interdiction of illegal drugs.

The public interest likewise demands effective measures to prevent the promotion of drug users to positions that require the incumbent to carry a firearm, even if the incumbent is not engaged directly in the interdiction of drugs. . . . We agree with the Government that the public should not bear the risk that employees who may suffer from impaired perception and judgment will be promoted to positions where they may need to employ deadly force. Indeed, ensuring against the creation of this dangerous risk will itself further Fourth Amendment values, as the use of deadly force may violate the Fourth Amendment in certain circumstances. . . .

Against these valid public interests we must weigh the interference with individual liberty that results from requiring these classes of employees to undergo a urine test. The interference with individual privacy that results from the collection of a urine sample for subsequent chemical analysis could be substantial in some circumstances. . . . We have recognized, however, that the "operational realities of the workplace" may render entirely reasonable certain work-related intrusions by supervisors and co-workers that might be viewed as unreasonable in other contexts. . . . While these operational realities will rarely affect an employee's expectations of privacy with respect to searches of his person, or of personal effects that the employee may bring to the workplace, . . . it is plain that certain forms of public employment may diminish privacy expectations even with respect to such personal searches. Employees of the United States Mint, for example, should expect to be subject to certain routine personal searches when they leave the workplace every day. Similarly, those who join our military or intelligence services may not only be required to give what in other contexts might be viewed as extraordinary assurances of trustworthiness and probity, but also may expect intrusive inquiries into their physical fitness for those special positions. Cf. *Snepp v. United States*, 444 US 507 (1980). . . .

We think Customs employees who are directly involved in the interdiction of illegal drugs or who are required to carry firearms in the line of duty likewise have a diminished expectation of privacy in respect to the intrusions occasioned by a urine test. Unlike most private citizens or government employees in general, employees involved in drug interdiction reasonably should expect effective inquiry into their fitness and probity. Much the same is true of employees who are required to carry firearms. Because successful performance of their duties depends uniquely on their judgment and dexterity, these employees cannot reasonably expect to keep from the Service personal information that bears directly on their fitness. . . .

Without disparaging the importance of the governmental interests that support the suspicionless searches of these employees, petitioners nevertheless contend that the Service's drug testing program is unreasonable in two particulars. First, petitioners argue that the program is unjustified because it is not based on a belief that testing will reveal any drug use by covered employees. In pressing this argument, petitioners point out that the Service's testing scheme was not implemented in response to any perceived drug problem among Customs employees, and that the program actually has not led to the discovery of a significant number of drug user. . . . Counsel for petitioners informed us at oral argument that no more

than 5 employees out of 3,600 have tested positive for drugs. . . . Second, petitioners contend that the Service's scheme is not a "sufficiently productive mechanism to justify [its] intrusion upon Fourth Amendment interests," . . . because illegal drug users can avoid detection with ease by temporary abstinence or by surreptitious adulteration of their urine specimens. . . . These contentions are unpersuasive.

Petitioners' first contention evinces an unduly narrow view of the context in which the Service's testing program was implemented. Petitioners do not dispute, nor can there be doubt, that drug abuse is one of the most serious problems confronting our society today. There is little reason to believe that American workplaces are immune from this pervasive social problem, as is amply illustrated by our decision in *Railway Labor Executives*. . . . Detecting drug impairment on the part of employees can be a difficult task, especially where, as here, it is not feasible to subject employees and their work-product to the kind of day-to-day scrutiny that is the norm in more traditional office environments. . . . In light of the extraordinary safety and national security hazards that would attend the promotion of drug users to positions that require the carrying of firearms or the interdiction of controlled substances, the Service's policy of deterring drug users from seeking such promotions cannot be deemed unreasonable.

The mere circumstance that all but a few of the employees tested are entirely innocent of wrongdoing does not impugn the program's validity. The same is likely to be true of householders who are required to submit to suspicionless housing code inspections, see *Camara v. Municipal Court*, 387 US 523, . . . (1967), and of motorists who are stopped at the checkpoints we approved in *United States v. Martinez-Fuerte*, 428 US 543, . . . (1976). The Service's program is designed to prevent the promotion of drug users to sensitive positions as much as it is designed to detect those employees who use drugs. . . .

We think petitioners' second argument—that the Service's testing program is ineffective because employees may attempt to deceive the test by a brief abstention before the test date, or by adulterating their urine specimens—overstates the case. As the Court of Appeals noted, addicts may be unable to abstain even for a limited period of time, or may be unaware of the "fade-away effect" of certain drugs. . . .

In sum, we believe the Government has demonstrated that its compelling interests in safeguarding our borders and the public safety outweigh the privacy expectations of employees who seek to be promoted to positions that directly involve the interdiction of illegal drugs or that require the incumbent to carry a firearm. We hold that the testing of these employees is reasonable under the Fourth Amendment.

C

We are unable, on the present record, to assess the reasonableness of the Government's testing program insofar as it covers employees who are required "to handle classified material." . . . We readily agree that the Government has a compelling interest in protecting truly sensitive information from those who, "under compulsion of circumstances or for other reasons, . . . might compromise [such] information." . . . We also agree that employees who seek promotions to positions where they would handle sensitive information can be required to submit to a urine test under the Service's screening program, especially if the positions covered under this category require background investigations, medical examinations, or other intrusions that may be expected to diminish their expectations of privacy in respect of a urinalysis test. . . .

It is not clear, however, whether the category defined by the Service's testing directive encompasses only those Customs employees likely to gain access to sensitive information. Employees who are tested under the Service's scheme include those holding such diverse positions as "Accountant," "Accounting Technician," "Animal Caretaker," "Attorney (All)," "Baggage Clerk," Co-op Student (All)," "Electric Equipment Repairer," "Mail Clerk/Assistant," and "Messenger." . . . We assume these positions were selected for coverage under the Service's testing program by reason of the incumbent's access to "classified" information, as it is not clear that they would fall under either of the two categories we have already considered. Yet it is not evident that those occupying these positions are likely to gain access to sensitive information, and this apparent discrepancy raises in our minds the question whether the Service has defined this category of employees more broadly than necessary to meet the purposes of the Commissioner's directive.

We cannot resolve this ambiguity on the basis of the record before us, and we think it is appropriate to remand the case to the court of appeals for such proceedings as may be necessary . . .

It is so ordered.

Justice Marshall, with whom Justice Brennan joins, dissenting.

. . . [T]he Court's abandonment of the Fourth Amendment's express requirement that searches of the person rest on probable cause is unprincipled and unjustifiable. But even if I believe that balancing analysis was appropriate under the Fourth Amendment, I would still dissent from today's judgment, for the reasons stated by Justice Scalia in his dissenting opinion. . . .

Justice Scalia, with whom Justice Stevens joins, dissenting.

The issue in this case is not whether Customs Service employees can constitutionally be denied promotion, or even dismissed, for a single instance of unlawful drug use, at home or at work. They assuredly can. The issue here is what steps can constitutionally be taken to *detect* such drug use. The Government asserts it can demand that employees perform "an excretory function traditionally shielded by great privacy," *Skinner v. Railway Labor Executives' Assn.*, . . . 103 L Ed 2d 639, 109 S Ct —, . . . The Court agrees that this constitutes a search for purposes of the Fourth Amendment—and I think it obvious that it is a type of search particularly destructive of privacy and offensive to personal dignity.

Until today this Court had upheld a bodily search separate from arrest and without individualized suspicion of wrongdoing only with respect to prison inmates, relying upon the uniquely dangerous nature of that environment. See *Bell v. Wolfish*, 441 US 520 . . . (1979). Today, in *Skinner*, we allow a less intrusive bodily search of railroad employees involved in train accidents. I joined the Court's opinion there because the demonstrated frequency of drug and alcohol use by the targeted class of employees, and the demonstrated connection between such use and grave harm, rendered the search a reasonable means of protecting society. I decline to join the Court's opinion in the present case because neither frequency of use nor connection to harm is demonstrated or even likely. In my view the Customs Service rules are a kind of immolation of privacy and human dignity in symbolic opposition to drug use.

. . . While there are some absolutes in Fourth Amendment law, as soon as those have been left behind and the question comes down to whether a particular search has been "reasonable," the answer depends largely upon the social necessity that prompts the search. Thus, in upholding the administrative search of a student's purse in a school, we began with the observation (documented by an agency report to Congress) that "[m]aintaining order in the classroom has never been easy, but in recent years, school disorder has often taken particularly ugly forms: drug use and violent crime in the schools have become major social problems." *New Jersey v. T.L.O.*, 469 US 325 . . . (1985). When we approved fixed checkpoints near the Mexican border to stop and search cars for illegal aliens, we observed at the outset that "the Immigration and Naturalization Service now suggests there may be as many as 10 or 12 million aliens illegally in the country," and that "[i]nterdicting the flow of illegal entrants from Mexico poses formidable law enforcement problems." *United States v. Martinez-Fuerte*, 428 US 543 (1976). . . .

The Court's opinion in the present case, however, will be searched in vain for real evidence of a real problem that will be solved by urine testing of Customs Service employees. Instead, there are assurances that "[t]he Customs Service is our Nation's first line of defense against one of the greatest problems affecting the health and welfare of our population;" . . . that "[m]any of the Service's employees are often exposed to [drug smugglers] and to the controlled substances they seek to smuggle into the country"; . . . To paraphrase Churchill, all this contains much that is obviously true, and much that is relevant; unfortunately, what is obviously true is not relevant, and what is relevant is not obviously true. The only pertinent points, it seems to me, are supported by nothing but speculation, and not very plausible speculation at that. It is not apparent to me that a Customs Service employee who uses drugs is significantly more likely to be bribed by a drug smuggler, any more than a Customs Service employee who wears diamonds is significantly more likely to be bribed by a diamond smuggler—unless, perhaps, the addiction to drugs is so severe, and requires so much money to maintain, that it would be detectable even without benefit of a urine test. Nor is it apparent to me that Customs officers who use drugs will be appreciably less "sympathetic" to their drug-interdiction mission, any more than police officers who exceed the speed limit in their private cars are appreciably less sympathetic to their mission of enforcing the traffic laws. . . . Nor, finally, is it apparent to me that urine tests will be even marginally more effective in preventing gun-carrying agents from risking "impaired perception and judgment" than is their current knowledge that, if impaired, they may be shot dead in unequal combat with unimpaired smugglers—unless, again, their addiction is so severe that no urine test is needed for detection.

What is absent in the Government's justifications—notably absent, revealingly absent, and as far as I am concerned dispositively absent—is the recitation of *even a single instance* in which any of the speculated horribles actually occurred: an instance, that is, in which the cause of bribe-taking, or of poor aim, or of unsympathetic law enforcement, or of compromise of classified information, was drug use. Although the Court points out that several employees have in the past been removed from the Service for accepting bribes and other integrity violations, and that at least nine officers have died in the line of duty since 1974, . . . 103 L Ed 2d 704, there is no indication whatever that these incidents were related to drug use by Service employees. Perhaps concrete evidence of the severity of a problem is unnecessary when it is so well known that courts can almost take judicial notice of it; but that is surely not the case here. . . .

. . . The only plausible explanation, in my view, is what the Commissioner himself offered in the concluding sentence of his memorandum to Customs Service employees announcing the program: "Implementation of the drug screening program would set an important example in our country's struggle with this most serious threat to our national health and security." . . . Or as respondent's brief to this Court asserted: "if a law enforcement agency and its employees do not take the law seriously, neither will the public on which the agency's effectiveness depends." . . . What better way to show that the Government is serious about its "war on drugs" than to subject its employees on the front line of that war to this invasion of their privacy and affront to their dignity? To be sure, there is only a slight chance that it will prevent some serious public harm resulting from Service employee drug use, but it will show to the world that the Service is "clean," and—most important of all—will demonstrate the determination of the Government to eliminate this scourge of our society! I think it obvious that this justification is unacceptable; that the impairment of individual liberties cannot be the means of making a point; that symbolism, even symbolism for so worthy a cause as the abolition of unlawful drugs, cannot validate an otherwise unreasonable search.

There is irony in the Government's citation, in support of its position, of Justice Brandeis's statement in *Olmstead v. United States*, 277 US 438 . . . (1928) that "[f]or good or for ill, [our Government] teaches the whole people by its example." . . . Brandeis was there *dissenting* from the Court's admission of evidence obtained through an unlawful Government wiretap. He was not praising the Government's example of vigor and enthusiasm in combatting crime, but condemning its example that "the end justifies the means." . . . An even more apt quotation from that famous Brandeis dissent would have been the following:

> "[I]t is . . . immaterial that the intrusion was in aid of law enforcement. Experience should teach us to be most on our guard to protect liberty when the Government's purposes are beneficent. Men born to freedom are naturally alert to repel invasion of their liberty by evil-minded rulers. The greatest dangers to liberty lurk in insidious encroachment by men of zeal, well-meaning but without understanding." Id., at 479. . . .

Those who lose because of the lack of understanding that begot the present exercise in symbolism are not just the Customs Service employees, whose dignity is thus offended, but all of us—who suffer a coarsening of our national manners that ultimately give the Fourth Amendment its content, and who become subject to the administration of federal officials whose respect for our privacy can hardly be greater than the small respect they have been taught to have for their own.

Anti-Discrimination Law

Title VII of the Civil Rights Act of 1964, as amended, prohibits discrimination on the basis of color, race, religion, sex, or national origin in employment decisions. The act affects both hiring and firing decisions. The statute itself states no concrete definition of discrimination, although it does expressly prohibit discriminating against employees or job applicants who have protested or otherwise tried to correct alleged discrimination. Thus the courts have borne the main task of formulating the specific meaning of discrimination and shaping the evidence that those alleging discrimination must prove to sustain their case. In *McDonnell Douglas Corp. v. Green* the Supreme Court stated that an individual plaintiff charging racial discrimination under Title VII must show *prima facie* (1) that he or she belongs to a racial minority; (2) that he applied and was qualified for a job the employer was trying to fill; (3) that he was rejected; (4) that thereafter the employer continued to seek applicants with the plaintiff's qualifications.[9] *Green* involved a private corporation, but the same rules of proof apply in nearly all respects to public employers. However, as the next case, *Washington v. Davis* (1976), indicates, the standards for proving discrimination are not always the same for the public and private sector (but see Justice Brennan's dissent).

Washington v. Davis

Did not use Title VII to see if they could stretch Constitutional protection

426 U.S. 229 (1976) 7–2

+ Burger, Stewart, White, Blackmun, Powell, Rehnquist, Stevens
– Brennan, Marshall

[The Washington, D.C., Police Department administered a standardized test (Test 21) developed by a neutral third party, the United States Civil Service Commission, to all applicants for a position on the force as a policeman. The test, used to measure verbal ability, vocabulary, and reading skills, was also used as an examining tool by the federal government. A minimum passing grade of 40 out of 80 was required along with high school graduation and the meeting of specified physical and character requirements before an applicant would be considered for a position. Davis, a rejected black applicant, brought suit claiming that the cultural bias of the test allowed whites to pass more frequently than blacks and that the test had not been validated by showing it was a good predictor of on-the-job performance. The district court found for the city, here represented by Mayor Washington. The D.C. Circuit reversed.]

Justice White delivered the opinion of the Court.

[T]he finding . . . of the District Court . . . warranted three conclusions: "(a) The number of black police officers, while substantial, is not proportionate to the population mix of the city. (b) A higher percentage of blacks fail the Test than whites. (c) The Test has not been validated to establish its reliability for measuring subsequent job performance." This showing was deemed sufficient to shift the burden of proof to the defendants in the action, petitioners here; but the court nevertheless concluded that on the undisputed facts respondents were not entitled to relief. The District Court relied on several factors. Since August 1969, 44% of new police force recruits had been black; that figure also represented the proportion of blacks on the total force and was roughly equivalent to 20- to 29-year-old blacks in the 50-mile radius in which the recruiting efforts of the Police Department had been constructed. It was undisputed that the Department had systematically and

affirmatively sought to enroll black officers many of whom passed the test but failed to report for duty. The District Court rejected the assertion that Test 21 was culturally slanted to favor whites and was "satisfied that the undisputable facts prove the test to be reasonably and directly related to the requirements of the police recruit training program and that it is neither so designed nor operates [sic] to discriminate against otherwise qualified blacks." It was thus not necessary to show that Test 21 was not only a useful indicator of training school performance but had also been validated in terms of job performance. . . .

[The Court of Appeals] held that the statutory standards elucidated in that case were to govern the due process question tendered in this one. . . . The court went on to declare that lack of discriminatory intent in designing and administering Test 21 was irrelevant; the critical fact was rather that a far greater proportion of blacks—four times as many—failed the test than did whites. This disproportionate impact,

[9] 411 U.S. 792 (1973).

standing alone and without regard to whether it indicated a discriminatory purpose, was held sufficient to establish a constitutional violation, absent proof by petitioners that the test was an adequate measure of job performance in addition to being an indicator of probable success in the training program, a burden which the court ruled petitioners had failed to discharge. . . .

[W]e have never held that the constitutional standard for adjudicating claims of invidious racial discrimination is identical to the standards applicable under Title VII, and we decline to do so today. . . . [O]ur cases have not embraced the proposition that a law or other official act, without regard to whether it reflects a racially discriminatory purpose, is unconstitutional solely because it is has a racially disproportionate impact. . . .

Necessarily, an invidious discriminatory purpose may often be inferred from the totality of the relevant facts, including the fact, if it is true, that the law bears more heavily on one race than another. It is also not infrequently true that the discriminatory impact — in the jury cases for example, the total or seriously disproportionate exclusion of Negroes from jury venires — may for all practical purposes demonstrate unconstitutionality because in various circumstances the discrimination is very difficult to explain on nonracial grounds. Nevertheless, we have not held that a law, neutral on its face and serving ends otherwise within the power of government to pursue, is invalid under the Equal Protection Clause simply because it may affect a greater proportion of one race than of another. Disproportionate impact is not irrelevant, but it is not the sole touchstone of an invidious racial discrimination forbidden by the Constitution. . . .

[V]arious Courts of Appeals have held in several contexts, including public employment, that the substantially disproportionate racial impact of a statute or official practice standing alone and without regard to discriminatory purpose, suffices to prove racial discrimination violating the Equal Protection Clause absent some justification going substantially beyond what would be necessary to validate most other legislative classifications. The cases impressively demonstrate that there is another side to the issue; but, with

all due respect, to the extent that those cases rested on or expressed the view that proof of discriminatory racial purpose is necessary in making out an equal protection violation, we are in disagreement. . . .

[Test 21] seeks to ascertain whether those who take it have acquired a particular level of verbal skill; and it is untenable that the Constitution prevents the Government from seeking modestly to upgrade the communicative abilities of its employees rather than to be satisfied with some lower level of competence, particularly where the job requires special ability to communicate orally and in writing. Respondents, as Negroes, could no more successfully claim that the test denied them equal protection than could white applicants who also failed. The conclusion would not be different in the face of proof that more Negroes than whites had been disqualified by Test 21. That other Negroes also failed to score well would, alone, not demonstrate that respondents individually were being denied equal protection of the laws by the application of an otherwise valid qualifying test being administered to prospective police recruits.

Nor on the facts of the case before us would the disproportionate impact of Test 21 warrant the conclusion that it is a purposeful device to discriminate against Negroes. . . . [T]he test is neutral on its face and rationally may be said to serve a purpose the Government is constitutionally empowered to pursue. Even agreeing with the District Court that the differential racial effect of Test 21 called for further inquiry, we think the District Court correctly held that the affirmative efforts of the Metropolitan Police Department to recruit black officers, the changing racial composition of the recruit classes and of the force in general, and the relationship of the test to the training program negated any inference that the Department discriminated on the basis of race or that "a police officer qualifies on the color of his skin rather than ability."

Under Title VII Congress provided that when hiring and promotion practices disqualifying substantially disproportionate numbers of blacks are challenged, discriminatory purpose need not be proved, and that it is an insufficient response to demonstrate some rational basis for the challenged practice. It is necessary, in addition, that they be "validated" in terms of job performance in any one of several ways, perhaps by ascertaining the minimum skill, ability, or potential necessary for the position at issue and determining whether the qualifying tests are appropriate for the selection of qualified applicants for the job in question. However this process proceeds, it involves a more probing judicial review of, and less deference to, the seemingly reasonable acts of administrators and executives than is appropriate under the Constitution where special racial impact, without discriminatory purpose, is claimed. We are not disposed to adopt this more rigorous standard for the purposes of applying the Fifth and the 14th Amendments in cases such as this.

A rule that a statute designed to serve neutral ends is nevertheless invalid, absent compelling justification, if in practice it benefits or burdens one race more than another would be far reaching and would raise serious questions about, and perhaps invalidate, a whole range of tax, welfare, public service, regulatory, and licensing statutes that may be more burdensome to the poor and to the average black than to the more affluent white.

Given that rule, such consequences would perhaps be likely to follow. However, in our view, extension of the rule beyond those areas where it is already applicable by reason of statute, such as in the field of public employment, should await legislative prescription. . . .

The judgment is reversed.

Justice Stewart joins Parts I and II of the Court's opinion.
Justice Stevens, concurring [omitted].

Justice Brennan, with whom Justice Marshall joins, dissenting.
. . . It is hornbook law that the Court accord deference to the construction of an administrative regulation when that construction is made by the administrative authority responsible for the regulation. *E.g., Udall v. Tallman,* 380 U.S. 1, 16 (1965). It is worthy of note, therefore, that the brief filed by the [Civil Service Commission] CSC in this case interprets the instructions in a manner directly contrary to the Court, despite the Court's claim that its result is supported by the Commissioners' "current views."

"Under Civil Service Commission regulations and current professional standards governing criterion-related test validation procedures, the job-relatedness of an entrance examination may be demonstrated by proof that scores on the examination predict properly measured success in job-relevant training (regardless of whether they predict success on the job itself).

"The documentary evidence submitted in the district court demonstrates that scores on Test 21 are predictive of Recruit School Final Averages. There is little evidence, however, concerning the relationship between the Recruit School tests and the substance of the training program, and between the substance of the training program and the post-training job of a police officer. *It cannot be determined, therefore, whether the Recruit School Final Averages are a proper measure of success in training and whether the training program is job-relevant."* Brief for CSC 14-15 (emphasis added).

The CSC maintains that a positive correlation between scores on entrance examinations and the criterion of success in training may establish the job relatedness of an entrance test—thus relieving an employer from the burden of providing a relationship to job performance after training—but only subject to certain limitations.

"Proof that scores on an entrance examination predict scores on training school achievement tests, however, does not, by itself, satisfy the burden of demonstrating the job-relatedness of the entrance examination. There must also be evidence—the nature of which will depend on the particular circumstances of the case—showing that the achievement test scores are an appropriate measure of the trainee's mastery of the material taught in the training program and that the training program imparts to a new employee knowledge, skills, or abilities required for performance of the post-training job." *Id.*, at 24–25. . . .

The CSC's standards thus recognize that Test 21 can be validated by a correlation between Test 21 scores and recruits' averages on training examinations only if (1) the training averages predict job performance or (2) the averages are proved to measure performance in job-related training. There is no proof that the recruits' average is correlated with job peformance after completion of training. . . . And although a positive relationship to the recruits' average might be sufficient to validate Test 21 if the average were proved to reflect mastery of material of the training curriculum that was in turn demonstrated to be relevant to job performance, the record is devoid of proof in this regard. First, there is no demonstration by petitioners that the training-course examinations measure comprehension of the training curriculum; indeed, these examinations do not even appear in the record. Furthermore, the Futransky study simply designated an average of 85 on the examination as a "good" performance and assumed that a recruit with such an average learned the material taught in the training course. Without any further proof of the significance of a score of 85, and there is none in the record, I cannot agree that Test 21 is predictive of "success in training."

Today's decision is also at odds with [Equal Employment Opportunity Commission] EEOC regulations issued pursuant to explicit authorization in Title VII. . . . Although the dispute in this case is not within the EEOC's jurisdiction, . . . the proper construction of Title VII nevertheless is relevant. Moreover, the 1972 extension of Title VII to public employees gave the same substantive protection to those employees as had previously been accorded in the private sector, *Morton v. Mancari*, 417 U.S. 535 . . . (1974), and it is therefore improper to maintain different standards in the public and private sectors. . . .

As with an agency's regulations, the construction of a statute by the agency charged with its administration is entitled to great deference. *Trafficante v. Metropolitan Life Ins. Co.*, 409 U.S. 205 . . . (1972). . . . The deference due the pertinent EEOC

regulations is enhanced by the fact that they were neither altered nor disapproved when Congress extensively amended Title VII in 1972. . . .

The EEOC regulations require that the validity of a job qualification test be proved by "empirical data demonstrating that the test is predictive of or significantly correlated with important elements of work behavior which comprise or are relevant to the job or jobs for which candidates are being evaluated." 29 CFR § 1607.4 (c) (1975). This construction of Title VII was approved in *Albemarle*, where we quoted this provision and remarked that "[t]he message of these Guidelines is the same as that of the *Griggs* case." 442 U.S., at 431. The regulations also set forth minimum standards for validation and delineate the criteria that may be used for this purpose.

> "The work behaviors or other criteria of employee adequacy which the test is intended to predict or identify must be fully described; and, additionally, in the case of rating techniques, the appraisal form(s) and instructions to the rater(s) must be included as a part of the validation evidence. Such criteria may include measures other than actual work proficiency, such as training time, supervisory ratings, regularity of attendance and tenure. Whatever criteria are used they must represent major or critical work behaviors as revealed by careful job analyses." 29 CFR § 1607.5 (b) (3) (1975).

. . . If we measure the validity of Test 21 by this standard, which I submit we are bound to do, petitioners' proof is deficient in a number of ways similar to those noted above. First, the criterion of final training examination averages does not appear to be "fully described." Although the record contains some general discussion of the training curriculum, the examinations are not in the record, and there is no other evidence completely elucidating the subject matter tested by the training examinations. Without this required description we cannot determine whether the correlation with training examination averages is sufficiently related to petitioners' need to ascertain "job-specific ability." . . . Second, the EEOC regulations do not expressly permit validation by correlation to training performance, unlike the CSC instructions. Among the specified criteria the closest to training performance is "training time." All recruits to the Metropolitan Police Department, however, go through the same training course in the same amount of time, including those who experience some difficulty. Third, the final requirement of § 1607.5 (b) (3) has not been met. There has been no job analysis establishing the significance of scores on training examinations, nor is there any other type of evidence showing that these scores are of "major or critical" importance.

Accordingly, EEOC regulations that have previously been approved by the Court set forth a construction of Title VII that is distinctly opposed to today's statutory result.

The Court also says that its conclusion is not foreclosed by *Griggs* and *Albermarle*, but today's result plainly conflicts with those cases. *Griggs* held that "[i]f an employment practice which operates to exclude Negroes cannot be shown to be *related to job performance*, the practice is prohibited." 401 U.S., at 431 (emphasis added). Once a discriminatory impact is shown, the employer carries the burden of proving that the challenged practice "bear[s] a *demonstrable relationship to successful performance of the jobs* for which it was used." *Ibid.* (emphasis added). We observed further:

> "Nothing in the Act precludes the use of testing or measuring procedures; obviously they are useful. What Congress has forbidden is giving these devices and mechanisms controlling force unless they are demonstrably a reasonable measure of job performance. . . .

What Congress has commanded is that any tests used must measure the person for the job and not the person in the abstract." *Id.*, at 436.

Albemarle read *Griggs* to require that a discriminatory test be validated through proof "by professionally acceptable methods" that it is " 'predictive of or significantly correlated with *important* elements of work behavior *which comprise or are relevant to the job or jobs* for which candidates are being evaluated.' " 422 U.S., at 431 (emphasis added), quoting 29 CFR § 1607.4 (c) (1975). Further, we rejected the employer's attempts to validate a written test by proving that it was related to supervisors' job performance ratings, because there was no demonstration that the ratings accurately reflected job performance. We were unable "to determine whether the criteria *actually* considered were sufficiently related to the [employer's] legitimate interest in job-specific ability to justify a testing system with a racially discriminatory impact." 422 U.S., at 433 (emphasis in original). To me, therefore, these cases read Title VII as requiring proof of a significant relationship to job performance to establish the validity of a discriminatory test. See also *McDonnell Douglas Corp. v. Green*, 411 U.S. 792, 802, and n. 14 (1973). Petitioners do not maintain that there is a demonstrated correlation between Test 21 scores and job performance. Moreover, their validity study was unable to discern a significant positive relationship between training averages and job performance. Thus, there is no proof of a correlation — either direct or indirect — between Test 21 and performance of the job of being a police officer. . . .

White employees have challenged affirmative actions plans to redress discriminatory employment practices as violating their Fourteenth Amendment equal protection rights. These anti-discrimination policies were dubbed "reverse discrimination" in the famous case *Regents of the University of California v. Bakke* (1978)[10] where a divided Supreme Court struck down racial quotas as unconstitutional but affirmed the use of race as one of many factors universities may consider in making admission decisions. Since the *Bakke* decision, the Court's constitutional and statutory interpretations of equal protection have given mixed messages about affirmative action programs. For example, in 1980, the Court held that government contract programs setting

[10]438 U.S. 265.

aside a certain percentage of contracts for minority bidders did not violate the equal protection component of the due process clause of the Fifth Amendment.[11] However, in 1989, the Court, in *City of Richmond v. Croson*,[12] appeared to back away from its earlier support for affirmative action in government contracting. The Court ruled that Richmond violated the Fourteenth Amendment's equal protection clause because the city required that nonminority-owned prime contractors on city construction contracts must provide at least a 30 percent set-aside for minority subcontractors.

The next case, *Martin v. Wilks* (1989), addresses a slightly more complex aspect of antidiscrimination policies—the legal force of consent decrees which create affirmative action programs. Often affirmative action programs result from discrimination suits. In these instances, both parties will agree to certain hiring and promotion practices to remedy employment discrimination. In *Firefighters Local Union No. 1784 v. Stotts* (1984),[13] the Supreme Court held that a consent decree entered into by parties to a discrimination suit and establishing remedies to past discrimination against minorities in hiring and promotion in the Memphis, Tennessee, Fire Department could not preempt the seniority system use by the City to lay off employees as a result of budgetary shortfall. The Court reasoned that because consent decrees are "voluntary" agreements between parties, the terms of the agreement cannot cover new circumstances (layoffs) to which the parties had not initially agreed. Consent decrees are a procedure for resolving antidiscrimination litigation, yet this procedural mechanism provides the framework for designing substantive policies.

Martin v. Wilks

109 S. Ct. 2180 (1989) 5–4

+ Rehnquist, White, O'Connor, Scalia, Kennedy
- Brennan, Marshall, Blackmun, Stevens

[A group of white firefighters sued the City of Birmingham, Alabama, and the Jefferson County Personnel Board alleging that the city and the board made promotion decision on the basis of race in reliance on certain consent decrees and that these decision violated their constitutional and statutory rights. The district court held that the white firefighters were precluded from challenging employment decisions taken pursuant to the decrees, even though they had not been parties to the proceeding in which the decrees were entered. The Eleventh Circuit Court of Appeals reversed and the Supreme Court granted certiorari.]

Chief Justice Rehnquist delivered the opinion of the Court.

. . . We think [the District Court's] holding contravenes the general rule that a person cannot be deprived of his legal rights in a proceeding to which he is not a party.

The litigation in which the consent decrees were entered began in 1974, when the Ensley Branch of the NAACP and seven black individuals filed separate class-action complaints against the City and the Board. They alleged that both had engaged in racially discriminatory hiring and promotion practices in vari-

[11] *Fullilove v. Klutznick*, 448 U.S. 448 (1980).

[12] 109 S.Ct. 706.

[13] 104 S.Ct. 2576.

ous public service jobs in violation of Title VII of the Civil Rights Act of 1964 . . . and other federal law. After a bench trial on some issues, but before judgment, the parties entered into two consent decrees, one between the black individuals and the City and the other between them and the Board. These proposed decrees set forth an extensive remedial scheme, including long-term and interim annual goals for the hiring of blacks as firefighters. The decrees also provided for goals for promotion of blacks within the department.

The District Court entered an order provisionally approving the decrees and directing publication of notice of the upcoming fairness hearings. . . . Notice of the hearings, with a reference to the general nature of the decrees, was published in two local newspapers. At that hearing, the Birmingham Firefighters Association (BFA) appeared and filed objections as *amicus curiae*. After the hearing, but before final approval of the decrees, the BFA and two of its members also moved to intervene on the ground that the decrees would adversely affect their rights. The District Court denied the motions as untimely and approved the decrees. *United States v. Jefferson County,* 28 FEP Cases 1834 (ND Ala. 1981). Seven white firefighters, all members of the BFA, then filed a complaint against the City and the Board seeking injunctive relief against enforcement of the decrees. The seven argued that the decrees would operate to illegally discriminate against them; the District Court denied relief. . . .

Both the denial of intervention and the denial of injunctive relief were affirmed on appeal. *United States v. Jefferson County,* 720 F. 2d 1511 (CA11 1983). The District Court had not abused its discretion in refusing to let the BFA intervene, thought the Eleventh Circuit, in part because the firefighters could "institut[e] an independent Title VII suit, asserting specific violations of their rights." . . . And, for the same reason, petitioners had not adequately shown the potential for irreparable harm from the operation of the decrees necessary to obtain injunctive relief. . . .

A new group of white firefighters, the *Wilks* respondents, then brought suit against the City and the Board in district court. They too alleged that,

because of their race, they were being denied promotions in favor of less qualified blacks in violation of federal law. The Board and the City admitted to making race conscious employment decisions, but argued the decisions were unassailable because they were made pursuant to the consent decrees. A group of black individuals, the *Martin* petitioners, were allowed to intervene in their individual capacities to defend the decrees.

The defendants moved to dismiss the reverse discrimination cases as impermissible collateral attacks on the consent decrees. The District Court denied the motions, ruling that the decrees would provide a defense to claims of discrimination for employment decisions "mandated" by the decrees, leaving the principal issue for trial whether the challenged promotions were indeed required by the decrees. . . . After trial the District Court granted the motion to dismiss. . . . The court concluded that "if in fact the City was required to [make promotions of blacks] by the consent decree, then they would not be guilty of [illegal] racial discrimination" and that the defendants had "establish[ed] that the promotions of the black individuals . . . were in fact required by the terms of the consent decree." . . .

. . . All agree that "[i]t is a principle of general application in Anglo-American jurisprudence that one is not bound by a judgment *in personam* in a litigation in which he is not designated as a party or to which he has not been made a party by service of process." *Hansberry v. Lee,* 311 U.S. 32, 40 (1940). . . . This rule is part of our "deep-rooted historic tradition that everyone should have his own day in court." 18 C. Wright, A. Miller, & E. Cooper, Federal Practice and Procedure § 4449, p. 417 (1981) (18 Wright). A judgment or decree among parties to a lawsuit resolves issues as among them, but it does not conclude the rights of strangers to those proceedings. . . .

. . . We begin with the words of Justice Brandeis in *Chase National Bank v. Norwalk,* 291 U.S. 431 (1934):

"The law does not impose upon any person absolutely entitled to a hearing the burden of voluntary intervention in a suit to which he is a stranger. . . . Unless duly summoned to appear in a legal proceeding, a person not a privy may rest assured that a judgment recovered therein will not affect his legal rights." *Id.* at 441.

While these words were written before the adoption of the Federal Rules of Civil Procedure, we think the Rules incorporate the same principle; a party seeking a judgment binding on another cannot obligate that person to intervene; he must be joined. . . . Against the background of permissive intervention set forth in *Chase National Bank*, the drafters cast Rule 24, governing intervention, in permissive terms. See Fed. Rule Civ. Proc. 24(a) (intervention as of right) ("[u]pon timely application anyone shall be permitted to intervene"); Fed. Rule Civ. Proc. 24(b) (permissive intervention) ("[u]pon timely application anyone may be permitted to intervene"). They determined that the concern for finality and completeness of judgments would be "better [served] by mandatory joinder procedures." . . . Accordingly, Rule 19(a) provides for mandatory joinder in circumstances where a judgment rendered in the absence of a person may "leave . . . persons already parties subject to a substantial risk of incurring . . . inconsistent obligations. . . . " Rule 19(b) sets forth the factors to be considered by a court in deciding whether to allow an action to proceed in the absence of an interested party.*

Joinder as a party, rather than knowledge of a lawsuit and an opportunity to intervene, is the method by which potential parties are subjected to the jurisdiction of the court and bound by a judgment or decree. The parties to a lawsuit presumably know better than anyone else the nature and scope of relief sought in the action, and at whose expense such relief might be granted. It makes sense, therefore, to place on them a burden of bringing in additional parties where such a step is indicated, rather than placing on potential additional parties a duty to intervene when they acquire knowledge of the lawsuit. The linchpin of the "impermissible collateral attack" doctrine—the attribution of preclusive effect to a failure to intervene—is therefore quite inconsistent with Rule 19 and Rule 24. . . .

. . . Petitioners contend that a different result should be reached because the need to join affected parties will be burdensome and ultimately discouraging to civil rights litigation. Potential adverse claimants may be numerous and difficult to identify; if they are not joined, the possibility for inconsistent judgments exists. Judicial resources will be needlessly consumed in relitigation of the same question.

Even if we were wholly persuaded by these arguments as a matter of policy, acceptance of them would require a rewriting rather than an interpretation of the relevant Rules. But we are not persuaded that their acceptance would lead to a more satisfactory method of handling cases like this one. It must be remembered that the alternatives are a duty to intervene based on knowledge, on the one hand, and some form of joinder, as the Rules presently provide, on the other. No one can seriously contend that an employer might successfully defend against a Title VII claim by one group of employees on the ground that its actions were required by an earlier decree entered in a suit brought against it by another, if the later group did not have adequate notice or knowledge of the earlier suit.

The difficulties petitioners foresee in identifying those who could be adversely affected by a decree granting broad remedial relief are undoubtedly present, but they arise from the nature of the relief sought and not because of any choice between mandatory intervention and joinder. Rule 19's provisions for joining interested parties are designed to accom-

---

*Rule 19(b) provides that:

"If a person . . . cannot be made a party, the court shall determine whether in equity and good conscience the action should proceed among the parties before it, or should be dismissed, the absent person being thus regarded as indispensable. The factors to be considered by the court include: first, to what extent a judgment rendered in the person's absence might be prejudicial to the person or to those already parties, second, the extent to which, by protective provisions in the judgment, by the shaping of relief, or other measures, the prejudice can be lessened or avoided; third, whether a judgment rendered in the person's absence will be adequate; fourth, whether the plaintiff will have an adequate remedy if the action is dismissed for nonjoinder."

modate the sort of complexities that may arise from a decree affecting numerous people in various ways. We doubt that a mandatory intervention rule would be any less awkward. As mentioned, plaintiffs who seek the aid of the courts to alter existing employment policies, or the employer who might be subject to conflicting decrees, are best able to bear the burden of designating those who would be adversely affected if plaintiffs prevail; these parties will generally have a better understanding of the scope of likely relief than employees who are not named but might be affected. . . .

Nor do we think that the system of joinder called for by the Rules is likely to produce more relitigation of issues than the converse rule. The breadth of a lawsuit and concomitant relief may be at least partially shaped in advance through Rule 19 to avoid needless clashes with future litigation. And even under a regime of mandatory intervention, parties who did not have adequate knowledge of the suit would relitigate issues. Additional questions about the adequacy and timeliness of knowledge would inevitably crop up. We think that the system of joinder presently contemplated by the Rules best serves the many interests involved in the run of litigated cases, including cases like the present one.

Petitioners also urge that the congressional policy favoring voluntary settlement of employment discrimination claims, referred to in cases such as *Carson v. American Brands, Inc.* 450 U.S. 79 (1981), also supports the "impermissible collateral attack" doctrine. But once again it is essential to note just what is meant by "voluntary settlement." A voluntary settlement in the form of a consent decree between one group of employees and their employer cannot possibly "settle," voluntarily or otherwise, the conflicting claims of another group of employees who do not join in the agreement. . . .

Affirmed.

Justice Stevens, with whom Justice Brennan, Justice Marshall, and Justice Blackmun join, dissenting.

As a matter of law there is a vast difference between persons who are actual parties to litigation and persons who merely have the kind of interest that may as a practical matter be impaired by the outcome of a case. Persons in the first category have a right to participate in a trial and to appeal from an adverse judgment; depending on whether they win or lose, their legal rights may be enhanced or impaired. Persons in the latter category have a right to intervene in the action in a timely fashion, or they may be joined as parties against their will. But if they remain on the sidelines, they may be harmed as a practical matter even though their legal rights are unaffected. One of the disadvantages of sideline sitting is that the bystander has no right to appeal from a judgment no matter how harmful it may be.

In this case the Court quite rightly concludes that the white firefighters who brought the second series of Title VII cases could not be deprived of their legal rights in the first series of cases because they had neither intervened nor been joined as parties. . . . There is no reason, however, why the consent decrees might not produce changes in conditions at the white firefighters' place of employment that, as a practical matter, may have a serious effect on their opportunities for employment or promotion even though they are not bound by the decrees in any legal sense. The fact that one of the effects of a decree is to curtail the job opportunities of nonparties does not mean that the nonparties have been deprived of legal rights or that they have standing to appeal from that decree without becoming parties.

Persons who have no right to appeal from a final judgment—either because the time to appeal has elapsed or because they never became parties to the case—may nevertheless collaterally attack a judgment on certain narrow grounds. . . . This rule not only applies to parties to the original action, but also allows interested third parties collaterally to attack judgments. In both civil and criminal cases, however, the grounds that may be invoked to support a collateral attack are much more limited than those that may be asserted as error on direct appeal. Thus, a person who can forsee that a lawsuit is likely to have a practical impact on his interests may pay a heavy price if he elects to sit on the sidelines instead of intervening and taking the risk that his legal rights will be impaired. . . .

. . . Regardless of whether the white firefighters were parties to the decrees granting relief to their black co-workers, it would be quite wrong to assume that they could never collaterally attack such a decree. If a litigant has standing, he or she can always collaterally attack a judgment for certain narrowly defined defects. . . .

. . . That the decree may not directly interfere with any of respondents' legal rights does not mean that it may not affect the factual setting in a way that negates respondents' claim. The fact that a criminal suspect is not a party to the issuance of a search warrant does not imply that the presence of a facially valid warrant may not be taken as evidence that the police acted in good faith. . . . Similarly, the fact that an employer is acting under court compulsion may be evidence that the employer is acting in good faith and without discriminatory intent. . . .

The predecessor to this litigation was brought to change a pattern of hiring and promotion practices that had discriminated against black citizens in Birmingham for decades. The white respondents in this case are not responsible for that history of discrimi-nation, but they are nevertheless beneficiaries of the discriminatory practices that the litigation was designed to correct. Any remedy that seeks to create employment conditions that would have obtained if there had been no violations of law will necessarily have an adverse impact on whites, who must now share their job and promotion opportunities with blacks. Just as white employees in the past were innocent beneficiaries of illegal discriminatory practices, so is it inevitable that some of the same white employees will be innocent victims who must share some of the burdens resulting from the redress of the past wrongs.

There is nothing unusual about the fact that litigation between adverse parties may, as a practical matter, seriously impair the interests of third persons who elect to sit on the sidelines. Indeed, in complex litigation this Court has squarely held that a sideline-sitter may be bound as firmly as an actual party if he had adequate notice and a fair opportunity to intervene and if the judicial interest in finality is sufficiently strong. . . .

Like the civil rights movement, the women's movement has sought to eradicate discrimination against women in the workplace by using litigation and building on the antidiscrimination provisions in Title VII of the Civil Rights Act of 1964. The women's movement has specifically attacked discrimination in wages. In 1963, as a result of long and difficult negotiations in Congress, the Equal Pay Act was passed as an amendment to the Fair Labor Standards Act. It provides:

No employer having employees subject to any provisions of this seciton shall discriminate, within any establishment in which such employees are employed, between employees on the basis of sex by paying wages to employees in such establishment at a rate less than the rate at which he pays wages to employees of the opposite sex in such establishment for equal work on jobs the performance of which requires equal skill, effort, and responsibility, and which are performed under similar working conditions, except where such payment is made pursuant to (i) a seniority system; (ii) a merit system; (iii) a system which measures earnings by quantity or quality of production; or (iv) a differential based on any other factor other than sex: *Provided,* That an employer who is paying a wage rate differential in violation of this subsection shall not, in order to comply with the

provision of this subsection, reduce the wage rate of any employee.
29 U.S.C. sec. 206(d)

Despite legislative reform, the gap in wages between men and women has not decreased significantly over the past thirty years. In 1955, the median income of full-time female workers was 64.3 cents to every male dollar. By 1977, it was 58.5 cents to every male dollar, and current figures show roughly the same disparity.[14] Beginning in the early 1980s the women's movement, frustrated by the narrow scope of the Equal Pay Act, which only protects against differential pay for identical jobs, began to mobilize to achieve equal pay for comparable work in a movement called *comparable worth*.[15] The argument for comparable worth is that since 75 percent of working women are employed in jobs where more than 80 percent of the workers are female (i.e., women's jobs), efforts to redress the gross inequities between male and female wages must go beyond attacking pay differentials for identical jobs and get at the root of the problem—sex-segregated employment. You probably can think of numerous "female jobs" that pay substantially less than "male jobs." In Los Angeles County, female librarians employed by the county threatened to bring a comparable worth suit in the late 1980s because they were paid 20 percent less than gardeners and maintenance workers, almost all of whom were male. The union and the county resolved this conflict through negotiation. Other female workers (e.g., clerical workers) have not been as successful in labor negotiation or in the courts. In *Spaulding v. University of Washington*, 740 F.2d 686 (1984), the Ninth Circuit Court of Appeals dismissed a comparable worth claim by nursing faculty who were paid substantially less than predominant male faculty who, they alleged, were doing comparable work, such as faculty in "health services, social work, architecture, urban planning, environmental health, speech and hearing, rehabilitative medicine, and pharmacy practice."[16] The Ninth Circuit held that the nursing faculty had not presented sufficient evidence to demonstrate that the University of Washington discriminated intentionally.[17] The "disparate impact" theory, advanced by the plaintiffs in this case, and in other comparable worth suits, would require that the "plaintiff must show only disparate *effect* of facially neutral wage policies on members of a protected class."[18] Courts have been unwilling to accept the disparate impact analysis in comparable worth cases; hence the judiciary is not a fruitful avenue for such antidiscrimination reform efforts as comparable worth. What about personnel managers in local government: Are they any more likely to implement comparable worth in their hiring policies? This is the question Professors Davis and West ask us to consider below.

[14] Margaret A. Berger, *Litigation on Behalf of Women* (New York: Ford Foundation, 1980), 10.

[15] See Ronnie Steinberg, "The Debate on Comparable Worth," *New Politics* 1 (1986): 108.

[16] 740 F.2d 686, at 696.

[17] The U.S. Supreme Court denied certiorari, 105 S.Ct. 511 (1984).

[18] Judith Olans Brown, Phyllis Tropper Baumann, and Elaine Millar Melnick, "Equal Pay for Jobs of Comparable Worth: An Analysis of the Rhetoric," *Harvard Civil Rights-Civil Liberties Law Review* 21 (1986): 146. Also see Janice R. Bellace, "Comparable Worth: Proving Sex-Based Discrimination," *Iowa Law Review* 69 (1984): 655.

Jobs, Dollars & Gender: An Analysis of the Comparable Worth Issue in Urban Areas

Charles Davis and Jonathan West
Polity 18 (1985): 138

A political issue of increasing importance to organizations representing the interests of working women is comparable worth, or the idea that equal pay should be received for work of comparable value. It represents a legislative, or in some cases, an administrative response to the allegation that jobs staffed primarily by women are undervalued in the marketplace, a charge bolstered by considerable empirical evidence which indicates that female workers fare less well than male employees for positions requiring similar levels of responsibility, training, skill, and experience.[*]

This tendency is especially pronounced when the jobs under scrutiny are sex-segregated; that is, when 70 percent of the incumbents are of the same gender. In examining the relationship between positional importance (as measured by a factor point evaluation system), job segregation, and pay under the Washington state civil service, Helen Remick concluded that existing rates of return were "separate and unequal."[†] Women employees generally received about 80 percent of the salary obtained by male workers for positions with an equivalent number of points. These results are echoed in studies by labor economists which frequently report a tendency for such wage differentials to persist after controlling for individual differences in productivity-related characteristics.[‡]

Despite the emergence of this issue as a social policy concern of some consequence, there seem to be no studies that examine the attitudes of administrators with responsibilities for its implementation and, where necessary, for designing appropriate programs. Such neglect is significant since newer programs, in the words of Sabatier and Mazmanian, "require implementors who are not merely neutral but sufficiently persistent to develop new regulations and standard operating procedures, and to enforce them in the face of resistance from target groups and from public officials reluctant to make the mandated changes." Personnel administrators are especially important in this regard since they assume a major role in the preparation of job analyses, classification plans, and compensation packages which would be directly affected by the adoption of a comparable worth policy.

. . . Do these administrators agree that women's jobs are typically undervalued in the marketplace? [T]o what extent is comparable wage legislation favored by local governmental personnelists? Whether these attitudes are shaped by the legal, institutional, organizational, or personal background characteristics of the personnel managers is also considered. Significant relationships are then controlled for managerial perceptions of financial barriers and the possibility of opposition from labor organizations or rank and file employees.

. . . Since the fundamental problem leading to proposals for comparable worth legislation is sex-based wage inequality which has become institutionalized over the years, our respondents are asked to consider a variety of alternative corrective strategies that might involve less controversy and/or expense. Of particular concern is whether this type of policy problem is best handled by legislation, administrative action, or judicial decree. Relevant policy implications are discussed in the concluding section.

I. Research Expectations

Whether personnel managers in local government are favorably predisposed toward wage equity legislation is generally unclear. For some of them comparable worth issues are best viewed within the context of progressive social policy; that is, strong action is

[*]E. H. Phelps-Brown, *The Inequality of Pay* (Berkeley, Calif.: University of California Press, 1977); David L. Featherman and Robert M. Hauser, "Sexual Inequalities and Socioeconomic Achievement in the U.S., 1962–1973," *American Sociological Review* 41 (June 1976): 462–483.

[†]Helen Remick, "The Comparable Worth Controversy," *Public Personnel Management Journal* 19 (Winter 1981): 371–383.

[‡]See, e.g., Francine D. Blau, *Equal Pay in the Office* (Lexington, Mass.: Lexington Books, 1977); Charles N. Halaby, "Sexual Inequality in the Workplace: An Employer-Specific Analysis of Pay Differences," *Social Science Research* 8 (March 1979): 79–104.

needed to overcome economic inequities rooted in long-standing social mores and institutional practices. On the other hand, administrative support may be diluted by a preference for alternative values such as economic efficiency or employee fairness. Personnelists, for example, may be sympathetic to the philosophical rationale for comparable wage legislation but frightened by the financial implications of corrective adjustments during a period of shrinking revenues and general fiscal austerity. Finally, the issue of fairness is likely to arise if the recommended program calls for a combination of selected wage hikes for women and a freeze on the pay of comparable occupational classes dominated by men. The latter concerns prompted some urban leaders such as Mayors Coleman Young and Richard Hatcher to remark that the impact of comparable worth on the collective bargaining process and the economy as a whole could be troublesome.[*]

Given the absence of attitudinal research on comparable worth policy issues, specific research expectations are largely based on evidence gleaned from studies of related policy areas, such as affirmative action. The importance of both environmental and personal background characteristics in shaping perceptions of administrative actors toward these subjects has been consistently demonstrated in the literature. One such influence is the presence or absence of a statute which cloaks an otherwise risky point of view with an aura of greater respectability.[†] Population size and governmental form may likewise affect the local policy agenda and subsequent policy actions; for instance, a number of researchers have found an empirical link between urbanization and mayor-council governmental systems on the one hand and greater receptivity to redistributive policy issues. In short, we expect to find greater support for comparable worth among personnel managers residing in states with such legislation in place and in local jurisdictions characterized by increasing population and a mayor-council form of government.

Managerial attitudes may also be affected by the adoption of related personnel policies. However, the specific effects of a collective bargaining system or an affirmative action program on perceptions of comparable worth are difficult to foresee. For example, a strong endorsement for more equitable job restructuring has been received from the leadership of the largest public sector union, the American Federation of State, County, and Municipal Employees (AFSCME). On the other hand, the political price for implementing a comparable worth policy may well entail a temporary freeze or short-term "scaling back" of wage increases for governmental employees in male-dominated occupations to permit those in historically underpaid job slots an opportunity to catch up. Since labor leaders retain support on the basis of an ability to provide continuing pay and benefit increases to their members, it is not hard to envision a gap between accepting comparable worth conceptually and the actual negotiations required to achieve a settlement acceptable to all parties.

On the other hand, there is greater reason to expect support for wage equity issues in communities with an affirmative action program in place. With collective bargaining systems, the expression of pro-comparable views is complicated by the prospective conflict between varying interpretations of employee fairness. However, the possibility of philosophical compatibility is enhanced if the notion of equal employment opportunity, which prompted the use of affirmative action programs to foster the recruitment and selection of women and minority job candidates, is extended to include financial compensation on the job as well. Both policies, after all, are essentially designed to reduce sources of employment discrimination rooted deeply in institutional patterns of work. A link between programs-in-place and support is further suggested by a recent study which found a significant relationship between the presence of an affirmative action plan and a favorable inclination toward such issues among urban personnel administrators.[‡]

[*]John H. Bunzel, "To Teach According to Her Worth?" *The Public Interest* 67 (Spring 1982): 77–93.

[†]Theodore L. Becker and Malcolm M. Feeley, *The Impact of U.S. Supreme Court Decisions* (New York: Oxford University Press, 1973).

[‡]Charles E. Davis and Jonathan P. West, "Implementing Public Programs: Equal Employment Opportunity, Affirmative Action, and Administrative Policy Options," *Review of Public Personnel Administration* 4 (Summer 1984): 16–30.

Finally, the potential importance of personal background characteristics in helping to account for attitudes toward comparable worth cannot be ignored. On one level, it seems plausible to assume the administrators perceive wage equity measures within a framework of social liberalism. Thompson and Browne, for example, concluded that a more liberal stance on several sociopolitical issues was associated with support for the recruitment of minorities as were sex and professionalism.[*] Attitudes toward comparable worth may thus be shaped by a general belief that corrective action is required to redress prior job discrimination against women. Such views may also be reinforced by expectations of gain or loss.[†] Hence we expect to find women personnel managers to be more supportive of wage equity issues than men and other background attributes — education and income — to be negatively associated with support.

II. Data

The data used in our research were obtained from questionnaires mailed to personnel directors in 1,026 municipalities. A sample stratified by geographic region and city population size was drawn from a membership roster of the International Personnel Management Association (IPMA) and a separate listing in the 1982 Municipal Yearbook. The dual sampling strategy was necessitated by the underrepresentation of IPMA members in certain regions and political jurisdictions within selected population categories.

The response rate was 35 percent, yielding a final data base of 357 valid cases. In general, a somewhat higher proportion of respondents came from larger cities and from the western region of the United States. As a group, the responding personnel managers were male (73 percent) between 35 and 54 years of age

(55 percent), and had earnings of greater than $20,000 annually (86 percent). Sixty percent had completed post-graduate training and the same proportion had more than ten years experience in the public sector.

III. Findings

We initially sought to examine the general level of support for comparable worth issues among local personnel managers. . . . [T]he data reveals moderate support (67 percent) for the premise that traditionally female jobs are "typically undervalued" in relation to present pay scales while slightly better than half (52 percent) favor expanding the concept of "equal pay for equal jobs" to include "equal pay for comparable jobs." Attitudes toward one are significantly associated with the other (gamma = +.34); that is, personnelists who perceive gender-based wage inequities tend to be more supportive of a comparable worth policy.

The relationships between contextual factors and managerial attitudes toward comparable worth are summarized in Table 12.1. In general, results are mixed. As expected, jurisdictional population size was found to be moderately associated with support; that is, personnel managers in metropolitan areas tend to be more favorably inclined toward comparable worth than their counterparts in smaller communities. This lends additional weight to the generalization that women, as a group, tend to receive a more sympathic hearing from urban policymakers; other studies have established a link between city size and the proportion of female employees[‡] and the adoption of newer, more objective forms of job analysis.[§] On the other hand, the data indicate that individual perceptions of wage equity issues are largely unaffected by the presence or absence of a state policy or by the form of government.

The data presented in Table 12.1 also indicate that having an affirmative action program or collective bargaining system in place provides a decision-making

---

[*]Frank J. Thompson and Bonnie Browne, "Commitment of the Disadvantaged among Urban Administrators: The Case of Minority Hiring," *Urban Affairs Quarterly* 13 (March 1978): 355–377.

[†]Charles E. Davis and Jonathan P. West, "Support for Affirmative Action in a Metropolitan Bureaucracy: An Analysis of Nonminority Administrators," in Steven W. Hays and Richard C. Kearney, eds., *Public Personnel Administration: Problems and Prospects* (Englewood Cliffs, N.J.: Prentice-Hall, 1983), 262–273.

[‡]John T. Marlin, "City Affirmative Action Efforts," *Public Administration Review* 37 (September/October 1977): 508–511.

[§]Gary Craver, "Job Evaluation Practices in State and County Government," in Harold Suskin, ed., *Job Evaluation and Pay Administration in the Public Sector* (Chicago: International Personnel Management Association, 1977), 427–441.

Table 12.1 Relationships of Contextual Factors, Institutional Policies, and Personal Background Characteristics to Support for Comparable Worth among Local Personnel Managers

	Support for Comparable Worth	
	Equal Pay for Comparable Jobs?	Womens' Jobs Are Typically Undervalued?
Contextual Factors		
Presence of State Comparable Worth Law	.06[a]	−.12
Governmental Form[b]	.08[c]	.05
Population Size	.33**	.30**
Institutional Policies		
Presence of an Affirmative Action Program	−.30*	−.15
Presence of Formal Collective Bargaining Arrangements	−.14	−.16
Personal Background Characteristics		
Sex	−.33	−.41*
Age	−.05	.17
Education	.08	−.05
Salary	.28**	.52**
Public Sector Experience	.07	.26**
(N = 357)		

  * Statistically significant at the .05 level.
 ** Statistically significant at the .01 level.
    a. *Gamma* coefficient.
    b. Coded as 1 = mayor-council, 2 = council-manager, and 3 = other.
    c. Cramer's *V* is employed as the statistical measure of association since governmental form is a nominal variable.

climate that is somewhat unfavorable to proponents of comparable worth issues. Although the strength of the bivariate pairings is not sufficiently pronounced to achieve statistical significance in three of the four relationships examined, the direction of these findings is uniform. In other words, there is a slightly greater tendency for public personnel managers residing in communities without either policy to express support for comparable worth.

Our third set of independent variables redirects attention from the environmental or policy characteristics of communities to the managers' personal background characteristics. A glance at the associa-

tions between socioeconomic indicators and comparable worth issues does not reveal a clear trend (see Table 12.1). Educational attainment is not related to either issue position. Nor did we find evidence of a generation gap. Younger respondents and those with less governmental experience are somewhat more likely to agree that women's jobs are undervalued but do not differ significantly on the issue of expanding the concept of equal pay for equal work to include equal pay for work of comparable value. On the other hand, salary level of public personnel managers is moderately associated with support, thus suggesting that the subjective calculus of gain or loss from the implementation of a comparable worth policy is of some importance. This interpretation is reinforced by a glance at the relationships between gender and issue positions. Not surprisingly, women administrators tend to be more supportive of comparable worth than their male counterparts.

Controlling for Financial and Political Barriers

Assuming that policy-related attitudes are occasionally shaped by an assessment of what is feasible as well as by the merits of a given issue, we decided to test significant bivariate relationships for both economic and organizational factors, using partial *gamma* coefficients (see Table 12.2 . . .). Control variables included the perceived importance of (a) the financial costs of implementing comparable worth legislation, (b) opposition from public sector labor organizations, and (c) opposition from rank and file employees. The data generally indicate that the associations of contextual, institutional, and personal background characteristics with either wage equity issue are largely unaffected when attitudes toward prospective financial and political barriers are held constant.

Preferred Options for Attaining Wage Equity Objectives

While support for comparable worth among those with implementional responsibilities is a useful—if not essential—precondition for the attainment of policy objectives, it represents but one piece of a much larger puzzle. Political as well as administrative acceptance is required, and the critical question of economic resources must be considered in determining the most appropriate means of achieving wage equity within personnel systems and the institutional arenas where decisions are made. [Also] personnel administrators opt for a less activist approach. An in-depth study of the personnel classification system is supported by most respondents while a somewhat lower proportion tends to favor expanded use of factor-based methods of job analysis and evaluation.

Table 12.2 Relationships of Contextual, Institutional, and Personal Background Characteristics to Agreement among Local Personnel Managers that Women's Jobs Are Typically Undervalued, Controlling for Perceptions of Financial Barriers and Opposition from Labor Organizations or Rank-and-File Employees

Contextual, Institutional, and Personal Background Characteristics	Bivariate Relationships	First Order Gamma Controls		
	B1	C1	C2	C3
Population Size	.30	.27	.29	.27
Sex	−.41	−.36	−.35	−.40
Salary	.52	.42	.52	.52
Public Sector Experience	.26	.28	.30	.23

(N = 357)

B1: Women's jobs are typically undervalued in the marketplace (agree-disagree).

C1: Do you think financial costs are a major barrier to the passage of comparable worth legislation, somewhat troublesome, or of little consequence?

C2: Do you think that opposition from public sector labor organizations is a major barrier to the passage of comparable worth legislation, somewhat troublesome, or of little consequence?

C3: Do you think that opposition from rank-and-file employees is a major barrier to the passage of comparable worth legislation, somewhat troublesome, or of little consequence?

A surprisingly small number of individuals surveyed selected either the legislative strategy or class action lawsuits as the most appropriate means of addressing comparable worth issues. In short, our data reveal a pattern of uncertainty about this issue which is reflected in the rather conservative distribution of preferred options.

IV. Summary and Conclusion

We initially sought to examine the degree of support for comparable worth among local governmental personnel managers and the kinds of strategies preferred for dealing with discriminatory job classification systems. Generally speaking, administrators agree that women's jobs are undervalued but are somewhat less inclined to favor the inclusion of equal pay for work of comparable value. Proponents of comparable worth are more apt to live in larger cities and in communities lacking an affirmative action plan or a collective bargaining agreement. On the basis of background characteristics, supporters include a disproportionate number of women as well as managers within the lower end of the salary range. These results were not appreciably altered by controls for managerial perceptions of financial or political barriers to the implementation of comparable worth policies.

What do our findings suggest for the prospect of greater managerial involvement in comparable worth policymaking processes? The distribution of respondent attitudes toward wage equity policy options reveals a marked preference for an administrative rather than a legislative or judicial approach to problem resolution. While this response is self-serving to some extent, there are a number of advantages to the utilization of local personnel administrators as the initial point of entry in the development of a comparable worth policy.

First, it is evident that personnelists (in comparison with most legislators and judges) have the appropriate training to undertake a thorough examination of the merits and shortcomings of a comparable worth program. Analyzing the relative worth of jobs, is, after all, a matter of assessing the usefulness of existing job classification structures within a given jurisdiction. Such an analysis could aid in structuring subsequent discussion or debate of alternative programmatic responses within the executive branch by indicating the degree of inequality within the system and the number and magnitude of changes required to bring about the desired balance.

A technically sound study of the job classification system might also lay the foundation for a political response based upon the need for administrative reform rather than an impromptu reaction to the demands of a particular constituency group. . . . It is often easier to fashion a legislative majority on behalf of a broad, recurring issue in state and local politics such as civil service reform than a redistributive social policy issue with clearly identifiable winners and losers. In short, our analysis suggests that personnelists may indeed be able and willing to play a constructive role in the development and/or implementation of gender-based wage equity policy options. However, the extent of their actual influence in this process will depend on the interaction of political, economic, and sociological forces operating outside the administrative arena and on the nature and direction of their own strategic calculations.

Employers—and one suspects most particularly personnel managers—probably lose as much sleep over the problem of discrimination as over any single issue they face. But the universality and seriousness of the problem have stimulated consultants to specialize in advising managers how to avoid such problems. And the standard journals for managers carry articles stating steps that management can take to avoid these problems. Here is one such article. As you read it put yourself in the position of a manager looking for ways to avoid discrimination charges. Do you feel the following suggestions are practical, that is, doable? If so, do you think practicing these suggestions would actually reduce the tensions or attitudes that might trigger a racial or sexual discrimination charge?

Coping with Anti-Discrimination Laws[19]

Lester E. Mood
Administrative Management
July, 1980: 31

Enforcement of anti-discrimination laws has been part of the employment scene ever since the introduction of Title VII. This part of the 1964 Civil Rights Act prohibiting discrimination in employment because of race, religion, sex, national origin, or ancestry, set up the Equal Employment Opportunity Commission, which enforces Title VII. At least 38 states and many city governments also have agencies that administer similar laws. Consequently, few managers will avoid an investigation conducted by at least one of these agencies.

Despite some local variations in jurisdisction and specific procedures, the system is highly standardized. A complaint is filed, an investigation conducted, and a finding made. In about half the cases, the findings are in favor of the respondent—the employer who has been charged. In those cases, where the finding is in favor of the charging party, an attempt is made to resolve the case through conciliation, a negotiation process. In only a very small percentage of the cases is legal action actually commenced, and only after attempts at negotiations have failed.

Generally speaking, it's the investigation that causes most concern for managers. The expense—in terms of time and resources—required to participate in the investigation is frequently greater than any liability involved. Much of the expense and aggravation can be alleviated when a manager knows what the investigator is seeking and why it is important.

Virtually all agencies have placed restrictions on investigators by defining what constitutes an acceptable investigation. If certain criteria are not met, the investigator must return and obtain additional information until his or her supervisor is satisfied. This is not a litigative process. Lawyers will rarely be in-volved in an investigation unless voluntary cooperation cannot be obtained. Therefore, an understanding of the investigator's needs is frequently more important than understanding the technicalities of the statute.

Three Categories

All charges of employment discrimination can be broken down into three distinct categories, although many charges will contain elements from more than one category. The first is *Evil Motive*, which simply means a person has done something to another person because of that other's race or sex, etc. It's this area that most laymen think of as discrimination.

This allegation is usually part of many of the charges filed, but is difficult to prove since it requires unmistakable evidence of the motive of the alleged perpetrator. To substantiate, it is necessary for the investigation to show that the person accused was disposed to discriminate. One form of proof is documented use of derogatory racial statements or epithets.

It should be noted that the documented use of *racial slurs* by a representative of the employer—or by co-workers where tolerated by the employer—is a violation in and of itself. This applies to *sexual harassment*. The only defense is to show that as soon as the employer became aware of the activity, immediate action was taken to end it and discipline the persons involved.

In this type of charge, the investigator will also attempt to determine if there has been a history of discriminatory behavior on the part of the person accused, or by the employer generally, revealing a predisposition to discriminate. The investigator would look for evidence, either records or testimony of co-workers, that persons of the same class as the changing party consistently fared worse in their relationship (or treatment) with the accused. This might take the form of a higher discipline rate, higher termination rate, or witnessed acts of harassment.

It is damaging to the charging party's case if it can be shown that other persons of the same class were similarly situated, but were not damaged or subjected to the alleged unfair treatment. This is only true for an Evil Motive charge, where one is dealing with the actions and motivations of an individual.

The investigator will be looking for the following in a charge of this nature:

- Documented use of racial (sexual, etc.) slurs.
- Evidence that employees of the same class as the charging party consistently fared worse than others.
- Testimony of witnesses to apparently racially motivated actions on the part of the person accused.
- Documented history of previous discriminatory behavior on the part of the person or employer accused.

The second category of discrimination is much more common: the *Differential Treatment* charge. It means that an individual is treated differently than persons of another class have been treated under similar circumstances.

This is the most frequent type of charge filed and investigated. It also places the greatest burden on the respondent because of the need to base the investigation on comparative evidence from company records. For large employers or large departments, the comparison of records can become extensive and troublesome.

An example best illustrates this type of charge. A black man alleges he was terminated after being absent from work, while whites who were absent were not. Investigation shows that the charging party had missed work five times before being fire for absenteeism. While most whites had fewer absences, several had missed work five or more times and retained their jobs. Barring other factors, these facts would indicate differential treatment.

They key to proving or disproving charges of this nature lies in the comparative evidence. In the example cited, this consists of attendance records and race of other employees, and records indicating the treatment they received. Every investigator is required to seek evidence comparing what happened to the charging party with what happened to other employees.

An error many managers make in trying to defend themselves against a charge of this nature is to assume that a comparison can be made between treatment of the charging party and company policy. In the example, the policy might have been to terminate after five absences. But if some whites were allowed to surpass this and the charging party was not, it still would have been a case of differential treatment, no matter what the policy. The investigation will probe what actually happened, not what should have happened.

Further, similar circumstances do not necessarily mean identical. The investigator frequently generalizes circumstances in order to obtain a body of data large enough to draw comparisons. If the charging party were fired for absenteeism and there were no other employees with absence records, the investigator might look at persons who had committed the offenses that would ordinarily be grounds for termination. The less similar the circumstances used for comparison, the less solidly based is the case, whether for or against the respondent. This emphasizes the need to keep detailed and accurate records.

An invesigation of Differential Treatment will have to answer the following questions:

- Precisely what happened to the charging party?
- What were the circumstances that gave rise to this action?
- What other employees were in similar circumstances?
- What happened to these other employees?

The third type of charge is concerned with actions that are fair in form and application, but that have a *Disparate Impact*. In this situation, a particular employment mechanism adversely affects a particular racial, sexual, or ethnic group—even though all groups are treated the same.

The best illustration of this comes from the classic court case of *Griggs v. Duke Power Co.* Here, all persons, regardless of race, were required to have a high school diploma to be eligible for certain company promotions. It was shown, however, that in North Carolina where the Duke Power plant was located, 34 percent of the white males had completed high school, while only 12 percent of the black males had done so. Consequently, far fewer blacks were eligible for higher ranking jobs. It was also shown that *high school graduation did not affect the ability of a person to perform the jobs in question*. What was present, then, was a policy that had a negative racial effect without a valid business motive.

The most common applications of this concept is in the area of employment testing. If a required test is shown to have a disparate impact on a particular racial, ethnic, or sexual group, the employer must be able to show it is job related, and no nondiscriminatory alternative is available that would serve the same purpose.

In this context, any preemployment or promotional requirement is considered a test. An example is the use of arrest records, without convictions, for screening. Since blacks, as a class, have significantly higher numbers of arrests without convictions, this is a "test" with a disparate impact—without a valid business motive. Another example is the use of height and weight requirements, which have a tendency to screen out women, where these requirements cannot be shown to be necessary for the successful performance of the job.

One misunderstanding many managers have in this area is that every test must be validated for job relatedness. This is true only when the test has been shown to have a negative impact. If an employer decides to hire the next person coming in wearing brown shoes, this would be an obviously invalid test. But it would not be illegal, since it could not be shown that this would have a disparate effect on any particular group.

As soon as a statistically valid impact has been shown, *the burden of proof in the case shifts to the respondent to prove that the "test" has been validated for job relatedness.* It is not necessary for the investigator to prove that it is not valid; the employer must show that it is. Requirements for validating a test are described in detail in the Federal guidelines, and taken from the standards for educational testing published by the American Psychological Association.

Most of these cases require a statistical analysis determining whether there is significant impact. This means the investigator must obtain information on everyone who has been subject to the mechanism in question, categorize them, then utilize statistical tests to determine the impact. The investigator is not highly concerned with the outcome of any one incident, except as it may relate to another part of the charge.

To complete an investigation of Disparate Impact, an investigator will have to obtain the following:

- Is there a negative impact that is statistically significant?
- What is the mechanism or test that causes this effect?
- Has it been validated for job-relatedness and business necessity?
- Is there a nondiscriminatory alternative available?

Almost every agency administering an antidiscrimination law is required to deliver a copy of each charge to the respondent before commencing an investigation. Due to the backlog of cases with which most agencies are faced, this frequently occurs well in advance. The manager charged should make use of this time to analyze the complaint and evaluate his or her position.

Once the manager has determined the nature of the charge, an internal investigation can be conducted to determine the extent of liability. There are several options available at this point.

The respondent can resist the investigation and refuse to cooperate. This course will almost certainly result in a long, and frequently costly, legal battle which the respondent frequently loses—without ever determining the merits of the charge. *One of the most common mistakes is trying to keep information from the investigator that will usually exonerate.*

Another option available is to simply throw open the doors—and the files—to the investigator. Investigators love this type of respondent because it makes their life easier. The main problem with this particular approach is that a sloppy investigator will simply gather everything in sight and sort out what is needed later.

A better approach is one of informed cooperation. If the manager understands what the charge is about and what will be necessary to prove or disprove it, it is possible to cooperate without running the risk of being taken advantage of. This allows the respondent to protect his rights without running up expenses. In taking this approach, the respondent makes available only those items for which there is justifiable need—preferably in writing. This has the added advantage of increasing the skills of the investigator.

Another option to consider is making an immediate offer of settlement, thus eliminating investigation. Agencies encourage this, since it reduces their workload with a minimum expenditure of time and resources.

Many managers also find this option advantageous because it saves the expense of responding to an investigation. Such settlements are usually quite reasonable. If the respondent is in violation, a settlement made prior to the investigation will almost always be less than what would be negotiated afterwards.

The primary disadvantage is that this approach may encourage other employees to file excessive charges for monetary gain. Another disadvantage: a respondent may end up "paying off" on a case that might otherwise be decided in his or her favor. Even here, however, it may be considered a potential savings because it avoid participating in a lengthy investigation.

A manager should regard every discrimination charge as an individual event. Any action taken should follow an informed analysis of the charge and the individual circumstances. Increased use of this form of redress by disgruntled employees makes it necessary for managers to enter the investigation process with a completely businesslike approach.

Exercises and Questions for Further Thought

1. Public employees are joining unions in increasing numbers. Even in jurisdictions that prohibit public employees from striking, union membership may give employees the benefits of more standardized and equitable grievance procedures. In such cases the collective bargaining agreement between union and management may make the union the employee's representative in a grievance procedure. But what happens if the union in effect concedes that the termination was warranted and refuses to pursue a fired employee's claim to the end? Does the employee's membership in the union waive any rights to notice and hearing? See *Winston and Cummings v. U.S. Postal Service*, 585 F.2d 198 (1978).

(handwritten: (Not now required) Both could be afforded:)

2. Recall Ms. Horowitz, the medical student expelled from the Missouri medical school before earning her degree. Does the fact that she was academically terminated communicate information to the public that will make it harder for her to gain admission to another medical school? On what grounds, if any, should the law offer stronger due process protections to terminated employees than terminated students?

(handwritten: 1. Facts 2. How facts fare w/ standards 3. Prove mistakes occurred.)

3. The personnel administrator for the state of Massachusetts has for years followed the policy of granting a preference to United States veterans in choosing public employees from among many job applicants. Since the vast majority of veterans are males, does this policy constitute illegal sex discrimination? See *Personnel Administrator of Massachusetts v. Feeney*, 99 S. Ct. 2282 (1979).

4. Do you think employers should be able unilaterally to implement drug and alcohol testing of public employees? Or should such a program be negotiated between the unions which represent public employees and the government? See *Johnson-Bateman Co.*, National Labor Relations Board, 295 NLRB No. 26 (1989), and *Minneapolis Star Tribune*, National Labor Relations Board, 295 NLRB No. 63 (1989).

(handwritten: more needs to be shown that it's a good idea.)

5. Affirmative action employment policies are often misunderstood. Many programs seek no more than to equalize racial or sexual balance in employment where occupational tests have little or no predictive power on job performance. Is there any legal or moral objection to such programs? What principles of justice, if any, support such affirmative action policies? In your reflection on such principles of justice as individual liberty, equality of opportunity, or the Marxist notion that from each according to abilities, to each according to needs, consider a range of foundations for social justice.

6. Assume that the Fourth Amendment limits mandatory warrentless drug testing to cases where the employees work in sensitive or dangerous jobs. Would such a rule prevent the state from testing all *applicants* for any position of public employment? Why or why not?

You can treat everyone the same but that does not waive your Constitutional rights.

PART IV
Evaluating Administrative Law

CHAPTER 13

Six Blind People and an Elephant—A Hypothetical Symposium on the Future of Administrative Law

The following transcript reports the remarks of participants in a conference sponsored in May 1990, by the American Administrative Law Association (AALA). The conference, held at a prestigious hotel in Washington, D.C., attracted an audience of over 150. The audience consisted primarily of attorneys practicing privately and with the federal government, but it also included several judges, some representatives of business, teachers of administrative law, and a variety of students.[1]

CHAIR: Good morning. I'm Sandra Mann, Executive Director of the AALA. We are delighted to welcome so many friends of administrative law. I've gotten a preview from our speakers during our breakfast meeting, and I'm confident you will find their remarks provocative. We have asked each of our speakers to talk for about ten minutes. We shall take a short coffee break at that point and then the six will comment on each other's remarks. We'll open it up afterward, time permitting, for questions and comments from the floor.

 Since we have much ground to cover, let me briefly introduce our panelists. On my far right, Professor Ruth Rimhorn, Chenery Professor of Administrative

---

[1] All of the named participants in this hypothetical symposium, their organizational affiliations (except for those of the judge and the congressman), and the AALA are fictitious. Any reader who tries to identify any real-world person or agency will only miss the point of the discussion, which is to set forth a variety of perspectives, criticisms, and hints at solutions to weaknesses in administrative law. Each of the six speakers has a vision of administrative law that is partially, but not entirely, valid.

 The idea for the hypothetical symposium originated from a remarkable conference "Workshop on Teaching Administrative Law," sponsored by the Association of American Law Schools, held March 4–6 1982, at the Hyatt Regency, New Orleans, Louisiana. Some of the ideas in the hypothetical symposium are composite positions inspired by the formal presentations and many informal conversations that occurred during the conference, in which Lief Carter participated. The comments of Richard Stewart, Arthur Bonfield, Antonin Scalia, Martin Shapiro, Paul Verkuil, Clark Byse, Jerry Mashaw, and Peter Barton Hutt proved particularly helpful. Mr. Hutt, former General Counsel of the FDA and now with Covington and Burling, Washington, D.C., inspired comments by Maverick, Smite, and, Horsefield.

Law at the Langdell Law School. Moving left, in space but not ideology, is a man familiar to many of you, Judge William Busselot of the District of Columbia Circuit Court of Appeals. Next to him is the honorable Martin Maverick, member of the U.S. House of Representatives from Austin, Texas. On my immediate left is Stephen Smite, general counsel of the Federal Commerce Administration. Next we have Paula Proffitt, chief executive officer of VitaMax Corporation, the nation's largest producer of over-the-counter health food products. And on the far left, Herbert Horsefield, senior partner in the D.C. law firm of Bovington and Hartman. Professor Rimhorn will lead off.

RIMHORN: When I first received the invitation to join you this morning, I was honored and eager for the chance to step back and look at the whole moving picture that may reveal where administrative law is going. But as I began to prepare, this euphoria gave way first to a quiet anxiety and then to near panic. I realized that I cannot say much about the future of administrative law because I'm not sure I can tell you what administrative law is now, much less where it might go. The field is in a frustrating condition. Sandy referred to us as friends of administrative law, but I must confess to some pretty hostile and belligerent feelings toward it. Trying to predict the future of administrative law is a little bit like hearing the first two or three notes of an entirely unfamiliar song and then having to predict where the rest of the notes in the melody will fall. So instead of making predictions I shall explain why I find prediction so difficult. There are two basic reasons.

The first reason is not unique to the field. *Administrative law* is an umbrella term like many terms in law such as *tort* or *criminal law*. It would make much more sense to talk about the future of no-fault insurance or the future of punishment for sex offenders than to talk about the future of something so general as tort law or criminal law, and the same is true of administrative law. The field encompasses everything from disciplinary procedures in schools to the legality of OSHA's or the NRC's or the EPA's rules for entire industries covering highly complex and scientifically open-ended matters. The label may encompass too much to be meaningful.

The second problem *is* unique to administrative law. The more I study and teach in the field the more I realize that, unlike tort law or contract law, administrative law has failed to develop core principles around which to focus the debate. We *could* intelligently discuss the future of tort law or contract law because these fields have centers, cores, like the principle of consideration in contract law, the principle of personal responsibility in tort, or the principle in property that emphasizes the need to preserve the integrity of title. Where would criminal law be without the principle of criminal intent? The principle by itself doesn't resolve cases, but it focuses the search for specific rules and decisions. Principles give us the security of an unquestioned moral starting point. Administrative law today possesses few such principles.

Now you may say to yourself that rulemaking and adjudication and the constitutional distinction between them provide the principles we need. Indeed the Supreme Court had given us the beginnings of such a tool in cases like *Goldberg* and *Sindermann*. And the APA seems to reinforce that principle. But the Court today seems busily trying to balance such principles down to nothing. At least that's what I get from *Mathews*, *Bishop v. Wood* and *Loudermill*. Even the old standby, the *Bi-Metallic/Londoner* distinction between rulemaking and adjudication, has fallen apart as we find adjudication settings that require no administrative due process, like school spanking, and some rulemaking settings that affect specific interests and do therefore require some due process. To make matters worse, the Court seems bent on evaporating away primary Bill of Rights protections. I refer to cases like *INS v. Lopez-Mendoza*, which dilute search and seizure and self-incrimination protections. I admit courts are making some progress in governmental tort liability, but I still find it difficult to justify the amount of governmental immunity that remains.

Administrative law ought to be a search for coherent theories of public decision-making and problem-solving. As such it ought to contain principles as do other fields of law and policy. We ought to possess some principles that state in a plausible way why, if Kelly deserves a pretermination hearing, officer Bishop doesn't. About the only explanation we get is that Bishop could go on welfare. Such a view fails to realize that treating Bishop fairly has value in its own right and that dismissing him from the force surely could hurt him by hindering his chances for a job in the future.

I can't say where administrative law is going if I'm not sure it exists. Yes, we can identify a trend. We find it in what we might call the retreat cases, cases like *Vermont Yankee* and *Chevron v NRDC*, but the trend only reinforces the idea that the field does not exist, as Gertrude Stein said of Oakland, "there is no there, there." Rather than helping create moral confidence, rather than playing a leadership role in the face of highly complex issues, the Court seems to be giving up because it can't find easy and obvious principles. What does it want, a silver platter?

Now if there is any cure to this ailment, and I think it a serious ailment indeed, it seems to me it must come from Congress and state legislatures. If Congress could take the lead by legislating wisely and in detail, as it surely has not in the Freedom of Information Act, Occupational Safety and Health Act, and many parts of the APA itself, attorneys and their clients, agencies and their staffs could function more efficiently and effectively. Society needs to develop a consensus about deep value problems, such as fairness in school discipline, and legislatures are the proper place to do the job. The same democratic premise calls for clarity and direction in liquor laws, zoning laws, policies to reduce the mayhem caused by drunk drivers on the highway, and other state and local policy matters. Legislatures must provide administrative principles or I fear we must prepare to live with pallid, judge-made mush.

I fear this prospect because societies need to maintain a collective sense of morality in order to survive. In the modern state the bureaucracy dominates. If we lose confidence that government can operate on a morally acceptable foundation, I fear society is doomed to disillusion and decay.

CHAIR: Thank you, Professor Rimhorn. Let me say that I found your remarks not just provocative. They are downright scary. Judge Busselot, you need no introduction.

BUSSELOT: I do appreciate the chance to share ideas with you this morning. It is refreshing to appear before many of you in, if you'll pardon the expression, a disrobed condition for a change. At the outset let me pick up on several implications of Professor Rimhorn's remarks. First, I appreciate her candor and I shall try to identify and voice my own deepest thoughts and concerns as she has. Second, I certainly agree that Congress could make our lives easier by giving us clearer statutory law. I agree that the results of legislative deliberations often give little guidance, and I would urge legislative reform. However, in my years on the bench I have come to learn that statutory ambiguity tends to come with the territory, and I am not holding my breath waiting for reform to occur.

It is easy in thinking about a subject like administrative law to focus exclusively or at least heavily on the United States Supreme Court and its doctrines. After all, the Court does state controlling law for the nation, and its opinions are, for better or worse, what teachers feel obliged to teach. But frankly, I believe we overemphasize the impact and significance of the Supreme Court. At the same time, the work of the lower courts gets less attention than it deserves. After all, the large bulk of administrative law cases in litigation never reach the Supreme Court.

But there's another reason not to take the Court too seriously. Lower court judges, particularly those on my bench whose docket administrative law cases dominate, are neither dummies nor slavish subordinates to the High Court. We and our clerks read the law reviews. When a case like *Vermont Yankee* comes along and its reasoning fails to persuade, we can in future instances usually find legal ways to distinguish it. In other words, judges and practitioners working in the trenches just don't find either the absence of principles or the uncertain line of Supreme Court precedent so terribly bothersome. A judge who is worth anything soon learns that his role is primarily that of problem solver. Indeed I agree with Professor Howard of Johns Hopkins University whose study of three federal appellate circuits, including our own, finds that the problem-solving attitude shows up rather strongly.[2] A lot of what we do simply exploits the loose framework the Congress and Court have given us in order to reach what strike us as acceptable solutions to often difficult and intractable problems. We have considerable discretion within the present state of administrative law and, frankly, I like it that way. It is just that flexibility that allows the lower courts to require a full hearing in a complex pollution case without getting bogged down requiring the same expensive and time-consuming process in minor matters such as the imposition of routine fines for small oil spills by the Coast Guard.

But now let me describe two kinds of problems that cause me difficulty, problems that I'm not sure we have solved very effectively. These tend to be at opposite ends of the spectrum. At one end, and these are often, but not always, relatively insignificant cases from a public policy point of view, we have situations where something subtle leads you to suspect that an official wasn't really paying attention to the law and the facts in the case. Maybe the subject matter in the case is prone

---

[2]J. Woodford Howard, *Courts of Appeals in the Federal Judicial System* (Princeton, N.J.: Princeton University Press, 1981).

to improper political pressures and influences. Maybe the complaining party is from an unpopular minority, or for other reasons the case resembles instances where deciders tend to jump to conclusions too quickly. What bothers me in such cases is that, while the record (or the very absence of a record, as in the *Overton Park* case) has an odor about it, simply running through the litany of *Goldberg* requirements, requirements for a full hearing on the record and so on, won't necessarily correct the problem. That is, even when the agency follows many due process protections it is not clear that the substantive outcomes are any fairer to the citizen. If we reverse and give the citizen a second shot, that citizen may or may not win, but even when he or she wins and the agency adopts a more thorough procedure in future cases, it's not clear they don't just manipulate the procedure to get the results they want. Al Kahn, to his great credit, blew the whistle over at the CAB, where that sort of thing was going on.

So I often think the best kind of administrative law comes not from judges perfunctorily humming the *Goldberg* variations but from judges who dig deeply into the record, who go past formalities and satisfy themselves that the agency has made the most sensible decision under the circumstances. And in most cases we can usually tell when that has happened.

The problem at the other end is what to do when judges can't tell what's sensible because nobody can—cases where the evidence is not just complex but fundamentally unsettled, unresolved. In such cases when I don't know an answer, digging into the record won't help because all you find there are two or more attorneys arguing about things they don't understand any better than I do. How can you make "correct" law about benzene? It could be the most harmful thing since Thalidomide. My heavens, some evidence exists that high tension electric lines set up a magnetic field that can harm those who live near them. Socrates said that wisdom is the recognition of how much one does not know.[3] I often think this is the only wisdom I possess, but when I look at the record in such cases I get the feeling that the administrators are just as much in the dark as I. I am saying, in other words, that where an agency's authority and reason for being depends on its expertise, courts should find some reason in the record to believe that expertise has been put to good use before accepting the agency's conclusion. In the case of benzene and the need for protection from the risks of toxic chemicals, the scientific state of the art is really primitive. There are, I am told, Democratic and Republican risk-assessment models. The one you use determines the result you get. About all you can say in such cases is that judicial assessment of policy probably, on the average of all the cases, won't make worse policy because it's a toss-up anyway. At least the threat of judicial intervention can work to keep bureaucrats honest and prevent some litigation from happening in the first place.

Well, I hope my effort to be candid hasn't shocked you. I shall stop now and look forward to the discussion later.

---

[3] This sentence is a direct quote from Judge David Bazelon, whom in nearly all respects Judge Busselot is not designed to resemble. See *International Harvester v. Ruckelshaus*, 478 F.2d 615 (1973).

CHAIR: Thank you very much, Judge Busselot. It is now my pleasure indeed to introduce Congressman Maverick, one of the great legislative legends of our time.

MAVERICK: You all probably have heard that my reputation as a Texas liberal sort of fits my name. That's true, but it's pure coincidence, folks, I assure you. The professor and the judge have given you some deep and candid ideas to think about, and I'll try to do the same. Let me give you some straight shooting descriptions about the ways of the United States Congress, descriptions you don't always read in textbooks.

First off, the professor is going to have to wait till hell freezes over before she will get the kind of clear and principled statutory language that will solve modern administrative law problems. The reasons are simple. If we in Congress knew what the policy ought to be and could agree on what it ought to be and knew how to put the ideas in plain words, we would do it, assuming we did anything at all, of course. The reason for all the vague statutes floating around is either that nobody in Congress knows what to do, or that nobody agrees. Often all we agree about is that we would rather have an agency take the time to figure out what to do than take all the time to do it ourselves.

You see, Congress just isn't designed to operate in a way that turns out detailed, clear, consistent, and scientifically sound policy at the level you're talking about. I don't mean this as a criticism, either. Most of the people I know in the Congress, in the House particularly, work hard and honestly. And, despite what you read in the press, the pay for the amount of effort most of us put in and for the responsibilities we bear is so low now relative to business and law practice that I fear the caliber may decline and turnover increase. But I digress. What happens is that the incentive system in Congress pushes us toward either of two extremes.

The incentive system I'm talking about is getting reelected, which is of course just what representation is all about. But the desire to get reelected means we have to spend some time on the big issues that everybody knows about and that have to get resolved by deadlines. I'm talking about things like the budget. Of course right now the budget is all tied in with what we do about the deficit, which has everybody confused and worried. And then of course we struggle with defense policy and nuclear weapons. Of course the committee system and to some extent the party leadership divides the labor and makes the load more manageable. But we all serve on several subcommittees, and of course big budget decisions can involve all of us. Besides, when the White House calls you on something and people in the press are clamoring for statements, it takes a lot of emotional energy for us to handle these pressures.

The rest of time we tend to spend at the other extreme, trying to take care of the complaints of the folks back home. Thirty or forty years ago, probably a third of the seats in Congress, particularly in the South, were safe seats. Reelection didn't pose any threat to a Sam Rayburn or a Wilbur Mills or an Everett Dirksen, and they could spend a lot of time putting together acceptable national policies. Today hardly anyone has a safe seat. The two-party system is more competitive and voters less predictable, and this means a person who wants to get reelected simply has to work harder at helping the folks at home. Often this is little stuff, but it's time-consuming. I know of one case where the trade negotiators agreed to eliminate the duty on imported water chestnuts. Well, it turned out that a couple of fellows in my district had invested thousands of dollars to develop the only producing water chestnut farm in the United States and the trade agreement would bankrupt them. They went to their Senator, and the Senator's staff got that part of the trade agreement removed.

And here's another interesting change. Nearly all of us have computer hookups in our offices and we get a lot more information about how proposed legislation would affect folks back home, and we can't ignore that.

Congress has always wanted to duck the hot moral issues, like school desegregation, but today it's getting harder to see the forest because more effective constituent pressure gets us all the more interested in looking at the trees. As a result, and it is unfortunate, the Congress is often paralyzed. Individual representatives try to do what's best for their constituents, and this seems morally right, but the collective result is people scrambling for their own angle so much that you can't put together the coalition to pass the bill at all, or when you do the bill only passes the buck to the agency. And sometimes we make plain dumb mistakes, like the time the House voted down a fine bill to improve information on the labels of over-the-counter health aids because the docket got confused and the majority of the members on the floor thought they were voting against a law to extend daylight savings time.

Increasing constituent responsiveness of course means that when an interest back home stands to lose before an agency, particularly in a major rulemaking situation like the FTC's efforts to limit children's television advertising, representatives are going to do what they can to help clients out. Believe me, there's no realistic way courts are going to eliminate ex parte contacts in major rulemaking cases. There's just too much at stake.

So practical legislative politics often blocks us from getting real hands-on control of the administrative process. But a fundamental constitutional confusion keeps us off balance, too. So far nobody today has said much about the role of the president in controlling administrative choices. Doesn't a Ronald Reagan or a George Bush have some constitutional power to shape administrative policy, policy made by the executive branch? After all, we haven't created a completely independent fourth branch of government, here. Unfortunately, the Constitution isn't very clear about how much the president can behave like "the commander in chief" toward executive agencies. So this nagging feeling persists that if Congress can control the administrative process, so can the president.

To put this another way, if the president (or, say, the Office of Management and Budget) has some constitutional power to act here, can't the president get on the phone with someone like the secretary of agriculture and, in a completely ex parte way, order the secretary to issue certain policies or squelch others? That sounds logical, and it causes no problem in Congress when you have one party controlling both the White House and the Hill. But it's like poking at a nest of yellow jackets when a Democratic Congress knows damn well that a Republican president like Reagan might just love to start dismantling the very regulatory protections of health and the environment the Democrats have fought for since the New Deal just by getting on the phone and making a few calls.

So bottom line is the agencies have potentially two bosses, plus the courts looking over their shoulders and making them act like courts a lot of the time, and you end up with a standoff. This basic constitutional confusion inclines us to take issues one at a time, with a lot of compromises with all the interests concerned, rather than provoking a constitutional confrontation with the White House.[4]

I'll just make two more points. Many of the toughest issues today depend on complicated scientific data. A lot of folks are under the impression that the legislature is the place to get all the data and analyze it. Well, for the reasons I've given, the incentives just don't make us care to do that. About all we do is find some scientific study to throw in to support the conclusion we've already reached, which is very different from weighing the evidence in an open-minded way. Of course much science, particularly what passes for "policy evaluation research" is really bad, and even when it's done well, the agencies and the courts are much more likely to act on it than the Congress.

Finally, I think the search for administrative justice really matters. As we become more and more bureaucratized at federal and state levels, administrative justice becomes more and more important, just as important as fairness and justice in criminal law. Justice comes down to a few simple things. One of my staff gave me a copy of something Dean Paul Verkuil of the Tulane Law School wrote: "Administrative procedure should be concerned with the overall fairness and accuracy of decisions, with their efficiency and low-cost resolution, and, in a democratic society, with participant satisfaction with the process."[5] I think this kind of justice is more attainable than many people seem to think. Cynicism is the biggest threat we face because it produces a powerful self-fulfilling prophecy. But, as Faulkner said, people aren't evil, they just don't have enough sense. There are ways to help make policy more fairly and efficiently and accurately. I supported the efforts of my friend, John Moss who, as a Congressman, struggled to improve the system. But in the short run the search for justice is up to you folks, lawyers, administrators, and judges, because Congress isn't going to give you much help.

Well, thanks for your attention. Thank God I was raised a Texan. A maverick like me couldn't get reelected anywhere else.

CHAIR: Thank you, Congressman. I'd vote to reelect an honest man like you any time. Next we shall hear from Steve Smite, General Counsel of the Federal Commerce Administration (FCA). Steve.

SMITE: Let me begin by thanking Sandy Mann for sparing us from the vapid and often long-winded introductions of speakers so common at events such as this. I

---

[4]See Martin Shapiro, *Who Guards the Guardians?* (Athens: University of Georgia, 1988), esp. 108–112, *infra* 526.

[5]Paul Verkuil, "The Emerging Concept of Administrative Procedure," *Columbia Law Review* 78 (1978): 279. See also Christopher F. Edley, Jr., *Administrative Law* (New Haven: Yale University Press, 1990).

wish I could claim a connection, coincidental or otherwise, between my name and my role as does the congressman. Unfortunately we at the FCA too often feel the political forces squeeze and frustrate our power to regulate in the public interest. I'll come back to this in a minute because I believe the courts unintentionally support and reinforce the capacity of private interests to frustrate the making of sound public policy.

Let me start by taking one step further Judge Busselot's suggestion, in which I generally concur, that we should downplay the importance of the Supreme Court. We are a pretty typical regulatory agency and I maintain that in the typical case before our agency you can forget about the courts and administrative law altogether. Sure, our authorizing statute is vague, but over the years we and the industries we affect have come to agree about what our role is and how we should go about performing it. In the typical case we get a complaint, we check it out informally, and if the complaint uncovers something pretty serious we can usually convince the business or businesses at which the complaint is directed to make a change. In the majority of cases no one ever mentions the APA or goes crying to the court about some ex parte conversation at the golf club. Usually what we work out is plausibly beneficial in the long run to all concerned. And even when companies don't like it, they often feel they can't afford the adverse publicity that might come from fighting the case. So, we work something out.

I have just described the typical case, but that doesn't mean I think a conference like this is a waste of time. The current state of administrative law deeply troubles me because in a minority of cases it causes unnecessary complications. For starters I take issue with Judge Busselot's rather cavalier attitude toward the absence of administrative law principles. We are now under a recent legislative mandate, the Widget Control Act of 1981, to seek ways of improving the design and safety record of widgets. Congress hasn't used the magic words, so we have to decide what shape the hearings, if any, will take. The courts simply haven't given us any kind of rule, guide, principle, or whatever that will let us get on with the job. I have nightmares where, after a year of work on widgets, some court tells us to go back and do it over a different way. That just wastes taxpayers' money.

The same lack of clarity causes problems at the level of state and local administration, though the problems are a little different. The principal at my daughter's middle school knows I'm in this line of work and collared me after a PTA meeting last year. He had, somewhat belatedly, but this is how things get disseminated, read about *Goss v. Lopez*, which requires some kind of presuspension hearing. "What kind of hearing?" he asked me. He was full of intelligent questions. He wanted to know whether you could isolate disciplinary problem students in a cubicle for a week and avoid the hearing requirement. He's concerned about how public suspension procedures might affect other students and student discipline in general. He is aware of the availability of new drugs that may really help hyperactive children who cause trouble. It is of course encouraging that he is thinking about these things, but ultimately the law should try to help answer them, and it's failing in that important responsibility.

My other complaint is probably more serious. Congressman Maverick spoke of the incentive system in Congress, quite accurately from what I observed over the years. He correctly suggests that the bureaucratic incentive system is better suited to the systematic development of justifiable policy that looks realistically at the data, whatever it may be worth, and weighs fairness and efficiency effectively. Agencies are like any other human organization. They contain people of all kinds, competent and incompetent, creative and rigid, with all sorts of human strengths and weaknesses, but in a properly led organization they can roughly share a sense of the organization's mission and try to contribute to it. When a major regulatory issue comes along and the corporations and lobbies start dragging their feet and putting up a fight, suddenly the vagueness in administrative law puts a cloud over the whole enterprise that undercuts the quality of what we do. This is because lawyers can use the uncertainties as a delaying and obstructing weapon. The credible threat to take us to court and force us to do the process over again from scratch has a demoralizing effect on all of us. For example, the law today in the OSHA cases leaves us somewhat in the dark about the extent to which we may properly use cost-benefit analyses and risk-assessment models in our work. The brown-lung decision helps, but it still leaves a lot of unanswered questions. It's stressful, and I mean in a personal immediate way, to adopt one cost-benefit approach and embark on a major rulemaking effort knowing that it may all be a waste of time. Often in those circumstances we don't develop our best case precisely because we know we may have to do it all over in the future. And we write what someone uncharitably once called "contrived and formless" opinions with our eyes on the courts, instead of on the substance of the policy problem before us. And I admit that sometimes this same uncertainty, in a contested case, pushes us to jump to conclusions, to assume that all the businesses out there are fast buck cheaters and bad guys. We too can exploit uncertainty in the law by using threats that may not have sound legal bases. Of course it's the little guys who most commonly feel this kind of pinch.

Maybe I only complain about the old saw that hard cases make bad law, but why do so many cases turn out to be so hard and the law so bad? My friend John Quarles over at EPA years ago practically had to run the whole EPA pesticide program out of the General Counsel's office, sidetracking a big staff, because the legal complications were so great that only the lawyers could make the final decisions.

One final set of observations. The congressman said our capacity to make sense of complex technical and social science facts exceeded the Congress's, which I believe is true. But let's not overestimate what science can do for us. When the Federal Trade Commission went after the Kroger supermarket chain for deceptive advertising—you may remember the Kroger Price Patrols on TV a few years back— they couldn't really say who, if anybody, was actually deceived. Deception is damn tough to measure. In many cases it all comes down to the fact that an agency has a mission from Congress, to support the environment or protect against consumer fraud or whatever, and when in doubt the agency tilts in the direction of its statutory obligation. In judgment-call cases like this I'm not sure lobbying and pressure is such a bad thing. These decisions where science doesn't help and everything depends on values ought to depend on consensus and public perceptions. As long as the various public groups—the Sierra Club and Ralph Nader groups as well as the business lobbies—have a balanced chance to be heard in rulemaking, I don't think the public interest suffers. But we must remember that in other cases our legislative mandate is clear, the data from the real world are pretty straightforward, and the policy choices pretty obvious. In circumstances like these, mushy administrative law only gives private interests an opportunity to delay and frustrate good public policy. Thank you.

CHAIR: Thank you, Steve. You may feel your agency isn't powerful enough, but your remarks certainly are. We turn next to a spokesperson for the corporate world, Paula Proffitt.

PROFFITT: Since there are some interesting conjunctions between names and roles here, let say that I don't really think of myself as a spokeswoman for the corporate world, and I am not in my line of work merely to show a profit. I am excited about the things I've heard this morning. (I've always wondered why the health product labeling bill failed!) But before I get into that, since I am less well known than some speakers, I'd better tell you a little about my background to let you know where I've come from. I was active in the civil rights movement in the early sixties and active in the antiwar movement while I was in graduate school in Berkeley in the late sixties.

VitaMax, my employer, is the largest producer of nonprescription health products in the United States. It is also the largest successful black-owned and black-managed business I know of. I have been with the company since 1974, and I believe in our work, not because it's a success story for my race but because we try to serve people, to make their lives better. Many business people, particularly younger ones, get a bum rap for simply chasing dollars. Our company believes that profit should measure how well we meet human needs, and that we are all called on this earth to try to meet the needs of our brothers and sisters as best we can. But that's enough soapbox oratory for now.

I said I was excited about what I've heard here this morning. The more I listened, the more fascinated I became because something unusual is happening. I find myself agreeing with just about everything everybody has said so far. How can that be? You're all saying different things, and you're contradicting each other in much of what you say. The amazing thing here is that you all care about justice. I think you all really, *really* agree with one of my favorite quotations, something I heard and used back in the sixties, from Justice Frankfurter, that our system must keep alive "the feeling, so important to a popular government, that justice has been done."[6]

I think the concern for the integrity and dignity of the individual should dominate our thinking in administrative law, which is, after all, a set of theories, many of them in pretty sorry shape today, for making decisions about people. Because I work in the human health business I have come across enough research reports to convince me that the way people are treated by others has a real effect on their

---

[6] *Joint Anti-Fascist Committee v. McGrath,* 341 U.S. 123 172 (1951).

physical as well as their mental health. John Thibaut and Laurens Walker have reported that different procedures evoke different levels of approval and satisfaction.[7] However, I refer more importantly to the pioneering work of Hans Selye, who shows the effects of stress on human tissues and relates stress in large part to the absence of feelings of gratitude and the presence of such feelings as revenge.[8] The feeling of gratitude, I am convinced, is fundamental to maintaining a healthy person and a healthy society. Today the interaction between government officials and citizens is so frequent that administrative law cannot neglect this important aspect. Procedures must not simply perpetuate the faceless indifference of a welfare office. People face to face need to maintain their souls and their generosity or justice as a psychological reality cannot occur.

I must say that as a businessperson I have been involved in several regulatory procedures, most of them oriented toward rulemaking. I have little to complain about from personal experience. We are an honest company, and agencies like Steve's have worked on the whole constructively with us. But I agree that the law seems full of unnecessary uncertainties. I guess I'm a strange hybrid of liberal and conservative, but I honestly do believe that those *Wall Street Journal* editorials are often correct when they complain that the social costs of public regulation outweigh the social benefits. I sense we are paying a lot of money for attorneys to work out purely procedural things. And when the case gets into the courts, what comes out in court often does not resemble the problem we were wrestling with it all. I have the general impression that the usual method of problem solving in business, where you get what facts you can and get together for hours and hammer something out with the sleeves rolled up, works better than a complicated trial.

In closing, if I could have one wish granted for the system of administrative justice, it would be that we all remember what Learned Hand once said: "Of those qualities on which civilization depends, next after courage, it seems to me, comes an open mind. . . ."[9] Procedures must work to help participants keep an open mind. Sometimes I know a formal trial-type proceeding is the best way to achieve that. But I often feel that the appellate courts that declare administrative law principles are way off in right field somewhere. The real issues of fairness have to do not with catch phrases like *hearing on the record* or *right to cross examine* or *failure to exhaust administrative remedies*. They depend on respect and constructive attitudes face to face, and that requires open minds.

CHAIR: Thank you. Those remarks have, I can tell, our sincere gratitude. Our final speaker is Herbert Horsefield. Herb.

HORSEFIELD: The most useful thing I can add to what has been a very stimulating set of remarks indeed is a brief list of the informal operating procedures that I use

---

[7]"A Theory of Procedure," *California Law Review*, 66 (1978):541.

[8]Hans Selye, *The Stress of Life* (New York: McGraw-Hill, 1956), 285–286. See also Joseph Sittler, *Grace Notes and Other Fragments*, Herhold and Delloff, eds. (Philadelphia: Fortress Press, 1981), 116. (My thanks to Rev. Ken Kinnett for bringing these sources to my attention., *LHC*).

[9]In Irving Dillard, ed., *The Spirit of Liberty* (New York: Vintage, 1959), 148.

in my practice of administrative law. At the outset I should say I took administrative law in school and don't remember a thing about it, except that the book cover was red. I have practiced for twenty years and have never taken part in a formal trial-type hearing. I don't remember ever hearing an APA issue arise in a case I've handled.

You see, I start with a client who has a problem. If I solve that problem successfully, and so far I have, it's at the informal level. Now here are five of Horsefield's homilies:

1. Always keep up with the *New York Times*, the *Washington Post*, and the *Federal Register*. These documents contain the main warning signs of trouble for your client. If you know about them at the outset, you ought to be able to manage the problem successfully.

2. Know the staff of the agency you're dealing with and its history, and know which of several possible agencies and people in them have the attitude most favorable to your client. In my field it's essential to know that the Bureau of Drugs is a tough enforcement agency, but the Bureau of Biologics, with overlapping jurisdiction, has a totally different approach because of its history and leadership.

3. Understand, as Judge Busselot and Steve Smite have already stated, that policy drives procedure in this town. Nobody reads the APA, and nobody stays awake nights worrying about due process. The question in this town is, first: Will it get the job done? and second: Is it acceptable to the parties involved? The cases that get to court are those where the parties botched the job of answering these questions.

4. Know how to write indignant but not personally insulting or accusatory letters. There ought to be a course in law school on such things, since I spend 95 percent of my time working out problems on the telephone or in diplomatically indignant letters.

5. Finally, and most important of all, anyone who practices well in this town learns that the lawyer must get to know the muddy details of the case better than anyone else involved. If you handle benzene *you* must become a benzene expert, which means a statistical expert, a chemist, and a lot of other things. Oliver Wendell Holmes once said, "For the rational study of law the black-letter man may be the man of the present, but the man of the future is the man of statistics and the master of economics." Believe it or not, he said that in 1897, but only in the last decade or so has his description become a true description of the way we practice law, at least in this town.

Now let me step back a bit. I found Ms. Proffitt's remarks morally valid, even inspiring, but we cannot fool ourselves. People are not by nature narrowly selfish or instinctively mean and competitive. But they are rationally self-interested. Nobody in this town wants to give things away for nothing. People on all sides of issues, in Congress, in public interest and special interest lobbies, everywhere, operate by making their own cost-benefit calculations, and the trick is to work them out in a jointly satisfying way. I think Congressman Maverick was making this very point about decisionmaking in the House. Cost-benefit calculations occur best when people know clearly what the costs and benefits are.

Now the important point is this: The greatest cost that we can threaten an agency with is going to court if they are not reasonable. From our perspective, informal problem solving can and will work *only* so long as the threat to go to court, though we hardly ever mention it, remains credible. That is why I feel uncomfortable with the implications of cases like *Vermont Yankee*, cases that support administrative discretion. I welcome the development of administrative common law, not because it directly affects my clients but because the possibility of going to court keeps the parties in informal negotiations more honest. From an absolutist point of view Judge Wright's decision in the *Moss* case was pretty naive. We all knew that the industry was potentially competitive and if they couldn't compete on price they would compete with service — flying piano bars and the like. And this made all those formalities a waste of time. But from another point of view it really helps to have judicial intervention from time to time. The biggest impact of *Moss* was, perhaps unwittingly, to shine a little more light on the CAB's decisionmaking process and hasten the day of deregulation, which was certainly long overdue.

Well, I am eager to see what the discussion period will bring up, so I'll stop now.

CHAIR: Thank you, Herb, and thanks to all of you for touching on so many difficult and important aspects of administrative law. We will now take ten minutes for a coffee break.

[*Here the transcript ends.*]

Exercises and Questions for Further Thought

1. The remainder of the transcript of the conference was destroyed when the secretary who had transcribed the conference accidentally erased, in the middle of the chair's remarks, the magnetic floppy disk on which the word processor had stored the rest of the transcript. The original audio tapes had by this time been used to record another conference. Therefore, it is up to readers to role-play the rest of the conference. What comments might each of the six make to the others about their presentations? Who might most vigorously disagree with whom, and why? What points might come from the floor, for example, what points of view and what ideas may the six speakers have missed altogether?

2. How does each of the six speakers implicitly or explicitly define justice? How compatible are their definitions?

CHAPTER 14

Principles and Policies in Administrative Law

At many points in the first three parts of this book we have introduced difficult evaluative questions about administrative law without resolving them. The hypothetical symposium set forth in the last chapter has, we trust, summarized these questions for you. This final chapter pushes us as far as possible down the road toward resolution of these difficult issues.

At this point, the beginning of the end, let us restate a premise embedded in this book that distinguishes it from many other textbooks you may have read. Instead of laying out the alternatives in a bland and neutral way, this textbook proposes and advocates a particular way of looking at its subject matter. It suggests that we examine the "ideal of legality" in administrative law. Therefore we present criticisms of the ideal of legality in what follows. If the components of the ideal of legality have faded in your memory since you encountered them at the beginning of this book, please review them, starting on page 70.

Pinpointing the Critical Issues

Each of the symposium speakers make important, valid, yet incomplete statements and observations about administrative law. Their beliefs, for example, about the importance of having and using clear principles of administrative law, conflict. The practitioners, Smite and Horsefield, wish for predictability in law so they can anticipate and prevent problems. The judge, on the other hand, prefers a legal ambiguity that give him flexibility to solve legal problems wisely. Yet no speaker is totally right or wrong. Each "partially blind" speaker struggles to understand a different part of the elephant.

This section begins to pinpoint the major evaluative questions in administrative law by identifying those parts of the administrative law elephant that we should treat as understood, beyond dispute. We can then treat these settled points as a framework in which to fit other more debatable recommendations for improving administrative law.

Settled Points

1. *Administrative law exists.* Administrative law is a continuing search for coherent models of public decisionmaking. These models should, as Paul Verkuil has urged, accommodate the claims of accuracy, fairness to and satisfaction of individuals, and efficency. The search requires us to ask fundamentally political questions: What is government? How does it work in practice? What characteristics of the practical operation of government tend, if uncorrected, to produce unfair, inaccurate, inefficient and/or ineffective decisions and policies? The failure of the field to develop such models arises from the fact that modern administrative government contributes to ongoing political debates about regulation and democracy.

No one doubts the existence of these political and philosophical problems. The fact that courts seem to search for solutions to these problems under the name of *administrative law* is equally clear. It is not, however, settled or certain that a consensus about government will ever emerge permitting adoption of solutions that will reach the level of principle that Professor Rimhorn seeks. Professor Martin Shapiro presents a prognosis for the future of administrative law principles later in this chapter.

2. *The judicial system has over time taken primary responsibility for the development of coherent administrative law.* We should not assume that Congress can or will create by statute the models of administrative decisionmaking that minimize arbitrariness for at least four reasons.

- Congressman Maverick's description (p. 488) of the incentive system and its consequences is correct. Legislative politics are not in all respects democratic, far-sighted, or rational. In May 1982 Congress for the first time vetoed, under the authority of 1980 legislation, a rule promulgated by the FTC. The rejected rule required full auto dealer disclosure of the known condition of their used cars. Think of all the incentives for special interest lobbying this new congressional willingness to overturn administrative rules creates. As Representative Toby Moffett (D-Connecticut) pointed out on the CBS Morning News (May 27, 1982), the prospect that the Congress *might* overturn *any* FTC rule is an open invitation to those affected to make large contributions to congressional campaigns. The computer printout of car dealers who had recently contributed to congressional campaigns was produced on this CBS news broadcast. It was many feet long.

- The detailed features of decisionmaking procedures are tailored to conform to the great variety of decisionmaking environments, but congressional policy at its best is broad-brushed and general. It cannot provide the details. The loopholes and ambiguities in the FOIA and in OSHA's enabling legislation are stereotypes of post-New Deal regulatory legislation. Agencies have primary responsibility to do this tailoring, but courts, not Congress, intervene more frequently to affect the results.

- The courts in common law systems assume responsibility for developing detailed legal rules and procedures that emerge from deciding concrete legal disputes.

A constitutional system that commands the courts to insure that government treat its citizens according to due process of law amplifies the judicial responsibility to articulate workable principles of administrative law.

- Finally, the courts operate in the center stage of administrative law. The raw material for administrative principles already exists.

3. *Democratic theory imposes few specific limitations on the propriety of judicial development of administrative law.* The critical issues of administrative law rarely surface on the list of agendas that concern the voting public. It is of course vital that government respond to strong popular feelings in a democracy when they occur. Some political campaigns might, of course focus on subject matter that administrative law principles have helped shape, and in turn been shaped by; environmental law is a good example here. There is, however, no "majority" public opinion or even awareness of the more procedural concerns of administrative law.

4. *Administrative realities often encourage inadequate decisionmaking.* In general, people are, as Mr. Horsefield stated, rationally self-interested. People tend to make individual decisions based on self-centered and often rough (or "satisficing") calculations of the costs and benefits to themselves of a potential choice. What Mr. Horsefield did not mention is the process by which people put prices tags on costs and benefits. A person's perceptions of his or her role play a major part in cost/benefit calculations. In organizational roles one of the most critical calculations concerns how much information about a problem a person chooses to collect. . . . The information cost deriving from the desire for perfect information is sometimes costly, if obtainable. The incentives influencing individual decisionmakers easily steer them toward making decisions without gathering or thinking hard about the available information.[1] However, the same trade-offs, the same causes of administrative error, make it impossible for courts and judges to insist on totally informed or error-free decisions.

Nevertheless, the differences in the incentive system between judges and administrators are highly significant. A person who internalizes the role of judge and the values of impartiality that go with it attaches a presumably very high cost to the possibility of accepting money for a favor. A businessperson whose role justifies making a profit may attach no cost to the same behavior, only a benefit. More to the point judges in a trial setting pay minimal costs for information gathering because the adversary system does that for them. While the role of administrative law judge in federal formal adjudication may so shape cost/benefit calculations that we can take judges' fairness for granted, the roles of most bureaucrats do not provide the same assurance. Commissioner Dixon and Pertshuk, the employer who fired office Bishop, the welfare worker in *Goldberg*, and so on, do not occupy roles that reward them for paying attention to the values Paul Verkuil has identified.

Let us therefore accept as settled that the following forces may deflect an administrative decision away from our decisionmaking standards:

a. Individual laziness, including the "burn-out" phenomenon (decisionmaker not rewarded for fairness, accuracy, etc.)

[1] Anthony Downs, *An Economic Theory of Democracy* (New York: Harper & Row, 1957), 210–16.

b. No sanction (no risk that negligently made decision will be reviewed or published)

c. Personal financial gain from one outcome independent of its merit

d. Prejudgment of facts, perhaps based on prior experience with similar cases

e. Insufficient time or budgetary support for full review of case

f. Conflicts between organizational rewards, e.g., promotion chances, and professional standards

g. Policy conflicts within agency

h. Need perceived by decisionmakers to maintain "face" or "credibility" by taking unwavering positions in cases whose specific facts dicatate a different result

i. Decisionmaking procedures unsuited to the effective interpretation of the kinds of facts that bear on the decision

j. Perception of facts relevant to decision distorted by "capture" of agency or lobbying and pressure from legislature or other politically powerful groups

k. Failure of decisionmaking procedures to afford access for new groups and/or ideas

This list is not exhaustive. Administrative law, defined as the search for processes of decisionmaking that assure accuracy, fairness, efficiency, and satisfaction, must try to minimize the effect these factors may have on judgment. It must therefore develop methods consistent with these values that help determine whether and when these forces have affected the decisionmaking process.

5. Administrative law models have implicit and explicit political philosophies. This does not mean, however that administrative law is predisposed to consistently reach "liberal" or "conservative" ideological outcomes. As McCraw's article on regulation and politics demonstrates (*supra* at p. 13), and other important review essays detail, administrative law embodies political views *and* contributes to shaping American politics.[2] We have not simply reduced administrative law to "politics" by identifying the political perspectives allied with various reforms in administrative law (e.g., New Deal, the public interest movement, deregulation). Although particular political tendencies are evident in the development of administrative law, it remains a contested terrain—an arena *for* the articulation of differing conceptions of economic and social justice.

Important Unsettled Questions

Assuming these five settled points, let us now turn to the open questions, the questions about administrative law that reasonable and conscientious thinkers might answer differently. These questions focus the rest of the material in this book.

1. To what extent should administrative law labor to generate core principles? Is Judge Busselot correct that incremental judicial problem solving provides the best strategy to attain the goals of administrative law? Does not his position require fairly deep judicial review of the facts of many cases? Is this desirable?

2. To the extent core principles are appropriate, what, roughly, should they look like?

[2] For example, see Richard B. Stewart, "The Reformation of American Administrative Law," *Harvard Law Review* 88 (1975): 1669: Gerald E. Frug, "The Ideology of Bureaucracy in American Law," *Harvard Law Review* 97 (1984): 1276; Robert L. Rabin, "Federal Regulation in Historical Perspective," *Stanford Law Review* 38 (1986): 1189; and Mark Tushnet, "The Constitution of the Bureaucratic State," in *Red, White, and Blue: A Critical Analysis of Constitutional Law* (Cambridge: Harvard University Press, 1988), 214–46.

3. How useful is the rulemaking/adjudication distinction in modern administrative law? Should we bemoan or welcome the blurring of the lines between them?

4. How can courts effectively review administrative handling of scientific materials when judges lack the training necessary to comprehend either the scientific issues themselves or the statistical methods by which scientists express their conclusions?

5. Finally, are face-to-face relationships between citizens and bureaucrats in "frontline" human service agencies governed so fully by deep cultural patterns and beliefs that courts can do nothing to change them? That is, can courts do much to satisfy Ms. Profitt's plea for administrative procedures that preserve dignity?

6. What is deregulation? How has this current trend in regulatory reform altered the core principles of administrative law? To what extent has administrative law been an ideological resource for deregulation advocates?

Principles in Administrative Law

A body of law serves the function of helping people plan their affairs. This is not law's only function, but it is as important as any. No body of law can do that—can help people make contracts or decide what insurance to carry or stay clear of criminal arrests—unless it states principles coherently. Principles of contract, tort, and wills and estate planning allow most people most of the time to make choices about their affairs with some degree of certainty about the consequences of their choices.

While problem-solving judges may feel that ambiguity and lack of principles give them a flexibility that improves justice, in specific cases this point of view neglects all the problems that Mr. Smite describes: uncertainty in designing agency procedures, delay, and reduction in bureaucratic morale and commitment to the task. In other words, an administrative law that merely encourages courts to review case-by-case and make hip-pocket judgments may not fully meet *any* of our standards for administrative law.

The Shape of Core Principles

Let us review the standards. *Administrative procedure should be concerned with the overall fairness and accuracy of decisions, with their efficiency and low-cost resolution, and, in a democratic society, with participant satisfaction with the process.* These standards present us immediately with the familiar trade-off problem. Getting perfectly accurate information is very time-consuming, costly, and inefficient. Participant satisfaction depends on many factors. The most important—winning the case—really has no place in any principle of law. Of course a court can say that the core of administrative law is "balancing" among these standards, but that approach is worthy only of the Queen in *Alice Through the Looking Glass*. Balancing creates no guides to action and makes no law at all. Therefore we must refine the meaning of these terms and put them in some order of priority.

First, with the exception of the factors discussed by Paula Proffitt (that is, the degree of dignity, respect, and helpfulness in the interpersonal relationship between citizen and bureaucrat), personal satisfaction turns out to be no evaluative standard at all. Personal satisfaction hinges on selfish motives, like winning the case, which obviously cannot concern us.

What, then, about fairness and accuracy? What is fairness? We are not about to provide the conclusive answer to that timeless question, but some elements of administrative fairness can be identified if we assume that the Constitution itself exemplifies the concept of fairness. Administrative decisions, then, are unfair if they violate the primary civil liberties of the Bill of Rights and if they do not demonstrably conform to the agency's statutory authority to make them. Administrative decisions must respect constitutional standards of free speech, religion, privacy, and equal protection, for example. Just as these questions of fairness involve general principles of constitutional law that overlay administrative law, so the issues of statutory interpretation are not specific to administrative law. Courts must interpret statutes by identifying the problem or problems the legislation seeks to correct and to determine whether the case in court is or is not such a problem.

Once an agency satisfies civil liberties and statutory standards, once its authority to proceed is clear, then questions of fairness and accuracy merge. Whether an administrative procedure is fair depends on whether it is accurate. At this point in our development of a core of administrative law principles we meet again the "ideal of legality," introduced near the beginning of the book. The ideal of legality, as we have seen, is not and cannot be an ideal of "following the law." The law is too general and too unsettled to follow. Cases always raise unique angles, new wrinkles, uncertain facts. The ideal of legality pushes decisionmakers toward the standard of accuracy.

Thus a central problem does exist for administrative law. This problem calls on judges to construct principles that lead the way to the creation of specific working rules of administrative action. The problem, as you may already have recognized, is to develop principles for resolving the trade-off between accuracy and the costs of gathering and analyzing information. We must locate principles that reduce arbitrariness without imposing on the judiciary the impossible task of remaking the administrative decision from scratch.

A previous section of this chapter listed many of the forces that push toward arbitrariness and against accurate information gathering and analysis. Some Supreme Court Justices have argued recently that the cost is too high. If every employee threatened with termination, every student or driver threatened with suspension, every rule protecting consumer or environmental interests is subject to the careful scrutiny of court-like procedures, the administrative burden would outweigh the social and individual interests at stake.

This solution however, might also contradict the social and political reasons for creating an administrative government in the first place. Recall from chapter 1 that courts are not themselves well organized and structured to develop the elaborate and often technically complex public policies modern times require. Thus the core of administrative law principles must determine for varying circumstances cost-effective methods that satisfy the need for accuracy. Leaving the issue to case-by-case balancing will not do.

A democracy should not trade off civil liberties for efficient and affordable administration. Separating the process of doing justice from substantive justice forces us to confront this dilemma, but we think administrative law can work to minimize the dilemma by insisting, for starters, that arbitrariness be eradicated. Administrators must justify their decisions, and their justifications must at minimum meet tests of prudence and common sense. An accurate decision is not arbitrary, and a nonarbitrary decision is simply a decision based on a plausible and reasoned argument showing how the facts of the case support the choice. For example, when we examine many of the major administrative law cases in this book, some fascinating transformations begin to take place. At the outset, the Supreme Court's retreat from *Goldberg* does, up to a point, make some sense. As Judge Busselot observed, merely providing these procedural formalities does not go to the heart of the matter, does not guarantee a fit between the facts and the administrative decision. Thus *Overton Park* (p. 355), not *Goldberg,* may illuminate the principles modern administrative law should adopt. *Overton Park* stands for the proposition that, regardless of the formal procedures used to make it, a decision cannot stand if the decisionmaker cannot plausibly demonstrate to a judge that it is logically consistent with the facts of the case and meets whatever legal standards the agency's authorizing statute and the constitution impose.

Notice that by placing the emphasis not on the form of the procedure but on its justifiability, administrators might have more flexibility to design and select procedures and methods for gathering information that suit the nature of the problem they face. It also takes away the opportunity for delay through litigation over the form of the procedure because the courts will not rigidly insist on procedural forms for their own sake. This may reinforce administrator morale and incentive by assuring them that *their* efforts to develop defensible policy at the front end will increase, and perhaps insure, judicial acceptance of the result.

Reducing Arbitrariness in Rulemaking and Adjudication

The perspective we have just outlined makes less critical the distinction between rulemaking and adjudication. It reinforces *Florida East Coast R.R.'s* conclusion (p. 270) that rulemaking belongs in administrative government. It provides a principle that justifies the judicial call for extra procedural protections in *Sangamon* (p. 273) and relatively few formal protections in *Horowitz* (p. 210) despite the fact that the first was technically rulemaking, the second adjudication. Some applications of the distinction to cases previously covered will help clarify it.

Bishop v. Wood

A principle of administrative law designed to minimize arbitrariness would not necessarily change the results in personnel cases like *Bishop* or school suspension and dismissal cases like *Horowitz,* but it would quite dramatically change the analysis. The perspective recognizes that in both these cases the plaintiffs were deprived of something of presumably substantial importance to their well-being and personal dignity. Government cannot deprive citizens of something of substantial immediate importance arbitrarily. To fire an employee or to expel a student imposes costs far greater than many criminal proceedings impose.

Two procedural tracks permit firing employees or suspending students with justification, that is, nonarbitrarily. The first we may call the *contractual* track. The other track calls for a hearing.

In employment contexts it is not arbitrary to fire someone without any form of hearing if by explicit agreement the employee has agreed that the employer may terminate him or her at any time at the employer's discretion. This agreement is of course made whenever an employee serves a probationary period. The year-to-year employment of untenured college professors fits the same category. But when a contract states or implies that termination may occur only for certain behaviors or in certain conditions, then the employer must, under the ideal of legality, be prepared to demonstrate plausible evidence that those behaviors or conditions have occurred. To argue that "the employer made no public accusations, therefore officer Bishop suffered no impairment of his chances for future employment," is false on its face, given the nature of his employment contract. The argument that he deserves no hearing is even weaker, since the real harm arises from the possibility that his employer fired him from *this* job arbitrarily, without plausible reasons. Note once again that we do not necessarily conclude that employers must follow all of the *Goldberg* formalities. The procedures in *Goldberg* may be less critical and substantive rationality more important.

Academic settings, like employment settings, permit dismissal on either contractual or due process bases, and neither is necessarily arbitrary. A student entering a university agrees that if he or she fails to earn a minimum grade average, he or she will be dismissed. Students also know that the assignment of grades depends ultimately on professional judgment. The student agrees to abide by these conditions and must accept dismissal if the grade average falls below the stated level. In these circumstances no hearing is required. In Ms. Horowitz's case, however, the medical school dismissed her on admittedly subjective grounds. She did not flunk out by falling below a published grade minimum. The Supreme Court's conclusion (that the medical school did not violate due process in dismissing her) in our judgment might be correct, but not for the *ad hominem* reasons advanced by the majority. Rehnquist's distinction—that a student's relationship to a medical school is nonadversarial but a client's relationship to a welfare office is adversarial—is absolutely irrelevant to the problem of arbitrariness. The threat of a loss of something valuable can convert *any* situation into an adversarial one.

More important, as Paula Proffitt suggests in the previous chapter, reasoned explanation that respects individual dignity has important moral value in its own right, regardless of the adversarial relationship between the parties. If you doubt the point, reflect on the value of discussion, explanation, and tolerance in parental nurturing of children. Justice Rehnquist would surely not call the familial relationship adversarial, though we all know it can and does become so from time to time.

In sum, Ms. Horowitz was dismissed fairly not because of the presence or absence of some legal abstraction. The school dismissed her fairly, the Court should have found, because the process the school used to evaluate her in fact put her on notice of her deficiencies and gave her ample opportunity to demonstrate her competence as measured by medical school policy.

But surely we are not arguing for amending formal adjudication out of the Administrative Procedure Act [APA] altogether, or against the value of the *Goldberg* protections in some circumstances. Congress may legally call for formal adjudication under the APA in whatever circumstances it chooses. In most cases, however, Congress does not do so. In these cases it is not clear that due process *Goldberg* protections need apply *except* in instances in which an agency seeks to impose a punishment, deprivation, or other substantial and inevitably harmful sanction against someone on the basis of allegations about that person's own past conduct.[3] It is in circumstances where the decision may depend on facts *uniquely* within the experience of the citizen that administrative law must preserve his or her full participation to avoid arbitrariness. In other words *all* formalities may be required only when the citizen can plausibly claim that the agency decision rests on information that he, the citizen, possesses—information that the agency could not independently acquire and assess.

In the absence of either a statutory requirement for a full hearing or a decision imposing a substantial punishment for past conduct, administrative law should require equally of rulemaking and adjudication the elements of APA Section 553—notice, written comments, and reasons. These should should be supplemented with oral presentation of evidence, cross-examination, and the remaining formalities at agency discretion or when the decision rests on significant facts uniquely within the experience of the citizen.[4] As we have suggested above, the courts take up the slack that relaxed formalities might create by applying the APA Section 706 substantial evidence test aggressively across the board. The emphasis throughout must avoid empty legal formulas and intellectually groundless excuses to approve agency discretion. Citizens must demand that agencies demonstrate the factual justifications for their decisions. This approach does not shackle the agencies. Again, Congress usually leaves agencies with discretion as to whether to justify by full evidentiary record, formal findings, or a less formal statement of reasons.

The following case demonstrates this approach in action.

District of Columbia Federation of Civic Associations v. Volpe

459 F.2d 1231, U.S.C.A., D.C. Cir. (1971) 3–0

[Recall the statutory standard that arose in *Overton Park*. Section 138 of Title 23 of the United States Code directs that the secretary of transportation withhold approval for the construction of a highway that would involve the use of parkland unless he finds that there exists no feasible and prudent alternative to the use of the parkland and is satisfied that the plans minimize harm to such parkland. In 1969 the Three

[3] Paul Verkuil, "The Emerging Concept of Administrative Procedure," *Columbia Law Review* 78 (1978): 321.

[4] Verkuil, 322–25.

Sisters Bridge, which would connect the District of Columbia with Virginia across the Potomac River, was added to the Interstate Highway System only after Representative Natcher, the chairman of the House Subcommittee on appropriations for the District, made it plain that his committee would not approve funds for the new D.C. subway system unless the bridge were built. Note Judge Bazelon's realistic reading of the political situation, and note also his solution: the creation of a formal record that justifies the secretary's decision on grounds free from political pressure.]

Bazelon, Chief Judge.

Our review of the Secretary's determination is hindered not only by the lack of any formal findings, but also by the absence of a "meaningful administrative record within the Department of Transportation evidencing the fact that proper consideration has been given to . . . [statutory] requirements. . . ." However regrettable, the failure to provide explicit findings indicating why all possible alternatives to the bridge would be unfeasible or imprudent does not, in itself, invalidate the Secretary's action. But the complete non-existence of any contemporaneous administrative record is more serious. Absent a record, judicial review of the Secretary's action can be little more than a formality unless the District Court takes the disfavored step of requiring the Secretary to testify as to the basis of his decision. And even the Secretary's *"post hoc rationalizations,"* filtered through a factfinder's understandable reluctance to disbelieve the testimony of a Cabinet officer, will rarely provide an effective basis for review. Furthermore, it is hard to see how, without the aid of any record, the Secretary could satisfactorily make the determinations required by statute. The absence of a record, in other words, simultaneously obfuscates the process of review and signals sharply the need for careful scrutiny. . . .

[T]he District Court approved the § 138 determination on the basis of the Secretary's testimony that a "minimum of parkland would be taken" for the ramps and interchanges. . . .

Absent a finalized plan for the bridge, it is hard to see how the Department could make a meaningful evaluation of "harm." . . . His approval of the project under § 138, was, in short, entirely premature, and we hold that he must make new determinations consistent with the statutory standards.

. . . Taken as a whole, the defects in the Secretary's determinations—in particular, his effort to make the determinations before plans for the bridge were complete—lend color to plaintiff's contention that the repeated and public threats by a few Congressional voices did have an impact on the Secretary's decisions. . . . When funds for the subway were, in fact, blocked, Representative Natcher made his position perfectly clear, stating that "as soon as the freeway project gets under way beyond recall then we will come back to the House and recommend that construction funds for rapid transit be approved."

. . . [T]he pressure exerted by Representative Natcher and others did have an impact on Secretary Volpe's decision to approve the bridge. . . . The Secretary's testimony indicated . . . that "his decision was based on the merits of the project and not *solely* on the extraneous political pressures."

. . . The [District] Court determined as a matter of law that since the Secretary was not acting in a judicial or quasi-judicial capacity, his decision would be invalid only if based *solely* on these extraneous considerations. I cannot accept that formulation of the applicable legal principle. . . . [T]he decision would be invalid if based in whole or in part on the pressures emanating from Representative Natcher.

. . . [W]e therefore hold that on remand the Secretary must make new determinations based strictly on the merits and completely without regard to any considerations not made relevant by Congress in the applicable statutes.

. . . The Secretary plainly understood that the price of abandoning, modifying, or even delaying construction of the bridge was the loss of appropriations for the District's subway. . . . We cannot agree, however, that a determination grounded on that reasoning would satisfy the requirements of § 138.

. . . We are persuaded . . . that holding these pressures relevant would effectively emasculate the statutory scheme. . . . [T]he Secretary must himself decide, bearing in mind the statute's mandate for the preservation of parkland, whether a prudent alternative is available. . . . Our interpretation of § 138 is essential if the Secretary is to be insulated from extraneous pressures that have no relevance to his assigned statutory task.

. . . [W]e emphasize that we have not found— nor, for that matter, have we sought—any suggestion of impropriety or illegality in the actions of Representative Natcher and others who strongly advocate the bridge. They are surely entitled to their own views on the need for the Three Sisters Bridge, and we indicate no opinion on their authority to exert pressure on Secretary Volpe. Nor do we mean to suggest that Secretary Volpe acted in bad faith or in deliberate disregarded of his statutory responsibilities. He was placed, through the action of others, in an extremely treacherous position. Our holding is designed, if not to extricate him from that position, at least to enhance his ability to obey the statutory command notwithstanding the difficult position in which he was placed.

We conclude that the case should be remanded to the District Court with directions that it return the case to the Secretary for him to perform his statutory function in accordance with this opinion. It seems clear that even though formal administrative findings are not required by statute, the Secretary could best serve the interests of the parties as well as the reviewing court by establishing a full-scale administrative record which might dispel any doubts about the true basis of his action. Accordingly, the District Court is directed to enjoin construction of the bridge until the defendants have complied with the applicable statutory provisions as set forth in our opinion.

Reversed and remanded.

This opinion nicely illustrates the essential features of administrative law in the best sense. The court does not take over responsibility for highway policy, but it does insist that when pressures of the kind that create unjustified decisions are present, the agency must show a justification in fact.

Science, Technology, and Administrative Law

Major administrative policy decisions do involve complex scientific questions and evidentiary methods. The question often comes up about how we can expect judges with no training in science or statistics to review decisions that may be scientifically or statistically arbitrary? In one scenario the courts, confronted with administrative decisions based on scientific or statistical findings, would in effect give up. They could rule that decisions with a scientific basis are presumptively not arbitrary. They might rule that agencies have scientific and statistical analytical skills that are so superior to those of the courts that courts must defer to agency superiority. Such a development in administrative law would be about as wise as the adolescent's thoughtless adoption of the latest fad in dress or popular music.

People untrained in scientific and statistical matters tend to overestimate the power of science for several reasons:

1. Numbers by themselves prove nothing. Without training in statistics it is very easy to assume that something causes something else when numbers assertedly fit together. In fact, developing proofs sufficient to justify casual inferences is one of the

trickiest and most demanding of all methodological and scientific operations.[5] The real temptation to find causation where it had not actually been established arises because every public policy choice rests on presumptions about casual relationships. Perhaps, to be safe, one should always bear in mind Mark Twain's taxonomy of "lies, damn lies, and statistics."

2. The same forces that promote arbitrary administrative decisionmaking can affect scientific and statistical inquiry. Science, like playing the piano, parenting children, playing basketball, or anything else, is done well in some circumstances by some people, badly by others in other circumstances. The scientific world, particularly the world of social science, is full of trivial, misleading, and improperly substantiated assertions—often happily published by leading journals in the field. Just as we cannot trust conclusions merely because they involve assertions about numbers so we should not trust conclusions because a so-called scientist has published them.

3. Today, economists are offering adminstrators the promise of improving public policy.[6] The economists claim their tools do not merely help determine how great a budget deficit is consistent with controlling inflation. They use cost/benefit analysis and risk assessment models to make judgments about optimal resource allocation in all policy fields. In criminal justice one can compare the costs of imprisonment against the cost of crimes committed by those on bail or probation. In the cotton dust case OSHA could make comparisons of the cost of reducing particulates in the air to the benefits of better health and fewer health care expenditures. Yet economic tools are so useful that it is easy to overlook or to manipulate away the policy issues that economic analysis does not and cannot resolve.[7] Here are some of the limitations inherent in economic analysis:

a. Measuring almost anything involves normative judgments. Should one or should one not calculate the aesthetic costs of the offensiveness of cigarette smoke and add them to the measurable health hazards?

b. Public preferences in a democracy properly help determine normative decisions in economic analysis, but these preferences are both very difficult to measure and subject to unpredictable changes that quickly outdate estimates of preferences, even if accurate when made.

c. Economists can say little about deep and enduring questions of political philosophy, e.g., the morally correct distribution of wealth in society. Economics provides no uncontroversial way to compare the value of an extra dollar given

[5] Beginners should examine Darrell Huff, *How to Lie with Statistics* (New York: Norton, 1954).

[6] See Stephen Breyer, "Analyzing Regulatory Failure: Mismatches, Less Restrictive Alternatives, and Reform," *Harvard Law Review* 92 (1979): 547, and Colin Diver, "Policymaking Paradigms in Administrative Law," *Harvard Law Review* 95(1981): 393, *supra*, at p. 284 Diver believes we may be entering an age in which government actually can make comprehensively rational policy changes rather than slow incremental adjustments. For an elegant statement of the normative problems that confound even simple empirical policy research questions, see William Popkin, "Effect of Representation on a Claimant's Success Rate," *Administrative Law Review* 31 (1979): 449. For a general overview of political perspectives in public policy analyses see Carl E. Van Horn, Donald C. Baumer, and William T. Goemley, Jr., *Politics and Public Policy* (Washington, D.C.: Congressional Quarterly Press, 1989).

[7] Steven E. Rhoads, "How Much Should We Spend to Save a Life?" *The Public Interest* 51 (1978): 1.

by public policy to a welfare mother, to an unemployed skilled craftsman, or to a needy college student.

d. How does one value life itself? What weights should a policymaker put on pain, fear of death or injury, the loss of a loved one or the fear of such a loss? Even when an individual can tell the relative importance of such intangibles as these in their own lives, by what techniques do public policymakers aggregate these feelings?

Given these realistic limits on science's contribution to policy, judges cannot automatically accept conclusions just because they are dressed out in the trappings of science. The danger is, of course, that untrained judges may, indeed probably will, do *worse* science if they question administrative decisions at all. OSHA's scientific approach in the benzene case may have been questionable, but Justice Steven's opinion is scientific nonsense because it assumes that science knows much more about the health risks of benzene than in fact it did know or could in the short run learn. The hard and measurable data, their great power to reduce our uncertainty, seduce us into neglecting the unmeasurable but vitally important normative side of questions. In the benzene case the real question is: Under what circumstances is it permissible for Congress, in the *absence* of persuasive scientific evidence, to protect citizens by adopting a deliberate policy of "playing it safe"? Our political system needs answers to such profound questions as this. The courts in our system ought properly to provide such answers.

On one dimension the scientific challenge to administrative law can be met. It can be met because of one fascinating characteristic of the scientific enterprise. While it is very difficult to prove convincingly by scientific methods that X is true, it is not nearly so difficult to identify a policy conclusion that *cannot* logically follow from the evidence, the science, offered to support it.[8] Thus in *Craig v. Boren*, 429 U.S. 190 (1976), the Court overturned a gender-based statute because the underlying data simply did not support the policy expressed in the law.

If, as Herbert Horsefield stated, lawyers can and do master the scientific characteristics of the problems they handle, there is no reason to believe that, in the long run at least, judges—former lawyers—cannot do so too. At least judges can learn enough statistics to spot, with the aid, perhaps, of expert testimony, studies that cannot logically yield the results the policymaker has presumed they do.[9]

Learning statistics is not the key to resolving the problem of judging conflicting scientific data and ambiguous congressional statutes. Albert Matheny and Bruce

[8] See Gary C. Bryner, "Scientific and Economic Analysis in Administrative Rule Making," *Bureaucratic Discretion: Law and Policy in Federal Regulatory Agencies* (New York: Pergamon Press, 1987), 41–64.

[9] Other interfaces between law and science are less easily resolved. In the early 1980s there was considerable debate over the creation of a "science court" to resolve scientifically complex contested matters. Arthur Kantrowitz, Professor of Engineering at Dartmouth College, endorsed such a court for resolving only the scientific issues disputed by parties in legal cases (see *The Science Court* [Cambridge: Abt Books, 1980], 53–58). For a related solution, see Joel Yellin, "High Technology and the Courts: Nuclear Power and the Need for Institutional Reform," *Harvard Law Review* 94 (1981): 489. Albert Matheny and Bruce Williams, presented convincing arguments against Kantrowitz's proposal in "Scientific Disputes and Adversary Procedures in Policy-Making," *Law & Policy* 3 (1981): 341.

Williams, two political scientists, make this point very clear as they delineate the political, scientific, and legal issues surrounding OSHA's Cancer Policy in the following essay. They emphasize the incongruities among these fields and assess the difficulties the Supreme Court has faced in addressing conflicts over OSHA's policy. In light of these factors, Matheny and Williams also consider the prospects for regulatory reform.

The New Social Regulation Under Review: The Supreme Court and Occupational Safety and Health*

Albert R. Matheny and Bruce A. Williams
(1990)

Among commentators on administrative law, much has been made over the last two decades on the changing relationship between courts and administrative agencies. Always an intensely political relationship,† its contours have nevertheless been defined by an admixture of legal and technical discourse. This admixture sometimes obscures the fact that each interaction between the agencies and the federal judiciary has political consequences. No one would argue that point: when judges apply legal doctrine to evaluate the exercise of technical expertise by agency decision-makers, some consequences—a substantive

---

*This essay is a revision of an earlier article published as "Regulation, Risk Assessment, and the Supreme Court: The Case of OSHA's Cancer Policy," *Law and Policy* 6 (1984): 425–449.

†One need only think of the Supreme Court's narrowing of the Sherman Anti-Trust Act [*U.S. v. E.C. Knight Co.*, 156 U.S. 1 (1895)], the nondelegation crisis that led to Franklin Roosevelt's "court-packing" plan [*Panama Refining Co. v. Ryan*, 293 U.S. 398, and *Schechter Poultry Corp. v. U.S.*, 295 U.S. 495 (1935)], the struggles over passage of the Administrative Procedures Act [*Wong Yang Sung v. McGrath*, 339 U.S. 33 (1950) and *Universal Camera Corp. v. NLRB*, 340 U.S. 474 (1951)], and the subsequent struggles over its toleration of an expansive interpretation of the National Environmental Policy Act [*Calvert Cliffs Coordinating Comm., Inc. v. AEC*, 449 F. 2d 1109 (D.C.Cir. 1971)] and its contraction of that interpretation in less than a decade [*Vermont Yankee Nuclear Power Corp. v. NRDC, Inc.*, 435 U.S. 519 (1978)]. For an argument directly connecting the evolution of administrative law to the development of American political theory, see Shapiro, 1982.

outcome—is inevitable. A far more controversial point, presented here, is that the judiciary, and particularly the Supreme Court over the last twenty years, has been guided more by the consequences of its rulings, than by a discernible trend in the judicial review of agency action.

William Rodgers has put the matter bluntly, but well:

> The Supreme Court encouraged intervention [strict scrutiny of administrative action] in its 1972 *Overton Park* decision [401 U.S. 402], cited hundreds of times by the lower federal courts, but called for deference [to administrative expertise] in its unanimous 1978 *Vermont Yankee* decision [435 U.S. 519], cited on scores of occasions since. All the while the suspicion has arisen, certainly among the practitioners who can say such things, that the grand synthesizing principle that tells us whether the court will dig deeply or bow cursorily depends exclusively on whether the judge agrees with the result of the administrative decision. This harsh descent to legal realism—and a cynical version at that—does not lack empirical ammunition. . . . Consistency and neutral principles are not problems until there are many occasions for decision; the reach and complexity of contemporary administrative law have made them problems (1981:302).

This article focuses precisely on "the reach and complexity of contemporary administrative law," as it was shaped by two seemingly contradictory decisions, and we argue that the U.S. Supreme Court has taken advantage of that reach and complexity in order to enhance its political power over administrative agencies.

The Court has accumulated this power through its willingness to maintain simultaneously competing and contradictory lines of precedent defining the extent of its reviewing powers over agency action, particularly over agency interpretations of congressional commands. At any moment in reviewing an agency's interpretation, the Court now has at its disposal equally convincing and lively sets of precedent that allow it a wide freedom to uphold or strike down agency action. As a result, either choice has doctrinal justification. The Court can "bow cursorily" to uphold agency action, or it can "dig deeply" to strike it down. Practically, this permits the Court to review agency action according to its majority's fundamental agreement or disagreement with the substantive impact of the action in question upon the parties involved. Cutting a result-oriented swath through the complex thicket of administrative action has contributed to a lack of doctrinal predictability in administrative law over the last twenty years. But the doctrinal chaos has been more than made up for, we submit, by an emerging substantive predictability that sends a fairly clear message to administrative agencies: consider the target of your actions as much as the source of your legislative authority, if you wish to have your policies upheld on review.

Conventional commentary on administrative law shies away from this "harsh descent to realism," embracing instead the "complexity" of administrative law, and urging that the legitimating doctrine is there, if only we are intelligent enough and willing to dig for it. But the search for a generalizable pattern in this particular area of administrative law leads scholars to an ever-increasing fragmentation of the field. Justice Scalia, writing as a professor in 1982, celebrated the "wondrous diversity" of administrative law and practice with this curious statement," . . . [J]udicial review makes more sense . . . when one considers a series of decisions dealing with a single agency rather than cases ranging from the Department of Defense to the FCC . . . " (1982: vii).

Arguably, Justice Scalia is right, but his agency-specific approach to administrative law is simply a restatement of the chaos in the field, unless there is some sort of principle underlying how the courts will deal with the actions of different agencies under similar circumstances. This article illustrates how the Supreme Court has actively contributed to the chaos in this field by its refusal to recognize the historical and institutional bases for the different standards of review that have evolved in response to the changing nature of regulation in American administrative government.

To establish our argument, we first examine the Supreme Court's exploitation of the duality of administrative law through a brief comparison of its decisions in *Industrial Union Department, AFL-CIO v. American Petroleum Institute*, 448 U.S. 607 (1980), commonly referred to as the *Benzene* case, and *Chevron, U.S.A., Inc. v. Natural Resources Defense Council, Inc.*, 467 U.S. 837 (1984), hereafter, *Chevron*. Next, we consider the regulatory context of the court's *Benzene* decision as a case study of the complexity of administrative regulation regarding workplace carcinogens and, more importantly, as an indication of the problem of inappropriate judicial review in an important area of government regulation. Drawing upon this case study, we conclude with some suggestions for doctrinal consistency to guide judicial review across a range of administrative action.

Benzene v. Chevron: A Summary of Conflicting Decisions

The particulars of *Benzene* and *Chevron* have been covered elsewhere in this text (pp. 122–132 and 136–141 respectively), so we address here only the contrast between the Justices' attitude toward the uncertainty the OSHAct's approach to workplace carcinogen regulation and the Court's approach to the uncertainty of the Clean Air Act Amendments' definition of "source" for the EPA's regulation of air pollution. The former delegation, in singling out workplace carcinogens for special regulation, was confusing in its command that the Secretary of Labor:

> . . . shall set the standard which most adequately assures, to the extent feasible, on the basis of the best available evidence, that no

employee will suffer material impairment of health or functional capacity. . . . 29 U.S.C.A., 655 (b) (5).

The command that "no employee will suffer material impairment of health" implies the promulgation of standards strongly protective of workers, but the insertion of "to the extent feasible" compromises that protectiveness in unclear ways, as discussed below.

The Clean Air Act Amendments of 1977 did not make clear Congress' intent regarding the regulation of a "new or modified major stationary source", 45 U.S.C.A., 7502 (b) (5)–(6), of pollution emission for determining attainment of national ambient air quality standards under the Act. Was regulation to be addressed to each pollution emission point within a given facility, or was the entire facility (or even a series of discrete facilities) to be considered as a source (under a "bubble"), within which cleaner, new emission points could counterbalance older, dirtier points? To compare the two cases: in the OSHAct Congress sent mixed messages to OSHA about workplace carcinogen regulation, and, in the Clean Air Act Amendments, it failed to convey any preference at all for the definition of "source."

The Supreme Court's reaction to these two nebulous delegations is a study in contrasts, even though the two cases were decided within four years of one another, and the author of the plurality opinion in *Benzene*. Justice Stevens, was also the author of the unanimous decision in *Chevron*. The standard under review in *Benzene* resulted from OSHA's so-called "Cancer Policy," discussed in detail below, which was an effort to interpret a practical agency policy out of the uncertainty of Congress' delegation in the area. As we shall see, the Cancer Policy was not lightly considered by the agency. But Justice Steven's did not "bow cursorily" to OSHA's efforts, and the tone of his rejection of the standard comes through quite clearly:

> . . . it is unreasonable to assume that Congress intended to give the Secretary [of Labor] the unprecedented power over American industry that would result from the Government's [OSHA's] view of [sections] 3(8) and 6 (b) (5), coupled with OSHA's Cancer Policy.

Expert testimony that a substance is probably a human carcinogen—either because it has caused cancer in animals or because individuals have contracted cancer following extremely high exposures—would justify the conclusion that the substance poses some risk of serious harm no matter how minute the exposure and no matter how many experts testified that they regarded the risk as insignificant. That conclusion would in turn justify pervasive regulation limited only by the constraint of feasibility. In light of the fact that there are literally thousands of substances used in the workplace that have been identified as carcinogens or suspect carcinogens, the Government's theory would give OSHA power to impose enormous costs that might produce little, if any, discernible benefit (448 U.S. at 645).

Now compare the tone of that statement by Justice Stevens to one he made in support of the EPA's conclusion that pollution sources could be regulated within the "bubble concept." Remember, the "bubble" permitted more air pollution. It would, thereby, make it more difficult to bring noncomplying areas under existing air quality standards, and it eased considerably the cost of pollution abatement on polluting industries.* But the courts recognized that the 1977 Amendments were, after all, *revisions* of the Clean Air Act, adding counterbalancing priorities to the agency's earlier mandate to promote clean air. These included preserving flexibility for the states in regulating air pollution and encouraging economic development in a time of recession. As a result, the court was sympathetic to the EPA's balancing of these competing demands:

> "Our review of the EPA's varying interpretations of the word "source"—both before and after the 1977 Amendments—convinces us that the agency primarily responsible for ad-

---

*According to Landau (1985), using the bubble to construct compliance with the Clean Air Act could save industry more than half in its compliance costs. DuPont Chemical alone would have to spend $106 million by the end of the decade to reduce emissions without the bubble, but only $43 million with it.

ministering this important legislation has consistently interpreted it flexibly—not in a sterile textual vacuum, but in the context of implementing policy decisions in a technical and complex arena. . . .

In this case, the [EPA] Administrator's interpretation represents a reasonable accommodation of manifestly competing interests and is entitled to deference. . . . Perhaps [Congress] consciously desired the Administrator to strike the balance at this level, thinking that those with great expertise and charged with responsibility for administering the provision would be in a better position to do so; . . . and perhaps Congress was unable to forge a coalition on either side of the question, and those on each side [in Congress] decided to take their chances with the scheme devised by the agency. For judicial purposes, it matters not which of these things occurred. . . .

When a challenge to an agency construction of a statutory provision, fairly conceptualized, really centers on the wisdom of the agency's policy, rather than whether it is a reasonable choice within a gap left open by Congress, the challenge must fail. In such a case, federal judges—who have no constituency—have a duty to respect legitimate policy choices made by those who do (467 U.S. at 863–866).

Taken out of context, Justice Steven's opinion for the unanimous court in *Chevron* reads almost like a dissent against his own plurality opinion in *Benzene*. Had the reasoning in *Chevron* been applied to the facts in *Benzene*, the Court's ruling would almost certainly have supported OSHA's benzene standard, and, indirectly, its Cancer Policy. What distinguishes the two cases, is that OSHA's benzene standard would have imposed significant costs on industry on the basis of a largely speculative policy balancing of unclear congressional intent. The "bubble concept" interpretation in *Chevron* relieved industry of significant costs on the basis of the EPA's largely speculative policy balancing of a congressional intent even less clear than

that of "feasibility" in the OSHAct. In effect, then, the Court seems to be telling agencies, "If you develop interpretive policies in response to uncertain congressional mandates, make sure those policies are cheaper for industry than the alternatives, or risk unfavorable review from this court."*

The Case of OSHA's Cancer Policy

The "policy considerations" underlying the EPA's choice of the "bubble concept" are extensively documented in the *Chevron* case itself, excerpted in this text (pp. 136–141). It is useful here to discuss in the same detail OSHA's attempt to deal with its ambiguous mandate from Congress as an illustration of the remarkable complexity of agency policymaking, carried out in an atmosphere of scientific and technical uncertainty. The Cancer Policy represents a pragmatic mixture of political, scientific, and legal judgment, all relevant to the agency's complex task of assessing and regulating the risks of carcinogens in the workplace. Our inquiry isolates each of these aspects of the policy for analysis. In practice, such analytical distinctions are almost impossible to maintain, yet each has its own separate logic and sometimes competing sources of legitimate authority.

THE POLITICAL CONTEXT. Much of the literature on regulation and regulatory reform treats risk assessment as if it were simply a technical means of distributing the equities of regulation. But further examination reveals that risk assessment is in large part a political question. Lowrance (1976) points out that risk assessment combines risk measurement (a technical issue) with the determination of the level of risk "acceptable" (a political issue). If one considers that the choice among measurement techniques is

*This cynical interpretation of current state of the art in scope-of-review has for the most part borne out in later cases. For example, the next direct application of *Chevron* came in *Young v. Community Nutrition Institute*, 106 S.Ct. 2360 (1986), in which an eight-member majority deferred the Food and Drug Administration's (FDA's) reluctance to promulgate "tolerance levels" for the carcinogen aflatoxin in feed corn. Interestingly, Justice Stevens wrote a bitter dissent, arguing that the court had misapplied the *Chevron* framework. As expected, the beneficiaries here avoided the expense of compliance with an FDA regulation.

also a political decision and that this choice generally affects the quantity of risk revealed, then even the ostensibly technical aspect of risk assessment is politically saturated.

The political balancing in risk assessment is captured in Lave's (1981) catalog of "decision frameworks" implicit in federal regulation. These frameworks range all the way from "market" regulation (leaving the private market to determine the level of acceptable risk) to an absolute "no risk" position (in which all risks are avoided by regulatory ban). Rodgers (1980) has developed a similar catalog for health and safety legislation by interpreting risk assessment as the relative balancing of costs and benefits expressed in statutory directives for regulation. The "cost-oblivious" directive weights public health and safety so heavily as to exclude all other considerations, whether related to economic costs or other competing benefits. "Cost-effective" directives set certain health and safety values as goals to be attained, not at all costs, but as efficiently as possible. "Cost-sensitive" is the most problematic of the four types, because it calls for the achievement of only those benefits that can be attained within certain cost constraints other than economic efficiency. "Cost-benefit" directives resemble economic decision criteria, in which the costs and benefits of regulation are compared indifferently. If the benefits outweigh the costs, then regulation should proceed.

Depending upon the political interpretation of "feasibility" in the OSHAct, OSHA's regulation of workplace carcinogens might be classified somewhere between a "cost-effective" directive (within technological limitations) and a "cost-benefit" directive (with the addition of a qualitative or quantitative risk factor). The indeterminate position of OSHA's directive reflects Congress' apparent uncertainty in striking the proper political balance in risk assessment. This uncertainty prompted Rodgers to create the "cost-sensitive" category between the cost-effective and cost-benefit categories. From this perspective, Congress simply asked OSHA to "play it by ear" regarding the definition of "feasibility" in risk-assessment terms.

THE TECHNICAL CONTEXT. The OSHAct posed a problem for OSHA because the "political conflicts" were unresolved when Congress asked OSHA to establish the "technical means" for regulating workplace carcinogens. As a result, OSHA was making *political* policy with *technical* decision criteria. The problems for OSHA were exacerbated by the fact that the technical criteria—scientific data on carcinogenesis—were just as uncertain as Congress' risk assessment directives. Essentially, the question comes down to whether or not there is a "safe" level of exposure to any documented carcinogen. At issue is whether carcinogenesis is a "one-hit" phenomenon in which one molecule of a carcinogenic substance is believed to be enough to interact with cell DNA to produce cancer or whether there are "threshold" levels below which cells can resist the mutagenic effects of carcinogenic substances.

The effect of exposure to suspected carcinogens is always a matter of extrapolation. "Biologic extrapolation" involves making inferences from "mouse to man," or scaling the results of laboratory animal experiments to fit human physiology. "Numeric extrapolation" refers to estimating the probability of cancer in humans at doses below experimental levels (Lashof et al., 1981: 12). Both types of extrapolation are essential in *measuring* risks as the "technical" component of any risk assessment regarding the regulation of carcinogens. Yet, particularly with numeric extrapolation, the method chosen will produce a systematic effect on the quantity of risk measured.

Such was the technical context within which OSHA interpreted the "feasibility" requirement of section 6 (b) (5) of the OSHAct, 29 U.S.C.A. sec. 655 (b) (5), and developed its risk assessment assumptions and procedures in its generic Cancer Policy, first proposed in 1977 (42 Fed. Reg. 54148) and finally promulgated three years later with over 200 pages of discussion and comment in the Federal Register (45 Fed. Reg. 5002). The policy embraced the conservative "risk averse" posture agreed upon by the Interagency Regulatory Liaison Group (IRLG), made up of the Environmental Protection Agency, the Food and Drug Administration, the Consumer Product Safety Commission, and OSHA. The IRLG issued a statement in 1979 (44 Fed. Reg. 39858) setting forth a policy on carcinogenic substances. The policy catalogued the assumptions under which the agencies would proceed in assessing the risks of human exposure to carcinogens. Among other things, it was assumed:

1. that there was no "safe level" of human exposure to carcinogenic substances;
2. that animal studies with positive cancer results were applicable to humans;
3. that substances causing either benign or malignant tumors in animals should be considered a cancer risk for humans; and
4. that human epidemiological studies are a useful but insufficient means of assessing carcinogenicity.

Specifically, OSHA's origin (1980) and later modified (1981) Cancer Policy classified potential carcinogens into one of three categories depending upon whether scientific data (1) indicated, (2) suggested, or (3) failed to demonstrate substances' carcinogenicity. "Category I potential carcinogens" were so designated if at least one "adequately conducted long-term bias-say" of a single mammalian species (with replication or supporting positive results from other tests) indicated carcinogenicity (29 C.F.R. 1990.112). In that event, the Cancer Policy required that worker exposure be reduced

> . . . to the lowest feasible level, primarily through the use of engineering or work practice controls. This is predicated in part upon the finding that no methods have been demonstrated for establishing exposure levels for carcinogens, acting singly or in combination, below which risks to exposed workers should be absent (45 Fed. Reg. 5284).

After OSHA determined that a substance was a Category I potential carcinogen, it was to conduct a "feasibility analysis" to determine the proper permanent standard for limiting worker exposure to the substance. OSHA's feasibility analysis incorporated risk assessment in a four-step process (MacCarthy, 1981–82: 807). First, OSHA determined whether the substance is hazardous (as in the Category I classification). If not, OSHA did nothing. If so, OSHA determined the exposure level at which "no employee will suffer material impairment of health." In the case of Category I substances, this level was presumed to

be zero unless a safe level of exposure above zero can be documented. Next, OSHA determined whether or not a zero-level standard was technologically feasible. If not, then OSHA selected the lowest level of exposure possible with available or conceivable* authorized technology. Finally, OSHA determined whether or not the industry as a whole could sustain the economic dislocation produced by complying with the exposure standard. If not, then OSHA set the exposure standard at the lowest level that was economically feasible for the entire industry.

Despite the technical trappings of OSHA's feasibility analysis, in essence it betrays a political *balancing* qualified in favor of workers (those exposed to the risks) by forcing industry (those generating the risks) to internalize, up to a point, the cost of the risks of workplace carcinogens. It is crucial to note that, in the absence of clearer congressional intent, OSHA could not escape making some political decisions as it chose among alternative technical strategies for setting its carcinogen standards. It could have justified more risk-tolerant standards under the vague feasibility directive. It should be noted that the inseparability of fact (technical) and value (political) in OSHA's Cancer Policy makes it a characteristic "regulatory question" (Matheny and Williams, 1981). Agencies routinely invoke their quasi-legislative authority to blend political policy with scientific fact in the forging of regulatory standards. It is the uncertainty of this blending, as discussed below, that made OSHA's Cancer Policy controversial. And, for regulatory purposes, it is within the legal context that this uncertainty is ultimately resolved.

THE LEGAL CONTEXT. Apart from the lack of clarity regarding workplace carcinogen regulation, the OSHAct complicates judicial review of OSHA standard setting, thus encouraging the courts to interpret policy and science as well as law. The nub of the legal problem with OSHA standard setting is a matter of administrative procedure. The OSHAct is a self-contained statute insofar as it specifies the procedures

---

*This is called "technology-forcing" and has been favorably reviewed in *Society of the Plastics Industry, Inc. v. OSHA*, 509 F. 2d 1301 (2d Cir. 1975).

for agency rulemaking; thus the Administrative Procedure Act does not apply. But in specifying these procedures and the criteria for judicial review of OSHA rulemaking, Congress created an "administrative mismatch" (Elliott, 1979: 226–228). Section 6 (b) (3) of the OSHAct, 29 U.S.C.A. 655 (b) (3), provides for *hearing procedures* customarily associated with informal agency rulemaking in the pursuit of quasi-legislative authority (Verkuil, 1974: 206).

Section 6 (f) 29 U.S.C.A. 655 (f), contradicts this interpretation by requiring that OSHA's rulemaking be "supported by substantial evidence in the record considered as a whole" upon judicial review, a *standard of review* normally required in formal rulemaking or adjudication. The origins of this mismatch are the result of congressional compromise best described in Judge McGowan's opinion in *Industrial Union Department, AFL-CIO v. Hodgson*, 499 F.2d 467 (D.C. Cir. 1974):

> The hybrid nature of OSHA in this respect can be explained historically, if not logically, as a legislative compromise. The Conference Report reflects that the Senate bill called for informal rulemaking, but the House version specified formal rulemaking and substantial evidence review. The House receded on the procedure for promulgating standards, but the substantial evidence standard of review was adopted (499 F.2d at 473).

The administrative mismatch in the OSHAct is important to the fate of the Cancer Policy because the standard that the reviewing court chooses to apply determines whether OSHA or those challenging OSHA standards must bear the burden of proof as to the validity of the standards. An informal rulemaking standard would require only that OSHA proceed in a nonarbitrary and noncapricious manner. Standards would be presumed valid, thus placing the burden of proof squarely upon the challenger. A formal rulemaking standard would require the rule to be reasonably related to evidence presented in the record, thus placing the burden of proof upon OSHA.

Because the Cancer Policy is based upon a series of political assumptions about scientific and technical criteria, none of which is subject to proof, assignment of the burden of proof essentially determines whether the policy stands or falls. At this point, the political, technical, and legal contexts of the Cancer Policy are in wondrous juxtaposition, and what is a *procedural* matter at law (informal vs. formal rulemaking) becomes a *methodological* criterion for establishing the technical bases of OSHA standard setting and a *substantive* criterion for discerning the political balancing intended by Congress in passing the OSHAct.

In response to the administrative mismatch in the OSHAct, OSHA has "formalized" its rulemaking proceedings (29 C.F.R. 1911.15) well beyond those prescribed in the legislation, in order to establish the exhaustive record necessary for meeting the substantial evidence standard. Judicial reception of OSHA's effort in the circuits was mixed. The Fifth Circuit Court of Appeals decided *American Petroleum Institute v. OSHA*, 581 F.2d 493 (5th Cir. 1978), holding that OSHA had to prove that the "lowest feasible level" was a reasonable level of benzene exposure, based upon substantial evidence in the record. The circuit court interpreted "reasonable" to mean that there must be a rational relationship between the expected reduction in employee cancers and the costs of implementing the new standard, demonstrated quantitatively through some form of cost-benefit analysis. The circuit court determined that "feasible" actually means "reasonable," suggesting that OSHA's regulatory directive is cost-benefit balancing, rather than cost-sensitive, based upon the standard of review required of OSHA by the circuit court.

As the Fifth Circuit was making its decision, the Third Circuit decided *American Iron and Steel Institute v. OSHA*, 577 F.2d. 825 (3rd Cir. 1978), using the accommodative standard of review to uphold OSHA's new coke oven emission standards. Here, the circuit court did not require a substantiated connection between the hazard and a resulting increase in safety. All that was necessary was a showing that a hazard existed (i.e., that coke oven emissions cause cancer), that the standard would lower employee exposure to emissions, that the technology was available to achieve lower exposure, and that implementation would not cause industry-wide economic dislocation.

As it granted review in the *Benzene* case, the U.S. Supreme Court received a chorus of dissonance and uncertainty from the circuit courts on the issue of OSHA's Cancer Policy. At stake was whether or not the courts had fundamentally distorted the political and technical aspects of OSHA's carcinogen regulation by applying different standards of judicial review.

THE SUPREME COURT AND "SIGNIFICANT RISK".

The Supreme Court was asked to resolve two issues in the *Benzene* case: (1) the validity of OSHA's permanent standard reducing concentrations of benzene in the workplace from ten parts per million (ppm) to one ppm and (2) whether OSHA was required to demonstrate a "reasonable relationship" between the expected benefits of the new standard and the costs of implementing it. Both of these issues arose from the Fifth Circuit's opinion that section 3(8) of the OSHAct (the "reasonably necessary or appropriate" definition), 29 U.S.C.A. 652 (8), should be read as controlling the "feasibility" requirement of section 6 (b) (5), 29 U.S.C.A. 655 (b) (5). The Court upheld the Fifth Circuit's judgment on the first issue and found it therefore unnecessary to reach a decision on the second. But the Fifth Circuit had answered both issues together, holding that OSHA has the burden of proving the new standard to be reasonably necessary or appropriate and that meant proving the benefits of the standard to be reasonably related to the costs (581 F.2d at 503–504).

In order to avoid the second issue while yet answering the first, the Supreme Court developed another criterion for proof. The plurality read sections 3(8) and 6 (b) (5) as requiring OSHA to make a threshold determination that workplace conditions prior to regulation present a "significant risk of material health impairment" (448 U.S. at 639). While "significant risk" language can be found nowhere in the OSHAct, the plurality supported its "amendment" by arguing that a "safe" workplace under section 3(8) does not mean a "risk-free" workplace.

The plurality's logic specifically contradicts Congress' obvious intent in singling out "toxic materials and harmful physical agents" for especially protective treatment (Ashford, 1976). As a result of the plurality's logic, section 6 (b) (5) is meaningless, thus violating the most basic rules of statutory construction: (1) that courts should attempt to give equal weight to all provisions in a statute, unless instructed otherwise, and (2) that specific provisions in a statute generally alter general definitions (Scorcia, 1980: 450). Finally, the plurality's position seems to ignore the established distinctions in statutory interpretation identified by Rodgers (1980). Justice Stevens' opinion likens OSHA's feasibility analysis to a "cost-oblivious" congressional directive, when, comparatively, feasibility (as a "cost-sensitive" directive) is not only more restrictive of agency action than a cost-oblivious, or "risk-free," directive, but also more restrictive than a "cost-effective" directive. The plurality's conflation of "feasible" and "reasonable" in its significant risk test is, then, a major shift of the political balance, however vague, originally struck by Congress in the OSHAct, and a point-black rejection of OSHA's intepretation of that balance in its Cancer Policy.

What appears to have happened in *Benzene* is that plurality simply did not like the political implications of OSHA's Cancer Policy and the "policy judgments" that it entailed. The "significant risk" test reinterprets the political and scientific assumptions of OSHA's Cancer Policy, regardless of the precise definition of "significant." Simply shifting the burden of proof to OSHA is enough to stop most regulation of low-level exposure to workplace carcinogens in its tracks. The vitality of the Cancer Policy was severely threatened in the *Benzene* case. And the Supreme Court had yet to answer the question of whether OSHA was required to relate the expected benefits of its standards to the costs of implementation. The Court's response was soon in coming, but did little to clarify the future of OSHA's Cancer Policy.

THE COTTON DUST CASE.

The majority in the *Cotton Dust* case, while apparently defending OSHA's regulatory scheme, unwittingly preserved a major obstacle to future OSHA regulation of carcinogens. The issue in the case is clear-cut. The Court was asked to determine whether or not the feasibility requirement of section 6 (b) (5) required OSHA to perform cost-benefit analysis in order to justify the promulgation of a standard. After addressing this issue, the

Court was asked to determine whether or not OSHA had developed "substantial evidence" in support of its cotton dust standards and their feasibility.

In a straightforward opinion, Justice Brennan, joined by the rest of the *Benzene* minority and Justice Stevens, stated simply that cost-benefit analysis is not required; rather, that "feasibility analysis is" (452 U.S. at 509). The majority then went on to hold that the lower court had not "misapprehended or grossly mis-applied" the OSHAct's substantial evidence test in upholding OSHA's findings in the promulgation of cotton dust standards (452 U.S. at 522–536). The result of the Court's decision was to leave OSHA's cotton dust standards substantially in place.

While the Court's ruling is fairly simple, it presents several complications for predicting the future of OSHA's carcinogen regulations. First, the government and OSHA did not challenge the significant risk standard. It had been incorporated into a revised OSHA Cancer Policy (46 Fed. Reg. 5878), despite the fact that only a plurality of the Court supported invention in the *Benzene* case, and despite the fact that a *majority* in the *Benzene* case refused to support the plurality's grafting of section 3(8)'s reasonableness definition onto section 6 (b) (5)'s feasibility criterion.* Second, the *Cotton Dust* majority's opinion completely destroys the statutory basis of the significant risk standard, holding:

> We cannot believe that Congress intended the general terms of [section] 3(8) to counter-mand the specific feasibility requirement of [section] 6 (b) (5). Adoption of petitioners' interpretation would effectively write [section] 6 (b) (5) out of the Act. We decline to render Congress' decision to include a feasibility requirement nugatory, thereby offending the well-settled rule that all parts of a statute, if possible, are to be given effect (452 U.S. at 513).

But in a footnote immediately following this statement, the majority reiterates the *Benzene* plurality's assertion that "all [section] 6 (b) (5) standards must be addressed to 'significant risks' of material health impairment" (452 U.S. at 513–514, n. 32).

It is difficult to understand how the Supreme Court could allow the crucial burden of proof question raised in the *Benzene* case to be answered effectively by default, with the support of only a minority of the justices. The *Cotton Dust* majority simply assumed the validity of the significant risk threshold, while, in the same breath, attacked the very underpinnings of that threshold. Granted, the *Cotton Dust* case clarifies the risk assessment balance implied in the OSHAct by holding that feasibility does not require cost-benefit analysis.† But this accomplishment perishes in the fact that the Court leaves unexamined the significant risk standard. This standard is much more crucial to the fate of OSHA's Cancer Policy that the cost-benefit issue because it erects a threshold test for regulation. If OSHA is unable to carry the initial burden of proving a significant risk, then, as in the *Benzene* case, it is irrelevant what particular type of risk assessment balancing is employed. As it stands now, the Cancer Policy is held in jeopardy by a judicial decision; a decision without a defensible statutory basis and without the explicit backing of a majority of the Court to support it.

The Supreme Court has, in essence, resolved the political, technical, and legal complexities of OSHA's workplace carcinogen regulation by deciding not to decide. The Court has left the uncertain future of a weakened Cancer Policy up to OSHA, just as Congress earlier had saddled the agency with uncertainties regarding risk assessment. But the Court's work has also made the Cancer Policy extremely vulnerable to the effects of economic recession and to the threats of regulatory reform under the Reagan and Bush administrations.

---

*Justice Rehnquist concurred in the *Benzene* plurality's rejection of OSHA's benzene standard, but on grounds that section 6 (b) (5) was an unconstitutional delegation of legislative power, which could not be saved by any attempt to modify section 6 (b) (5) with section 3(8) (448 U.S. at 686–688).

†Justice Rehnquist introduces a troublesome point in dissent, however. He argues that the court's opinion interprets the OSHAct as not *requiring* cost-benefit analysis and that this means OSHA would be *permitted* to conduct cost-benefit analysis if it were to choose to do so (452 U.S. at 544).

UNMAKING OSHA'S CANCER POLICY. As the *Benzene* and *Cotton Dust* cases place the burden of proving "significant" cancer risks on OSHA instead of the regulated industry, the research capacity of OSHA—its ability to develop the evidence necessary to pursue carcinogen regulation in the workplace and to meet the burden of proof in court—became crucial. Equally important to the future of workplace carcinogen regulation was OSHA's reaction to the influence of the Reagan and Bush administrations' increasingly persistent calls for regulatory reform, and the difficulties posed by economic recession.

On July 12, 1981, OSHA proposed a reduction in the requirement for companies to keep medical records on employees exposed to hazardous substances. The number of workers covered would be reduced from 28 million to 17 million. The number of substances would be reduced from 39,000 to about 3,500. The period for retaining records was also slightly reduced and modified (47 Fed. Reg. 30420). This proposal came at the same time as Reagan administration proposals to reduce funding for OSHA's research and monitoring activities under the National Institute of Occupational Safety and Health (NIOSH). From a budget base of $76,217,000 for research in FY 1981, NIOSH was to experience a 36.4 percent reduction in funding by FY 1983. NIOSH's budget for training inspectors ($20,926,000 in FY 1981) was to be entirely phased out by FY 1983, with the states presumably picking up the slack. Finally, NIOSH's budget for scientific and technical services ($5,287,000 in FY 1981) was to be reduced by 60.6 percent over the same period (Office of Management and Budget, 1982: I-K8).

Given the scientific uncertainties and the obvious need for more data on workplace carcinogenesis, it is difficult to imagine how OSHA could meet the threshold determination (significant risk) required in the *Benzene* and *Cotton Dust* cases in future regulatory efforts, even under the best of circumstances. But the addition of a "reconsidered" Cancer Policy, research budget cutbacks, and reduced monitoring and manpower capacities make OSHA's failure to do so a near certainty (Bosker, 1982). The Supreme Court has given OSHA the burden of proof, and the

Reagan administration reduced OSHA's research ability to meet that burden, placing OSHA's Cancer Policy in a legal and scientific "double-bind" with the political consequence of reduced regulatory capacity. Workplace carcinogen regulation is now a "no-win" proposition. The *Benzene* case illustrates particularly well the political consequences of treating political conflicts as if they were simply issues of science and legal procedure. *Benzene's* significant standard, shifting the burden of proof to OSHA, was the linchpin of the Cancer Policy's effective demise.

In the Wake of Benzene and Chevron: An End to Judicial Duplicity

In order to appreciate the extent of the Supreme Court's "hard look" in *Benzene* compared to its "soft look" in *Chevron*, consider that, in the decade since *Benzene* was decided, regulation of workplace carcinogens has gone almost nowhere. No matter how unclear Congress' delegation to OSHA, Congress must have envisioned some meaningful regulation of occupational disease in passing section 6 (b) (5) of the OSHAct. Yet because of the technical and scientific uncertainties and the Reagan administration's early efforts to weaken federal regulation of occupational disease, OSHA as been paralyzed in its regulatory efforts. The Supreme Court simply did not permit OSHA to make the policy (read: value-laden) decisions necessary to go beyond the inherent scientific limitations in the area. Further, *Benzene's* establishment of the significant risk threshold, and the dismantling of the Cancer Policy, have made it virtually impossible for interests supporting worker health to challenge the agency's inactivity in court as a means of forcing OSHA to take occupational disease seriously.

In order to bring some consistency to the Supreme Court's choice of "administrative deference" and "hard-look" approaches to judicial review, we should remember that the two standards of review developed in response to entirely different eras in the emergence of administrative government in America. Perhaps the most useful way to capture these eras is to begin by identifying generic categories of regulation based upon the several commonly accepted purposes of regulation, as practiced in American government. These are: (1) regulation to restore *efficiency* in economic markets, often called economic regulation; (2) regulation to promote *equity*, or nonmarket, political goals in society, sometimes referred to as social regulation; and (3) regulation to capture *externalities* as they occur through subtle failures of the market, referred to here as the "new" social regulation. These categories, while failing perhaps to describe any particular regulatory program, usefully define the modal tendencies of most of the government's regulatory efforts. What's more, they nicely coincide with the historical and institutional development of the American administrative state.

Early federal regulation was mostly economic regulation, centering on efforts to achieve efficiency in the operation of American markets. Modern administrative government, born at the turn of the century, at first existed in a hostile legal and political environment, an environment that did not change until the late 1930s with eventual victory of Franklin Roosevelt's New Deal. Essentially, judicial deference to agency expertise emerged with the expansion of administrative authority accompanying the New Deal. A solicitous judiciary, wary of the power of regulated interests to inhibit effective regulation by the fledgling "alphabet agencies," bent over backward to support administrative authority.* A deferential standard of review was compatible with the Progressive political vision of the era, suggesting that expertise was the key legitimating ingredient of administrative governance, thus requiring as little intrusion as possible from political and judicial influences.

By the 1960s, a series of developments transformed the foundations underlying the legitimacy of adminis-

trative government. First, as noted by McCraw earlier in the text (pp. 13-23), the dominant image of neutral agency expertise in the area of economic regulation had been replaced by a perception of "regulatory capture." Second, the regulatory agenda of American government had been expanded to include a significant commitment to regulation in pursuit of equity values (e.g., the civil rights legislation of the mid-1960s) and in pursuit of the reduction of negative externalities in the operation of economic markets. The perception of regulatory capture and government involvement in pursuit of equity values, particularly those aimed at expanding the franchise to vote, were indicative of a change in public and judicial perceptions about the legitimate operation of administrative agencies. This presaged the development of a new attitude among the judiciary toward agency decisionmaking, leading to the establishment of "hard-look" review.† The judiciary was apparently inspired by a belief that administrative expertise could no longer be accepted uncritically and should at least be tempered by an openness in administrative proceedings and a serious examination of the data used by the experts to arrive at their decisions. One result was the courts' relaxation of standing requirements to permit much greater public involvement as a check on the undue influence of regulated interests in agency decisionmaking.

An important part of this shift in consciousness about administrative government had to do with the recognition by the judiciary that agencies weren't simply making technical decisions about the efficiency of market competition anymore. Those decisions, in themselves, were influenced by politics, and now agencies were increasingly asked to make explicitly political decisions involving the equitable goals of social regulation. If agency fare were increasingly (seen as) political, then judicial review should reflect that perception with a more penetrating examination of agency action to insure public input (since participa-

---

*Such solicitude inspired the passage of the Administrative Procedure Act in 1946, in which Congress attempted to channel agency power and strengthen judicial review of agency action in order to place systematic controls on agency government. But the tradition of judicial deference continued for at least another twenty years. The discussion presented here reflects our larger examination of regulation in *Democracy, Dialogue, and Regulation: Being Fair versus Being Right* now under review for publication. We also rely on Shapiro (1982) and Harris and Milkis (1989).

†And, we might add, the shortlived attempt to expand the procedural requirements in agency rule-making beyond the APA minimum, ended by *Vermont Yankee.*

tion is a legitimating norm of political decisionmaking) and careful scrutiny of the basis of agency policy (to guard against "agency bias"). The judiciary was faced with a tough choice in developing a suitable standard of review. If they abandoned the earlier deferential approach, they would leave agencies open to the powerful second-guessing of regulated interests. But failing to embrace the new standard of review would leave the prospects of regulatory capture undisturbed and would deny public access to the admittedly political decisions of administrative government.

As an illustration of this judicial dilemma, it is educational to read Justice Marshall's tortured opinion in the *Overton Park* case, as he develops the basics of the "hard-look" doctrine, while trying desperately to leave administrative deference in general undisturbed. Unfortunately for students of administrative law, the problems skirted by Justice Marshall in *Overton Park* are only exacerbated when agencies are assigned the responsibility of implementing the new social regulation, including environmental regulation, occupational safety and health regulation, toxic substances regulation, and a variety of consumer regulation, etc. The distinguishing characteristics of this sort of regulation are: (1) *redistributive effects*, caused by the internalization of market externalities; (2) explicitly *political weighting* of otherwise undervalued commodities, like clean air or worker health; and (3) policymaking based upon *incomplete scientific and technical data.*

The key problem with the pursuit of the new social regulatory agenda is straightforward. It attempts to impose the concentrated costs of internalizing the externalities of past market practices on identifiable and intensely organized interests, while surrendering the benefits of these impositions on to a diffuse, unorganized general population. Because the intense and organized "cost-bearers" have a strong incentive to resist the redistributive effects of such regulation, and because the calculus of that redistribution is either politically determined or incompletely specified by scientific and technical data, the thrust of such regulation is likely to be compromised in the policy process. As a result, agencies are likely to be similarly compromised in their efforts to develop and implement the policies commanded by the new social regulation. And compromised agency action is very vulnerable to judicial review, particularly if the courts have not clearly articulated when they will "bow cursorily" or "dig deeply" into administrative action.

When we combine the criticism underlying the ideologies of regulatory capture (the need to correct for undue influence of regulated interests), social regulation (the need for more egalitarian involvement in American life), and the new social regulation (the need to protect undervalued commodities from the operation of the market), a solution to the problem of judicial review of agency action suggests itself. Essentially, these criticisms reflect the demands of those interests that are structurally inhibited from expressing themselves in the operation of economic markets and in the American political system.

The recognition of structural constraints on political participation in the sphere of constitutional law has been dealt with successfully, though controversially, through the famous convention introduced in Justice Stone's "footnote four" of *U.S. v. Carolene Products Co.*, 304 U.S. 144 (1938). Perhaps it is time to govern the choice of deference or scrutiny in administrative law using a similar logic. The burden of structural constraint could be used to identify interests underrepresented in the administrative process, and then the appropriate standard of review could be applied to insure that those interests were, in fact, adequately represented. This proposal goes beyond Richard Stewart's (1975) "interest representation" model, which covers regulatory capture and the new ethic of participatory politics in agency policymaking, and suggests a generalizable way of handling the increasingly difficult problems of the new social regulation, e.g., protecting the policy judgments of administrators which are based upon incomplete and unattainable scientific and technical evidence. The courts would first make a threshold judgment as to whether the policy is aimed at the protection or promotion of a structurally constrained interest that would not normally find expression in the operation of the market or the political process. Following that determination, the courts would then choose between the "hard-look" and administrative deference standard of review. A retrenchment by the agency in a consumer protection program would be scrutinized carefully, while an inventive, but only scantily documented, agency policy designed to redress the effects of acid rain might receive a cursory bow.

The suggestion here is entirely speculative, particularly considering the current composition of the Supreme Court. It is a provocative suggestion, nonetheless, because it so clearly marks the judicial review of administrative action in a value-laden way. It can certainly be attacked for allowing the intrusion of nonlegal values into administrative law, but that intrusion is no less apparent in footnote four's similar foray into constitutional law. Further, those values are at least declared explicitly at the outset, and by comparison with the Supreme Court's recent behavior in reviewing agency action, such a declaration is, by itself, a distinct improvement on present practice. As it stands now, the Court dodges the political implications of its review policy, burying its agenda within "the reach and complexity of contemporary administrative law."

References

AIHC (1978) *American Industrial Health Council Recommended Alternative to OSHA's Generic Carcinogen Proposal*. Scarsdale, N.Y.: AHIC.

ASHFORD, N.A. (1976) *Crisis in the Workplace: Occupational Disease and Injury*. Cambridge, Mass.: MIT Press.

BOSKER, G. (1982) "Stepping Backward on the Environment," Editorial, *Gainesville Sun*, p. 2A, December 27.

DONIGER, D.D. (1978) "Federal Regulation of Vinyl Chloride: A Short Course in the Law and Policy of Toxic Substances Control," 7 *Ecology Law Quarterly* 497.

ELLIOTT, C.A. (1979) "A Model for Judicial Review of OSHA Standards," 5 *Journal of Corporation Law* 222.

FREEMAN, A.M. (1980) "Technology-Based Effluent Standards: The U.S. Case," 16 *Water Resources Research* 21.

FRIES, M.L. (1981) "Searching for Scientific Certainty in the Enigma of Carcinogenecity," 8 *Ohio Northern University Law Review* 179.

HARRIS, R.A., and S.M. MILKIS (1989) *The Politics of Regulatory Change: A Tale of Two Agencies*. New York: Oxford University Press.

LANDAU, J. (1985) "*Chevron, U.S.A. v. NRDC:* The Supreme Court Declines to Burst EPA's Bubble Concept," 15 *Environmental Law* 285.

LASHOF, J.A. *et al.* (1981) *Assessment of Technologies for Determining Cancer Risks from the Environment*. Washington, D.C.: Office of Technology Assessment.

LAVE, L.B. (1981) *The Strategy of Social Regulation: Decision Frameworks for Policy*. Washington, D.C.: Brookings Institution.

LINDBLOM, C.E. (1982) "The Market as Prison," 44 *Journal of Politics* 324.

LOWRANCE, W.W. (1976) *Of Acceptable Risk*. Los Altos, Calif.: Kaufmann.

MacCARTHY, M. (1981-82) "A Review of Some Normative and Conceptual Issues in Occupational Safety and Health," 9 *Boston College Environmental Affairs Review* 773.

MATHENY, A.R. and B.A. WILLIAMS (1981) "Scientific Disputes and Adversary Procedures in Policy-Making," 3 *Law and Policy Quarterly* 341.

MAUGH, T.H. (1978) "Chemical Carcinogens: How Dangerous Are Low Doses?" 202 *Science* 37.

MILLER, G. (1981) "Occupational Safety: Real Costs, Real Benefits," 17 *Trial* 47.

MORELLI, J.C. (1980) "The *Benzene* Case: Life, Liberty and the Pursuit of Health," 3 *Western New England Law Review* 311.

OFFICE OF MANAGEMENT AND BUDGET (1982) *Budget of the United States-Appendix*. Washington, D.C.: Government Printing Office.

PERROW, C. (1982) "Not Risk But Power," 11 *Contemporary Sociology* 298.

RODGERS, W.H. (1980) "Benefits, Costs, and Risks: Oversight of Health and Environmental Decisionmaking," 4 *Harvard Environmental Law Review* 191.

RODGERS, W.H. *(1981)* "Judicial Review of Risk Assessments: The Role of Decision Theory in Unscrambling the Benzene Decision," 11 *Environmental Law* 301.

SCALIA, A. (1982) "Chairman's Message: Support Your Local Professor of Administrative Law," 34 *Administrative Law Review* v.

SCORCIA, M. (1980) "Section 6 (b) (5) of the Occupational Safety and Health Act of 1970: Is Cost-Benefit Analysis Required?" 49 *Fordham Law Review* 432.

SHAPIRO, M. (1982) "On Predicting the Future of Administrative Law," *Regulation* 18 (May/June).

STONE, P.F. (1981) "The Significant Risk Requirement in OSHA Regulation of Carcinogens," 33 *Stanford Law Review* 551.

STEWART, R.B. (1975) "The Reformation of American Administrative Law," 88 *Harvard Law Review* 1669.

VERKUIL, P. (1974) "Judicial Review of Informal Rulemaking," 60 *Virginia Law Review* 185.

VILLMOORE, A.H. (1982) "State and Legal Authority: A Context for the Analysis of Judicial Policy-Making, 4 *Law and Policy Quarterly* 5.

VOGEL, D. (1981) "The 'New' Social Regulation in Historical and Comparative Perspective," in T.K. McCraw (ed.) *Regu-lation in Perspective: Historical Essays.* Cambridge, Mass.: Harvard University Press, 155.

WEINBERG, A. (1972) "Science and Trans-Science," 10 *Minerva* 207.

WILLIAMS, B.A., and A.R. MATHENY (1990) *Democracy, Dialogue, and Regulation: Being Fair versus Being Right.* (Manuscript under review for publication).

Citizens, Bureaucrats, and Dignity

Some readers may object, observing that a shift in emphasis from the formal protections of a hearing to the substantive justifiability of the result will make front-line bureaucracies more impersonal, less respectful of the dignity of the individual. This criticism assumes that a person feels greater self-worth and dignity if he or she is heard, and heard orally, regardless of how much the hearing affects the outcome. Therefore hearings should be preserved for dignity's sake even when rationality will not increase and when hearings add time and money.

We should indeed take this criticism seriously. First, the problem of dignity goes much further than relationships in contested cases. Of the millions of citizens whose welfare, unemployment, personnel, disability, or licensing cases are reviewed each year, only a tiny handful raise even the possibility of a formal hearing. Policies that try to enhance dignity must cover the millions of cases, not just the handful.[10] Second, recall that in the most serious cases, where an agency imposes a specific sanction based on factual allegations about an individual's own actions, principles of administrative law should require hearings sufficiently formal to insure accuracy, and these will usually involve an oral hearing. Third, we are not convinced that offering reasons for a decision after notice and comment are substantially less respectful than maintaining the formalities of hearings, *as long as* the citizen can challenge the substance of the result.

Furthermore, three kinds of policies that we have not yet mentioned can and must be enhanced or preserved to help sustain dignity. The first concerns the the evidentiary process called "discovery." Parties who sense arbitrariness in government decisions may need access to the information the government possesses to prepare their case. In criminal procedure defendants have extensive access to the prosecution's evidence. The same benefits should be applied in administrative law.

The second policy seems at the moment reasonably secure. The justiciability principles of standing, ripeness, and exhaustion must continue to permit broad access to the courts. These principles give access to interest groups representing the poor, consumers, or other classes of people who do not possess the resources to finance their own lawsuits.

The third policy is in great danger, probably because, unlike the first two, courts have not chosen to support it. Poor people with individual grievances against their

[10]For example, see Jerry L. Mashaw's study of social security disability claims, *Bureaucratic Justice* (New Haven: Yale University Press, 1983).

treatment by the bureaucracy cannot rely on the private bar to assist them free of charge. The complexity of administrative structures and problems means that in many cases effective legal assistance will inevitably cost more than the poor can pay. It is therefore essential to maintain publicly funded legal services for the poor in noncriminal cases. President Reagan, since his first days as California's governor, tried to reduce or eliminate these programs.[11]

Deregulation: Law in Politics

Far more has been written about the politics of deregulation than about deregulation policy in administrative law.[12] In previous chapters, however, you have read cases and studied administrative law reforms that are part of deregulation. In the area of rulemaking, for example, the Supreme Court's decision not to support the National Highway Traffic and Safety Administration's procedure for deregulating (see *Motor Vehicles Manufactures Association v. State Farm Mutual Automobile Insurance Co.*, 1983, *supra* at p. 306), suggests that the Court still requires agencies to justify their policy choices despite who is in the White House (but see Justice Rehnquist's dissent, *supra* at p. 311). Regulatory negotiation is another example of deregulation in administrative law. While not all proponents of regulatory negotiation endorse deregulation, its emphasis on rulemaking through an informal bargaining process may lead to more privatized rulemaking compatible with the philosophy of deregulation. In the area of judicial review of agency discretion (chapter 9), you studied the trend toward greater judicial deference of agency interpretation and less support for the hard-look standard of review (e.g., see *Heckler v. Chaney*, 1985, *supra* at p. 366).[13] Finally, perhaps the failure to hold agencies liable for inaction (e.g., see *DeShaney v. Winnebago County Department of Social Services*, 1989, *supra* at p. 398), signifies a shift away from expanding the welfare state,[14] if not eroding the legal theory of the welfare state.

With these examples in mind, we conclude first by describing the political context of deregulation and then by providing two examples of how it has been implemented. We bring together three short descriptions of the ideology and actors in deregulation. Martin Shapiro, a law professor and political scientist at the University of California, Berkeley, argues that deregulation initially was supported by liberals and conservatives who viewed "old" regulation as inefficient. The turn toward the right is more evident

[11]For a comment on how the Legal Services Corporation has been "Reaganized" see Jane Bryant Quinn, "Justice for the Poor," *Newsweek*, April 12, 1982, p. 70.

[12]Stephen Breyer, *Regulation and Its Reform* (Cambridge: Harvard University Press, 1982); Martha Derthick and Paul J. Quirk, *The Politics of Deregulation* (Washington, D.C.: Brookings Institution, 1985); and Richard A. Harris and Sidney M. Milkis, *The Politics of Regulatory Change* (New York: Oxford University Press, 1989).

[13]Also see Cass R. Sunstein, "Deregulation and the Hard-Look Doctrine," 5 *Supreme Court Review* 5 (1984): 1977, and Merrick B. Garland, "Deregulation and Judicial Review," *Harvard Law Review* 98 (1985): 505.

[14]See Anthony Champagne and Edward J. Harpham eds., *The Attack on the Welfare State* (Prospect Heights, Ill.; Waveland Press, Inc., 1984).

once "new" social regulation is targeted by the Reagan administration. Two other political scientists, Martha Derthick and Paul Quirk, fill out the story on deregulation by tracing the formation of its political agenda and identifying its advocates. And Alfred Aman, a law professor at Cornell University, provides a concise summary on the economic discourse of deregulation. With this background, we return to Derthick and Quirk for a brief description of deregulation policy on air pollution.[15] We end with an essay by Robert Kuttner from the *New Republic* on the case for "re-regulate" the airlines, the first industry to be deregulated in 1980.[16]

Deregulation has affected many other policy areas in addition to the two (environmental protection and airline regulation) we focus on in this chapter. The collapse of the savings and loan industry, for example, is another fallout from deregulation. Richard Stevenson, a journalist for the *New York Times*, documents questionable investments made with government-insured deposits and fraud committed by the owners of savings and loan banks when federal regulations were rolled back:

> Carl M. Rheuban founded First Network Savings Bank in 1983, and for six years poured its Government-insured deposits into questionable real estate deals, a solar energy company and even a "museum of magic" in the savings and loan institution's headquarters [in Los Angeles]. . . . Mr. Rheuban, who paid himself $11 million in dividends over six years as the owner of 97 percent of First Network, filed for personal bankruptcy last month, listing few assets and tens of millions of dollar in debts.
>
> The rise and fall of First Network is a case history of how one institution, like hundreds of others, rushed to take advantage of the savings industry's deregulation during the early 1980s, only to end up contributing to the most costly financial crisis since the Depression.[17]

---

[15]For background on the role of courts in environmental policy see Lettie Wenner, *The Environmental Decade in Court* (Bloomington: Indiana University Press, 1982), and R. Shep Melnick, *Regulation and the Court: The Case of the Clean Air Act* (Washington, D.C.: Brookings Institution, 1983). Also see Doug Amy, *The Politics of Environmental Mediation* (New York: Columbia University Press, 1987), on the use of mediation to avoid litigation by resolving environmental disputes informally.

[16]See Linda E. Demkovich, "The Pros and Kahns of Airline Deregulation," *National Journal*, August 26, 1978, and Richard W. Hurd, "How PATCO Was Led into a Trap," *Nation*, December 26, 1981.

[17]Richard W. Stevenson, "How One Savings Institution Came Apart," *New York Times*, June 12, 1990.

Regulation and Deregulation

Martin Shapiro
*Who Guards the Guardians?: Judicial Control of
   Administration*
Athens: University of Georgia, 1988, 94–98

Sometime in the seventies, the green began to fade a little in American public life. The magnitude of this fading should not be overemphasized, and attempting to account for changes in public sentiment always involves more speculation than science. In part, there was a general loss of confidence in government throughout the Western democratic social-welfare nations during the late seventies and early eighties. Long periods of Socialist rule in a number of European countries were interrupted. In the United States Jimmy Carter and Ronald Reagan each became president by running against "Washington." Even incumbent congressmen often ran against Congress in their bids for reelection. Much of this unrest had no direct link to regulation. It seemed to arise largely from the increased perception that more and more government spending on social welfare programs did not seem to make people happier and happier or to end poverty.

One aspect of this general unrest did seem to be more closely linked to regulation. During the sixties, it was rather widely assumed that American and Western European economies had reached such high levels of productivity that they no longer needed to concern themselves primarily with further economic growth. They could tolerate some cutback in growth rates and even some reduction in overall production in order to achieve a cleaner, safer, healthier environment. We all appeared to have more than enough cars and refrigerators and TV sets. What we needed was more clean air and open space. We could easily absorb the costs of environmental improvement without really cutting into our standard of living. In the eighties, it suddenly became far less clear that the industrialized nations of the West were so rich and so far ahead of everybody else that they could shift radically from economic growth to improving the quality of life. We began worrying about the costs of government's regulatory programs as well as its welfare programs.

We have noticed that much of the cost of the new regulatory programs initially appeared acceptable to Congress because those costs were to be borne by the regulated, not the taxpayers. Once Americans began to worry about the national economy as a whole, however, this appearance of cost shifting disappeared. In the sixties, it was we, the people or the public or the consumers against them, the polluters or big business or special interests. We would get the benefits, and they would pay the costs. In the eighties, it became we, the American economy, against the economies of the rest of the world with the fear that industrial production and jobs and money would shift abroad, threatening the living standards of all Americans. If environmental and safety regulation made American products more costly, discouraged investment, and threatened economic growth, then we, the Americans paid the cost and they, the Japanese and the Koreans and the Germans benefited. In the sixties, we worried about saving the environment for our children. Today, we worry about whether they will manage to have a standard of living as high as their parents. Today, the endangered species we may worry about most are the steel worker and the farmer. Government is seen as imposing regulatory costs that must be balanced against regulatory benefits.

A general loss of confidence in government as the solution to all our problems and a general anxiety about national economies occurred throughout the Western world and led to a more critical attitude toward government regulation of the economy. This critical attitude flowered into the "deregulation" movement that has captured so much political support in recent years.

To speak of a deregulation movement is a bit too simple. It disguises the basic fact that while we have been doing away with some regulation of a few industries, the total amount of government regulation has continued to increase. Indeed, even the Reagan administration can only brag that it has decreased the

Deregulation targeted old, single theme agencies- ie regulation of truckers.

New regulation is seen as focusing on business.

rate at which new regulations are enacted, not that it has decreased the total amount of regulation.

One way to unravel this complexity is to distinguish between old and new regulation. We have seen that a kind of corollary of capture theory was a life-cycle model. As agencies got older, they lost their early regulatory vigor and became more subject to capture. It also just so happened that the older regulatory agencies were single-industry regulators and thus more likely to acquire a certain sympathy for the industry regulated than the newer all-industry agencies such as OSHA and EPA. Much of the deregulation movement has been aimed at the old single-industry regulators and has been occurring at a time when there is still considerable enthusiasm for the new health, safety, and environmental regulation. Thus an apparent paradox of more regulation and less regulation is resolved in part into an off-with-the-old, on-with-the-new phenomenon.

The moves to deregulate long-haul trucking, radio, airlines, and natural gas, and to reduce regulation of railroads, banking, and television are largely built around a common rationale. Many years ago, Congress was confronted by quasi-natural monopolies or situations where a small number of operators with reduced competition appeared to be desirable even if not inevitable. In response, Congress passed regulatory legislation that legitimated the quasi-monopoly but substituted regulatory controls in the public interest for the market place controls that would have operated had the industry been more competitive.

Over time, however, these regulatory controls had come to serve the public badly for a number of reasons. In some instances, agencies had been captured and their regulations had come to favor the industry against the public. In others, the regulations had been well-intended but turned out to be wrong. They led to inefficient investment and the unwarranted cross-subsidization of some classes of customers or industries or parts of the country by others. In other instances yet, economic or technological changes had ended the necessity or desirability of a particular quasi-monopoly. It would have been replaced by healthy and economically efficient competition but for the legal regimes of regulation that were needlessly preserving monopoly.

It is not clear that deregulators were always correct in their analysis or solely devoted to serving the public good as opposed to the interests of specific sectors of the economy. Nevertheless, their common claim was that certain bodies of regulation were artificially maintaining monopolies where free competition would yield better results. Merely by sweeping away the regulation, the public good would be better served.

This facet of deregulation accounts for some political phenomena that might otherwise have appeared rather strange. In Congress, deregulation often brought together liberals and conservatives at the very time when the same liberals continued to champion newer forms of regulation. It permitted liberal Democrats associated in the public mind with now disreputable "big government" to show that they too were against big government. And it tended to render defenseless even the spokesmen of those big industries that really, deep down would have preferred to remain regulated. After all, they had been among the most prominent critics of such regulation in the past.

Until the Reagan administration, the deregulation campaign had moved chiefly against segments of the old regulation. Gradually, however, attacks began to mount against the new regulation as well. They came largely, but not entirely, from Republican and conservative sources.

The problem began, in a sense, in the earliest days of OSHA, which started off with an extremely mechanical mode of safety enforcement. It instructed its inspectors to cite every violation no matter how minor, and it wrote many of its own regulations in extremely rigid ways. Tales were soon rife of OSHA inspectors insisting that every fire extinguisher in a huge plant be moved six inches because OSHA regulations required that they be mounted three feet above the floor and the plant's were two feet six inches. If the change was not made, the inspector would issue six hundred citations each time he visited the plant, one for each extinguisher. OSHA soon engendered a considerable spirit of resistance in the private sector which, finding it could not reason with the inspectors, took to fighting out a high proportion of the citations in court.

OSHA's problem served as a kind of prelude to the increased worries about the new regulation that almost necessarily followed from the shift in public concerns that occurred in the 1980s. If there is a general concern about "big government" and about maintaining an efficient economy with a substantial

rate of growth, the new regulation cannot go entirely unscathed.

The attacks on the new regulation did not take the form of questioning its basic values of health, safety and environmental purity. Those retained a strong hold on the minds of most Americans. Instead they came in the form of questioning the efficiency of the new regulations and of counterbalancing another value, economic prosperity, against the new regulatory values.

The Reform Idea

Martha Derthick and Paul J. Quirk
The Politics of Deregulation
Washington, D.C.: Brookings Institution, 1985, 39–56

It was the happy fate of the advocates of deregulation in 1974–75 to make the best matches with officeholders that anyone could have conceived of—first with the most publicized Democrat in the Senate, Edward M. Kennedy, and soon thereafter with the new Republican president, Gerald R. Ford, who succeeded the disgraced Richard M. Nixon in the late summer of 1974. Both men espoused procompetitive deregulation as a policy choice and by their own actions and advocacy turned it into a political symbol of moderate potency.

Kennedy and Consumerism

Kennedy became involved when one of the expert advocates of regulatory reform, Stephen G. Breyer, became special counsel to the Subcommittee on Administrative Practice and Procedure of the Judiciary Committee, which Kennedy chaired. A professor of administrative and antitrust law at Harvard, Breyer had worked in the Justice Department's Antitrust Division in the late 1960s at the time it was

beginning to get involved in regulatory proceedings, and with the economist Paul MacAvoy he was coauthor of a book that argued for deregulation of natural gas.* Though not an economist himself, he was very much part of the academic community that had built the analytic case for reform, and his arrival on Capitol Hill substantially bolstered the forces of advocacy in Washington.

Upon joining the subcommittee staff in the spring of 1974, Breyer urged Kennedy to consider airline regulation as a subject of investigative hearings, with the expectation that this would set the theme—regulation versus competition—for a whole series of investigations. He wanted to begin with the airlines because he believed that the analytic case for reform had been especially well established for that industry. Kennedy showed routine interest rather than great enthusiasm for the subject; he was willing to let the staff see what they could make of it. . . .

Breyer told him, not altogether correctly, [it] would be "nonglamorous." But it is more likely that Kennedy was attracted to the subject because he saw in it a response to consumerism, the political movement that addressed the interests of the consumer against big business or, in the case of regulatory regimes, the com-

---

*Stephen G. Breyer and Paul W. MacAvoy, *Energy Regulation by the Federal Power Commission* (Washington, D.C.: Brookings, 1974).

bination of big business and big government. As possible themes of the hearings, Breyer had suggested "help the consumer," "free the captive agency," or "more competition," and his memoranda to Kennedy defined prices as the central issue. Kennedy's opening statement in the hearings did so too: "Regulators all too often encourage or approve unreasonably high prices, inadequate service, and anticompetitive behavior. The cost of this regulation is always passed on to the consumer. And that cost is astronomical." "The way to get the press's and the public's and the senator's attention," a staff aide later said, "was with the consumer stuff," not just high prices, but also lost luggage and the suffering of household pets shipped as freight. . . .

The themes that anticompetitive regulation had a probusiness bias and that regulatory agencies were at best incompetent and at worst "captured" and corrupt had been driven home quite widely by the mid-1970s, even if price and entry deregulation was not, strictly speaking, a mass issue. Anyone who had an informed opinion on the subject could hardly have failed to have that opinion. Academic analysis played a part in this. While economists purported to show, with ever-increasing analytic sophistication, that anticompetitive regulation was inefficient and therefore contrary to the public interest, the literature of political science and history provided an explanation of why this outcome had occurred. Overwhelmingly, it portrayed regulatory agencies as excessively subject to the interests of regulated industries, although the authors differed over whether government regulation had been inspired by business interests in the first place or only succumbed to them with time through a combination of internal decay and the default of public supervision.

Having gained considerable currency in academic settings, the view that regulatory agencies served the interests of the regulated was greatly amplified in the late 1960s and early 1970s by Ralph Nader and the political movement that formed around his person, purporting to speak for consumers generally. Nader's Raiders, Ivy League graduate students who were eager to expose the wrongdoing of regulators, fanned out through government agencies and produced a series of books on the incompetence and probusiness bias they believed they found there. These books had surprisingly large sales, partly as a result of their use as college texts. Nader's Raiders took the critique of regulatory agencies out of learned journals and gave it a semipopularized, widely accessible form. . . .

. . . Eventually the idea that government regulation served business interests penetrated mass attitudes. In 1977 a poll for *U.S. News & World Report* showed that 81 percent agreed and only 8 percent disagreed with the statement that "large companies have a major influence on the government agencies regulating them." . . .

Kennedy's hearings on the CAB, held early in 1975 after a half year of preparation by Breyer and a very able staff, were an outstanding dramatic success. They set forth anew the academic findings about the adverse effects of airline regulation, uncovered abundant evidence of the agency's anticompetitive policies, and combined the two in a setting that exposed the CAB's inability to answer its critics. One whole day of hearings was devoted, for example, to showing that intrastate fares in Texas and California, for flights not subject to CAB regulation, were less than fares for comparable interstate flights, which were subject to regulation. This difference, which academic literature had already called attention to, appeared to constitute one of the most vivid and compelling indictments of regulation, but the CAB and the regulated airlines denied that regulation was the cause of it, arguing instead that differences in weather conditions, traffic densities, and aircraft types were to blame. The subcommittee staff gathered evidence with which to confirm regulation as the leading cause.

Ford and Inflation

Except for the need to combat inflation, President Ford might not have become an advocate of deregulation. When he took office in the summer of 1974, inflation was the leading domestic problem, and his administration began with a series of summit meetings of influential citizens to discuss remedies for it. Nearly all economists at these meetings agreed on one thing only—that government itself was contributing to inflation with a variety of anticompetitive restrictions on the operation of markets. Hendrik Houthakker, a former member of the CEA, prepared a long list of offending yet well-established government policies, so-called sacred cows, that were potential objects of reform, such as the monopoly of the U.S. Postal Service, minimum wage laws, and subsidies for ship construction and operation.

Slaughtering sacred cows is hard political work, and no one in the Ford administration could quite figure out in the fall of 1974 what to do next. The administration's initial response was vague and vacuous compared with its later effort. . . .

This was not a prescription for fast or effective action, and it may have been a blessing for the executive branch proponents of regulatory reform that Congress did not act on the president's recommendation for a commission. Had it done so, policy change would probably have been delayed rather than advanced. Instead, an administration task force—the Domestic Council Review Group on Regulatory Reform (DCRG)—emerged in the summer as an analyst and advocate, less prestigious and less publicized than a national commission would have been, but also more cohesive, committed, expeditious, and effective, even though lacking a formal charter. The group met once a week in the White House, bringing together reform proponents from the Department of Justice, Council of Economic Advisers, Office of Management and Budget, Domestic Council, and Council on Wage and Price Stability. . . .

By the spring of 1975, Ford was speaking of regulatory reform as if it were an end in itself, not just one element in an anti-inflation program, and he was rationalizing it on grounds that mixed popular culture, individual psychology, and economics: "Reduced competition hurts . . . the entire free enterprise system," he told an audience in New Hampshire. . . .

Thus, whereas Senator Kennedy had hewed consistently to a proconsumer theme, Ford's criticisms of regulation were variously addressed to consumer interests, business interests, the traditional American attachment to free enterprise, and popular hostility to big government. Mass distrust of government was growing, and so was resentment of the costs of supporting it and bearing its intrusions on private activity. A policy stance that promised to reduce government activity therefore had some potential for mass appeal (and some potential utility for a president who would soon be asking the national electorate to return him to office). Ford found that his speeches attacking big government and promising regulatory reform elicited a warm response. . . .

Progress was uneven, and priorities were unclear. The Domestic Council Review Group's interest in reform covered a very wide range of activities. For some—railroads, natural gas, financial institutions, repeal of "fair trade" laws—legislation was already pending before Congress when the DCRG was formed. For others—the Davis-Bacon Act, ocean shipping, insurance, agricultural cooperatives, the Postal Service, the activities generally of the "dependent" (or line) agencies—the DCRG made forays into regulatory terrain but achieved no progress substantial enough to approach the submission of bills. The greatest concentration of effort was on airlines and trucking, for which the administration submitted reform bills in 1975, and cable television and the Robinson-Patman Act (enacted during the Depression as a price-stabilizing measure to protect small grocers against supermarket chains), for which it came very close to doing so. These were subjects on which a good deal of preparatory work had been done even before the DCRG was formed and for which it was possible to use the expertise of line or presidential staff agencies to challenge independent regulatory commissions. . . . Because the DCRG had no staff capacity for the preparation of bills, it depended very heavily on task forces drawn from executive agencies. This may have been one of the reasons why the Ford administration found that it was harder to make headway with regulatory reform in the line agencies than in the independent regulatory commissions. Departmental secretaries generally were inclined to resist reform of regimes over which they presided, whereas Ford's secretary of transportation, William T. Coleman, actively cooperated in the administration's effort to modify the regimes of the CAB and ICC.

The Gathering Momentum of Reform

As work progressed and reform gained momentum and adherents, the goals of reform advocates became more ambitious. Within Kennedy's subcommittee, Breyer had initially had in mind rather modest procedural revisions of airline regulatory statutes that would have involved the Department of Justice and Department of Transportation more formally in regulatory proceedings. The committee report went further, calling for legislation designed to limit the CAB's powers to control prices, restrict entry, and confer antitrust immunity. In the hearings, Ralph Nader argued for abolishing the CAB. "Throughout the land," he said, "people are repulsed by arrogant and unresponsive bureaucracies serving no useful public purpose, and they are looking to this Congress to get on with the national housecleaning job that is needed. Can you think of a better place to start than the Civil Aeronautics Board?" More important and surprising, in the summer of 1975 a study done within the CAB staff called flatly for ending entry, exit, and price regulation within three to five years. What once had seemed impossible or absurd, and then unlikely, was now beginning to seem within reach after all—and it was beginning to be spoken of as "deregulation" rather than the more vague and ambiguous "regulatory reform," which was initially the prevalent term.

Not that "deregulation" failed to cloak a good deal of ambiguity. So remarkable was the convergence of the Ford and Kennedy positions that it became easy to overlook the fact that the convergence was in fact quite specific and delimited. It was confined to procompetitive deregulation—the removal of restrictions on price and entry. As a conservative, Ford sought to embrace deregulation much more broadly and to reduce government intervention in business conduct on a wide front, but the consumerist orientation of Kennedy meant that his advocacy was much more narrowly confined. This was true for liberal Democrats in Congress generally and for Jimmy Carter, the Democrats' presidential nominee in 1976. In a campaign appearance at a Public Citizens' Forum chaired by Ralph Nader, Carter categorized his own beliefs as those of "consumerism," embraced the view that the economic regulatory agencies created during the New Deal had been captured by regulated interests, and called for reducing anticompetitive regulation—but said he wanted to strengthen regulation for consumer and environmental protection.

Within the sphere of their agreement—airline deregulation being the immediate, specific case—the actions of Kennedy's subcommittee and the administration importantly reinforced each other. Breyer drew likeminded members of the administration into collaboration with the subcommittee staff, and the hearings helped to precipitate the formulation of an administration position. . . . When Kennedy's subcommittee issued its report, the senator and the president exchanged mutually encouraging letters that were made public, and the administration and the senator's staff continued to collaborate. A genuine alliance formed across the division of governmental branches and political parties, so strong was the shared commitment to a policy goal.

On the other hand, the symbolic, evocative power of the term "deregulation" did not lose much from the fact that the Democratic and Republican leaders of the gathering drive were far from fully agreed on their goals. Ambiguity is a great advantage in political symbols, and here was one that in a single phrase could be made to serve in two quite different ways. It could be used to affirm the traditional values of competition, free enterprise, and limited government, which were still widely held among conservatives and were enjoying a modest rediscovery among liberals. In a more polemical fashion, it expressed a deep cynicism about government institutions that was central to the ethos of consumerism, was fast spreading to the public at large, and was injecting a new ambivalence into the policy positions of liberals. The development of deregulation as a political symbol associated with powerful political figures was a necessary precondition to the next stage of its evolution, as a fashion in policy choice. . . .

Within a very short time, deregulation was transformed from a lonely cause with poor political prospects into a buzzword and bandwagon. Once coined—it first appeared as an entry in the *New York Times* index in 1976—the term entered swiftly into common and often gratuitous usage in Washington. Thus, for example, an extensive and varied reform of federal banking laws, under consideration for many years and with only one title of six having much to do with deregulation, was in 1980 entitled the Depository Institutions Deregulation and Monetary Control Act—much as the Federal Aid Highway Act of 1956 authorized a "national system of interstate and defense highways." Just as everyone in 1956 was in favor of defense, everyone in 1980 was in favor of deregulation.

The making of fashions in policy choice is more than a little mysterious, as is the making of fashions generally, but much can be inferred from what we have already said. Here was an idea, encompassable in a single if slightly awkward phrase, that responded to widely shared values, moods, and beliefs. That it could mean very different things to different people was an asset, not a liability; it suggested something worthwhile to virtually everyone. It also had very powerful and highly placed sponsors, and it suffered little or no loss in that respect when Jimmy Carter defeated Gerald Ford in the presidential election of 1976.

Whereas deregulation was manifestly congenial to Ford, a conservative Republican who rejected the notion that presidents are to be judged by their success in expanding the reach of federal government activity, a Democrat might have been expected to drop the issue in favor of giving priority to new programs. Carter did not say much about deregulation in his campaign, yet he promptly took up the cause after entering office and in early March 1977 endorsed airline deregulation in a brief message to Congress, signifying his interest in swift action. In its procompetitive form, deregulation was thoroughly consistent with Carter's professed commitment to consumerism, and, thanks to the efforts of his predecessor, it was a ripe issue to which he conveniently fell heir. Beyond that, the opportunity for fresh assertions of government power had been sharp-

ly reduced from the previous decade by budget deficits, stagflation, public disillusionment with big government, and liberals' loss of nerve and self-confidence. Increasingly, the activism of presidents was being channeled into rationalizing government rather than expanding it; hence the abiding interest in some version of regulatory reform.

In addition to having acquired very powerful political sponsors, deregulation—again, it its distinctively procompetitive form—continued to benefit from having a broad base of support in academic opinion and analysis. In one way or another, the intellectual premises of this policy prescription had been adopted to an exceptional degree by academics, especially in the elite universities. The economists who argued for such deregulation, though perhaps not a large number, could not truly be called lonely. Virtually the whole profession agreed with them, as they rightly were pleased to point out to congressional committees. . . .

Not only were economists agreed among themselves to an exceptional degree, but the agreement ranged, again to an exceptional degree, across the social sciences. The work of political scientists and historians had entered into the critique of regulatory conduct, and all of this work had had a telling influence on law schools, which were important because the practice of regulation had been the province of lawyers. Future regulators were trained here, and until the late 1960s and early 1970s they were generally trained in administrative law courses whose subject matter was overwhelmingly procedural and technical. But as the social sciences began to take up the study of regulation, their intellectual products began to invade law school curricula and publications. Some of the pioneering and influential critiques of public utility regulation appeared in law journals, and some of the influential advocates of reform—Breyer is the leading example—were members of law school faculties. Thus people who take their cues from the luminaries of the academic world would have come to think of procompetitive deregulation as a desirable thing, as would those who take cues from holders of the highest offices. Inside Washington, very few people indeed are impervious to both of these sets of cue givers. The press is attentive to both, and everyone is attentive to the press.

Apart from the properties of the fashionable idea itself and the properties of its sponsors, the creation of this policy fashion is to be understood also by reference to the nature of the community in which it reigned. Washington as the governing city is highly susceptible to fashions because it *is* a community—a collectivity overwhelmingly preoccupied with a common interest, the activities of government and politics, and positively saturated with internal communication. As a community, it is also internally competitive, intensely present-oriented, and status-conscious, which is to say responsive to the cues of leaders. Officeholders, thousands who serve them, and hundreds more who write and talk about them compete for political and policy successes. In this general quest, ideas as policy prescriptions are propounded in bewildering variety, and some succeed in the sense that they cease to be merely ideas; they are so widely approved within the Washington community, so often propounded, and so readily seized upon, that by sheer incantation they come to define styles in policy choice.

Though it puts us a bit ahead of our story, it is important finally to note that the appeal of deregulation as a policy fashion was immeasurably increased when its potential for political success began to be demonstrated. Incantation alone is unlikely to establish a fashion; some payoff in action is required. When Alfred E. Kahn as chairman of the CAB achieved well-publicized successes in deregulating through administrative action and when Congress then endorsed what he had done and carried it farther, deregulation became more than the policy preference of all right-thinking people. It became a proven winner in the competitive struggle for policy and political achievements, and everyone in Washington who wished to leave his mark on history could see that this was so. . . .

"There is a saying," Merton J. Peck observed in a gathering of lawyers and economists who were discussing regulatory reform, "that economists make bullets that lawyers fire at one another." In the late 1950s, Peck, an economist, had done research on the regulation of transportation, "and at that time no lawyers were taking the bullets." Peck thought that "what really dictates their demands for information are matters outside the purview of economists and their profession. . . . Changes in economic knowledge are less important in precipitating regulatory reform than events outside of economics."*

Much of our analysis supports this view. Economists had begun making the bullets of procompetitive regulatory reform fifteen years before politicians found them to be usable in particular battles they wished to fight. Drawing on the developing academic critique of transportation regulation, the Kennedy administration had sent a procompetitive reform bill to Congress in 1962 but elicited no response. In neither house was the bill even reported to the floor. What ultimately, in the mid-1970s, made the economists' arguments relevant to politics were events that no one could have foreseen: the development of severe inflation, the rise of consumerism, and a vague but widely diffused disaffection with a government that seemed to grow uncontrollably and irreversibly. Ironically, the economists' arguments became relevant then largely because the profession was so thoroughly at a loss to offer any better, more plausible cure for inflation, and not because anyone seriously thought that the inefficiencies created by public utility regulation were a significant cause of the inflationary spiral.

Unsettled Questions on Regulatory Reform (Washington, D.C.: American Enterprise Institute for Public Policy Research, 1978), 13.

Administrative Law in a Global Era: Progress, Deregulatory Change, and the Rise of the Administrative Presidency

Alfred C. Aman, Jr.
Cornell Law Review 1101; 1154–58 (1988):73

The political rhetoric that surrounds deregulation often implies that deregulation is clearly defined. Taken on its own terms, deregulation is the antithesis of regulation. Among those favoring deregulation, regulation stands for the heavy, inefficient, all-too-visible hand of the federal government, while deregulation represents individual liberty and a free marketplace. Those advocating deregulation often approach reform as if regulation and deregulation were opposites and as if the debate were truly dialectical.

This, however, is an oversimplified view, particularly for deregulation that occurs at the agency level. Deregulation is not simply the antithesis of regulation. Rather, deregulation can and does implement a variety of policy goals and aspirations. It is not a monolithic concept. Deregulation may be advocated for theoretical, normative, or pragmatic reasons, or for combinations of all of these kinds of reasons.

Micro-economic theory forms the underlying theoretical basis for deregulation. This kind of deregulatory logic typically argues as follows: Government intervention is unnecessary where markets can or do exist and where they can function reasonably freely. Markets can best allocate society's scarce resources to their highest and best use. Law is only necessary to bolster or help create a market. From an economic, theoretical point of view, law should not try to undo, substantially change, or modify the results a freely functioning market would otherwise produce. Thus, according to this view, there is no need to control the price of natural gas or oil because competition exists at the production level and the law of supply and demand will reach an equilibrium by means of the pricing mechanism. Those who cannot afford to pay will simply fall off the demand curve.

Closely related to the theoretical aspects of micro-economics which argue in favor of deregulation are the normative or philosophical reasons favoring deregulation. A market approach not only furthers efficency, but arguably furthers such values as liberty, creativity, decentralized government, and the excellence that comes with maximum individual freedom of choice. Thus, for example, Milton Friedman writes: "The preservation of freedom is the protective reason for limiting and decentralizing governmental power. But there is also a constructive reason. The great advances of civilization, whether in architecture or painting, in science or literature, in industry or agriculture have never come from centralized government." Friedman goes on to note that, while some governmental regulation might improve the standard of living of many individuals, "in the process, government would replace progress with stagnation . . . [and] . . . substitute uniform mediocrity for the variety essential for that experimentation which can bring tomorrow's laggards above today's mean." In short, the market is intrinsically good. The market leads to efficiency, and this, in turn, enables other positive values and individual economic rights to flourish.

Viewed in these theoretical and normative ways, the regulation-deregulation debate is a dialectical one. Government intervention stands as the antithesis of the free market. The process of deregulation, however, is political and the political reasons for advocating a market regime as opposed to a regulatory approach usually are based on pragmatic, often short-run policy goals. The market, like the law, is viewed and used instrumentally; that is to say, advocating and adopting market approaches to problems is not a return to nature, but the use of an impersonal regulatory tool, particularly appropriate, for example, for allocating shortages of energy supplies for which no politician particularly wants to take responsibility. Therefore, when the market reaches or promises politically popular results it is embraced. When the market's results are not politically popular, the market is rejected, regardless of the underlying theoretical or normative views of regulation. In short, behind the pragmatic use of the market is the same view of theory that underlies Keynes' famous dictum: "In the long run, we are all dead."

At the congressional level, for example, deregulation is often presented in a manner that resembles consumer legislation. Airline deregulation, for example, was aimed at lowering air fares and increasing services for consumers. Advocates of oil decontrol pitched it as a conservation measure and coupled the initiative with a stiff windfall profits tax to redistribute wealth in a politically acceptable manner. Such goals are similar to the policy aspirations and goals of traditional New Deal statutes. Though the means for achieving these ends is the market, the process of implementing this approach is the same as implementing any other government programs. Laws must be passed, speeches given, positions established, and votes taken. In the process, legislators' identities are sharpened. Deregulation is, in short, a political process and what it promises has much to do with whether or not it will succeed legislatively.

Viewed in this manner, it is impossible to see the regulation-deregulation issue simply in either/or terms. Nor does decontrol represent a simple regime. Control and decontrol, and regulation and deregulation are the same side of the same coin. To decontrol, one must first control. To deregulate, one must first regulate. Both actions require affirmative governmental proceedings and much of the decontrol that has occurred to date continues to focus attention on the federal government. In some cases, decontrol may actually increase federal power, particularly if the area decontrolled cannot constitutionally be regulated by the states. In short, even if one thinks of decontrol in normative and theoretical terms, it is nonetheless, ironically, another kind of government program as well, albeit one that does not necessarily require any expenditure of federal funds. Decontrol, therefore, need not be, and seldom is, the antithesis of control. It is, rather, a continuation of the same kind of political, regulatory processes as before. This is particularly the case in deregulation that occurs at the agency level. . . .

The Limits of Deregulation

Martha Derthick and Paul J. Quirk
The Politics of Deregulation
Washington, D.C.: Brookings Institution,
1985, 212–18

Air Pollution

In the wave of health and safety regulation newly authorized by Congress in the 1960s and 1970s—often loosely called "social" regulation to distinguish it from the "economic" regulation that accumulated earlier—by far the most costly both to governments and businesses was that designed to control air and water pollution. A survey of forty-eight companies released by the Business Roundtable in March 1979

found that 77 percent of the costs of the six regulatory programs selected for study stemmed from environmental rules. . . .

The need to cut back on environmental regulation had been one of [Reagan's] campaign themes. He had called for returning the primary responsibility for environmental regulation to the states. "They've got rules that would practically shut down the economy if they were put into effect," David Stockman remarked of the EPA soon after the election. As director-designate of the Office of Management and Budget, Stockman wrote an apocalyptic memorandum warning that the recent buildup of industrial regulation would "sweep through the industrial economy with near gale force, pre-empting multi-billions in investment capital, driving up operating costs and

Most expensive regulations are those that protect air & water.

siphoning off management and technical personnel in an incredible morass of new controls and compliance procedures." . . . The Clean Air Act was the leading target, not just because it was very costly in the aggregate and very burdensome to particular major industries that were in serious trouble (steel and autos), but also because it was due to be renewed in 1981 and because it prohibited the EPA from considering costs in setting national ambient air quality standards. This law epitomized for the economically oriented the irrationality and extremism of much of the social regulation.

No important legislative reforms occurred, however, and none were proposed by the administration. Rather than submit legislation, in the summer of 1981 the president sent Congress a set of eleven broadly worded principles to guide legislation. Their tone was much more moderate than what had been anticipated from the administration and had in fact been leaked in an early draft. Perceiving that there was not enough support for a major reduction of air pollution regulation, the administration chose not to risk a public defeat on the issue—a "shrewd political move," according to Robert T. Stafford, Republican of Vermont, chairman of the Senate Committee on Environment and Public Works. The lack of support was in fact remarkably pervasive, embracing different strata of the population and both political parties.

Critical though many were of air pollution regulation, expert analysts nonetheless had not mounted against it the kind of fundamental assault that they had brought to bear on controls of price, entry, and exit in multifirm markets. One after another, analyses of these regulatory regimes yielded findings that were unusually stark and sweeping: there was no justification for regulation, and no public benefits were realized from it. The policy recommendation was correspondingly extreme and unambiguous: regulation should be eliminated. By contrast, expert critiques of air pollution regulation accepted the underlying rationale for it—to take account of externalities— but argued that costs were not sufficiently being taken into account or that benefits had not been shown to justify the costs. Arguments revolved around the

rationale and procedures for standard setting, the quality of scientific evidence used, the logic with which it was applied, and marginal differences in allowable amounts of particular pollutants. The issue was not whether to deregulate; it was how, and how extensively, to regulate. Prescriptions for reform resulted in a stream of presidential contrivances for achieving better analysis and review.

If expert analysts failed to support deregulation, so did the public, with even greater visibility. The passage of air pollution control legislation in 1970 owed a great deal to a surge of public opinion in support of clean air, and a decade later pollsters reported that the country had not changed its collective mind on this question. The CBS News-*New York Times* poll in the fall of 1981 found that nearly two-thirds of adult Americans wanted to keep clean air laws "as tough as they are now" even if "some factories might have to close." . . . No important subgroup favored relaxation, not even conservatives or voters for Reagan. Questions on environmental issues elicited no important differences among age, income, occupation, or partisan and ideological groups, except that people of low socioeconomic status were more likely than others to profess unfamiliarity with the issues. Poll results, besides being exceptionally consistent among polls and among population subgroups, were exceptionally well publicized. . . .

. . . An ideological close cousin of the environmental movement, sharing with it sponsorship, leadership, goals, and adversaries in industry, the consumer movement was most strongly moved to protest the costs of regulation to consumers when government collaborated with business in imposing those costs. It was this collaboration in support of industry-serving ends, and not the higher prices per se, that made anticompetitive regulation outrageous to the neopopulists in the consumer movement.

Observing this array of forces—disinterested critics whose criticism focused on technical and procedural issues, a public overwhelmingly favorable to pollution control, an environmental movement not yet spent, and a business community in less than unanimous opposition—Republicans in Congress did not rush to support the Reagan administration in an attempt at relaxing controls. Nor had Republicans in Congress stood for weak controls in the past. In sharp contrast with natural gas pricing, pollution control measures had not elicited a clear and consistent pattern of party differences. President Nixon had sponsored clean air legislation in 1970, and the two houses of Congress had passed it with only one dissenting vote between them. . . .

Unable to win regulatory relief from Congress and unwilling, as things turned out, even to invest political resources in the attempt, the Reagan administration was forced to pursue its goals through executive action. In so doing, it had the advantage, by comparison with its predecessor, of internal cohesion. The Carter administration's attempts to have professional inflation fighters in the president's office supervise regulation touched off a round of fights in 1978-79 between the White House and the executive agencies as well as oversight hearings by agency protectors in Congress and court suits brought by agency allies in organized labor and the environmental movement, all challenging the right of the president to intervene or the economic logic on which intervention was based. James C. Miller III, the OMB official who initially headed the Reagan administration's attempts at economic oversight of rule making, told Congress that his task would be "hopelessly impossible" if he had to deal with Carter's regulatory appointees instead of Reagan's.

Even with the advantages of internal cohesion, the Reagan administration, relying on executive powers alone, made limited and halting headway against the established body of environmental regulation. It refrained from promulgating some regulations that the Carter administration had prepared, and the rate at which new regulations were issued slowed down, but other branches delayed or thwarted substantive changes of major importance. When the EPA under Reagan sought to extend application of the "bubble" concept—an EPA scheme, instituted under Carter, that gave firms increased flexibility in managing factory emissions—the U.S. Court of Appeals of the District of Columbia found the change impermissible,

although the Supreme Court subsequently overturned its decision.* The Senate Environment and Public Works Committee, proceeding with its markup of amendments to the Clean Air Act, not only failed to endorse changes the administration wanted, but approved by wide margins two amendments that were specifically designed to block pending EPA proposals to relax emission controls for trucks.

To the extent that deregulation of pollution control occurred under Reagan, it resulted from the one kind of action that the executive could take unilaterally. Reductions in personnel and in levels of enforcement occurred in the EPA and other regulatory agencies throughout the federal executive branch. For this, the administration did receive indirect congressional endorsement in the form of cuts in appropriations. Budget reductions, which the administration sought for their own sake, constituted a crude, backdoor approach to deregulation even when it could not be achieved directly.

The politics of deregulation with respect to health, safety, and the environment—the subjects of the post-1967 wave of new regulation—were entirely different from the politics of procompetitive deregulation. Even Reagan in his earliest statements drew a distinction. "We have no intention of dismantling the regulatory agencies," he told the nation within three weeks of taking office, "especially those necessary to protect [the] environment and to ensure the public health and safety." No one advocated deregulation, if by that one means literally the abolition of regulatory regimes. Industry opponents asked for less exacting standards or delays in enforcement; disinterested critics asked for more rationality in regulatory decisions. But with respect to pollution control,

---

* *Natural Resources Defense Council v. Gorsuch*, 685 F. 2d 718 (D.C. Cir., 1982); and *Chevron, U.S.A. v. Natural Resources Defense Council*, 44 *Supreme Court Bulletin* (Commerce Clearing House, 1984), p. B3841–43. Under the "bubble" concept, EPA applied emission limits to an entire plant rather than to each pollution source, such as a smokestack or vent, within it. Application of this concept meant that a reduction in pollution from one source within the plant could offset an increase from another source.

Copyright © 1986 by Universal Press Syndicate. Reprinted by permission.

even piece-meal relaxations and procedural reforms were resisted by the environmental movement and were subject to delay or defeat by the courts and a bipartisian majority in the Senate.

. . . [D]eregulation succeeded best with respect to regulatory regimes in which government agencies were allied with producers in such a way as to foster an-ticompetitive pricing and hence to inflate consumers' costs. It was only this pattern of regulation that plainly elicited deregulation as a policy prescription from disinterested analysts and brought liberals (attentive to consumerism) and conservatives (attentive to free enterprise) together in a bipartisian coalition for reform. . . .

Plane Truth: The Case for Re-regulating Airlines

Robert Kuttner
The New Republic, July 17 and 24, 1989, pp. 21–23

Something has gone disastrously wrong with airline deregulation. Fares have been rising far faster than inflation. Most of the small, upstart airline companies launched in the early 1980s have gone broke or been gobbled up by the big carriers. The top five airlines control more of the market (71 percent) than they did in 1977, the last year of the fully regulated regime. The turbulence of a free market has produced precisely the reconcentration and gouging that skeptics predicted.

Deregulation was supposed to bring a closer correspondence between costs and fares, but fares have become a crazy quilt. On routes with shared monopolies and many business travelers, like New York-Washington, the airlines charge an astronomical 50 to 60 cents per seat mile; their costs are about 11 cents. On comparable, highly competitive routes, fares drop dramatically. A one-way coach ticket from Oakland, California, to San Diego, 448 miles away, costs $49. A one-way Washington-Boston ticket, a 406-mile trip, costs $219.

Two passengers sitting next to each other can pay wildly different fares . . .

Admittedly, there are often good economic reasons why the price should vary over time for a commodity. Airlines reward passengers who are willing to book early and risk a penalty, or to fly stand-by and bear the risk of delay. They understandably offer price inducements to attract passengers to fly at off-peak times when seats go begging, just as vendors offer steep discounts for day-old bread, overripe vegetables, rush tickets for concerts, and weekend hotel specials.

But nothing else comes close to the price bazaar of deregulated airlines. It seems patently unfair when Smith and Jones, seated in 22A and 22B, pay $1,020 and $318 for the same product. What's worse, airlines evidently have designed a byzantine pricing structure not mainly to attract the discretionary flyer, but to insulate themselves from price competition and make it possible to soak captive customers.

The airlines have invented several measures to thwart the free market environment of deregulation. These include: mergers (the time-tested way to neutralize a competitor is to buy it); frequent flyer gimmicks to train the customer to value mileage credits and brand loyalty over comparison shopping (with the customer's employer often footing the bill); airline-owned computer systems that offer the parent company instant intelligence on the pricing strategy of competitors and facilitate the use of kickbacks ("override commissions") to encourage travel agents to book passengers on the parent airline; ties between major carriers and commuter lines (which frustrate inter-airline competition); and a little-appreciated monster of route manipulation known as the hub-and-spoke system.

Hubs are a good place to begin, because they are so wonderfully misleading. With more people flying, one would expect greater economies of scale in the form of more wide-body planes and more non-stop flights. After all, a 747 can carry passengers coast to coast non-stop at far greater comfort and lower cost than a 727 making a stopover in Minneapolis or St. Louis. . . . Yet under deregulation, there are relatively fewer non-stops and more retooled 727s, and passengers find increasingly that they must squeeze into a cramped plane and endure a time-consuming stopover at Pittsburgh, Charlotte, Denver, or some other hub. . . .

Hubs have been touted as instruments of greater efficiency, flexibility, and choice. Supposedly, the new system of short hauls is a faithful reflection of consumer preference and entrepreneurial ingenuity newly liberated by the free market. but it is a dirty little secret that hubs—known in the industry as "fortress hubs"—are mainly a device for increasing market power. If TWA can dominate St. Louis, or Northwest/Republic monopolizes Minneapolis, or USAir/Piedmont controls Charlotte, and if an increasing fraction of flights are routed to require a stopover, then price competition is restricted and the airline is free to charge whatever the (rigged) market will bear.

A recent study by the General Accounting Office found that profits at "high concentration" hub airports (dominated by one or two airlines) were 27 percent higher than at competitive airports. TWA controls 82 percent of departures at St. Louis's Lambert Airport, flights that produce 28 cents per passenger mile. Delta flights originating at Atlanta, a hub dominated by two carriers, produce 27 cents per passenger mile, versus an average of 15 cents at a sample of 38 airports not dominated by one or two airlines. Between May 1985 and May 1988, the number of airports served by as many as four airlines dropped by 52 percent, while the number served by only one carrier increased by 25 percent. . . .

The hub phenomenon also leads to a fascinating statistical aberration in the claims made for deregulation. You now fly more miles to get to the same place. For example, Boston-San Francisco direct is a distance of 2,429 miles. Via Dallas, the trip is 3,024 miles, and takes about four hours longer. This extra mileage is known in the business as "circuity." The statistics showing that air fares have dropped thanks to deregulation are based on actual passenger miles flown—which exceed what they ought to be. Actual costs, and hence fares, could be that much cheaper if deregulation hadn't demolished so many non-stops.

Some historical perspective: in 1887, Congress regulated the railroads because of a range of monopoly abuses, which included discriminatory pricing, kickbacks, predation, outright and shared monopolies, and price-gouging on short hauls. . . .

The early experience of the airlines was similar. In the 1920s a series of "spoils conferences" divided up routes and rigged fares, with the blessing of the postmaster general, who was the airlines' biggest customer. In 1938 Congress formally regulated the airlines as quasi-public utilities. A new Civil Aeronautics Board treated the airlines as a regulated cartel, granting shared route monopolies and specifying fares. This security stabilized profits, and also limited them. It allowed airlines to invest in new generations of equipment, and despite regulation (or perhaps because of it), fares gradually dropped in real terms as planes became more efficient.

But there were plainly excesses. No new major carrier was allowed into the interstate airline business for 40 years. Fares on intrastate flights within Texas and California were a lot cheaper than on regulated instate flights. As airlines seeking market share tried to substitute things like free champagne for price competition, regulation sometimes went to hilarious extremes. Delta, for example, filed a laborious complaint before the CAB against Northeast's promotion offering steaks "cooked to order" on its New York-Florida flights. Delta alleged that the steaks were cooked in advance, and merely reheated to order. This dispute consumed several months of solemn deliberation—and was abruptly mooted when Delta bought Northeast.

In the 1960s and 1970s a wave of research, relying both on new economic theory and on the Texas and California experiences, held that airlines were not, after all, natural monopolies requiring regulation as quasi-utilities, but were really naturally competitive. After all, their sunk capital was portable, and it could be bought and sold. In principle, a skyway

was not like a pipeline; it could accommodate many new competitors. Bipartisan support for this view emerged in celebrated hearings conducted by Ted Kennedy's Senate Judiciary subcommittee. Critics held that the regulators invariably got captured by the regulated. An anti-business populism exemplified by Ralph Nader, who supported deregulation, combined with the pro-business populism of the economists, who foresaw a new day of enterpreneurial innovation, price competition, and cheap fares. This culminated in the Airline Deregulation Act of 1978, birthed by economist Alfred Kahn, who was Jimmy Carter's CAB chairman.

Economists predicted that new airline companies with lower costs and closer-to-the-market pricing strategies would drive down fares, and that monopoly pricing and inefficient labor and management practices would be competed away. They didn't anticipate the computer and the Reagan administration. Several upstart airlines entered the market, but the computer allowed the established carriers to match their discount prices on just enough seats to drive the upstart company's "load factor" (the fraction of seats filled) below the break-even point. That sounds a lot like predatory pricing, but the Reagan administration was dominated by antitrust theorists who believe, Chicago-fashion, that such a thing cannot exist. Moreover, the administration took an extremely liberal view of mergers, so that as the big carriers drove their new competitors toward bankruptcy, they were free to buy them out. By the mid-1980s the industry was in a frenzy of buy-or-be-bought, which led to the re-emergence of an airline cartel.

To appreciate that deregulation has misfired is not to be confident of the remedy. Many leading students of the problem, such as Michael Levine, dean of the Yale School of Management, initially an eager advocate of deregulation, now hold that airlines do not follow the naturally competitive behavior that was predicted. Much entrepreneurial energy has been directed at creating subtle barriers to competition. But Levine warns against a return to pre-1978 style route and fare regulation. Alfred Kahn, the architect of the present regime, says the main thing that undermined his scheme was the Reagan administration's failure to enforce the antitrust laws, and its slowness to build more airport capacity. Kahn continues to be a champion of deregulation.

Ted Harris, who heads a Washington-based airline consulting firm, is one of the few industry insiders who unequivocally favors reregulation. He argues that with expensive capital equipment the airlines really can't stand free price competition, and that deregulation spawned the cartelization that one would expect in an industry with characteristics of a natural monopoly. "The industry has forgone profits in the first years of deregulation to put itself in a shared monopoly that it is just now beginning to exploit," he says. . . .

The great promise of deregulation was its populism. Its honeymoon phase made it possible for whole new classes of people to fly. Supposedly, critics of deregulation are simply elitists seeking lower fares and emptier skies for the business class. However, today's fares are a jumbled blend of vanishing bargains and skyway robbery—and the bargains don't always go to the deserving cases. When bleeding-heart liberals propose that society's less fortunate should pay on a sliding scale for medical treatment, housing, or child care, it is denounced as inefficient so-cialism. But when the free market dispenses $1,000 tickets with one invisible hand, and $300 tickets with the other, it is hailed as efficiently redistributive.

Economic analysis needs to concede that in monopolistic industries, entrepreneurial innovation is often aimed at complicating pricing and retarding consumer choice, rather than serving it; and that there are limits to the efficiencies gained from managing more cleverly, shaving maintenance costs, and hammering down wages. Ultimately, the task of carrying a passenger from point A to point B is a straightforward one. Over time, the surest efficiency gains are to be had from the development of more efficient planes. Deregulation doesn't necessarily serve that goal.

Here we have another good lesson in the hubris of standard economics. There is no such thing as a naturally free market. All markets are social constructs, anchored in law. Antitrust is as much a regulatory intervention as rate regulation. Nor, in the real world, is every posted price continuously renegotiable. Despite deregulation, the airline passenger cannot go up to a ticket counter with knowledge of load factors and offer to pay $19 for a seat to Seattle that would otherwise go begging. The airline business, it turns out, is not a flea market.

Some Concluding Questions and Answers

Administrative law, as you know all too well by now, covers a tremendously broad and varied territory. Since administrative government touches nearly all aspects of a complex society and since administrative law states standards of fairness and rationality with which government should comply, the breadth of the field can't be helped. Covering all this terrain in one book is no easy task, and the unconvincing and sometimes garbled quality of much of administrative law today only heightens the task's difficulty. Rather than attempting to write a neat concluding section to a topic that has no neat conclusions, we shall close by anticipating some questions readers may now want to ask, questions that we have not managed to address or answer clearly enough in the earlier part of the book. We have phrased these questions so that you, the reader, are the person who asks them.

Q: We are still uncertain as to how deeply reviewing courts must examine the facts. It seems that to assure that the decision is not arbitrary, courts must review all the facts from scratch. But doesn't that put us right back where we started from, with courts making time-consuming decisions that they are structurally unsuited to make and creating further opportunities for people to delay enforcement?

A: No, courts do not need to reexamine the facts from scratch. Judge Bazelon in the Vermont Yankee did not review whether the facts supported licensing the nuclear power plant. But he searched carefully for evidence that the agency had weighed the facts, done the homework, and reached a decision the facts supported. The question about delay is a somewhat tougher one. Some people are bent on delaying enforcement by any possible means. They use the opportunity for review merely to delay the day of final judgment. The only way to reduce this delay is to reduce the opportunity for judicial review. This price is, of course, too high to pay because the availability of judicial review plays a pivotal role in keeping administrative conscientiousness alive.

Do note, however, that the approach we suggest does eliminate one source of uncertainty that can cause delay. This uncertainty exists today under the unpredictable (one might say "lawless") balancing tests in such cases as *Mathews*. Consider the confusion balancing creates, not only in the minds of bureaucrats and private parties who may want to get on with the job of working something out, but also in the trial judge. The Supreme Court may sit back and philosophize about balancing, but this hardly tells a trial judge how to decide the case before her or him.

Or put yourself in Ms. Horowitz's shoes when she was dismissed from medical school. Is it not likely that uncertainties about the formalities courts might require in her case encouraged her to fight her case to the Supreme Court? Could not this case have been settled more efficiently by a rule requiring the university to put its reasons in writing, to then give her a chance to dispute the factual basis for these reasons, and finally to be prepared to defend in court its reasons as rational (not necessarily perfect, just rational)? The principle we endorse communicates a straightforward message to bureaucrats: "Be prepared to defend your decision as a plausible application of acceptable legal policy to believable facts and we, the courts, will leave you alone." Recall the reference to Mencken's statement that conscience is the small voice that tells us someone may be looking. When courts take the substantial evidence test seriously they become the "someone looking" that in turn stimulates administrative conscientiousness. This consequence in its turn lowers the number of instances where people need to seek judicial review to resolve uncertainties.

Q: Explain why you say a court isn't organizationally well suited to deciding for itself problems such as whether to put highways in parks. Why isn't this a function of how honest and intelligent the decider is, regardless of his role as judge or administrator?

A: The issues of administrative law in *Overton Park,* are somewhat different from the regulatory issues, the questions about the highways and the parks themselves. Whether a highway ought to cut through and destroy part of a park depends on a highly complex and interrelated set of data. These include information about traffic safety, pollution, predicted demographic changes with and without the highway, cost comparisons, and so forth. It is a "polycentric" problem, to use current political science jargon, and polycentric problems require different specialists on one staff to evaluate many factors and then combine their findings. Judges do not wrap all the necessary skills in one person, but perhaps the real problem, at least in the two "highways in the park" cases, is that the decider *should* consider local political opinion. Indeed the statute obligates the Secretary to consider the desires of local government in making the final decision. Sniffing political winds is, however, not part of a judge's official fact-finding role. Notice that in the District of Columbia case Judge Bazelon properly concludes that the pressure from Congressman Natcher prevented the secretary from considering the opinions of the local District of Columbia political leadership. These people approved the bridge "under protest." They stated publicly that they opposed the bridge but voted for it, under the coercive pressure from Natcher, to save the subway. Judge Bazelon did not need to sniff the wind to reach that conclusion. It was presented to him, uncontradicted, by the testimony in the case before him.

Q: The Reagan administration sought to shift power from the federal government to the states. The Bush Administration is continuing this policy. Are state and local governments prepared to assume substantially more regulatory and other administrative duties? Are the principles and policies in state administrative law developed to the point where they can check arbitrariness effectively?

A: Ten years ago if we had asked this question we would not get an encouraging answer. Yes, the state Model Administrative Procedure Act has been around since 1961 and a fair number of states have enacted versions of it. Recall that in some respects the model state APA provides broader coverage than does the federal APA. But, in practice, ten years ago most lawyers and judges at the state and local levels had hardly heard of these statutes, and paid little attention to them even when they had. Fascinating developments, however, have occurred in the states in the past decades. They offer some hope that states can use administrative law effectively. Whether they will do so in fact depends on how effectively lawyers and judges learn to use principles.

There are some encouraging recent facts about administrative procedure in the states. Forty states now publish their administrative rules so that the benefits of the *Federal Register* system of communication now can work in the states if lawyers pay attention to them. The states have experimented with a variety of legislative and executive checks on administrative decisionmaking. For example, in many states a legislative committee screens agency rules before they can become effective. Two states give legislative committees standing to sue to challenge the legality of an administrative rule. A few states allow a legislative committee to suspend a rule at any time.

The point is not that all these mechanisms are necessarily valid or reliable methods of administrative rulemaking. They obviously open doors to reach expedient and politically manipulated results. Indeed courts in two states have struck down a committee veto system on constitutional grounds. The point is rather that by trying different methods, some of which involve legislative review and some of which involve executive review, some states may hit upon new procedures that more effectively assure fairness, accuracy and efficiency than that "Model T" of administrative procedure, the old federal APA.

One particularly promising innovation has occurred in California. This state now has an Office of Administrative Law. The office has authority to order an agency to cease any procedure not authorized by law and to nullify any new agency rule if it lacks statutory authority or is unclear or internally inconsistent. If the office nullifies a rule, the governor must specifically reverse the office or the rule is dead.

Overall the new Model Act, by stressing complete recordkeeping and documentation of decisions, by requiring openness of the process to meaningful public participation in rulemaking and wide ability to intervene in adjudication, offers great hope of reducing arbitrariness in bureaucratic government. If states attempt on short notice to assume vast new administrative responsibilities without adopting the procedures in the Model Act, arbitrary and perhaps even chaotic decisions will likely increase.

Q: Is the proposal that courts look more closely at the substantive rationality of results than at procedures a radical redefinition of the judical role? What guarantee have we that judges actually can or will retool to play this role effectively? It will take a major redirecting both of the American Bar Association and of the nature of American legal education from the bottom up. Isn't it unlikely that these old and cumbersome institutions will change enough to make substantive justice a reality? For that matter, will the public accept decisions in which judges give up the pretense of neutrality that procedural justice affords and start overtly examining policy itself?

A: We have no guarantees to offer. Legal institutions are actually fairly changeful. Law schools are teaching economic theories of law and using computer technology today to a degree few would have bet on a decade ago. But the problems raised by this set of questions are very uncertain. Martin Shapiro, as astute a political scientist as one can find on matters of public law, believe that the courts will ultimately fail at this task.[18]

---

[18] Martin Shapiro, "On Predicting the Future of Administrative Law," *Regulation*, May/June 1982, 18.

The Informality-Formality Continuum in Administrative Law

Informal Decisions:
Decisions made without significant legal rules governing the process

Adjudication

Formal Decisions:

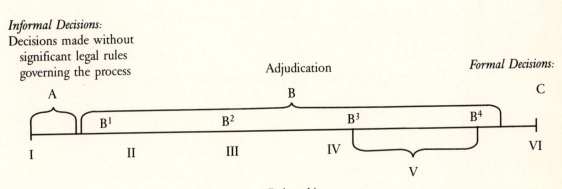

Rulemaking

Adjudication

A. Due process adjudication where no *Goldberg* ingredients are required. Rare, but *Ingraham* (the school "spanking" case) comes close.

B. Increasing due process formality under *Goldberg*.
B^1 *Horowitz*
B^2 *Goss*
B^3 Many licensing and personnel cases
B^4 All ten *Goldberg* ingredients

C. Full adjudicatory formality under federal and state Administrative Procedure Acts.

Rulemaking

I. Classical rulemaking under *BiMetallic* (agencies have same discretion as legislature).

II. "Notice and Comment" rulemaking under section 553, Federal Administrative Procedure Act.

III. Model State APA rulemaking, somewhat more formal than section 553.

IV. "Hybrid" FTC rulemaking under Magnuson-Moss statute.

V. Judicially applied due process standards in rulemaking that resembles adjudication in substance, *e.g., Sangammon Valley*.

VI. Full adjudicatory formality when statute requires hearing "on the record" in federal rulemaking (APA section 554).

APPENDIX B

Federal Administrative Procedure Act

P.L. 404, 60 Stat. 237 (1946), as amended through the conclusion of the 101st Congress, Second Session (1989).
5. U.S.C.A. § § 551–559, 701–706, 1305, 3105, 3344, 5372, 7521.

Title 5 — Government Organization and Employees

Part I — The Agencies Generally

Chapter 5 — Administrative Procedure
Subchapter II — Administrative Procedure

§ 551. Definitions

For the purpose of this subchapter—

(1) "agency" means each authority of the Government of the United States, whether or not it is within or subject to review by another agency, but does not include—

(A) the Congress;

(B) the courts of the United States;

(C) the governments of the territories or possessions of the United States;

(D) the government of the District of Columbia; or except as to the requirements of section 552 of this title—

(E) agencies composed of representatives of the parties or of representatives of organizations of the parties to the disputes determined by them;

(F) courts martial and military commissions;

(G) military authority exercised in the field in time of war or in occupied territory; or

(H) functions conferred by secions 1738, 1739, 1743, and 1744 of title 12; chapter 2 of title 41; or sections 1622, 1884, 1891–1902, and former section 1641 (b)(2), of title 50, appendix;

(2) "person" includes an individual, partnership, corporation, association, or public or private organization other than an agency;

(3) "party" includes a person or agency named or admitted as a party, or properly seeking and entitled as of right to be admitted as a party, in an agency proceeding, and a person or agency admitted by an agency as a party for limited purposes;

(4) "rule" means the whole or a part of an agency statement of general or particular applicability and future effect designed to implement, interpret, or prescribe law or policy or describing the organization, procedure, or practice requirements of an agency and includes the approval or prescription for the future of rates, wages, corporate or financial structures or reorganizations thereof, prices, facilities, appliances, services or allowances therefor or of valuations, costs, or accounting, or practices bearing on any of the foregoing;

(5) "rule making" means agency process for formulating, amending, or repealing a rule;

(6) "order" means the whole or a part of a final disposition, whether affirmative, negative, injunctive, or declaratory in form, of an agency in a matter other than rule making but including licensing;

(7) "adjudication" means agency process for the formulation of an order;

(8) "license" includes the whole or a part of an agency permit, certificate, approval, registration, charter, membership, statutory exemption, or other form of permission;

(9) "licensing" includes an agency process respecting the grant, renewal, denial, revocation, suspension, annulment, withdrawal, limitation, amendment, modification, or conditioning of a license;

(10) "sanction" includes the whole or a part of an agency—

(A) prohibition, requirement, limitation, or other condition affecting the freedom of a person;

(B) withholding of relief;

(C) imposition of penalty or fine;

(D) destruction, taking, seizure, or withholding of property;

(E) assessment of damages, reimbursement, restitution, compensation, costs, charges, or fees;

(F) requirement, revocation, or suspension of a license; or

(G) taking other compulsory or restrictive action;

(11) "relief" includes the whole or a part of an agency—

(A) grant of money, assistance, license, authority, exemption, exception, privilege, or remedy;

(B) recognition of a claim, right, immunity, privilege, exemption, or exception; or

(C) taking of other action on the application or petition of, and beneficial to, a person;

(12) "agency proceeding" means an agency process as defined by paragraphs (5), (7), and (9) of this section;

(13) "agency action" includes the whole or a part of an agency rule, order, license, sanction, relief, or the equivalent or denial thereof, or failure to act; and

(14) "ex parte communication" means an oral or written communication not on the public record with respect to which reasonable prior notice to all parties is not given, but it shall not include requests for status reports on any matter or proceeding covered by this subchapter.

§ 552. *Public Information; Agency Rules, Opinions, Orders, Records, and Proceedings*

(a) Each agency shall make available to the public information as follows:

(1) Each agency shall separately state and currently publish in the Federal Register for the guidance of the public—

(A) descriptions of its central and field organization and the established places at which, the employees (and in the case of a uniformed service, the members) from whom, and the methods whereby, the public may obtain information, make submittals or requests, or obtain decisions;

(B) statements of the general course and method by which its functions are channeled and determined, including the nature and requirements of all formal and informal procedures available;

(C) rules of procedure, descriptions of forms available or the places at which forms may be obtained, and instructions as to the scope and contents of all papers, reports, or examinations;

(D) substantive rules of general applicability adopted as authorized by law, and statements of general policy or interpretations of general applicability formulated and adopted by the agency; and

(E) each amendment, revision, or repeal of the foregoing.
Except to the extent that a person has actual and timely notice of the terms thereof, a person may not in any manner be required to resort to, or be adversely affected by, a matter required to be published in the Federal Register and not so published. For the purpose of this paragraph, matter reasonably available to the class of persons affected thereby is deemed published in the Federal Register when incorporated by reference therein with the approval of the Director of the Federal Register.

(2) Each agency, in accordance with published rules, shall make available for public inspection and copying—

(A) final opinions, including concurring and dissenting opinions, as well as orders, made in the adjudication of cases;

(B) those statements of policy and interpretations which have been adopted by the agency and are not published in the Federal Register; and

(C) administrative staff manuals and instructions to staff that affect a member of the public;

unless the materials are promptly published and copies offered for sale. To the extent required to prevent a clearly unwarranted invasion of personal privacy, an agency may delete identifying details when it makes available or publishes an opinion, statement of policy, interpretation, or staff manual or instruction. However, in each case the justification for the deletion shall be explained fully in writing. Each agency shall also maintain and make available for public inspection and copying current indexes providing identifying information for the public as to any matter issued, adopted, or promulgated after July 4, 1967, and required by this paragraph to be made available or published. Each agency shall promptly publish, quarterly or more frequently, and distribute (by sale or otherwise) copies of each index or supplements thereto unless it determines by order published in the Federal Register that the publication would be unnecessary and impracticable, in which case the agency shall nonetheless provide copies of such index on request at a cost not to exceed the direct cost of duplication. A final order, opinion, statement of policy, interpretation, or staff manual or instruction that affects a member of the public may be relied on, used, or cited as precedent by an agency against a party other than an agency only if—

(i) it has been indexed and either made available or published as provided by this paragraph; or

(ii) the party has actual and timely notice of the terms thereof.

(3) Except with respect to the records made available under paragraphs (1) and (2) of this subsection, each agency, upon any request for records which (A) reasonably describes such records and (B) is made in accordance with published rules stating the time, place, fees (if any), and procedures to be followed, shall make the records promptly available to any person.

(4)(A)(i) In order to carry out the provisions of this section, each agency shall promulgate regulations, pursuant to notice and receipt of public comment, specifying the schedule of fees applicable to the processing of requests under this section and establishing procedures and guidelines for determining when such fees should be waived or reduced. Such schedule shall conform to the guidelines which shall be promulgated, pursuant to notice and receipt of public comment, by the Director of the Office of Management and Budget and which shall provide for a uniform schedule of fees for all agencies.

(B) On complaint, the district court of the United States in the district in which the complainant resides, or has his principal place of business, or in which the agency records are situated, or in the District of Columbia, has jurisdiction to enjoin the agency from withholding agency records and to order the production of any agency records improperly withheld from the complainant. In such a case the court shall determine the matter de novo, and may examine the contents of such agency records in camera to determine whether such records or any part thereof shall be withheld under any of the exemptions set forth in subsection (b) of this section, and the burden is on the agency to sustain its action.

(C) Notwithstanding any other provision of law, the defendant shall serve an answer or otherwise plead to any complaint made under this subsection within thirty days after service upon the defendant of the pleading in which such complaint is made, unless the court otherwise directs for good cause shown.

(D) [Repealed, P.L. 98–620, 98 Stat. 2428].

(E) The court may assess against the United States reasonable attorney fees and other litigation costs reasonably incurred in any case under this section in which the complainant has substantially prevailed.

(F) Whenever the court orders the production of any agency records improperly withheld from the complainant and assesses against the United States reasonable attorney fees and other litigation costs, and the court additionally issues a written finding that the circumstances surrounding the withholding raise questions whether agency personnel acted arbitrarily or capriciously with respect to the withholding, the Special Counsel shall promptly initiate a proceeding to determine whether disciplinary action is warranted against the officer or employee who was primarily responsible for the withholding. The Special Counsel, after investigation and consideration of the evidence submitted, shall submit his findings and recommendations to the administrative authority of the agency concerned and shall send copies of the findings and recommendations to the officer or employee or his representative. The administrative authority shall take the corrective action that the Special Counsel recommends.

(G) In the event of noncompliance with the order of the court, the district court may punish for contempt the responsible employee, and in the case of a uniformed service, the responsible member.

(5) Each agency having more than one member shall maintain and make available for public inspection a record of the final votes of each member in every agency proceeding.

(6)(A) Each agency, upon any request for records made under paragraph (1), (2), or (3) of this subsection, shall—

(i) determine within ten days (excepting Saturdays, Sundays, and legal public holidays) after the receipt of any such request whether to comply with such request and shall immediately notify the person making such request of such determination and the reasons therefor, and of the right of such person to appeal to the head of the agency any adverse determination; and

(ii) make a determination with respect to any appeal within twenty days (excepting Saturdays, Sundays, and legal public holidays), after the receipt of such appeal. If on appeal the denial of the request for records is in whole or in part upheld, the agency shall notify the person making such request of the provisions for judicial review of that determination under paragraph (4) of this subsection.

(B) In unusual circumstances as specified in this subparagraph, the time limits prescribed in either clause (i) or clause (ii) of subparagraph (A) may be extended by written notice to the person making such request setting forth the reasons for such extension and the date on which a determination is expected to be dispatched. No such notice shall specify a date that would result in an extension for more than ten working days. As used in this subparagraph, "unusual circumstances" means, but only to the extent reasonably necessary to the proper processing of the particular request—

(i) the need to search for and collect the requested records from field facilities or other establishments that are separate from the office processing the request;

(ii) the need to search for, collect, and appropriately examine a voluminous amount of separate and distinct records which are demanded in a single request; or

(iii) the need for consultation, which shall be conducted with all practicable speed, with another agency having a substantial interest in the determination of the request or among two or more components of the agency having substantial subject-matter interest therein.

(C) Any person making a request to any agency for records under paragraph (1), (2), or (3) of this subsection shall be deemed to have exhausted his administrative remedies with respect to such request if the agency fails to comply with the applicable time limit provisions of this paragraph. If the Government can show exceptional circumstances exist and that the agency is exercising due diligence in responding to the request, the court may retain jurisdiction and allow the agency additional time to complete its review of the records. Upon any determination by an agency to comply with a request for records, the records shall be made promptly available to such person making such request. Any notification of denial of any request for records under this subsection shall set forth the names and titles or positions of each person responsible for the denial of such request.

(b) This section does not apply to matters that are—

(1)(A) specifically authorized under criteria established by an Executive order to be kept secret in the interest of national defense or foreign policy and (B) are in fact properly classified pursuant to such Executive order;

(2) related solely to the internal personnel rules and practices of an agency;

(3) specifically exempted from disclosure by statute (other than section 552b of this title), provided that such statute (A) requires that the matters be withheld from the public in such a manner as to leave no discretion on the issue, or (B) establishes particular criteria for withholding or refers to particular types of matters to be withheld;

(4) trade secrets and commercial or financial information obtained from a person and privileged or confidential;

(5) inter-agency or intra-agency memorandums or letters which would not be available by law to a party other than an agency in litigation with the agency;

(6) personnel and medical files and similar files the disclosure of which would constitute a clearly unwarranted invasion of personal privacy;

(7) records or information compiled for law enforcement purposes, but only to the extent that the production of such law enforcement records or information (A) could reasonably be expected to interfere with enforcement proceedings, (B) would deprive a person of a right to a fair trial or an impartial adjudication, (C) could reasonably be expected to constitute an unwarranted invasion of personal privacy, (D) could reasonably be expected to disclose the identity of a confidential source including a

state, local, or foreign agency or authority or any private institution which furnished information on a confidential basis, and, in the case of a record compiled by a criminal law enforcement authority in the course of a criminal investigation, or by an agency conducting a lawful national security intelligence investigation, information furnished only by the confidential source, (E) would disclose techniques and procedures for law enforcement investigations or prosecutions, or would disclose guidelines for law enforcement investigations or prosecution if such disclosures could reasonably be expected to risk circumvention of the law, or (F) could reasonably be expected to endanger the life or physical safety of any individual;

(8) contained in or related to examination, operating, or condition reports prepared by, on behalf of, or for the use of an agency responsible for the regulation or supervision of financial institutions; or

(9) geological and geophysical information and data, including maps, concerning wells.

Any reasonably segregable portion of a record shall be provided to any person requesting such record after deletion of the portions which are exempt under this subsection.

(c)(1) Whenever a request is made which involves access to records described in subsection (b)(7)(A) and—

(A) the investigation or proceeding involves a possible violation of criminal law; and

(B) there is reason to believe that (i) the subject of the investigation or proceeding is not aware of its pendency, and (ii) disclosure of the existence of the records could reasonably be expected to interfere with enforcement proceedings, the agency may, during only such time as that circumstance continues, treat the records as not subject to the requirements of this section.

(2) Whenever informant records maintained by a criminal law enforcement agency under an informant's name or personal identifier are requested by a third party according to the informant's name or personal identifier, the agency may treat the records as not subject to the requirements of this section unless the informant's status as an informant has been officially confirmed.

(3) Whenever a request is made which involves access to records maintained by the Federal Bureau of Investigation pertaining to foreign intelligence or counterintelligence or international terrorism, and the existence of the records is classified information as provided in subsection (b)(1), the Bureau may, as long as the existence of the records remains classified information, treat the records as not subject to the requirements of this section.

(d) This section does not authorize withholding of information or limit the availability of records to the public, except as specifically stated in this section. This section is not authority to withhold information from Congress.

(e) On or before March 1 of each calendar year, each agency shall submit a report covering the preceding calendar year to the Speaker of the House of Representatives and President of the Senate for referral to the appropriate committees of the Congress. The report shall include—

(1) the number of determinations made by such agency not to comply with request for records made to such agency under subsection (a) and the reasons for each such determination;

(2) the number of appeals made by persons under subsection (a)(6), the result of such appeals, and the reason for the action upon each appeal that results in a denial of information;

(3) the names and titles or positions of each person responsible for the denial of records requested under this section, and the number of instances of participation for each;

(4) the results of each proceeding conducted pursuant to subjection (a)(4)(F), including a report of the disciplinary action taken against the officer or employee who was primarily responsible for improperly withholding records or an explanation of why disciplinary action was not taken;

(5) a copy of every rule made by such agency regarding this section;

(6) a copy of the fee schedule and the total amount of fees collected by the agency for making records available under this section; and

(7) such other information as indicates efforts to administer fully this section. The Attorney General shall submit an annual report on or before March 1 of each calendar year which shall include for the prior calendar year a listing of the number of cases arising under this section, the exemption involved in each case, the disposition of such case, and the cost, fees, and penalties assessed under subsections (a)(4)(E), (F), and (G). Such report shall also include a description of the efforts undertaken by the Department of Justice to encourage agency compliance with this section.

(f) For purposes of this section, the term "agency" as defined in section 551(1) of this title includes any executive department, military department, Government corporation, Government controlled corporation, or other establishment in the executive branch of the Government (including the Executive Office of the President), or any independent regulatory agency.

§ 552a. Records Maintained on Individuals [Also known as the Privacy Act.]

(a) Definitions. For purposes of this section—

(1) the term "agency" means agency as defined in section 552(e) of this title;

(2) the term "individual" means a citizen of the United States or an alien lawfully admitted for permanent residence;

(3) the term "maintain" includes maintain, collect, use, or disseminate;

(4) the term "record" means any item, collection, or grouping of information about an individual that is maintained by an agency, including, but not limited to, his education, financial transactions, medical history, and criminal or employment history and that contains his name, or the identifying number, symbol, or other identifying particular assigned to the individual, such as a finger or voice print or a photograph.

(5) the term "system or records" means a group of any records under the control of any agency from which information is retrieved by the name of the individual or by some identifying number, symbol, or other identifying particular assigned to the individual;

(6) the term "statistical record" means a record in a system of records maintained for statistical research or reporting purposes only and not used in whole or in part in making any determination about an identifiable individual, except as provided by section 8 of title 13;

(7) the term "routine use" means, with respect to the disclosure of a record, the use of such record for a purpose which is compatible with the purpose for which it was collected.

(A) means computerized comparison of—

(i) two or more automated systems of records or a system of records with non-Federal records for the purpose of—

(I) establishing or verifying the eligibility of, or continuing compliance with statutory and regulatory requirements by, applicants for, recipients or beneficiaries of, participants in, or providers of services with respect to, cash or in-kind assistance or payments under Federal benefit programs, or

(II) recouping payments or delinquent debts under such Federal benefit programs, or

(ii) two or more automated Federal personnel or payroll systems of records or a system of Federal personnel or payroll records with non-Federal records,

(B) but does not include—

(i) matches performed to produce aggregate statistical data without any personal identifiers;

(ii) matches performed to support any research or statistical project, the specific data of which may not be used to make decisions concerning the rights, benefits, or privileges of specific individuals;

(iii) matches performed, by an agency (or component thereof) which performs as its principal function any activity pertaining to the enforcement of criminal laws, subsequent to the initiation of a specific criminal or civil law enforcement investigation of a named person or persons for the purpose of gathering evidence against such person or persons;

(iv) matches of tax information (I) pursuant to section 6103(d) of the Internal Revenue Code of 1986, (II) for purposes of tax administration as defined in section 6103(b)(4) of such Code, (III) for the purpose of intercepting a tax refund due an individual under authority granted by section 464 or 1137 of the Social Security Act; or (IV) for the purpose of intercepting a tax refund due an individual under any other tax refund intercept program authorized by statute which has been determined by the Director of the Office of Management and Budget to contain verification, notice, and hearing requirements that are substantially similar to the procedures in section 1137 of the Social Security Act;

(v) matches—

(I) using records predominantly relating to Federal personnel, that are performed for routine administrative purposes (subject to guidance provided by the Director of the Office of Management and Budget pursuant to subsection (v)); or

(II) conducted by an agency using only records from systems of records maintained by that agency;

if the purpose of the match is not to take any adverse financial, personnel, disciplinary, or other adverse action against Federal personnel; or

(vi) matches performed for foreign counterintelligence purposes or to produce background checks for security clearances of Federal personnel or Federal contractor personnel;

(9) the term "recipient agency" means any agency, or contractor thereof, receiving records contained in a system of records from a source agency for use in a matching program;

(10) the term "non-Federal agency" means any State or local government, or agency thereof, which receives records contained in a system of records from a source agency for use in a matching program;

(11) the term "source agency" means any agency which discloses records contained in a system of records to be used in a matching program, or any State or local government, or agency thereof, which discloses records to be used in a matching program;

(12) the term "Federal benefit program" means any program administered or funded by the Federal Government, or by any agent or State on behalf of the Federal Government, providing cash or in-kind assistance in the form of payments, grants, loans, or loan guarantees to individuals; and

(13) the term "Federal personnel" means officers and employees of the Government of the United States, members of the uniformed services (including members of the Reserve Components), individuals entitled to receive immediate or deferred retirement benefits under any retirement program of the Government of the United States (including survivor benefits).

(b) Conditions of disclosure. No agency shall disclose any record which is contained in a system of records by any means of communication to any person, or to another agency, except pursuant to a written request by, or with the prior written consent of, the individual to whom the record pertains, unless disclosure of the record would be—

(1) to those officers and employees of the agency which maintains the record who have a need for the record in the performance of their duties;

(2) required under section 552 of this title;

(3) for a routine use as defined in subsection (a)(7) of this section and described under subsection (e)(4)(D) of this section;

(4) to the Bureau of the Census for purposes of planning or carrying out a census or survey or related activity pursuant to the provisions of title 13;

(5) to a recipient who has provided the agency with advance adequate written assurance that the record will be used solely as a statistical research or reporting record, and the record is to be transferred in a form that is not individually identifiable;

(6) to the National Archives of the United States as a record which has sufficient historical or other value to warrant its continued preservation by the United States Government, or for evaluation by the Administrator of General Services or his designee to determine whether the record has such value;

(7) to another agency or to an instrumentality of any governmental jurisdiction within or under the control of the United States for a civil or criminal law enforcement activity if the activity is authorized by law, and if the head of the agency or instrumentality has made a written request to the agency which maintains the record specifying the particular portion desired and the law enforcement activity for which the record is sought;

(8) to a person pursuant to a showing of compelling circumstances affecting the health or safety of an individual if upon such disclosure notification is transmitted to the last known address of such individual;

(9) to either House of Congress, or, to the extent of matter within its jurisdiction, any committee or subcommittee thereof, any joint committee of Congress or sub-committee of any such joint committee;

(10) to the Comptroller General, or any of his authorized representatives, in the course of the performance of the duties of the General Accounting Office; or

(11) pursuant to the order of a court of competent jurisdiction.

(12) to a consumer reporting agency in accordance with section 3711 (f) of title 31.

(c) Accounting of certain disclosures. Each agency, with respect to each system of records under its control, shall—

(1) except for disclosures made under subsections (b)(1) or (b)(2) of this section, keep an accurate accounting of—

(A) the date, nature, and purpose of each disclosure of a record to any person or to another agency made under subsection (b) of this section; and

(B) the name and address of the person or agency to whom the disclosure is made;

(2) retain the accounting made under paragraph (1) of this subsection for at least five years or the life of the record, whichever is longer, after the disclosure for which the accounting is made;

(3) except for disclosures made under subsection (b)(7) of this section, make the accounting made under paragraph (1) of this subsection available to the individual named in the record at his request; and

(4) inform any person or other agency about any correction or notation of dispute made by the agency in accordance with subsection (d) of this section of any record that has been disclosed to the person or agency if an accounting of the disclosure was made.

(d) Access to records. Each agency that maintains a system of records shall—

(1) upon request by any individual to gain access to his record or to any informa-tion pertaining to him which is contained in the system, permit him and upon his request, a person of his own choosing to accompany him, to review the record and have a copy made of all or any portion thereof in a form comprehensible to him, ex-cept that the agency may require the individual to furnish a written statement authorizing discussion of that individual's record in the accompanying person's presence;

(2) permit the individual to request amendment of a record pertaining to him and—

(A) not later than 10 days (excluding Saturdays, Sundays, and legal public holi-days) after the date of receipt of such request, acknowledge in writing such receipt; and

(B) promptly, either—

(i) make any correction of any portion thereof which the individual believes is not accurate, relevant, timely, or complete; or

(ii) inform the individual of its refusal to amend the record in accordance with his request, the reason for the refusal, the procedures established by the agency for the individual to request a review of that refusal by the head of the agency or an officer designated by the head of the agency, and the name and business address of that official;

(3) permit the individual who disagrees with the refusal of the agency to amend his record to request a review of such refusal, and not later than 30 days (excluding Saturdays, Sundays, and legal public holidays) from the date on which the individual requests such review, complete such review and make a final determination unless, for good cause shown, the head of the agency extends such 30-day period; and if, after his review, the reviewing official also refuses to amend the record in accordance with the request, permit the individual to file with the agency a concise statement setting forth the reasons for his disagreement with the refusal of the agency, and notify the individual of the provisions for judicial review of the reviewing official's determination under subsection (g)(1)(A) of this section;

(4) in any disclosure, containing information about which the individual has filed a statement of disagreement, occurring after the filing of the statement under paragraph (3) of this subsection, clearly note any portion of the record which is disputed and provide copies of the statement and, if the agency deems it appropriate, copies of a concise statement of the reasons of the agency for not making the amendments requested, to persons or other agencies to whom the disputed record has been disclosed; and

(5) nothing in this section shall allow an individual access to any information compiled in reasonable anticipation of a civil action or proceeding.

(e) Agency requirements. Each agency that maintains a system of records shall—

(1) maintain in its records only such information about an individual as is relevant and necessary to accomplish a purpose of the agency required to be accomplished by statute or by executive order of the President;

(2) collect information to the greatest extent practicable directly from the subject individual when the information may result in adverse determinations about an individual's rights, benefits, and privileges under Federal programs;

(3) inform each individual whom it asks to supply information, on the form which it uses to collect the information or on a separate form that can be retained by the individual—

(A) the authority (whether granted by statute, or by executive order of the President) which authorizes the solicitation of the information and whether disclosure of such information is mandatory or voluntary;

(B) the principal purpose or purposes for which the information is intended to be used;

(C) the routine uses which may be made of the information, as published pursuant to paragraph (4)(D) of this subsection; and

(D) the effects on him, if any, of not providing all or any part of the requested information;

(4) subject to the provisions of paragraph (11) of this subsection, publish in the Federal Register upon establishment or revision a notice of the existence and character of the system of records, which notice shall include—

(A) the name and location of the system;

(B) the categories of individuals on whom records are maintained in the system;

(C) the categories of records maintained in the system;

(D) each routine use of the records contained in the system, including the categories of users and the purpose of such use;

(E) the policies and practices of the agency regarding storage, retrievability, access controls, retention, and disposal of the records;

(F) the title and business address of the agency official who is responsible for the system of records;

(G) the agency procedures whereby an individual can be notified at his request if the system of records contains a record pertaining to him;

(H) the agency procedures whereby an individual can be notified at his request how he can gain access to any record pertaining to him contained in the system of records, and how he can contest its content; and

(I) the categories of sources of records in the system;

(5) maintain all records which are used by the agency in making any determination about any individual with such accuracy, relevance, timeliness, and completeness as is reasonably necessary to assure fairness to the individual in the determination;

(6) prior to disseminating any record about an individual to any person other than an agency, unless the dissemination is made pursuant to subsection (b)(2) of this section, make reasonable efforts to assure that such records are accurate, complete, timely, and relevant for agency purposes;

(7) maintain no record describing how any individual exercises rights guaranteed by the First Amendment unless expressly authorized by statute or by the individual about whom the record is maintained or unless pertinent to and within the scope of an authorized law enforcement activity;

(8) make reasonable efforts to serve notice on an individual when any record on such individual is made available to any person under compulsory legal process when such process becomes a matter of public record;

(9) establish rules of conduct for persons involved in the design, development, operation, or maintenance of any system of records, or in maintaining any record, and instruct each such person with respect to such rules and the requirements of this section, including any other rules and procedures adopted pursuant to this section and the penalties for noncompliance;

(10) establish appropriate administrative, technical, and physical safeguards to insure the security and confidentiality of records and to protect against any anticipated threats or hazards to their security or integrity which could result in substantial harm, embarrassment, inconvenience, or unfairness to any individual on whom information is maintained; and

(11) at least 30 days prior to publication of information under paragraph (4)(D) of this subsection, publish in the Federal Register notice of any new use or intended

use of the information in the system, and provide an opportunity for interested persons to submit written data, views, or arguments to the agency; and

(12) if such agency is a recipient agency or a source agency in a matching program with a non-Federal agency, with respect to any establishment or revision of a matching program, at least 30 days prior to conducting such program, publish in the Federal Register notice of such establishment or revision.

(f) Agency rules. In order to carry out the provisions of this section, each agency that maintains a system of records shall promulgate rules, in accordance with the requirements (including general notice) of section 553 of this title, which shall—

(1) establish procedures whereby an individual can be notified in response to his request if any system of records named by the individual contains a record pertaining to him;

(2) define reasonable times, places, and requirements for identifying an individual who requests his record or information pertaining to him before the agency shall make the record or information available to the individual;

(3) establish procedures for the disclosure to an individual upon his request of his record or information pertaining to him, including special procedure, if deemed necessary, for the disclosure to an individual of medical records, including psychological records, pertaining to him;

(4) establish procedures for reviewing a request from an individual concerning the amendment of any record or information pertaining to the individual, for making a determination on the request, for an appeal within the agency of an initial adverse agency determination, and for whatever additional means may be necessary for each individual to be able to exercise fully his rights under this section; and

(5) establish fees to be charged, if any, to any individual for making copies of his record, excluding the cost of any search for and review of the record.

The Office of the Federal Register shall annually compile and publish the rules promulgated under this subsection and agency notices published under subsection (e)(4) of this section in a form available to the public at low cost.

(g)(1) Civil remedies.

(1) Whenever any agency

(A) makes a determination under subsection (d)(3) of this section not to amend an individual's record in accordance with his request, or fails to make such review in conformity with that subsection;

(B) refuses to comply with an individual request under subsection (d)(1) of this section;

(C) fails to maintain any record concerning any individual with such accuracy, relevance, timeliness, and completeness as is necessary to assure fairness in any determination relating to the qualifications, character, rights, or opportunities of, or benefits to the individual that may be made on the basis of such record, and consequently a determination is made which is adverse to the individuals; or

(D) fails to comply with any other provision of this section, or any rule promulgated thereunder, in such a way as to have an adverse effect on an individual, the individual may bring a civil action against the agency, and the district courts of the United States shall have jurisdiction in the matters under the provisions of this subsection.

(2)(A) In any suit brought under the provisions of subsection (g)(1)(A) of this section, the court may order the agency to amend the individual's record in accordance with his request or in such other way as the court may direct. In such a case the court shall determine the matter de novo.

(B) The court may assess against the United States reasonable attorney fees and other litigation costs reasonably incurred in any case under this paragraph in which the complainant has substantially prevailed.

(3)(A) In any suit brought under the provisions of subsection (g)(1)(B) of this section, the court may enjoin the agency from withholding the records and order the production to the complainant of any agency records improperly withheld from him. In such a case the court shall determine the matter de novo, and may examine the contents of any agency records in camera to determine whether the records or any portion thereof may be withheld under any of the exemptions set forth in subsection (k) of this section, and the burden is on the agency to sustain its action.

(B) The court may assess against the United States reasonable attorney fees and other litigation costs reasonably incurred in any case under this paragraph in which the complainant has substantially prevailed.

(4) In any suit brought under the provisions of subsection (g)(1)(C) or (D) of this section in which the court determines that the agency acted in a manner which was intentional or willful, the United States shall be liable to the individual in an amount equal to the sum of—

(A) actual damages sustained by the individual as a result of the refusal or failure, but in no case shall a person entitled to recovery receive less than the sum of $1,000; and

(B) the costs of the action together with reasonable attorney fees as determined by the court.

(5) An action to enforce any liability created under this section may be brought in the district court of the United States in the district in which the complainant resides, or has his principal place of business, or in which the agency records are situated, or in the District of Columbia, without regard to the amount in controversy, within two years from the date on which the cause of action arises, except that where an agency has materially and willfully misrepresented any information required under this section to be disclosed to an individual and the information so misrepresented is material to establishment of the liability of the agency to the individual under this section, the action may be brought at any time within two years after discovery by the individual of the misrepresentation. Nothing in this section shall be construed to authorize any civil action by reason of any injury sustained as the result of a disclosure of a record prior to September 27, 1975.

(b) Rights of legal guardians. For the purposes of this section, the parent of any minor, or the legal guardian of any individual who has been declared to be incompe-

tent due to physical or mental incapacity or age by a court of competent jurisdiction, may act on behalf of the individual.

(i)(1) Criminal penalties. Any officer or employee of an agency, who by virtue of his employment or official position, has possession of, or access to, agency records which contain individually identifiable information the disclosure of which is prohibited by this section or by rules or regulations established thereunder, and who knowing that disclosure of the specific material is so prohibited, willfully discloses the material in any manner to any person or agency not entitled to receive it, shall be guilty of a misdemeanor and fined not more than $5,000.

(2) Any officer or employee of any agency who willfully maintains a system of records without meeting the notice requirements of subsection (e)(4) of this section shall be guilty of a misdemeanor and fined not more than $5,000.

(3) Any person who knowingly and willfully requests or obtains any record concerning an individual from an agency under false pretenses shall be guilty of a misdemeanor and fined not more than $5,000.

(j) General exemptions. The head of any agency may promulgate rules, in accordance with the requirements (including general notice) of sections 553(b)(1), (2), and (3),(c), and (e) of this title, to exempt any system of records within the agency from any part of this section except subsections (b), (c)(1) and (2), (e)(4)(A) through (F), (e)(6), (7), (9), (10), and (11), and (i) if the system of records is—

(1) maintained by the Central Intelligence Agency; or

(2) maintained by an agency or component thereof which performs as its principal function any activity pertaining to the enforcement of criminal laws, including police efforts to prevent, control, or reduce crime or to apprehend criminals, and the activities of prosecutors, courts, correctional, probation, pardon, or parole authorities, and which consists of (A) information compiled for the purpose of identifying individual criminal offenders and alleged offenders and consisting only of identifying data and notations of arrests, the nature and disposition of criminal charges, sentencing, confinement, release, and parole and probation status; (B) information compiled for the purpose of a criminal investigation, including reports of informants and investigators, and associated with an identifiable individual; or (C) reports identifiable to an individual compiled at any stage of the process of enforcement of the criminal laws from arrest or indictment through release from supervision.At the time are adopted under this subsection, the agency shall include in the statement required under section 553(c) of this title, the reasons why the system of records is to be exempted from a provision of this section.

(k) Specific exemptions. The head of any agency may promulgate rules, in accordance with the requirements (including general notice) of sections 553 (b)(1), (2), and (3), (c), and (e) of this title, to exempt any system of records within the agency from subsections (c)(3), (d), (e)(1), (e)(4)(G), (H), and (I) and (f) of this section if the system of records is—

(1) subject to the provisions of section 552(b)(1) of this title;

(2) investigatory material compiled for law enforcement purposes, other than material within the scope of subsection (j)(2) of this section: *Provided, however,* That if any individual is denied any right, privilege, or benefit that he would otherwise be entitled by Federal Law, or for which he would otherwise be eligible, as a result of the maintenance of such material, such material shall be provided to such individual, except to the extent that the disclosure of such material would reveal the identity of a source who furnished information to the Government under an express promise that the identity of the source would be held in confidence, or, prior to the effective date of this section, under an implied promise that the identity of the source would be held in confidence;

(3) maintained in connection with providing protective services to the President of the United States or other individuals pursuant to section 3056 of title 18;

(4) required by statute to be maintained and used solely as statistical records;

(5) investigatory material compiled solely for the purpose of determining suitability, eligibility, or qualifications for Federal civilian employment, military service, Federal contracts, or access to classified information, but only to the extent that the disclosure of such material would reveal the identity of a source who furnished information to the Government under an express promise that the identity of the source would be held in confidence, or, prior to the effective date of this section, under an implied promise that the identity of the source would be held in confidence;

(6) testing or examination material used solely to determine individual qualifications for appointment or promotion in the Federal service the disclosure of which would compromise the objectivity or fairness of the testing or examination process; or

(7) evaluation material used to determine potential for promotion in the armed services, but only to the extent that the disclosure of such material would reveal the identity of a source who furnished information to the Government under an express promise that the identity of the source would be held in confidence, or, prior to the effective date of this section, under an implied promise that the identity of the source would be held in confidence.

At the time rules are adopted under this subsection, the agency shall include in the statement required under section 553(c) of this title, the reasons why the system of records is to be exempted from a provision of this section.

(l)(1) Archival records. Each agency record which is accepted by the Administrator of General Services for storage, processing, and servicing in accordance with section 3103 of title 44 shall, for the purposes of this section, be considered to be maintained by the agency which deposited the record and shall be subject to the provisions of this section. The Administrator of General Services shall not disclose the record except to the agency which maintains the record, or under rules established by that agency which are not inconsistent with the provisions of this section.

(2) Each agency record pertaining to an identifiable individual which was transferred to the National Archives of the United States as a record which has sufficient historical or other value to warrant its continued preservation by the United States Government, prior to the effective date of this section, shall, for the purposes of this

section, be considered to be maintained by the National Archives and shall not be subject to the provisions of this section, except that a statement generally describing such records (modeled after the requirements relating to records subject to subsections (e)(4)(A) through (G) of this section) shall be published in the Federal Register.

(3) Each agency record pertaining to an identifiable individual which is transferred to the National Archives of the United States as a record which has sufficient historical or other value to warrant its continued preservation by the United States Government, on or after the effective date of this section, shall, for the purposes of this section, be considered to be maintained by the National Archives and shall be exempt from the requirements of this section except subsections (e)(4)(A) through (G) and (e)(9) of this section.

(m) Government contractors.

(1) When an agency provides by a contract for the operation by or behalf of the agency of a system of records to accomplish an agency function, the agency shall, consistent with its authority, cause the requirements of this section to be applied to such system. For purposes of subsection (i) of this section any such contractor and any employee of such contractor, if such contract is agreed to on or after the effective date of this section, shall be considered to be an employee of an agency.

(2) A consumer reporting agency to which a record is disclosed under section 3711(f) of title 31 shall be considered a contractor for the purpose of this section.

(n) Mailing lists. An individual's name and address may not be sold or rented by an agency unless such action is specifically authorized by law. This provision shall not be construed to require the withholding of names and addresses otherwise permitted to be made public.

Matching agreements.

(1) No record which is contained in a system of records may be disclosed to a recipient agency or non-Federal agency for use in a computer matching program except pursuant to a written agreement between the source agency and the recipient agency or non-Federal agency specifying—

(A) the purpose and legal authority for conducting the program;

(B) the justification for the program and the anticipated results, including a specific estimate of any savings;

(C) a description of the records that will be matched, including each data element that will be used, the approximate number of records that will be matched, and the projected starting and completion dates of the matching program;

(D) procedures for providing individualized notice at the time of application, and notice periodically thereafter as directed by the Data Integrity Board of such agency (subject to guidance provided by the Director of the Office of Management and Budget pursuant to subsection (v)) . . . that any information provided by such applicants, recipients, holders, and individuals may be subject to verification through matching programs;

(E) procedures for verifying information produced in such matching program as required by subsection (p);

(F) procedures for the retention and timely destruction of identifiable records created by a recipient agency or non-Federal agency in such matching program;

(G) procedures for ensuring the administrative, technical, and physical security of the records matched and the results of such programs;

(H) prohibitions on duplication and redisclosure of records provided by the source agency within or outside the recipient agency or the non-Federal agency, except where required by law or essential to the conduct of the matching program;

(I) procedures governing the use by a recipient agency or non-Federal agency of records provided in a matching program by a source agency, including procedures governing return of the records to the source agency or destruction of records used in such program;

(J) information on assessments that have been made on the accuracy of the records that will be used in such matching program; and

(K) that the Comptroller General may have access to all records of a recipient agency or a non-Federal agency that the Comptroller General deems necessary in order to monitor or verify compliance with the agreement.

(p) Verification and opportunity to contest findings.

(1) In order to protect any individual whose records are used in matching programs, no recipient agency, non-Federal agency, or source agency may suspend, terminate, reduce, or make a final denial of any financial assistance or payment under a Federal benefit program to such individual, or take other adverse action against such individual as a result of information produced by such matching programs, until an officer or employee of such agency has independently verified such information. Such independent verficiation may be satisfied by verification in accordance with (A) the requirements of paragraph (2); and (B) any additional requirements governing verification under such Federal benefit program.

(2) Independent verification referred to in paragraph (1) requires independent investigation and confirmation of any information used as a basis for an adverse action against an individual including, where applicable—

(A) the amount of the asset or income involved,

(B) whether such individual actually has or had access to such asset or income for such individual's own use, and

(C) the period or periods when the individual actually had such asset or income.

(3) No recipient agency, non-Federal agency, or source agency may suspend, terminate, reduce, or make a final denial of any financial assistance or payment under a Federal benefit program to any individual described in paragraph (1), or take other adverse action against such individual as a result of information produced by a matching program, (A) unless such individual has received notice from such agency containing a statement of its findings and informing the individual of the opportunity to contest such findings, and (B) until the subsequent expiration of any notice period provided by the program's law or regulations, or 30 days, whichever is later. Such opportunity to contest may be satisfied by notice, hearing, and appeal rights governing such Fed-

eral benefit program. The exercise of any rights shall not affect any rights available under this section.

(4) Notwithstanding paragraph (3), an agency may take any appropriate action otherwise prohibited by such paragraph if the agency determines that the public health or public safety may be adversely affected or significantly threatened during the notice period required by such paragraph.

(q) Sanctions.

(1) Notwithstanding any other provision of law, no source agency may disclose any record which is contained in a system of records to a recipient agency or non-Federal agency for a matching program if such source agency has reason to believe that the requirements of subsection (p), or any matching agreement entered into pursuant to subsection (o), or both, are not being met by such recipient agency.

(2) No source agency may renew a matching agreement unless—

(A) the recipient agency or non-Federal agency has certified that it has complied with the provisions of that agreement; and

(B) the source agency has no reason to believe that the certification is inaccurate.

(r) Report on new systems and matching programs.

Each agency that proposes to establish or make a significant change in a system of records or a matching program shall provide adequate advance notice of any such proposal (in duplicate) to the Committee on Government Operations of the House of Representatives, the Committee on Governmental Affairs of the Senate, and the Office of Management and Budget in order to permit an evaluation of the probable or potential effect of such proposal on the privacy or other rights of individuals.

(s) Biennial Report.

The President shall biennially submit to the Speaker of the House of Representatives and the President pro tempore of the Senate a report—

(1) describing the actions of the Director of the Office of Management and Budget pursuant to Section 6 of the Privacy Act of 1974 during the preceding 2 years;

(2) describing the exercise of individual rights of access and amendment under this section during such years;

(3) identifying changes in or additions to systems of records;

(4) containing such other information concerning administration of this section as may be necessary or useful to the Congress in reviewing the effectiveness of this section in carrying out the purposes of the Privacy Act of 1974.

(t) Effect of other laws.

(1) No agency shall rely on any exemption contained in section 552 of this title to withhold from an individual any record which is otherwise accessible to such individual under the provisions of this section.

(2) No agency shall rely on any exemption in this section to withhold from an individual any record which is otherwise accessible to such individual under the provisions of section 552 of this title.

(u) Data Integrity Boards.

(1) Every agency conducting or participating in a matching program shall establish a Data Integrity Board to oversee and coordinate among the various components of such agency the agency's implementation of this section.

(2) Each Data Integrity Board shall consist of senior officials designated by the head of the agency, and shall include any senior official designated by the head of the agency as responsible for implementation of this section, and the inspector general of the agency, if any. The inspector general shall not serve as chairman of the Data Integrity Board.

(3) Each Data Integrity Board—

(A) shall review, approve, and maintain all written agreements for receipt or disclosure of agency records for matching programs to ensure compliance with subsection (o), and all relevant statutes, regulations, and guidelines;

(B) shall review all matching programs in which the agency has participated during the year, either as a source agency or recipient agency, determine compliance with applicable laws, regulations, guidelines, and agency agreements, and assess the costs and benefits of such programs;

(C) shall review all recurring matching programs in which the agency has participated during the year, either as a source agency or recipient agency, for continued justification for such disclosures;

(D) shall compile an annual report, which shall be submitted to the head of the agency and the Office of Management and Budget and made available to the public on request, describing the matching activities of the agency . . .

(E) shall serve as a clearinghouse for receiving and providing information on the accuracy, completeness, and reliability of records used in matching programs;

(F) shall provide interpretation and guidance to agency components and personnel on the requirements of this section for matching programs;

(G) shall review agency recordkeeping and disposal policies and practices for matching programs to assure compliance with this section; and

(H) may review and report on any agency matching activities that are not matching programs.

(4)(A) Except as provided in subparagraphs (B) and (C), a Data Integrity Board shall not approve any written agreement for a matching program unless the agency has completed and submitted to such Board a cost-benefit analysis of the proposed program and such analysis demonstrates that the program is likely to be cost effective.

(B) The board may waive the requirements of subparagraph (A) of this paragraph if it determines in writing, in accordance with guidelines prescribed by the Director of the Office of Management and Budget, that a cost-benefit analysis is not required.

(C) A cost-benefit analysis shall not be required under subparagraph (A) prior to the initial approval of a written agreement for a matching program that is specifically required by statute. Any subsequent written agreement for such a program shall not be approved by the Data Integrity Board unless the agency has submitted a cost-benefit analysis of the program as conducted under the preceding approval of such agreement.

(5)(A) If a matching agreement is disapproved by a Data Integrity Board, any party to such agreement may appeal the disapproval to the Director of the Office of Management and Budget. Timely notice of the filing of such an appeal shall be provided by the Director of the Office of Management and Budget to the Committee on Governmental Affairs of the Senate and the Committee on Government Operations of the House of Representatives.

(B) The Director of the Office of Management and Budget may approve a matching agreement notwithstanding the disapproval of a Data Integrity Board if the Director determines . . .

(C) The decision of the Director to approve a matching agreement shall not take effect until 30 days after it is reported to committees described in subparagraph (A).

(D) If the Data Integrity Board and the Director of the Office of Management and Budget disapprove a matching program proposed by the inspector general of an agency, the inspector general may report the disapproval to the head of the agency and to the Congress.

(6) The Director of the Office of Management and Budget shall, annually during the first 3 years after the date of enactment of this subsection and biennially thereafter, consolidate in a report to the Congress the information contained in the reports from the various Data Integrity Boards under paragraph (3)(D). Such report shall include detailed information about costs and benefits of matching programs that are conducted during the period covered by such consolidated report, and shall identify each waiver granted by a Data Integrity Board of the requirement for completion and submission of a cost-benefit analysis and the reasons for granting the waiver.

(7) In the reports required by paragraphs (3)(D) and (6), agency matching activities that are not matching programs may be reported on an aggregate basis, if and to the extent necessary to protect ongoing law enforcement or counterintelligence investigations.

(v) *Office of Management and Budget responsibilities.* The Director of the Office of management and Budget shall—

(1) develop and, after notice and opportunity for public comment, prescribe guidelines and regulations for the use of agencies in implementing the provisions of this section; and

(2) provide continuing assistance to and oversight of the implementation of this section by agencies.

§ 552b. Open Meetings

(a) For purposes of this section—

(1) the term "agency" means any agency, as defined in section 552(e) of this title, headed by a collegial body composed of two or more individual members, a majority of whom are appointed to such position by the President with the advice and consent of the Senate, and any subdivision thereof authorized to act on behalf of the agency;

(2) the term "meeting" means the deliberations of at least the number of individual agency members required to take action on behalf of the agency where such deliberations determine or result in the joint conduct or disposition of official agency business, but does not include deliberations required or permitted by subsection (d) or (e); and

(3) the term "member" means an individual who belongs to a collegial body heading an agency.

(b) Members shall not jointly conduct or dispose of agency business other than in accordance with this section. Except as provided in subsection (c), every portion of every meeting of an agency shall be open to public observation.

(c) Except in a case where the agency finds that the public interest requires otherwise, the second sentence of subsection (b) shall not apply to any portion of an agency meeting, and the requirements of subsections (d) and (e) shall not apply to any information pertaining to such meeting otherwise required by this section to be disclosed to the public, where the agency properly determines that such portion or portions of its meeting or the disclosure of such information is likely to—

(1) disclose matters that are (A) specifically authorized under criteria established by an Executive order to be kept secret in the interests of national defense or foreign policy and (B) in fact properly classified pursuant to such Executive order;

(2) relate solely to the internal personnel rules and practices of an agency;

(3) disclose matters specifically exempted from disclosure by statute (other than section 552 of this title), provided that such statute (A) requires that the matters be withheld from the public in such a manner as to leave no discretion on the issue, or (B) establishes particular criteria for withholding or refers to particular types of matters to be withheld;

(4) disclose trade secrets and commercial or financial information obtained from a person and privileged or confidential;

(5) involve accusing any person of a crime, or formally censuring any person;

(6) disclose information of a personal nature where disclosure would constitute a clearly unwarranted invasion of personal privacy;

(7) disclose investigatory records compiled for law enforcement purposes, or information which if written would be contained in such records, but only to the extent that the production of such records or information would (A) interfere with enforcement proceedings, (B) deprive a person of a right to a fair trial or an impartial adjudication, (C) constitute an unwarranted invasion of personal privacy, (D) disclose the identity of a confidential source and, in the case of a record compiled by a criminal law enforcement authority in the course of a criminal investigation, or by an agency conducting a lawful national security intelligence investigation, confidential information furnished only by the confidential source, (E) disclose investigative techniques and procedures, or (F) endanger the life or physical safety of law enforcement personnel;

(8) disclose information contained in or related to examination, operating, or condition reports prepared by, on behalf of, or for the use of an agency responsible for the regulation or supervision of financial institutions;

(9) disclose information the premature disclosure of which would—

(A) in the case of an agency which regulates currencies, securities, commodities, or financial institutions, be likely to (i) lead to significant financial speculation in currencies, securities, or commodities, or (ii) significantly endanger the stability of any financial institution; or

(B) in the case of any agency, be likely to significantly frustrate implementation of a proposed agency action, except that subparagraph (B) shall not apply in any instance where the agency has already disclosed to the public the content or nature of its proposed action, or where the agency is required by law to make such disclosure on its own initiative prior to taking final agency action on such proposal; or

(10) specifically concern the agency's issuance of a subpena, or the agency's participation in a civil action or proceeding, an action in a foreign court or international tribunal, or an arbitration, or the initiation, conduct, or disposition by the agency of a particular case of formal agency adjudication pursuant to the procedures in section 554 of this title or otherwise involving a determination on the record after opportunity for a hearing.

(d)(1) Action under subsection (c) shall be taken only when a majority of the entire membership of the agency (as defined in subsection (a)(1)) votes to take such action. A separate vote of the agency members shall be taken with respect to each agency meeting a portion or portions of which are proposed to be closed to the public pursuant to subsection (c), or with respect to any information which is proposed to be withheld under subsection (c). A single vote may be taken with respect to a series of meetings, a portion or portions of which are proposed to be closed to the public, or with respect to any information concerning such series of meetings, so long as each meeting in such series involves the same particular matters and is scheduled to be held no more than thirty days after the initial meeting in such series. The vote of each agency member participating in such vote shall be recorded and no proxies shall be allowed.

(2) Whenever any person whose interests may be directly affected by a portion of a meeting requests that the agency close such portion to the public for any of the reasons referred to in paragraph (5), (6), or (7) of subsection (c), the agency, upon request of any one of its members, shall vote by recorded vote whether to close such meeting.

(3) Within one day of any vote taken pursuant to paragraph (1) or (2), the agency shall make publicly available a written copy of such vote reflecting the vote of each member on the question. If a portion of a meeting is to be closed to the public, the agency shall, within one day of the vote taken pursuant to paragraph (1) or (2) of this subsection, make publicly available a full written explanation of its action closing the portion together with a list of all persons expected to attend the meeting and their affiliation.

(4) Any agency, a majority of whose meetings may properly be closed to the public pursuant to paragraph (4), (8), (9)(A), or (10) of subsection (c), or any combination thereof, may provide by regulation for the closing of such meetings or portions thereof in the event that a majority of the members of the agency votes by recorded vote at the beginning of such meeting, or portion thereof, to close the exempt portion or portions of the meeting, and a copy of such vote, reflecting the vote of each member on the question, is made available to the public. The provisions of paragraphs (1), (2), and (3) of this subsection and subsection (e) shall not apply to any portion of a meeting to which such regulations apply: *Provided*, That the agency shall, except to the extent that such information is exempt from disclosure under the provisions of subsection (c), provide the public with public announcement of the time, place, and subject matter of the meeting and of each portion thereof at the earliest practicable time.

(e)(1) In the case of each meeting, the agency shall make public announcement, at least one week before the meeting, of the time, place, and subject matter of the meeting, whether it is to be open or closed to the public, and the name and phone number of the official designated by the agency to respond to requests for information about the meeting. Such announcement shall be made unless a majority of the members of the agency determines by a recorded vote that agency business requires that such meeting be called at an earlier date, in which case the agency shall make public announcement of the time, place, and subject matter of such meeting, and whether open or closed to the public, at the earliest practicable time.

(2) The time or place of a meeting may be changed following the public announcement required by paragraph (1) only if the agency publicly announces such change at the earliest practicable time. The subject matter of a meeting, or the determination of the agency to open or close a meeting, or portion of a meeting, to the public, may be changed following the public announcement required by this subsection only if (A) a majority of the entire membership of the agency determines by a recorded vote that agency business so requires and that no earlier announcement of the change was possible, and (B) the agency publicly announces such change and the vote of each member upon such change at the earliest practicable time.

(3) Immediately following each public announcement required by this subsection, notice of the time, place, and subject matter of a meeting, whether the meeting is open or closed, any change in one of the preceding, and the name and phone number of the official designated by the agency to respond to requests for information about the meeting, shall also be submitted for publication in the Federal Register.

(f)(1) For every meeting closed pursuant to paragraphs (1) through (10) of subsection (c), the General Counsel or chief legal officer of the agency shall publicly certify that, in his or her opinion, the meeting may be closed to the public and shall state each relevant exemptive provision. A copy of such certification, together with a statement from the presiding officer of the meeting setting forth the time and place of the meeting, and the persons present, shall be retained by the agency. The agency shall maintain a complete transcript or electronic recording adequate to record fully the proceedings of each meeting, or portion of a meeting, closed to the public, except that in the case of a meeting, or portion of a meeting, closed to the public pursuant to paragraph (8), (9)(A), or (10) of subsection (c), the agency shall maintain either such a transcript or recording, or a set of minutes. Such minutes shall fully and clearly describe all matters discussed and shall provide a full and accurate summary of any actions taken, and the reasons therefor, including a description of each of the views expressed on any item and the record of any rollcall vote (reflecting the vote of each member on the question). All documents considered in connection with any action shall be identified in such minutes.

(2) The agency shall make promptly available to the public, in a place easily accessible to the public, the transcript, electronic recording, or minutes (as required by paragraph (1)) of the discussion of any item on the agenda, or of any item of the testimony of any witness received at the meeting, except for such item or items of such discussion or testimony as the agency determines to contain information which may be with-

held under subsection (c). Copies of such transcript, or minutes, or a transcription of such recording disclosing the identity of each speaker, shall be furnished to any person at the actual cost of duplication or transcription. The agency shall maintain a complete verbatim copy of the transcript, a complete copy of the minutes, or a complete electronic recording of each meeting, or portion of a meeting, closed to the public, for a period of at least two years after such meeting, or until one year after the conclusion of any agency proceeding with respect to which the meeting or portion was held, whichever occurs later.

(g) Each agency subject to the requirements of this section shall, within 180 days after the date of enactment of this section, following consultation with the Office of the Chairman of the Administrative Conference of the United States and published notice in the Federal Register of at least thirty days and opportunity for written comment by any person, promulgate regulations to implement the requirements of subsections (b) through (f) of this section. Any person may bring a proceeding in the United States District Court for the District of Columbia to require an agency to promulgate such regulations if such agency has not promulgated such regulations within the time period specified herein. Subject to any limitations of time provided by law, any person may bring a proceeding in the United States Court of Appeals for the District of Columbia to set aside agency regulations issued pursuant to this subsection that are not in accord with the requirements of subsections (b) through (f) of this section and to require the promulgation of regulations that are in accord with such subsections.

(h)(1) The district courts of the United States shall have jurisdiction to enforce the requirements of subsections (b) through (f) of this section by declaratory judgment, injunctive relief, or other relief as may be appropriate. Such actions may be brought by any person against an agency prior to, or within sixty days after, the meeting out of which the violation of this section arises, except that if public announcement of such meeting is not initially provided by the agency in accordance with the requirements of this section, such action may be instituted pursuant to this section at any time prior to sixty days after any public announcement of such meeting. Such actions may be brought in the district court of the United States for the district in which the agency meeting is held or in which the agency in question has its headquarters, or in the District Court for the District of Columbia. In such actions a defendant shall serve his answer within thirty days after the service of the complaint. The burden is on the defendant to sustain his action. In deciding such cases the court may examine in camera any portion of the transcript, electronic recording, or minutes of a meeting closed to the public, and may take such additional evidence as it deems necessary. The court, having due regard for orderly administration and the public interest, as well as the interests of the parties, may grant such equitable relief as it deems appropriate, including granting an injunction against future violations of this section or ordering the agency to make available to the public such portion of the transcript, recording, or minutes of a meeting as is not authorized to be withheld under subsection (c) of this section.

(2) Any Federal court otherwise authorized by law to review agency action may, at the application of any person participating in the proceeding pursuant to the other

applicable law, inquire into violations by the agency of the requirements of this section and afford such relief as it deems appropriate. Nothing in this section authorizes any Federal court having jurisdiction solely on the basis of paragraph (1) to set aside, enjoin, or invalidate any agency action (other than an action to close a meeting or to withhold information under this section) taken or discussed at any agency meeting out of which the violation of this section arose.

(i) The court may assess against any party reasonable attorney fees and other litigation costs reasonably incurred by any other party who substantially prevails in any action brought in accordance with the provisions of subsection (g) or (h) of this section, except that costs may be assessed against the plaintiff only where the court finds that the suit was initiated by the plaintiff primarily for frivolous or dilatory purposes. In the case of assessment of costs against an agency, the costs may be assessed by the court against the United States.

(j) Each agency subject to the requirements of this section shall annually report to Congress regarding its compliance with such requirements, including a tabulation of the total number of agency meetings open to the public, the total number of meetings closed to the public, the reasons for closing such meetings, and a description of any litigation brought against the agency under this section, including any costs assessed against the agency in such litigation (whether or not paid by the agency).

(k) Nothing herein expands or limits the present rights of any person under section 552 of this title, except that the exemptions set forth in subsection (c) of this section shall govern in the case of any request made pursuant to section 552 to copy or inspect the transcripts, recordings, or minutes described in subsection (f) of this section. The requirements of chapter 33 of title 44, United States Code, shall not apply to the transcripts, recordings, and minutes described in subsection (f) of this section.

(l) This section does not constitute authority to withhold any information from Congress, and does not authorize the closing of any agency meeting or portion thereof required by any other provision of law to be open.

(m) Nothing in this section authorizes any agency to withhold from any individual any record, including transcripts, recordings, or minutes required by this section, which is otherwise accessible to such individual under section 552a of this title.

§ 553. Rule Making

(a) This section applies, according to the provisions thereof, except to the extent that there is involved—

(1) a military or foreign affairs function of the United States; or

(2) a matter relating to agency management or personnel or to public property, loans, grants, benefits, or contracts.

(b) General notice of proposed rule making shall be published in the Federal Register, unless persons subject thereto are named and either personally served or otherwise have actual notice thereof in accordance with law. The notice shall include—

(1) a statement of the time, place, and nature of public rule-making proceedings;

(2) reference to the legal authority under which the rule is proposed; and

(3) either the terms or substance of the proposed rule or a description of the subjects and issues involved.

Except when notice or hearing is required by statute, this subsection does not apply—

(A) to interpretative rules, general statements of policy, or rules of agency organization, procedure, or practice; or

(B) when the agency for good cause finds (and incorporates the finding and a brief statement of reasons therefor in the rules issued) that notice and public procedure thereon are impracticable, unnecessary, or contrary to the public interest.

(c) After notice required by this section, the agency shall give interested persons an opportunity to participate in the rule making through submission of written data, views, or arguments with or without opportunity for oral presentation. After consideration of the relevant matter presented, the agency shall incorporate in the rules adopted a concise general statement of their basis and purpose. When rules are required by statute to be made on the record after opportunity for an agency hearing, sections 556 and 557 of this title apply instead of this subsection.

(d) The required publication or service of a substantive rule shall be made not less than 30 days before its effective date, except—

(1) a substantive rule which grants or recognizes an exemption or relieves a restriction;

(2) interpretative rules and statements of policy; or

(3) as otherwise provided by the agency for good cause found and published with the rule.

(e) Each agency shall give an interested person the right to petition for the issuance, amendment, or repeal of a rule.

§ 554. *Adjudications*

(a) This section applies, according to the provisions thereof, in every case of adjudication required by statute to be determined on the record after opportunity for an agency hearing, except to the extent that there is involved—

(1) a matter subject to a subsequent trial of the law and the facts de novo in a court;

(2) the selection or tenure of an employee, except administrative law judge appointed under section 3105 of this title;

(3) proceedings in which decisions rest solely on inspections, tests, or elections;

(4) the conduct of military or foreign affairs functions;

(5) cases in which an agency is acting as an agent for a court; or

(6) the certification of worker representatives.

(b) Persons entitled to notice of an agency hearing shall be timely informed of—

(1) the time, place, and nature of the hearing;

(2) the legal authority and jurisdiction under which the hearing is to be held; and

(3) the matters of fact and law asserted.

When private persons are the moving parties, other parties to the proceeding shall give prompt notice of issues controverted in fact or law; and in other instances agencies may by rule require responsive pleading. In fixing the time and place for hearings, due regard shall be had for the convenience and necessity of the parties or their representatives.

(c) The agency shall give all interested parties opportunity for—

(1) the submission and consideration of facts, arguments, offers of settlement, or proposals of adjustment when time, the nature of the proceeding, and the public interest permit; and

(2) to the extent that the parties are unable to determine a controversy by consent, hearing and decision on notice and in accordance with sections 556 and 557 of this title.

(d) The employee who presides at the reception of evidence pursuant to section 556 of this title shall make the recommended decision or initial decision required by section 557 of this title, unless he becomes unavailable to the agency. Except to the extent required for the disposition of ex parte matters as authorized by law, such an employee may not—

(1) consult a person or party on a fact in issue, unless on notice and opportunity for all parties to participate; or

(2) be responsible to or subject to the supervision or direction of an employee or agent engaged in the performance of investigative or prosecuting functions for an agency. An employee or agent engaged in the performance of investigative or prosecuting functions for an agency in a case may not, in that or a factually related case, participate or advise in the decision, recommended decision, or agency review pursuant to section 557 of this title, except as witness or counsel in public proceedings. This subsection does not apply—

(A) in determining applications for initial licenses;

(B) to proceedings involving the validity or application of rates, facilities, or practices of public utilities or carriers; or

(C) to the agency or a member or members of the body comprising the agency.

(e) The agency, with like effect as in the case of other orders, and in its sound discretion, may issue a declaratory order to terminate a controversy or remove uncertainty.

§ 555. Ancillary Matters

(a) This section applies, according to the provisions thereof, except as otherwise provided by this subchapter.

(b) A person compelled to appear in person before an agency or representative thereof is entitled to be accompanied, represented, and advised by counsel or, if permitted by the agency, by other qualified representative. A party is entitled to appear in person or by or with counsel or other duly qualified representative in an agency proceeding. So far as the orderly conduct of public business permits, an interested person may appear before an agency or its responsible employees for the presentation, adjustment, or determination of an issue, request, or controversy in a proceeding, whether interlocutory, summary, or otherwise, or in connection with an agency function. With due regard for the convenience and necessity of the parties or their representatives and within a reasonable time, each agency shall proceed to conclude a matter presented to it. This subsection does not grant or deny a person who is not a lawyer the right to appear for or represent others before an agency or in an agency proceeding.

(c) Process, requirement of a report, inspection, or other investigative act or demand may not be issued, made, or enforced except as authorized by law. A person compelled to submit data or evidence is entitled to retain or, on payment of lawfully prescribed costs, procure a copy or transcript thereof, except that in a nonpublic investigatory proceeding the witness may for good cause be limited to inspection of the official transcript of his testimony.

(d) Agency subpenas authorized by law shall be issued to a party on request and, when required by rules of procedure, on a statement or showing of general relevance and reasonable scope of the evidence sought. On contest, the court shall sustain the subpena or similar process or demand to the extent that it is found to be in accordance with law. In a proceeding for enforcement, the court shall issue an order requiring the appearance of the witness or the production of the evidence or data within a reasonable time under penalty of punishment for contempt in case of contumacious failure to comply.

(e) Prompt notice shall be given of the denial in whole or in part of a written application, petition, or other request of an interested person made in connection with any agency proceeding. Except in affirming a prior denial or when the denial is self-explanatory, the notice shall be accompanied by a brief statement of the grounds for denial.

§ 556. Hearings; Presiding Employees; Powers and Duties; Burden of Proof; Evidence; Record as Basis of Decision

(a) This section applies, according the provisions thereof, to hearings required by section 553 or 554 of this title to be conducted in accordance with this section.

(b) There shall preside at the taking of evidence—

(1) the agency;

(2) one or more members of the body which comprises the agency; or

(3) one or more administrative law judges appointed under section 3105 of this title. This subchapter does not supersede the conduct of specified classes of proceedings, in whole or in part, by or before boards or other employees specially provided for by or designated under statute. The functions of presiding employees and of employees participating in decisions in accordance with section 557 of this title shall be conducted in an impartial manner. A presiding or participating employee may at any time disqualify himself. On the filing in good faith of a timely and sufficient affidavit of personal bias or other disqualification of a presiding or participating employee, the agency shall determine the matter as a part of the record and decision in the case.

(c) Subject to published rules of the agency and within its powers, employees presiding at hearings may—

(1) administer oaths and affirmations;

(2) issue subpenas authorized by law;

(3) rule on offers of proof and receive relevant evidence;

(4) take depositions or have depositions taken when the ends of justice would be served;

(5) regulate the course of the hearing;

(6) hold conferences for the settlement or simplification of the issues by consent of the parties;

(7) dispose of procedural requests or similar matters;

(8) make or recommend decisions in accordance with section 557 of this title; and

(9) take other action authorized by agency rule consistent with this subchapter.

(d) Except as otherwise provided by statute, the proponent of a rule or order has the burden of proof. Any oral or documentary evidence may be received, but the agency as a matter of policy shall provide for the exclusion of irrelevant, immaterial, or unduly repetitious evidence. A sanction may not be imposed or rule or order issued except on consideration of the whole record or those parts thereof cited by a party and supported by and in accordance with the reliable, probative, and substantial evidence. The agency may, to the extent consistent with the interests of justice and the policy of the underlying statutes administered by the agency, consider a violation of section 557(d) of this title sufficient grounds for a decision adverse to a party who has knowingly committed such violation or knowingly caused such violation to occur. A party is entitled to present his case or defense by oral or documentary evidence, to submit rebuttal evidence, and to conduct such cross-examination as may be required for a full and true disclosure of the facts. In rule making or determining claims for money or benefits or applications for initial licenses an agency may, when a party will not be prejudiced thereby, adopt procedures for the submission of all or part of the evidence in written form.

(e) The transcript of testimony and exhibits, together with all papers and requests filed in the proceeding, constitutes the exclusive record for decision in accordance with section 557 of this title and, on payment of lawfully prescribed costs, shall be made available to the parties. When an agency decision rests on official notice of a material fact not appearing in the evidence in the record, a party is entitled, on timely request, to an opportunity to show the contrary.

§ 557. Initial Decisions; Conclusiveness; Review by Agency; Submissions by Parties; Contents of Decisions; Record

(a) This section applies, according to the provisions thereof, when a hearing is required to be conducted in accordance with section 556 of this title.

(b) When the agency did not preside at the reception of the evidence, the presiding employee or, in cases not subject to section 554(d) of this title, an employee qualified to preside at hearings pursuant to section 556 of this title, shall initially decide the case unless the agency requires, either in specific cases or by general rule, the entire record to be certified to it for decision. When the presiding employee makes an initial decision, that decision then becomes the decision of the agency without further proceedings unless there is an appeal to, or review on motion of, the agency within time provided by rule. On appeal from or review of the initial decision, the agency has all the powers which it would have in making the initial decision except as it may limit the issues on notice or by rule. When the agency makes the decision without having presided at the reception of the evidence, the presiding employee or an employee qualified to preside at hearings pursuant to section 556 of this title shall first recommend a decision, except that in rule making or determining applications for initial licenses—

(1) instead thereof the agency may issue a tentative decision or one of its responsible employees may recommend a decision; or

(2) this procedure may be omitted in a case in which the agency finds on the record that due and timely execution of its functions imperatively and unavoidably so requires.

(c) Before a recommended, initial, or tentative decision, or a decision on agency review of the decision of subordinate employees, the parties are entitled to a reasonable opportunity to submit for the consideration of the employees participating in the decisions—

(1) proposed findings and conclusions; or

(2) exceptions to the decisions or recommended decisions of subordinate employees or to tentative agency decisions; and

(3) supporting reasons for the exceptions or proposed findings or conclusions. The record shall show the ruling on each finding, conclusion, or exception presented. All decisions, including initial, recommended, and tentative decisions, are a part of the record and shall include a statement of—

(A) findings and conclusions, and the reasons or basis therefor, on all the material issues of fact, law, or discretion presented on the record; and

(B) the appropriate rule, order, sanction, relief, or denial thereof.

(d)(1) In any agency proceeding which is subject to subsection (a) of this section, except to the extent required for the disposition of ex parte matters as authorized by law—

(A) no interested person outside the agency shall make or knowingly causes to be made to any member of the body comprising the agency, administrative law judge, or other employee who is or may reasonably be expected to be involved in the decisional process of the proceeding, an ex parte communication relevant to the merits of the proceeding;

(B) no member of the body comprising the agency, administrative law judge, or other employee who is or may reasonably be expected to be involved in the decisional process of the proceeding, shall make or knowingly cause to be made to any interested person outside the agency an ex parte communication relevant to the merits of the proceeding;

(C) a member of the body comprising the agency, administrative law judge, or other employee who is or may reasonably be expected to be involved in the decisional process of such proceeding who receives, or who makes or knowingly cause to be made, a communication prohibited by this subsection shall place on the public record of the proceeding:

(i) all such written communications;

(ii) memoranda stating the substance of all such oral communications; and

(iii) all written responses, and memoranda stating the substance of all oral responses, to the materials described in clauses (i) and (ii) of this subparagraph;

(D) upon receipt of a communication knowingly made or knowingly caused to be made by a party in violation of this subsection, the agency, administrative law judge, or other employee presiding at the hearing may, to the extent consistent with the interests of justice and the policy of the underlying statutes, require the party to show cause why his claim or interest in the proceeding should not be dismissed, denied, disregarded, or otherwise adversely affected on account of such violation; and

(E) the prohibitions of this subsection shall apply beginning at such time as the agency may designate, but in no case shall they begin to apply later than the time at which a proceeding is noticed for hearing unless the person responsible for the communication has knowledge that it will be noticed, in which case the prohibitions shall apply beginning at the time of his acquisition of such knowledge.

(2) This subsection does not constitute authority to withhold information from Congress.

§ 558. Imposition of Sanctions; Determination of Applications for Licenses; Suspension, Revocation, and Expiration of Licenses

(a) This section applies, according to the provisions thereof, to the exercise of a power or authority.

(b) A sanction may not be imposed or a substantive rule or order issued except within jurisdiction delegated to the agency and as authorized by law.

(c) When application is made for a license required by law, the agency, with due regard for the rights and privileges of all the interested parties or adversely affected persons and within a reasonable time, shall set and complete proceedings required to be conducted in accordance with sections 556 and 557 of this title or other proceedings required by law and shall make its decision. Except in cases of willfulness or those in which public health, interest, or safety requires otherwise, the withdrawal, suspension, revocation, or annulment of a license is lawful only if, before the institution of agency proceedings therefor, the license has been given—

(1) notice by the agency in writing of the facts or conduct which may warrant the action; and

(2) opportunity to demonstrate or achieve compliance with all lawful requirements.

When the licensee has made timely and sufficient application for a renewal or a new license in accordance with agency rules, a license with reference to an activity of a continuing nature does not expire until the application has been finally determined by the agency.

§ 559. Effect on Other Laws; Effect of Subsequent Statute

This subchapter, chapter 7, and sections 1305, 3105, 3344, 4301(2)(E), 5372, and 7521 of this title, and the provisions of section 5335(a)(B) of this title that relate to administrative law judges, do not limit or repeal additional requirements imposed by statute or otherwise recognized by law. Except as otherwise required by law, requirements or privileges relating to evidence or procedure apply equally to agencies and persons. Each agency is granted the authority necessary to comply with the requirements of this subchapter through the issuance of rules or otherwise. Subsequent statute may not be held to supersede or modify this subchapter, chapter 7, sections 1305, 3105, 3344, 4301(2)(E), 5372, or 7521 of this title, or the provisions of section 5335(a)(B) of this title that relate to administrative law judges, except to the extent that it does so expressly.

Subchapter III—Administrative Conference of the United States

§ 571. Purpose

It is the purpose of this subchapter to provide suitable arrangements through which Federal agencies, assisted by outside experts, may cooperatively study mutual problems, exchange information, and develop recommendations for action by proper authorities to the end that private rights may be fully protected and regulatory activities and other Federal responsibilities may be carried out expeditiously in the public interest.

§ 572. Definitions

For the purpose of this subchapter—

(1) "administrative program" includes a Federal function which involves protection of the public interest and the determination of rights, privileges, and obligations of private persons through rule making, adjudication, licensing, or investigation, as those terms are used in subchapter II of this chapter, except that it does not include a military or foreign affairs function of the United States;

(2) "administrative agency" means an authority as defined by section 551(1) of this title; and

(3) "administrative procedure" means procedure used in carrying out an administrative program and is to be broadly construed to include any aspect of agency organization, procedure, or management which may affect the equitable consideration of public and private interests, the fairness of agency decisions, the speed of agency action, and the relationship of operating methods to later judicial review, but does not include the scope of agency responsibility as established by law or matters of substantive policy committed by law to agency discretion.

§ 573. Administrative Conference of the United States

(a) The Administrative Conference of the United States consists of not more than 101 nor less than 75 members appointed as set forth in subsection (b) of this section.

(b) The Conference is composed of—

(1) a full-time Chairman appointed for a 5-year term by the President, by and with the advice and consent of the Senate. The Chairman is entitled to pay at the highest rate established by statute for the chairman of an independent regulatory board or commission, and may continue to serve until his successor is appointed and has qualified;

(2) the chairman of each independent regulatory board or commission or an individual designated by the board or commission;

(3) the head of each Executive department or other administrative agency which is designated by the President, or an individual designated by the head of the department or agency;

(4) when authorized by the Council referred to in section 575(b) of this title, one or more appointees from a board, commission, department, or agency referred to in

this subsection, designated by the head thereof with, in the case of a board or commission, the approval of the board or commission;

(5) individuals appointed by the President to membership on the Council who are not otherwise members of the Conference; and

(6) not more than 40 other members appointed by the Chairman, with the approval of the Council, for terms of 2 years, except that the number of members appointed by not be subject to judicial review. When an action for judicial review of a rule is instituted, any regulatory flexibility analysis for such rule shall constitute part of the whole record of agency action in connection with the review.

(c) Nothing in this section bars judicial review of any other impact statement or similar analysis required by any other law if judicial review of such statement or analysis is otherwise provided by law.

§ 612. Reports and intervention rights

(a) The Chief Counsel for Advocacy of the Small Business Administration shall monitor agency compliance with this chapter and shall report at least annually thereon to the President and to the Committees on the Judiciary of the Senate and House of Representatives, the Select Committee on Small Business of the Senate, and the Committee on Small Business of the House of Representatives.

(b) The Chief Counsel for Advocacy of the Small Business Administration is authorized to appear as amicus curiae in any action brought in a court of the United States to review a rule. In any such action, the Chief Counsel is authorized to present his views with respect to the effect of the rule on small entities.

(c) A court of the United States shall grant the application of the Chief Counsel for Advocacy of the Small Business Administration to appear in any such action for the purposes described in subsection (b).

Chapter 7 — Judicial Review

Sec.

§ 701. Applications; Definitions

(a) This chapter applies, according to the provisions thereof, except to the extent that—
(1) statutes preclude judicial review; or
(2) agency action is committed to agency discretion by law.
(b) For the purpose of this chapter—

(1) "agency" means each authority of the Government of the United States, whether or not it is within or subject to review by another agency, but does not include—

(A) the Congress,

(B) the courts of the United States;

(C) the governments of the territories or possessions of the United States;

(D) the government of the District of Columbia;

(E) agencies composed of representatives of the parties or of representatives of organizations of the parties to the disputes determined by them;

(F) courts martial and military commissions;

(G) military authority exercised in the field in time of war or in occupied territory; or

(H) functions conferred by sections 1738, 1739, 1743, and 1744 of title 12; chapter 2 of title 41; or sections 1622, 1884, 1891–1902, and former section 1641(b)(2), of title 50, appendix; and

(2) "person," "rule," "order," "license," "sanction," "relief," and "agency action" have the meanings given them by section 551 of this title.

§ 702. *Right of Review*

A person suffering legal wrong because of agency action, or adversely affected or aggrieved by agency action within the meaning of a relevant statute, is entitled to judicial review thereof. An action in a court of the United States seeking relief other than money damages and stating a claim that an agency or an officer or employee thereof acted or failed to act in an official capacity or under color of legal authority shall not be dismissed nor relief therein be denied on the ground that it is against the United States or that the United States is an indispensable party. The United States may be named as a defendant in such action, and a judgment or decree may be entered against the United States: *Provided,* That any mandatory or injunctive decree shall specify the Federal officer or officers (by name or by title), and their successors in office, personally responsible for compliance. Nothing herein (1) affects other limitations on judicial review or the power or duty of the court to dismiss any action or deny relief on any other appropriate legal or equitable ground; or (2) confers authority to grant relief if any other statute that grants consent to suit expressly or impliedly forbids the relief which is sought.

§ 703. *Form and Venue of Proceedings*

The form of proceeding for judicial review is the special statutory review proceeding relevant to the subject matter in a court specified by statute or, in the absence of inadequacy thereof, any applicable form of legal action, including actions for declaratory judgments or writs or prohibitory or mandatory injunction or habeas corpus, in a court of competent jurisdiction. If no special statutory review proceeding is applicable, the action for judicial review may be brought against the United States, the agency by its official title, or the appropriate officer. Except to the extent that prior, adequate, and exclusive opportunity for judicial review is provided by law, agency action is subject to judicial review in civil or criminal proceedings for judicial enforcement.

§ 704. *Actions Reviewable*

Agency action made reviewable by statute and final agency action for which there is no other adequate remedy in a court are subject to judicial review. A preliminary, procedural, or intermediate agency action or ruling not directly reviewable is subject to review on the review of the final agency action. Except as otherwise expressly required by statute, agency action otherwise final is final for the purposes of this section whether or not there has been presented or determined an application for a declaratory order, for any form of reconsideration, or, unless the agency otherwise requires by rule and provides that the action meanwhile is inoperative, for an appeal to superior agency authority.

§ 705. *Relief Pending Review*

When an agency finds that justice so requires, it may postpone the effective date of action taken by it, pending judicial review. On such conditions as may be required and to the extent necessary to prevent irreparable injury, the reviewing court, including the court to which a case may be taken on appeal from or on application for certiorari or other writ to a reviewing court, may issue all necessary and appropriate process to postpone the effective date of an agency action or to preserve status or rights pending conclusion of the review proceedings.

§ 706. *Scope of Review*

To the extent necessary to decision and when presented, the reviewing courts shall decide all relevant questions of law, interpret constitutional and statutory provisions, and determine the meaning or applicability of the terms of an agency action. The reviewing court shall—

(1) compel agency action unlawfully withheld or unreasonably delayed; and

(2) hold unlawful and set aside agency action, findings, and conclusions found to be—

(A) arbitrary, capricious, an abuse of discretion, or otherwise not in accordance with law;

(B) contrary to constitutional right, power, privilege, or immunity;

(C) in excess of statutory jurisdiction, authority, or limitations, or short of statutory right;

(D) without observance of procedure required by law;

(E) unsupported by substantial evidence in a case subject to sections 556 and 557 of this title or otherwise reviewed on the record of an agency hearing provided by statute; or

(F) unwarranted by the facts to the extent that the facts are subject to trial de novo by the reviewing court.

In making the foregoing determinations, the court shall review the whole record or those parts of it cited by a party, and due account shall be taken of the rule of prejudicial error.

Part II—The United States Civil Service Commission

Chapter 13—Special Authority

§ 1305. Administrative Law Judges

For the purpose of sections 3105, 3344, 4301(2)(D), and 5372 of this title and the provisions of section 5335(a)(B) of this title that relate to administrative law judges, the Office of Personnel Management may, and for the purpose of 7521 of this title, the Merit Systems Protection Board may investigate, require reports by agencies, issue reports, including an annual report to Congress, prescribe regulations, appoint advisory committees as necessary, recommend legislation, subpena witnesses and records, and pay witness fees as established for the courts of the United States.

Part III—Employees

Subpart B—Employment and Retention

Chapter 31—Authority for Employment

§ 3105. Appointment of Administrative Law Judges

Each agency shall appoint as many administrative law judges as are necessary for proceedings required to be conducted in accordance with sections 556 and 557 of this title. Administrative law judges shall be assigned to cases in rotation so far as practicable, and may not perform duties inconsistent with their duties and responsibilities as administrative law judges.

Chapter 33—Examination, Selection, and Placement

§ 3344. Details; Administrative Law Judges

An agency as defined by section 551 of this title which occasionally or temporarily is insufficiently staffed with administrative law judges appointed under section 3105 of this title may use administrative law judges selected by the Office of Personnel Management from and with the consent of other agencies.

Subpart D — Pay and Allowances

Chapter 53 — Pay Rates and Systems

§ 5372. *Administrative Law Judges*

Administrative law judges appointed under section 3105 of this title are entitled to pay prescribed by the Office of Personnel Management independently of agency recommendations or ratings and in accordance with subchapter III of this chapter and chapter 51 of this title.

Subpart F — Employee Relations

Chapter 75 — Adverse Actions

§ 7521. *Actions Against Administrative Law Judges*

(a) An action may be taken against an administrative law judge appointed under section 3105 of this title by the agency in which the administrative law judge is employed only for good cause established and determined by the Merit Systems Protection Board on the record after opportunity for hearing before the Board.

(b) The actions covered by this section are —

(1) a removal;

(2) a suspension;

(3) a reduction in grade;

(4) a reduction in pay; and

(5) a furlough of 30 days or less;

but do not include —

(A) a suspension or removal under section 7532 of this title;

(B) a reduction-in-force action under section 3502 of this title; or

(C) any action initiated under section 1206 of this title [i.e., by the Special Counsel of the Board].

APPENDIX C

Uniform Law Commissioners' Model State Administrative Procedure Act (1981)

Article I General Provisions

§ 1-102. [Definitions]

As used in this Act:

(1) "Agency" means a board, commissions, department, officer, or other administrative unit of this State, including the agency head, and one or more members of the agency head or agency employees or other persons directly or indirectly purporting to act on behalf or under the authority of the agency head. The term does not include the [legislature] or the courts [, or the governor] [, or the governor in the exercise of powers derived directly and exclusively from the constitution of this State]. The term does not include a political subdivision of the state or any of the administrative units of a political subdivision, but it does include a board, commission, department, officer, or other administrative unit created or appointed by joint or concerted action of an agency and one or more political subdivisions of the state or any of their units. To the extent it purports to exercise authority subject to any provision of this Act, an administrative unit otherwise qualifying as an "agency" must be treated as separate agency even if the unit is located within or subordinate to another agency.

(2) "Agency action" means:

(i) the whole or a part of a rule or an order;

(ii) the failure to issue a rule or an order; or

(iii) an agency's performance of, or failure to perform, any other duty, function, or activity, discretionary or otherwise.

(3) "Agency head" means an individual or body of individuals in whom the ultimate legal authority of the agency is vested by any provision of law.

(4) "License" means a franchise, permit, certification, approval, registration, charter, or similar form of authorization required by law.

(5) "Order" means an agency action of particular applicability that determines the legal rights, duties, privileges, immunities, or other legal interests of one or more specific persons. . . .

(6) "Party to agency proceedings," or "party" in context so indicating, means:

(i) a person to whom the agency action is specifically directed;

or

(ii) a person named as a party to an agency proceeding or allowed to intervene or participate as a party in the proceeding.

(7) "Party to judicial review or civil enforcement proceedings," or "party" in context so indicating, means:

(i) a person who files a petition for judicial review or civil enforcement or

(ii) a person named as a party in a proceeding for judicial review or civil enforcement or allowed to participate as a party in the proceeding.

(8) "Person" means an individual, partnership, corporation, association, government subdivision or unit thereof, or public or private organization or entity of any character, and includes another agency.

(9) "Provision of law" means the whole or a part of the federal or state constitution, or of any federal or state (i) statute, (ii) rule of court, (iii) executive order, or (iv) rule of an administrative agency.

(10) "Rule" means the whole or a part of an agency statement of general applicability that implements, interprets, or prescribes (i) law or policy, or (ii) the organization, procedure, or practice requirements of an agency. The term includes the amendment, repeal, or suspension of an existing rule.

(11) "Rule making" means the process for formulation and adoption of a rule.

§ 1-103. [Applicability and Relation to Other Law]

§ 1-104. [Suspension of Act's Provisions When Necessary to Avoid Loss of Federal Funds or Services] . . .

§ 1-105. [Waiver]

Except to the extent precluded by another provision of law, a person may waive any right conferred upon that person by this Act.

§ 1-106. [Informal Settlements]

Except to the extent precluded by another provision of law, informal settlement of matters that may make unnecessary more elaborate proceedings under this Act is encouraged. Agencies shall establish by rule specific procedures to facilitate informal settlement of matters. This section does not require any party or other person to settle a matter pursuant to informal procedures.

§ 1-107. [Conversion of Proceedings]

(a) At any point in an agency proceeding the presiding officer or other agency official responsible for the proceeding:

(1) may convert the proceeding to another type of agency proceeding providing for by this Act if the conversion is appropriate, is in the public interest, and does not substantially prejudice the rights of any party; and

(2) if required by any provision of law, shall convert the proceeding to another type of agency proceeding provided for by this Act.

(b) A conversion of a proceeding of one type to a proceeding of another type may be effected only upon notice to all parties to the original proceeding.

(c) If the presiding officer or other agency official responsible for the original proceeding would not have authority over the new proceeding to which it is to be converted, that officer or official, in accordance with agency rules, shall secure the appointment of a successor to preside over or be responsible for the new proceeding.

(d) To the extent feasible and consistent with the rights of parties and the requirements of this Act pertaining to the new proceeding, the record or the original agency proceeding must be used in the new agency proceeding.

(e) After a proceeding is converted from one type to another, the presiding officer or other agency official responsible for the new proceeding shall:

(1) give such additional notice to parties or other persons as is necessary to satisfy the requirements of this Act pertaining to those proceedings;

(2) dispose of the matters involved without further proceedings if sufficient proceedings have already been held to satisfy requirements of this Act pertaining to the new proceedings; and

(3) conduct or cause to be conducted any additional proceedings necessary to satisfy the requirements of this Act pertaining to those proceedings.

(f) Each agency shall adopt rules to govern the conversion of one type of proceeding to another. Those rules must include an enumeration of the factors to be considered in determining whether and under what circumstances one type of proceeding will be converted to another.

§ 1-108. [Effective Date]

This Act takes effect on [date] and does not govern proceedings pending on that date. This Act governs all agency proceedings, and all proceedings for judicial review or civil enforcement of agency action, commenced after that date. This Act also governs agency proceedings conducted on a remand from a court or another agency after the effective date of this Act.

§ 1-109. [Severability]

If any provision of this Act or the application thereof to any person or circumstance is held invalid, the invalidity does not affect other provisions or applications of the Act which can be given effect without the invalid provision or application, and for this purpose the provisions of this Act are severable.

Article II Public Access to Agency Law and Policy

§ *2-101. [Administrative Rules Editor; Publication, Compilation, Indexing, and Public Inspection of Rules]*

(a) There is created, within the executive branch, an [administrative rules editor]. The governor shall appoint the [administrative rules editor] who shall serve at the pleasure of the governor.

(b) Subject to the provisions of this Act, the [administrative rules editor] shall prescribe a uniform numbering system, form, and style for all proposed and adopted rules caused to be published by that office [, and shall have the same editing authority with respect to the publication of rules as the [reviser of statutes] has with respect to the publication of statutes].

(c) The [administrative rules editor] shall cause the [administrative bulletin] to be published in pamphlet form [once each week]. For purposes of calculating adherence to time requirements imposed by this Act, an issue of the [administrative bulletin] is deemed published on the later of the date indicated in that issue or the date of its mailing. The [administrative bulletin] must contain:

(1) notices of proposed rule adoption prepared so that the text of the proposed rule shows the text of any existing rule proposed to be changed and the change proposed;

(2) newly filed adopted rules prepared so that the text of the newly filed adopted rule shows the text of any existing rule being changed and the changes being made;

(3) any other notices and materials designated by [law] [the administrative rules editor] for publication therein; and

(4) an index to its contents by subject.

(d) The [administrative rules editor] shall cause the [administrative code] to be compiled, indexed by subject, and published [in loose-leaf form]. All of the effective rules of each agency must be published and indexed in that publication. The [administrative rules editor] shall also cause [loose-leaf] supplements to the [administrative code] to be published at least every [3 months]. [The loose-leaf supplements must be in a form suitable for insertion in the appropriate places in the permanent [administrative code] compilation.]

(e) The [administrative rules editor] may omit from the [administrative bulletin or code] any proposed or filed adopted rule the publication of which would be unduly cumbersome, expensive, or otherwise inexpedient, if:

(1) knowledge of the rule is likely to be important to only a small class of persons;

(2) on application to the issuing agency, the proposed or adopted rule in printed or processed form is made available at no more than its costs of reproduction; and

(3) the [administrative bulletin or code] contains a notice stating in detail the specific subject matter of the omitted proposed or adopted rule and how a copy of the omitted material may be obtained.

(f) The [administrative bulletin and administrative code] must be furnished to [designated officials] without charge and to all subscribers at a cost to be determined by the [administrative rules editor]. Each agency shall also make available for public inspection and copying those portions of the [administrative bulletin and administrative code] containing all rules adopted or used by the agency in the discharge of its functions, and the index to those rules.

(g) Except as otherwise required by a provision of law, subsections, (c) through (f) do not apply to rules governed by Section 3–116, and the following provisions apply instead:

(1) Each agency shall maintain an official, current, and dated compilation that is indexed by subject, containing all of its rules within the scope of Section 3–116. Each addition to, change in, or deletion from the official compilation must also be dated, indexed, and a record thereof kept. Except for those portions containing rules governed by Section 3–116(2), the compilation must be made available for public inspection and copying. Certified copies of the full compilation must also be furnished to the [secretary of state, the administrative rules counsel, and members of the administrative rules review committee], and be kept current by the agency at least every [30] days.

(2) A rule subject to the requirements of this subsection may not be relied on by an agency to the detriment of any person who does not have actual, timely knowledge of the contents of the rule until the requirements of paragraph (1) are satisfied. The burden of proving that knowledge is on the agency. This provision is also inapplicable to the extent necessary to avoid imminent peril to the public health, safety, or welfare.

§ 2–102. [Public Inspection and Indexing of Agency Orders]

(a) In addition to other requirements imposed by any provision of law, each agency shall make all written final orders available for public inspection and copying and index them by name and subject. An agency shall delete from those orders identifying details to the extent required by any provision of law [or necessary to prevent a clearly unwarranted invasion of privacy or release of trade secrets]. In each case the justification for the deletion must be explained in writing and attached to the order.

(b) A written final order may not be relied on as precedent by an agency to the detriment of any person until has been made available for public inspection and indexed in the manner described in subsection (a). This provision is inapplicable to any person who has actual timely knowledge of the order. The burden of proving that knowledge is on the agency.

§ 2–103. [Declaratory Orders] omitted

§ 2–104. [Required Rule Making]

In addition to other rule-making requirements imposed by law, each agency shall:

(1) adopt as a rule a description of the organization of the agency which states the general course and method of its operations and where and how the public may obtain information or make submissions or requests;

(2) adopt rules of practice setting forth the nature and requirements of all formal and informal procedures available to the public, including a description of all forms and instructions that are to be used by the public in dealing with the agency; [and]

(3) as soon as feasible and to the extent practicable, adopt rules, in addition to those otherwise required by this Act, embodying appropriate standards, principles, and procedural safeguards that the agency will apply to the law it administers [; and][.]

[(4) as soon as feasible and to the extent practicable, adopt rules to supersede principles of law or policy lawfully declared by the agency as the basis for its decisions in particular cases.]

§ 2–105. [Model Rules of Procedure]

In accordance with the rule-making requirements of this Act, the [attorney general] shall adopt model rules of procedure appropriate for use by as many agencies as possible. The model rules must deal with all general functions and duties performed in common by several agencies. Each agency shall adopt as much of the model rules as is practicable under its circumstances. To the extent an agency adopts the model rules, it shall do so in accordance with the rule-making requirements of this Act. Any agency adopting a rule of procedure that differs from the model rules shall include in the rule a finding stating the reasons why the relevant portions of the model rules were impracticable under the circumstances.

Article III Rule Making

Chapter 1–Adoption and Effectiveness of Rules

§ 3–101. [Advise on Possible Rules Before Notice of Proposed Rule Adoption]

(a) In addition to seeking information by other methods, an agency, before publication of a notice of proposed rule adoption under Section 3–103, may solicit comments from the public on a subject matter of possible rule making under active consideration within the agency by causing notice to be published in the administrative bulletin of the subject matter and indicating where, when, and how persons may comment.

(b) Each agency may also appoint committees to comment, before publication of a notice of proposed rule adoption under Section 3–103, on the subject matter of a possible rule making under active consideration within the agency. The membership of those committees must be published at least annually in the administrative bulletin.

§ 3–102. [Public Rule-Making Docket]

(a) Each agency shall maintain a current, public rule-making docket.

(b) The rule-making docket [must] [may] contain a listing of the precise subject matter of each possible rule currently under active consideration within the agency for proposal under Section 3–103, the name and address of agency personnel with whom persons may communicate with respect to the matter, and an indication of the present status within the agency of that possible rule.

(c) The rule-making docket must list each pending rule-making proceeding. A rule-making proceeding is pending from the time it is commenced, by publication of a notice of proposed rule adoption, to the time it is terminated, by publication of a notice of termination or the rule becoming effective. For each rule-making proceeding, the docket must indicate:

(1) the subject matter of the proposed rule;

(2) a citation to all published notices relating to the proceeding;

(3) where written submissions on the proposed rule may be inspected;

(4) the time during which written submissions may be made;

(5) the names of persons who have made written requests for an opportunity to make oral presentations on the proposed rule, where those requests may be inspected, and where and when oral presentations may be made;

(6) whether a written request for the issuance of a regulatory analysis of the proposed rule has been filed, whether that analysis has been issued, and where the written request and analysis may be inspected;

(7) the current status of the proposed rule and any agency determinations with respect thereto;

(8) any known timetable for agency decisions or other action in the proceeding;

(9) the date of the rule's adoption;

(10) the date of the rule's filing, indexing, and publication; and

(11) when the rule will become effective.

§ 3-103. *[Notice of Proposed Rule Adoption]*

(a) At least 30 days before the adoption of a rule an agency shall cause notice of its contemplated action to be published in the administrative bulletin. The notice of proposed rule adoption must include;

(1) a short explanation of the purpose of the proposed rule;

(2) the specific legal authority authorizing the proposed rule;

(3) subject to Section 2–101(e), the text of the proposed rule;

(4) where, when, and how persons may present their views on the proposed rule; and

(5) where, when, and how persons may demand an oral proceeding on the proposed rule if the notice does not already provide for one.

(b) Within 3 days after its publication in the administrative bulletin, the agency shall cause a copy of the notice of proposed rule adoption to be mailed to each person who has made a timely request to the agency for a mailed copy of the notice. An agency may charge persons for the actual cost of providing them with mailed copies.

§ 3-104. *[Public Participation]*

(a) For at least 30 days after publication of the notice of proposed rule adoption, an agency shall afford persons the opportunity to submit in writing, argument, data, and views on the proposed rule.

(b)(1) An agency shall schedule an oral proceeding on a proposed rule if, within 20 days after the published notice of proposed rule adoption, a written request for an oral proceeding is submitted by the administrative rules review committee, the administrative rules counsel, a political subdivision, an agency, or 25 persons. At that proceeding, persons may present oral argument, data, and views on the proposed rule.

(2) An oral proceeding on a proposed rule, if required, may not be held earlier than 20 days after notice of its location and time is published in the administrative bulletin.

(3) The agency, a member of the agency, or another presiding officer designated by the agency, shall preside at a required oral proceeding on a proposed rule. If the

agency does not preside, the presiding official shall prepare a memorandum for consideration by the agency summarizing the contents of the presentations made at the oral proceeding. Oral proceedings must be open to the public and be recorded by stenographic or other means.

(4) Each agency shall issue rules for the conduct of oral rule-making proceedings. Those rules may include provisions calculated to prevent undue repetition in the oral proceedings.

§ 3–105. [Regulatory Analysis]

(a) An agency shall issue a regulatory analysis of a proposed rule if, within 20 days after the published notice of proposed rule adoption, a written request for the analysis is filed in the office of the secretary of state by the administrative rules review committee, the governor, a political subdivision, an agency, or 300 persons signing the request. The secretary of state shall immediately forward to the agency a certified copy of the filed request.

(b) Except to the extent that the written request expressly waives one or more of the following, the regulatory analysis must contain: [omitted]

(c) Each regulatory analysis must include quantification of the data to the extent practicable and must take account of both short-term and long-term consequences.

(d) A concise summary of the regulatory analysis must be published in the administrative bulletin at least 10 days before the earliest. [omitted]

(e) The published summary of the regulatory analysis must also indicate where persons may obtain copies of the full text of the regulatory analysis and where, when, and how persons may present their views on the proposed rule and demand an oral proceeding thereon if one is not already provided.

(f) If the agency has made a good faith effort to comply with the requirements of subsections (a) through (c), the rule may not be invalidated on the ground that the contents of the regulatory analysis are insufficient or inaccurate.

§ 3–106. [Time and Manner of Rule Adoption]

(a) An agency may not adopt a rule until the period for making written submissions and oral presentations has expired.

(b) Within 180 days after the later of (i) the publication of the notice of proposed rule adoption, or (ii) the end of oral proceedings thereon, an agency shall adopt a rule pursuant to the rule-making proceeding or terminate the proceeding by publication of a notice to that effect in the [administrative bulletin].

(c) Before the adoption of a rule, an agency shall consider the written submissions, oral submissions or any memorandum summarizing oral submissions, and any regulatory analysis, provided for by this Chapter.

(d) Within the scope of its delegated authority, an agency may use its own experience, technical competence, specialized knowledge, and judgment in the adoption of a rule.

§ 3–107. [Variance Between Adopted Rule and Published Notice of Proposed Rule Adoption] omitted

§ 3–108. [General Exemption From Public Rule-Making Procedures]

(a) To the extent an agency for good cause finds that any requirements of Sections 3–103 through 3–107 are unnecessary, impracticable, or contrary to the public interest in the process of adopting a particular rule, those requirements do not apply. The agency shall incorporate the required finding and a brief statement of its supporting reasons in each rule adopted in reliance upon this subsection.

(b) In an action contesting a rule adopted under subsection (a), the burden is upon the agency to demonstrate that any omitted requirements of Section 3–103 through 3–107 were impracticable, unnecessary, or contrary to the public interest in the particular circumstances involved.

(c) Within 2 years after the effective date of a rule adopted under subsection (a), the administrative rules review committee or the governor may request the agency to hold a rule-making proceeding thereon according to the requirements of Sections 3–103 through 3–107. The request must be in writing and filed in the office of the secretary of state. The secretary of state shall immediately forward to the agency and to the administrative rules editor a certified copy of the request. Notice of the filing of the request must be published in the next issue of the administrative bulletin. The rule in question ceases to be effective 180 days after the request is filed. However, an agency, after the filing of the request, may subsequently adopt an identical rule in a rule-making proceeding conducted pursuant to the requirements of Sections 3–103 through 3–107.

§ 3–109. [Exemption for Certain Rules]

(a) An agency need not follow the provisions of Sections 3–103 through 3–108 in the adoption of a rule that only defines the meaning of a statute or other provision of law or precedent if the agency does not possess delegated authority to bind the courts to any extent with its definition. A rule adopted under this subsection must include a statement that it was adopted under this subsection when it is published in the administrative bulletin, and there must be an indication to that effect adjacent to the rule when it is published in the administrative code.

(b) A reviewing court shall determine wholly de novo the validity of a rule within the scope of subsection (a) that is adopted without complying with the provisions of Sections 3–103 through 3–108.

§ 3–110. [Concise Explanatory Statement]

(a) At the time it adopts a rule, an agency shall issue a concise explanatory statement containing:

(1) its reasons for adopting the rule; and

(2) an indication of any change between the text of the proposed rule contained in the published notice of proposed rule adoption and the text of the rule as finally adopted, with the reasons for any change.

(b) Only the reasons contained in the concise explanatory statement may be used by any party as justifications for the adoption of the rule in any proceeding in which its validity is at issue.

§ 3–111. [Contents, Style, and Form of Rule] omitted

§ 3–112. [Agency Rule-Making Record]

(a) An agency shall maintain an official rule-making record for each rule it (i) proposes by publication in the [administrative bulletin] of a notice of proposed rule adoption, or (ii) adopts. The record and materials incorporated by reference must be available for public inspection.

(b) The agency rule-making record must contain:

(1) copies of all publications in the [administrative bulletin] with respect to the rule or the proceeding upon which the rule is based;

(2) copies of any portions of the agency's public rule-making docket containing entries relating to the rule or the proceeding upon which the rule is based;

(3) all written petitions, requests, submissions, and comments received by the agency and all other written materials considered by the agency in connection with the formulation, proposal, or adoption of the rule or the proceeding upon which the rule is based;

(4) any official transcript of oral presentations made in the proceeding upon which the rule is based or, if not transcribed, any tape recording or stenographic record of those presentations, and any memorandum prepared by a presiding official summarizing the contents of those presentations;

(5) a copy of any regulatory analysis prepared for the proceeding upon which the rule is based;

(6) a copy of the rule and explanatory statement filed in the office of the [secretary of state];

(7) all petitions for exceptions to, amendments of, or repeal or suspension of, the rule;

(8) a copy of any request filed pursuant to Section 3–108(c);

(9) a copy of any objection to the rule filed by the administrative rules review committee pursuant to Section 3-204(d) and the agency's response, and

(10) a copy of any filed executive order with respect to the rule.

(c) Upon judicial review, the record required by this section constitutes the official agency rule-making record with respect to a rule. Except as provided in Section 3–110(b) or otherwise required by a provision of law, the agency rule-making record need not constitute the exclusive basis for agency action on that rule or for judicial review thereof.

§ 3–113. [Invalidity of Rules Not Adopted According to Chapter; Time Limitation] omitted

§ 3–114. [Filing of Rules] omitted

§ 3–115. [Effective Date of Rules] omitted

§ 3–116. [Special Provision for Certain Classes of Rules] omitted

§ 3–117. [Petition for Adoption of Rule]

Any person may petition an agency requesting the adoption of a rule. Each agency shall prescribe by rule the form of the petition and the procedure for its submission, consideration, and disposition. Within [60] days after submission of a petition, the agency shall either (i) deny the petition in writing, stating its reasons therefor, (ii) initiate rule-making proceedings in accordance with this Chapter, or (iii) if otherwise lawful, adopt a rule.

Chapter II—Review of Agency Rules

§ 3–201. [Review by Agency]

At least annually, each agency shall review all of its rules to determine whether any new rule should be adopted. In conducting that review, each agency shall prepare a written report summarizing its findings, its supporting reasons, and any proposed course of action. For each rule, the annual report must include, at least once every 7 years, a concise statement of:

(1) the rule's effectiveness in achieving its objectives, including a summary of any available data supporting the conclusions reached;

(2) criticisms of the rule received during the previous 7 years, including a summary of any petitions for waiver of the rule tendered to the agency or granted by it; and

(3) alternative solutions to the criticisms and the reasons they were rejected or the changes made in the rule in response to those criticisms and the reasons for the changes. A copy of the annual report must be sent to the administrative rules review committee and the administrative rules counsel and be available for public inspection.

[§ 3–202. [Review by Governor; Administrative Rules Counsel]

(a) To the extent the agency itself would have authority, the governor may rescind or suspend all or a severable portion of a rule of an agency. In exercising this authority, the governor shall act by an executive order that is subject to the provisions of this Act applicable to the adoption and effectiveness of a rule.

(b) The Governor may summarily terminate any pending rule-making proceeding by an executive order to that effect, stating therein the reasons for the action. The executive order must be filed in the office of the [secretary of state], which shall promptly forward a certified copy to the agency and the [administrative rules editor]. An executive order terminating a rule-making proceeding becomes effective on [the date it is filed] and must be published in the next issue of the [administrative bulletin].

(c) There is created within the office of the governor, an administrative rules counsel to advise the governor in the execution of the authority vested under this Article. The governor shall appoint the administrative rules counsel who shall serve at the pleasure of the governor.]

§ 3–203. [Administrative Rules Review Committee] omitted

§ 3–204. [Review by the Administrative Rules Review Committee] omitted

Article IV Adjudicative Proceedings

Chapter I—Availability of Adjudicative Proceedings; Applications; Licenses

§ 4–101. [Adjudicative Proceedings; When Required; Exceptions]

(a) An agency shall conduct an adjudicative proceeding as the process for formulating and issuing an order, unless the order is a decision:

(1) to issue or not to issue a complaint, summons, or similar accusation;

(2) to initiate or not to initiate an investigation, prosecution, or other proceeding before the agency, another agency, or a court; or

(3) under Section 4–103, not to conduct an adjudicative proceeding.

(b) This Article applies to rule-making proceedings only to the extent that another statute expressly so requires.

§ 4–102. [Adjudicative Proceedings; Commencement]

(a) An agency may commence an adjudicative proceeding at any time with respect to a matter within the agency's jurisdiction.

(b) An agency shall commence an adjudicative proceeding upon the application of any person, unless:

(1) the agency lacks jurisdiction of the subject matter;

(2) resolution of the matter requires the agency to exercise discretion within the scope of Section 4–101(a);

(3) a statute vests the agency with discretion to conduct or not to conduct an adjudicative proceeding before issuing an order to resolve the matter and, in the exercise of that discretion, the agency has determined not to conduct an adjudicative proceeding before issuing an order to resolve the matter and, in the exercise of that discretion, the agency has determined not to conduct an adjudicative proceeding;

(4) resolution of the matter does not require the agency to issue an order that determines the applicant's legal rights, duties, privileges, immunities, or other legal interests;

(5) the matter was not timely submitted to the agency; or

(6) the matter was not submitted in a form substantially complying with any applicable provision of law.

(c) An application for an agency to issue an order includes an application for the agency to conduct appropriate adjudicative proceedings, whether or not the applicant expressly requests those proceedings.

(d) An adjudicative proceeding commences when the agency or a presiding officer:

(1) notifies a party that a pre-hearing conference, hearing, or other state of an adjudicative proceeding will be conducted; or

(2) begins to take action on a matter that appropriately may be determined by an adjudicative proceeding, unless this action is:

(i) an investigation for the purpose of determining whether an adjudicative proceeding should be conducted; or

(ii) a decision which, under Section 4–101(a), the agency may make without conducting an adjudicative proceeding.

§ 4–103. [Decision Not to Conduct Adjudicative Proceeding.]

If an agency decides not to conduct an adjudicative proceeding in response to an application, the agency shall furnish the applicant a copy of its decision in writing, with a brief statement of the agency's reasons and of any administrative review available to the applicant.

§ 4-104. [Agency Action on Applications]

(a) Except to the extent that the time limits in this subsection are inconsistent with limits established by another statute for any stage of the proceedings, an agency shall process an application for an order, other than a declaratory order, as follows:

(1) Within 30 days after receipt of the application, the agency shall examine the application, notify the applicant of any apparent errors or omissions, request any additional information the agency wishes to obtain and is permitted by law to require, and notify the applicant of the name, official title, mailing address and telephone number of an agency member or employee who may be contacted regarding the application.

(2) Except in situations governed by paragraph (3), within [90] days after receipt of the application or of the reponse to a timely request made by the agency pursuant to paragraph (1), the agency shall:

(i) approve or deny the application, in whole or in part, on the basis of emergency or summary adjudicative proceedings, if those proceedings are available under this Act for disposition of the matter;

(ii) commence a formal adjudicative hearing or a conference adjudicative hearing in accordance with this Act; or

(iii) dispose of the application in accordance with Section 4-103.

(3) If the application pertains to subject matter that is not available when the application is filed but may be available in the future, including an application for housing or employment at a time no vacancy exists, the agency may proceed to make a determination of eligibility within the time provided in paragraph (2). If the agency determines that the applicant is eligible, the agency shall maintain the application on the agency's list of eligible applicants as provided by law and, upon request, shall notify the applicant of the status of the application.

(b) If a timely and sufficient application has been made for renewal of a license with reference to any activity of a continuing nature, the existing license does not expire until the agency has taken final action upon the application for renewal or, if the agency's action is unfavorable, until the last day for seeking judicial review of the agency's action or a later date fixed by the reviewing court.

§ 4-105. [Agency Action Against Licensees] omitted

Chapter II – Formal Adjudicative Hearing

§ 4-201. [Applicability]

An adjudicative proceeding is governed by this chapter, except as otherwise provided by:

(1) a statute other than this Act;

(2) a rule that adopts the procedures for the conference adjudicative hearing or summary adjudicative proceeding in accordance with the standards provided in this Act for those proceedings;

(3) Section 4–501 pertaining to emergency adjudicative proceedings; or

(4) Section 2–103 pertaining to declaratory proceedings.

§ 4–202. [Presiding Officer, Disqualification, Substitution]

(a) The agency head, one or more members of the agency head, one or more administrative law judges assigned by the office of administrative hearings in accordance with Section 4–301 . . . in the discretion of the agency head, may be the presiding officer.

(b) Any person serving or designated to serve along or with others as presiding officer is subject to disqualification for bias, prejudice, interest, or any other cause provided in this Act or for which a judge is or may be disqualified.

(c) Any party may petition for the disqualification of a person promptly after receipt of notice indicating that the person will preside or promptly upon discovering facts establishing grounds for disqualification, whichever is later.

(d) A person whose disqualification is requested shall determine whether to grant the petition, stating facts and reasons for the determination.

(e) If a substitute is required for a person who is disqualified or becomes unavailable for any other reason, the substitute must be appointed by:

(1) the governor, if the disqualified or unavailable person is an elected official; or

(2) the appointing authority, if the disqualified or unavailable person is an appointed official.

(f) Any action taken by a duly-appointed substitute for a disqualified or unavailable person is as effective as if taken by the latter.

§ 4–203. [Representation]

(a) Any party may participate in the hearing in person or, if the party is a corporation or other artificial person, by a duly authorized representative.

(b) Whether or not participating in person, any party may be advised and represented at the party's own expense by counsel or, if permitted by law, other representative.

§ 4–204. [Pre-hearing Conference—Availability, Notice

The presiding officer designated to conduct the hearing may determine, subject to the agency's rules, whether a pre-hearing conference will be conducted. If the conference is conducted:

(1) The presiding officer shall promptly notify the agency of the determination that a pre-hearing conference will be conducted. The agency shall assign or request the office of administrative hearings to assign a presiding officer for the pre-hearing conference, exercising the same discretion as is provided by Section 4–202 concerning the selection of a presiding officer for a hearing.

(2) The presiding officer for the pre-hearing conference shall set the time and place of the conference and give reasonable written notice to all parties and to all persons who have filed written petitions to intervene in the matter. The agency shall give notice to other persons entitled to notice under any provision of law.

(3) The notice must include:

(i) the names and mailing addresses of all parties and other persons to whom notice is being given by the presiding officer;

(ii) the name, official title, mailing address, and telephone number of any counsel or employee who has been designated to appear for the agency;

(iii) the official file or other reference number, the name of the proceeding, and a general description of the subject matter;

(iv) a statement of the time, place, and nature of the prehearing conference;

(v) a statement of the legal authority and jurisdiction under which the pre-hearing conference and the hearing are to be held;

(vi) the name, official title, mailing address and telephone number of the presiding officer for the pre-hearing conference;

(vii) a statement that at the pre-hearing conference the proceeding, without further notice, may be converted into a conference adjudicative hearing or a summary adjudicative proceeding for disposition of the matter as provided by this Act; and

(viii) a statement that a party who fails to attend or participate in a pre-hearing conference, hearing, or other state of an adjudicative proceeding may be held in default under this Act.

(4) The notice may include any other matter that the presiding officer considers desirable to expedite the proceedings.

§ 4–205. [Pre-hearing Conference – Procedure and Pre-hearing Order]

(a) The presiding officer may conduct all or part of the pre-hearing conference by telephone, television, or other electronic means if each participant in the conference has an opportunity to participate in, to hear, and, if technically feasible, to see the entire proceeding while it is taking place.

(b) The presiding officer shall conduct the pre-hearing conference, as may be appropriate, to deal with such matters as conversion of the proceeding to another type, exploration of settlement possibilities, preparation of stipulations, clarification of issues, ruling on identity and limitation of the number of witnesses, objections to proffers of evidence, determination of the extent to which direct evidence, rebuttal evidence, or cross-examination will be presented in written form, and the extent to which telephone, television, or other electronic means will be used as a substitute for proceedings in person, order of presentation of evidence and cross-examination, rulings regarding issuance of subpoenas, discovery orders and protective orders, and such other matters as will promote the orderly and prompt conduct of the hearings. The presiding officer shall issue a pre-hearing order incorporating the matters determined at the pre-hearing conference.

(c) If a pre-hearing conference is not held, the presiding officer for the hearing may issue a pre-hearing order, based on the pleadings, to regulate the conduct of the proceedings.

§ 4–206. [Notice of Hearing]

(a) The presiding officer for the hearing shall set the time and place of the hearing and give reasonable written notice to all parties and to all persons who have filed written petitions to intervene in the matter.

(b) The notice must include a copy of any pre-hearing order rendered in the matter.

(c) To the extent not included in a pre-hearing order accompanying it, the notice must include:

(1) the names and mailing addresses of all parties and other person to whom notice is being given by the presiding officer;

(2) the name, official title, mailing address and telephone number of any counsel or employee who has been designated to appear for the agency;

(3) the official file or other reference number, the name of the proceeding, and a general description of the subject matter;

(4) a statement of the time, place, and nature of the hearing;

(5) a statement of the legal authority and jurisdiction under which the hearing is to be held;

(6) the name, official title, mailing address, and telephone number of the presiding officer;

(7) a statement of the issues involved and, to the extent known to the presiding officer, of the matters asserted by the parties; and

(8) a statement that a party who fails to attend or participate in a pre-hearing conference, hearing, or other state of an adjudicative proceeding may be held in default under this Act.

(d) The notice may include any other matters the presiding officer considers desirable to expedite the proceedings.

(e) The agency shall give notice to persons entitled to notice under any provision of law who have not been given notice by the presiding officer. Notice under this subsection may include all types of information provided in subsections (a) through (d) or may consist of a brief statement indicating the subject matter, parties, time, place, and nature of the hearing, manner in which copies of the notice to the parties may be inspected and copied, and name and telephone number of the presiding officer.

§ 4–207. [Pleadings, Briefs, Motions, Service]

(a) The presiding officer, at appropriate stages of the proceedings, shall give all parties full opportunity to file pleadings, motions, objections and offers of settlement.

(b) The presiding officer, at appropriate stages of the proceedings, may give all parties full opportunity to file briefs, proposed findings of fact and conclusions of law, and proposed initial or final orders.

(c) A party shall serve copies of any filed item on all parties, by mail or any means prescribed by agency rule.

§ 4–208. [Default]

(a) If a party fails to attend or participate in a pre-hearing conference, hearing, or other stage of an adjudicative proceeding, the presiding officer may serve upon all parties written notice of a proposed default order, including a statement of the grounds.

(b) Within 7 days after service of a proposed default order, the party against whom it was issued may file a written motion requesting that the proposed default order be vacated and stating the grounds relied upon. During the time within which a party may file a written motion under this subsection, the presiding officer may adjourn the proceedings or conduct them without the participation of the party against whom a proposed default order was issued, having due regard for the interests of justice and the orderly and prompt conduct of the proceedings.

(c) The presiding officer shall either issue or vacate the default order promptly after expiration of the time within which the party may file a written motion under subsection (b).

§ 4–209. [Intervention] omitted

§ 4–210. [Subpoenas, Discovery and Protective Orders] omitted

§ 4–211. [Procedure at Hearing]

At a hearing:

(1) The presiding officer shall regulate the course of the proceedings in conformity with any pre-hearing order.

(2) To the extent necessary for full disclosure of all relevant facts and issues, the presiding officer shall afford to all parties the opportunity to respond, present evidence and argument, conduct cross-examination, and submit rebuttal evidence, except as restricted by a limited grant of intervention or by the pre-hearing order.

(3) The presiding officer may give nonparties an opportunity to present oral or written statements. If the presiding officer proposes to consider a statement by a nonparty, the presiding officer shall give all parties an opportunity to challenge or rebut it and, on motion of any party, the presiding officer shall require the statement to be given under oath or affirmation.

(4) The presiding officer may conduct all or part of the hearing by telephone, television, or other electronic means, if each participant in the hearing has an opportunity to participate in, to hear, and, if technically feasible, to see the entire proceeding while it is taking place.

(5) The presiding officer shall cause the hearing to be recorded at the agency's expense. The agency is not required, at its expense, to prepare a transcript, unless required to do so by a provision of law. Any party, at the party's expense, may cause a reporter approved by the agency to prepare a transcript from the agency's record, or cause additional recordings to be made during the hearing if the making of the additional recordings does not cause distraction or disruption.

(6) The hearing is open to public observation, except for the parts that the presiding officer states to be closed pursuant to a provision of law expressly authorizing closure. To the extent that a hearing is conducted by telephone, television, or other electronic means, and is not closed, the availability of public observation is satisfied by giving members of the public an opportunity, at reasonable times, to hear or inspect the agency's record, and to inspect any transcript obtained by the agency.

§ 4–212. [Evidence, Official Notice] omitted

§ 4–213. [Ex parte Communications]

(a) Except as provided in subsection (b) or unless required for the disposition of ex parte matters specifically authorized by statute, a presiding officer serving in an adjudicative proceeding may not communicate, directly or indirectly, regarding any issue in the proceeding, while the proceeding is pending, with any party, with any person who has a direct or indirect interest in the outcome of the proceeding, or with any person who presided at a previous stage of the proceeding, without notice and opportunity for all parties to participate in the communication.

(b) A member of a multi-member panel of presiding officers may communicate with other members of the panel regarding a matter pending before the panel, and any presiding officer may receive aid from staff assistants if the assistants do not (i) receive ex parte communications of a type that the presiding officer would be prohibited from receiving or (ii) furnish, augment, diminish, or modify the evidence in the record.

(c) Unless required for the disposition of ex parte matters specifically authorized by statute, no party to an adjudicative proceeding, and no person who has a direct or indirect interest in the outcome of the proceeding or who presided at a previous stage of the proceeding, may communicate, directly or indirectly, in connection with any issue in that proceeding, while the proceeding is pending, with any person serving as presiding officer, without notice and opportunity for all parties to participate in the communication.

(d) If, before serving as presiding officer in an adjudicative proceeding, a person receives an ex parte communication of a type that could not properly be received while serving, the person, promptly after starting to serve, shall disclose the communication in the manner prescribed in subsection (e).

(e) A presiding officer who receives an ex parte communication in violation of this section shall place on the record of the pending matter all written communications received, all written responses to the communications, and a memorandum stating the substance of all oral communications received, all responses made, and the identity of each person from whom the presiding officer received an ex parte communication, and shall advise all parties that these matters have been placed on the record. Any party desiring to rebut the ex parte communication must be allowed to do so, upon requesting the opportunity for rebutall within [10] days after notice of the communication.

(f) If necessary to eliminate the effect of an ex parte communication received in violation of this section, a presiding officer who receives the communication may be disqualified and the portions of the record pertaining to the communication may be sealed by protective order.

(g) The agency shall, and any party may, report any willful violation of this section to appropriate authorities for any disciplinary proceedings provided by law. In addition, each agency by rule may provide for appropriate sanctions, including default, for any violations of this section.

§ 4–214. [Separation of Functions]

(a) A person who has served as investigator, prosecutor or advocate in an adjudicative proceeding or in its pre-adjudicative stage may not serve as presiding officer or assist or advise a presiding officer in the same proceeding.

(b) A person who is subject to the authority, direction, or discretion of one who has served as investigator, prosecutor, or advocate in an adjudicative proceeding or in its pre-adjudicative stage may not serve as presiding officer or assist or advise a presiding officer in the same proceeding.

(c) A person who has participated in a determination of probable cause or other equivalent preliminary determination in an adjudicative proceeding may serve as presiding officer or assist or advise a presiding officer in the same proceeding, unless a party demonstrates grounds for disqualification in accordance with Section 4–202.

(d) A person may serve as presiding officer at successive stages of the same adjudicative proceeding, unless a party demonstrates grounds for disqualification in accordance with Section 4–202.

§ 4–215. [Final Order, Initial Order]

(a) If the presiding officer is the agency head, the presiding officer shall render a final order.

(b) If the presiding officer is not the agency head, the presiding officer shall render an initial order, which becomes a final order unless reviewed in accordance with Section 4–216.

(c) A final order or initial order must include, separately stated, findings of fact, conclusions of law, and policy reasons for the decision if it is an exercise of the agency's discretion, for all aspects of the order, including the remedy prescribed and, if applicable, the action taken on a petition for stay of effectiveness. Findings of fact, if set forth in language that is no more than mere repetition or paraphrase of the relevant provision of law, must be accompanied by a concise and explicit statement of the underlying facts of record to support the findings. If a party has submitted proposed findings of fact, the order must include a ruling on the proposed findings. The order must also include a statement of the available procedures and time limits for seeking reconsideration or other administrative relief. An initial order must include a statement of any circumstances under which the initial order, without further notice, may become a final order.

(d) Findings of fact must be based exclusively upon the evidence of record in the adjudicative proceeding and on matters officially notice in that proceeding. Findings must be based upon the kind of evidence on which reasonably prudent persons are accustomed to rely in the conduct of their serious affairs and may be based upon such evidence even if it would be inadmissible in a civil trial. The presiding officer's experience, technical competence, and specialized knowledge may be utilized in evaluating evidence.

(e) If a person serving or designated to serve as presiding officer becomes unavailable, for any reason, before rendition of the final order or initial order, a substitute presiding officer must be appointed as provided in Section 4–202. The substitute presiding officer shall use any existing record and may conduct any further proceedings appropriate in the interests of justice.

(f) The presiding officer may allow the parties a designated amount of time after conclusion of the hearing for the submission of proposed findings.

(g) A final order or initial order pursuant to this section must be rendered in writing 90 days after conclusion of the hearing or after submission of proposed findings in accordance with subsection (f) unless this period is waived or extended with the written consent of all parties of for good cause shown.

(h) The presiding officer shall cause copies of the final order or initial order to be delivered to each party and to the agency head.

§ 4–216. [Review of Initial Order; Exceptions to Reviewability]

(a) The agency head, upon its own motion may, and upon appeal by any party shall, review an initial order, except to the extent that:

(1) a provision of law precludes or limits agency review of the initial order; or

(2) the agency head, in the exercises of discretion conferred by a provision of law,

(i) determines to review some but not all issues, or not to exercise any review,

(ii) delegates its authority to review the initial order to one or more persons, or

(iii) authorizes one or more persons to review the initial order, subject to further review by the agency head.

(b) A petition for appeal from an initial order must be filed with the agency head, or with any person designated for this purpose by rule of the agency, within 10 days after rendition of the initial order. If the agency head on its own motion decides to review an initial order, the agency head shall give written notice of its intention to review the initial order within 10 days after its rendition. The 10-day period for a party to file a petition for appeal or for the agency head to give notice of its intention to review an initial order on the agency head's own motion is tolled by the submission of a timely petition for reconsideration of the initial order pursuant to Section 4–218, and a new 10-day period starts to run upon disposition of the petition for reconsideration. If an initial order is subject both to a timely petition for reconsideration and to a petition for appeal or to review by the agency head on its own motion, the petition for reconsideration must be disposed of first, unless the agency head determines that action on the petition for reconsideration has been unreasonably delayed.

(c) The petition for appeal must state its basis. If the agency head on its own motion gives notice of its intent to review an initial order, the agency head shall identify the issues that it intends to review.

(d) The presiding officer for the review of an initial order shall exercise all the decision-making power that the presiding officer would have had to render a final order had the presiding officer presided over the hearing, except to the extent that the issues subject to review are limited by a provision of law or by the presiding officer upon notice to all parties.

(e) The presiding officer shall afford each party an opportunity to present briefs and may afford each party an opportunity to present oral argument.

(f) Before rendering a final order, the presiding officer may cause a transcript to be prepared, at the agency's expense, of such portions of the proceeding under review as the presiding officer considers necessary.

(g) The presiding officer may render a final order disposing of the proceeding or may remand the matter for further proceedings with instructions to the persons who rendered the initial order. Upon remanding a matter, the presiding officer may order such temporary relief as is authorized and appropriate.

(h) A final order or an order remanding the matter for further proceedings must be rendered in writing within [60] days after receipt of briefs and oral argument unless that period is waived or extended with the written consent of all parties or for good cause shown.

(i) A final order or an order remanding the matter for further proceedings under this section must identify any difference between this order and the initial order and must include, or incorporate by express reference to the initial order, all the matters required by Section 4–215(c).

(j) The presiding officer shall cause copies of the final order or order remanding the matter for further proceedings to be delivered to each party and to the agency head.

[Sections 4-217 through 4-220 are omitted.]

§ 4–221. [Agency Record]

(a) An agency shall maintain an official record of each adjudicative proceeding under this Chapter.

(b) The agency record consists only of:

(1) notices of all proceedings;

(2) any pre-hearing order;

(3) any motions, pleadings, briefs, petitions, requests, and intermediate rulings;

(4) evidence received or considered;

(5) a statement of matters officially noticed;

(6) proffers of proof and objections and rulings thereon;

(7) proposed findings, requested orders, and exceptions;

(8) the record prepared for the presiding officer at the hearing, together with any transcript of all or part of the hearing considered before final disposition of the proceeding;

(9) any final order, initial order, or order on reconsideration;

(10) staff memoranda or data submitted to the presiding officer, unless prepared and submitted by personal assistants and not inconsistent with Section 4–213(b); and

(11) matters placed on the record after an ex parte communication.

(c) Except to the extent that this Act or another statute provides otherwise, the agency record constitutes the exclusive basis for agency action in adjudicative proceedings under this Chapter and for judicial review thereof.

Chapter III Office of Administrative Hearings [omitted]

Chapter IV Conference Adjudicative Hearing [omitted]

Chapter V Emergency and Summary Adjudicative Proceedings [omitted]

Article V Judicial Review and Civil Enforcement

Chapter I—Judicial Review

§ 5–101. *[Relationship Between This Act and Other Law on Judicial Review and Other Judicial Remedies]*

This Act establishes the exclusive means of judicial review of agency action, but:

(1) The provisions of this Act for judicial review do not apply to litigation in which the sole issue is a claim for money damages or compensation and the agency whose action is at issue does not have statutory authority to determine the claim.

(2) Ancillary procedural matters, including intervention, class actions, consolidation, joinder, severance, transfer, protective orders, and other relief from disclosure of privileged or confidential material, are governed, to the extent not inconsistent with this Act, by other applicable law.

(3) If the relief available under other sections of this Act is not equal or substantially equivalent to the relief otherwise available under law, the relief otherwise available and the related procedures supersede and supplement this Act to the extent necessary for their effectuation. The applicable provisions of this Act and other law must be combined to govern a single proceeding, or if the court orders, 2 or more separate proceedings, with or without transfer to other courts, but no type of relief may be sought in a combined proceeding after expiration of the time limit for doing so.

§ 5–102. *[Final Agency Action Reviewable]*

(a) A person who qualifies under this Act regarding (i) standing (Section 5–106), (ii) exhaustion of administrative remedies (Section 5–107), and (iii) time for filing the petition for review (Section 5–108), and other applicable provisions of law regarding bond, compliance, and other pre-conditions is entitled to judicial review of final agency action, whether or not the person has sought judicial review of any related non-final agency action.

(b) For purposes of this section and Section 5–103:

(1) "Final agency action" means the whole or a part of any agency action other than non-final agency action;

(2) "Non-final agency action" means the whole or a part of an agency determination, investigation, proceeding, hearing, conference, or other process that the agency intends or is reasonably believed to intend to be preliminary, preparatory, procedural, or intermediate with regard to subsequent agency action of that agency or another agency.

[Sections 5–103 through 5–115 are omitted.]

§ 5–116. *[Scope of Review; Grounds for Invalidity]*

(a) Except to the extent that this Act or another statute provides otherwise:

(1) The burden of demonstrating the invalidity of agency action is on the party asserting invalidity; and

(2) The validity of agency action must be determined in accordance with the standards of review provided in this section, as applied to the agency action at the time it was taken.

(b) The court shall make a separate and distinct ruling on each material issue on which the court's decision is based.

(c) The court shall grant relief only if it determines that a person seeking judicial relief has been substantially prejudiced by any one or more of the following:

(1) The agency action, or the statute or rule on which the agency action is based, is unconstitutional on its face or as applied.

(2) The agency has acted beyond the jurisdiction conferred by any provision by law.

(3) The agency has not decided all issues requiring resolution.

(4) The agency has erroneously interpreted or applied the law.

(5) The agency has engaged in an unlawful procedure or decision-making process, or has failed to follow prescribed procedure.

(6) The persons taking the agency action were improperly constituted as a decision-making body, motivated by an improper purpose, or subject to disqualification.

(7) The agency action is based on a determination of fact, made or implied by the agency, that is not supported by evidence that is substantial when viewed in light of the whole record before the court, which includes the agency record for judicial review, supplemented by any additional evidence received by the court under this Act.

(8) The agency action is:

(i) outside the range of discretion delegated to the agency by any provision of law;

(ii) agency action, other than a rule, that is inconsistent with a rule of the agency; [or]

(iii) agency action, other than a rule, that is inconsistent with the agency's prior practice unless the agency justifies the inconsistency by stating facts and reasons to demonstrate a fair and rational basis for the inconsistency. [; or][.]

(iv) [otherwise unreasonable, arbitrary or capricious.]

§ 5–117. [Type of Relief]

(a) The court may award damages or compensation only to the extent expressly authorized by another provision of law.

(b) The court may grant other appropriate relief, whether mandatory, injunctive, or declaratory, preliminary or final; temporary or permanent; equitable or legal. In granting relief, the court may order agency action required by law, order agency exercise of discretion required by law, set aside or modify agency action, enjoin or stay the effectiveness of agency action, remand the matter for further proceedings, render a declaratory judgment, or take any other action that is authorized and appropriate.

(c) The court may also grant necessary ancillary relief to redress the effects of official action wrongfully taken or withheld, but the court may award attorney's fees or witness fees only to the extent expressly authorized by other law.

(d) If the court sets aside or modifies agency action or remands the matter to the agency for further proceedings, the court may make any interlocutory order it finds necessary to preserve the interests of the parties and the public pending further proceedings or agency action.

[§ 5–118. [Review by Higher Court]

Decisions on petitions for review of agency action are reviewable by the [appellate court] as in other civil cases.

Occupational Safety and Health Act (1970)*

§ *651. Congressional statement of findings and declaration of purpose and policy*

(a) The Congress finds that personal injuries and illnesses arising out of work situations impose a substantial burden upon, and are a hindrance to, interstate commerce in terms of lost production, wage loss, medical expenses, and disability compensation payments.

(b) The Congress declares it to be its purpose and policy, through the exercise of its power to regulate commerce among the several States and with foreign nations and to provide for the general welfare, to assure so far as possible every working man and woman in the Nation safe and healthful working conditions and to preserve our human resources—

(1) by encouraging employers and employees in their efforts to reduce the number of occupational safety and health hazards at their places of employment, and to stimulate employers and employees to institute new and to perfect existing programs for providing safe and healthful working conditions;

(2) by providing that employers and employees have separate but dependent responsibilities and rights with respect to achieving safe and healthful working conditions;

(3) by authorizing the Secretary of Labor to set mandatory occupational safety and health standards applicable to businesses affecting interstate commerce, and by creating an Occupational Safety and Health Review Commission for carrying out adjudicatory functions under this chapter;

(4) by building upon advances already made through employer and employee initiative for providing safe and healthful working conditions;

(5) by providing for research in the field of occupational safety and health, including the psychological factors involved, and by developing innovative methods, techniques, and approaches for dealing with occupational safety and health problems;

(6) by exploring ways to discover latent diseases establishing causal connections between diseases and work in environmental conditions, and conducting other research relating to health problems, in recognition of the fact that occupational health standards present problems often different from those involved in occupational safety;

*We have reprinted only the first seven sections of this act; there are twenty-eight sections in the act.

(7) by providing medical criteria which will assure insofar as practicable that no employee will suffer diminished health, functional capacity, or life expectancy as a result of his work experience;

(8) by providing for training programs to increase the number and competence of personnel engaged in the field of occupational safety and health;

(9) by providing for the development and promulgation of occupational safety and health standards;

(10) by providing an effective enforcement program which shall include a prohibition against giving advance notice of any inspection and sanctions for any individual violating this prohibition;

(11) by encouraging the States to assume the fullest responsibility for the administration and enforcement of their occupational safety and health laws by providing grants to the States to assist in identifying their needs and responsibilities in the area of occupational safety and health, to develop plans in accordance with the provisions of this chapter, to improve the administration and enforcement of State occupational safety and health laws, and to conduct experimental and demonstration projects in connection therewith;

(12) by providing for appropriate reporting procedures with respect to occupational safety and health which procedures will help achieve the objectives of this chapter and accurately describe the nature of the occupational safety and health problem;

(13) by encouraging joint labor-management efforts to reduce injuries and disease arising out of employment.

(Pub. L. 91-595, § 2, Dec. 29, 1970, 84 Stat. 1590).

§ 652. Definitions

For the purposes of this chapter—

(1) The term "Secretary" means the Secretary of Labor.

(2) The term "Commission" means the Occupational Safety and Health Review Commission established under this chapter.

(3) The term "commerce" means trade, traffic, commerce, transportation, or communcation among the several States, or between a State and any place outside thereof, or within the District of Columbia, or a possession of the United States (other than the Trust Territory of the Pacific Islands), or between points in the same State but through a point outside thereof.

(4) The term "person" means one or more individuals, partnerships, associations, corporations, business trusts, legal representatives, or any organized group of persons.

(5) The term "employer" means a person engaged in a business affecting commerce who has employees, but does not include the United States or any State or political subdivision of a State.

(6) The term "employee" means an employee of an employer who is employed in a business of his employer which affects commerce.

(7) The term "State" includes a State of the United States, the District of Columbia, Puerto Rico, the Virgin Islands, American Samoa, Guam, and the Trust Territory of the Pacific Islands.

(8) The term "occupational safety and health standard" means a standard which requires conditions, or the adoption or use of one or more practices, means, methods, operations, or processes, reasonably necessary or appropriate to provide safe or healthful employment and places of employment.

(9) The term "national consensus standard" means any occupational safety and health standard or modification thereof which (1) has been adopted and promulgated by a nationally recognized standards-producing organization under procedures whereby it can be determined by the Secretary that persons interested and affected by the scope or provisions of the standard have reached substantial agreement on its adoption, (2) was formulated in a manner which afforded an opportunity for diverse views to be considered and (3) has been designated as such a standard by the Secretary, after consultation with other appropriate Federal agencies.

(10) The term "established Federal Standard" means any operative occupational safety and health standard established by any agency of the United States and presently in effect, or contained in any Act of Congress in force on December 29, 1970.

(11) The term "Committee" means the National Advisory Committee on Occupational Safety and Health established under this chapter.

(12) The term "Director" means the Director of the National Institute for Occupational Safety and Health.

(13) The term "Institute" means the National Institute for Occupational Safety and Health established under this chapter.

§ 653. Geographic applicability; judicial enforcement; applicability to existing standards; report to Congress on duplication and coordination of Federal laws; workmen's compensation law or common law or statutory rights, duties, or liabilities of employers and employees unaffected

(a) This chapter shall apply with respect to employment performed in a workplace in a State, the District of Columbia, the Commonwealth of Puerto Rico, the Virgin Islands, American Samoa, Guam, the Trust Territory of the Pacific Islands, Lake Island, Outer Continental Shelf Lands defined in the Outer Continental Shelf Lands Act [43 U.S.C. 1331 et seq.], Johnston Island, and the Canal Zone. The Secretary of the Interior shall, by regulation, provide for judicial enforcement of this chapter by the courts established for areas in which there are no United States district courts having jurisdiction.

(b)(1) Nothing in this chapter shall apply to working conditions of employees with respect to which other Federal agencies, and State agencies acting under section 2021 of title 42, exercise statutory authority to prescribe or enforce standards or regulations affecting occupational safety or health.

(2) The safety and health standards promulgated under the Act of June 30, 1936, commonly known as the Walsh-Healey Act [41 U.S.C. 35 et seq.], the Service Contract Act of 1965 [41 U.S.C. 351 et seq.], Public Law 91–54, Act of August 9, 1969, Public Law 85–742, Act of August 23, 1958, and the National Foundation on Arts and Humanities Act (20 U.S.C. 951 et seq.] are superseded on the effective date of corresponding standards, promulgated under this chapter, which are determined by the Secretary to be more effective. Standards issued under the laws listed in this para-

graph and in effect on or after the effective date of this chapter shall be deemed to be occupational safety and health standards issued under this chapter, as well as under such other Acts.

(3) The Secretary shall, within three years after the effective date of this chapter, report to the Congress his recommendations for legislation to avoid unnecessary duplication and to achieve coordination between this chapter and other Federal laws.

(4) Nothing in this chapter shall be construed to supersede or in any manner affect any workmen's compensation law or to enlarge or diminish or affect in any other manner the common law or statutory rights, duties, or liabilities of employers and employees under any law with respect to injuries, diseases, or death of employees arising out of, or in the course of, employment. . . .

§ 654. Duties of employers and employees

(a) Each employer—

(1) shall furnish to each of his employees employment and a place of employment which are free from recognized hazards that are causing or are likely to cause death or serious physical harm to his employees;

(2) shall comply with occupational safety and health standards promulgated under this chapter.

(b) Each employee shall comply with occupational safety and health standards and all rules, regulations, and orders issued pursuant to this chapter which are applicable to his own actions and conduct. . . .

§ 655. Standards

(a) Promulgation by Secretary of national consensus standards and established Federal standards; time for promulgation; conflicting standards

Without regard to chapter 5 of title 5 or to the other subsections of this section, the Secretary shall, as soon as practicable during the period beginning with the effective date of this chapter and ending two years after such date, by rule promulgate as an occupational safety or health standard any national consensus standard, and any established Federal standard, unless he determines that the promulgation of such a standard would not result in improved safety or health for specifically designated employees. In the event of conflict among any such standards, the Secretary shall promulgate the standard which assures the greatest protection of the safety or health of the affected employees.

(b) Procedure for promulgation, modification, or revocation of standards

The secretary may by rule promulgate, modify, or revoke any occupational safety or health standard in the following manner:

(1) Whenever the Secretary, upon the basis of information submitted to him in writing by an interested person, a representative of any organization of employers or employees, a nationally recognized standards-producing organization, the Secretary of Health and Human Services, the National Institute for Occupational Safety and Health, or a State or political subdivision, or on the basis of information developed

by the Secretary or otherwise available to him, determines that a rule should be promulgated in order to serve the objectives of this chapter, the Secretary may request the recommendations of an advisory committee appointed under section 656 of this title. The Secretary shall provide such an advisory committee with any proposals of his own or of the Secretary of Health and Human Services, together with all pertinent factual information developed by the Secretary or the Secretary of Health and Human Services, or otherwise available, including the results of research, demonstrations, and experiments. An advisory committee shall submit to the Secretary its recommendations regarding the rule to be promulgated within ninety days from the date of its appointment or within such longer or shorter period as may be prescribed by the Secretary, but in no event for a period which is longer than two hundred and seventy days.

(2) The Secretary shall publish a proposed rule promulgating, modifying, or revoking an occupational safety or health standard in the Federal Register and shall afford interested persons a period of thirty days after publication to submit written data or comments. Where an advisory committee is appointed and the Secretary determines that a rule should be issued, he shall publish the proposed rule within sixty days after the submission of the advisory committee's recommendations or the expiration of the period prescribed by the Secretary for such submission.

(3) On on before the last day of the period provided for the submission of written data or comments under paragraph (2), any interested person may file with the Secretary written objections to the proposed rule, stating the grounds therefor and requesting a public hearing on such objections. Within thirty days after the last day for filing such objections, the Secretary shall publish in the Federal Register a notice specifying the occupational safety or health standard to which objections have been filed and a hearing requested, and specifying a time and place for such hearing.

(4) Within sixty days after the expiration of the period provided for the submission of written data or comments under paragraph (2), or within sixty days after the completion of any hearing held under paragraph (3), the Secretary shall issue a rule promulgating, modifying, or revoking an occupational safety or health standard or make a determination that a rule should not be issued. Such a rule may contain a provision delaying its effective date for such period (not in excess of ninety days) as the Secretary determines may be necessary to insure that affected employers and employees will be informed of the existence of the standard and of its terms and that employers affected are given an opportunity to familiarize themselves and their employees with the existence of the requirements of the standard.

(5) The Secretary, in promulgating standards dealing with toxic materials or harmful physical agents under this subsection, shall set the standard which most adequately assures, to the extent feasible, on the basis of the best available evidence, that no employee will suffer material impairment of health or functional capacity even if such employee has regular exposure to the hazard dealt with by such standard for the period of his working life. Development of standards under this subsection shall be based upon research, demonstrations, experiments, and such other information as may be appropriate. In addition to the attainment of the highest degree of health and safety protection for the employee, other considerations shall be the latest available scientific data in the field, the feasibility of the standards, and experience gained under this and

other health and safety laws. Whenever practicable, the standard promulgated shall be expressed in terms of objective criteria and of the performance desired.

(6)(A) Any employer may apply to the Secretary for a temporary order granting a variance from a standard or any provision thereof promulgated under this section. Such temporary order shall be granted only if the employer files an application which meets the requirements of clause (B) and establishes that (i) he is unable to comply with a standard by its effective date because of unavailability of professional or technical personnel or of materials and equipment needed to come into compliance with the standard or because necessary construction or alteration of facilities cannot be completed by the effective date, (ii) he is taking all available steps to safeguard his employees against the hazards covered by the standard, and (iii) he has an effective program for coming into compliance with the standard as quickly as practicable. Any temporary order issued under this paragraph shall prescribe the practices, means, methods, operations, and processes which the employer must adopt and use while the order is in effect and state in detail his program for coming into compliance with the standard. Such a temporary order may be granted only after notice to employees and an opportunity for a hearing: *Provided*, That the Secretary may issue one interim order to be effective until a decision is made on the basis of the hearing. No temporary order may be in effect for longer than the period needed by the employer to achieve compliance with the standard or one year, whichever is shorter, except that such an order may be renewed not more than twice (I) so long as the requirements of this paragraph are met and (II) if an application for renewal is filed at least 90 days prior to the expiration date of the order. No interim renewal of an order may remain in effect for longer than 180 days.

(B) An application for a temporary order under this paragraph (6) shall contain:

(i) a specification of the standard or portion thereof from which the employer seeks a variance,

(ii) a representation by the employer, supported by representations from qualified persons having firsthand knowledge of the facts represented, that he is unable to comply with the standard or portion thereof and a detailed statement of the reasons therefor,

(iii) a statement of the steps he has taken and will take (with specific dates) to protect employees against the hazard covered by the standard,

(iv) a statement of when he expects to be able to comply with the standard and what steps he has taken and what steps he will take (with dates specified) to come into compliance with the standard, and

(v) a certification that he has informed his employees of the application by giving a copy thereof to their authorized representative, posting a statement giving a summary of the application and specifying where a copy may be examined at the place or places where notices to employees are normally posted, and by other appropriate means.

A description of how employees have been informed shall be contained in the certification. The information to employees shall also inform them of their right to petition the Secretary for a hearing.

(C) The Secretary is authorized to grant a variance from any standard or portion thereof whenever he determines, or the Secretary of Health and Human Services certifies, that such variance is necessary to permit an employer to participate in an experiment approved by him or the Secretary of Health and Human Services designed to demonstrate or validate new and improved techniques to safeguard the health or safety of workers.

(7) Any standards promulgated under this subjection shall prescribe the use of labels or other appropriate forms of warning as are necessary to insure that employees are apprised of all hazards to which they are exposed, relevant symptoms and appropriate emergency treatment, and proper conditions and precautions of safe use or exposure. Where appropriate, such standard shall also prescribe suitable protective equipment and control or technological procedures to be used in connection with such hazards and shall provide for monitoring or measuring employee exposure at such locations and intervals, and in such manner as may be necessary for the protection of employees. In addition, where appropriate, and such standard shall prescribe the type and frequency of medical examinations or other tests which shall be made available, by the employer or at his cost, to employees exposed to such hazards in order to most effectively determine whether the health of such employees is adversely affected by such exposure. In the event such medical examinations are in the nature of research, as determined by the Secretary of Health and Human Services, such examinations may be furnished at the expense of the Secretary of Health and Human Services. The results of such examinations or tests shall be furnished only to the Secretary or the Secretary of Health and Human Services, and, at the request of the employee, to his physician. The Secretary, in consultation with the Secretary of Health and Human Services, may by rule promulgated pursuant to section 553 of title 5, make appropriate modifications in the foregoing requirements relating to the use of labels or other forms of warning, monitoring or measuring, and medical examinations, as may be warranted by experience, information, or medical or technological developments acquired subsequent to the promulgation of the relevant standard.

(8) Whenever a rule promulgated by the Secretary differs substantially from an existing national consensus standard, the Secretary shall, at the same time, publish in the Federal Register a statement of the reasons why the rule as adopted will better effectuate the purposes of this chapter than the national consensus standard.

(c) Emergency temporary standards

(1) The Secretary shall provide, without regard to the requirements of chapter 5 of title 5, for an emergency temporary standard to take immediate effect upon publication in the Federal Register if he determines (A) that employees are exposed to grave danger from exposure to substances or agents determined to be toxic or physically harmful or from new hazards, and (B) that such emergency standard is necessary to protect employees from such danger.

(2) Such standard shall be effective until superseded by a standard promulgated in accordance with the procedures prescribed in paragraph (3) of this subsection.

(3) Upon publication of such standard in the Federal Register the Secretary shall commence a proceeding in accordance with subsection (b) of this section, and the standard as published shall also serve as a proposed rule for the proceeding. The Secre-

tary shall promulgate a standard under this paragraph no later than six months after publication of the emergency standard as provided in paragraph (2) of this subsection.

(d) Variances from standards; procedure

Any affected employer may apply to the Secretary for a rule or order for a variance from a standard promulgated under this section. Affected employees shall be given notice of each such application and an opportunity to participate in a hearing. The Secretary shall issue such rule or order if he determines on the record, after opportunity for an inspection where appropriate and a hearing, that the proponent of the variance has demonstrated by a preponderance of the evidence that the conditions, practices, means, methods, operations, or processes used or proposed to be used by an employer will provide employment and places of employment to his employees which are as safe and healthful as those which would prevail if he complied with the standard. The rule or order so issued shall prescribe the conditions the employer must maintain, and the practices, means, methods, operations, and processes which he must adopt and utilize to the extent they differ from the standard in question. Such a rule or order may be modified or revoked upon application by an employer, employees, or by the Secretary on his own motion, in the manner prescribed for its issuance under this subsection at any time after six months from its issuance.

(e) Statement of reasons for Secretary's determinations; publication in Federal Register

Whenever the Secretary promulgates any standard, makes any rule, order, or decision, grants any exemption or extension of time, or compromises, mitigates, or settles any penalty assessed under this chapter, he shall include a statement of the reasons for such action, which shall be published in the Federal Register.

(f) Judicial review

Any person may be adversely affected by a standard issue under this section may at any time prior to the sixtieth day after such standard is promulgated file a petition challenging the validity of such standard with the United States court of appeals for the circuit wherein such person resides or has his principal place of business, for a judicial review of such standard. A copy of the petition shall be forthwith transmitted by the clerk of the court to the Secretary. The filing of such petition shall not, unless otherwise ordered by the court, operate as a stay of the standard. The determinations of the Secretary shall be conclusive if supported by substantial evidence in the record considered as a whole.

(g) Priority for establishment of standards

In determining the priority for establishing standards under this section, the Secretary shall give due regard to the urgency of the need for mandatory safety and health standards for particular industries, trades, crafts, occupations, businesses, workplaces or work environments. The Secretary shall also give due regard to the recommendations of the Secretary of Health and Human Services regarding the need for mandatory standards in determining the priority for establishing such standards.

§ 656. Administration

(a). National Advisory Committee on Occupational Safety and Health; establishment; membership; appointment; Chairman; functions; meetings; compensation; secretarial and clerical personnel

(1) There is hereby established a National Advisory Committee on Occupational Safety and Health consisting of twelve members appointed by the Secretary, four of whom are to be designated by the Secretary of Health and Human Services, without regard to the provisions of title 5 governing appointments in the competitive service, and composed of representatives of management, labor, occupational safety and occupational health professions, and of the public. The Secretary shall designate one of the public members as Chairman. The members shall be selected upon the basis of their experience and competence in the field of occupational safety and health.

(2) The Committee shall advise, consult with, and make recommendations to the Secretary and the Secretary of Health and Human Services on matters relating to the administration of this chapter. The Committee shall hold no fewer than two meetings during each calendar year. All meetings of the Committee shall be open to the public and a transcript shall be kept and made available for public inspection.

(3) The members of the Committee shall be compensated in accordance with the provisions of section 3109 of title 5.

(4) The Secretary shall furnish to the Committee an executive secretary and such secretarial, clerical, and other services as are deemed necessary to the conduct of its business.

(b) Advisory committees; appointment; duties; membership; compensation; reimbursement to member's employer; meetings; availability of records; conflict of interest

An advisory committee may be appointed by the Secretary to assist him in his standard-setting functions under section 655 of this title. Each such committee shall consist of not more than fifteen members and shall include as a member one or more designees of the Secretary of Health and Human Services, and shall include among its members an equal number of persons qualified by experience and affiliation to present the viewpoint of the employers involved, and of persons similarly qualified to present the viewpoint of the workers involved, as well as one or more representatives of health and safety agencies of the States. An advisory committee may also include such other persons as the Secretary may appoint who are qualified by knowledge and experience to make a useful contribution to the work of such committee, including one or more representatives of professional organizations of technicians or professionals specializing in occupational safety or health, and one or more representatives of nationally recognized standards-producing organizations, but the number of persons so appointed to any such advisory committee shall not exceed the number appointed to such committee as representatives of Federal and State agencies. Persons appointed to advisory committees from private life shall be compensated in the same manner as consultants or experts under section 3109 of title 5. The Secretary shall pay to any State which is the employer of a member of such a committee who is a representative of the health or safety agency of that State, reimbursement sufficient to cover the actual cost to the State resulting from such representative's membership on such committee. Any meeting of such committee shall be open to the public and an accurate record shall be kept and made available to the public. No member of such committee (other than representatives of employers and employees) shall have an economic interest in any proposed rule.

(c) Use of services, facilities, and personnel of Federal, State, and local agencies; reimbursement; employment of experts and consultants or organizations; renewal of contracts; compensation; travel expenses

In carrying out his responsibilities under this chapter, the Secretary is authorized to—

(1) use, with the consent of any Federal agency, the services, facilities, and personnel of such agency, with or without reimbursement, and with the consent of any State or political subdivision, thereof, accept and use the services, facilities, and personnel of any agency of such State or subdivision with reimbursement; and

(2) employ experts and consultants or organizations thereof as authorized by section 3109 of title 5, except that contracts for such employment may be renewed annually; compensate individuals so employed at rates not in excess of the rate specified at the time of service for grade GS-18 under section 5332 of title 5, including travel-time, and allow them while away from their homes or regular places of business, travel expenses (including per diem in lieu of subsistence) as authorized by section 5703 of title 5 for persons in the Government service employed intermittently, while so employed.

§ 657. Inspections, investigations, and recordkeeping

(a) Authority of Secretary to enter, inspect, and investigate places of employment; time and manner

In order to carry out the purposes of this chapter, the Secretary, upon presenting appropriate credentials to the owner, operator, or agent in charge, is authorized—

(1) to enter without delay and at reasonable times any factory, plant, establishment, construction site, or other area, workplace or environment where work is performed by an employee of an employer; and

(2) to inspect and investigate during regular working hours and at other reasonable times, and within reasonable limits and in a reasonable manner, any such place of employment and all pertinent conditions, structures, machines, apparatus, devices, equipment, and materials therein, and to question privately any such employer, owner, operator, agent, or employee.

(b) Attendance and testimony of witnesses and production of evidence, enforcement of subpoena

In making his inspections and investigations under this chapter the Secretary may require the attendance and testimony of witnesses and the production of evidence under oath. Witnesses shall be paid the same fees and mileage that are paid witnesses in the courts of the United States. In case of a contumacy, failure, or refusal of any person to obey such an order, any district court of the United States or the United States courts of any territory or possession, within the jurisdiction of which such person is found, or resides or transacts business, upon the application by the Secretary, shall have jurisdiction to issue to such person an order requiring such person to appear to produce evidence if, as, and when so ordered, and to give testimony relating to the matter under investigation or in question, and any failure to obey such order of the court may be punished by said court as a contempt thereof.

(c) Maintenance, preservation, and availability of records; issuance of regulations; scope of records; periodic inspections by employer; posting of notice by employer; notification of employee of corrective action

(1) Each employer shall make, keep and preserve, and make available to the Secretary or the Secretary of Health and Human Services, such records regarding his activities relating to this chapter as the Secretary, in cooperation with the Secretary of Health and Human Services, may prescribe by regulation as necessary or appropriate for the enforcement of this chapter or for developing information regarding the causes and prevention of occupational accidents and illnesses. In order to carry out the provisions of this paragraph such regulations may include provisions requiring employers to conduct periodic inspections. The Secretary shall also issue regulations requiring that employers, through posting of notices or other appropriate means, keep their employees informed of their protections and obligations under this chapter, including the provisions of applicable standards.

(2) The Secretary, in cooperation with the Secretary of Health and Human Services, shall prescribe regulations requiring employers to maintain accurate records or, and to make periodic reports on, work-related deaths, injuries and illnesses other than minor injuries requiring only first aid treatment and which do not involve medical treatment, loss of consciousness, restriction of work or motion, or transfer to another job.

(3) The Secretary, in cooperation with the Secretary of Health and Human Services, shall issue regulations requiring employers to maintain accurate records of employees exposures to potentially toxic materials or harmful physical agents which are required to be monitored or measured under section 655 of this title. Such regulations shall provide employees or their representatives with an opportunity to observe such monitoring or measuring, and to have access to the records thereof. Such regulations shall also make appropriate provision for each employee or former employee to have access to such records as will indicate his own exposure to toxic materials or harmful physical agents. Each employer shall promptly notify any employee who has been or is being exposed to toxic materials or harmful physical agents in concentrations or at levels which exceed those prescribed by an applicable occupational safety and health standard promulgated under section 655 of this title, and shall inform any employee who is being thus exposed of the corrective action being taken.

(d) Obtaining of information

Any information obtained by the Secretary, the Secretary of Health and Human Services, or a State agency under this chapter shall be obtained with a minimum burden upon employers, especially those operating small businesses. Unnecessary duplication of efforts in obtaining information shall be reduced to the maximum extent feasible.

(e) Employer and authorized employee representatives to accompany Secretary or his authorized representative on inspection of workplace; consultation with employees where no authorized employee representative is present

Subject to regulations issued by the Secretary, a representative of the employer and a representative authorized by this employees shall be given an opportunity to accompany the Secretary or his authorized representative during the physical inspection of any workplace under subsection (a) of this section for the purpose of aiding such inspection. Where there is no authorized employee representative, the Secretary or his authorized representative shall consult with a reasonable number of employees concerning matters of health and safety in the workplace.

(f) Request for inspection by employees or representative of employees; grounds; procedure; determination of request; notification of Secretary or representative prior to or during any inspection of violations; procedure for review of refusal by representative of Secretary to issue citation for alleged violations

(1) Any employees or representative of employees who believe that a violation of a safety or health standard exists that threatens physical harm, or that an imminent danger exists, may request an inspection by giving notice to the Secretary or his authorized representative of such violation or danger. Any such notice shall be reduced to writing, shall set forth with reasonable particularity the grounds for the notice, and shall be signed by the employees or representative of employees, and a copy shall be provided the employer or his agent no later than at the time of inspection, except that, upon the request of the person giving such notice, his name and the names of individual employees referred to therein shall not appear in such copy or on any record published, released, or made available pursuant to subsection (g) of this section. If upon receipt of such notification the Secretary determines there are reasonable grounds to believe that such violation or danger exists, he shall make a special inspection in accordance with the provisions of this section as soon as practicable, to determine if such violation or danger exists. If the Secretary determines there are no reasonable grounds to believe that a violation or danger exists he shall notify the employees or representative of the employees in writing of such determination.

(2) Prior to or during any inspection of a workplace, any employees or representative or employees employed in such workplace may notify the Secretary or any representative of the Secretary responsible for conducting the inspection, in writing, of any violation of this chapter which they have reason to believe exists in such workplace. The Secretary shall, by regulation, establish procedures for informal review of any refusal by a representative of the Secretary to issue a citation with respect to any such alleged violation and shall furnish the employees or representative of employees requesting such review a written statement of the reasons for the Secretary's final disposition of the case.

(g) Compilation, analysis, and publication of reports and information; rules and regulations

(1) The Secretary and Secretary of Health and Human Services are authorized to compile, analyze, and publish, either in summary or detailed form, all reports or information obtained under this section.

(2) The Secretary and the Secretary of Health and Human Services shall each prescribe such rules and regulations as he may deem necessary to carry out their responsibilities under this chapter, including rules and regulations dealing with the inspection of an employer's establishment.

Credits and Acknowledgements
(continued from page ii.)

Martha Derthick and Paul J. Quirk. From "The Limits of Deregulation" and "The Reform Idea" in *The Politics of Deregulation*. Copyright 1985 by the Brookings Institution.

Colin S. Diver. From "Policymaking Paradigms in Administrative Law," *95 Harvard Law Review 393*, 1981. Reprinted by permission.

A. Lee Fritschler. From *Smoking and Politics: Policymaking and the Federal Bureaucracy*, 2nd ed., Copyright 1975, pp. 34–35. Reprinted by permission of Prentice-Hall, Inc., Englewood Cliffs, New Jersey.

George Getschow. Excerpted from "Houston's Tax Breaks Aimed at Business Require Immediate Remedy, Judge Rules," *The Wall Street Journal*. 14 September 1981. Reprinted by permission of *The Wall Street Journal*, Copyright Dow Jones and Company, Inc., 1981. All Rights Reserved.

Charles Goodsell. From "Looking Once Again at Human Service Bureaucracy," *The Journal of Politics*, August 1981, pp. 770–771. Reprinted by permission.

Christine B. Harrington. From "Regulatory Reform," *10 Law and Policy 293*, 1988. Reprinted by permission.

Louis L. Jaffe. From "The Illusion of the Ideal Administration," *86 Harvard Law Review 1183*, 1973. Reprinted by permission.

Charles H. Koch, Jr. and Barry R. Rubin. From "A Proposal for a Comprehensive Restructuring of the Public Information System," *The Duke Law Journal* 1 (1979). Copyright 1979, Duke University School of Law. Reprinted by permission.

Robert Kuttner. From "Plane Truth," 17 July and 24 July 1989. Copyright 1989, *The New Republic, Inc.* Reprinted by permission of *The New Republic*.

Theodore J. Lowi. From "Toward Judicial Democracy," *The End of Liberalism*, (New York: W. W. Norton, 1979). Reprinted by permission.

Jeffrey S. Lubbers. From "Federal Administrative Law Judges," *33 Administrative Law Review 109*, 1981. Reprinted by permission.

J. Mashaw and R. Merrill. From *Introduction to the American Public Law System* (St. Paul: West Publishing Company, 1975), Copyright 1975. Reprinted by permission.

Albert R. Matheny and Bruce A. Williams. From "Regulation, Risk Assessment and the Supreme Court," *6 Law and Policy 425*, 1984. Revised 1990. Reprinted by permission.

Thomas K. McCraw. From "Regulation in America," *159 Business History Review*, 1975. Reprinted by permission.

Philippe Nonet. From *Administrative Justice: Advocacy and Change in Government Agencies*, by Philippe Nonet. Copyright 1969 by Russell Sage Foundation. Reprinted by permission of the publisher.

Karen O'Connor and Lee Epstein. From "Bridging the Gap Between Congress and the Supreme Court," *Western Political Quarterly* Vol. 38: 2, June, 1985, pp. 238–249. Reprinted by permission of the University of Utah, copyright holder.

Robinson, Gelhorn, and Bruff. From *The Administrative Process* (St. Paul: West Publishing Company, 1980), Copyright 1980. Reprinted by permission.

John T. Scholz and Feng Heng Wei. From "Regulatory Enforcement in a Federal System," *80 American Political Science Review 1249*, 1986. Reprinted by permission.

621

CASE INDEX

Principal (excerpted) cases are boldfaced. Italicized page numbers refer to the pages where the excerpt occurs.